Praise for
THE OXFORD HANDBOO

HOLOCAUST STUDIES

"a pioneering achievement which sets the standard for future such handbooks by capturing the current major debates of the field in an incisive and insightful way."
K. Hannah Holtschneider, *Expository Times*

"The catalogue of the Library of Congress currently lists more than sixteen thousand books on the Holocaust...If I had to limit my own library to ten out of those sixteen thousand Holocaust books, this would be one of them."
Thomas Kühne, *H-Net Reviews in the Humanities and the Social Sciences*

"a tour de force scrupulously compiled by two acclaimed scholars...this is a magnificent reference tool"
Paul Vincent, *CHOICE*

"Oxford University Press promised that this disciplinary Handbook would both exhibit the diversity of approaches to Holocaust studies and testify to the field's complexity. [It] largely realizes its promise and accomplishes its purposes...the Handbook provides a valuable introduction to Holocaust studies as a discipline."
Jay Geller, *Journal of Religion*

Peter Hayes is Theodore Z. Weiss Professor of Holocaust Studies, Northwestern University.
John K. Roth is Edward J. Sexton Professor Emeritus of Philosophy, Claremont McKenna College.

THE OXFORD HANDBOOK OF

HOLOCAUST STUDIES

Edited by

PETER HAYES

and

JOHN K. ROTH

OXFORD
UNIVERSITY PRESS

OXFORD

UNIVERSITY PRESS

Great Clarendon Street, Oxford, OX2 6DP,
United Kingdom

Oxford University Press is a department of the University of Oxford.
It furthers the University's objective of excellence in research, scholarship,
and education by publishing worldwide. Oxford is a registered trade mark of
Oxford University Press in the UK and in certain other countries

Published in the United States of America by Oxford University Press
198 Madison Avenue, New York, NY 10016, United States of America

British Library Cataloguing in Publication Data
Data available

Library of Congress Cataloging in Publication Data
Data available

ISBN 978-0-19-966882-3

Links to third party websites are provided by Oxford in good faith and
for information only. Oxford disclaims any responsibility for the materials
contained in any third party website referenced in this work.

In Memoriam

Gerald D. Feldman
1937–2007

Frederick E. Sontag
1924–2009

The teaching of the wise is a fountain of life . . .
Proverbs 13:14

Contents

List of Contributors   xi

Introduction   1
PETER HAYES AND JOHN K. ROTH

PART I ENABLERS

1. Antisemitism   23
   RICHARD S. LEVY

2. Science   39
   PATRICIA HEBERER

3. Nationalism   54
   ERIC D. WEITZ

4. Colonialism   68
   A. DIRK MOSES

5. Fascism   81
   PHILIP MORGAN

6. World Wars   95
   DORIS L. BERGEN

PART II PROTAGONISTS

7. Hitler and Himmler   113
   ALAN E. STEINWEIS

8. Problem Solvers   128
   CHRISTOPHER R. BROWNING

9. Killers   142
   EDWARD B. WESTERMANN

10. On-Lookers   156
    PAUL A. LEVINE

11. Rescuers   170
    DEBÓRAH DWORK

12. Jews   185
    DAN MICHMAN

13. Women   203
    LENORE J. WEITZMAN

14. Children   218
    NICHOLAS STARGARDT

15. Catholics   233
    KEVIN P. SPICER

16. Protestants   250
    ROBERT P. ERICKSEN

17. The Allies   265
    SHLOMO ARONSON

18. Gypsies, Homosexuals, and Slavs   274
    JOHN CONNELLY

PART III SETTINGS

19. Greater Germany   293
    WOLF GRUNER

20. Living Space   310
    WENDY LOWER

21. Occupied and Satellite States   326
    RADU IOANID

22. Ghettos   340
    MARTIN C. DEAN

23. Labor Sites   354
    MARK SPOERER

24. Camps   364
    KARIN ORTH

PART IV REPRESENTATIONS

25. German Documents and Diaries   381
    PETER FRITZSCHE

26. Jews' Diaries and Chronicles   397
    AMOS GOLDBERG

27. Survivors' Accounts   414
    HENRY GREENSPAN

28. Literature   428
    SARA R. HOROWITZ

29. Film   444
    LAWRENCE BARON

30. Art   461
    DORA APEL

31. Music   478
    BRET WERB

32. Memorials and Museums   490
    JAMES E. YOUNG

PART V AFTEREFFECTS

33. Liberation and Dispersal   509
    ARIEH J. KOCHAVI

34. Punishment   524
    REBECCA WITTMANN

35. Plunder and Restitution   540
    PETER HAYES

36. Denial   560
    DEBORAH E. LIPSTADT

37. Israel   575
    BOAZ COHEN

38. Jewish Culture   590
    JEFFREY SHANDLER

39. Judaism   607
    MICHAEL BERENBAUM

40. Christianity   620
    STEPHEN R. HAYNES

41. Germany   635
    JEFFREY HERF

42. Europe   650
    JAN-WERNER MÜLLER

43. The Social Sciences   667
    JAMES E. WALLER

44. The Humanities   680
    BEREL LANG

45. Education   695
    SIMONE SCHWEBER

46. Human Rights Law   709
    DAVID H. JONES

47. Ethics   722
    JOHN K. ROTH

    Epilogue   737
    PETER HAYES AND JOHN K. ROTH

Index   741

List of Contributors

Dora Apel is Associate Professor and holds the W. Hawkins Ferry Chair of Modern and Contemporary Art History at Wayne State University.

Shlomo Aronson is Professor Emeritus of Political Science and Holocaust History at the Hebrew University, Jerusalem, and Visiting Professor at Tel-Aviv University and the Tel-Aviv-Yaffo Academic College.

Lawrence Baron is the Abraham Nasatir Professor of Modern Jewish History at San Diego State University.

Michael Berenbaum is Professor of Jewish Studies at the American Jewish University and Director of the Sigi Ziering Institute: Exploring the Ethical and Religious Implications of the Holocaust.

Doris L. Bergen is the Chancellor Rose and Ray Wolfe Professor of Holocaust Studies at the University of Toronto.

Christopher R. Browning is the Frank Porter Graham Professor of History at the University of North Carolina at Chapel Hill.

Boaz Cohen heads the Holocaust studies program of the Western Galilee College, Acco, teaches Jewish studies at Shaanan College, Haifa, and pursues Holocaust-related research at Bar Ilan University.

John Connelly teaches the history of East Central Europe at the University of California, Berkeley.

Martin C. Dean is Applied Research Scholar at the United States Holocaust Memorial Museum's Center for Advanced Holocaust Studies in Washington, DC.

Debórah Dwork is the Rose Professor of Holocaust History and Director of the Strassler Center for Holocaust and Genocide Studies at Clark University.

Robert P. Ericksen is Kurt Mayer Professor of Holocaust Studies at Pacific Lutheran University.

Peter Fritzsche is Professor of European History at the University of Illinois.

Amos Goldberg teaches Holocaust studies at the Hebrew University of Jerusalem.

Henry Greenspan is Consulting Psychologist and Senior Lecturer in Social Theory and Practice at the University of Michigan in Ann Arbor.

Wolf Gruner is Shapell-Guerin Chair in Jewish Studies and Professor of History at the University of Southern California, Los Angeles.

Peter Hayes is Professor of History and Theodore Zev Weiss Holocaust Educational Foundation Professor of Holocaust Studies at Northwestern University.

Stephen R. Haynes is Professor of Religious Studies at Rhodes College.

Patricia Heberer is a historian with the Center for Advanced Holocaust Studies at the United States Holocaust Memorial Museum in Washington, DC.

Jeffrey Herf is Professor of Modern European History at the University of Maryland, College Park.

Sara R. Horowitz directs the Israel and Golda Koschitzky Centre for Jewish Studies, and is Professor of Humanities, at York University (Toronto).

Radu Ioanid is Director of International Archival Programs at the United States Holocaust Memorial Museum in Washington, DC.

David H. Jones is Professor of Philosophy Emeritus at the College of William and Mary.

Arieh J. Kochavi is Professor of Modern History and head of the School of History at the University of Haifa, where he directs the Institute of Holocaust Studies.

Berel Lang is Visiting Professor of Philosophy and Letters at Wesleyan University.

Paul A. Levine is Senior Lecturer in Holocaust History at The Hugo Valentin Centre (formerly the Programme for Holocaust and Genocide Studies), Uppsala University, Sweden.

Richard S. Levy is Professor of German History and the History of the Holocaust at the University of Illinois at Chicago.

Deborah E. Lipstadt is Dorot Professor of Modern Jewish and Holocaust Studies at Emory University.

Wendy Lower is Research Fellow and Lecturer in the Department of Eastern European History at the Ludwig Maximilian University, Munich, Germany.

Dan Michman is Professor of Modern Jewish History and Chair of the Arnold and Leona Finkler Institute of Holocaust Research at Bar-Ilan University, Israel, and Chief Historian at the Yad Vashem International Institute of Holocaust Research.

Philip Morgan is Senior Lecturer in Contemporary European History at the University of Hull, United Kingdom.

A. Dirk Moses teaches history at the University of Sydney.

Jan-Werner Müller teaches in the politics department at Princeton University.

Karin Orth is a Research Fellow in the Historical Seminar of the University of Freiburg.

John K. Roth is the Edward J. Sexton Professor Emeritus of Philosophy and the Founding Director of the Center for the Study of the Holocaust, Genocide, and Human Rights (now the Center for Human Rights Leadership) at Claremont McKenna College.

Simone Schweber is the Michael S. and Judith B. Goodman Professor of Education and Jewish Studies at the University of Wisconsin-Madison.

Jeffrey Shandler is Professor of Jewish Studies at Rutgers University.

Kevin P. Spicer is Associate Professor of History at Stonehill College, Easton, MA, where he chairs the Catholic-Jewish Dialogue Committee.

Mark Spoerer, an economic and social historian, is Visiting Fellow at the German Historical Institute in Paris.

Nicholas Stargardt teaches modern European history at Magdalen College, Oxford.

Alan E. Steinweis is Professor of History at the University of Vermont, where he also directs the Carolyn and Leonard Miller Center for Holocaust Studies.

James E. Waller, an Affiliated Scholar with the Auschwitz Institute for Peace and Reconciliation, holds the Cohen Chair of Holocaust and Genocide Studies at Keene State College.

Eric D. Weitz is Distinguished McKnight University Professor of History at the University of Minnesota.

Lenore J. Weitzman has been a professor at Stanford University, the University of California, Harvard University, and George Mason University as well as a scholar in residence at Brandeis University.

Bret Werb is Musicologist and Music Collection Curator for the United States Holocaust Memorial Museum in Washington, DC.

Edward B. Westermann is a retired Colonel in the United States Air Force and has taught courses on European history, the Holocaust, and military history at the United States Air Force Academy and Air University. He is currently teaching at Texas A&M University-San Antonio.

Rebecca Wittmann is Associate Professor of History at the University of Toronto.

James E. Young is Distinguished University Professor of English and Judaic Studies at the University of Massachusetts, Amherst.

INTRODUCTION

PETER HAYES

JOHN K. ROTH

EVERY book begins before its first page. This volume's immediate origins lie in a message that John Roth received from Lucy Qureshi on 5 September 2005. Then the commissioning editor for religion and theology at Oxford University Press, Qureshi wanted to know about the feasibility of an Oxford Handbook of Holocaust Studies. Primarily focused on Nazi Germany's genocidal assault against the Jews, such a work, she indicated, would be a tall order, for it would need to be an authoritative, up-to-date guide to both the state of the interpretive art and the salient issues and debates that have driven research about the Holocaust to date and are likely to do so in the future. Discussion between Qureshi and Roth soon included Peter Hayes. In mid-November 2005, Hayes and Roth submitted a proposal to Qureshi, who obtained a number of very helpful readers' reports that prompted the editors to think boldly about the proposed structure of the work. Then contributors were invited; chapters written, critiqued, and redone; kind agreement was obtained from Ava Schieber, a Holocaust survivor, to let us use her art for the book's cover; and under the direction of the editorial team at Oxford University Press—Tom Perridge, Elizabeth Robottom, Jenny Wagstaffe, Tessa Eaton, and the copyeditor Malcolm Todd—publication of *The Oxford Handbook of Holocaust Studies* followed.

Because the subject at hand is a historical one, however, its beginnings obviously antedate 2005. Without earlier developments, no *Handbook of Holocaust Studies* could exist. Even the name is a historical product. In Israel and some European countries, the preferred umbrella term for the events treated here is the Hebrew word *Shoah*, signifying catastrophic destruction. Many scholars favor this term because *Holocaust* derives from an ancient Greek word used to denote offerings made by fire unto God and thus carries religious and/or sanctifying connotations. Nonetheless, since its introduction in the 1950s, *Holocaust* has become the most prevalent and widely recognized descriptor and been adopted as such by many languages. Rather like the term "Renaissance," which many specialists think has misleading implications, Holocaust has taken root nonetheless both in English and elsewhere. Although the editors of this volume believe that neither name—Holocaust or Shoah—takes the measure of the onslaught perpetrated by Nazi Germany, they also think that *Holocaust studies* has become and is likely to remain the most commonly understood heading for work in the area and therefore the appropriate title rubric.

Terminology aside, the origins of Holocaust studies are coeval with the events they treat. As numerous contemporary documents and diaries demonstrate, recording and reflecting upon the destruction unleashed by Adolf Hitler (1889–1945), his followers, and their collaborators began while it raged. Subsequent efforts by survivors and scholars, artists and filmmakers, research centers and museums, teachers and students have extracted and expanded the meaning of these records and produced the field of Holocaust studies, its focus scholarly but not confined to universities and colleges, its scope international, and its vitality robust. Although memory, memories, and remembering have been watchwords of this development and given it powerful and positive impetus, they also played catastrophic roles in bringing on the Holocaust itself. That circumstance represents another respect in which the origins and nature of the field remain entwined and subjects of constant reflection.

In recent decades, few scholarly fields have developed more rapidly and vigorously than this one. Building on formidable, often underestimated beginnings during the Holocaust and in the early postwar decades, scholarship about the persecution and murder of the European Jews and its aftereffects has generated an enormous literature in multiple academic disciplines. Indeed, the Holocaust has become a touchstone of public and intellectual discourse—political, ethical, and religious—in the early twenty-first century. As the importance of the field has grown, so has the recognition that, if the Holocaust was the quintessential genocide—defined as the intended destruction, in whole or in part, of a national, ethnic, racial, or religious group—it was neither the first nor the last. How the field of Holocaust studies and the more recently emerging field of genocide studies should relate to one another is work in progress, not least because the issue raises complicated, sometimes charged issues of comparing and contrasting. Arguably even more demanding is the challenge of making the ethical "lessons" of the Holocaust, if they exist, credible and compelling in a world from which genocide and other inflictions of mass violence show too few signs of disappearing.

Taking stock of a field that both crosses and respects the traditional boundaries of academic disciplines, the forty-seven essays in this book summarize the state of knowledge and debate about their respective topics and interpret the issues at hand and the challenges for research that lie ahead. The volume differs from related books in at least three respects. First, by primarily featuring chapters by the second and third generations of Holocaust scholars, rather than direct contributions by the pioneers in the field—for example, Yehuda Bauer (b. 1926), Henry Friedlander (b. 1930), Saul Friedländer (b. 1932), Raul Hilberg (1926–2007), and Gerhard Weinberg (b. 1928)—or by other significant senior figures who have retired from teaching (works by some of these senior scholars figure prominently in many of the essays), the book seeks to represent the field at a key juncture in its own evolution.

Second, the book bridges a perhaps widening gap between various disciplinary approaches to the study of the Holocaust. In particular, the preoccupations of Holocaust historians frequently differ greatly from those of colleagues whose interests arise out of somewhat more theoretical or artistic fields. Indeed, the principal books that might be likened to this one fall decisively on one side or another of this divide. Michael Marrus, *The Holocaust in History* (1987), Michael Berenbaum and Abraham J. Peck (eds.), *The Holocaust and History* (1998), Dan Stone (ed.), *The Historiography of the Holocaust* (2004), Donald Bloxham and Tony Kushner, *The Holocaust: Critical Historical Approaches* (2005), and Dan Stone, *Histories of the Holocaust* (2010) all focus mainly on historical issues and historians' concerns. Neil Levi and Michael Rothberg (eds.), *The Holocaust: Theoretical Readings* (2003) and R. Clifton Spargo and Robert M. Ehrenreich (eds.), *After Representation? The Holocaust, Literature, and Culture* (2010) are representative examples of similar sorts of work focused on literary or cultural studies. Michael L. Morgan (ed.), *A Holocaust Reader: Responses to the Nazi Extermination* (2001), Eve Garrard and Geoffrey Scarre (eds.), *Moral Philosophy and the Holocaust* (2003), David Patterson and John K. Roth (eds.), *After-Words: Post-Holocaust Struggles with Forgiveness, Reconciliation, Justice* (2004), and David Patterson and John K. Roth (eds.), *Fire in the Ashes: God, Evil, and the Holocaust* (2005) explore philosophical and religious reflections on the Holocaust, but none of these volumes does the bridgework found here, which encourages readers to rethink and extend what they "know" about the Holocaust and its aftereffects. Third, a substantial portion of the book is devoted to the Holocaust's aftermath, engaging issues that the historically-oriented titles just mentioned do not emphasize. Thus, the *Handbook* addresses those interested in the Holocaust's implications for postwar political, philosophical, judicial, ethical, and religious developments.

Conventional treatments of the Holocaust often emphasize a three-dimensional analysis that concentrates on perpetrators, victims, and bystanders. Gestures are made to the pre-1933 context and to some of the post-Holocaust implications and reverberations of the Nazi genocide, but typically the latter topics are not discussed in much detail. Without abandoning insights from the perpetrator–victim–bystander rubric, the organization and content of *The Oxford Handbook of Holocaust Studies* call for reevaluation, stress new historical findings, encourage exploration of heretofore unraised questions, advance interdisciplinary perspectives and integrative approaches, and expand the contextual horizons—before and after the Holocaust—in order to increase understanding of the genocide and its implications.

ENABLERS

Part I of the book consists of six chapters that concentrate on *enablers*, the broad and necessary contextual conditions for the Holocaust, and stresses the ways in which attitudes or experiences associated with each of the title terms were linked by particular actors to the occurrence of the Holocaust. These chapters, like all good historical analysis of causation, seek to strike the appropriate interpretive balance between individual agency and the force of influential currents of opinion at a given time and place. A governing theme throughout the book, supported by and influencing research, is that specific conditions, decisions, and actions were necessary for the Holocaust to happen, but it was neither fated nor determined. The Holocaust happened because humans made certain choices and rejected others, often abetted by intellectual environments that narrowed their horizons and disposed them in cruel directions. Thus, human agency, accountability, and responsibility loom large in the chapters that follow, including those on the enablers of the Holocaust.

Antisemitism, science, nationalism, colonialism, fascism, and the world wars were all contributors to the occurrence of the Holocaust, but issues remain and debates swirl regarding exactly how so. Richard Levy's opening chapter addresses the phenomenon of organized antisemitism in the sixty years preceding the "Final Solution," primarily in Germany but with comparisons to contemporaneous developments elsewhere in Europe. The author assesses theories that attempt to account for the appearance of political movements aimed at disempowering Jews, profiles the creators and proponents of antisemitic ideology, identifies the social groups they sought to mobilize, and notes the widespread failure of these movements to achieve their goals prior to 1933. Levy finds that decades of organized antisemitism prepared the way for the Holocaust chiefly by eroding popular willingness to defend, indeed to care about, the rights and fates of Jews.

Patricia Heberer's chapter shows how science and medicine, as practiced by influential researchers and physicians in Nazi Germany, were also among the enablers of the Holocaust. The discussion explores a disturbing paradox that remains at the center of research in this area of Holocaust studies: National

Socialism's aim to destroy Jews and other "inferior" groups was legitimated and promoted by respected members of one of the world's preeminent scientific communities. This reality raises a vexing question: Was there such a thing as Nazi science, and, if so, what were its defining features? Investigation of those issues reveals how Nazi authorities harnessed the efforts of scientists and physicians, not only to fuel Germany's war machine and to advance its prestige abroad, but also to achieve the regime's ideological goals and to implement many of its most radical racialist policies.

National Socialism sought a radical restructuring of the European population. The drive to assert German domination over the continent entailed not only territorial conquest and political dictatorship but also demographic engineering, in which the annihilation of the Jews was the core aspiration. Eric Weitz shows that a program of this sort was one possible outcome of nationalism, since that idea and race thinking are closely linked. Both forms of understanding human diversity and defining community developed from the fifteenth and especially the eighteenth century onward in the western world. National Socialism provided particularly intertwined and vicious definitions of nation and race that reveal in stark terms how nationalism, which always carries an exclusionary component, was a necessary enabling condition for the Holocaust.

A long tradition of scholarship has posited colonialism and "racial imperialism" as an enabler of the genocide against European Jewry, though often in imprecise ways. In response, critics of this view have insisted that antisemitism and World War I were the salient enablers, and Germany's colonial experience was too ephemeral to have had serious causal importance. Dirk Moses's chapter changes the terms of debate by presenting the murderous National Socialist program as a colonial and imperial project executed in Europe to compensate for the loss of Germany's empire abroad and in central Europe in 1919. He argues that the style of occupation and warfare Germany conducted in realizing this project was colonial in nature and inspiration, and the Holocaust of European Jewry can be understood in terms of colonial logics as well. At least in part, the Holocaust was, for the Nazis, the attempt of an indigenous people—the Germans—to cast off the perceived exploitative rule of a foreign people: Jews.

Nazism is often distinguished from other European fascist movements, especially Italian fascism, on the grounds that racist antisemitism distinctively defined Nazi ideology and policy. While taking the importance of antisemitism to Nazism as a given, Philip Morgan maintains that racism and antisemitism were implicit in all fascist ideology, although articulated in different forms and ways by individual fascist movements. His analysis emphasizes the common population policies of the fascist regimes in Italy and Germany and evaluates recent scholarship that has changed our understanding of Italian fascist antisemitism and the role of fascism in making the Holocaust possible.

Doris Bergen brings Part I to a close by tracing the complex relationships between the two world wars and the Holocaust, as seen by contemporaries and as understood in hindsight. Jewish diarists knew their fates were linked to the war's outcome; some also noted that atrocity propaganda during the previous world war predisposed the Allies to dismiss evidence of the destruction of Jews. Hitler and other Nazis believed in the stab-in-the-back myth as an explanation of Germany's defeat in World War I and prepared for and fought their own war accordingly, using massive plunder and slave labor to keep the home front happy and coming to insist on the total annihilation of all Jews everywhere as the only way to prevent another defeat. War enabled mass killing of disabled people and brought an ever-widening circle of victims into German hands: Poles, black French soldiers, Soviet POWs, and millions of Jews, although the effects of specific military developments on the fate of Jews were often neither intended nor foreseeable.

PROTAGONISTS

Part II, which concentrates on the principal *protagonists* in the Holocaust, reflects this book's effort to disaggregate the conventional interpretive categories of perpetrator, victim, and bystander. The section explores not only the agency of Nazi leaders and the killers who showed initiative even as they executed orders from above, but also the efforts of Jews, including children and women, to resist and survive the onslaught against them, even as this assault struck them in distinct ways. The chapters under this heading also examine the motives and actions of institutions, such as the Christian churches and Allied and neutral governments, whose behavior affected the course of the Holocaust and its aftereffects. Taking the time-worn term *bystander* to be too general and vague, this section suggests that the term *on-lookers* may do better justice to the internal diversity of the category and includes a chapter on a subgroup that hardly fits under the usual tripartite division, namely those who risked their lives to rescue Jews.

Any credible account of the Holocaust's protagonists must begin with Hitler and Heinrich Himmler (1900–1945), the subjects of Alan Steinweis's chapter. Although research has shown that Nazi anti-Jewish policy was propelled by a complex interaction between the "center" and the "periphery," Hitler remained the decisive figure on key questions. When he did not issue specific instructions, he set the direction and goals of policy, permitting his subordinates to "work toward the Führer." At pivotal moments, such as the launchings of the November pogrom of 1938 and the "Final Solution" in 1941, Hitler acted decisively to move anti-Jewish measures to a higher level of brutality. Although Himmler did not play a key role in

Nazi anti-Jewish policy before World War II, he eventually came to be instrumental in translating Hitler's will into action. Himmler received this role because he had molded the SS into a cadre of hardened, dependable ideological soldiers who possessed the wherewithal and the motivation to undertake the difficult task of mass murder.

Looking beyond Hitler and the most prominent Nazi leaders, Christopher Browning demonstrates how lesser-known "problem solvers" were essential Holocaust protagonists during four phases of Nazi Jewish policy: 1933–1939, when the regime disemancipated, isolated, and impoverished the Jews of Greater Germany and drove over half of them abroad; 1939–1940, when the regime sought to clear its expanding empire of Jews through schemes of massive ethnic cleansing; 1941, when the definition of a "Final Solution" to the self-imposed Jewish Question became systematic and total mass murder; and 1942–1945, when the Third Reich tried to achieve this goal. At every turn, the regime encountered myriad problems. In a political culture encouraging activism and initiative, cadres of middle-echelon experts, functionaries, and technocrats "working toward the Führer" made many of the decisions and devised many of the measures that drove this lethal radicalization.

These problem solvers included the killers who are the subject of Edward Westermann's chapter. The victims of the Holocaust died not only by the thousands in gas chambers and in mass shootings, but also daily in small groups or alone during cold-blooded reprisals or at the whim of soldiers, policemen, and Nazi administrators. The executioners included the various forces of Himmler's SS and police empire, ethnic German and indigenous auxiliaries, and units of the German armed forces. Westermann lays bare the complex dispositional and situational factors that made these organizations so devastating to the regime's putative political, social, and racial enemies.

Absent "bystanders," the perpetrators of the Holocaust could not have inflicted such harm on their victims. Yet that claim, which has been a chief ingredient of the conventional tripartite classification of actors in the genocide, obscures as much as it reveals. A key reason is that the "bystander" category embraces a larger and more heterogeneous population than its counterparts. Just as the category's boundaries are imprecise and fluctuating, so are the theoretical and methodological discussions about bystanders, all the more so because their passivity seems to arouse especially intense moral outrage in retrospect. Paul Levine explores how a different concept, "on-lookers," may deepen scholarly analysis by directing attention to protagonists who "viewed" the Holocaust in various ways, at different times, and in diverse political and social contexts, and then *acted* accordingly. Exploring how these on-lookers, whether citizens of democracies or authoritarian states, faced similar dilemmas when formulating their responses to mass murder sheds light not only on key aspects of Holocaust history but also on the important role of effective teaching about this subject in education to prevent genocide.

Some witnesses to the plight of Jews under the swastika decided to intervene by becoming rescuers. Debórah Dwork shows that their actions evolved as the Nazi persecution radicalized: whereas "rescue" in the prewar years meant helping "refugees," it meant hiding Jews and assisting their flight once Nazism expanded. Common to both periods, however, was the fact that rescuers—male and female, urban and rural, gentile and Jewish, of all ages, social classes, and degrees of religious observance—stepped forward individually and collectively, despite all odds, to save lives. The rescuers did not derail the Holocaust, but without them the number of Jewish deaths would have been larger and the genocide's aftereffects more devastating.

Identifying Jews solely as *victims* of the Holocaust, a classification long employed in Holocaust studies, begs more questions than it answers because this approach tends to underplay the active and even proactive stance of Jews who at every turn did what they could to defend and preserve their lives. At times paralleling Dwork's findings but also extending them, Dan Michman surveys the multiple ways in which Jews confronted the Holocaust. Following background discussion about Judaism and modern Jewish history, he examines how Jews in the 1930s and 1940s comprehended and reacted to the Nazi onslaught, examining Jewish leadership within and outside of Europe, ways of perseverance and resistance, and modes of documenting the Jewish experience. His chapter concludes with an account of Jewish losses and the Holocaust's impact on Jewish culture and peoplehood.

Holocaust studies recognized only haltingly the impact of gender differences on the roles of Jews as protagonists during the genocide, and correcting this shortcoming remains a work in progress. Lenore Weitzman advances that work by concentrating on the experiences of Jewish women during the Holocaust and comparing their predicaments with those of Jewish men. She highlights three topics: the initial responses of Jewish men and women to Nazi persecution, which reflected the traditional roles women played before World War II and therefore prioritized women's responsibilities as mothers, wives, and daughters; the Nazi policies and rules that treated men and women differently and created distinctive constraints and options for women; and the effect of specific problems in the ghettos and camps on women's coping strategies. Her analysis gives special attention to the fraught topic of the incidence of rape of Jewish women during the Holocaust.

That the Holocaust took an immense toll on children is a fact both well-known and under-researched in Holocaust studies. Typically overlooking how children took action rather than were acted upon, the popular depiction of children in the Holocaust tends toward the sentimental, with murdered innocence at its center. Nicholas Stargardt explores how historians, at least since the late 1980s, have subjected the experience of children to more searching analysis, without making their fate any less shocking. Nazism had a special interest in children, both in shaping the next generation of German children and in eliminating the offspring of

Jews, Sinti, Roma, and other so-called degenerates. At every stage of persecution, children were targeted in specific ways, from "Jew benches" in schools, through the medical killing of children in psychiatric asylums, to selection in the death camps. Children, however, were anything but passive victims. New research has revealed much about their experience of ghettoization, in particular their adeptness at smuggling, hiding, and adopting new identities, languages, and religious beliefs. Investigating children's relationships and roles helps delineate the forms and limits of youthful adaptation in extremity.

Catholic and Protestant churches were on-lookers and sometimes worse, as their responses to persecution included forms of inaction that spilled over into complicity. Beginning with an examination of the corrupting influence of Catholic antisemitism on European Christians through the centuries and the role of religious prejudice in advancing racial antisemitism, Kevin Spicer explores the controversial choices and modulated actions of the Catholic Church. He devotes particular attention to German Catholicism's response to the question, "who is my neighbor?" and assesses the reaction and attitude of the Church hierarchy, especially Pope Pius XII (1876–1958), to Nazi acts of persecution.

Robert Ericksen takes up the so-called *Kirchenkampf* (Church Struggle) waged by German Protestants in the Third Reich and finds that it hardly represented forthright opposition to the Nazi state, as claimed by some of its veterans after World War II. According to Ericksen, most Protestants were more supportive than resistant to the Nazi regime. Even the Confessing Church, once considered a resistance movement, showed considerable support for Hitler and little concern for the Jewish victims of his policies. The other side in the church struggle, the *Deutsche Christen*, sought to prove their Nazi credentials by separating Christianity from its Jewish roots, even suggesting an "Aryan Jesus." Some Protestant individuals, such as Martin Niemöller (1892–1984) and Dietrich Bonhoeffer (1906–1945), did oppose Nazi policies at risk to their lives. More typical, however, was Gerhard Kittel (1888–1948), a renowned theologian who joined the Nazi Party in 1933, claimed a natural affinity between Christianity and Nazism, and engaged in polemics against Jews.

The Big Three Allies—Great Britain, the United States, and the Soviet Union—ultimately brought vast military power to bear against the Third Reich, thus obtaining its unconditional surrender. But as Nazi pressure on Jews turned into the "Final Solution," the Allies' actions usually did not assign priority to defending or rescuing the victims. Shlomo Aronson explains this pattern with reference to the Allies' prewar immigration and refugee policies, political and military objectives during World War II, and concerns about domestic public opinion. He finds that the Jewish fate was determined largely by the continuous interplay between Nazi Germany's antisemitic propaganda and the Allies' desire to avoid the impression that they were fighting to benefit the Jews.

Other groups—for example, Sinti and Roma, homosexuals, and Slavs—were swept up in the maelstrom of the Holocaust, but not for the same reasons as Jews and not with the same consequences. John Connelly shows that despite the absence of guidelines in the ideological writings of the top Nazi leadership, the Nazi regime raised popular German resentments and prejudices toward these groups to the level of policy, thus denying millions of human beings their elemental rights, often even their lives. In none of these cases, however, was the target group considered dangerous or coherent enough to warrant complete or immediate extirpation. This circumstance constitutes a significant difference from policies pursued toward the Jews, a difference that helps to clarify and define the Holocaust itself.

SETTINGS

Because the actions of the Holocaust's protagonists and the forms the persecution took literally were grounded in particular places, sites, and physical circumstances, Part III concentrates on key Holocaust *settings*. Wolf Gruner begins by surveying the concept and reality of "Greater Germany." After World War I, the idea of bringing all European Germans together in a single political entity was shared by many people, including Hitler. This "folkish" project entailed the expulsion of the Jews, but detailed directives from above for anti-Jewish policy were lacking when the Nazis first came to power in 1933, so central, regional, and local administrations enjoyed enormous freedom of action. Many mayors and city officials, both National Socialists and non-Party members among them, introduced measures excluding Jews from public facilities. Often extending beyond the few new national anti-Jewish laws, such actions, coordinated by the German Council of Municipalities, were tolerated by the Nazi government. This controlled decentralization of anti-Jewish policy dominated until 1938, when the annexation of Austria prompted a centralization of persecution and the increasing likelihood of war fostered radical new ideas, such as ghettoization and forced labor. Municipalities carried out the former, and the ministerial bureaucracy the latter, as well as the deportations of 1941–1943 that allowed Hitler and his government to realize, if only briefly, their Pan-German dream.

That dream envisioned an expansion of "living space," which oriented Hitler's regime eastward. Wendy Lower assesses Nazi intentions for eastern Europe, which were colonial by design, and discusses how Nazi leaders sought to restructure Germanized "living space" economically and racially. While underscoring the importance of the imperial context in which the Holocaust occurred, Lower also cautions that causally linking the campaigns of genocide and ethnic German resettlement can be misleading. She shows that the two processes were synchron-ized in wartime Poland, but far less so in Belorussia, Ukraine, and the Baltic states. Although settler colonialism and antisemitism were European traditions that the Nazis forged into one genocidal ideology, these two policy tracks often diverged in practice because of regional peculiarities, the changing conditions of the war, and the behavior of local collaborators.

Radu Ioanid's chapter on "Occupied and Satellite States" also underlines the many paradoxes that accompanied the destruction of European Jewry during World War II. Aside from Germany, no country was so directly involved in killing Jews as Romania, yet half of that country's Jewish population, the third largest in Europe, survived the Holocaust. Hungary participated in murdering most of its Jewish community near the end of the war, even after Germany's defeat and the likelihood of retribution for genocide had become clear. Bulgaria, another German ally, destroyed "only" the Jews from its newly acquired territories. In spite of prevalent and intense antisemitism, Croatia massacred more Serbs then Jews. The Netherlands, a country with relatively weak antisemitic traditions, lost a much larger share of its Jews than France, the home of the Dreyfus Affair, and Italy, although a German ally, was disinclined to let Jews under its jurisdiction be killed. In a chapter that helps to map the vastness of the Holocaust, Ioanid reveals how contemporary Holocaust scholarship interprets the origins and unfolding of these counterintuitive variations in behavior.

Every analysis of the Holocaust must deal with places such as ghettos, labor sites, and camps, but what are the most current findings and issues about them? Narratives about the ghettos in Warsaw and Łódź have dominated the depiction of Jewish ghettoization during the Holocaust, but Martin Dean shows that these two cases diverged considerably and were hardly representative. The Germans created more than 140 ghettos in the Polish territories incorporated into the Reich, approximately 380 in the General Government, and more than 600 in other occupied territories. Dean explores the similarities and differences that characterized this ghastly and still incompletely researched aspect of the Holocaust. Meanwhile, recent studies show that forced labor sites were far more numerous than previously thought. While maintaining that the term "slave labor" understates the condition of Jewish workers during the Nazi era, Mark Spoerer provides a taxonomy of the Nazi regime's use of forced, especially Jewish, labor from 1938 to 1945 and outlines the circumstances that made such labor lethal to greater or lesser degrees in particular times and places. Concluding Part III, Karin Orth shifts the focus on Holocaust settings to the evolution of the Nazi concentration camp system. She discusses how this system evolved from a relatively small network of installations dedicated to punishing "unreliable" Germans prior to World War II into an empire under the control of the Inspectorate of Concentration Camps (IKL) and the Economic Administration Main Office (WVHA) of the SS. Eventu-ally, this system encompassed more than twenty main camps, some 900 satellite installations, and a prisoner population that peaked in 1944 at over 700,000. Six of these camps became devoted to the mass murder of the European Jews in ways and numbers that Orth summarizes.

REPRESENTATIONS

The Holocaust's magnitude and devastation are known from documents and diaries, testimonies and trials, and artifacts and places, and because literature, film, art, music, memorials, museums, and other acts of remembering keep directing attention toward those realities. At every turn, however, questions remain about how the Holocaust can and should be grasped—detailed, described, depicted—for the event's vastness and particularity, its horrors and implications seem to confound articulation and comprehension. In response to those challenges, Holocaust studies rely on historical analysis, interpretation of texts, artistic creation and criticism, and philosophical and religious reflection to find the most adequate, if always fallible and limited, ways to state what happened and what the meaning of the event(s) or lack of meaning may be. Part IV turns to such issues by considering *representations* of the Holocaust.

Without documentation provided by German sources, understanding of the Holocaust would be severely hampered. Peter Fritzsche amplifies this point by showing that German government offices and private diarists and correspondents kept widely scattered but extensive records of the unfolding of the "Final Solution." Anti-Jewish legislation ensured that the paper trails of persecution ran to the far corners of the German bureaucracy. Moreover, the perpetrators of anti-Jewish actions at the local and national level commemorated their deeds, in effect preparing initial drafts for a victorious history of the destruction of Jewish life. Private diaries and letters not only confirm the widespread knowledge that Germans came to share about the "Final Solution," but also the process by which many of them came to endorse cruelty toward Jews.

Without documentation provided by Jewish sources, understanding of the Holocaust would be equally impaired. Arguably diary and memoir writing by Jews was the most significant and typical literary phenomenon of the Holocaust period. Amos Goldberg shows that Jews from almost all ages and cultural backgrounds wrote such documents in nearly all locations of persecution, including Auschwitz. Treating the "Holocaust diary" as a linguistic-cultural phenomenon, this chapter offers a typology: the "documentary diary" focuses on recording events and raises the question of cultural continuity; the "synecdochical diary" concentrates on the writer's individual experience and its relation to history; the "reflective diary" explores existential and semi-philosophical issues. Goldberg concludes by examining the reception of diaries and commenting on whether these texts bear witness to the persistence of the human spirit or precisely the opposite.

Jews who fled or hid from the Nazis, endured the ghettos and camps, and survived shooting squadrons have provided eyewitness testimony that is invaluable for glimpsing what the Holocaust was and how it happened. But, as Henry Greenspan's chapter emphasizes, hearing or reading survivor testimony, really hearing or reading it, requires careful attention to detail, nuance, and even silence. Greenspan traces the history of survivors' recounting, from the testimony-gathering projects immediately after liberation to the emergence of survivors in the public role of "witness" in recent decades. Throughout, the survivors' audiences (readers and listeners) have played a central, sometimes inhibiting, and sometimes facilitating role in retelling. Greenspan maintains that the core task of recounting is, as one survivor put it, to "make a story of what is 'not a story.'" He reviews the use of survivors' narratives in historiography but rejects the proposition that recounting is simply "oral history." Containing a wide range of personal responses to the destruction, survivor accounts equally include informative reflection on the processes of remembering and retelling.

Compared to accounts and documents from the Holocaust years or later testimony from survivors, most forms of Holocaust-related literature, film, art, and music involve perspectives and sensibilities that stand at various levels of distance from the Holocaust itself. Sara Horowitz's chapter discusses the development of literature of the Holocaust since World War II and endorses a broad definition of Holocaust literature that embraces a range of genres, subject positions, and literary traditions. Horowitz argues that such works both resist and embrace integration into the continuum of Jewish and western thought and expression. Holocaust literature mediates life and death, survival and memory, during and after the war, through indirection, fragmentary narratives, and other literary strategies. Self-reflexively ambivalent about literary representation, works of Holocaust literature negotiate the inherent contradictions between historical and imaginative discourses, paradoxically insisting on the need to narrate the events and inner experiences of the Nazi genocide and the impossibility of doing so adequately. As Holocaust imagery increasingly permeates western culture, literature offers not only an ethical discourse of mourning and commemoration but also metaphors for psychological states, social and political issues, and contemporary evil.

In the cinematic world, Lawrence Baron observes, the representation of the Holocaust began with the Third Reich's propaganda films and the footage taken by the Allies at liberated concentration camps. In the early postwar period, European filmmakers exaggerated resistance against Nazi Germany's policies and obscured the specificity of Jewish victimization, while Hollywood avoided the topic, allegedly because it was too depressing and parochial. The NBC miniseries *Holocaust* (1978) and Claude Lanzmann's documentary *Shoah* (1985) shattered these patterns, and *Schindler's List* (1993) and *Life Is Beautiful* (1997) stimulated a second round of Holocaust-related cinema and scholarship on it, along with considerable controversy. Baron's analysis shows that studies of Holocaust films made in particular nations have been a staple of research in the field, but that scholarship has shifted since 2000 toward analysis of the cinematic qualities of Holocaust-related film, the impact of globalization, comparisons with portrayals of other genocides, and the use of film in Holocaust education.

Dora Apel's chapter on Holocaust-related art connects with Baron's study of film because she argues that Theodor Adorno's (1903–1969) postwar rejection of aesthetics led to indirect, allusive, and elegiac forms of Holocaust representation until the 1980s and 1990s, when artists born after World War II began to rebel against this paradigm and to address the Holocaust as they encountered it through media representation. Incorporating irony and satire, their new strategies of representation focus on contemporary uses of Holocaust meaning, such as the continuing presence of fascist aesthetics in advertising or the exploitation of memory in contemporary political policies. Apel's discussion draws on the controversy surrounding the 2002 exhibition *Mirroring Evil* at the Jewish Museum in New York to analyze the continuing debate between those who believe that Auschwitz is owned by its victims and those who believe that an ossified and sacralized pedagogy of the Holocaust does not engage newly constituted global contexts.

Few artistic expressions stir human feeling more than music. Not surprisingly, therefore, music played key parts in the Holocaust. Richard Wagner's (1813–1883) operas deeply affected Hitler. The Nazis suppressed music by Jewish composers and dismissed Jewish professional musicians. In Theresienstadt and other ghettos, concerts were given, operas staged, and musical works were written by Jewish musicians. As the "Partisans' Song" illustrates, music encouraged Jewish resistance as well. Music continues to be important in relation to the Holocaust, posing and responding to challenges and prospects for representing that event. Bret Werb surveys the repertoire of Holocaust-related music—a category encompassing commemorative music, musical settings of relevant texts, and works dramatizing events in Holocaust history—in classical and popular genres, and places these works in the context of stylistic trends and cultural-political developments. He also identifies the repertoire's most frequently employed subjects and texts—the Warsaw ghetto, Auschwitz, Anne Frank (1929–1945), children's poetry from Theresienstadt—and discusses Holocaust representation in folk song, topical song, rock and roll, jazz, and rap.

Holocaust memorials and museums depend on all the forms of representation noted above, but as James Young indicates, they become places and provide occasions that represent the Holocaust in their own distinctive ways. Public memorialization of the Holocaust era began early, with every affected group remembering its own fate. The more events of World War II and the Holocaust recede in time, the more prominent museums and memorials about them become. As survivors have struggled to bequeath memory of their experiences to the next generations and governments have sought to unify disparate polities with "common" national narratives, a veritable "Holocaust memorial and museums boom" has occurred. Since 1990, hundreds of museums and institutions have been established worldwide to remember and tell the history of Nazi Germany's destruction of the European Jews. Young emphasizes that depending on who builds these memorials and museums and where, they recollect this past according to particular national myths, ideals, and political needs. At a more specific level, these museums also reflect the temper of the memory-artists' time, their architects' schools of design, and their physical locations in national memorial landscapes.

AFTEREFFECTS

Interpretation of documents and diaries, survivor testimony, literature and film, art and music, memorials and museums—all are part of the Holocaust's reverberations. Part V, focused on *aftereffects*, explores the Holocaust's impact on politics and ethics, education and religion, national identities and international relations, the prospects for genocide prevention, and the defense of human rights. The Holocaust has shattered cherished assumptions about human goodness and optimistic hopes about progress. For that reason, the Holocaust's aftereffects contain immense challenges. Reflection about them, informed by multiple disciplines and approaches, rightly has become an increasingly important aspect of Holocaust studies.

Some of the Holocaust's aftereffects came soon, others later, but whenever they were felt, they have lingered and often intensified. An immediate aftereffect was the liberation and dispersal of Holocaust survivors, the topic of Arieh Kochavi's chapter. When World War II ended, Germany contained fewer than 28,000 German Jews and 60,000 Jewish survivors from other countries. By the end of 1947, approximately 250,000 Jews constituted some 25 percent of all the Displaced Persons (DPs) in the British, French, and American occupation zones of Germany. Most of this influx of refugees came from Soviet bloc countries with Moscow's knowledge and consent, and the overwhelming majority concentrated in American-occupied territory, where they received preferential treatment. In contrast, Britain's restrained policy toward the Jewish DPs stemmed first and foremost from its efforts to keep them from entering Palestine. For their part, the Jewish DPs created self-governing Jewish camps and started their long process of mental and physical rehabilitation with the aid of refugee organizations. Many had to stay in Germany and Austria for years, at least until the establishment of the State of Israel, because the western democracies were ambivalent about admitting them.

While Jewish DPs acted on the available options, the victorious Allies launched what became a series of postwar judicial proceedings against accused war criminals that continues more than sixty years after World War II ended. Rebecca Wittmann's chapter points out, however, that the most famous postwar trials seldom centered on the Holocaust. Although the indictments of Nazi leaders, followers, bureaucrats, camp guards, lawyers, doctors, and businessmen prompt most people nowadays to think primarily of the "Final Solution," virtually all postwar prosecutions categorized the offenses at issue as war crimes, crimes against peace, crimes against humanity, or ordinary murder and manslaughter. The importance of these trials remains, as does that of the sometimes appropriate but often mild punishments meted out. However, recognition of the significance and distinctiveness of the Holocaust mainly came about in other ways.

Massive theft, a key aspect of the Holocaust itself, was among the most widespread offenses committed by Hitler's regime and its collaborators, and ever since World War II ended, international negotiations and legal proceedings have generated a halting and incomplete process of compensating or restituting the losses of successive categories of Holocaust victims. Peter Hayes surveys the methods and extent of the Nazi plunder from Jews and the reasons why recovering it or obtaining recompense has been so drawn out and, in the end, only partially successful. He concludes that the quest for "justice" in this sphere was flawed in a number of respects, but as necessary as it was impossible.

As restitution cases indicate, some aftereffects have brought increased attention and visibility to the Holocaust, but Deborah Lipstadt's chapter examines efforts by those who would do the opposite by denying that the genocide took place. Holocaust denial pivots around and is defined by the claim that the Jews invented the story of the Holocaust to win sympathy from the world, money from Germany, and land in the Middle East. Deniers contend that the Nazis sought to uproot the Jewish community, not to kill it, that the gas chambers did not exist, that the number of Jews killed by Nazis was substantially smaller than six million, and that those who did die perished because they were partisans, criminals, or spies, not because they were Jews. Historians who have traced deniers' claims back to their supposed proofs have found repeated distortions, inventions, and fabrications, and in a celebrated British legal case involving Lipstadt and David Irving (b. 1938), the British judge ruled that denial is based on a "distortion and manipulation of historical evidence." Unfortunately, Holocaust denial continues to be persistent and pernicious, courtroom proceedings against deniers notwithstanding, as it morphs into current forms that include fueling hostility toward Israel in ongoing Middle East conflicts.

Nowhere have the Holocaust's impacts been more decisive and long-lasting than in the State of Israel, Jewish culture, and Judaism. Taking up the first of those topics, Boaz Cohen shows how Zionists wanted to make *Eretz-Israel* a haven for Jews, a need exacerbated by the Holocaust. Israel's establishment in 1948 both moved in that direction and intensified debate about how the Holocaust should be remembered. Underscoring the survivors' contributions to Israeli commemoration of the Holocaust, Cohen assesses the dynamics of Holocaust memorialization in Israel, showing how memory of the Holocaust remains decisive in Israeli identity and policy.

Expanding the horizon beyond contested Israeli borders, Jeffrey Shandler maintains that the Holocaust not only has become a mainstay of Jewish culture but also has engendered an array of cultural practices across the spectrum of Jewish ideological and geographical diversity. At the same time, the subject has prompted debates over the nature—or even the possibility—of "proper" Holocaust remembrance. Jewish culture is engaged in forging new, definitional narratives of Jewish experience that respond to the Holocaust and in establishing new cultural practices of Holocaust remembrance. Some of these rest on precedents for Jewish responses to calamity and others on the influence of new authorities, notably Holocaust survivors. Implicated in this discovery process are new forms of engagement between Jews and other religious and national groups, especially as Jews consider the implications of the wide embrace of Holocaust remembrance beyond their own communities, where it often figures as a master moral paradigm.

Relationships between Jewish culture and Judaism have been immensely complicated by the Holocaust. The two are intertwined but not identical. If the Holocaust continues to inform and challenge what being Jewish can and should mean, those issues embed themselves deeply in ongoing reflection about the implications of the Holocaust for Judaism. Michael Berenbaum contends that the impact of the Holocaust on Judaism and particularly on Jewish theological reflection did not reach full force until the 1960s. Since that time, attention to the Shoah's implications for Jewish religious thought and practice has been intense and widespread. Emphasizing the post-Holocaust reflection of David Weiss Halivni (b. 1927), this chapter explores key currents and debates in post-Holocaust Judaism as it wrestles with questions about God and Jewish life. The role of Holocaust survivors looms large in these issues. Their example enlarges senses of conscience and responsibility, decency and dignity, suggesting that if the Holocaust itself was devoid of God, that absence need not characterize the Shoah's aftermath.

Absent Christianity and its centuries-long hostility toward Jews and Judaism, the Holocaust scarcely would have been possible. What difference has that recognition made to Christian traditions, institutions, and Christians themselves? Stephen Haynes addresses these aftereffects of the Holocaust, underscoring how reflection on Christianity and the Holocaust has produced challenging questions, fierce debates, and a voluminous literature. As with Holocaust studies generally, perspectives have evolved steadily in the decades since the end of World War II, with new developments catalyzed by important publications. Haynes tracks what he takes to be the three salient issues in Christianity's unsettling and unfinished encounter with the Holocaust: the relationship between Christian belief and anti-semitism, the role of Christian people and institutions during the Nazi era, and the post-Holocaust need to change Christian understandings of Jews and Judaism.

The Holocaust emerged out of Christendom, and Germany has been a key part of that cultural, political, and religious reality. But what of the Holocaust's impact on postwar German politics, identity, and international conduct? Tracking such issues, Jeffrey Herf shows that a distinctive form of memory of the Holocaust arose in Germany following World War II as a byproduct of total military defeat, Allied occupation, and the restoration of previously suppressed German political trad-itions. In East Germany, the memory of the suffering and triumph of the Soviet Union loomed far larger in "anti-fascist" political culture than the fate of Europe's Jews. The limits of justice and memory in the two Germanys after 1945 are striking in view of the enormity of the crime of the Holocaust. However, compared with the amnesia and paucity of justice that often have followed other criminal dictator-ships, the West German and then unified German confrontation with the crimes of the Nazi era have yielded a distinctive mixture of some truth telling, some judicial reckoning, some excellent historical scholarship, and some compassion for the survivors of the Holocaust.

Not only Germany but virtually all of Europe was implicated if not complicit in the Holocaust. Jan-Werner Müller examines the Holocaust's aftereffects on Euro-pean sensibilities. Noting that the National Socialists frequently invoked a value-laden, antisemitic, and anti-Bolshevik conception of "Europe" to justify their creation of a "New Order" that subjugated nations and exterminated races, he observes that this European dimension of the Holocaust was often forgotten after World War II. The construction of the European Community from the 1950s onwards was presented as a means to prevent the recurrence of war between European nation-states; references to the Holocaust were notable for their absence. That situation began to change with the end of the Cold War and the supposed legitimacy crisis of what had by 1992 become the European Union (EU), which tried to link its value to remembrance of the Holocaust and specific moral and political lessons derived from the genocide. This project found its clearest practical expression in the sanctions against Austria when Jörg Haider's nationalist Freedom Party (FPÖ) entered government in 2000. Müller argues that any European politics of memory centered on the Holocaust should be approached very carefully and counsels against treating the Holocaust as a kind of "founding myth" for the EU.

The Holocaust's aftereffects have spread far and wide, influencing, for example, academic fields in the social sciences and humanities and the theory and practice of Holocaust-related education. James Waller's chapter assesses where the field of Holocaust studies has been and is going with respect to sociology, psychology, anthropology, political science, and economics. Following an analysis of social scientific approaches, methods, and issues that have been engaged in understanding perpetrator behavior, Waller examines relationships between Holocaust studies and the broader field of comparative genocide studies. His account discusses the emergence of social scientists as scholar-activists in Holocaust and genocide studies and outlines challenges that await current and future social scientific approaches to Holocaust studies.

Turning to the humanities, Berel Lang's chapter begins by emphasizing that the concepts of truth, fact, and verifiability—mainstays in the modern history of the humanities as well as of science—came under the increasing pressure of skepticism in the late nineteenth and twentieth centuries. This trend was exemplified in such otherwise different perspectives as those of existentialism, analytic philosophy, historicism, pragmatism, post-structuralism, and postmodernism as those outlooks shaped literary studies, historiography, philosophy, and the humanities in general. The Holocaust poses a distinctive, if not unique, testing point for these fields, since they all, whether in writing about the Holocaust or not, face (at times explicitly, but always tacitly) the challenge of Holocaust-denial: the "either/or" question of the epistemic status of the Holocaust that asks whether it *did* occur or not, with no available third option. How one responds to this question has important consequences for every area of the humanities and the principles of interpretation and explanation on which they depend. The occurrence of the Holocaust has become a line of demarcation for all reflection in the humanities that comes after it.

Simone Schweber scrutinizes Holocaust education, which now takes place across continents and grade-levels and through diverse programs and pedagogies. She argues that research about these efforts and their effects has been underdeveloped, partly because the approaches, objectives, and challenges of Holocaust education necessarily reflect cultural and national differences. While taking these into account, her chapter explores recurrent themes and practices in Holocaust pedagogy, identifying what is underscored and underplayed. Her discussion stresses that the currently predominant context for Holocaust education is the repeated threat of genocidal violence, and she therefore examines how Holocaust education and research about it can foster a sense of global citizenship.

As one looks forward, arguably no aspect of the Holocaust's impact is more important than its influence on reflection, education, and action concerning human rights and ethics. Addressing what David Jones calls the "promise of Nuremberg," which began in 1945 with the Charter of the International Military Tribunal, his chapter argues that the Charter, partly as a response to the evil of the Holocaust, broke dramatically with traditional international law by mandating "individual responsibility" for crimes against peace, war crimes, and crimes against humanity (including extermination) committed by the leaders of the Axis Powers. The Nuremberg Principles were codified into international law by the United

Nations General Assembly in 1946; the Universal Declaration of Human Rights and the Convention on the Prevention and Punishment of Genocide followed in 1948. However, the promise of Nuremberg remains largely unfulfilled. None of these post-World War II documents included mechanisms for executive or judicial enforcement, the UN Security Council was stymied by the power of the veto held by its permanent members, and the UN became a community of bystander states that has allowed numerous genocides and mass killings to occur. Jones contends that among the possibilities for making the world safer for human rights are reform of the Security Council, creation of an international Rapid Response Force, the spread of democracy, and a reduction of poverty in the underdeveloped world.

Echoing a variety of aftereffect themes stressed in Part V, John Roth's concluding chapter argues that absent the overriding of moral sensibilities, if not the collapse or collaboration of ethical traditions, the Holocaust could not have happened. Although the Shoah did not pronounce the death of ethics, it showed that ethics is vulnerable, subject to misuse and perversion, and that no simple reaffirmation of pre-Holocaust ethics, as if nothing disastrous had happened, will do any longer. Exploring those realities and focusing on some of the most important issues they contain, Roth stresses that the Holocaust did not have to happen. It emerged from human choices and decisions. Those facts mean that nothing human, natural, or divine guarantees respect for the ethical values and commitments that are most needed in contemporary human existence, but nothing is more important than our commitment to defend them, for they remain as fundamental as they are fragile, as precious as they are endangered. Ethics may not be enough, but failures notwithstanding, it still provides our best post-Holocaust compass.

Each and all, the contributors have tried to fulfill the tall order that Oxford University Press placed when it commissioned *The Oxford Handbook of Holocaust Studies* as an authoritative, up-to-date guide to the most important issues and salient debates that inform research—currently and yet to come—about the Holocaust. The book's readers will decide how well the following pages meet the challenges of that assignment.

PART I

ENABLERS

CHAPTER 1

....

ANTISEMITISM

....

RICHARD S. LEVY

THE classic definition of *antisemitism* as "any expression of hostility, verbal or behavioral, mild or violent, against the Jews as a group, or against an individual Jew because of his belonging to that group" (Ackermann and Jahoda 1950: 19) is not of much use in the exploration of the Holocaust's ideological underpinnings. Formulated for clinical psychiatric purposes, this, like many other broadly conceived definitions, does not differentiate between the casually prejudiced and the dedicated "full-time" enemies of Jews, between the millions of passive onlookers and those who took the lead in genocide. A conception more historical and more precise, one that considers changing context and functionality, is required to untangle the relationship between antisemitism and mass murder. Constructing this analytical tool ought to begin with distinguishing between an amorphous, ancient, and adaptable body of attitudes regarding Jews, on the one hand, and the willingness to act against Jews for any number of reasons, on the other.

Anti-Jewish sentiments are so readily detectable in history and they vary so greatly in intensity that they are not reliable indicators of antisemitism. Antisemitism is often driven by hatred, but its exponents and exploiters can also be cold-blooded, even indifferent to Jews. Several men responsible for sending thousands of Jews to their deaths during the Holocaust had never expressed animosity toward them prior to it. In contrast, some prominent rescuers of Jews had long records of speaking out against them. In the twentieth as in earlier centuries, negative feelings about Jews did not automatically translate into action.

Antisemites are distinguishable from Jew-haters, whatever their level of affect, by the determination to act decisively. The men who ultimately resolved upon and implemented the extermination of Jewry were animated, at least in part, by the desire to deal with the "problem of the Jews" in a final, irreversible way. No doubt, the anti-Jewish stereotypes elaborated over time affected the mentalities of these individuals, providing their antisemitism with content and context. But, unlike the majority of their contemporaries who shared negative feelings and images regarding Jews, antisemites were not satisfied with mere prejudice or the antagonism usually embedded in it. The ideology that helped move some of them toward murder is what this essay denotes as *antisemitism*.

What follows is an attempt to investigate the connections between organized antisemitism and the genocide of the Jews, giving the greatest weight to the German variant but occasionally comparing it to other contemporaneous antisemitisms. Before the Nazis, antisemitism may have been more deadly in the Russian Empire, more politically charged in France, more empowered in Austria, more socially entrenched in England. Nevertheless, the Holocaust was German in inspiration, so that German history is the place to search for its causes.

Adhering to the distinction between the way Jews were perceived and the way they were acted upon reduces the scope of an investigation of antisemitism as an enabler of the Holocaust from the seemingly impossible to the almost manageable. Concentrating on its activist nature anchors the historian in the sixty years before the execution of the "Final Solution." Jew-haters certainly had acted against Jews well before this time, sometimes producing a murderous violence. These occurrences, however, were usually short-lived, punctuating long periods of co-existence between Jews and non-Jews that were peaceful enough to have left no imprint on the historical record. Only in the last third of the nineteenth century, beginning in Germany but rapidly spreading beyond its borders, did anti-Jewish impulses become institutionalized in political parties, voluntary associations, newspapers, and other publishing ventures. No longer episodic or "defensive," antisemitism entered the political culture of many nations with the stated purpose of disempowering the Jews.

It is surely not coincidental that the word *antisemite* also took root in Germany at this time, appearing in an advertisement announcing an Antisemites' League in late 1879. Self-identified enemies of the Jews, Jews and their non-Jewish defenders, and neutral observers soon began using the new term and the abstraction *antisemitism*. Its swift adoption after 1879—absorption into all the major European languages was complete by 1894—reflected a wide, although sometimes imprecise, recognition that traditional patterns of anti-Jewish persecution had so changed that a special word was now needed to describe a new sort of anti-Jewish activity and activist. Before describing the unfolding of the antisemitic movement in Germany during the 1880s, however, a prior issue needs to be addressed.

Industrial Capitalism, Emancipation, and Antisemitism

Jews had lived dispersed among the nations for nearly two millennia. While subject to discrimination and occasional aggression, they had not had to confront an ideologically driven movement aimed at their systematic ruination. Why then did antisemitism emerge in Europe—and where Europeans settled elsewhere in the world—at this particular moment in history? The near-simultaneous appearance of organized political antisemitism in widely separated places, the homogeneity of its social bases, and the similarity of its charges against Jews point to causes larger than the circumstances of a given country, the dynamic leadership of individual antisemites, or the persuasiveness of antisemitic ideologues. The most likely such large cause, in fact, the only readily identifiable common denominator for disparate movements, was the emergence of industrial capitalism during the nineteenth century. In dissolving the economic and social order of traditional societies and transforming the everyday lives of millions of people, industrial capitalism created new categories of winners and losers in the competition for status and wealth.

In Germany—and in Austria and Hungary as well—the transition from an agricultural to an industrial market economy was proving unsettling even before the crash of 1873. The *Krach*, followed by twenty years of economic uncertainty, took a heavy toll on peasants and the petty bourgeoisie, prompting elements of these groups to take flight into what Hans Rosenberg labeled "the politics of paranoia." He first called attention to the effects of structural economic changes on the lower middle class, particularly its loss of faith in liberalism and consequent opening to several forms of extremism, including antisemitism (Rosenberg 1967: 62–78, 88–9). Although the economic restructuring of the modern era hit these vulnerable strata hard, certain sectors responded to the lure of antisemitism more strongly than others. One such reaction can be seen as a result of the new mass-circulation daily newspapers that began to thrive in the 1870s. German Jews were closely identified with this media revolution, which put many veteran journalists out of work while reducing the status of others to hired hands; several key figures in the developmental stage of the antisemitic movement were disgruntled newspapermen, embittered by what "the Jews" had done to their profession. Similarly, big department stores, another innovation in which German Jews were decisive, put small retailers under heavy competitive pressure: many found their way into antisemitic politics. Cause and effect were not always as striking as in these two examples, but the fluctuating mass appeal of antisemitism, the heightening and slackening of agitation, voting results, and overall size of the movement faithfully reflected the general health of economic life. In Germany, the antisemitic parties and clubs took shape in the wake of the crash of 1873 and expanded during the lingering slump of the next two decades. Economic recovery starting in the mid-1890s gradually sapped the strength of the antisemitic organizations by 1914.

Much recommends an analysis of antisemitism in socio-economic terms, and many scholars in the last few decades have followed Rosenberg's lead. But a purely social-historical approach is at a loss to answer some important questions. For example, it can account for the thriving of antisemitism in periods of crisis but cannot explain why it survived, even at diminished levels of intensity, when good times returned. Perhaps the most serious defect of the approach is its inability to deal with variations of responsiveness among people who experienced the same social and economic conditions. The Protestant peasants of Hesse in central Germany and their Catholic neighbors offer a case in point. While probably sharing the same hostile view of the Jewish middlemen they depended upon, and certainly suffering from the same general economic woes, they behaved in far different ways when it came to politics. The Protestant farmers became the loyal electoral base of the antisemitic parties in the region; the Catholics never elected a candidate of an antisemitic party. Germany's Catholics, who might also be counted among those adversely affected by a modernizing economy, found other ways of dealing with their problems. Extraordinarily vigorous Catholic grassroots organizations regularly resorted to anti-Jewish themes, as did several newspapers and much devotional literature (Blaschke 1997: 61, 117–22). But, with few exceptions, Catholic political leaders refrained from targeting Jews for special legislation or supporting it when advocated by others. Social history obscures rather than illuminates these contrasting expressions of anti-Jewish hostility among Protestants and Catholics.

Social history also fails to explain why all Jews became the objects of social protest. Antisemites did not single out Jews at the forefront of economic change who might be expected to awaken enmity among the cast-offs of a dynamic capitalism. *All* Jews, living and dead, came under attack. Without attention to cultural and psychological factors, and the long history of interaction between Jews and non-Jews, social history can see Jews only as essentially accidental victims of anonymous economic processes. Jews appear in the story most often as scapegoats, an "explanation" of antisemitism that actually denies historical context and explains too little.

Reinhard Rürup (1975), attempting to account for the appearance of antisemitic political movements, gave due recognition to the socio-economic context but sought also to explain why Jews became the targets of protest. By the mid-nineteenth century, freeing Jews from age-old restrictions on citizenship, habitation, and occupation had come to be seen as one of a number of self-evident necessities for a modern country, at least to the governing elite that eventually carried out these changes. The turmoil of the 1870s subjected this reform agenda and especially its liberal champions to a series of challenges. The politicization of the *Jewish question*, a term that came out of the century-long debate over emancipation, and the rise of an organized antisemitic movement can best be understood, according to Rürup, as a somewhat belated reaction to the achievement of Jewish equality in Germany (1869–1871) and in the Habsburg Empire (1867). Emancipation provided the catalyst for the development of antisemitism because it seemed to signal a portentous reversal in the relations between Jews and non-Jews. Jews had not merely gained *equality*, they had been *empowered*, thanks to their liberal allies or pawns. From this time forward, antisemitic movements everywhere hinged on fantasies of enormous Jewish power, acquired in wholly illegitimate ways and used with cold efficiency to subvert all that was holy and good.

Although Rürup's tying of emancipation to the origins of the antisemitic political movement works well for central Europe, it is less satisfactory when applied elsewhere. In France, for example, emancipation dated back to 1791, but an organized antisemitism is difficult to discern there before the 1880s. In the Russian Empire, on the other hand, Jews had to wait until 1917 before winning equal rights, and only when Poland regained its sovereign statehood in 1918 did its Jews also become equal citizens. By these dates, however, organized antisemitism had already been active for many years.

A more flexible formulation for explaining the appearance of antisemitic political movements is offered by Albert Lindemann (1997: 20–3). The "rise of the Jews," rather than any specific legislative or executive granting of equal rights, is what prompted the birth of antisemitic organizational forms. Both Jews and non-Jews were astonished by the upward mobility of the Jewish population during the nineteenth century: as contributors to the arts and sciences, accumulators of wealth, leaders of political parties, and holders of public offices. At the end of the eighteenth century, an estimated 80 percent of German Jews lived in poverty. By 1900, Jews in Frankfurt am Main were paying four times more taxes than Protestants and eight times more than Catholics, a sure sign of their greater income levels. In Hungary during the emancipation era, the Jewish minority provided 50 percent of the medical practitioners, 45 percent of the lawyers, 40 percent of the journalists, and 25 percent of those professionally engaged in the arts. In 1892, just before the Dreyfus Affair broke, three hundred Jewish officers were serving in the French army.

The "rise of the Jews," although indisputable, was far from even and far from universal, as Lindemann notes. Well into the twentieth century, Jewish slums remained in many European cities where eastern European immigrants often had to rely on Jewish welfare agencies. Those Jews who had stayed in the east were "prosperous" only relative to the crushing poverty of their neighbors. In many countries, in defiance of the law, Jews were excluded from or denied advancement in the professional civil service, academia, and the military. This counter-evidence to their seemingly unstoppable advancement made no impression on their enemies, however. Antisemites did not draw fine distinctions, nor were they inclined to balanced judgments. They clung to overdrawn images of Jewish power because such exaggerations lent credibility to their warnings. The relentless advance of the Jews had to be halted or Christians would fall under their yoke for all time. The prospering of Jews also substantiated what was already widely believed concerning the defects of Jewish character. Traditionalists were satisfied to condemn Jews for violating Christian ethical norms. But other antisemites, using fashionable theories of race, rushed to explain the rise of the Jews as the product of inherited "genetic" traits: heartless realism, lust for revenge, soulless materialism—all buttressed by a religion that inculcated dishonesty—had armed the Jews for success in the modern world. The same genetic arsenal that fitted them for worldly riches was leading them to victory in their covert war against the non-Jewish world. Finally, harping on the "rise of the Jews" generated a sense of urgency and stimulated mass mobilization. A people long regarded as morally and physically inferior was seen to be flourishing while honest, hard-working natives suffered. Anger and moral outrage that alien Jews rather than real Germans should be doing so well pervaded the meeting halls and rallies of the organizing movement, a pattern eventually repeated with Romanians, Poles, Frenchmen, and Americans of both hemispheres.

The organizational model designed to remedy this injustice was established in Germany, however. Antisemitic reform clubs, patriotic societies, youth groups, and political parties drew the bulk of their membership from those who felt threatened by modern developments, primarily the until now scarcely organized and at-risk elements of the lower middle classes in town and countryside. Despite the movement's pronounced lower-middle-class character, the appeal of antisemitism reached beyond these groups to a great variety of people, no matter where they stood on the social scale. Those who did the recruiting, edited the newspapers, and placed themselves at the head of the organizations did not always act out of obviously economic grievances or anxieties about declining status, although these motives were often present. For leaders, as well as many of the led, the movement came to define its adherents to themselves and to others. As Shulamit Volkov observed, pre-Nazi antisemitism served them as a cultural code, part of a "cluster of ideas, values, and norms . . . a permanent fixture in the aggressively nationalistic and anti-modern discourse" (2006: 116). Integral nationalists, cultural pessimists, ultraconservatives, anti-socialists and anti-liberals, misogynists, and homophobes were also likely antisemites. Although Volkov's assessment tends to downplay the conscious aim of antisemitism to harm Jews, it usefully points out that "pure antisemitism" was a rarity. The ideology's ability to bond with and energize other causes was and remains part of its power.

WHO WERE THE ANTISEMITES?

The movement everywhere attracted opportunists who had taken notice of antisemitism's mobilizing potential among certain social strata. Powerful men, their purposes sometimes obvious for all to see, tried to exploit antisemitism to defend or increase their power. Another segment of the movement consisted of "situational antisemites," people who attended meetings, sometimes voted for antisemitic candidates, joined various voluntary associations, dropped out, and then joined again. In certain circumstances, they could be persuaded to take action against Jews. At other times, they could not be engaged for such projects, although they probably never abandoned their anti-Jewish prejudices. The mixture of motives in this group makes it difficult to see what bound them together or to measure the degree of priority they gave to combating Jewish power.

The movement's true believers were more persistent and decisive. The antisemites who wanted to act against Jews in a systematic way and for as long as necessary to neutralize the peril they claimed to see were far fewer in number than those who voted for their parties or occasionally attended their meetings. Those who fashioned the movement and remained loyal to its goals through good times and bad shared several traits, no matter what their national origins or personal idiosyncrasies. First, most made a lifelong commitment to the cause. The rare individual might recant, declaring that antisemitism had been a childhood disease, now thankfully outgrown. But the typical "sincere" antisemite was beyond learning or changing. The personal testimonies of several of them speak to the discovery of antisemitism as a consciousness-changing event that made sense out of an entire life and then lent that life purpose. Having unearthed the truth about what mystified so many of their naive compatriots—the dark inner workings of history, politics, society, and culture—these antisemites could not surrender the magical explanation. On the other hand, even though—or perhaps because—antisemites possessed a store of esoteric knowledge, they were often extraordinarily pessimistic about ultimate victory over the Jews. Far into the 1920s, leading voices in the movement could be heard prophesying defeat and future enslavement. The march of Jewish power was so relentless, the defenses of their intended victims were so feeble, the witting and unwitting allies of the Jews were so numerous that the prognosis appeared dismal indeed.

The creators and proponents of the ideology were, for the most part, powerless "little people," who convinced themselves, mistakenly in most cases, that antisemitism could give them a yearned-for importance, avenge insults, or assure their place in history. Thwarted intellectuals were numerous, with irascible academics overrepresented in the group; career failures, frustrated social dropouts, struggling businessmen, déclassé noblemen, and a disproportionate number of the mentally unhinged showed up repeatedly at the national and local levels of antisemitic politics. Yet some of the best known antisemites were models of success. The renowned composer Richard Wagner (1813–1883), Hohenzollern Court Chaplain Adolf Stoecker (1835–1909), the American industrialist Henry Ford (1863–1947), and many internationally known artists and authors had achieved worldly fame and wielded considerable influence in public life before making their significant contributions to organized antisemitism. In Austria, Hungary, Germany, Poland,

and Romania, university student elites became early converts to antisemitism and helped carry its messages to the broad public. Clearly, antisemitism was not exclusively a protest movement mounted by the casualties of modern life.

Those who shaped antisemitic ideology and who led the organized attack against Jews were not, as a rule, stupid or uneducated, nor were they extraordinarily evil. They left the world few great ideas, but they understood how to articulate powerful myths and, at least for short periods of time, rally sizable parts of the public behind their cause. Although they dreamt of a mass movement uniting all their country-men against the common enemy, they found most of their followers on the right side of the political spectrum, among Christian conservatives, extreme nationalists, and violence-prone reactionaries. Radical democrats and socialists might harbor and give voice to many anti-Jewish prejudices, but rarely did they become antisemites. They did not take or urge action against Jews or, with occasional exceptions, attempt to exploit generalized anti-Jewish feelings for political ends. The reason for this difference, however, is not to be found in any greater or lesser appreciation of Jews. The left as well as the right was fettered to traditional anti-Jewish stereotypes, from which only a few broke free. The difference between the two groups had to do, not with Jews, but with contrasting views of the masses of humanity and their potential for democratic emancipation. Antisemites, no matter their other differences, were united in the rejection of democracy. In fact, political antisemitism appealed to them precisely because they saw in it a new and better way of harnessing the power of the people.

THE SOURCES AND STRATEGIES OF ANTISEMITISM

The anti-democratic thought and action that typified the antisemitic movement issued from many sources. A major impulse came from the churches. By the time antisemitism emerged as a political force, militant Christians had come to identify democracy as one of the modern secular evils undermining religion. They put no faith in the autonomous decision-making capacity of the masses, certain that the common people required hierarchy and authority to be truly happy and good. A second strand of anti-democratic thinking was the work of several one-time liberal or democratic intellectuals who had come to antisemitism after having experienced a loss of faith in the people's political capacities. The weak-mindedness of the people, almost as much as Jewish evil itself, was responsible for the Jewish problem. One of their standing complaints was the inability of feckless Germans to see the true dimensions and dangers of the Jewish conspiracy.

At times, antisemites appeared in the guise of populists or as protectors of the defenseless or as fearless critics of the established authorities. Nevertheless, their programs were uniformly antidemocratic. They promised prosperity, national power, or moral regeneration, once the Jews were disempowered, but none envisioned a democratic future as desirable. The masses were too fickle, too undiscerning, to be trusted with their own governance. That they had been invested with voting rights in the first place—thanks to Jewish radicals and revolutionaries—was one reason that the absolutely crucial battle against Jewry had such uncertain prospects.

Despite misgivings about the political intelligence of their countrymen and disdain for democracy, the antisemites' weapon of choice in the struggle against Jewry was political organization. Popular expressions of anti-Jewish feeling had been frequent enough in Germany during the nineteenth century to convince them that the basis of a successful mass mobilization was already in place. They did not have to begin from scratch in educating the public about Jewish evil. The *Volk* could be won over initially through its historic anti-Jewish instincts, rather than its weakly developed rational faculties. Still, much "enlightenment" work remained to be done before this potential could be channeled into effective action against Jews with long-lasting results. The common herd's casual prejudices and occasional outbursts of violence might once have been sufficient to keep the Jews at bay. No longer. In light of the breathtaking growth in Jewish power since emancipation, what was needed now, at the last hour, was not mindless mob violence but a leadership with the virtues rarely found in the *Volk*—scientific rigor, disciplined behavior, and stamina. Combating the Jews by winning elections could begin immediately, but no victory would be permanent until ordinarily prejudiced Germans could be made over into authentic antisemites.

At least to begin with, there was a consensus among antisemites to follow conventional, nonviolent paths to political power: form parties, put up candidates, campaign for them vigorously, and gather strength in successive elections until a parliamentary majority of antisemites or a sufficiently strong bloc of them could win enough allies to legislate Jews out of national life. Petitions organized by activists and circulated by university students in 1880 and 1881, having gathered nearly a quarter million signatures, enunciated what became the basic program for all the German antisemitic parties before World War I: limitation or prevention of Jewish immigration, occupational exclusions—particularly, in the judicial and educational systems—and a special census to determine the "real" number of Jews in the country. This set of demands, modest by twentieth-century standards, nevertheless amounted to revocation of Jewish emancipation and would have required a constitutional amendment, a very ambitious goal.

Organized antisemitism in the German empire accomplished neither this nor any of its other objectives. It reached its high-water mark in the national elections of 1893, in which approximately 350,000 votes (4.4 percent) were cast for identifiable antisemites from all parties, enough to win the three specifically antisemitic parties 16 of the 397 seats in the Reichstag. Uniting themselves into a single party between 1894 and 1900 did not increase their percentage of the vote or number of deputies in the parliament. During the war, all the parties ceased being able to function independently (although some of their content and style migrated in 1917 to the powerful far right and diehard Fatherland Party).

Unable to achieve their major goal, the revocation of emancipation, the anti-semitic parties also failed to pass any overtly anti-Jewish legislation through the national parliament. Many factors contributed to this outcome. Leadership resided in a few fractious individuals who spent much time protecting their power against each other. The movement produced a few notable orators, but they lacked sufficient knowledge or organizational skill to become productive members of a parliament where their allegations of Jewish conspiracy often met with ridicule. Despite being great believers in the power of newspapers to mold public opinion and relentless in their criticism of the "Jewish press hydra," the antisemites were never able—not even after the rise of the Nazis—to produce journals able to rival the big dailies or the papers of their political competitors. The movement's major failing, however, was its inability to expand its constituency. Catholic voters remained steadfastly loyal to the Catholic party. Socialist voters, too, kept aloof from the antisemitic movement. The antisemites could rely only on the lower middle classes, who were numerous but weak in resources and deeply divided in their political loyalties.

This story of futility was repeated virtually wherever antisemites sought to solve the Jewish question within the framework of conventional politics. Hungarian antisemites organized a political party in the aftermath of a sensational ritual murder case and university disturbances in the early 1880s. In close contact with German colleagues and following their example, the Hungarians developed a press, circulated petitions, and proposed legislation. Having succeeded in seizing public attention, their party won a modest electoral success in 1884, gaining seventeen seats (7 percent) in the parliament. But this achievement proved to be their high point of electoral effectiveness; after remaining a factor in Hungarian politics for about a decade, organized antisemitism withered, although it never entirely dis-appeared. Antisemitism in France took shape in the wake of corruption scandals in the 1880s and culminated in the decade-long crisis of the Dreyfus Affair. Although antisemitism played a more significant role in French intellectual life than in other national settings, its drive for political power was no more successful. Taking advantage of the uproar surrounding the second trial of Alfred Dreyfus (1859–1935) and helping to foment violence in several locales, the antisemites won twenty-two seats in the French Chamber of Deputies in the elections of May 1898. But, as elsewhere, they could not build upon this impressive beginning. Their legislative efforts also met with defeat.

The partial exception to this record of ineffectiveness was Austria, one of the only places where antisemites wielded governmental power before the war. In the mid-1880s, the Austrian antisemitic movement produced both a conservative Christian and a radical racist attack on recently emancipated Jews. The pan-German racist movement of Georg von Schönerer (1842–1921) antagonized too many Austrians with its stridently anti-Habsburg, anti-Catholic politics to attract a large following. But the Christian Socials, led by their "uncrowned king" and gifted demagogue, Karl Lueger (1844–1910), ruled Vienna from 1897 onward; after Lueger's death in 1910, his party continued to play a major role in the capital and in Austrian national politics into the 1930s. The sessions Lueger chaired in the city council, reported and seconded by the antisemitic press, vilified Jews in every conceivable way. The diffuse charges, complaints, and insinuations coalesced into an implicit demand for their rigorous exclusion from Austrian society. Yet despite all the passion and posturing, the Christian Socials lacked the power to undo Jewish emancipation and were therefore unable to damage the careers, social standing, or cultural presence of Austria's Jews.

Austrian antisemitism, although exercising governmental power, proved no more effective against its enemies than the German, Hungarian, or French. But was the failure complete? Richard Geehr has argued (1990) that the extremist rhetoric of the Pan-Germans and the Christian Socials, ranging from vulgar insults to threats of death, inspired the next generation of antisemites to act far more decisively against Jews. Although difficult to prove, the proposition merits consideration. For among this next generation was Adolf Hitler (1889–1945), a reader of the antisemitic press and an avid observer of Viennese politics in Lueger's last years. Normally stingy with his praise of predecessors, Hitler expressed special admiration in *Mein Kampf* for both Schönerer and Lueger, "the greatest German mayor."

REVOLUTIONARY ANTISEMITISM

Mainstream antisemites in Imperial Germany had looked to parliamentary politics to curtail Jewish influence in public life. Disempowering the Jews, along with some socio-economic fine-tuning, would strengthen "truly German" peasants, shop-keepers, and artisans, and allow the nation once again to flourish. But the lack of progress in this direction forced antisemites to reevaluate their strategy. Apparently, state and society were more deeply flawed than they had at first wanted to believe. As they lost ground at the polls, they began bitterly criticizing the empire's judicial, educational, and financial institutions, its foreign and domestic policy-making agencies, universal suffrage, and the monarchy itself. Rather than question the truth of their ideology or confront its inability to win over the people, antisemites gravitated toward revolutionary politics.

A general recognition among antisemites that new strategies were needed, combined with the deaths of many of the old leaders just before the war, emboldened those who had stood at the fringes of the movement to take charge. Men who had always derided parliamentary politics, writers, culture critics, and independent activists now seized the opportunity to present much more radical solutions to the Jewish question. Few in number and with little or no organizational underpinnings, they were nevertheless heard from more frequently, scorning the errors of the conventional antisemites, both personal and ideological, that had led a noble cause to stagnation, if not defeat. These newly prominent spokesmen for the cause were not restrained by even nominal respect for the empire's basic institutions. Talk of vigilante violence, calls for the expropriation of the property of Jews, their segregation or even expulsion, and the urgent need to form conspiratorial cadres surfaced amid the ruins of the movement. Mere "adjustments" would no longer suffice to defeat the ever-growing power of the Jews. The crisis situation called for thorough, top-to-bottom transformation, a "revolutionizing of German values" and the institutions that supported them. Only then could the problem of the Jews be dealt with decisively. As Hitler emerged politically during the chaotic early years of the Weimar Republic, the vocabulary of a more radical antisemitism was already prevalent. He needed to invent nothing.

Another consequence of the failure of conventional antisemitism was the growing influence of several extraparliamentary voluntary associations. In Germany, the Agrarian League, the German-National White Collar Employees Association, and a number of small, conspicuously anti-parliamentary "cultural" organizations, with names like the Reich Imperial League or the German Union or the Alliance against the Arrogance of Jewry, took over as the major disseminators of antisemitism, reaching a wider public than ever before. With greater resources and operational competence than the antisemitic political parties, these groups had the potential to do greater harm to Jews. Leaders of the organizations, recognizing the potential of antisemitism to seize public attention and energize the rank and file, quickly moved to incorporate it into their programs, publications, and lobbying activities. For most, antisemitism was essentially instrumental, a means of bringing pressure to bear on government or drumming up public support for the group's special interests. A specific organization's use of antisemitism could therefore vary over time, depending on conditions and calculations that had little to do with "solving the Jewish question." The Agrarian League remained doggedly antisemitic, but the white collar association occasionally wavered when it found antisemitism an impediment to advancing the economic interests of its membership.

Overall, these groups spoke to the same constituency as had the antisemitic parties, the rural and urban lower middle classes. But, as we have seen, antisemitism had never been confined to these threatened social groups. University students had shown an interest in the movement from its beginnings in the early 1880s. In the following decades, graduates embarking on careers entered associations with an established middle-class social makeup where antisemitism was considered intellectually respectable. The Pan-German League, with its relatively small membership of professionals, kept its distance from the vulgar, politically engaged antisemites, although it found room in its ranks for the most well-behaved among them. Becoming steadily more disenchanted with the Kaiser and his government, the group's dynamic leader Heinrich Class (1868–1953) mounted a crusade for far-reaching changes. The Pan-Germans flirted with antisemitism from the 1890s until the last year of the war and then finally embraced it openly, motivated both by a heartfelt Jew-hatred and a cynical appreciation of its potential as a tool of anti-democratic mobilization. Still, before the war, the League's antisemitism had been far from typical of extraparliamentary associations and lobbying groups in the German empire. This leaves open the question of just how deeply and broadly antisemitism had permeated these organizations and how large a role it played beyond the lower middle classes.

On the eve of World War I, despite these new departures, it is doubtful that organized antisemitism was headed toward great new successes in Germany. Although many Jews may have been psychologically wounded by the antisemites' lies and threats, they continued to prosper and play a significant role in public life, their physical safety assured by a powerful state. Indeed, Germany still beckoned as a place of refuge to many Jews living in far less hospitable lands.

What, then, did this record of quite limited effectiveness contribute to the Holocaust? For several years after World War II, historians commonly assumed that a straight path led from the imperial era to the "Final Solution." The progress of popular antisemitism, so it was argued, was unbroken; nurtured by parties, organizations, and individuals, it spread ever more widely in German society from the late 1870s until it resulted finally and inevitably in the Holocaust. This is no longer the consensus view. The continuity between previous forms of political antisemitism and those that led the Nazis to genocide is not obvious. The evidence strongly suggests that the road to Auschwitz was a twisted one.

To begin with, the links in personnel are tenuous. Only a few of the antisemites prominent in the earlier era played significant roles in Weimar or the Third Reich. Hitler and several leading Nazis lionized the stalwart Theodor Fritsch (1852–1933) toward the end of his long career, but through most of the 1920s there was a good deal of mutual contempt expressed by Hitler and Fritsch for one another (Zumbini 2003: 626–34). More generally, veteran activists bore the stigma of failure too clearly to be taken as role models by the new generation; for their part, the old-timers were jealous of the Nazis' successes and/or scandalized by their recklessness. Nazi histories of the early movement spoke of courageous leaders who sounded the first warnings about the Jewish danger to a sleeping nation, but then dismissed these same leaders as lacking correct ideology or political savvy or sufficient will to act. Without Hitler, nothing would have come of their well-meant but bungled attempts. Most importantly, the parliamentary solution of the Jewish question, the hallmark of conventional antisemitism, had been a fool's errand, a wrong turn. Parliament was no place to defend the nation against Jewish conspiracy. It was part of the conspiracy. If Hitler ever entertained the idea of parliamentarizing the Jewish question, he soon dropped it. However committed he was to bringing the Jews to account, his rhetorical antisemitism was primarily a tool of mobilization, a tool he used only as long as it could advance his designs on power. After he achieved power, his solution of the Jewish question eventually bypassed mass participation and all the problems related to "enlightening" the Germans, with whom he grew increasingly impatient when it came to their grasp of what was at stake. In effect, Hitler rejected most of the strivings and strategies of those who had gone before.

In a context radically altered by war and revolution, violent antisemitism dominated the Weimar Republic. The Nazis and their many rivals on the radical right spoke and wrote openly of murder, assaulted Jews in the streets, vandalized their businesses, desecrated cemeteries and synagogues, and reviled the laws and institutions of the republic as they did so (Walter 1999: 38–51, 97–102, 151–76). Before the lost war, legal self-defense had been at least partially effective against the antisemites, because conviction in the Kaiser's courts had brought public disgrace and occasionally even ended political careers. But the republic's courts no longer had credibility with the German people. The unending crises of the 1920s undermined authority and destroyed the Germans' confidence in the state. Antisemitic thugs and libelers now wore their conviction by the "Jew republic" as a badge of honor.

Political antisemitism, pushed to the margins of Imperial Germany, was now much more central to the everyday experience of Germans. The relatively restrained public sphere of the prewar era had produced a self-limiting, unimaginative antisemitism that struck the new revolutionaries as simply passé. In its extremist programs and actions, its rhetorical excess and will to violence, the revolutionary antisemitism of the Weimar era amounted to a virtual new beginning.

All this argues against the idea that the development from the Second to the Third Reich was linear in nature or that the Nazis simply studied the precedents of the past and applied them more diligently and ruthlessly than their predecessors. Yet it defies reason to think that the theories and practices of the conventional antisemites contributed nothing at all to the genocide of the Jews. For despite their lack of accomplishment and the decline of organized antisemitism before World War I, antisemitic propaganda continued unabated. The volume and ready availability of printed matter perpetuated anti-Jewish stereotypes and broadcast them all over the world. The audience for libelous newspapers, offensive caricatures, and inflammatory speeches may not have believed all it heard or read. Relatively few people positioned Jews at the center of universal evil or believed that a solution of the Jewish problem would greatly improve their lives. But the hammering away at Jews had pernicious effects, and the anti-Jewish feelings they kept alive had destructive consequences.

A likely effect of the propaganda barrage was to obscure the line between anti-Jewish feeling and antisemitism. More people may have become willing to act against Jews during the interwar era or to tolerate others acting for them. Certainly the willingness to defend Jewish rights diminished, and in some countries disappeared altogether. Put briefly, the decades of calumny had taken their toll. It had become difficult to imagine Jews as totally blameless or to think of them as people for whom one was obliged to take risks. They had been objects of suspicion for centuries, and received wisdom told one to be cautious in their presence. Antisemitic propaganda reinforced these prejudices. Further, by the 1920s, after four decades of exposure, the public had become accustomed to seeing Jews singled out for political attack. The passive acceptance of political antisemitism had become routine in Germany well before the Nazis. Germans may not have joined Hitler's party or voted for him because of what he threatened against the Jews. But neither did they find it unusual, let alone offensive enough to deny him their support or reject his leadership after 1933.

Before Hitler, organized antisemitism had set out to convert prejudiced people into authentic antisemites who placed paramount importance on the struggle against Jewish power and stood ready to act. Although that plan fell short, these antisemites were successful in another way. They helped isolate Jews from other Germans, psychologically and emotionally, well before the Nazis did so physically. They contributed significantly to the Germans' indifference toward the rights of Jews and then their fates. This apathy may well have been antisemitism's largest contribution to the Holocaust.

REFERENCES

ACKERMANN, N. and JAHODA, M. (1950). *Anti-Semitism and Emotional Disorder: A Psycho-analytic Interpretation*. New York: Harper.

BLASCHKE, O. (1997). *Katholizismus und Antisemitismus im Deutschen Kaiserreich*. Göttingen: Vandenhoeck & Ruprecht.

GEEHR, R. (1990). *Karl Lueger: Mayor of Fin de Siècle Vienna*. Detroit, MI: Wayne State University Press.

LINDEMANN, A. (1997). *Esau's Tears: Modern Anti-Semitism and the Rise of the Jews*. Cambridge: Cambridge University Press.

ROSENBERG, H. (1967). *Grosse Depression und Bismarckzeit*. Berlin: W. de Gruyter.

RÜRUP, R. (1975). "Emancipation and Crisis. The 'Jewish Question' in Germany 1850–1890." *Leo Baeck Yearbook* 20: 13–25.

VOLKOV, S. (2006). *Germans, Jews, and Antisemites: Trials in Emancipation*. Cambridge: Cambridge University Press.

WALTER, D. (1999). *Antisemitische Kriminalität und Gewalt: Judenfeindschaft in der Weimarer Republik.* Bonn: Verlag J.H.W. Dietz Nachf.

ZUMBINI, M. (2003). *Die Würzeln des Bösen: Gründerjahre des Antisemitismus von der Bismarckzeit zu Hitler.* Frankfurt am Main: Vittorio Klostermann.

OTHER SUGGESTED READING

BEIN, A. (1990). *The Jewish Question: Biography of a World Problem.* Madison, NJ: Fairleigh Dickinson University Press.

BLOBAUM, R. (ed.) (2005). *Antisemitism and Its Opponents in Modern Poland.* Ithaca, NY: Cornell University Press.

BOYER, J. (1998). *Culture and Political Crisis in Vienna: Christian Socialism in Power, 1897–1918.* Chicago, IL: University of Chicago Press.

EVANS, R. (2004). *The Coming of the Third Reich.* New York: Penguin Press.

HOFFMANN, C., BERGMANN, W., and SMITH, H. (eds.) (2002). *Exclusionary Violence: Antisemitic Riots in Modern German History.* Ann Arbor, MI: University of Michigan Press.

KATZ, J. (2006). *From Prejudice to Destruction: Anti-Semitism, 1700–1933.* Cambridge, MA: Harvard University Press.

LEVY, R. (ed.) (2005). *Antisemitism: A Historical Encyclopedia of Prejudice and Persecution.* 2 vols. Santa Barbara, CA: ABC-Clio Press.

NIEWYK, D. (1990). "Solving the 'Jewish Problem': Continuity and Change in German Antisemitism, 1871–1945." *Leo Baeck Year Book* 35: 335–70.

SEGEL, B. (1995). *A Lie and a Libel: The History of the Protocols of the Elders of Zion.* Ed. R. Levy. Lincoln, NE: University of Nebraska Press.

CHAPTER 2

···

SCIENCE

···

PATRICIA HEBERER

IN 1937, the prominent German pathologist Otmar von Verschuer (1896–1969) published *Erbpathologie* (Hereditary Pathology), an important work that emphasized the genetic origins of many common and widespread diseases. Director of the newly founded Institute for Hereditary Biology and Racial Hygiene at the University of Frankfurt since 1935 and the author of widely respected and well funded clinical studies, Verschuer was a leading scientific figure in a nation that stood in the vanguard of medical research, public health, and preventive medicine. As one of the foremost advocates of the hereditary principles inherent in eugenics, Verschuer was deeply involved in twin research, utilizing it as a method to trace the genetic origins of diseases such as tuberculosis. Twin research was seen at the time as the ideal tool in weighing the variant factors of heredity and environment and was handsomely funded during the era of the Third Reich. No scientist was more associated with this "sovereign method" of genetic research than Verschuer, whose data derived from years of careful study of thousands of identical and fraternal twins.

In 1942, Verschuer succeeded his friend Eugen Fischer (1874–1967) as director of the prestigious Kaiser Wilhelm Institute for Anthropology. This advancement brought Verschuer into close proximity with the racial policies of the Nazi regime. Although he joined the Nazi Party only in 1940 and, like many prominent physicians and scientists in the Third Reich, considered himself above the political fray, Verschuer's convictions were much in keeping with the guiding principles of National Socialist racial hygiene measures. For years prior to his 1942 appointment, he had been the editor of *Der Erbarzt* (The Hereditary Physician), a supplement to Germany's leading medical journal, which served as a professional forum for the implementation of Germany's forced sterilization policy. In 1937, the same year in which he published *Erbpathologie*, he supported the expansion of racial hygiene instruction in German medical school curricula. He also wrote extensively on the "Jewish issue," placing the "racial biology" of Jews within the context of his formative research in hereditary pathology. In 1941, his *Leitfaden der Rassenhygiene* (Primer to Racial Hygiene) called for a "complete solution to the Jewish Question" (Proctor 1988: 211).

As the German war effort deteriorated after 1941, Verschuer encountered difficulties in obtaining materials for his research, but discovered an unlikely solution in the form of his former graduate student and protégé, Josef Mengele (1911–1979). Since September 1937, Mengele had served as Verschuer's assistant in Frankfurt, and even in Mengele's new post at Auschwitz as of spring 1943, he continued to serve his old professor in singular fashion. On 20 March 1944, Verschuer informed his funding agency, *Die Deutsche Forschungsgemeinschaft* (German Research Foundation or DFG), that "my assistant Dr. Mengele . . . has joined me in this branch of research. He is at present assigned as SS-*Hauptsturmführer* and camp physician at the Auschwitz concentration camp. With the permission of SS-*Reichsführer* [Heinrich Himmler], anthropological investigations of the most diverse racial groups are being conducted, and the blood samples sent for processing to my lab" (Klee 1997: 458). Mengele's notorious human experimentation in Auschwitz was funded in part by the DFG, while the young and ambitious physician sent his master a vast variety of "research material," including the skeletons of murdered Jews, the internal organs of Roma ("Gypsy") victims, the severed heads of Roma children, and blood samples of various prisoners, including twins whom Mengele had infected with typhus. There is no question that Verschuer, in Berlin, knew the origin of this "genetic material" and the circumstances under which it was procured.

After World War II, while his protégé fled to South America, Verschuer remained in Germany, where a denazification court adjudged him a *Mitläufer* (collaborator), thus removing any stain of direct culpability in Nazi crimes. Although unpleasant allegations of involvement in criminal medical experimentation eventually surfaced, Verschuer assumed a coveted position as professor of genetics at the university in Münster, which he developed into a leading center for genetic research in the new Federal Republic of Germany. His earlier "work" in racial biological principles translated neatly and without taint into the expanding study of human genetics. In 1954, Verschuer published an important work on this topic, and became dean of the medical faculty. When he died in 1969, eulogists made no reference to his Nazi past.

SCIENCE IN NAZI GERMANY

As practiced by influential researchers and physicians in Nazi Germany, the disciplines of science and medicine were among the key enabling agents of the Holocaust. In many ways, the career and fate of Otmar von Verschuer confirm that claim, illustrating as well a disturbing paradox that properly remains at the center of research in this area of Holocaust studies: National Socialism's aim to destroy Jews and other "inferior" groups was advanced by respected members of one of the world's preeminent scientific communities. Verschuer's case also illustrates the tension that existed between valid scientific inquiry and the racialist theories that made the Holocaust possible. Like many fellow researchers, Verschuer grounded his exploration of the pathology of diseases in clinical trials and empirical study, yet he endorsed and employed the notions of racial hygiene that were integral to Nazi principles and practice. Verschuer's body of work combined "pure" science and what has come to be seen as pseudoscience. Like many of his colleagues, he refrained from active participation in political affairs, yet his work brought him into direct contact with the ideological and practical implications of Nazi policy. As a scientist in the Nazi era, Verschuer straddled the bounds of legitimate research and unethical and inhumane experimentation. He was complicit in some of the regime's most heinous crimes, yet, like most in his milieu, he eluded prosecution and blended seamlessly back into professional life and civil society when World War II ended. Verschuer's experiences emblematize the ambiguous course that the scientific disciplines took during the Nazi years.

Such developments raise a vexing question: Was there such a thing as Nazi science? If so, what features defined it? At first glance, scientific activity under the swastika appears to belong predominantly to the domain of the pseudosciences. Governed by the dictates of a racialist ideology, many such efforts lacked rational approach and empirical method and have earned comparison to contemporaneous Soviet "scientific" dogmas such as Lysenkoism. "Nazi science" typically underscored National Socialist beliefs and stereotypes, highlighted the superiority of the "Nordic race," and embraced the element of struggle. An example in this vein was the so-called *Welteislehre* (World Ice Theory), a concept asserting that ice was the basic substance of all cosmic matter. The theory, developed in 1894 by Austrian engineer Hanns Hörbiger (1860–1931), suggested that the earth's solar system originated from a collision between the sun and smaller masses of celestial ice. Thereafter, the source of existence had been formed in the eternal struggle between the elements of fire and ice, which provided the explanation for all observable cosmic phenomena. During the Nazi era, the *Welteislehre* received powerful patronage from Heinrich Himmler (1900–1945); under his aegis the concept became the regime's sanctioned cosmological model, and Himmler made efforts to silence or discredit its detractors. Many proponents noted the strong similarities between the tenets of *Welteislehre* and Norse mythology; more conveniently, the ice construct challenged the prevailing theory of relativity proposed by the German-Jewish scientist Albert Einstein (1879–1955). Roundly rejected by the international scientific community and quickly discarded in postwar Germany, world ice theory was not the only Nazi doctrine plied to counter "Jewish influence" in the scientific sphere. The fields of psychology and psychotherapy, pioneered by the Austrian Sigmund Freud (1856–1939), would be forced to take root outside the borders of their birthplace in German-speaking Europe because Nazi leaders dismissed the new disciplines as "Jewish sciences" (Friedlander 1995: 79).

The SS sponsored many of the scientific theories and methods that aimed to counteract "Jewish manipulation" and challenge the "materialistic" liberal sciences. Himmler's expanding SS empire provided an early opportunity to found—and fund—research projects in areas significant to the development and support of Nazi ideology (Szöllösi-Janze 2001). The scientific research institute *Ahnenerbe* (Ancestral Heritage), founded in 1935 by Himmler and Reich agricultural minister Richard Walther Darré (1895–1953), boasted forty academic divisions dedicated to advancing research about the anthropological and cultural history of the "Aryan race" and to accumulating scientific data in support of the National Socialist worldview. With what can only be described as a holistic and interdisciplinary approach, *Ahnenerbe* scholars were also making forays by the late 1930s into the natural and medical sciences. SS funding for all these academic endeavors continued until quite late in the war effort. Until 1944, for example, SS coffers funded the compilation of a comprehensive codex on the persecution of witches, based on the hypothesis that the central European "witch craze" of the sixteenth and seventeenth centuries had represented an attack, under the auspices of the Catholic Church and "the Jews," to destroy a still intact German pagan culture.

Nazi Party and SS subventions often financed scientific enterprises which furthered National Socialist beliefs and aims. Until circumstances intervened, powerful forces in the Nazi Party supported the notion of "Aryan Physics," a movement led by physicists Johannes Stark (1874–1957) and Philipp Lenard (1862–1947). Stark hoped to reorganize and ground his discipline along nationalistic and *völkisch* lines. His 1941 work, *Jüdische und Deutsche Physik* (Jewish and German Physics) elucidated the "Aryan" scientific worldview, in which Jewish contributions to physics had inflicted untold damage to the field in the first decades of the twentieth century. Now that the Nazi era had come, Stark argued, the German physics community was obliged to eliminate these degenerate influences from its ranks. The antisemitic activism of "Aryan physics" and the Nazi policy of *Gleichschaltung* (synchronization) worked hand in hand; and if, as Alan Beyerchen (1977) has suggested, "Aryan physics" alone did not account for the German failure to match American efforts in the race for the atomic bomb, certainly the purge of prize-winning and promising Jewish and leftist scientists worked to the detriment of the German nuclear program.

But "Nazi science" was not confined to such empirically questionable and ideologically loaded disciplines as "Aryan physics." Nazi Germany could not have conducted its ambitious war effort wholly on the basis of fleeting and aberrant scientific theories. It could not have succeeded in waging six years of armed conflict against such a range of formidable and powerful opponents without the aid and support of a rational, resourceful, and dynamic scientific community. Many of the same funds that fostered scientists pursuing the Nazi ideal of a racially pure German society also supported advances in aeronautics, biochemistry, and the production of synthetic materials. Germany, already in the forefront of the international medical community before the Nazi era, forged ahead during this period in such areas as virology and cancer research. Not latter-day health-conscious Americans but "Nazi scientists" discovered the vital causal connection between smoking and lung cancer. In the years before World War II, German scientists even recognized the dangers of "second-hand smoke" (passive smoking) and documented the carcinogenic effects of heavy metals and asbestos, as well as of tobacco products (Proctor 1999). Progressive public health measures, such as prenatal screening, public awareness campaigns against smoking and alcohol abuse, and advances in occupational health and safety standards, certainly coincided with the Nazi pursuit of racial hygiene, but they also followed a line of continuity from the Weimar era, in which Germany had dominated the field of preventive medicine.

So perhaps, in the context of weighing the ephemeral and the efficacious, the aberrant and the accepted, pseudoscience and "pure" science, an exploration of the defining theme in the evolution of science under the swastika should ask not, "What was Nazi science?" but rather, "*Which* was Nazi science?"

One of the keys to this riddle lies in an examination of the way in which the National Socialist hierarchy regarded science and scientists. Many people believe that the Nazi leadership, which embraced racial theory and *völkisch* ideals of irrationalism and anti-materialism, manifestly rejected legitimate science. But was the Nazi movement fundamentally unscientific? Undoubtedly National Socialist ideology and practice were antithetical to science in many ways. In disciplines where free inquiry and open dialogue concerning theories and methods are invaluable and even indispensable, the Nazi dictatorship muzzled dissent and discouraged alternative opinions. This was especially the case in medicine and parallel fields where eugenic and racial hygiene constructs permeated scientific discourse. Nazi authorities also worked to create a society in which ideological imperatives often trumped practical considerations. The Law for the Restoration of the Professional Civil Service of April 1933, which forced the dismissal of

Jews and "politically unreliable" individuals from government posts, affected some 15 percent of university lecturers in Germany. This and subsequent discriminatory measures compelled a large number of scholars and scientists to emigrate throughout the 1930s, among them numerous future Nobel Prize winners. Nazi authorities may not have bemoaned this loss at the time, but their actions clearly diminished a vibrant and vigorous scientific community. Historians ever since have debated the degree to which this "brain drain" diminished Germany's predominance in the sciences and tempered the country's ability to wage war successfully.

But to suggest that the Nazi regime was fundamentally unreceptive to science or that it was the single-minded patron of ideologically skewed and pseudoscientific endeavors is incorrect. The Nazi state was not a monolithic entity, but a polycratic and multifaceted enterprise. The excellent research conducted under the aegis of a German Presidential Commission concerning the history of the Kaiser Wilhelm Society from 1933 to 1945 demonstrates the extent to which significant institutions of German research and scholarship gained in prestige and funding during the era of the Third Reich (Rürup and Schneider 2000–2007). In matters of science, the Nazi hierarchy looked forward as much as backward (Herf 1986). It put great faith in scientists, researchers, and technocrats, not only to modernize the nation and to advance its military technologies, but also to vindicate its ideological beliefs by scientific method. Most German scientists during the Nazi era were not ideologically motivated but politically neutral and research-driven (Beyerchen 1977). The Nazi regime needed this sort of individual to fuel its war machine, advance its prestige in the scientific disciplines, and to carry out its ideological goals, such as the massive population transfers envisioned by planners of Germanization policy. To subjugate and deport millions of indigenous Slavs, the *Generalplan Ost* (General Plan East) harnessed not only the efforts of Party ideologues but also those of academically trained geographers, demographers, space specialists, and urban planners (Aly and Heim 2002). Nazi authorities were not always steadfastly ideological but pragmatic and utilitarian when necessary, adopting alternative strategies and makeshift solutions as the need arose. Sensibly, they employed those sciences that were useful to the regime's objectives, engaging professionals in these areas with a modicum of indoctrination. This was particularly true for fields such as biology, chemistry, biotechnology, geography, and engineering. The applied sciences were less subject than the life sciences to the inroads of ideology and thus to characterization as "Nazi science."

Thus, the science practiced during the National Socialist era had a legitimate side, if legitimacy refers to the measurement of progress by the standards of the field and not by conformity to Nazi ideological imperatives. At the opposite end of the continuum were scientific endeavors that were exploited to manifest the goals of the regime and to implement its racial policies.

THE EUGENICS MOVEMENT

Many of the scientific theories associated with National Socialism sprang neither from the dictates of Nazi leaders nor from their ideological canon, but from the theory of *eugenics*, an international movement that gained currency with the flourishing of the natural sciences at the end of the nineteenth century. The term, from Greek roots meaning "good birth," was coined in 1883 by the English naturalist Francis Galton (1822–1911); its German counterpart *Rassenhygiene* (racial hygiene) was first employed by economist Alfred Ploetz (1860–1940) in 1895. At the core of the movement's belief system was the conviction that human heredity was fixed and immutable, a concept that gained adherence with the advent of Darwinist theory and with the rediscovery of Mendelian genetics in the late nineteenth century. For eugenicists, the social ills that attended modern society—mental illness, alcoholism, prostitution, criminality, and even poverty—stemmed from hereditary factors. Proponents of eugenic theory were not prepared to attribute the origins of societal problems to environmental causes, such as the rapid industrialization and urbanization that marked the last half of the nineteenth century in western Europe and the United States. Perceiving a rising tide of "degeneration," advocates hoped to mobilize the modern science of eugenics to arrest the cycle of decay. In doing so, eugenicists championed three primary objectives: to discover and enumerate "hereditary" characteristics contributing to the social ills, to develop biomedical solutions for these scourges, and to campaign actively for public health measures that might combat these dangers.

Although eugenics found its most radical interpretation in Germany, its influence was by no means limited to that nation alone. Throughout the late nineteenth and early twentieth centuries, eugenics societies and research institutions sprang up throughout most of the industrialized world, most notably in the United States and Great Britain as well as Germany. Whatever their setting, most supporters before World War I endorsed the call from American advocate Charles Davenport (1866–1944) for the development of eugenics as a science devoted to the improvement of the human race through superior breeding. They lobbied for "positive" eugenic policies, which aimed to support physically, racially, and hereditarily "healthy" individuals and encouraged these "valuable" members of society to reproduce. Dovetailing with efforts to support the "productive" came negative eugenic measures: initiatives to exclude society's "unproductive" elements and to redirect social and economic resources from these "less valuable" to the "worthy."

In Germany as well as in the United States, many proponents of eugenics promoted strategies to marginalize segments of society with limited mental or social capacity and to restrict their reproduction through voluntary or compulsory sterilization. Eugenicists targeted the mentally ill and developmentally disabled, asserting a direct link between diminished capacity and depravity, promiscuity, and criminality. They viewed the racially "inferior" and the poor as menaces who ostensibly passed on their deficiencies to offspring who burdened the public till. Each of these groups, tainted through inherited deficiencies, endangered the national gene pool and placed a financial burden on the society that maintained them. More often than not, eugenicists' "scientific" conclusions about disabled individuals or ethnic and racial minorities merely recapitulated popular prejudice. Yet the employment of "research" and "theory" gave eugenics the appearance of cutting-edge science and its practitioners' notions of human inferiority and superiority the pretense of scientific fact.

With the advantage of hindsight, we know that the German eugenics effort ultimately pursued a separate and terrible course, but before 1914—and in some cases before 1933—the German racial hygiene movement did not differ appreciably from its American and British counterparts. Yet three important circumstances distinguished the German eugenics establishment from those of other countries, particularly the United States, its closest rival for leadership of the movement. First, German scientists and medical professionals generally enjoyed greater prestige within the German academic structure and in popular perception than did their American colleagues. The establishment of medicine and hygiene on scientific bases in German lands between 1850 and 1875 rapidly formed an academically trained medical community with unparalleled public recognition and corresponding political power. Significantly, the vast majority of Germany's eugenics leadership had training and careers in medicine. Moreover, more physicians and scientists holding academic appointments played an active role in the new movement than did their American counterparts.

A second important matter was centralization. America's Eugenics Record Office in Cold Spring Harbor, New York, represented the central nerve point of the American eugenics effort, but the scientific landscape was dotted with countless local and independent chapters that bespoke the heterogeneous nature of the field. In Germany, one society held sway: *Die Deutsche Gesellschaft für Rassenhygiene* (The German Society for Racial Hygiene), established by the movement's national leader Alfred Ploetz in 1905.

Finally, a genuine radicalization of Germany's eugenics community arose from the devastating effects of World War I. The Great War brought not only humiliating defeat. The unprecedented carnage on the battlefield and the economic and social upheaval of the interwar years also served to underscore the division between the "fit" and "useful" Germans who had died at the front, and the "unproductive" Germans left at home. Whereas their hereditarily "valuable" countrymen had sacrificed their lives for the Fatherland, these "impaired" individuals had remained behind to reproduce, maintained by the slender resources of the state. A eugenicist version of the "stab-in-the-back" legend emerged and resurfaced again and again in the Weimar and Nazi eras to justify increasingly extreme measures against institutionalized and "socially disabled" persons.

FROM PRINCIPLE TO POLICY

Any discussion that explores the progression of an idea from principle to policy must be careful to differentiate theory from practice. Thus it is important to separate the advocacy of eugenic strategies in an era where they enjoyed limited political or public support from the translation of those ideas into state-enforced measures in the years of the Nazi dictatorship. Nonetheless, by 1933, theories of racial hygiene had become embedded in professional and public attitudes and in the thinking of Adolf Hitler (1889–1945) and many of his supporters. Dedicated to an ideology that incorporated eugenic doctrine, the Hitler regime provided the context and latitude for realizing the most extreme racial hygiene measures: compulsory sterilization, the Nuremberg Laws, the killing of the institutionalized mentally and physically disabled, the destruction of Roma communities through-out Europe, and, in its last and most terrible manifestation, the genocide of European Jewry.

On 2 June 1933 an Expert Advisory Council on Questions of Population and Racial Policy met for the first time. Its chairman was Arthur Gütt (1891–1949), head of the Reich Interior Ministry's Department of Public Health. The council assem-bled the foremost figures of the nation's racial hygiene movement, including Alfred Ploetz, the father of German eugenics; Ernst Rüdin (1874–1952), director of the Kaiser Wilhelm Institute for Genealogy in Munich; Gerhard Wagner (1888–1939), leader of the Reich Physicians' Chamber; and Hans F. K. Günther (1891–1968), a leading racial anthropologist. At its first meeting the council announced its inten-tion to forge a strategy that would reverse the dwindling birth rate, stem Jewish immigration from eastern and central Europe, and halt the birth of "degenerate," "hybrid," and "genetically diseased" offspring. A comprehensive strategy of "gene and race cultivation" was envisioned; at its core were measures intended to advance the reproductive capacity of racially and genetically "healthy" Germans and to proscribe the propagation of the "hereditarily compromised."

An immediate outgrowth of the council's work was the Law for the Prevention of Progeny with Hereditary Diseases (*Gesetz zur Verhütung erbkranken Nachwuchses*) of 14 July 1933, which ordered the compulsory sterilization of German citizens suffering from certain "hereditary" afflictions. Five of the diseases designated in the decree represented psychiatric or neurological disorders, including schizophrenia, bipolar disorder, hereditary epilepsy, Huntington's chorea, and "hereditary feeble-mindedness." Physical conditions that warranted sterilization under the new legis-lation were hereditary deafness, hereditary blindness, serious hereditary physical deformity, and severe alcoholism. Medical professionals were now obligated by law to report patients who exhibited these illnesses or disabilities. As a result, the majority of proposals for sterilizations came from physicians—from state medical offices or from directors or chief physicians of mental health institutions—but also

from social workers and welfare agencies. Adjudication of sterilization proceedings—for these were legal suits—came within the jurisdiction of newly constructed
hereditary health courts (*Erbgesundheitsgerichte*). By 1936, some 230 of these tribunals had been established throughout Germany. Because each tribunal comprised
two physicians and one jurist, medical professionals on the bench held the balance
of authority for each verdict.

The new law took effect in January 1934. Under its aegis some 400,000 Germans
were forcibly sterilized before war's end in May 1945 (Bock 1989: 230–46). This
figure does not include the thousands of Jews, Roma, Poles, and other victims
sterilized outside the law's parameters during the war years. The great majority of
German sterilization victims were persons suffering from mental illness, with
schizophrenia and "hereditary feeblemindedness" representing the most common
diagnoses warranting the procedure. Particularly these illnesses, whose definitions
were elastic, permitted physicians and psychiatrists to include in their dragnet not
only the mentally ill and developmentally disabled but also those judged socially
aberrant or "asocial": vagrants, prostitutes, mothers with illegitimate children,
petty criminals, juvenile delinquents, and in large numbers, German Roma and
Sinti, whom Nazi officials viewed at once as a racial menace and as an ethnic
criminal element on German soil.

Medical professionals played an indispensable role in the development and
implementation of forced sterilization policy: in the drafting of legislation and
legal commentaries; as informers against potential victims to public health offices;
as judges on hereditary health tribunals; and as individual physicians performing
the procedures at designated hospitals and clinics. To be sure, the German scientific
community's support for the sterilization measure was not unprecedented. Apart
from the magnitude of the German effort, the United States and Germany, both
leaders in the eugenics movement, shared a very similar experience in this sphere.
In 1907, the U.S. state of Indiana enacted the very first sterilization law. By the mid-
1930s, more than half of all American states had similar legislation; and some
60,000–70,000 U.S. citizens were compulsorily sterilized before individual states
began removing such laws from their books in the 1950s. Yet in Nazi Germany
compulsory sterilization was only the first of many ways in which German medical
professionals acted as mediators, planners, and perpetrators of Nazi racial policy.

Already in the 1920s, intellectuals in Weimar Germany had begun to discuss the
legalization of mercy killing and, more significantly, of state intervention in the
euthanasia process. Until 1920, the concept of euthanasia had remained at the outer
margins of the eugenics dialogue, but in the context of dwindling resources in the
unstable Weimar years, discourse began to radicalize. The publication *Die Freigabe
der Vernichtung lebensunwerten Lebens* (The Authorization of the Destruction of
Life Unworthy of Life) by jurist Karl Binding (1841–1920) and psychiatrist Alfred
Hoche (1865–1943), both prominent in right-wing nationalist circles, soon framed
the debate in the German-speaking world. Certain forms of life, Hoche and

Binding argued, have "so far forfeited the character of something entitled to enjoy the protection of the law that its prolongation represents a perpetual loss of value, both for its bearer and for society as a whole" (Burleigh 1994: 17–18). After careful medical evaluation, they contended, the state should have the right to intercede for the death of these "ballast existences," even if relatives opposed the measure. The Hoche–Binding treatise had immediate impact and was widely discussed in medical and scientific circles. Although it produced more detractors than defenders, the tract, with its utilitarian arguments for redirecting resources from "incurables" to the less impaired, made an impression upon physicians, psychiatrists, and caregivers already instilled with eugenicist principles.

In the late 1930s, as Nazi racial and territorial goals radicalized, voices within a Nazified medical community began to call for the elimination of severely disabled patients living in institutional settings, arguing that such individuals imposed a genetic threat and a financial burden on a society now committed to war. In the spring and summer months of 1939, planners led by Philipp Bouhler (1899–1945), the director of Hitler's private chancellery (the Führer Chancellery), and Karl Brandt (1904–1948), Hitler's attending physician, began to organize a secret killing operation targeting disabled children. On 18 August 1939, the Reich Interior Ministry circulated a decree compelling all physicians and midwives to report newborn infants and children under the age of 3 who showed signs of severe mental or physical disability. At first restricted to infants and toddlers, the scope of the measure eventually widened to include juveniles up to 17 years of age in the killings. Conservative estimates suggest that at least 5,000 disabled children were murdered at specially designated children's killing wards through starvation or lethal overdoses of medication (Burleigh and Wippermann 1991: 144).

By January 1940, an adult "euthanasia" program paralleled the killing of German infants, toddlers, and juveniles. Code-named Operation T4 after the address of its Berlin headquarters at Tiergartenstrasse 4 near Potsdamer Platz, the program organized the registration of severely mentally and physically disabled patients, especially those who had been institutionalized for five years or more, as well as "non-German" (i.e., Jewish) patients, and prisoners who had been remanded to institutional settings for crimes committed under diminished capacity. Teams of "medical experts"—prominent physicians and psychiatrists recruited for the secret killing program—reviewed the registration forms and selected individuals for inclusion in the "euthanasia" effort, often without seeing the patients in question. In January 1940, these "lives unworthy of life," as Nazi authorities described them, began to be transferred from their home institutions to one of eventually six centralized killing centers throughout Germany and Austria. Within hours of their arrival, these patients were murdered in specially designed gas chambers and their bodies destroyed in nearby crematory ovens. Faithful to the injunction of T4 administrator Viktor Brack (1904–1948), who insisted that the handle of the gas valve belonged in the hands of a medical professional, the attending physicians at these facilities gave doomed patients a superficial examination, conducted the actual gassing, and supplied the fictive causes and dates of death that appeared on the victims' death certificates and official papers. According to T4's own internal statistics, 70,273 mentally and physically disabled persons perished at the six gassing installations between January 1940 and August 1941 (Friedlander 1995: 109).

Although the program was a clandestine one, it quickly became an open secret. Fearing popular unrest at a critical point in the war effort, Adolf Hitler himself called a halt to the T4 effort on 24 August 1941. For roughly one year, the adult "euthanasia" program lingered in a kind of stasis. During this time, more than one hundred T4 functionaries were dispatched to Poland to serve as German personnel in the death camps of Belzec, Sobibor, and Treblinka, where approximately 1.7 million Jews were murdered. In the summer months of 1942, the planners of the "euthanasia" effort, led by physician Karl Brandt, reinstated the killing of adult patients, albeit in a more decentralized format. Murder by lethal overdose and starvation, those modes of killing that had proven so successful in the child "euthanasia" effort, continued at a broad range of German institutions until the spring of 1945. By war's end, the Nazi "euthanasia" program had claimed the lives of an estimated 200,000 disabled patients living in institutional settings in Germany and German-controlled territories.

The Nazi persecution of persons with disabilities fit within an overarching framework of radical public health strategies that aimed at excluding hereditarily "compromised" Germans from the national community. These eugenic measures, born of scientific discourse, began with sterilization and led to the destruction of roughly 60 percent of the institutionalized population as it had existed in prewar Germany. What seems particularly horrific to later generations of observers is that the "euthanasia" campaign, the Nazis' first program of systematic mass murder, was implemented not by the SS or by fanatical ideologues, but by medical professionals who murdered their patients, the very individuals they had been enjoined to care for and protect.

Scientists, and especially medical professionals, proved integral to shaping and implementing antisemitic and racialist policies, often reaping benefit from the fruits of their terrible labor through professional acknowledgment and career advancement. At Auschwitz they played a crucial role in the genocide of European Jewry. There, physicians oversaw the murders of the 1.1 million individuals— mainly Jews—delivered to the gas chambers. As a requisite feature of their "rounds," medical staff performed "selections" of prisoners on the ramp, determining from among the mass of humanity arriving at Auschwitz-Birkenau who would live and who would die. Physicians consistently supervised the application of *Zyklon* at the gassing sites, and, as with the "euthanasia" program, officially pronounced their victims dead before *Sonderkommando* units disposed of the bodies. As one survivor noted, physicians presided at the beginning and end of the destruction process. Particularly in Auschwitz, but wherever in the concentration camp system camp doctors performed periodic "selections" of ill and exhausted prisoners, the introduction of the physician in the routine of mass murder created the impression of a medicalized killing process, which lent a perverse rationalization to the destruction of hundreds of thousands of human beings.

Physicians and scientists also made their mark upon the "concentration camp universe" through grisly experimentation, conducted upon nearly every representative group within the Nazi camp system. In 1931, the Weimar government had issued a decree, based on an earlier Prussian state directive, which helped to codify medical ethics in the German context, particularly with regard to the issue of informed consent for subjects of human experimentation. Long before the United States had similar guidelines, Germany established restrictions safeguarding the rights and safety of test subjects; indeed the codex provided the model for the 1947 Nuremberg Code, a convention of ethical standards developed in response to the crimes committed in the name of medicine under National Socialism. Yet during the Nazi years, German researchers and scientists, in direct violation of the 1931 decree, forced prisoners—among them Jews, Roma, Poles, political prisoners, and Soviet prisoners of war—to participate in dangerous and painful experimentation against their will. Many prisoners died as a direct result of the proceedings or were murdered to facilitate a post-mortem examination.

Unethical human medical experimentation carried out by Nazi scientists can be classified into three categories. The first grouping consisted of experiments designed to help German military personnel survive under dangerous wartime conditions. An example was the work of Drs. Siegfried Ruff (1907–?) and Hans Romberg (1911–1981) of the German Experimental Institute for Aviation and Luftwaffe physician Siegfried Rascher (1909–1945), who conducted high-altitude experiments in order to determine suitable conditions from which crews of damaged aircraft could parachute to safety. Some seventy to eighty prisoners perished from asphyxiation and internal injuries in low-pressure chambers that simulated atmospheric conditions at high altitudes.

A second broad sphere of Nazi experimentation focused on developing and testing pharmaceuticals and treatment methods for injuries and illnesses that German soldiers might encounter in the field. Some of the most grisly such efforts were conducted by Karl Gebhardt (1897–1948), whose research in the areas of bone-grafting, tissue transplants, and early sulfa drug trials resulted in the death and disfigurement of dozens of Polish female prisoners at Ravensbrück and Hohenly-chen. In these instances, Nazi scientists pursued research meant to advance the health and safety of German military and civilian personnel, a goal that conformed to professional standards, even as the methods they employed breached all norms of medical practice and violated basic codes of ethical conduct.

In the third realm of Nazi experimentation, neither ends nor means were legitimate. This genre embraces Josef Mengele's horrifying experiments upon twins at Auschwitz and his serological trials, utilizing Roma, which aimed to determine how different "races" withstood infectious diseases. Similar efforts to further Nazi racial goals included a series of sterilization experiments, undertaken primarily at Auschwitz and Ravensbrück, where physicians Karl Clauberg (1898–1957) and Horst Schumann (1906–1983) endeavored to develop an efficient and inexpensive procedure for the mass sterilization of Jews, Gypsies, and other groups that the National Socialists' leaders considered racially undesirable.

Medical perpetrators of Nazi crimes were tried in the immediate postwar period. At the Nuremberg "Doctors' Trial" in 1946, American prosecutors, focusing principally upon inhumane experimentation, sought to emphasize the most macabre aspects of Nazi medical crimes. Their efforts helped give rise to the myth that the German physicians and scientists responsible for these atrocities has been quacks and charlatans operating on the margins of the scientific establishment. This perception—still widely held—attests to the paradox with which this chapter has wrestled. In reality, most physicians and scientists who adjudged sterilization proceedings, participated in grisly human medical experimentation, implemented "euthanasia" policy, and helped to plan the destruction of the European Jewish and Roma communities were integrated members of one of the world's preeminent scientific communities. In the service of National Socialism, illegitimate scientific endeavors obtained almost unlimited license, and science was harnessed and misused to do the unthinkable. The last word on how and why these developments took place has not been written. Scholars must continue to explore the tension between legitimate science and "racial hygiene" in the German context in order to gain a more nuanced perspective of the role of the scientific disciplines under National Socialism and to comprehend more fully the contribution of science and scientists to the crimes of the Holocaust.

REFERENCES

ALY, G. and HEIM, S. (2002). *Architects of Annihilation: Auschwitz and the Logic of Destruction*. Princeton, NJ: Princeton University Press.

BEYERCHEN, A. (1977). *Scientists under Hitler: Politics and the Physics Community in the Third Reich*. New Haven, CT: Yale University Press.

BOCK, G. (1989). *Zwangssterilisation im Nationalsozialismus: Studien zur Rassenpolitik und Frauenpolitik*. Opladen: Westdeutscher Verlag.

BURLEIGH, M. (1994). *Death and Deliverance: Euthanasia in Germany, 1900–1945*. Cambridge: Cambridge University Press.

——and WIPPERMANN, W. (1991). *The Racial State: Nazi Germany, 1933–1945*. Cambridge: Cambridge University Press.

FRIEDLANDER, H. (1995). *The Origins of Nazi Genocide: From Euthanasia to the Final Solution*. Chapel Hill, NC: University of North Carolina Press.

HERF, J. (1986). *Reactionary Modernism: Technology, Culture, and Politics in Weimar and in the Third Reich.* Cambridge: Cambridge University Press.

KLEE, E. (1997). *Auschwitz, die NS-Medizin und ihre Opfer.* Frankfurt am Main: S. Fischer Verlag.

PROCTOR, R. (1988). *Racial Hygiene: Medicine under the Nazis.* Cambridge, MA: Harvard University Press.

——(1999). *The Nazi War on Cancer.* Princeton, NJ: Princeton University Press.

RÜRUP, R. and SCHNEIDER, W. (eds.) (2000–2007). *Die Kaiser-Wilhelm-Gesellschaft im Nationalsozialismus.* 17 vols. Göttingen: Wallstein Verlag.

SZÖLLÖSI-JANZE, M. (ed.) (2001). *Science in the Third Reich.* New York: Berg.

OTHER SUGGESTED READING

ALY, G., CHROUST, P., and PROSS, C. (1994). *Cleansing the Fatherland: Nazi Medicine and Racial Hygiene.* Baltimore, MD: Johns Hopkins University Press.

DEICHMANN, U. (1986). *Biologists under Hitler.* Cambridge, MA: Harvard University Press.

GOULD, S. J. (2008). *The Mismeasure of Man.* Rev. edn. New York: W. W. Norton.

KATER, M. H. (1989). *Doctors under Hitler.* Chapel Hill, NC: University of North Carolina Press.

KEVLES, D. J. (1995). *In the Name of Eugenics: Genetics and the Uses of Human Heredity.* Cambridge, MA: Harvard University Press.

KÜHL, S. (2002). *The Nazi Connection: Eugenics, American Racism, and German National Socialism.* 2nd edn. New York: Oxford University Press.

KUNTZ, D. (ed.) (2004). *Deadly Medicine: Creating the Master Race.* Washington, DC: United States Holocaust Memorial Museum.

MOSSE, G. (1985). *Toward the Final Solution: A History of European Racism.* Madison, WI: University of Wisconsin Press.

MÜLLER-HILL, B. (1998). *Murderous Science: The Elimination by Scientific Selection of Jews, Gypsies, and Others in Germany, 1933–1945.* Plainview, NY: Cold Spring Harbor Laboratory Press.

SCHMIDT, U. (2007). *Karl Brandt: The Nazi Doctor.* New York: Continuum.

CHAPTER 3

··

NATIONALISM

··

ERIC D. WEITZ

NATIONAL Socialism sought a radical restructuring of the European population. The drive to assert German domination over the continent entailed not only territorial conquest and political dictatorship but also a concerted effort of demographic engineering. Annihilating the Jews constituted the core aspiration of this program, which was surrounded by an array of policies to promote the health and fertility of the so-called Aryan population and to purge it of other unwanted groups. The Nazi state sterilized and then murdered people thought to be genetic carriers of mental and physical handicaps, sterilized Afro-Germans, exterminated hundreds of thousands of Roma and Sinti, and carried out near-genocidal policies against Poles, Russians, and other Slavs. These deadly measures were intended to redesign the populations of Germany and Europe.

Demographic engineering of this sort was one possible outgrowth of nationalism, the ideological and political movement that was born in the French Revolution and still serves as the underpinning of the nation-state. The prevalent form of political organization in the modern world, nationalism is usually distinguished from racism or, to use Hannah Arendt's more open-ended term, race thinking (Arendt 1958). Nationalism often evokes positive connotations of patriotism and popular sovereignty along the lines of the American and French Revolutions, while race thinking conjures up mythologies of blood-line purity and exploitative, repressive, and lethal forms of social and political organization, from Jim Crow America and the Third Reich to apartheid South Africa (Kohn 1944; B. Anderson 1991; Fredrickson 2002). However, nationalism is often divided into good and bad variants, the civic and the ethnic. The positive sort is associated, again, with the French and the American Revolutions and centers on republican citizenship. The negative sort is linked with organic, essentialist, often blood-line understandings of community derived from German theorists such as Johann Gottlieb Fichte (1762–1814).

The classic scholarly commentaries of the 1930s and 1940s, as well as the most sophisticated recent studies, identify a distinctive chronological and spatial character to these two variants of nationalism. The positive version emerged in the late eighteenth and early nineteenth centuries along the Atlantic seaboard in western Europe and North America. As nationalism moved west to east across Europe and into the late nineteenth century and twentieth centuries, it degenerated in form and content and became more exclusive and irrational, as well as an expression of mass rather than liberal politics. This sort of "bad" nationalism inclined to chauvinism and racism and culminated in fascism and Nazism (Kohn 1944; Gellner 1983; Hobsbawm 1990; B. Anderson 1991; Brubaker 1992).

Or so goes the standard story. Nation and race, however, often are not distinguishable; they slide easily the one into the other, as do civic and ethnic nationalisms (Yack in Beiner 1998; Brubaker 2004). Nation and race are modern forms of understanding human diversity and defining community. They are not unmediated reflections of nature; rather, they are human-made expressions of difference.

Necessarily, the act of constructing nation and race means establishing boundaries of inclusion and exclusion, of defining who is fit to be a member of a particular nation or race, and who must be kept out or purged. Constructions of nation and race typically rest upon and rigidify senses of ethnic identity, that is, the belief in a group of people that it possesses common origins, language, and customs (Fredrickson 2002; Weitz 2003).

National Socialism developed particularly vicious definitions of nation and race and their interrelationship. Although those definitions were not rooted in Nazism alone—they stemmed from the ways human diversity and political community had come to be understood in the western world since the late fifteenth century— the history of Nazism shows in stark terms that nationalism always carries an exclusionary component.

THE RISE OF NATION AND RACE

Concepts of nation and race emerged together in the western world in the late Middle Ages. Philologists have demonstrated that the word *race* did not exist in European languages until the fourteenth century. Although *nation* has older roots in the Latin *natio*, the term traditionally meant any kind of group: students, cobblers, and the Saxons were each termed a *natio* in the original usage. Profound changes in Europe during the fifteenth and sixteenth centuries fundamentally altered the meaning of *natio*, giving it a recognizably modern significance, and brought race into the forefront of the ways Europeans and Americans came to understand difference. The rise of powerful states, overseas exploration, and New World slavery marked the shift into the modern world. A few pioneering states (England, France, the Netherlands) began to take on something of a national character in the sense that each was understood to be the representative of a particular ethnic group—the English, the French, the Dutch. At the same time, slavery in the New World came to be the condition of a single, phenotypically distinct group, black Africans. Previously, slavery had been a practice in almost all human societies and the tragic fate of diverse peoples. Race as a hierarchical way of understanding difference developed in association with New World slavery, as the claim that African and African-descended populations were collectively and eternally inferior became the major way of explaining and justifying their servitude.

Not until the eighteenth-century Enlightenment, however, did the decisive movement toward modern definitions of race and nation take place. Here especially one can see how permeable the boundary is between those concepts and between civic and ethnic understandings of the nation. The Enlightenment sought to spread liberty and humanitarian ways of living by calling for representative government, religious toleration, the abolition of torture, and rights of free speech. But Enlightenment figures also sought to understand the broad diversity of the human species, something that had become much more apparent to Europeans during the age of exploration and its aftermath, as more Europeans took seaborne journeys and travel writing developed into a popular genre. As a result, several notable philosophers and scientists, including Immanuel Kant (1724–1804), Carolus Linnaeus (1707–1778), and Johann Friedrich von Blumenbach (1752–1840), invented an anthropology that classified humanity into distinct races, each with its own inheritable characteristics. In varied but persistent ways, this anthropology understood racial classification as a hierarchical system, with Europeans or Caucasians, as Blumenbach dubbed them, at the pinnacle (Hannaford 1996).

Then came the French Revolution, whose protagonists radicalized the concept of the nation, making it the focus of the political order. No longer was the king the embodiment of the nation; "the people" constituted the nation and created the state as its representative, a perspective famously inscribed in Article 3 of the Declaration of the Rights of Man and Citizen (26 August 1789): "The principle of all sovereignty resides essentially in the nation." The French Revolution thereby linked the strands of state and nation, weaving them into one powerful concept: the nation-state. The French revolutionary and Napoleonic armies spread this idea throughout Europe; it coursed throughout the world in the nineteenth and twentieth centuries and retains its power in the twenty-first.

Every national movement that developed in the nineteenth century—Greek, Italian, Hungarian, Jewish, German, and many others—strove to create a compact, territorially defined state that would be the representative of one national group. But the great problem for every nationalist movement already had emerged in the French Revolution: Who, precisely, constituted the nation? How was membership in the national community to be defined? While the French generally provided a civic definition—loyalty to the constitution of the Republic—strains of ethnic and even racial understandings emerged as well. Slavery in the French empire was hotly debated, and although the National Assembly finally abolished it in the wake of uprisings in the Caribbean, many revolutionaries gave voice to decidedly racial notions that barred blacks from the national community (Peabody and Stovall 2003). Meanwhile, the Abbé Sieyès (1748–1836), one of the great expositors of revolutionary principles, depicted a France divided between the "true" French and a divergent race of aristocratic exploiters and their minions that had to be purged from the body of the people (Sewell 1994). For all of its democratic principles, the nationalism of the French Revolution also contained a strong "racially purifying" strain.

Inspired by the French example, all across the continent educated individuals, such as teachers, writers, philosophers, and priests, led the way in forging national identities. Usually they claimed to be rediscovering a timeless community that had been corrupted and diluted over the course of centuries by external powers. Language was seen as the critical marker of the collectivity. Nationalists argued that a language literally bespeaks the essential nature of the people that developed it and, therefore, that the boundaries of the national community should be identical with the reach of the common tongue. They wrote dictionaries, reformed grammars, and resurrected (or invented) epic poems. They also established schools and publishing houses. The new media of the nineteenth century, notably the telegraph and mass-circulation newspapers, enabled them to propagate their ideas far more widely than in the past. In the established states of western Europe, public schools and the army taught young people the ideology of the nation and tried to drum out of them regional dialects and identities. The nation had to be one. When nationalists did not have their own state, they often established movements and parties, most with "Young" in the title—for example, Young Italy or Young Croatia—to symbolize the hopeful and activist elements of the national movements. Many fomented armed rebellions against the ruling dynasties that still governed much of the European land mass, which added instability to domestic and international politics, especially in eastern and southeastern Europe.

As nation became an ever more powerful and prevalent form of defining human difference, so did race, and the line between the two concepts blurred. New World slavery peaked in numbers and economic significance in the first half of the nineteenth century, especially in North America. This growth gave added sustenance to the ideology of race, as did the spread of European colonial domination in Africa and Asia during the century's second half. Concurrently, race thinking appeared to be ever more firmly "scientific," thanks to interpretations of emerging Darwinian evolutionary theory and other developments in the biological sciences.

In *On the Origin of Species* (1859), Charles Darwin (1809–1882) did not use the term *race*. His thought, moreover, revolved around the mutability of species. But his later work, *The Descent of Man* (1871), proved more useful to race theorists as they took Darwin's ideas down paths he had not imagined. These interpreters applied to the human world his understanding of evolution as a brutal struggle of species for resources in a harsh environment. According to this social Darwinism, as it came to be called, all of history was depicted as a struggle among nations and races in which only the strong prevail or survive. Such interpretations also imagined the possibility of perfecting nations and races by weeding out the bearers of unwanted characteristics. These views were common by the turn into the twentieth century, and they pulsed later through every aspect of Nazi thinking.

In association with the ascent of race thinking and nationalism, two new words appeared in the last third of the nineteenth century. In 1879, the German journalist Wilhelm Marr (1819–1904) popularized the term *antisemitism*, and Darwin's cousin, Francis Galton (1822–1911), introduced the word *eugenics* in 1881. Marr's term, emerging alongside the first explicitly anti-Jewish political parties in Germany, signified the rise of a modern, racially-based hostility toward Jews to accompany old-style, religious Judaeophobia. Traditionally, Jews were condemned in Christian Europe for their refusal to accept Jesus as the Messiah and their supposed role in his crucifixion. However, the path of conversion and acceptance into the Christian fold lay open to Jews for the most part. To racially motivated antisemites, however, Jewish guilt was not a product of belief, but lay "in the blood," and the Jews' nefarious traits could never be removed by baptism. Jews themselves were a constant and irredeemably corrupting danger to society.

Galton's term referred to the selective breeding of human populations for favored characteristics and against traits deemed unworthy and dangerous. Botanists and herders had long pursued such results; Galton now promoted a similar program for human beings. Those endowed with "good" characteristics—productivity or beauty, as conventionally defined—should be encouraged to reproduce. Lesser beings, as evidenced by alcoholism, aversion to work, and in women, sexual promiscuity, should be discouraged or prohibited from reproducing. With the advance of biological knowledge and surgical techniques around the turn into the twentieth century, eugenicists envisaged radical interventions into the body, such as compulsory sterilization to prevent the reproduction of weak or disabling traits. A healthy, productive society, they argued, could be achieved only by the application of racial-biological programs. Galton's views developed a substantial following, including in Germany, where Alfred Ploetz (1860–1940) founded the *Journal for Racial and Social Biology* as one of the main scientific venues for the spread of eugenicist thinking.

NATION AND RACE IN GERMANY

Germany became a unified nation-state in 1871, when combinations of race think-ing and nationalism were reaching hegemonic status in Europe. Prior to the nineteenth century, "Germany" had been a linguistic and cultural term, not one that designated a single political entity. The German states constituted a loose collection of major and near-major powers, such as Austria, Prussia, and Bavaria, and hundreds of smaller principalities, dukedoms, prince-bishoprics, free cities, and knightly estates, all enjoying degrees of sovereignty within the Holy Roman Empire. Napoleon Bonaparte (1769–1821) consolidated many of these entities and abolished the Empire in 1806. After his fall in 1815, the European powers undid his work only partially, creating a German Confederation with thirty-nine largely independent members.

This Confederation was still not a nation-state and, in fact, very little desire existed for such a creation. For most Germans in the late eighteenth and early nineteenth centuries, religion, locality, and region were the primary foci of identity. Only a few intellectuals, responding to the great force of the French Revolution and Napoleon, had begun to posit the idea of a unified state embracing all Germans. Usually, this aspiration was articulated in conjunction with liberalism: the new German state would have a constitution and representative government, male property holders would have suffrage rights, and political liberties would be respected. This German nationalism, like others during the nineteenth century, exuded a Romantic and utopian sensibility, a pathos about the nation as the end goal of history and the nation-state as the political form that would allow Germans to reach new heights of prosperity and cultural achievement. Moreover, the first expressions of German nationalism contained a harshly exclusionary tone, an assertion of German superiority in a world of difference. All of these elements are evident to differing degrees in the statements of early advocates of the nation, among them not only Fichte but also Friedrich Ludwig Jahn (1778–1852) and various gymnastics and student associations inspired by him.

The Revolution of 1848 was a defining moment for German nationalism. By this time, that ideology had spread beyond the intellectuals who had posited the notion in the immediate post-Napoleonic years. Now the first factories and the general expansion of production and trade led the growing commercial bourgeoisie to demand a political setting more conducive to a modernizing, industrial, market-based economy. These developments required, most fundamentally, the lowering or elimination of barriers to trade, such as customs duties and tariffs imposed on goods crossing the borders between any of the German Confederation states and a multiplicity of currencies and systems of weights and measures. Those demands led to the creation in 1834 of the Zollverein, the Customs Union among many of the German states, which fostered their economic integration.

In popular demonstrations and the Frankfurt Parliament, as well as in numerous individual state constitutional assemblies that convened in 1848 and 1849, liberal nationalism came to the fore. Activists demanded a German nation-state, representative government, political liberties, and policies conducive to economic development. But just as during the French Revolution, the crucial issue of inclusion and exclusion framed much of the discussion. Who, precisely, belonged to the nation? Czech or Polish speakers who lived within member states of the Confederation? Austria, with an empire that extended into southeastern Europe and included so many diverse populations? While the debates about citizenship did not focus as much on Jews as was later the case, always lurking was a discomfort with Jewish difference. According to many liberal nationalists in the years through 1848, Jews could become German but only by giving up their beliefs and customs or at least shedding Orthodoxy for less visible, less distinctive practices. The nation could be open and inclusive but at the expense of difference.

The Revolution of 1848 did not succeed in Germany or anywhere else, with the partial exception of France. Royal and imperial power proved more potent and suppressed the popular movement, but not for long. The era from the 1860s to the 1880s became the heyday of state- and constitution-building and liberal reform in Europe and beyond, typified by the British Reform Act of 1867, the unifications of Germany and Italy, the Austro-Hungarian federal compromise, the reconstitution of the American republic in the Civil War and Reconstruction, the abolition of serfdom in Russia, and the Meiji Restoration in Japan. German unification and German nationalism were of a piece with these broader developments.

Ultimately, the creation of the nation-state was the work of Prussia, Germany's second largest state (after Austria), under its Minister President, Otto von Bismarck (1815–1898), and its Hohenzollern king, Wilhelm I (1797–1888). Bismarck understood that the preservation of Prussia's power in central Europe and beyond required placing it at the head of the movement for national unification. Otherwise, liberals or socialists might be the pacesetters of the nation. Moreover, a Prussian-directed unification would secure the power of the nobility and put to rest the specter of the French Revolution and its elimination of aristocratic privilege.

The German Empire that Bismarck created was a hybrid of authoritarian and liberal elements. Historians still debate whether the tendencies toward liberal reform could have triumphed over conservative authoritarianism anchored in the imperial family, the officer corps, and a government answerable not to the parliament but to the throne (M. L. Anderson 2000; Röhl 2001). They argue about whether the German model was *sui generis*, a deviation from a common western pattern of liberal reform and democratic advance whose distinctiveness resulted, finally, in the Third Reich (Blackbourn and Eley 1984; Wehler 1985).

Although the latter perspective is too teleological, the formation of the German nation-state certainly provided a strong platform for the growth of nationalism as well as a modern economy. By the turn into the twentieth century, Germany had developed a thriving industrial system and substantial, vibrant cities and towns that were the settings for probably the most developed educational and research systems in the world and a vigorous cultural life. Germany's urbanization also set the stage for intense social conflict as the burgeoning industrial working class struggled against often miserable living and working conditions. The German Social Democratic Party became the world's largest and most prestigious socialist organization and a model of the modern, mass movement that deployed demonstrations, an extensive press, and youth and cultural organizations in an integrated fashion.

Jewish life thrived in the new German Empire. The French revolutionary and Napoleonic conquest of Germany in the late eighteenth and early nineteenth centuries had fostered the emancipation of the Jews—that is, the removal of legal disabilities upon them and the establishment of Jewish equality under the law. Although some of these measures were rolled back in 1815, most German states reinstated emancipation during the ensuing decades, and the Constitution of the German Empire of 1871 completed the process of extending full legal equality. Jews still faced substantial prejudice in certain sectors of society, however. The state bureaucracy, the officer corps, and managerial positions in heavy industry were largely closed to them. But in professions such as law and medicine and the new, rapidly expanding arenas of the press and the cultural world, Jews found a prominent place. Although assimilation and outmarriage were significant trends, Jewish life and communal institutions flourished. Jews, in turn, gave their fervent loyalty to Germany, most of them choosing one or another of the liberal parties on election days. Through World War I, Jewish nationalism in the German Empire was largely German nationalism, not Zionism.

Overall, German nationalism retained many of its liberal features from the Revolution of 1848 and earlier. The Constitution of 1871 provided the firm basis for Jewish men to become full-fledged citizens of Germany. Even some Africans who hailed originally from the German colonies could become citizens via military service. There were no formal color or religious bars to citizenship, and in that sense, the German Empire was a solidly liberal political order.

At the same time, the more exclusionary strains of nationalism, often mingled with racism, were audible, especially after 1890, as the social and political tensions caused by rapid industrialization became palpable, and Germany under the new Kaiser (emperor), Wilhelm II (1859–1941), projected its power on the global stage. The first antisemitic parties had proven a flash in the pan, but after 1890, zealous expressions of antisemitism appeared in the platforms and statements of the conservative parties and innumerable conservative associations, such as the Agrarian League and the Navy League. Although led by established nobles, officers, businessmen, and academics, these associations developed mass followings and forged a mass politics that made them harbingers of twentieth-century European political action (Eley 1980). All of these groups targeted Jews as the source of Germany's woes, which were often, in fact, the woes of specific segments of society—the low commodity prices and indebtedness faced by farmers, the competition from department stores (often Jewish-owned) that confronted small shopkeepers, and the discomfort with the incipient signs of a modern mass consumer culture felt by many religious Germans. The Jewish presence in urban society, in the professions, and in the cultural realm, made Jews the symbols of a modern world that many Germans disliked intensely.

Some of the associations, the Navy League being a prime example, had close ties to the very upper reaches of the German state. Wilhelm II and his hangers-on maintained their support for the League even when its lobbying for a powerful fleet sometimes seemed uncouth. Indeed, the other impetus to a more stringent, shrill nationalism came directly from the state and from the man who acceded to the imperial throne in 1888. A decade later, the Kaiser officially launched Germany's "world policy," which sought to extend German power abroad, most notably in Anatolia and the Middle East. Little of liberal nationalism's emancipatory, humanistic element could be heard as Wilhelm and his minions, along with troops of intellectuals, publicists, and businessmen, proclaimed the virtues of German world power. That power was also tied to the colonial empire that Germany began to secure in 1884. Southwest Africa (today Namibia) and East Africa (today Tanzania, excluding the island of Zanzibar) were the major sites of German imperial activity, but Togo, Cameroon, and Samoa were also significant, and Germany, along with the other European powers, also established a sphere of influence in China.

Germany's African colonies incubated a specifically anti-black racism that functioned to legitimate exploitative and brutal behavior by settlers and officials, which then set off revolts by the indigenous populations that were cruelly suppressed. In Southwest Africa, the German army pursued a campaign of deliberate annihilation against the Herero and Nama peoples, thereby creating the first genocide of the twentieth century (Hull 2005). Between 1904 and 1908, 60 to 80 percent of the Herero and 40 to 60 percent of the Nama died in combat, from starvation and thirst in the Omaheke desert, into which the German army drove them, and in concentration camps.

When the fighting ended, Germany imposed an apartheid system that expropriated all land and cattle from the surviving Herero and Nama, retroactively banned marriages between Germans and Africans, and ordered Africans (with the exception of the "mixed race" Reheboth Bastards) to wear passports around their necks, all as parts of an effort to track and control the movement of Africans and to reduce a largely pastoral people to the status of wage laborers. In short, Germany's first racial state and society took shape, not under the Third Reich, but under Imperial Germany in its prime African colony. The German army, colonial administrators, and settlers learned that against Africans they could practice the most brutal measures possible, and could do so with the active support of the very center of German state power, the Kaiser, the military staff, and the civilian government. As Hannah Arendt wrote:

African colonial possessions became the most fertile soil for the flowering of what later was to become the Nazi elite. Here they had seen with their own eyes how peoples could be converted into races and how, simply by taking the initiative in this process, one might push one's own people into the position of the master race....When the European mob discovered what a "lovely virtue" a white skin could be in Africa, when the English conqueror in India became an administrator who no longer believed in the universal validity of law, but was convinced of his own innate capacity to rule and dominate ... the stage seemed to be set for all possible horrors. Lying under anybody's nose were many of the elements which gathered together could create a totalitarian government on the basis of racism. (Arendt 1958: 206–7, 221)

German nationalism, then, was articulated in racial terms in relation to Africans, and colonial culture was reproduced in novels, stories, advertisements, and carnival displays of Africans and African villages, all depicting their inferiority, which was presumed to be "in the blood" and transmitted through the generations. All of this occurred at precisely the same time that antisemitism targeted Jews as the source of German ills and called for the exclusion of Jews from German society. In short, an intermingling of images, characterizations, and policy prescriptions for Jews and Africans took place within the German domain. Especially on the part of Germany's large and varied right wing—which would become even bigger and more complex after World War I—Jews and Africans were seen as threatening to the German nation and way of life. Both groups had to be subdued and segregated, albeit in different fashions.

Moreover, rivalries among states intensified in the two decades prior to World War I. At sea and on land, the major powers competed for imperial domination and on more than one occasion came close to combat. Germany began to build a much larger, more powerful navy and to challenge Britain's control of the seas. On the fringes of Europe, Japan and the United States emerged as major powers, hinting at a world that might no longer be dominated by Europe. These developments contributed a much more aggressive tone to nationalism all across Europe. German publicists and statesmen spoke scathingly of Britain as a mere "shopkeeper" nation, of "effeminate" Frenchmen, and of "mongrel" Americans.

From War to Race War

World War I accentuated these tendencies. Although the picture of universal support for war on 4 August 1914 is exaggerated, the majority of Germans did rally to the flag with nationalist zeal. They were fighting, so they were told and many believed, barbaric Russians who threatened to overrun German soil, Belgians and French who coveted German land and German women, and the British (and later Americans as well) who feared Germany's economic prowess. Moreover, what began as a war among states became a war among peoples, often defined in racial terms (Mosse 1990). Total war required the mobilization of all societal resources, including public morale. Every belligerent nation developed a propaganda apparatus that depicted the enemy in fearsome terms. More importantly, in eastern Europe German soldiers and officials obtained the direct experience of ruling subject populations, somewhat akin to the experience in the overseas colonies. Occupation was a heady experience, one that inspired thoughts of a grand German imperium across the continent. Those visions flourished among the Kaiser and his staff, the officer corps, and the civilian government. They were relayed to the population at large through the promise of victory, the pledge that all of the great sacrifices borne in war would be recompensed by the prosperity that Germans would reap through their domination of Europe. Although a humanistic core to German nationalism still existed among many people, nationalism had also come to mean subjugation of others.

The Fatherland Party emerged on the extreme right, advocating a massive annexationist program and a military-political dictatorship and blaming the nation's beleaguered military situation on the Hohenzollern monarch and Germany's civilian leaders. The Party's rapid growth signaled the eclipse of traditional, aristocratic conservatism by a radical, populist conservatism that propelled the fascist movements of the postwar era. On the Left, the war bred division, frustration, and mounting labor unrest. Germany's politics became even more fragmented and more radical. In short, the legacy of World War I to the German nation was intense political polarization.

More than any other period in German history, the postwar era was riven with contradictions. Between 1917 and 1923, a democratic movement swept through every sector of German society. Largely working class and socialist in origin, it spread in 1918–19 to soldiers and sailors, artists and intellectuals, and even to some peasants, and it toppled the imperial regime and established representative government. Although the new democracy was founded in the worst conditions imaginable—the war left two million Germans dead, four million wounded, and the population at home impoverished and dispirited—the proclamation of the Weimar Constitution in August 1919 heralded the possibility of a resurgence of liberal nationalism in Germany, one linked to social solidarity rather than inter-state rivalry (Weitz 2007).

Yet the war's bitter legacy stalked such hopeful prospects. The Allies' imposition of the Versailles Treaty in 1919 stripped Germany of border regions that virtually all Germans considered intrinsic to the nation, placed the nation's former colonies under the victorious powers, limited the size of its armed forces, compelled it to accept responsibility for the outbreak of the war, and saddled the country with the obligation to pay the victors reparations of a not yet specified amount. As a result, the peace terms became a focal point of aggrieved nationalism in Germany. From all political corners thundered rhetorical depictions of Germany as a victim of the rapacious Allies, aided, in the communist version, by the collusion of homegrown capitalists or, in the Nazi version, by that of the Jews.

Resentment of the "dictate of Versailles" fit easily with the "stab-in-the-back" legend, the military's self-serving tale that Germany had not been defeated in battle but betrayed at home by socialists and Jews. Indeed, at the time of the armistice on 11 November 1918 German troops still occupied parts of France, Belgium, and Russia, which seemed to lend credence to the claim that they remained unbeaten. But on the western front, those troops were in irreversible retreat, and the two supreme commanders of the military, Field Marshal Paul von Hindenburg (1847–1934) and General Erich Ludendorff (1865–1937), knew that the army was at the breaking point. Ludendorff's first formulations of the stab-in-the-back in October 1918 were a brazen effort to cover up his own failures, but the charge carried far and wide and had special resonance with the multitudinous right wing.

The nationalism of the war years had been infused with the allure of domination; that of the postwar years became infused with a pathos of victimhood. The Nazis proved particularly adept at fusing both elements into a vision of German power and racial purity. Master political rhetoricians and organizers, the Nazis appropriated the heady vocabulary of the German right wing and carried out the virtually complete merger of race thinking and nationalism. *Volkstum* and *Deutschtum* (roughly, "peopleness" and "German-ness") conveyed belief in a German essence that was found "in the blood" and transmitted through the generations. The "people's body" (*Volkskörper*) was productive, disciplined, and creative, but threatened with corruption by diverse foreign bodies, notably Jews, but also Slavs and Gypsies, and by Germans who were deficient in specified ways. These foes were the perpetrators of the *Dolchstoß* (stab-in-the-back), and they were the true beneficiaries of the postwar "profiteers'" or "Jews'" Republic (*Schieber-* or *Judenrepublik*). With Germans' victory over the Jews, a Third Reich (*Drittes Reich*) would arise to succeed its medieval and Wilhelminian forerunners and to last for a thousand years.

The endpoint of this vicious fantasizing was not utopia but annihilation of the Jews and a swath of destruction through Europe that ultimately rebounded upon Germany and its people. This history was neither predetermined nor an aberration from some imagined normal course of German or European development. The Holocaust emerged as a particular manifestation of the intermingling of race thinking and nationalism, the predominant ways of understanding difference and political community in the modern world.

New Directions in Research

For the most part, nation and race have been the subjects of distinct lines of scholarly inquiry. Many historians and social scientists have posited strict boundaries between the two forms of defining difference. But more may be gained in the future by examining the intersecting development of ideologies of nation and race, especially under the influence of colonialism. Scholars working on Germany have begun to explore what specialists in French, British, Dutch, Portuguese, and Spanish history have appreciated for a generation, namely that colonies were not mere appendages to European nation-states, but an intrinsic aspect of their history in the nineteenth and twentieth centuries. The metropole not only shaped the colony; the colony profoundly influenced the culture and society of the dominating country. One of the ways it did so was in contributing to the racialization of national identities. In the German case, that process produced hitherto almost unimaginable degrees of destruction and death.

References

Anderson, B. (1991). *Imagined Communities: Reflections on the Origin and Spread of Nationalism.* Rev. edn. London: Verso Books.

Anderson, M. (2000). *Practicing Democracy: Elections and Political Culture in Imperial Germany.* Princeton, NJ: Princeton University Press.

Arendt, H. (1958). *The Origins of Totalitarianism.* New York: Meridian Books. (Orig. pub. 1951.)

Beiner, R. (ed.) (1998). *Theorizing Nationalism.* Albany, NY: SUNY Press.

Blackbourn, D. and Eley, G. (1984). *The Peculiarities of German History: Bourgeois Society and Politics in Nineteenth-Century Germany.* New York: Oxford University Press.

Brubaker, R. (1992). *Citizenship and Nationhood in France and Germany.* Cambridge, MA: Harvard University Press.

——(2004). *Ethnicity without Groups.* Cambridge, MA: Harvard University Press.

Eley, G. (1980). *Reshaping the German Right: Radical Nationalism and Political Change after Bismarck.* New Haven, CT: Yale University Press.

Fredrickson, G. (2002). *Racism: A Short History.* Princeton, NJ: Princeton University Press.

Gellner, E. (1983). *Nationalism.* Ithaca, NY: Cornell University Press.

Hannaford, I. (1996). *Race: The History of an Idea in the West.* Washington, DC: Woodrow Wilson Center Press.

Hobsbawm, E. (1990). *Nations and Nationalism since 1780: Programme, Myth, Reality.* Cambridge: Cambridge University Press.

Hull, I. (2005). *Absolute Destruction: Military Culture and the Practices of War in Imperial Germany.* Ithaca, NY: Cornell University Press.

KOHN, H. (1944). *The Idea of Nationalism: A Study in its Origins and Background*. New York: Macmillan.

MOSSE, G. (1990). *Fallen Soldiers: Reshaping the Memory of the World Wars*. New York: Oxford University Press.

PEABODY, S. and STOVALL, T. (eds.) (2003). *The Color of Liberty: Histories of Race in France*. Durham, NC: Duke University Press.

RÖHL, J. (2001). *Wilhelm II: Der Aufbau der Persönlichen Monarchie, 1888–1900*. Munich: C. H. Beck.

SEWELL, W., JR. (1994). *A Rhetoric of Bourgeois Revolution: The Abbé Sieyes and "What Is the Third Estate?"* Durham, NC: Duke University Press.

WEHLER, H. (1985). *The German Empire, 1871–1918*. Leamington Spa: Berg Publishers.

WEITZ, E. (2003). *A Century of Genocide: Utopias of Race and Nation*. Princeton, NJ: Princeton University Press.

——(2007). *Weimar Germany: Promise and Tragedy*. Princeton, NJ: Princeton University Press.

OTHER SUGGESTED READING

GEWALD, J. (1999). *Herero Heroes: A Socio-Political History of the Herero of Namibia, 1890–1923*. Oxford: James Currey.

KING, R. and STONE, D. (eds.) (2007). *Hannah Arendt and the Uses of History: Imperialism, Nation, Race, and Genocide*. New York: Berghahn Books.

MOSSE, G. (1975). *The Nationalization of the Masses: Political Symbolism and Mass Movements in Germany from the Napoleonic Wars through the Third Reich*. New York: Howard Fertig.

PULZER, P. (1964). *The Rise of Political Anti-Semitism in Germany and Austria*. New York: Wiley.

VOLKOV, S. (2006). *Germans, Jews, and Antisemites: Trials in Emancipation*. Cambridge: Cambridge University Press.

WEBER, E. (1976). *Peasants into Frenchmen: The Modernization of Rural France, 1870–1914*. Stanford: Stanford University Press.

ZIMMERER, J. (2002). *Deutsche Herrschaft über Afrikaner: Staatlicher Machtanspruch und Wirklichkeit im kolonialen Namibia*. Münster: Lit Verlag.

CHAPTER 4

···

COLONIALISM

···

A. DIRK MOSES

IDENTIFYING colonialism as an enabler of the Holocaust invites the objection that antisemitism and World War I were more powerful progenitors. Colonialism usually refers to maritime or blue water empires, and Germany held its seven major overseas possessions in Africa and the Pacific region only from the 1880s until the Treaty of Versailles in 1919. How could such an ephemeral episode be of great consequence? Even the proposition that colonialism enabled fascism faces problems: For a long time, Britain and France had large empires, but those nations did not go the way of Italy or Germany. Besides, did not Adolf Hitler (1889–1945) shun colonialism in Africa as a distraction from hegemony in Europe?

These objections slight some sixty years of fruitful analysis of National Socialism's relationship to colonial expansion and imperialism (Neumann 1944; Arendt 1951; Césaire 1955; Dallin 1981; Koehl 1957; Fanon 1963). Nevertheless, challenges remain in demonstrating significant *empirical* links between late nineteenth- and early twentieth-century colonialism and the Holocaust. Imperial Germany's colonial possessions and the associated governmental infrastructure were relatively small. The number of former colonial officials, soldiers, and scientists who became Nazis also was not large. Much has been made of the facts that Heinrich Göring (1839–1913), the infamous Hermann's father, had been a colonial administrator in Southwest Africa and that Franz Ritter von Epp (1868–1946), an officer of the German forces that crushed the Herero, became a Freikorps leader who nurtured the young Hitler. Also, the anthropologist Eugen Fischer (1874–1967) conducted field work in Southwest Africa for studies that Hitler apparently read, thus laying the basis for an influential career under the Nazis, during which Fischer advocated the sterilization of the children fathered in western Germany during the 1920s by occupation forces from French West Africa (Madley 2005). Much could be made of the fact that in the early 1940s SS men commonly called their Ukrainian auxiliaries "askari," which was the Swahili term used decades earlier for the indigenous troops of German East Africa. Still, such direct linkages seem more arresting than consequential.

The tenuous nature of these connections has led some recent scholarship to emphasize morphological rather than empirical continuity. Jürgen Zimmerer, the most prominent exponent of this contemporary school, highlights the "structural parallels" of "race and space" shared by the Holocaust and the genocidal counter-insurgency against the Herero and Nama people in German Southwest Africa between 1904 and 1907. On the basis of these parallels, he claims that the Nazi campaign "against Poland and the USSR was without doubt the largest colonial war of conquest in history" (in Moses 2004: 49). The African case was an "important precedent" for "race war," without which the Holocaust "would probably not have been thinkable." Breaking the taboo against destroying entire peoples, it showed that a colonial war and a war of extermination could be one and the same (Zimmerer 2008). Isabel Hull reasons similarly, but from an earlier starting point that leads her to a different conclusion. She finds the historical precursor of the Holocaust and especially German military brutality toward civilians during World War II in a specifically Prussian-German military doctrine that was forged during the war against France in 1870–71. That doctrine stressed massive and concentrated violence to achieve "absolute destruction" of enemies, particularly those operating behind German lines. Thus, in her view, the murderous campaign in Southwest Africa was less a cause than a result, and the real harbinger of German viciousness in World War II lay further back in history (Hull 2005).

To demonstrate how colonialism enabled the Holocaust requires yet another approach, one that focuses on how the generic concept illuminates broader and deeper connections. This perspective directs attention to the totality of European imperial history since the late nineteenth century. Imperial centers and their colonial peripheries were porous economic, cultural, and military domains that contended with one another in fields of action governed by philosophies of struggle and survival. Because Europe comprised colonial powers and continental empires, Nazi Germany cannot be understood outside a colonial or imperial frame. To understand how the guerrilla wars, racism, colonial rule, and settlement patterns of the imperial era are related to the Nazi conquest of Europe and the destruction of Jews, Roma, and Slavs entails examining German expansionism in relation to European empire in general, as well as determining the colonial and imperial features of the Holocaust.

GERMAN EMPIRES, AFRICAN AND EUROPEAN

German colonialism, like that of other nations, was an expression of aspirations for power, prosperity, security, and status. Expansionism to these ends could aim just as well at contiguous as remote lands, providing a country was willing to pay the price in conflict. For this reason, applying the term "colonialism" only to maritime empires is misleading. "Modern colonialism," as one scholar put it recently, "can be defined as the annexation of a territory by people with ties to a foreign state who perceive the conquered population as culturally distant and inferior. Annexation is followed by efforts to appropriate the resources of the colony and to dominate its inhabitants in an ongoing way, that is, by a state apparatus" (Steinmetz 2007). *Weltpolitik* (the acquisitions of extra-European colonies with a strong navy) and *Ostpolitik* (eastern Europe as Germany's imperial space) represented flipsides of the same coin (Liulevicius 2000: 166–7).

The affinity between these notions accounts for the ease with which Hans Grimm's book about German colonialism in Africa, *Volk ohne Raum* (People without Space), published in 1926, morphed in the public mind into a book about Germany's possibilities in eastern Europe (W. D. Smith 1986). That region long had been regarded, in the words of General Erich Ludendorff (1865–1937), as "primal German settlement territory," because German settlers had colonized it centuries earlier and in some places still constituted the leading social stratum (Koehl 1953: 56). Furthermore, Imperial Germany already was a continental land empire that, like its Russian and Austro-Hungarian counterparts, included national minorities—above all Poles, who composed more than 6 percent of the population, mainly in Prussian border regions, where they often constituted a majority. Attempts to drive these people out and replace them with German speakers enjoyed considerable support. Indeed, Chancellor Otto von Bismarck (1815–1898) launched the Royal Prussian Colonization Commission in 1886 to acquire Polish-owned estates for German farmers as part of an effort to change the ethnic composition of Germany's eastern provinces, and the Society for the Support of Germandom in the Eastern Marches was established in 1894 to advance similar aims. The latter group (nicknamed the H-K-T Society or *Hakatisten* after the initials of its founders) depicted Poles and Slavs as primitive people who deserved to be supplanted by Germans and modernity (Eley 1980, Tims 1941).

Before as well as during the Nazi period, a versatile form of colonial rhetoric saturated political discourse. *Lebensraum*, a term coined in the 1890s by the political geographer Friedrich Ratzel (1844–1904), became the chief rationale of German overseas and continental expansion. Ratzel literally rooted success in the Darwinian struggle for collective survival in a people's possession of sufficient land to provide prosperity. *Lebensraum* became a slogan for the political right in the 1920s and a central concept of the new academic discipline of "geopolitics," which explained national foreign policies as responses to the location and resources of states. Via Rudolf Hess (1894–1987) and Alfred Rosenberg (1893–1946), such thinking influenced Hitler, who concluded that Germany's *Lebensraum* lay in eastern Europe (W. D. Smith 1986).

COLONIAL RULE AND ANTISEMITISM

By the end of the nineteenth century, antisemitism and colonial racism were intertwined, especially in the right-wing milieu of the Pan-German League (Eley 1980). In the period prior to World War I, this group's understanding of a future German empire in Europe was influenced by contemporaneous discussions about German colonialism in Africa and the Pacific. Upset by the success of Jewish integration into German society, the Pan-Germans became obsessed with racial mixing, contending that such "bastardization" had brought about the fall of the Roman Empire. Their ideal of a "tribal empire" (*Stammesreich*) in Europe posited a racially pure utopia of German rule over Slavs (von Joeden-Forgey in King and Stone 2007: 31).

German rule over Africans provided the model of racial subjugation, segregation, and oppression. In the 1890s, for instance, German antisemites simultaneously demanded that Jews be placed under a special alien law and that Africans be subjected to a separate "native law." They defended Carl Peters (1856–1918), the German colonial adventurer whose brutal treatment of the locals in German East Africa scandalized sensibilities at home, by insisting that European norms of war could not apply to Africans, who inhabited an inferior moral universe. Above all, the Jewish presence in Germany became understood in the context of a race-conscious worldview in which conquest and colonization of foreign peoples, hierarchies of civilization, progress and decline, survival and extinction were central elements. In 1912, Heinrich Class (1868–1953), who led the Pan-German League from 1908 to 1939, published *Wenn ich der Kaiser wäre* (If I Were the Emperor), which called for banning Jews from public office, the legal profession, and any position that might give them dominance over Germans. During World War I, Class advocated German expansion and annexation in eastern Europe, complete with "an ethnic housecleaning" to ensure German control in that region, including the expulsion of all Jews. By then, such ideas had moved from the periphery to the mainstream of conservative nationalist thinking, a trend illustrated by the German acquisition of territory, at least for a time, in the Baltic region, Belarus, Ukraine, and even the Caucasus after the defeat of the Russian army in 1917 (Liulevicius 2000; H. Smith 2008: 222–3).

An important distinction between colonial racism and antisemitism pivoted on the facts that Jews were *in* Germany and doing well. These circumstances inverted the framing dichotomy of colonizer–colonized in Germany. Especially during World War I, German antisemites played up Jewish success and non-Jewish German suffering and construed both as results of Jewish domination over non-Jewish Germans. Already during the 1912 national elections, right-wing Germans had decried supposed Jewish control of international communism and capitalism. In Austria, antisemites complained that Jews owned more than 50 percent of the banks and held 80 percent of the key positions in banking. The development of capitalism was presented as a Jewish imposition, a "control system" over gentiles (Mosse 1964: 142). During the war, the military, in particular, complained about shirking and profiteering by Jews. No less a figure than General Ludendorff leveled an accusation that became common during the Weimar Republic. "They [Jews] acquired a dominant influence in the 'war corporations' . . . which gave them the occasion to enrich themselves at the expense of the German people and to take possession of the German economy, in order to achieve one of the power goals of the Jewish people" (quoted in Friedländer 1997: 74).

Many Germans regarded themselves as an "indigenous" people who were being slowly colonized by foreigners, namely Jews. Indicative of this outlook was a *völkisch* obsession with "ancient German tribes" whose virtues of simplicity and honesty were contrasted with the decadent civilization of the French and British. This ideology culminated in the "blood and soil" rhetoric of the Nazis, who idealized the peasant rooted in the land. Nomadic peoples—such as Arabs and Jews—were parasites, whereas settlers, such as the "Nordic" colonists in North America, spread civilization and advanced humanity (Mosse 1964: 67–71).

Anxiety about "colonization" by Jews was compounded after World War I when parts of the Rhineland were occupied by French troops from Africa. The imperial rivals that had stripped Germany of its overseas possessions now added insult to injury by making Germany the colonized, not the colonizer (Poley 2005). Right-wing Germans launched a massive propaganda campaign against the "black disgrace" of the occupation, replete with lurid tales of rapes and violence against local women. In thrall to conspiracy theories, they believed the occupation was an international plot to contaminate Germans with "inferior blood." Foreign Minister Adolf Köster (1883–1930) spoke for many when he complained, "the German *Volkskörper* was facing permanent annihilation on its western front" (Koller in Hagemann and Schüler-Springorum 2002: 145–7). In short, the occupation was portrayed as an act of premeditated genocide against Germans, as by Hitler in *Mein Kampf*:

It was and is the Jews who bring the negro to the Rhine with the same concealed thought and clear goal of destroying, by the bastardization which would necessarily set in, the white race which they hate, to throw it down from its cultural and political height and in turn to rise personally to the position of master. (1940: 448–9)

Hitler's sense of panic about reverse colonization was palpable. Jews, a "foreign people," had erected a "tyranny" over Germany, enslaving it through the stock exchange, the media, cultural life, and the governmental machinery of the Weimar Republic (Hitler 1940: 426–33). His arguments that Jews had infiltrated the ruling strata by intermarriage later were shared by many, including the National Socialist *Sippenforscher* (genealogical researcher) Heinrich Banniza von Bazan (1904–1950), who deplored the "flood" of Jewish immigration from Poland and complained that, "Following the collapse of the German people after the world war, [Jewish] domination over the political fate of the nation became totally naked. A racially alien stratum developed that arrogated to itself the power to codetermine the welfare and direction of the German people." Moreover, Bazan fearfully calculated that by the Nazi seizure of power in 1933, "some 2.5 million residents had Jewish blood coursing through their veins" (Bazan 1937: 92–3).

Hitler's "indigenous" response to this perceived colonization and foreign rule was to expel the Jewish colonists and establish an autarkic economy removed from "international finance control"—that is, from their influence (Hitler 1940: 380). Otherwise the fate that met other peoples in the past awaited Germany: "Carthage's fall is the horrible picture of such a slow self-earned execution of a nation" (Hitler 1940: 969). Time was short. The alleged Jewish colonizer was pressing its rule over the world: "The British Empire is slowly becoming a colony of the American Jews!" (Hitler 1980: 305).

HITLER'S IMPERIALISM

The loss of Germany's colonies in World War I occasioned a persistent effort to win them back, especially since the great powers remained unremittingly imperialist. Much was at stake. Article 22 of the Treaty of Versailles disqualified Germans from governing "natives" by highlighting, somewhat hypocritically, German colonial abuses. Driven by German colonial associations, the counter-campaign used trade fairs, exhibitions, publications, and lobbying to raise consciousness in the German population, to restore national honor, and to advance the cause in the international community. Hitler was no enthusiast for this colonial revisionism, although he rhetorically supported the return of German colonies. He saw no point in challenging the British maritime empire. The ambition to do so after the 1890s had led to a disastrous war, and the German colonial possessions were not worth the sacrifice. He greatly admired the British Empire, which he thought was based not on the professed humanitarian ideals of its apologists, but on the "capitalist exploitation of 350 million slaves" (Hitler 1953: 193). Long rule in India had inculcated in the British a racial arrogance and born-to-rule mentality that he wanted Germans to emulate.

In the 1920s, Hitler's eclectic reading and exposure to the new discipline of geopolitics and its concepts of continental domination and *Lebensraum* (living space) led him to conclude that Germany's future lay in a European empire. Analogies with past empires—Greek, Persian, Mongol, Aztec, Inca, and Spanish—were integral to Hitler's worldview. He attributed Rome's success to the absorption of Aryan blood by its ruling strata and Rome's decline to racial intermixing and Christianity, with its pernicious doctrine of racial equality. According to Hitler, Bolshevism, another Jewish invention, performed the same corrosive, leveling function in his own time (Hitler 1953: 78).

Traumatized by Germany's loss in World War I and convinced that Germans faced extinction, Hitler applied the lessons of a world history that he imagined imperialistically and without sentimentality. Germany must never again be vulnerable to internal colonization by a foreign people (Jews) or at the mercy of foreign powers in the manner of the Weimar Republic. Salvation lay in founding a self-sufficient, continental, Germanic empire, eradicating opposition, clearing away superfluous Slavs, and settling the new border regions with "Aryan" colonists (Lower 2005). His imperial commissars in Ukraine should act like viceroys (Dallin 1981: 103). The essence of National Socialism was imperial expansion (W. Smith 1986: 231).

Hitler has been interpreted as being, in principle, against far-off colonies, but a careful reading of his texts shows that he admired how the British used their colonies for both settlement and resource exploitation. The problem with Germany's former African colonies was that their climates and soils were ill-suited to North American- or Australian-style settler colonialism (Hitler 2003: 77). By 1936, Hitler had recommitted to *Weltpolitik*, but now on the assumption that Africa would be a source of raw materials and eastern Europe a receiver of German settlers (Schmokel 1964: 51). A "folkish land and space policy" for Germany must be based, therefore, on contiguous territory in eastern Europe. Germany needed to colonize this space as it had so successfully in the past (Hitler 1944: 26–7). Dismissing the western rhetoric of civilizing uplift as brazen hypocrisy, Hitler enjoined ruthless exploitation to match how he thought the western powers actually governed their colonial possessions (Hitler 1944: 353). He wanted an extractive empire as the British had in India, but also settler colonies—enriched by plunder—as had developed in North America. In Hitler, the imperial models of centuries of human history congealed into a single, total, imperial outlook that entailed genocidal conquest, colonization, and exploitation.

As a result, Nazi occupation policy in eastern Europe had three central and incompatible agendas—economic exploitation (which included slave labor), population resettlement, and security—that also were characteristic of colonial rule. In practice, even in occupied Poland, which was the object of more sustained occupation and planning than the Soviet Union, reconciling these competing agendas was impossible because ruthless exploitation and forced resettlement gave Slavs no incentive to harvest their crops and drove them into the hands of partisans. Hitler's imperialism was internally incoherent.

German plans for the racial restructuring of Polish and later Soviet territory were certainly colonial in style and form (Müller in Boog et al. 1998: 118–224). Whether in the prewar Polish territories annexed to Germany or in those grouped into the General Government or captured from the USSR in 1941, the German occupiers consistently referred to the land and their mission in colonial terms, depicting the Poles and Jews as backward and uncivilized and the land as undeveloped (Aly and Heim 2002). Demographic planners revived and extended the program of the *Hakatisten* and set out to make room for German settlers by removing Poles and Jews (Browning 2004). The authors of the *Generalplan Ost* and later the *General-Siedlungsplan,* the long-term Nazi plans for the German East, envisaged not only the largest genocide in history—the anticipated deportation and starvation of tens of millions of Slavs to "modernize" the economic structure—but also the permanent rule of German colonists, who would occupy fortified settlements whence they would rule over a "helot" population of denationalized "slaves" (Kay 2006). In other parts of eastern Europe, "native non-Bolshevik governments" would govern on behalf of Germans, and the Slavic population would be mobilized against Jews in the manner of colonial divide-and-rule tactics (Förster in Boog et al. 1998: 481).

Jews were barely mentioned in the *Generalplan Ost* because they had no long-term future within occupied Poland's General Government, even though—against the will of its governor, Hans Frank (1900–1946)—Jews from elsewhere in German-occupied Europe were temporarily ghettoized there. Still, the fact that the systematic mass killing of Jews did not begin until the invasion of the USSR in mid-1941 indicates that settlement policy alone cannot account for the Holocaust. Moreover, Heinrich Himmler (1900–1945), who was in charge of German settlement, largely abandoned those demographic plans after the defeat at Stalingrad in 1943 (Madajczyk in Michalka 1989: 849). Henceforth ready to compromise about population policies toward Slavs, he remained relentless regarding the extermination of Jews.

The role of security proved to be more decisive in shaping policy toward the Jews. Reinhard Heydrich (1904–1942) summarized this outlook when he remarked that "*political* pacification is the first prerequisite for *economic* pacification" (quoted in Kay 2006: 105). Political pacification meant the elimination of actual or even potential resistance to German rule. Jews were particularly suspect, above all Soviet Jews, because Nazism defined them as congenitally hostile to Germans. The Nazis had convinced themselves that Jews were responsible for the traumatic collapse of the German home front and military morale in 1917 and 1918, as well as the short-lived postwar socialist government in Munich (Hitler 1944: 246;

Förster in Boog et al. 1998: 498). As the supposed bearers of Bolshevism, Jews were linked by Nazis to both insurrection at home and the terrorist regime in the USSR that had exterminated classes and peoples in an "Asiatic" manner. There could be no place for such a dangerous people in the German empire.

This worldview had much to do with colonialism and, in particular, colonial-style warfare, which had been characterized by disregard for the conventional laws of war. By criminalizing Soviet and Jewish enemies, the German state authorized its military to conduct the eastern campaign as a colonial conflict in which the laws of war regarding treatment of combatants and civilians did not apply. All resistance was regarded as illegitimate, and civilians were targeted *pre-emptively* and often *collectively* to forestall future resistance, just as in colonial wars of "pacification" against unruly tribes. Hitler rejected the application of the laws of war in the Soviet campaign with the infamous "commissar order" of 6 June 1941, which permitted the summary execution of Bolshevik functionaries. Three million Russian POWs subsequently were allowed to perish. Soviet Jewish men, and eventually women and children, were murdered by Einsatzgruppen acting according to the formula "Jew equalled Bolshevik equalled partisan" (Shepherd 2004: 88).

Meanwhile, in orders and reports German military officials routinely associated Jews with other security threats: "It is ultimately of the utmost importance to eradicate the influence of the Jews and deploy the most radical measures to eliminate these elements, because they in particular . . . maintain contacts with the Red Army and the bandits we are fighting"; "The Jewish class, which forms the largest section of the population in the towns, is the driving force behind the growing resistance movement in some areas" (quoted by Heer in Heer and Naumann 2000: 103–4). The Nazi ideal of "preventative security" rested on the notion that Communist Party functionaries and Red Army officers would form the nucleus of organized resistance after German military victory. Such potential insurgents were to be hunted down in rear areas and liquidated (Förster in Boog et al. 1998: 48, 491–2, 1189; Shepherd 2004: 75).

By the end of the war, the logic of pacification meant that in parts of the Soviet Union everyone except active collaborators was considered a criminal resister. On 23 October 1942, the commissioner for "anti-bandit warfare" in central Russia, General Curt von Gottberg (1896–1945), criminalized the entire civilian population with the following order: "bandits, a population of bandit suspects and bandit sympathizers, Jews, Gypsies, horse-riders and juveniles to be considered spies" (Heer in Heer and Naumann 2000: 113). Hitler approved of such methods. To crush the resistance, he insisted, "barbaric methods" were justified, especially as the death of so many fine German soldiers tipped the demographic balance in favor of criminal elements at home who might support Bolshevism and insurrection, his greatest fear since the leftist uprising in 1919 (Hitler 1980: 348). Colonialism and the Holocaust are linked by the well-known formula of "race and space" and by common inflationary quests for security.

CONCLUSION

The Holocaust was not a classical case of "colonial genocide," that is, of a colonizer destroying the colonized. Nevertheless, the colonial experience was relevant to the fate of the Jews. German Jews were killed *as colonizers* who had—in the Nazi imagination—dominated Germany and led it to the brink of extinction. Eastern European Jews had to die because they provided the "breeding ground" for those colonists. Simultaneously, Hitler regarded Germans as a colonizing people. His administrators and soldiers were taught to think of eastern Jews in terms of colonial stereotypes: as dirty, lazy, and uncivilized. For that reason, they had no place in greater Germany's future. Like many other colonized people, these Jews were murdered or worked to death. Soviet Jews were labeled as security threats to the conquest of the east and therefore murdered *pre-emptively*. The Holocaust arose out of the union of imperial and colonial impulses. It was born of a frustrated imperial nation struggling against a perceived colonizer, and it fed on the compensatory fantasies of many Germans during the interwar period, fantasies of achieving invulnerability through a new empire, colonies, and the expulsion and later elimination of "enemy peoples."

Recent research has highlighted Nazism's colonial aspirations and imperial dimensions (Lower 2005; Zimmerer 2008). Integrating the Holocaust into this picture has been challenging because Jews, especially assimilated ones, do not fit conventional images of a colonized people. But the key fact is that many Germans believed that *they* were being colonized *by* Jews. Antisemitism and the outcome of World War I did not so much eclipse colonialism as a salient enabler of the Holocaust as become entwined with it in a new, unprecedentedly vicious form of aggression.

German antisemitism radicalized during and after World War I primarily because many right-wing Germans believed that Jews not only profited from the conflict, but also used it to take control of the Weimar Republic. Such beliefs, as real as they were paranoid and fantastic, need to be reconstructed, explained, and contextualized in a world of empires in which one either colonized or was colonized and condemned to slavery or extinction. In this apocalyptic scenario, a Holocaust could be conceived and perpetrated. Research that highlights personal and institutional continuities between German colonialism and Nazi genocide can continue to show important empirical connections between the two, but what most deserves emphasis is that the Holocaust was rooted in a Nazi imperial vision that sought to correct the mistakes of Wilhelmine colonialism by forging an empire in which inner enemies were exterminated and foreign regimes were powerless to interfere.

REFERENCES

ALY, G. and HEIM, S. (2002). *Architects of Annihilation: Auschwitz and the Logic of Destruction*. London: Phoenix.

ARENDT, H. (1951). *The Origins of Totalitarianism*. New York: Harcourt Brace.

BAZAN, H. BANNIZA VON (1937). *Das deutsche Blut im deutschen Raum: Sippenkundliche Grundzüge des deutschen Bevölkerungswandels in der Neuzeit*. Berlin: Alfred Messner Verlag.

BOOG, H., FÖRSTER, J., HOFFMANN, J., KLINK, E., MÜLLER, R., and UEBERSCHÄR, G. (1998). *Germany and the Second World War*. Vol. 4, *The Attack on the Soviet Union*. Oxford: Clarendon.

BROWNING, C. (2004). *The Origins of the Final Solution: The Evolution of Nazi Jewish Policy, September 1939–March 1942*. With contributions by J. Matthäus. Lincoln, NE: University of Nebraska Press.

CÉSAIRE, A. (1955). *Discourse on Colonialism*. New York: Monthly Review Press. (Repr. 1972.)

DALLIN, A. (1981). *German Rule in Russia, 1941–1945*. 2nd edn. London: MacMillan.

ELEY, G. (1980). *Reshaping the German Right: Radical Nationalism and Political Change after Bismarck*. New Haven, CT: Yale University Press.

FANON, F. (1963). *Wretched of the Earth*. New York: Grove Press.

FRIEDLÄNDER, S. (1997). *Nazi Germany and the Jews*. Vol. 1, *The Years of Persecution, 1933–1939*. New York: HarperCollins.

HAGEMANN, K. and SCHÜLER-SPRINGORUM, S. (eds.) (2002). *Home/Front: The Military, War and Gender in Twentieth-Century Germany*. Oxford and New York: Berg.

HEER, H. and NAUMANN, K. (eds.) (2000). *The War of Extermination: The German Military in World War II, 1941–1944*. New York: Berghahn Books.

HITLER, A. (1940). *Mein Kampf*. New York: Reynal and Hitchcock.

——(1944). *Hitler's Words: Two Decades of National Socialism, 1923–1943*. Ed. G. W. Prange, intro. F. Schuman. Washington, DC: American Council on Public Affairs.

——(1953). *Hitler's Table-Talk, 1941–1945*. Introd. H. R. Trevor-Roper. Oxford: Oxford University Press.

——(1980). *Monologe im Führer-Hauptquartier, 1941–1945*. Ed. W. Jochmann. Hamburg: Albrecht Knaus.

——(2003). *Hitler's Second Book: The Unpublished Sequel to Mein Kampf*. Ed. G. L. Weinberg. New York: Enigma.

HULL, I. (2005). *Absolute Destruction: Military Culture and the Practices of War in Imperial Germany*. Ithaca, NY: Cornell University Press.

KAY, A. (2006). *Exploitation, Resettlement, Mass Murder: Political and Economic Planning for German Occupation Policy in the Soviet Union, 1940–1941*. New York: Berghahn Books.

KING, R. and STONE, D. (eds.) (2007). *Hannah Arendt and the Uses of History: Imperialism, Nation, Race, and Genocide*. New York: Berghahn Books.

KOEHL, R. (1953). "A Prelude to Hitler's Greater Germany," *American Historical Review* 59/1: 43–65.

——(1957). *RKFDV: German Resettlement and Population Policy 1939–1945: A History of the Reich Commission for the Strengthening of Germandom*. Cambridge MA: Harvard University Press.

LIULEVICIUS, V. (2000). *War Land on the Eastern Front: Culture, National Identity and German Occupation in World War I.* Cambridge and New York: Cambridge University Press.

LOWER, W. (2005). *Nazi Empire-Building and the Holocaust in Ukraine.* Chapel Hill, NC: University of North Carolina Press.

MADLEY, B. (2005). "From Africa to Auschwitz: How German South West Africa Incubated Ideas and Methods Adapted and Developed by the Nazis in Eastern Europe." *European History Quarterly* 35/3: 429–64.

MICHALKA, W. (ed.) (1989). *Der Zweite Weltkrieg: Analysen, Grundzüge, Forschungsbilanz.* Munich and Zurich: Piper.

MOSES, D. (ed.) (2004). *Genocide and Settler Society: Frontier Violence and Stolen Indigenous Children in Australian History.* New York: Berghahn Books.

MOSSE, G. (1964). *The Crisis of the German Ideology.* London: Weidenfeld and Nicolson.

NEUMANN, F. (1944). *Behemoth: The Structure and Practice of National Socialism, 1933–1944.* Chicago: Ivan R. Dee. (Repr. 2009.)

POLEY, J. (2005). *Decolonization in Germany: Weimar Narratives of Colonial Loss and Foreign Occupation.* Bern: Peter Lang.

SCHMOKEL, W. (1964). *Dream of Empire: German Colonialism, 1919–1945.* New Haven, CT: Yale University Press.

SHEPHERD, B. (2004). *War in the Wild East: The German Army and Soviet Partisans.* Cambridge, MA: Harvard University Press.

SMITH, H. (2008). *The Continuities of German History: Nation, Religion, and Race across the Long Nineteenth Century.* Cambridge: Cambridge University Press.

SMITH, W. (1986). *The Ideological Origins of Nazi Imperialism.* New York and Oxford: Oxford University Press.

STEINMETZ, G. (2007). *The Devil's Handwriting: Precoloniality and the German Colonial State in Qingdao, Samoa, and Southwest Africa.* Chicago, IL: University of Chicago Press.

TIMS, R. (1941). *Germanizing Prussian Poland: The H-K-T Society and the Struggle for the Eastern Marches in the German Empire.* New York: Columbia University Press.

ZIMMERER, J. (2008). *Von Windhuk nach Auschwitz? Beiträge zum Verhältnis von Kolonialismus und Holocaust.* Münster: Lit-Verlag.

OTHER SUGGESTED READING

AMES, E., KLOTZ, M., and WILDENTHAL, L. (eds.) (2005). *Germany's Colonial Pasts.* Lincoln, NE and London: University of Nebraska Press.

BLOXHAM, D. and MOSES, A. (eds.) (2010). *The Oxford Handbook of Genocide Studies.* New York: Oxford University Press.

BRANDON, R. and LOWER, W. (eds.) (2008). *The Shoah in Ukraine: History, Testimony, Memorialization.* Bloomington, IN: Indiana University Press.

ELEY, G. and NARANCH, B. (eds.) (2009). *German Cultures of Colonialism: Race, Nation, and Globalization, 1884–1945.* Durham, NC: Duke University Press.

GANN, L. and GUIGNAN, P. (1977). *The Rulers of German Africa, 1884–1914.* Stanford, CA: Stanford University Press.

LANGBEHN, V. and SALAMA, M. (eds.) (2009). *Colonial (Dis)-Continuities: Race, Holocaust, and Postwar Germany.* New York: Columbia University Press.

MANN, M. (2005). *The Dark Side of Democracy: Explaining Ethnic Cleansing.* New York: Cambridge University Press.

MAZOWER, M. (2008). *Hitler's Empire.* New York: Penguin.

MOSES, A. (ed.) (2008). *Empire, Colony, Genocide: Conquest, Occupation and Genocide and World History.* New York: Berghahn Books.

NELSON, R. (2009). *Colonialism in Europe? Germany's Expansion to the East.* Basingstoke: Palgrave Macmillan.

ROSSINO, A. (2003). *Hitler Strikes Poland: Blitzkrieg, Ideology, and Atrocity.* Lawrence, KS: University of Kansas Press.

ZANTOP, S. (1997). *Colonial Fantasies: Conquest, Family, and Nation in Precolonial Germany, 1770–1870.* Durham, NC: Duke University Press.

CHAPTER 5

FASCISM

PHILIP MORGAN

POINT 4 of the original German Nazi Party platform of February 1920 proclaimed that "only members of the nation may be citizens of the State. Only those of German blood, whatever their creed, may be members of the nation. Accordingly, no Jew may be a member of the nation" (Noakes and Pridham 1999: 14). Point 7 of the manifesto of November 1943 of the Republican Fascist Party, and hence of the Fascist Italian Social Republic set up under Benito Mussolini (1883–1945) in Nazi-occupied northern and central Italy, declared that "all those who belong to the Jewish race are foreigners. For the duration of the war, they shall be regarded as being of enemy nationality" (Delzell 1971: 239).

More than twenty years separated these programmatic statements. The first appeared at the very start of Adolf Hitler's political career, the second at the very end of Mussolini's. Much has been made of the long interval between these comparable commitments to the exclusion of Jews from national life. The centrality of antisemitism to Nazi ideology and the extremism and finality of its culmination in the genocide of Europe's Jews have strengthened the assumption that German Nazism was *sui generis*, a unique phenomenon separate from generic European interwar and wartime fascism. That Italian Fascism appeared to be an opportunistic late-comer to antisemitism has been taken to mean that neither that movement nor Italians bore responsibility for the Holocaust.

Recent work on Italian Fascist racism has reduced the perceived distance between the two most significant fascist movements and regimes (Centro Furio Jesi 1994; Sarfatti 1994, 2006; Burgio 2000). In so doing, it has restored credibility to the still controversial view that a general phenomenon called fascism existed in interwar and wartime Europe, rather than an assortment of radical ultra-nationalisms far surpassed in evil ideology and deeds by Adolf Hitler (1889–1945) and German Nazism. In this chapter, the first fascist movement, that of Italy, is referred to as "Fascism," and the term "fascism" denotes the broad family of ultra-nationalist cross-class parties that shared distinctive militarist organizations and activist political styles and sought to regenerate their nations through the violent destruction of all perceived anti-national forces and the formation of a new totalitarian order.

ANTISEMITISM—INTEGRAL TO FASCISM

Antisemitism was an inherent element of fascist ideology during the interwar and wartime periods, although its articulation by fascist movements and regimes varied according to national contexts. As a result, fascism contributed profoundly to creating the environment in which the Holocaust was possible.

All fascist movements, as well as the German and Italian fascist regimes, understood antisemitism as a dimension of the racism and xenophobia that each cultivated. Racism was always present in fascist ideology as an expression of hyper-nationalism. Fascists assigned political priority to creating and sustaining a strong and cohesive national community, which involved the removal of alien and non- or anti-national elements. Fascists also readily appropriated the millennial stereotype of the "wandering Jew," a being without a nation or a homeland, a member of a rootless community that battened parasitically on other people's nations. This prejudice was reinvigorated by the emergence in the nineteenth and early twentieth centuries of rival and competitive national states across Europe and the concomitant emancipation of European Jews, now recognized as full citizens of the countries where they resided. The Romanian Iron Guard, for example, was systemically anti-democratic and anti-parliamentary on the sole ground that the country's post-World War I constitution had granted rights of citizenship to Jews.

Fascist antisemitism also gained resonance in society at large during the interwar period as a result of two watershed events. The Bolshevik revolution in Russia in 1917 and the emergence of the communist Soviet Union posed a revolutionary challenge to the political systems and the territorial integrity of all European countries. The Great Depression of the late 1920s and early 1930s presented a parallel challenge to the global capitalist economy. Fascist movements in the early 1920s and the 1930s were an explicit response to and resolution of what seemed to be the collapse of European civilization. The presence of Jews in the leaderships of the Soviet and other communist parties, and the Jews' alleged dominance of bank and finance capitalism in the United States and worldwide, lent themselves easily to scapegoating and to crude depictions of a linked international Bolshevik and "plutocratic" Jewish conspiracy.

Since racism was intrinsic to fascist ideology, such antisemitism was always part and parcel of a more general racist outlook and politics. A few fascist movements, such as the *Danmarks Nationalsocialistiske Arbejderparti* (National Socialist Workers' Party of Denmark or DNSAP) and the *Nationaal Socialistische Beweging* (National Socialist Movement or NSB) in the Netherlands, explicitly imitated the German National Socialist Party, practically reproducing the latter's platform as their own, antisemitism and all. In early 1930s France, a small fascist movement called *Francisme* offered a racism tailored to the defense of a nation that was the seat of an overseas empire, condemning black African immigration in the same breath as it castigated French Jews for being inassimilable aliens. Italian Fascism provided the other example of the extension of colonial "white" on "black" racism to metropolitan antisemitism. Finland's fascist movement of the 1930s, *Isänmaallinen kansanliike* (Patriotic People's Movement or IKL), which oxymoronically regarded the Finns as a pure racial cross between Scandinavian and Baltic peoples, wanted to take away the rights not only of the country's Jews, but also of its Swedish-speaking minority as part of the realization of a Greater Finland that was to include Estonia and parts of the USSR (Morgan 2003: 86–90).

Ferenc Szálasi (1897–1946), the leader and ideologue of the late 1930s Hungarian fascist movement, the Arrow Cross, regarded himself as a "purer" National Socialist than Hitler. He developed so-called Hungarism, his view of the Magyars as Europe's Asiatics, a branch, along with the Japanese, of the "Turanians," and envisaged a global division into racial regional empires, with the Magyars dominating a Carpathian–Danubian Greater Fatherland in southeastern and eastern Europe. His purportedly "a-semitic" policy involved the deportation of Jews from Europe and the "Magyarization" of Jewish property and assets. This independently Hungarian or "Turanian" racial fantasy was one reason why Szálasi and Hitler could not cooperate until the Germans occupied Hungary in face of a Soviet invasion in 1944 and then backed an Arrow Cross takeover of the Hungarian government. The Arrow Cross militia, which earlier had participated in the Nazi German-led ghettoization and deportation of Hungary's provincial Jews, then conducted a violent pogrom and round-up of Budapest's large and assimilated Jewish population as a contribution to both the Nazi Holocaust and the realization of the "a-semitic" Turanian empire.

A similar process marked the *Ustasha* fascist movement's creation of a "Greater Croatia." Once the small state of Croatia was formed following the Axis' defeat of Yugoslavia in 1941, the *Ustasha* began clearing its territory of Serbs, Muslims, and Gypsies, as well as Jews, in a murderous campaign that was independent of the Nazi Holocaust.

The Italian Fascist regime pursued racist policy before and after it became overtly antisemitic. It attempted to impose assimilation on Italy's "inferior" ethnic and linguistic French, German, and Slav minorities, which were majorities in the sensitive northwestern and northeastern border regions of the country. The brutal, colonizing behavior of Italian military and civilian authorities in the parts of Yugoslavia that Fascist Italy annexed or occupied during World War II was but an escalation of the country's interwar efforts to destroy Slav culture and create a racially homogenous "Italianized" territory adjacent to mainland Italy (Rodogno 2006: 47–54, 258–76). The Italian Fascist regime called its Slavs and Germans "alien foreigners." Moreover, Mussolini authorized Pietro Badoglio (1871–1956) and Rodolfo Graziani (1882–1955), the Italian military governors of the North African colony of Libya, to carry out a genocidal pacification of the territory in the late 1920s. This campaign utilized a war of terror, deliberate destruction of the animal herds that were the nomadic tribes' livelihood, and desert concentration camps to prepare the colony for future Italian emigration and settlement.

Fascist Demography

One of the clearest indications that antisemitism was a component of a broad fascist racism was the common demographic policy of the Italian Fascist and German Nazi regimes. Public and governmental concern about differential patterns of fertility was widespread in all modern or modernizing societies in the early twentieth century (Quine 1996). A perceived combination of a falling birth rate among the educated and well-off classes and a rising one among the poorer and unhealthy industrial working classes was seen as threatening to social morality and to national security and survival. Population policy connected fascist policies and action on everything from social welfare to empire building and embodied fascism's aspirations to a "totalitarian" control and full mobilization of national human and material resources. Despite variations between the two fascist regimes in this sphere, similarities in aim and approach were far more significant than differences. Both Hitler and Mussolini consistently made improving the "race" a core matter of public policy, and Mussolini self-consciously placed this task in the global context of defending the "white" races from being overwhelmed by the "black" and "yellow" races. Just as national race policies were promoted as contributions to the regeneration of a declining or threatened European civilization, the Nazis "Europeanized" the Jewish question during the war, projecting their "solution" in the wartime occupied territories as an act of continental self-defense through quantitative and qualitative racial improvement. Both the German and Italian regimes stressed that the trend of declining fertility had to be reversed and the racial health of the population had to be improved to generate sufficient numbers of racially fit Italians and Germans to conquer and settle the "living space" (*Lebensraum* in German and *spazio vitale* in Italian) deemed essential to survival and dominance.

Thus, measures to encourage early marriage and prolific families, to provide pre- and post-natal care to mothers, to ban abortion and access to contraceptive advice and means, to drive women out of the labor force and into the home, where they could perform their national duty as wives and mothers, were all, ultimately, driven by fascist racial imperialism. The same went for punitive and discriminatory measures against those considered anti-social or "asocial" (e.g., criminals, drop-outs), models of "deviant" and "unnatural" behavior (bachelors, the childless, homosexuals), racially "degenerate" (Gypsies and Jews), and in the Nazi German though not the Italian Fascist case, hereditarily mentally or physically disabled (Horn 1994; Ipsen 1996; Noakes and Pridham 2000: 254–76).

That antisemitism was an aspect of a general fascist racism is also apparent from the links of both ideologies to the emerging science of genetics, i.e., the study of hereditary transmission of physical and behavioral traits, and Social Darwinism, the application to contemporary human societies of Charles Darwin's theory of evolution by a process of natural selection in which the individuals in a plant or animal population that are best adapted to the demands of their environment are most likely to live and procreate and thus to define the attributes of succeeding generations of the species. This doctrine, a commonplace of European culture by the early twentieth century, provided a pseudoscientific rationale for ideas of cultural and racial superiority and for state policies of imperialism and war. Respectively, Social Darwinism and genetics seemed to furnish explanatory frameworks for global economic, military, and territorial competition among Europe's and the world's industrial and industrializing powers, and for the apparently rising incidence of the social and moral pathologies, such as alcoholism and criminality, that seemed to accompany the transition to a modern urban and industrial civilization. Above all, these thought systems legitimated a harsh view of life as governed by relentless struggle and competition in which only the "fittest" can and should survive and in which the commingling of races or species was defined as a threat to this fitness.

Ultimately, the point for fascists was the utility of racial scientific thinking in creating and maintaining a powerful, unifying sense of national identity and togetherness. Mussolini obviously felt that his insistence on the Italians being an "Aryan" race would enhance their sense of dignity and worth. So Mussolini talked about the Italians as "Aryans of a Mediterranean type." But even Italian anthropologists who believed that the Italians were a distinctively "Mediterranean" race firmly opposed the miscegenation of Italians with Africans and Jews and endorsed laws that prohibited marriage and sexual relations between the races. In Nazi ideology, the boundaries of "Aryan" status also were imprecise, but the need to police these boundaries was equally undisputed.

FASCIST RACISM RECONSIDERED

....

The common sourcing of fascist race ideology in late nineteenth- and early twentieth-century science undercuts the view that German Nazism or any other fascism was "anti-modern." Demarcating a modern, forward-looking Italian Fascism from a regressive, backward-looking German Nazism, especially on the ground that the Nazis were intrinsically racist and the Fascists not, is erroneous (cf. Gregor 1974; De Felice 1977). Both Hitler and Mussolini subscribed to a racism that purported to be modern and "scientific." Similarly overdrawn are my own attempts to distinguish fascist movements whose racism was based on a biologically determined racial identity (e.g., in Germany, Austria, Hungary, Norway, and Finland) from those whose racism rested on a less deterministic sense of cultural, religious, and economic differences (e.g., the British Union of Fascists and French fascist movements), with Italian Fascism and the Romanian Iron Guard representing hybrids of the two forms (Morgan 2003: 176).

A policy based on the biological concept of race had clear implications. Such an idea served to freeze in place a perceived or presumed hierarchy of races, since the qualities and demerits that made a race "superior" or "inferior" were biologically inherited and in the nature of things. Racial improvement was a matter of literally getting rid of inherited "bad" genes by preventing their reproduction. What was biologically determined could not really be changed, only eradicated. Thus, biologically racist fascists were likely to pursue antisemitism beyond discrimination and persecution to the point of actually killing Jews, removing for good one of the sources of racial contamination and hence of racial decline. In other words, at least according to some interpretations of these views, the Holocaust was embedded from the start in German Nazism, and its form of antisemitism was intrinsically "eliminationist" (Goldhagen 1997).

Fascist racism, however, was both biological and cultural, in that it made a causal connection between a people's physical and biological traits and its collective moral and psychological ones, which were taken to constitute "soul" or "spirit." This sort of reasoning specified history, in the form of a people's past geographical, climatic, and cultural environment, as the shaper of each "race." Thus, Giuseppe Sergi (1841–1936), Italy's most influential anthropologist, saw the Italians as a "Mediterranean" race, descended directly from the ancient Romans and having all their qualities and virtues. Centuries of foreign invasion and conquest since the collapse of the Roman empire had made no difference to the racial composition of the Italian people, who had assimilated their conquerors and had been "spiritually" unified and shaped as a race over time by living continuously from generation to generation in the same territory and sharing the same geographical and cultural environment and historical development (Gillette 2002: 28–32). This concept of the Italian race Mussolini expressed as his own even before it became the centerpiece of his speeches launching and justifying the Fascist state's official antisemitism in 1938 (Delzell 1971: 94–5; Sarfatti 1994: 47; Gillette 2002: 38–9). Race was seen as a synthesis through time, a magical and natural combination of a people's history, physical and cultural environment, and inheritance, a fusion of "spirit" and "blood."

As for the relationship of racist ideology to practice under Italian Fascism, consider the extreme violence perpetrated in Libya in the late 1920s, Ethiopia in the late 1930s, and in annexed and occupied Yugoslavia in the early 1940s. Being at war both covered and justified extreme actions otherwise unjustifiable in peacetime conditions. But the Fascist round-ups and internment in concentration camps of Slavs and Jews in ex-Yugoslavia cannot be explained just as a counter-insurgency operation against partisans resisting Italian occupation and local populations that supported them. The massive Italian army campaign in the summer and autumn of 1942 depopulated entire areas of annexed Slovenia, as some 65,000 Italian troops destroyed villages, farms, and livestock, killed peasants, and captured many others for internment. Between 1941 and the fall of Mussolini in July 1943, about 25,000 Slovene men, women, and children, approximately 8 percent of the population of Lubiana (Ljubljana) province, were put in camps nearby or in mainland Italy (Capogreco 2001: 220). This operation was an act of Fascist racist imperialism, designed to achieve, as Mussolini put it, an alignment of political with racial frontiers (Capogreco 2001: 209). The goal was to clear territory identified as belonging to Italy in order to open the way to settlement by Italian colonists.

Even less can the Italian wartime internment of Jews, as opposed to the Nazi deportations to death camps, be viewed as a measure of the qualitative difference in Fascist and Nazi race ideologies or in Italian and German national characters or cultures (cf. Steinberg 1990). The claim that Italian military commanders dragged their feet in occupied Yugoslavia in 1942–43 in response to German requests for the handing over of Jews for deportation because Italians wanted to save Jews from the "Final Solution" is simply not accurate. The Italian authorities demonstrated in their words and actions that they had internalized Fascism's racist and imperialist plan for the area. They closed their borders to all refugees, including Jews, and expelled Jews entering their territory illegally, knowing that returning those refugees to the *Ustasha* or the Germans was tantamount to a death sentence (Rodogno 2006: 362–85). Similar steps were taken in Italian-occupied southeastern France in the summer of 1943, just before Mussolini's dismissal by the king. Jews were to be interned in camps, and the Italian police were ordered to transfer to the German authorities those German refugee Jews living in the Italian occupation zone and to repatriate Italian Jews. The orders were withdrawn after Mussolini's first fall from power; but the Fascist government clearly was about to sanction sending foreign and refugee Jews to the death camps (Morgan 2004: 216; Rodogno 2006: 393–400).

Of course, internment was "better" than deportation and death. The internment policy was probably a preparation for eventual deportation or expulsion from Europe after the war, which was consistent with the likely aim of Fascist antisemitic legislation in Italy from 1938. Meanwhile, the policy enabled the Italian Fascist regime to assert sovereignty over occupied territories and keep control of Jewish policy in the areas it governed, exactly as Vichy France sought to do in distinguishing between French and foreign Jews from early 1942. But the policy hardly shows that Fascism and Italians were more humane towards Jews than Nazism or Germans or that cultural factors made Italian Fascism less antisemitic than German Nazism.

Conversely, the argument that biological German Nazi racism was inherently "eliminationist" needs to be qualified. The Nazi regime was not "eliminationist" in its treatment of the Jews until the invasion and occupation of the USSR in mid-1941. The laws and measures that enabled discrimination against and persecution of German, and then ex-Austrian and ex-Czech Jews, in the 1930s broadly paralleled in intent and impact the antisemitic legislation enacted in the prewar period by the Italian Fascist regime and non-fascist authoritarian governments in Hungary, Romania, and Poland (Cohen 1988). Before the war, enforced emigration seemed to be the preferred "Final Solution" in all of these places. The Nazis' decision to kill Jews systematically was a function of wartime pressures and problems, characteristically enlarged to the point of requiring urgent resolution by the Nazis' own methods of invasion and occupation of eastern Europe and western Russia. The decision was also the radical outcome of the internal dynamism and momentum of the Nazi totalitarian system, which generated and then generalized local and improvised initiatives to confront and overcome apparently insuperable logistical difficulties.

To illustrate the same point in another way, the Romanian Iron Guard was a fascist movement that acted in "eliminationist" fashion before the Nazi regime did. The Guard's visceral antisemitism reflected a conviction that Romanian ethnic and religious identity was threatened by the influx of Jews who inhabited the formerly Hungarian and Russian territories incorporated into Greater Romania as a result of the country's alliance with the victorious Allied side in World War I. The movement's homicidal intentions toward Jews were not expressed in the same systematic manner as the Nazi "Final Solution." Guardists preferred pogroms and a deliberate strategy of tension and terror, revolving around spectacular public assassinations of Jews and government ministers and officials who allowed Jews to reside in Romania. The Iron Guard developed an idiosyncratic cult of martyrdom, which transformed deaths in service to the purity of the Romanian nation into a kind of redemptive spiritual capital at the disposal of the Romanian people. Accordingly, the Guard's idea of a coup, as staged against the military dictator Ion Antonescu (1882–1946) in January 1941, was to storm the Bucharest Jewish district, kill scores of Jews and hang their bodies like carcasses in a slaughterhouse, and then to go down in a hail of police and army bullets as the church bells rang.

Fascist racism—typically a complex mixture of biological and cultural elements—generated and justified discrimination, persecution, segregation, murder, and genocide. Scholarship, however, needs to contextualize the ways and moments in which individual European fascist movements articulated and implemented their common racism and antisemitism. Researchers should not assume that biological racism invariably led in one direction, non-biological racism in another. An appropriately nuanced approach casts the antisemitic policies of the Italian Fascist regime in a very different light than heretofore.

THE ITALIAN HOLOCAUST

Although race was central to the mix of pronatalist and socially punitive measures and initiatives that the Fascist regime enacted during the 1920s to increase the population and improve the racial health of the Italian people, antisemitism became incorporated into this population strategy somewhat later. The key stimulus came from the Fascist invasion and conquest of the East African country of Ethiopia in 1935–36, which had considerable impact on the expression of both the "spiritual" and biological elements of Fascist racist ideology. For Mussolini and the Fascist regime, the extension of Italy's East African empire from Somalia and Eritrea to Ethiopia necessitated the inculcation among Italians of a proper sense of racial prestige or consciousness, without which Italy could not expect to retain or exploit its African empire. The Italians had to be and behave as a "master race," as a "superior" people ruling over "inferior" peoples.

From the perspective of the Fascist regime, the enlargement of empire in the late 1930s impelled, then, a stepped-up "fascistization" of the Italian people. This was why the onset of official antisemitism in 1938–39 coincided and interacted with a sometimes grotesque "anti-bourgeois" campaign, which was a concerted attempt on many fronts to harden the Italians' psyche and mentality by driving out so-called defeatist and sentimental attitudes and behavior patterns. Thus, proclaimed the regime, to sympathize with the fate of the Jews on the announcement and enactment of antisemitic measures was to think and behave in an un-Fascist, un-Italian way, inappropriate to being a "master race" (Ben-Ghiat 2001: 157; Morgan 2004: 196–9). As Mussolini put it to a Fascist Party meeting in October 1938, the race laws were meant to be "a heavy punch in the stomach," a salutary jolt to Italians' reprehensible complacency and humanitarianism (Sarfatti 1994: 47).

The conquest of Ethiopia also made urgent the defense of the "master race" against the threat of degeneration. The first Italian measures against miscegenation were taken in Italy's African empire, including the refusal to offer automatic citizenship to mixed race children when the white father was unknown and the attempt to stamp out the tendency of Italian civilian and military officials to

cohabit with black African women. These measures were accompanied and followed by a deliberate policy of segregating the "superior" white race from the
"inferior" black race, sexually, socially, and spatially.

Extending the African empire's anti-miscegenation measures and general racial
segregation policy to metropolitan Italy appeared logical and appropriately totalitarian to the Fascist regime. The leap was made because the Ethiopian invasion put
Italian Jews into an invidious position in other ways, too. Mussolini had long
identified Jews at home and abroad with anti-Fascism. His belief that "international Jewry" had solicited and backed League of Nations sanctions against Fascist
Italy in response to the invasion of Ethiopia strengthened this assumption
and prompted some explicitly antisemitic propaganda from the regime during
the sanctions crisis. Because Fascist Italy was now under threat internationally,
Mussolini could reveal his doubts about whether the basic loyalties of Italian Jews
lay with an international anti-Fascist front or with the nation.

The other important contextual element in releasing the Fascist regime's official
antisemitism was the prominence of the Jewish issue in continental Europe.
Discriminatory and persecutory measures against Jews were introduced in the
mid- to late 1930s not only in an enlarged Nazi Germany but also in Romania,
Hungary, and Poland. The Jewish question was being raised across the continent
and was affecting the politics of all European countries, including Fascist Italy. One
result was a serious international refugee problem, as now often stateless Jews fled
the countries enforcing discriminatory legislation. Fascist Italy received an influx of
about 14,000 foreign refugee Jews in the late 1930s.

The invasion and conquest of Ethiopia and the spread of state antisemitism
across central and eastern Europe thus created a conjuncture that made Italy's own
small Jewish population and the growing number of foreign Jews appear to the
Fascist regime as pressing problems requiring urgent resolution. No evidence
documents any direct pressure from Nazi Germany for the introduction of anti-
Jewish measures in Fascist Italy. Possibly Mussolini felt indirect pressure as his Axis
alliance with Nazi Germany, another byproduct of the Ethiopian invasion and
League of Nations sanctions, tightened. Enthusiasm for that alliance may have
contributed to Mussolini's decision to make antisemitism an explicit part of public
policy. But such thinking could be influential only in the context of the fatal
conjuncture of 1935 to 1938.

The opening salvo of the regime's antisemitic campaign, the Race Manifesto of
July 1938, was a statement of biological racism. The Italians were declared a purely
Aryan race of Indo-European descent, while the Jews were denounced as members
of another, inassimilable race, and, therefore, as incapable of being Italian, just as
black Africans were. A steady stream of antisemitic declarations, speeches, laws,
and decrees followed throughout the autumn of 1938 and seriously damaged the
position of both foreign and Italian Jews in Italy. Foreign Jews were to be expelled,
both those who were refugees from other countries' punitive legislation and those

who had immigrated since 1919 and taken out Italian citizenship, which was now revoked. Further entry of foreign Jews to Italy was banned.

The same strategy of isolation, exclusion, and segregation initially applied in the African empire was now carried out in mainland Italy. Italians could not have sexual relations with or marry "non-Aryans," an important prohibition because intermarriage already had led to a considerable degree of assimilation. The livelihoods of Italian Jews also were attacked through exclusions from state employment and restrictions on property and business ownership. Jewish teachers, pupils, lecturers, and students were removed from the state school and university systems, and Jewish communities were confined to separate Jewish schools.

The census of Jews undertaken in August 1938 by the newly created race agency (*Demorazza*) in the Interior Ministry applied biological and racial, not religious and cultural, criteria. It led to a legal definition of Jewishness that was primarily based on parental ancestry as a means of identifying who was subject to discriminatory measures. As in Nazi Germany, a complicated system of racially classifying the offspring of "mixed race" marriages was devised. At its core was the biological concept of race, and as a result, the near-automatic determination of racial identity and belonging. Partial exemptions were granted to Italian Jews who could demonstrate national and/or Fascist "merits," but such credentials were severely circumscribed. The right to apply for exemption did not contradict the racial criteria being applied to Italian Jews. Even exempted Jews were subject to the segregating measures being enforced with regard to education and to sexual and marital relations.

Above all, the Fascist regime's antisemitic measures were imposed energetically and remorselessly, and not, as much previous scholarship has argued or assumed, *all'italiana*, in a haphazardly or corruptly humane way. Exemptions were not the norm. Requests for partial exemption from the laws for families claiming exceptional mitigating national or Fascist service affected some 15,000 people, but by January 1943 only about 6,500 people benefited from official acceptance of such requests. Although *Demorazza* had the power to reclassify "Jews" as "Aryan," it did so between 1939 and mid-1942 in only 145 cases (Sarfatti 2006: 134, 137). Even "mixed race" people officially classified as Aryan rather than Jewish were kept under police surveillance, in case of any regression to "Jewishness."

The effective "Aryanization" of the two government ministries most associated with the preparation, implementation, and promotion of the antisemitic agenda, the Interior Ministry and the Ministry of Popular Culture, was more or less "totalitarian," as it was also in the Education Ministry and in the armed forces. Indeed, the competitive energy and decisiveness with which the Fascist ministers emptied their bureaucracies of Jewish employees resembled the radicalizing process of "working towards the *Führer* (leader)" that characterized the Nazi German system of rule (Noakes and Pridham 2000: 13). The Interior Ministry even instructed the prefects, the agents of state authority in the provinces, to check on whether any Jews were being employed as municipal firemen (Sarfatti 2006: 100–1).

The rigorous enforcement of anti-Jewish measures meant that the antisemitic campaign penetrated deep into Italian society. The police, responsible to the Interior Ministry, readily took an anti-Jewish stance in day to day policing and deployed their wide discretionary and administrative powers to harass and restrict Jews and Jewish activity. The refusal to renew local business and trading licenses was a low-level but cumulative contribution to the "Aryanization" of the Italian economy, and some Italians, at least, were aware of the commercial advantage to be gained from the official antisemitic campaign. Window signs saying that "this shop is Aryan" were photographed and reproduced throughout the country in the national press (Tannenbaum 1973: 344–5).

The overall intention of the Italian Fascist regime's antisemitic campaign was clearly to make life for Jews in Italy so uncomfortable and uncongenial that they would feel obliged to leave. The impact of the campaign was to drive Jews out of many sectors of national life and to isolate Jews from contact with "Aryan" Italians. Primo Levi, the chemist and writer who survived the Holocaust, described the creeping social ostracism of Jews as a result of these antisemitic measures. He could not remember "a hostile word or gesture" from his "Christian classmates," only a sense of reciprocal distancing, of exclusion and self-exclusion: "every look exchanged between me and them was accompanied by a miniscule but perceptible flash of mistrust and suspicion"(Sarfatti 2006: 168).

The round-up and internment of Italian Jews and the foreign Jews still in Italy began in the summer of 1940, when Fascist Italy entered World War II. The largest of the camps, at Ferramonti di Tarsia, in south central Italy, effectively became a transit or holding camp for something worse. After the Allied invasion of Sicily and the south, and on the very day when Mussolini was overthrown by a royal coup, 25 July 1943, the order was given for the transfer of the camp's large contingent of foreign Jews to Bolzano on the northeastern border. Presumably, if Mussolini had stayed in power, they would have been handed over to the Germans for deportation to the death camps (Sarfatti 2006: 161). Once the Fascist Social Republic was installed in northern Italy in late 1943, with antisemitism formally part of its political platform, that fate awaited *all* interned Jews. The Fascist authorities and German police operated independently or in tandem in the hunt for and internment of Jews until early in 1944, when the Germans took over the running of the main internment camp, to which the Fascist police and militias consigned their haul of Jews for deportation and death (Picciotto Fargion 1986).

NOT BY NATIONAL SOCIALISM ALONE

During the war, throughout the Nazi-occupied territories of northern and western Europe, collaboration between the Nazi authorities and organizations and the national fascist movements was more troublesome that one might have expected. Indigenous fascist leaders expected to be raised to power by the Nazi occupiers, but Hitler distrusted them for their lack of popular support and for their nationalism, which made them anticipate a more independent status for their countries in the Nazi New Order than he was prepared to concede. Nothing divided the two sides on the Jewish issue, however. Local fascist gangs participated in the "Final Solution" from 1942, making good the manpower shortages of the German police and assiduously tracking down Jews who had gone into hiding. The fascists of wartime Nazi-occupied Europe were ultimately all the Germans could count on once the war turned against them. Although the fascists' Jew-hunting was undertaken to realize the German Nazi "Final Solution," that does not mean these fascists were antisemitic merely by proxy or imitation. Nazi racism alone could not account for the Holocaust. Arguably, the Holocaust was generically fascist rather than specifically National Socialist because racism was integral to the hyper-nationalism of all European fascist movements. In fact, some fascist movements, such as the Arrow Cross, the Iron Guard, and the *Ustasha*, were "eliminationist" antisemites before the German Nazis moved explicitly in that direction.

REFERENCES

BEN-GHIAT, R. (2001). *Fascist Modernities: Italy, 1922–1945*. Berkeley, CA: University of California Press.

BURGIO, A. (ed.) (2000). *Nel nome della razza: Il razzismo italiano nella storia d'Italia, 1870–1945*. Bologna: il Mulino.

CAPOGRECO, C. (2001). "Una Storia rimossa dell'Italia fascista: L'internamento dei civili jugoslavi (1941–1943)." *Studi Storici* 42: 204–30.

CENTRO FURIO JESI (ed.) (1994). *La menzogna della razza: Documenti e immagini del razzismo e dell' anti-semitismo fascista*. Bologna: Grafis.

COHEN, A. (1988). "La politique antijuive en Europe (Allemagne exclue) de 1938 à 1941." *Guerres mondiales e conflits contemporains* 150: 45–59.

DE FELICE, R. (1977). *Interpretations of Fascism*. Cambridge, MA and London: Harvard University Press.

DELZELL, C. (ed.) (1971). *Mediterranean Fascism, 1919–1945: Selected Documents*. London: Macmillan.

GILLETTE, A. (2002). *Racial Theories in Fascist Italy*. London: Routledge.

GOLDHAGEN, D. (1997). *Hitler's Willing Executioners: Ordinary Germans and the Holocaust*. London: Abacus.

GREGOR, A. (1974). *Interpretations of Fascism*. Morristown, NJ: General Learning Press.

HORN, D. (1994). *Social Bodies: Science, Reproduction, and Italian Modernity*. Princeton, NJ: Princeton University Press.

IPSEN, C. (1996). *Dictating Demography: The Problem of Population in Fascist Italy*. Cambridge: Cambridge University Press.

MORGAN, P. (2003). *Fascism in Europe, 1919–1945*. London: Routledge.

——(2004). *Italian Fascism, 1915–1945*. 2nd edn. Basingstoke: Palgrave Macmillan.

NOAKES, J. and PRIDHAM, G. (eds.) (1999). *Nazism, 1919–1945*. Vol. 1, *The Rise to Power, 1919–1934*. Exeter: University of Exeter Press.

——————(eds.) (2000). *Nazism, 1919–1945*. Vol. 2, *State, Economy and Society*. Exeter: University of Exeter Press.

PICCIOTTO FARGION, L. (1986). "Anti-Jewish Policy of the Italian Social Republic, 1943–1945." *Yad Vashem Studies* 17: 17–49.

QUINE, M. (1996). *Population Politics in Twentieth Century Europe: Fascist Dictatorships and Liberal Democracies*. London: Routledge.

RODOGNO, D. (2006). *Fascism's European Empire: Italian Occupation during the Second World War*. Cambridge: Cambridge University Press.

SARFATTI, M. (1994). *Mussolini contro gli ebrei: Cronaca dell' elaborazione delle leggi del 1938*. Turin: Zamorani.

——(2006). *The Jews in Mussolini's Italy*. Madison, WI: University of Wisconsin Press.

STEINBERG, J. (1990). *All or Nothing: The Axis and the Holocaust, 1941–1943*. London: Routledge.

TANNENBAUM, E. (1973). *Fascism in Italy: Society and Culture, 1922–1945*. London: Allen Lane.

OTHER SUGGESTED READING

KNOX, M. (2000). *Common Destiny: Dictatorship, Foreign Policy, and War in Fascist Italy and Nazi Germany*. Cambridge: Cambridge University Press.

MANN, M. (2004). *Fascists*. Cambridge: Cambridge University Press.

MICHAELIS, M. (1978). *Mussolini and the Jews: German–Italian Relations and the Jewish Question in Italy, 1922–1945*. Oxford: Clarendon Press.

PAXTON, R. (2004). *The Anatomy of Fascism*. London: Allen Lane.

WEINDLING, P. (1988). "Fascism and Population in Comparative European Perspective." *Population and Development Review* 14: 102–21.

WILDVANG, F. (2007). "The Enemy Next Door: Italian Collaboration in Deporting Jews during the German Occupation of Rome." *Modern Italy* 12: 189–204.

ZIMMERMAN, J. (2005). *Jews in Italy under Fascist and Nazi Rule*. New York: Cambridge University Press.

ZUCCOTTI, S. (1987). *The Italians and the Holocaust: Persecution, Rescue and Survival*. New York: Basic Books.

CHAPTER 6

....

WORLD WARS

....

DORIS L. BERGEN

THE relationship among three major events of the twentieth century—World War I, World War II, and the Holocaust—is assumed more often than it is analyzed. Most histories and popular treatments of these cataclysms examine them in isolation, as if they occurred in separate worlds, or connect them superficially, as if World War I and the peace settlement that followed somehow made World War II and the Holocaust inevitable. Only a few scholars, led by Gerhard Weinberg, have considered the world wars and the Holocaust as intertwined subjects (Weinberg 1994 and 1995, McKale 2002, Bergen 2009). This chapter follows Weinberg to present World War I, World War II, and the Holocaust as inextricably linked, not in a simple, monocausal way, but in a tangled knot of perceptions and misperceptions; causes, effects, and unintended consequences; violence, shocks, and aftershocks.

This analysis also builds on the work of Saul Friedländer (1997 and 2007), who has demonstrated the value of integrating Jewish sources into the master narrative of the Holocaust. The concerns, even obsessions, of the victims who are Friedländer's main informants reveal the omnipresence of the war in their experience of the Shoah. Numerous diaries reveal that European Jews followed the course of World War II intently, knowing that their survival and that of any Jewish remnant depended upon Germany's defeat (Frank 1995; Sierakowiak 1996; Klemperer 1998–1999; Garbarini 2006). Even when that defeat was certain, they realized it might come too late. On 23 July 1944, for example, Herman Kruk, a Warsaw librarian who kept a detailed chronicle of life in the Vilna ghetto and an Estonian labor camp, gave voice to this torturous mix of hope and fear:

Since the latest events on the Eastern Front, since the assassination attempt on H. [Hitler], since Estonia and the entire Baltic has [*sic*] been surrounded, our situation seems to be coming to a head. We are so upset, our nerves choke us, and every day is superfluous. Everything is more and more irritating. We count not just the days, but the hours and minutes: any minute we may get out of hell. When I write about it, I can hardly believe it. (Kruk 2002: 697–8)

The outcome was all too typical: Kruk was not liberated but killed, and his body burned on a garbage heap one day before the Red Army reached his camp. Kruk's fate shows in microcosm the Nazi German war effort and mass murder as two sides of the same coin, mutually reinforcing parts of an escalating dynamic of destruction.

LESSONS OF WORLD WAR I

Contemporaries of the world wars noted and acted on connections between war and genocide that scholars' hindsight has tended to overlook. Adolf Hitler (1889–1945) built his vision of world domination on the interlocking goals of "purifying" the "Aryan" German race and expanding its living space. Both aims, he was convinced, would be achieved through wars of conquest that Germany would win by learning from the war it had lost in 1918. One thing Hitler took from the preceding war was the lesson of impunity. Who today remembers the Armenians, he asked in August 1939, as he contemplated the destruction of Poland and the killing of countless Poles?

The Great War's lesson of impunity was not lost on the targets of Nazi German violence, but unlike Hitler, they learned it with horror. Jews saw a different parallel, between the destruction of the Armenians in Anatolia during World War I and their own annihilation. In the ghettos of Białystok, Warsaw, and Kovno, Franz Werfel's 1933 novel, *Forty Days of Musa Dagh*, became a sought-after book, passed from hand to hand by Jews who must have felt kinship with the defiant Armenians Werfel depicted, besieged on a mountaintop and ready, like the heroes of Masada, to embrace death by suicide before accepting surrender (Auron in Bartov and Mack 2001: 279–81).

In 1942, two Jews at opposite ends of Europe recalled with dismay the cynical disbelief bred by World War I. A prominent publicist in London lamented that the debunking after the war of tales of German atrocities in Belgium in 1914–1918—some of which have been confirmed by subsequent research (Horne and Kramer 2001)—predisposed people in the English-speaking world to miss current accounts of atrocities against Jews (Gollancz 1942). In the ghetto of Otwock, near Warsaw, a Jewish policeman watched his wife and young daughter loaded onto a transport to Treblinka. He imagined the disbelief with which the wider world would receive news of their fates:

Where is Konigsberg? Where is Rybak? You ran away from Treblinka in order to tell the world untrue things about Greater Germany! You will be preaching *Greuelpropaganda* [atrocity stories]? No, Germans don't worry about escapees. They will come with a transport of Jews from another town. (Perechodnik 1996: 51)

For these observers, the Great War was present in the catastrophe of their own time as a brutalizing force and a harbinger of indifference to suffering (Becker in Bergen 2008).

The Great War taught Hitler another imperative: total destruction of the enemy, including the enemy within. He believed that Germany owed its defeat in 1918 to Jews and Marxists who had undermined the war effort at home. By extension, winning the next war, or more precisely, the series of wars Hitler planned, required preventing a similar "stab in the back" (Hitler 2003). To Hitler, the vital preconditions of military success were keeping the home front loyal and ensuring that Jews were in no position to engage in sabotage. These objectives propelled Nazi Germany's appetite for plunder and slave labor (Tooze 2007) and its attempts, first, to drive the Jews from Germany and, later, to annihilate them.

Hitler knew that over the centuries Jews had been expelled from many places, and they had always returned. This time, he insisted, they would not come back because none of them would remain alive. Expressed in numerous speeches from January 1939 on, Hitler's commitment to the elimination of Jews and the link to the stab-in-the-back myth were echoed in the propaganda of Joseph Goebbels (1897–1945) and the exhortations of Heinrich Himmler (1900–1945). In October 1943, Himmler's infamous speech to SS leaders in Posen explicitly justified destruction of Jews by referring to World War I:

for we know how difficult we would have made it for ourselves if, on top of the bombing raids, the burdens and the deprivations of war, we still had Jews today in every town as secret saboteurs, agitators and troublemakers. We would now probably have reached the 1916–17 stage when the Jews were still part of the body of the German nation. (Noakes and Pridham 2001: 618)

The specter of the lost World War served the Nazi regime as a call to world domination, a threat, and a rationalization for murder of Jews and anyone else cast in the role of the shirker, traitor, or defeatist. By all indications, the Nazi elite, many of its members shaped by World War I and participation in suppressing leftists during its bloody aftermath, took the stab-in-the-back myth seriously (Theweleit 1987; Wildt 2009).

PERSECUTION AND PREPARATION FOR WAR

In Germany after 1933, preparations for war and attacks on Jews and other target populations proceeded in tandem. To Hitler, "redistributing" Jewish property and isolating German Jews from their neighbors were as necessary as constructing tanks because victory depended as much on preserving the iron will of the home front as on military training or weapons.

War, Hitler believed, would enable the fulfillment of key Nazi goals. In 1935 Germany's full rearmament, including conscription, was revealed. At the Nazi Party rally that year, Hitler promised the Reich Physicians' Leader Gerhard Wagner (1888–1939) that once war began, the "problem" of the disabled would be resolved (Noakes and Pridham 2001: 396). At the same time, Hitler proclaimed the Nuremberg Laws, defining who counted as a "Jew" in Germany, prohibiting marriage and sexual relations between Jews and so-called Aryans, and depriving most Jews of the rights and protections of German citizenship. A few months earlier, the Nazi leadership had excluded men defined as Jewish from the Wehrmacht, adding "proof" to the antisemitic notion that Jews were cowardly and unfit for military service and, in a maneuver typical of Nazism's penchant for self-fulfilling prophecies, preventing Jews from demonstrating otherwise. Not coincidentally, 1935 also brought intensified persecution of Jehovah's Witnesses, who refused to serve in the military, and of men accused of homosexuality. Himmler and others feared that their presence in the armed forces would endanger national security by spreading weakness and inviting blackmail.

By 1938, Hitler was spoiling for war, and attacks on Jews were part of the plan. At a meeting in November 1937, he presented his program for a series of wars to top military and state officials. Those who seemed unconvinced soon fell prey to a purge that removed the war, economics, and foreign ministers, along with the army commander-in-chief and dozens of senior generals. The regime stepped up the pace of "Aryanization" in the ensuing months, imposed stigmatizing measures such as the "J" stamp on passports and obligatory middle names for Jews, and redoubled its efforts to induce the supposed Jewish "fifth column" to leave the country, especially after Adolf Eichmann (1906–1962) developed the mechanisms in Vienna during the spring of 1938 to retain most of the property of emigrants.

The following summer, the Germans provoked a crisis over the Sudetenland, which Hitler hoped would lead to war with Czechoslovakia. When the result instead was the diplomatic settlement brokered at the Munich Conference, a disappointed Hitler vowed not to be cheated out of war again. In late 1938, as he and his inner circle planned the demolition of Czechoslovakia and the invasion of Poland, both of which followed in 1939, they also engineered a massive assault on the Jews of the newly enlarged Germany, the *Kristallnacht* pogrom of 9–10 November 1938.

Hitler's regime benefited in numerous ways from this purportedly spontaneous but carefully coordinated attack on Jews, Jewish property, and sites of Jewish worship and communal life. Impatient Nazis satisfied their thirst for action. German gentiles, initially uncomfortable with the brutal tactics of their government, found that paying rock-bottom prices for property from Jews eager to get out of the country fostered a new loyalty to the Nazi system. Still, many Germans grumbled about public disorder, and international observers decried the level of violence in Hitler's Germany. Why were Hitler and Goebbels, generally so keen to maintain a positive image at home and abroad, willing to take this public relations risk? The timing suggests that a key reason was their desire to force Jews out of Germany before launching into war. By Nazi logic, every Jew gone meant one less traitor who would stab Germany in the back.

This line of reasoning implied another self-fulfilling prophecy. The more than 200,000 Jews who fled Germany between 1933 and 1939 (Kaplan 1998: 132) settled where they could: elsewhere in Europe or in England and its dominions, the United States, Palestine, China, the Caribbean, India, and Africa. From those new homes, Nazi conspiracy theorists claimed, Jews would plot against Germany and lead an international effort to destroy the Aryan race. By making it impossible for Jews to live in Germany but simultaneously increasing their numbers abroad, Nazi Germans fed their own paranoia about international isolation and hardened their emerging conviction that what was needed was total destruction of the Jewish threat.

Even before Hitler's war began, it was a war against the Jews. "Europe cannot find peace until the Jewish question has been solved," Hitler told the Reichstag on 30 January 1939, less than three months after Nazi thugs had torched synagogues and pillaged Jewish homes and businesses all over Germany. War, Hitler had already decided, was to start that year. "In the course of my life I have very often been a prophet," he continued, "and have usually been ridiculed for it." Now, he concluded, things were different: "Today I will once more be a prophet: if the international Jewish financiers in and outside Europe should succeed in plunging the nations once more into a world war, then the result will not be the bolshevizing of the earth, and thus the victory of Jewry, but the annihilation of the Jewish race in Europe!" (Noakes and Pridham 2001: 441) During the war, Hitler, Goebbels, and others often quoted this "prophecy," consistently misdated to coincide with the German invasion of Poland on 1 September 1939.

HITLER'S WAR AND THE WIDENING CIRCLE OF VICTIMS

Examining the war and the Holocaust together reveals connections between the numerous National Socialist programs of killing. State-sponsored murder began with people deemed handicapped (H. Friedlander 1995). The euphemistically labeled "euthanasia" program started in 1939 with the murder of institutionalized children and soon expanded to include adults. When some of the professionals involved requested legal cover, Hitler obliged with an authorization typed on his personal notepaper and backdated to 1 September 1939—the day Germany invaded Poland. That chronological sleight-of-hand cloaked the killings in military necessity, and this rationalization appeared in everything from doctors' letters to math problems for schoolchildren. Of course the war did not require tens of thousands of children and adults in hospitals and mental institutions across Germany to be starved to death, killed by lethal injection, or suffocated with gas. But, as Hitler had promised in 1935, war enabled realization of a scheme that in peacetime seemed unthinkable.

The Germans attacked and occupied Poland with a brutality that marked 1939 as the onset of a war of annihilation (Rossino 2003). SS, police, and soldiers, aided by militia units of ethnic Germans from inside Poland, rounded up and shot thousands of Poles, including more than a thousand Roman Catholic priests and many university professors, journalists, and schoolteachers, on the false pretext that they had massacred tens of thousands of *Volksdeutsche* (ethnic German) residents of Poland during the early days of the war and were plotting a nationalist resistance.

The war pulled new victims into the machinery of destruction as the Germans in Poland learned murder was not just acceptable but the preferred solution to problems generated by conquest. Under the terms of the Hitler—Stalin Pact signed in August 1939, ethnic Germans in territories in the Soviet sphere of control were to be resettled in German lands. Eager to prove their efficiency and please their Führer, German administrators, SS experts, and military men rushed to implement a series of massive population transfers (Aly 1999). Unprepared for the arrival of hundreds and sometimes thousands of "fellow Germans" from eastern Poland, northern Romania, and the Baltic states, officials in incorporated and occupied Poland applied the methods of the "euthanasia" program. In late 1939, SS men outfitted a van to pipe bottled carbon monoxide gas into the cargo compartment, disguised it with a sign reading "Kaiser's Coffee," and used it to murder inmates of Polish mental hospitals to free up accommodations for incoming *Volksdeutsche* (Noakes and Pridham 2001: 412). Using this equipment or simply bullets, the Germans added thousands of institutionalized Poles to the roster of victims.

Military conquest in 1939 put approximately two million Polish Jews in German hands, and Nazi ideology plus years of antisemitic rhetoric and action inside Germany made these Jews targets against whom anything and everything was permitted. Random shootings, rape, public humiliation, hostage taking, and robbery were commonplace. To the Germans in Poland, Jews embodied both the racial threat to "Aryan" blood and a major obstacle to German order. When a Wehrmacht general complained that participation in atrocities was brutalizing soldiers and undermining morale, Hitler invoked military necessity: "One can't fight a war with Salvation Army methods," he retorted (Noakes and Pridham 2001: 333).

Hitler's global ambitions required subordination of France and Britain, so with Poland defeated and divided between German and Soviet occupation, German attention turned westward. Even in the west, where German warfare was less vicious than in the east, the nexus of Nazi racial ideology, war, and murder was evident. On Hitler's instructions, German soldiers invading France in 1940 were deluged with propaganda that focused on France's use of native troops from its colonies and played on stereotypes of Africans as savages. In May and June 1940, Germans killed between one and four thousand black Africans serving in the French army. In most cases, German officers ordered the execution of all black prisoners, and even when individual soldiers initiated the murders, they had their superiors' tacit approval (Scheck 2006).

In 1941, the Wehrmacht again turned east, first to the Balkans. In Yugoslavia, which capitulated in April, the Germans matched or even surpassed their brutality in Poland. The practice of exacting reprisals echoed and anticipated methods used to crush Jewish resistance in the ghettos of Poland and Lithuania and provoked a flow of people into partisan groups. For every German wounded or killed, up to two hundred Yugoslavs were executed, women and in some cases children as well as men. In the Balkans, the Wehrmacht, not special SS units, carried out mass shootings of civilians. No German soldiers were forced to participate, but there were always enough volunteers, including many who sent photographs of their exploits back home. Often they chose their first victims from local Jewish and Roma ("Gypsy") populations, but they also targeted Serbs, Croats, and Bosnian Muslims. In April and May 1941, the Wehrmacht overran Greece and there too assaulted civilians accused of partisan activity, sometimes wiping out entire towns (Mazower 1993). The Wehrmacht's ruthlessness in the Balkans reflected a military culture that took shape in Imperial Germany and rewarded—even demanded—absolute destruction of the enemy (Hull 2005).

On 22 June 1941, German forces invaded Soviet territory. The objectives were the destruction of the Soviet Union, seizure and colonization of its land, and enslavement of its people. In instructions to the military and SS, Hitler, Himmler, and Heydrich made clear that no mercy was to be shown Germany's enemies. Their plans envisioned "Germanization" of a vast territory from the Reich to the Ural Mountains, where ethnic Germans were to settle and produce food and babies for the Nazi Empire. The tens of millions of people who already inhabited those lands were to be expelled, exploited, or exterminated, some of them immediately, the rest as the growth of the German population permitted. To hasten that growth, German planners proposed taking "racially valuable" children away from their parents. From the outset, killing, starving, and kidnapping characterized an occupation that convinced most of those subjected to it that even Stalin was preferable to Hitler.

The first areas the Germans entered in June 1941 were the regions of Poland and the Baltic states that the Soviet Union had seized in 1939 and 1940 pursuant to the secret codicils of the German–Soviet Non-Aggression Pact. Probably unforeseen by those who masterminded the agreement was the way its aftermath exacerbated hostilities between gentiles and Jews in Poland, Latvia, Lithuania, and Estonia. In 1939 and 1940, the Soviet occupiers arrested, dispossessed, and tortured many of their new subjects and shipped hundreds of thousands of them to Siberia for forced labor. Such oppression, added to the ravages of preceding years, among them the famine in Ukraine, fed anti-Russian and anti-communist passions. The Soviet retreat in mid-1941 gave local populations a chance for revenge, which they took, not on the departing occupiers but on Jews, a target pre-approved by the new German overlords. In 1941–42, local nationalists proved willing to make common cause with the Germans, so long as they could harbor the illusion that cooperation might win them autonomy. For Jews in eastern Europe, the Soviet Union was the lesser of two evils, but for many nationalists, at least initially, the Germans appeared preferable.

In Lwów in Eastern Galicia, Ukrainians greeted the arrival of the Germans with a massive pogrom that left thousands of Jews dead. Similar events took place in Lithuania and eastern Poland, most famously in Jedwabne, where local Poles slaughtered hundreds of Jews on 10 July 1941. Poles accused Jews of having collaborated with the Soviets, but often those gentiles most implicated in Soviet crimes led attacks on Jews both to deflect the anger of their neighbors and to curry favor with the new occupiers (Gross 2001). That the carnage also made goods of all kinds available for transfer from the victims to their killers added another incentive.

Characteristic of Nazi German warfare was the use of special killing squads, the SS-Einsatzgruppen and the associated Order Police. These units advanced directly behind the Wehrmacht with instructions to kill Jews, communists, and anyone suspected of anti-German activity. During the summer of 1941, in the Baltic states, Belorussia, Ukraine, and other Soviet territories, these squads slaughtered Jewish men, women, and children. They also killed Roma and inmates of mental hospitals, albeit less systematically. Using threats, bribes, alcohol, and promises of privilege for recruits and their families, the Germans found local collaborators to help with the dirty work. At Babi Yar, near Kiev, in just two days in September 1941, mobile killing units shot more than 30,000 Jews and an unknown number of other victims.

The regular military cooperated with the Einsatzgruppen and Order Police by providing supplies, security, and intelligence. Knowing they were backed by orders from above must have helped ease soldiers' misgivings. In October 1941, in the wake of the Babi Yar massacre, Field Marshal Walter von Reichenau (1884–1942) issued a directive to address "uncertainty regarding the behavior of the troops" in the east. To destroy the "Jewish-Bolshevist system," he assured his men, Germany was compelled to break the rules of war and show no mercy, above all to "Jewish subhumans" (Noakes and Pridham 2001: 494). Reichenau's army group commander found the order so excellent he distributed copies to all the other armies in his group and to rear area headquarters.

Soviet prisoners of war, often forgotten in western accounts, were major victims of the German war of annihilation. Between 22 June 1941 and the war's end, approximately 5.7 million Red Army soldiers became German prisoners. By early 1945, more than 3.3 million of them were dead. Some were shot upon surrender, others died of starvation, neglect, disease, or mistreatment in labor and concentration camps, many of them run by the Wehrmacht; still others were hanged or gassed (Streit 1997). To German authorities, Soviet POWs posed a particular threat, not only as Slavic "subhumans" but also as part of the "Bolshevik menace."

After June 1941, antisemitic themes became ubiquitous in German propaganda as Goebbels and his underlings found endless grist for their mills in the notion of a Jewish–Bolshevik conspiracy (Herf 2006). When the war was going well for Germany, propaganda trumpeted the impending defeat of the diabolical foe. Military setbacks, for their part, served to "prove" just how fearsome the Jewish enemy was and therefore to justify the most extreme measures against a menace that allied itself with the hammer and sickle and pulled the strings of its "puppets," Churchill and Roosevelt. In this view of the world, no Jew was innocent, and any appearance of harmlessness was just another cunning ploy.

This ideology and the war it fueled created a deathtrap for Jews (Aronson 2004). As Nazi propaganda and practice elided the categories of "Jew," "Bolshevik," and partisan, Germany's war of annihilation not only provided cover for mass murder of Jews; it became a war on Jews. The German police regulation of September 1941 requiring all those inside the Reich who were defined as Jews to wear a Star of David badge reinforced the obvious: stigmatized as enemies, Jews everywhere were open targets. Systematic transports of Jews from Germany and western Europe for killing in the east began the next month. Meanwhile, persecution of Jews exploded inside Romania, where that country's decision to join in the invasion of the USSR, along with the precedent set by their German allies, gave antisemites license to live out their hatreds (Ioanid 2000). Romanian authorities forced Jews across the border into Ukraine, where Germans and their accomplices slaughtered them in the killing fields of Transnistria. For Romanians and other German allies and partners—in Slovakia, Croatia, Italy, and Hungary—attacks on Jews became an easy way to win German favor and position themselves for present and future rewards.

As the dynamic of the war generated ever more victims, it produced a host of practiced killers invested in mass murder and in some cases massively enriched by it, and an expanding network of collaborators and enablers. Some of these people shared the ideological commitments of Nazism, many did not, but all were pulled by the aligned forces of self-interest, greed, opportunism, fear, peer pressure, and family and community ties toward involvement in or at least facilitation of the robbing and killing of Jews. It was not impossible to help Jews and other victims, and individuals did so in courageous and resourceful ways. But the obstacles, risks, and costs for members of conquered and subject peoples were terrifyingly high.

UNFORESEEN CONSEQUENCES: MILITARY DEVELOPMENTS, MASS KILLING, AND REPERCUSSIONS

The years 1942 and 1943, when German power reached its apex, were also the peak period of killing, when extreme violence culminated in the death camps that have become emblematic of the Holocaust. By mid-February 1943, 75 percent of the Jews murdered in the Holocaust were already dead. Within the preceding eleven months alone, Germans and their accomplices had murdered three million Jews. Military conquest brought victims into the Nazi orbit in the first place: 95 percent of Jews murdered in the Holocaust came from outside Germany's 1933 borders. War itself produced radicalization, and the Nazi principles of spatial expansion and "racial purification" meant that more and more killing was a goal as well as a result of the German war effort.

Hindsight allows us to identify specific links between events in the war and the Holocaust, chains of cause and effect that were neither expected nor understood by the people who set them in motion. Although details of German atrocities in the Soviet Union were available to British intelligence almost as they occurred (Breitman 1998), Allied military planners devoted little thought to what seemed bizarre sideshows on the Germans' part, in particular the mass murder of Jews. Nevertheless, Allied military decisions and (in)actions had repercussions for Jews that far exceeded any intentions. Developments in the Soviet Union, North Africa, and Italy in 1942–43 illustrate this point. The extent to which mass killing was entangled in the war is evident in the fact that even German setbacks often worsened the situation of those targeted for destruction.

Germany's defeat at Stalingrad in early 1943 may have been the beginning of the end for the Third Reich, but it did not bring immediate relief for Europe's remaining Jews. The surrender of Germany's Sixth Army did help convince Bulgarian and Romanian authorities to renege on promises to start deporting Jews for killing, and it strengthened the Hungarian government's unwillingness to agree to deportations. But the plight of those Jews still trapped under German control in occupied Poland, the western Soviet Union, the Baltic States, and most of central and western Europe became ever more catastrophic. The outcome of the war was far from a foregone conclusion, and the Germans retained a solid eastern front and the capacity for successful offensives. In the autumn of 1943, they destroyed nearly all of the remaining Jewish communities in Poland, sweeping aside the fact that most of these were engaged in production for the German war effort. Meanwhile, the SS men, guards, and bureaucrats responsible for killing Jews found a new reason to step up their efforts: they would rather stay safely behind the lines slaughtering unarmed people than face the advancing Red Army. By the end of the year, the few Jews left were living targets: scattered in work camps, fighting in partisan units, passing as "Aryans," hiding in barns, attics, and wardrobes, even inside tombs.

By May 1943, the Allies had driven the Germans out of North Africa, and here too, the repercussions were immense, complex, and unanticipated. On the one hand, the Axis, aided by Vichy France, had managed to hold the Allies in Tunisia long enough to make an Allied landing impossible on the European continent in 1943. As a result, the Germans were able to kill hundreds of thousands more Jews. At the same time, the Allied victory quite unintentionally preserved the Jews in Palestine, who, as Hitler had promised the prominent Arab leader and Mufti of Jerusalem, Hajj Amin Al-Husseini (1895–1974), were to have been killed. These were no mere words: a murder squad attached to Field Marshall Erwin Rommel's headquarters had been created to do the job, an indication that the goal of annihilating Jews reached beyond Europe.

North Africa also provided a jumping-off point for the Allied landings in Sicily and then the Italian peninsula in the summer of 1943, which prompted the overthrow of Mussolini and Italy's surrender. In response, German troops occupied Rome, disarmed and interned Italian soldiers, and began sending them to Germany as forced laborers. These events had devastating effects on civilians in Yugoslavia, Albania, Greece, and France, where the former Italian occupation zones ceased to provide relative refuge for many Jews. In late 1943 and 1944, Germans destroyed the ancient Sephardic Jewish communities in Greece and Yugoslavia, even sending boats to pick up the last old Jews from remote Greek islands, described on German plans as located in Asia, before shipping them to Auschwitz to be killed.

From 1944 until May 1945, the last stage of the war in Europe brought German retreat, defeat, and collapse, but the Nazi Empire remained bloody and destructive until its end. In its death throes, the Third Reich devoured not only civilian victims and Allied soldiers but also many ordinary Germans. One factor in that spiral of violence was the dynamic produced by mass killing programs in the preceding years.

Well into 1945, Nazi programs of mass murder continued in the ever-shrinking German-controlled territories. In March 1944, German forces occupied Hungary, their ally, to prevent it from suing for peace, safeguard access to resources, and enforce murder of the Hungarian Jews, the largest national community of Jews left in Europe. Between mid-May and early July 1944, German and Hungarian police, led by experts including Adolf Eichmann (1906–1962), crammed some 437,000 Jews into trains and sent them to Auschwitz-Birkenau, where functionaries murdered as many as 12,000 arriving Jews per day.

During 1942 and 1943, as the Germans concentrated their energies on killing Jews, they had backed off in targeting other populations. German priorities were clear: killing facilities, experienced killers, even trains and trucks were to be devoted first to the central target and number one enemy: the Jews. The death rate of Soviet POWs slowed noticeably, and new programs were introduced to provide incentives for certain categories of prisoners to work for the war effort. On Himmler's instructions, many concentration camps opened brothels to reward inmates deemed productive, even as they punished the women consigned to sexual slavery within them (Schikkora in Herzog 2006). So-called experts offered some "Aryan" men charged with homosexuality the chance to be released into the military, often into notoriously dangerous units, sometimes on the condition that they allow themselves to be castrated (Giles 1992). The Roma incarcerated in the "Gypsy camp" at Auschwitz, scheduled for gassing in May 1944, received a brief reprieve when they offered resistance. During the summer and fall of 1944, most of the Slavic prisoners in Auschwitz were transferred to work camps in Germany.

By the end of 1943, most of the Jews within Germany's reach had been killed, and in the eyes of the Germans, those still alive in Europe were nothing but an accident or temporary convenience; in essence they were already dead. The killers remained, however: thousands of experts in mass murder, skilled and hardened by years on the job. Many of them had plied their trade against more than one target group: SS racial experts had dumped Roma into Jewish ghettos all over Poland, and the Order Police who shot Jews into mass graves also massacred Red Army commissars, inmates of mental hospitals, and Gypsies. Franz Stangl (1908–1971), commandant of the killing centers of Sobibor and Treblinka, had started his career in the murderous "euthanasia" program; so had Christian Wirth, his predecessor at Treblinka, and many others (Sereny 1983). The gas chambers at Auschwitz first used to kill Soviet POWs had been expanded and perfected as instruments of murdering Jews.

By 1944, men who had spent the previous years hunting and killing Jews had almost done themselves out of a job, and during the last two years of the war, the rate of murdering Jews actually fell. In search of ways to continue to earn the promotions, rewards, and power that their work had brought, the killers turned to the remaining targets. Thus, as soon as transports of Jews from Hungary to Auschwitz ceased in July 1944, camp personnel busied themselves with murdering those Gypsy inmates who had been allowed to languish during the preceding hectic months. Similarly, the interminable German retreats westward through Belorussia and north through the Italian peninsula were marked by horrific brutality against local populations. Stangl, Wirth, and others who had killed Jews at Chelmno, Treblinka, Sobibor, Belzec, and elsewhere moved on, when those sites closed, to fight "partisans" in areas still in German hands. Men who had solved every "problem" through total destruction were unlikely to unlearn that lesson merely because their problems were now called "bandits" not Jews.

Only the shrinking reach of the German military and the associated decrease in German diplomatic and economic influence, not any change of heart, ultimately limited the perpetrators' destructive power. Even defensive measures had deadly effects. In response to Allied air raids, the Germans used slave labor to produce arms in large, new plants concentrated in Upper Silesia and later in underground factories at Dora/Mittelbau. Both "solutions" proved fatal for many prisoners consigned to them.

As the Germans retreated, they evacuated camps and killing centers and marched the remaining inmates in guarded columns away from the ever-advancing front. Throughout late 1944 and early 1945, trails of half-dead prisoners made their way through the Polish, German, and Czech countryside. For the guards, their enfeebled, starving charges remained the ticket toward home and safety. Meanwhile, Nazi authorities and activists introduced draconian measures against accused deserters and traitors in the German military, an estimated 30,000 of whom were shot over the course of the war, most of them in its last months. SS and police also executed defeatist German civilians as the Allies advanced (Fritz 2004). The "all or nothing" Nazi mentality and the years of war eventually made all lives, including German lives, cheap. Long after the cause was lost, knowledge of the staggering crimes committed by Germans and in their name, along with fear that revenge on a comparable scale might follow, kept many Germans fighting for Hitler. In this way, ordinary Germans' awareness of the Holocaust, if not by that name, was itself a factor in prolonging the war.

WHY THE SEPARATION BETWEEN WAR AND HOLOCAUST?

Given the myriad connections between the world wars and the Holocaust, one might ask why the tendency to separate these events has been so strong in popular as well as scholarly accounts. The development of two distinct historiographies— one of World War II, the other of the Holocaust, each with its own set of sources, methodologies, and questions—offers a partial explanation, although it is more a symptom of the separation than its cause. The fact that scholarly interest in the Holocaust burgeoned during the Cold War provides another clue: while archives in eastern Europe were closed, and it was unpopular in the west to acknowledge the Soviet contributions to defeating Nazi Germany and impossible in the east bloc to mention the cooperation between Hitler and Stalin from August 1939 to June 1941, crucial aspects of the war–genocide nexus were off limits.

Scholarship is an ongoing conversation, and topics not addressed tend to be forgotten. A sort of inertia seems to have been at play in this case. Just as Allied policy makers during the war considered the Holocaust to be separate from the conflict, regarding mass murder as a sideshow and defining Auschwitz as a non-military target, so people continued to reproduce this distinction in subsequent studies. The magnitude and complexity of the war and the scale and horror of the Holocaust presented additional barriers; separating events was a way to domesticate this painful past and relegate it to the status of a chess game or a fable about the triumph of the human spirit.

The Jewish chroniclers who recognized the inextricability of their fate from the course of the war knew that the history they lived and died was neither a game nor an object lesson. From his hiding place in Warsaw in 1943, the Jewish policeman Calel Perechodnik described how he and his bunker mates responded to news of the Italian surrender: "The same thought came to our minds: We longed for the end of the war, prayed for its early termination, and at the same time, trembled at the thought that the war would end. Where would we go then? With whom would we celebrate?" (Perechodnik 1996: 187).

Perechodnik's questions point toward a void, an abyss of death, broken hopes, shame, and terrible loneliness. Like his countryman Herman Kruk and three million other Polish Jews, he did not survive the war. A Polish patriot who fought in the Warsaw uprising, Perechodnik committed suicide in September or October 1944. His life and death and the bitter, wrenching manuscript he left behind suggest some of the many gaps that remain in our knowledge of the war and the Holocaust. What roles did Jews play in national resistance movements in Poland and elsewhere? What national, regional, and even local factors shaped relations between Jews and the many other targets of the Nazi German war of annihilation? How was information—and misinformation—about military developments communicated to and among participants and victims of war and genocide? How did outcomes of the war affect antisemitism afterward? It is probably the final phase of entangled war and genocide and the period of the immediate aftermath that is in most urgent need of careful study.

REFERENCES

ALY, G. (1999). *"Final Solution": Nazi Population Policy and the Murder of the European Jews.* London: Arnold.

ARONSON, S. (2004). *Hitler, the Allies, and the Jews.* New York: Cambridge University Press.

BARTOV, O. and MACK, P. (eds.) (2001). *In God's Name: Genocide and Religion in the Twentieth Century.* New York: Berghahn.

BERGEN, D. (ed.) (2008). *Lessons and Legacies VIII: From Generation to Generation.* Evanston, IL: Northwestern University Press.

——(2009). *War and Genocide: A Concise History of the Holocaust.* Lanham, MD: Rowman & Littlefield.

BREITMAN, R. (1998). *Official Secrets: What the Nazis Planned, What the British and Americans Knew.* New York: Hill and Wang.

FRANK, A. (1995). *The Diary of a Young Girl.* New York: Doubleday.

FRIEDLANDER, H. (1995). *The Origins of Nazi Genocide: From Euthanasia to the Final Solution.* Chapel Hill, NC: University of North Carolina Press.

FRIEDLÄNDER, S. (1997). *Nazi Germany and the Jews.* Vol. 1, *The Years of Persecution, 1933–1939.* New York: HarperCollins.

——(2007). *The Years of Extermination: Nazi Germany and the Jews, 1939–1945.* New York: HarperCollins.

FRITZ, S. (2004). *Endkampf: Soldiers, Civilians, and the Death of the Third Reich.* Lexington, KY: The University Press of Kentucky.

GARBARINI, A. (2006). *Numbered Days: Diaries and the Holocaust.* New Haven, CT: Yale University Press.

GILES, G. (1992). "'The Most Unkindest Cut of All': Castration, Homosexuality, and Nazi Justice." *Journal of Contemporary History* 27/1: 41–61.

GOLLANCZ, V. (1942). *"Let My People Go": Some Practical Proposals for Dealing with Hitler's Massacre of the Jews and an Appeal to the British Public.* London: V. Gollancz.

GROSS, J. (2001). *Neighbors: The Destruction of the Jewish Community in Jedwabne, Poland.* Princeton, NJ: Princeton University Press.

HERF, J. (2006). *The Jewish Enemy: Nazi Propaganda During World War II and the Holocaust.* Cambridge, MA: Belknap Press of Harvard University Press.

HERZOG, D. (ed.) (2006). *Lessons and Legacies VII: The Holocaust in International Perspective.* Evanston, IL: Northwestern University Press.

HITLER, A. (2003). *Hitler's Second Book: The Unpublished Sequel to Mein Kampf.* Ed. G. L. Weinberg. New York: Enigma.

HORNE, J. and KRAMER, A. (2001). *German Atrocities, 1914: A History of Denial.* New Haven, CT: Yale University Press.

HULL, I. (2005). *Absolute Destruction: Military Culture and the Practices of War in Imperial Germany.* Ithaca, NY: Cornell University Press.

IOANID, R. (2000). *The Holocaust in Romania: The Destruction of Jews and Gypsies under the Antonescu Regime, 1940–1944.* Chicago, IL: Ivan R. Dee.

KAPLAN, M. (1998). *Between Dignity and Despair: Jewish Life in Nazi Germany.* New York: Oxford University Press.

KLEMPERER, V. (1998–1999). *I Will Bear Witness: A Diary of the Nazi Years.* 2 vols. New York: Random House.

KRUK, H. (2002). *The Last Days of the Jerusalem of Lithuania: Chronicles from the Vilna Ghetto and the Camps, 1939–1944.* Ed. Benjamin Harshav. New Haven, CT: Yale University Press.

McKALE, D. (2002). *Hitler's Shadow War: The Holocaust and World War II.* New York: Cooper Square.

MAZOWER, M. (1993). *Inside Hitler's Greece: The Experience of Occupation.* New Haven, CT: Yale University Press.

NOAKES, J. and PRIDHAM, G. (eds.) (2001). *Nazism, 1919–1945: A Documentary Reader.* Vol. 3, *Foreign Policy, War and Racial Extermination.* Exeter: University of Exeter Press.

PERECHODNIK, C. (1996). *Am I a Murderer? Testament of a Jewish Ghetto Policeman.* Ed. and trans. F. Fox. Boulder, CO: Westview.

ROSSINO, A. (2003). *Hitler Strikes Poland: Blitzkrieg, Ideology, and Atrocity.* Lawrence, KS: University Press of Kansas.

SCHECK, R. (2006). *Hitler's African Victims: The German Army Massacres of Black French Soldiers in 1940.* New York: Cambridge University Press.

SERENY, G. (1983). *Into that Darkness: An Examination of Conscience.* New York: Random House.

SIERAKOWIAK, D. (1996). *The Diary of Dawid Sierakowiak: Five Notebooks from the Łódź Ghetto.* Oxford: Oxford University Press.

STREIT, C. (1997). *Keine Kameraden: Die Wehrmacht und die sowjetischen Kriegsgefangenen 1941–1945.* 2nd edn. Bonn: Dietz.

THEWELEIT, K. (1987). *Male Fantasies.* Vol. 1, *Women, Floods, Bodies, History.* Minneapolis, MN: University of Minnesota Press.

TOOZE, A. (2007). *The Wages of Destruction: The Making and Breaking of the Nazi Economy.* New York: Penguin.

WEINBERG, G. (1994). *A World at Arms: A Global History of World War II.* Cambridge: Cambridge University Press.

——(1995). *Germany, Hitler, and World War II.* Cambridge: Cambridge University Press.

WILDT, M. (2009). *An Uncompromising Generation: The Nazi Leadership of the Reich Security Main Office.* Madison, WI: University of Wisconsin Press.

OTHER SUGGESTED READING

ARAD, Y. (2009). *The Holocaust in the Soviet Union.* Lincoln, NE: University of Nebraska Press.

BARTOV, O. (1991). *Hitler's Army: Soldiers, Nazis and War in the Third Reich.* New York: Oxford University Press.

——(2001). *The Eastern Front, 1941–1944: German Troops and the Barbarization of Warfare.* New York: Palgrave Macmillan.

BROWNING, C. (1993). *Ordinary Men: Reserve Police Battalion 101 and the Final Solution in Poland.* New York: Harper Perennial.

DEAN, M. (2000). *Collaboration in the Holocaust: Crimes of the Local Police in Belorussia and Ukraine, 1941–44.* New York: St. Martin's Press.

DESBOIS, P. (2008). *The Holocaust by Bullets: A Priest's Journey to Uncover the Truth behind the Murder of 1.5 Million Jews.* New York: Palgrave Macmillan.

EVANS, R. (2009). *The Third Reich at War.* New York: Penguin Press.

HEER, H. and NAUMANN, K. (eds.) (2000). *War of Extermination: The German Military in World War II, 1941–1944.* New York: Berghahn Books.

PART II

PROTAGONISTS

CHAPTER 7

....

HITLER AND HIMMLER

....

ALAN E. STEINWEIS

THE causes of the Holocaust cannot be reduced to the biographies and actions of the Nazi leadership. Mass murder was propelled by the government of Nazi Germany, executed by tens of thousands of Germans and their collaborators, and facilitated by an even larger number of other Europeans with disparate motives. Moreover, the causes and characteristics of the Holocaust were interwoven with salient features of World War II, including ethnic conflict (inflected in the German case by modern biological racism), a colonialist drive to acquire territory, resources, and geopolitical advantage, and a fanatical desire to eradicate Bolshevism. Clearly, the persecution and murder of the Jews developed as the result—although by no means the inevitable result—of long-term historical patterns and forces.

Yet, the historical background presented necessary but not sufficient conditions for a genocide of such magnitude. The mass murder of the Jews stemmed from decisions and actions by powerful individuals who willed it to happen, first and foremost Adolf Hitler (1889–1945) and Heinrich Himmler (1900–1945). Hitler set the antisemitic priorities of the regime, overcame the reservations of German elites about some of his methods, and deployed his oratorical skill and persona as "Führer" to secure the support or acquiescence of most Germans. Himmler, for his part, emerged over time as the chief organizer and implementer of the "Final Solution" in his capacities as *Reichsführer* of the SS and Chief of the German Police. By virtue of his direct role in organizing and supervising the killing, Himmler was the "architect of genocide" (Breitman 1991). Recognition of this fact does not diminish, however, the absolutely central role played by Hitler. He was the chief decider in matters of Nazi Jewish policy, the driving force behind it, and its most important source of legitimacy inside the regime. Hitler was the "prime mover" of the Holocaust (Burrin 1994).

Early biographies and interpretations did not grasp Hitler's decisive role in the Holocaust. Scholars such as Alan Bullock (1952) and A. J. P. Taylor (1961) depicted the Führer as a traditional, albeit extreme, megalomaniac, for whom ideology was a tool rather than a driving motivation. Totalitarianism theory, which was influential in western academic life during the Cold War, gave short shrift to the antisemitic component of Hitler's ideology, focusing instead on structural parallels between Nazi Germany and the Soviet Union (Friedrich and Brzezinski 1956). The author of one of the great early syntheses of the Nazi phenomenon recognized the centrality of antisemitism to Hitler and Nazism, but did little to document Hitler's driving role in anti-Jewish policy (Bracher 1970). In the 1970s and 1980s, the tendency to de-center Hitler received new impetus from the "functionalist" school of scholarship, which emphasized the polycratic power structure of the Nazi regime and portrayed Hitler as a "weak dictator." More recently, a shift of scholarly emphasis toward the role of "the periphery" in radicalizing Nazi policy toward Jews has been led by a generation of young German historians who exploited archives in central and eastern Europe opened only after the Cold War ended (Gerlach 1999).

Starting in the 1990s, a "re-Hitlerization" took place in research about Nazi anti-Jewish policy. Released from postwar concealment in Soviet archives, segments of Joseph Goebbels' (1897–1945) diaries contained new evidence of Hitler's importance in major decisions related to the Holocaust (Eckert 2004). A second illuminating document to emerge from the former Soviet Union, Himmler's appointment calendar for the years 1941 and 1942, also revealed similarly significant new information (Himmler 1999). In addition, scholars began to reevaluate the meaning of Hitler's known public statements about his intentions for the Jews (Friedländer 1997, 2007). The most recent and thorough major biography of Hitler (Kershaw 1998, 2000) places antisemitism at the core of Hitler's motivations and actions and Hitler at the center of the Nazi regime's decision-making process regarding the Jews.

COMPLEMENTARY ATTRIBUTES

In important respects, Hitler and Himmler were very different personalities. Whereas Hitler was the dynamic, charismatic leader who often acted impulsively and showed impatience with bureaucracy, the more introverted Himmler approached his responsibilities methodically and with careful attention to detail.

These complementary character attributes help to explain Hitler's readiness to delegate ever more power to Himmler and his SS (*Schutzstaffel*) after 1933 and ultimately to entrust them with the murder of the Jews.

Although both men hailed from southern Germany (in Hitler's case, from just across the border, in Austria), joined the Nazi movement in its early days in Munich, and achieved great power at relatively young ages—Hitler was 43 when he became Chancellor of Germany at the end of January 1933, Himmler barely 40 when he was placed in charge of the murder of millions of people during World War II—their backgrounds diverged somewhat. Hitler had not grown up amidst hardship, as he later claimed, but stemmed from a modest middle-class back-ground and had no advanced education. He spent his formative years as a Bohe-mian in Vienna, imbibing his racial consciousness from contacts with the Austrian capital's polyglot population and from lowbrow racist publications such as *Ostara* (Kershaw 1998: 49–51). In contrast, Himmler's youth was decidedly *haute bourgeois*, as his father directed a *Gymnasium* in Munich, and Heinrich earned a degree in agriculture from the Technical Academy there (Longerich 2008: 18–52).

Moreover, their difference in ages had profound consequences. Hitler's service as a front fighter (*Frontkämpfer*) during World War I molded his worldview and his subsequent political career. By all accounts he served with distinction, displaying poise and courage under fire as a courier. Injured by mustard gas toward the end of the war, he learned of the German defeat while recuperating in a military hospital. These experiences of combat, personal sacrifice, and national loss help explain his fanatical devotion to the "Fatherland," his tendency to regard opponents and critics as enemies who had to be removed or destroyed, and his conviction that Germany had not been defeated, but stabbed in the back by traitors, especially Jews and Marxists. Hitler's status as a wounded, decorated war veteran also lent him status and legitimacy in many circles of German society as he pursued power in the 1920s (Kershaw 1998: 73–105). Himmler's military experience, in contrast, was confined to officer training that was interrupted by the end of the war and brief service in a Free Corps unit that helped suppress the left-wing regime set up by Kurt Eisner (1867–1919) in Bavaria.

The nature and depth of Hitler's antisemitism before 1919 remain obscure, and the distaste for the Jews of prewar Vienna that he later expressed may have been a retrojection. Only from the outset of his political career in 1919 does the evidence of his virulently anti-Jewish speeches and correspondence confirm that antisemitism had become a central element of his worldview. His particular form of that hatred synthesized long-standing stereotypes and modern-sounding notions about race. He believed that Jews were best understood as a race that had lost its ancestral homeland and lived ever since parasitically, weakening host nations as it nourished itself. Although widely scattered, the Jews of the world, Hitler maintained, thought and acted in concert, constituting a single entity that he and other Nazis usually referred to as "World Jewry" or "International Jewry." Efforts to convert or assimilate the Jews were therefore worse than misguided because they granted Jews access to positions of influence in the host societies and opportunities to promote degeneracy, decay, and chaos. Their tools included finance capitalism and Bolshevism, which they deployed in tandem to create suffering among the working classes and then to exploit it, as well as domination of the press, the professions, and the arts. The recent tragedies that had befallen Germany, Hitler insisted, were the results of Jewish treachery. Together with their Marxist allies, Jews had stabbed Germany in the back in 1918, betrayed Germany's interests by agreeing to the Treaty of Versailles, and installed the Weimar Republic, a "system" characterized by chaos, weakness, and decadence.

Hitler thus subscribed to a "redemptive antisemitism" that saw the cure for the ills of Germany, Europe, and the world in the defeat of Jewish power (Friedländer 1997: 73–112). But how this view was to translate into policy remained vague. The Party program of 1920 merely pledged to combat the "Jewish-materialist spirit," stated that "only those of German blood, whatever their creed, may be members of the nation" and "accordingly, no Jew may be a member of the nation," and stipulated that Jews, as racial aliens, should not be allowed to hold official appointments or edit or contribute to newspapers (Noakes and Pridham 1998: 14–16). Until Hitler began to deploy the word "extermination" (*Vernichtung*) publicly in 1939, he did not speak or write about murdering the Jews, only about disfranchising them, removing them from positions of influence, and ultimately getting rid of them through emigration or expulsion. Rather atypical was a passage in *Mein Kampf* in which Hitler observed that the sacrifices of the 1914–1918 war would have been justified if "twelve or fifteen thousand of these Hebrew corrupters of the people had been held under poison gas" (Kershaw 1998: 244). Nonetheless, Hitler's long-term aspiration to conquer "living space" in eastern Europe, where the Jewish population numbered in the millions, implied the potential for an ethnic cleansing of enormous proportions.

Himmler belonged to what one historian has termed the "generation of the unbound," a cohort of adolescents during World War I who felt cut loose during its tumultuous aftermath from familiar traditions, institutions, and expectations. Such men gravitated toward the Nazi movement, notably to the police and intelligence services collected into the SS, and aspired to the toughness and soldierly virtues of the "Front Generation" to which Hitler belonged (Wildt 2009). In Himmler's case, the move into the orbit of the *völkisch* movement was accompanied by the transformation of his traditionally Catholic form of antisemitism into a racialist ideology. Unlike Hitler's visceral loathing of Jews, however, Himmler's antisemitism was largely a product of a rigidly ideological worldview, not unlike his parallel obsession with the history, rites, and racial purity of the Germanic cult (Longerich 2008: 265–308).

After Himmler joined the Nazi Party in the summer of 1923, he participated in the failed *Putsch* in Munich that November. In 1925, he entered the SS, which then functioned as little more than the praetorian guard of the movement, and began to rise within its thin ranks. Upon becoming *Reichsführer-SS* in 1929, he commanded fewer than 300 members within a party that remained on the margins of German politics (Longerich 2008: 122). But this narrow platform proved quite sufficient, as Himmler superimposed his racial fanaticism onto the organization and gradually increased its size. That the SS later morphed into the chief agent of genocide reflected Hitler's confidence in Himmler's ideological dependability, his own proficiency as a manager, and, not least, his determination to see the "Jewish Question" solved once and for all.

No Blueprint for Persecution

Hitler came to power on 30 January 1933 without a blueprint for the so-called de-Jewification of Germany. Nazi anti-Jewish policy unfolded thereafter as a grand improvisation. The disfranchisement of the Jews and their removal from Germany were priorities for Hitler, but they had to be balanced against other concerns, such as reviving the nation's economy, strengthening the Nazi regime's popular support, and not arousing international opposition at a time when the country was militarily vulnerable, diplomatically isolated, and still dependent on international trade. Accordingly, Hitler did not create a central ministry or agency for the "Jewish question." Instead, he set the general direction and pace of persecution and expected existing organs of government to devise rules and regulations that executed his wishes. Because the same expectation applied to non-governmental institutions, such as business enterprises, professional associations, and sport clubs, the purge of Jews and the adoption of antisemitic policies became essential elements of "coordination," the gradual Nazification of German society after 1933. Far from indicating that Hitler was a "weak dictator," this ruling technique succeeded in mobilizing German officialdom and German society behind the antisemitic program. Whether impelled by conviction, opportunism or both, Germans swiftly recognized the advantages of "working toward the Führer" (Kershaw 1998: 527–31).

These circumstances did not mean that Hitler remained aloof from anti-Jewish measures during the 1930s. Quite the contrary, when subordinates disagreed over policy, which they often did, or when inconsistencies arose in the practices of various agencies, Hitler had to intervene. He had a hand in the creation of the Nuremberg Laws in 1935, which resulted from the need for a standard set of racial categories to replace the *ad hoc* definitions that had prevailed since 1933. Until 1938, he partially restrained his more zealous followers' desire to "Aryanize"

Jewish-owned property and deferred to the advice of his Economics Minister, Hjalmar Schacht (1877–1970), who urged a more cautious approach. Similarly, on several occasions during the 1930s, the Führer ordered crackdowns against acts of anti-Jewish street violence committed by the Storm Troopers of the SA (*Sturmabteilung*) and other elements of the Nazi Party, lest these harm his regime's image.

Hitler's balancing act came to an end between November 1937, when he removed Schacht as Economics Minister, informed his generals that they needed to prepare for a European war, and dismissed those commanders who balked at the prospect, and November 1938, when the Nazi regime unleashed a violent pogrom on the Jews of Germany. In the interim, Germany annexed Austria and the border regions of Czechoslovakia, and Hitler became convinced that Germany's war for "living space" was imminent. Emboldened by his recent successes, Hitler was also troubled by a lesson he drew from Germany's last reach for world power. He blamed the Jews for the defeat of 1918, and he therefore considered the departure of Germany's remaining Jews as a vital preparatory step for the coming conflict. Largely for these reasons, Hitler authorized the massive pogrom of 9–10 November 1938, the so-called *Kristallnacht*. Although the massive assault on Jews and their homes, synagogues, and businesses was the brainchild of Joseph Goebbels, the Minister of Propaganda, he cleared it with the Führer in advance. Hitler also assented to the concurrent arrest of roughly 30,000 Jewish men and their incarceration (for the most part temporary) in concentration camps. In comparison with the mass murder that came later, a pogrom that cost hundreds of lives might seem a minor event, but it signaled the end of Jewish life in Germany. As a series of new ordnances assured the rapid completion of "Aryanization," Jews intensified their efforts to emigrate from the country.

With the memory of the pogrom fresh, Hitler addressed the Reichstag on 30 January 1939, the sixth anniversary of his accession to power, and delivered these chilling words:

I have very often in my lifetime been a prophet and was mostly derided. In the time of my struggle for power it was in the first instance the Jewish people who received only with laughter my prophesies that I would some time take over the leadership of the state and of the entire people in Germany and then, among other things, also bring the Jewish problem to its solution. I believe that this once hollow laughter of Jewry in Germany has meanwhile already stuck in the throat. I want today to be a prophet again: if international finance Jewry inside and outside Europe should succeed in plunging the nations once more into a world war, the result will not be the bolshevization of the earth and thereby the victory of Jewry, but the annihilation (*Vernichtung*) of the Jewish race in Europe! (Kershaw 2000: 152–3)

Several historians have interpreted this prophecy as a merely tactical move, designed to encourage western nations to accept larger numbers of Jewish refugees or intended to exploit Jews as hostages (Mommsen 1997). Although these calculations may have figured in Hitler's thinking, the fact that he reiterated or referred back to the prophecy several times later, when the mass murder of Europe's Jews was in progress, suggests that he had intended his speech as a warning to "international Jewry" and a signal to the German people about the future.

Meanwhile, the development of the SS into, among other things, the principal security organization of the Nazi Reich began with the unit's formal separation from the SA after the "Night of the Long Knives" of 30 June 1934. Himmler quickly proved so successful in pulling a decentralized collection of police and intelligence agencies together under his command that Hitler made him "Chief of the German Police" in June 1936. By creating the RSHA (*Reichssicherheitshauptamt* or Reich Security Main Office) three years later, Himmler centralized control over the security sector under the command of SS-General Reinhard Heydrich (1904–1942), who had served as Himmler's chief deputy in security matters since 1936. Among the agencies collected within the RSHA were the Gestapo (*Geheime Staatspolizei* or Secret State Police), which had responsibility for suppressing domestic dissent, and the SD (*Sicherheitsdienst* or Security Service), which had originated as an organ of the Nazi Party responsible for gathering intelligence about its ideological enemies.

Prior to the outbreak of World War II in September 1939, Himmler was not instrumental in shaping anti-Jewish policy. Nevertheless, departments within Himmler's security empire played important roles in the implementation of that policy. The Gestapo monitored Jewish life and Jewish organizations inside Germany, enforced racial legislation (Gellately 1991), and exercised important powers regarding emigration. Meanwhile, a group of young SD functionaries developed expertise in matters of Jewish policy and attempted to promote a putatively more rational, unified official approach to the "Jewish Question" (Wildt 2009). One of these men, Adolf Eichmann (1906–1962), took over a new office intended to facilitate Jewish emigration after the annexation of Austria in March 1938. During the war, Eichmann headed up the Jewish desk of the Gestapo (Office IV.B.4 of the RSHA) and acted as the chief organizer of deportations to the ghettos, labor camps, and extermination centers in the east (Cesarani 2007).

Eichmann's trajectory from antisemitic functionary to murderer was not atypical. As Himmler built his security empire during the 1930s, he placed a premium on ideology in recruiting, promoting, and training the men under his authority (Matthäus et al. 2003). Thus, by the time Hitler decided to undertake the annihilation of European Jewry, entrusting the coordination and implementation of that task to Himmler and the hardened ideological soldiers under his command seemed the logical course. The Gestapo and the SD, in addition to other units of the SS, eventually provided much of the personnel to carry out the "Final Solution." In particular, the prewar concentration camps served as a training ground for men who rose to become important figures in the extermination camps. Rudolf Höss (1900–1947), for example, under whose command hundreds of thousands of Jews were murdered at Auschwitz, served as an officer at both Dachau and Sachsenhausen during the 1930s.

Moreover, the rhetoric of the SS at times foreshadowed the antisemitic barbarism of World War II. On the eve of *Kristallnacht*, Himmler described the Jews as "the source of everything negative in the world" and promised to "chase them out with unprecedented ruthlessness" (Breitman 1991: 50–2). In the wake of the pogrom, the official newspaper of the SS, *Das Schwarze Korps*, contemplated the "hard necessity of exterminating the Jewish underworld" by means of "fire and sword." "The result," the newspaper noted, "would be the actual and final end of Jewry in Germany, its absolute annihilation" (Breitman 1991: 58).

TOWARD THE "FINAL SOLUTION"

Despite such ominous prewar rhetoric, most historians agree that the decision to murder every single Jew within reach of German power emerged in response to situations that arose between September 1939 and the end of 1941. First, the conquest of Poland left the Reich in control of many times more Jews than on the eve of the war. Second, the ghettos created in Poland to concentrate and exploit Jews were not viable over the long term and were conceived as holding pens for further deportations. Third, the prospect of dispatching millions of European Jews to Madagascar or some other distant location proved impractical (Brechtken 1997). Fourth, the desire to remove the Jews from eastern Europe was reinforced by a more general ambition to transform that region into a zone of Germanic colonization (Lower 2007). Fifth, the so-called T4 program, in which the Nazi regime carried out the eugenically motivated murder of tens of thousands of mentally disabled Germans between 1939 and 1941, showed the Nazi leadership that large numbers of people could be exterminated systematically (Friedlander 1995).

Exactly when and how the decision for genocide was taken in response to these circumstances has been a matter of some disagreement among specialists. Some have argued that the decision preceded the German invasion of the Soviet Union in June 1941 (Breitman 1991). One much discussed intervention holds that the decision came much later, in December 1941 after the United States entered the war and the Jews of Europe had lost their value as hostages against American involvement (Gerlach 1998). Still another authority dates the decision to the autumn of 1941 and attributes it to Hitler's resolve to punish the Jews for German military reverses (Burrin 1994). The most thoroughly documented and persuasive account maintains that the decision emerged from a "euphoria of victory" that took hold in the Nazi leadership during the summer and autumn of 1941 (Browning 2004).

Hitler and Himmler are the decisive figures in Browning's interpretation of the origins of the "Final Solution." In December 1940, Hitler ordered his military commanders to prepare for the invasion of the Soviet Union by the end of May 1941. As preparations proceeded, he made clear to his generals that the conflict in the east would not be a traditional one, but rather a war of annihilation against a bitter ideological foe. The Soviet regime would have to be destroyed, along with the "Jewish-Bolshevik intelligentsia" at its helm. While the Wehrmacht conducted military operations, "special tasks" of a political and ideological nature were to be entrusted to Himmler, operating independently and on his own authority. In the spring of 1941, Himmler charged his deputy Heydrich with the organization of "special task forces"—Einsatzgruppen—required for the mission. Their personnel was drawn from diverse branches of the security and police apparatus within the SS and supplemented by battalions of the Order Police and the Waffen-SS (Browning 2004: 215–25).

Ambiguity remains regarding the orders given to these units on the eve of their deployment (Earl 2009). They probably were not instructed to kill all Jews, but only communist officials as well as Jews who held positions in the party and government. Nevertheless, as these units followed the Wehrmacht into Soviet-occupied Poland and the Soviet Union proper in late June 1941, they lost little time in carrying out mass shootings of Jews and inciting massacres by the local populations. Although the operation had not begun officially as an attempt to murder all of the Jews in the Soviet Union, it quickly evolved into that. Many commanders of the individual murder units interpreted their orders broadly, reasoning that all Jews constituted a threat to the security of the German occupation. This escalation was not much of a logical leap for men who had internalized a belief in the threat posed by "Judeo-Bolshevism."

Himmler was present on the ground as German forces drove eastward. As commander of several Waffen-SS cavalry brigades, totaling around 25,000 men, during the invasion of the USSR, he played an important role in transforming a political liquidation action into a "racial" cleansing operation. He made inspection visits to several of his special task forces during the first weeks of the invasion, personally sanctioning mass executions of adult Jewish men and implementing a strategy of "controlled escalation" (Matthäus in Browning 2004: 263).

On 16 July 1941, three and a half weeks into the invasion, Hitler offered a number of "fundamental observations" to a group of top leaders of the Nazi Party and the German military. The Führer was elated by the rapid progress of the German advance and determined to transform the occupied east into a "Garden of Eden." This goal would be accomplished through "all necessary measures," including shootings and resettlements. That the Soviet regime had called for its population to engage in partisan warfare against the Germans, Hitler explained, "gives us the opportunity to exterminate anyone who is hostile to us." In the days following, Himmler diverted a significant number of Order Police battalions and other units to support the Einsatzgruppen in their tasks. The murder of Jews escalated in short order to include women and children (Browning 2004: 309–12).

Hitler's thinking at this juncture was reflected in his announcement to the visiting Croatian Defense Minister, Slavko Kvaternik (1878–1947), a few days later that Germany would approach every state in Europe with the demand that their Jews be evacuated. On 31 July, Heydrich received the authorization to undertake "all necessary preparations" and to draft a comprehensive plan for a "Final Solution to the Jewish question" in German-controlled Europe. The authorization did not stipulate that all of the Jews of Europe were to be killed. A "Final Solution" still could take the form of mass deportations to a faraway place. But the Rubicon had already been crossed in the case of the Soviet Union, and a convergence of events in the latter months of 1941 soon led the Nazi leadership to extend the mass murder of Jews to the remainder of the German sphere of influence.

Once again, Hitler acted as the prime mover. After meeting with him in August 1941, Goebbels noted in his diary:

The Führer is convinced his prophecy in the Reichstag, that should Jewry succeed once again in provoking a world war, this would end in their annihilation, is being confirmed. It is coming true in these weeks and months with a certainty that appears almost sinister. In the east the Jews are paying the price, in Germany they have already paid in part and will have to pay still more in the future.

In the same conversation, Hitler referred approvingly to the mass execution of Jews by Romanian troops in the Soviet Union, and then assured Goebbels that "I will not rest or be idle until we too have gone all the way with the Jews" (Browning 2004: 320–1).

During the autumn of 1941, Nazi regional leaders (*Gauleiter*) and other Nazi officials inundated Hitler with requests that the Jews of Germany be deported. Hitler authorized the deportations in mid-September, but the problem was where to send them. Hans Frank (1900–1946), the Nazi official in charge of the General Government in Poland, resisted the shipment of yet more Jews into his territory. Meanwhile, lower-level officials in the RSHA began to consider methods of achieving the "total eradication" of the Jews. As early as July 1941, discussions took place about using poison gas, a method that had been employed for some time in the T4 program to kill disabled Germans. Even in the absence of instructions from above, problem solvers in the SS and elsewhere were seeking to respond to circumstances in a manner consistent with the ideological goals of Nazism; they were, once again, "working toward the Führer."

Himmler gave impetus to such initiatives after witnessing a mass shooting in Minsk in mid-August 1941 and being struck by the emotional and psychological burden on the killers. In mid-October, he approved a plan presented by Odilo Globocnik (1904–1945), the SS Police Leader in Lublin, to construct a camp at Belzec that would kill Jews by poison gas. Simultaneously, Heydrich arranged the delivery of specially designed gas vans for use against Jews at Chelmno. Experiments with killing by gas also had begun at Auschwitz. Meanwhile, deportations of large numbers of Jews from the Reich and Prague to ghettos in Poland increased in frequency. By the end of October 1941, then, the basic pattern of the "Final Solution" was in place: the Jews of Europe would be deported to Poland and killed by poison gas in special facilities (Browning 2004: 319–73).

On 12 December 1941, Hitler received government and party leaders at his Berlin residence. Although he did not go into details, he confirmed that a comprehensive "Final Solution" was under way. In his diary, Goebbels summarized the Führer's remarks as follows:

Concerning the Jewish Question, the Führer is determined to make a clean sweep. He prophesied to the Jews that if they were once again to cause a world war, the result would be their own destruction. That was no figure of speech. The world war is here, the destruction of the Jews must be the inevitable consequence. The question must be viewed without sentimentality. (Browning 2004: 407)

Hitler's comments on 12 December (among other pieces of evidence) shed important light on the infamous Wannsee Conference of 20 January 1942. The purpose of that meeting, over which Heydrich presided with Eichmann's assistance, was not to make policy, which already had been set at the top, but to coordinate implementation by a host of government and Nazi party agencies and to assure that they recognized the primacy of the RSHA in the operation.

On 30 January 1942, when Hitler delivered his annual speech in the Reichstag commemorating his appointment in 1933, he signaled a shift in his main function with regard to the "Final Solution." In remarks broadcast on German radio and printed in the nation's newspapers, he again highlighted his "prophecy" of January 1939, declaring that "the result of this war will be the annihilation of Jewry" and assuring his listeners that "the hour will come when the most evil world enemy of all time, at least in the last thousand years, will be finished off" (Herf 2006: 143–4). Having made the key decisions and delegated the implementation to Himmler, Heydrich, and others, Hitler took on the role of propagandist for the genocide. To be sure, the "Final Solution" was in theory secret, and steps were taken to prevent details of the mass murders from leaking out. But killing on such a scale and involving the participation of so many Germans could not be kept under wraps. The Nazi leadership—especially Hitler and Goebbels—therefore set out to convince the German people that the fate befalling the Jews of Europe was retribution for their crimes and misdeeds over the centuries. In the process, the German people would be drawn further into the circle of moral responsibility for the killing, bound more closely to the ideological aims of the regime, and made more fearful of the consequences of defeat at the hands of "World Jewry" and its allies in Washington and Moscow (Herf 2006).

As the "Final Solution" unfolded and expanded, Himmler's hands-on management continued. He spent much time in the east, receiving briefings from subordinates, coordinating operations, and inspecting facilities. In July 1942, for example, he inspected Auschwitz, where he observed the "selection" and murder of Dutch Jews. Telling insight into his mentality emerges from a surviving sound recording of his speech to SS generals in Posen in October 1943. "Most of you know what it's like," he said, "when 100 corpses lie next to each other, or 500 or 1,000." He praised his men for having "persevered through this" and nevertheless "remained respectable," and he reminded them, "We had the moral right, we had the duty to our people, to kill this race that wanted to kill us." This was how Himmler motivated and flattered his men and himself: by emphasizing their common self-sacrifice (Longerich 2008: 709–10).

Hitler continued to deliver speeches blaming the war on the Jews and warning his listeners of the dire consequences of defeat. On 30 January 1944, he told the German people that the goal of "International Jewry" was "the complete extermination of the German nation." Although calculated to rally the nation behind the leadership and to justify the removal of the Jews, such comments were not mere propaganda. Hitler had been animated by such ideas from the beginning of his political career, and he thought the occurrence of the war validated them. In his Political Testament, dictated on 29 April 1945, the Führer once more asserted that the war had been "desired and launched exclusively by those international statesmen who either were of Jewish origin or worked for Jewish interests." He referred to his prophecy one final time, observing that he had "left no doubt" that Jewry would be "called to account" for plunging the world into war. He had made clear that Jewry, which was the "real culprit" behind the war, would have to "atone for its guilt." The next day he killed himself.

CONCLUSION

Research published during the last two decades has produced a precise and nuanced picture of the decision-making processes that culminated in the "Final Solution" (Longerich 2010). Policy emerged from interaction between the "center" and the "periphery," i.e., between the top Nazi leadership and lower-level officials in the bureaucracies and in German-occupied Europe. Several impressive studies, notably by a generation of young German scholars, have enhanced understanding of how initiatives and improvisations by functionaries and field commanders percolated upward and shaped the choices available to the leaders (Pohl 1997; Gerlach 1999). Nonetheless, Hitler remains the central figure. When he did not issue specific instructions, he set the direction and goals of policy that oriented his subordinates as they "worked toward the Führer." The ultimate prerogative always rested with him, and at pivotal points—the *Kristallnacht*, for example, or the launching of the continental-wide genocide—he acted decisively to bring anti-Jewish measures to a more brutal level. Himmler was instrumental in transforming the Führer's will into action as the war of annihilation against "Judeo-Bolshevism" escalated, first into an ethnic cleansing of the Jews of the Soviet Union, and ultimately into an all-encompassing genocide of European Jews. He won this role because he had molded and hardened the SS into a cadre of ideologically dependable men who possessed the capacity and motivation to carry out this demanding mission.

Although major new documentation is unlikely to emerge in the future, the potential for research on Hitler's and Himmler's roles in the Holocaust has not been exhausted. The picture currently available is an enormous puzzle comprising thousands of pieces of evidence, and future historians may find cause to arrange those pieces in ways that challenge the current state of knowledge. For example, adjusting the timing of Hitler's "Final Solution" decision forward or backward by just a few weeks in 1941 has implications for interpreting the Führer's priorities, motives, and mindset at the decisive moment. Similarly, reexamining how the chronology of the "Final Solution" correlated with that of the SS-supervised ethnic resettlement project in eastern Europe may yield insight into Himmler's view of the relationship between anti-Jewish policy and German territorial expansion.

In the case of Hitler, the most fruitful areas for new research regarding his role in bringing on the Holocaust may lie in a reassessment of the effectiveness of his antisemitic rhetoric during the Nazi rise to power, a subject that has not received sufficient attention. The most influential work on Nazi propaganda before 1933 tended to play down the significance of its antisemitic component (Childers 1983), but the matter has acquired renewed importance as historians reconsider the degree of continuity of popular antisemitism in German society in the decades preceding Nazi rule (Smith 2008). Himmler offers even more research opportunities, and the recent full-scale biography, the first of its kind, offers a fine platform for further work (Longerich 2008). That book's depiction of the many policy fronts on which Himmler was active simultaneously provides essential context for assessing his actions toward the Jews.

A final promising area for new research relates to the increasingly comparative nature of Holocaust studies. With regard to such matters as ideology, temperament, and management style, did Hitler and Himmler exhibit characteristics apparent in their counterparts in other genocides? Were the roles they played in the Holocaust unique or paradigmatic? Patterns of leadership among the perpetrators of genocide cry out for comparison, all the more so as the number of relevant cases is tragically large.

REFERENCES

BRACHER, K. (1970). *The German Dictatorship: The Origins, Structure and Effects of National Socialism*. New York: Praeger.

BRECHTKEN, M. (1997). *"Madagaskar für die Juden": Antisemitische Idee und politische Praxis 1885–1945*. Munich: Oldenbourg.

BREITMAN, R. (1991). *The Architect of Genocide: Himmler and the Final Solution*. New York: Knopf.

BROWNING, C. (2004). *The Origins of the Final Solution: The Evolution of Nazi Jewish Policy, September 1939–March 1942*. With contributions by J. Matthäus. Lincoln, NE: University of Nebraska Press.

BULLOCK, A. (1952). *Hitler: A Study in Tyranny*. New York: Harper.

BURRIN, P. (1994). *Hitler and the Jews: The Genesis of the Holocaust*. London: Edward Arnold.

CESARANI, D. (2007). *Becoming Eichmann: Rethinking the Life, Crimes, and Trial of a "Desk Murderer"*. Cambridge, MA: Da Capo Press.

CHILDERS, T. (1983). *The Nazi Voter: The Social Foundations of Fascism in Germany, 1919–1933*. Chapel Hill, NC: University of North Carolina Press.

EARL, H. (2009). *The Nuremberg SS-Einsatzgruppen Trial, 1945–1958: Atrocity, Law, and History*. New York: Cambridge University Press.

ECKERT, A. (2004). "Glasplatten im märkischen Sand: Zur Überlieferungsgeschichte der Tageseinträge und Diktate von Joseph Goebbels." *Vierteljahrshefte für Zeitgeschichte* 52: 479–526.

FRIEDLANDER, H. (1995). *The Origins of Nazi Genocide: From Euthanasia to the Final Solution*. Chapel Hill, NC: University of North Carolina Press.

FRIEDLÄNDER, S. (1997). *Nazi Germany and the Jews*. Vol. 1, *The Years of Persecution, 1933–1939*. New York: HarperCollins.

——(2007). *The Years of Extermination: Nazi Germany and the Jews, 1939–1945*. New York: HarperCollins.

FRIEDRICH, C. and BRZEZINKSI, Z. (1956). *Totalitarian Dictatorship and Autocracy*. Cambridge, MA: Harvard University Press.

GELLATELY, R. (1991). *The Gestapo and German Society: Enforcing Racial Policy, 1933–1945*. New York: Oxford University Press.

GERLACH, C. (1998). "The Wannsee Conference, the Fate of German Jews, and Hitler's Decision in Principle to Exterminate all German Jews." *Journal of Modern History* 70: 759–812.

——(1999). *Kalkulierte Morde: Die deutsche Wirtschafts- und Vernichtungspolitik in Weißrußland 1941 bis 1944*. Hamburg: Hamburger Edition.

GOEBBELS, J. (1993–2008). *Die Tagebücher von Joseph Goebbels*. 32 vols. Ed. E. Fröhlich et al. Munich: Saur.

HERF, J. (2006). *The Jewish Enemy: Nazi Propaganda during World War II and the Holocaust*. Cambridge, MA: Harvard University Press.

HIMMLER, H. (1999). *Der Dienstkalender Heinrich Himmlers 1941/42*. Ed. P. Witte, M. Wildt, M. Voigt, D. Pohl, P. Klein, C. Gerlach, C. Dieckman, and A. Angrick. Hamburg: Christians.

KERSHAW, I. (1998). *Hitler 1889–1936: Hubris*. New York: Norton.

——(2000). *Hitler 1936–1945: Nemesis*. New York: Norton.

LONGERICH, P. (2008). *Heinrich Himmler: Biographie.* Munich: Siedler.

——(2010). *Holocaust: The Nazi Persecution and Murder of the Jews.* New York: Oxford University Press.

LOWER, W. (2007). *Nazi Empire-Building and the Holocaust in Ukraine.* Chapel Hill, NC: University of North Carolina Press.

MATTHÄUS, J., KWIET, K., FÖRSTER, J., and BREITMAN, R. (2003). *Ausbildungsziel Judenmord? "Weltanschauliche Erziehung" von SS, Polizei und Waffen-SS im Rahmen der "Endlösung".* Frankfurt: Fischer.

MOMMSEN, H. (1997). "Hitler's Reichstag Speech of 30 January 1939." *History and Memory* 9: 147–61.

NOAKES, J. and PRIDHAM, G. (eds.) (1998). *Nazism, 1919–1945: The Rise to Power 1919–1934.* Exeter: University of Exeter Press.

POHL, D. (1997). *Nationalsozialistische Judenverfolgung in Ostgalizien 1941–1944: Organisation und Durchführung eines staatlichen Massenverbrechens.* Munich: Oldenbourg.

SMITH, H. (2008). *The Continuities of German History: Nation, Religion, and Race across the Long Nineteenth Century.* New York: Cambridge University Press.

TAYLOR, A. (1961). *The Origins of the Second World War.* London: Hamilton.

WILDT, M. (2009). *An Uncompromising Generation: The Nazi Leadership of the Reich Security Main Office.* Madison, WI: University of Wisconsin Press.

OTHER SUGGESTED READING

BLOXHAM, D. (2009). *The Final Solution: A Genocide.* Oxford: Oxford University Press.

EVANS, R. (2009). *The Third Reich at War.* New York: Penguin Press.

GREGOR, N. (2005). *How to Read Hitler.* New York: Norton.

HAMANN, B. (1999). *Hitler's Vienna: A Dictator's Apprenticeship.* New York: Oxford University Press.

KERSHAW, I. (1997). *The Hitler Myth: Image and Reality in the Third Reich.* New York: Oxford University Press.

KOEHL, R. (1983). *The Black Corps: The Structure and Power Struggles of the Nazi SS.* Madison, WI: University of Wisconsin Press.

REDLICH, F. (1999). *Hitler: Diagnosis of a Destructive Prophet.* New York: Oxford University Press.

ROSENBAUM, R. (1998). *Explaining Hitler: The Search for the Origins of His Evil.* New York: Random House.

SAFRIAN, H. (2010). *Eichmann's Men.* New York: Cambridge University Press.

STEINWEIS, A. (2009). *Kristallnacht 1938.* Cambridge, MA: Harvard University Press.

WEINBERG, G. (1995). *Germany, Hitler, and World War II: Essays in Modern German and World History.* New York: Cambridge University Press.

CHAPTER 8

....

PROBLEM SOLVERS

....

CHRISTOPHER R. BROWNING

IN the course of a monologue at his headquarters in the early hours of 14 October 1941, Adolf Hitler (1889–1945) is quoted as saying: "Where would I be if I did not find trusted men to do the work that I cannot do, hard men . . . who act as radically as I would. The best man for me is he who bothers me least, in that he takes 95 out of 100 decisions on himself" (Jochmann 1980: 82). When an atypically timid SS officer asked Heinrich Himmler (1900–1945) for clarification about the uncertain jurisdiction of his new appointment, the *Reichsführer*-SS answered scornfully that "a National Socialist makes out of his position what he himself is worth" (Indictment of Arpad Wigand, Hamburg Staatsanwaltschaft 147 Js 8/75, 35). Thus, alongside their emphasis on the "Leadership Principle" (*Führerprinzip*), Nazi leaders encouraged a culture of activism, initiative, and local problem solving by those beneath them.

In the Third Reich, one of the problems most urgently requiring a solution was the Jewish Question (*Judenfrage*) that the very presence of Jews allegedly posed. Clearly Hitler and other top leaders of the regime did not solve this self-imposed problem by themselves. They relied on subordinates—often relatively young men in their thirties and early forties—to make decisions and take action on their own. Who were these indispensable helpers? How did they arrive at systematic mass murder as the "Final Solution" to the issue they confronted? Answering these questions is all the more important in view of the fact that in the years 1933–1939, these problem solvers not only achieved the definition, disemancipation, segregation, expropriation, and partial expulsion of the German Jews, but also did so with the tacit acceptance and increasing complicity of the initially skeptical German public.

DEVELOPMENTS IN GERMANY, 1933–1939

The isolation, impoverishment, and partial expulsion of German Jews first was analyzed in detail as a complex, pluralistic, and unplanned political process along "the twisted road to Auschwitz" in the pioneering works of Karl Schleunes (1970) and Uwe Dietrich Adam (1972). Their findings have been supplemented more recently with greater emphasis on Nazi ideology and the role of Hitler by Saul Friedländer (1997) and on party activism and public opinion by Peter Longerich (2010). During the interval between these two pairs of fundamental books, historiographical debate over Nazi Jewish policy polarized around "intentionalist" and "functionalist" interpretations, the former emphasizing Hitler's premeditation and grand design, the latter depicting the "Final Solution" not as the result of a master plan but as the byproduct of initiatives emanating from diffuse Nazi power structures. The dominant paradigm of Nazi decision- and policy-making that has crystallized since then reconciles these polarities. This consensus view sees Hitler as a key legitimizing and frequently decisive figure but not a micro-manager, ideology as providing direction but not a concrete blueprint of action, antisemitism as but one among a number of driving motives, and a wide array of participants as engaged in an interactive process of initiation and response from both above and below.

Most historians also portray developments in 1933–1939 as following a pattern in which waves of activism and intensified legislative and administrative persecution by the ministerial bureaucracy alternated with brief periods of deceptive calm. In early 1933, party activists took direct action against Jewish lawyers and department stores and instigated a nationwide boycott of Jewish businesses even before the first wave of legislation purged Jews from the civil service, professions, and cultural life, thus achieving, in effect, the disemancipation and "civic death" of German Jewry. In 1935, Julius Streicher (1885–1946) and the party activists pursued "wild actions" against Jewish individuals and businesses before Hitler gratified them with the Nuremberg Laws that banned intermarriage and even sexual relations between Germans and Jews, thus completing the isolation and "social death" of German Jewry. And in 1938, violence mounted in the summer and fall before exploding in the *Kristallnacht* riots, which Hermann Göring (1893–1946) seized upon to complete his systematic expropriation of Jewish property—thus achieving the "economic death" of German Jews—and Himmler and Reinhard Heydrich (1904–1942) used to solidify SS control over both the remnant Jewish community and its emigration.

Additional research has filled out this traditional scenario in three important ways. First, new work on the "Aryanization" of Jewish property in Germany has modified Helmut Genschel's pioneering study (1966), which emphasized the state-enforced, top-down, and centralized expulsion of Jews from the economy in 1938, by showing that "creeping" and decentralized "Aryanization" from below put an end to two-thirds of Jewish-owned enterprises in Germany between 1933 and 1937 and made the expropriations of 1938 a final sprint to the finish line (Barkai 1989). Examinations of various enterprises and banks have illuminated corporate culpability in the rush for spoils (Hayes 1987, 2004), and local studies have exposed the grass roots mechanisms of enrichment and corruption (Bajohr 2002). Second, research on municipal governments and the Council of German Municipalities has revealed an additional layer of actors who initiated and experimented with various forms of persecution locally, and then pressed for their nationwide adoption (Gruner 1999 and in Bankier 2000: 78–105). Third, various organizational histories have shown that the successive waves of legal measures against the Jews led to the institutionalization of continuous persecution. Every Berlin ministry and party organization appointed people to deal with the consequences of anti-Jewish measures relevant to their jurisdictions. Thus the bureaucracy spawned a new phenomenon—a network of "Jewish desks" staffed by self-made "Jewish experts" who protected their agency's turf, offered initiatives to assert their agency's power, and periodically met in conferences to amend each other's proposals and hammer out new legislation. The growth of this cadre of officials from the lowest to the highest levels explains in part the bureaucratic momentum behind Nazi Jewish policy. Once these positions had become established, the flow of discriminatory measures was virtually self-sustaining: the mere existence of the jobs themselves saw to that.

Scholars know too little about this shadowy collection of young officials who staffed the Jewish desks of the German bureaucracy. Often their initial appointment was haphazard. In March 1933, Foreign Office State Secretary Bernhard von Bülow (1885–1936) asked his cousin, Vicco von Bülow-Schwante (1891–1970), to collect materials to defend Germany against foreign criticism of its Jewish policy (Browning 1978: 11–13). In April 1933, Interior Ministry State Secretary Hans Pfundtner (1881–1945) asked Bernhard Lösener (1890–1952), a party member since December 1930 who had just transferred into the ministry, to answer a pile of letters proposing and protesting anti-Jewish legislation (Schleunes 2001: 35–6). In both cases a ministerial "Jewish desk" (*Judenreferat*) had been born. Likewise that spring, Rudolf Hess (1894–1987) appointed 29-year-old physician and party member Dr. Walter Gross (1904–1945) to head the new National Socialist Office for Enlightenment on Population Policy and Racial Welfare (Koonz 2003: 108). The new Foreign Office Jewish desk advised against unnecessary provocations but wrapped Nazi Jewish policy in the flag of German patriotism and held fast to Bülow-Schwante's principle that the greater the criticism from abroad, "the less shall a compromise be thought of in the Jewish question." Lösener helped draft the Nuremberg Laws and subsequent legal definition of Jews but advised the regime on the adverse effect of including people with one or two Jewish grandparents in the persecution. And Gross, while vehemently antisemitic in internal discussions, put on a benign face of scientific dispassion and objectivity in public. In short, each of these "experts" not only furthered persecution of the Jews but also facilitated broader acceptance by restraining the regime's worst instincts. After the war, only Lösener among them could claim with some justification that he had clung to his position to prevent worse results.

None of these men belonged to the SS, but within that organization a similar development occurred, as Reinhard Heydrich created his own Jewish desk within the SD (Security Service). Ideologically self-conscious and committed, these SD Jewish experts defined the goal of Nazi Jewish policy as making Germany "free of Jews" (*judenrein*) through emigration. The lives of Jews in Germany were to be rendered so miserable and hopeless that they would realize they had no future there and leave the country. The SD looked down on the instigation of pogroms, which Julius Streicher and the party radicals wanted, as simplistic and emotional, and the legislative approach of the bureaucrats as cumbersome and inhibited. While priding themselves on their dispassionate, rational approach to removing the Jewish problem, they had no compunction about exploiting violence as a means toward their goal. In November 1937, a workshop of all the SD Jewish experts and their staffs in both the main and regional offices brought together no fewer than sixty-six people, including the young and as yet inconspicuous Adolf Eichmann (1906–1962), who had been recruited in 1935 (Wildt 1995 and 2009; Lozowick 2002). Among the cadre of "Jewish experts" from the party, SS, ministerial bureaucracy, and municipal governments, his name alone was destined to become a household word.

The belated centralization of Nazi Jewish policy following the pogrom of November 1938 and the intensified focus on the primacy of emigration could not overcome, however, the central contradiction that impoverishing the Jews reduced their chances of going elsewhere. For all practical purposes, the increasingly elderly and female Jewish population remaining in Germany was trapped. And as war loomed, the Nazis faced a second paradox, namely that, as with the annexation of Austria and the Protectorate earlier, each successful territorial gain would increase the number of Jews within the expanding German empire. Military victory and expansion stood at cross purposes with solving the Jewish problem. Not oblivious to these dilemmas, Hitler prophesied, in a speech to the Reichstag on 30 January 1939, that the outbreak of another world war would mean the destruction of the Jewish race in Europe. Hitler thus signaled his followers that once the war he was determined to wage had started, the Jews in all of Europe under German control—not just the remnant still in Germany—would have to disappear from the continent. The problem solvers had been put on notice to meet this new challenge.

NEW SCALE, NEW ANSWERS

As a result of the division of Poland in September 1939 according to the terms of the Nazi–Soviet Non-Aggression Pact, the German empire acquired 1.7–1.8 million Jews, even after some 200–300,000 Jews escaped over the demarcation line to the Soviet sphere. The presence of these Polish Jews was not the only demographic challenge the Nazis faced, however. With the annexation of western Poland (eastern Upper Silesia, West Prussia, and the so-called *Warthegau*) to the Third Reich, German-occupied Poland was destined to become the laboratory for Nazi experiments in racial engineering, characterized by ever vaster schemes to remake the ethnic map of eastern Europe. Many technocratic and academic experts contributed eagerly to the realization of German expansion and colonization in the east, but ultimately Himmler and the SS remained dominant, though certainly not alone, in shaping Nazi racial imperialism.

The German occupiers tried to pursue simultaneously four different programs that were in some ways complementary but in other ways contradictory. First, they attempted to destroy Polish national consciousness by eliminating the nation's elites. Second, they sought to "cleanse" the annexed or "incorporated" territories of western Poland of 7.5 million Poles and half a million Jews. Third, they endeavored to repopulate and "Germanize" these lands by bringing in "ethnic Germans" repatriated from Soviet territory. Fourth, they envisaged deporting all Jews from not only annexed and occupied Poland but also the entire German Reich to a "Jewish reservation" in the Lublin District along the demarcation line with the Soviet Union. In the judgment of the district governor, this area suited the purpose because its extremely marshy nature would "induce a severe decimation of the Jews." The head of the General Government, Hans Frank (1900–1946), was even more explicit concerning the Jews' fate: "The more that die, the better" (Browning 2004: 45). Indeed, recent scholarship has emphasized the genocidal implications of German behavior in Poland and its continuity with subsequent German behavior in the Soviet Union (Rossino 2003; Longerich 2010).

Recurrent attempts to "resettle" or expel the Jews produced more frustration than success. In October 1939, the SS expulsion expert, Adolf Eichmann, experimented with transports of Jews from Vienna, Mährisch Ostrau in the Protectorate, and Katowice in the "incorporated territory" of eastern Upper Silesia to the village of Nisko on the San River, where some Jews were made to construct a transit camp while others were chased eastward into the Lublin District. In Eichmann's words, he did this "to collect experiences, in order . . . to be able to carry out evacuations of much greater numbers" (Browning 2004: 37). However, Himmler quickly closed down Eichmann's Nisko experiment in order to concentrate on expelling Poles and Jews from the *Warthegau* and thus to make room for repatriated Baltic Germans. The attempt to clear the "incorporated" territories of all Poles and Jews foundered on the growing opposition of Hans Frank and Hermann Göring to the logistical difficulties and economic consequences of Himmler's attempted demographic revolution in the midst of an unfinished war. By the spring of 1940, the expulsion of both Poles and Jews had been sharply scaled back, and Hitler disowned the plan for a Jewish reservation in the Lublin District.

The quick German conquests of Denmark, Norway, the Netherlands, and Belgium and imminent victory over France emboldened Himmler in late May 1940 to suggest to Hitler that the French empire in Africa might provide a place to send all European Jews. The new Foreign Office Jewish expert, Franz Rademacher (1906–1973), came to the same idea independently and proposed Madagascar as the destination. Hitler approved in principle, and Rademacher and Eichmann worked feverishly over the summer of 1940 to produce their respective versions of a Madagascar Plan. With Germany's defeat in the Battle of Britain, however, these schemes became moot. The Jews of Europe could not be shipped en masse to Madagascar while the Royal Navy blocked the way.

Hitler's decision to attack the Soviet Union without first vanquishing Great Britain, finalized in December 1940, opened up yet another possibility to the Nazi demographic engineers who were increasingly frustrated by the continuing existence of numerous Jews within the German sphere. SS and Foreign Office officials began to discuss resettling the Jews of Europe in a "territory yet to be determined" after the upcoming victory. This was a coded reference to the Arctic and Siberian wastelands of a conquered Soviet Union, which military secrecy ruled out mentioning by name (Aly 1999: 124–6, 172–3).

While Nazi Jewish experts worked on this sequence of unrealized expulsion plans, occupation officials in Poland had to cope with the consequences of Germany's inability to carry them out. In September 1939, Heydrich had ordered Polish Jews concentrated in cities to facilitate their subsequent deportation. At different times in different places, and often citing divergent reasons—for example, to extract Jewish wealth, protect public health, alleviate housing shortages, or beautify cities—local authorities gradually confined the Jews of German-occupied Poland to crowded ghettos that were isolated from surrounding areas with varying degrees of strictness. The larger the ghetto and the more hermetically it was sealed, the more intense the ensuing starvation and epidemics among the ghettoized Jews. Thus, in the two largest and most tightly enclosed ghettos of Łódź and Warsaw, rising death rates and looming catastrophe sparked a debate among local German authorities between "productionists" and "attritionists." The former advocated harnessing Jewish labor so that the ghettoized Jews could feed themselves at no cost to the Reich, while the latter urged letting malnutrition run its lethal course. In Łódź, the 38-year-old Hans Biebow (1902–1947)—former Hamburg businessman, party member since 1937, and now ghetto manager—successfully argued that every effort must be made "to facilitate the self-maintenance of the Jews through finding them work." He prevailed over his adversary, ideological zealot Alexander

Palfinger, who asserted that "a rapid dying out of the Jews is for us a matter of total indifference, if not to say desirable" (Browning 2004: 119–20). Palfinger went off to Warsaw in November 1940 and allied with the like-minded Waldemar Schön. Together they instituted an "attritionist" policy until replaced in April 1941 by Viennese banker Max Bischof as economic controller and Heinz Auerswald (1908–1970) as ghetto manager, respectively, who were directed to achieve ghetto self-sufficiency.

Ghetto managers generally agreed on two matters, however: the cynical use of Jewish councils to save German manpower and fan antagonism among the ghettoized Jews and the ultimate desirability of dissolving the ghettos and sending their inhabitants elsewhere. In the meantime, ghetto economies could be improvised out of marginal resources not claimed by others. Along with the German managers, district civil administrations played a key role in facilitating the ghettoization, expropriation, and labor exploitation of Polish Jews within the General Government.

THE TURN TOWARD MURDER

In the spring of 1941, as Germany prepared for the invasion of the Soviet Union, Hitler once again set the tone, emphasizing that this would not be a conventional conflict but rather an ideological and racial struggle to the death, a "war of destruction" (*Vernichtungskreig*). German planners in various agencies were delegated the task of turning this vision into reality. The army amended its martial law to leave Soviet civilians unprotected, ordered the summary execution of captured communist functionaries, mandated collective reprisal for acts of resistance or sabotage, gave free rein and logistical support to SS execution squads operating up to the front, and made no provisions to care for the large number of Soviet POWs that inevitably resulted from German encirclement tactics. Economic experts laid the basis for such extensive looting that millions of Soviet citizens surely would starve to death. The SS created special mobile Operations Groups (Einsatzgruppen) to eliminate potential enemies and envisioned lowering the population of the conquered territories by 30–40 million. In short, German behavior in the Soviet Union was not a situational response to the ferocity of resistance on the eastern front. Rather that ferocity was a reaction to the premeditated savagery with which the principal German organizations involved in planning Hitler's "war of destruction" set out to realize it.

At first, only adult male Jews, especially those deemed community leaders, were among the potential enemies targeted by the Einsatzgruppen. However, after

Germany's spectacular initial victories prompted Hitler to proclaim in mid-July 1941 that the conquered territories must be transformed into a German "Garden of Eden," Himmler multiplied the number of killing units behind German lines and authorized the recruiting of auxiliary police from the borderland populations, thus providing sufficient manpower to move from selective to mass murder. During visits to many of these units, he and other top SS leaders sanctioned and approved the killing initiatives of some commanders and goaded or reproached others, thereby initiating a gradual but pervasive re-targeting to include Jewish women, children, and elderly as well. Though no single comprehensive order was disseminated to that effect, by the end of the summer the systematic mass murder of all Soviet Jews was under way almost everywhere behind the advancing eastern front.

For the problem solvers, carrying the genocide of Soviet Jews to completion was an immense logistical task that took a somewhat different course in different regions. Many of these developments have been the subject of regional studies made possible only after 1989 by the opening of archives in eastern Europe. Until then, the role of the four Einsatzgruppen, revealed by extensive surviving documentation and in postwar trials, dominated the portrayal of the Holocaust of Soviet Jews. Now the role of the German Order Police and its regional auxiliaries, both in battalion formations and local precincts, has become increasingly recognized. Given the immense manpower demands for round-ups, mass executions by firing squad, and the pursuit of Jews who fled to the forests, the use of native auxiliary police units (*Schutzmannschaften*) was both widespread and crucial. Local commanders developed different methods to expedite mass killing by gunfire. Some preferred salvo fire from a distance at victims lined up at the edge of mass graves to depersonalize the killing. Some forced victims into lines to file past "specialists" who delivered "neck shots" in rapid succession. Some forced victims to enter the mass graves and lie down upon the previous round of victims, head to toe, layer by layer, with shooting done by automatic weapons from the grave's edge—a method gruesomely referred to as "sardine-packing" because it maximized the number of bodies that could be interred in each mass grave. This method also increased the number of wounded victims buried alive.

Moreover, the German army became involved in the "war of destruction" and the genocide of the Jews. The military's participation in mass shootings of Jews usually occurred in the guise of reprisal or anti-partisan actions, indicating a broad acceptance in the Army of the equation communist=partisan=Jew. Supposedly on the basis of military necessity rather than an overtly racist goal of genocide, Wehrmacht massacres of Jews reached their peak in Serbia and Belarus in the fall of 1941 and claimed tens of thousands of Jewish victims.

If the destruction of Soviet Jewry was decided in mid-July 1941 (in the sense that Himmler and others correctly understood what Hitler expected of them) and fully under way by the end of the summer, the fate of all other European Jews still hung in the balance. On 31 July 1941, Göring instructed Heydrich in writing to draft a solution—characterized as "total" in one sentence and "final" in another—to the Jewish question throughout the European territories within the German sphere of power. Here the Nazis were moving into truly uncharted territory, but many people were eager to help find a course of action that did not merely replicate the mass executions by firing squads behind the eastern front. On Soviet territory the killers came to the victims, but from the rest of Europe, the victims had to be brought to the killers (Hilberg 2003).

Ultimately, three groups of experts pooled their experience to implement the "Final Solution." First, there was the expulsion apparatus of Eichmann and his staff, which had coordinated the efforts of local authorities and railway officials to deport large numbers of people during earlier Nazi programs of ethnic cleansing (Cesarani 2004; Safrian 2010). Second, there were the concentration camp commanders and guards who could erect new facilities in Poland that afforded relative secrecy in comparison to the open air mass shootings witnessed by thousands of troops and civilians in the east. Third, there were the euthanasia experts who had killed some 70,000 physically and mentally handicapped Germans by the summer of 1941, mostly with bottled carbon monoxide released into gas chambers. Experiments in September 1941 by crime lab chemist Dr. Albert Widmann (1912–?) near Minsk and euthanasia official Christian Wirth (1885–1944) near Lublin proved that ordinary exhaust gas from internal combustion engines could serve just as well. Experimental gassing with the fumigant Zyklon also took place in September at Auschwitz, and Mogilev and Riga were also briefly considered as sites for camps with gassing facilities.

Three crucial steps taken in mid-October 1941 indicate that systematic mass murder had been set in motion as the problem solvers' ultimate answer to the hitherto intractable Jewish question. On 13 October, Himmler met with his top SS men from the General Government following Wirth's poison gas experiments in the Lublin District. Construction of the prototype death camp with stationary gas chambers began at Belzec two weeks later and of a second camp, utilizing mobile gas vans whose development traced back to Widmann's experiments in Belarus, at Chelmno near Łódź shortly thereafter. On 15 October, a transport of some 1,000 Jews from Vienna, organized by Eichmann, departed for Łódź, marking the onset of the eastward deportation of 58,000 Jews from the Reich by late February 1942. On 17 October, Heydrich rejected a Spanish proposal to evacuate Spanish Jews from German-occupied France to North Africa because they would then be "too much out of the reach of measures for a basic solution to the Jewish question" (Browning 2004: 325, 368), and the next day he and Himmler decided to halt even the last trickle of Jewish emigration from the German sphere. Henceforth, the goal of Nazi Jewish policy was not to expel Jews but to hold them for asphyxiation once the necessary facilities were in place. Thus, in the fateful months from July to October 1941 the problem solvers of the Nazi regime had arrived at their "Final

Solution" in the form of a conscious plan and a developing capacity to murder all the Jews in the German grasp (Breitman 1991; Burrin 1994; Gerlach 1998; Browning 2004; and Longerich 2010 present differing accounts).

ADMINISTERING DEATH

The invention of the death camp provided an exponential increase in lethality over the firing squad massacres on Soviet territory. Whereas thousands of killers fanned out in the east for several years in pursuit of their quarry, at just one of the major death camps, Treblinka, 30 Germans and 120 Ukrainian guards, utilizing the physical labor of 800 Jewish prisoners, killed some 950,000 Jews in scarcely more than a year. But the new killing system required a vast logistical network to provide a steady supply of victims to the killing factories. At the Wannsee Conference on 20 January 1942, Heydrich obtained the cooperation of key Berlin ministries in this process and recognition of his leading position. Eichmann's staff arranged for transport on one-way charter trains at group discount rates, with children under 10 at half fare and under 4 at no charge (Hilberg 1981). In Germany, a wide array of participants at the municipal level prepared each transport down to the minutest detail. Their measures included even the overtime hiring of cleaning women to strip-search female deportees and the collection for the German Red Cross of perishables left behind.

In the "semi-circular arc" of countries from Norway to Greece, the problem solvers faced a different set of challenges, since local assistance, especially in the forms of preparatory legislation and local police round-ups, was always useful and often essential. In conjunction with the Foreign Office's Jewish desk, Eichmann sent traveling emissaries—especially Theo Dannecker (1913–1945) and Dieter Wisliceny (1911–1948)—to give advice and exert pressure. Specific arrangements had to be tailored to a dizzying array of regimes, ranging from allied Italy and quasi-autonomous Denmark through willing or expedient allies (Romania, Bulgaria, and Hungary) and dependent satellites (Slovakia and Croatia) to military administrations (France, Belgium, Serbia, and Greece) and party fiefdoms (the Netherlands, Norway).

Because the areas of direct German domination contained the largest concentrations of Jews, by mid-February 1943—after the ghetto liquidation campaign in Poland, the second sweep on Soviet territory, and the first deportation wave from the "semi-circular arc"—some 75–80 percent of all Jews killed in the Holocaust already had perished. However, as the Nazi regime strove to complete the genocide, problem solvers faced two complications that arose from the deteriorating military situation after the German defeat at Stalingrad. First, Germany's allies and satellites became less cooperative and more insistent on drawing a distinction between "alien" and native Jews. Thus, Hungary had expelled its foreign Jews into Ukraine to be massacred in 1941, Romania had carried out its own "parallel" genocide against the Jews of the conquered regions of Bessarabia, Bukovina, and Transnistria in 1941–42, and Bulgaria had handed over to the Germans the Jews of annexed Thrace and Macedonia in early 1943. But with the changing tide of war, each declined to deport its native Jews. Italy went a step further, protecting even foreign Jews in its occupation zones. Mismanaged attempts to switch sides in the war opened both Italy and Hungary to German intervention that proved fatal to most of the Jews of Hungary in 1944, but the native Jews of Romania and Bulgaria (and most Italian Jews) survived. Deportations from the west also slackened in 1943 and 1944, particularly as the capacity of the Vichy regime in France to round up and deport its Jews steadily declined.

Second, the deteriorating military situation intensified Germany's shortage of labor and thus confronted the Reich with the economic costs of mass murder. The difference between the Nazi problem solvers' political and economic priorities now seemed increasingly irreconcilable. Although some working Jews were granted brief stays of execution, Himmler sooner or later pushed for murder regardless of the cost. Thus, he had the entire Jewish labor force in the Lublin District of Poland—42,000 Jews—killed in the "Harvest Festival" (*Erntefest*) massacre on 3–4 November 1943, the largest single killing action of the entire Holocaust, as the climax of his campaign to eliminate all Jewish labor camps in the east. Thereafter, however, military and economic necessity began to prevail and the labor camp complexes of Plaszow, Auschwitz, and eastern Upper Silesia, the industrialized ghetto of Łódź, and the Jewish labor camps of the munitions industries in the Radom District survived until the arrival of the Soviet army appeared imminent.

CONTESTED INTERPRETATIONS

Certainly one contested area in scholarship on the Nazi experts, functionaries, and technocrats of racial persecution concerns the relationship between economics and ideology in motivating the perpetrators, along with the related issue of the relative costs and benefits of the Holocaust to the Third Reich. Götz Aly has argued that the regime's need for popular support catalyzed the initial measures against German Jews as a means of redistributing their jobs and property, that a demographic reconfiguration deemed necessary by technocrats for the economic modernization of Germany's new east European empire sparked the "Final Solution," and that the

systematic plunder of Europe—including Jewish property—by Germany's inge-
nious accounting and economic experts helped buy the regime popular support to
the very end. In comparison to such material considerations, Aly characterizes
ideology as "propaganda" and "rhetoric" (Aly and Heim 2002; Aly 2007). Michael
Thad Allen (2002) has argued that a first generation of SS concentration camp
personnel viewed inmate labor as a useful means of torment and torture, not profit
and productivity, but later SS technocrats took the economic return on camp labor
as seriously as their racist ideology.

How vital was the seizure and distribution of Jewish property, first in Germany
and then throughout Europe, to gaining the support of both Germans and
collaborators? How much did the regime lose through its destruction of Jewish
labor, not just economically but also as a result of the resistance to German
occupation stirred up by the draconic round-ups of forced labor from other
populations? That the seizure of Jewish property facilitated the Nazi persecution
of the Jews and ultimately the "Final Solution" seems clear. But the economic
and political balance sheet of the Nazi liquidation of Jewish labor, plunder of
property, and round-up of non-Jewish forced labor throughout its empire remains
unwritten.

For the moment, scholars agree on a consensus paradigm regarding the decision-making process that produced the Holocaust. Decisions were not simply
handed down from above. Rather they emerged and crystallized through interaction between senior and junior officials occupying both central and peripheral
posts, all of whom operated within a broad consensus about the existence of a
Jewish problem and the need to solve it. Responding to Hitler's exhortations, often
given in the form of prophecies and visions, eager problem solvers "worked toward
the Führer" (Kershaw 1998: 527). They experimented and proposed and stood ready
to act when the next signal came from above. Often, they took the initiative,
sensing what was expected of them and confident of obtaining sanction and
approval after the fact. But the relationship between this decision-making pattern
and the course of the war is still disputed. Browning has argued that at each peak of
victory euphoria—September 1939 over Poland, May/June 1940 over France, July
1941 in the full flush of blitzkrieg success, and yet again the first weeks of October
1941 when the end of Soviet resistance and the capture of Moscow seemed imminent—Hitler felt emboldened to escalate and radicalize Nazi Jewish policy. In
contrast, others have emphasized frustration over the simultaneous failure of the
blitzkrieg in the Soviet Union and the entry of the United States into the widening
war as catalytic (Burrin 1994; Gerlach 1998).

Above all, the motivation of the problem solvers remains an elusive and open
issue. They were so diverse that their driving impulses defy easy analysis. Even as
individuals, they exhibited "hybrid behavior" that blended numerous mutually
reinforcing motives: self-conscious ideological conviction, hero-worshipping identification with Hitler, a sense of professional fulfillment in displaying technocratic

skill, the intoxication of exercising unfettered power over others, and the experiential high (what Raul Hilberg dubbed the *Erlebnis*) of making history and doing what no one had dared before, alongside such mundane factors as career advancement, material gain, and the comforts of conformity (Bajohr 2006: 184). One thing we do know for certain: Whatever the mixture of motivations, one challenge the problem solvers did not face was an insufficient supply of themselves.

REFERENCES

ADAM, U. (1972). *Judenpolitik im Dritten Reich*. Düsseldorf: Droste.

ALLEN, M. (2002). *The Business of Genocide: The SS, Slave Labor, and the Concentration Camps*. Chapel Hill, NC: University of North Carolina Press.

ALY, G. (1999). *"Final Solution": Nazi Population Policy and the Murder of the European Jews*. London: Arnold.

——(2007). *Hitler's Beneficiaries: Plunder, Racism, and the Nazi Welfare State*. New York: Metropolitan.

ALY, G. and HEIM, S. (2002). *Architects of Annihilation: Auschwitz and the Logic of Destruction*. London: Phoenix.

BAJOHR, F. (2002). *"Aryanisation" in Hamburg: The Economic Exclusion of Jews and the Confiscation of their Property in Nazi Germany*. New York: Berghahn Books.

——(2006). "The 'Folk Community' and the Persecution of the Jews: German Society under National Socialist Dictatorship, 1933–1945." *Holocaust and Genocide Studies* 20/2: 183–206.

BANKIER, D. (ed.) (2000). *Probing the Depths of German Antisemitism: German Society and the Persecution of the Jews, 1933–1941*. New York: Berghahn Books.

BARKAI, A. (1989). *From Boycott to Annihiliation: The Economic Struggle of German Jews 1933–1943*. Hanover, NH: University Press of New England.

BREITMAN, R. (1991). *The Architect of Genocide: Heinrich Himmler and the Final Solution*. New York: Knopf.

BROWNING, C. (1978). *The Final Solution and the German Foreign Office: A Study of Referat D III of the Abteilung Deutschland, 1940–43*. New York: Holmes & Meier.

——(2004). *The Origins of the Final Solution: The Evolution of Nazi Jewish Policy, September 1939–March 1942*. With contributions by J. Matthäus. Lincoln, NE: University of Nebraska Press.

BURRIN, P. (1994). *Hitler and the Jews: The Genesis of the Holocaust*. London: Edward Arnold.

CESARANI, D. (2004). *Becoming Eichmann: Rethinking the Life, Crimes, and Trial of a "Desk Murderer."* London: William Heinemann.

FRIEDLÄNDER, S. (1997). *Nazi Germany and the Jews*. Vol. 1, *The Years of Persecution, 1933–1939*. New York: HarperCollins.

GENSCHEL, H. (1966). *Die Verdrängung der Juden aus der Wirtschaft im Dritten Reich*. Göttingen: Musterschmidt.

GERLACH, C. (1998). *Krieg, Ernährung, Völkermord*. Hamburg: Hamburger Edition.

GRUNER, W. (1999). "The German Council of Municipalities (*Deutscher Gemeindetag*) and the Coordination of Anti-Jewish Local Politics in the Nazi State." *Holocaust and Genocide Studies* 13/2: 171–99.

HAYES, P. (1987). *Industry and Ideology: IG Farben in the Nazi Era*. New York: Cambridge University Press.

——(2004). *From Cooperation to Complicity: Degussa in the Third Reich*. New York: Cambridge University Press.

HILBERG, R. (1981). *Sonderzüge nach Auschwitz*. Mainz: Dumjahn.

——(2003). *The Destruction of the European Jews*. 3 vols. 3rd edn. New Haven, CT: Yale University Press.

INDICTMENT OF ARPAD WIGAND, Hamburg Staatsanwaltschaft 147 Js 8/75.

JOCHMANN, W. (ed.) (1980). *Adolf Hitler: Monologe im Führerhauptquartier 1941–1944: Die Aufzeichnungen Heinrich Heims*. Hamburg: Albrecht Knaus Verlag.

KERSHAW, I. (1998). *Hitler, 1889–1936: Hubris*. London: Norton.

KOONZ, C. (2003). *The Nazi Conscience*. Cambridge, MA: Harvard University Press.

LONGERICH, P. (2010). *Holocaust: The Nazi Persecution and Murder of the Jews*. New York: Oxford University Press.

LOZOWICK, Y. (2002). *Hitler's Bureaucrats: The Nazi Security Police and the Banality of Evil*. London: Continuum.

ROSSINO, A. (2003). *Hitler Strikes Poland: Blitzkrieg, Ideology, and Atrocity*. Lawrence, KS: University Press of Kansas.

SAFRIAN, H. (2010). *Eichmann's Men*. New York: Cambridge University Press.

SCHLEUNES, K. (1970). *The Twisted Road to Auschwitz: Nazi Policy Toward German Jews 1933–1939*. Urbana, IL: University of Illinois Press.

——(ed.) (2001). *Legislating the Holocaust: The Bernard Loesener Memoirs and Supporting Documents*. Boulder, CO: Westview Press.

WILDT, M. (ed.) (1995). *Die Judenpolitik des SD 1935 bis 1938: Eine Dokumentation*. Munich: Oldenbourg.

——(2009). *An Uncompromising Generation: The Nazi Leadership of the Reich Security Main Office*. Madison, WI: University of Wisconsin Press.

OTHER SUGGESTED READING

BROWNING, C. (1992). *Ordinary Men: Reserve Police Battalion 101 and the Final Solution in Poland*. New York: HarperCollins.

——(2000). *Nazi Policy, Jewish Workers, German Killers*. New York: Cambridge University Press.

FRIEDLÄNDER, S. (2007). *The Years of Extermination: Nazi Germany and the Jews, 1939–1945*. New York: HarperCollins.

GRUNER, W. (2006). *Jewish Forced Labor Under the Nazis: Economic Needs and Racial Aims, 1938–1944*. New York: Cambridge University Press.

ROSEMAN, M. (2002). *The Villa, the Lake, the Meeting: Wannsee and the Final Solution*. London: Penguin.

CHAPTER 9

···

KILLERS

···

EDWARD B. WESTERMANN

VIOLENCE and murder were defining characteristics of the Third Reich. From 1933 on, the National Socialist government deployed them while incarcerating thousands of its putative political, social, and racial enemies in concentration camps and prisons (Orth 1999; Wachsmann 2004). The outbreak of war in September 1939, however, gave a mammoth impetus to Nazism's lethal impulse. Mass murder became a routine instrument for achieving the regime's political, military, and racial goals and part of a larger strategy of conquest and cumulative annihilation. The primary executors of this murderous strategy were the various forces in the SS and police empire of Heinrich Himmler (1900–1945), assorted ethnic German and indigenous auxiliaries, and units of the German armed forces (Wehrmacht). Himmler's "political soldiers," notably the Waffen-SS, the Death's Head formations, the Order Police, the Security Police, and the notorious Einsatzgruppen, stood in the vanguard of genocide. They also usually supervised and directed the ethnic German and indigenous auxiliaries that played an important role in beating, terrorizing, guarding, and slaughtering target populations in German-occupied territories. Wehrmacht forces, operating sometimes independently and sometimes in coordination with SS and police forces, made a major contribution to the death toll, especially in the occupied east. Although Nazi barbarity fell most heavily on the inhabitants of Poland and the Soviet Union, the execution of black French colonial troops by German forces in 1940, the brutal anti-partisan campaign in southeast Europe, and the ruthless reprisal policies carried out in Italy and France demonstrate that large-scale killing characterized German occupation policy throughout Europe (Manoschek 1993; Andrae 1995; Scheck 2006; Lieb 2007).

Even as new evidence of atrocities committed by German forces and their auxiliaries continues to come to light, the matter of their motivation remains subject to debate and dispute. Because the variety of organizations and individuals involved in mass murder was as great as the range of situational and dispositional factors that influenced their actions, several theories of perpetrator motivation have arisen. Fortunately for scholars and students trying to assess these interpretations, new scholarship on organizations such as the Security Police, the Security Service, the Order Police, the Command Staff of the SS, the Einsatzgruppen, and specific Wehrmacht units provides a wealth of clarifying information. Moreover, multiplying regional studies, facilitated by the opening of Russian and east European archives, offer additional perspectives on the functioning of Nazi administration in the occupied territories and the relationship between the Party and civil bureaucracies, the SS and police apparatus, and the Wehrmacht in these areas.

CONTESTING MOTIVATION

In the early 1980s, academicians engaged in a contentious debate centering on the nature of the power and influence exercised by Adolf Hitler (1889–1945) within the Nazi dictatorship. Was Hitler "Master of the Reich" or a "weak dictator"? This dispute had profound implications for the interpretation of both the Führer's role in the "Final Solution" and that of the state apparatus. The competing perspectives became embodied in intentionalist and functionalist positions, the former contending, in its strictest form, that Hitler pursued a premeditated path to genocide as set forth in *Mein Kampf* (1925), and the latter insisting upon "a twisted road to Auschwitz" created in a process of cumulative radicalization by Hitler's paladins and Nazi functionaries as they "worked towards the Führer." This was no arcane academic feud. It raised crucial issues of agency and personal responsibility, and the reverberations of the argument continue to inform contemporary interpretations of perpetrator motivation and the larger question of German guilt (Marrus 1987; Kershaw 2000).

In 1996, political scientist Daniel J. Goldhagen ignited an acrimonious dispute over the driving impulse behind Nazi Germany's attempt to annihilate the European Jews. On the basis of his examination of Germans associated with the Order Police battalions, labor camps, and the forced death marches in 1945, Goldhagen concluded that an "eliminationist anti-Semitic German political culture" was the "prime mover of both the Nazi leadership and ordinary Germans in the persecution and extermination of the Jews" (1996: 454). Goldhagen's use of the term "ordinary Germans" reflected two critical aspects of his argument. On the one hand, he contended, "Being ordinary in the Germany that gave itself to Nazism was to have been a member of an extraordinary, lethal political culture." On the other hand, his word choice was a rejoinder to, and rejection of, the historian Christopher Browning's book *Ordinary Men* (1992), which located the motives of the largely middle-aged members of a reserve police battalion that shot Jews in Poland in considerations that were hardly specific to Germans, including group solidarity, peer pressure, respect and deference for authority, and desire for career advancement.

The "Goldhagen controversy" gave renewed impetus to the study of perpetrator motivation, notably among social psychologists, who approached the issue through comparison and generalization in order to situate cases of mass killing and atrocity in the broad context of human behavior. James Waller (2007) examined cases of mass murder from the Holocaust, Cambodia, Guatemala, and the Balkans and found a convergence of dispositional (internal influences), situational (external influences), and social factors that led "ordinary people" to commit mass atrocity. Similarly, Harald Welzer (2005) highlighted a process of "social restructuring" in which the identification of Jews as the foreign "other" furnished an in-group of "Aryan" Germans with the necessary justification to initiate a process of incremental radicalization on the path to genocide. Ultimately, the identification, definition, and reinforcement of the Jews as an "out-group" provided the dynamic for exclusion, expropriation, and eventually annihilation.

In contrast, contemporary historical studies have scrutinized the actions of specific organizations, institutions, and units within the National Socialist system to discern the rationale for mass murder. For example, Michael Wildt (2009) examined the leadership, structure, and actions of the Reich Security Main Office (RSHA) and its role and importance in formulating and prosecuting National Socialist racial policies. Established in September 1939, the RSHA encompassed the Gestapo, the Criminal Police, and the Security Service and assumed a key role in the "Final Solution." Within the leading ranks of the RSHA, Wildt identified a highly educated cohort of men born between 1900 and 1910 and characterized by activism, ambition, and ideological commitment. These men did not fit the caricature of myopic desk-bound bureaucrats and proved equally at ease drafting racial policy or holding a pistol to the heads of the Third Reich's putative political and racial enemies in the occupied east. Another organizational study of mid-level SS functionaries within the Business Administration Main Office (WVHA) also rejected the conventional depiction of amoral cogs in the machinery of industry, slave labor, and annihilation. On the contrary, the WVHA personnel were dedicated to SS ideals and a "plexus of ideologies" that included technological modernization, Nazi racism, and the creation of an SS "New Order." These officials "believed in the legitimacy of murder and the forced labor of Jews and whoever did not count as 'Aryan'" (Allen 2002: 15). As the organizational histories of the

RSHA and WVHA demonstrate, the prosecution of genocide required both the "right men" and the "right institutions."

Browning's pioneering study of Reserve Police Battalion 101 focused attention on an organization, the Order Police, that had escaped not only the reach of Nuremberg but also scholarly examination for almost five decades. Members of this force murdered over 500,000 persons in the occupied territories and proved a key instrument of annihilation in the east (Breitman 1998). Recent studies of these policemen's willingness to dispense death have emphasized several key ways in which their behavior was molded. Jürgen Matthäus focused on the effects of SS indoctrination and specifically the portrayal of the "Jewish question" in SS and police literature, but also highlighted the importance of social factors, including the use of organized entertainment activities and professional and social "fellowship evenings" to build unit cohesion and a sense of shared purpose among deployed police units. The resulting "internalization of an attitude" legitimized the use of violence against the "Jewish enemy" (Matthäus et al. 2003: 85). Edward B. Westermann's analysis underlined the importance of the senior leadership of the Order Police in creating, even prior to the war, an "organizational culture" that glorified the concepts of military identity and duty and wedded them to the fulfillment of Nazi racial philosophy. On his showing,

the impetus for genocide came from within an organization that established and promoted its own values, beliefs, and standards for behavior, that created an environment in which persecution, exploitation, and murder became both acceptable and desirable attributes of a police corps charged with preserving the German *Volk* and locked in an apocalyptic battle against the internal and external enemies of the Reich. (Westermann 2005: 239)

DRESS REHEARSAL FOR ANNIHILATION

Renewed scholarly attention to the opening campaign of World War II, the German invasion of Poland, recently has led to three important insights into the nature and conduct of the war in the east (Rossino 2003; Mallmann and Musial 2004; Böhler 2006). First, this scholarship demonstrates that the actions of German military and SS and police forces in Poland in many respects constituted a dress rehearsal for the war of annihilation that began two years later against the Russian colossus. Second, the nature and evolution of the relationship between these German entities demonstrate their high degree of complicity from the beginning of the war. Finally, these studies of the Polish campaign highlight the ideological dimensions of Hitler's first blitzkrieg.

In a path-breaking study, Alexander Rossino outlined the German preparations for a premeditated *Volkstumskampf* (ethnic battle) against the Polish population. This ethnic battle involved mass murder by Wehrmacht and SS and police forces, and their joint enforcement of draconian reprisal policies, the brutal treatment of Polish civilians, and the ghettoization and deportation of Jews. The initiation of severe reprisals against the Polish population by the German army set an ominous precedent and became "a critical component of the racial-ideological warfare waged by the Third Reich" (Rossino 2003: 121). In a pattern that was repeated in the Soviet Union, Einsatzgruppen consisting of SS and police forces under the command of specially selected leaders became the primary instruments for eliminating the political and racial enemies of the Third Reich, including Polish nationalists, Catholic clergy, members of the nobility and the intelligentsia, and Jews (Krausnick 1981).

The invasion of Poland tested relationships and forged partnerships between the organizations that constituted a deadly triad in the east: the SS and Police, the Wehrmacht, and indigenous auxiliaries. Wehrmacht and SS and police forces dealt ruthlessly with cases of actual or perceived resistance from Polish "irregulars," including Jews, and murdered more than 16,000 civilians in September and October 1939 (Böhler 2006: 241). Despite concerns expressed by some senior leaders of the Wehrmacht about the effect of such killings on order and discipline, operations in Poland proceeded smoothly at the unit level. Possessed by an almost psychotic fear of guerrillas, army units advanced and relied on SS and police forces to provide rear area security and protect key lines of communication, a pattern that fostered mutual dependence between the two organizations.

BARBAROSSA AND BARBARISM

The invasion of the Soviet Union in June 1941 cemented the increasingly symbiotic relationship among Wehrmacht and SS and police forces with respect to security and "pacification" duties. In part, this relationship was a marriage of necessity, the consequence of the vastness of the east and casualties that stretched available army manpower to the limit. Nonetheless, the anti-partisan campaign of 1941 provided the pretext for the *Ostheer*'s increasing reliance on SS and police forces and for the army's increasing cooperation with these forces in the conduct of mass murder and atrocity. The hand-in-glove relationship of military and security units was symbolized by the fact that the Wehrmacht "created the necessary conditions" for the murder of the Russian Jews in the first few months of the invasion (Wette 2006: 107). Whether the Wehrmacht conducted an "anti-partisan war without partisans"

(Heer and Naumann 2000: 97) or acted in response to a real or honestly perceived threat remains contested by historians. The fact, however, that the Jewish population of the Soviet Union became a major target of the anti-partisan campaign is indisputable. Likewise, the active participation and cooperation of both the Wehrmacht and SS and police forces in this campaign are equally apparent (Cüppers 2005).

The Nazi administration in the east employed a dual approach of direct and indirect murder to support its program of cumulative annihilation. Direct murder primarily involved mass shootings and gassing. The principal method of indirect murder was mass starvation of all those viewed as racial or political threats or economic burdens to the Third Reich, including Soviet prisoners of war (POWs) and large portions of the Soviet population. As early as 1957, Alexander Dallin drew attention to the German "geopolitics of starvation," the Reich's premeditated policy of "immediate and maximum exploitation of the occupied areas," and "the extinction of industry as well of a large percentage of human beings" within Russia (1957: 309–11). Recent scholarship has uncovered more detailed information on the formulation of German intentions and the Reich's adoption of a "Hunger Plan." During a pre-invasion meeting of German State Secretaries on 2 May 1941 to discuss the planned economic and agricultural expropriation of the Soviet Union, a group of senior German bureaucrats agreed in principle that "the war can only continue to be waged if the entire Wehrmacht is fed from Russia" and accepted that "as a result, x million people will doubtlessly starve" (Kay 2006: 686). In short order, the assembled officials, like their counterparts who convened at the Wannsee villa eight months later to discuss the "final solution to the Jewish question," reached agreement on a policy of wiping out millions, perhaps tens of millions, of people as a means of achieving the regime's military and racial goals.

If the blueprint for mass starvation was drawn in Berlin, the practical implementation of this plan was left to German occupation authorities, who encountered many difficulties. These did not prevent Nazi administrators, Wehrmacht commanders, and senior SS and police officials from embracing their task. They pursued a policy of "calculated murder" toward the civilian population of Belorussia (Gerlach 1999). In Ukraine, the German administration banned the supply of food to the city of Kiev at the end of September 1941, resulting in the deaths of thousands of people (Berkhoff 2004: 164–86). The starvation policy exacted a particularly horrific toll on Soviet POWs, thousands of whom perished daily from a lack of food and the aggravating factors of forced labor, abuse, and disease. By the end of the war, an estimated 3.3 million Soviet POWs out of a total of 5.7 million fell victim to direct and indirect murder at the hands of the Wehrmacht and SS and police forces (Streit 1978).

HELPING HANDS

Regional and sub-regional histories have provided key detail on the mundane and horrific aspects of the daily face of Nazi administration throughout occupied Europe (e.g., Mazower 1993 and Pohl 1996). These studies increase our understanding of the Holocaust by highlighting the continuities and disruptions of National Socialist racial policy and by advancing a more nuanced understanding of the roles played by specific persons, policies, organizations, and chronology in the implementation of genocide at the local level. With respect to the perpetrators, these accounts offer especially important insights into the behavior of indigenous auxiliaries. Two interrelated questions surround the participation of these local inhabitants in the killing of their countrymen. First, were these killings spontaneous expressions of hatred toward the local Jewish population or were they orchestrated by German forces? Second, what motivated collaborating inhabitants of occupied countries to kill Jews, "Gypsies," and other "undesirables"?

Clearly, the Einsatzgruppen sought to encourage local inhabitants to conduct "spontaneous" pogroms. In the words of the head of Einsatzgruppe A, Dr. Franz Walter Stahlecker (1900–1942):

The task of the security police was to set these purges in motion and put them on to the right track so as to ensure that the liquidation goals that had been set might be achieved in the shortest possible time. It was equally essential to create an established and provable fact for the future that the liberated population had taken the hardest measures against their Bolshevik and Jewish adversaries of their own accord without directions from German authorities being discernible. (Klee et al. 1991: 27)

The rationale for such efforts appears to have been threefold. First, the SS and police leadership wanted to create "plausible deniability" regarding German involvement. Second, they believed that apparently impulsive acts of popular retribution aimed at the Jewish "oppressors" would lend credibility to Nazi propaganda concerning the ubiquity and depth of antisemitism. Third, the murder of the Jews by local inhabitants and auxiliaries would reduce the workload of SS and police units later.

The success of the Einsatzgruppen in promoting pogroms proved mixed and depended in large part on the identification of "reliable" local auxiliaries and the varying levels of antisemitism present in occupied areas. In Lithuania, the inhabitants of Kaunas/Kovno welcomed the withdrawal of Soviet forces, and local vigilante groups enthusiastically participated in the murder of Jews prior to the entry of German forces into the city. These murders continued thereafter and appear to have been propelled by widespread perceptions of allegedly "treasonous" behavior by the Lithuanian Jewish community in welcoming the Soviet occupation of the country in June 1940. The Nazi linkage of Jews and Bolshevism found a receptive audience and produced numerous Lithuanian volunteer killers (Mallmann et al. 2003: 61–7). In contrast, neighboring Latvia offers a different picture of local participation in the murder of the Jews. According to one authoritative study, the "assertion that there was a spontaneous killing of the Jews in Latvia, and that the Latvians carried out murders without German orders is patently wrong." German propaganda, obedience to higher authority, and the harsh realities of Nazi occupation policy only eventually induced local collaboration in the annihilation of the Jews and the mass murder of communists and "Gypsies." This study concludes: "Above all, the Germans obtained Latvian participation in the killings by popularizing the idea of Jewish Bolshevism" (Ezergailis 1996: 18–19). In Ukraine, German officials and Einsatzgruppe C initially found little local support for the murder of Jews. However, SS and police leaders succeeded in instigating pogroms and mass killings by Ukrainian and ethnic German militias not only by playing on antisemitic and anti-Bolshevik feelings but also by offering opportunities for plunder and promotion at a time when such things were scarce (Lower 2005).

The organization and use of ethnic Germans (*Volksdeutsche*) in the conduct of mass murder is a topic that deserves greater scholarly attention. The precedent for using such auxiliaries emerged during the invasion of Poland in 1939, once again highlighting the importance of this campaign in setting the stage for later annihilationist policy in the east. SS and police forces assumed the lead in organizing detachments of ethnic German auxiliaries from the earliest days of the invasion, not least because Himmler viewed these men as valuable recruits for his "black corps" for whom he did not have to compete with the Wehrmacht. In Poland, approximately 100,000 men served with the ethnic German auxiliaries, many as members of death squads that routinely participated in the torture of Polish gentiles and Jews and the summary execution of an estimated 10,000 persons (Jansen and Weckbecker 1992).

Reprisal and revenge catalyzed by real and alleged Polish atrocities against ethnic Germans constituted the primary motivations for the murderous activity of these auxiliaries in the early weeks of the war, but their continued participation in the abuse and killing of Poles and Jews points to an acceptance of Nazi anti-Slav and antisemitic propaganda and a willingness to follow these precepts to their logical extreme. Likewise the readiness of ethnic Germans to join the German administration in Ukraine and to identify and kill Jews demonstrates that this phenomenon was not found only in Poland. In the end, Himmler and the senior SS and police leadership not only enlisted the support of ethnic Germans in the conduct of genocide but also mobilized ethnic Germans into the Waffen-SS, providing them with an opportunity to commit mass murder under the auspices of the "antipartisan" campaign (Lumans 1993).

After the German invasions in southeast Europe and the Soviet Union in 1941, the need for "helping hands" in the pacification and control of the occupied territories became a critical issue for their German political and military administrations (Quinkert et al. 2003). Hitler supported the enlistment of local auxiliaries and the creation of paramilitary battalions and companies (*Schutz-mannschaften*) composed of men from the indigenous populations to supplement existing SS and police forces. The vast extent of the territory under German control and the chronic manpower shortage faced by German forces in the east made the enlistment of these auxiliaries imperative. Furthermore, the local knowledge and the willingness of these units to participate in actions aimed at partisans and Jews made them a valuable instrument for the realization of Nazi racial policies. Thus, in 1941–42 the number of auxiliaries serving in the occupied Soviet territories exploded from some 45,000 to over 300,000, an increase that corresponded to a massive wave of killing aimed at Jews and the growing partisan movement. Like their ethnic German counterparts, these forces indulged in atrocity and mass murder for both affective and instrumental reasons, ranging from anti-communism and/or Jew hatred to expectations of material gain. Supervised and encouraged by the SS and police authorities, these auxiliaries emerged as key instruments of the overall strategy of cumulative annihilation in the east (Westermann 2005: 195–9).

THE WEHRMACHT AND THE "FINAL SOLUTION"

If the functionalist versus intentionalist dispute dominated the scholarly discourse of the 1970s and the 1980s, the 1990s witnessed a heated debate over the role of the German army in the National Socialist war of annihilation in the east. Omer Bartov (1992) led the way toward a fundamental reexamination of the actions and motivations of the German *Landser* (infantryman) on the eastern front. A few years later, the first photographic exhibition highlighting the crimes committed by "Hitler's Army" in the occupied territories traveled to cities in Germany and Austria and sparked a major public and scholarly controversy. Contemporary scholarship has debunked the myth of a "clean Wehrmacht" and demonstrated not only the army's complicity but also its initiative in spreading atrocity and mass murder throughout Europe.

Bartov's study of the German army outlined the process by which "ordinary men" became "highly professional and determined soldiers, brutalized instruments of a barbarous policy, and devoted believers in a murderous ideology" (1992: viii). In his view, the transformation of the *Landser* into an instrument of annihilation resulted from the "demodernization" of the war in the east caused by the destruction of primary groups, a "perversion of discipline" enforced through draconian punishments, and the politicization of an army that came to deify Hitler and embrace Nazi ideology. Another study published a few years later identified the importance of comradeship and training in shaping the actions of the common soldier, but also noted the brutalizing effect of Nazi ideology as it "seeped into the consciousness of the rank and file" (Fritz 1995: 242). Still a third, more recent analysis of German military conduct focused on the importance of male gender roles and group dynamics in forging an ideal of soldierly camaraderie and conformity. Soldierly comradeship, operating within a general atmosphere of racial and antisemitic beliefs in the Wehrmacht, helps to explain both the participation of the *Landser* in mass murder and the willingness of these men to fight until the final collapse of the Third Reich (Kühne 2006).

In contrast to these examinations of the German army as a whole, several recent studies of the actions and motivations of the common soldier have focused on specific geographical areas or individual units. For example, a history of the 253rd Infantry Division examined the unit's enlisted soldiers, including their social and demographic make-up, the methods used to bind them to the regime, and the individual and institutional freedom of action they enjoyed during the war. Despite spending four years on the eastern front, this unit maintained its "primary groups" consisting of soldiers bound together by shared socialization and experience and common social and regional affinities. Their participation in a war of annihilation and the conduct of genocide resulted from the overrepresentation of an age cohort born between 1910 and 1920 that experienced the full strength of National Socialist indoctrination, the widespread presence of officers and senior enlisted leaders committed to the Nazi leadership model and the regime's racial ideals, and a diverse system of punishment and reward designed to promote group conformity (Rass 2003). Another unit level study examined the actions of the 221st Security Division, a collection of Wehrmacht "third stringers" charged with rear area pacification duties in the Soviet Union. This over-aged, undersized cohort that "fell far short of the yardstick of military excellence with which the Wehrmacht is so widely associated" pursued policies that alternated between extermination and the creation of "dead zones" on the one hand and the use of inducements and a policy of "constructive engagement" on the other in an attempt to pacify the unit's area of responsibility (Shepherd 2004: 48). This study offers a balanced discussion of the range of ideational and empirical determinants of unit behavior, including Nazi ideology, institutional mentality, demographics, policy guidelines, and wartime conditions.

Studies of the Wehrmacht as an organization and of its individual units show the difficulty of ascribing motivation to an organization that probably included 17 to 18 million men between 1935 and 1945. If the motivations of these men remain debatable and disparate, the widespread tacit and explicit cooperation of the German armed forces in the conduct of mass murder and genocide in the occupied territories of eastern and southeastern Europe, and to a lesser degree in Italy and France, is clear. The image of a supposedly heroic and apolitical Wehrmacht has been dashed permanently by the evidence of its complicity in the prosecution of the political and racial aims of the National Socialist regime.

A STRATEGY OF CUMULATIVE ANNIHILATION

Over the course of the Third Reich, individuals and organizations within the National Socialist regime murdered as many as 31,595,000 persons, including an estimated 19,315,000 persons in occupied Europe alone (Rummel 1992: 11–13). The victims died not only by the thousands in gas chambers and mass shootings, but also daily in small groups or alone during cold-blooded reprisals or at the whim of soldiers, policemen, and Nazi administrators. Despite the dramatic increase in Holocaust research, the activities of some perpetrator groups still require further study, including the Wehrmacht's Secret Field Police, the military police (*Feldgendarmerie*), local auxiliaries, and the Axis-allied militaries. Likewise, the role of female perpetrators deserves greater attention, even if the opportunity for their participation was circumscribed by the regime's own gender norms (Harvey 2003). In the end, only after all these stories are told will the entire scope of the National Socialist strategy of cumulative annihilation be apparent.

REFERENCES

ALLEN, M. (2002). *The Business of Genocide: The SS, Slave Labor, and the Concentration Camps*. Chapel Hill, NC: University of North Carolina Press.

ANDRAE, F. (1995). *Auch gegen Frauen und Kinder: Der Krieg der deutschen Wehrmacht gegen die Zivilbevölkerung in Italien, 1943–1945*. Munich: Piper.

BARTOV, O. (1992). *Hitler's Army: Soldiers, Nazis, and War in the Third Reich*. Oxford: Oxford University Press.

BERKHOFF, K. (2004). *Harvest of Despair: Life and Death in Ukraine under Nazi Rule*. Cambridge, MA: Harvard University Press.

BÖHLER, J. (2006). *Auftakt zum Vernichtungskrieg: Die Wehrmacht in Polen, 1939*. Frankfurt am Main: Fischer.

BREITMAN, R. (1998). *Official Secrets: What the Nazis Planned, What the British and Americans Knew*. New York: Hill & Wang.

BROWNING, C. (1992). *Ordinary Men: Reserve Police Battalion 101 and the Final Solution in Poland*. New York: Harper Collins.

CÜPPERS, M. (2005). *Wegbereiter der Shoah: Die Waffen SS, der Kommandostab Reichsführer-SS und die Judenvernichtung, 1939–1945*. Darmstadt: Wissenschaftliche Buchgesellschaft.

DALLIN, A. (1957). *German Rule in Russia, 1941–1945: A Study of Occupation Policies*. New York: St. Martin's Press.

EZERGAILIS, A. (1996). *The Holocaust in Latvia, 1941–1944: The Missing Center.* Riga: The Historical Institute of Latvia.

FRITZ, S. (1995). *Frontsoldaten: The German Soldier in World War II.* Lexington, KY: University Press of Kentucky.

GERLACH, C. (1999). *Kalkulierte Morde: Die deutsche Wirtschafts- und Vernichtungspolitik in Weißrußland 1941 bis 1944.* Hamburg: Hamburger Edition.

GOLDHAGEN, D. (1996). *Hitler's Willing Executioners: Ordinary Germans and the Holocaust.* New York: Alfred A. Knopf.

HARVEY, E. (2003). *Women and the Nazi East: Agents and Witnesses of Germanization.* New Haven, CT: Yale University Press.

HEER, H. and NAUMANN, K. (eds.) (2000). *War of Extermination: The German Military in World War II, 1941–1944.* New York: Berghahn.

JANSEN, C. and WECKBECKER, A. (1992). *Der "Volksdeutsche Selbstschutz" in Polen, 1939/40.* Munich: Oldenbourg.

KAY, A. (2006). "Germany's Staatssekretäre, Mass Starvation and the Meeting of 2 May 1941." *Journal of Contemporary History* 41: 685–700.

KERSHAW, I. (2000). *The Nazi Dictatorship: Problems and Perspectives of Interpretation.* New York: Oxford University Press.

KLEE, E., DRESSEN, W., and RIESS, V. (eds.) (1991). *"The Good Old Days": The Holocaust as Seen by Its Perpetrators and Bystanders.* New York: The Free Press.

KRAUSNICK, H. (1981). *Hitlers Einsatzgruppen: Die Truppen des Weltanschauungskrieges, 1938–1942.* Frankfurt am Main: Fischer.

KÜHNE, T. (2006). *Kameradschaft: Die Soldaten des nationalsozialistischen Krieges und das 20. Jahrhundert.* Göttingen: Vandenhoeck & Ruprecht.

LIEB, P. (2007). *Konventioneller Krieg oder NS-Weltanschauungskrieg?: Kriegführung und Partisanenbekämpfung in Frankreich 1943/44.* Munich: Oldenbourg.

LOWER, W. (2005). *Nazi Empire-Building and the Holocaust in Ukraine.* Chapel Hill, NC: University of North Carolina Press.

LUMANS, V. (1993). *Himmler's Auxiliaries: The Volksdeutsche Mittelstelle and the German National Minorities of Europe, 1933–1945.* Chapel Hill, NC: University of North Carolina Press.

MALLMANN, K. and MUSIAL, B. (2004). *Genesis des Genozids, Polen, 1939–1941.* Darmstadt: Wissenschaftliche Buchgesellschaft.

—— RIEß, V., and PYTA, W. (2003). *Deutscher Osten, 1939–1945: Der Weltanschauungskrieg in Photos und Texten.* Darmstadt: Wissenschaftliche Buchgesellschaft.

MANOSCHEK, W. (1993). *"Serbien ist Judenfrei": Militärische Besatzungspolitik und Judenvernichtung in Serbien 1941/42.* Munich: Oldenbourg.

MARRUS, M. (1987). *The Holocaust in History.* Hanover, NH: University Press of New England.

MATTHÄUS, J., KWIET, K., FÖRSTER, J., and BREITMAN, R. (2003). *Ausbildungsziel Judenmord?: "Weltanschauliche Erziehung" von SS, Polizei und Waffen-SS im Rahmen der "Endlösung."* Frankfurt am Main: Fischer.

MAZOWER, M. (1993). *Inside Hitler's Greece: The Experience of Occupation, 1941–1944.* New Haven, CT: Yale University Press.

ORTH, K. (1999). *Das System der nationalsozialistischen Konzentrationslager: Eine politische Organisationsgeschichte.* Hamburg: Hamburger Edition.

POHL, D. (1996). *Nationalsozialistische Judenverfolgung in Ostgalizien, 1941–1944.* Munich: Oldenbourg.

QUINKERT, B., DIECKMANN, C., and TÖNSMEYER, T. (2003). *Kooperation und Verbrechen: Formen der "Kollaboration" im östlichen Europa, 1939–1945.* Göttingen: Wallstein.

RASS, C. (2003). *"Menschenmaterial": Deutsche Soldaten an der Ostfront.* Paderborn: Schöningh.

ROSSINO, A. (2003). *Hitler Strikes Poland: Blitzkrieg, Ideology, and Atrocity.* Lawrence, KS: University Press of Kansas.

RUMMEL, R. (1992). *Democide: Nazi Genocide and Mass Murder.* New Brunswick, NJ: Transaction Publishers.

SCHECK, R. (2006). *Hitler's African Victims: The German Army Massacres of Black French Soldiers in 1940.* Cambridge: Cambridge University Press.

SHEPHERD, B. (2004). *War in the Wild East: The German Army and Soviet Partisans.* Cambridge, MA: Harvard University Press.

STREIT, C. (1978). *Keine Kameraden: Die Wehrmacht und die Sowjetischen Kriegsgefangenen, 1941–1945.* Stuttgart: Deutsche Verlags-Anstalt.

WACHSMANN, N. (2004). *Hitler's Prisons: Legal Terror in Nazi Germany.* New Haven, CT: Yale University Press.

WALLER, J. (2007). *Becoming Evil: How Ordinary People Commit Genocide and Mass Killing.* 2nd edn. Oxford: Oxford University Press.

WELZER, H. (2005). *Täter: Wie aus ganz normalen Menschen Massenmörder werden.* Frankfurt am Main: Fischer.

WESTERMANN, E. (2005). *Hitler's Police Battalions: Enforcing Racial War in the East.* Lawrence, KS: University Press of Kansas.

WETTE, W. (2006). *The Wehrmacht: History, Myth, Reality.* Cambridge, MA: Harvard University Press.

WILDT, M. (2009). *An Uncompromising Generation: The Nazi Leadership of the Reich Security Main Office.* Madison, WI: University of Wisconsin Press.

OTHER SUGGESTED READING

BLOOD, P. (2006). *Hitler's Bandit Hunters: The SS and Nazi Occupation of Europe.* Dulles, VA: Potomac Books.

BLOXHAM, D. (2009). *The Final Solution: A Genocide.* Oxford: Oxford University Press.

BROWN, P. (2003). "The Senior Leadership Cadre of the Geheime Feldpolizei, 1939–1945." *Holocaust and Genocide Studies* 17: 278–304.

DEAN, M. (2000). *Collaboration in the Holocaust: Crimes of the Local Police in Belorussia and Ukraine, 1941–44.* New York: St. Martin's Press.

HACHTMANN, R. and SÜß, W. (2006). *Hitlers Kommissare: Sondergewalten in der national-sozialistischen Diktatur.* Göttingen: Wallstein.

HARTMANN, C., HÜRTER, J. and JULREIT, U. (2005). *Verbrechen der Wehrmacht: Bilanz einer Debatte.* Munich: C. H. Beck.

HORNE, J. and KRAMER, A. (1994). "German 'Atrocities' and Franco-German Opinion, 1914: The Evidence of German Soldiers' Diaries." *Journal of Modern History* 66: 1–33.

KOONZ, C. (2003). *The Nazi Conscience.* Cambridge, MA: Harvard University Press.

MANN, M. (2005). *The Dark Side of Democracy: Explaining Ethnic Cleansing.* New York: Cambridge University Press.

MEGARGEE, G. (2006). *War of Annihilation: Combat and Genocide on the Eastern Front, 1941.* Lanham, MD: Rowman & Littlefield.

NEUMAIER, C. (2006). "The Escalation of German Reprisal Policy in Occupied France, 1941–42." *Journal of Contemporary History* 41: 113–31.

PEZZINO, P. (2007). "The German Military Occupation of Italy and the War against Civilians." *Modern Italy* 12: 173–88.

RUTHERFORD, P. (2007). *Prelude to the Final Solution: The Nazi Program for Deporting Ethnic Poles, 1939–1941.* Lawrence, KS: University Press of Kansas.

CHAPTER 10

....

ON-LOOKERS

....

PAUL A. LEVINE

OF the three basic research categories that often structure Holocaust studies, "bystanders" is in many ways the most problematic. Not only does the term embrace an even more internally diverse group of people than "perpetrators" and "victims," but also "bystanders" arouse a more complex set of moral reactions. After several decades in which the "bystanders" were understood to consist primarily of the western Allies, the neutral states, the churches (especially the Vatican), elements of the western press, and international institutions, such as the International Committee of the Red Cross (ICRC), researchers have begun to question the boundaries of the category and even the value of a simplistic umbrella term for such a diffuse and heterogeneous assortment of people and institutions. Indeed, two recent studies have called for either a thorough reevaluation of the concept or its outright rejection (Cesarani and Levine 2002; Bloxham and Kushner 2005). Meanwhile, the anger that long propelled research into those who stood by as Europe's Jews were assaulted has given way to a more nuanced, less blanket assessment of actions and decisions that is informed by Primo Levi's (1919–1987) concept of "the gray zone" (Levi 1988: 36–69).

One indication of the category's daunting nature is numerical. The number of perpetrators ran to hundreds of thousands, and that of the victims to approximately six million, but the bystanders were almost countless, amounting to hundreds of millions of people. They included significant segments of the citizenry and governments in the United States, Great Britain and its dominions, most of Latin America, and the former Soviet Union, not to mention a majority of Christians throughout the world. Significant segments of the civilian populations of Germany, occupied Poland, the Baltic states, Vichy France, "Quisling" Norway,

Hungary, the Balkan states, and the rest of occupied Europe had knowledge of one or another aspect of the genocide. As the doyen of Holocaust scholars pointed out, "Many were remote from the scene of anti-Jewish activity; many others were neighbors of the victims... Even if one looked away, asked no questions, and refrained from talk in public, a dull awareness remained. The disappearance of the Jews, or the appearance of their property, was a signal of what was happening. The event could not be stamped out completely" (Hilberg 1992: 195). How is one to generalize about the motivations of such different populations living under such different circumstances?

METHODOLOGICAL ISSUES AND TERMINOLOGY

The unifying principle of writing on bystanders is, of course, their lack of active solidarity with Jews being subjected to persecution. Retrospective revulsion with this indifference or passivity largely has driven research on the topic, but such passions, as one astute observer has warned, can be highly distorting, for they raise the "great danger that the historian will apply... the standards, value systems, and vantage point of the present, rather than those of the period being discussed" in assessing what happened (Marrus 1987: 156). The intensity of this temptation springs from a number of aspects of contemporary culture, especially in liberal democratic societies. Many inhabitants of such societies assume, largely as a precondition for their smooth functioning and despite much evidence to the contrary, that the automatic and proper response to another person's distress is and should be to come to his or her aid or, at the very least, to show concern. When history disappoints, undermines, or complicates such expectations, the effect is frightening, which fuels the impulse to condemn, rather than explain. The conviction that institutions and individuals must be held morally accountable for their action or inaction intensifies such reactions. If passivity increased the number of victims of the Holocaust, then it amounted to complicity in murder, and if an institution or country with which one identifies engaged in that complicity, the shock can be disorienting. Some early writing on bystanders thus made them nearly as guilty as perpetrators. More nuanced attitudes now generally prevail, but the trope of bystander guilt persists. The founders of the United States Holocaust Memorial Museum, for example, maintained that, "one of the Holocaust's fundamental lessons is that to be a bystander is to share in the guilt. This lesson is applicable to the contemporary problems of society and to the behavior of individuals... Only the intervention of the bystander can help society to become more human" (Bloxham and Kushner 2005: 175).

Writing on bystanders faces multiple, layered methodological challenges. They include evaluating the range of bystanders' opportunities, the consequences of their choices, and the degree to which bystanders were sufficiently informed to understand the consequences of inaction. Tracing the acquisition and impact of information on either an individual or institution is only one of the imposing tasks. Judging the degree to which persons or entities made adequate or reasonable efforts to inform themselves about what was happening to Jews further complicates the required scholarship. That knowledge of the depth and extent of the Holocaust was highly uneven among bystanders is a truism that calls for painstaking investigation of each kind of bystander.

Despite the daunting odds, scholars have made considerable progress in this field of Holocaust studies in recent decades. This research reveals the need for new terminology. Now that historians have demonstrated the degree to which the persecution, plunder, deportation, and murder of the Jews was knowable, indeed in many respects public, the term "on-looker" seems more precise than "bystander" to designate those who did not prevent or intervene against those events. "On-looker" underscores the act and proximity of witnessing and suggests greater responsibility for outcomes, even perhaps a greater emotional range of available responses to them and a greater implicit reinforcement to the perpetrators, than does the more neutral-sounding "bystander."

BRITAIN AND THE UNITED STATES

Not until the mid-1960s did historians and journalists in the United States and Britain begin exploring the reactions of their nations' governments, media, and some specific interest groups to the Nazi genocide. In Britain, Andrew Sharf's *The British Press and Jews under Nazi Rule* (1964) was one of the first studies that asked the still critical question "who knew what, and when?" and in the United States, journalist Arthur Morse published *While Six Million Died: A Chronicle of American Apathy* (1967), which sharply attacked the response of Franklin Roosevelt's (1882–1945) administration to Nazi Germany's anti-Jewish policies. These and others researchers wanted to know why the great liberal democracies had responded tepidly to the plight of Jews seeking refuge from Germany and, later, to the continent-wide slaughter of those caught in Nazi-occupied Europe. David Wyman offered a partial answer in *Paper Walls: America and the Refugee Crises, 1938–1941* (1968), his influential portrayal of a cold-hearted government bureaucracy.

A consensus soon took shape that, rather than having tried to ease the plight of the persecuted, British and American officials worked assiduously to block emigration to their countries, backed by an unsympathetic public and politicians unwilling to consider the humanitarian aspects of the situation. When the mass killing began, the two belligerent democracies seemingly failed to do much to impede it. By failing to offer refuge before the Holocaust began and relief while it was happening, the U.S. and U.K. allegedly contributed to the extent of the Nazi massacre. Numerous follow-up studies exploring the procedures and decisions of government leaders, their bureaucracies, what newspapers reported, and the responses of other segments of society generally confirmed this depiction. By the 1980s, the most prominent publications on the subject consisted largely of "charge sheets," as such studies as Wyman's *The Abandonment of the Jews: America and the Holocaust, 1941–1945* (1984) and M. N. Penkower's *The Jews were Expendable: Free World Diplomacy and the Holocaust* (1988) accused the western Allies in emotive terms of complicity in the genocide through suppression of information about the escalating scale of deportation and slaughter and high-level decisions not to intervene. To most scholars and much of the public in this period, the explanation for Anglo-American inaction was that those being persecuted, deported, and exterminated were Jews—that is, a latent or at times obvious antisemitism.

Deborah Lipstadt's *Beyond Belief: The American Press and the Coming of the Holocaust, 1933–1945* (1986) extended this line of argument by exploring the contribution of influential newspapers to American passivity regarding the persecution of the Jews. Her study revealed both how much information was in the public realm and known to governments and yet how poorly newspapers appreciated the scope of the Nazi genocide. She and other examiners of British and American journalism argued that greater attention to the subject would have generated stronger popular pressure on leaders such as Roosevelt and Winston Churchill (1874–1965) to do something to help the Jews. That these figures were preoccupied with the vast military conflict they were guiding did not go unmentioned in such studies, but the implication was that the desperate struggle to defeat Nazi Germany should not have blotted out attention to mass murder. Raul Hilberg (1926–2007), however, touched on the reasons why that was exactly what happened, when he observed, "the Western Allies did not want the war to be perceived by their own populations as an effort for the deliverance of Jewry. There was to be no hint or implication that Allied soldiers were mercenaries in a Jewish cause" (1992: 255).

Increasingly during the 1980s and into the 1990s, the tone of work on Anglo-American policy toward the Holocaust became more measured, as more archival records became available. Such historians as Henry Feingold, Walter Laqueur, Yehuda Bauer, Richard Breitman and Alan Kraut, Bernard Wasserstein, and Martin Gilbert asked some of the same questions as the pioneers in the field, but provided more subtle and measured responses. Though the thrust of their conclusions remained similar to those of the earlier studies, the work of these figures was less heated and emotional and more tightly focused on analyzing governmental decisions and media responses in relation to such key events as the passage in September 1935 of the Nuremberg Laws, the Evian Conference of July 1938, the pogrom of November 1938 in Germany, the Bermuda Conference of April 1943, the establishment of President Roosevelt's War Refugee Board in January 1944, and the response to the genocide of Hungarian Jewry.

Much of the newer scholarship pivoted on establishing the state of knowledge on the part of the western Allies at any given time, as in Breitman's *Official Secrets: What the Nazis Planned, What the British and Americans Knew* (1998) and Louise London's *Whitehall and the Jews 1933–1948: British Immigration Policy and the Holocaust* (2001). B. A. Zucker's *In Search of Refuge: Jews and U.S. Consuls in Nazi Germany 1933–1941* (2001) exemplifies the empirical depth and methodological precision that research in this field has achieved. English historian Tony Kushner sharpened theoretical understanding of the response to genocide in the democracies with *The Holocaust and the Liberal Imagination: A Social and Cultural History* (1994).

For the war years, the pivotal question is whether the Allies, including the Soviet Union, could have done more to impede the slaughter of the Jews. Rescue advocates, Jewish groups, and many others argued at the time that this was possible, and they achieved a modest success in 1944 with the founding of America's War Refugee Board, whose sole purpose was to assist and rescue Jews. By the end of the war, its dedicated and effective staff could point to some accomplishments in saving human lives. On the whole, however, the western Allies argued that the military struggle against Nazi Germany was paramount, and that the best way to help Europe's remaining Jews was to concentrate all efforts on defeating Nazi Germany. Under Josef Stalin (1879–1953), the Soviet Union declined altogether to address the issue of helping Jews, as Jews, during the war. Among historians, the greatest controversy in this connection concerns the Anglo-American decision in 1944 not to bomb the Auschwitz-Birkenau concentration camp systematically, lest the effort "divert" military resources. Although "this debate has helped clarify the technical issues of bombing and has raised interesting new insights into broader questions of the overall Allied attitudes to the fate of the Jews" (Neufeld and Berenbaum 2000: 5), the issue should not be allowed to obscure the sad fact that the geographical concentration and temporal compression of the Nazi murder campaign made the Allies almost powerless to obstruct it until after most of the Jewish victims had been killed.

Inquiry about Anglo-American on-lookers came also to include the Jewish communities in the two democracies and in Palestine, which Britain controlled from 1919 to 1948. Yehuda Bauer broke important archival and conceptual ground with his *American Jewry and the Holocaust: The American Jewish Joint Distribution Committee, 1933–45* (1981). A decade later, Dina Porat's *The Blue and Yellow Stars of David: The Zionist Leadership in Palestine and the Holocaust, 1939–1945* (1990) and

Dalia Ofer's *Escaping the Holocaust: Illegal Immigration to the Land of Israel, 1939–1944* (1990) pioneered the exploration of the acts and attitudes of Jews in Palestine (the Yishuv). Both studies presented surprising and somewhat disturbing pictures of a setting in which many leaders and individuals were horrified by what they knew and eager to do something, yet the communities continued, in the main, to go about their daily lives even as the "Final Solution" raged. Richard Bolchover's *British Jewry and the Holocaust* (1993) competently surveyed that nation's Jewish community, but examinations of American Jewry and the Holocaust are both legion and highly variable in quality. One provocative analysis of this community of on-lookers, including the war years but with greater focus on the memory of the event, is Peter Novick's *The Holocaust in American Life* (1999).

THE EUROPEAN NEUTRALS

Gradually, the questions put to western democracies about political, diplomatic, and economic responses to genocide were also directed to European nations that remained neutral during the war. These included the Vatican (discussed elsewhere in this volume), and the peripheral states of Ireland, Portugal, and Turkey. A German ally during World War I, Turkey had been transformed thereafter by Mustafa Kemal Atatürk (1881–1938) into a secular state, which declared its neutrality upon the outbreak of World War II in 1939. The country's location assured, however, that some Jews would seek to use it as an escape route to Palestine, especially after the Turkish government permitted various rescue committees to operate from Istanbul. Altogether, at least 16,000 Jews escaped the Holocaust via Turkey and some estimates run much higher. Moreover, the country provided refuge and employment to over one thousand Jewish academicians dismissed from posts in Germany after 1933 (Epstein in Berenbaum and Peck 1998: 536–50) and extended diplomatic protection to its own Jewish citizens living in Vichy France (Shaw 1993). Dubbed by one historian the "long haul neutrals" (Wylie 2003), Ireland and Portugal had limited contact with the Nazi genocide, except insofar as Portugal became a point of departure from Nazi-controlled Europe. In June 1940, as tens of thousands of refugees fled Germany's advance into France, the Portuguese consul general in Bordeaux, Aristedes de Sousa Mendes (1885–1954), courageously issued thousands of entry visas to both Jews and non-Jews in defiance of his government's wishes. Recalled home and dismissed from the diplomatic service, he died penniless.

The most significant European neutrals were Sweden, Switzerland, and Spain. Sweden and Switzerland responded to the Holocaust in several parallel ways, and historians have treated these histories rather similarly. In both societies after World War II, intellectual and political elites quickly established enduring narratives that presented their nations as under great pressure throughout the conflict, but adroit in preserving their autonomy and generally uninformed about the ongoing genocide. Praise for national leaders who made the "right" choices was virtually unstinting, and for decades professional historians in both countries declined to explore either the restrictive refugee policies practiced by both countries before the war or their extensive and mutually vital trade relationships with Nazi Germany almost until it collapsed. Though Switzerland's financial utility to Germany was guessed at and Sweden's indispensable iron ore and ball-bearing shipments to Germany were well known, critical analyses rarely disturbed the national mythologies that enveloped public discourse about the Holocaust.

The process of revision commenced in Switzerland with Alfred A. Hasler's *Das Boot ist voll: Die Schweiz und die Flüchtlinge 1933–1945* (1967) and in Sweden with Hans Lindberg's doctoral dissertation *Svensk flyktingpolitik under internationellt tryck, 1936–1941* (1973), both of which demonstrated that the respective countries' positive self-image regarding refugee policies was unwarranted. Both books also documented similarities between the responses of their nations and those of the western democracies: bureaucratic cold-heartedness toward the plight of the Jews was informed by antisemitic attitudes. Not until 1988, however, did the first monograph illuminate Sweden's response to the Holocaust itself. American historian Steven Koblik's *The Stones Cry Out: Sweden's Response to the Persecution of the Jews, 1933–1945* (1988) broke the long silence about the subject and challenged the dominant narrative that Swedish neutrality had benefited humanity at large, as many Swedes still wish to believe.

In fact, as ever more German Jews had sought refuge, Switzerland and Sweden had strengthened their own "paper walls." Their foreign ministries collaborated with Germany by making separate requests that passports held by Jews become easily identifiable. The result was the infamous large red "J" stamped into passports held by German and (after the *Anschluss*) Austrian Jews. During the war, however, the two countries' responses to genocide diverged: Switzerland doggedly maintained its policy of refusing Jews asylum, even sending thousands back into the hands of the Nazis and their collaborators, but Sweden eventually responded far more generously.

Switzerland's history of on-looking was unveiled in a spectacular way in the mid-1990s. Following revelations about the country's economic collaboration with Nazi Germany and difficulties encountered by survivors seeking to gain access to bank accounts their families may have held at Swiss financial institutions, international pressure forced many bank and government archives to reveal their "secrets." Although many Swiss deeply resented the process, some twenty volumes exploring these issues had been published by the turn of the century under the aegis of "The Independent Commission of Experts Switzerland–Second World War," along with a summary volume in English (Independent Commission of Experts 2002). Most of this literature remains in German and French, but a compressed version of historian Jacques Picard's study *Die Schweiz und die Juden 1933–1945* (1994) has appeared in English (Picard in Cesarani and Levine 2002: 103–45).

Sweden felt compelled to reappraise its response to the ongoing genocide in autumn 1942, when the Germans and their Norwegian collaborators assaulted Norway's tiny Jewish population. That Scandinavian Jews now were under attack aroused Sweden's collective conscience, and the government concluded that it could not continue merely looking on. Never before had a "*broderfolk*" (a fraternal people) been threatened. On the basis of that understanding, Swedish diplomats throughout Europe, led from Stockholm by Gösta Engzell (1897–1997), head of the Foreign Ministry's Legal Division, used normative diplomatic procedures as a form of "bureaucratic resistance" and protected thousands of Jews in several countries (P. Levine 1998). Sweden had abandoned its "on-looker" status in favor of human-itarian activism. Subsequently, when Denmark's Jews were targeted in October 1943, Sweden announced publicly that any Jew reaching its borders would be welcomed. This stance reached its substantive and symbolic peak in Budapest in 1944, when businessman and amateur diplomat Raoul Wallenberg (1912–?) worked with his professional counterparts Carl Ivan Danielsson (1880–1963) and Per Anger (1913–2002) and with other neutral diplomats, such as the experienced Swiss consul Karl Lutz (1895–1975), Swedish Red Cross representative Valdemar Langlet (1872–1960), and Papal Nuncio Angelo Rotta (1872–1965), who was making his own shift from being an on-looker to a rescuer, in issuing protective papers, flags, and building plaques that rescued tens of thousands of Budapest Jews from German and Hungarian perpetrators.

During the war's final weeks, Sweden's paramilitary "White Busses" expedition rescued thousands of Jews and non-Jews from German concentration camps. Led by Count Folke Bernadotte (1895–1948), this episode recently stimulated fierce historical controversy after evidence came to light that Swedish personnel com-plied with a German request that they transport some 2,000 non-Scandinavian camp prisoners from the Neuengamme concentration camp in order to make room there for the Danish and Norwegian prisoners designated for rescue. Many of the people being removed died while in Swedish custody, which cast a shadow over the humanitarianism of Bernadotte's mission. Both quantitatively and quali-tatively, the historiography concerning Sweden and the Holocaust has made extraordinary advances during the past fifteen years, as at least a score of new publications have examined various aspects of Sweden's response to the nearby genocide.

Spain's choices during the Holocaust also illuminate many issues related to on-lookers. Ruled after the civil war of 1936–39 by fascist dictator Francisco Franco (1892–1975), Spain was sought after as an ally by Nazi Germany. However, when World War II began in 1939, Franco declared the country neutral, a status he later shifted to "non-belligerent." Nonetheless, the country was an important economic partner of Nazi Germany, in particular as a source of tungsten ore, which was vital to the production of weapons. Labeled the "Axis neutral" by one historian (Leitz 2000: 114), Spain contributed the Blue Division to the June 1941 invasion of the Soviet Union. It is likely that some soldiers witnessed episodes of mass murder of Jews, making some Spaniards literally on-lookers to genocide. The country's response to the plight of Jewish refugees shifted several times during the war. In 1940–41, tens of thousands of Jews gained refuge, with most eventually departing overseas. However, Spanish authorities were reluctant to allow humanitarian organizations to operate in the country, thus worsening the plight of Jews who remained there. As Germany's military situation deteriorated in 1943–44, Spain once again allowed a few thousand Jewish survivors to enter the country. By the end of the war, Spain had let in some 40,000 Jewish refugees (Yahil 1990: 602). In occupied or Nazi-allied Europe, Spain also extended diplomatic protection to 4,000–5,000 Jews, primarily those with Spanish citizenship (Avni 1981; Payne 2008). The most notable Spanish rescue work was that of the diplomat Angel Sanz Briz (1910–1980), whose efforts in Budapest in 1944–45, with little assistance from Madrid, accounted for much of that total.

The conduct of these three neutral nations exemplifies the ambiguous moral calculus of on-looking during the Holocaust. For while they collectively saved the lives of thousands of Jews, the economic assistance each country provided to Germany undoubtedly lengthened the war and with it, the Third Reich's capacity to carry out the "Final Solution."

NAZI EUROPE

The study of on-lookers has expanded in recent years to include previously neglected groups, especially the civilian populations of the Greater German Reich and Nazi-occupied Europe. Studying what these groups knew about the Holocaust and the effect their knowledge had on their behavior at the time illuminates many significant methodological problems and suggests further research possibilities. This broadening of scope has blurred the borders between on-lookers and perpetrators on the continent, revealing those boundaries to be more permeable than they seemed before.

How can the scholar compare, contrast, and comprehend the responses of such different people and groups as Poles living and farming near a death camp or German civilians eagerly bidding for the furniture of deported Jews or Budapest policemen carrying out their duties? How are the reactions of widespread groups of

Europeans who were proximate witnesses to persecution, state-sponsored thievery, deportation in broad daylight, and even the erection and operation of death camps to be understood? How can people living in the relatively secure environment of contemporary democracies interpret and assess the conduct of people subjected to constant and arbitrary police terror? Historians today understand in a very different light than previously the actions and decisions of, for example, the German civilian in Stuttgart or Bochum; the long-serving policemen in Vichy France, Quisling's Norway, and Belgium; the clergyman in Zagreb or Kraków; the railroad man in Slovakia or Holland; and the ethnic German populations throughout eastern Europe. The depth and breadth of continent-wide on-looking emerges from numerous recent studies, effectively summarized in D. Bankier and I. Gutman's *Nazi Europe and the Final Solution* (2003).

In the case of Germany, the bystander formerly was understood by some as a physical presence at scenes of murder, as seen for example in the essential collection of documents, *"The Good Old Days": The Holocaust as Seen by Its Perpetrators and Bystanders* (Klee, Dressen, and Riess, eds. 1988). But these on-lookers were directly complicit, even if at least some were horrified by what they were viewing. More recent studies of German domestic police forces, including the Gestapo, leave no doubt that the regime was far more sensitive to public opinion than was long understood and that greater popular opposition to Nazi policies might have altered them. David Bankier's *The Germans and the Final Solution: Public Opinion under Nazism* (1992) was both preceded and followed by Robert Gellately's *The Gestapo and German Society: Enforcing Racial Policy 1933–1945* (1990) and *Backing Hitler: Consent and Coercion in Nazi Germany* (2001). All three works demonstrated the widespread acceptance, even approval, of the regime's antisemitic measures by the vast majority of the population and highlighted the invaluable aid widespread denunciations of Jews and their helpers gave the Gestapo. Such denunciations were almost always voluntary and anonymous, and without them the regime's ability to persecute and deport its Jewish population would have been much diminished.

The effect that the "on-looking" German population might have had is illustrated in the history of the so-called euthanasia or T4 program. Targeting mostly handicapped and "asocial" non-Jews, this system of officially sanctioned murder became an open secret and provoked open protest, epitomized by the sermon of Archbishop Clemens August Graf von Galen (1878–1946) in August 1941. His protest, knowledge of which reached the British, who spread word of it, compelled the regime to appear to halt the killings. However, von Galen never protested against the treatment of German or European Jews (Griech-Polelle 2002). The fate of Father Bernhard Lichtenberg (1875–1943), Provost of St. Hedwig's Cathedral in Berlin, who prayed publicly for the Jews every day and was therefore arrested, imprisoned, and finally beaten to death on his way to incarceration in Dachau, suggests that the regime might have responded harshly to religious intervention on behalf of non-Aryans. Of course, keeping silent in the face of persecution is different from doing so when genocide is being perpetrated, but the one usually precedes and fosters the other. Particularly disturbing about the on-looking German civilian population is the possibility that its acquiescence to genocide was literally purchased with plunder. What is today recognized as one of history's greatest robberies, the vast amount of goods plundered from murdered Jews, was made available to Germany's civilian population by the regime and accepted without apparent qualms (Aly 2007).

Surrounded by such public tragedy, a few German civilians did try to help a miniscule number of Jews in need. Historian Beate Kosmola writes movingly about some German rescuers, including one who explained to his Gestapo interrogators his decision to help a Jew "because we'd known each other since we were kids and now he's all alone" (in Bankier and Gutman 2003: 103). Important to our understanding of the German "on-looker" is Kosmala's conclusion that "no evidence has been found . . . to confirm suspicions that provision of help for Jews was punished in Nazi Germany by the death penalty" (in Bankier and Gutman 2003: 105).

Killing centers on Polish soil and terror against the non-Jewish population complicate evaluation of Poland's on-lookers, a task entailing analysis of multiple factors in a fraught equation (Steinlauf 1997). For decades, the conventional wisdom held that the Polish population's endemic antisemitism explained the prevailing indifference to the fate of the Jews, but that few Poles actively collaborated in murder. Moral and interpretive suspicions between Jewish and non-Jewish historians of the Holocaust ran deep, with fruitful discussions made even more difficult by the Soviet bloc's highly ideological view of the Jewish tragedy. In 2001, the publication of Jan Gross's *Neighbors: The Destruction of the Jewish Community of Jedwabne, Poland* ignited a furious political debate in Poland. His research, which depicted murderous and on-looking Poles in a village occupied by the Germans in June 1941, outraged many but also forced a reconsideration of what the "average" Polish civilian knew and did during the war. Continuing the revision of long accepted "truths," G. Steven Paulsson's *Secret City: The Hidden Jews of Warsaw, 1940–1945* (2002) demonstrated that tens of thousands of Jews survived in "Aryan" Warsaw, largely with the help of Christian Poles. Though the population was severely brutalized for years by the Nazi occupation, the Polish underground formed an organization, called *Zegota*, whose task was specifically to aid Jews, making it the only group of its kind in all of Nazi-occupied Europe. Current research does not reduce the complexity of the relationships between Poland's Jewish and non-Jewish populations during and after the Holocaust, but it continues to clarify that history and its legacy (Zimmerman 2003; Cherry and Orla-Bukowska 2007).

Hungary presents yet a different sort of case regarding on-lookers. Although successive right-wing Hungarian governments adopted antisemitic laws and Hungary was a close German economic and military ally during World War II, the nation's leadership resisted pressure to hand its Jews over to Germany. Everything changed, however, in March 1944. Following Germany's invasion and occupation of the country, the Hungarian state and people turned viciously on the almost 800,000 Jews surviving on Hungarian soil and helped the Germans carry out one of the Holocaust's most murderous episodes during spring 1944. Yet in Budapest numerous Hungarian officials aided resident neutral diplomats in assisting thousands of Jews to survive until the Soviet Red Army liberated them. How then does one consistently define and evaluate Hungarian on-lookers?

Another significant on-looker during the Holocaust was the International Committee of the Red Cross (ICRC), which groped for a way to assist Jews in concentration camps during the war without provoking the Nazi regime to restrict ICRC access to Allied soldiers in German prisoner of war camps. Faced with Nazi resistance to the ICRC's rather cautious initiatives, the organization's leadership took the position that the Jews were stateless civilians and thus not eligible for assistance by the ICRC. Only in Budapest in the second half of 1944 did the organization finally engage in effective humanitarian aid and diplomacy on behalf of threatened Jews (Favez 1999).

CONCLUSION

The ubiquity in Europe of public theft, concentration camps, deportation sites, and killing fields underlines the physical connection of millions of on-lookers to genocide. This documented proximity permits the final rejection of both the notion that nothing was known and the moral refuge offered by alleged ignorance. Yet the causal impact of this proximity remains difficult to understand and evaluate. Further complicating historical evaluation today is the continuing sense of shame felt by descendants of on-lookers for what their parents or grandparents did and did not do. Many such people remain reluctant to accept the legacy of moral failure during the Holocaust, and this reluctance has implications for the possibilities of objective research and its acceptance by the public, especially in countries that were occupied by the Germans.

Nonetheless, this category of Holocaust studies undoubtedly will continue to develop, driven by the need to understand why the wartime generation showed so little solidarity with innocent Jewish and Romani neighbors. Since definitional boundaries will continue to shift, teaching this category of Holocaust studies with precision and nuance will become more difficult than in the past and thus pose a particular challenge for educators. Teaching the history of on-lookers must have an articulated social utility, and if it is to have any impact, educators must not shy away from presenting the acute moral and ethical dilemmas that confronted the on-looker—even if doing so upsets grandparents and parents.

The most urgent task for both scholar and citizen remains to understand why during a genocidal moment most people and governments remained passive or indifferent to the plight of their fellow human beings. Evidence from the Holocaust and other genocides makes clear that not acting is the product of a conscious decision. Nonetheless, many citizens in many nations, not least representative democracies, maintain the expectation that their governments will react positively when a humanitarian crisis breaks out. The globalization of information made possible by technology may spur people in the future to positive action, and more rapidly than during the Holocaust. Today, even authoritarian governments have much greater difficulty keeping immoral actions secret than during World War II. If an antidote to on-looking exists, information is among its chief ingredients. Building on that recognition and on solid historical research, effective education about on-looking may increase awareness that the choice—and chance—to do something helpful during a genocide is as present as other, less risky or more convenient options.

REFERENCES

ALY, G. (2007). *Hitler's Beneficiaries: Plunder, Racial War and the Nazi Welfare State.* New York: Metropolitan Books.

AVNI, H. (1981). *Spain, the Jews, and Franco.* Philadelphia, PA: Jewish Publication Society.

BANKIER, D. and GUTMAN, I. (eds.) (2003). *Nazi Europe and the Final Solution.* Jerusalem: Yad Vashem.

BERENBAUM, M. and PECK, A. (eds.) (1998). *The Holocaust and History.* Bloomington, IN: Indiana University Press.

BLOXHAM, D. and KUSHNER, T. (2005). *The Holocaust: Critical Historical Approaches.* Manchester: Manchester University Press.

CESARANI, D. and LEVINE, P. (eds.) (2002). *"Bystanders" to the Holocaust: A Re-evaluation.* London: Routledge.

CHERRY, R. and ORLA-BUKOWSKA, A. (eds.) (2007). *Rethinking Poles and Jews: Troubled Past, Brighter Future.* Lanham, MD: Rowman & Littlefield.

FAVEZ, J. (1999). *The Red Cross and the Holocaust.* Cambridge: Cambridge University Press.

GRIECH-POLELLE, B. (2002). *Bishop von Galen: German Catholicism and National Socialism.* New Haven, CT: Yale University Press.

HILBERG, R. (1992). *Perpetrators, Victims, Bystanders: The Jewish Catastrophe, 1933–1945.* New York: HarperCollins.

INDEPENDENT COMMISSION OF EXPERTS SWITZERLAND—SECOND WORLD WAR (2002). *Switzerland, National Socialism and the Second World War. Final Report.* Zurich: Pendo Verlag.

LEITZ, C. (2000). *Nazi Germany and Neutral Europe during the Second World War.* Manchester: Manchester University Press.

LEVI, P. (1988). *The Drowned and the Saved.* New York: Vintage.

LEVINE, P. (1998). *From Indifference to Activism: Swedish Diplomacy and the Holocaust, 1938–1945.* Uppsala: Almqvist & Wiksell Intl.

MARRUS, M. (1987). *The Holocaust in History.* Hanover, NH: University Press of New England.

NEUFELD, M. and BERENBAUM, M. (eds.) (2000). *The Bombing of Auschwitz.* New York: St. Martin's Press.

PAYNE, S. (2008). *Franco and Hitler: Spain, Germany, and World War II.* New Haven, CT: Yale University Press.

SHAW, S. (1993). *Turkey and the Holocaust.* New York: Macmillan.

STEINLAUF, M. (1997). *Bondage to the Dead: Poland and the Memory of the Holocaust.* Syracuse, NY: Syracuse University Press.

WYLIE, N. (ed.) (2003). *European Neutrals and Non-Belligerents during the Second World War.* Cambridge: Cambridge University Press.

YAHIL, L. (1990). *The Holocaust: The Fate of European Jewry.* Oxford: Oxford University Press.

ZIMMERMAN, J. (ed.) (2003). *Contested Memories: Poles and Jews during the Holocaust and Its Aftermath.* New Brunswick, NJ: Rutgers University Press.

OTHER SUGGESTED READING

ARONSON, S. (2004). *Hitler, the Allies, and the Jews.* Cambridge: Cambridge University Press.

BARNETT, V. (2000). *Bystanders: Conscience and Complicity during the Holocaust.* Westport, CT: Praeger.

BREITMAN, R. and KRAUT, A. (1987). *American Refugee Policy and European Jewry, 1933–1945.* Bloomington, IN: Indiana University Press.

KREIS, G. (1999). *Switzerland in the Second World War: Responding to the Challenges of the Time.* Zurich: Pro Helvetia.

LONDON, L. (2001). *Whitehall and the Jews 1933–1948: British Immigration Policy and the Holocaust.* New York: Cambridge University Press.

PENKOWER, M. N. (1988). *The Jews were Expendable: Free World Diplomacy and the Holocaust.* Detroit, MI: Wayne State University Press.

WYMAN, D. (1984). *The Abandonment of the Jews: America and the Holocaust, 1941–1945.* New York: Pantheon.

....

CHAPTER 11

RESCUERS

....

DEBÓRAH DWORK

RESCUERS did not derail the Holocaust, but without them the number of Jews murdered would have been greater. Acts of rescue illuminate how people transcended hardships and organized help for others and for themselves. Not everyone stood by silently; not everyone participated in genocide. Other forms of behavior were practicable and feasible.

Rescue encompassed diverse forms of aid during the Nazi era: asylum, passage across borders, transportation, food, clothing, and shelter. A range of actors took part: governments, organizations, institutions, individuals, and the victims themselves. Their efforts ranged from legal measures to clandestine operations and changed in form over time (Dwork and van Pelt 2009).

PREWAR PREDICAMENTS AND RESPONSES

....

When the Nazis came to power in 1933, many governments understood that "rescue" meant admitting refugees, but the Depression fanned fears that immigrants would take away jobs or add to the welfare rolls. Nevertheless, 37,000 to 45,000 Jewish Germans and 10,000 gentile Germans found safe havens that year (Bentwich 1936: 33; Simpson 1939: 140, 148, 562; Rosenstock 1956: 377; Strauss 1980: 326). Often in physical danger, these refugees typically were urban, male, and renowned politicians, intellectuals, and artists who capitalized on their international contacts to leave. Most imagined only a temporary need for asylum (Bentwich 1936: 36), as did the countries that opened their doors, even though strict currency restrictions meant that refugees usually brought few possessions and little money. The French government, cherishing the ideal of asylum, waived its visa restrictions and admitted 25–30,000 Germans (Bentwich 1936: 38; Caron 1999: 14). The Netherlands and Czechoslovakia also dropped paperwork and admitted 6,000 and 5,000 refugees, respectively (Bentwich 1936: 44–6; Grossmann 1969: 34–6).

Holland's tiny Jewish community established a Committee for Jewish Refugees, which found employment for numerous refugees and set up an agricultural training program for the younger Jews among them (Baert 1938; D. Cohen 1955; Moore 1986). But elsewhere refugees usually were not allowed employment and soon ran out of funds. By autumn 1933, the situation in France had become so desperate that, a Quaker aid group reported, the government provided "five barracks in which to house some hundreds of refugees, mostly young men. Conditions in the barracks were at first appalling, there being no heat or light, no tables, chairs or beds, and very poor food. Most of the men were without occupation of any kind" (Darnton 1954: 18).

The British spared themselves such scenes. A cabinet committee met in April to consider an urgent proposal from the newly organized Jewish Refugees Committee (JRC) that all German Jewish refugees "should be admitted without distinction, and that German Jews already admitted for the purpose of visits or who may be admitted in the future, should be allowed, during the present emergency, to prolong their stay indefinitely" (Public Record Office 1933). The JRC pledged that "all expense, whether in respect of temporary or permanent accommodation or maintenance will be borne by the Jewish community without ultimate charge to the State" (Public Record Office 1933). Unimpressed, the Minister of Labor declared that he "was not prepared to take the responsibility of agreeing to any measures involving a perceptible increase in the unemployment figures," and predicted "that a number of refugee Jews would, in the course of a few months, either apply for permission to take up employment in this country, or take up employment without that permission." The committee also discounted the idea that the new-comers might bring advantageous skills and expertise. All things considered, the government decided "that there can be no question at the present time of relaxing the restrictions on the entry of aliens," although it accepted the Jewish community's financial guarantee, primarily in order to finance extensions of residence for Jews who already had fled to Britain (Sherman 1973: 31–5; Gottlieb 1998: 7–31; London 2000: 27–30).

As the screws tightened on Jews in Germany, economic considerations replaced fear of arrest as the major stimulus for emigration, and the expectation that exile would be temporary gave way to acknowledgment of permanent relocation. Whereas in 1933, 19 percent of German-Jewish refugees went to Palestine but only 8 percent of Jews leaving Germany went to other places overseas, in 1935 the latter percentage equaled that of Jews going to Palestine (36 percent), in 1936 the figure reached 43 percent, and in 1937, 60 percent, compared to only 15 percent going to Palestine and 25 percent to other parts of Europe (Rosenstock 1956: 381–2). For a time, South Africa, the first of the British dominions to recover from the Depression, glimmered brightly. Some 3,350 German Jews landed in 1936, and others wished to follow. Local Nazi anti-Jewish agitation soon closed that door, however, and in 1937 immigration to South Africa dropped to 900 (Wischnitzer 1948: 187f.). Although South American countries generally did not welcome refugees, appeared religiously intolerant, and were insufficiently industrialized to accommodate middle-class settlers, tens of thousands immigrated to that continent in the mid-1930s thanks to the efforts of South American Jewish communities (Tartakower and Grossmann 1944: 314–17).

The pogrom of 9–10 November 1938 proved a turning point. It made clear that the sole hope for the Jews of Greater Germany lay in emigration, and the door to Britain cracked open. In a powerful speech to the House of Commons, Philip Baker (1889–1982) detailed the Nazis' antisemitic program of the past five years, described the violence of the pogrom, and asked "Where is this going to end? . . . What is it going to mean to us before it is ended?" (Great Britain 1938: 1437–8). Home Secretary Samuel Hoare (1880–1959) spoke in response. Britain would do more. To mollify critics, Hoare explained a new policy aimed at easing the way for "transmigrants" who could furnish proof that they would not become a burden on the state. "While the absorptive powers of this country might be limited as far as permanent residents are concerned, we certainly could take in larger numbers of refugees for a temporary period, provided they were eventually to be settled in some other part of the world" (Great Britain 1938: 1472–73).

Thousands of German, Austrian, and Czech Jews who had obtained an American quota number valid for immigration in 1940 or 1941 now could move to Britain immediately. Other groups were eligible for entry as well. Children under the age of 18 qualified for a temporary stay, as did people between 16 and 35 who were to attend a vocational training program to prepare them for emigration overseas. Persons over 60 with guaranteed support qualified for permanent residence. And London unofficially relaxed the rules so that imprisoned Jewish men could get visas urgently and be released from concentration camps. In January 1939, the Council for British Jewry agreed to establish a refugee camp to house the men, and Whitehall agreed to add them to the officially identified categories of refugees (Gottlieb 1998: 135–45).

The plight of children struck an especially resonant chord in Britain and Holland. If admitting them came at a price for Britain, Hoare observed, "I could not help thinking what a terrible dilemma it was to the Jewish parents in Germany to have to choose between sending their children to a foreign country, into the unknown, and continuing to live in the terrible conditions to which they are now reduced." Yet, he had learned that "Jewish parents were almost unanimously in favour of facing this parting" (Great Britain 1938: 1474). Supported by many gentiles, the Anglo-Jewish community marshaled its resources to rescue as many youngsters as possible. All told, the *Kindertransports* (train- and then boatloads of children) brought nearly ten thousand children to Britain (Gottlieb 1998: 103–4). The Dutch government also approached the Nazi regime about "the children problem" and swiftly received assurances that the Reich would issue passports and exit visas to all the youngsters the Netherlands was willing to admit. Their number came to 1,500, and thousands more traveled through Holland on their way to England (Berghuis 1990: 30, 89–90).

Jewish communities under Nazi rule and the British philanthropic organization, the Movement for the Care of Children from Germany, faced an agonizing task in choosing from among the 60,000 Jewish children in Germany and Austria "the limited number that safely could be gathered in" (Movement for the Care of Children 1938–39: 4). The organization decided to rely upon the judgment of the *Reichsvertretung* (Central Organization of German Jews) in Berlin, the *Kultusgemeinde* (Jewish Community) in Vienna and, as there was no centralized Jewish body in Bohemia and Moravia, a small group of English representatives in Prague, including Nicholas Winton (b. 1909), a young stockbroker who persistently intervened on behalf of the Czech Jewish children. Community officials in the first instance chose healthy, physically fit youngsters at greatest risk: "danger of internment, death of parents, absence of any means of livelihood" (Movement for the Care of Children 1938–39: 4–6; Presland 1944: 4–5).

THE IMPACT OF WAR

With the outbreak of war in September 1939, many countries closed their borders, and the *Kindertransports* ended. Previously legal or semi-legal emigration efforts became increasingly clandestine and illicit, in the east of Europe as well as in the west. Although the Soviets had given Jews little reason to seek asylum in the USSR before the war began, the partition of Poland changed the situation. Some 300,000 Jews fled east to join the 1.2 million Jews who lived in the Soviet-occupied part of the country (Pinchuk 1978: 143). Overwhelmed by these numbers and by efforts to smuggle still more refugees across the German–Soviet demarcation line, the Soviet authorities grew still more irritated at the ungrateful response of the refugees to Stalin's offer of citizenship. What the Soviets saw as a gift, the vast majority of Jewish refugees considered the dashing of hope for returning to home and family or emigrating. Although refusal meant forced removal deep into the

Soviet Union, which commenced in June 1940 and involved over 250,000 refugees (Weinryb 1953: 348), those deported were not unduly alarmed, and some actively sought transport to the east. They believed (correctly, as it happened) that their relocation would be temporary while they worked in the Soviet heartland and awaited the collapse of the Third Reich (Levin 1995: 194–7). Most went to internment camps and collective farms in the Arctic region of European Russia, Siberia, or the Soviet Republics of central Asia. Many died, but the great majority thus were saved.

The tide of war also affected decisions about rescue. By September 1943, Germany clearly was headed for defeat. Formerly "Axis-neutral" nations shifted to a more "Allies-neutral" stance and stood willing to participate in rescue efforts. And ordinary people from all walks of life in occupied or collaborating nations were emboldened by the prospect of a German defeat. This is nowhere illustrated better than in the celebrated rescue of the Danish Jews, which depended upon the actions of all manner of people, but turned on timing.

Werner Best (1903–1989), the German Plenipotentiary in Denmark, had long resisted pressure from the Reich Security Main Office in Berlin to get on with the antisemitic program, largely because he thought harsh measures directed at the seven to eight thousand Jews in the country would upset the smooth functioning of the occupation. But rising popular unrest prompted the Germans to impose martial law in August 1943 and the Danish government to resign. Best thereupon embarked on a double game. Perhaps to improve his standing with Berlin, he got the Reich Security Main Office to set October 2 as the date to deport the Jews under the pretext of the emergency situation. But to strengthen the position of those Danes who still were willing to work with him, he leaked word of the plans to his aide Georg Duckwitz (1904–1973), who passed the information to Rabbi Marcus Melchior (1897–1969). He alerted his congregants at the morning service on 29 September, thus activating the "mouth-radio" as Rosh Hashanah was about to begin. Also tipped off by Duckwitz, the Swedish government broadcast its willingness to admit Jews, and the Danish resistance movement began hiding them in homes near the shore.

Throughout October, rescuers aided by the Danish coastguard and police ferried people to Sweden in small boats carrying up to twelve at a time. The German navy did not intervene, and Best forbade the Gestapo and military police to enter Jewish homes by force. Even so, the exodus became a perilous and frightening business, undertaken at mortal risk under cover of darkness. Close to 6,000 Jews, 1,300 "part-Jews," and 686 non-Jewish spouses were ferried to safety. The police, the church, and the people of Denmark defied the Gestapo, which succeeded in shipping only 477 Jewish Danes, some 6 percent of the Jewish population, to Theresienstadt (Yahil 1969; Kirchhoff 1994; Jensen and Jensen 2003).

"PASSING" AND HIDING

In late 1941, the Germans prohibited further emigration of Jews from Nazi-controlled Europe, began the mass murder of all Jews in reach, and turned a European conflict into World War II by declaring war on the United States. Escape from Hitler's realm became increasingly difficult, and "to rescue" now meant "to hide." Tens of thousands of Jews illicitly crossed the Alps into Switzerland or the Pyrenees to reach Spain or fled east to Asiatic Russia. But for most Jews, the only way out was to disappear.

Faced with *razzias* (dragnet operations), deportations, and horrifying rumors about "unknown destinations" to which Jews were shipped, rescue networks emerged, started by individuals, families, or disparate people united by their concern about Jews. A number of entities across Europe—charitable organizations, scouting associations, university student clubs, and the apparatus of political parties, especially the Communist Party—took on hiding as part of resistance or reshaped previously legal functions into "illegal" systems to help those in need. How did this happen?

The Boogaards, like many other rescuers, came to hide Jews more or less by happenstance. The elderly farmer Hannis Boogaard and the members of his extended family were anti-Nazis who had engaged in acts of economic sabotage during the first two years of the German occupation of the Netherlands. Then, early in 1942, they took in, first, a young gentile man who had been called up for forced labor service in Germany but refused to go and, then, a Jew in the same predicament. When the Jew asked if his endangered parents also could hide on the farm, the Boogaards agreed. From then on, Hannis Boogaard traveled throughout the country making contact with Jews who wished to hide. Aided by two women, Truus de Swaan-Willems and Lies de Jong, he also found a way to help orphaned children in Amsterdam. A former resident of the orphanage, de Jong knew the institution and its personnel. She picked up children as they walked to school and on outings and passed them on to de Swaan-Willems, who got them to Boogaard and his farm (van Ommeren and Scherphuis 1985; van Stam 1986).

Other groups did not grow from a familial nucleus, as the Boogaards' operation had. People who were unrelated to each other, and indeed shared nothing except their common cause, came together to establish organizations to aid and assist Jews. Their motivations varied from political ideology to humanitarian beliefs to religious principles (Tec 1986; Oliner and Oliner 1988). Thus, for example, in Poland late in September of 1942, people as different as Zofia Kossak-Szczucka (1889–1968), a well-known novelist and president of the conservative Catholic social organization, the Front for Reborn Poland, and the democrat Wanda Krahelska-Filipowiczowa (1886–1968) worked together to found the (clandestine) Temporary Committee to Help Jews. The Committee's activities were centered in

Warsaw, with branches in Kraków and Lwów. Within months, representatives of all the political parties of the *Delegatura* (the official body delegated to represent the Polish-government-in-exile on Polish soil) joined this new initiative, now called the Council for Aid to Jews (*Rada Pomocy Żydom* or RPZ) and known by the cryptonym *Zegota*.

Jews given away by accent or appearance were spirited into hiding. Jews who looked and sounded like Catholic Poles needed housing and false documents in order to pass as such. This sort of "normal" life was as perilous as hiding, but it offered independence. With the required identification (*Kennkarte*) and a good biographical story, a Jew could obtain an employment card for work and ration cards for shopping. To get a *Kennkarte*, however, one needed a birth certificate, and in Poland, priests registered most births and deaths. Sympathetic clergy passed hundreds of legal birth certificates to *Zegota* and then destroyed the paired death certificates. *Zegota* matched, as best it could, the sex and age of the deceased with a live Jew. This supply was augmented by fictitious or forged birth certificates and counterfeit *Kennkarten*. Many Poles needed false papers—the resistance, the underground army, Jews—and clandestine document production flourished, facilitating escapes to the "Aryan" side, which rose dramatically with the Warsaw ghetto uprising in April 1943.

Child rescue emerged as a central focus for *Zegota*, and a Children's Bureau was established in July 1943 under the direction of Irena Sendlerowa (1910–2008). In 1939, Sendlerowa worked in the Social Welfare Department of Warsaw's Municipal Administration, and thereafter she used her position to create a network that provided financial and material assistance to Jews. After the ghetto was sealed on 15 November 1940, she obtained entry documents for herself and her close colleague Irena Schultz and established contact with Eva Rechtman, who organized a secret network of women employed by the Jewish charitable organization, CENTOS (Federation of Associations for the Care of Orphans in Poland). Thus, Sendlerowa and Schultz managed to bring money, food, medicine, and clothing (all of which they obtained by presenting false documentation to the Social Welfare Department) into the ghetto, where it was distributed by Rechtman and her associates. The mass deportations from Warsaw in 1942 spurred Sendlerowa and Schultz to smuggle children out of the ghetto and hide them with willing families, orphanages, and convents on the "Aryan" side. According to Sendlerowa, "The children were usually brought out of the ghetto through the underground corridors of the public courts building and through the tram depot in Muranow district." Over time, some 2,500 children were registered by the Warsaw branch of *Zegota* (Bartoszewski in Bartoszewski and Lewin 1969: xliv–lii; Sendler in Bartoszewski and Lewin 1969: 41–62; Kermish in Gutman and Zuroff 1977: 367–98; Prekerowa in Abramsky et al. 1986: 161–76).

Grassroots networks such as the Boogaards' or *Zegota*'s developed spontaneously, but some established organizations responded as well. The Jewish philanthropic organization, *Oeuvre de Secours aux Enfants* (OSE or Children's Aid Organization) is one of a number of groups that disprove the notion that only gentiles rescued Jews. Founded by Jewish physicians in Russia in 1912 and successively moved to Berlin after 1917 and to Paris after 1933, the OSE designated protecting Jewish children as its chief mission during the 1930s. With the fall of France in June 1940 and division of the country into the northern "occupied" zone and the southern "free" zone under the collaborationist government of Marshal Philippe Pétain (1856–1951) in Vichy, OSE emptied its orphanages in the Parisian suburbs and fled to the south (Lazare 1996; Paul 2002). OSE-Sud became responsible for the activities carried out in the unoccupied zone. Two officers, Falk Walk (1883–1943) and Eugène Minkovski (1885–1972), carried on in Paris and kept the OSE-Nord office at 92 Champs-Elysées open throughout the war, supporting Jews hiding in the city.

Soon realizing that foreign Jews were at greater risk than their French-born co-religionists, OSE-Nord turned to smuggling central and eastern European children across the demarcation line. OSE staff in the "free" zone (like everyone else) believed that a French government would deal more kindly with its Jewish citizens and refugees than the German invaders, and OSE-Sud developed a legal network of services. The August 1942 razzias proved otherwise, and OSE-Sud began underground operations. The legal structure of children's homes and health care centers remained intact, but they also served as a screen for the organization of secret border crossings, for laboratories to produce false identity papers, and for hiding those in imminent danger of arrest. Following the German occupation of Vichy in November, the OSE directorate decided on "the systematic camouflage of children sheltered in the various children's homes" (Dwork 1991: 55–64). One network, run by Georges Garel (1909–1979), hid children who could pass as gentiles. They got false identity cards or birth certificates and doctored ration cards for food and clothing and were dispersed among the French population. Another network, operated by Andrée Salomon (1908–1985), hid children who could not pass because of religious practice, inability to speak French, or appearance. When possible, these children were smuggled over the border into Switzerland or Spain.

INSTITUTIONAL FAILURE AND PERSONAL INITIATIVE

Rescue efforts before and during the Holocaust did not come from politicians, as demonstrated by the Evian Conference of July 1938 and the Bermuda Conference convened by the British and American governments on 19 April 1943. While the

Warsaw ghetto went up in flames and facts about the "Final Solution" were known, the delegates in Bermuda were more concerned that Berlin would dump Jewish refugees on the Allies than they were about saving them. Nor, with few exceptions such as in Denmark and Bulgaria, did help come from the Protestant, Catholic, or Orthodox churches or directly from any but one of the regular armies at the front and throughout occupied Europe. Perhaps because other interests took precedence, their own antisemitic factions bred quiescence, and they simply were too inflexible to respond promptly, institutions largely failed the Jews of Europe. But across Europe, a few people within each of these institutions did not.

Franklin D. Roosevelt (1882–1945), whose administrations spanned the Nazi era, inherited American immigration policies that were unfriendly to Jewish refugees and maintained that the best way to save Jews was to force Germany's unconditional surrender. Nevertheless, private American volunteer organizations launched rescue efforts when and where they could. For example, the New York-based Emergency Rescue Committee (ERC), particularly through the work of Varian Fry (1907–1967), aided Jewish refugees who were stranded in France after the German invasion in June 1940 (Fry 1997). A journalist and editor, Fry became the ERC's representative in Marseilles and established a legal entity, the American Relief Organization, as a front for illegal work that enabled hundreds of endangered refugees—Jews and anti-fascists—to escape from France. In September 1941, the Vichy government forced him to return to the United States, where the Federal Bureau of Investigation kept him under surveillance and hampered his career options. Fry was the first American to be named "Righteous Among the Nations" when Yad Vashem, Israel's Holocaust Heroes and Martyrs Remembrance Authority, so honored him posthumously in 1996.

Japan's consul in Kaunas, Lithuania, Chiune Sugihara (1900–1986), disagreed with his country's policy of non-intervention with regard to Jews, hundreds of whom gathered outside his office every day during the summer of 1940, pleading for help. Realizing that he might well suffer consequences, he nevertheless decided to provide thousands of visas, each allowing a whole family transit through Japan (Levine 1996; Sakamoto 1998: 101–57). Similarly, Aristedes de Sousa Mendes (1885–1954), the Portuguese Consul General in Bordeaux, issued thousands of visas until the government in Lisbon realized what he was doing and swiftly recalled him on 24 June 1940 (Franco 2000). Both men had no reason to get involved, both defied their orders, both stood to lose a career, and both did. Sugihara was dismissed upon his return to Japan after the war, de Sousa Mendes immediately following his recall to Lisbon.

Many more diplomats stepped forward in Budapest in March 1944, when Germany had all but lost the war yet remained determined to annihilate the last remaining major Jewish community in its grasp, that of Hungary. Desperate Jews besieged the Swedish Legation in Budapest hoping for asylum. Although the Legation was supposed to protect only Swedes and citizens of other countries represented by Sweden, the diplomats went to work. First, they issued provisional passports and negotiated with the Hungarian authorities to ensure that Jews holding them would be treated as Swedish citizens and exempted from wearing the yellow Star of David. But the need exceeded the capacities of the Legation's staff, which requested help from Stockholm. It appointed Raoul Wallenberg (1912–?), a 32-year-old businessman and member of a prominent family of Swedish financiers, as Secretary of the Swedish Legation in Budapest. Arriving in July, he had the support of the War Refugee Board, a new American organization established by President Roosevelt under duress only a few months earlier.

In the ensuing months, Wallenberg, whose personal fate remains uncertain (Levine 2010: 373–75), created a rescue organization with a special department to fabricate a new protective passport. His staff quickly grew to some 400 people, primarily Jews who were exempt from wearing the star and, in theory, protected against deportation. With their help, the Legation distributed some fifteen to twenty thousand passports. When the collaborationist Arrow Cross Party took power in October 1944 and violence against Jews spread throughout Budapest, the protective passports sometimes no longer deterred the Germans and their Hungarian allies. Wallenberg organized checkpoints on the major roads out of Budapest and at the border to demand the release of Jews who had been picked up despite having these papers. His personnel, people brave enough to confront the German authorities directly, even dared to disburse passports on the spot. Altogether, he and his collaborators protected some 70,000 Jews until the Red Army arrived in January 1945 (Anger 1981; Barany in Braham and Pók 1997; Levine 1998). With varying degrees of support from home, the Swiss, Spanish, and Portuguese Legations in Budapest also were heavily involved in efforts to save Jews, as was the Papal Nuncio, Angelo Rotta (1872–1965).

In contrast to these largely individual initiatives, the entire Italian army in Italian-occupied Croatia, Greece, and France flouted the Germans. In the early 1940s, Italians grew increasingly unhappy with their alliance with Germany, disgusted with the war, and hopeful for an Allied victory. When Jews began fleeing from the new anti-Serb, antisemitic Croatian state into the Italian-annexed areas of former Yugoslavia in 1942, the local governor wanted to throw them back. But Italy's commanding general refused, and the Foreign Ministry in Rome ruled against expelling Jews "for obvious reasons of political prestige and humanity" (Steinberg 1990: 54). A number of Jews and Serbs had been transferred to the Dalmatian island of Arbe by the time Benito Mussolini (1883–1945) was overthrown in July 1943, but after Italy surrendered to the Allies in September, nearly all of them were allowed to escape and join the partisans. Because of the Italian army's policies, 3,000 of the 3,500 Jewish refugees who remained in the Italian zone of Yugoslavia survived as a group, and thousands more slipped over the border into Italy, helped by local army commanders who did not stop them (Carpi in Gutman and Zuroff 1977: 468–506; Garti 1996). Similarly, in the eight departments of France placed under Italian military occupation, the commanders decided that round-ups and deportations of Jews were "irreconcilable with the dignity of the Italian army" (Steinberg 1990: 112).

Although the Catholic and Protestant church hierarchies largely failed in their key tasks of serving as the public conscience and the voice of morality, many nuns, priests, ministers, prelates, and laypersons throughout Europe spoke out against the evil they witnessed and engaged in many clandestine rescue activities. A few, like Monsignor Jules-Gérard Saliège (1870–1956), the elderly, partly paralyzed, and popular archbishop of Toulouse, were high-ranking religious authorities. Appalled by the razzias sweeping through France in the summer of 1942, Saliège released a pastoral letter that was read in every parish of his archdiocese on 23 August. He reminded his flock in no uncertain terms that "Jews are men, Jews are women. Foreigners are men, foreigners are women. It is forbidden to harm them, to harm these men, to harm these women, to harm these fathers and mothers of families. They are part of the human race; they are our brothers like all others. A Christian may not forget this" (A. Cohen 1993: 305). Saliège's statement marked the first public criticism of Vichy's and Germany's racist policies by an important religious figure since 1940. Three other bishops in the free zone made similar pronouncements in the following weeks, each acting independently of Rome and of each other. The thirty-one other French bishops said nothing.

If few in high religious positions were willing to speak or act against antisemitic policies, many subordinate figures committed themselves to all kinds of rescue initiatives. Perhaps two-thirds of the seventy-four female religious communities in Poland took in Jews, adults, and children alike (Kurek-Lesik 1988). In Rome, where the silence and passivity of Pope Pius XII (1876–1958) amounted to tacit collusion in the persecution, a number of monasteries and convents offered refuge after the razzia in Rome's ancient ghetto in October 1943 (Friedländer 1966; Phayer 2000; Zuccotti 2000; Rittner and Roth 2002). When more than a quarter (1,259) of the neighborhood's inhabitants were scooped up and 1,007 ultimately deported, shocked convents and monasteries opened their doors to the hunted, often asking nothing in return.

On the local level, Protestants were as active as Catholics. Grassroots religious organizations of many denominations often worked together, as the case of Le Chambon-sur-Lignon illustrates (Hallie 1994; Henry 2007). The inhabitants of this small Huguenot village in southern France shared one basic principle: they believed that needy persons should be offered refuge. Resistance groups throughout France brought Jews to Le Chambon, and Jews made their way there themselves. A few thousand either hid there throughout the war or were passed over the border to Switzerland. Many were harbored by individual families, others in seven group homes supported by a range of philanthropic organizations, including the Society of Friends, the American Congregationalists, and le Secours Suisse aux Enfants (Swiss Relief for Children), and national governments, notably those of

Switzerland and Sweden. A small, poor Protestant parish, inspired by a deeply principled pastor, André Trocmé (1901–1971), managed what the universal, Catholic church, led by a highly politicized pope, did not undertake: to rescue Jews from the Germans.

Discussions of rescue during the Holocaust usually focus on the rescuers and, in so doing, elide the role of victims in their own rescue. Jews become passive participants in these narratives, stripped of agency, energy, or insight. Yet at no point was this depiction true. Every Jew who sought—successfully or unsuccessfully—to go into hiding, pass as gentile, join the partisans, escape Nazi Europe, and help fellow Jews to do any of these things was involved in rescue. Although no Jew survived without the help of gentiles, and sometimes literally hundreds of them over the course of years, Jews actively participated in the process, striving to save themselves and each other as best they could. To cross national boundaries, to pass, and to disappear, to live as if one had vanished from the face of the earth, and yet remain alive—none of this was easy.

CONCLUSION

During the Holocaust, rescue was a complex affair in an unprecedented situation. Few Jews or gentiles had experience in clandestine operations, and few could comprehend that millions of ordinary civilians were being murdered. Who in the west could envision a razzia or life in a Nazi ghetto—let alone the fate of the Germans' victims? Even as information became available to the free world through smuggled reports and photographs, few people could absorb it as knowledge. Thus, while rescuers strove persistently and in diverse circumstances, albeit with odds against them at every turn, the limits of the imagination as well as a lack of political will worked for the Germans and their allies in the genocide. Future research needs to highlight the diversity of rescue efforts and circumstances, the dilemmas faced by rescuers and those they helped, and the roles that rescuers play in Holocaust education.

REFERENCES

Abramsky, C., Jachimczyk, M., and Polonsky, A. (eds.) (1986). *The Jews in Poland.* London: Basil Blackwell.

Anger, P. (1981). *With Raoul Wallenberg in Budapest.* New York: Holocaust Library.

Baert, J. (1938). *De vluchteling in Nederland, met een overzicht van het aantal en de aard der vluchtelingencomité's.* Assen: van Gorcum.

BARTOSZEWSKI, W. and LEWIN, Z. (eds.) (1969). *Righteous Among Nations: How the Poles Helped the Jews, 1939–1945.* London: Earlscourt Publications.

BENTWICH, N. (1936). *The Refugees from Germany, April 1933 to December 1935.* London: George Allen & Unwin.

BERGHUIS, C. (ed.) (1990). *Joodse Vluchtelingen in Nederland, 1938–1940: Documenten betreffende toelating, uitleiding en kampopname.* Kampen: J. H. Kok.

BRAHAM, R. and PÓK, A. (eds.) (1997). *The Holocaust in Hungary: Fifty Years Later.* New York: Columbia University Press.

CARON, V. (1999). *Uneasy Asylum: France and the Jewish Refugee Crisis, 1933–1942.* Stanford, CA: Stanford University Press.

COHEN, A. (1993). *Persécutions et sauvetage: Juifs et Français sous l'occupation et sous Vichy.* Paris: Cerf.

COHEN, D. (1955). *Zwervend en Dolend: De joodsche vluchtelingen in Nederland in de jaren 1933–1940.* Haarlem: De Erven F. Bohn.

DARNTON, L. (1954). *Friends Committee for Refugees and Aliens, 1933–1950.* London: Friends Committee for Refugees and Aliens.

DWORK, D. (1991). *Children With A Star: Jewish Youth in Nazi Europe.* New Haven, CT: Yale University Press.

——and VAN PELT, R. (2009). *Flight from the Reich: Refugee Jews, 1933–1946.* New York: W. W. Norton.

FRANCO, M. (ed.) (2000). *Spared Lives: The Actions of Three Portuguese Diplomats in World War II.* Lisbon: Instituto Diplomatico-Ministerio dos Negócios Estrangeiros.

FRIEDLÄNDER, S. (1966). *Pius XII and the Third Reich.* New York: Alfred A. Knopf.

FRY, V. (1997). *Surrender on Demand.* Boulder, CO: Johnson Books.

GARTI, I. (1996). "The Living Conditions of Jewish Refugees from Yugoslavia Held as Civilian Prisoners of War in Fascist Italy up to the Fall of the Regime in July 1943." *Yad Vashem Studies* 25: 343–60.

GOTTLIEB, A. (1998). *Men of Vision: Anglo-Jewry's Aid to Victims of the Nazi Regime, 1933–1945.* London: Weidenfeld and Nicolson.

GREAT BRITAIN (1938). *Parliamentary Debates: House of Commons Official Report,* 5th series, 341 (8 November–25 November 1938).

GROSSMANN, K. (1969). *Emigration: Geschichte der Hitler-Flüchtlinge 1933–1945.* Frankfurt am Main: Europäische Verlagsanstalt.

GUTMAN, Y. and ZUROFF, E. (eds.) (1977). *Rescue Attempts During the Holocaust.* Jerusalem: Yad Vashem.

HALLIE, P. (1994). *Lest Innocent Blood Be Shed: The Story of the Le Chambon and How Goodness Happened There.* New York: Harper & Row.

HENRY, P. (2007). *We Only Know Men: The Rescue of Jews in France during the Holocaust.* Washington, DC: Catholic University of America Press.

JENSEN, S. and JENSEN, M. (2003). *Denmark and the Holocaust.* Copenhagen: Danish Institute for International Studies.

KIRCHHOFF, H. (1994). "*SS-Gruppenführer* Werner Best and the Action Against the Danish Jews." *Yad Vashem Studies* 24: 195–222.

KUREK-LESIK, E. (1988). "The Conditions of Admittance and the Social Background of Jewish Children Saved by Women's Religious Orders in Poland from 1939–1945." *Polin* 3: 244–75.

LAZARE, L. (1996). *Rescue as Resistance.* New York: Columbia University Press.

LEVIN, D. (1995). *The Lesser of Two Evils: Eastern European Jews Under Soviet Rule, 1939–1941.* Philadelphia, PA: Jewish Publication Society.

LEVINE, H. (1996). *In Search of Sugihara.* New York: The Free Press.

LEVINE, P. (1998). *Indifference to Activism: Swedish Diplomacy and the Holocaust, 1938–1944.* Uppsala: Uppsala University Library.

——(2010). *Raoul Wallenberg in Budapest: Myth, History and Holocaust.* Portland, OR: Vallentine Mitchell.

LONDON, L. (2000). *Whitehall and the Jews, 1933–1948: British Immigration Policy and the Holocaust.* Cambridge: Cambridge University Press.

MOORE, B. (1986). *Refugees from Nazi Germany in the Netherlands, 1933–1940.* Dordrecht: Martinus Nijhoff.

MOVEMENT FOR THE CARE OF CHILDREN FROM GERMANY, LTD. (1938–39). *First Annual Report: November 1938–December 1939.* London: Central British Fund for Jewish Relief Archive. Reel 153.

OLINER, S. and OLINER, P. (1988). *The Altruistic Personality.* New York: The Free Press.

OMMEREN, A. VAN and SCHERPHUIS, A. (1985). "De Onderduikers in de Haarlemmermeer." *Vrij Nederland,* 16 March: 1–25.

PAUL, C. (2002). *Rescuing the Children.* Madison, WI: University of Wisconsin Press.

PHAYER, M. (2000). *The Catholic Church and the Holocaust, 1930–1965.* Bloomington, IN: Indiana University Press.

PINCHUK, B.-C. (1978). "Jewish Refugees in Soviet Poland, 1939–1941." *Jewish Social Studies* 40: 141–58.

PRESLAND, J. (1944). *A Great Adventure: The Story of the Refugee Children's Movement.* London: Bloomsbury House.

PUBLIC RECORD OFFICE (1933). Cabinet Committee 27/549 10686. Cabinet Committee on Aliens Restrictions, Report, 3 [circa 6 April 1933]. "Proposals of Jewish Community as Regards Jewish Refugees from Germany," being an appendix to a memorandum entitled "The Present Position in Regard to the Admission of Jewish Refugees from Germany to This Country," by the Home Secretary for the Cabinet Committee on Aliens Restrictions.

RITTNER, C. and ROTH, J. (eds.) (2002). *Pope Pius XII and the Holocaust.* New York: Continuum.

ROSENSTOCK, W. (1956). "Jewish Emigration from Germany." *Leo Baeck Institute Yearbook* 1: 373–90.

SAKAMOTO, P. (1998). *Japanese Diplomats and Jewish Refugees.* Westport, CT: Praeger.

SHERMAN, A. (1973). *Island Refuge: Britain and Refugees from the Third Reich, 1933–1939.* Berkeley, CA: University of California Press.

SIMPSON, J. (1939). *The Refugee Problem: Report of a Survey.* London: Oxford University Press.

STAM, C. VAN (1986). *Wacht Binnen de Dijken.* Haarlem: Uitgeverij de Toorts.

STEINBERG, J. (1990). *All or Nothing: The Axis and the Holocaust 1941–1943.* New York: Routledge.

STRAUSS, H. (1980). "Jewish Emigration from Germany: Nazi Policies and Jewish Responses (1)." *Leo Baeck Institute Yearbook* 25: 313–61.

TARTAKOWER, A. and GROSSMANN, K. (1944). *The Jewish Refugee.* New York: Institute of Jewish Affairs.

TEC, N. (1986). *When Light Pierced the Darkness: Christian Rescue of Jews in Nazi-occupied Poland.* New York: Oxford University Press.

WEINRYB, B. (1953). *The Jews in the Soviet Satellites.* Syracuse, NY: Syracuse University Press.

WISCHNITZER, M. (1948). *To Dwell in Safety: The Story of Jewish Migration Since 1800.* Philadelphia, PA: Jewish Publication Society.

YAHIL, L. (1969). *The Rescue of Danish Jewry: Test of a Democracy.* Philadelphia, PA: Jewish Publication Society.

ZUCCOTTI, S. (2000). *Under His Very Windows: The Vatican and the Holocaust in Italy.* New Haven, CT: Yale University Press.

OTHER SUGGESTED READING

GUSHEE, D. (2003). *Righteous Gentiles of the Holocaust: Genocide and Moral Obligation.* 2nd edn. St. Paul, MN: Paragon House.

MOORE, B. (2010). *Survivors: Jewish Self-help and Rescue in Nazi-occupied Western Europe.* New York: Oxford University Press.

OLINER, P. (2004). *Saving the Forsaken: Religious Culture and the Rescue of Jews in Nazi Europe.* New Haven, CT: Yale University Press.

PALDIEL, M. (2007). *The Righteous Among the Nations.* New York: HarperCollins.

SATLOFF, R. (2007). *Among the Righteous: Lost Stories from the Holocaust's Reach into Arab Lands.* New York: Public Affairs.

TEC, N. (2009). *Defiance.* New York: Oxford University Press.

TODOROV, T. (2001). *The Fragility of Goodness: Why Bulgaria's Jews Survived the Holocaust.* Princeton, NJ: Princeton University Press.

CHAPTER 12

....

JEWS

....

DAN MICHMAN

Jewry and Judaism began some three thousand years ago with the crystallization of a distinct identity among twelve tribes in Canaan (the old name for Palestine) around the belief in one abstract, invisible, and infinite God. In 722 BCE, the Assyrians conquered and scattered a majority of the ten tribes that inhabited the northern Kingdom of Israel, but the Kingdom of Judea (Yehuda in Hebrew) remained until the destruction of the First Temple in Jerusalem by the Babylonians in 586 BCE. For roughly fifty years, the population was exiled, and this was when it acquired the name "Jews" (Yehudim, i.e., descendants of the tribe of Juda/Yehuda). The main contours of Jewish faith, ritual, and scripture—what is collectively known as "rabbinical Judaism"—took shape in the so-called Mishnaic and Talmudic Period from the third century BCE through the fifth century CE, i.e., the Hellenistic and Roman periods in Mediterranean history. Following the destruction of the Second Temple (70 CE) by the Romans, the Bar Kokhba revolt against them (132–135 CE), and the economic waning of Palestine in the first centuries of the Common Era, the historic locus of the Jewish people and Judaism declined. Ever since, most Jews have lived outside Palestine in lands dominated by Christianity (Europe and, later, the United States) and Islam (the Middle East and North Africa).

The diaspora Jews regarded themselves—and so did their surrounding populations—as a distinct people (nation), defined largely by religion and living in communities with special legal and partially autonomous status. Relations with gentiles varied considerably with time and place, but periodically erupted in outbreaks of anti-Jewish hostility and violence. Community councils, supplemented by the spiritual authority of the rabbis, governed most of the Jewish communities.

Dispersion, however, also produced differentiation, exemplified in a major way by the development of Sephardic ("Spanish") and Ashkenazi ("German") traditions, which diverged significantly from the sixteenth century onward. Whatever their differences, Jews approached life in "Galut" (exile/diaspora) as an anomaly that would end in Messianic times with the ingathering of all exiles into the Land of Israel (Ben-Sasson 1976).

Developments during the eighteenth and nineteenth centuries transformed European Jewry. More rapid rates of democratization and emancipation from occupational and political restrictions in western Europe created the cultural and mental divide between so-called *Westjuden* (i.e., West and Central European Jews) and *Ostjuden* (East European Jews). Especially among the *Westjuden*, expanded rights and opportunities, secularizing trends, and expectations that newly acquired citizenship entailed adaptation to national standards of language and education weakened traditional community and religious structures. The tendency increased among Jews and governments to see Jewry as a religion, rather than a people, giving rise both to Reform (Liberal-Religious or Neolog) Jewry and to the use in most European languages of the term *Israelites* instead of Jews. Wherever liberalism and industrialization grew, new career avenues opened for Jews, and their swift advance made them socially conspicuous, despite their relatively small numbers. Likewise, democratization increased Jewish political involvement, within and outside Jewish society, often splitting Jews into diverse and rival groups, socialists and communists among them. European nationalism invigorated varied forms of modern Jewish nationalism, including Zionism, the drive for a national home in Palestine, which gained traction in response to increasingly vocal and sometimes violent antisemitism in the decades just prior to World War I.

Traditional Jewry reacted to these trends by redefining itself as "faithful" Jewry. Many currents rippled through this "orthodoxy," as some called it, including the vigorous rivalry in eastern Europe during the eighteenth and nineteenth centuries between *Chassidic* sects and their fierce *Mitnaggedic* (also called "Lithuanian") opponents. Because of enormous Jewish emigration from eastern Europe after the 1880s, these many religious and political cleavages spread to other countries. Consequently, in no country were all Jews united in one organization and able to speak in one voice about politics or religion (Friesel 1990; Michman 2003: 59–66).

According to Jewish religious law (*Halachah*) a person's Jewishness is established by birth to a Jewish mother or by religious conversion. However, the different standards and categorizations applied by national censuses make precise Jewish population figures elusive. Demographers, nevertheless, generally accept the following figures for the worldwide Jewish population: 4.5 million in 1840 (88 percent in Europe), 11 million in 1900 (81 percent in Europe), and 16.7 million in 1939 (57 percent in Europe) (Friesel 1990). The major concentrations of Jews in the 1930s were in Poland (3.3 million) and the Soviet Union (3 million), but communities of 100,000 to 700,000 people also existed in Hungary, Romania, Germany,

Czechoslovakia, France, Great Britain, and the Netherlands, and smaller communities were present in almost all other European and North African countries.

ATTACK AND RESPONSE

Whereas Jews in the 1930s were scattered and disunited, Adolf Hitler (1889–1945) and Nazi ideology perceived "world Jewry" and its "spirit" as conspiratorial, powerful, and cohesive forces that had to be erased from the earth for the sake of German hegemony and human survival. Though Jews were not the only group persecuted by Nazi Germany, they were the victims perceived as most threatening. Nazi antisemitism transformed centuries-long hostility to Jews and Jewry into an apocalyptic, life-or-death battle against a parasitic and corrupting enemy. Above all, the Jews stood for the "unnatural" and corrosive principle of human equality, which underlay the pernicious beliefs of Christianity, liberalism, democracy, internationalism, capitalism, and communism and undermined the hierarchical principle of nature, according to which the "Aryans" should be the world's dominant race (Levy 1991: 213). The SS-man Dieter Wisliceny (1911–1948) described this outlook as a "mythical religious perception" of a struggle between evil (the Jews) and good that could not be understood by logic or reason, but only by analogy with such phenomena as the exorcising of witches (Michman in Matthäus and Mallmann 2006: 209–10). For Hitler, the war against the Jews was an obsession, expressed most tellingly in his speech to the German parliament on 30 January 1939, when he foretold that in case of another world war, "the result will not be the bolshevization of the earth, and thus the victory of Jewry, but the annihilation of the Jewish race in Europe!" and in the political testament he wrote shortly before his suicide on 29 April 1945, which called on future generations "to fight mercilessly against the poisoners of all the peoples of the world, international Jewry" (Arad et al. 1981: 134–5, 162).

The evolution of Nazi anti-Jewish policies should be seen in this context. Until November 1938, different authorities pursued differing strategies. Their varying approaches and intentions sometimes collided on the bureaucratic level, but for the Jews this made little difference: they experienced the avalanche of anti-Jewish measures and growing estrangement from the rest of the German population as the creation of a new ghetto or even as a destruction before that word got its murderous meaning (Arad et al. 1981: 61; Michman 2003: 207). From the end of 1937, anti-Jewish policy escalated rapidly, primarily because Hitler stepped up his timetable for expansion and saw Jews as potential fifth columnists at home and influential opponents abroad. Each step in German conquest from the annexation of Austria in March 1938 to the invasion of the Soviet Union in June 1941 was accompanied by intensified and broadening persecution of Jews. Everywhere they were registered, humiliated, impoverished, and rapidly excluded from the educational systems, civil services, professions, and the cultural sphere. Other restrictions encroached on religious life, such as the prohibition of kosher slaughtering and limitations on prayer in synagogues. In occupied Poland, the medieval practices of marking Jews and confining them to ghettos were given the modern form of badges or armbands and specified residential areas, where living conditions quickly deteriorated, resulting in epidemics, malnutrition, and high mortality rates. Extensive imposition of forced labor added to the death toll during this period.

The decisive and peak stage of persecution began with the invasion of the Soviet Union and the onset of mass shootings of Jews in the regions conquered. By the fall of 1941, plans had crystallized for the deportation and annihilation of the rest of European Jewry, and these became operational in the spring of 1942. By the end of 1943, the murder campaign within German-controlled Europe was largely complete, but even in 1944, long after the tide of war had turned, the "sacred mission" of erasing Jewry continued in the swift deportation of most of Hungarian Jewry in April–July and of the small Jewish communities of Rhodes and Kos in July–August (Browning 2004; Friedländer 2007). The last stage of massive killing of Jews, more than 200,000 (alongside close to half a million non-Jews), occurred during the last weeks of 1944 and the first months of 1945, in the so-called death marches of concentration camp inmates away from the advancing Allied armies (Yahil 1990: 526–42).

After 1945, many Jews reproached themselves and even the victims of the Nazi onslaught for not having been able to prevent the carnage. In the first edition of his path-breaking and influential study of the Holocaust, Raul Hilberg (1926–2007) asserted:

> if we . . . look at the whole Jewish reaction pattern, we notice that in its two salient features it is an attempt to avert action and, failing that, automatic compliance with orders. . . . Why did the Jews act in this way? . . . They hoped that somehow the German drive would spend itself. This hope was founded on a two-thousand-year-old experience. In exile the Jews had . . . learned that they could avert danger and survive destruction by placating and appeasing their enemies. . . . This experience was so ingrained in the Jewish consciousness as to achieve the force of law. . . . A two-thousand-year-old lesson could not be unlearned; the Jews could not make the switch [to resistance when their leadership realized] . . . that the modern machine-line destruction process would engulf European Jewry. (1961: 666)

Others, especially in Zionist circles, depicted European, particularly German, Jews of the 1930s as blinded by an unfounded faith in liberalism, enlightenment, and progress and unable to see the supposedly clear signs of impending disaster.

These views rest on erroneous assumptions: that anti-Jewish policies developed linearly toward a murderous goal recognizable from the outset; that Jews were a uniform group and behaved homogeneously; and that the besieged Jews generally reacted in servile, compliant ways. Other chapters in this volume make clear that the first assumption is untenable, and the initial pages of this essay refute the second. As to the behavior of Jews in- and outside of Nazi-controlled areas in response to Germany's unfolding policies, it varied immensely, evolved over the time, and often was active, prompt, and resistant, depending on the possibilities at hand. However, actions were taken on the basis of the existing state of knowledge about what was going on, interpretive models shaped by persecutions of earlier decades, and the recognition that Jews were *not* unified and uniform. That an all-encompassing, systematically organized extermination campaign against Jews and Jewry was humanly possible was beyond the capacity of contemporaries to envisage—at least, until the Nazis themselves did so.

Jews' comprehension of and reactions to Nazi policies went through six stages, as knowledge of these policies and the level of institutional and individual analysis changed (Michman 2003: 179–214). Stage 1 lasted for three to four months after Hitler ascended to power in January 1933 and was characterized by shock on the part of German Jews and a first wave of emigration from Germany that peaked in April, as well as by protests, the creation of first assistance organizations, and even demonstrations by Jews abroad. Stage 2, which stretched from the summer of 1933 to the beginning of 1938, was a relatively long period of fading initial panic but enduring tension. Anti-Jewish policies escalated, but in fits and starts, which fed the feeling that coping was possible and that Jewish life could be maintained to some extent. The rapid escalation of anti-Jewish policies in 1938–39 gave rise to stage 3, a period of reconceptualization. Jewish hope for political change in Germany declined, and recognition of the need for speedy though organized emigration spread. Jewish delegations proposed solutions at the Evian conference (6–15 July 1938), and international Jewish organizations reacted both politically and philanthropically to the plight of Jews, especially after the November pogrom in Germany. Nevertheless, most of those involved still lacked a common sense of utmost urgency.

The first months of World War II in fall 1939 brought on stage 4, another round of profound shock. Now the enormous and vibrant Jewish community of Poland came under the rule of Nazis (more than 2 million Jews) and Soviets (more than 1 million). As anti-Jewish policies became more brutal, many Jews fled to Soviet-occupied territories, such as Lithuania. Chaim Kaplan (1880–1942/43), a Warsaw Jewish teacher, wrote in his diary, "the Jews of Poland are faced with total extermination. If no sudden means of salvation appears *force majeure* or otherwise . . . , we will witness a catastrophe unprecedented in Jewish history, overflowing with the torments of Hell—the total destruction and eradication of a Jewish community that played such a vital role in our history. It will vanish from the Jewish stage" (in Gutman 1982: 36). Outside the Nazi orbit, other Jews feared for the Polish Jewish community. Consequently, international Jewish relief organizations now focused on Poland, and special new aid committees, such as those in the Yishuv (Jewish organized community) in Palestine, came into being. But aid organizations, the most important of which was the American Joint Distribution Committee (JDC), had very limited access to the oppressed Jewish communities (Bauer 1981).

Stage 5 started at the beginning of 1940 and continued into late 1941. As German expansion continued, beleaguered Jews tried to cope with their rapidly deteriorating situation, which the Warsaw historian Emanuel Ringelblum (1900–1944) already grasped as "exterminationist in nature." The strategy was "to hold on" ("*tsu iberleybn*"), to be steadfast and outlast the Nazi occupation, which was expected to collapse in due course. In western Europe, where segregation of the Jews increased slowly and no ghettos were established, conditions were more deceptive than in Poland. Thus, in these areas Jews struggled to survive primarily by legal means, while in Poland much was done by illegal and underground action. In the free world, Jews had to monitor the situation with even less information, but as a result of what leaked out, they tried with some success to establish contact with and send material aid to European Jews through the regular mail, diplomatic representations, and enterprises that maintained economic ties with Germany. But large-scale rescue operations still were not considered necessary.

Stage 6 was the period of extermination. Slowly but surely, awareness spread that an extraordinary murder campaign had begun. Through intercepted German radio transmissions, British intelligence knew of mass shootings by the Einsatzgruppen by the late summer of 1941 but did not publicize the information or relay it to Jewish leaders (Breitman 1998; Terry 2004). On 7 January 1942, after the first Soviet counter-offensive, Soviet Foreign Minister Vyacheslav Molotov (1890–1986) revealed that the Germans had carried out extensive massacres of "civilians" on Soviet soil, but not that Jews in particular had been targeted, although internal reports by Red Army and partisan intelligence and inquiry teams so indicated. At the end of June 1942, eleven months before he committed suicide to protest the lack of intervention to save Polish Jewry, Szmul Zygielbojm (1895–1943), the representative of the Bund (Polish Jewish Socialist Party) in the Polish government-in-exile in London, submitted a report on the systematic murder of Jews in Poland that was published in the press and broadcast on the BBC news. Only in the second half of 1942 did information accumulate sufficiently for a clear picture of events to emerge. Consequently, the Jewish Agency issued an official announcement of the systematic extermination of Jews by Nazi Germany on 23 November, and the Allies made an official condemnation on December 17. Only in the final months of 1942 did comprehension of the "Final Solution" jell outside of Germany (Laqueur 1980; Porat 1990).

In the territories under Nazi control, the expansion of knowledge about the extermination was much delayed due to censorship and the limited communication among Jewish communities. A declaration of 1 January 1942, formulated by

Abba Kovner (1918–1987) after several weeks of deliberation by members of the underground movement in the Vilna (Vilnius) ghetto, included the statement that "Hitler aims to destroy all the Jews of Europe" (Arad et al. 1981: 433). However, in January 1943, a special team of the Amsterdam *Joodsche Raad* (Jewish Council) analyzed mail sent from Auschwitz by Dutch Jews and concluded that they were alive and working in a labor camp. The Jews of Salonica knew nothing of Auschwitz before their deportation there from March to August 1943 (Michman 2003: 195). Lack of knowledge hampered the development of response strategies. Nevertheless, in many cases even scraps of information were enough to make people seek to evade deportation, although the possibilities of doing so were scarce when Germany was at the peak of its power, that is, before the tide of war turned at the beginning of 1943.

PROTESTS, AID, AND RESCUE EFFORTS BY JEWS IN THE FREE WORLD

From the outset of Hitler's regime, Jews outside Nazi Germany sought to counteract its anti-Jewish activities. Protests and demonstrations, interventions through diplomatic channels, and the establishment of special committees to aid German Jews began soon after Hitler came to power and continued thereafter. Most of these responses were organized locally, but other initiatives were international and expressed a rising sense of Jewish solidarity with persecuted German Jews. Among the initiatives undertaken in 1933 were the establishment of committees to boycott German goods and tourism, the founding of a special information bureau by Alfred Wiener (1885–1964) in Amsterdam (which later became the Wiener Library), the submission of the "Bernheim petition" to the League of Nations demanding the revocation of anti-Jewish legislation in Upper Silesia, the negotiations by the Zionist movement to enhance emigration of German Jews to Palestine, which culminated in the controversial *Ha'avara* ("Transfer") agreement between the Jewish Agency and the German Ministry of Economics, and the lobbying that ultimately prompted the League of Nations to name a High Commissioner for Refugees Coming from Germany (Jewish and Other). The JDC intensified its support for German Jewry and supplied a major part of the budget of the National Representation of German Jews (*Reichsvertretung der deutschen Juden*). After its establishment in 1936, the World Jewish Congress persistently attempted to use diplomatic channels to mitigate the persecutions (Yahil 1990: 88–122).

Once anti-Jewish policies escalated in 1938–39, Jewish agencies outside Germany concentrated increasingly on helping Jews leave that nation, which entailed lobbying against the restrictive immigration policies of many countries. Jewish organizations also supported refugee German Jews, especially in countries neighboring the Reich. Some Jewish groups explored the establishment of an autonomous Jewish region in Australia or South America (Tartakower and Grossmann 1944; Wischnitzer 1956).

Relief efforts ramped up after World War II began, many of them to assist Polish Jews, but just as war increased Jewish need, it also constrained the delivery of aid. Only the American-based JDC, which had an extensive European network, continued effective intervention in occupied areas. Those initiatives were curtailed when the United States entered the war in December 1941, although the JDC was still able to function to some extent in satellite and neutral counties thereafter (Bauer 1981). The major international Jewish organizations, including the JDC, the World Jewish Congress, the Zionist movement, and the orthodox Agudath Israel, maintained offices or emissaries and representatives in neutral but strategically important European states (Switzerland, Portugal, Sweden, and Turkey), as well as in London and New York. These outposts gathered information about the fate of Jews in occupied Europe and tried to aid them by supplying food, passports, and visas (forged or authentic) and by lobbying the most influential governments.

Accumulating significantly in the second half of 1942, documentation about the carnage intensified appeals for Allied intervention. Although these pleas contributed to the issuing of the official Allied protest of 17 December 1942, which identified and condemned Nazi Germany's exterminationist policies and affirmed that the perpetrators would not escape retribution, the Allies did not increase significantly aid or rescue efforts for European Jews. Jewish leaders and organizations continued to plead and cajole, but deep differences over ideology and tactics hindered coordination as mass murder raged.

Pressure from such diverse sources as Hillel Kook (alias Peter Bergson, 1915–2001) and U.S. Secretary of the Treasury Henry Morgenthau, Jr. (1891–1967) was instrumental in the establishment in January 1944 of the U.S. War Refugee Board, which advanced rescue activity, especially in Hungary, in the war's latter months, but Jewish efforts to convince the Allies to bomb Auschwitz in the summer of 1944 were unsuccessful (Wasserstein 1979; Wyman 1984; Marrus 1987: 168–73; Porat 1990; Yahil 1990: 573–630; Aronson 2004; Friling 2005; Kushner in Stone 2004: 253–75). Other intervention initiatives included occasions when Jews tried to negotiate with the Germans for the release of Jews, the dispatching of parachutists to southeast Europe by the Yishuv in 1943, and the Jewish Brigade of soldiers from Palestine who enlisted in the British army and fought in Europe during the last stages of the war (Bauer 1994; Porat 1990). In the USSR, the state-sponsored Jewish Anti-Fascist Committee, established in 1942 to gain political and financial support for the communist ally among Jews in the west, assembled information on the

Germans' atrocities in the occupied Soviet Union and made some of it public. The Committee gradually became a mouthpiece for Jews in the Soviet Union, which eventually led to its brutal dissolution (Redlich 1995).

The Options of the Trapped: Perseverance, Flight, Resistance, Hiding, and Documentation

For some thirty years after World War II ended in 1945, critics targeted the Jewish leadership in Europe during the Holocaust. The Jewish philosopher Hannah Arendt (1906–1975) led the charge when she asserted:

> ... Wherever Jews lived, there were recognized Jewish leaders, and this leadership, almost without exception, cooperated in one way and another, for one reason or another, with the Nazis. The whole truth was that if the Jewish people had really been unorganized and leaderless, there would have been chaos and plenty of misery but the total number of victims would hardly have been between four and a half and six million people. (1963: 125)

Who were these "leaders"? Drawing on Hilberg's pioneering *The Destruction of the European Jews* (1961), Arendt pointed to the Jewish Councils (*Judenräte*) that the Germans appointed to head Jewish communities under Nazi control. But she thus repeated a fundamental misunderstanding that remains common in the academic literature (Gutman 1979). The Jewish Councils were an example of what sociologists call "headships," which derive their authority from a source external to the group being governed. Although their members were Jews and often had held leading positions in Jewish organizations prior to the German occupation, their compulsory appointment and dependence on the constantly threatening authorities curtailed their maneuvering ability and deprived them of the status of representative leadership.

Moreover, most evaluations of the Jewish Councils make the mistakes of viewing them through the prism of the "Final Solution" and generalizing from too few examples. Jewish "headships" were not devised as cogs in a machinery of destruction, but as an administrative convenience gradually introduced by the Jewish Department of the SD (*Sicherheitsdienst* or SS Security Service) after 1937, long before the "Final Solution" was conceived or initiated. The councils were established only where the SS was influential and were used for some time for purposes unrelated to the later murder campaign. The Holocaust occurred in many places, especially in the Soviet Union, without the help of Councils. Where they existed, their composition was subject to frequent change by the German authorities. In fact, the conditions and places where the many hundreds of Councils operated were so divergent that generalization about their behavior is problematic, if not impossible (Trunk 1972; Gutman 1979; Bauer 1981; Weiss in Gutman 1990: 762–71; Michman 2003: 159–75).

The conventional overemphasis on the responsibility of the Jewish Councils also often obscures the leadership roles of many other groups in Jewish communities during the Nazi assault. They included political parties, youth movements, rabbis, welfare institutions (especially the *Yiddishe Sotziale Alaynhilf* in Poland during the first two years of the German occupation), communal boards that continued to exist after the establishment of headships as in France and the Netherlands, and even non-affiliated and converted Jews who had been active in non-Jewish (especially political) movements (Michman in Stone 2004: 319–40).

Until 1938 most German Jewish organizations tried to adapt to their increasingly dire situation by reorganizing and persevering during what they still took to be a temporary crisis, supported in these efforts by Jews abroad (Bauer 1974). Impressive welfare, educational, and cultural activities were developed (Paucker 1986; Benz 1988; Barkai 1989; Barkai and Mendes-Flohr 1998: 195–388; Miron et al. 2006). But many individual Jews decided to emigrate, and some Jewish organizations, both Zionist and non-Zionist, set up training systems to facilitate adaptation to other societies. Émigrés from Germany totaled approximately 37,000 in 1933, 23,000 in 1934, 21,000 in 1935, 25,000 in 1936, 23,000 in 1937, 47,000 in 1938, and 68,000 in 1939, bringing the overall total to about 245,000 or some 45 percent of the German Jewish population when Hitler came to power in 1933; from Austria alone, more than 50,000 Jews emigrated between March and December 1938 (Benz 1988; Michman 2003: 183). Among those who fled earliest were many intellectuals and political activists (Jackman and Borden 1983).

Jewish flight from other states took place as a first response to German occupation. Some 300,000 Polish Jews fled east until the Soviets closed the demarcation line at the end of 1939. Tens of thousands fled the Low Countries to southern (later, Vichy) France in May–June 1940. However, the war made organized emigration and even individual flight extremely difficult, since most neutral countries closed their borders as much as possible, and the states at war with Germany feared the entry of a "fifth column." Thus, after 1940 the prospect of escape from Nazi-controlled Europe declined and became marginal to the Jewish response to the Holocaust.

Strategies of perseverance (*iberleybn*, or *amida* in Hebrew) were now developed to cope with hunger, epidemics, and lack of housing, especially in the overcrowded ghettos that were established in Poland, where the death rates rose drastically. Everywhere Jewish communities and organizations put emphasis on developing mutual assistance and social relief. Where the Germans established Jewish Councils, these included in their activities the establishment and maintenance of public health and of educational, artistic, and religious institutions. That many Jews were well educated enabled them to organize this infrastructure despite the context of persecution and segregation (Trunk 1972; Yahil 1990: 186–224). Daily life in these circumstances was scarcely "normal" or free of corruption, crime, class struggle, social and personal rivalries, and many other social maladies. Nevertheless, Jewish communities did not atomize and fall apart in spite of the enormous pressure on them.

Within the besieged Jewish communities self-questioning and crises of faith and identity were widespread experiences (Aschheim in Zimmermann 2006: 17–32). Orthodox Jews questioned divine providence and the credibility of Jewish chosenness or election (Katz et al. 2007). Reform and liberal Jews wondered whether fraternity among religions and ecumenism had a future (Meyer in Zimmermann 2006: 281–95). Assimilationists pondered the reality of integration, noting that their adopted national and ideological commitments continued to be challenged and "their Jewishness kept in mind by others" (Friedländer in Zimmermann 2006: 3–16). Bundists and communists recognized how little solidarity their gentile counterparts offered despite the fact that they were persecuted, too (Bankier in Timms and Hammel 1999: 229–42). Zionists feared that their dreams of a national Jewish renaissance were doomed by the assault. Despair grew; so did the number of Jewish suicides, especially in Germany and western European countries. But many other Jews, perceiving humankind's failure as greater than God's, took a renewed interest in Judaism and Jewish identity, even in religiosity (Michman 2003: 284–99).

Unfortunately, perseverance strategies availed the Jews little once their annihilation became Nazi policy. With the beginning of the mass murders and mass deportations in 1941–42, many Jews sensed the crisis and tried to go into hiding or to reach partisan-controlled areas. Hiding, primarily in the houses of gentiles, bunkers, and forests, became the most important means of individual rescue during the Holocaust. Jews helped other Jews as best they could, but success depended largely on help and goodwill from gentiles. Although rescuers were only a tiny minority in Europe, tens of thousands of non-Jews were involved in life-saving activity (Gutman 2003–2008; Grabowski 2008).

Clandestine activities, which resisted the Nazi onslaught in one way or another, began even before the "Final Solution" started, especially among politically involved Jews. Jewish youth movements, first and foremost the Zionist ones, played a strong role in this development. Their ideological spirit and energy, together with the cohesion fostered in the prewar years, turned them into activists from the first hour. Once the "Final Solution" began, they helped fellow Jews flee to free or satellite countries, such as Switzerland, Spain, and Hungary, prepared armed resistance, and participated significantly when ghetto uprisings and partisan raids took place. The Warsaw ghetto uprising in April–May 1943 was brutally suppressed by the Germans but left a deep imprint on Jewish consciousness during and after the Holocaust. Armed resistance by Jews in partisan units—some of them Jewish-led, such as the group headed by the Bielski brothers—emerged first and foremost in occupied areas of the Soviet Union, but also in parts of Poland, Slovakia, Belgium, France, and Greece (Gutman 1982; Cohen and Kochavi 1995; Tec in Laqueur 2001: 543–50; Tzur in Laqueur 2001: 550–6; Blatman 2003; Michman 2003: 217–48; Rozett in Stone 2004: 341–63).

From the onset of the Nazi era, Jews documented what was happening to them and used sophisticated means of doing so. Thus, in addition to the documentation center initiated by Wiener in 1933, underground archives were established in several places in the 1940s, the best known and equipped documentation effort being the *Oneg Shabbat* archive, organized in Warsaw by historian Ringelblum and other scholars. Archives also were set up in the Łódź, Białystok, and Vilna ghettos. A document collection begun in Grenoble, France, in 1943 was intended to lay the groundwork for eventual lawsuits and compensation for confiscation and looting of Jewish property (Bensoussan in Bankier and Michman 2009: 245–54). All of these collections were founded to provide evidence for postwar historians, authors, and prosecutors; those who created these archives took their work as tantamount to a sacred mission.

The traditional Jewish imperative to remember produced a multitude of writings, including periodicals, official correspondence, and artistic works, that have become part of the historical record of the Holocaust. Numerous individuals wrote letters (Bacharach 2004) and diaries (Goldberg 2004). In religious circles, sermons, religious commentaries on scriptures, and Halachic treatises and responsa were prepared by both rabbis and non-ordained believers; these documents show how Jewish traditions were used to cope with contemporary problems and dilemmas (Schindler 1990; Polen 1998; Michman 2003: 270–99; Farbstein 2007).

Jewish artists, such as Felix Nussbaum (1904–1944) in Brussels, put art in the service of memory, working openly or secretly as circumstances required (Blatter and Milton 1981; Milton in Laqueur 2001: 26–32; Rosenberg 2003). In the case of the Jewish writer and painter Bruno Schulz (1892–1942), art discovered in 2001 bears distinctive witness to the Holocaust, for at a German officer's behest Schulz produced murals in Drohobycz, Ukraine, for the playroom of that man's children. The faces depicted in those long-lost paintings include those of murdered Jews, among them Schulz himself, who was shot to death in 1942 (Ficowski 2003). Music (classical, popular, and religious) was composed for performances within the state-supervised Jewish *Kulturbund* in Germany in the 1930s and in some of the major ghettos, in Amsterdam and Paris, and in the Westerbork, Theresienstadt, and Bergen-Belsen camps in the 1940s. Literature, too, was written by Jews under the Nazi regime or by refugees, some of it printed in Jewish papers at the time, much of it lost or unpublished until after the war. All these modes of expression served survival strategies as well as documentary purposes. They reveal deep feelings and agonizing crises as Jews struggled to endure and survive and provide insight into the peculiar sense of time that developed among Jews subjected to persecution (Marrus in Almog et al. 2001: 10–38; Goldberg 2004).

CONSEQUENCES

For several reasons, the exact number of Jews and others who perished at the hands of Germany and its allies from murder, starvation, maltreatment, medical experimentation, and death marches will never be known. First, an accurate tally of the number of Jews in Europe as of 1939 does not exist, since the various prewar censuses that compiled this information used different principles of inclusion and exclusion. Second, border changes during the 1930s and 1940s make the avoidance of double-counting or omissions very difficult. Third, many murders were never recorded: Einsatzgruppen commanders, for example, often reported their mass executions only in general terms; not until the early twenty-first century did inquiries and excavations in Ukraine reveal numerous, hitherto unknown execution sites; and no exact tabulation of the people gassed at Auschwitz appears ever to have been made. Fourth, while the Holocaust was in process, the Jewish population changed in normal as well as murderous ways: some Jews died natural deaths, others were born (and then killed), but registrations of these demographics are scarcely to be found. Fifth, many thousands died from consequences of the Holocaust during the first weeks and months after liberation in 1945, and exactitude about those statistics is unavailable.

Nevertheless, scholarly research, aided by recently opened archives and computerized data processing capacities, has put statistical estimates on a firmer footing than was possible in earlier decades. In previous stages of research, estimates of the Jewish victims ranged from 4,202,000–4,575,400 (Reitlinger 1961: 533-46), to 5.1 million (Hilberg 1961: 767), to 5,820,960 (Robinson 1971: 889), to 6,093,000 (Lestchinsky 1948: 60). At the end of the 1980s two different teams, one headed by a German scholar, another by an Israeli, meticulously reviewed all the available data and arrived at the following numbers for Jewish fatalities during the Holocaust: 5,596,000 to 5,860,149 (Gutman 1990: 1799) and 5.29 million to slightly more than 6 million (Benz 1991: 17). The new Yad Vashem museum, which opened in 2005, mentions 5,786,748 Jewish victims. One can be skeptical of such precision, but the most current research reliably calculates a total number of victims close to the now iconic figure Six Million, a number used by the Jewish resistance leader and writer Abba Kovner in a speech to Jewish Brigade soldiers at Tarvisio, Italy, on 17 July 1945, picked up intuitively among survivors immediately after the Holocaust, and reinforced by estimates made during the International Military

Tribunal proceedings at Nuremberg in 1945–46 (International Military Tribunal 1947–49, 22: 496, 31: 85–7; Gutman and Rothkirchen 1976: 673).

About a third of the world's approximately 17 million Jews (as of 1939) lost their lives in the Holocaust, but the consequences were far more devastating than the numerical loss alone can convey. The demographic wellspring of world Jewry, centered culturally and religiously in eastern Europe before World War II, had all but disappeared. The majority of post-Holocaust world Jewry (about 13.3 million people) now lives in immigration countries (primarily in Israel and the United States, approximately 5.3 and 5.2 million, respectively), and the leading languages among Jews are not Yiddish, Ladino, or most other European languages but English, Hebrew, and Russian. This transformation of environments and cultural settings has deeply harmed the continuity of Jewish culture as it had developed for centuries on European soil (Halevi 1963).

In popular consciousness, casually formed, uncritical assumptions link the Holocaust and the establishment of the State of Israel, even though the relationship between these events is, in fact, complex and contested. In one way or another, diverse groups, such as Religious Zionist thinkers, Zionist educators, Holocaust "revisionists" (i.e., Holocaust deniers), east European post-communist ultra-nationalists, many Arab and especially Palestinian and pro-Palestinian commentators, and Israeli so-called Post-Zionists have advanced misleading and simplistic narratives about the connections between those events.

These narratives often assume, for example, that international guilt feelings about the Holocaust contributed significantly to the creation of a Jewish state in Palestine. However, careful examination and analysis of political developments between 1945 and 1948, the positions and beliefs of the major powers, and the broader historical context (including such elements as the history of Zionist settlement in Palestine, the ongoing decolonization process, the lack of unity in the Arab world, and the still weak sense of Palestinian nationalism) show that international remorse about the Holocaust played little, if any, role in supporting the creation of a Jewish state in Palestine. In fact, the extent of Jewish losses in the Holocaust undermined the establishment of a state, rather than aided it. At most, the Holocaust significantly advanced the popularity of Zionism among Jews, and groupings that had been non- or anti-Zionist in the past reversed themselves in the 1940s. Among survivors the support for a Jewish state was especially high, even if many of them preferred to reunite with remnants of their families living elsewhere. The decisive role in the creation of Israel was played by the Zionist infrastructure that had been built in Palestine since the end of the nineteenth century and that was almost entirely detached from Holocaust-related issues (Michman 2003: 303–28).

REFERENCES

ALMOG, S., BANKIER, D., BLATMAN, D., and OFER, D. (eds.) (2001). *The Holocaust: History and Memory. Essays Presented in Honor of Israel Gutman.* Jerusalem: Yad Vashem and Avraham Hartman Institute of Contemporary Jewry/The Hebrew University.

ARAD, Y., GUTMAN, I., and MARGALIOT, A. (eds.) (1981). *Documents on the Holocaust.* Lincoln, NE and Jerusalem: University of Nebraska Press and Yad Vashem.

ARENDT, H. (1963). *Eichmann in Jerusalem: A Report on the Banality of Evil.* New York: Viking Press.

ARONSON, S. (2004). *Hitler, the Allies and the Jews.* New York: Cambridge University Press.

BACHARACH, Z. (ed.) (2004). *Last Letters from the Shoah.* Jerusalem: Yad Vashem.

BANKIER, D. and MICHMAN, D. (eds.) (2009). *Holocaust Historiography in Context: Emergence, Challenges, Polemics and Achievements.* New York: Berghahn.

BARKAI, A. (1989). *From Boycott to Annihilation: The Economic Struggle of German Jews 1933–1943.* Hanover, NH: University Press of New England.

——and MENDES-FLOHR, P. (1998). *Renewal and Destruction 1918–1945.* New York: Columbia University Press.

BAUER, Y. (1974). *My Brother's Keeper: A History of the American Jewish Joint Distribution Committee 1929–1939.* Philadelphia, PA: The Jewish Publication Society of America.

——(1981). *American Jewry and the Holocaust: The American Jewish Joint Distribution Committee, 1939–1940.* Detroit, MI: Wayne State University Press.

——(1994). *Jews for Sale? Nazi-Jewish Negotiations, 1933–1945.* New Haven, CT: Yale University Press.

BEN-SASSON, H. (ed.) (1976). *A History of the Jewish People.* Cambridge, MA: Harvard University Press.

BENZ, W. (ed.) (1988). *Die Juden in Deutschland 1933–1945.* Munich: C. H. Beck.

——(ed.) (1991). *Dimension des Völkermords: Die Zahl der jüdischen Opfer des Nationalsozialismus.* Munich: R. Oldenbourg.

BLATMAN, D. (2003). *For Our Freedom and Yours: The Jewish Labor Bund in Poland, 1939–1949.* London: Vallentine Mitchell.

BLATTER, J. and MILTON, S. (1981). *Art of the Holocaust.* London: Orbis Publishing.

BREITMAN, R. (1998). *Official Secrets: What the Nazis Planned, What the British and Americans Knew.* New York: Hill and Wang.

BROWNING, C. (2004). *The Origins of the Final Solution. The Evolution of Nazi Jewish Policy, September 1939–March 1942.* With contributions by Jürgen Matthäus. Lincoln, NE and Jerusalem: University of Nebraska Press and Yad Vashem.

COHEN, A. and KOCHAVI, Y. (eds.) (1995). *Zionist Youth Movements during the Shoah.* New York: Peter Lang.

FARBSTEIN, E. (2007). *Hidden in Thunder: Perspectives on Faith, Halachah and Leadership during the Holocaust.* Jerusalem: Feldheim.

FICOWSKI, J. (2003). *Regions of Great Heresy: Bruno Schulz, a Biographical Portrait.* New York: W. W. Norton.

FRIEDLÄNDER, S. (2007). *The Years of Extermination: Nazi Germany and the Jews, 1939–1945.* New York: HarperCollins.

FRIESEL, E. (1990). *Atlas of Modern Jewish History.* New York: Oxford University Press.

FRILING, T. (2005). *Arrows in the Dark: David Ben-Gurion, the Yishuv Leadership, and Rescue Attempts during the Holocaust.* Madison, WI: University of Wisconsin Press.

GOLDBERG, A. (2004). *Holocaust Diaries as "Life Stories."* Jerusalem: Yad Vashem.

GRABOWSKI, J. (2008). *Rescue for Money: Paid Helpers in Poland, 1939–1945.* Jerusalem: Yad Vashem.

GUTMAN, I. (ed.) (1979). *Patterns of Jewish Leadership in Nazi Europe, 1933–1945.* Jerusalem: Yad Vashem.

——(1982). *The Jews of Warsaw 1939–1943: Ghetto, Underground, Revolt.* Bloomington, IN: University of Indiana Press.

——(ed.) (1990). *Encyclopedia of the Holocaust.* 4 vols. New York: Macmillan.

——(ed.) (2003–2008). *Encyclopedia of the Righteous Among the Nations.* Jerusalem: Yad Vashem.

——and ROTHKIRCHEN, L. (eds.) (1976). *Catastrophe of European Jewry: Antecedents—History—Reflection.* Jerusalem: Yad Vashem.

HALEVI, H. (1963). *The Influence of World War II on the Demographic Characteristics of the Jewish People.* Ph.D. thesis, The Hebrew University of Jerusalem (in Hebrew).

HILBERG, R. (1961). *The Destruction of the European Jews.* New York: Harper and Row.

INTERNATIONAL MILITARY TRIBUNAL (1947–49). *Trial of the Major War Criminals before the International Military Tribunal: Nuremberg 14 November 1945–1 October 1946* (Blue Series). 42 vols. Nuremberg.

JACKMAN, J. and BORDEN, C. (1983). *The Muses Flee Hitler: Cultural Transfer and Adaptation 1930–1945.* Washington, DC: Smithsonian Institution Press.

KATZ, S., BIDERMAN S., and GREENBERG, G. (eds.) (2007). *Wrestling with God: Jewish Theological Responses during and after the Holocaust.* New York: Oxford University Press.

LAQUEUR, W. (1980). *The Terrible Secret.* London: Weidenfeld and Nicolson.

——(ed.) (2001). *The Holocaust Encyclopedia.* New Haven, CT: Yale University Press.

LESTCHINSKY, J. (1948). *Crisis, Catastrophe and Survival: A Jewish Balance Sheet 1914–1948.* New York: Institute of Jewish Affairs.

LEVY, R. (ed.) (1991). *Antisemitism in the Modern World: An Anthology of Texts.* Lexington, MA: D.C. Heath and Company.

MARRUS, M. (1987). *The Holocaust in History.* Hanover, NH: University Press of New England.

MATTHÄUS, J. and MALLMANN, K.-M. (eds.) (2006). *Deutsche, Juden, Völkermord: Der Holocaust als Geschichte und Gegenwart.* Darmstadt: WBG.

MICHMAN, D. (2003). *Holocaust Historiography: A Jewish Perspective.* London: Vallentine Mitchell.

MIRON, G., BORUT, J., and ELKIN, R. (2006). *Aspects of Jewish Welfare in Nazi Germany.* Jerusalem: Yad Vashem.

PAUCKER, A. (ed.) (1986). *Die Juden im Nationalsozialistischen Deutschland/The Jews in Nazi Germany.* Tübingen: J. C. B. Mohr (Paul Siebeck).

POLEN, N. (1998). *The Holy Fire: The Teachings of Rabbi Kalonymus Kalman Shapira, the Rebbe of the Warsaw Ghetto.* Northvale, NJ: Jason Aronson.

PORAT, D. (1990). *The Blue and Yellow Stars of David: Zionist Leadership in Palestine and the Holocaust.* Cambridge, MA: Harvard University Press.

REDLICH, S. (1995). *War, Holocaust and Stalinism: A Documented Study of the Jewish Anti-Fascist Committee in the USSR.* Luxembourg: Harwood Academic.

REITLINGER, G. (1961). *The Final Solution.* South Brunswick, NJ: Thomas Yoselohf.

ROBINSON, J. (1971). "Holocaust." *Encyclopedia Judaica.* Jerusalem: Keter Publishing House, 8: 828–917.

ROSENBERG, P. (2003). *L'Art des Indésirables: L'art dans les camps d'internement français 1939–1944.* Paris: L'Harmattan.

SCHINDLER, P. (1990). *Hasidic Responses to the Holocaust in the Light of Hasidic Thought.* New York: Ktav.

STONE, D. (ed.) (2004). *The Historiography of the Holocaust.* Houndmills: Palgrave Macmillan.

TARTAKOWER, A. and GROSSMANN, K. (1944). *The Jewish Refugee.* New York: Institute of Jewish Affairs of the American Jewish Congress and World Jewish Congress.

TERRY, N. (2004). "Conflicting Signals: British Intelligence on the 'Final Solution' through Radio Intercepts and Other Sources." *Yad Vashem Studies,* 32: 351–96.

TIMMS, E. and HAMMEL, A. (eds.) (1999). *The German-Jewish Dilemma, From the Enlightenment to the Shoah.* New York: Edwin Mellen Press.

TRUNK, I. (1972). *Judenrat: The Jewish Councils in Eastern Europe under Nazi Occupation.* New York: Macmillan.

WASSERSTEIN, B. (1979). *Britain and the Jews of Europe 1939–1945.* London and Oxford: Institute of Jewish Affairs and Clarendon Press.

WISCHNITZER, M. (1956). *Visas to Freedom: The History of HIAS.* Cleveland, OH and New York: The World Publishing Company.

WYMAN, D. (1984). *The Abandonment of the Jews: America and the Holocaust 1941–1945.* New York: Pantheon Press.

YAHIL, L. (1990). *The Holocaust: The Fate of European Jewry 1932–1945.* New York: Oxford University Press.

ZIMMERMANN, M. (ed.) (2006). *On Germans and Jews under the Nazi Regime: Essays by Three Generations of Historians.* Jerusalem: Magness Press.

OTHER SUGGESTED READING

BANKIER, D. and GUTMAN, I. (eds.) (2003). *Nazi Europe and the Final Solution.* Jerusalem: Yad Vashem.

BAUER, Y. (2010). *The Death of the Shtetl.* New Haven, CT: Yale University Press.

FEINSTEIN, M. (2010). *Holocaust Survivors in Postwar Germany, 1945–1957.* New York: Cambridge University Press.

FRIEDLÄNDER, S. (1997). *Nazi Germany and the Jews.* Vol. 1, *The Years of Persecution, 1933–1939.* London: Weidenfeld and Nicolson.

GIGLIOTTI, S. (2010). *The Train Journey: Transit, Captivity, and Witnessing in the Holocaust.* New York: Berghahn Books.

GOESCHEL, C. (2009). *Suicide in Nazi Germany.* New York: Oxford University Press.

KAPLAN, C. (1973). *The Warsaw Diary of Chaim A. Kaplan.* New York: Collier Books.

KUSHNER, T. (1994). *The Holocaust and the Liberal Imagination: A Social and Cultural History.* Oxford: Blackwell.

MATTHÄUS, J. and ROSEMAN, M. (2009). *Jewish Responses to Persecution, 1933–1946.* Vol. 1, *1933–1938.* Lanham, MD: Rowman & Littlefield.

ROSKIES, D. (1984). *Against the Apocalypse: Responses to Catastrophe in Modern Jewish Culture.* Cambridge, MA: Harvard University Press.

ROTH, J. and MAXWELL, E. (eds.) (2001). *Remembering for the Future: The Holocaust in an Age of Genocide.* 3 vols. Houndmills: Palgrave.

SEGEV, T. (1993). *The Seventh Million: The Israelis and the Holocaust.* New York: Hill and Wang.

WEINBERG, G. (1995). *Germany's War of World Conquest and the Extermination of the Jews.* Washington, DC: United States Holocaust Memorial Museum.

CHAPTER 13

....

WOMEN

....

LENORE J. WEITZMAN

THIS chapter concentrates on Jewish women, comparing their Holocaust experiences with those of Jewish men. It focuses primarily on three topics: the initial responses of Jewish men and women to Nazi persecution, which reflected the traditional roles women played before World War II and therefore prioritized women's responsibilities as mothers, wives, and daughters; the Nazi policies that treated men and women differently and created distinctive constraints and options for women; and how particular problems in the ghettos and camps affected women's coping strategies. Such matters were scarcely on the agenda during the first fifty years of postwar scholarship on the Holocaust. The male experience, vividly portrayed in memoirs such as those by Primo Levi (1996) and Elie Wiesel (2006), was assumed to exemplify the experience of all survivors. Two events—a major conference in 1983 on women's experiences in the Holocaust, organized by Esther Katz and Joan Ringelheim, and the publication of *Different Voices: Women and the Holocaust* (Rittner and Roth 1993)—called that paradigm into question and opened the door for new scholarship on women, which has been growing ever since (Baumel 1998; Gurewitsch 1998; Ofer and Weitzman 1998; Fuchs 1999; Littell 2001; Baer and Goldenberg 2003; Tec 2003; Bock 2005; Hertzog 2008; Hedgepeth and Saidel 2010).

At first, scholarship about Jewish women's experiences in the Holocaust faced resistance and hostility because some survivors, scholars, and Jewish intellectuals feared that a focus on women would deflect attention from the single Nazi aim of brutalizing and killing all Jews (Rittner and Roth 1993: 3–4; Ofer and Weitzman 1998; Schoenfeld 1998). But equally important was a simple mistake: many of those who feared that feminist scholars were "hijacking" the Holocaust with their gendered perspectives were probably unaware that documents, especially diaries and memoirs, made clear that the experience of Jewish women during the Holocaust was distinctive and worthy of further research. In May 1942, Emanuel Ringelblum (1900–1944), the Warsaw ghetto archivist and historian, underscored the key point: "The future historian," he wrote, "would have to dedicate a proper page to the Jewish woman during this war. She will capture an important part in this Jewish history for her courage and ability to survive. Because of her, many families were able to get over the terrors of these days" (Ringelblum 1992: 380). In fact, because Ringelblum saw gender as important in shaping the everyday lives of Jews, he commissioned a special study of women's experiences in the Warsaw ghetto (Ofer in Ofer and Weitzman 1998: 43–67). Today, his view that chronicling the experiences of women is vital to a full understanding of the Holocaust is widely accepted (Heschel 2000; Heschel in Diefendorf 2004: 300–21).

EARLY GENDERED RESPONSES TO NAZI PERSECUTION

Before the Holocaust, in the 1920s and 1930s, most Jewish men and women followed traditional gender patterns that made men responsible for economic support while women looked after the home, children, and family. These traditional roles endowed men and women with different spheres of knowledge, expertise, and social networks. It is therefore not surprising that Jewish men and women responded to the early Nazi laws in gender-specific ways (Kaplan in Ofer and Weitzman 1998: 39–45). For example, Ruth Bondy, a Czech survivor, observed the different reactions of middle-class Jewish men and women in Prague during the first years under German occupation:

Both men and women experienced a profound crisis, but for opposite reasons. The men lost their work and with it they lost both their economic security and their status; compelled to be idle or to work in forced labor-squads, shoveling snow or building roads, they felt degraded. The women, in contrast, had to cope with a new and growing burden of work: most Jewish families in Prague had been middle class and had employed a Czech housekeeper. By the spring of 1939, Jews could no longer afford to employ "Aryans"—and were forbidden to do so in any case. Now the women of the house had to do all the work, to stoke the coal-fires, wash the clothes, prepare the meals from the scarce rations available for Jews, and knit and sew clothes for the family by recycling old material. (Bondy in Ofer and Weitzman 1998: 311)

Similar patterns existed among middle-class families in Germany. When anti-Jewish legislation left Jewish men unemployed and depressed by their loss of status, salary, and self-esteem, their wives had to make things work by managing their households with less money and no help, shopping for food in hostile stores, helping their frightened children to cope with antisemitic harassment, and raising their family's spirits (Kaplan in Ofer and Weitzman 1998: 39–45; Kaplan 1998: 42, 50–73).

If these examples suggest that women's prewar roles gave them advantageous coping skills, the same roles also created restrictions. In Germany, for example, women's adherence to their traditional roles helps to explain the disproportionate number of Jewish women who did not escape the country. Although many reasons explain the sharp gender difference between Jews who left Germany in the mid-1930s and those who stayed, including the Nazi targeting of men and the labor skills that gave men advantages in obtaining immigration visas, one of the most important considerations was the unwillingness of many Jewish women to leave aging parents. The Jewish population that remained in Germany thus became increasingly female.

In Poland, where the early German assault on the Jews was much more violent than in Germany, Jewish men, especially those who were most visible because of their beards and traditional clothing, were immediately targeted for degradation, mockery, and harassment. They were not only cut off from their jobs, businesses, and professions, and left without a means of supporting a family, but also "captured" on the streets and put into forced labor brigades, which led to further humiliation and beatings. Many Jewish men responded by retreating from the streets. Their wives, in contrast, took on new responsibilities to spare their husbands exposure to Nazi treatment. Women stood in bread lines, attempted to retrieve property from confiscated homes, traded family belongings for food, tried to find work to support their families, and represented the family in dealings with public officials. As Ringelblum summarized the situation in Warsaw: "Men don't go out....She stands on the long line....When there is need to go to the Aleja Szucha [the Gestapo] the daughter or wife goes....The women are everywhere...[Women] who never thought of working [out of their homes] are now performing the most difficult physical work" (Ringelblum 1992: 51–2).

Adam Czerniakow (1880–1942), head of the Warsaw ghetto's Jewish Council, also observed the assertiveness of Jewish women, noting their tenacity in arguing with Germans and their occasional success in stopping the Germans from confiscating family belongings or seizing their husbands for forced labor. Czerniakow was so impressed by their fearlessness in the face of danger that he took notes on the techniques they used with the Germans (Hilberg et al. 1979: 88, 92–3, 102–3, 122, 162–3, 184–6, 202–5).

Ironically, the new roles of Jewish women in Germany and Poland also reflected traditional norms of "chivalry" in German culture, which dictated that the Germans should be gentler with women and refrain from arresting or assaulting them. While Jewish women in both Germany and Poland took advantage of this chivalry, no presumptions about it were certain. For example, on 16 July 1942, the day of massive round-ups in Paris that became known as "Black Thursday," many men were prepared and escaped, but women and children stayed home because they assumed that only the men were in danger. But the police had orders to arrest all the Jews, including the women and children they found at home. Most were sent to Auschwitz (Zuccotti 1993: 107). As the "Final Solution" went into effect, Nazi policy abandoned "chivalry" and murdered women and children with chilling barbarity.

German Policies and Treatment of Men and Women

Eventually Nazi policy called for the annihilation of all Jews without exception, but prior to the implementation of the "Final Solution," many of the Germans' anti-Jewish rules and regulations embodied cultural assumptions that led to different treatment for Jewish men and women. The nature and scope of these differences were important because they affected the quality and duration of the lives of Jewish men and women before they were killed.

Early Nazi policy subjected Jewish men, but usually not Jewish women, to arrest and imprisonment. For example, in Germany, during the *Kristallnacht* pogrom of November 1938, only Jewish men were arrested and sent to concentration camps. Similarly, as noted above, when Germany invaded Poland, Jewish men (but usually not Jewish women) were physically assaulted, arrested, sent to forced labor or incarceration, and murdered. Although Jewish women were assaulted less frequently, they were not immune from humiliating treatment on the street and in their homes. On 18 December 1939, for instance, the young Jewish diarist Mary Berg (b. 1924) noted that two of her classmates in Łódź had been terrorized by Nazis who stormed into their apartment, beat their parents, and forced the girls to strip, play the piano, and dance (Berg 1945: 23–4).

Despite such harassment, violent attacks on women in public were comparatively rare until the mass shootings in the summer of 1941 and the deportations from the ghettos thereafter. From then on, nothing was taboo. In Warsaw, for example, during the deportations to Treblinka in the summer of 1942, children were hurled out of windows and smashed against walls; old women who did not move quickly enough were shot on the spot; and young women in the process of giving birth were forced from their hospital beds. Even the ghetto diarists who had spent three years documenting Nazi atrocities could scarcely find words to describe the cruelty toward women and children during the deportations (Levin 1969: 104).

A second difference in the German treatment of men and women was their singling out of Jewish men, sometimes for positions of authority and sometimes for attack. The Jewish Councils in the ghettos were almost entirely male; the few exceptions among the members, such as Gisi Fleischmann (1892–1944), a leader of the Slovakian Jewish community, and Dr. Olia (Olga) Goldfein (1889–1964), a member of the Jewish Council in Pruzhany, Belorussia, proved the rule (Bauer in Ofer and Weitzman 1998: 253–64; Gurewitsch 1998: 357). The Germans also targeted the male Jewish leaders, especially rabbis, in order to terrorize the rest of the population (Yahil 1990: 195–210). At times, Germans executed male Jewish officials to ensure the compliance of the men appointed to replace them (Trunk 1972: 22–3).

German forced labor policy also perpetuated the traditional division of labor between the sexes and the higher value accorded to male labor. Factories that used Jewish slave labor typically paid the SS (who supplied the workers) less for women, normally two-thirds or three-quarters of what they paid for men, even if they were doing similar work (Karay in Ofer and Weitzman 1998: 285–6).

The most devastating German policy towards the two sexes involved the treatment of mothers—as distinct from fathers. At Auschwitz-Birkenau, for example, mothers with small children were automatically condemned to death and sent to the gas chambers. In contrast, fathers with young children might be spared for labor. If a father and son were in the selection line, and the boy was deemed too young for forced labor, the boy would be sent to the group of women and children destined to be killed, but the boy's father would not be sent to the gas chambers with him. Thus, fathers with young children were allowed to live, but mothers with young children were condemned to die, even if the mothers were young and strong and would have otherwise been selected for forced labor.

After seeing so many young Jewish women condemned to death because they were mothers (and would, supposedly, keep their children calm and make it easier for the Nazis to kill them), the Jews who worked on the arrival ramp at Auschwitz sought a way to save the lives of some mothers by advising them, in a whisper, to "give their children to the grandmother who would take care of them" because the ramp workers knew that the older women and the children would be killed anyway. The Jewish workers engaged in a similar form of effort to save the lives of boys by advising them to say that they were older than they were and their fathers by advising them to say that they were younger so both would be selected for work (Wiesel 2006: 30).

Pregnancy was also a death sentence at Auschwitz: any visibly pregnant woman was sent immediately to the gas chambers. If a woman in the early months of pregnancy managed to escape detection and be sent to slave labor, and if she somehow managed to survive the remaining months and (secretly) deliver in the camp, she again risked immediate death for herself and the child. Some women prisoners who were physicians tried to save the mother by poisoning the child—as the only way to prevent the deaths of both (Lengyel 1947: 110–13; Perl 1984: 80–6; Tedeschi 1992: 44–5; Goldenberg in Ofer and Weitzman 1998: 335–6).

A few Jewish women, not visibly pregnant at first but later identified as pregnant, were put under the supervision of Nazi doctors who subjected them to cruel experiments. After the women gave birth, the doctors taped the mothers' breasts to prevent them from breast feeding their babies and then measured the endurance of the mother and the baby. The agonized mothers were forced to participate until their babies starved to death (Elias 1998).

German policy on Jewish pregnancy was not as uniform in the ghettos, but forced abortion was common. In Theresienstadt, for example, an order for compulsory abortion was issued in July 1943: any Jewish woman who gave birth after that date was sent to certain death, with her baby and her husband, on the next "transport to the East" (Bondy in Ofer and Weitzman 1998: 289–90). In the Lithuanian ghettos, the Germans required Jewish doctors to report all pregnancies and to abort them. One unusual form of resistance to this policy involved Dr. Aharon Peretz, a physician in the Kovno ghetto who conspired with a group of young women to circumvent the Nazi edict (Preis in Hyman and Ofer 2006; Ben-Sefer in Hedgepeth and Saidel 2010). The women begged the doctor to help them have their babies as a way of resisting the Nazi effort to dehumanize them. They said that as long as they were alive they wanted to experience their full womanhood by giving birth and becoming mothers. Even though the young women knew that the Nazis would probably kill them and their children, they did not want to allow the Nazis to dictate this most intimate aspect of their lives. Peretz risked his life to help them.

Abortion was scarcely an option in most labor camps because there were no facilities to perform them. As a result, a pregnancy in a work camp automatically condemned the woman to death. Felicja Karay, who writes about the importance of "romantic liaisons" between Jewish men and women in the labor camps as manifestations of their will to live, also describes the draconian consequences that these "bunk romances" could have for the women who became pregnant. As soon as a woman became visibly pregnant, she—but not her male partner—was singled out for death (Karay in Ofer and Weitzman 1998: 289; Tedeschi 1992: 116–17, 164–7).

Some German practices, such as forcing Jews to undress in front of male German guards, nominally subjected men and women to the same treatment, but were clearly intended to be more degrading, humiliating, and traumatic for women because of Jewish and German cultural expectations about how women should be treated (Gurewitsch 1998: xvii). As a pioneering article on women in the Holocaust states, "Almost every woman referred to the humiliating feelings and experiences surrounding her entrance to the camp [Auschwitz] . . . being nude, being shaved all over . . . being observed by men . . . Their stories demonstrate shared fears about and experiences of sexual vulnerability as women, not only about mortal danger as

Jews" (Ringelheim in Rittner and Roth 1993: 376). Holocaust survivor Cecilie Klein's description illustrates the point:

First, we were ordered to strip naked. . . . Then the women and girls were lined up on one side and were ordered to lie on our sides on a wooden table. While an SS officer gawked and jeered, a woman with a stick poked around our private parts. My burning cheeks betrayed my sense of shame and humiliation. I sobbed for my mother, subjected to this bestial invasion. (Klein 1988: 73)

While Jewish men also describe the shock of forced nakedness and the degrading process of being stripped of their personhood, their accounts do not reflect the same level of emotional trauma, shame, and mortification as the women's accounts. Nor do the men replicate the women's feelings of sexual assault when they recall body searches and invasive "examinations." Instead, the most emotional parts of the men's diaries and memoirs are those that describe the outrage they felt because of the way their wives, mothers, and daughters were being treated. In fact, the men reacted as if they were personally assaulted by the humiliation of their women.

RAPE: THE "MINIMALISTS" AND THEIR CRITICS

Another key difference is commonly assumed to characterize German treatment of Jewish men and women during the Holocaust: Jewish women were raped, not just sexually abused in other ways. Rape of Jewish women was not German policy, but currently issues surrounding this topic are among the most fraught and intensely debated in Holocaust studies regarding Jewish women, partly because precise empirical data cannot be obtained. Two points of view focus the controversy— one of them "minimalist," the other contesting that position (Ofer and Weitzman 1998; Goldenberg in Mazur 2007: 159–69; Hedgepeth and Saidel 2010).

Maintaining that rape of Jewish women by Germans was rare, those who take a minimalist perspective point to Nazi ideology, which emphasized racial purity and the threat of racial pollution, and to German law that forbade sexual relations with Jews as acts of *Rassenschande*, disgracing one's race. According to the minimalist outlook, the taboo against racial contamination from having sex with a Jewish woman had deep traction in the Third Reich. Even if a German soldier did not consider sexual relations with Jews polluting, he was likely to want to avoid disapproval from his peers or being charged with race defilement. Moreover, Germans probably were unlikely to engage in sexual relations with Jewish women when women of other nationalities in German-occupied territory were "available" and likely to be more attractive than the emaciated and impoverished Jewish women the Germans encountered in ghettos and camps.

Furthermore, the minimalist perspective tends to claim, relatively few reports of rape appear in the large number of survivor memoirs and testimonies collected since the end of World War II. If widespread rapes occurred, the facts that they were rarely mentioned, acknowledged, or discussed, not even with a sister or best friend or in a personal diary or memoir, and that few people saw, heard, inferred, or were told about the rape either at that time or later are rather surprising. Very different patterns have been found elsewhere. For example, the German women who were raped by Russian soldiers at the end of the war were also ashamed and without power to prosecute, yet reports about what happened to them from the abused women, their relatives and neighbors, and physicians, to say nothing of boastful Russian soldiers, were plentiful at the time and have surfaced in memoirs and testimonies often since.

While emotional factors such as shame make the absence of contemporary evidence of rape easy to understand, minimalists stress that the absence of later testimony or secondary sources in the postwar years is difficult to explain. What, they go on to ask, explains the persistence of the assumption that rape of Jewish women by Germans was common? The response is that at least four factors contribute to the misunderstanding. First, many Jewish women were terrorized by rumors of rape, even if the rumors were unfounded. Second, many Jewish women felt and were sexually humiliated in various ways by the Germans. Expressions of these fears and feelings may have led to the interpretation that widespread rape actually took place. Third, although relatively small in number, testimonies about rape probably have been given disproportionate prominence. For example, drawing on multiple eyewitness accounts, Felicja Karay describes the rape of Jewish women by German officers in the Skarzysko labor camp (Karay 1996: 289–90). The eyewitness reports are so graphic as to be remembered disproportionately, as though they were the norm and not the exception to the rule. If events similar to those at Skarzysko had occurred in other settings, they eventually would have come to light in like fashion. Fourth, blurring of identities may have produced some testimonies that attribute to Germans abusive acts that were actually done by their surrogates and collaborators (Fein 1999).

Granting that German policies and pressures may have had a restraining effect on the number of Jews raped by the SS or men in the German army during the Holocaust, critics of the minimalist position emphatically dissent from the conclusion that evidence of widespread rape of Jewish women during the Holocaust remains scant. One fundamental difference between the two outlooks involves the assessment of oral and written testimony during and after the Holocaust. The minimalists' analysis notwithstanding, one can argue that references, explicit and implicit, to German sexual exploitation, including rape, of Jewish women are persistent and widespread in oral and written testimony during and after the

Holocaust (Hedgepeth and Saidel 2010). In addition to assessing testimony differently, those who reject the minimalist perspective and believe that rape was common and widespread emphasize that shame led Jewish women to underreport rape and avoid explicit discussion of its occurrence. In addition, since such women had no power, they saw little point in accusing rapists at the time. Furthermore, most Jewish women who were raped were also killed, sooner or later, and therefore could give no testimony after the war.

Critics of the minimalist outlook find further support in documentation about past and contemporary settings in which rape has been a spoil or an instrument of war. One thinks of Russian soldiers who raped women in occupied Germany at the end of World War II or campaigns of ethnic cleansing and genocide in the late twentieth and early twenty-first centuries. The minimalists counter that these situations differ significantly from the Holocaust. The rape of German women by Russian soldiers was often condoned by their commanders and almost never punished. Perpetrators of recent ethnic cleansing and genocide have made rape a part of their methods. But rape of Jewish women by German men was explicitly condemned and forbidden during the Holocaust.

The persuasiveness of this minimalist line of argumentation, however, depends on the degree to which one believes that the Holocaust differed fundamentally from other genocides and the extent to which one accepts that rules and prohibitions against sexual exploitation, including rape, were sufficient to curb if not prevent it during the Holocaust. Even if the rape of Jewish women was not part of Nazi policy, the conditions of violence, brutality, and genocide in multiple and diverse circumstances during the Holocaust scarcely produced a one-size-fits-all obedience to ideological norms. The tensions between "center" and "periphery" that have been influential and important in other areas of Holocaust studies may have their place in considerations concerning the rape of Jewish women (Sinnreich in Hedgepeth and Saidel 2010). Closure in the debate about rape during the Holocaust should not be expected any time soon. To the contrary, the issues have not been moved to the fore until fairly recently. They ought to compel further research.

COPING STRATEGIES IN THE GHETTOS AND CAMPS

The coping strategies of Jewish men and women in ghettos and camps reveal further gender differentiation. Women's coping strategies in the ghettos followed three distinct paths: Jewish women drew on and expanded their traditional home-making skills to make do with less (or no) income when their husbands lost their jobs and businesses; departing from tradition, they assumed new roles as the family's representative to the outside world, becoming the family "spokesmen" who stood up to the Jewish police and risked danger to negotiate with the Germans; and they took over the husband's/father's responsibility for supporting the family. The latter role was a radical departure from their prewar lives, because most Jewish women had no experience in the paid labor force before the war.

Ghetto existence offered two main ways for a Jewish woman to support her family. She could obtain a job in the "official" ghetto labor force by working in the ghetto factories or outside labor brigades or in the ghettos' kitchens, laundries, orphanages, and other services run by the Jewish Councils. The second option was to find or invent *ad hoc* or illegal means to secure money and food. Within these parameters, women's work experience was diverse, as research on the Łódź and Warsaw ghettos shows. In Łódź, which was a major textile center before the war, an unusually high 37 percent of Jewish women were employed before the war. That percentage skyrocketed thereafter. In 1944, when the final census was taken, almost all the remaining women in the Łódź ghetto were working, and women made up half of the ghetto's labor force (Unger 1997: 65; Unger in Ofer and Weitzman 1998: 123–42).

In Warsaw, by contrast, only 20 percent of Jewish women were in the labor force before the war. Women's lack of labor experience, coupled with the severe job shortage in the Warsaw ghetto—in September 1941, for example, about half of the 200–250,000 inhabitants lacked income-producing jobs and most were starving to death—meant that finding a life-sustaining job was extremely difficult for women (Ofer in Ofer and Weitzman 1998: 152–62). Most of the unemployed were women, and women without a job had no way to feed their children. A majority of the starving families consisted of women and children. But even women with jobs had a hard time feeding their children. They tried to save some of the food they received at work for their children's meal, but there was never enough. Even families with two working parents were in dire straits and had to supplement the food they received by selling what remained of their belongings. This task often fell to women who, little by little, had to part with their favorite clothes and the bedding from their dowries (Ofer in Ofer and Weitzman 1998: 150–1).

The draconian conditions in the Warsaw ghetto led many Jewish women to seek other, sometimes illegal ways to support their families. We know about these activities because Ringelblum commissioned the journalist Cecilia Slepak (d. 1943) to write about the experiences of women in the Warsaw ghetto (Ofer in Ofer and Weitzman 1998: 143–67; Ofer in Baumel and Cohen 2003: 29–50; Ofer in Hyman and Ofer 2006). Although Slepak interviewed only sixteen women (in early 1942), she found that each showed remarkable determination to support her family. Some, for example, took up the dangerous "occupation" of smuggling, which entailed trading on the "Aryan side" and the risky escape from and reentry to the ghetto that such clandestine work required. Their ingenuity enabled them to renew past contacts and exchange clothing, jewelry, and linens for food and other scarce resources.

While Jewish mothers resisted German policies by striving to keep their families alive, ghettoized women also played other critical resistance roles such as maintaining illegal schools and helping to rescue and save lives. Younger Jewish women, especially those without children, were prominent when armed resistance movements in the ghettos rose up against the Nazis. A combination of factors, including wartime chaos, constraints on Jewish men, and the revolutionary egalitarian ideology of the Jewish youth movements, not only created opportunities for women in the armed resistance but also facilitated women's assuming key roles in the organizations' leadership. In several ghettos, including Warsaw, women were among the leaders of the central command. In the Bendin ghetto, they led the fighters.

The *kashariyot* (couriers) played an especially significant role in the Jewish resistance (Weitzman in Diefendorf 2004: 112–52; Weitzman in Hyman and Ofer 2006). Unconventional fighters, their weapons were not guns but false papers and disguises that enabled clandestine travel outside the ghettos, and smuggling, which brought news, forged documents, money, food, and medical supplies into the ghettos. Their most important missions included warning the ghettoized Jews about the Germans' highly secret mass killings. They also inspired and helped organize resistance, smuggled weapons into the ghettos, and saved lives by rescuing Jews from those doomed places (Weitzman in Hyman and Ofer 2006).

The courage and heroism of the *kashariyot* add a new dimension to roles Jewish women played during the Holocaust because these couriers were not primarily defined by their family positions as wives, mothers, and daughters. The activities of the *kashariyot* also challenge conventional wisdom about "fighting" and "resistance" and suggest a more gender-neutral framework for conceptualizing resistance. This framework interprets resistance as any act that sought to defy, subvert, thwart, oppose, or disobey the Nazis, an interpretation congruent with the behavior that survivors defined as resistance in the concentration camps. In the camps, simple acts of humanity, such as sharing bread or helping someone stand up during inspection, were seen as ways to subvert and defeat the Nazis' goal of brutalizing and dehumanizing all Jews.

Turning from the ghettos to the camps, three types of gender-specific coping strategies loom large. First, Jewish women persistently tried, as best they could, to maintain their personal appearance, hygiene, grooming, and clothing, which helped to sustain their "human" dignity. Although this behavior is not always explicitly identified as a coping strategy, most women's memoirs refer to women's efforts to look more attractive by washing their faces, combing their hair, mending their clothing, and caring for other aspects of personal grooming as circumstances permitted. While some of their efforts to look healthier (pinching their cheeks, for example, or rubbing black coal into their graying hair) were intended to improve the women's chances of being selected for work instead of death, survivor accounts state that these actions were also motivated by the women's desire to maintain their dignity. Some men also made a point of washing (even in dirty water and without soap) "for dignity and propriety" so that the Germans do not "reduce us to beasts" and "to remain alive, not to begin to die" (Levi 1996: 41). But the memoir literature suggests that this behavior—or at least expressed concern about it—was more common among women than men.

Differences between the grooming habits of women and men in the camps may have enhanced women's survival chances and hastened men's deaths (Karay in Ofer and Weitzman 1998: 285–309). One scholar, a survivor of three camps, puts the point as follows:

Men who ceased to wash and shave soon forfeited their human semblance and hastened their death...Women paid more attention to personal hygiene than the men; they kept their bodies and hair clean and mended their clothing....This had major consequences on all levels....[One example was] in the factory [where] their nearly normal appearance induced their overseers to give them more assistance, subject them to fewer beatings and, most important, treat them more humanely. (Karay in Ofer and Weitzman 1998: 305)

A second gender-specific coping skill noted in many memoirs was the sharing of recipes as a response to hunger and an affirmation of identity. Sharing recipes and cooking techniques in the face of planned starvation was no trivial matter: "It had a powerful psychological effect because it reflected a commitment to purposefulness, affirmed the will to live, and assumed that there would be a future" (Goldenberg in Ofer and Weitzman 1998: 335; Goldenberg in Baer and Goldenberg 2003: 161–78). Such sharing apparently helped women to mitigate the harsh reality of their surroundings by recalling and affirming their identities as mothers, daughters, and wives and by imagining themselves in these roles in the future, in their kitchens preparing for joyous occasions.

Once again, one may ask whether this gender difference is supported by the evidence and, if so, whether the practice was unique to women, or just more common among them, or more clearly remembered by women survivors. While we can point to reports of similar discussions about food (and restaurants) among men in the camps, the topic of food, and the discussions about its preparation do appear to be more prevalent and prominent in women's memoirs. However, some scholars still question the portrait of women survivors that these accounts of food memories present. Na'ama Shik, for example, argues that the struggle to obtain food transcended gender lines; women fought for food like men did (Shik in Bergen 2008: 125–56). She points to early memoir writers such as Gisella Perl (1907–1988) and Olga Lengyel (1908–2001), who described the despair to which hunger brought them and the "bestial" fights that broke out over it. While Shik concludes that women's homemaking skills, like the ability to sew a pocket to keep one's bread, could have contributed to their survival, she finds, at least with regard to Auschwitz, that "the claim that women dealt with hunger better is too general, somewhat superficial, and overlooks the reality of daily life" (Shik in Bergen 2008: 134). Yet others, including a number of survivors, attest to the power of the mind and of the community to help satiate hunger.

Third, women in the camps often formed intense bonds that supported and sustained two or more women in what came to be called a "camp-sister" relationship. Bonnie Gurewitsch states: "the term *Lager-Schwestern* (camp sisters), coined by women in the concentration camps, referred to the close 'family-like' ties the women formed for mutual assistance and strength. The term is unique to women. A parallel term, describing male friendships as 'brotherly' does not exist for men." Sometimes these camp sisters were relatives—mothers and daughters, sisters, or cousins—and sometimes they were prewar friends, but many of these women met and bonded in the camps, forming "little families" that provided mutual help (Gurewitsch 1998: xviii–xix; Gurewitsch in Littell 2001: 49–61). Camp sisters were usually emotionally close and intensely loyal to each other. They often shared food and other resources, protected one another from threats and assaults as best they could, and sacrificed for each other when one of them became sick. Many memoirs refer to a camp sister as the person who "kept me alive" (both physically and emotionally) or provided a reason to go on living (Klein 1988).

The intense bond and the feeling that one is responsible for and cannot leave a more vulnerable member of one's family were characteristic not only of camp sisters but also of daughters' powerful attachment to their mothers and mothers' passionate attachment to their children. For example, Karay describes the heart-wrenching scenes of women who refused to abandon their mothers during the final selection in the Skarzysko labor camp and chose to accompany them to their death (1996: 160, 225). Another instance of this passionate attachment involves mothers in the "family camp" at Auschwitz in June 1944 who were given the choiceless choice of appearing for selection, where they could be chosen as workers, or staying with their children who were being sent to the gas chambers. The "choice" was one that only women faced because it seemed natural, for both the Nazis and the Jews, to link the destinies of women and children. "Only two of about six hundred mothers of young children appeared for the selection; all the others decided to stay with their children to the end" (Bondy in Ofer and Weitzman 1998: 324). Reference to that sad event makes a fitting conclusion for this chapter, for the dilemma that confronted those women underscores how the Nazis often structured different experiences, if not outcomes, for Jewish women and men during the Holocaust.

REFERENCES

BAER, E. and GOLDENBERG, M. (eds.) (2003). *Experience and Expression: Women and the Holocaust.* Detroit, MI: Wayne State University Press.

BAUMEL, J. (1998). *Double Jeopardy: Gender and the Holocaust.* Portland, OR: Vallentine Mitchell.

——and COHEN, T. (eds.) (2003). *Gender, Place and Memory in Modern Jewish Experience: Replacing Ourselves.* London: Vallentine Mitchell.

BERG, M. (1945). *Warsaw Ghetto Diary.* Ed. S. Shneidemian. New York: L. B. Fischer.

BERGEN, D. (ed.) (2008). *Lessons and Legacies VIII: From Generation to Generation.* Evanston, IL: Northwestern University Press.

BOCK, G. (ed.) (2005). *Genozid und Geschlecht: Judische Frauen im Nationalsozialistischen Lagersystem.* Frankfurt am Main: Campus.

DIEFENDORF, J. (ed.) (2004). *Lessons and Legacies VI: New Currents in Holocaust Research.* Evanston, IL: Northwestern University Press.

ELIAS, R. (1998). *Triumph of Hope: From Theresienstadt and Auschwitz to Israel.* New York: John Wiley.

FEIN, H. (1999). "Genocide and Gender: The Uses of Women and Group Destiny." *Journal of Genocide Research* 1: 43–63.

FUCHS, E. (ed.) (1999). *Women and the Holocaust: Narrative and Representation.* Lanham, MD: University Press of America.

GUREWITSCH, B. (ed.) (1998). *Mothers, Sisters and Resisters: Oral Histories of Women Who Survived the Holocaust.* Tuscaloosa, AL: University of Alabama Press.

HEDGEPETH, S. and SAIDEL, R. (eds.) (2010). *Sexual Violence against Jewish Women during the Holocaust.* Waltham, MA: Brandeis University Press.

HERTZOG, E. (ed.) (2008). *Life, Death and Sacrifice: Women and Family in the Holocaust.* Jerusalem and New York: Geffen Publishing House.

HESCHEL, S. (2000). "Beyond Heroism and Victimhood: Gender and Holocaust Scholarship." *Studies in Contemporary Jewry* 16: 294–304.

HILBERG, R., STARON, S., and KERMISZ, J. (eds.) (1979). *The Warsaw Diary of Adam Czerniakow: Prelude to Doom.* Trans. S. Staron. New York: Stein and Day.

HYMAN, P. and OFER, D. (eds.) (2006). *Jewish Women: A Comprehensive Historical Encyclopedia.* Jerusalem: Shalvi Publishing Ltd, electronic edition: <http://jwa.org/encyclopedia>.

KAPLAN, M. (1998). *Between Dignity and Despair: Jewish Life in Nazi Germany.* New York: Oxford University Press.

KARAY, F. (1996). *Death Comes in Yellow: Skarzysko-Kamienna Slave Labor Camp.* Amsterdam: Harwood Academic Press.

KATZ, E. and RINGELHEIM, J. (eds) (1983). *Proceedings of the Conference on Women Surviving the Holocaust.* New York: The Institute for Research in History.

KLEIN, C. (1988). *Sentenced to Live: A Survivor's Memoir.* New York: Holocaust Library.

LENGYEL, O. (1947). *Five Chimneys.* Chicago, IL: Ziff-Davis Publishing Company.

LEVI, P. (1996). *Survival in Auschwitz.* Trans. S. Woolf. New York: Simon & Schuster.

LEVIN, A. (1969). *Warsaw Diary.* Tel Aviv: Ha Kibbutz Ha Meuchad.

LITTELL, M. (ed.) (2001). *Women in the Holocaust: Responses, Insights and Perspectives.* Merion Station, PA: Merion Westfield Press International.

MAZUR, Z. (ed.) (2007). *The Legacy of the Holocaust: Women and the Holocaust.* Kraków: Jagiellonian University Press.

OFER, D. and WEITZMAN, L. (eds.) (1998). *Women in the Holocaust.* New Haven, CT: Yale University Press.

PERL, G. (1984). *I Was a Doctor in Auschwitz.* Salem, NH: Ayer.

RINGELBLUM, E. (1992). *Diary and Notes from the War Period: Warsaw Ghetto, September 1939–December 1942.* Ed. Y. Gutman, Y. Kermisz, and I. Sham. Jerusalem: Yad Vashem.

RITTNER, C. and ROTH, J. (eds.) (1993). *Different Voices: Women and the Holocaust.* New York: Paragon House.

SCHOENFELD, G. (1998). "Auschwitz and the Professors." *Commentary* 105/6: 42–6.

TEC, N. (2003). *Resilience and Courage: Women, Men and the Holocaust.* New Haven, CT: Yale University Press.

TEDESCHI, G. (1992). *There Is a Place on Earth: A Woman in Birkenau.* New York: Random House.

TRUNK, I. (1972). *Judenrat: The Jewish Councils in Eastern Europe under Nazi Occupation.* New York: Macmillan.

UNGER, M. (1997). *The Internal Life in the Lodz Ghetto, 1940–1944.* Ph.D. dissertation, The Hebrew University of Jerusalem (in Hebrew).

WIESEL, E. (2006). *Night.* Trans. M. Wiesel. New York: Hill and Wang.

YAHIL, L. (1990). *The Holocaust.* New York: Oxford University Press.

ZUCCOTTI, S. (1993). *The Holocaust, the French, and the Jews.* New York: Basic Books.

OTHER SUGGESTED READING

BRENNER, R. (2003). *Writing as Resistance: Four Women Confront the Holocaust: Edith Stein, Simone Weil, Anne Frank, and Etty Hillesum.* University Park, PA: Pennsylvania State University Press.

HERZOG, D. (ed.) (2009). *Brutality and Desire: War and Sexuality in Europe's Twentieth Century.* New York: Palgrave Macmillan.

KREMER, S. (2001). *Women's Holocaust Writing: Memory and Imagination.* Lincoln, NE: University of Nebraska Press.

MEDDING, P. (ed.) (1998). *Coping with Life and Death: Jewish Families in the Twentieth Century.* New York: Oxford University Press.

READING, A. (2002). *The Social Inheritance of the Holocaust: Gender, Culture, and Memory.* New York: Palgrave Macmillan.

RITVO, R. and PLOTKIN, D. (1998). *Sisters in Sorrow: Voices of Care in the Holocaust.* College Station, TX: Texas A & M University Press.

ROTH, J. and MAXWELL, E. (eds.) (2001). *Remembering for the Future: The Holocaust in an Age of Genocide.* 3 vols. New York: Palgrave.

SAIDEL, R. (2004). *The Jewish Women of Ravensbrück Concentration Camp.* Madison, WI: University of Wisconsin Press.

CHAPTER 14

....

CHILDREN

....

NICHOLAS STARGARDT

KILLING children lay at the heart of the Nazi project of racial extermination. This focus was already clear in the milder forms of racial obliteration, such as sterilization, that were discussed in relation to children of "mixed blood" and practiced against Sinti and Roma, German psychiatric patients, and juvenile delinquents deemed "hereditarily feeble-minded." The "science" in Nazi persecution always justified destruction as a means of stemming demographic trends that threatened to overwhelm "healthy Aryans" with Jews, criminals, and idiots. Children were central to policies that sought to control the racial character of the future.

Some 1.1 million Jews composed the largest number of child victims, but systematic racial murder neither began nor ended with them. On the eve of World War II, the medical murder of child psychiatric patients started in Germany and was rapidly extended to occupied western Poland in the autumn of 1939. There Einsatzgruppen, police units, and ethnic German militias included infants and school children in the mass executions they carried out in the first few months of the occupation, especially in the region around Bromberg/Bydgoszcz. When the greatly expanded Einsatzgruppen swept through the western Soviet Union in the summer of 1941, they executed Jewish and Roma children and women alongside their main target, Jewish men. By spring 1942, Jews of all ages from eastern and western Europe were being gassed in the Operation Reinhard death camps—Belzec, Sobibor, and Treblinka—in Poland. Even after the mixed death and labor camps at Majdanek and Auschwitz began operating, children were amongst those least likely to be spared the gas chambers: generally, they had to pass as able-bodied men and women to do so.

Killing children spread into other areas of Nazi activity, providing a critical measure of the increasingly genocidal conduct of the war. As civilian forced labor became scarcer from 1943 onwards, pregnant women were no longer sent home but forced to stay in Germany and have their babies in so-called delivery units. Mothers were routinely separated from their babies and sent back to their place of work within two days of giving birth. Daily rations for the infants—half a liter of milk and one and a half lumps of sugar—were so low that most died within a few months. Even the hard-headed leader of the National Socialist People's Welfare, SS Lt-Gen. Erich Hilgenfeldt (1897–1945) noted to SS leader Heinrich Himmler (1900–1945) in August 1943:

On these rations the infants must perish from under-nourishment within a few months. I was informed that there is a difference of opinion regarding the care of the infants. On the one side, to let the children of the women workers from the East die; on the other, to rear them. (Reiter 1993: 249–50)

Hilgenfeldt's observation made no difference. Postwar testimony revealed that doctors also carried out medical experiments on the children or gave them lethal injections. "Undesirable" children had been subjected to such practices in concentration camps and psychiatric asylums, and as these deeds spread, so did public knowledge. In Bad Gandesheim, infants born to forced laborers in the old convent "home" of Brunshausen were sent "down the canal," as the common slang put it. German children playing in the ditch beside the road came upon the corpse of one such infant, who had fallen from a burial cart. Another local remembered how an elderly German foreman came to their farmstead to threaten a mother with sending her child to the unit if she were late for work again (Reiter 1993).

Forcing parents to work for the German military by holding their children hostage was also a policy pioneered by the Ninth Army on the eastern front: it established special camps for children, so that the parents would not run away to the forests. The policy quickly spread within the Wehrmacht in 1944, in its last desperate attempts to maintain control of the western Soviet territory of Belorussia (Gerlach 1999: 1010–35, 1085–9).

Research on the so-called "euthanasia" killings, the persecution of Sinti and Roma, and the occupation policies in the Soviet Union has expanded historians' awareness of the range of the victims of the Holocaust. As a result of the increasing diversity of those recognized as victims, constructing a unitary, collective narrative of what happened to "children" has become correspondingly difficult. Their experience of persecution differed dramatically, depending on whether they were Jewish or Roma, *Mischlinge* or disabled, and from Belorussian villages or Belgian cities. Nor is it possible to provide statistically representative testimony: some camps had numerous survivors; a major death camp like Belzec, only two adults. In general, the materials we possess from western Europe disproportionately outweigh the published documentation from the occupied Soviet Union, despite the far greater number of victims there.

Scholarly interest in children as protagonists in the Holocaust is also relatively recent, having risen markedly during the last two decades with the publication of a number of diaries, memoirs, and historical studies. The change parallels the rise of interest in gender history, cultural life, and subjective experience. The passing of generations also has played a part here, with children born in 1930 now featuring amongst the older survivors of the Holocaust. Perhaps the most important question is whether children are the subjects or objects of this history-writing. Can one write a collective history of children as subjects and *protagonists* within the Holocaust or only a history of their persecution and victimhood? What kinds of sources do scholars have to draw upon?

Diaries, interviews, and memoirs count as the best-known sources for children's experience, but they are not the only ones: historians have scoured ghetto chronicles and adult diaries for evidence about children's activities, have read the medical files of child psychiatric patients to reconstruct their games and snatches of their conversations with their nurses, and looked for surviving letters and children's artwork. Children's games and artworks expand the range of potential sources children left behind. Whereas child diarists are unusual and almost no children below the age of 10 write diaries, drawing and play start much earlier and are universal.

Play, Art, and Rupture

In Vilna, Jewish children used to linger near the ghetto's single gate, hoping to be thrown some food by the adults returning from the workshops on the Lithuanian side of town. This activity furnished the material for a popular game, which children called "Going through the Gate," the drama revolving around the real attempts by the workers to smuggle food past the gate guards into the starving ghetto. As one child survivor recalled:

Two main characters were selected; [Meir] Levas, the hated head of the Jewish gate guards, and Franz Murer, one of the most murderous Gestapo men. The rest of the children played the Jewish workers who tried to smuggle some food into the starving ghetto and the guards who attempted to find the contraband. While the Jewish gate guards search everyone "Murer" comes, which propels the Jewish police to intensify its brutality and, at the same time, precipitates a tumult and panic among the "workers." They try desperately to toss away the small food packages, but "Murer" finds some with the incriminating evidence and the "workers" are put aside and later are whipped by the police. (Kuretzka in Eisen 1988: 76–8)

The two biggest boys got to play Murer and Levas, leaving the smaller ones to take the roles of the Jewish workers, who, in reality, often included their own older relatives. Like the adults they were playing, they were powerless to protect themselves from the blows rained upon them, in this case by the bigger, stronger children.

Such games were by no means rare. In Vilna, children continued to play "Going through the Gate" until the ghetto was destroyed by the Germans in 1944. Similar games were played elsewhere. Henryk Ross (1910–1991), a Jewish photographer in the Łódź ghetto, captured a game in which a boy in the uniform of a ghetto policeman "arrests" another boy. In the "Family Camp," a special section of Birkenau where Jewish families from Theresienstadt were held (from September 1943 to July 1944) in readiness for a possible inspection by the International Red Cross, children played "Roll Call," "Camp Elder and Block Elder," and "Hats Off," assuming the roles of guards and camp functionaries who bullied and humiliated ordinary prisoners. Children also played the sick who were beaten for fainting during roll call and the doctor who took food away and refused to help inmates if they had nothing to give him in return (Stargardt 2005: plate 11, 174–5, 216–18).

Almost all of these games derived from generic models, which continued to be played by children in other contexts: the war game, cops and robbers, hide and seek. Some had prominent survival-oriented elements, as children turned hide and seek into "Blockade" or "*Aktion*," and practiced the skills they would need— remaining still and quiet for long periods of time—to hide from real ghetto round-ups. But even in these games, children faced the choice that was closed to them in reality, namely, who would they rather be.

Games in concentration camps did not protect children from the reality around them by preserving an ideal world of make-believe. On the contrary, the children reshaped their games to incorporate that reality. In so doing, they drew the most extreme conclusion from the key lessons defeat and occupation taught. The first thing that defeated children witnessed was the sudden impotence of the adults they had grown up thinking were all-powerful. Power and success were suddenly embodied in their enemies. In some cases, children could imagine themselves as partisan fighters or members of one of the underground armies of the resistance. But complete defeat and capitulation left few positive role models. During the war years, conquered children did not just fear and hate their enemies. They also profoundly envied them, often preferring to imagine themselves in the position of their enemies rather than their parents or their elder brothers and sisters.

Yet, the very fact of children's play leaves a degree of openness and ambiguity about the meaning of their games: what does it mean for children to enact such scenarios? When, in May 1940, Emanuel Ringelblum (1900–1944) overheard an

8-year-old Jewish boy in the Warsaw ghetto screaming, "I want to steal, I want to rob, I want to eat, I want to be a German," he was hearing the voice of pure desperation and rage (Sloan 1958: 39). But to *play* at robbing, stealing, and being German was somehow different from this starving child's scream. Children knew it was a game, the one scenario that they could control, however powerless they might be in other respects.

And then there were things they did not play at directly. The "Family Camp" in Birkenau was situated within sight of three crematoria whose chimneys belched out three and four meter high flames when in constant use. Whereas the adults attempted to ignore their proximity to the gas chambers, the children drew them directly into the fabric of their daily lives. The older ones played games with death, daring each other to run up to the electric fence and touch it with their fingertips, knowing the high voltage current was usually switched off during the daytime. One day one of the kindergarten teachers came upon the younger children playing "Gas Chamber" outside their block. They had dug a hole and were throwing in one stone after the other. These stones were to be the people who were going into the crematorium, and the children mimicked their cries. In one significant way, their game broke down here. Whereas in their normal games of "Roll Call," the little children may have had to submit to beatings for "fainting," here no one jumped into the hole that was the gas chamber. They used stones instead (Hoffmann-Fischel in Deutschkron 1985: 54). Clearly none of the children could be those people: we may surmise that pretending to be so would have been too psychologically self-destructive, the equivalent in play of dreaming one's own death.

Play is as natural to children as conversation is to adults. An inability to play marks a greater psychological disturbance than participation even in games such as these. The ability to play points to one of the great dividing lines between children and adults. Children sought to express the difficulties and tensions and, by the very act of dramatizing them, to overcome them. How they played—which roles they vied for, and the limits to who they could be—provides unusual evidence of how children made sense of their predicament, simultaneously protecting themselves from and adapting to a reality in which they recognized their enemies as the image of victorious strength and their parents as impotent failure. But perhaps more important here is the fact of play itself: even in the brutally regimented context of the "Family Camp," children preserved that extraordinary capacity to "lose themselves" in play, as if the normal forward movement of time had been—temporarily—suspended. Other sources created by individual children, such as their diaries or artwork, also preserve something of the reveries, the complete absorption in the activity, which went into shaping them.

Among the 4,000 children's pictures preserved from Theresienstadt are many drawings that depict daily life in the ghetto or recreate images of "home" from the pre-ghetto world, whose archetypal family living rooms contrasted starkly with the triple bunks and single-sex dormitories of the ghetto's segregated children's homes

(Stargardt 1998). Despite the Jewish Council's efforts to protect children and allot them special rations, hunger forms a major theme within the art works. In Ilona Weissová's drawing, the 11-year-old stands smiling pensively surrounded by the most remarkable foods: a not very kosher pig and a hedgehog bearing fruits with forks stuck in them; a fish on a platter and impaled on a fork, chickens walking up to her with forks sticking out of them, a winged figure delivering a basket of eggs from above, a bottle on a low trolley, jars of cocoa and coffee, sardines, cheese, sweets, cake, milk, and an apple. To remove any lingering doubt, the sign behind the girl reads "Fantasy land. Entry 1 Crown". This picture is full of pleasurable, rounded shapes, and the girl is decked out in a party dress with her hair done in bunches. She smiles as if at her own reverie.

In genre, the drawing is reminiscent of the themes of Breughel's *Schlaraffenland*, where pigs fly into the mouths of sleeping peasants (a theme given prominence in the nineteenth-century collections of fairy tales and their renditions for children). However, whereas in these tales, as in the early modern myth, *Schlaraffenland* provides the carnivalesque contours of a "world turned upside down," here the utopian land of dreams belongs firmly to that past golden age before Ilona was deported to Theresienstadt. Though fragmentary, these sources show how little their creators knew of their future and how, instead, they recorded the dislocations of their present by reference to their recent past, depicting, for example, the direction of traffic in a bustling, pre-ghetto street by a ghetto policeman.

Close scrutiny reveals intrusions of the ghetto even into idealized visions of the orderly prewar "home": in one drawing by Zuzana Winterová, while the children sit at table and the mother cleans, the father reads the daily paper in his armchair: The banner on his newspaper reads, not *Tageszeitung* (Daily News), but *Tagesbehfel*, a misspelling of "Order of the Day." Posted in the ghetto by the Council, in response to verbal instructions from the SS, the Order of the Day would have been read out to Zuzana in the morning assembly by the head of her home. With the Freudian slip of "News" into "Order," Winterová's family idyll dissolved back into the dormitory space she occupied in the ghetto (Stargardt 1998).

Drawings are fragmentary sources. Like games, letters, school work, and even some diaries, they convey at most frozen moments of time. Deeply rooted in their immediate context, they are open to interpretation only when we are able to recreate the micro-world of that particular ghetto or children's home, that section of the Birkenau "Family Camp" or that asylum. The accidental and fragmented character of the sources that survive accentuates the children's tendency to see the Holocaust not as a unity but as a fractured set of events, a succession of ruptures, in which nothing that came next had any precedent in the worlds children had experienced up to that point. This fractured perspective contains much truth, as many memoirs and survivor interviews emphasize. Nothing could prepare children for deportation, for ghettoization, for further deportation, or for the camps. For children, whose frame of comparative reference was often so much narrower than that of adults, this sense of rupture between one location and another was even more dramatic.

Shocked by the speed with which children adjusted to each new setting, many adults assumed at the time that children had no sense of the past. Ghetto chroniclers oscillated between experiencing uplifting feelings of excitement after watching children's theatrical and musical performances and deep pessimism when confronted with the wild play of gangs of starving and thieving children on the streets. As hope for the future vied with fear of destruction, adult contemporaries frequently projected both onto children, adding the prospect of cultural degeneration to their premonitions of physical annihilation.

ADAPTING: ROLE REVERSALS AND RESPONSIBILITIES

Children's ability to adapt to conditions for which nothing could have prepared them remains one of the most striking characteristics of their experience. The German occupation of eastern Europe not only undermined parental authority; it also thrust new responsibilities upon children. A round-up by the Polish welfare authorities in January 1942 confirmed that just over half the child beggars picked up on the streets on the "Aryan" side of Warsaw—forty-nine out of ninety-six— were Jewish. They were washed, fed, and sent back to the ghetto. The non-Jewish children were medically examined and questioned; all but one of the thirty-six families they came from had no adult male breadwinner. Unemployment, war deaths, deportation to Germany, disability, and the concentration camps had taken their toll. Most of these Polish children were seriously underweight, suffering from scabies, fungal growths on the skin, and tooth decay, and they all showed signs of tuberculosis. Nevertheless, they were the principal bread-winners for their families. The German authorities in Warsaw accepted the Polish report and quietly dropped the issue of child begging (Szarota 1985: 103–5).

Similar motives drove Jewish children into begging, but their conditions and role reversals were more extreme. The memoir of one of the Warsaw ghetto's child smugglers recounts both his pride in becoming the family's primary support and the anguish this caused his father. By September 1941, his father and mother had died, and the 10-year-old became the major provider for his sister and two brothers (Klajman 2000: 20–37). In other cases, as Jewish children lost their families, they adapted by turning to each other. Street gangs became surrogate families. In one extraordinary case, a gang of Jewish children managed to ply their trade as cigarette sellers in the heart of German-occupied Warsaw during the entire period between the ghetto's destruction in May 1943 and the Warsaw uprising in August 1944 (Ziemian 1970).

As children adapted to extremity by taking on ever greater responsibilities, they inadvertently contributed to an inversion of parent–child relations. Becoming beggars and smugglers to feed their families was a logical progression from looking after younger siblings while their effectively single mothers went out to work. Hordes of street children, child beggars, and smugglers in the Jewish ghettos confronted Jewish adults with spectacles of children dying of starvation on the streets, whilst others fought pitched battles around them, or aped the behavior of prosperous adult black marketeers. Small wonder that the Jewish authorities in almost all the larger ghettos and transit camps attempted to replace some of the destroyed structures of childhood by organizing playgrounds and nurseries, some-times even childcare. At the same time, these authorities worried about how little they could remedy. Thus, Adam Czerniakow (1880–1942), head of the Jewish Council in the Warsaw ghetto, took his own life when he received deportation orders that left him helpless to save the ghetto's children. Less drastically, after watching the children who performed the invaluable task of collecting coal and firewood in the Łódź ghetto, diarist Jozef Zelkowicz (1897–1944) reflected on the growth of "a deformed, crippled generation, which the enemies of the Jewish people are so eager to see, in order to tell the whole world: 'See, we were right, weren't we?'" (Adelson and Lapides 1989: 136). By 1946, German children were plying their black market, too. Hunger drove them to progress from playing "Coal Thief and Engine Driver" to stealing coal and becoming smugglers across the German–Belgian border, just as other children had done under German occupation during the war.

Viewed as protagonists, children—even in their most maligned activities—kept adapting to the responsibilities that necessity thrust upon them. Many children of different nationalities across Europe were forced to take care of younger or sicker siblings and to beg, trade, and steal to feed their families. The change in family relationships that this premature assumption of responsibility entailed had enduring emotional effects. In most of Europe, the family—however battered and dysfunctional—survived the war. By contrast, many Jewish families had been destroyed by the extremities of hunger and deprivation within the ghettos even before the deportations to the death camps. Of the relatively small number of Jewish children who survived the Holocaust, most were orphans: their lives as street hawkers or forest children became just one of the many transformations they had been forced to undergo.

IDENTITIES

In the cases of children of so-called mixed race, the boundaries between "Jew" and "Aryan," "Gypsy" and "German" ran within the family, and children's senses of identity often were upset by searing family conflicts. Alfred Völkel, for example, was 14 when, in June 1943, he was sent from a children's home in Nuremberg to the psychiatric asylum at Hadamar, a center of medical killing. Völkel was given the task of sorting children's clothes in one of the attics. On his way there, he had to walk through a ward where he heard hungry and exhausted children battling for breath against the fluid flooding their lungs: the trional or luminal that they had been given induced symptoms of acute pneumonia or bronchitis, dragging their deaths out over several days. Völkel managed to smuggle a letter to his maternal uncle, who was able to prove that he retained legal guardianship over the boy and to have him released. (Völkel was not mentally disabled. He was half-Jewish, but his Bavarian Catholic family kept that fact from him. After the war Völkel immigrated to the United States. In 1996, he returned to Hadamar, contacted the local archive, and read a copy of his medical file. Only then did he realize that his father—whom he had never known—was Jewish.) On his release in October 1943, Völkel returned to Nuremberg, was readmitted to the Hitler Youth, and fought in the *Volkssturm* at the end of the war. Like many "Aryan" children taken into German children's homes, he saw his predicament as a family tragedy, not as a case of racial persecution. "All I could see," Völkel wrote in a short memoir, "was that my mother chose others over me—a 'stepfather' and later two half siblings" (Völkel 1998: n. p.). Völkel may have owed his life to the persistence of his mother's brother, but for him, Nazi racism primarily affected the most intimate of all relationships—mother and child.

Völkel's experiences were extreme, but it was no accident that he first suffered racial exclusion within his Bavarian Catholic family, anxious as his mother no doubt was to avoid public opprobrium for having had an illegitimate child by a Jewish man. Similar pressures were brought to bear on Angela Reinhardt, a girl with a Sinti father and an "Aryan" German mother, who narrowly escaped being sent from a Swabian children's home, the St. Josefspflege, to Auschwitz in May 1944, thanks to the quick thinking of one of the nuns. Reunited with her mother, Erna Schwartz, Angela clung to her Sinti roots in spite of her mother's evident hostility. After the war, she eventually learned the fate of her father and of the other St. Josefspflege children and took her father's name, Reinhardt: ahead of her lay a lifetime of scrimping at the margins of German society (Krausnick 2001: 77–135).

Other children were brought to Germany to be "Germanized." Anna, Marie, and Vaclav Hanf and Alusia and Darya Witaszek were among those selected for the SS's *Lebensborn* scheme after their fathers had been executed and their mothers sent to the Ravensbrück concentration camp. The Witaszeks were involved in the Polish underground; the Hanfs fell victim to the Lidice massacre, carried out in reprisal for the Czech assassination of Reinhard Heydrich (1904–1942). Their destiny was linked with the racial-biological commissions that searched Belorussian orphanages for Jews and for children whose visibly "Aryan" characteristics made them candidates for Germanization (Henry and Hillel 1976: 239–40; Lilienthal 1993; Chiari 1998: 197–98). The dual role of these commissions reflected Nazi thinking about "positive" and "negative" eugenics, but for the children who were to be saved and, in Nazi-speak, "re-Germanized," the experience of positive eugenic selection was brutal and to young children, unintelligible. Sent to special homes in Łódź and Kalisz, where they were forced to speak German and assessed for conduct, cleanliness, and "positive attitude," the minority who qualified were given new names and birth certificates and placed with proper Reich families as "ethnic German orphans." The majority who failed the screening—these included many of the older children who clung to their Polish or Czech identities—often were sent from one home to another or to concentration camps. For the children who survived the selection and training procedures, liberation often compounded their problems. Marie Meierhofer, a Swiss psychiatrist who worked with war orphans after 1945, considered the difficulties faced by the young children who had been "Germanized" to be greatest of all, because twice they had to change "their language, social environment, culture, religion and, indeed, nationality." She found that "their memory holds no past on which it might be possible to build" (Brosse 1950b: 27).

The experience of rapid and wholesale makeovers of their identity also affected Jewish children who went into hiding. One of the greatest difficulties for such children was to learn and maintain their cover stories. In Lwów, Nelly Toll was first entrusted by her parents to the Krajteróws, who passed her off as a niece. She became Marysia, and she had to learn Catholic prayers, the catechism, and the stories of the New Testament. Not only had she been placed with strangers, but the 6-year-old had to act the part convincingly when her fictitious "mother" came to visit the family. Anxious overacting by Nelly was enough to convince the Krajteróws that they had to let her go back to her parents in the ghetto (Toll 1993: 32–41).

People watching for children with Jewish "looks," "sad" or frightened eyes, and the wrong speech mannerisms and gestures routinely asked, "Are you going to school?" or "What was your name before?" But even if a child passed all these tests, an inadvertent slip could spell disaster. A 5-year-old boy had been playing the part of a Christian very well until the grandfather told a story over dinner about the horse-drawn trams on the streets of Warsaw in his youth. Forgetting that these trams now existed only in the ghetto, the child chimed in that he had seen a horse-drawn tram in Zamenhoff Street. He had to be moved (Ringelblum 1976: 144–5; Paulsson 2002: 105–11).

Unlike Anne Frank (1929–1945) and her family, most families had to split up and keep moving from one hiding place to another. The profile of those willing to hide

Jews was even more heterogeneous than those ready to denounce them. Janina Bauman (née Lewinson, b. 1926) gives a vivid picture of the motley array of people who helped her family: a Polish aristocrat, Andrej Szawernowski, and Lily, a German prostitute, whose brother worked on the railways as a policeman catching smugglers and Jews. Janina was helped by at least two ethnic Germans and a number of working-class Poles as well as by members of the right-wing—and politically antisemitic—Polish resistance. Some ran the risk out of idealism, others for money, while some commercial relationships developed into friendships, with hosts going on protecting the family even when it had nothing left to give in return. Each time a hiding place was discovered by blackmailers, new havens had to be found. Janina moved thirteen times (Bauman 1986; Paulsson 2002: 49–53).

Although neither the resistance organizations nor the Catholic and Protestant churches were committed to hiding Jewish children, individuals and small groups within these entities did so, including Jules-Gérard Saliège (1870–1956), the Catholic archbishop of Toulouse, and the small French Protestant community. But the bulk of assistance was undertaken by predominantly Jewish organizations, such as *Oeuvre de Secours aux Enfants* (OSE) (Klarsfeld 1984; Cohen 1993). After the great deportation from the Warsaw ghetto in 1942, the Jewish leadership apparently discussed an offer to hide children in Polish Catholic institutions but rejected the proposal for fear of Christian conversion (Ringelblum 1976: 150–1; Paulsson 2002: 87–88). Some parents were able to make private arrangements, and a number of survivor memoirs deal with the experience of being hidden in Catholic boarding schools, showing that the parents had to consent to their children's conversion in advance to secure a place. These documents also reveal that the children were often deeply attracted to the new religion. Feeling that the Old Testament God had rejected the Jews might go hand in hand with the desire to belong to the secure, national majority rather than the persecuted minority, just as German Jewish children often had wanted to join the Hitler Youth in the 1930s. But at least some Jewish children were also profoundly attracted to Catholicism, especially to the cult of the Virgin Mary. Recalling the power of this attraction in his memoir of being hidden as a child in France, Saul Friedländer (b. 1932) wondered whether he found in Mary—after effectively losing his parents—"something of the presence of a mother" (Friedländer 1979: 122; also David 1966; Weinstein 1985: 82; Dwork 1991).

Children may have been easier to hide than adults, but the new identities the children adopted changed them and became part of their growing up. Being hidden from the Germans in occupied Europe also hid children from their own former selves. If, against all the odds, children survived the genocide, little remained to which they could return. They emerged with new names, even new languages, and, in the cases of very young children, often with no sense of who they had once been.

THE CULT OF THE CHILD

When Anne Frank's diary first appeared as a book in the summer of 1947, Contact Publishers in Amsterdam produced just 1,500 copies. In 1953, the diary appeared in the United States with a brief introduction by Eleanor Roosevelt (1884–1962), praising Anne Frank as a heroic young victim of war and commending the diary as an anti-war document. The stage play based on the diary swept Broadway in 1955 and soon came to Europe (including West Germany), bringing her story to a mass audience and inspiring a generation of young people to identify with her, to write to her, and to form Anne Frank clubs. In 1959, the play provided the script for a Hollywood film: both play and film took much further the general, humanitarian gloss on Anne Frank's life presaged by Eleanor Roosevelt's remarks, expunging Frank's comments on antisemitism and Hitler's brutality, lest they detract from the affirmation of her faith in human nature. In their emotional high points, both the play and film closed with a fictitious speech that embellished the most famous line in the diary: "... in spite of everything, I still believe that people are really good at heart." What appeared in the diary as a painful dialectical self-interrogation between "ideals, dreams and cherished hopes," on the one hand, and "the horrible truth" of "confusion, misery and death," on the other, was flattened out and simplified in the play and film. That reworking has been criticized since the 1990s for promoting a liberal universalism that erased what was emotionally complex or specifically Jewish in her experience. Be this as it may, the freshness of Anne Frank's teenage writing survived the editing and made hers the most popular of all Holocaust diaries, to the point that she became a proxy in the popular mind for all children's experience during the Holocaust.

Meanwhile, in a country like Poland, children featured prominently in their twin roles as victims of Nazi policies and as heroic resisters. The example of Aleksander Kamiński, who progressed through the Grey Ranks of the illegal boy scouts to fight in the Warsaw uprising of 1944, is still studied by 12-year-olds in Polish schools. In 1946, the Warsaw illustrated magazine *Przekrój* promised a kilo of sweets to the winner of an art competition for children. The published drawings mingled pictures of civilian executions in Warsaw with the striped clothing of the concentration camps, quickly establishing a pattern that would prove particularly resilient: the suffering and persecution of Jewish children would be recorded but also nationalized and subsumed within the greater Polish whole, often without specific reference to their Jewish identity (Stargardt 2005: 362–3). This nationalization of all Polish victims was a tradition that continued into the 1980s, including the way the victims of the death camps were commemorated in Poland (Young 1993), and it influenced the early Polish scholarship on child victims of Nazism.

These developments went together with forgetting many of the anxieties adults had entertained about children during and immediately after the war. In 1945, the

Polish State Institute of Mental Hygiene studied the war's moral and psychological effects through a large-scale questionnaire. The results showed that many children claimed to have learned patriotic virtues from their parents, teachers, and the resistance. But just as many children admitted that they had learned to lie, steal, and deceive, to hate, treat authority with contempt, feel indifferent to all ideals, and even to have lost faith in the sanctity of human life (Brosse 1950a: 19–20, 77–100). Matters were little different in defeated Germany, where the authorities responded to a postwar wave of theft, prostitution, and black-marketeering by sending large numbers of young teenagers to reformatories (Stargardt 2005). Set against the evidence of teenage drinking, sex, absenteeism from work, theft, and black market-eering, which welfare workers, juvenile courts, and psychologists were reporting across the European continent, such surveys confirmed the belief that the war had destroyed children's innocence.

As heroic resisters, children could serve as classic redemptive role models, carrying hope for the future; and virtually all chroniclers from the ghettos lauded children's play and theatrical events as evidence of spiritual resistance and hoped-for survival. But, as the objects whose childhood was being destroyed, children were also seen during and immediately after the war as dangerous and threatening. In hindsight, both these social anxieties and the symbolic frameworks of represent-ing children appear to have drawn upon a common core of nineteenth- and twentieth-century ideas about childhood. Whether the overall message was an exclusive and nationalist or a liberal and universalist one, the cultural symbolism deployed in the postwar years, despite the dissonance caused by children's danger-ous and threatening behavior, remained broadly similar: children tended to sym-bolize innocence and suffering, sacrifice and heroism, redemption and regeneration. What varied was whether the subject of suffering, sacrifice, and redemption was humanity as a whole or a particular nation. For children to be rediscovered as active subjects in their own right had to wait for a different generation and a different age.

REFERENCES

ADELSON, A. and LAPIDES, R. (eds.) (1989). *Lodz Ghetto: Inside a Community under Siege*. New York: Viking.

BAUMAN, J. (1986). *Winter in the Morning: A Young Girl's Life in the Warsaw Ghetto and Beyond, 1939–1945*. New York: Free Press.

BROSSE, T. (1950a). *War-handicapped Children: Report on the European Situation*. Paris: UNESCO.

——(1950b). *Homeless Children: Report of the Proceedings of the Conference of Directors of the Children's Communities, Trogen, Switzerland*. Paris: UNESCO.

CHIARI, B. (1998). *Alltag hinter der Front: Besatzung, Kollaboration und Widerstand in Weissrussland 1941–1944*. Düsseldorf: Droste Verlag.

COHEN, A. (1993). *Persécutions et sauvetages: Juifs et Français sous l'Occupation et sous Vichy.* Paris: Editions du Cerf.

DAVID, J. (1966). *A Touch of Earth: A Wartime Childhood.* London: Hutchinson.

DEUTSCHKRON, I. (1985). *. . . denn ihrer war die Hölle: Kinder in Gettos und Lagern.* Cologne: Verlag Wissenschaft und Politik.

DWORK, D. (1991). *Children with a Star: Jewish Youth in Nazi Europe.* New Haven, CT: Yale University Press.

EISEN, G. (1988). *Children and Play in the Holocaust: Games Among the Shadows.* Amherst, MA: University of Massachusetts Press.

FLINKER, M. (1971). *Young Moshe's Diary: The Spiritual Torment of a Jewish Boy in Nazi Europe.* Jerusalem: Yad Vashem.

FRIEDLÄNDER, S. (1979). *When Memory Comes.* New York: Farrar, Straus and Giroux.

GERLACH, C. (1999). *Kalkulierte Morde: Die deutsche Wirtschafts- und Vernichtungspolitik in Weissrussland 1941 bis 1944.* Hamburg: Hamburger Edition.

HENRY, C. and HILLEL, M. (1976). *Children of the SS.* London: Hutchinson.

KLAJMAN, J. (2000). *Out of the Ghetto.* London: Vallentine Mitchell.

KLARSFELD, S. (1984). *Les enfants d'Izieu: Une tragédie juive.* Paris: B. Klarsfeld Foundation.

KRAUSNICK, M. (2001). *Auf Wiedersehen im Himmel: Die Geschichte der Angela Reinhardt.* Munich: Elefanten.

LILIENTHAL, G. (1993). *Der "Lebensborn e.V.": Ein Instrument nationalsozialistischer Rassenpolitik.* Frankfurt: Fischer.

PAULSSON, G. S. (2002). *Secret City: The Hidden Jews of Warsaw, 1940–1945.* New Haven, CT: Yale University Press.

REITER, R. (1993). *Tötungsstätten für ausländische Kinder im Zweiten Weltkrieg: Zum Spannungsverhältnis von kriegswirtschaftlichem Arbeitseinsatz und nationalsozialistischer Rassenpolitik in Niedersachsen.* Hannover: Hahn.

RINGELBLUM, E. (1976). *Polish–Jewish Relations During the Second World War.* Ed. J. Kermish and S. Krakowski. New York: Fertig.

SLOAN, J. (ed.) (1958). *Notes from the Warsaw Ghetto: The Journal of Emmanuel Ringelblum.* New York: McGraw-Hill.

STARGARDT, N. (1998). "Children's Art of the Holocaust." *Past and Present* 161: 192–235.

——(2005). *Witnesses of War: Children's Lives under the Nazis.* London: Jonathan Cape.

SZAROTA, T. (1985). *Warschau unter dem Hakenkreuz: Leben und Alltag im besetzten Warschau 1.10.1939 bis 31.7.1944.* Paderborn: Schöningh.

TOLL, N. (1993). *Behind the Secret Window: A Memoir of a Hidden Childhood during World War Two.* New York: Dial Books.

VÖLKEL, A. (1998). "Not just because I was a 'bastard.'" MS, 1 August 1998. Landeswohlfahrtsverband Hessen, K 12/ 5031.

WEINSTEIN, F. (1985). *A Hidden Childhood: A Jewish Girl's Sanctuary in a French Convent, 1942–1945.* New York: Hill and Wang.

YOUNG, J. (1993). *The Texture of Memory: Holocaust Memorials and Meaning.* New Haven, CT: Yale University Press.

ZIEMIAN, J. (1970). *The Cigarette Sellers of Three Crosses Square.* London: Vallentine Mitchell.

OTHER SUGGESTED READING

BAR-ON, D. (1989). *Legacy of Silence: Encounters with Children of the Third Reich.* Cambridge, MA: Harvard University Press.

BERG, M. (2009). *The Diary of Mary Berg: Growing Up in the Warsaw Ghetto.* Ed. S. Pentlin. Oxford: Oneworld Publications.

DWORK, D. and VAN PELT, R. (2009). *Flight from the Reich: Refugee Jews, 1933–1946.* New York: W. W. Norton.

FRANK, A. (1997). *A Diary of a Young Girl: The Definitive Edition.* Trans. S. Massoty. London: Viking.

HOCHBERG-MARIAŃSKA, M. and GRÜSS, N. (eds.) (1996). *The Children Accuse.* London: Vallentine Mitchell.

KLÜGER, R. (1992). *Weiter Leben: Eine Jugend.* Göttingen: Wallstein.

RUDASHEVSKI, Y. (1973). *The Diary of the Vilna Ghetto: June 1941–April 1943.* Tel Aviv: Ghetto Fighters' House.

SIERAKOWIAK, D. (1996). *The Diary of Dawid Sierakowiak: Five Notebooks from the Łódź Ghetto.* Ed. A. Adelson. New York: Oxford University Press.

VICE, S. (2004). *Children Writing the Holocaust.* New York: Palgrave Macmillan.

ZAPRUDER, A. (ed.) (2002). *Salvaged Pages: Young Writers' Diaries of the Holocaust.* New Haven, CT: Yale University Press.

CHAPTER 15

....

CATHOLICS

....

KEVIN P. SPICER

EUGENIO Pacelli (1876–1958; Pope Pius XII 1939–1958) has become a conspicuous symbol of the Catholic Church's alleged "indifference" to the plight of Jews during the Holocaust. This development has hindered historians' efforts to avoid polemics and to analyze Pacelli's record objectively. Continued restrictions on access to Vatican archives also have aroused mistrust and muddied the historical waters. Preoccupation with Pacelli, however, should not deflect scholarly attention from the biblical and patristic texts that formed Catholic doctrine and inclined Catholics to negative images of Jews and of Judaism for nearly two millennia.

In a spiritual guidebook for the laity published in 1927, Monsignor Maximilian Kaller (1880–1947), who later became the Bishop of Ermland (1930–1945), wrote that Catholics have "a very strong dislike of Jewry" (1927: 264). Not every Catholic fit this description, but at the time very few German Catholic leaders would have challenged Kaller's statement. Behind this prejudice lay centuries of Christians portraying Jews as the people who rejected Christ and crucified him. Christian scripture, especially the Gospel of John, which was proclaimed regularly during Mass and in popular Catholic liturgical texts, included conspicuously negative depictions of Jews (Ruether 1974; Flannery 1985; Carroll 2001; Cohen 2007). Consequently, in the 1930s and 1940s, Catholics had immense difficulty distancing themselves from the tradition of Christian antisemitism. Moreover, many Catholics accused "unfaithful, secular" Jews of betraying the basic tenets of their own revealed faith by becoming obsessed with money and material goods. The Church asserted that these individuals exploited the Enlightenment and modernity and used their "pernicious influence" in business, culture, and politics to attack and undermine Christian moral and religious teaching.

Nonetheless, the Church rejected the racial antisemitism that made descent the indelible marker of Jewish identity and thus rendered baptism null and void. In the late 1920s, some Church leaders, including officials at the Vatican, issued statements that condemned antisemitism but still characterized "Jews as blind for rejecting their messiah and as the former people of God" (Brechenmacher 2005: 161; Phayer 2000: 1). Even when Catholics tried to disown antisemitism or demonstrate moral sympathy toward Jews, theological sympathy toward them remained in short supply. This lack of theological sympathy led Catholics to a reductive appraisal of Jews as persistent non-believers, too alien and obstinate for the Church's leaders to include in the gospel mandate to "love thy neighbor." As a result, for the ordinary Catholic, various forms of antisemitism—racial, theological, economic, and cultural—became indistinguishable and mutually reinforcing.

The German Catholic Church and National Socialism

After the Nazi Party's political breakthrough in the Reichstag elections of 1930, Nazi calls for the creation of a schismatic German national church, the "purification" of the Old Testament, and the sanctification of race aroused concern in the church hierarchy. Hitler's refusal to clarify these issues and to define the Party's profession of "positive Christianity" only increased this mistrust. Therefore, beginning in the fall of 1930, the German bishops individually issued pastoral guidelines that, in general, forbade Catholics to join the Nazi Party. In some dioceses, the directives even ordered priests not to provide the sacraments to Party members (Müller 1963: 21–37). But many Catholics were drawn to the Nazis' emphasis on nationalism, and the appointment of Adolf Hitler (1889–1945) as Chancellor on 30 January 1933 intensified this trend. As National Socialists took over national and local leadership positions, Catholics feared being left out of the political process, labeled traitors by the new government, and being subjected to a second *Kulturkampf* (culture war) like the one Chancellor Otto von Bismarck (1815–1898) had waged against the Church in 1871–1887. Speaking to the Reichstag on 23 March 1933, Hitler tried to calm these fears and win support for an Enabling Act, which would allow his cabinet to rule by decree, by promising Catholic and Lutheran churches that Christianity would be the German nation's underlying foundation. A few days later, on 28 March, the German bishops lifted their ban on Nazi Party membership and publicly acknowledged Hitler's promise, but they did not revoke their condemnation of the religious and moral errors they perceived in National Socialist ideology.

On 20 July 1933, the German government and the Vatican concluded a Concordat (i.e., a papal treaty on ecclesiastical affairs) that recognized and promised to protect the Catholic Church and its institutions in Germany, something the German Reich never had done before (Biesinger in Coppa 1999; Brechenmacher 2007). The document stipulated that the bishops henceforth could and would challenge the state only in those areas where its actions contradicted Church teaching and encroached upon the bishops' freedom to exercise their ministry. In subsequent years, when the bishops protested that the state had not kept its end of the bargain, they usually achieved little except to alarm the authorities. Thus, a legalistic approach that many historians have perceived "as capitulation or, at the very least, lack of resistance, was viewed by Nazi leaders as posing a very serious threat" (Dietrich 1988: 182).

In overseeing its daily liturgies and educating its members in the faith, the Catholic Church provided a worldview that stood in stark contrast to National Socialism's. Some commentators have suggested that this worldview and the parochial associations of Catholics enabled them to resist National Socialist ideology (von Hehl 1996: 41), and even scholars who do not entirely agree concede that the Church insulated its followers from Nazism's worst ideological seductions (Löwenthal in Bracher et al. 1986: 627; Lönne in Claussen and Schwarz 1986: 178). Nonetheless, although proclaiming the Christian faith forced many Catholic bishops and priests to make statements and engage in activities that government officials labeled political resistance, most Church leaders rejected any association with or connection to resistance—the term or reality—and nationalistically pledged their allegiance to their German fatherland. They also insisted that they had to act solely to protect the interests of their Church and to secure pastoral freedom. In their preaching and rebuttals of local Nazi officials, Catholic bishops and priests were, from their sacramental perspective, primarily fulfilling a mandate instituted by Christ to proclaim the gospel and administer the sacraments. Any limitation placed on the exercise of these ministries threatened that mission, so bishops and priests seldom ran the risk of speaking about political issues that did not concern their Church's welfare. According to their worldview, Catholics took care of Catholics, Protestants took care of Protestants, and Jews took care of Jews. Their parallel worlds rarely converged.

Franz Schubert (1876–1937), a professor of pastoral theology at the University of Breslau, emphasized these points. He encouraged seminarians to establish a relationship of "peace, mutual respect and mutual appreciation" with the secular authority (whose decrees must always be honored), to "refrain from disrespectful censure and offensive criticism," and to promote "responsible obedience toward authority" among their parishioners. By contrast, priests "should and must reject harmful discourteous treatment" by state authorities, but never dishonor their office while doing so (Schubert 1935: 147, 176–7). The German hierarchy long had taught, as Bishop Christian Schreiber (1872–1933) of Berlin stated in November 1930, that God granted and "vested in the legal bearer of state authority" the power to rule the state and therefore Catholics had to "submit to state authority." He stressed that Church and state were "independent in their area of power," but also that the Church had "no right in any way to interfere in the purely political affairs of the state" because the state was "independent in purely civic things" (*Germania*: 15 November 1930).

Some scholars have concluded that such thinking led Catholics to question and resist the state only when they perceived that it was jeopardizing their institutions (Lewy 1964; Conway 1968; Denzler 1984; Scholder 1988). But the Church clearly made profound emotional and psychological demands on its members (Spicer 2004). The Church made God present in the sacraments, elucidated the faith of believers, and was the extension of the heavenly Christ himself. Only by being grafted into this Church could people be saved. Consequently, preservation of this institution required an uncommonly loyal and disciplined following. Instead of causing the Church to succumb to Nazism, the spiritual practices and programs of the Church sometimes provoked Catholic bishops and priests to confront the state directly and often to see the dangerous implications for the faithful of Nazi ideology. Unfortunately, Jews were not normally in the sphere of the Church's concern and rarely benefited from such "pastoral confrontations."

The Catholic Church's interaction with Hitler's government varied over time. One generally sound analysis identifies three principal phases: 1933–1935, when Church leaders were under the illusion that they would be able to work with the state; 1936–1940, when the state attacked the Church's value system and worked to remove it from "individual and societal life"; and 1940–1945, when the state engaged in "new unparalleled radicalization of domestic policy," namely the "murder of the mentally ill and the deportation and subsequent murder of the Jews" (Gotto et al. in Gotto and Repgen 1990: 175–6, 179, 189). During the third period, the state also threatened the future existence of the Church in Germany and its occupied territories (Hürten 1985). Reliable as this time division is, one might add that the murder of Erich Klausener (1885–1934), the politically outspoken director of Berlin's Catholic Action group, on 30 June 1934 during the Röhm Purge was also a significant turning point. Thereafter, the bishops focused even more on self-preservation and safeguarding their ecclesial freedoms and turned a blind eye to injustices and human rights violations that did not affect the Church directly (Spicer 2004: 38–40).

THE CHURCH AND THE PERSECUTION OF GERMAN JEWS

Although the German Catholic bishops never sanctioned National Socialist racism, they never specifically discussed the persecution of the Jews in pastoral letters or public statements (Tinnemann 1984). Instead, they expressed the belief that Jews could take care of themselves. In April 1933, for example, Munich's Cardinal Michael von Faulhaber (1869–1952) wrote to Vatican Secretary of State Cardinal Eugenio Pacelli, making this very point with reference to the 1 April boycott of Jewish-owned businesses: "It is at this time not possible to intervene because the struggle against the Jews would at the same time become a struggle against the Catholics and because the Jews can help themselves, as the hasty breaking off of the boycott shows" (quoted in Stasiewski 1968: 54). Concurrently, many members of the hierarchy firmly believed that Jews had inordinate influence in the world, especially regarding the press, and had used it to propagate socialist ideas at the expense of Catholic concerns. Again the events of 1 April revealed such thinking. On 31 March 1933, Oscar Wassermann (1869–1934), the director of the Deutsche Bank and President of the Inter-Denominational Working Group for Peace, met with Cardinal Adolf Bertram (1859–1945) to request the Church's intervention against the planned boycott. Immediately following the meeting, Bertram wrote to his fellow bishops and informed them that the boycott was solely an economic matter and as such outside the bishops' sphere of activity. Bertram added, "the press that is predominantly in Jewish hands has been totally silent regarding the persecution of Catholics in various countries" (Stasiewski 1968: 42–3).

Throughout 1933, the German bishops continued their hands-off stance toward Nazi Jewish policy. During Advent, for example, Cardinal Faulhaber preached a series of sermons that challenged the Nazi assault on the Old Testament. Subsequently, the Basel *National Zeitung* published an additional sermon falsely attributed to Faulhaber, which directly contradicted National Socialist racial teaching. Members of the budding World Jewish Congress, who were meeting in Geneva, publicly endorsed the falsely attributed sermon. Soon thereafter, Faulhaber's secretary publicly disassociated the Cardinal from the *National Zeitung* sermon and declared that Faulhaber had only defended the integrity of the Old Testament and "took no position on the Jewish question of today" (Beilage, *Amtsblatt* Archdiocese of Munich and Freising, 15 November 1934). Such statements reveal that Church leaders feared aligning themselves too closely with Judaism or emerging as defenders of Jews, lest the National Socialists turn on Catholicism as well.

The German Catholic hierarchy did not change this stance after the Reich enacted the infamous Nuremberg Laws in November 1935. Instead of protesting this institutionalization of discrimination, the bishops preoccupied themselves with the repercussions of a 15 July 1935 article in *L' Osservatore Romano*, a semi-official Vatican newspaper, concerning the German government's infringements on the Reich–Vatican Concordat and its toleration of the anti-Catholic writings of Nazi Party ideologist Alfred Rosenberg (1893–1946). In response, Prussian Minister-President Hermann Göring (1893–1946) decreed on 16 July that the German government would no longer tolerate political dissent from the Catholic Church and called on government officials and state police to employ "the full severity of existing punishment" in order to counter any challenge to the state. Göring's decree led to increasing arrests of clergy, primarily for criticism of the state in their sermons and pastoral work. In the summer of 1935, Minister of Propaganda Joseph Goebbels (1897–1945) worked to break the "political" activity of Catholics by creating scandals involving members of the clergy. First, he initiated legal action against diocesan clergy and religious communities that allegedly had violated Germany's complex foreign exchange regulations (Hoffmann and Janssen 1967; Rapp 1981). Then Goebbels sensationalized sexual assault charges brought against some members of the St. Francis Waldbreitbach religious community in the Rhineland and expanded the scope of similar accusations to a number of priests throughout Germany (Hockerts 1971). Since there was some truth to the latter charges, the German bishops did not denounce the legal proceedings; however, they did challenge, both individually and jointly, the press's propaganda attacks on all German religious and clergy as an attempt to delegitimate the Church.

Such continued assaults on the Church eventually led the German bishops to ask Pope Pius XI (1857–1939; reigned 1922–1939) to address the situation. The result was a 14 March 1937 encyclical entitled *Mit brennender Sorge* (With Burning Concern). Working from Cardinal Faulhaber's rough draft, Vatican Secretary of State Eugenio Pacelli crafted a version for Pope Pius XI, who issued the final rendition in his own name. The encyclical primarily encouraged Christians to stand firm in their faith and to reject everything that challenged or attacked it. Although Pius XI also questioned National Socialism's exaltation of race, people, and state, the encyclical did not speak directly in behalf of Jews nor condemn the Nazi legislation against them (Spicer 2004: 55–8). Despite these limitations, when priests throughout Germany read the encyclical during Sunday Mass, it "struck like a bomb," and the German government viewed it as a direct assault (Leiber 1961/62). Its appearance also disquieted the German hierarchy, whose members overwhelmingly wished to avoid being labeled unpatriotic or adversarial. Very few bishops, for example, concurred with Konrad von Preysing (1880–1950), bishop of Berlin, who declined to limit his pastoral concerns to issues affecting only the Church and wanted the bishops to address matters of personal freedom. Thus, the majority of German bishops supported Cardinal Bertram's *Eingabenpolitik* (policy of suggestion), which trusted in the state's willingness to abide by the Concordat and the Church's prerogative to write letters to high-ranking Nazi officials as a means of redressing violations (Leugers 1996: 84–93).

Despite their reluctance to challenge the state directly or to speak against its anti-Jewish legislation, some of the German bishops realized that they needed to provide pastoral services for Catholics of Jewish heritage. Once again, Bishop Preysing exercised leadership, founding on 24 August 1938 the *Hilfswerk beim bischöflichen Ordinariat Berlin* (Relief Agency of the Berlin Chancery) (Phayer 1990: 204–24). In its first years, the *Hilfswerk* procured financial support and food, oversaw arrangements for emigration, and provided counsel. In the war years, as threats to Jews heightened, the agency also assisted in hiding the persecuted, helping families prepare for deportation, and accompanying them to deportation sites. Preysing's assistant, Monsignor Bernhard Lichtenberg (1875–1943), administered the *Hilfswerk* until his arrest in the fall of 1941, when Preysing himself took over. The *Hilfswerk*'s heart, however, was Dr. Margarete Sommer (1893–1965), a devout Catholic laywoman, who courageously risked her life to run the organization until the end of the war. She not only endeavored to ensure that the *Hilfswerk* met the material and spiritual needs of Catholics of Jewish heritage and, at times, Jews, but also established contacts that informed her about the Holocaust. Risking her own life, Sommer dauntlessly passed this information to Preysing and his fellow bishops (Phayer and Fleischner 1997; Herzberg 2000). Despite such efforts to alert the German hierarchy to the plight of European Jews, the staff of the *Hilfswerk* primarily assisted Catholics of Jewish heritage (Leichsenring 2007). Though no other diocese matched the Berlin *Hilfswerk*, several bishops elsewhere enlisted Catholic laywomen to reach out to Catholics of Jewish heritage. In Breslau, for example, Gabriele Gräfin Magnis (1896–1976) took on this role for Cardinal Bertram (Leichsenring 2000), and in Freiburg, Gertrud Luckner (1900–1995) acted in behalf of Bishop Conrad Gröber (1872–1948) (Wollasch 1999 and 2005). Generally, however, the German bishops remained indifferent to anyone outside their religious tradition.

Similarly, the fact that some bishops responded pastorally to the situation of Catholics of Jewish heritage did not translate into overt resistance against the Nazi state or public criticism of the Reich government for its anti-Jewish actions. Even following the horrific pogrom of November 1938, only one priest—Monsignor Lichtenberg—spoke out. In St. Hedwig's Cathedral, he proclaimed from the pulpit: "We know what happened yesterday. We do not know what tomorrow holds. However, we have experienced what happened today. Outside, the synagogue burns. That is also a house of God" (Mann 1977: 9). Lichtenberg began to pray daily during the cathedral services for both Jews and Christians of Jewish heritage, as well as for imprisoned priests and religious, until his arrest in 1941. After enduring excruciating interrogations, prison, and torture, he died in November 1943 while being deported to Dachau (Spicer 2004: 160–82). No other German priest offered such a clear witness in behalf of Jews.

During World War II, the majority of German bishops did their part morally and spiritually to support the war effort, often by giving nationalistic sermons and speeches, especially at the onset of Operation Barbarossa in June 1941 (Zahn 1962). Although military bishop Franz Rarkowski (1873–1950) played an outspoken role in promoting a war of annihilation (Missalla 1982, 1997, 1999), the rest of the hierarchy in no way advocated the segregation, deportation, or murder of European Jews. Instead, for a number of reasons it remained silent on this issue. At root was the bishops' fear of appearing unpatriotic during wartime. The Reich viewed anything that smacked of defeatism as treasonous and acted accordingly.

In addition, the earlier divisions between the bishops had not lessened. Their leader, Cardinal Bertram, refused to veer from his conciliatory course and infuriated many by his willingness to send Hitler annual birthday greetings. Of course, the deep-seated antisemitism of the Catholic tradition cannot be discounted either. By December 1942, armed with Margarete Sommer's well informed reports, Bishop Preysing demanded that the German bishops address the injustices committed by their countrymen and composed a dramatic Advent letter for this purpose. Though initially supported by the West German Bishops' Conference (Cologne, Aachen, Limburg, Mainz, Münster, Osnabrück, and Paderborn), Preysing's version went through significant rewrites and was read in full only in the dioceses of Berlin, Limburg, and Mainz. Ultimately, it declared the sovereignty of God's law and proclaimed that an "individual cannot and must not be permitted to be completely absorbed by the state or by the nation or by the race. . . . Primeval rights enjoyed by mankind, the right to live, to exist unharmed, to be free" did not depend "upon the arbitrary dictum of governments" and could not be "taken from anyone who [was] not of our blood" or who did "not speak our language" (Spicer 2004: 67–70).

Although Preysing's Advent letter did not go so far as to address the plight of European Jews specifically, he became on 9 March 1941 in a sermon at St. Hedwig's Cathedral the first bishop to denounce state-imposed euthanasia. In even stronger terms, Bishop Clemens von Galen (1878–1946), preaching at St. Lambert's Church in Münster on 3 August 1941, also spoke out forcefully against the state's murderous policy toward those it categorized as "life unworthy of life." This intervention has both earned him praise as a great resister (Kuropka 1993, 1998) and attracted attention to his antisemitism and the gap between his concern for "Aryan" Germans murdered under the "euthanasia" program and his silence on the plight of German Jews (Griech-Polelle 2002). The latter point reveals that one could be both anti-Nazi and antisemitic.

The bishops criticized the Nazi state, at times strongly, but their lack of common and comprehensive action undercut their message. And although the Advent letter of 1942 and a subsequent one the following year alluded to the gross infractions of human rights that individuals witnessed daily in the Third Reich, neither addressed the suffering of Jews directly. Instead, the German hierarchy viewed earthly existence primarily as a stepping stone to eternal life. Earthly life was a time of testing, a time of turmoil that also might be filled with joy and peace, with signs of the coming Kingdom of God. In 1944, for example, even in the midst of a losing war and rumors about atrocities on the eastern front, a bishop as courageous as Preysing could ask Berlin Catholics only to turn to the mercy of God and reconsecrate their diocese and each parish to the Most Sacred Heart of Jesus. Not surprisingly, the bishops had not yet come to practice a theology that encouraged Catholics to use the gospel as a means to confront social and political ills. Instead, the bishops emphasized a pietistic sharing in the sufferings of Christ until the Second Coming.

PIUS XII AND THE EUROPEAN JEWS

In his work on the papacy and the Holocaust, Frank J. Coppa (2006) portrayed Pope Pius XI as a feisty and increasingly bold antagonist of Nazism and Pope Pius XII as a placatory diplomat who failed to stand up to Nazism. Some evidence supports such claims. For example, in June 1938, Pope Pius XI invited the Jesuit priest John LaFarge (1880–1963) to draft an encyclical condemning antisemitism and racism. Assisted by fellow Jesuits Gustav Gundlach (1892–1963) and Gustave Desbuquois (1869–1959), LaFarge created drafts in French, English, and German of an encyclical tentatively entitled *Humani Generis Unitas* (The Unity of the Human Race). Though the drafts condemned racism and antisemitism, they also included traditional expressions of Christian antisemitism, including the deicide charge. Apparently, internal Jesuit politics at the highest level delayed delivery of the drafts to Pius XI until his deteriorating health made him too weak to work on them. He died on 10 February 1939. The first encyclical issued by his successor, Pius XII, entitled *Summi Pontificatus* (On the Unity of Human Society) and issued on 20 October 1939, included significant material from the drafts of *Humani Generis* but not the sections that addressed antisemitism (Passelecq and Suchecky 1997). Critics of Pius XII have taken the omission as evidence of the Pope's indifference to the plight of European Jews.

But Pius XII was a complex individual who cannot be easily categorized. Consider two little-known illustrations of this complexity. In July 1935, while Vatican Secretary of State (1930–1939), he pushed the candidacy of von Preysing, then bishop of Eichstätt, for the bishopric of Berlin. The future Pope was well aware of Preysing's outspoken criticism of the National Socialist government (Spicer 2004: 45–6). Conversely, pro-Nazi German priests blamed the former Cardinal Pacelli for the "oppositional" course of the German Catholic Church. Writing in despair of his election as Pope in 1939, one of these prelates lamented that "the most dangerous opponent of the new Germany in our Church, Pacelli, has today, already, in the third ballot, been elevated by two-thirds of the College of Cardinals to become the head of our Church, under the thunderous applause of an entire world that is set against us Germans" and called this action "the most official insult of the official Church 'leadership' against Adolf Hitler and Benito Mussolini . . . synonymous with a Church-historical catastrophe" (Spicer 2008: 174).

Neither of these tales frees Pius XII of the charge of antisemitism, even in its primarily religious form. Richard Rubenstein takes that position when he implies that Pius XII "regarded the political emancipation of the Jews as a tragic mistake" that, over time, would endanger Christianity, and thus would not speak up against a process that was putting an end to this emancipation (Rubenstein in Roth and Maxwell 2001, 2: 476). Not straying far from Rubenstein's thesis, John Cornwell's biography of Pius XII (1999) portrays the Pope as a lifelong antisemite who supported Hitler and the Nazis' annihilative policies toward Jews. Both Rubenstein and Cornwell, however, offer little concrete evidence for their claims. By contrast, David I. Kertzer (2001) convincingly uncovers the recurrent vehemence of the Holy See's antisemitism through a close analysis of the Vatican's pronouncements and those of publications closely linked to it.

Certainly, traditional Christian antisemitism, which some authors refer to as anti-Judaism, figured in the theological mindset of most pre-Vatican II Catholics, including Pius XII. As Michael Marrus explains:

Traditional Catholic teaching saw the Jews as the people who had rejected Christ, who had conspired in his execution, and who sought to undermine or obstruct the teachings of the Church. Often linked with these views were the associations many Catholics had of Jews as champions of modernity: Bolshevism, secularism, materialism, atheism, rationalism, liberalism, capitalism, democracy were all, at one time or another, seen as inspired, invented, or promoted by the Jews. (Marrus in Rittner and Roth 2002: 44)

However, this does not mean that Pius XII was "an antisemite and 'uninterested' in the fate of European Jewry," an argument that Suzanne Brown-Fleming reminds us has been "rejected by nearly all scholars of the subject" (2006: 128). Instead, as Michael Phayer suggests,

the Christian tradition of supersessionism allowed the pope to regret the Holocaust as it took place while at the same time allowing him to concentrate on preserving the Church that had inherited the Jews' birthright. Supersessionism . . . left Pius XII free not to dwell on the disaster and to move on to preserve the treasure given to the new chosen people, about whom he wrote so explicitly in [the encyclical] *Mystici Corporis Christi* [The Mystical Body of Christ, 1943] while the Holocaust was under way. (Phayer 2008: 258–9)

In that document, Pius XII made the doctrine of supersession explicit when he wrote: "On the Cross then the Old Law died, soon to be buried and to be a bearer of death, in order to give way to the New Testament" (Phayer 2008: 68).

Although Phayer stresses that he wishes to study Pius XII only as a political leader, by underlining the importance of supersessionism he adopts the perspective of historians who incorporate Catholic theology in their analysis of the actions of Church leaders under National Socialism. During this tumultuous period, Pius XII's primary concern remained, as always, the care, protection, and continuation of the visible Church, especially in Rome and Vatican City, and its mission to bring salvation to its members (Spicer 2004; Besier 2007: 199; Phayer 2008). Unfortunately, the care and concern of those who were not members of the Catholic Church was secondary. Similarly, the visible institution itself, which Pius XII likened to "the mystical Body of Christ," and the freedom of this institution to continue its otherworldly mission to aid Catholics to salvation through the administration of the sacraments also took precedence over the life and well-being of any individual Catholic. This posture may account for the silence of the official Church about the thousands of priests and religious who were sent to concentration camps, where many of them perished.

Other considerations also guided Pius XII's actions during the Holocaust. Pius at times feared communism more than National Socialism (Friedländer 1966; Graham 1996). Phayer even dubs Pius XII the "world's first Cold War warrior" and ties his Germanophile behavior after the war (e.g., appointing the bishops of Berlin and Münster as cardinals, sending care packages to German POWs, and petitioning for clemency for select German war criminals) to his profound anti-communism (2008: 134, 160). Moreover, Pius XII's experience as Papal Nuncio to Germany and then Vatican Secretary of State led him to prefer behind-the-scenes diplomacy to bold, public actions. He thwarted during the early 1930s a group in the Roman Curia around Bishop Alois Hudal (1885–1963) that sought to condemn a significant number of National Socialist writings by placing them on the Vatican Index (Burkard 2007). Though this example illustrates Pacelli's preference for undemonstrative methods in dealing with Nazism, it does not allow a simple interpretation, since Hudal was a problematic character. He believed that National Socialism was salvageable and differentiated between "good" and "dangerous" Nazis. Following World War II, aided by a cadre of like-minded Catholic clergy and laypeople, he helped reprehensible Nazi war criminals, such as Eduard Roschmann (1908–1977), Adolf Eichmann (1906–1962), Franz Stangl (1908–1971), and Josef Mengele (1911–1979), to escape Europe and prosecution (Klee 1991; Goñi 2002; Phayer 2008: 203, 206; Steinacher 2008). Historians have been unable to show that Pius XII had any direct knowledge of this "ratline."

The literature on Pius XII and the Holocaust is vast, growing, and multifarious. It includes a significant number of apologetic works whose authors abuse the historical method by selectively deploying or distorting primary sources to defend Eugenio Pacelli and have him canonized. Even after that matter is resolved, debate over Pius XII's wartime interventions—or lack of them—against Germany's persecution and slaughter of the European Jews surely will continue. José Sánchez (2002) provides a helpful synthesis of this controversy and adds his own analysis, which should be read in light of the criticisms offered by Suzanne Brown-Fleming

(2006: 128–9). Sánchez argues that Pius XII refused to issue a broad condemnation of the Holocaust, not because he was an antisemite or he feared imprisonment or the destruction of Rome and the Vatican, but because he worried about the likely repercussions, especially for Catholics in Germany, but also for the Jews. Sánchez stresses that Pius XII recalled the protest of the Dutch Catholic bishops against the rounding up of Jews in their country in July 1942, which led to increased deportations, specifically of Catholics of Jewish heritage. When Bishop von Preysing personally asked Pius XII in April 1943 to intercede for Jews facing deportation from Germany, the Pope responded:

Regarding pronouncements by the bishops We leave it to local senior clergymen to decide if, and to what degree, the danger of reprisals and oppressions, as well as, perhaps, other circumstances caused by the length and psychological climate of the war may make restraint advisable—despite the reasons for intervention—in order to avoid greater evils. This is one of the reasons why We limit ourselves in Our proclamations. (Zuccotti 2000: 311)

Whether or not the events following the protest of the Dutch bishops motivated Pius XII to withhold public pronouncements on the Holocaust, an examination of the Holy See's diplomatic efforts during the Holocaust led John F. Morley to conclude that "Vatican diplomacy only rarely acted on behalf of Jews as Jews, and this usually only for specific individuals" (1980: 196). At most, Vatican nuncios focused on sacramental concerns relating to intermarriage, conversion, and the efficacy of baptism for Catholics of Jewish heritage. In a rare exception to this pattern, in March 1942 Cardinal Luigi Maglione (1877–1944), the Vatican Secretary of State, protested the deportation of 80,000 Slovak Jews to Charles Sidor, the Slovak minister to the Holy See. The protest, however, failed to head off not only the deportation, but also the willingness of priests in the Slovak parliament to help pass legislation two months later that authorized the deportations, deprived Slovak Jews of citizenship, and expropriated their property. Perhaps both outcomes were assured by the fact that the Slovak Prime Minister was an antisemitic priest, Monsignor Josef Tiso (1887–1947), and by a pastoral letter from the Slovak bishops a month earlier that reaffirmed "the need to act humanely toward the Jews," while labeling them a "cursed people because of their deicide" and the "economic and financial" ruin they had supposedly brought to the Slovak nation (Morley 1980: 85–6).

In her study of the Vatican and the Holocaust in Italy, Susan Zuccotti (2000) finds no evidence that Pius XII offered a clear protest to the Nazi round-up of Italian Jews in October 1943. She admits that the Vatican-sponsored *L'Osservatore Romano* ran occasional articles critical of actions against Jews, such as the "infamous order number five of December 1, 1943, which declared that all Jews in Italy were to be arrested by Italian police and carabinieri and interned in camps within the country" (Zuccotti 2000: 306). But, she notes, such intercessions were not repeated and failed to produce significant results. Zuccotti also states that the

Vatican issued no official order to Italian convents and monasteries to hide Jews. On the contrary, Vatican officials often criticized individual priests who tried to rescue Jews for jeopardizing Vatican neutrality or bringing retaliation upon the city of Rome. In 2006, however, an anonymous chronicle from the Augustinian nuns of the Santi Quattro Coronati in Rome came to light that includes the following entry:

Having arrived at this month of November [1943] we must be ready to render services of charity in a completely unexpected way. The Holy Father Pius XII, of paternal heart, feels in himself all the sufferings of the moment. Unfortunately with the Germans' entry into Rome, which happened in the month of September, a ruthless war against the Jews has begun, whom they wish to exterminate by means of atrocities prompted by the blackest barbarities. . . . In this painful situation the Holy Father wants to save his children, also the Jews, and orders that hospitality be given in the convents to these persecuted, and that the cloisters must also adhere to the wish of the Supreme Pontiff. (30 Days 2006)

Doubts about the date of origin of the document have been raised, however, and it awaits verification.

The most potentially disruptive issue concerning Catholics, Jews, and the Holocaust is the postwar and contemporary posture of a Holy See that does not seem to comprehend what Jews have suffered and lost as a result of centuries of antisemitism culminating in the Holocaust. In a study of the Vatican and custody of Jewish children who survived the Holocaust under the protection of Catholic institutions, Michael Marrus noted that although "there was no campaign at the very highest levels of the Catholic Church to 'kidnap' Jewish children in 1945 and 1946 . . . neither was there a clear call from that quarter to come to terms with the suffering Jewish people" (Marrus 2007: 397). Such a pattern continues even today. The push by some Catholics to have Pope Pius XII canonized offers evidence of such lack of empathy on the part of Catholics toward Jews. Whether historians can uncover new information exalting or exculpating Pius XII's actions during the Holocaust remains to be seen. However, for many people, Jews and Christians alike, Pius XII stands for the indifference of the Church toward the murder of six million Jews and, in that context, represents both theologically and ideologically nearly two millennia of Christian antisemitism that led to the Holocaust. Until the Catholic Church accepts this fact and faces its antisemitism, both past and present, there will be no historical consensus on Pius XII.

REFERENCES

30 Days (2006). "The Unpublished memorial of the Augustinian nuns of the convent of the Santi Quattro Coronati in Rome." *30 Days in the Church and the World* 19/8. Available at: <http://www.30giorni.it/us/articolo_ stampa.asp?id=11037>. Accessed 20 May 2009.

Besier, G. (2007). *The Holy See and Hitler's Germany*. New York: Palgrave Macmillan.

BRACHER, K., FUNKE, M., and JACOBSEN, H. (eds.) (1986). *Nationalsozialistische Diktatur 1933–1945: Eine Bilanz.* Ulm: Franz Spiegel.

BRECHENMACHER, T. (2005). *Der Vatikan und die Juden: Geschichte einer unheiligen Beziehung.* Munich: C. H. Beck.

——(ed.) (2007). *Das Reichskonkordat 1933: Forschungsstand, Kontroversen, Dokumente.* Paderborn: Ferdinand Schöningh.

BROWN-FLEMING, S. (2006). *The Holocaust and Catholic Conscience: Cardinal Aloisius Muench and the Guilt Question in Germany.* Notre Dame, IN: University of Notre Dame Press.

BURKARD, D. (2007). "Alois Hudal—ein Anti-Pacelli? Zur Diskussion um die Haltung des Vatikans gegenüber dem Nationalsozialismus." *Zeitschrift für Religions- und Geistesgeschichte* 59: 61–89.

CARROLL, J. (2001). *Constantine's Sword: The Church and the Jews: A History.* Boston, MA: Houghton Mifflin.

CLAUSSEN, R. and SCHWARZ, S. (eds.) (1986). *Von Widerstand lernen: Von der Bekennenden Kirche bis zum 20. Juli 1944.* Bonn: Bouvier.

COHEN, J. (2007). *Christ Killers: The Jews and the Passion from the Bible to the Big Screen.* New York: Oxford University Press.

CONWAY, J. (1968). *The Nazi Persecution of the Churches 1933–45.* New York: Basic Books.

COPPA, F. (ed.) (1999). *Controversial Concordats: The Vatican's Relations with Napoleon, Mussolini, and Hitler.* Washington, DC: The Catholic University of America Press.

——(2006). *The Papacy, the Jews, and the Holocaust.* Washington, DC: The Catholic University of America Press.

CORNWELL, J. (1999). *Hitler's Pope: The Secret History of Pius XII.* New York: Viking.

DENZLER, G. (1984). *Widerstand oder Anpassung? Katholische Kirche und Drittes Reich.* Munich: Piper.

DIETRICH, D. (1988). "Catholic Resistance in the Third Reich." *Holocaust and Genocide Studies* 3: 171–86.

FLANNERY, E. (1985). *The Anguish of the Jews: Twenty-Three Centuries of Antisemitism.* Rev. edn. Mahwah, NJ: Paulist Press.

FRIEDLÄNDER, S. (1966). *Pius XII and the Third Reich: A Documentation.* New York: Alfred A. Knopf.

GOÑI, U. (2002). *The Real Odessa: Smuggling the Nazis to Perón's Argentina.* New York: Granta.

GOTTO, K. and REPGEN, K. (eds.) (1990). *Die Katholiken und das Dritte Reich.* Mainz: Matthias-Grünewald.

GRAHAM, R. (1996). *The Vatican and Communism During World War II: What Really Happened?* San Francisco: Ignatius.

GRIECH-POLELLE, B. (2002). *Bishop von Galen: German Catholicism and National Socialism.* New Haven, CT: Yale University Press.

HEHL, U. VON. (1996). *Nationalsozialistische Herrschaft.* Munich: R. Oldenburg.

HERZBERG, H. (2000). *Dienst am Höheren Gesetz: Dr. Margarete Sommer und das "Hilfswerk beim Bischöflichen Ordinariat Berlin."* Berlin: Servi.

HOCKERTS, H. (1971). *Die Sittlichkeitsprozesse gegen katholische Ordensangehörige und Priester 1936/1937: Eine Studie zur nationalsozialistischen Herrschaftstechnik und zum Kirchenkampf.* Mainz: Matthias-Grünewald.

HOFFMANN, E. and JANSSEN, H. (1967). *Die Wahrheit über die Ordensdevisenprozesse 1935/36.* Bielefeld: Hausknecht.

HÜRTEN, H. (1985). "Endlösung für den Katholizismus? Das nationalsozialistische Regime und seine Zukunftspläne gegenüber der Kirche." *Stimmen der Zeit* 203: 534–46.

KALLER, M. (1927). *Unser Laienapostolat: Was es ist und wie es sein soll.* Leutesdorf am Rhein: Johannesbund.

KERTZER, D. (2001). *The Popes against the Jews: The Vatican's Role in the Rise of Modern Anti-Semitism.* New York: Knopf.

KLEE, E. (1991). *Persilscheine und falsche Pässe: Wie die Kirchen den Nazis halfen.* Frankfurt: Fischer.

KUROPKA, J. (ed.) (1993). *Clemens August Graf von Galen: Neue Forschung zum Leben und Wirken des Bischofs von Münster.* 2nd edn. Münster: Regensberg.

——(ed.) (1998). *Clemens August Graf von Galen: Menschenrechte—Widerstand—Euthanasie—Neubeginn.* Münster: Regensberg.

LEIBER, R. (1961/62). "Mit brennender Sorge. März 1937–März 1962." *Stimmen der Zeit* 87: 417–26.

LEICHSENRING, J. (2000). *Gabriele Gräfin Magnis, Sonderbeauftragte Kardinal Bertrams für die Betreuung der Katholischen Nichtarier Oberschlesiens: Auftrag-Grenzüberschreitung-Widerstand?* Stuttgart: Jan Thorbecke.

——(2007). *Die Katholische Kirche und "ihre Juden": Das "Hilfswerk beim bischöflichen Ordinariat Berlin" 1938–1945.* Berlin: Metropol.

LEUGERS, A. (1996). *Gegen eine Mauer bischöflichen Schweigens: Der Ausschuß für Ordensangelegenheiten und seine Widerstandskonzeption 1941 bis 1945.* Frankfurt: Josef Knecht.

LEWY, G. (1964). *The Catholic Church and Nazi Germany.* New York: McGraw-Hill.

MANN, H. (1977). *Prozeß Bernhard Lichtenberg: Ein Leben in Dokumenten.* Berlin: Morus.

MARRUS, M. (2007). "The Vatican and the Custody of Jewish Child Survivors after the Holocaust." *Holocaust and Genocide Studies* 21: 378–403.

MISSALLA, H. (1982). *Für Volk und Vaterland: Die kirchliche Kriegshilfe im Zweiten Weltkrieg.* Bodenheim: Athenäum.

——(1997). *Wie der Krieg zur Schule Gottes wurde: Hitlers Feldbischof Rarkowski: Eine notwendige Erinnerung.* Oberursel: Publik-Forum.

——(1999). *Für Gott, Führer und Vaterland: Die Verstrickung der katholischen Seelsorge in Hitlers Krieg.* Munich: Kösel.

MORLEY, J. (1980). *Vatican Diplomacy and the Jews during the Holocaust 1939–1943.* New York: KTAV.

MÜLLER, H. (1963). *Katholische Kirche und Nationalsozialismus: Dokumente 1930–1935.* Munich: Nymphenburger.

PASSELECQ, G. and SUCHECKY, B. (1997). *The Hidden Encyclical of Pius XI.* New York: Harcourt Brace & Company.

PHAYER, M. (1990). *Protestant and Catholic Women in Nazi Germany.* Detroit, MI: Wayne State University Press.

——(2000). *The Catholic Church and the Holocaust, 1930–1965.* Bloomington, IN: Indiana University Press, 2000.

——(2008). *Pius XII, the Holocaust, and the Cold War.* Bloomington, IN: Indiana University Press.

——and FLEISCHNER, E. (1997). *Cries in the Night: Women who Challenged the Holocaust.* Kansas City, MO: Sheed & Ward.

PIUS XII. (1943). *Mystici Corporis Christi*. <http://www.vatican.va/holy_father/pius_xii/en-cyclicals/documents/hf_p-xii_enc_29061943_mystici-corporis-christi_en.html>. Accessed 13 May 2009.

RAPP, P. (1981). *Die Devisenprozesse gegen katholische Ordensangehörige und Geistliche im Dritten Reich*. Bonn: Universidad Bonn.

RITTNER, C. and ROTH, J. (eds.) (2002). *Pope Pius XII and the Holocaust*. New York: Continuum.

ROTH, J. and MAXWELL, E. (eds.) (2001). *Remembering for the Future: The Holocaust in an Age of Genocide*. 3 vols. New York: Palgrave Macmillan.

RUETHER, R. (1974). *Faith and Fratricide: The Theological Roots of Anti-Semitism*. New York: Seabury.

SÁNCHEZ, J. (2002). *Pius XII and the Holocaust: Understanding the Controversy*. Washington, DC: The Catholic University of America Press.

SCHOLDER, K. (1988). *The Churches and the Third Reich*. Vol. 1, *Preliminary History and the Time of Illusions 1918–1934*. Philadelphia, PA: Fortress.

SCHUBERT, F. (1935). *Grundzüge der Pastoraltheologie*. Vol. 3, *Theorie der Seelsorge*. Leipzig: Ulrich Mosers.

SPICER, K. (2004). *Resisting the Third Reich: The Catholic Clergy in Hitler's Berlin*. DeKalb, IL: Northern Illinois University Press.

——(2008). *Hitler's Priests: Catholic Clergy and National Socialism*. DeKalb, IL: Northern Illinois University Press.

STASIEWSKI, B. (ed.) (1968). *Akten deutscher Bischöfe über die Lage der Kirche 1933–1945*. Vol. 1, *1933–1934*. Mainz: Matthias-Grünewald.

STEINACHER, G. (2008). *Nazis auf der Flucht: Wie Kriegsverbrecher über Italien nach Übersee entkamen*. Innsbruck: Studier.

TINNEMANN, E. (1984). "The German Catholic Bishops and the Jewish Question: Explanation and Judgment." *Holocaust Studies Annual* 2: 55–85.

WOLLASCH, H. (ed.) (1999). *Betrifft: Nachrichtenzentrale des Erzbischof Gröber in Freiburg. Die Ermittlungsakten der Geheimen Staatspolizei gegen Gertrud Luckner 1942–1944*. Konstanz: UVK.

——(2005). *Getrud Luckner: "Botschafterin der Menschlichkeit."* Freiburg: Herder.

ZAHN, G. (1962). *German Catholics and Hitler's Wars*. New York: Shed & Ward.

ZUCCOTTI, S. (2000). *Under His Very Windows: The Vatican and the Holocaust in Italy*. New Haven, CT: Yale University Press.

OTHER SUGGESTED READING

CARGAS, H. (ed.) (1998). *Holocaust Scholars Write to the Vatican*. Westport, CT: Greenwood Press.

GODMAN, P. (2004). *Hitler and the Vatican*. New York: The Free Press.

RITTNER, C. and SMITH, S. (eds.) (2009). *No Going Back: Letters to Pope Benedict XVI on the Holocaust, Jewish–Christian Relations and Israel*. London: Quill in association with The Holocaust Centre.

RUBENSTEIN, R. and ROTH, J. (2003). *Approaches to Auschwitz: The Holocaust and Its Legacy.* Rev. edn. Louisville, KY: Westminster John Knox Press.

SPICER, K. (ed.) (2007). *Antisemitism, Christian Ambivalence, and the Holocaust.* Bloomington, IN: Indiana University Press.

UNITED STATES CATHOLIC CONFERENCE (1998). *Catholics Remember the Holocaust.* Washington, DC: USCCB Publishing.

CHAPTER 16

···

PROTESTANTS

···

ROBERT P. ERICKSEN

DURING the immediate postwar years, Protestant Christians in Germany tried, like most Germans, to wash their hands of responsibility for or connection to the Holocaust. In doing so, Protestants had several advantages. Along with Catholics, they could claim the traditional mantle of Christian morality and maintain that no Christian would have done such things. This claim exploited the need among Christians in the Allied west to think the best about Christianity. Moreover, Protestant Christians could highlight one of the most famous political prisoners of the Nazi state, Pastor Martin Niemöller (1892–1984). Imprisoned since 1937, he had become widely known in the west as a martyr to Nazi oppression. Another Protestant pastor and theologian, Dietrich Bonhoeffer (1906–1945), although less known until the 1950s, suited the Christian martyr's role even better. As a participant in the anti-Nazi conspiracy associated with Admiral Wilhelm Canaris (1887–1945), the enigmatic head of the Abwehr intelligence agency, Bonhoeffer had tried to overthrow Adolf Hitler (1889–1945). Because his arrest in 1943 led to execution in April 1945, he actually died for what could be seen as the Christian cause (Bethge 1970).

For several decades Protestant Germans nurtured this sort of narrative and built a better reputation than their conduct deserved, not unlike their Catholic counterparts. Some historians still depict Christians as opposed to the Nazi state, either secretly and quietly in some form of inner emigration or dangerously and courageously in resistance activity. However, although the courage and suffering of Niemöller and Bonhoeffer were real, these men were by no means typical. On the contrary, scholarship has increasingly laid bare the widespread complicity of German Protestants in the Nazi state.

The *Kirchenkampf*

Protestants experienced a *Kirchenkampf* (church struggle) during the Nazi period, but the conflict was an ecclesiastical struggle *within* the Protestant church, not a political struggle *against* the Nazi state (Ericksen and Heschel in Stone 2004: 296–318). One faction, the *Deutsche Christen* (DC or German Christians), tied itself directly and enthusiastically to the Nazi movement. The DC praised Hitler, waved the swastika, tried to convince other Germans that Protestant Christian faith constituted a natural ally and appropriate partner to the Nazi movement, and sought to modify church doctrine in compliance with Nazi opposition to all things Jewish (Bergen 1996). Although the German Christians were opposed by members of the Confessing Church (*Bekennende Kirche* or BK), that does not mean that most of these believers were also opponents of Hitler and National Socialism.

During the first months of Nazi rule, the German Christians seemed ascendant. First, they convinced Protestant regional churches (*Landeskirchen*) to sacrifice their accustomed independence in favor of a national church structure. Then they succeeded in placing their candidate, Ludwig Müller (1883–1945), in the new position of Reich Bishop. In this case, they received assistance from Hitler, who gave a national radio address on behalf of DC the night before church elections in July. Large DC majorities across Germany resulted in Müller's selection as Prussian Bishop in early September and Reich Bishop on 27 September. However, these DC successes were certain to provoke discontent. A national church could not be created without reducing the authority of twenty-eight regional bishops, potentially exacerbating deep-seated feelings of regional difference and threatening the confessional purity of two major groups, Lutheran and Reformed, some of whose followers took their historic differences very seriously. Blatant political interference in church elections also aroused concern. Opponents of Reich Bishop Müller saw no significant qualifications in his candidacy beyond his distant acquaintance with Hitler and the political benefits that it might bring.

Tensions worsened when the DC tried to modify traditional faith and practice in line with the antisemitic ideology of the Nazi state. Not wanting to stir up a religious quarrel, the regime had not tried to make clergy subject to the "Aryan Paragraph" of the new Civil Service Law (7 April 1933), which excluded people with a Jewish parent or grandparent from many professions. DC leaders, however, called for a self-imposed culling process to demonstrate the church's enthusiasm for the Nazi ideology. Though Protestant pastors of Jewish descent represented a tiny number—three dozen or fewer out of 18,000—the DC passed a demand at a Prussian synodical meeting in September 1933 that the Aryan Paragraph be applied within the church. Martin Niemöller, pastor of a congregation in the Berlin suburb of Dahlem, responded by creating a "Pastors' Emergency League" to fight this policy. Niemöller shared the DC's enthusiasm for Nazi politics (Schmidt 1971;

Bentley 1984). However, implementation of the Aryan Paragraph raised doctrinal issues for him, since it would negate ordinations of clergy and call into question the efficacy of the sacrament of baptism. The DC aroused further consternation with the "Sports Palace scandal" of 13 November 1933. Celebrating the 450th anniversary of Martin Luther's birth, a rally of 20,000 people heard the DC's most flamboyant speaker, Reinhold Krause (1893–1980), call for implementation of the Aryan Para-graph, removal of the Old Testament from the Christian Bible, and the filtering of "Jewish elements" out of the New Testament. The Pastors' Emergency League expanded quickly as clergy responded to what they viewed as heresy. Some five thousand pastors soon held membership cards (Niemöller 1969: 53).

Tensions increased throughout the fall of 1933, especially when Müller tried to claim the "*Führer* principle" for himself. In December, he merged Protestant youth groups into the Hitler Youth. He also imposed a "muzzling decree" that forbade clergy to criticize his policies in sermons or in print. Members of the Pastors' Emergency League began calling for Müller's resignation and appealing directly to Hitler and to President Paul von Hindenburg (1847–1934). Under pressure, Hitler invited a group of discontented Protestant leaders to what became an explosive meeting with him in the Berlin Chancellery on 25 January 1934. A dozen Protestant leaders, including bishops Theophil Wurm (1868–1953) of Württemberg, August Marahrens (1875–1950) of Hanover, and Hans Meiser (1888–1956) of Bavaria, barely had sat down when Hitler cued Hermann Göring (1893–1946) to report on a telephone call intercepted earlier that day in which Martin Niemöller had made an unguarded prediction that President von Hindenburg would exercise influence in this matter. Hitler angrily called this a plot to create division between the Chancellor and the President. In response, only Niemöller held his ground. The others, outmaneuvered by this questioning of their *political* loyalty, immediately gave up their ecclesiastical complaints. Shortly thereafter they signed a statement that left no doubt where their true loyalties lay:

Under the impression of the great occasion on which the leaders of the German Evangelical Church met with the Reich Chancellor, they unanimously affirm their unconditional loyalty to the Third Reich and its Leader. They most sharply condemn any intrigues or criticism against the State, the People or the [Nazi] Movement . . . In particular they deplore any activities on the part of the foreign Press which seek falsely to represent the discussions within the Church as a conflict against the State. (Conway 1968: 74)

These dozen leaders represented the Protestant "opposition," but they openly, explicitly, and fervently denied that their stance included any sort of opposition to Hitler. Almost all subsequent quarrels within the *Kirchenkampf* can be under-stood within these parameters.

By May 1934 the internal church struggle against the DC found its primary expres-sion in the Barmen Declaration, a document drafted by Karl Barth (1886–1968) that stated six points of disagreement with the beliefs of *Deutsche Christen*. Those who accepted the Barmen Declaration now designated themselves the *Bekennende Kirche* (BK) or Confessing Church. For several decades after 1945, many imagined that this Confessing Church was an opposition movement against Hitler, but that idealized image is flawed. The Barmen Declaration did not mention Jews or express the slightest critique of Nazi antisemitism. Furthermore, the Declaration did not criticize Adolf Hitler, the Nazi state, and the enthusiasm felt by so many Germans for the "renewal" of Germany under Nazi auspices. On the contrary, the preface included this warning: "Be not deceived by loose talk, as if we meant to oppose the unity of the German nation!" (Cochrane 1962: 237–42).

The closest the Barmen Declaration came to a political statement is found in point 5: "We reject the false doctrine, as though the State, over and beyond its special commission, should and could become the single and totalitarian order of human life, thus fulfilling the Church's vocation as well." Some postwar commentators read this as a warning to the Nazi state. However, the document added, "We reject the false doctrine, as though the Church, over and beyond its special commission, should and could appropriate the characteristics, the tasks, and the dignity of the State," and this follows a statement describing the state's "divine appointment" to provide "justice and peace . . . by means of the threat and exercise of force," adding that "[t]he Church acknowledges the benefit of this divine appointment in gratitude and reverence before him [God]."

The Barmen Declaration was written so that Nazis could sign the document in good conscience. It scrupulously avoided the criticism that might have been leveled by an unrestrained Karl Barth or Dietrich Bonhoeffer. Barth left Germany in 1935 for his more politically bearable home in Switzerland, and both Bonhoeffer and Niemöller came to be seen as radicals on the fringe of the Confessing Church. Contrary to postwar mythology, the Confessing Church did not view itself as a resistance movement or even an opponent of the Nazi state. Rather, its battle was fought within the church over matters of church doctrine and church governance.

THE PROTESTANT CENTER OF GRAVITY

Protestant enthusiasm for the Nazi regime and acceptance of its anti-Jewish policies were apparent in many ways. Voting records indicate that heavily Protestant regions of Germany voted strongly for the Nazi Party (Lehmann 1998: 130–52). Professor Paul Althaus (1888–1966) of Erlangen University, perhaps the most prominent Luther scholar of his day, declared in 1933, "We Christians greet the rise of Adolf Hitler as a gift and miracle from God" (Althaus 1934: 5). From the Protestant Church of Bavaria came a statement to be read in all Protestant churches in the region: "A state which begins once again to govern according to God's command may expect not just the applause but the joyous cooperation of the church" (*AELKZ* 1933b). An important weekly newspaper of German Lutherans, the *Allgemeine Evangelisch-Lutherische Kirchenzeitung* (AELKZ), rejoiced on 10 February: "We still stand in astonishment before the great turning point brought by January 30th ... Now democracy in all its shades has been struck down by its own weapons, and one can well imagine the disappointment [of its supporters]" (*AELKZ* 1933c). An editorial in April acknowledged that some might question certain aspects of Nazi policy, but warned that: "We get no further if we get stuck on little things that might displease us, failing to value the great things God has done for our *Volk* through them [the Nazis]" (*AELKZ* 1933a).

The vast majority of Protestants had resented the Versailles Treaty and rejected democracy and the Weimar Republic. They appreciated Point 24 in the Nazi program, which proclaimed "positive Christianity" as the foundation of German life. They also responded to the "values" preached by Hitler (Koonz 2003). After 1945 many Protestants attributed their early membership in the Nazi Party or other incriminating evidence of support to idealism. The belief that Hitler represented their values permeated Protestant sermons, church newspapers, and theological journals in 1933. Furthermore, this early enthusiasm was never questioned or rejected later by any significant group of church leaders in public, even though Hitler's "values" included harsh and brutal treatment of Jews and other minorities from the very beginning and such brutality steadily increased.

Individual Protestant opponents of the Nazi state emerged, but one searches almost in vain for official Protestant criticism or opposition to the regime. Two noteworthy exceptions indicate that public opposition was possible, that it did not necessarily result in punishment, and that it could produce results. The first example originated in the fall of 1934, when Reich Bishop Müller and his legal assistant, August Jäger, tried to remove bishops Wurm and Meiser and replace them with clergy from the DC. Both were placed under house arrest, and in each case parishioners attended protest services and marched in the streets. Because many of the protestors were influential Nazis, Hitler soon received warnings that Jäger and Müller had gone too far. In late October, he invited Wurm and Meiser to Berlin to reassure them of their reinstatement. He made certain that Jäger was fired and resisted only the request that Müller be replaced as well (Scholder 1988b: 225–82). Seven years later, Bishop Wurm joined the Catholic Bishop Clemens August Graf von Galen (1878–1946) of Münster in protest against the Nazi euthanasia campaign, which targeted Germans with mental and physical disabilities. Once again, parishioners demonstrated and marched in the streets, and the government backed down.

These two incidents show that protest was possible in Nazi Germany. However, similar public protests against the mistreatment of Jews and other ethnic, political, and cultural minorities or against waging aggressive war were almost non-existent.

The "Niemöller wing" of the Confessing Church raised a tentative critique of the Nazi state on two occasions and thus provided partial exceptions. However, the denouement in each case proves the rule that most Protestants supported Hitler and neither endorsed nor countenanced criticism of the Nazi state.

The first event began in 1935, when Hitler created a Ministry of Church Affairs under Hanns Kerrl (1887–1941), hoping it would reduce conflict with the churches. Large segments of the Confessing Church, including the churches under bishops Marahrens, Wurm, and Meiser, proved willing to cooperate with Kerrl. Martin Niemöller did not, and he led a rump group which formed the "Provisional Church Administration" of the Confessing Church. This was often called the "Niemöller wing" or the "Dahlemites," named for Dahlem, the place where Niemöller served as pastor. In May 1936, this group sent a letter to Hitler complaining about limitations placed upon churches by Nazi agencies and the efforts by some Nazis to "de-Christianize" Germany, and asking whether such policies represented his wishes or whether he would repudiate them. Then, uniquely in the experience of the Confessing Church, this letter also complained about the brutality of concentration camps and even criticized Nazi Jewish policy: "If Christians are pressed to adopt an antisemitic attitude as part of the National Socialist ideology, which will incite them to hate the Jews, then this is against the Christian commandment to love one's neighbor" (Conway 1968: 162).

Hitler chose not to respond. Soon, however, one of Niemöller's associates, Friedrich Weissler (1891–1937), a convert from Judaism later arrested and murdered at Sachsenhausen, smuggled a copy of the letter to Switzerland, where its publication provoked international criticism of the Third Reich. Embarrassed, the Dahlemites quickly recanted. They produced a pastoral letter in August that complained of some Nazi restraints on church activities and criticized attempts by Alfred Rosenberg (1893–1946) to make paganism a core part of Nazi ideology, but included no criticism of concentration camps or antisemitism. Bishops Marahrens, Meiser, and Wurm then issued a declaration of solidarity with the Nazi state (Conway 1968: 164).

At the highpoint of the Sudetenland crisis of 1938, the Niemöller wing of the Confessing Church prepared a liturgy of repentance that described war as a punishment. Although the Munich Pact assured that the liturgy never was used, it was attacked as disloyal, and Protestant bishops issued a statement: "We hereby declare that the circular published by the 'Provisional Church Administration' . . . is repudiated by us on religious and patriotic grounds . . . We condemn the attitude made public here most strongly and dissociate ourselves entirely from those persons responsible for this publication" (Conway 1968: 222). When war actually did break out on 1 September 1939, the German Protestant Church proclaimed its support, not just for the troops but for the aggressive purposes behind the attack: "Since yesterday our German people have been called on to fight for the land of their fathers *in order that German blood may be reunified with German blood* [emphasis added]...The Church has added to the weapons of steel her own invincible weapons from the Word of God" (Conway 1968: 234).

THE "JEWISH QUESTION"

The general support of Protestants for Hitler included a widespread willingness to accept the anti-Jewish policies of the Nazi state. Otto Dibelius (1880–1967), an important figure in the Confessing Church, wrote to fellow pastors in 1928: "I have always considered myself an antisemite. It cannot be denied that Judaism plays a leading role in all the corruptive phenomena of modern civilization." Later, defending the 1 April 1933 boycott against Jews, Dibelius wrote in Berlin's *Evangelische Sonntagsblatt*: "The last fifteen years in Germany have strengthened Jewry's influence to an extraordinary degree. The number of Jewish judges, Jewish politicians, and Jewish civil servants in influential positions has grown measurably. Public sentiment turns against this" (Gerlach 2000: 14–15).

A similar anti-Jewish argument was more systematically presented by Gerhard Kittel (1888–1948), a professor of theology at the University of Tübingen and the founding editor of an important reference work, *The Theological Dictionary of the New Testament*. Like Dibelius, Kittel accepted the Nazi claim that Jews were a problem. In a public lecture on 1 June 1933, he dismissed as impractical the possible solutions of murdering Jews or forcing their emigration to Palestine. He also condemned assimilation as a process that allowed Jews to become more secretive and dangerous. His preferred approach was to assign Jews "guest status," take away their citizenship, create restrictions that applied only to them, and remove them from every important niche within German life and culture. Kittel's remedy echoed Nazi planning documents at the time and thus anticipated the Nuremberg racial laws by more than two years (Kittel 1933).

Kittel recognized how hard his proposal would hit Jews, and he noted it might give some Christians, "one is almost inclined to say, a bad conscience" (8). Kittel assured his audience, however, "that the fight against Jews can be conducted from the platform of a conscious and clear Christianity. It is not enough to base this battle on racial points of view or current attitudes alone. *The actual, complete answer can only be found where one succeeds in giving the Jewish question a religious foundation, giving the battle against the Jews a Christian interpretation*" (8, emphasis in the original). Natural Christian sympathy for individual Jews, he said, "must never lead to a sentimental softening and paralysis" (62). Furthermore, "We must not allow ourselves to be crippled because the whole world screams at us of barbarism and a reversion to the past...How the German *Volk* regulates its own cultural affairs does not concern anyone else in the world" (39).

Various versions of Kittel's deep-seated prejudice and his rhetoric about a "Jewish question" permeated the Protestant church in 1933. Even Dietrich Bonhoeffer could not entirely escape such notions. Bonhoeffer rightly is celebrated for his defense of Jews. In April 1933, he wrote a paper calling upon Christians to bind up the wounds of Jewish victims. He even suggested that Christians might find it necessary to "place a spoke in the wheel" of the vehicle crushing Jews, an early nod to political resistance. However, in the midst of this morally perceptive statement, Bonhoeffer accepted the specious antisemitic view that Jews represented a "problem" and, in keeping with his understanding of Luther's theology of "two kingdoms," he acknowledged the right of the state to deal with the problem. He explained Jewish suffering over the centuries as God's punishment for unbelief and suggested that the real solution to the "Jewish question" would come when Jews accepted Jesus as the Messiah (Barnes in Ericksen and Heschel 1999: 110–28). It seems clear that Bonhoeffer moved past such supersessionist Christian ideas in subsequent years, as his human sympathy for Jewish suffering increased (Bethge in Godsey and Kelly 1981: 43–96). The same cannot be said for most of his co-religionists.

Several indicators suggest that Protestant anti-Jewish attitudes exhibited in 1933 continued unabated. All Protestant pastors of Jewish descent were gone by 1938, despite early enthusiasm on their behalf by the Pastors Emergency League (Lindemann 1998). By April 1939, a group of DC produced the Godesberg Declaration, a statement meant to resist the claim by some Nazis that Christian beliefs were ultimately Jewish. On the contrary, this statement asserted, Christianity always had stood in "irreconcilable opposition" to Judaism. One month later a majority of Protestant regional churches agreed to create an institute to prove the case. The "Institute for the Study and Eradication of Jewish Influence in German Religious Life" was offered a home in Eisenach, the birthplace of Martin Luther (1483–1546). Walter Grundmann (1906–1976), a former student of Kittel, became its director. This institute hosted conferences attended by dozens of Protestant theologians and hundreds of Protestant clergy. It also produced a Bible "cleansed" of the Old Testament. The resulting volume, printed in large numbers and given to at least some German troops at the front, also stripped the New Testament of all references to Jewish texts, Jewish ideas, and Jewish words. Grundmann himself took up the problem of Jesus, claiming that his origins in Hellenized Galilee suggested that Jesus was almost certainly of "Aryan" birth (Bergen 1996; Heschel 2008). This idea, often argued in the Protestant church of Nazi Germany (Hirsch 1939: 158–65), has maintained no traction since 1945. Speculative claims about the demographics of ancient Galilee can hardly refute the overwhelming evidence that Jesus was a Jew—brought to the Temple, circumcised by Jewish custom, and a teacher steeped in Jewish scripture. Yet many Protestants in Hitler's Germany accepted the strange and radical idea of an "Aryan" Jesus.

Kittel illustrates the tenacity of Protestant antisemitism during the Third Reich. As a founding member of Walter Frank's "Institute for the History of the New Germany," he shifted from normal theological scholarship to an attempt to prove how and when Jews became racially mongrelized and spiritually corrupted (Ericksen 1985). By 1943, he knew about the annihilation of Jews on the Russian front (Kittel 1945: 27). In 1944, he still described the Nazi state and the Christian church as "twin bulwarks" against the Jewish menace. He argued that Christians during the Middle Ages had accurately recognized the threat of Jews and placed them in ghettoes. The Enlightenment, with its rationalism and democratic values, then weakened the Christian church, so that now it required the Nazi Party to reinvigorate and lead Christians in a necessary battle against Jewish threats (Kittel 1944). From his prominent place in a renowned theological faculty and as the mentor of a significant number of Protestant pastors, Kittel wanted to prove that Christians could be Nazis. He never placed Jews into the category of "neighbor" to be loved. By accepting the language of a "Jewish problem" or a "Jewish question," he and his Protestant colleagues became much more inclined to rationalize Nazi behavior than to criticize it.

Gerhard Kittel's is not the entire Protestant story. Individual Christians besides Bonhoeffer and Niemöller disliked or grew to distrust the Nazi regime, and a few became "Righteous Gentiles," hiding Jews and saving Jewish lives at extreme risk to themselves. Cioma Schönhaus (b. 1922), a young Jewish man in Berlin who used his artistic skills to forge identity papers for German Jews, depended for raw material on legitimate passes dropped into a collection box by members of Martin Niemöller's congregation (Schönhaus 2007: 75–165). Elisabeth Schmitz (1893–1977), a member of the Confessing Church who acquired a special sensitivity to the plight of Christians of Jewish descent, as well as Jews, through her close friendship with one of the victims, compiled stories of individual suffering for a paper circulated among potentially receptive Confessing Church members. Schmitz recognized the moral horror of Nazi anti-Jewish policy, saw the victims as human beings, and tried to alert her fellow Protestants (Gailus 2008). Other Protestants participated in the Canaris Conspiracy or the Kreisau Circle, an opposition group centered around Helmuth James Count von Moltke (1907–1945) until his arrest in January 1944 and execution a year later (Ringshausen 2007). Nonetheless, while accounts of these heroic people are valuable to show how and why resistance became possible and to inspire contemporary readers, the grim reality remains that such courage and moral clarity was rare.

POSTWAR DISTORTION AND REPRESSION

The tendency toward postwar mythology and misrepresentation did not occur by accident. Wilhelm Niemöller (1898–1983)—Protestant pastor, younger brother of Martin, and participant in the church struggle—became perhaps the single most important historian of the *Kirchenkampf* in the first decades after 1945. He used his connections and personal experience to create an archive at his parish in Bielefeld that continues to be the locus for much research, and he edited collections of documents and wrote books about specific events and the church struggle as a whole—always as if an admiring depiction of the Confessing Church represented the entire story (Ericksen in Gailus and Lehmann 2005: 433–51).

That the Confessing Church maintained the allegiance of only 20 percent of Protestants in Nazi Germany by Niemöller's own count (in Littell and Locke 1974: 43) did not stop him from presenting this part as the whole of his subject, even when he gave his works titles such as *The Protestant Church in the Third Reich: Handbook of the Kirchenkampf* (1956). Niemöller described his approach shortly after World War II in words likely to raise red flags for readers today: "As I began to write this book, I did not think to walk with historians. . . . Rather, I wanted to testify that God still does miracles today . . . push[ing] a tired and satisfied, a battle weary and passionless church to become a confessing church" (1948: 9). Two decades later, having recognized but rejected an alternative to his spiritual, theological approach, he reaffirmed his desire to write history to glorify God (1969: 15).

Wilhelm Niemöller not only left most Protestants out of his story but also ignored his own enthusiasm for Hitler and early membership in the Nazi Party. He and Martin had fought in the rightwing *Freikorps* at the beginning of the Weimar Republic. Wilhelm had joined the Nazi Party in 1923. Although Martin was never a Nazi Party member, both brothers voted for and vigorously supported the rise of Hitler. Only disgruntlement over the regime's church politics finally tempered their enthusiasm (Schmidt 1971: 91 n. 127; Bentley 1984: 24–5, 39–43). This aspect of the Niemöller political stance never became part of the story told by Wilhelm, even though we now know, and he knew, that attraction to Hitler represented a large part of the Protestant experience. As long as Wilhelm Niemöller and the Bielefeld Archive dominated postwar church history, the story of Protestant enthusiasm for Hitler remained well out of sight.

The stance of the postwar church on Allied denazification gives more evidence of self-conscious distortion. During the war, the Allies planned a "cleansing" process, based on the assumption that Germany had become widely "nazified." Clemens Vollnhals has shown that Protestant church leaders joined the large number of Germans who complained that this policy was too harsh and broad (1989). When brought to account, virtually no German admitted to having been a "real" or committed Nazi. Nearly everyone claimed that available evidence—membership in the Nazi Party, officer status in the SS, enthusiastic statements in support of the Nazi ideology—merely represented behavior necessary to keep one's job or avoid persecution under a dictatorial regime. Protestants had never really supported Hitler but only used their position within the Nazi apparatus to try to protect Christian or academic or traditional values (Ericksen 1994).

These widespread distortions of the past came not only from individuals in their own cause but also in letters by third parties, references so uniformly favorable to the accused that they became known derisively as *Persilscheine*, "detergent certificates" designed to wash the record clean. Protestant pastors wrote such *Persilscheine* by the basketful. Ernst Klee has found startling examples. Otto Fricke (1902–1954), a Confessing Church pastor, wrote for Otmar Freiherr von Verschuer (1896–1969), the racial scientist who inspired Joseph Mengele (1911–1979) in his research on twins at Auschwitz:

He and his family belong to my confessional congregation and he supported me most energetically during the difficult years of struggle over the Confessing Church . . . Professor von Verschuer belongs among those modern natural scientists who undertake their profession in responsibility to the living God and our Lord Jesus Christ . . . People of his type and his character are suited to guide the redirection of the German academic world onto a Christian foundation and promote the rebuilding of German life. (Klee 1991: 128)

Bishop Wurm wrote on behalf of SS *Hauptsturmführer* Karl Sommer, a man sentenced to death for his crimes. Wurm noted Sommer's six years as a member of the Organization of Young Christian Men in Cologne, ignored his withdrawal from the church in 1933, and accentuated his reading of the New Testament while incarcerated by the Allies: "I must therefore believe that Sommer, if he really committed crimes worthy of death, must have done so under the pressure of especially unfortunate circumstances, so that . . . as a believing Christian [he] is worthy of a show of mercy" (Klee 1991: 101). Most Protestant leaders opposed the entire concept of denazification, claiming that it would remove good Christians from positions of authority and leave Germany in the hands of socialists and communists. When Bishop Wurm protested against the harshness of Allied policy, he was, among other things, defending his own son, who had falsified his *Fragebogen* to hide an enthusiastic association with the Nazi Party dating back to 1922 (Klee 1991: 15).

Throughout the process of denazification, Protestants ignored the seriousness of German crimes and regarded their pastors as defenders of the German people against former enemies unjustly trying to inflict punishment. Although one document produced by the *Evangelische Kirche in Deutschland* in October 1945, the Stuttgart Declaration of Guilt, superficially suggests otherwise, a closer look leads to a different conclusion. First, the Declaration was forced upon German Protestants by the World Council of Churches as a precondition for receiving assistance and being allowed a place in future ecumenical activities. Also, the men who signed this document, including Martin Niemöller, were soon chastised in public settings all across Germany for taking the side of the enemy. Finally, the Declaration's language is problematic. Placing the church alongside the German people within a "community of suffering" and a "solidarity of guilt," it claims much in terms of resistance and offers little in terms of repentance: "Certainly we have fought for many long years in the name of Jesus Christ against the spirit which found its horrible expression in the National Socialist regime of violence, but we charge ourselves for not having confessed more courageously, prayed more faithfully, believed more joyously, and loved more fervently" (Besier and Sauter 1985: 62). One finds no mention of enthusiastic support for the Nazi regime and no word about crimes against Jews.

THE RISE OF CRITICAL SCHOLARSHIP

A few decades after the collapse of the Nazi state, histories of the *Kirchenkampf* began to be less defensive, less rooted in the church itself, and more based on extensive archival research (Conway 1968; Helmreich 1979; Scholder 1988a). Such authors aspired to the claim, "Nowhere have I spared anything, but have named blindness and lies, arrogance, stupidity and opportunism for what they were" (Scholder 1988a: x). But the sympathy for the church of these scholars led to certain interpretive decisions. The most important of these were to emphasize Nazi "persecution" of Christians rather than their complicity and to suggest that Christians were so targeted by the Nazi ideology that they were likely to be next in line after Jews for annihilation. Is that assertion credible? Jews suffered a thoroughgoing and relentless rhetorical, legal, and then physical attack, whereas Christians suffered some criticism from the Nazi theoretician Alfred Rosenberg and others, plus some restrictions upon church activities. Some Christians resisted Nazism and were imprisoned and killed for doing so, but at the same time, the Nazi state collected taxes for the church, paid the churches' bills, continued to fund theological faculties at universities, and maintained religious education in the schools. The attraction of highlighting and claiming Christian victimhood is clear but suspect: depicting Christians as among the victimized separates them from the perpetrators and bystanders.

Scholarship since the 1970s has tended to associate Christians more and more with the perpetrators. The anti-Jewish role of Kittel drew early attention (Ericksen 1977; Siegele-Wenschkewitz 1978 and 1980), as did the pro-Hitler enthusiasms of three major Protestant theologians (Ericksen 1985). These works showed that support for Nazi ideology ran deep among the heirs of Martin Luther and many students of the German theological tradition. Local studies of the Hanoverian and Bavarian Protestant churches discovered how widespread Nazi enthusiasm got washed out of sight in the process of "self-cleansing" allowed to the churches in lieu of denazification (Besier 1986; Vollnhals 1989). Several studies have shown that the DC cannot simply be dismissed as a minor, heretical fringe group (Bergen 1996), that one of the DC tropes, the "Aryan Jesus," demonstrates the embeddedness of prejudice against Jews within the Christian tradition (Heschel 2008), and that support for Nazi ideas ran deep among Protestants in Berlin, a city long considered a stronghold of Martin Niemöller and his supporters (Gailus 2001).

The most important lessons for historians of this topic since 1945 seem to mandate a methodology long known but only sometimes practiced: a careful and comprehensive reading of sources, a willingness to be honest, and a refusal to sweep unpleasant evidence under the carpet. Those commitments plus energetic research should increase understanding of how Germans committed genocide against European Jews and the role of Protestant Christians in that process.

References

AELKZ (1933a). "Kirche und Nationalsozialismus." *Allgemeine Evangelisch-Lutherische Kirchenzeitung* 66/14: 328.

——(1933b). "Kirchliche Nachrichten." *Allgemeine Evangelisch-Lutherische Kirchenzeitung* 66/16: 379.

——(1933c). "Wochenschau." *Allgemeine Evangelisch-Lutherische Kirchenzeitung* 66/18: 138.

ALTHAUS, P. (1934). *Die deutsche Stunde der Kirche*. Göttingen: Vandenhoek & Ruprecht.

BENTLEY, J. (1984). *Martin Niemöller 1892–1984*. New York: Free Press.

BERGEN, D. (1996). *Twisted Cross: The German Christian Movement in the Third Reich*. Chapel Hill, NC: University of North Carolina Press.

BESIER, G. (1986). *"Selbstreinigung" unter britischer Besatzungsherrschaft: Die Evangelisch-Lutherische Landeskirche Hannovers und ihr Landesbischof Marahrens, 1945–1947*. Göttingen: Vandenhoek & Ruprecht.

——and SAUTER, G. (1985). *Wie Christen ihre Schuld bekennen: Die Stuttgarter Erklärung 1945*. Göttingen: Vandenhoek & Ruprecht.

BETHGE, E. (1970). *Dietrich Bonhoeffer: Theologian, Christian, Contemporary*. New York: Collins.

COCHRANE, A. (1962). *The Church's Confession under Hitler*. Philadelphia, PA: Westminster Press.

CONWAY, J. (1968). *The Nazi Persecution of the Churches*. New York: Basic Books.

ERICKSEN, R. (1977). "Theologian in the Third Reich: The Case of Gerhard Kittel." *Journal of Contemporary History* 12: 595–622.

——(1985). *Theologians under Hitler: Gerhard Kittel, Paul Althaus and Emanuel Hirsch*. New Haven, CT: Yale University Press.

——(1994). "Religion und Nationalsozialismus im Spiegel der Entnazifizierungsakten der Göttinger Universität." *Kirchliche Zeitgeschichte* 7/1: 83–101.

——and HESCHEL, S. (eds.) (1999). *Betrayal: German Churches and the Holocaust*. Minneapolis, MN: Fortress Press.

GAILUS, M. (2001). *Protestantismus und Nationalsozialismus: Studien zur nationalsozialistischen Durchdringung des protestantischen Sozialmilieus in Berlin*. Cologne: Böhlau Verlag.

——(ed.) (2008). *Elisabeth Schmitz und ihre Denkschrift gegen die Judenverfolgung: Konturen einer vergessenen Biographie (1893–1977)*. Berlin: Wichern-Verlag.

——and Lehmann, H. (eds.) (2005). *Nationalprotestantische Mentalitäten: Konturen, Entwicklungslinien und Umbrüche eines Weltbildes.* Göttingen: Vandenhoeck & Ruprecht.

Gerlach, W. (2000). *And the Witnesses Were Silent: The Confessing Church and the Persecution of the Jews* (German orig. 1987). Trans. and ed. V. J. Barnett. Lincoln, NE: University of Nebraska Press.

Godsey, J. and Kelly, G. (eds.) (1981). *Ethical Responsibility: Bonhoeffer's Legacy to the Churches.* New York: Edwin Mellen Press.

Helmreich, E. (1979). *The German Churches under Hitler.* Detroit, MI: Wayne State University Press.

Heschel, S. (2008). *The Aryan Jesus: Christian Theologians and the Bible in Nazi Germany.* Princeton, NJ: Princeton University Press.

Hirsch, E. (1939). *Das Wesen des Christentums.* Weimar: Deutsche Christen Verlag.

Kittel, G. (1933). *Die Judenfrage.* Stuttgart: W. Kohlhammer Verlag.

——(1944). "Das Rassenproblem der Spätantik und das Frühchristentum," a lecture delivered at the University of Vienna, 15 June 1944; typescript in the theological library at Tübingen University.

——(1945). "Meine Verteidigung," a typescript by Kittel dated June 1945, copies of which were sent to friends abroad. I am indebted to the late Dr. Herman Preus, Luther Seminary, St. Paul, MN, for access to the document. An expanded version dated Nov/Dec 1946 is in the Tübingen University Archive.

Klee, E. (1991). *Persilscheine und falsche Pässe: Wie die Kirchen den Nazis halfen.* Frankfurt am Main: Fischer Taschenbuch Verlag.

Koonz, C. (2003). *The Nazi Conscience.* Cambridge, MA: Harvard University Press.

Lehmann, H. (1998). *Protestantische Weltsichten: Transformationen seit dem 17. Jahrhundert.* Göttingen: Vandenhoek & Ruprecht.

Lindemann, G. (1998). *"Typisch Jüdisch": Die Stellung der Ev.-luth. Landeskirche Hannovers zu Antijudaismus, Judenfeindschaft und Antisemitismus 1918–1949.* Berlin: Duncker & Humblot.

Littell, F. and Locke, H. (eds.) (1974). *The German Church Struggle and the Holocaust.* Detroit, MI: Wayne State University Press.

Niemöller, W. (1948). *Kampf und Zeugnis der Bekennenden Kirche.* Bielefeld: Bechauf Verlag.

——(1956). *Die Evangelische Kirche im Dritten Reich: Handbuch des Kirchenkampfes.* Bielefeld: Bechauf Verlag.

——(1969). *Wort und Tat im Kirchenkampf: Beiträgen zur neuesten Kirchengeschichte.* Munich: Kaiser Verlag.

Ringshausen, G. (2007). *Widerstand und christlicher Glaube angesichts des Nationalsozialismus.* Berlin: LIT Verlag.

Schmidt, J. (1971). *Martin Niemöller im Kirchenkampf.* Hamburg: Leibniz Verlag.

Scholder, K. (1988a). *The Churches and the Third Reich.* Vol. 1, *Preliminary History and the Time of Illusions 1918–1934* (German orig. 1977). Philadelphia, PA: Fortress Press.

——(1988b). *The Churches and the Third Reich.* Vol. 2, *The Year of Disillusionment 1934: Barmen and Rome* (German orig. 1985). Philadelphia, PA: Fortress Press.

Schönhaus, C. (2007). *The Forger.* Cambridge, MA: Da Capo Press.

SIEGELE-WENSCHKEWITZ, L. (1978). "Die Evangelisch-theologische Fakultät Tübingen in den Anfangsjahren des Dritten Reichs II. Gerhard Kittel und die Judenfrage." *Zeitschrift für Theologie und Kirche* 4: 53–80.

——(1980). *Neutestamentliche Wissenschaft vor der Judenfrage: Gerhard Kittels theologische Arbeit im Wandel deutscher Geschichte.* Munich: Kaiser Verlag.

STONE, D. (ed) (2004). *The Historiography of the Holocaust.* London: Palgrave Macmillan.

VOLLNHALS, C. (1989). *Evangelische Kirche und Entnazifizierung, 1945–1949: Die Last der nationalsozialistischen Vergangenheit.* Munich: R. Oldenbourg.

OTHER SUGGESTED READING

BARNETT, V. (1992). *For the Soul of the People: Protestant Protest against Hitler.* New York: Oxford University Press.

HAYNES, S. (2006). *The Bonhoeffer Legacy: Post-Holocaust Perspectives.* Minneapolis, MN: Fortress Press.

HOCKENOS, M. (2004). *A Church Divided: German Protestants Confront the Nazi Past.* Bloomington, IN: Indiana University Press.

HOLTSCHNEIDER, K. (2001). *German Protestants Remember the Holocaust: Theology and the Construction of Collective Memory.* New Brunswick, NJ: Transaction Publishers.

JANTZEN, K. (2008). *Faith and Fatherland: Parish Politics in Hitler's Germany.* Minneapolis, MN: Fortress Press.

RUBENSTEIN, R. and ROTH, J. (2003). *Approaches to Auschwitz: The Holocaust and Its Legacy.* Rev. edn. Louisville, KY: Westminster John Knox Press.

STEIGMANN-GALL, R. (2004). *The Holy Reich: Nazi Conceptions of Christianity, 1919–1945.* Cambridge: Cambridge University Press.

CHAPTER 17

....

THE ALLIES

....

SHLOMO ARONSON

BETWEEN 1933 and 1945, the interaction of German policies and Allied responses to them—primarily those of Britain, the United States, and the Soviet Union—drove European Jews into the Holocaust. Although Nazi Germany bore primary responsibility for the genocide, the Allies' motives and calculations led to acts of omission and commission that reinforced and channeled the Third Reich's escalating violence against European Jewry. Particularly important in shaping Allied behavior were three sets of circumstances: the evolving nature of Nazi Germany's policy toward the Jews, which left the Allies guessing during the 1930s about its scope and purpose; the global scale of the conflict with Nazi Germany, which introduced geopolitical considerations into Allied policy regarding Nazi persecution, notably the need to maintain Muslim support; and the emergence of the alliance between the western powers and the Soviet Union, which added grounds for Allied caution in responding to the plight of the European Jews.

Attention to German planning and policy is a precondition for understanding the dilemmas that Nazi Germany's anti-Jewish posture created for the Allies. The Nazi regime sought continuously to make political use of the "Jewish question." Both before and after World War II began, the Germans repeatedly invoked the Jewish issue as a means of driving wedges between their former enemies in World War I (notably Britain, France, and the United States) and their respective governments and populations. Nazi propaganda incessantly depicted these states as dominated by "world Jewry" and seized on every humanitarian statement or intervention on behalf of Jews as proof of the allegation. In other words, Nazi propaganda about the Jews maneuvered the Allies gradually and deftly into a "trap" that left them frequently concluding that their best course regarding the persecution of the Jews was to do nothing and change the subject.

In assessing how the Allies dealt with these challenges, historians must take into account when credible information about the "Final Solution" was available to the Allies and how it was disseminated and processed in their huge bureaucracies and among policy makers wrestling with the global scale of World War II (Laqueur 1980; Gilbert 1981; Weinberg 2005). Even after the Allies realized that Nazi Germany intended the destruction of the European Jews, however, the preferred terminology for expressing Allied war aims—"freedom" or stopping the Axis bid for world domination—was too universal to allow emphasis on the plight of Jews. When the Nazis kept depicting Allied behavior as reflecting enslavement to Jewish interests, the Allies redoubled their efforts to disprove that charge, further universalizing the rhetoric of their war objectives. Meanwhile, Nazi Germany's military control of Europe enabled it to carry out genocide without significant Allied interference because most of the murders took place out of the reach of Allied forces and while they were still on the defensive. But even after the tide of war turned, the Allies found making the rescue of Jews a priority too impractical and risky, as well as potentially politically counterproductive.

POLICIES THAT DOOMED THE JEWS

Arguably, the Holocaust began with Adolf Hitler's (1889–1945) forced emigration policy, which commenced with his appointment as Chancellor of Germany in 1933 and intensified in the wake of the November pogrom in 1938. Until late 1940, this policy had two interrelated goals: forcing Jews to find refuge wherever they could and exporting antisemitism (Aronson 2004). The assumption behind the second goal was that the Third Reich would benefit whether or not western nations admitted Jewish refugees. If they did, that action would increase hatred of Jews in the rest of the population, and if the doors were barred, the resulting clamor by resident Jews would set off a public debate that could be used to foster antisemitism. In particular, the Nazis calculated that a flow of Jewish refugees into Palestine, which had already prompted the Arab rebellion of 1936–39, would add to Britain's difficulties with the Arabs and possibly with Muslims generally, thus fanning British antisemitism. At the very least, British officials in London and the Middle East might conclude that providing a haven in Britain or Palestine for Jewish refugees would impede mobilizing the British people against German expansionism.

German calculations did not control the situation entirely, but along with lingering economic problems from the Great Depression and currents of antisemitism in the west, Nazi policy and propaganda produced responses from London and Washington that were unfriendly to the interests of Jewish refugees. The British saved some Jewish children in the *Kindertransport* program, but Britain, including the British government of Palestine, and the United States refused to admit Jews in large numbers during most of their moments of dire prewar need, when rescue was much easier than it became during wartime (Wyman 1984; Kushner 1989; Dinnerstein 1994). The exception that proved the rule came in the six months after the November pogrom in Germany and Austria, when the U.S. and U.K. each admitted fully half of the Jewish refugees who made it to each country between 1933 and 1939.

The Nazi policy of forced emigration continued after war began on 1 September 1939. With the capitulation of France in June 1940, Hitler expected the British to yield and offered them as "racial brethren" what he thought were generous terms: retention of most of their empire in return for becoming his vassals. This "offer" was coupled in Nazi planning with a far-reaching, violent "solution" to the "Jewish question": the deportation of the millions of Jews already under Hitler's control to the island of Madagascar, where their hostage status would guarantee the good behavior—neutrality—of their fellow Jews in America.

Together with the Allies' misgivings that immigrant Jews might include willing or coerced espionage agents, the potential use of Jews as hostages contributed to an Allied reluctance to move directly and explicitly against the Nazis' anti-Jewish posture. At the same time, Sir Alexander Cadogan (1884–1968), Permanent Under-Secretary of State in the British Foreign Office, attested to the impact of Nazi propaganda when he remarked that it was "necessary, at all costs, to avoid anything that would give strength to the Jews' War accusations" (Kushner 1989: 157). Nonetheless, Hitler scarcely got his way with the British, who wanted none of his "offer," took the fight to him with a naval blockade and bombings of Germany, and used American aid to avoid capitulation. When domination of Britain eluded him, Hitler decided to destroy the Soviet Union, which he considered not only an untrustworthy ally but also an obstacle to his territorial aims. Conquest of the USSR would permit the elimination of the standing threat that its Jewish population represented, a prospect made more appealing by the realization that the American commitment to the British largely negated the value of holding Jews hostage. As a result, between the fall of 1941 and the early months of 1942, the "Final Solution" was applied, first, to the Jews of the USSR and, then, extended to all of the European Jews.

With the United States' entry into the war in December 1941, the world war that Hitler had forecasted in early 1939 became a reality, bringing with it further issues for the Allies regarding Jews. In August 1941, for instance, British intelligence intercepted numerous field reports from Einsatzgruppen units and thus learned of mass killings of Jews in Soviet-occupied territories. Prime Minister Winston Churchill (1874–1965) publicly referred to the mass shootings in the Soviet Union as early as 24 August 1941, without, however, identifying Jews as victims (Breitman

1998: 88–109). This statement was followed by a deliberate refusal to disseminate the information, partly for fear of revealing how it had been acquired and prompting the Germans to change their codes and transmission methods. In any case, no further public statements about these matters were made by the western Allies until late in 1942.

On 17 December 1942, the British Foreign Secretary Anthony Eden (1897–1977) told the House of Commons about the mass murder of Jews by the Germans and read an Allied statement condemning the "bestial" extermination and promising to hold the perpetrators accountable. In response, the House rose for a minute of silence in respect for the victims. Nevertheless, Eden's utterance "was regarded as a mistake by the Foreign Office, for it raised public expectations of government action in aiding the Jews of Europe, when no such policy was intended" (Wasserstein 1979: 183–221). Reflecting establishment concerns, British officials worried about how to manage public opinion that encompassed both antisemitism and sympathy for the beleaguered Jews. Such figures therefore both displayed humane concern and decided against more demonstrative measures in order to avoid domestic repercussions, forestall turmoil with Arabs, and preclude trouble with Joseph Stalin (1879–1953), who was known to be worried that the western Allies might negotiate separately with the Germans, possibly under Jewish pressure. To officials such as Eden, giving greater attention to the Jewish plight entailed unwarranted risks, ranging from having to make concessions to Hitler or his allies to creating the impression that the war was being fought primarily on behalf of Jews.

Several British politicians made their views clear in this regard. In a letter to Chaim Weizmann (1874–1952), president of the World Zionist Organization, dated 4 March 1943, Ronald I. Campbell (1890–1983), a British diplomat in Washington, DC, responded on behalf of the ambassador, Lord Halifax (1881–1959), and Foreign Secretary Eden to Weizmann's offer to facilitate the emigration to Palestine of 70,000 Romanian Jews in exchange for a large payment to the Romanian government. Campbell wrote as follows:

His Majesty's Government has no evidence to show whether or not the Rumanian proposal is meant to be taken seriously. But if it is, it would still be a piece of blackmail which, if successful, would open up the endless prospect, on the part of Germany and her satellites in Southeastern Europe, of unloading at a given price all their unwanted nationals on overseas countries. (Central Zionist Archive, Jerusalem, file S25/7570)

Campbell went on to say that Britain, in conjunction with others, would continue to give earnest consideration regarding all "practical means" to alleviate the refugees' circumstances so long as those steps were consistent with the success of the war effort, but that acceding to blackmail did not meet that test. He added that his political superiors saw an Allied victory as the only feasible answer to the humanitarian problems raised by the German domination of Europe, of which the Jewish question was but one aspect.

The trap that gripped the Jews was evident: Among the western Allies, the Jews were viewed as a potential obstacle to destroying the German machine, even though that machine was bent on their utter destruction. Among the Nazis and their allies, the Jews were blamed for the western effort to destroy the German Reich. As the trap's jaws continued to close, the Jews paid the price.

The Soviets also felt compelled to respond to German propaganda that linked Bolshevism and Jewry by "proving" that theirs was not a "Jewish war." Thus, Stalin muted attention to the "Final Solution," although the fate of Jews in the occupied USSR was mentioned officially from time to time. Both during and after the war, Soviet commentary lumped the Jewish dead into the vast number of victims of Nazi atrocities and treated Jews as just further examples of those who suffered under Nazi brutality. To the western Allies, especially the Americans, who were determined to maintain the grand alliance with Stalin, Soviet censorship of the Jewish issue dictated, among other things, extra caution in the west about possible deals with Nazi Germany to rescue Jews.

British policy continued to reflect such attitudes. By the end of 1943, when military victory began to appear more likely, the British allowed some Jews who had escaped occupied Europe on their own to enter Palestine. At that time, Churchill created a cabinet committee to discuss the future of that part of the Middle East (Porath 1985: 235). But after radical Zionist groups launched attacks on British forces in Palestine, the committee ceased activity. Meanwhile, rescue efforts undertaken by the Zionists were perceived by Allied intelligence agencies as threats to the united war effort, and, indeed, Nazi overtures in the spring of 1944 to exchange Hungarian Jews in return for war materiel and other goods were ploys to split the Allies (Aronson 2004: 227–47).

FRANKLIN D. ROOSEVELT, THE JEWS, AND THE U.S. WAR REFUGEE BOARD

Hitler, Churchill, and Stalin played key roles in the Holocaust, and so did the American president Franklin D. Roosevelt (1882–1945), who also found himself snared by the "Jewish question." His public criticism of Nazi Germany's prewar persecution of Jews produced no direct intervention, and his various attempts to deal with Jewish refugees and to relieve the Jewish plight, including international deliberations at Evian (1938) and Bermuda (1943), reflected ambiguous commitment and produced scant success (Feingold 1970; Wyman 1984; Breitman and Kraut 1987).

Roosevelt's unwillingness or inability to do more with regard to the "Jewish question" did not stem entirely from American antisemitism, although it was strong and vocal in the 1930s and extended significantly into the military (Bendersky 2000). Dilemmas pertaining to the Nazis themselves were also relevant. If Roosevelt openly addressed the rescue issue and embraced that cause, Hitler's likely responses had to be anticipated and taken into account. Nazi rhetoric alleged that Jews had brought on the war and that Roosevelt was their tool. If he really wanted to curb Nazi Germany's harsh treatment of the Jews, the Allies should stop their war against the Third Reich and come to terms with Hitler. That outcome was unthinkable because it opened the door for German territorial expansion and even world domination, but the Nazi propaganda line made Roosevelt cautious about giving Jewish affairs priority. He was trapped if he made concessions to Hitler on behalf of Jews, but if he fought openly to defend Jews, the allegation that he was waging a Jewish war could gain traction. That trap had to be avoided to keep the home front supportive of the war effort. Explicit concern for the Jews thus had to take a back seat in Roosevelt's wartime policies. Therefore, among other things, restrictive immigration policies remained in place.

Roosevelt had no intention of demanding less than unconditional surrender from Nazi Germany. Nor would he endanger the coalition with the Soviets or risk unnecessary domestic controversy. Roosevelt was well aware that he and his administration were perceived as pro-Jewish by some American critics. The New Deal, after all, was often called the "Jew Deal." Hence, direct negotiations with the Germans for the purpose of rescuing Jews were out of the question, and Jewish issues, including Zionist initiatives for a Jewish state in Palestine, were sidelined in favor of insistence that the key objective was to win the war. As circumstances permitted or required, that objective was also touted as the best way to serve Jewish interests. These policies and outcomes were expedient for Roosevelt's management of the political situation at home, relations with the Allies, and the conduct of the war overseas, but they gave little comfort to the Jews.

Meanwhile, Jews had relatively little influence on American foreign and military policies. But when Jews organized rescue attempts of their own, those initiatives also got little support from the American and other Allied governments. Anti-semitism, reluctance to arouse Arabs in and around Palestine, and the Allied war aim of completely destroying the Third Reich combined to make aid for Jewish self-rescue efforts almost anathema. Separate Jewish efforts to deal with Germany or Germans in order to save Jews were regarded by the Allies as endangering strategic-political priorities, which to some extent had been dictated by the enemy, especially through allegations of Jewish responsibility for the war (Aronson 2004).

As the destruction of the European Jews became increasingly apparent, Roosevelt probably did not "abandon" the Jews (Wyman 1984). Instead, he may have thought that by leaving the Jewish catastrophe unmentioned in public and not intervening in favor of the Jews in imprudent ways, he was actually serving their cause while advancing his own priorities. Roosevelt may have believed that if he emphasized the Jewish plight in public, he would only arouse more Nazi wrath, further hurt the Jews, and confirm for the German home front Hitler's claims that the war was being fought by the Allies "for the Jews." Certainly the Nazis' objective in tainting the war as "Jewish" was in large measure to cement their home front. Roosevelt may have calculated that helping to encourage the German home front could only create problems for him at home, within the grand alliance, and even on the battlefield, where the war might be needlessly prolonged.

American opinions were indeed various and conflicting—some expressed deep concern about the escalating violence against the Jews, many others did not, and still others loudly articulated antisemitic conspiracy theories centering on the president himself. If Roosevelt appeared unmoved by such attacks, his posture regarding issues such as the rescue of Jews suggests that anti-Jewish pressures influenced the priority he assigned to maintaining a consensus about the war at home, ensuring his continuance in office in order to achieve victory and Nazi Germany's unconditional surrender, sustaining the grand alliance, and working to secure a better world order.

Roosevelt's posture changed somewhat in early 1944. Throughout World War II, the administrators of U.S. immigration law tightly restricted entry to refugees for reasons that included fear of spies and saboteurs, xenophobia, and antisemitism (Wyman 1984). As a result, between December 1941 and May 1945, only 21,000 refugees entered the United States, a total that equaled only 10 percent of the allotted quotas of immigrants from all Axis-controlled countries during that period (Wyman 1984: 136). Treasury department officials John W. Pehle (1909–1999), Randolph Paul (1890–1956), and Josiah DuBois, Jr. (1913–1983) documented the Department of State's foot dragging concerning the predicament of the European Jews. DuBois drafted the key document on Christmas Day 1943 under the title "Report to the Secretary on the Acquiescence of This Government in the Murder of the Jews." Secretary of the Treasury Henry Morgenthau, Jr. (1891–1967) toned down the heading and submitted a "Personal Report to the President" in mid-January 1944. His hand forced, Roosevelt issued an executive order on 22 January 1944, which established the War Refugee Board (WRB).

The WRB's mandate was to provide relief and assistance, consistent with the American war effort, that would help people whose lives were threatened by enemy persecution. Underfunded and relatively toothless though it was, the WRB had a role in rescuing a significant number of Jews, particularly through interventions on behalf of Hungarian Jews in 1944. The WRB's impotence had various causes. Other American agencies gave the Board little practical support because they had different war priorities and feared either trouble with the Soviets or German exploitation of rescue efforts. Indeed, the destruction of the Hungarian Jews was accompanied by unprecedented German overtures aimed at exchanging Hungarian Jews for Allied goods or even peace itself (Bauer 1994). The western Allies correctly interpreted these German initiatives as further attempts to drive wedges between them and the Soviets and rejected the proffered deals. A corollary of those decisions was that Jews who attempted to facilitate such negotiations were declared to be "enemy tools" and "enemy agents" (Aronson in Bankier 2006: 65–104).

The WRB explored and advocated the bombing of the rail routes to the killing center at Auschwitz. Scholarly debate about the feasibility of this undertaking continues (Neufeld and Berenbaum 2000). The Allies had air superiority in the region, as well as aerial reconnaissance photos of Auschwitz-Birkenau, and bombed the IG Farben factory at nearby Monowitz during the summer of 1944, but decided to leave the death camp alone, arguing that attacking it would represent a diversion of military resources from the war effort and endanger the lives of the inmates.

As the war ground to a close, recurrent Allied radio broadcasts threatening war criminals with postwar punishment did have an intimidating effect on the German personnel, especially at Auschwitz in the autumn of 1944. But the Allies worried that Hitler's last stand might jeopardize the lives of Allied POWs and entail protracted acts of vengeance. These concerns, intensified in part by the expectation that assistance to Jews would enrage the Nazis further, also militated against direct action in support of Jews, indicating that, to the very end, the Allies never made relief for Jews a high priority, let alone a foremost concern.

CONCLUSION

Dated 29 April 1945, the day before Hitler committed suicide in his Berlin bunker, the Führer's "Political Testament" denied that he had wanted war, blamed the Jews for starting and prolonging the conflict, predicted a rebirth of National Socialism, urged the German people to uphold the race laws, and defended the "Final Solution" by urging continued merciless resistance against "international Jewry." Hitler had entrapped the Allies and the Jews in more ways than one. Despite his defeat and the Allies' triumph, the war he waged on the Jewish "front," a war in which the Allies were complicit protagonists, made him, even in death, hugely victorious.

REFERENCES

ARONSON, S. (2004). *Hitler, the Allies, and the Jews*. Cambridge: Cambridge University Press.
BANKIER, D. (ed.) (2006). *Secret Intelligence and the Holocaust*. New York: Enigma Books.
BAUER, Y. (1994). *Jews for Sale?: Nazi–Jewish Negotiations, 1933–1945*. New Haven, CT: Yale University Press.
BENDERSKY, J. (2000). *The "Jewish Threat": Anti-Semitic Politics of the U.S. Army*. New York: Basic Books.

BREITMAN, R. (1998). *Official Secrets: What the Nazis Planned, What the British and Americans Knew*. New York: Hill and Wang.

——and KRAUT, A. (1987). *American Refugee Policy and European Jewry, 1933–1945*. Bloomington, IN: Indiana University Press.

DINNERSTEIN, L. (1994). *Antisemitism in America*. New York: Oxford University Press.

FEINGOLD, H. (1970). *The Politics of Rescue: The Roosevelt Administration and the Holocaust, 1938–1945*. New Brunswick, NJ: Rutgers University Press.

GILBERT, M. (1981). *Auschwitz and the Allies*. New York: Holt, Rinehart, and Winston.

KUSHNER, T. (1989). *The Persistence of Prejudice: Antisemitism in British Society during the Second World War*. Manchester: Manchester University Press.

LAQUEUR, W. (1980). *The Terrible Secret: Suppression of the Truth about Hitler's "Final Solution"*. Boston: Little, Brown.

NEUFELD, M. and BERENBAUM, M. (eds.) (2000). *The Bombing of Auschwitz: Should the Allies Have Attempted It?* New York: St. Martin's Press.

PORATH, Y. (1985). *In the Test of Political Praxis: Palestine, Arab Unity and British Policy 1930–1945*. Jerusalem: Yad Itzhak Ben-Zvi.

WASSERSTEIN, B. (1979). *Britain and the Jews of Europe 1939–1945*. London: Institute of Jewish Affairs.

WEINBERG, G. (2005). *A World at Arms: A Global History of World War II*. 2nd edn. Cambridge: Cambridge University Press.

WYMAN, D. (1984). *The Abandonment of the Jews: America and the Holocaust 1941–1945*. New York: Pantheon.

OTHER SUGGESTED READING

ABZUG, R. (1999). *America Views the Holocaust, 1933–1945: A Brief Documentary History*. New York: St. Martin's Press.

ARAD, Y. (2009). *The Holocaust in the Soviet Union*. Lincoln, NE: University of Nebraska Press.

ARONSON, S.(ed.) (2002). *New Records—New Perspectives: Lectures on the Holocaust, the Birth of Israel, and the Contemporary Middle East: Published in Honor of Emmanuel Sella*. Sedeh Boker: Ben-Gurion University of the Negev Press.

BESCHLOSS, M. (2002). *The Conquerors: Roosevelt, Truman, and the Destruction of Hitler's Germany*. New York: Simon & Schuster.

BREITMAN, R., GODA, N., NAFTALI, T., and WOLFE, R. (2005). *U.S. Intelligence and the Nazis*. Cambridge: Cambridge University Press.

CHEYETTE, B. (1993). *Constructions of "the Jew" in English Literature and Society: Racial Representations, 1875–1945*. Cambridge: Cambridge University Press.

COHEN, M. (1985). *Churchill and the Jews*. London: Frank Cass.

DALLEK, R. (1995). *Franklin D. Roosevelt and American Foreign Policy, 1932–1945*. New York: Oxford University Press.

HAMEROW, T. (2008). *Why We Watched: Europe, America, and the Holocaust*. New York: W. W. Norton.

REES, L. (2008). *World War II behind Closed Doors: Stalin, the Nazis and the West*. New York: Pantheon.

CHAPTER 18

··

GYPSIES, HOMOSEXUALS, AND SLAVS

··

JOHN CONNELLY

GYPSIES, homosexuals, and Slavs were among the most victimized groups in Nazi-ruled Europe, yet they were not targeted in the major tracts of Nazi ideology, such as *Mein Kampf*. How was that possible? How did the Nazis go from an apparent ideological vacuum to methodical destruction? What caused Party leaders to incarcerate and murder members of these groups by the thousand? If one sets these cases against the background of the "Final Solution of the Jewish Question," they appear especially baffling. A Jew among the Nazi leaders was inconceivable, yet several leading figures in the Nazi movement were homosexual, including the movement's top paramilitary leader, Ernst Röhm (1887–1934), the only Nazi so intimate with Hitler that he used the informal *Du*. Röhm viewed the Nazi seizure of power as a revolution against petty-bourgeois sexual mores. In the case of Gypsies—this word is used interchangeably with "Roma and Sinti" here—supposed "pure-bloods" were thought to possess particular racial value, but Gypsy "hybrids" (*Mischlinge*) were thought to be a mortal threat, which was exactly the opposite of Nazi racial logic regarding Jews. Perhaps most confusing was the victimization of Slavs, which was highly variable. At one extreme, the Bulgarians were treated as an ally and spared German occupation; at the other, the Russians suffered brutal invasion and policies that aimed at enslavement. Czechs experienced a relatively mild occupation, while German behavior in Poland cost two million ethnic Poles their lives (Friszke 2003: 50). Slovakia and Croatia were granted "independent" puppet states, the first nation-states these peoples had ever known.

This chapter attempts to account for these apparent incongruities. According to rough estimates, up to 500,000 Roma and Sinti lost their lives as a result of Nazi policies (Bastian 2001: 79). Victims among Slavic peoples of the Nazi racial crusade went into many millions, with the total number of dead Soviet citizens alone (including non-Slavs) reaching some 25 million (Barber and Harrison in Suny 2006: 217). Some 50,000 persons were convicted of homosexuality under the Nazi regime, of whom 5,000 to 15,000 were sent to concentration camps (Jellonnek 1990: 328).

"Gypsies"

Roma and Sinti, originally from the Punjab region of north India, came to Germany in the late fifteenth century. Thereafter, most of them lived itinerant lives and protected a distinctive culture. In 1933, the approximately 35,000 Gypsies in Germany were perhaps the country's most vilified ethnicity, primarily because their ideas of hygiene and means of subsistence differed substantially from those of the majority population. Even before the Nazis came to power, German Gypsies attracted the attention of experts on criminology and so-called racial science. Theories emerged asserting their racial inferiority, and laws targeted Gypsies for discrimination, the most infamous example being the Bavarian "Law for Combating Gypsies, Vagabonds and Work-shy" of 1926. Beginning in 1929, this law was taken as a federal norm, and other German states developed their own restrictions on Gypsies' freedom of movement and choices of profession, even though these provisions contradicted the constitution of the Weimar Republic (Wippermann 2005: 31).

The history of the Roma and Sinti under Nazi rule seems to validate a "functionalist" interpretation of the origins of mass murder. No signs of a preconceived "intention" to kill appear in the writings of Adolf Hitler (1889–1945) or Alfred Rosenberg (1893–1946), the man regarded as the Nazi Party's chief ideologue. From 1933 onward, anti-Gypsy initiatives emerged from numerous agencies, above all the police and SS, but also the academic community. A leading student of the Nazi persecution of the Gypsies concludes that it never developed into a Europe-wide plan to do away with all of them (Lewy 2000).

Yet even if the Nazi program of 1920 and Hitler's *Mein Kampf* fail to mention Gypsies, no one in the Party doubted that they constituted an "inferior" people that should not intermarry with Germans. In 1935, medical doctor Robert Ritter (1901–1951) began assembling a team of researchers that theorized that most of the originally pure Aryan Gypsy people had interbred with dangerous, lower world elements after entering Europe. These "mixed breeds" tended toward crime, whereas the "pure-blooded" derived from a "primitive" Indian tribe and merited protection. Ritter estimated that about 90 percent of the German Gypsy population was of mixed ancestry (Wippermann 2005: 29).

State agencies coordinated the anti-Gypsy initiatives inherited from earlier regimes and applied new regulations, some of which made no mention of Gypsies, in discriminatory fashion. For example, the law on the "Prevention of Genetically Diseased Offspring" of 14 July 1933 was invoked by the Hereditary Health Courts (*Erbgesundheitsgerichte*) as a basis for the sterilization of large numbers of Roma and Sinti. The provisions of the Nuremberg Laws of 1935 that regulated sexual relations between Germans and those "not of German blood" were interpreted as binding on Gypsies. The view that Gypsies shared pariah status with Jews also was reflected in the commentary on racial legislation that Hans Globke (1898–1973) wrote in 1936. According to him, "In Europe only the Jews and the Gypsies are of racially foreign [*artfremd*] blood" (Wippermann 2005: 26). The same perception was common in the medical community. In 1939, Dr. Kurt Hannemann wrote the following in the journal of the National Socialist Union of Doctors, *Ziel und Weg* (Goal and Path):

Rats, insects, and fleas are part of nature just like Gypsies and Jews. They are beings willed by God, but cannot be improved, regardless of how much considerate attention one devotes to them. We cannot shield ourselves from such individuals through quarantine, the way we do a-socials or those who are abnormal, egomaniacal, and criminally unrestrained. All life is struggle. Therefore we must gradually eliminate these pests through biological means. (Bastian 2001: 31–2)

In 1936 Heinrich Himmler (1900–1945) became head of the newly centralized German police and pressured both Reich and Prussian interior ministers to order "preventive incarceration" of all those who committed "minor but persistent acts of illegal behavior." Among the targets mentioned were "vagabonds (gypsies)" (Wippermann 2005: 33–4). As a result, thousands of Gypsies were deported to Buchenwald, Dachau, and Sachsenhausen. The interior ministry and local agencies were also active on their own accord. In June of that year the various anti-Gypsy laws that had been enacted regionally were extended to the entire territory of the Reich. Gypsies were now officially called "racially foreign" (*artfremd*) and incarcerated in work camps in Berlin, Frankfurt, Cologne, Düsseldorf, Essen, Gelsen-kirchen, and Königsberg.

Robert Ritter now became director of the Research Institute for Racial Hygiene and Population Biology in the Ministry of Health. He and his team began performing "racial" evaluations of some 30,000 German Gypsies, making use of information held by both state agencies and the churches. No new law had been passed to regulate Gypsy policy, and Sinti and Roma technically still enjoyed a somewhat higher legal status than Jews as *Reichsbürger*, not simply *Staatsbürger*. This situation persisted until 25 April 1943, when all "Jews and Gypsies" were denied the status of "citizens" or even "dependents" of Germany. They were to enjoy no legal protections at all. In the meantime, if the growing exclusion of Gypsies resembled that of Jews, few Gypsies were able to escape by going abroad. But some of them evaded detection by Ritter's Institute and managed to pass as "Aryan," and others successfully claimed citizenship of countries allied with Germany.

One leading authority on the subject dates a worsening of Gypsies' position from the outbreak of World War II (Wippermann 2005: 38). On 17 October 1939, Himmler released a statement predicting that "shortly the Gypsy question in Germany will be settled in a basic way." Gypsies were restricted to their places of residence, and plans emerged among high SS officials to deport Gypsies along with Jews to occupied Poland. Although the Nazi governor there, Hans Frank (1900–1946), resisted letting them into his sphere of influence, some 2,800 German Gypsies—men, women, and children—were sent to Lublin in 1940, and approximately 5,000 German, Hungarian, Romanian, and Austrian Gypsies to the Łódź ghetto in 1941. Many in this latter group became victims of the gas trucks at Chelmno.

During the attack on the Soviet Union, Gypsies were targeted by the Einsatzgruppen, without a special order having been given or required. This, after all, was a racial war. In December 1941, Heinrich Lohse (1896–1964), the Reich Commissar for Belarus and the Baltic region, ordered that "Gypsies and Jews will be treated equally." His nominal superior, Alfred Rosenberg, the Reich Commissar for the Eastern Territories, objected to this formulation, but only because he saw it as a usurpation of his authority. Himmler then achieved a temporary resolution: the commanders of the Security Police and the SS Security Service were to decide how to proceed on their own.

In their eyes, no reason seemed too weak to justify killing Roma: they were "pests" or "useless mouths" or "bearers of illness." Perhaps most fatefully, German troops believed Gypsies, with their itinerant lifestyle, made perfect spies. Germans, therefore, took connections to the partisans for granted. Moreover, the antipathy toward Gypsies in German society was perhaps more pervasive and visceral than hatred toward Jews (Wippermann 2005: 13–25).

Still, these killing operations were marked by an inconsistency not seen in the murder of the Jews. Take the army. In February 1941, an order was issued that contradicted Ritter's categorization: it required the release from service of "full-blooded" Gypsies. Many army offices then assumed that those of "mixed blood" could remain. Not until February 1942 was the criminal police directed to find out how many Gypsies of either description were in the Wehrmacht. After consultations with the Reich interior ministry, the Wehrmacht High Command issued new orders in July 1942 that all "Gypsy hybrids" were to be dismissed from duty. The number released is not known. One knowledgeable scholar writes that by early 1943 the armed forces of Germany were "mostly 'free of Gypsies.'" He notes that according to a directive of September 1943 on the use of "non-Jewish foreign-blooded German citizens," "Gypsies" as well as "Gypsy hybrids" were to be released from duty "as a rule," but those who had proved themselves in combat could remain. Yet these exceptions were reversed in a further order of July 1944 (Zimmermann 1996: 198–9).

Because of the decision to leave Gypsy policy in the hands of local authorities, its execution also differed throughout the occupied Soviet Union. In July 1942, the Ministry of Eastern Territories drafted a decree according to which Gypsies were to be treated like Jews, with no distinction made between sedentary and itinerant Gypsies. But later drafts called for "concentrating Gypsies in separate camps . . . under supervision" and stated that Gypsies were "not to be on the same basis as Jews." Finally, on 15 November 1943 the Ministry decreed that Gypsies, whether "hybrid" or not, would be left alone if sedentary. Itinerant Gypsies were to be "assigned the same status as the Jews and are to be put into concentration camps." As Guenter Lewy comments: "the decree . . . did not really establish anything new. The decree put into formal language the existing situation: itinerating Gypsies were regularly shot when apprehended; sedentary Gypsies had a chance to survive" (2000: 127). This policy may have saved lives in the western USSR, but did not help the Crimean Gypsies, who were practically wiped out. As a rule the killings included men, women, and children and were carried out with great brutality.

Himmler believed that "pure blooded" Gypsies had to be preserved because of their magical powers. Yet his plan to set up a reservation for Gypsies was canceled by Hitler in December 1942. In the early months of 1943, practically all German Gypsies who had been identified were sent to Auschwitz, where they were kept in a separate "Gypsy family camp" under conditions calculated to kill; many died of disease and starvation. When the SS decided to liquidate the camp in the summer of 1944, armed opposition arose, which delayed plans to murder the inmates in the gas chambers. Of the 23,000 Roma and Sinti sent to Auschwitz, more than 20,000 are thought to have perished (Lewy 2000: 166).

Elsewhere in Europe the fate of Gypsies depended upon local circumstances. Most Gypsies lived in southeastern Europe. Croatia, Romania, Bulgaria, Slovakia, and Hungary had pro-German regimes, and their anti-Gypsy policies radicalized during World War II. Yet none of these countries had precise definitions of who counted as Gypsy, nor did they know how many Gypsies lived on their territories. Many Roma had become experts in blending into the local population over centuries of persecution.

Croatia, which went furthest in copying Germany's racism, murdered between 25,000 and 50,000 Roma, most of them in the camp at Jasenovac. Most Muslim Roma were excepted. Up to 20,000 of the 150,000 Gypsies living in Serbia were killed by the German occupiers, some in camps, many in reprisal for attacks on Germans. In 1941, the Romanian regime deported between 20,000 and 26,000

Gypsies to Transnistria, where they were left to their fates, with no housing or employment. This group is thought to have included more itinerant than sedentary Gypsies. Perhaps 2,000 returned in 1944 when Soviet forces liberated Romania. The prosecution at Romanian war crimes trials after World War II estimated that 8–9,000 of the deportees had died. The Bulgarian regime had plans to force a sedentary lifestyle upon the country's approximately 100,000 Roma, but these were not carried out. Instead, several thousand became forced laborers in agriculture and on various building projects. The Slovak regime, which had identified its Jewish population as "alien elements," permitted Roma to be citizens if they could speak Slovak and produce a permanent address. "Travelers," as the Gypsies were sometimes called, were thus considered "foreign elements." Some men identified as Gypsies were pressed into special labor battalions for "reeducation." Others were interned in labor camps, along with Slovak "asocials," and put to work building railroad tracks and dams. After the Slovak uprising of 1944, German and Slovak troops employed special severity against the Gypsy population, which was suspected of sympathizing with the partisans. Up to 1,000 Gypsies may have been killed (Zimmermann 1996: 284–92).

The authoritarian regime in Hungary had little in the way of Gypsy policy, despite the desires and efforts of many of its racist local prefects, and despite a decree of 1938 declaring the Gypsies "suspicious" and requiring police surveillance. Prior to 1941, about 100,000 of them lived in Hungary, to which some 200,000 were added with the annexation of Yugoslav and Romanian territories in that year. Discussions followed in parliament about placing "work shy" elements in labor camps, but little came of this. In the summer of 1944, Roma in five counties were subjected to "labor duty" in agriculture.

The Hungarian fascists ("Arrow Cross"), whom the Germans placed in power that October, also had no thought-out Gypsy policy. They fell back upon familiar stereotypes, and as the Russian army approached, the interior minister ordered the arrests of Roma living in the southern military districts. Thousands more were arrested along with communists, partisans, and deserters in the western and southwestern districts and sent on murderous foot marches to a prison at Komarom in Northern Hungary. From there many were deported to German camps at Buchenwald and Ravensbrück. During military operations in 1945 many Roma were shot for supposed sympathy with the enemy. Reports of losses vary dramatically. While early reports estimated numbers of deportees at 25–30,000, more recent studies by Laszlo Karsai of reparation materials kept in Budapest archives place the figure for Gypsies victimized in the closing days of the war at some 5,000, of whom perhaps 1,000 died (Zimmermann 1996: 284–92).

Some 6,500 Roma and Sinti lived in the Protectorate of Bohemia and Moravia in 1939, when the German authorities introduced measures to restrict this population's mobility. On 31 May 1939—less than two months after the German rule began—an order was released forbidding travelers to move about in "hordes."

In November the interior ministry instructed police to settle Gypsies forcibly within two months, which proved impossible, thus triggering a further order in February 1940 for the incarceration of those who continued to travel. Some five camps were established by the fall of 1940 where "traveling Gypsies" joined "do-nothings" and "vagabonds." With the arrival of Reinhard Heydrich (1904–1942) as temporary *Reichsprotektor* the situation worsened. He subordinated Czech administration to German directors. Further Roma were placed in camps as "asocials." In December 1942, a transport of ninety Czech Gypsies was sent to Auschwitz; three months later only twenty were still alive.

In July 1942, authorities in the Protectorate moved to bring their practice closer to that of the Reich by issuing the order for "Combating the Gypsy Plague." This reversed the previous Czech practice of registering the Gypsy population by sociological rather than racial criteria. By early 1943, some 11,886 persons had been counted, often according to skin and hair color, as "Gypsies," "Gypsy hybrids," and "persons traveling like Gypsies." The first two categories included 5,830 persons. Of these, 2,625 persons were interned in the camps at Lety (Bohemia) and Hodonin (Moravia) for reeducation. They were made to accomplish hard labor without pay, wear prison garb, and have their heads shaven. Provisions were substandard, housing overcrowded. Only 783 persons are known to have survived these camps; the others either died there or were deported to Auschwitz (Zimmermann 1996: 217–22).

Of the 28,000 Gypsies in prewar Poland, approximately 8,000 died of a variety of causes during the war. Some were forced to live in the Warsaw ghetto, including a self-anointed "king" of "all Gypsy tribes in Europe," Rudolf Kwiek. Those who had lived in western Polish areas appended to the Reich were deported to central Poland (the *Generalgouvernement*). Gypsies were often seized in reprisal for attacks on German forces, and many who died in summary executions were recorded as "Poles." Although sedentary Gypsies generally were left in peace, those who roamed were often incarcerated, and many died in Treblinka, Sobibor, Majdanek, and Belzec.

The situation of Gypsies in Belgium, the Netherlands, and France did not greatly concern the Germans. Populations in the former two countries were relatively small (about 1,000). Suspected of communist sympathies and of harboring "alien elements," these Gypsies were first forbidden to itinerate, then forced to relocate into special zones. From 1940 on, the Germans attempted to transfer these Roma and Sinti to collection camps, and none appear to have survived the war (Lutz and Lutz 1995: 351). In most French departments, the Germans permitted local officials to decide who was Gypsy. Like their Czech counterparts, these bureaucrats had a more sociological than racial understanding of their target group and tended to apprehend persons defined as "nomads" or prostitutes. As elsewhere, sedentary Gypsies as a rule were left alone. Even the decree forbidding itineration of 6 April 1940 was not strictly enforced. How many French Gypsies were interned is difficult to ascertain. Some 3,000 "nomads" are believed to have perished in camps from

1940 to 1944, primarily because of harsh conditions. Of a prewar population of 40,000, some 15,000 French Gypsies are thought to have died during World War II (Lutz and Lutz 1995: 349).

Because historians are uncertain about how many Gypsies lived in Europe before the Nazi onslaught, specifying how many died is difficult. Overall estimates of Gypsies killed in what the Roma language calls *Porajmos* (the Devouring) vary between 220,000 (Gilbert 1988: 141) and 500,000 (Wippermann 2005: 47). Though the toll was heavy, mortality rates varied greatly by country, and the Germans did not pursue a policy of comprehensive destruction.

HOMOSEXUALS

Homosexuals in Germany long had confronted discrimination, anchored most notoriously in Paragraph 175 of the Reich legal code of May 1871, which read: "Unnatural sexual offenses that are committed between persons of the male sex are to be punished with imprisonment" (Bastian 2000: 14). But the story was not simply of repression; this law also called forth resistance. For example, in the 1890s some 6,000 prominent intellectuals, as well as the Social Democratic Party of Germany (SPD), called for an end to the criminalization of homosexual relations. In the more liberal Weimar Republic, German gays organized in their own interest, yet they were never free from fears of prosecution, and prominent figures often became targets of smear campaigns by a sensationalist press.

Just as German society was marked by ambivalent attitudes toward homosexuality, so was the Nazi Party. Hitler does not seem to have had strong views for or against, but his lieutenants Himmler and Rosenberg expressed antipathy, while SA-chief Ernst Röhm publicly admitted to being "bisexual." The NSDAP became an object of gay-bashing by liberal and Social Democratic newspapers for its supposed encouragement of homoeroticism. On 22 June 1931, the *Münchener Post*, which was close to the SPD, drew attention to Röhm's sexual behavior in an article headlined "Gay Fraternity in the Brown House" (*Warme Brüderschaft im Braunen Haus*) (Bastian 2000: 29).

Homosexuals were not targeted for victimization in the first year of Nazi rule. Indeed, Nazi judges later complained that they initially feared the consequences of enforcing Paragraph 175. For his part, Röhm declared that victory had not been won by "apostles of morality," and that further revolutionary steps would not be impeded by "petty bourgeois" (*spiessbürgerliche*) elements. His SA (*Sturmabteilung*) would ensure that the German revolution was not "stopped half way . . . betrayed by non-fighters." When he was murdered and the SA purged in June 1934, the cause was not his unconventional sexuality, but the threats he was thought to pose to public order and Germany's traditional military leadership (Bastian 2000: 34–6).

The removal of Röhm opened the way for Party members who wanted to suppress homosexuality. Perhaps sensing the discomfort Röhm had caused, Hitler struck a new tone, telling the Council of Ministers on 3 July—two days after Röhm was shot—that this SA clique had consisted of "inferior, homosexual elements." The moment had arrived for homophobic SS chief Himmler to assert a new policy. He later boasted that in the six weeks after the Röhm putsch more cases were tried under Paragraph 175 than in the entire previous twenty-five years combined. When he moved from Munich to Berlin, Himmler brought along inspector Josef Meisinger (1899–1947), who gathered data from police offices throughout the Reich on everyone accused of "homosexual activity." He then began purging high-ranking officials from the state bureaucracy, for example the main inspector of the elite Party schools (NAPOLA), Joachim Haupt (1900–1989), and the Gauleiter of Silesia, Helmuth Brückner (1896–1954). About a year after Röhm's murder, the Nazi revision of Paragraph 175 declared all homosexual acts punishable, not just those involving intercourse. The result was a jump in convictions from 3,907 in the years 1933–35 to 22,153 in the years 1936–38. Between 1933 and 1945 some 100,000 persons were tried for homosexual activity, about half of whom were convicted (Bastian 2000: 55).

As with regard to Gypsies, Himmler's rise to head of the German police in 1936 resulted in a centralization of persecution of homosexuals. In 1937, the Prussian criminal police saw its competence extended to cover all of Germany. Two years later, this all-German force created a "Reich Central Office for Combating Homosexuality and Abortion." The "old fighter" Meisinger was now transferred to the occupied east and replaced by the young technocrat Erich Jacob, who within a year had compiled registrations of 42,000 homosexuals (Bastian 2000: 57). In July 1940, Himmler ordered that "all homosexuals who have seduced more than one partner are to be taken into preventive detainment after their release from prison" (Bastian 2000: 58). How many men this measure affected is unclear: the total number of homosexuals put in concentration camps is estimated at between 5,000 and 15,000 (Bastian 2000: 73). This is a relatively small share of all concentration camp inmates (over 1.65 million during Nazi rule, not including death camps) and all German gay men (presumably over one million). The inmates were identified by pink triangles sewn onto their clothing and occupied nearly the bottom of the camp hierarchy as objects of special contempt, a fact reflected in a high death rate, though here, too, numbers are elusive. Some of those killed were victims of gruesome experiments involving the injection of hormones to cure their "disease."

The Nazi regime was less concerned about sexual relations between women. It inherited a legal understanding that did not criminalize such relations, and in 1935 officials in the Ministry of Justice decided to adhere to that practice. Policy makers believed that homosexuality among women was less common than among men, weaker in intensity, largely hidden from public display and thus less likely to encourage imitation, and usually temporary and confined to prostitutes and thus no real barrier to sexual reproduction (Schoppmann in Jellonnek and Lautmann 2002).

Subjective adherence to homosexuality was not a strict requirement for classification as homosexual; at times allegations sufficed and were used to strengthen other accusations against Roman Catholic priests or leftist intellectuals. At the same time, homosexual inclinations alone were not enough to justify arrest: "whoever could credibly assure the Gestapo during interrogation that he was homosexual but was not homosexually active was spared further persecution" (Jellonnek 1990: 327). And indeed, well-known persons of homosexual tendency, such as the writer Friedo Lampe (1899–1945) were not harassed because of their sexuality during the Third Reich. This pattern highlights a difference between the persecutions of gays and of ethnic minorities: personal behavior could influence a gay individual's fate, which was unthinkable for Jews, unlikely for Gypsies, and unusual for persecuted Slavs, such as captured Soviet soldiers.

Nazi leaders believed that the tendency of homosexuals to engage in illicit acts (*Unzucht*) could be controlled by radical measures short of incarceration and murder. Thus, two laws passed in 1933 permitted the state to castrate individuals considered likely to produce "hereditarily diseased offspring" (homosexuality was regarded as an inheritable disease) or to become "dangerous habitual criminals" ("morality criminals" had to be stopped before spoiling otherwise "healthy young men"). Some 2,000 men were castrated between 1933 and 1940 under the latter provision (Bastian 2000: 68). Plans to enact a further law expediting castration for those "alien to the community" were shelved during the war as less than urgent. In fact, some homosexuals were released from camps in the war's last stages and inducted into the Wehrmacht. How many castrations took place according to the law on "hereditarily diseased offspring" is not known.

SLAVS

Germans understood the category "Slavs" to mean "speakers of Slavic languages." Not even Nazi racial scientists considered them a racial group. Their treatment had varied considerably between the German states governed from Berlin and Vienna. Otto von Bismarck (1815–1898) had used economic and educational policies to Germanize the Poles living in West Prussia and other eastern provinces. In Austria-Hungary, the state traditionally recruited functionaries from every Slavic group, though after 1867 attempts were made to Magyarize Slavs living under Hungarian rule. Probably the two most feared and distrusted Slavic populations in German central Europe were the Russians and Serbs.

Like homosexuals and Gypsies, Slavs had an insignificant place in Hitler's world view. Despite denigrating the role they had played in the Habsburg empire, Hitler did not make them a clear target of his racial hatred in his two books. And indeed, the state he led pursued ambivalent and opportunistic policies toward Slavic peoples. Propaganda Minister Joseph Goebbels called the Bulgarians "friends," and Bulgaria became a German ally, was never occupied by German troops, and maintained diplomatic relations with the Soviet Union until September 1944. The Slovaks and the Croats were permitted to have their own puppet states with fully native governments, police forces, educational systems (including universities), and elite military units modeled on the SA and SS. Croatia's borders were extended to include Bosnia-Herzegovina, and the fascist *Ustasha* regime implemented policies of racist extermination against another Slavic people: the Serbs. The Czechs were subjected to a "Protectorate" and six years of German occupation, and the Czech intelligentsia suffered severe repression. Yet for the overwhelming majority of the population life went on in relatively normal fashion: businessmen continued making profits, working class earnings increased thanks to wartime demand, and the birthrate edged upward. The rations allotted to Czech workers were on a par with those of German workers.

Slavic groups living in the Soviet Union—Russians, White Russians, and Ukrainians—were subjected to annihilation from the moment German troops crossed the Soviet boundaries in 1941. Among the earliest victims were Bolshevik commissars, who were summarily executed, and millions of captured troops, who were starved to death. The goals were short-term exploitation and preparation for German settlement, made possible by the expulsion of entire populations. Millions of Soviet citizens were transported to the Reich as slave laborers. The remaining population lived under conditions of semi-starvation. The brutality of the German occupation called forth resistance, and a "vicious cycle of violence and murder" evolved, with the Germans eradicating villages suspected of aiding partisans or withholding grain, thereby further decreasing productivity and driving more people into the underground (Connelly 1999: 7).

Yet here, too, variation is apparent. Ukrainians living in former Soviet territories were under the direction of East Prussian Gauleiter Erich Koch (1896–1986) and subjected to his contempt as "racial inferiors." Though Ukrainians found Nazi rule "one hundred times worse" than under the Bolsheviks, such sentiments did not concern Koch, who vowed to "pump every last thing out of this country" (Connelly 1999: 7). Ukrainians in the former Polish territories (eastern Galicia) fared better, however. In 1939 the Germans permitted the formation of a Ukrainian Relief Committee to oversee a strengthening of Ukrainian social, cultural, and economic life within the *Generalgouvernement*. Whereas before the war 2,510 Ukrainian language schools dotted the region, by 1942–43 the number had increased to 4,173. The German Academic Exchange Service (DAAD) extended scholarships for study in Germany to Ukrainian students, and in April 1943 the SS formed a Ukrainian Division ("Galicia") that attracted 80,000 volunteers.

Ukrainians in the *Generalgouvernement* enjoyed these relative "privileges" because the Germans hoped to play them off against the Poles. Soon after crossing the Polish border in 1939, the Nazis began mass executions of Polish intellectuals and others considered potentially hostile to Germany. Throughout the war no Polish government or even administration existed above the level of municipality, and the Nazis imposed forced labor even for teenagers and starvation rations and permitted practically no autonomous Polish cultural life. The occupiers closed universities and secondary schools. Random and pervasive terror kept "order." On any given day, a Pole might be apprehended in a mass street arrest (*lapanka*) as the Nazis routinely cordoned off sections of cities and rounded up anyone who happened to be there. If not shot as hostages, those so captured were sent to camps. As in Soviet territories, Nazi brutality called forth vigorous partisan activity, culminating in the Warsaw uprising of 1944 that left over 250,000 civilians dead.

Poland endured Nazi destruction longer than any other area in Europe. But the apparently scripted, methodical brutality of German troops was not necessarily predictable from National Socialist policy toward Poland before 1939 or in Hitler's writings and speeches. Although Hitler thought of Poles as "racially foreign elements," the Poles' victory against Russia in 1920 had made it difficult for him to conceive of Polish racial inferiority. Poland was above all a "border state" to be courted for alliance against "enemy No. 1": the Soviet Union. In January 1934, Germany and Poland concluded a non-aggression pact, and the Nazis reversed the anti-Polish policies of the Weimar Republic. Some Nazi leaders respected their Polish counterparts; Hermann Göring (1893–1946), who visited Poland repeatedly on hunting excursions, even wrote an introduction for the German edition of the collected works of the Polish leader Jozef Pilsudski (1867–1935) (Connelly 1999: 11).

Poland became an enemy of Nazi Germany not because of underlying ideological animus but because the Polish government and people refused to do Hitler's bidding. Following the Munich crisis in 1938, the Germans made three demands of Poland: the surrender of Danzig, the construction of an extraterritorial railroad and highway through the "Polish Corridor," and Polish collaboration in the Anti-Comintern Pact. In return, they offered to guarantee Poland's borders and dangled a share of the spoils of war with the Soviet Union. Poland rejected these proposals and received promises of support from Great Britain in late March 1939 in the event that Polish sovereignty was "clearly threatened." The following month, Hitler renounced the pact of 1934 and began planning Poland's destruction. Only after launching the war against Poland did the Nazi leadership and the supporting scientific community convince themselves of Polish racial inferiority. With the ruins of Warsaw still smoldering, leading Eastern expert and historian Albert Brackmann (1871–1952) hurried a booklet into print relegating the Poles and other Slavs to non-European status. Later that fall, Joseph Goebbels (1897–1945) noted after a visit to Poland that it was already "Asia" (Connelly 1999: 13–14).

Further evidence of Nazi willingness to adjust policies and ideology to changing circumstance is provided by the cases of the Czechs, the Croats, and the Ukrainians. As an Austrian, Hitler bore greater enmity toward the first-named group, but unlike in Poland, no spark of defiance arose in the Czech lands. In 1939, the Germans completed their destruction of Czechoslovakia with virtually no opposition. Neither Czechs nor Germans ever had an incentive to upset the relative calm that settled on the "Protectorate." The Germans valued the steady production of war materials from Czech industry, and the Czechs the significant room that remained for pursuit of economic and cultural interests. Though Hitler harbored the strongest suspicions of Germanizing foreign populations, he ruled in September 1940 that the assimilation of the "greater part of the Czech people is possible for historical and racial reasons."

Hitler also came to view the cooperative Croats as fully assimilable. With time, he saw even Ukrainians in a more favorable light. Though he continued to rule out Ukrainian statehood, Hitler's views on Ukrainians' racial character softened. In September 1941, he approved the use of women from the east as domestic servants in Germany, and he instructed aides to revise "school knowledge about the great migration of peoples," because the many blond, blue-eyed Ukrainians might be "peasant descendants of German tribes who never migrated." In August 1942, Hitler came out in support of assimilating Ukrainian women, who would help foster a "healthy balance" among the Germans. The superficiality of Nazi racial science made such opportunism all but inevitable. The only "scientific" tools the Nazis possessed to discover "valuable blood" among the Slavs were eye color, hair color, physical dimensions (e.g., skull), and various measures of intelligence (Connelly 1999: 14–15).

In the case of Russians, Nazi willingness to compromise was limited. The reason lay in part in long-standing anti-Russian sentiments in the German population, but also in the destiny assigned to Russians by the Nazi strategy of attaining living space: their cities and industry were to be destroyed to make way for German rural settlements. According to the *Generalplan Ost*, the Russian population was to be largely resettled beyond the Ural mountains. Yet here, too, German policy stopped short of complete destruction. In 1941, Hitler gave strict orders that Russians were not to be used as soldiers, yet by the end of the war tens of thousands were fighting on the German side. The breakdown of his injunction was gradual and opportunistic: first, German troops began using Russian POWs as helpers of all kinds and learned that giving proper rations resulted in better work. As early as 1941, these *Hilfswillige* were used for guard and police functions, then as soldiers. Beginning in 1943, the Nazis offered land grants to "Eastern soldiers"—many of them Russian— who had distinguished themselves in service. These compromises were necessitated by the fact that the German military and administrative presence was insufficient to oversee the local population. The use of supposed "subhumans" as soldiers increased as the situation on Germany's many fronts became more desperate and the killing of Jews continued.

What if the Nazis had won the war? All available evidence suggests that massive use of Slavic people as laborers would have continued. In 1940, a confident Himmler predicted that Slavs would become a "leaderless work force . . . and be called upon, under the strict, consistent, and fair direction of the German people, to help in the construction of its eternal cultural deeds and monuments." Millions of foreign workers were destined for yearly planting and harvests. In October 1943, the SS leader said in Poznan: "If we treat it properly, we can mine endless quantities of value and energy from the human mass of this Slavic people" (Connelly 1999: 28).

When imagining the consequences of a Nazi victory, historians tend to think of the Third Reich as all-powerful, somehow relieved of its endemic confusion and a hostile surrounding world. But Nazi planners anticipated challenges. The greatest would be finding colonists for Bohemia and Moravia, all of Poland, the Baltic States, much of Ukraine and Russia. Experiences during the war did not inspire confidence about finding enough Germans to settle an area previously inhabited by over 100 million Slavs. Only a few hundred thousand "Germans" proved willing to settle western Poland—and most of these had been taken from Ukraine to begin with! They thus continued an old tradition of German migration to economically more developed western areas, for example from Silesia to the Ruhr.

Even during the war the Nazis did not approach success in eradicating the part of Slavic populations that was slated for immediate destruction: the intelligentsia. Although Hitler declared in the fall of 1940 that "all members of the Polish intelligentsia must be killed," the wartime losses, including Jews, amounted to 57 percent of all lawyers, 39 percent of all physicians, 29.5 percent of all university teachers; and in general 37.5 percent of all Polish citizens with higher education (Connelly 1999: 31). Many of the 20,000 Polish officers captured by the Germans in 1939 belonged to the intelligentsia, but the Nazis did not attempt to kill them off, though they remained in POW camps throughout the war.

CONCLUSION

In April 1942, Director of the Advisory Board of the Office of Racial Politics of the NSDAP Dr. Erhard Wetzel (1903–1975) included the following among his "thoughts" on the *Generalplan Ost*:

it should be obvious that the Polish question cannot be solved by liquidating the Poles in the way the Jews are being liquidated. Such a resolution of the Polish question would weigh upon the German people deep into the future and cost us sympathies everywhere because neighboring peoples would have to figure on being dealt with the same way, when their time came. (Connelly 1999: 31)

His point was that killing Poles as such was not an issue: if killing them advanced Nazi goals, it was good; when it ceased to advance such goals, it should stop.

An important lesson about Nazi persecution of Gypsies, homosexuals, and Slavs is that, in each case, it was undertaken not as an end in itself, but as a means to achieve other goals. Here the difference from the murder of Europe's Jews is basic: killing Jews was an ideological end in itself, requiring no further justification and permitting no let-up or exception. To think of Jews as divided between acceptable and unacceptable (as were Gypsies), as tolerable or fixable (as were some homosexuals), and as bearing useful "blood" that might be ascertained by looking at eye and hair color (as were some Slavs)—all of this was inconceivable. The Jew was thought to pose an evil going beyond the evidence of the senses (Connelly 1999: 33).

The question remains as to why these groups—Gypsies, homosexuals, and (especially eastern) Slavs—became targets of mass murder. One basic answer is the misanthropy in the words of Wetzel: Poles would be killed, in fact annihilated, if they got in the way of Nazi expansion. But there is more to the story: France and Belgium also impeded Nazi goals but neither French nor Belgians were targeted for genocide. In their crusade against Gypsies, homosexuals, and Slavs, the Nazi leadership also indulged the hatreds and fears of the Nazi movement. Ian Kershaw has written of the impulse guiding Nazi bureaucrats in a world often lacking clear guidance that they "worked toward the Führer" (1998: 529–31). In the case of Slavs, Roma, and gay men, the Führer worked toward his movement, creating spaces in which hatred of others could be released without any limits other than the practical ones to which Wetzel alludes. Hitler may not have borne particular hatred toward homosexuals or Poles, but very many members of his Party did. In 1934 and in 1939, the Führer lifted the door to a cage in which the energies of destruction had been trapped.

REFERENCES

BASTIAN, T. (2000). *Homosexuelle im Dritten Reich: Geschichte einer Verfolgung*. Munich: C. H. Beck.

——(2001). *Sinti und Roma im Dritten Reich: Geschichte einer Verfolgung*. Munich: C.H. Beck.

CONNELLY, J. (1999). "Nazis and Slavs: From Racial Theory to Racist Practice." *Central European History* 32: 1–33.

FRISZKE, A. (2003). *Polska: Losy panstwa i narodu 1939–1989*. Warsaw: Wydawnictwo Iskry.

GILBERT, M. (1988). *Atlas of the Holocaust*. Oxford: Pergamon Press.

JELLONNEK, B. (1990). *Homosexuelle unterm Hakenkreuz: Die Verfolgung von Homosexuellen im Dritten Reich.* Paderborn: Schöningh.

——and LAUTMANN, R. (eds.) (2002). *Nationalsozialistischer Terror gegen Homosexuelle.* Paderborn: Schöningh.

KERSHAW, I. (1998). *Hitler 1889–1936: Hubris.* New York: W. W. Norton.

LEWY, G. (2000). *The Nazi Persecution of the Gypsies.* New York: Oxford University Press.

LUTZ, B. and LUTZ, J. (1995). "Gypsies as Victims of the Holocaust." *Holocaust and Genocide Studies* 9: 346–59.

SUNY, R. (ed.) (2006). *Russia: The Twentieth Century.* Cambridge: Cambridge University Press.

WIPPERMANN, W. (2005). *Auserwählte Opfer? Shoah und Porrajmos im Vergleich: Eine Kontroverse.* Berlin: Frank & Timme.

ZIMMERMANN, M. (1996). *Rassenutopie und Genozid: Die nationalsozialistische "Lösung der Zigeunerfrage".* Hamburg: Christians.

OTHER SUGGESTED READING

BERKHOFF, K. (2004). *Harvest of Despair: Life and Death in Ukraine under Nazi Rule.* Cambridge, MA: Harvard University Press.

BLOXHAM, D. (2009). *The Final Solution: A Genocide.* Oxford: Oxford University Press.

BRYANT, C. (2007). *Prague in Black: Nazi Rule and Czech Nationalism.* Cambridge, MA: Harvard University Press.

BURLEIGH, M. and WIPPERMANN, W. (1991). *The Racial State: Germany 1933–1945.* New York: Cambridge University Press.

DALLIN, A. (1981). *German Rule in Russia 1941–1945.* 2nd edn. New York: Macmillan.

GILES, G. (2001). "The Institutionalization of Homosexual Panic in the Third Reich," in R. Gellately and N. Stolzfus (eds.), *Social Outsiders in Nazi Germany.* Princeton, NJ: Princeton University Press, 233–55.

GROSS, J. (1979). *Polish Society under German Occupation: The Generalgouvernement, 1939–1944.* Princeton, NJ: Princeton University Press.

HARVEY, E. (2003). *Women and the Nazi East: Agents and Witnesses of Germanization.* New Haven, CT: Yale University Press.

HERBERT, U. (1997). *Hitler's Foreign Workers.* New York: Cambridge University Press.

MAZOWER, M. (2008). *Hitler's Empire: How the Nazis Ruled Europe.* New York: Penguin Press.

PART III

SETTINGS

CHAPTER 19

....

GREATER GERMANY

....

WOLF GRUNER

FOR decades before Adolf Hitler (1889–1945) came to power, extreme German nationalists harbored the dream of uniting within a Greater German Reich all the regions of Europe in which Germans ever had settled. Hitler, who was born and socialized in Habsburg Austria, a hotbed of such sentiments, believed fervently in this vision (Hamann 1999). Indeed, the very first point of the program of his National Socialist German Workers Party (NSDAP), formulated in 1920, called for the unification of all Germans within a Greater Germany. Conversely, Jews, as the alleged cause of national decline since 1918, were to be separated from the "people's community," stripped of their German citizenship and by way of a "carefully planned legal struggle" in the end totally removed (Jäckel 1980: 89–90).

Between 1933 and 1945, the Nazi regime came remarkably close to realizing both of these objectives. In 1933, some 500,000 persons of the Jewish faith lived among 65 million people in Germany. By the end of World War II twelve years later, expulsion, deportation, and mass murder had reduced the total number of Jews on German soil to only 15,000, most of them married to non-Jews (Benz 1991: 52).

How could a democratic Germany turn into a genocidal society in barely one decade? Since World War II, historians have offered a variety of answers. Many such explanations center on the fierce antisemitism of Hitler or Joseph Goebbels (1897–1945) and conceive of the persecution of Jews primarily as a matter of orchestration from Berlin. Developments at lower levels of government generally play little role in these analyses. Only a few historians (Schleunes 1970; Pätzold 1975; Friedländer 1997) have paid attention to the numerous local studies that since the 1960s have provided compelling evidence of anti-Jewish municipal initiatives (e.g., Kommission zur Erforschung 1963; Sauer 1966; Fliedner 1971). Such actions affected the daily life of many Jews, since 70 percent of them lived in the nation's fifty largest cities.

From 1933 onwards, persecution developed as a process in which far more authorities participated than previously assumed. Hitler's new government, including traditional conservatives, the Reich ministries, and the Nazi Party leadership, determined anti-Jewish policy. However, the governments of the German states, such as Bavaria or Saxony, and cities also played important roles. The dynamic interaction of local, regional, and central German authorities constituted a major element in the rapid radicalization of persecution.

CENTRAL AND LOCAL PERSECUTION POLICIES, 1933–1937

Within a month of Hitler's accession to power on 30 January 1933, local SA or SS gangs attacked the Jewish personnel of courts and universities and organized boycotts of "Jewish" stores and businesses. Such pressure increased in mid-March, when the Nazi leadership launched a national media campaign against Jews in certain professions. Acting on their own authority, some mayors expelled Jewish municipal personnel and/or dissolved business relationships with firms owned by Jews. These actions reflected, in part, the rapid increase of Nazi influence within local governments as many mayors, especially in the big cities, were forcibly replaced or subordinated to special state commissioners. Veteran National Socialists, such as Karl Fiehler (1895–1969) in Munich and Julius Lippert (1895–1956) in Berlin, took office this way. This process accelerated in March with the dissolution of existing town councils and the holding of new municipal elections in Prussia, which the Nazi party won almost everywhere.

When journalists, politicians, emigrants, and representatives of Jewish organizations abroad spoke up against these developments, Hitler used their criticism as a pretext to justify a national anti-Jewish boycott. The headline of the *Völkischer Beobachter* on 1 April 1933, read: "War Declared on Jewish World Power." Everywhere, the SA set up guard units with warning posters in front of stores, law firms, and medical offices. Shops were plundered, people attacked, and several Jews murdered. Part of the population viewed the actions with dismay; some even expressed solidarity with the persecuted (Bankier 1995: 95; Longerich 2006: 65–6). Although some victims of the terror told themselves that it would blow over, many others decided to flee the country during the ensuing months, including 13,000 Jews from Berlin alone in 1933 (Gruner 2009: 170).

With the nationwide boycott, the Nazi leadership succeeded in synchronizing SA violence and municipal initiatives and creating an atmosphere in which the first anti-Jewish laws could be enacted. These excluded Jews from certain professions, such as the law and the civil service. The infamous Professional Civil Service Law of 7 April 1933, which aimed to "cleanse" the public administration of communists, socialists, and Jews, legalized the earlier dismissals by some municipalities and provided a tool for further discrimination at all administrative levels in the form of the notorious "Aryan paragraph," which defined Germans who had one Jewish grandparent as non-Aryan.

During the ensuing months, central, regional, and local authorities dismissed most of their Jewish employees, as did universities, medical insurance agencies, banks, savings and loan associations, and public transportation companies. Various municipalities introduced new restrictions on Jews. Prohibitions of visits to public swimming pools or markets were particularly damaging because the segregation was advertised in public, it stigmatized all Jews without distinction, and municipal actions were perceived as acts of state authority. Local restrictions, national laws, and the steady propaganda produced pressure for people to conform. Political parties, social clubs, and private organizations now became closed to Jews with few exceptions (Gruner 2000b: 75–88).

Jewish individuals and organizations protested against the spreading discrimination in letters to Reich ministries or Nazi leaders. Later, the *Reichsvertretung der deutschen Juden*, the new umbrella organization of the German Jews headed by Rabbi Leo Baeck (1873–1956), raised its voice several times. Foreign consulates intervened frequently on behalf of their citizens. Perhaps as a result, in late summer 1933, the National Socialist leadership chose to slow down the persecution and ordered the repeal of local restrictions not sanctioned by law, in particular those refusing Jews entrance to public baths or entire localities (Mommsen and Willems 1988: 429). Despite the supposed existence of a dictatorial "Führer state," the decree produced little effect: few towns withdrew their measures, and some cities even introduced new ones (Gruner 2000b: 86). Although further instructions criticized the widespread use of the "Aryan Paragraph," in January 1934 Reich interior minister Wilhelm Frick (1877–1946) underlined his unwillingness to impede initiatives that aimed at "treating non-Aryans in a special way" (Pätzold 1983: 70). His stance reflected a policy of controlled decentralization, in which the arena of persecution changed from the national to the local level.

Developments at the local level were hardly spontaneous. Many of the activities were coordinated by the German Council of Municipalities (*Deutscher Gemeinde-tag*) that the Nazi regime founded in May 1933 as a compulsory membership organization for town governments. Thanks to the resulting flow of information, exclusion reached previously unimaginable proportions during the following year. By the end of 1934, the city of Berlin had alone enacted more than fifty-five restrictions on Jews (Gruner 2002 and 2009). Rabbi Joachim Prinz (1902–1988) summarized the situation of the city's Jews with the remarkable words: "Outside is the ghetto for us. At the public markets, on the road, in the restaurants, everywhere there's the ghetto. It is indicated by a sign. The sign reads: neighborless" (*Jüdische Rundschau*, 17 April 1935).

In January 1935, most inhabitants of the Saar, which had been governed since 1919 by the League of Nations, opted for union with Germany. The Nazi leadership celebrated this first step toward the realization of Greater Germany by putting more pressure on the Jews. Propaganda was reintensified, and the SA and SS engaged in violent attacks in various regions. New laws excluded Jewish men from the German army and the Reich Labor Service. During that summer, newspaper propaganda depicted Jews as criminals, stigmatized relationships with Jews, and promoted new municipal restrictions (Gruner 2000b: 95).

Despite countless local, regional, and central initiatives Hitler remained the supreme authority over anti-Jewish policy, and he intervened in it frequently and powerfully (Longerich 2001). As new laws were being contemplated, he forbade further anti-Jewish actions that had not been approved by Berlin. With the enactment of the notorious Nuremberg Laws, which had been under discussion since 1933, central policy reached a new stage in September 1935. By means of a racial definition, Germans of Jewish origin (now defined as people with three or four grandparents of Jewish faith) were stripped of political and civil rights. Plans for a law excluding them from parts of the German economy were dropped, however (Pätzold 1975: 272–80; Essner 2002: 113–54). As in the spring of 1933, no simple welling up of local party pressure pushed the government to introduce new laws, as some historians contend (e.g., Longerich 1998: 25–41, 71–101). The facts clearly point to an intertwined process of central and local administrative radicalization.

While the Nazi government issued further restrictions on Jews' access to professions and education in 1936–37, and the Gestapo and the Security Service of the SS coordinated their anti-Jewish tasks (Wildt 1995), municipalities—encouraged by the German Council of Municipalities—now extended bans for Jews to parks, pawnshops, hospitals, theaters, zoos, and shelters for the homeless. Local welfare offices reduced assistance for poor Jews. By the end of 1937, anti-Jewish regulations were common in German cities, but the degree of segregation varied according to the ambitions of the local personnel (Gruner 2000b and 2002).

The law evolved similarly. Initially, German courts issued contradictory rules in labor, criminal, or civil matters regarding Jews. Judges, prosecutors, and lawyers at local courts first showed more restraint in applying Nazi interpretations of the law than the personnel at regional or national courts, but slowly adopted increasingly antisemitic behavior (Noam and Kropat 1975; Majer 2003). New court rulings often triggered new legislation, and the combined result was the gradual construction of a "special law" for Jews (Blau 1954; Walk 1981).

Displacement of Jews from the economic sphere proceeded similarly. In 1933, many Jewish members of the business elites were induced to resign from their firms. Later, increasing local pressure drove Jewish entrepreneurs to close their businesses or sell them to "Aryan" competitors. Local studies have shown that the process developed often faster in small towns than in big cities (e.g., Bajohr 2002). No law had sanctioned the "Aryanization" of property, stores, and enterprises so far. Fear of disruptions in the economy even led the Nazi leadership to intervene several times to slow down the process (Genschel 1966; Barkai 1988; Wojak and Hayes 2000). Nonetheless, neither in general, nor in local settings did Jews experience a "quiet" interlude during 1936 and 1937. As a result of relentless but decentralized persecution, unemployment and pauperization increased dramatically (Barkai 1988; Benz 1988; Gruner 2002).

In the summer of 1937, after the expiration of the 1922 treaty between Poland and Germany that had governed the treatment of minorities, riots took place and anti-Jewish laws were introduced in Upper Silesia. Now, the Nazi leadership set out to fulfill two of the preconditions for building a Greater Germany by forcing the expulsion of the more than 350,000 remaining Jews within the Reich's borders and conquering Austria and Bohemia. The combination of a projected war, a predictable massive increase of the Jewish population as a result of annexations, and limited prospects for emigration fundamentally changed the framework of Nazi anti-Jewish policy in 1938.

THE CREATION OF GREATER GERMANY AND THE COORDINATION OF ANTI-JEWISH POLICY

Only days after the annexation of Austria in March 1938, when Hitler dissolved the German parliament and called for elections to a new representative body for "Greater Germany," his moment of glory had an ironic side: the gains of five years of anti-Jewish policy had vanished, since the 190,000 Jews in annexed Austria outnumbered those who had been driven from Germany since 1933. On 26 March 1938, Hermann Göring (1893–1946) publicly demanded that Vienna, where 90 percent of the Austrian Jews dwelt, should be made "free of Jews" within four years. The hasty process of catching up with the anti-Jewish standards of Germany, as well as the first weeks of institutional confusion, triggered brutal attacks on Jews and their property by the Nazi Party formations in Vienna. The new mayor, Hermann Neubacher (1893–1960), swiftly purged the municipality's Jewish employees, and during the next months, other public agencies and private enterprises followed suit. The Nazi activists achieved in weeks what had taken years to accomplish in Germany. But Austrians also pushed anti-Jewish policy even beyond German standards. The mayors of Vienna and Linz ordered the segregation of Jewish pupils in public schools, and the Austrian Ministry of Education promptly legalized those measures in June 1938 (Rosenkranz 1978; Gruner 2000a). A corresponding decree for the German Reich was issued only six months later.

Reacting to the disturbing economic and political effects of the radical attacks in Austria, Göring undertook to centralize anti-Jewish policy. A decree of 26 April 1938 mandated the registration of Jewish property throughout Greater Germany. During the following months, Jews were excluded from additional professions and commercial activities. Reich ministries banned public contracts with Jewish enterprises and isolated Jews in public hospitals, thus extending the policies of municipalities to the entire nation. Most measures drastically impoverished many Jews and thus reduced their chances of emigrating. To break this impasse, the state responded with violence and sent thousands of German and Austrian Jews with minor criminal records to concentration camps (Gruner 2000a and 2000b).

To force emigration from Vienna and to organize this process effectively, a Central Office for Jewish Emigration was established in mid-1938 under Adolf Eichmann (1906–1962) and the SS Security Service. However, this organization did not command anti-Jewish policy there, as some historians assume (e.g., Anderl 1994; Safrian 2010: 19–27). Instead, it participated in a division of labor with the NSDAP district leaders, the Reich Commissar Joseph Bürckel (1895–1944), and the Vienna municipality (Gruner 2000a: 23–30).

In mid-September 1938, the annual Nazi party rally in Nuremberg was heralded as "the convention of Greater Germany". Hitler demanded the revision of the Versailles treaty and an end to the supposed oppression of the 3.5 million Germans in Czechoslovakia. Through the Munich Agreement a few weeks later, Germany gained the Czech border territories, the so called *Sudeten* area, inhabited by many Germans. Nevertheless, Hitler was still plotting to annex Bohemia and Moravia. In the face of a possible war with the rump Czech Republic, the Gestapo and the SS Security Service, as well as the Reich ministries, began to discuss ghettoization and conscript labor as new forms of anti-Jewish policy (Gruner 2000b). Force was a possible means. At the end of October 1938, the German state expelled 17,000 Jews of Polish origin. Among the deportees were the parents of a young man whose response was to assassinate a German diplomat in Paris. This act presented Hitler with a welcome pretext to instigate a pogrom in Greater Germany. During the night of 9–10 November, SA and SS members set synagogues ablaze and invaded and looted countless apartments, homes, Jewish institutions, and shops. Many Jews committed suicide, more than 100 people were murdered, and as many as 30,000 men were clapped into concentration camps where many died. Yet, force could not resolve the contradiction built into the German persecution policy: the more it took from the Jews, the less chance they had of emigrating.

After the pogrom, the Nazi leadership therefore began preparing to segregate the remaining Jews from the rest of society. Greater Germany imposed a special head tax on the Jews, put the "Aryanization" of Jewish property under state control, and prohibited commercial or professional activity by Jews. Jews were banned from public schools, the poor excluded from public welfare, and the unemployed forced to perform manual labor. Under Göring's supervision, the Security Main Office took charge of emigration issues and all Jewish institutions were subordinated to a new compulsory organization called the *Reichsvereinigung der Juden in Deutschland*. No comparable entity was established in Austria, since the Gestapo's control of the Jewish community already seemed complete.

While the ministries controlled "Aryanization" and the collection of special taxes, a law of 30 April 1939 gave the cities the authority to create segregated residences, the so-called *Judenhäuser*. The pace and manner of the segregation depended on the degree of local zeal. In May, the municipality of Vienna began forcing thousands to move to apartments in buildings owned by Jews in certain districts, and Leipzig and Dresden "purged" whole districts of Jews by the end of 1939. Göttingen, by contrast, began to set up separate housing in fall 1940, and the city of Hanover waited until mid-1941 (Exenberger et al. 1996; Gruner 2000a and 2000b).

In addition, the cities retained autonomy over the implementation of national policies. In spring 1939, when Jews were forced to sell their precious metals and jewelry, the municipal pawnshops had considerable leeway concerning the process of collection and the purchase prices. Following the decree of 19 November 1938 on the exclusion from state welfare benefits, municipal welfare offices frequently shed their Jewish clients, even when local Gestapo offices opposed this for fear that Jewish agencies could not carry the resulting burden. In Berlin, however, the obligation to provide assistance for tens of thousands of Jewish needy was not transferred to the Jewish community until 1940 (Gruner 2002: 235–94).

Following an idea developed in Vienna in September, the national labor administration on 20 December 1938 obligated all Jews receiving unemployment benefits to accept work assignments issued by local labor exchanges. By the summer of 1939, more than 20,000 Jewish males were performing heavy manual labor on local, regional, and supra-regional construction projects for public bodies and private enterprises. Cities exploited Jews at garbage dumps, gasworks, streets, and parks. Some employers paid the minimum wage for unskilled labor, while others paid nothing (Barkai 1988; Gruner 2006).

As Nazi leaders planned the occupation of Bohemia and Moravia, representatives of the army and the Gestapo discussed "the service of Jews in case of war" with the Reich Interior Ministry, projecting that some 200,000 Jewish males could be put to forced labor (Kwiet 1991: 408–10). However, after Germany occupied the western part of the Czechoslovakian Republic without incident on 15 March 1939, the planning was suspended. The next day, Hitler declared the territory a part of the German Reich and dubbed it the Protectorate of Bohemia and Moravia. Inhabitants of German ancestry became German citizens, but Czechs and Jews only citizens of the Protectorate. The at least 118,310 Jews (Kárný 1986) were now subjected to anti-Jewish policies shaped by four different groups: the Czech Government headed by Alois Eliaš (1890–1942), the German Reich Protector Konstantin von Neurath (1873–1956), the German security police, and the local authorities.

Immediately after the occupation, Jews were attacked and synagogues burned. As had happened in Germany and Austria, the Czech government quickly cut off Jews from many employment opportunities (Rothkirchen 2005: 99–101). In May 1939, the Czech government informed the Germans of its intention to exclude Jews from citizenship and public life. But the Reich Protector insisted on even more radical regulations. His decree of 21 June defined Jews racially according to the Nuremberg Laws and ordered the registration of their property as had occurred in Germany and Austria. This started a rush to "Aryanize" Jewish assets. The Czech Ministry of Interior instructed local authorities on 3 August 1939 to segregate Jews in swimming pools, restaurants, and coffee houses and to label all Jewish businesses. Reinhard Heydrich (1904–1942), head of the security police, initially had instructed the Prague police to stop Jewish emigration because Czech Jews would reduce German Jews' chances to depart. However, by July 1939, a Central Office for Jewish Emigration, subordinated to the Security Main Office in Berlin, was established in Prague on the Austrian model. Its aim was to force expulsion from the newest part of Greater Germany, but with the additional stipulation that money taken from Czech Jews would be used to increase the emigration of German Jews (Gruner in Milotová and Wögerbauer 2005: 34–6).

THE WAR AND RESETTLEMENT

Prior to the outbreak of World War II, more than 250,000 Jews were able to flee Germany out of a population of 500,000 in 1933; of the 320,000 Jews of Austria and Bohemia-Moravia in 1938, only 128,000 escaped by September 1939, when all borders were closed. The resulting situation prompted a radical new decision: Shortly after the fall of Warsaw, Hitler gave the order to "resettle" 300,000 Jews from Greater Germany on a "reservation" in eastern Poland. This meant almost all Jews, probably excepting only the elderly, since the total number of members of Jewish religious communities still living in Germany, Austria, and the Protectorate at that moment came to 326,000, and the number of Jews according to the Nazi racial criteria to about 430,000.

Eichmann, the chief organizer of the upcoming transports, promptly compiled lists of all registered Jews in the three territories. Soon, the recently established Reich Security Main Office in Berlin gave the green light for transports. After several thousand Jews from the Protectorate, Austria, and eastern Upper Silesia had been deported in October 1939, and shortly before the first transports from Germany were scheduled to leave, SS chief Heinrich Himmler (1900–1945) suspended the operation for technical reasons. Transports resumed on 13 February 1940, when over 1,000 German Jews from Stettin and a dozen other Pomeranian towns were deported to locations near Lublin, now in the so-called General Government. Only because Göring and Heydrich then decided to assign priority to the "cleansing" of the annexed Polish territories (the *Warthegau* and East Upper Silesia) did these deportations from Germany cease (Gruner in Kundrus and Meyer 2004: 32–40).

"Resettlement" thus replaced forced labor as the centerpiece of Nazi planning immediately after the war began. So long, however, as the transports did not roll, the labor administration wished to exploit the available manpower. All able-bodied Jews, not just the unemployed, were put to forced labor in spring 1940, primarily in war industries (Gruner 2006). In the meantime, some municipalities intensified the segregation of the Jews by restricting them to separate shops or limited shopping hours, as in Vienna in September 1939 or in Berlin in July 1940. That same month, in response to local demands, the Czech Interior Minister decreed a limitation of shopping hours for the Protectorate (Gruner in Milotová and Wögerbauer 2005: 41–3).

After the quick victory over France in June 1940, deportation planning took on fantastically ambitious dimensions, as Nazi authorities envisioned exiling millions of European Jews to a French colony, the island of Madagascar (Brechtken 1997: 221–83). That pipedream dissolved, however, when Germany failed to bomb Britain into suing for peace during the fall of 1940. The Reich Security Main Office was allowed to deport 6,500 German Jews from Baden and the Palatinate to France on 22 and 23 October 1940, but the near-term solution appeared once again to be transports to Poland. In early December, Hitler ordered all 60,000 Jews still living in Vienna deported. Yet, even this plan could not be implemented fully; only 5,000 Jews had reached the General Government by March 1941, when a new stop took effect (Rosenkranz 1978: 258–61; Gruner in Kundrus and Meyer 2004: 41–3). Meanwhile, an eleventh supplementary decree to the Reich citizenship law was discussed among the Reich ministries. It would revoke the citizenship of German Jews who had taken "residence" abroad and declare their property automatically forfeit to the Reich (Adam 1972: 292–9; Dean 2008: 161–71).

German planning for an attack on the Soviet Union made further "evacuation" of Jews from the Reich impossible for the moment, but officials continued to lay the basis for that process. On 26 March 1941, Heydrich presented to Göring a new plan that designated the Soviet Union as the future destination of mass transports (Aly 1999: 171–7). This strategic shift set off a reshuffling within the Reich Security Main Office, a Gestapo drive to close down most Jewish organizations and hand over the former employees for forced labor, and the removal of thousands of Jewish families from their dwellings to forty new camps, where most of them were consigned to forced labor (Gruner 2000b and 2006).

Meanwhile, compulsory labor had been introduced in the Protectorate, and by the summer of 1941, a total of 11,700 Jews, mostly men between the ages of 16 and 60, had been conscripted for that purpose, which brought the total of Jews toiling in Greater Germany to 70,000 (Gruner 2006: 152–67). The increasing importance of their forced labor did not conflict with the overall plan to remove the Jews because an infinite quantity of manpower was expected after the victory against the Soviet Union, which had been invaded on 22 June 1941. Hence, at the end of July, the Nazi leadership decided on new deportations. Hitler assured Goebbels that the Jews would be "expelled from Berlin to the East as soon as possible" (Goebbels 1996: 266). Following an initiative from the Protectorate, and to facilitate the impending deportations, Heydrich issued a police order on 1 September 1941, requiring Jews in Greater Germany to wear a yellow star on their outermost garments and prohibiting them from leaving their places of residence without a permit (Pätzold 1983: 294).

The slowing of the German advance into Russia led the impatient regime to search for intermediate destinations as it "cleansed" the Reich. Thus, Himmler agreed in early September 1941 to send 60,000 Jews from Greater Germany to the ghetto of Łódź/Litzmannstadt in the annexed *Warthegau* (Witte et al. 1999: 205). Now, the Jewish communities of Vienna, Berlin, and Prague were informed of the imminent "evacuation." Since the prospective destination was within the German Reich, the contemplated automatic loss of citizenship when crossing the nation's borders could not be applied to these deportees, so the Reich Security Main Office ordered the "collective confiscation" of their property on the grounds that the Jews' "aspiration" to be expelled to the Litzmannstadt ghetto was "hostile to the state." In mid-October 1941, the first trains left Vienna, Prague, and Berlin, but they carried "only" 20,000 Jews because the Łódź ghetto could not cram in any more.

Responding to the need for other destinations, Hitler chose Riga and Minsk. On 23 October, Eichmann notified the regional Gestapo offices of the next "evacuation" wave of 50,000 Jews from Greater Germany (Gruner in Kundrus and Meyer 2004: 50–2). At this point, the Nazi leadership considered expanding the previously scattered and limited shipments into a continuous outflow. On 10 October, Heydrich, the new Deputy Reich Protector in Prague, mentioned Hitler's instruction to get "as many Jews as possible out of German space" by the end of 1941 (Kárný 1997: 137–41). To that end, they were tallied: 150,925 persons defined as Jews still lived in Germany, 47,578 in Austria, and 83,961 in the Protectorate (*Reichsvereinigung* statistics, 1 November 1941). Since the new destinations, Riga and Minsk, were located outside Greater German boundaries, on 25 November 1941, the eleventh supplementary decree to the Reich citizenship law finally was announced, depriving Jews of their citizenship and confiscating their property at the moment they exited the country (Essner 2002: 292–305; Dean 2008: 161–71).

In the meantime, the Nazi leadership had decided on the "resettlement" of all Jews in occupied Europe in the near future. On 23 October 1941, Himmler notified the relevant offices in Greater Germany and occupied Belgium and France that he forbade any further "emigration of Jews." On 29 November, Heydrich issued invitations for an interministerial conference to be held in Berlin-Wannsee (Gruner in Kundrus and Meyer 2004: 54–5).

The Organization of Deportation, Expropriation, and Mass Murder

Heydrich revealed at the notorious Wannsee conference of 20 January 1942 that 537,000 Jews had been driven from Greater Germany since 1933. With Hitler's approval, emigration now had been superseded by "evacuation" to the east. This "Final Solution" was to encompass 11 million European Jews. Although historians long believed that this meeting made the decision for genocide, they now recognize that its purpose was to secure the cooperation of all relevant agencies with the mass murder project (Roseman 2002). The fundamental decision had been made earlier, although whether it occurred in the summer of 1941 amidst euphoria about the likelihood of victory in the Soviet Union (Browning 2004), in the fall as a result of disillusion over the slowing of Germany's offensive (Burrin 1994), or in December in reaction to America's entry into the war (Gerlach 1998) is still contested.

Jews from Greater Germany were the first to be deported to the east. On 6 March 1942, Eichmann declared that the transports interrupted since January for military reasons would resume with 55,000 more Jews (Adler 1974: 193). For the sake of speed and efficiency, Eichmann and his staff bypassed traditional administrative channels, communicated by radio and phone, and traveled by car and airplane to talk in person to the local authorities in the annexed and occupied territories. In contrast to most anti-Jewish measures, local initiatives played no role in the progress of the deportations. The Reich Security Main Office determined the where, how, and when of the transports. The local Gestapo took care of the selection, collection, expropriation, and removal of the victims in close collaboration with the labor offices, Wehrmacht armaments inspection offices, police, municipalities, local courts, tax offices, and railway directorates (Adler 1974; Kenkmann 1999; Gruner in Kundrus and Meyer 2004).

In response to requests from the army and the labor administration after the first transports, the Gestapo agreed to spare Jews employed in war industries until they could easily be replaced. In the Protectorate, labor offices even expanded their forced labor program as other Jews were being deported, with the result that over 16,000 women and men toiled at construction sites and in Czech industry in spring 1942 (Gruner 2006).

An arson attack on the Berlin propaganda exhibit "Soviet Paradise" and the assassination of Heydrich apparently spurred a decision among the Nazi leaders to accelerate the deportations. On 29 May 1942, representatives of the *Reichsvereinigung* and the Jewish communities of Berlin, Prague, and Vienna were summoned by Eichmann and told that the "total evacuation of the Jews" was now under way. All Jews under the age of 65 would be sent from Greater Germany to the occupied east, the elderly and veterans to "permanent residence" in the ghetto Terezin (*Theresienstadt*) in the Protectorate (Safrian 2010: 118). The resulting process of removing the Jews illustrates both the extent of Hitler's power and its limitations. Within a few months, most regions of Greater Germany were "cleansed." At the end of 1942, out of an original population of over 800,000 Jews, merely 74,959 remained (51,327 in Germany, 8,102 in Austria, 15,530 in the Protectorate), almost half of whom were married to non-Jews (Inspekteur für Statistik beim RFSS, "Die Endlösung der europäischen Judenfrage," 1 April 1943: 4–5). Yet, despite Hitler's wish for Berlin to be the first city "free of Jews," the majority of those remaining in Germany still inhabited the heart of the Nazi empire. The reason: 15,000 Jews toiled in Berlin's industries. Only in February 1943, when hundreds of thousands of workers brought from all over Europe relieved the German labor market, did the Reich Security Main Office feel free to deport most of the remaining Jews and their families from Berlin and the Reich to Auschwitz (Gruner 2006).

In mid-May 1943, Himmler set the end of June as the date for the last transports from Greater Germany (Lozowick 2002: 107–8, 113). The *Reichsvereinigung* was dissolved and only a minor office remained for the Jews living in mixed marriages. Already at the end of 1942 and the beginning of 1943, the Jewish community offices in Vienna and Prague had been closed and "councils of elders" appointed (Benz 1988: 690–700; Gruner 2000a: 264–71; Rothkirchen 2005: 130). The last big transport left Berlin for Auschwitz on 28 June 1943, with some 300 victims, most of them former employees of Jewish organizations (Gottwaldt and Schulle 2005: 421–2). Exactly at this moment, when the nation was being described as "free of Jews," Hitler demanded that diplomatic communications refer to him as "the leader of the Greater German Reich," and the appellation "Greater German Reich" appeared for the first time, five years after the annexation of Austria, in international treaties and on national stamps. Only a dwindling number of Jews remained within the country, some protected, though ever less well, by their "mixed marriages" and others in hiding.

CONCLUSION

After World War I, the racist vision of a Greater Germany constituted one of the driving political forces, especially in "folkish" circles and the National Socialist movement. However, in addition to antisemitic ideology, many

interests—personal and bureaucratic, political and economic—shaped anti-Jewish
policy once Nazism came to power. Because Hitler did not outline exactly how to
achieve the stated goal of expelling the Jews, he opened the way for authorities at
every state level to act. Political decisions emerged from open discussions, pragmatic choices, institutional compromises, and individual initiatives rather than a
long-term master plan. Conflicts between party and state never dominated the
political arena, as suggested by one famous interpretation (Fraenkel 1941), nor did
polycratic chaos, as argued by others (cf. Hüttenberger 1976).

Hitler, the Reich ministries, and other central agencies were responsible at the
national level for the persecution policy. While Hitler usually based his decisions
on the preparatory work of the ministries, he retained final say on the formulation
of laws and on the moment for introducing them. He personally decided on the
1933 boycott, the Nuremberg Laws, the 1938 pogrom, and the deportations. Nonetheless, a dynamic relationship between periphery and center shaped the persecution process in a special way. At the regional and local level, party leaders and state
administrations developed their own initiatives, and municipalities played a key
role, more so than the local NSDAP. The German Council of Municipalities, as well
as regional authorities, often backed city initiatives against ministerial reservations.
Thus, the persecution did not follow a top-down model; rather for long periods it
testified to a policy of controlled decentralization. Dynamic interaction among
local, regional, and central administrations was a common feature not only in
Germany but also in Austria and the Protectorate. Moreover, the policies developed
in the annexed territories had effects on the decision-making process in Berlin.
While Austria has always been regarded as a catalyst for radicalization, the influence of developments in Bohemia and Moravia has been overlooked.

Just as historians have underestimated the radicalizing impact of local and
regional initiatives on the central decision-making process, they have overesti-
mated the influence of the Gestapo and the SS Security Service. Their part in
implementing the persecution increased after the mid-1930s, but remained limited
and shared with the ministries and municipalities. At the end of 1938, when Göring
centralized anti-Jewish policy in reaction to events in annexed Austria, both
organizations gained full control of the Jewish institutions and emigration, while
ministries supervised forced labor and expropriation and the cities handled ghettoization. Only in the context of mass deportations from Greater Germany during
1941 could the Reich Security Main office partly abrogate this division of labor.

Many Germans and Austrians, but also Czechs, profited from the expulsion of
the Jews from Greater Germany, first with jobs or better career chances, later with
bigger apartments and expropriated property. Only a decreased solidarity on the
part of the non-Jewish population, in conjunction with the systematic segregation
of the Jews on the local level, could create the social, psychological, and organizational preconditions for Hitler's decision in 1939 for total deportation of the Jews to
the occupied east. The "twisted road" that led to Auschwitz (Schleunes 1970) was

built by many people at multiple levels of government, but its direction was determined by the idea of a Greater Germany.

REFERENCES

ADAM, U. (1972). *Judenpolitik im Dritten Reich*. Düsseldorf: Droste Verlag.

ADLER, H. (1974). *Der verwaltete Mensch: Studien zur Deportation der Juden aus Deutschland*. Tübingen: Mohr.

ALY, G. (1999). *"Final Solution": Nazi Population Policy and the Murder of the European Jews*. London: Arnold.

ANDERL, G. (1994). "'Die Zentralstellen für jüdische Auswanderung' in Wien, Berlin und Prag—ein Vergleich." *Tel Aviver Jahrbuch für deutsche Geschichte* 23: 276–99.

BAJOHR, F. (2002). *"Aryanisation" in Hamburg: The Economic Exclusion of Jews and the Confiscation of their Property in Nazi Germany*. New York: Berghahn Books.

BANKIER, D. (1995). *Die öffentliche Meinung im Hitler-Staat: Die "Endlösung" und die Deutschen. Eine Berichtigung*. Berlin: Spitz.

BARKAI, A. (1988). *From Boycott to Annihilation: The Economic Struggle of German Jews, 1933–1943*. Hanover, NH: University Press of New England.

BENZ, W. (ed.) (1988). *Die Juden in Deutschland 1933–1945: Leben unter nationalsozialistischer Herrschaft*. With Volker Dahm et al. Munich: C.H. Beck.

——(ed.) (1991). *Dimension des Völkermords: Die Zahl der jüdischen Opfer des Nationalsozialismus*. Munich: Oldenbourg Verlag.

BLAU, B. (ed.) (1954). *Das Ausnahmerecht für die Juden in Deutschland 1933–1945*. 2nd edn. Düsseldorf: Allgemeine Wochenzeitung der Juden in Deutschland.

BRECHTKEN, M. (1997). *"Madagaskar für die Juden": Antisemitische Idee und politische Praxis 1885–1945*. Munich: Oldenbourg.

BROWNING, C. (2004). *The Origins of the Final Solution: The Evolution of Nazi Jewish Policy, September 1939–March 1942*. With contributions by J. Matthäus. Lincoln, NE: University of Nebraska Press.

BURRIN, P. (1994). *Hitler and the Jews: The Genesis of the Holocaust*. London: Edward Arnold.

DEAN, M. (2008). *Robbing the Jews. The Confiscation of Jewish Property in the Holocaust, 1933–1945*. New York: Cambridge University Press.

ESSNER, C. (2002). *"Die Nürnberger Gesetze" oder die Verwaltung des Rassenwahns 1933–1945*. Paderborn: Schöningh.

EXENBERGER, H., KOSS, J., and UNGAR-KLEIN, B. (1996). *Kündigungsgrund Nichtarier: Die Vertreibung jüdischer Mieter aus den Wiener Gemeindebauten in den Jahren 1938–1939*. Vienna: Picus-Verlag.

FLIEDNER, H. (1971). *Die Judenverfolgung in Mannheim 1933–1945*. Vol. 2, *Dokumente*. Stuttgart: Kohlhammer.

FRAENKEL, E. (1941). *The Dual State: A Contribution to the Theory of Dictatorship*. New York: Oxford University Press.

FRIEDLÄNDER, S. (1997). *Nazi Germany and the Jews*. Vol. 1, *The Years of Persecution, 1933–1939*. New York: HarperCollins.

GENSCHEL, H. (1966). *Die Verdrängung der Juden aus der Wirtschaft im Dritten Reich.* Göttingen: Musterschmidt.

GERLACH, C. (1998). "The Wannsee Conference, the Fate of German Jews, and Hitler's Decision in Principle to Exterminate All European Jews." *Journal of Modern History* 70/4: 759–812.

GOEBBELS, J. (1996). *Die Tagebücher von Joseph Goebbels: Teil II: Diktate 1941–1945,* Vol. 1. Ed. E. Fröhlich. Munich: Saur Verlag.

GOTTWALDT, A. and SCHULLE, D. (2005). *Die "Judendeportationen" aus dem Deutschen Reich 1941–1945: Eine kommentierte Chronologie.* Wiesbaden: Marixverlag.

GRUNER, W. (2000a). *Zwangsarbeit und Verfolgung: Österreichische Juden im NS-Staat 1938–1945.* Innsbruck: StudienVerlag.

——(2000b). "Die NS-Judenverfolgung und die Kommunen: Zur wechselseitigen Dynamisierung von zentraler und lokaler Politik 1933–1941." *Vierteljahrshefte für Zeitgeschichte* 48/1: 75–126.

——(2002). *Öffentliche Wohlfahrt und Judenverfolgung: Wechselwirkungen lokaler und zentraler Politik im NS-Staat (1933–1942).* Munich: Oldenbourg Verlag.

——(2006). *Jewish Forced Labor under the Nazis: Economic Needs and Racial Aims 1938–1944.* New York: Cambridge University Press.

——(2009). *Judenverfolgung in Berlin 1933–1945: Eine Chronologie der Behördenmaßnahmen in der Reichshauptstadt.* Rev. edn. Berlin: Hentrich.

HAMANN, B. (1999). *Hitler's Vienna: A Dictator's Apprenticeship.* New York: Oxford University Press.

HÜTTENBERGER, P. (1976). "Nationalsozialistische Polykratie." *Geschichte und Gesellschaft* 2: 417–42.

JÄCKEL, E. (ed.) with KUHN, A. (1980). *Hitler: Sämtliche Aufzeichnungen 1905–1924.* Stuttgart: Deutsche Verlagsanstalt.

KÁRNÝ, M. (1986). "Zur Statistik der jüdischen Bevölkerung im sogenannten Protektorat." *Judaica Bohemiae* 22/1: 9–19.

——(ed.) (1997). *Deutsche Politik im "Protektorat Böhmen und Mähren" unter Reinhard Heydrich 1941–1942: eine Dokumentation.* Berlin: Metropol-Verlag.

KENKMANN, A. (ed.) (1999). *Verfolgung und Verwaltung: Die wirtschaftliche Ausplünderung der Juden und die westfälischen Finanzbehörden.* Münster: Villa ten Hompel.

KOMMISSION ZUR ERFORSCHUNG DER GESCHICHTE DER FRANKFURTER JUDEN (ed.) (1963). *Dokumente zur Geschichte der Frankfurter Juden.* Frankfurt am Main: Kramer.

KUNDRUS, B. and MEYER, B. (eds.) (2004). *Beiträge zur Geschichte des Nationalsozialismus.* Vol. 20, *Die Deportation der Juden aus Deutschland: Pläne, Praxis, Reaktionen 1938–1945.* Göttingen: Wallstein Verlag.

KWIET, K. (1991). "Forced Labor of German Jews in Nazi Germany." *Leo Baeck Institute Year Book* 23: 389–410.

LONGERICH, P. (1998). *Politik der Vernichtung: Eine Gesamtdarstellung der nationalsozialistischen Judenverfolgung.* Munich: Piper.

——(2001). *The Unwritten Order: Hitler's Role in the Final Solution.* Stroud: Tempus.

——(2006). *"Davon haben wir nichts gewußt": Die Deutschen und die Judenverfolgung 1933–1945.* Munich: Siedler Verlag.

LOZOWICK, Y. (2002). *Hitler's Bureaucrats: The Nazi Security Police and the Banality of Evil.* London and New York: Continuum.

MAJER, D. (2003). *"Non-Germans" under the Third Reich*. Baltimore, MD: Johns Hopkins University Press.

MILOTOVÁ, J. and WÖGERBAUER, M. (eds.) (2005). *Theresienstädter Studien und Dokumente 2005*. Prague: Sefer-Institut Theresientädter Initiative.

MOMMSEN, H. and WILLEMS, S. (eds.) (1988). *Herrschaftsalltag im Dritten Reich: Studien und Texte*. Düsseldorf: Schwann.

NOAM, E. and KROPAT, W. (1975). *Juden vor Gericht 1933–1945: Dokumente aus hessischen Justizakten*. Wiesbaden: Kommission für die Geschichte der Juden in Hessen.

PÄTZOLD, K. (1975). *Faschismus, Rassenwahn, Judenverfolgung: Eine Studie zur politischen Strategie und Taktik des faschistischen Imperialismus (1933–1935)*. Berlin: Deutscher Verlag der Wissenschaften.

——(ed.) (1983). *Verfolgung, Vertreibung, Vernichtung: Dokumente des faschistischen Antisemitismus 1933–1942*. Leipzig: Reclam Verlag.

ROSEMAN, M. (2002). *The Villa, the Lake, the Meeting: The Wannsee Conference and the "Final Solution."* Harmondsworth: Penguin.

ROSENKRANZ, H. (1978). *Verfolgung und Selbstbehauptung: Die Juden in Österreich 1938–1945*. Wien: Herold.

ROTHKIRCHEN, L. (2005). *The Jews of Bohemia and Moravia: Facing the Holocaust*. Lincoln, NE: University of Nebraska Press.

SAFRIAN, H. (2010). *Eichmann's Men*. New York: Cambridge University Press.

SAUER, P. (ed.) (1966). *Dokumente über die Verfolgung der jüdischen Bürger in Baden-Württemberg durch das nationalsozialistische Regime 1933–1945*. Stuttgart: Kohlhammer.

SCHLEUNES, K. (1970). *The Twisted Road to Auschwitz: Nazi Policy towards German Jews 1933–1939*. Urbana, IL: University of Illinois Press.

WALK, J. (ed.) (1981). *Das Sonderrecht für die Juden im NS-Staat: Eine Sammlung der gesetzlichen Maßnahmen—Inhalt und Bedeutung*. Heidelberg-Karlsruhe: Müller.

WILDT, M. (ed.) (1995). *Die Judenpolitik des SD 1935 bis 1938: Eine Dokumentation*. Munich: Oldenbourg.

WITTE, P. et al. (eds.) (1999). *Der Dienstkalender Heinrich Himmlers 1941/42*. Edited for the Forschungsstelle für Zeitgeschichte in Hamburg. Hamburg: Christians.

WOJAK, I. and HAYES, P. (eds.) (2000). *"Arisierung" im Nationalsozialismus: Volksgemeinschaft, Raub und Gedächtnis*. Jahrbuch 2000 zur Geschichte und Wirkung des Holocaust des Fritz Bauer Instituts. Frankfurt am Main and New York: Campus.

OTHER SUGGESTED READING

ADLER, H. (1955). *Theresienstadt 1941–1945: Das Antlitz einer Zwangsgemeinschaft. Geschichte, Soziologie, Psychologie*. Tübingen: Mohr (Siebeck).

EVANS, R. (2005). *The Third Reich in Power 1933–1939*. New York: Penguin Press.

GELLATELY, R. (2001). *Backing Hitler: Consent and Coercion in Nazi Germany*. New York: Oxford University Press.

GRUNER, W. (ed.) (2008). *Die Verfolgung und Ermordung der europäischen Juden durch das nationalsozialistische Deutschland 1933–1945*, ed. G. Aly, W. Gruner et al. Vol. 1, *Deutsches Reich 1933–1937*, Munich: R. Oldenbourg Verlag.

KERSHAW, I. (1998). *Hitler 1889–1936: Hubris*. London: Penguin Press.

——(2000). *Hitler 1936–1945: Nemesis.* London: Penguin Press.

WILDT, M. (2007). *Volksgemeinschaft als Selbstermächtigung: Gewalt gegen Juden in der deutschen Provinz 1919 bis 1939.* Hamburg: Hamburger Edition.

——(2009). *An Uncompromising Generation: The Nazi Leadership of the Reich Security Main Office.* Madison, WI: University of Wisconsin Press.

....

CHAPTER 20

LIVING SPACE

....

WENDY LOWER

CENTRAL to the ideology of Nazi imperialism was the joining of race and space. The "New Order" the Nazis sought entailed a racial classification and "cleansing" of Europe, especially its eastern reaches, which Nazi leaders envisioned as the ideal German "living space" (*Lebensraum*). Yet between Hitler's utopian vision of the eastern territories as a "Garden of Eden" and the implementation of the Holocaust and Nazi resettlement programs in Poland, the Baltic states, Belorussia, and Ukraine lay many gray areas. This chapter examines the interrelationship of Nazi expansionism, anti-Jewish policies, and schemes to resettle ethnic Germans (*Volksdeutsche*) in eastern Europe in an effort to assess the extent to which the history of the Shoah should be understood in the context of Nazi dreams and schemes of *Lebensraum*.

THE IDEOLOGY

....

The term *Lebensraum* appeared in 1901 in the title of an essay by the zoologist and geographer Friedrich Ratzel (1844–1904), who touted the importance of "species migration" through colonization and cultivation. Ratzel saw nations as organisms whose health hinged on expansion. Evincing an agrarian bias, he presented the ideal "living space" of humans as cultural and organic (Smith 1986: 146–52). His school of thought, called political geography, gained a following after World War I with the establishment of an institute of geopolitics at the University of Munich. Among Germans, the humiliating loss of territory in 1919 increased the popularity of the claim that they were a *Volk ohne Raum*, a people without adequate space, which was the title of Hans Grimm's bestselling novel in the 1920s.

At first a serious, albeit flawed academic theory, Ratzel's concept of "living space" lent legitimacy to the Nazi movement's imperial aspirations in eastern Europe. While imprisoned for the attempted coup of 1923, Adolf Hitler (1889–1945) read Ratzel's work and discussed it with his private secretary Rudolf Hess (1894–1987), a devotee of Karl Haushofer's (1869–1946) geopolitical theories. Also influential in shaping Hitler's thinking was Alfred Rosenberg (1893–1946), a German émigré from Estonia, who related his experiences fleeing Bolshevism and gave the Nazi leader a copy of the fabricated *Protocols of the Elders of Zion*. During this formative period, Hitler adopted a land policy that staked Germany's territorial claims in eastern Europe, where mounting Jewish influence supposedly threatened the future existence of the German *Volk*.

In the "bible" of the Nazi movement, *Mein Kampf*, Hitler declared:

Just as our ancestors . . . had to fight for [soil] at the risk of their lives, in the future no *völkish* grace will win soil for us and hence life for our people, but only the might of a victorious sword. For it is not in colonial acquisitions that we must see the solution of this problem, but exclusively in the acquisition of a territory for settlement, which will enhance the area of the mother country . . . And so we National Socialists consciously draw a line beneath the foreign policy tendency of our pre-War period. We take up where we broke off six hundred years ago. We stop the endless German movement to the south and west of Europe, and turn our gaze toward the land in the east. At long last we break off the colonial and commercial policy of the pre-War period and shift to the soil policy of the future . . . If we speak of soil in Europe today, we can primarily have in mind only Russia and her vassal border states. (Hitler 1971: 654)

During the 1930s a growing cadre of specialists in "eastern research" (*Ostforschung*), including economists, agronomists, and population planners, maintained that the eastern territories were Germany's historically "destined space" (Burleigh 1988; Haar and Fahlbusch 2005). In 1940, Professor Dr. Heinrich Hunke (1902–2000), an economics advisor to the Nazi Party in Berlin, member of the Reichstag, head of the foreign department in the propaganda ministry, and board member of the Deutsche Bank, called for the revival of the Hanseatic model, which he described as a civilized, peaceful, and productive version of "eastern colonization" and contrasted with the British Empire with its "stark naked imperialism, outright plundering, and essentially brutal dominance." "For centuries and today we battle over these two approaches," Hunke wrote, but with the Nazi revolution this struggle for economic hegemony over Europe would come to an end. He asked, "Why do we accept the poor plight of the German child born into a narrow household" with no space and light "destined to spend his day in a small workshop instead of an expansive farm and open field?" The world had deprived Germans by severing them from the global economy and blocking territorial expansion since World War I, but no longer. As Hunke's book indicated, the Nazi grasp for *Lebensraum* was not only about race and space but also about economic growth and conceived as part of a competitive, zero sum game of national survival among the Great Powers of Europe (Hunke 1940: 149, 162).

Like the utopianism of the "people's community" (*Volksgemeinschaft*) at home, the vision of *Lebensraum* to the east was supposed to galvanize Germans to conquer, colonize, and exploit the newly won territories. Yet regional variation marked how German officials viewed and transformed eastern Europe. In the north, the history of the coveted space contained the Hanse trading ports, medieval towns, Baltic barons, and the Teutonic knights. In the south, Ukraine was home to clusters of German pioneers and peasants in Volhynia, along the Volga River, and by the Black Sea. In Poland, the Nazis aimed to "liberate" their brethren who were "victims" of the Versailles Treaty in eastern Upper Silesia, Pomerania, and Posen. According to Nazi researchers in the 1930s, about ten million ethnic Germans needed to be "rescued" in these parts of eastern Europe, as well as in Romania and Hungary. Swastika-adorned patriots, careerists, and adventurers from myriad professions and academic disciplines, across generations, men and women alike, were mobilized for this "liberation" struggle in the east. They contributed their ingenuity and diligence to one of history's most morally misguided and violent attempts at empire-building.

"HEIM INS OSTLAND": NAZI SCHEMES OF CONQUEST, COLONIZATION, AND MURDER

In November 1937, Hitler met with his top military commanders and his foreign minister, Konstantin von Neurath (1873–1956), to unveil his plans for war and spoke specifically of the German need for living space. According to the minutes of the meeting, Hitler declared that "the aim of German policy was to make secure and to preserve the racial community and to enlarge it. It was therefore a question of space. The German racial community comprised over 85 million people and, because of their number and the narrow limits of habitable space in Europe, constituted a tightly packed racial core such as was not to be met in any other country and such as implied the right to a greater living space than in the case of other peoples." For the present, Hitler prioritized the task of annexing Austria and the Czech lands. However, parts of Poland (East Prussia, Pomerania, and Upper Silesia) also would "have to be reckoned with," entailing an eventual military confrontation with Russia (Noakes and Pridham 2001: 72, 77–8).

By September 1939, Hitler had arrived at the second stage of the program he outlined in 1937, the reckoning with Poland, whose territory Germany and the Soviet Union had agreed to divide between them. Late in that month, the Germans and Soviets signed a secret supplementary protocol that provided for the resettlement within German territory of ethnic Germans scattered across the Soviet "sphere of influence." To manage these transfer operations, Hitler appointed Heinrich Himmler (1900–1945), who was already *Reichsführer* of the SS and Police and Chief of the SS Race and Settlement Office, as the Reich Commissar for the Strengthening of Germandom. He thus acquired plenary authority over the processes of not only repatriating and resettling ethnic Germans, but also "eliminating the harmful influence of those alien sections of the population which constitute a danger to the Reich and German national community" (Noakes and Pridham 2001: 322).

The Germanization Himmler envisioned was "not in the old sense of bringing the German languages and laws to the people dwelling in that area, but to ensure that in the East only people of genuinely Germanic, Teutonic blood shall live" (Lemkin 1944: 21). He began with a plan to resettle Baltic Germans from Estonia and Latvia to the parts of Poland that Germany had annexed, especially the area now dubbed the *Warthegau*, from which Jews and Poles were to be expelled into the remainder of the country, the General Government. A reservation for the Jews was to be set up between the Bug and Vistula rivers. In plans already sketched out before the Nazi invasion of Poland, Germans in Italian-controlled South Tirol also were relocated forcibly to Poland. By 1944, one million ethnic Germans from eastern Europe, Italy, Yugoslavia, and former colonies overseas had been uprooted and moved to the annexed Polish territories. To "cleanse" the resettlement areas of "harmful elements," roughly three million Poles were dumped in the General Government or shipped to the Reich as forced laborers. Nearly all the 600,000 Jews in the annexed territories were eventually confined to camps and ghettos. Some 200,000 Jews and 5,000 Roma passed through the Łódź ghetto before being gassed at the nearby Chelmno facility or sent to Auschwitz. Nazi Party and state officials seized over three billion reichsmarks in property from the resettled *Volksdeutsche* and billions more from the expelled Poles and Jews (Aly 1999: 3, 7, 25, 47; Lumans in Steinweis and Rodgers 2003: 87, 95).

About a dozen agencies, most of them under Himmler's command, were involved in these resettlement actions. In December 1940, Hitler gave Himmler full authority over the Ethnic German Liaison Office (*Volksdeutsche Mittelstelle*), an instrument of foreign policy that lobbied on behalf of Germans abroad in the 1930s, and also served as a base for Nazi Party and Secret Service operatives outside of Germany. SS-police personnel, who had passed extensive genealogical background checks, in turn examined individuals for their Germanic features, categorized their racial worth, evaluated and confiscated the property of those to be resettled, and assigned work to the evacuees. Within the expanding bureaucracy of SS-police operations in Europe, certain pivotal figures had enormous power over the movement and ultimate fate of millions. For example, Adolf Eichmann (1906–1962) was responsible initially for the evacuations of Jews and Poles from the annexed territories as the coordinator of the Central Resettlement Office for ethnic Germans located in Łódź; when he was also named Section Chief of Emigration and Evacuation Matters in the Reich Security Main Office, he became responsible for deportations of Jews across Europe. Himmler's deputy, Reinhard Heydrich (1904–1942), who oversaw the Central Immigration and Central Resettlement Offices for Poland and southeastern Europe, also supervised the Einsatzgruppen and was later charged with devising a plan for the "Final Solution of the Jewish Question." Thus, many officials in the SS-police administration pursued simultaneously the evacuation and destruction of "inferior" races and the registration and "rehabilitation" of their "racial brethren."

As these social engineers carried out the violent and discriminatory resettlement operations, "creative" specialists in Himmler's offices of space planning, building, and landscaping drafted grand plans for transforming the *Lebensraum*. The architect of these plans was SS-*Standartenführer* Professor Konrad Meyer (1901–1973), the director of the Institute for Agrarian Science and Agrarian Policy at the University of Berlin. The marshaling of German intellectual talent for such a massive, criminal undertaking has been the subject of many studies that link the academic tradition of *Ostforschung* to the genocidal plans and practices of the Third Reich (Haar and Fahlbusch 2005). Between 1940 and 1943, at least five versions of the *Generalplan Ost* were produced, each one more elaborate and encompassing than the last and eventually covering the vast space from the Reich's eastern border to the Ural Mountains. A November 1941 version predicted that a twenty-year campaign to Germanize the east would result in the deportation or murder of 31 million Poles, Balts, Ukrainians, and Belorussians. This estimate was raised to 50 million in 1942. An estimated 14 million "foreign peoples" (excluding Jews) were to serve as worker slaves for the 4 million resettled Reich and ethnic Germans. The "removal" of Jews was barely mentioned in the plans, but assumed as a precondition for German resettlement. Since the Jews were depicted as obstacles to development, their pauperization and eventual disappearance were necessary steps in securing and improving the territory (Aly and Heim 2002).

Himmler, Meyer, and their cadre of academics and technicians viewed the east as a *tabula rasa* on which they could inscribe their own utopia of agrarian swathes of settlement grouped around thirty-six centers and populated by soldier-peasants. The carefully chosen names of these colonies were meant to reclaim Germany's historical roots. St. Petersburg and its surroundings were to be renamed "Ingermanland," the Crimea "Gotengau." As Hitler had said in *Mein Kampf* and numerous speeches, *Lebensraum* could be realized only through the plough and the sword and would function both to ensure German economic self-sufficiency and to serve as a bulwark against the "Asiatic Hordes."

To what extent were these colonial fantasies realized? Postwar scholarship has confirmed that the population exchanges carried out by the Axis powers became a significant factor in radicalizing anti-Jewish measures and expanding the scope of the Holocaust (Koehl 1957; Müller 1991; Madajczyk 1994; Heinemann 2003). On its face, the logic of the destruction seems clear and consistent with an imperial pattern of conquest followed by mass migration, forced deportation, and genocidal displacement of the "native" population. However, the ideological and causal links between Nazi resettlement programs, which were limited to certain areas and populations, and the scale of the Holocaust with its numerous perpetrators and victim groups across Europe were more tenuous. Even within the eastern European region, where nearly all of the mass murder and colonization occurred, the history of these two campaigns diverged significantly. Poland, however, with its clearly defined topography of Nazi killing-centers and German colonies offers the most persuasive case for causally linking the two.

Germanization and Murder in Poland

From the start, the Nazi leadership portrayed the invasion of Poland in September 1939 as a rescue of the *Volksdeutsche*. Indeed, Germans often legitimated brutality toward Poles and Jews as revenge for their alleged persecution or murder of *Volksdeutsche*, for example in the "Bloody Sunday" massacres in Bromberg (Bydgoszcz) (Rossino 2003). In the annexed territories, a priority area for "ethnic cleansing," the Holocaust and ethnic German resettlement programs literally intersected, as making room for repatriated Germans became a rationale for slaughtering Jews. In the General Government, the Lublin district became a cross-roads and an end station for many victims of Nazi social engineering schemes. The central figure in these operations was SS-Police Leader Odilo Globocnik (1904–1945), Himmler's point person for Operation Reinhard, the Nazi campaign to wipe out Polish Jews. In October 1941, he initiated a colonial experiment near his Lublin headquarters by establishing a resettlement planning office and hiring a team of academicians, architects, timber specialists, and construction engineers. Their work led to the expulsion between November 1942 and July 1943 of over 48,000 Poles and Jews from 300 villages in and around Zamosc. Polish children, kidnapped at night, were shipped to orphanages in Germany. Those deemed racially unfit were abandoned in camps, where many succumbed to the harsh conditions, or brought to Majdanek and Auschwitz with their parents and killed there. In January 1943, about 1,000 Poles from the Zamosc action arrived in Berlin "to take the jobs of 'armaments Jews.'" The same train that brought these Poles was used to transport those Jews to Auschwitz, then to bring ethnic German settlers to Zamosc, and finally to carry Poles categorized as "undesirable" by the security police and racial examiners to Auschwitz. This hideous movement of human cargo epitomized the Nazi machinery of "resettlement and removal, selection and genocide, the intrinsic logic of 'human deployment', and the planning and organizational unity of so-called positive and negative population policy" (Aly 1999: 248–9).

While Eichmann and Globocnik boasted of the "smooth" coordination of these "shipments," the entire Zamosc action was both a tragedy and a failure. Only 28 percent of the designated *Volksdeutsche* made it to the colony, while the rest languished in transit camps. The upheaval caused many Poles to engage in retaliatory attacks against the local German farmers and Ukrainian laborers, whom the Germans strategically housed in a band around the colony. The Germans responded by escalating the violence. In Operation Werwolf, German SS and police razed nearby villages and shot inhabitants, increasing the toll of those killed or deported in the region to 100,000 persons (Heinemann 2003: 403–15).

Although Auschwitz-Birkenau seemed to operate in secret isolation, this killing center should be seen in the broad context of German colonization schemes. The town of Auschwitz, where many private and state officials associated with the camp resided, developed along a model of "industrialization, urban improvement and population restructuring." Industrialists who arrived for the ceremonial establishment of the new IG Farben plant in 1941 lined the streets of the town to watch the deportations of the local Jews. The remaining Poles and the new elite of German developers financed by Farben demolished the Jewish quarter and cemetery, using the gravestones for road building, turning the synagogue into a storage house, and erecting on the site a cinema, a Nazi Party building, and a hotel. But as this boomtown developed, the smell of burning corpses from the nearby crematoria permeated the atmosphere. Local residents complained that the SS camp did not fit "organically" into the town's surroundings. The deprivation and misery in the camp contrasted sharply with the debauchery and liveliness in the town, providing a stark display of the link between "negative" Nazi population policies and "positive" development work (Steinbacher 2005: 62–78).

GERMANIZATION AND MURDER
IN THE SOVIET UNION

The true "proving ground" of German racial superiority lay less in a model town annexed to the Reich, such as Auschwitz, than farther east in the lands of the Soviet Union. Secret plans for Operation Barbarossa, the Nazi-led invasion of the

Soviet Union, included unprecedented harshness in the name of military security, economic exploitation, and planned depopulation. While the SS and army reached agreement on the treatment of racial and political enemies, the Reich Ministry for Food and Agriculture opined that food shortages at home could be avoided by confiscating the grain and livestock in the Soviet Union and letting some 20–30 million Slavs starve to death. Hermann Göring's (1893–1946) Four Year Plan personnel and the Wehrmacht's Economic Staff East divided the Soviet territories into two zones: the forest regions and the black soil area. Because the former could produce no food surplus for the Reich, the population was to experience famine or be expelled to Siberia. Most urban dwellers also were branded "useless eaters" and condemned to starvation-level rations (Gerlach 1999: 46–59).

On 21 June 1941, the day before the Nazi invasion of the Soviet Union, Himmler lunched with Hitler, met with an official in the Reich Ministry for Food and Agriculture about "resettlement issues," and then ordered Meyer to draw up a new version of the *Generalplan Ost* that covered the territory of the Soviet Union. A few weeks later, in the euphoria of victory, Hitler convened his top leaders at his headquarters and spoke at length about his vision of the east. In this new "Garden of Eden," the Crimea was to be transformed into a German Riviera and incorporated into the Reich along with the Baltic states. Parts of Belorussia and the Ukraine were to be reserved for Germans only, and the city of Leningrad was to be leveled and given to Finland. Accordingly, on 6 September 1941, Hitler extended Himmler's authority as Reich Commissioner for the Strengthening of Germandom to the conquered Soviet territories (Witte et al. 1999: 177, 205; Kay 2006: 180–7).

These high level meetings and sweeping plans translated into carnage on the ground. The systematic mass murder of Jews began in Ukraine, Lithuania, and other parts of the Soviet territories in the summer of 1941. Initially all male Jews were targeted. Then the killing expanded to entire communities, most markedly after mid-August. The four Einsatzgruppen (A, B, C, D) followed on the heels of the military units or advanced alongside them and fanned out to the villages and towns. In the first six months of the occupation, hundreds of thousands of Jews were killed in mass shootings, the largest of which occurred in Kamianets'-Podil's'kyi and in Kiev at the Babi Yar, where 33,771 people were gunned down on 29 and 30 September 1941, according to the report that Einsatzgruppe C sent to Berlin. By way of such shootings, pogroms, and mobile gas vans, the Einsatzgruppen slaughtered at least 1.25 million Jewish men, women, and children, along with hundreds of thousands of POWs, mentally and physically disabled people, Roma and Sinti, "Asiatics," communist officials, and others branded racial or political "undesirables." Altogether, at least 2.2 million Jews died during the Nazi occupation of the Soviet Union, including an estimated 1.5 million in Ukraine, 500,000 in Belorussia, 210,000 in Lithuania, 70,000 in Latvia, and 2,000 in Estonia (Gerlach 1999; Herbert 2000; Arad 2005; Friedländer 2007; Brandon and Lower 2008).

In this part of Europe, the Germans could rely on most Ukrainians, Poles, Latvians, Estonians, and Lithuanians to remain indifferent to anti-Jewish violence, to serve as police auxiliaries in the actions, and to carry out pogroms, especially in the border-lands that the Soviet Union had taken over in 1939–40. The largest pogroms occurred in L'viv, Kovno, and Iasi where tens of thousands of Jews were brutally massacred by local residents acting on a lethal mix of nationalism, anti-Bolshevism, and greed. In smaller places, such as the Polish town of Jedwabne, which came under German control during the invasion of Soviet-held territory in the summer of 1941, the local population, not the German occupiers, initiated the massacre of Jews (Gross 2001). In Lithuania, the fascist Activist Front announced that anyone suspected of having aided the Soviet occupiers could exonerate himself by providing evidence of having killed or helped kill a "Bolshevik Jew." In Belorussia, however, Einsatzgruppen leaders complained that the local population was less supportive and in rare cases even resistant to German demands to hand over or assault "their" Jews. In Minsk in July 1941, some Belorussians refused German orders to bury Jews alive, prompting the *Einsatzkommando* unit there to shoot both groups (Epstein 2008).

Volksdeutsche also aided and abetted the killings on former Soviet territory. In addition to the Einsatzgruppen, Himmler deployed other mobile forces code-named *Sonderkommando R* (Special Command Russia). Consisting of some 277 SS and police personnel, these units were responsible for resettlement operations, beginning with the registration of the *Volksdeutsche*. From headquarters in Odessa, Kiev, Mogilev, and Riga, these forces pursued their tasks of identifying "valuable German blood" and fertile land for colonization and of recruiting auxiliaries. For instance, around Zhytomyr, where the task forces reported that few of the 40,000 scattered *Volksdeutsche* could speak German, and 40 percent of them were unskilled day laborers, those few individuals who could serve as translators or local administrators were immediately put to use. Thus, a newly installed ethnic German mayor, helped by a Ukrainian police chief, supervised the destruction of Berdychiv's Jewish community. One of the more notorious ethnic Germans in Einsatzgruppe C was Dr. Arthur Boss, a 33-year-old neurologist from Odessa who spoke Russian and German. He helped Paul Blobel's (1894–1951) *Sonderkommando 4a* with the massacre of Zhytomyr's 3,000 Jews on 19 September 1941. According to eyewitness accounts, Boss was Blobel's right hand man, identifying the Jews, accompanying Blobel to the killing site, and afterwards helping with the distribution of Jewish clothing and linens to local *Volksdeutsche*. Boss also set up a medical practice in Zhytomyr and provided Blobel's shooters with injections to calm their nerves after the killing actions. Like Arthur Boss, the brothers Paul and Edmund Becker, who were in their teens and came from a nearby ethnic German community called Alter Huette, were also recruited to help implement the "Final Solution." They were transferred later to the SS training center at Trawniki, where they learned Nazi methods for guarding ghettos and death camps (Lower in Petropoulos and Roth 2005: 191).

Unlike in Poland, however, in Ukraine Heydrich's Einsatzgruppen and Rosenberg's commissars rarely used propaganda about the *Volksdeutsche* to stir up anti-Jewish or anti-Ukrainian violence. The Germans did not want to antagonize the large Ukrainian population in a colonial territory that was not slated for full Germanization. Instead, anti-Bolshevik themes were deployed to explain the sorry plight of the *Volksdeutsche* and incite anti-Jewish violence. At the highest levels of the leadership, Reich Minister Rosenberg lobbied Hitler in early September 1941 to push all central European Jews into Russia's interior in retaliation for Stalin's order to deport Volga Germans. In the killing fields of Ukraine, German and non-German perpetrators brutalized and killed Jews for a variety of motives, not the least of which was to make Jews pay for the sad state of the ethnic German minority.

By the end of 1941, at least 500,000 Ukrainian Jews were dead, most of them from the urban centers east of the Zhytomyr district, but more than 900,000 remained in towns such as Rivne, Vinnytsia, Pinsk, Luts'k, Kowel, and Letychiv (Kruglov in Brandon and Lower 2008: 272–91). Thousands were scattered in small rural ghettos, and hundreds of orphans roamed the countryside in search of food and shelter. For the completion of the "Final Solution" in the area, the SS-police and German civilian rulers relied upon Ukrainian and ethnic Germans as translators and police auxiliaries in the gendarmerie. One such ethnic German policeman, 19-year-old Ernst Hering from the Ustynivka district in the Nikolaev Commissariat, was asked in spring 1942, after a few months of service in the police, to shoot the Jews of his hometown. His unit, which included his cousin Gustav, rounded up and killed about twenty-five Jewish men, women, and children and twenty half-Jewish children and babies from the surrounding area, with the help of the district leader and local police chief, who also were *Volksdeutsche* (Dean in Brandon and Lower 2008: 248–9). At nearby Halbstadt Colony, even German Mennonite young men reacted against Stalinism by joining the Hilter Youth or the Waffen-SS and fighting the partisans. By war's end many had blood on their hands.

While Nazi leaders drew upon existing German colonies in the Black Sea region, they experimented near Zhytomyr with the creation of a new colony at Hegewald, not far from Himmler's regional headquarters. In fall 1942, over 10,000 ethnic Germans were concentrated there into twenty-eight villages and collective farm communities, and thousands of Ukrainians were pushed out, many of them into labor camps closer to the front. The final killing sweeps against Jews in this area had occurred the preceding summer. For the arriving *Volksdeutsche*, the SS and Nazi Party established occupational training programs, kindergartens, shooting ranges, athletic routines, and Hitler Youth gatherings. Special rations and household goods, including many items sent from Auschwitz, were distributed by Nazi Party welfare workers. Nazi planners envisioned Hegewald as the first of several settlement "pearls" that would form a "necklace" connecting Himmler's compound with Hitler's at Vinnytsia (Lower 2007: 171–7).

By the end of 1942, the SS controlled nearly 600,000 hectares of farmland between the Black and Baltic seas. Some of these went to disabled SS veterans as a reward for good service and loyalty to the Reich. Many German civilian developers and aristocrats sought to reclaim a Prussian estate or take over a formerly Polish one. Ordinary Germans could also dream of such wealth, though few would actually obtain it, and most were not eager to relocate to the east while the war raged. In Eastern Galicia one poor Thuringian farmer named Horst managed to rise from a simple Nazi Party member in 1932 to the master of his own estate. After joining the SS and completing some military training in 1941, he was sent with his wife Erna and small son to the Grzenda manor. They possessed seventy Polish, Ukrainian, and Jewish forced laborers, a lavish, white-pillared house with multiple terraces, horse-drawn coaches, rolling farmland, livestock, stables, and gardens. They wined and dined ranking SS-police and army officials who passed through the area, including the SS and Police Commander for Galicia and his wife. The estate was located a few kilometers from the L'viv–Lublin railway line, a route used to send Galician Jews to the killing centers in Poland. During 1943, when young, starving, and naked Jews escaped the railway cars and sought refuge on the grounds of the Grzenda estate, this farmer and his wife shot them down (USHMM Archive).

While plantations in Ukraine satisfied *völkisch* peasants, the Baltic region, historically home to the "upper crust of Germandom," was to serve, in Hitler's words, as the foundation for "German ascendancy over all European nations" (Housden 2000: 37–8). On 30 October 1941, Nazi ministers met in Rosenberg's Ministry for the Occupied Eastern Territories to discuss territorial plans. A native of Tallin in Estonia, Rosenberg was especially excited about Germany's conquest of this area. As he stated:

you all recall the year 375 as a year in the history of Europe of a great change, when after 200 years of Gothic dominance between the Baltic and Black Sea, the Huns swept away their empire in a matter of a few months. Many Germans lived in this space in fortressed strongholds and scattered settlements. What is happening *today* is the revision of this invasion of the Huns…We have three great tasks before us now: the expansion and securing of the empire, the economic independence of Germany and Europe, and the Germanization of certain territories and creation of a settlement space for 15–20 million Germans. (Müller 1991: 161–2)

According to the *Generalplan Ost*, the border area of Latvia and Estonia was a priority target for Germanization, as befit the historic patrimony of the thirteenth- and fourteenth-century Livonian Order of German Knights. One-third of the Latvian population was considered "Germanizable." Space and population planning offices gathered statistics and made projections, such as the proposal that 5–6 million people be resettled from Germany to the Ostland, beginning with 200,000 farmers from Baden and Westphalia "who were slated to lose their farms because of industrial development in the Reich." Three million Dutch colonists, presumably experts in the dredging of swamps and building of canals, were to develop the Polesje-Prypiat marshland bordering the Reich Commissariat Ostland and the Reich Commissariat Ukraine. Some 4–5,000 Dutch colonists arrived and ended up working as agricultural estate managers, officials in the Central Trading Society East, and as master craftsmen in the Reich Commissariant Ostland and Ukraine. In a little known German–Finnish treaty on population exchange, 65,000 Finns were forcibly "repatriated" to Finland from Estonia in 1943, and Estonians with Swedish "blood" were shipped to Sweden. However, except for the return of some Baltic Germans, the only mass resettlement of Reich citizens to the Baltic region was the shipment of German Jews to Riga and Kovno, where most of them were killed (Dallin 1957: 281–2; Friedländer 2007: 262–3, 266–7).

Nazi leaders alleged that a glorious history of the German race could be revived in Poland, Ukraine, the Baltic region, and East Prussia, but in Belorussia only the formerly Polish districts were deemed "Germanizable." Because this swampy and forested region lacked fertile farmland and was home to some of the worst poverty in Europe, the area did not figure in the various versions of the *Generalplan Ost* as a destination for German settlers. Nevertheless, the territory was to be cleared of its Jewish population, which was about 820,000 when the Germans swept in during 1941. Forty percent of these people were killed in the first six months. Ghettos were short-lived and remained by 1943 only in Minsk, Glubokoye, and Lida. Nazi leaders accelerated the killing to make room for Jews being shipped from the Reich, Bohemia-Moravia, Poland, Austria, and the Netherlands. Most of these went first to the Minsk ghetto, and then to the shooting sites in the nearby village of Maly Trostinets, where about 200,000 perished. The bloody history of Trostinets did not deter the local commander of the Sipo-SD in Minsk, Eduard Strauch (1906–1955) from dreaming of establishing his own estate there after the war (Gerlach 1999: 122). Otherwise, Nazi officials treated Belorussia as a colony of extraction from which to suck all resources for the military and motherland. In the course of anti-partisan warfare entire villages were razed, their populations killed or deported, and parts of the country turned into "dead zones." These "reprisals" dovetailed with the aim of "preparing" the space for later settlement by Nazi elites, but not by *Volksdeutsche* (Gerlach 1999).

As German military setbacks mounted in the east during 1943, *Volksdeutsche* resettlement programs were scaled back, but the Nazi war against the Jews continued. Soviet propaganda incited civilians and the Red Army to take revenge on all Germans, including the *Volksdeutsche* retreating westwards with the Wehrmacht. Those interned by the Red Army or repatriated to the Soviet Union after World War II under the terms of the Yalta Agreement ended up in the trans-Ural region, where up to 45 percent of them perished. Nazi resettlement policies and the war resulted in the displacement of 15 million *Volksdeutsche* and the deaths of 2 million (de Zayas 2006).

THE HOLOCAUST, GERMANIZATION, AND THE
LOGIC OF GENOCIDAL COLONIALISM

The Nazi attempt to Germanize eastern Europe was a catastrophe for the region's Jews and costly to millions of Poles, Belorussians, Latvians, Estonians, Lithuanians, Finns, and Ukrainians as well. Though ostensibly the beneficiaries of this sinister racial reshuffling, millions of ethnic Germans also suffered from it. Once implemented, the *Generalplan Ost* and other resettlement experiments caused upheaval that intensified the spiraling violence. Jews and other minorities found themselves caught in the middle of interethnic struggles and partisan warfare that engulfed these resettlement regions. The forced relocation of populations from various borderlands in eastern Europe was not only the work of the SS but also the subject of formal agreements among the Axis powers, such as the Second Vienna Award, that entwined the fate of Romanian, Hungarian, and Slovakian Jews with diplomatic agreements intended to solve the "nationalities problem" through border changes and population exchanges.

German administrators in the various occupation agencies complained that resettlement of *Volksdeutsche* disrupted the economy and antagonized the majority of the "native" population. Even Hitler agreed that the experiments should be postponed until after the war. After the conflict turned against Germany, Nazi leaders could no longer inspire their "pioneers of Germandom" with pep talks about the unlimited opportunities in the east. Though Rosenberg's commissars and Himmler's SS-policemen were compared to frontiersmen who settled the American West, German colonizers were racially selected by the Reich, ideologically tested, and placed into an ethnically "cleansed" and artificial society. Most of the transplanted *Volksdeutsche* ended up in transit camps and makeshift housing. By summer 1943, major resettlement experiments were shelved and attention turned to evacuation. By contrast, the Nazi deportation and mass murder of Jews continued and even expanded to Greece, Bulgaria, and Hungary. In short, by then, "far more Jews were being deported and killed than the logistical imperatives of the resettlement required" (Lumans in Steinweis and Rogers 2003: 95; Bergen in Steinweis and Rogers 2003: 101–9).

Many senior officials in the SS and police, above all Himmler and Heydrich, but also Eichmann and Globocnik, managed the deportations and mass murder of Jews, the expulsion of Poles and other so-called undesirables from the designated *Lebensraum*, and the selection and forced resettlement of the *Volksdeutsche*. When viewed from the perspective of the Nazi leadership and the central "race and space" planning offices, the destructive logic of the Third Reich seems to suggest that the "Final Solution" was a function or byproduct of Nazi resettlement operations. The Nazi "rescue" of the *Volksdeutsche* and utopian development fantasies may have offered many Germans a positive rationale for mass murder. However, the pogroms and mass shootings in the Soviet Union do not seem to have been motivated by widespread empathy for the *Volksdeutsche* or committed as acts of revenge on their behalf. The same regional commissars in Rosenberg's administration, SS-policemen in Himmler's agencies, and economic "developers" in Göring's Four Year Plan who rarely questioned the eradication or enslavement of those deemed unfit to inhabit or live freely on the *Lebensraum*, remained uncertain, skeptical, and less enthusiastic about their role in developing the war-torn east. Rather than serving as an ideological motivation, the *Volksdeutsche* offered Nazi regional leaders a critical source of manpower to carry out the Holocaust. This minority had access to newfound power, especially within the lower ranks of the Nazi system where the genocide was realized. Some, such as the Becker brothers, Ernst Hering, and Arthur Boss in Ukraine, became perpetrators and integrated parts of the system of destruction.

Nazi leaders largely succeeded in carrying out the first step of their larger plan to remap and Germanize Europe. More than 80 percent of the Jews who were killed in the Holocaust resided in the eastern territories intended to be the new German "living space." Nazi leaders, ideologues, technocrats, engineers, economists, SS-police, military personnel, and academicians accepted or rationalized the murders as a means to a much larger end of securing a German empire in Europe and beyond. Conversely, many Germans, including the *Volksdeutsche* and most non-German collaborators who stole Jewish property, brutalized Jews in pogroms, and assisted in ghetto liquidations, deportations, and mass shootings against innocent women, children, the elderly and infirm, were not driven by Hitlerian fantasies of an Aryan *Lebensraum*, but by their own antisemitic desires, vendettas, and goals.

Although understanding that the Holocaust occurred in the context of Nazi occupation policies and goals is important, causally linking the two programs of genocide and ethnic German resettlement can mislead. Although these two policies were synchronized in Poland, such coordination does not lie behind the deaths of millions of Jews, Soviet prisoners of war, Roma, and the mentally and physically disabled killed in the fields, ravines, and camps across eastern Europe. Settler colonialism and antisemitism were European traditions that the Nazis forged into one genocidal ideology. In practice, however, these two tracks of the movement often diverged by region and according to the changing conditions of the war and calculations of local collaborators.

References

ALY, G. (1999). *"Final Solution": Nazi Population Policy and the Murder of the European Jews.* New York: Oxford University Press.

—— and HEIM, S. (2002). *Architects of Annihilation: Auschwitz and the Logic of Destruction.* Princeton, NJ: Princeton University Press.

ARAD, Y. (2005). "The Murder of the Jews in German-Occupied Lithuania (1941–1944)," *Zeitschrift für Ostmitteleuropa-Forschung* 54: 56–79.

BRANDON, R. and LOWER, W. (eds.) (2008). *The Shoah in Ukraine: History, Testimony, Memorialization.* Bloomington, IN: Indiana University Press.

BURLEIGH, M. (1988). *Germany Turns Eastward: A Study of Ostforschung in the Third Reich.* Cambridge: Cambridge University Press.

DALLIN, A. (1957). *German Rule in Russia, 1941–1945.* New York: St. Martin's Press.

EPSTEIN, B. (2008). *The Minsk Ghetto, 1941–1943: Jewish Resistance and Soviet Internationalism.* Berkeley, CA: University of California Press.

FRIEDLÄNDER, S. (2007). *The Years of Extermination: Nazi Germany and the Jews, 1939–1945.* New York: HarperCollins.

GERLACH, C. (1999). *Kalkulierte Morde: die deutsche Wirtschafts-und Vernichtungspolitik in Weissrussland 1941 bis 1944.* Hamburg: Hamburger Edition.

GROSS, J. (2001). *Neighbors: The Destruction of the Jewish Community in Jedwabne Poland.* Princeton, NJ: Princeton University Press.

HAAR, I. and FAHLBUSCH, M. (eds.) (2005). *German Scholars and Ethnic Cleansing, 1920–1945.* New York: Berghahn Books.

HEINEMANN, I. (2003). *"Rasse, Siedlung, deutsches Blut": Das Rasse-und Siedlungshauptamt der SS und die rassenpolitische Neuordnung Europas.* Göttingen: Wallstein Verlag.

HERBERT, U. (ed.) (2000). *National Socialist Extermination Policies: Contemporary German Perspectives and Controversies.* New York: Berghahn Books.

HITLER, A. (1971). *Mein Kampf.* Boston, MA: Houghton Mifflin.

HOUSDEN, M. (2000). *Hitler: Study of a Revolutionary?* London: Routledge.

HUNKE, H. (1940). *Hanse, Downing Street, und Deutschlands Lebensraum.* Berlin: Haude & Spenersche Verlag.

KAY, A. (2006). *Exploitation, Resettlement, Mass Murder.* New York: Berghahn Books.

KOEHL, R. (1957). *RKFDV: German Resettlement and Population Policy, 1939–1945.* Cambridge, MA: Harvard University Press.

LEMKIN, R. (1944). *Axis Rule in Occupied Europe: Laws of Occupation, Analyses of Government, Proposals for Redress.* Washington, DC: Carnegie Endowment for International Peace.

LOWER, W. (2007). *Nazi Empire Building and the Holocaust in Ukraine.* Chapel Hill, NC: University of North Carolina Press.

MADAJCZYK, C. (ed.) (1994). *Vom Generalplan Ost zum Generalsiedlungsplan.* Munich: Saur.

MÜLLER, R. (1991). *Hitlers Ostkrieg und die deutsche Siedlungspolitik.* Frankfurt am Main: Fischer Verlag.

NIEWYK, D. and NICOSIA, F. (2000). *The Columbia Guide to the Holocaust.* New York: Columbia University Press.

NOAKES, J. and PRIDHAM, G. (eds.) (2001). *Nazism 1919–1945.* Vol. 3, *Foreign Policy, War and Racial Extermination.* Exeter: University of Exeter Press.

PETROPOULOS, J. and ROTH, J. (eds.) (2005). *Gray Zones: Ambiguity and Compromise in the Holocaust and its Aftermath.* New York: Berghahn Books.

ROSSINO, A. (2003). *Hitler Strikes Poland.* Lawrence, KS: University Press of Kansas.

SMITH, W. (1986). *The Ideological Origins of Nazi Imperialism.* New York: Oxford University Press.

STEINBACHER, S. (2005). *Auschwitz: A History.* New York: Harper Collins.

STEINWEIS, A. and RODGERS, D. (eds.) (2003). *The Impact of Nazism: New Perspectives on the Third Reich and its Legacy.* Lincoln, NE: University of Nebraska Press.

USHMM (UNITED STATES HOLOCAUST MEMORIAL MUSEUM) Archive. RG 14.068, Fiche 565, Archives of BStU Berlin, file number Eft.AU 403/63 GA 1, East German War Crimes Trial of Horst and Erna P.

WITTE, P. et al. (eds.) (1999). *Der Dienstkalender Heinrich Himmlers 1941/1942*. Hamburg: Hans Christians Verlag.

ZAYAS, A. DE (2006). *A Terrible Revenge: The Ethnic Cleansing of the East European Germans.* New York: Palgrave Macmillan.

OTHER SUGGESTED READING

ARAD, Y. (2009). *The Holocaust in the Soviet Union.* Lincoln, NE: University of Nebraska Press.

DESBOIS, P. (2008). *The Holocaust by Bullets: A Priest's Journey to Uncover the Truth behind the Murder of 1.5 Million Jews.* New York: Palgrave Macmillan.

HARVEY, E. (2003). *Women and the Nazi East: Agents and Witnesses of Germanization.* New Haven, CT: Yale University Press.

HIDEN, J. and HOUSDEN, M. (2007). *Neighbours or Enemies? Germans, the Baltic and Beyond.* Amsterdam/New York: Rodopi.

KAMENETSKY, I. (1961). *Secret Nazi Plans for Eastern Europe: A Study of Lebensraum Policies.* New York: Bookman Associates.

SNYDER, T. (2010). *Bloodlands: Europe between Hitler and Stalin.* New York: Basic Books.

WESTERMANN, E. (2005). *Hitler's Police Battalions: Enforcing Racial War in the East.* Lawrence, KS: University Press of Kansas.

....

CHAPTER 21

OCCUPIED AND SATELLITE STATES

....

RADU IOANID

THE destruction of European Jewry during World War II is full of paradoxes. Aside from Germany, no country was so directly involved in killing Jews as Romania, yet half of that country's Jewish population, the third largest in Europe, survived the Holocaust. Hungary participated in murdering most of its Jewish community at the end of the war, even after Germany's defeat and the likelihood of retribution for genocide had become clear. Bulgaria, another German ally, destroyed "only" the Jews from its newly acquired territories. In spite of locally prevalent and intense antisemitism, Croatia massacred more Serbs then Jews. The Netherlands, an occupied country with a relatively weak antisemitic tradition, was much more efficient than France, the home of the Dreyfus Affair, in delivering Jews to death, and Italy, although a German ally, was disinclined to let Jews under its jurisdiction be killed. What accounts for such counterintuitive variations in behavior?

THE OPPORTUNISTIC SATELLITES: ROMANIA, HUNGARY, AND BULGARIA

....

In the three countries that Raul Hilberg (1926–2007) called "the opportunistic satellites of Nazi Germany," namely Romania, Bulgaria, and Hungary, the fate of Jews depended heavily on where they lived and when their government was most committed to the German war effort (1985, 2: 742). Jews were killed first and most thoroughly in territories that changed hands during the Nazi era. In Romania, deported and murdered Jews came overwhelmingly from Bukovina and Bessarabia, areas lost to the Soviet Union in 1940 and regained from it in 1941, and from Transnistria, formerly Soviet land occupied when Romania took part in the Nazi invasion of the USSR. In Hungary, Jews who were viewed as non-Hungarian were deported from or killed first in the newly acquired territories of Carpatho-Ruthenia, taken from Czechoslovakia in 1939; Northern Transylvania, taken from Romania in 1940; and Voievodina, taken from Yugoslavia in 1941. In Bulgaria, Jews from Thrace and Macedonia, regions annexed from Greece and Yugoslavia in 1941, were sent to the German extermination camps. Moreover, most of the deaths of Jews in Romania and Bulgaria occurred prior to the fall of 1942, when the German advance into the Soviet Union bogged down at Stalingrad and the tide of war began to turn in eastern Europe, and most of those in Hungary took place in the same early period or in the spring of 1944, after German troops occupied the country as the Soviet army reached its eastern border. In other words, the opportunism of which Hilberg wrote was political: murder occurred under these governments where and when it seemed to suit their interests.

In 1930, Romania contained 756,000 Jews; about 375,000 remained in 1945. About 135,000 of those who came under Hungarian control in 1940 perished in German camps in 1944. More than 45,000 Romanian Jews—probably closer to 60,000—were killed in Bessarabia and Northern Bukovina by Romanian and German troops in 1941 during the first days of the war against the Soviet Union and another 154,000 Jews from these regions were pushed into Transnistria, of whom 105,000 died from hunger, disease, mistreatment, and execution (Friling et al. 2005: 178). In that region, another 130,000 indigenous Jews also were liquidated, especially in the city of Odessa and the districts of Golta and Berezovka. Altogether, the regime of Marshall Ion Antonescu (1882–1946) killed some 280,000 Jews (Friling et al. 2005: 179). Roma were also deported: of 25,000 sent to Transnistria, only about 11,000 returned (Friling et al. 2005: 236). Sometimes Romanian officials worked with German help, but more often they required no outside guidance and, in fact, spurned it. As a result, even in this early phase of joint engagement in slaughter, Romanian and German agencies did not work together well or consistently. Irreconcilable differences of style, timing, and methodology triggered negative reactions, especially from the Germans, who often expressed anger at the Romanians' inefficient pogrom "techniques," improvised "death marches," hasty dumping of huge groups of deportees across the Dniester River in 1941 and the Bug River in 1942, and tendency to act without clear plans. Sometimes the Romanians conducted expulsions and simply expected the Germans to handle the consequences.

The initial round of slaughter reflected Antonescu's obsession with purging Romania of minorities, who represented in his eyes a "danger" to the state, especially in border areas. His antisemitism was economic, political, and social, however, not mystical and religious, like that of the members of the Legion of the Archangel Michael (Iron Guard). His hatred was not that of the middle-class man, armed with a truncheon; rather, it was that of the bureaucrat, pretending to solve a problem in a fundamental, reasonable, nuanced, and legal fashion. The Jews might have fared worse if the Legionnaire government of 1940–41 had lasted longer; the Legionnaires surely would have been more closely aligned with Germany. Nonetheless, Antonescu deployed the Romanian military, police, and judicial apparatus to advance an ideology that mixed the fascism of the Iron Guard with the fascist tenets of the National Christian party, to which many mid-level civil servants formerly had belonged. The antisemitic legislation enacted was hate-inspired, hypernationalist, and often imitative of Nazi racial laws (Shapiro 1974). A few thousand Jews were permitted to emigrate in return for substantial payments, but the rest were subjected to arbitrary execution, deportation, forced labor, and starvation. Because enforcement was erratic, pragmatic, and corrupt, however, the results were both a tragedy for innumerable Romanian Jews and a chance at salvation for many others. As one famous scholar summarized the situation:

Romania was a corrupt country. It was the only Axis state in which officials as high as minister and mayor of the capital city had to be dismissed for "dark" transactions with expropriated Jewish property. The search for personal gain in Romania was so intensive that it must have enabled many Jews to buy relief from persecution....In examining the Romanian bureaucratic apparatus, one is therefore left with the impression of an unreliable machine that did not properly respond to command and that acted in unpredictable ways, sometimes balking, sometimes running away with itself. That spurting action, unplanned and uneven, sporadic and erratic, was the outcome of an opportunism that was mixed with destructiveness, a lethargy periodically interrupted by outbursts of violence. The product of this mixture was a record of anti-Jewish actions that is decidedly unique. (Hilberg 1985, 2: 759–60)

Several examples attest to the stop and go character of Romanian persecution. Because the haste to destroy the Jews of Bessarabia and Bukovina was equaled only by the chaotic implementation of that goal, delays arose that opened opportunities to survive. Although Romanian Jews were deported en masse to Transnistria, selected thousands later were repatriated in late 1943 and early 1944. When Antonescu realized that "Romanization" (i.e., dispossessing Jews of their livelihoods and property) was damaging the economy, he slowed down the process. Romania initially approved the deportation of Jews with Romanian citizenship from Germany and the territories it occupied, which resulted in the death of about 4,500 people (Ioanid 2000: 259–70), but then restored diplomatic protection to Romanian Jews living abroad, when Antonescu noticed that Hungarian Jews in the Nazi sphere were being treated better than "his" Jews.

Above all, Romania backtracked in October 1942 on a plan to deport Jews living in the Regat, the original, core provinces of the country, to Belzec. The same leaders who had carried out the deportation and killing of the Jews of Bessarabia, Bukovina, and Transnistria refused German pressure to condemn more of their country's Jews to death. That decision came in response to a series of external and internal appeals triggered by the vicious treatment meted out to the Jews of Bessarabia, Bukovina, and Transnistria. Clergymen, diplomats from Switzerland and Sweden, representatives of American agencies (especially the War Refugee Board in Istanbul), the International Committee of the Red Cross, and the Vatican all participated. Various liberal or simply decent Romanian politicians and public figures also intervened on behalf of the Jews, including Iuliu Maniu (1873–1953), Constantin I. C. Bratianu (1866–1950), Nicolae Lupu (1884–1944), and Queen Mother Elena (1896–1982). Misunderstandings in relations with Germany, vice-prime-minister Mihai Antonescu's (1904–1946) realization—even before the outcome of Stalingrad had become fully clear—that the situation on the eastern front was not what had been envisioned, and perhaps Antonescu's pride (dictators do not like to be dictated to) also now argued for a less murderous course. Finally, even in some right-wing circles, German pressure to hand over the Jews of the Regat backfired: no foreign power was going to tell Romanian nationalists what to do with *their* Jews. Thus, in the fall of 1942, a second phase, one offering meaningful chances for Jewish survival, arrived. Even Heinrich Himmler (1900–1945) seems in 1943 to have lost all hope of Romanian collaboration in the destruction of the country's Jews and planned to withdraw his representatives (Hilberg 1985, 2: 790).

Antonescu remained a violent antisemite, but as the war dragged on, ideological criteria inspired his policy less. At the beginning of the war, Antonescu believed that he could resolve "the Jewish question" once and for all, as well as that of the other minorities, especially Ukrainians. But he maintained contact with minority leaders in his own country and with the Allies via Cairo and Stockholm, which suggests that he had a realistic streak. After the end of 1942, he imagined, like many other Romanian politicians, that he could use the Romanian Jews as capital in negotiating Romania's postwar status with the United States and England. While acknowledging that "bloody repression" had occurred under Romanian aegis during the war, Antonescu nevertheless declared that under his authority, there had been no massacres: "I passed a lot of repressive laws, [but] we did not execute a single Jew. . . . I gave orders for reprisals, not for perpetrating massacres" (*Procesul marii tradari nationale*, 1946: 51).

Equally contradictory is the history of the destruction of Hungarian Jewry. As the leading scholar on the subject has pointed out, "the Jewish community of Hungary, which enjoyed an unparalleled level of development after its legal emancipation of 1867, was the first to be subjected to a discriminatory legislation in post-World War I Europe" (Braham 1994, 1: xxix). Virtually from its inception in 1919, the conservative regime of Regent Miklos Horthy (1868–1957) had introduced antisemitic measures and laid the basis for increasing social and economic pressure on Hungary's Jews. The trend accelerated as Nazi Germany became a patron of Hungary's desire to reverse its territorial losses as a result of World War I. Thus, the acquisition in 1938–39 of new territories from Czechoslovakia, the Upper Province

(*Felvidek*), or Carpatho-Ruthenia, coincided with the enactment of the first and second anti-Jewish laws, and the third anti-Jewish law followed around the time of the annexation of Northern Transylvania from Romania in 1940. Persecution and then murder of "alien" Jews began shortly after Hungary joined in the invasion of Russia in mid-1941. During that summer, 16,000–18,000 Polish Jewish refugees and Hungarian Jews who could not prove their citizenship were deported to the Kamenets-Podolsk area of occupied Ukraine and killed by Einsatzgruppen. Later that year, Hungarian troops executed 6,000 Serbs and 4,000 Jews in the *Delvidek* region annexed from Yugoslavia (Hilberg 1985, 2: 811–13).

As in Romania, "the destruction of the Hungarian Jews began as a voluntary Hungarian venture, and the first Hungarian measures were enacted without much German prodding and without any German help" (Hilberg 1985, 2: 799). Both countries were eager to carry out ethnic cleansings of newly acquired territories. The Germans, however, blocked immediate expulsions of ethnic Germans or even Ukrainians. Disposing of the Jews was a different matter: the Nazis not only gave the green light to radical planning but also offered their support. But the process of destruction was not linear: "there was a close correlation between the succession of Hungarian rulers and the pacing of the anti-Jewish action. The moderate prime ministers slowed down and arrested the catastrophe; the extremists hurried it along ... near tranquility alternated with outbursts of destructive activity" (Hilberg 1985, 2: 799). As a result, most Hungarian Jews were still alive in May 1944, when they were suddenly subjected to a massive destruction process of unparalleled efficiency and speed.

Like Romania, Hungary had assumed that it would solve the "Jewish problem" at its own pace and without direct German involvement. But a number of differences between the two countries' situations invalidated this assumption. Romania had a more favorable geostrategic position in relation to Germany, and the Nazi leaders held Antonescu in higher regard than Horthy. In Hungary, moreover, local, radically antisemitic collaborators were available in the form of the Arrow Cross movement, whereas in Romania the Iron Guard had been crushed in 1941, ironically with Hitler's blessing. Thus, in the aftermath of the German military occupation on 18 March 1944, undertaken to counter the Soviet threat that had now reached Hungary's borders, the country did not have the strength or resolve to refuse the application of the "Final Solution." Instead, Horthy "legitimized the [German] occupation and contributed to the placement of the entire Hungarian state apparatus at the service of the Germans" (Braham 1994, 1: 392).

During April 1944, Hungarian authorities, working closely with German representatives, prepared a sweeping plan of ghettoization and deportation. For administrative purposes, the country was divided into six zones. Jews in small settlements were rounded up, locked in community buildings and synagogues while their valuables were confiscated, and then transferred to ghettos in larger localities.

Jews in towns and cities were put directly into ghettos, which were often located in brickyards and warehouses. Once the process of concentration was completed, deportation started. According to a German report dated 13 June 1944, 289,357 Jews from Zones I and II (Carpatho-Ruthenia and Northern Transylvania) were sent to Auschwitz. By the time the deportations ended on 30 June, another 92,304 Jews had been dispatched from Zones III (northern Hungary) and IV (southern Hungary) and another 55,741 Jews from Zone V (western Hungary and the suburbs of Budapest), making the total number of Jews deported to the concentration camps, primarily Auschwitz, and then gassed 437,402 (Braham 1994, 1: 792). Jews from Budapest escaped deportation primarily because Horthy ordered an end to the transports on 7 July 1944. Prime Minister Dome Sztojay (1883–1946) justified this measure to the Germans by noting that the Romanian and Slovak governments were expressing similar reservations, mentioning Papal, Turkish, Swiss, and Spanish interventions on behalf of the Jews, and expressing concern about future retribution. After a German-backed coup on 15 October resulted in the appointment of the Hungarian Arrow Cross leaders to a new government headed by Ferenc Szalasi (1897–1946), deportations resumed in the form of forced marches, to which 27,000 Jews were subjected in November.

The leading historians of the Hungarian Holocaust agree that 550,000 Hungarian Jews perished in it, 502,000 of them after the German military occupation of March 1944. In addition to the killings in the newly acquired territories and the deportations, the total includes 42,000 victims of forced labor. In 1941, Hungary's population included 725,005 Jews, of whom 324,026 lived in territories recently annexed from Czechoslovakia, Romania, and Yugoslavia, the areas affected first by the deportations. In 1945, 255,500 Jews remained alive in Hungary, of whom 190,000 lived within the country's former borders (Braham 1994, 2: 1296–7). In short, the survival rate, as in Romania, was higher in the core provinces (almost 50 percent) than in the annexed regions (20 percent).

In spite of its alliance with Nazi Germany, Bulgaria took care not to antagonize the Allies. No Bulgarian troops fought against the Soviet Union, propaganda against Stalin was forbidden, and hostilities against U.S. and Great Britain were confined to downing a few Allied bombers that flew over Bulgaria to attack Romanian oil fields. The first Bulgarian anti-Jewish law dated from January 1941, later than in Romania or Hungary, and defined Jews less strictly than in the two neighboring countries. However, Bulgaria did impose the yellow star, create an Office of the Commissar of Jewish Affairs headed by Alexander Belev (d. 1944), and deport under his direction 7,122 Jews from Macedonia and 4,221 from Thrace to Treblinka in April 1943. But when Belev presented plans for deporting Jews from Sofia either to Poland or to the provinces, the Bulgarian authorities chose the latter alternative. Consequently, 25,743 Jews from Sofia were sent to the countryside, along with another few hundred Jews from Stara Zagora and Kazanlak (Hakov

1998: 129). Dimiter Peshev (1894–1973), the deputy chairman of the Bulgarian parliament, protested against the deportations from Thrace and Macedonia. His resolution accusing the government of atrocities during the deportations won the support of forty-three deputies (Hilberg 1985, 2: 755–6). As a result, Peshev was suspended as deputy chairman, and some of his supporters were forced to withdraw their signatures (Hakov 1998: 127). The Holy Synod of the Bulgarian Orthodox Church also pleaded with the Bulgarian authorities for decent treatment of the Jews, converts or not. Asked in April 1943 by German Foreign Minister Joachim von Ribbentrop (1893–1946) why Bulgaria was delaying the deportation of its Jews to occupied Poland, King Boris III (1894–1943; reigned 1918–1943) responded that he intended to send "only a small number of Bolshevik-communist elements from Old Bulgaria because he needed the rest of the Jews for road construction." (USHMM/SRI, RG-25.004M, roll 31, fond 40010, vol. 1). In fact, as the German Foreign Office understood, the Bulgarians were afraid of the Allies and did not want to stand out as a country heavily involved in the persecution of the Jews (Hilberg 1985, 2: 758). Although the 50,000 Bulgarian Jews suffered greatly from discrimination, expulsions, and forced labor during World War II, with the exception of the approximately 15,000 Jews from Thrace and Macedonia not granted Bulgarian citizenship and thus deported, they survived the war. On 30 August 1944, nearly simultaneously with Romania, the Bulgarian cabinet repealed all antisemitic legislation.

THE CONTROLLED SATELLITES: SLOVAKIA, CROATIA, AND SERBIA

Even before the destruction of Czechoslovakia, representatives of the Slovak autonomous government promised Germany that they would subject the roughly 88,000 Slovakian Jews to the same antisemitic legislation that the Reich had enacted. Thus, when Slovakia proclaimed its independence in March 1939, the fate of the Slovak Jews was sealed. Anti-Jewish measures and the "Aryanization" of Jewish property followed rapidly. German diplomats and special envoys closely monitored these developments and occasionally exerted pressure for more rapid implementation. On 26 March 1942, the deportations began. Although approximately 7,000 Slovak Jews escaped to neighboring Hungary, 30,000 others had been shipped to Auschwitz and Lublin by mid-May 1942 (Hilberg 1985, 2: 730–3). By the end of June 1942, that number had risen to 52,000, and at the end of March 1943 it stood at 57,545 (Hilberg 1985, 2: 734–5). Informed about the fate of these people after reaching Poland, Papal Nuncio Giuseppe Burzio (1901–1966) questioned Slovak Prime Minister Vojtech Tuka (1880–1946) about their treatment and then wrote to Cardinal Luigi Maglione (1877–1944), the Vatican's secretary of state, describing the Slovak dignitary as "demented" (Hilberg 1985, 2: 737–8). In December 1943, Slovak President Josef Tiso (1887–1947), who was a Catholic priest, decided to place the remaining 16,000–18,000 unconverted Jews in concentration camps and the 10,000 Jewish converts to Catholicism in a separate internment camp (Hilberg 1985, 2: 739), but his government dragged its feet in conducting the round-ups. Labor camps for Jews also were established, the most important being Novaky, Sered, and Vihne (Kamenec 2007: 319). After the occupation of Slovakia by the Germans in September 1944, roughly 13,500 Slovak Jews were deported to Auschwitz, Sachsenhausen, and Terezin, of whom approximately 10,000 perished (Kamenec 2007: 337).

Croatia, a state with a Fascist-Catholic philosophy, was the Nazi "satellite par excellence" (Hilberg 1985, 2: 709). Created in March 1941 out of the ruins of defeated Yugoslavia, the new state wasted no time in enacting more severe anti-semitic legislation than Germany's and in interning Serbs, Gypsies, Jews, and Croat political prisoners in concentration camps guarded by Croat fascists. At two death camps, Jasenovac and Stara Gradiska, half of Croat Jewry was interned, including women and children, and subjected to shootings, typhus, starvation, and torture. According to postwar Yugoslav investigations, 25,000–26,000 Jews perished in the Croat concentration camps (Tomasevich 2001: 595). More recent research suggests that this number may be slightly too high. Of approximately 39,000 Jews living initially under Croat jurisdiction, 20 percent may have survived in the country until the end of the war, and thousands more escaped to Italian-occupied territory (Tomasevich 2001: 595). Thoroughly documented, however, are the deportations to German death camps: in August 1942, seven trains carrying at least 4,927 Croat Jews left Zagreb for Auschwitz, as did one transport directly from the camp of Lobograd; in March 1943, another 2,000 Croatian Jews were sent to the same destination (Hilberg 1985, 2: 714, 715, 717).

In August 1941, a Serbian puppet regime headed by General Milan Nedic (1877–1946) took shape, but the destruction of Jews and Roma in this occupied territory was carried out principally by German troops, with Nedic's uniformed men occasionally participating in round-ups. By mid-1942, this process of physical elimination was already over. The German army completed the execution of the last 4,000–5,000 Jewish men in December 1941, and the 6,000–7,500 remaining Jewish women and children were held at a camp at Semlin in Croat territory until the following spring, when they were killed in gas vans (Hilberg 1985, 2: 691–92; Manoschek in Herbert 2000: 179–80). Estimates by Yugoslav commissions investigating war crimes and other studies indicate that 15,000–16,000 Jews were killed in Serbia and Banat during the war (Tomasevich 2001: 588). Of the 75,000 Jews in all of prewar Yugoslavia, 63,000 perished during the war (Hilberg 1985, 2: 1048, 1220).

FRANCE: A COUNTRY UNDER DOUBLE JURISDICTION

··

No country in Europe posed such complexities in the territorial implementation of anti-Jewish measures as did France. The Vichy French legislation covered occupied as well as unoccupied territory, while the German regime was restricted to the occupied area. As a result, the Jews from the occupied zone suffered under a double oppression—French and German—while in the unoccupied zone Jews were exposed only to the regulations of the Vichy regime. In 1942 the demarcation line collapsed, and French and German measures alike were enforced in all France. (Hilberg 1985, 2: 615)

Beginning in 1940, immediately after the armistice that sealed Germany's victory over France, the collaborationist government headquartered at Vichy enacted and implemented comprehensive anti-Jewish legislation, including the denaturalization of certain categories of immigrant Jews and their children, followed by internment of foreign Jews. Under SS supervision, the Paris prefecture of police created a complex card index for these Jews, allowing efficient round-ups and internments in transit camps. Although some French Jews also were arrested and deported, the majority of those sent to Auschwitz were stateless or foreign Jews. Ultimately, perhaps 9–13 percent of French Jews and 42–45 percent of foreign Jews in France were deported from that country (Zuccotti in Berenbaum and Peck 1998: 493). Most of the foreign Jews had lost the protection of their countries of origin. Altogether, about 25 percent of the Jews living in France were transported to Auschwitz, usually in groups of 1,000 people from the transit camp at Drancy. The first transports left France in the summer of 1942 and the last ones in the summer of 1944, after the Allied invasion of Normandy. Of the 75,000 Jews deported from France, roughly 69,000 went to Auschwitz, 2,000 to Majdanek, another 2,000 to Sobibor, and 1,000 to Kovno. The survival rate of these deportees was minimal, at most a few dozen per transport.

Heavily involved in the round-ups of the foreign Jews, the confiscation of their property, their internment in transit camps, and the preparation of the transports were Vichy's Commissariat for Jewish Affairs, led successively by Xavier Vallat (1891–1972) and Louis Darquier de Pellepoix (1897–1980), and the Vichy French police. However, most of the approximately 200,000 Jews living in France prior to the outbreak of the war survived. Among the explanations for this extraordinary rate of survival were the desire of the Vichy authorities "to confine the destruction process to certain limits," their "uneasiness" and "defensiveness" about that process, and the Germans' inability to devote sufficient manpower to cover the territory of France on their own (Hilberg 1985, 2: 609, 625). Furthermore, the lack of cooperation from the Italian occupiers of southeastern France and the refusal of the Vichy authorities to allow the French police to participate in the deportation of French Jews forced the Germans to rely almost exclusively on their own forces in the round-ups of the Jews (Hilberg 1985, 2: 646, 654, 656).

BELGIUM: A COUNTRY UNDER GERMAN MILITARY OCCUPATION

Belgium and the part of France occupied initially constituted the Northern Zone of Occupation, which was under German military rule. The Jewish population of Belgium consisted of about 90,000 people, most of them recent immigrants, including 30,000 refugees from the Reich. When the German armies entered Belgium, many of these Jews either fled to southern France or were pushed in that direction by the occupation authorities. By the beginning of 1941, only 52,000 Jews remained in the country, and fewer than 5,000 of them held Belgian citizenship (Hilberg 1985, 2: 600–1). Beginning in November 1942, shortly after the "Aryanization" of Jewish property in Belgium ended, 15,000 Jews were deported eastwards. By the time of the country's liberation in September 1944, the German occupation authorities had sent 25,000 Jews to Auschwitz, most of them via Malines, the main Belgian transit camp, where Belgian members of the SS guarded the prisoners. The majority of these deportees were foreign, but some were Belgians caught not wearing the mandatory yellow star. The relatively high rate of survival of the Jews from Belgium can be explained by the "shortage" of German police forces and the lack of "understanding" that the Belgians showed to the Jewish question (Hilberg 1985, 2: 600). Numerous Jews were sheltered by Belgian families, and a report of the SS Security Service in 1944 claimed that 80 percent of the Jews living in Belgium had fake identity papers (Hilberg 1985, 2: 606, 608).

THE NETHERLANDS: A COUNTRY UNDER GERMAN CIVILIAN OCCUPATION

About 75 percent of the prewar Dutch Jewish population of approximately 140,000 was deported. "Aryanization" and liquidation of Jewish properties were swift, and forced labor of Jews was implemented in part. The main Dutch transit camps were Vught and Westerbork. The latter was under SS control and the source of the vast majority of Dutch transports to the death camps, although two transports to

Auschwitz left from Vught. Close to 5,000 "privileged Jews"—people who had been decorated in World War I or performed "services for Germany" or had relatives in the Terezienstadt ghetto in occupied Czechoslovakia—were sent to that destination, but most of the Dutch Jews went to Auschwitz (60,000) and Sobibor (34,000). Only about 5,000 of them returned. In spite of this merciless process of destruction, 12,000–16,100 Dutch Jews survived the war in hiding, protected by Christian friends and neighbors (Hilberg 1985, 2: 597; Croes 2006: 491). The motives of this rescue included "a sense of moral duty, even for the people who may have harbored a dislike for the Jews, and often enough it was money, some of which was still being paid after liberation" (Hilberg 1985, 2: 593). The Dutch churches protested publicly and often jointly against the anti-Jewish measures and especially against the forced sterilization of Jews (Paldiel 2006: 170–1). In February 1941, a general strike even occurred against their persecution.

Compared to other occupied countries from western Europe, the Germans were extremely effective in the destruction of the Dutch Jews. The geography of the Netherlands did not offer natural hiding places, such as forests or mountains. Dominated by Austrian Nazis, the German administration zealously implemented the Nuremberg Laws as it strove to prepare the Netherlands for incorporation into the Reich. In spite of the general strike in solidarity with the Jews and courageous acts of armed resistance, the fate of the Dutch Jewry was sealed by the high degree of Dutch administrative cooperation with the Germans and by the passivity of the majority of the Dutch Jews, who faced the deportations "with a residual faith in German civilization" (Hilberg 1985, 2: 591–7).

NORWAY AND DENMARK: "ARYAN" COUNTRIES UNDER OCCUPATION

Occupied on 9 April 1940, Norway and Denmark experienced different processes of destruction of their small Jewish communities. The leader of Norway's version of the Nazi Party, Vidkun Quisling (1887–1945), was tolerated more than embraced by the German occupiers, but Norwegian collaboration significantly aided and abetted the persecution of the country's approximately 1,700 Jews. As many as 930 Jews escaped from Norway to Sweden with help from the Norwegian underground, but following round-ups in late October 1942, coordinated by Norwegian police, the Germans deported about 770 Norwegian Jews by sea in late November 1942 and late February 1943. Only a handful of the deportees survived; most were gassed at Auschwitz. Norwegian church leaders protested against the deportations, and "many Norwegian officials—including members of the collaborationist leader

Vidkun Quisling's own political party and the Norwegian state police—found the persecution distasteful, and therefore refused to participate" (Hollander in Mazur et al. 2004: 129–30). Nevertheless, about 45 percent of Norway's Jews were killed in the Holocaust, a higher proportion than in some other Nazi-occupied countries.

Approximately 6,500 Jews lived in Denmark before the war. Their status worsened radically only in August 1943. A Nazi plan to deport them at the very end of 1943 was leaked by German diplomats in the country and sabotaged by the Danish population, churches, and police. Solidarity with Jews was greater in Denmark than in Norway, and it facilitated the escape by sea that took thousands of Danish Jews to safety in Sweden. "The Jews were moved to fishing ports north and south of the capital. At the northern-most point of Zealand Island, the town of Gilleleje, whose population consisted of 1,682 persons, harbored almost as many Jews as inhabitants . . . When the operation was over, 5,919 Jews, 1,301 part Jews, and 686 non-Jews who were married to Jews had been brought to shore in Sweden" (Hilberg 1985, 2: 567–8). This massive rescue operation was not without risks. In at least two instances, the Gestapo fired on vessels carrying refugees from Danish ports, and 57 rescuers were caught by the Gestapo in October 1943 (Morgensen in Jensen and Jensen 2003: 49–50). Only 477 Danish Jews, less than 10 percent of the country's total Jewish population, were arrested and deported to the Terezin ghetto. Fifty-two of them died there, but the Danish Red Cross continued to visit them and send them food packages for the duration of the war, and none were deported to Auschwitz.

ITALY: THE RELUCTANT ALLY

As in Romania, the first wave of antisemitic legislation affected Jews living in Italy in 1938. The enforcement of this legislation focused primarily on the 3,674 refugee and foreign Jews in the country as of 1941, out of a total Jewish population of 43,118 people. During the spring of 1942, Italian Jews also were forced into labor camps at Rome, Bologna, Milan, and in Libya. But despite heavy pressure from Berlin, Italy continued to decline to deport its Jews to Nazi concentration camps, a policy that extended to the Jews in the Italian-occupied areas of Greece, Yugoslavia, and France. This situation continued until July 1943, when Prime Minister Benito Mussolini (1883–1945) was overthrown. Only after Germany occupied the country and liberated Mussolini to create the Republic of Salo in northern Italy did the situation of the Italian Jews change. On 18 October 1943, German troops rounded up 1,007 Italian Jews in Rome and shipped them to Auschwitz. During the winter of 1944, Jews from Milan and Verona also were deported. A transit camp was created near Modena at Fossoli di Carpi, from which several transports left for Auschwitz during the winter and spring of 1944. Other transports followed during the summer. Estimates of the death toll vary from "about 6,800 Jews—about 20 percent of the total" (Breitman in Diefendorf 2004: 43) to approximately 9,000, including Jews from the island of Rhodes (Hilberg 1985, 3: 1220), but the most precise accounting is as follows: "the Jews in the territory of the Italian Social Republic numbered 32,307, of whom 8,529 were arrested. Of these 6,806 were deported, 322 were murdered or committed suicide during the imprisonment in Italy; the others comprised 950 non-identified deportees and 451 who were arrested but not deported" (Picciotto in Bankier and Gutman 2003: 518).

CONCLUSION

Nazi Germany, its allies, and its collaborators implemented the mass murder of European Jewry on a continental scale. In certain occupied areas of western Europe, Nazi Germany showed atypical restraint in setting the destruction process in motion or pressing it forward, usually because the Third Reich did not want to endanger the smooth operation of "collaboration." Thus, in western Europe, stateless Jews were dispatched to death in larger numbers and earlier than Jews still considered citizens of one or another country. Meanwhile, the process of destruction affected first the periphery of the east European states and advanced in time toward their capital cities. A full understanding of the complex unfolding of the Holocaust is still far off, but the huge quantity of archival documents unearthed during the last twenty years is bound to produce important new revelations.

REFERENCES

BANKIER, D. and GUTMAN, I. (eds.) (2003). *Nazi Europe and the Final Solution.* Jerusalem: Yad Vashem.

BERENBAUM, M. and PECK, A. (eds.) (1998). *The Holocaust and History: The Known, The Unknown, the Disputed, and the Reexamined.* Bloomington, IN: Indiana University Press.

BRAHAM, R. (1994). *The Politics of Genocide: The Holocaust in Hungary.* 2 vols. New York: Columbia University Press.

CROES, M. (2006). "The Holocaust in Netherlands and the Rate of Jewish Survival." *Holocaust and Genocide Studies* 20: 474–99.

DIEFENDORF, J. (ed.) (2004). *Lessons and Legacies VI: New Currents in Holocaust Research.* Evanston, IL: Northwestern University Press.

FRILING, T., IOANID, R., and IONESCU, M. (eds.) (2005). *International Commission on the Holocaust in Romania: Final Report*. Iasi: Polirom.

HAKOV, D. (1998). "The Fate of the Bulgarian Jews during World War II." *Etudes Balkaniques*, 24/1–2: 122–30.

HERBERT, U. (ed.) (2000). *National Socialist Extermination Policies: Contemporary German Perspectives and Controversies*. New York: Berghahn.

HILBERG, R. (1985). *The Destruction of the European Jews*. 2nd edn. 3 vols. New York: Holmes and Meier.

IOANID, R. (2000). *The Holocaust in Romania: The Destruction of Jews and Gypsies Under the Antonescu Regime, 1940–1944*. Chicago, IL: Ivan R. Dee.

JENSEN, M. and JENSEN, S. (eds.) (2003). *Denmark and the Holocaust*. Njalsgade: Institute for International Studies.

KAMENEC, I. (2007). *On the Trail of Tragedy: The Holocaust in Slovakia*. Bratislava: Hajko and Hajkova.

MAZUR, Z., KONIG, F., KRAMER, A., and WITALISZ, W. (eds.) (2004). *The Legacy of the Holocaust: National Perspectives*. Kraków: Jagiellonian University Press.

PALDIEL, M. (2006). *Churches and the Holocaust, Unholy Teaching, Good Samaritans, and Reconciliation*. Jersey City, NJ: KTAV Publishing House.

Procesul marii tradari nationale (1946). Bucharest [no publisher].

SHAPIRO, P. (1974). "Prelude to Dictatorship in Romania: The National Christian Party in Power, December 1937–February 1938." *Canadian-American Slavic Studies* 8: 45–88.

TOMASEVICH, J. (2001). *War and Revolution in Yugoslavia, 1941–1945, Occupation and Collaboration*. Stanford, CA: Stanford University Press.

USHMM (UNITED STATES HOLOCAUST MEMORIAL MUSEUM)/SRI, RG-25.004, Records from the Romanian Information Services, Roll 31, Fond 40010, v. 1.

OTHER SUGGESTED READING

GERLACH, C. and ALY, G. (2002). *Das letzte Kapitel: Der Mord an den ungarischen Juden*. Stuttgart: Deutsche Verlags Anstalt.

MARRUS, M. and PAXTON, R. (1981). *Vichy France and the Jews*. New York: Basic Books.

MOORE, B. (1997). *Victims and Survivors: The Nazi Persecution of the Jews in the Netherlands 1940–1945*. New York: Arnold.

SARFATTI, M. (2006). *The Jews in Mussolini's Italy*. Madison, WI: University of Wisconsin Press.

SNYDER, T. (2010). *Bloodlands: Europe between Hitler and Stalin*. New York: Basic Books.

ZIMMERMAN, J. (ed.) (2005). *Jews in Italy under Fascist and Nazi Rule, 1922–1945*. New York: Cambridge University Press.

CHAPTER 22

··

GHETTOS

··

MARTIN C. DEAN

From the Middle Ages until the mid-nineteenth century, specific residential areas for Jews existed in many European cities and towns. Known in most European languages as "ghettos," a word derived from the name of the island where Venetian Jews were forced to live, these sometimes walled-off spaces were intended to prevent Jews from mixing, trading, and socializing with non-Jews. Even after residential restrictions on Jews had disappeared throughout Europe, the name survived in loose parlance as a term for urban areas in which Jews were concentrated. The Nazis' appropriation of the term sought to delude the Jews with its familiarity and to legitimize new and extreme forms of racial persecution through allusion to historical precedents.

Discourse about ghettos surfaced in Nazi Germany during the autumn of 1938, when the regime recognized that its "Jewish problem" could not be solved through forced emigration. In October 1938, Hermann Göring (1893–1946) suggested that the nation would have to establish ghettos in an emergency situation because no foreign currency would then be available to finance the Jews' removal. Reinhard Heydrich (1904–1942) objected, however, citing the difficulty of policing the inhabitants (Corni 2002: 23).

PATTERNS OF GHETTOIZATION

··

After the German invasion of Poland in September 1939, Heydrich took the lead in ordering the ghettoization of Jews in the parts of that country annexed or occupied by the Reich. His plan was to concentrate the Polish Jews in urban areas near railway lines. The first of these ghettos was decreed on 8 October 1939 in Piotrków-Trybunalski. The Jews were given until the end of the month to move into an old and impoverished part of town. The ghetto's borders were marked by signposts bearing the word Ghetto (in gothic script) above a white skull and crossbones on a blue background, indicating that health reasons required ghettoization of the Jews. No fence or other barrier enclosed the ghetto (Kermish in Giladi 1991: 323–53).

Between January 1940 and the invasion of the Soviet Union on 22 June 1941, the Germans established more than seventy ghettos in occupied Poland, a figure that exceeded 200 by August 1942. Altogether during World War II, the Germans created more than 140 ghettos in the Polish territories incorporated into the Reich (*Warthegau, Regierungsbezirk* Zichenau, *Provinz* Oberschlesien, and *Distrikt* Białystok), about 380 ghettos in the occupied Polish areas grouped into the *Generalgouvernement*, and more than 600 ghettos in the occupied territories of the Soviet Union, specifically in *Reichskommissariat Ostland* (the Baltic States and much of western Belarus) and *Reichskommissariat Ukraine*, which were under civil administration, and in those regions further east that remained under military administration (Russia, Eastern Belarus, Eastern Ukraine, and Crimea). Additional ghettos were established by Germany's allies in Hungary, Romania, and Transnistria. The Germans, however, did not establish ghettos in the Old Reich (Germany's territory as of the end of 1937), western Europe, and most of southern Europe, although exceptions to this rule occurred in Thessaloniki (northern Greece) and Terezin (Theresienstadt in Bohemia).

Ghettoization was driven and justified by a variety of ideological, economic, health, and security reasons, and their relative weight resulted in many regional differences in implementation (Hilberg 2003: 216–36). Heydrich's ghettoization order of 21 September 1939 included no specific policy recommendations other than the establishment of Jewish Councils (*Judenräte*) to facilitate indirect rule of the ghettos by the Germans. Initially, the expectation was that all the Jews in the *Warthegau* soon would be deported eastward, but after an initial wave of expulsion at the end of 1939, these plans were repeatedly deferred (Browning 1992: 31).

Multiple approaches were taken to ghettoization in the *Warthegau* (Alberti 2006). Ghettos were not erected in every town, and in many places the Germans still had not isolated the Jews by spring 1942. In most of the more than fifty ghettos established in the region, the Jews retained some contact with the outside, a pattern that contrasted sharply with the high walls and strict security around the Łódź ghetto. Only a relatively small proportion of the *Warthegau* ghettos ever were enclosed—those in Kutno, Turek, Łęczyca, and Gostynin among them—and in cases such as Zduńska Wola, enclosure occurred only shortly before liquidation. In several districts, such as Turek and Konin, so-called village ghettos were populated by Jews moved from the main towns to villages where few if any Jews had lived before. Local German authorities pushed for the establishment of most *Warthegau* ghettos usually because of urban overcrowding or fear of epidemics. Another motive was to control Jewish black marketeering. Ghetto establishment also may have been driven by the resettlement of ethnic Germans into the region (Alberti 2006: 193–217). In any case, most of the *Warthegau* ghettos were short-lived. By the fall of 1942, the region had been largely cleared of Jews except for those in Łódź. Most deported Jews went to the Chelmno extermination facility, where they perished by asphyxiation in mobile gas vans.

Patterns of ghettoization also varied considerably within the *Generalgouvernement*, although the Germans ultimately established more than fifty ghettos in each of five administrative regions (*Distrikte*): Warsaw, Lublin, Radom, Kraków, and Eastern Galicia. In the Warsaw region, many of the small and medium-sized ghettos existed only until the Jews were moved into the vast Warsaw ghetto. For example, the Sochaczew ghetto lasted for less than one month before the Jews were sent to Warsaw in early 1941. The ghetto in Tłuszcz, however, existed from September 1940 until May 1942, when its Jews were transferred to Warsaw via Radzymin. A few, mostly larger, ghettos, such as those in Żelechów, Otwock, and Minsk Mazowiecki, were maintained until mass deportations in the summer and fall of 1942 dispatched their inhabitants to Treblinka.

These examples suggest considerable differences among the experiences of Jews in the largest ghettos, such as Warsaw and Łódź, whose peak populations numbered hundreds of thousands; those in medium-sized ghettos with populations exceeding 20,000, including Lwów, Kraków, Kovno, Vilna, Riga, Białystok, Lublin, Częstochowa, Grodno, and Pinsk; and those in the much smaller and lesser known ghettos. The narratives of the ghettos of Warsaw and Łódź, in particular, have come to dominate how historians depict the entire ghetto experience, but these two cases were different and scarcely representative of the small and short-lived ghettos.

Conditions in the smaller ghettos are difficult to describe in detail, as documentation, especially diaries or photographs, rarely survived. Despite strict prohibitions, some form of barter with the surrounding population took place in almost all ghettos and a major preoccupation for the Jews was obtaining food. Overcrowding within the ghettos was a particular source of stress, especially as furniture, fuel, cooking utensils, clothing, and toiletries were all in desperately short supply and had to be bartered away for food. Barter transactions were necessary for every ghetto's survival, but the terms of trade heavily favored the local peasants. Terror also played a part in steadily worsening conditions as the ghettos were enclosed.

Out of a total population of some 450,000 in the Warsaw ghetto, 43,239 deaths were officially registered in 1941 and 22,760 more during the first five months of 1942. Such mortality rates were not found in the smaller, rural ghettos where some access to food from the surrounding countryside persisted. Although other large ghettos, such as Lublin or Kielce, experienced mass starvation and severe epidemics (Bauer 1981: 76), this was not the case in most of the eastern ghettos, such as Brześć or Pinsk (Browning 2000: 131). In a few of the ghettos established in the larger cities in the east, such as those in Minsk, Mogilev, or Vitebsk, however, Jews did experience very high rates of mortality prior to the mass murder of the remaining inmates.

POLICIES AND PROCEDURES
IN OCCUPIED POLAND

Clashes among the Germans who administered the ghettos have been characterized as conflicts between "productionists" and "attritionists" (Browning 1992: 42). The former wished to exploit Jewish slave labor, which entailed at least minimal nourishment for the Jews, while the latter sought to starve them out, with no concern for loss of labor. This conflict demonstrates that the ghettos' physical impact on the Jewish population was clear to the German authorities from the start. However, some senior officials feared the consequences for the population outside the ghettos—especially Germans—if starvation and disease were allowed to run rampant inside. In 1940–41, this recognition prepared the way for a radical transition to ghetto liquidation and extermination of the Jews in regional killing centers. This new policy evolved from the summer of 1941 through the interaction of central and regional initiatives, which were influenced by the campaign of mass shooting conducted by the Einsatzgruppen and other agencies after the invasion of the Soviet Union began in late June 1941.

Meanwhile, a significant intention and impact of ghettoization was to drain remaining property and resources from the Jewish population by forcing ghettoized Jews to sell their last possessions for food. In January 1941, the Germans confiscated all Jewish property in Warsaw, save that inside the ghetto, which meant that many Jews lost in one blow most of their life savings. The affected properties included 1,700 grocery shops and 2,500 other businesses (Levine 2004: 69). In Łódź, the German ghetto administration under Hans Biebow (1902–1947) boasted of its success in extracting as much as possible in the way of cash, valuables, and labor from the Jews through a variety of schemes, including the introduction of a ghetto currency (valid only inside the ghetto) that was exchanged for remaining valuables, and repeated searches by the German police.

Inside the ghettos a harsh black market based on the barter of remaining mobile assets came to dominate the economic life that still existed. In the Warsaw ghetto, inflated prices of food soon drained people's reserves until only the "wealthiest" could afford to buy on the black market (Levine 2004: 18–19). In the smaller ghettos, the economic restrictions were sometimes easier to circumvent. For example, in the Glowno ghetto, established in April 1940, bribery gave some Jews access to the town and opportunities to trade on the black market and smuggle food into the ghetto. As a result, no large-scale starvation ravaged the Glowno ghetto before most of its inhabitants were deported to the Warsaw ghetto in February 1941 (Spector and Wigoder 2001: 435). Some Jews in ghettos in *Regierungsbezirk* Zichenau even managed to send food packages to relatives trapped in the Warsaw ghetto.

In the Lublin region (*Distrikt*), the German authorities established relatively few enclosed ghettos before mass deportations began in spring 1942. But an influx of

Jews—refugees and also deportees—meant that numerous de facto open ghettos came into existence, especially after the death penalty was introduced in October 1941 for Jews caught outside their residential quarters without permission (Musial 1999: 144). The town of Hrubieszów, where an open ghetto was established in 1942, provides a good example of the complexities of ghettoization in the Lublin region. Jews from surrounding villages were moved into Hrubieszów's Jewish quarter in May 1942, just before the first deportation of those without work permits took place in early June. After the June *Aktion*, the remaining Jews were moved into a reorganized smaller ghetto, which served mainly to dupe them into believing they would be kept alive as useful workers. In October 1942, this ghetto, in turn, was liquidated, except for a small clean-up squad. Hundreds of Jews discovered in hiding were shot at the Jewish cemetery in the weeks after the second *Aktion* (Kaplinsky 1962: xvi, 107). This region also contained transit ghettos, including Izbica Lubelski, Piaski Luterskie, and Dęblin-Irena, that held Jews deported from the Reich and other areas under German control until they could be deported again, this time to extermination camps (Kuwałek in Libionka 2004).

In the Radom region, the German civil administration systematically organized ghetto establishment and policy in 1941 and 1942. Until May 1942, for example, Jews were permitted to live in 150 towns and settlements in the Opatów district (*Kreis*) of the Radom region. Then, on 13 May, the German administrator Heinz Ritter ordered Jews restricted to only five towns and twelve settlements in that area as of 1 June, which gave the Jews just two and a half weeks to resettle. Those who did so before 28 May 1942 could transport their belongings with them; after that date, they could take only what they could carry. As of 1 June, the seventeen resettlement centers in the Opatów district were all recognized as ghettos (Urbański 2004: 152–3).

The deportations from the ghettos of the Radom region during the summer and fall of 1942 were particularly brutal. The Germans frequently shot hundreds of Jews deemed unfit for travel or caught in hiding after the *Aktionen*. By November 1942, the German authorities had decreed that only four "remnant ghettos" would remain in the region, including the ghetto in Sandomierz. In the weeks following this announcement, thousands of desperate Jews, suspicious of German intentions but unable to survive in hiding any longer, moved into Sandomierz, raising that ghetto's population to more than 6,000. One reason for their desperation was the hostile attitude of the many Polish partisan groups that turned Jews away or betrayed them as they fled to the forests. Jews who took flight from the ghettos were sometimes murdered by Poles for private gain, as demonstrated by several postwar Polish trials covering events in the Radom region (Skibińska and Petele-wicz 2005). Scant though they were, the best chances for survival by ghettoized Jews in this region and others included transfer to a forced labor camp or some other part of the vast Nazi concentration camp system.

Official German documentation sometimes used the term "Jewish Residential District" (*Jüdischer Wohnbezirk*) rather than ghetto, which implied a concentrated residential area reserved only for Jews and often not enclosed by a fence. At least ten of these open ghettos existed in the Kraków region. In Nowy Targ (Neumarkt) such a ghetto, approximately 1,000 square meters in size, was created in May 1941, holding about 2,000 Jews from that town and the surrounding area (Berenstein 1961: 64). Other open ghettos in the Kraków region included Grybów, Mszana Dolna, Stary Sącz, and Zmigród Nowy. In August 1942, the Security Police in Kraków decided to murder the Jews of Mszana Dolna on the spot, thus eliminating the problem of transporting the Jews to the nearest railway station some thirty miles away for deportation to the killing centers (Lehrer and Strassman 1997: 310–11).

In Eastern Galicia, a region annexed to the *Generalgouvernement* in the summer of 1941, the German authorities established a ghetto in Stanisławów and tried to ghettoize most of Lwów's 80,000 Jews in December 1941, following mass killings in the region during the summer and fall. In spring 1942, some Jews declared unfit for work were deported to the Bełżec extermination camp. Additional ghettos were set up throughout 1942, such as in Borszczów in April and Trembowla during the fall. In Skalat, for example, the ghetto was established in steps between April and December, accompanied by successive deportations and reductions in its size. On the order of Higher SS and Police Leader Friedrich Wilhelm Krüger (1894–1945), the number of ghettos (*Jüdische Wohnbezirke*) in Eastern Galicia was limited to thirty-two by 1 December 1942 (Berenstein 1961: 344–6). The ghettoization process in the summer and fall included the liquidation of a few smaller ghettos in conjunction with deportations to Bełżec. The remaining ghettos and forced labor camps represented a final effort to extract labor from those Jews still fit to work before the last ghettos in the region were liquidated in the summer of 1943 (Pohl 1996: 244).

Powerful evidence of the devastating effects of relocation on the smaller Jewish communities emerges from the unusual case of the Jews of Gliniany in Eastern Galicia. When the German authorities announced in November 1942 that all the Jews of the region were to be concentrated in the thirty-two designated ghettos by December, the Jewish Council, hoping to forestall the cruel fate of resettlement, attempted to bribe German officials to establish a ghetto in Gliniany. The attempt failed, and when the Jews left for nearby towns recognized as ghettos, Ukrainians robbed them and seized the property left behind. The Jews of Gliniany arrived at their new ghetto quarters in a particularly impoverished condition (*Hurbn Glinyane* n.d.: 260–1).

EAST OF THE *GENERALGOUVERNEMENT*

In the Baltic States, the Germans and local collaborators established many temporary "destruction ghettos," which were used mainly to contain the Jewish populations for a few days or weeks before their annihilation. Many of the small towns in

Lithuania reflected this policy. By the summer of 1942, only three main ghettos remained—Kovno, Siauliai, and Vilna—a considerable reduction from more than one hundred mostly temporary ghettos or improvised holding camps for Jews during the summer of 1941. In Kėdainiai, for example, the Lithuanian district chief ordered the establishment of a ghetto in early August 1941. The Jews were exploited briefly for forced labor, but by the end of August, forces composed mainly of local Lithuanians acting under the authority of *Einsatzkommando* 3 had murdered all the ghetto inhabitants, more than 2,000 people. In the summer of 1941, as news of mass shootings spread among the Lithuanian Jews, the authorities in Lithuania used the promise of ghettoization (usually fraudulent) to "reassure" the Jews that they would not be shot. By 1943, however, Jewish labor had become more valuable, and some of the last remaining ghettos, such as those in Kovno and in Riga in Latvia, together with their associated forced labor camps, were converted into concentration camps and subcamps and subordinated directly to the SS (Angrick and Klein 2006).

Mass shootings of Jews that took place in the summer of 1941 as the Wehrmacht moved east did not mean that ghettoization came to an end in those areas. For example, operating behind German Army Group Center, Einsatzgruppe B and the military administration established ghettos in more than twenty-five towns in the occupied territory of the Russian Federation. Some of these ghettos existed for several months. Following the German failure to capture Moscow in December 1941, the Red Army's counter-offensive resulted in the liberation of ghettoized Jews in Kaluga, I'lino, and in Kolyshki (Belarus) (Doubson 2000; Altman 2008: 324–6).

In *Generalkommissariat* Weissruthenien, the German authorities established approximately one hundred ghettos, in many cases moving Jews into them from the surrounding villages. The Jewish Council in Byten, for example, organized major efforts to prepare food, shelter, and medical care for hundreds of Jewish refugees who were driven out of the nearby town of Iwacewicze in March 1942 (Abramovitsh and Bernshtayn 1954: 221–4). The overcrowded conditions in Baranowicze, another ghetto in the region, have been described by one of the survivors, a doctor named Leon Berk:

We were given space to live in a small house, which already contained three other families. There were 27 of us all told. There was one kitchen, one bathroom and nine of us slept in each of the other small rooms in three-tiered bunks . . . The crowded conditions put a strain on us all but the women suffered the most and many of them came near to breakdown. Food was scarce, cooking utensils were at a premium, and competition for use of the stove and the bathroom was inevitable. Every day there were tears and screams. The struggle to keep a family fed and clothes clean and free of lice was a battle they had no hope of winning. (Berk 1992: 70)

Research has identified three types of relationship between the Jewish Councils in the ghettos in western Belarus (mostly in the *Generalkommissariat* Weissruthenien) and the region's Jewish underground organizations. In some ghettos, the underground's activities faced opposition. In Nowogródek, to prevent Jewish youths from fleeing to the forest, the Jewish police caught them and took away their shoes (Cholawsky 1998). In other places, a more ambivalent or sympathetic attitude about armed uprisings prevailed, characterized perhaps by the situation in Baranowicze, where the first date set for an uprising was postponed. A third type of relationship emerged where the Jewish Council itself assumed leadership of a full-scale uprising, as happened in Łachwa. At times, a compromise was reached, as in the ghettos at Szarkowszczyzna and Zdzięcioł (Levin in Gutman and Haft 1979: 133–50). In these cases, the underground waited until it knew that an *Aktion* was about to take place; then the whole ghetto fought back together, in the hope that at least some inhabitants might flee successfully to the partisans. Unlike the Warsaw ghetto uprising in April–May 1943, these battles were not prolonged. Bursts of armed ghetto resistance enabled hundreds of Jews to escape to the forests, but the success of armed resistance was always limited by the overwhelming odds against it.

The best of the meager chances that these ghettoized Jews had for survival was to escape the ghetto clandestinely and join Soviet partisans in the forest. A number of Jews escaped successfully from ghettos in Minsk (Belarus), Vilna (Lithuania), and other places. Perhaps the most effective mass escape was from the Mir ghetto in Belarus. Here a Jewish agent within the German police, Oswald Rufeisen (1922–1998), managed to organize the escape of about 200 mostly younger Jews while the Germans and local police were away following up on a fictitious report about Soviet partisans that he had planted. Nevertheless, the majority of the Jews— mostly women, children, and the elderly—remained behind because they could not see themselves surviving for long as fugitives in the forests, and German forces shot them all shortly afterwards. Even in Belarus (*Generalkommissariat* Weissruthenien and those parts under German military control further east), a sizable Soviet partisan movement that could give support to fleeing Jews did not emerge until the summer of 1942, just as the Germans started the final wave of liquidation against the remaining ghettos (Dean 2000: 90–2 and 119).

In Wolhynien-Podolien, Ukraine, the German civil administration adopted a similar policy, establishing numerous ghettos, usually in the small market towns where the local administration for each subdivision (*raion*) was based. Jews were brought into the ghettos in the *raion* centers from the surrounding villages some time before the liquidation actions. Reichskommissar Erich Koch (1896–1986) issued an order in September 1941 that no ghettos were to be established in places where the Jewish population was less than 200 (Lower in Sterling 2005: 134). In the fall of 1941, one of the first regulations issued by the new civil administration prohibited Jews from leaving their places of residence. The ghettos in Weissruthenien and Wolhynien-Podolien performed important functions in concentrating the Jews, facilitating the exploitation of Jewish labor, controlling the food supply, and preparing for the murders.

At the beginning of November 1941, the Jews of Łokacze (in Wolhynien-Podolien) were forced into an open ghetto. Half of their houses were confiscated, and about 800 Jews were brought into the village from the countryside, causing terrible over-crowding. On 5 January, the authorities ordered the Jewish Council to construct a two-meter high, wooden fence around the ghetto, which took one month. This constraint made trading with local peasants more difficult and caused blackmarket prices to rise. Ukrainian police made matters worse by shooting Jews caught outside the ghetto (Diment 1992: 38–72).

Inevitably, the shortages of food and material goods within the ghettos put added strain on the Jewish Councils and their administrative organs, especially if they tried to distribute fairly what remained. Inequalities in distribution, corruption, and harsh treatment of other Jews caused many to recall with considerable bitterness the activities of some Jewish Councils. In January 1942, for example, the Jewish Council in Łokacze received German instructions to collect a poll tax of twenty rubles from all of the ghetto inhabitants. One survivor described the situation as follows:

The Judenrat and the militia with an additional 15 Jewish muscle men called on those who had not contributed . . . They broke into homes shouting: "Give us the money!". . . All valuables found were confiscated; they also took food and flour . . . Everyone was very angry at the way the Judenrat handled the situation. They were very bitter but the money had to be turned over. (Diment 1992: 64–5)

Contradictory accounts, even about the same Jewish Council officials, exist among Jewish survivors, and no individual testimony should be given undue weight (Trunk 1996: 577–85). However, the multiple accounts available in many Yizkor books provide a broad base for assessing Jewish views on the character of particular Jewish Councils, reflecting also the sometimes strong emotions aroused by certain personalities (Spector 1990: 165–6).

The Yizkor book for Stepań (Ukraine), where Yosef Vaks ousted the chairman of the Judenrat, assumed his position, and apparently went so far as to turn an upper chamber of the synagogue into a jail for Jews who disobeyed the ghetto police, indicates that the majority of the Jews saw Vaks as arrogant and unsympathetic (Ganuz and Fri 1977: 244, 275, and 300–1). Another Yizkor book account from Wiśniowiec (Ukraine) tells a different story.

The chairman of the Judenrat, Koylnbrener, was a man from Łódź who had come to Wiśniowiec as a refugee after his hometown was conquered by the Germans near the end of 1939. He was a warm-hearted Jew, a lover of the Jewish people prepared to give his life for each and every Jew in the town. He was the central figure in those tragic days. He was everything to us. For his sake, every one of us was willing to go beyond his normal capabilities.

Koylnbrener knew German perfectly, was well liked by the Germans, and knew how to deal with them. At times it seemed that they did not want to kill him. However, they killed him later on during the liquidation of the ghetto. (Rabin 1979: 311–25)

Recent research has advanced understanding of the dilemmas faced by the Jewish Councils as they tried to address the needs of their communities. A study based on documentation from the Brest (Brześć) archives concerning economic and other aspects of life in the Pinsk (Wolhynien-Podolien) ghetto draws several significant conclusions about the activities of the Jewish Council during the last months of that community's existence:

> The documentation . . . permits us to sketch a portrait of the Judenrat and its activity on the Jews' behalf . . . It put the emphasis on sustaining daily life and spared no effort to seek ways and means to assure the Jewish population's survival. It attempted to maneuver between the authorities' demands and the Jews' needs and to repeal various decrees by petitioning the authorities repeatedly. It fought disease by hiring doctors, operating a hospital, and finding medicines, and resisted starvation by keeping the ghetto population employed, distributing ration cards, and improving food supplies. However, the Judenrat also pressured the Jews whenever contributions and confiscations of belongings were necessary. Its actions were surely criticized, but it operated under conditions of continual pressure and threats—from the August 1941 *Aktion*, continuing with ghettoization, and ending with the final liquidation *Aktion*. It was, in fact, a rump Judenrat, eviscerated after many of its members were murdered immediately after their appointment. (Fatal-Knaani 2001b: 182)

The Jewish Council in the Kovno (Lithuania) ghetto undertook numerous initiatives to help its inhabitants maintain their spirits and survive. It supplemented the official starvation rations by cultivating gardens and smuggling food. Transgressing German limitations on its power, the Council established schools, took preventive measures against the appalling health conditions, and tried to preserve at least a minimum of cultural life. In the Kovno ghetto, the police orchestra gave concerts, art exhibitions were staged, and religious holidays were observed (United States Holocaust Memorial Museum 1998).

In the Horochów ghetto (*Generalkommissariat* Wolhynien-Podolien), extra food was unobtainable, and starvation wracked the ghetto. People were shot if they tried to leave. Skilled workers received 300 grams of bread per day, while "useless" Jews received 150 grams. The food scarcity led twenty youngsters to tunnel under the ghetto fence, remove their yellow stars, and forage for food, bartering items such as clothing or jewelry in exchange for provisions that could keep their families alive. As in virtually every ghetto, the lack of adequate sanitation and hygiene led to disease and death and the stench that accompanied these conditions. In Rożyszcze (Wolhynien-Podolien), the bread allocation—fifty grams daily per person—was even less than in Horochów. To enhance opportunities to barter for food, one enterprising group of Jews risked going to the Kowel ghetto to obtain rare items, such as needles and thread, that were sought after by the local peasants. Jews caught smuggling were beaten severely by the Ukrainian police (Zik 1976: 33–4, 37).

In almost all ghettos, Jews were put to forced labor. Seeking to reduce the random seizure of Jews by the Germans, the Jewish Councils often made the labor assignments. Some Councils permitted wealthy Jews to pay for substitutes to take their places in the labor details, a policy that could raise money to supplement the workers' remuneration or provide social services for the community. For example, in Prużana (Belarus), the Jewish Council assigned ghetto inhabitants to forced labor, which included work outside the ghetto on road construction, clothing production, and domestic chores for German families. Jewish craftsmen also worked in the ghetto workshops, where their skills in carpentry, tailoring, and shoemaking helped to sustain life, at least for a time (Harshalom 1990: 44).

FOREBODING AND RESISTANCE

By 1942, contrary to the oft-stated view of Jews as unwitting and therefore largely helpless victims, most ghetto inmates had a strong sense of foreboding about what was coming. For example, Jews in the Kosów Lacki ghetto (Warsaw district) learned about mass murder at Treblinka from a few Jews who had escaped from deportation trains and even from the camp itself. Ghettoized Jews usually made extensive preparations for an expected *Aktion* in order at least to make the destructive task of the Germans and their local collaborators more difficult. As arms were almost impossible to obtain and the chances of a successful armed revolt miniscule at best, the most common form of resistance was the preparation of hiding places in concealed bunkers or behind false walls. Survivor accounts recall the incredible tension experienced by those in hiding, as they overheard the conversations of those searching the ghetto for Jews and loot after the initial clearance sweep.

The Białystok district in occupied Poland contained more than fifty ghettos, with Białystok and Grodno among the largest (Fatal-Knaani 2001a). Many of them were established shortly after the invasion of Soviet territory in June 1941. A few Jewish survivors fled from the ghetto liquidations in Weissruthenien and Wolhynien-Podolien to ghettos in the Białystok region, bringing reports of the destruction they had narrowly escaped. But their warnings were scarcely of help when the Germans quickly liquidated most of the Białystok region's ghettos in the autumn of 1942, dispatching their inhabitants to Treblinka and Auschwitz.

The Białystok ghetto, which had held 50,000 Jews, remained in existence, albeit with a reduced population, until the summer of 1943. Its Jewish Council was headed by an engineer named Ephraim Barash (1892–1943). A well-known advocate of the strategy of "rescue through work," Barash became convinced that the utility of Jewish labor in Białystok had improved the attitude of the Germans toward the ghetto. This personal conviction awakened in him the hope—it became almost a certainty to him—that the Białystok ghetto would survive the war intact (Bender 2008). The rapid liquidation of the ghetto in August 1943 proved him wrong. About one hundred Jews escaped during the uprising that broke out during the liquidation. In a pattern repeated in numerous ghettos, labor bought the Białystok ghetto some time but not rescue. Only in August 1944 did Soviet forces wrest the Białystok region from German control.

The ghettoized Jews' desperate efforts to survive reveal the hopelessness of their situation, which was increasingly dominated by the expectation, shared by non-Jews as well as Jews, that the ghettos would eventually be liquidated and their last inhabitants killed. Peasants often asked Jews to give them their remaining property, so that at least the Germans would not profit from it. Some younger Jews tried to flee to the partisans or offer armed resistance, but for the majority of ghetto inmates (mainly women, children, and the elderly) such plans offered no real hope. The last resort was to hide in some concealed compartment, trying to evade the repeated searches conducted by the local police. Thousands of ghettoized Jews did survive, usually with the help of several different neighbors, or even strangers who acted spontaneously when confronted with their plight. But every encounter with people outside the ghetto ran the risk of betrayal, and this constant fear was often too much to bear. The pervading attitude in the surrounding populations was hostility, spurred on by draconian German punishments of those helping Jews and generous rewards to those who betrayed them. Some escaped Jews even resignedly accepted false German promises of an amnesty and returned to the last remnant ghettos, despairing of life in the forests (Kaczerginski 1947: 155). On the eve of the major ghetto liquidations in 1942 and thereafter, most Jews knew what to expect and were largely reconciled to their fate.

Many historians have criticized the Jewish Councils strongly for failing to resist the Germans and even opposing the plans of the Jewish underground in many ghettos. However, even in such cases the motivation of the Jewish Council was usually its concern for the welfare of the whole community. The most vehement criticisms of the Jewish Councils target corruption, personal enrichment, and indifference to the fate of individual Jews in their community. Such accusations do not apply fairly to the majority of members of the Jewish Councils, who acted as best they could in impossible situations. Their survival strategies—appeasing the Germans with bribes or Jewish labor—ultimately not only proved unsuccessful but also cost their own lives.

REFERENCES

ABRAMOVITSH, D. and BERNSHTAYN, M. (eds.) (1954). *Pinkes Biten*. Buenos Aires: Bitener Landslayt in Argentine.

ALBERTI, M. (2006). *Die Verfolgung und Vernichtung der Juden im Reichsgau Wartheland 1939–1945*. Wiesbaden: Harrassowitz.

ALTMAN, I. (2008). *Opfer des Hasses: Der Holocaust in der UdSSR 1941–1945*. Zurich: Gleichen.

ANGRICK, A. and KLEIN, P. (2006). *Die "Endlösung" im Ghetto Riga: Ausbeutung und Vernichtung 1941–44*. Darmstadt: Wissenschaftliche Buchgesellschaft.

BAUER, Y. (1981). *American Jewry and the Holocaust: The American Jewish Joint Distribution Committee, 1939–1945*. Detroit, MI: Wayne State University Press.

BENDER, S. (2008). *The Jews of Bialystok during World War II and the Holocaust*. Waltham, MA: Brandeis University Press.

BERENSTEIN, T. (ed.) (1961). *Faschismus, Getto, Massenmord: Documentation über Ausrottung und Widerstand der Juden in Polen während des zweiten Weltkrieges*. Berlin: Rutten & Loenig.

BERK, L. (1992). *Destined to Live: Memoirs of a Doctor with the Russian Partisans*. Melbourne: Paragon Press.

BROWNING, C. (1992). *The Path to Genocide: Essays on Launching the Final Solution*. Cambridge: Cambridge University Press.

——(2000). *Nazi Policy, Jewish Workers, German Killers*. Cambridge: Cambridge University Press.

CHOLAWSKY, S. (1998). *The Jews of Bielorussia during World War II*. Amsterdam: Harwood.

CORNI, G. (2002). *Hitler's Ghettos: Voices from a Beleaguered Society, 1939–1944*. London: Oxford University Press.

DEAN, M. (2000). *Collaboration in the Holocaust: Crimes of the Local Police in Belorussia and Ukraine, 1941–44*. London and New York: Macmillan and St. Martin's in cooperation with the U.S. Holocaust Memorial Museum.

DIMENT, M. (1992). *The Lone Survivor: A Diary of the Lukacze Ghetto and Svyniukhy, Ukraine*. New York: Holocaust Library.

DOUBSON, V. (2000). "Ghetto na okkupirovannoy territorii rossiiskoy federatsii (1941–42)." *Vestnik. Evreyskogo Universiteta. Istoriya. Kultura. Tsivilizatsiya* 3/21: 157–84.

FATAL-KNAANI, T. (2001a). *Zo Lo Otah Grodnah, Kehilat Grodnah ve-Svivatah be-Milkhamah uve-Shoah 1939–1943*. Jerusalem: Yad Vashem.

——(2001b). "The Jews of Pinsk, 1939–1943 through the Prism of New Documentation." *Yad Vashem Studies* 29: 149–82.

GANUZ, Y. and FRI, Y. (eds.) (1977). *Ayartenu Stepan*. Tel Aviv: Irgun yots'e Stepan vehasevivah be-Yisra'el.

GILADI, B. (ed.) (1991). *A Tale of One City: Piotrków-Trybunalski*. New York: Shengold, in cooperation with the Piotrkow-Trybunalski Relief Association.

GUTMAN, Y. and HAFT, C. (eds.) (1979). *Patterns of Jewish Leadership in Nazi Europe, 1933–1945*. Jerusalem: Yad Vashem.

HARSHALOM, A. (1990). *Alive from the Ashes*. Tel Aviv: Hidekel.

HILBERG, R. (2003). *The Destruction of the European Jews*. 3rd edn. New Haven, CT: Yale University Press.

Hurbn Glinyane: lezikoren unzere doyshim (n.d.). New York: Emergency Relief Committee for Gliniany and Vicinity.

KACZERGINSKI, S. (1947). *Hurbn Vilne: umkum fun di Yidn in Vilne un Vilner gegnt . . . : zamlung fun eydus: bavayzn oder dokumentn*. New York: Aroysgegebn fun dem fareyniktn Vilner hilfs-komitet in Nyu-York durkh Tsiko bikher-farlag.

KAPLINSKY, B. (ed.) (1962). *Pinkas Hrubieshov: Memorial to a Jewish Community in Poland*. Organization of Former Jewish Inhabitants of Hrubieszow in Israel.

LEHRER, S. and STRASSMAN, L. (1997). *The Vanished City of Tsanz*. Southfield, MI: Targum.

LEVINE, I. (2004). *Walls Around: The Plunder of Warsaw Jewry during World War II and Its Aftermath*. Westport, CT: Praeger.

LIBIONKA, D. (ed.) (2004). *Akcja Reinhardt: Zagłada Żydów w Generalnym Gubernatorstwie*. Warsaw: Instytut Pamięci Narodowej.

MUSIAL, B. (1999). *Deutsche Zivilverwaltung und Judenverfolgung im Generalgouvernement: Eine Fallstudie zum Distrikt Lublin, 1939–1944*. Wiesbaden: Harrasowitz.

POHL, D. (1996). *Nationalsozialistische Judenverfolgung in Ostgalizien 1941–1944*. Munich: Oldenbourg.

RABIN, H. (ed.) (1979). *Vishnivits: sefer zikaron li-kedoshe Vishnivits she-nispu be-sho'at ha-natsim*. Tel-Aviv: Irgun 'ole Vishnivits.

SKIBIŃSKA, A. and PETELEWICZ, J. (2005). "Udział Polaków w zbrodniach na Żydach na prowincji regionu świętokrzyskiego." *Zagłada Żydów: studia i materiały*, vol. 1.

SPECTOR, S. (1990) *The Holocaust of Volhynian Jews, 1941–44*. Jerusalem: Achva Press.

——and WIGODER, G. (eds.) (2001). *The Encyclopedia of Jewish Life Before and During the Holocaust*. Jerusalem: Yad Vashem; New York: New York University Press.

STERLING, E. J. (ed.) (2005). *Life in the Ghettos During the Holocaust*. Syracuse, NY: Syracuse University Press.

TRUNK, I. (1996). *Judenrat: The Jewish Councils in Eastern Europe under Nazi Occupation*. Lincoln, NE: University of Nebraska Press.

UNITED STATES HOLOCAUST MEMORIAL MUSEUM (1998). *Hidden History of the Kovno Ghetto*. Boston: Little, Brown.

URBAŃSKI, K. (2004). *Zagłada Żydów w Dystrykcie Radomskim*. Kraków: Wydawnictwo Naukowe AP.

ZIK, G. (ed.) (1976). *Roz'ishts' 'ayarati/Mayn shtetl Rozshishtsh*. Tel Aviv: Irgun yots'e Roz'ishts' be-Yi'srael veha-irgunim be-Artsot ha-berit, Kanadah, Brazil, ve-Argentinah.

OTHER SUGGESTED READING

COLE, T. (2003). *Holocaust City: The Making of a Jewish Ghetto*. New York: Routledge.

KASSOW, S. (2007). *Who Will Write Our History? Emanuel Ringelblum, the Warsaw Ghetto, and the Oyneg Shabes Archive*. Bloomington, IN: Indiana University Press.

MEGARGEE, G. (ed.) (2009). *The United States Holocaust Memorial Museum Encyclopedia of Camps and Ghettos, 1933–1945*. Bloomington, IN: Indiana University Press.

MIRON, G. and SHULHANI, S. (eds.) (2010). *The Yad Vashem Encyclopedia of the Ghettos during the Holocaust*. 2 vols. New York: New York University Press.

PETROPOULOS, J., RAPAPORT, L., and ROTH, J. (eds.) (2010). *Lessons and Legacies IX: Memory, History, and Responsibility: Reassessments of the Holocaust, Implications for the Future*. Evanston, IL: Northwestern University Press.

ZAPRUDER, A. (ed.) (2002). *Salvaged Pages: Young Writers' Diaries of the Holocaust*. New Haven, CT: Yale University Press.

CHAPTER 23

LABOR SITES

MARK SPOERER

In December 1999, Germany decided to compensate former forced laborers of World War II, and Austria followed suit two months later. Only in the ensuing months did the scale of their undertaking become clear. Whereas the approximate number of forced laborers within Nazi Germany from 1933 to 1945, including Austria after March 1938, could be pegged at 12 million with the help of detailed contemporary labor records produced by the German labor and armaments administrations, a reliable tally of laborers forced to work for the German occupation forces in other countries was quite another matter. In eastern Europe alone, the number exceeded 20 million, according to rough estimates (Spoerer and Fleischhacker 2002), but comprehensive figures were impossible to assemble. How many of these millions of forced laborers were Jews (or defined as such by the Germans) proved even more difficult to establish. Most of them were deployed in mid-eastern and eastern Europe under circumstances that did not favor statistical record keeping. Many of the former laborers could not recall the particulars of their exploitation, since it was for them an episode overshadowed by other and more striking Holocaust memories. And the gradual recognition by researchers that earlier estimates of the number of possible Jewish Holocaust survivors were too low actually exerted an inhibiting effect on tabulation, since correcting these totals ran the risk of feeding deniers' claims that the number of Holocaust victims previously had been exaggerated.

These relatively recent quantitative realizations reflect the circumstance that for many years few historians of the Holocaust paid attention to the use of Jews as forced workers before their deaths or the fact that some of them survived precisely because of that role. These topics gained relevance only as academic interpretations of the origins of the Holocaust shifted from an exclusive focus on its ideological and "irrational" causes and began making allowance for the possibility that the attack on the Jews had "rational" drivers as well, that is, that it also was engineered to serve other ends. Since then, Jewish forced labor and concentration camp labor in general have been discussed under two overarching headings with somewhat different implications: "destruction through work" and "slave labor." Historians have debated whether Nazi perpetrators created compulsory labor for Jews merely as a means of annihilation—while extracting a last, welcome round of work along the way—or whether Jews at some point experienced a paradigm shift that, however briefly, elevated them to a factor of production that might be profitably exploited. Only in the latter case would calling them "slave workers" be appropriate, for slaveholders, in antiquity as well as in antebellum America, always had an economic interest in the manpower of the slaves and thus usually in their lives as well.

Broadly speaking, the academic literature dealing with Jewish forced labor developed in two stages. The first concerned forced labor in concentration camps, where Jewish inmates were usually a small minority, and initially concentrated on production facilities run by the SS before broadening to encompass sites that were guarded but not run by the SS. Well-balanced syntheses of this sort have been published by Karin Orth (1999) and Michael Allen (2002). In the second stage, beginning in the 1990s, an increasing number of authors researched Jewish forced labor camps in the General Government (roughly equivalent to the central part of occupied Poland) and the Reichskommissariat Ostland (roughly equivalent to the Baltic states) (Sandkühler and Pohl in Herbert et al. 1998), and made Jewish forced labor an important subject in more general case studies on the German occupation regime in eastern Europe (Browning 2000). At present, the most comprehensive and authoritative history of Jewish forced labor is that of Wolf Gruner (2006).

Jewish Forced Labor under Nazi Rule: An Overview

In the course of the Nazi persecution, the exploitation of Jewish labor took four successive, but overlapping forms. Jews were employed (1) as forced civilian workers, (2) as ghetto workers, (3) as Jewish labor camp inmates, and (4) as concentration camp inmates.

The origins of forced labor in Nazi Germany date from 1938 when German workers were forced to erect the *Westwall* along the nation's western border and Austrian workers were sent to armaments factories in central Germany against their will. As the Jews were systematically driven out of the German economy in the same year, many became jobless and dependent on public welfare. Nazi zealots insisted that if the state was going to coerce full-scale *Volksgenossen* to work against their will, then Jews, who were officially regarded as "subjects," not citizens, in Germany, should also perform forced labor. Despite this economic rationale, when Jewish forced labor began in the fall of 1938, the main motive was humiliation. Typical tasks were snow removal, street and park cleaning, and other forms of menial work. Starting in 1940, exploitation became more systematic, and the labor offices sent Jews to manufacturing firms, especially in the electrotechnical industry in Berlin, which employed a large share of the altogether approximately 52,000 German Jews engaged in forced labor in July 1941. Since these Jews were still German subjects who had been coerced into formal labor contracts, they may be classified as forced civilian workers.

When these Jewish laborers were deported to eastern Europe between fall 1941 and 1943, most of them ended up in ghettos, where they and other residents were assigned to workshops or sent on to labor camps outside. Often these workshops had been owned by Jewish proprietors and taken over by German firms that sought to employ cheap Jewish labor. Usually these firms were in the textiles and leather business or other light industries. The ghettos were dissolved between 1941 and 1944, and their inhabitants were either transferred to extermination camps or to Jewish forced labor camps where the inmates worked on road and water construction, forestry, and shop floors. In 1943 and 1944, most Jewish forced labor camps were dissolved and the surviving inmates transferred to extermination or concentration camps. In the latter they were grouped together with non-Jewish inmates and, from spring 1944 on, with Hungarian Jews, who became caught up in the Holocaust precisely when the German war economy was most short of labor. The Hungarian Jews were sent to Auschwitz, which served both as extermination camp and as a labor source for mining and manufacturing firms of the area. As these workplaces were usually far away from the concentration camps, satellite camps (*Aussenlager*) arose that in turn sent the concentration camp inmates (*Arbeitskommandos*) in labor gangs to the firms. Hence, when Jewish forced laborers were liberated, they were either in the status of concentration camp inmates or inmates of the few remaining Jewish forced labor camps, most of which were within the borders of Germany as of March 1938.

Another way to depict the history of Jewish forced labor is to look at the most meaningful variable for the victims: the probability of surviving. From this perspective, the four vital determinants were timing, place, occupation, and gender. With respect to timing, at the risk of some oversimplification, one can discern three phases of Jewish forced labor. The first started in late 1938 when German and Austrian Jews were registered and compelled to work in infrastructure and armaments firms. Even though many of these people had been driven out of their dwellings and into crowded "Jew houses," the prevailing conditions still allowed them to survive. Because they usually worked among non-Jewish Germans, and the regime dared not risk provoking a political backlash, they could not be treated with the same degree of cruelty as ghetto inhabitants and camp inmates later were. This inhibition provided a bit of protection not only to German and Austrian Jewish forced civilian workers but also to those in countries where the German occupants did not want to alienate the population, i.e., in the occupied areas outside Poland, the Soviet Union, and the Balkans. Czech Jews, for example, experienced comparatively moderate measures of the German occupation regime as long as they remained in the Protectorate, and the Jews in occupied Tunisia were treated similarly. From 1938 to summer 1941, when the transition to the systematic murder of Jews had not yet taken place, the persecutors were more interested in humiliation and exploitation than in killing.

The second phase began during the summer and autumn of 1941 with the onset of deportations of Jews from Germany and Austria and the emergence of a program of systematic mass murder. Although the killing frequently was indiscriminate, Jews judged able to work usually could survive longer than others. Conversely, even those Jews who had been used for productive purposes at the Siemens plants in Berlin or armaments factories in occupied Poland ultimately were deported to extermination camps or murdered on the spot. In this phase the fate of the Jewish forced laborers was foreseeable to the persons in charge. Hence they no longer cared about living and working conditions, which soon deteriorated. Even privately owned firms deliberately subjected Jewish workers to lethal conditions, with IG Farben and especially the less well known HASAG (*Hugo Schneider AG*) munitions firm being forerunners.

IG Farben came into being when a number of large chemical firms merged in 1925. It was one of the world's leading corporations and Germany's largest industrial enterprise in the early 1940s. When the firm sought a site for a new plant to produce synthetic rubber and synthetic oil, it opted for the vicinity of Auschwitz, which offered an excellent railway infrastructure and other natural advantages and where the SS had erected a concentration camp. The Auschwitz camp soon provided the Farben plant with fresh inmate labor. At the beginning, IG officials protested against the poor health status of the inmates but soon a process of habituation set in. In mid-1942 the Auschwitz camp erected a satellite camp in Monowitz next to the factory premises. Altogether IG Farben used about 35,000 inmates to construct its new factory, of whom some 23,000 died in the process. Counted together, all IG Farben plants employed at least 52,000 concentration camp inmates, several thousand of them Jewish (Hayes 1987: 343, 359).

The much smaller HASAG group with headquarters in Leipzig (Saxony) ran a number of plants in the Radom district of occupied Poland, where the workforce consisted mainly of Jews after the dissolution of most of the ghettos in the summer of 1942. Upon arrival at the plants, these Jews were plundered, and those unfit to work, such as pregnant women and the sick, were murdered by the factory guards. In the notorious Skarzisko-Kamienna plant, the weakest persons were made to work with highly toxic acids without protective equipment or clothing; their skin and hair became greenish-yellow. Within three months at the most, they died from emaciation or were murdered. The HASAG plants in Poland employed about 40,000 Jewish men and women, of whom at least 20,000 were worked to death or killed (Karay 1996).

In fall 1943, following a revolt in the Sobibor extermination camp, Heinrich Himmler (1900–1945) ordered the massacre of the remaining Jewish laborers in the Lublin district, who were mostly concentrated in the camps of Poniatowa, Trawniki, and Majdanek. The campaign, cynically called Operation Harvest Festival (*Erntefest*), resulted in the murder of 42,000–43,000 Jewish forced laborers in the first days of November 1943 and had very few survivors. However, this initiative was not the end of Jewish forced labor, even in Poland, since labor matters were not the exclusive province of the SS. Between 1939 and 1945 at least 1,300 Jewish forced labor camps in the Greater German Reich and the occupied Polish territories were outside the concentration camp system and maintained by a number of companies and institutions of which regional SS offices were just a part (Pohl in Herbert et al. 1998; Gruner 2006).

The third phase commenced in spring 1944 with the launching of the *Jägerstab-Programm*, a desperate effort to break allied air superiority by producing more and better fighter aircraft, mainly in subterranean plants. This new program intensified the use of concentration camp labor obtained from the last untapped labor reserve available to the Nazi regime, the Hungarian Jews. After a period of exploitation by the Hungarian labor system, the Hungarian Jews came within reach of the SS precisely at a moment when the urgent need for workers in the German armaments industry partially trumped the ideological aim to murder the Jews immediately. Thus, when the 435,000 Hungarian Jews deported to Auschwitz after May 1944 under the direction of Adolf Eichmann (1906–1962) were subjected to "selection" at the notorious ramp, those designated as fit to work, among them many girls and women, were sent to construction sites and manufacturing firms. The *Jägerstab* program was lethal and consumed at least ten thousand lives. For a portion of the Hungarian Jews, however, it offered a chance to survive. In the end, a high proportion of Holocaust survivors held Hungarian citizenship.

In addition to timing, the place of exploitation made a difference to Jews' survival prospects. Although reliable information is sparse, it suggests that Jews who worked in or close to their hometowns and lived in houses or flats in Germany, Austria, or the Protectorate did not experience greatly increased mortality in 1938–1941. To be sure, the suicide rate rose as a result of often humiliating living conditions, but probably not as a direct consequence of forced labor per se. However, the distinction between the workplace and the home as a place of respite was erased for Jewish forced laborers in ghettos, labor camps, and concentration camps. Here they faced poverty, malnutrition, confinement, cold, contagious diseases, and a high incidence of crime. In consequence, mortality increased enormously and independently of harassment and murder by guards. Moreover, generally speaking, perpetrators acted more relentlessly and brutally the further away from Germany and the more eastwards they were. Even Jews within Germany in 1940–41 experienced conditions that were relatively benign compared to what awaited them after deportation. The occupation regime in the annexed and occupied parts of Poland was much harsher. In the so-called *Warthegau*, as well as in and around East Upper Silesia, many Jews were driven into ghettos or forced labor camps, where the mortality rates were high even before the systematic murder of the Jews started.

In the occupied parts of the Soviet Union Jews also faced very harsh working and living conditions. Many were employed in road construction that, as Eichmann indicated at the Wannsee Conference (January 1942), was intended to achieve "destruction through work": "In pursuance of the final solution, the Jews will be conscripted for labour in the east under appropriate supervision. Large labour gangs will be formed from those fit for work, with the sexes separated, which will be sent to these areas for road construction and undoubtedly a large number of them will drop out through natural wastage" (Noakes and Pridham 2001: 538).

The German authorities had used road construction work to humiliate German and Austrian Jews as early as 1938. Beginning in late 1939, this way of exploiting the Jewish workforce was continued in Poland, where thousands of Polish Jews were employed to improve the transport infrastructure in preparation for the invasion of the USSR. This form of exhausting forced labor was extended to Galicia in summer 1941 and to Ukraine in early 1942. One of the most important routes developed was a transit road from Lviv to the Donezk basin, which ultimately was to be extended to the Caucasus (*Durchgangsstraße IV*). For this project alone, the German authorities employed 50,000 Ukrainian civil workers, 50,000 Soviet prisoners of war, and 10,000 Jewish forced workers who were brought in mainly from Galicia and Transnistria because most Ukrainian Jews already had been killed. Relative to the physical difficulty of the work, the food rations were lethally low. Moreover, if guards believed a Jew no longer fit to work, they could shoot him on the spot. Very few Jews survived.

The third variable with a decisive impact on survival chances was occupation. In general, the less exposed forced laborers were to the caprices of the weather, the higher the probability of survival. In other words, construction work was more fatal than assembly-line labor in most instances. In addition, semi-skilled or skilled work abilities made some forced laborers less easily replaceable than others. In such cases, the employer had an economic interest in not losing a valuable worker and thus was more likely to resist harsh measures that endangered labor productivity.

Finally, gender mattered to whether one lived or died. That female inmates were rarely employed on construction sites considerably enhanced their probability of surviving. Numerous accounts of female survivors also indicate that the foremen and guards usually treated female inmates better than males. Sometimes senior managers even behaved almost chivalrously toward female inmates (Hayes 2004: 267–8).

MOTIVES AND PROFITS

Economic motives clearly played a more important role in determining the fates of forced laborers than the early historiography of the Holocaust suggested. The Nazi economy was short of labor as early as 1936, and in some skilled professions as early as 1934, and conscription aggravated this situation. Thus, from the perspective of labor policy, the eviction of the Jews, the decision to transfer them to eastern Europe, and especially their murder were completely counterproductive. Nonetheless, many institutions remained able, at least temporarily, to obtain Jewish laborers. Since most of these entities, such as the waterways administration, suffered from the prevailing labor shortage, they were eager to fill their workforces with Jews who were deprived of all rights and deployable without any regard to safety. Other institutions acted like slave traders, for example the *Organisation Schmelt*, which in 1942 was able to divert Jews from the deportations to Auschwitz and lease them to local employers in Upper Silesia. Until 1942 concentration camp commanders were likewise in a position to lease inmates to nearby employers, even to peasants (Tuchel 1994: 135). Given the character of most camp commanders and the competition among employers for scarce labor, bribery may have played an important role in the allocation of such forced laborers.

For the employers, the Jews were a welcome relief from the constant labor shortage. Whether they were cheaper or costlier than German labor was beside the point. Indeed, concentration camp inmates were less expensive on an hourly basis than civilian workers would have been, but because their productivity was much lower as well, the financial balance sheet of using them was mixed. Employing skilled, semi-skilled, and female inmates was on average more profitable than employing civilian workers, but most unskilled male inmates were so unproductive that, despite the low rental fee that the employer had to pay to the SS, civilian workers would have generated higher returns. The important point, however, is that the standard of comparison at the time was not civilian workers, but no workers, since unforced ones were no longer available. Using more expensive workers was usually better than having no workers at all, especially since the employers were allowed to account for the low labor productivity when they billed the Reich for the goods produced (Spoerer 1999: 65–73).

An indicator of the profitability of forced labor is that the employers actively competed for foreign workers, prisoners of war, concentration camp inmates, and "work Jews." Admittedly, from 1943 onwards any firm that refused forced laborers risked difficulties with the bureaucracy and the security organs. Failing to man costly machinery would not have been tolerated. Indeed, to date no single medium or large-sized German manufacturing firm that did not employ civilian forced laborers or prisoners of war has been identified. In contrast, firms were usually in the position to avoid the use of concentration camp labor, if they wished so. Several cases are documented in which private enterprises declined to employ concentration camp inmates and went unharmed. However, most firms were eager to compete intensely for such laborers. To date only a single case has been well documented in which a firm, the Drägerwerke in Lübeck, actually was forced to employ concentration camp inmates (Lorentz 2001: 323–35). One can infer that this finding for concentration camp inmates also holds for those of Jewish forced labor camps.

In exceptional instances, Germans employing Jews went to great lengths to save them. The most famous case is that of Oskar Schindler (1908–1974), which even became the subject of a successful Hollywood film. Berthold Beitz (b. 1913), a young and aspiring German engineer who ran a large refinery in the Bukowina during the war, also saved many Jews from the gas chambers for as long as that lay within his power (Sandkühler 1996). Several other cases are known as well. But the overwhelming majority of employers actively took part in exploiting Jewish labor. When the managers of the IG Farben installations at Auschwitz claimed during the Nuremberg trials that working for them had spared the Jews the fate of being gassed in Auschwitz, this defensive maneuver was belied by the murderous working conditions at Farben's factory and mines near the camp.

Although some managers may have felt compelled to employ forced labor, whether Jewish or not, especially when other sources of labor were exhausted, the treatment of forced laborers reveals considerable variation and room for maneuvering. To forced laborers, food, housing, clothing, protective gear, and access to air raid shelters and medical care were the most important issues. In a war economy that rationed every important consumer good according to official guidelines that overtly discriminated against Jews, alleviating their fate was not easy. Nevertheless, some firms managed to plant vegetable gardens that added valuable vitamins to the meager daily diet. Others, in contrast, did not even take steps against the endemic corruption among the camp staff, which diverted and sold food intended for the inmate laborers. Similarly, some firms, engineers, and foremen paid attention to work safety, while many others did not and accepted a high incidence of work accidents. In general, the attitude of most German superiors to the welfare of forced laborers was indifference. The employers cared chiefly about keeping the war machinery running.

In this connection, one should recall that forced labor was not used only in production. Toward the end of the war, when the Allied intention to partition Germany became known to German industrialists, they started to relocate their valuable machinery westwards in an extraordinarily demanding effort that cost the lives of thousands of concentration camp inmates. Hence in the final episode of forced labor, human beings were sacrificed to preserve expensive capital investments (Spoerer 2001: 240–1).

CONCLUSION

....

Clearly, Nazism exploited the labor supply in regions under the Third Reich's control in anything but an economically optimal or even rational way. This evaluation holds in particular for the treatment of Jewish labor. The idea that the whole exploitation program cost more than it earned (Mommsen in Chickering et al. 2005: 177–86), however, is far off the mark. Without the initially voluntary and soon enforced help of millions of foreign workers, the Nazi economy never would have attained the peak production levels of summer 1944 (Herbert 1997). Moreover, after the currency reform of 1948, when German firms prospered during what became known as the "economic miracle," they relied on plants and machinery that often had been built by millions of forced laborers, among them several hundred thousand Jews, most of whom did not survive the war.

While "destruction through work" is not an appropriate term to describe the German forced labor system or even the concentration camp system as a whole, it certainly applies to the Jewish forced laborers after 1941 at the latest. Once the decision to murder the whole of European Jewry was made in late summer 1941, forced labor was meant to be only transitory. In this sense, politics took priority over all economic concerns. Therefore, Jewish forced laborers may be characterized as "slave laborers" only during the period preceding summer 1941 and intermittently thereafter. Benjamin Ferencz (b. 1920), Chief Prosecutor for the United States in the Einsatzgruppen Case at the Nuremberg Trials in 1946–47, coined a much more appropriate term to describe Jewish forced laborers at other times: they were, he said, "less than slaves" (Ferencz 2002).

REFERENCES

ALLEN, M. (2002). *The Business of Genocide: The SS, Slave Labor, and the Concentration Camps*. Chapel Hill, NC: University of North Carolina Press.

BROWNING, C. (2000). *Nazi Policy, Jewish Workers, German Killers*. New York: Cambridge University Press.

CHICKERING, R., FÖRSTER, S., and GREINER, B. (eds.) (2005). *A World at Total War: Global Conflict and the Politics of Destruction, 1937–1945*. Cambridge: Cambridge University Press.

FERENCZ, B. (2002). *Less Than Slaves: Jewish Forced Labor and the Quest for Compensation*. Bloomington, IN: Indiana University Press.

GRUNER, W. (2006). *Jewish Forced Labor Under the Nazis: Economic Needs and Racial Aims, 1938–1944*. New York: Cambridge University Press.

HAYES, P. (1987). *Industry and Ideology: IG Farben in the Nazi Era*. New York: Cambridge University Press.

——(2004). *From Cooperation to Complicity: Degussa in the Third Reich*. New York: Cambridge University Press.

HERBERT, U. (1997). *Hitler's Foreign Workers: Enforced Foreign Labor in Germany Under the Third Reich*. Cambridge: Cambridge University Press.

——ORTH, K., and DIECKMANN, C. (eds.) (1998). *Die nationalsozialistischen Konzentrationslager: Entwicklung und Struktur*. 2 vols. Göttingen: Wallstein.

KARAY, F. (1996). *Death Comes in Yellow: Skarzysko-Kamienna Slave Labor Camp*. Amsterdam: Harwood.

LORENTZ, B. (2001). *Industrieelite und Wirtschaftspolitik: Heinrich Dräger und das Drägerwerk*. Paderborn: Schöningh.

NOAKES, J. and PRIDHAM, G. (eds.) (2001). *Nazism 1919–1945*. Vol. 3, *Foreign Policy, War and Racial Extermination*. Exeter: University of Exeter Press.

ORTH, K. (1999). *Das System der nationalsozialistischen Konzentrationslager: Eine politische Organisationsgeschichte*. Hamburg: Hamburger Edition.

SANDKÜHLER, T. (1996). *"Endlösung" in Galizien: Der Judenmord in Ostpolen und die Rettungsinitiativen von Berthold Beitz 1941–1944*. Bonn: Dietz.

SPOERER, M. (1999). "Profitierten Unternehmen von KZ-Arbeit? Eine kritische Analyse der Literatur." *Historische Zeitschrift* 268: 61–95.

——(2001). *Zwangsarbeit unter dem Hakenkreuz: Ausländische Zivilarbeiter, Kriegsgefangene und Häftlinge im Dritten Reich und im besetzten Europa 1939–1945*. Stuttgart: DVA.

——and FLEISCHHACKER, J. (2002). "The Compensation of Nazi Germany's Forced Laborers: Demographic Findings and Political Implications." *Population Studies* 56: 5–21.

TUCHEL, J. (1994). *Die Inspektion der Konzentrationslager 1938–1945: Das System des Terrors*. Berlin: Edition Hentrich.

OTHER SUGGESTED READING

BROWNING, C. (2010). *Remembering Survival: Inside a Nazi Slave-labor Camp*. New York: W. W. Norton.

EIZENSTAT, S. (2003). *Imperfect Justice: Looted Assets, Slave Labor, and the Unfinished Business of World War II*. New York: Public Affairs.

FELDMAN, G. and SEIBEL, W. (eds.) (2006). *Networks of Nazi Persecution: Bureaucracy, Business, and the Organization of the Holocaust*. New York: Berghahn.

GREGOR, N. (1998). *Daimler-Benz in the Third Reich*. New Haven, CT: Yale University Press.

NEANDER, J. (2001). "Wie 'profitabel' waren KZ-Häftlinge wirklich? Versuch einer Annäherung." *Betriebswirtschaftliche Forschung und Praxis* 53: 281–92.

RAUH-KÜHNE, C. (2002). "Hitler's Hehler? Unternehmerprofite und Zwangsarbeiterlöhne." *Historische Zeitschrift* 275: 1–55.

CHAPTER 24

··

CAMPS

··

KARIN ORTH

DURING the first year of their regime, the National Socialists rounded up thousands of perceived political opponents and consigned them to "protective custody" at a number of new incarceration sites. The wave of unfettered violence marked a fundamental break with the Weimar Republic, but not necessarily the first step in a plan to establish a comprehensive system of terror and extermination. The early Nazi camps of 1933–34 were heterogeneous, improvised, and fundamentally different from those established after 1936. The profound differences in institutional support, organizational structures, persecution methods, groups targeted, prison conditions, and number of the victims before and after 1936 suggest that, strictly speaking, the true Nazi "concentration camp" system came into existence only in that year. By 1945, that system encompassed twenty-three major camps plus some nine hundred satellite installations (Megargee 2009).

Heinrich Himmler's (1900–1945) appointment in April 1934 as head of the Prussian Secret State Police Office (*Gestapa*) and the murder of Ernst Röhm (1887–1934) and the SA leadership in June laid the basis for the ultimate transformation. With these events, the Bavarian group of the SS leadership under Himmler and Reinhard Heydrich (1904–1942) prevailed over the SA, the newly appointed regional governors (*Reichstaathalter*), and Nazi Party provincial chiefs (*Gauleiter*) and set the stage for Himmler's unification of the political police forces throughout the Reich and subsequent unification of the existing camps and prisons. In July 1934, he named Theodor Eicke (1892–1943), the commandant of the earliest SS camp at Dachau, Inspector of Concentration Camps and instructed him either to dissolve the other existing camps or to restructure them according to the Dachau model. He also established a subordinate, initially small administrative office, the

Inspectorate of Concentration Camps (IKL), which developed into the central administrative body for the entire camp system. In time, the IKL regulated all matters related to the life or death of camp inmates with the exceptions of the admission and release of prisoners, which remained the province of the Political Police. While Eicke closed some camps and reorganized others, the number of prisoners sank to only 3,000 (compared to 45,000 in the first months of Nazi rule), and thought was given to dissolving the whole camp system and handing over the remaining subjects of "protective custody" to the judicial authorities for transfer to normal prisons. Adolf Hitler (1889–1945) decided, however, in 1935 to bring the camps within the state budget, to leave them and the prisoners under the authority of the SS, to turn the guard force into a military organization, and to keep the resulting organizations strictly separate from the judicial system (Tuchel 1991: 307–15; Herbert 1996: 168–70).

The consolidation process came to an end in the summer of 1936 with the appointment of Himmler as Chief of the German Police and the subordination of the Political Police and the Criminal Police (*Kripo*) to the Security Police (*Sipo*). Himmler, with the express support of Hitler, once again prevailed over the regional governors, the Ministry of the Interior, and the Ministry of Justice and thus put an end to the influence of traditional administrative agencies over the camps. Within a year, Himmler had dissolved all the existing sites with the exception of Dachau or handed them over to other institutions, such as the Gestapo or the judicial authorities. In their place appeared a new type of National Socialist concentration camp.

Dachau was significantly enlarged between 1936 and the beginning of the war, and five new IKL camps were established—Sachsenhausen, Buchenwald, Flossenbürg, Mauthausen, and Ravensbrück—all structured according to the Dachau model. Each installation subjected prisoners to the same "camp order," which systematized terror by standardizing it. The sharp growth in the camps' populations, especially in 1937–38, was closely connected with preparations for war as the regime felt less need to concentrate on political opponents and focused on groups deemed threatening to the *Volk* in socio-biological or racial ways. Criminals, the "work-shy," and "asocials" were favored targets initially (Ayaß 1995). The pogrom of November 1938, which was intended to increase pressure on Jews to emigrate from Germany, swept up some 30,000 Jews into concentration camps for six to eight weeks of barbarous treatment, from which the price of escape was usually the surrender of one's property. At the same time, the ways in which the SS exploited prisoners changed. Rather than continuing to apply the inmates' energies to camp improvements or pointless exercise, as in previous years, the SS began using the prisoners for money-making purposes, such as brick- and furniture-making and stone-quarrying, under the direction of Oswald Pohl (1892–1951), the organization's administrative head. Thus a "preventative measure to protect the racial community" dovetailed with the SS's appetite for forced labor (Broszat in Buchheim et al. 1982: 77).

The transfer of a comprehensive socio-biological and racial concept into the practice of the persecuting authorities proved to be a pivotal moment. Henceforth, the camp system persecuted both political and "racial" opponents. As the camps were transformed into sites of racial prophylaxis, the composition of the inmate population fundamentally changed.

THE INTERNATIONALIZATION OF THE CAMPS

The concentration camp system expanded anew once World War II began. During the first half of the war, the IKL opened five new concentration camps—Auschwitz, Neuengamme, Natzweiler, Groß-Rosen, and Majdanek—as well as two small camps at Niedernhagen near Paderborn and Hinzert in the Hunsrück that had special assignments. In less than three years the number of prisoners nearly quadrupled: from around 21,000 in August 1939 to an estimated 70,000–80,000 in the spring of 1942 (Kaienburg 1990: 229). The first numerical surge was the result of round-ups of actual or potential National Socialist opponents following the outbreak of the war. Included were people who had been in prison but subsequently set free, such as members of the labor movement or Jews who had not managed to emigrate after their release from concentration camps in 1938–39, as well as clerics and anyone else suspected of causing "unrest" in the population. The significant increase in prisoner numbers was, however, first and foremost the consequence of mass arrests in countries conquered by the Wehrmacht.

The incarcerations in western Europe were directed primarily against resistance groups and saboteurs; in eastern Europe the round-ups also were designed to support the implementation of Nazi population policy as well as the recruitment of labor. From 1940 on, non-Germans, especially Poles, constituted a significant percentage of the prisoners; in some concentration camps they composed the majority during the first half of the war. This relative decline of Germans and Austrians among the inmates continued throughout the war, so that by its end they accounted for only 5–10 percent of all concentration camp prisoners.

This increasing internationalization fundamentally transformed the internal structure of the prisoner population, possibly to an even greater degree than had occurred in 1937–38. The triangle marking system of the prewar period—criminals wore green upside-down triangles, political prisoners red, asocials black, homosexuals pink, and Jehovah's Witnesses purple—became less important than the national hierarchy of prisoner groups, based on "racial" criteria. For the most part, the SS gave the so-called Reich German camp prisoners privileged positions as prison functionaries or placed them in protected positions in a work detachment regardless of which triangle they wore. However, Slavic or Jewish prisoners received exceptionally rough treatment and the worst work detachments.

The outbreak of the war resulted in considerable worsening of the prisoners' conditions, and death rates increased dramatically, especially in winter (Pingel 1978: 81, 259–60). The effects of this worsening situation varied somewhat among the different national and social groups. Prisoners in the punishment companies, Jewish concentration camp inmates, Slavic prisoners, as well as the Spaniards in Mauthausen/Gusen who had fought for the Republic in the Spanish Civil War had the highest death rates. The SS exposed most of the prisoners to conditions that took them to the brink of death but did not pursue a policy of outright extermination. That was reserved for some prisoners of Slavic origin as well as for all Jews.

PLANNED MASS KILLINGS AND PILOT PROJECTS FOR USING LABOR

The year 1941 brought a new level of terror to the concentration camp system. The SS had used the camps from the beginning to kill individuals or particular prisoner groups, and at a few sites the murders became almost systematic. In the spring of 1941, however, the first planned and coordinated massacres occurred throughout the concentration camp system (Orth 2002: 113–31). A first round of murders was directed at sick and weakened prisoners, whom the SS increasingly regarded as a burden in the overcrowded camps. From April 1941 to April 1942, doctors attached to the T4 "euthanasia" operation visited at least ten concentration camps to select such prisoners, who then were killed by carbon monoxide in the "euthanasia institutions" at Bernburg, Sonnenstein, and Hartheim. The camp SS also used these killing actions to have certain Jewish and political prisoners murdered. At least 10,000 and possibly between 15,000 and 20,000 prisoners were killed in all (Orth 2002: 116). From the summer of 1941 on, this murder program, named "14 f. 13" after the associated IKL file, included a second set of targets, Soviet prisoners of war designated as "Russian commissars."

Himmler had made an agreement with the Wehrmacht that a portion of the Soviet soldiers captured in the invasion of Russia would be allotted to him. Beginning in October 1941, he ordered two large camp complexes established as holding pens, Majdanek and Birkenau. Both were subordinate to the IKL, Majdanek as an independent concentration camp and Birkenau as a subcamp of Auschwitz until 1943, when it became formally autonomous. In the autumn of 1941, the Wehrmacht handed over to Himmler tens of thousands of the promised Soviet prisoners, who were distributed among the existing concentration camps and so-called prisoner of war camps (or prisoner of war labor camps) that were now attached to all concentration camps. In essence, these were specially fenced off areas into which the SS crowded the Soviet soldiers, who were not entered in the camp registers. Apparently, Himmler planned to use the prisoners as a labor force, but in reality, they were left to languish unfed and die. Soviet soldiers were not only exposed to hunger and epidemics, but at least at Auschwitz a Gestapo special commission selected the so-called political commissars and shot some of them (Czech 1997: 107). Mass shootings began in all concentration camps in the late summer of 1941, taking the lives of at least 34,000 and perhaps as many as 45,000 Soviet prisoners of war (Orth 2002: 130–1).

During 1941, the foundations were laid for the use of concentration camp prisoners in industry (Orth 2002: 142–8), although only a few "pilot projects" took shape at this early juncture. Beginning in the spring of 1941, the IKL leased a few hundred prisoners from Auschwitz to IG Farben and three hundred prisoners from Mauthausen to Steyr-Daimler-Puch AG. Both companies were trying to offset the prevailing labor shortage by using forced laborers; both initially used the inmates solely for construction work and unskilled labor (Hayes 1987: 349–60; Perz 1991: 81–4). The SS leadership made prisoners available to interested companies for a fee per head, per day providing that doing so served its own purposes. In the case of Steyr-Daimler-Puch AG, Himmler hoped to obtain cheap armaments for the Waffen-SS in return for his help, and from IG Farben he wanted building materials for its nearby factory diverted to the expansion of the Auschwitz concentration camp. Moreover, the SS did not relinquish control over the prisoners, who continued to be accommodated in the respective main camps and guarded by SS men while working. From the companies' point of view, cooperation with the SS was anything but smooth. They complained that the daily transport of the prisoners to and from work reduced their output and that the prisoners were inefficiently used because of a shortage of guards. Similarly motivated protests against mistreatment of the prisoners had little effect. After about a year, both companies, acting independently, suggested that the prisoners be quartered near the construction sites. The SS agreed after some initial resistance. In general, during the first half of the war, cooperation with industry played a minor part in the concentration camp system. Only when the function of the camps changed again, and they came to be seen as a labor reservoir for the armaments industry, did the cases mentioned here come to be seen as models.

The reorganization of labor utilization that the IKL undertook in the autumn of 1941 was at first intended to serve Himmler's extensive plans for settlement "in the east," not war production. This geographical emphasis, along with a view to the "later settlement of the Danzig-West Prussian Gau," prompted Himmler at the end of 1941 to place the camp at Stutthof near Danzig, which had been established at the beginning of the war, under the control of the IKL.

FORCED LABOR AND GENOCIDE WITHIN
THE CAMP SYSTEM

Himmler changed the focus of his labor planning to the armaments sector when he realized during the winter of 1941–42 that the war against the Soviet Union would drag on. To increase his own power, he intended to turn the concentration camps, which had an apparently inexhaustible supply of workers, into a labor reservoir for the entire war economy. During the first half of 1942, a number of measures were introduced to restructure the camp system. In March, Himmler integrated the IKL into the recently established SS Business Administration Main Office (WVHA) as Office Group D. In doing so, he sought to prevent Fritz Sauckel (1894–1946), the recently appointed Plenipotentiary General for Labor Deployment, from seizing control of the concentration camp system. With Oswald Pohl's appointment as head of the WVHA and the subordination to him of the IKL, Himmler cemented Pohl's leading position in the concentration camp system.

Pohl set out to mobilize all prisoner labor and began negotiations with the Armaments Ministry and private industry about the most advantageous deployment of camp workers. Initial plans to produce weapons at the camps quickly foundered on the resistance of the Ministry, which feared the increase in Himmler's power and the SS's autonomy that would result. Instead, in September 1942, Hitler, Himmler, and Armaments Minister Albert Speer (1905–1981) agreed that camp prisoners would be leased to armaments firms and accommodated in specially constructed subcamps erected near the factories (Herbert 1993: 177–9). Only in the winter of 1942–43 did the IKL begin to open subcamps on any significant scale, and in 1944–45 their number increased exponentially.

The decision of autumn of 1942 had differing consequences for the various concentration camp prisoner groups. For Jews held in concentration camps within the Reich, it meant death. All camp commands were informed at the beginning of October 1942 that Himmler wished "to free the concentration camps within the Reich of Jews," with the result that at least 1,559 Jewish concentration camp prisoners (1,037 men and 522 women) were deported to Auschwitz and probably murdered (Orth 2002: 174). For non-Jewish prisoners, the decision meant condemnation to institutionalized compulsory labor in private or state armaments factories. In order to foster the use of prisoner labor, the SS command abandoned plans for two mass shootings of non-Jewish inmates. Moreover, it succeeded in significantly increasing the number of potential laborers at its disposal. In the winter of 1942–43, 12,000 so-called "preventive detainees" were transferred from the judicial system to the camp system. In addition, round-ups and mass arrests took place across the Reich, primarily of Polish and Soviet forced laborers who had been imported by Sauckel's organization and were now charged with offending against one or another regulation. Within six months, the number of concentration camp inmates almost doubled from around 110,000 in September 1942 to 203,000 in April 1943. By August 1943, the camps held 224,000 prisoners, and a year later the total came to 524,286 (Orth 2002: 174).

The restructuring of the concentration camp system into a labor reservoir for the war economy did not lighten the lot of the concentration camp inmates, despite many WVHA directives aimed at improving the efficiency of prisoners' deployment and increasing their productivity. Few of these orders were put into practice, and only two brought about better conditions: first, the SS introduced food supplements for prisoners doing heavy labor and second, beginning in the autumn of 1942, Himmler allowed food packages to be sent to the camps by relatives or friends of the inmates. Similarly, there was less to the apparently declining death rate than meets the eye. The WVHA explicitly instructed the camp doctors and commanders to lower the mortality rate, and it fell, in fact, from a monthly average of 10 percent of the camp population in the second half of 1942 to 2.8 percent in June 1943 (Pingel 1978: 182–83). However, three arguments undermine the conclusion that this reflected a general improvement in conditions. First, the absolute number of murdered camp prisoners declined far less than the percentages would suggest because of the large influx of new prisoners; second, the official figures were partially falsified in order to convince Himmler that his demands had been met; and third, the SS manipulated the rates by sending sick and dying arriving prisoners directly to the killing centers without registering them. So long as the flow of prisoners into the camp remained steady, the increased value of the inmates in the eyes of the SS did not translate into improved chances of survival. These remained dependent upon a prisoner's position in a work detachment or the prisoner hierarchy, which in turn depended on "racial" criteria. The only beneficiaries of improved conditions in 1942–43 were the minority of prisoners at the top of the camps' racial hierarchy or those with professional skills useful to the SS. These inmates gained from the introduction in May 1943 of the so-called bonus system, which offered financial incentives and improved conditions in return for special achievements. However, the idea for the system stemmed from the industries that were using the concentration camp prisoners, not from the WVHA.

Moreover, in the second half of the war the concentration camp system was characterized by the simultaneity of slave labor and genocide, the former applying chiefly to non-Jewish inmates, the latter to Jews. Along with the death camps of Operation Reinhard (Treblinka, Sobibor, and Belzec) along the Bug River in the General Government and the one located west of Łódź at Chelmno, Auschwitz-Birkenau and Majdanek developed into killing centers during this period. The principal differences between the former four and the latter two installations were in the methods of killing applied, the nature of the sites, and the survival rates. Chelmno and the Reinhard camps killed with carbon monoxide gas generated by diesel truck motors, whereas Auschwitz always and Majdanek usually gassed with a vaporizing granular pesticide named Zyklon B that was normally used to fumigate barracks. Moreover, Chelmno and the Reinhard camps were ramshackle installations built for the short term, since their target populations were the Jewish inhabitants of their immediate vicinities, and they had virtually no (Chelmno) or very few (the Reinhard camps) "inhabitants", i.e., prisoners allowed to remain alive for a time on the site to perform various functions for the SS. In contrast, Auschwitz especially and Majdanek to a lesser degree were installations built to last and to contain a continuing, if constantly turning over population because both were intended to be labor reservoirs and murder sites, not only for nearby Jews, but also for those transported from quite far away. Unsurprisingly, given these characteristics, the numbers of known survivors of Chelmno and the Reinhard camps are tiny; those who outlived Majdanek and Auschwitz are more numerous.

The organized murder of European Jews in Auschwitz-Birkenau began in early 1942 and took on systematic form the following summer (Piper 1991: 97). At first sporadically, but regularly after 4 July 1942, SS doctors and members of the command staff conducted "selections" of all Jews arriving at the camp complex (Czech 1997: 191–2). On average, probably around 80 percent of the people on each transport were sent directly to their deaths (Broszat 1992: 163–4). Those regarded as "capable of work" were deployed in Auschwitz or one of its numerous subcamps, where life expectancies were short, sometimes as little as four to six weeks (Hayes 1987: 359–60). By the time the SS evacuated the site in January 1945, at least 1.3 million people had been brought to Auschwitz, of whom only about 125,000 survived World War II. Some 90 percent of the victims were Jews (Hayes 2003: 330–3).

The history of Majdanek divides into four phases, and historians accurately have noted that the camp remained a "multi-functional provisional arrangement" because its chief function often changed, and it never really emerged from the planning stage (Kranz in Herbert et al. 1998: 381). The first period (October 1941 to the middle of 1942) saw the construction of the camp, the second (the second half of 1942) a marked increase in the number of prisoners as Jews and Poles from the Lublin area flowed in, along with Jews from the Warsaw and Białystok ghettos. Majdanek functioned as a killing center from 1943 on, while the SS also used it as a holding area for Polish and Soviet farmers. Simultaneously, Pohl was trying to integrate the few remaining Jewish prisoners in the General Government into the economic empire of the WVHA, but in the autumn of 1943, following the uprisings in the Warsaw ghetto and the Sobibor death camp, the Nazi leadership decided to murder these Jews. On 3–4 November 1943, the SS shot 40,000–43,000 Jewish laborers who had been gathered at three camps: Poniatowa, Trawniki, and Majdanek. At Majdanek, the toll came to 17,000 Jews (Hilberg 1985: 532; Gutman 1990, 3: 939). Operation Harvest Festival (*Aktion Erntefest*), the code name for the massacre, was one of the largest mass shootings in the history of the National Socialist extermination of the Jews. In the last phase of the camp's history, until the evacuation of Majdanek in the summer of 1944, while Pohl unsuccessfully attempted to reorganize the use of labor for the German Armaments Works (DAW) factories in the Lublin area, Majdanek functioned more as a place of execution for Polish civilians and a reception camp for sick and weakened prisoners sent from elsewhere. The total number of deaths at Majdanek lies between 170,000 and 250,000, of whom at least 90,000 were Jews (Kranz in Herbert et al. 1998: 373, 380–1).

A final expansion of the concentration camp system occurred in the course of 1943–44. In January, Pohl established in the occupied Netherlands the Herzogen-busch concentration camp, which functioned as a transit camp for Jewish prisoners on their way to the killing centers. Between July and September, he took control of the remaining Jewish ghettos, the Reichskommissariat Ostland's so-called forced labor camps (*Zwangsarbeitlager*) for Jews, and the Gestapo prison in Warsaw. These sites became the independent concentration camps Riga, Kaunas, Vaivara, and Warschau and brought the number of camps administered by the WVHA to twenty. And, in January 1944, he took over the forced labor camp for Jews in Kraków, renaming it Plaszów (Orth 2002: 213–21).

THE CAMP SYSTEM IN THE FINAL YEAR OF THE WAR

The last year of World War II was marked by a significant increase in the numbers of prisoners and new subcamps. Desperate attempts by the Nazi regime to ward off defeat by all possible means were accompanied by ever more urgent demands for labor for the war economy, which resulted in a broadening of the scope of arrests. As German troops retreated, round-ups, now also in western and northern Europe, drove up the total camp population from 524,286 in August 1944 to almost 715,000 in January 1945 (Nuremberg document NO-399; Bundesarchiv Berlin-Lichterfelde, Sammlung Schumacher 329).

In the spring of 1944, moreover, the demand for labor had led the authorities to abandon the principle of keeping the Reich "free of Jews." Himmler exempted some of the Hungarian Jews, who recently had fallen under German control, from immediate extermination, and transferred them from Auschwitz to concentration camps in the Reich. Starting in the summer of 1944, Pohl ordered the concentration camps in the Baltic region, which held Jewish prisoners almost exclusively, to be evacuated westward. As a result of both these actions, tens of thousands of Jewish prisoners reached camps in the Reich within a short period of time. The result was chaos. The drastic reduction in available resources, accompanied by an escalation of mistreatment and an intensification of forced labor, led to previously unknown levels of mass mortality.

The camp system was now characterized by four different sorts of installations: the killing center Auschwitz-Birkenau, the main concentration camps with their networks of subcamps, and two new types of site, the subterranean factory camps and the mass mortality camps. The genocide in Auschwitz-Birkenau reached its ghastly climax in the spring and summer of 1944, when the SS killed 350,000 Hungarian Jews, the inhabitants of the Theresienstadt Family Camp in Birkenau, the prisoners in the "Gypsy Camp" there, and the remnant population of the Łódź ghetto. However, the might of the SS had its limits. Resistance began to increase in 1944 (for example, the *Sonderkommando* uprising in the fall), as did the number of escape attempts. These developments and the approach of the Red Army caused the SS to relocate 70,000 prisoners from Auschwitz to concentration camps in the Old Reich in the second half of 1944 (Gutman 1990, 1; 116–17; Strzelecki in Dlugoborski and Piper 2000, 5: 21–4). In the last year of the war, the main concentration camps developed into reception and transit camps, that is, into labor distribution centers for their subcamps. With regard to relative populations of prisoners, the relationship between the main camps and the subcamps gradually reversed itself, so that both proportionately and in absolute numbers the subcamps came to predominate.

The subterranean factory camps (*KZ der Verlagerungsprojekte*) consisted of a complex of subcamps whose origins date from August 1943 (Orth 2002: 243–55). At first, they exclusively served the process of relocating the production of V-1 and V-2 "revenge weapons" (*Vergeltungswaffen*) to underground, bombproof sites. Himmler agreed to the use of concentration camp prisoners for this gigantic construction project and ordered the opening of a subcamp of Buchenwald at Mittelbau-Dora in the Harz, where the prisoners drove a gigantic cavern through a mountain in order to create space for an assembly line. Himmler also appointed Hans Kammler (1901–1945), until then head of the Office Group C (Construction) in the WVHA, as Special Emissary for Construction on the site. The organizational structure and expertise that developed at Mittelbau-Dora resembled those of existing concentration camps only to a limited degree, but developed into a model for the relocation underground of most of the German armaments industry. In 1944, this so-called Fighter Staff Program (*Jägerstab-Programm*) took on immense proportions. Half of the estimated 480,000 concentration camp prisoners classified by the SS at the end of 1944 as "capable of work" were leased to private industries, but virtually all of the remainder was involved in these massive factory relocation projects under the direction of Kammler or the Organisation Todt (Herbert 1993: 188–9).

The second new type of concentration camp that developed in the last year of the war was the "mass mortality camp" (Orth 2002: 260–9). By 1944, all main concentration camps and most subcamp complexes contained "zones of impoverishment" where newly delivered, severely overworked, sick, and completely weakened prisoners were simply left to die. The SS did not kill here with shootings or poison, but by withholding provisions and letting hunger, thirst, epidemics, and cold do their work. Only one of these camps was raised to the status of an independent concentration camp: Bergen-Belsen. Himmler founded it in 1943 as a holding camp (*Aufenthaltslager*) for certain groups of Jews he wanted to use as bargaining chips in possible exchanges for German citizens. In fact, such exchanges occurred only on a small scale. Beginning in 1944 and accelerating rapidly in the second half of the year, Bergen-Belsen became a receiving camp for a constant stream of the sick, the dying, and the dead shipped in from other camps. It became the infernal destination of the collapsing concentration camp system.

The Evacuation of the Concentration Camps

The evacuation of the concentration camps extended over more than a year and was marked by monstrous brutality and enormous carnage. Not for nothing were the "evacuation marches" immediately renamed "death marches." In the first stage of emptying camps in the latter half of 1944, Pohl ordered the evacuation of the Majdanek killing center, of the concentration camps in the Baltic States, and of the most westerly installations, Herzogenbusch and Natzweiler. The second stage of the evacuation was triggered by the Soviet winter offensive: from the middle of January the SS began marching at least 113,000 concentration camp prisoners in a westerly direction: 58,000 from Auschwitz, 11,000 from Stutthof (although a large number of prisoners remained there until April 1945), and 44,000 from Groß-Rosen in Silesia. At least 24,500 prisoners did not survive these marches; the total is probably higher as the figures are incomplete for the retreat from Groß-Rosen (Orth 2002: 286–7). In the interim between these withdrawals and the issuing of a general order to evacuate the remaining camps at the end of March 1945, the SS guards labored to prepare their own escapes and remove all traces of the crimes that had been committed. As part of this process, the SS executed two groups of prisoners: those who seemed unlikely to survive the exertions of an "evacuation march," and those who might prove "dangerous" when enemy troops approached.

Consideration was now given to murdering all concentration camp prisoners at the approach of Allied troops. Himmler rejected such ideas in March 1945 because he was attempting to begin negotiations with the Western Powers for a separate peace. Hoping to use the Jewish prisoners as hostages, he ordered that no more Jews be killed, but the edict had no effect on reality in the camps. During this period Himmler met with Carl J. Burckhardt (1891–1974), the President of the International Committee of the Red Cross, as well as Count Folke Bernadotte

(1895–1948), the Vice President of the Swedish Red Cross, and agreed to gather together all Scandinavian inmates and release them. In fact, the Scandinavian prisoners were relocated to Neuengamme and then taken to Sweden before the war ended. Altogether, more than 20,000 concentration camp inmates, including around 8,000 Scandinavians, gained their freedom through "Operation Bernadotte" (Gutman 1990, 1: 206).

The remaining concentration camps were dissolved at the beginning of April 1945. In the third stage of evacuations Pohl emptied Mittelbau-Dora, followed by Buchenwald (at least in part). American troops arrived at these two camps on April 11 and 13 respectively, and two days later the British reached Bergen-Belsen. Immediately thereafter, Himmler told the commanders of Flossenbürg and Dachau to set the prisoners in motion and to ensure that none of them fell into enemy hands alive (Zámečnik 1985: 219–31). At the remaining concentration camps the last non-ambulatory or dangerous prisoners were finished off, the destruction of camp files largely completed, and all remaining prisoners marched out. The columns from Flossenbürg and Dachau headed south toward the chimerical Alpine Fortress; those from Neuengamme, Sachsenhausen, Stutthof, and Ravensbrück went north in the direction of the Baltic coast and the less illusory Northern Fortress.

The SS made great efforts to keep the concentration camp prisoners under their control as they moved north. Although Allied formations liberated the prisoners from Sachsenhausen and Ravensbrück on the way to Schleswig-Holstein, the inmates from Neuengamme were taken via Lübeck to the Neustadt harbor, where at the end of April or the beginning of May they were loaded onto three ships. A short time later, the prisoners from Stutthof also arrived in the Bay of Lübeck on barges from across the Baltic. They were crammed into the same ships, where they remained for five days until British planes mistook the boats for warships and bombed them on 3 May 1945. Some 2,000 prisoners on one of the ships survived; virtually all of the unfortunates on the other craft were drowned or massacred on the beaches to which they swam (Orth 2002: 328–35).

THE VICTIMS—A BALANCE SHEET

The number of Holocaust victims is known: at least 5.29 million and perhaps just over 6 million Jews were murdered (Hilberg 1985: 1219–20; Benz 1991: 17). The various ways of killing are known: mass bludgeoning and shooting, starvation and mistreatment in the various places of detention, and poison gas. Almost three million Jews were asphyxiated. Around two million died from carbon monoxide poisoning in Chelmno and the killing centers of Operation Reinhard, and more than a million were murdered at Auschwitz-Birkenau and at least 50,000 in Majdanek with Zyklon B (Hilberg 1985: 1219; Benz 1991: 19; Piper 1991: 98). In addition, the SS murdered another 40,000 Jews in these concentration camps by means other than gas (Kranz in Herbert et al. 1998: 373, 380–1).

The figures for the total number of dead in the concentration camps are less certain. As of 2005, researchers have identified at least 1.8–2.0 million deaths in the concentration camps of the IKL and the WVHA, including Jews murdered in Auschwitz and Majdanek (Orth 2002: 345–7). The SS probably murdered many more prisoners, however. Only the number of registered deaths is known; beyond that, there are only estimates and sometimes not even those. The majority of the deaths among concentration camp inmates occurred in the second half of the war; outside of the death camps, the majority died from the catastrophic conditions of their confinement, not execution. During the final weeks of the war, the death rate reached a terrible crescendo. Between one-third and one-half of the more than 700,000 registered concentration camp prisoners in January 1945 expired thereafter on the death marches or in the mass mortality camps, and the fatalities among the Jewish prisoners came to an even higher fraction (Broszat in Buchheim et al. 1982: 132–3; Bauer in Marrus 1989, 9: 492).

REFERENCES

AYAß, W. (1995). *"Asoziale" im Nationalsozialismus*. Stuttgart: Klett-Cotta.

BENZ, W. (ed.) (1991). *Dimension des Völkermords: Die Zahl der jüdischen Opfer des Nationalsozialismus*. Munich: Oldenbourg.

BROSZAT, M. (ed.) (1992). *Rudolf Höß, Kommandant in Auschwitz, Autobiographische Aufzeichnungen des Rudolf Höss*. Munich: DTV.

BUCHHEIM, H., BROSZAT, M., JACOBSEN, H., and KRAUSNICK, H. (1982). *Anatomie des SS-Staates*. 2 Vols. Munich: DTV.

CZECH, D. (1997). *Auschwitz Chronicle 1939–1945*. New York: Owl Books.

DLUGOBORSKI, W. and PIPER, F. (eds.) (2000). *Auschwitz 1940–1945*. 5 vols. Oswiecim: Auschwitz-Birkenau State Museum.

GUTMAN, Y. (ed.) (1990). *Encyclopedia of the Holocaust*. 4 vols. New York: Macmillan.

HAYES, P. (1987). *Industry and Ideology: IG Farben in the Nazi Era*. New York: Cambridge University Press.

——(2003). "Auschwitz, Capital of the Holocaust." *Holocaust and Genocide Studies* 17: 330–50.

HERBERT, U. (1993). "Labour and Extermination. Economic Interest and the Primacy of Weltanschauung in National Socialism." *Past and Present* 138: 144–95.

——(1996). *Best: Biographische Studien über Radikalismus, Weltanschauung und Vernunft 1903–1989*. Bonn: Dietz.

——ORTH, K., and DIECKMANN, C. (eds.) (1998). *Die nationalsozialistischen Konzentrationslager: Entwicklung und Struktur*. 2 vols. Göttingen: Wallstein.

HILBERG, R. (1985). *The Destruction of the European Jews*. 2nd edn. New York: Holmes & Meier.

KAIENBURG, H. (1990). *"Vernichtung durch Arbeit": Der Fall Neuengamme. Die Wirtschaftsbestrebungen der SS und ihre Auswirkungen auf die Existenzbedingungen der KZ-Gefangenen.* Bonn: Dietz.

MARRUS, M. (ed.) (1989). *The Nazi Holocaust: Historical Articles on the Destruction of European Jews.* 9 vols. Westport, CT: Meckler.

MEGARGEE, G. (ed.) (2009). *The United States Holocaust Memorial Museum Encyclopedia of Camps and Ghettos, 1933–1945.* Vol. 1. Bloomington, IN: Indiana University Press.

ORTH, K. (2002). *Das System der nationalsozialistischen Konzentrationslager: Eine politische Organisationsgeschichte.* Zurich/Munich: Pendo.

PERZ, B. (1991). *Projekt Quarz: Steyr-Daimler-Puch und das Konzentrationslager Melk.* Vienna: Verlag für Gesellschaftskritik.

PINGEL, F. (1978). *Häftlinge unter SS-Herrschaft: Widerstand, Selbstbehauptung und Vernichtung im Konzentrationslager.* Hamburg: Hoffmann und Campe.

PIPER, F. (1991). "Estimating the Number of Deportees to and Victims of the Auschwitz-Birkenau Camp." *Yad Vashem Studies* 21: 49–103.

TUCHEL, J. (1991). *Konzentrationslager: Organisationsgeschichte und Funktion der "Inspektion der Konzentrationslager" 1934–1938.* Boppard: Edition Hentrich.

ZÁMEĆNIK, S. (1985). "'Kein Häftling darf lebend in die Hände des Feindes fallen': Zur Existenz des Himmler-Befehls vom 14./18. April 1945." *Dachauer Hefte* 1: 219–31.

OTHER SUGGESTED READING

ALLEN, M. (2002). *The Business of Genocide: The SS, Slave Labor, and the Concentration Camps.* Chapel Hill, NC: University of North Carolina Press.

ARAD, Y. (1987). *Belzec, Sobibor, Treblinka.* Bloomington, IN: Indiana University Press.

CAPLAN, J. and WACHSMANN, N. (2010). *Concentration Camps in Nazi Germany: The New Histories.* New York: Berghahn Books.

DWORK, D. and VAN PELT, R. (1996). *Auschwitz 1270 to the Present.* New York: W. W. Norton.

GUTMAN, Y. and BERENBAUM, M. (eds.) (1994). *Anatomy of the Auschwitz Death Camp.* Bloomington, IN: Indiana University Press.

KAIENBURG, H. (2003). *Die Wirtschaft der SS.* Berlin: Metropol.

REES, L. (2005). *Auschwitz: A New History.* New York: Public Affairs.

STEINBACHER, S. (2005). *Auschwitz: A History.* New York: Ecco Press.

WACHSMANN, N. (2006). "Looking into the Abyss. Historians and the Nazi Concentration Camps." *European History Quarterly* 36: 247–78.

PART IV

REPRESENTATIONS

CHAPTER 25

GERMAN DOCUMENTS AND DIARIES

PETER FRITZSCHE

HEINRICH Himmler's (1900–1945) notorious speech to high-ranking SS officers in Posen on 4 October 1943, in which he referred to "the annihilation of the Jewish people" as "an unwritten and never-to-be-written page of glory in our history," has often been cited to underscore the secretive nature of the Nazi program of murder. Indeed, once a territorial solution to the "Jewish problem" had given way to extermination in 1942, racial administrators enforced secrecy by continuing to use the now euphemistic terminology of "deportation," "resettlement," and "work service." Himmler even ordered corrections to the vocabulary of genocide in a report for Hitler by the SS's chief statistician, Richard Korherr (1903–?), who meticulously totaled the number of Jews killed by 31 December 1942: "He does not wish the words 'special treatment of Jews' to be used at all," wrote Himmler's personal assistant to Korherr; "on page 9, point 4, the text must read as follows: 'Number of those passed through the camps in the Generalgouvernement'" (Dwork and van Pelt 2002: 326). The regime also enforced slander laws against German civilians who gossiped about the murder of Jews (Dörner 1998: 233–41) and made strenuous efforts in 1943 and 1944 to dismantle death camps and erase the traces of other killing sites. The resulting "unspeakability" seemed to register the sublime quality that the perpetrators attached to the fact of annihilation (Haidu in Friedländer 1992; LaCapra 1994: 106). Since "the 'Jewish Question' has been solved in Germany and generally in German-occupied countries," as Himmler reported to military leaders in May 1944, the now superfluous signs prohibiting Jews entry to Germany's telephone booths, swimming pools, and restaurants gradually came down in the last years of the war (Steinert 1977: 145; Longerich 2008: 715). Germans who later claimed ignorance of the scale of the "Final Solution" in the years 1941 to 1945 eagerly cited such indications of Nazi efforts to keep the murders a secret.

Yet just two years after Himmler's declaration, the prosecution teams at the war crimes trials in Nuremberg were able to assemble a remarkable array of documents that the "Final Solution" had left behind. They included evidence of the relentless operations of an extensive bureaucracy, such as the Reich Ministry for Food and Agriculture's requests that postal officials inform local food offices about parcels sent to German Jews so that their rations could be reduced correspondingly (International Military Tribunal 1947–49, 27: 80). Prosecutors possessed Adolf Hitler's (1889–1945) order of September 1939 initiating the euthanasia program, Hans Frank's (1900–1946) diary recording his rule in the *Generalgouvernement*, and Alfred Rosenberg's (1893–1946) protocol of his discussions with Hitler on 14 December 1941, in which Rosenberg agreed "not to speak about the extermination of Jewry" in an upcoming speech at the Sportpalast (International Military Tribunal 1947–49, 26: 169, 27: 270). The Nuremberg documents also included material that might be considered rough drafts for a forthcoming history of the "Final Solution": excerpts from the "Stroop Report" on the destruction of the Warsaw ghetto in May 1943 with accompanying photographs, as well as a description of the stills of a film about the pogrom that followed the German occupation of Lemberg in early July 1941.

Some of the "pages of glory" were lying around the ruins of the Nazi empire. On the day American troops liberated Dora-Mittelbau concentration camp on 9 April 1945, one of the inmates, Lili Jacob (1926–1999) was rummaging around for warm clothes in an abandoned SS barracks when she found a photo album depicting the arrival and selection at Auschwitz of her own transport from Hungary on 26 May 1944. The thematic arrangement of snapshots and handwritten captions in the "Auschwitz Album" revealed perpetrators who took pride in their work and hoped to commemorate their achievements (Gutman and Gutterman 2002). It points to an archive of the "Final Solution" comprising not just orders, reports, and protocols passed along the bureaucratic chain of command, but also more vernacular texts that expose the documentary zeal of their creators. The hand-made quality of the "Auschwitz Album" suggests the ways ordinary citizens translated the "Final Solution" into their own hand. Photographs, diaries, and letters registered shock and remorse as well as commemoration. The destruction of Jewish communities occupied the farthest reaches of the German bureaucracy and left behind documentary traces in the folds of everyday life.

BUREAUCRATIC PAPER TRAILS

The entire German bureaucracy from the local to the national level, a structure in which millions of people worked, was the instrument and object of the first national anti-Jewish legislation. The Law for the Reestablishment of the Professional Civil Service, prepared by the Ministry of the Interior on 7 April 1933, authorized the forced retirement of Jews and political opponents of the Nazis. As a result, each office had to inspect, monitor, and cleanse itself of Jews who were defined as such on the basis of having one or more Jewish grandparents. Government ministries, town and county administrations, schools and universities, the courts, and the vast network of post offices and railway depots all became the subjects and objects of the self-administration of this extraordinary anti-Jewish measure. The fact that exceptions were made for those Jews already employed before World War I or who had fought in the war or who had lost fathers or sons in the conflict vastly expanded the documentation the law required. Emendations and clarifications regulating retirement, pensions, and the status and suitability for promotion of civil servants with Jewish spouses swelled the law's paper trails throughout 1933 and 1934. All these issues recurred when a new law mandated the forced retirement of all Jewish civil servants without exception in 1935. In sheer number of pages, the Law for the Reestablishment of the Professional Civil Service laid an extensive and sturdy foundation to the archive of the "Final Solution."

The Law for the Protection of German Blood and Honor, which the Ministry of the Interior promulgated on 15 September 1935, pushed racial paperwork into almost every German home. The Nuremberg Laws that withdrew full citizenship from anyone with three or four Jewish grandparents, prohibited sexual intercourse and marriage between Germans and Jews, and regulated the status of *Mischlinge* with one or two Jewish grandparents, required all Germans and Jews to prepare papers documenting their racial identities. Since the state did not issue *Ahnenpässe* or racial passports, Germans had to prove their "Aryan" identity by their own often considerable efforts. Individuals had to get in touch with civil registries as well as the church rectories that recorded births and marriages before 1875 in order to gain the necessary validations of the identity and religion of their parents and grandparents for a nominal fee, usually paid in postage stamps (Ehrenreich 2007; Fritzsche 2008: 77). Even the highest officials in the Third Reich prepared tables of ancestors: a detailed handwritten family tree, proving his "Aryan" descent back to the middle of the eighteenth century, can be found in the personnel file of General Alfred Jodl (1890–1946), later deputy chief of the Supreme Command of the Armed Forces (Friedländer 1997: 197). With the *Ahnenpässe* Germans inscribed for themselves their identity as "Aryans" and began seriously to think of themselves as such, noting the problems in the *Stammbaum*, or family tree, of acquaintances and breathing a sigh of relief when only a Jewish great-grandmother turned up in their own.

A collection of *Ahnenpässe* in the Landesarchiv Berlin (Sammlung F Rep. 240/1) reveals that individual identities, family archives, and racial categories became increasingly intermingled inside the pages of the *Ahnenpass* as Germans gathered all sorts of private papers there: the mandated labor books, four-leaf clovers, restaurant bills, marriage licenses, birth announcements, baptismal certificates, inoculation records, divorce papers, insurance cards, Winter Relief stamps, correspondence with sons at the front, official confirmations of soldiers missing in action, and even a letter from a fallen man's comrade describing the whereabouts of the dead man's grave. Some Germans continued to update their *Ahnenpässe* even when they had become defunct, noting down births and deaths of family members after 1945.

As the regime intensified its anti-Jewish policies after 1935, it mobilized bureaucratic offices where a vast number of civil servants worked on the "Jewish question" on a part-time basis (Hilberg 2003: 1075). Ministries appointed experts in Jewish affairs; the Foreign Office, the Ministry of the Interior, and the Ministry of Finance all created Jewish desks. And, of course, the Gestapo, the Security Service, and later the Reich Security Main Office had specialized offices to oversee Jewish affairs. But the number of officials involved in the "Jewish question" full-time was very small compared to the "part-timers." Especially in the Ministry of Finance and the Ministry of the Interior, "part-timers" were the ones who processed the growing raft of laws that regulated Jewish life in the Third Reich. Officials in the Ministry of Finance oversaw the estimation of the wealth of departing Jews and assessed the flight tax which they, along with all other emigrants, had to pay. Since hundreds of thousands of Jews left Germany in the late 1930s, the amount of paperwork increased substantially. The Ministry of Interior's decree stipulating that all Jewish men add the middle name "Israel" and Jewish women the name "Sara" generated a flurry of correspondence to hundreds of civil registrars across Germany. As Victor Klemperer (1881–1960) noted, "I myself have to notify the registry offices in Landsberg," where he was born, "and Berlin," where he was married, "as well as the town hall in Dölzschen," where he resided in August 1938 (1998: 264). Henceforth, Jews had to conduct all official correspondence in their new name, in Klemperer's case as Victor Israel, thereby marking the documents of their exchanges with the German bureaucracy as "Jewish." At the same time, in fall 1938, the Foreign Office invalidated all passports held by Jews in order to reissue them with a boldly stamped "J" and informed German consulates to reissue newly stamped passports to German Jews living abroad (Hilberg 2003: 175).

With the invasion of Poland in 1939, the Ministry of Food and Agriculture initiated an extensive correspondence with local offices concerning the limitations on and reduction of Jews' ration stamps, which after 1940 were stamped with a "J" (Walk 1981: 312, 318). Local town administrations and housing offices dealt with the relocation of Jews into "Jew houses." And after the deportation of German Jews in the years 1941–1943, a process directed by the Reich Security Main Office but dependent on the huge Reichsbahn administration to integrate transports into the regular assignment of rolling stock to tracks, local finance offices organized the redistribution and sale of Jewish property, though not before scooping the best items for their own purposes (Gottwaldt and Schulle 2005). Finance officials in Württemberg, for example, carried on a lively correspondence concerning the booty available in the town of Baisingen in May 1942: "Dr. Schmal's easy chair is probably not right for the main office; I suggest instead that we take Wolff's plush chair as well as Ebert's chaise lounge" (Becker 1994: 78). In one city, to take just one example, the file of one debtor was closed in July 1942 because the case worker assumed "that Steinweg will never return to Detmold" (Hartmann in Niebuhr and Ruppert 1998: 668). Thousands of railway, police, and finance officials worked part-time to process the business of persecuting and deporting the Jews. In these circumstances, "the boundaries dividing criminals from normal persons, the guilty from the innocent," had been completely effaced since so many people had been "forced to take part in one way or another in the workings of this machine of mass murder" (Arendt 1978: 229–30).

The identification of the "part-time" nature of dealing with the "Jewish question" exposes the breadth of the involvement of the civil service and the extent of documentation of the process leading to the "Final Solution." "Part-timers" may not, in all cases, have been fully aware of the comprehensive process of persecution in which they participated, but this partiality of perspective should not obscure the responsibility and initiative that civil servants demonstrated at every step. It was in the context of a big project that "the experienced functionary" came "into his own"; "a middle-ranking bureaucrat, no less than his highest superior was aware of currents and possibilities." As a result, "thousands of proposals were introduced in memoranda, presented at conferences, and discussed in letters. The subject matter ranged from dissolution of mixed marriages to the deportation of the Jews of Liechtenstein or the construction of some 'quick-working' device for the annihilation of Jewish women and children at Lodz" (Hilberg 2003: 1063). Since the presidential cabinets in the last years of the Weimar Republic, ministerial bureaucracies had become more powerful, more autonomous, and more accustomed to demonstrating initiative. They also agreed fundamentally with the Nazi aim to isolate Jews (Adam 1972: 109, 112–13). Just as countless Germans suddenly became expert at assessing Jewish influence, Jewish quotas, and other elements of the "Jewish question" in spring 1933, so bureaucratic offices increasingly based their activity on the National Socialist premise that the German body needed to be protected and that Jewish bodies needed to be expelled. This explains the bureaucratic zeal to carry out a "Jewish politics" from below in the most remote corners of German society and to give the harshest interpretation to ministerial directives regarding the Jews that came from above.

Small humiliations had profound effects when translated into social practice. After Berlin's municipal swimming pools were all "Aryanized" in summer 1935, one father wondered about the effect on his two Jewish stepchildren: "As soon as they met up with their swimming pool friends, the children were told, in a friendly way, about the non-Aryan sign at the South End pool. They do not quite know how to react, and it occupies them a great deal. Reni will probably no longer go, but the pool doesn't mean as much to her as it does to Brigitte." "Aryan" friends appeared willing to collude in the attempt to let Reni and Brigitte "pass," which neither girl necessarily wanted to do. In all probability, everyone was a little relieved not to be put to the test, a result that enforced the prohibition (Klepper 1955: 273). The "swimming pool friendship" dissolved.

The waves of anti-Jewish legislation were at first not uniform since they were the product of hundreds of initiatives, but gradually, as state and federal authorities stepped in, decrees and regulations left no realm of Jewish life untouched: Jewish lawyers were debarred, Jewish dental technicians prohibited from working with the public health care system, Jewish students denied certifications and continuing education courses, and Jewish youth groups disallowed from wearing uniforms or displaying badges and flags. All these directives left behind paper trails: most were published in the principal legal gazette, the *Reichsgesetzblatt*, or in the official publications of the various ministries. During the war, the Reich Security Main Office assumed leadership in dictating the conditions of Jewish life, confiscating cameras, typewriters, and electrical appliances, prohibiting Jews from using public telephones or keeping pets, terminating newspaper subscriptions, and drastically restricting access to public transportation. But the zeal, the attention to detail, and the restless refinement of what Hans Adler referred to as "the administered person" characterized all bureaucratic offices (1974).

COMMEMORATING THE "FINAL SOLUTION"

Such a level of activity called for some sort of recognition, and evidence suggests that the Nazis attempted to prepare a history of the "Final Solution." On 1 August 1941, just as the Einsatzgruppen in the Soviet Union began including women and children among their victims, Gestapo chief Heinrich Müller (1900–1945) ordered units to send "particularly interesting visual material" to Berlin "as quickly as possible," such as "photographs, placards, leaflets, and other documents" (Gerlach 1999: 574). The Einsatzgruppen reported daily on the numbers of mostly Jewish civilians being killed in the occupied territories of the Soviet Union; consolidated totals circulated in twenty-three and, by 1942, in seventy-five copies around the ministries in Berlin (Arad et al. 1989; Hilberg 2001: 61). Himmler went so far as to recruit novelists Hanns Johst (1890–1978) and Edwin Erich Dwinger (1898–1981) and filmmakers and photographers to accompany SS missions. A film probably was made to document the murder of Jews in Minsk that Himmler witnessed on 15 August 1941 (Gerlach 1999: 573–4; Düsterberg 2004; Hesse in Gaertringen 2007: 180–6). Stationed in Paris in spring 1942, Ernst Jünger (1895–1998) registered the accumulation of reports about SS massacres, which he described as "ghost festivals, with the murder of men, children, women. The gruesome booty is quickly interred, then other ghosts arrive to dig it out again; they film the dismembered, half-decomposed carcasses with a nightmarish glee. And then they screen these films for others" (1955: 90). Although such films likely were not intended for public consumption, they circulated well beyond Hitler's inner circle. Indeed, at almost every point in the deportation and murder process, filmmakers and photographers stood by: pogroms in Lemberg, streetlife in the Warsaw ghetto and in Theresienstadt, and deportations from Nuremberg and Stuttgart all were filmed. Carefully prepared photo albums depicted the deportation of Jews from Würzburg and Munich (Müller 1988: 405; Browning 2004: 385–6; Stargardt 2006: 154). In Bad Neustadt, local Nazis photographed elderly, malnourished Jews on 22 April 1942 as they stood before the fountain on the market place and arranged final group shots before marching them to the train station for deportation. They later enlarged the photographs and hung them in picture windows in the town center to document the successful action (Schultheis 1980: 467–8).

These efforts should be interpreted as part of a broader aim to create "war chronicles" in which German localities fitted themselves into the larger, presumably victorious war. In Münster, one writer of such a document played the flaneur on the eve of the first deportations of Jews on 12 December 1941: "Today I belonged to those who check out two more taverns and mix with the guests at the bar. In the second place, . . . as I stand among mid-level civil servants, artisans, and business-men, I hear that all the Jews will have to leave Münster by the 13th of this month. Animated discussion follows this news" (Longerich 2006: 195–6). The editor of the local paper chronicled his own archival work. "Last Friday," he wrote in his diary on 15 December 1941 about the same event, "Münster Jews under the age of 65, having had to assemble in the Gertruden Courtyard, are gone. I was in Berlin and so couldn't see for myself, but I want to still try to gather material and get details. Later, that will be very interesting" (Wantzen 2000: 651–2). No one ordered this man to gather documentary evidence, yet he shared the impulse to hold fast the historic moment for posterity. Even the director of Dortmund's municipal pawn-shop, which tallied gold and silver objects taken from Jews in 1939, concluded his 1941 report with a commemorative flourish: "If even in later years a researcher who is acquainted with Jews only through hearsay, would rummage in the records of the municipal archives of Dortmund, he will discover that the municipal pawnshops also did their small part in the solution of the Jewish question" (Hilberg 2001: 43).

Aside from the "Auschwitz Album," the most famous documentation of the "Final Solution" is probably the "Stroop Report," prepared by *Brigadeführer* Jürgen Stroop (1895–1952) to chronicle his defeat of the Warsaw ghetto uprising in May 1943. Stroop grandly titled his report "The Ghetto is No More," thereby distinguishing it from routine bureaucratic accounts (International Military Tribunal 1947–49, 26: 628–94). His was a special narrative to which he appended several dozen photographs, including the now iconic snapshot of a frightened boy with his hands raised at the point of a gun. This image was taken by a German photographer, and its inclusion in a German military report testified to the National Socialist desire to commemorate not only the "Final Solution" but the willingness of the SS to shoulder the burden of annihilating all Jewish life, including women and children, the possible "avengers" of the future. Even the verb in the photograph's caption, "produced out of the bunkers by force," signals the performative nature of the scene. The poignancy of the photograph served as the deliberate marker of the perpetrator's toughness. Indeed, half boastfully, half self-pityingly, Himmler himself repeatedly referred to the "difficult task" of murdering women and children (Longerich 2008: 556, 661). In one exchange, noted down by a German correspondent, a young SS shooter hoped to demonstrate his maturity to his girlfriend's mother by pointing out that "with the war he was no longer so young. At the age of 17 he had already helped shoot 200 Jewish women and children" (Kempowski Archive, 6257/1, Ella to Erich Neuss, 16 August 1943). How many others claimed this sort of distinction is unknown, but the Nazis' camera eye clearly sought out women and children.

In sum, the "Auschwitz Album," Münster's "war chronicles," and the "Stroop Report" constitute drafted, if scattered "pages of glory." Most documents reporting on the deportation and murder of European Jews employed deceptive and camouflaged language, yet the perpetrators plainly wanted to (and did) commemorate their activities.

Letters and diaries also reveal a widespread urge among German soldiers and civilians to document the history of the Third Reich. Of course, most correspondents did not concentrate on the Jews. Gossip was the main channel to broadcast rumors and news about the killings in the east. Indeed, diarists often recorded such information with the construction "one hears" or "it is said" (Wantzen 2000: 378, 407, 551). But even if they are unrepresentative, the letters and diaries that do refer to Jews and the "Final Solution" provide telling evidence of how Germans understood the knowledge of persecution, deportation, and murder. Gustav René Hocke has analyzed how in times of war and dictatorship diarists counterposed their private "I" to the overwhelming public "We," remarking that "'honest people' increasingly hole themselves up in their diaries" (Hocke 1963: 229). Despite, or precisely because of the "claims of the totality," wrote Ursula von Kardorff (1911–1988) during the war, the diary is "the way to oneself" (1942). This is undoubtedly true, but diaries also were written to witness or document the new epoch represented by the Nazis, especially new opportunities to travel. Other autobiographical writings exposed the difficulties the "I" had committing itself to the Nazi "We," although the desire was usually there, or the exuberant claims the "We" made on a still reluctant "I." In other words, diarists used writing to perform their struggle with (or for) National Socialism. To grasp how ego-documents represented the Holocaust, one needs to examine the impulse to document and the moral struggles of living in Nazi Germany.

What Germans Knew

The urge to document history in the making animated ordinary soldiers as much as it did the regime's elite. Utterly dazzled by the capture of Kiev at the end of 1941, a "heroes' epic, like none that has existed before," Hitler addressed his army on 2 October, exclaiming that "your names" will be "forever associated with the most tremendous victories in world history" (Hitler 1980: 71). Millions of soldiers composed their letters in the aural space of speeches such as this one. After listening to Hitler, a delicatessen owner from Münster wrote a long descriptive letter to his wife, intending "to provide a bit of insight into our experience" and detailed instructions on keeping mementoes of the war: "I am sending you 6 rolls of film to develop. I don't have to tell you how important these pictures are to me. Let me ask you to develop these pictures with *total care* in a 6 x 9 format. Preferably, silk smooth matte finish." Later he requested bigger 18 x 24 centimeter enlargements to provide "an ornament for our apartment" (Fritzsche 2008: 147–8). Especially at the beginning of the war, letters and photographs composed unofficial archives, indicating the extent to which soldiers deliberately placed themselves in German history and adopted the heroic vantage of the Third Reich.

Among the snapshots that the soldier from Münster had developed in 1941 was one ("roll XIII, 16") depicting Jewish women working under armed guard in a railway yard in Stolpce, most of whom were murdered one month later (Fritzsche 2008: 152). Photographs taken by other soldiers showed partisans hanged in market squares and Jewish civilians shot on the edges of town. That photographs of massacres often revealed soldiers holding cameras indicates the keen interest they took in documenting their part in the war—so much so that the army leadership felt it necessary to prohibit "Landser" from taking photographs. Nonetheless, "thousands of photographs, taken from dead or captured German soldiers by the Russians, or discovered among the possessions of veterans," continued to "record mass executions" (Burleigh 2000: 561). The camera facilitated a cool, distanced relationship to events, but photography remained basically commemorative:

photographs of the Holocaust exist because German soldiers took them and saw to it that they were developed and preserved. Often, the same person was behind the gun and the camera.

Photography in World War II underscored the confident, victorious posture of German soldiers, but letters and diaries expressed more doubt about the moral validity of Germany's "Final Solution." In most cases, doubt appeared as a glimmer to be snuffed out, but it existed nonetheless. At the very beginning of the Third Reich in April 1933, the pro-Nazi wife of the deputy mayor of the city of Braunschweig received a letter from her daughter, who was living in Holland and witnessing the arrival of Jewish refugees fleeing the violence in Germany. What about the "mean" and "horrible" "campaign against the Jews?" the daughter asked. Her mother conceded "sympathy" for *the fate of the individual*," but justified the boycott of Jewish businesses: "Germany is using the weapon it has" to respond to "the smear campaign" from abroad. In other words, Germans were the actual victims. The next word is predictable since discussions about Jewish suffering frequently switched to German suffering: "Versailles" had taken the "opportunities for life" away from Germans, who were now "completely understandably" fighting back on behalf of their "own sons." The mother's reasoning is faulty, but she argued that the Jews would have to make up for what the Allies had taken. Her rhetoric captures the work of becoming a Nazi. She confronted Nazi terror, hesitated momentarily, and dismissed the consequences as justified in the name of German suffering (Kalshoven 1995: 188, 190–1).

This is a model performance of how belief outmaneuvered doubt. It held in the war, when soldiers found themselves witnesses to mass murder and reacted with striking similarity. One reassured himself thusly in his wartime diary: "we heard the machine-gun and machine-pistol fire with which the SS 'wasted' everything Jewish." On the one hand, Tarnopol was "hell." On the other hand, "we also recognize that the root of all this evil is simply the Jews, whose spirit made it possible for Bolshevism to emerge in the first place" (Kempowski Archive, 6257/2, Erich Neuss's diary entry for 3 July 1941). Another found that "it was hard, very hard, but necessary"; "around the world, the Jews are attempting to mobilize everything they can against us" (Kempowski Archive, 6130/2, Walter to Mimi Solze, 31 July 1941). After the initial shock, a process of emotional armoring usually followed.

On the home front, a woman in one letter asked her husband stationed behind the front for "a silk 'Jewish dress'"—"but it's got to be plenty big!" because she wanted to give it to her aunt—yet struggled in a later missive with the news of the deportation of her Jewish neighbors:

They are being sent to Poland, to Lodz. In Bremen, in our neighborhood, they had to assemble in 2 big schools, right near Heinz and Alma. There they reside with kit and caboodle and they look just terrible. They are allowed 100 M travel money. The railway journey costs 90 M, so 10 M has to cover necessities for an 8-day period. They leave the Reich as the poorest of the poor . . . Many find this bitter hard and some were okay. But now they all have to take responsibility for their kind. Now I have given enough "honor" to the Jews, having sacrificed half a page of writing paper on their account. So let's change the subject. (Kempowski Archive, 5483, Isa to Fritz Kuchenbuch, 8 July and 23 November 1941)

The alleged sins of the collective repeatedly justified the acknowledged sufferings of individual Jews.

Letters and diaries such as these are probably skewed in their lack of empathy for Jews. This may be so because writing was a medium of confession and justification. Even so, they bespeak wide knowledge of a major, even systematic offensive against Jews. In 1941 and 1942, Germans knew brutal facts about the Einsatzgruppen: the inclusion of women and children in the ranks of innocents murdered, the procedures that left victims naked at the edge of pits, and the scale of massacres such as Babi Yar at the end of September 1941. They also suspected the entanglement of "ordinary Germans" serving in the Wehrmacht in the murders (Fritzsche 2008). But later on there were very few references to gas or to Auschwitz in contemporary letters and diaries. In some ways, the shock of Babi Yar blocked out the horrific news of Auschwitz. However, the news of the "Final Solution" was not just passively noted. As Kuchenbuch's case indicates, neighbors discussed and debated the fate of Jews; it was mulled over, and often justified. These conversations admitted a great deal of detail: "100 M travel money . . . 8-day period."

After the majority of Europe's Jews had been annihilated, they returned in abstract or camouflaged guises as Germans considered their own vulnerabilities in a war that from 1943 on increasingly threatened to kill them. The devastation of Allied air raids brought Germans to familiarize themselves with the crude Nazi stereotype of the all-powerful, menacing Jew. While Nazi propaganda simply put the blame for the raids on international Jewry, talk on the street went further and blamed the Jews for using their supposedly powerful positions abroad to avenge the cruel treatment Jews had suffered. Or else, the Allies or Providence were punishing Germany for persecuting the Jews. With this idea of retaliation, public opinion established a link between what had happened to Jews and what was happening to Germans. Both letters and security reports recorded rumors that cities such as Frankfurt had not been bombed because departed Jews wanted to "move back into their houses" (Kempowski Archive, 6257/1, Ella to Erich Neuss, 3 July 1943). These "urban legends" implied fundamental criticism of the deportations even as they relied on antisemitic caricatures. Interestingly, as the air raids grew worse, the German crime to which they were linked remained large enough to sustain the equivalency: few people ever said that persecuted Jews were overdoing their revenge. But if popular reactions to the air raids revealed guilty knowledge during the war, the association between persecution and bombing also enabled Germans to relieve themselves of guilt afterwards on the grounds that they had become victims too.

The Nazis actually came close to admitting that the Germans might be fitting objects of revenge. Throughout 1943, the motto "Only Those Who Fight, Can Escape the Revenge of the Jews" introduced the propaganda of "total war" (Dörner 2007: 467). Prominent Nazis fanned out across Germany using strikingly similar words to buttress civilian resolve about the "bridges" that Germany had burned behind itself. "A movement and a people who have burned the bridges behind them fight with much greater determination than those who are still able to retreat," noted Joseph Goebbels (1897–1945) in his diary (1994: II.7.454). Alfred Rosenberg told a *Gauschulungstagung* on 8 May in Trier, "Today our task is to make Germany and Europe clean again. After 2000 years of parasitical activity, Europe must be liberated from Jewish leprosy. That is not brutality, but clean, biological humanitarianism. Better that 8 million Jews disappear than 80 million Germans. The bridges have been broken behind us, and there is no way back anymore" (Wantzen 2000: 1093). These revelations did not reach all Germans, of course, but Goebbels published the frightening watchwords that the Germans had "broken the bridges behind us" in *Das Reich*, which had a circulation of 1.4 million (14 November 1943).

That burned bridges were an explicit reference to the "Final Solution" was unmistakable to ordinary Germans. What is remarkable about this propaganda is that it mocked conventional morality on the far side of the burnt bridge as "sentimentalism" in order to push Germans further into the moral calamity of the Third Reich. It thereby acknowledged that the Allies would treat German conduct as a great crime. "Goebbels has allowed so much information on German crimes to filter through," argued a Swedish correspondent in August 1943, "that everyone is conscious of shared responsibility and guilt, and afraid of personal retaliation" (Barth 2003: 238). Knowledge of the "Final Solution" had become inextricably tied to fear and guilt, which deformed the comprehension of the Holocaust for many decades after 1945.

At the end of the war, a gathering hysteria indicted Nazis for betraying the Third Reich. "Damn them," a 16-year-old swore at the Nazi pack in her diary in April 1945, "these war criminals and Jew murderers," but she disbelieved that all the struggles had been in vain; it could not be "Germany's end, even if it is ours." Like many other diarists, she blamed the Nazis for destroying Nazism (Hammer and Nieden 1992: 309). Feelings of betrayal also explain why postwar affirmation of the accomplishments of the Third Reich, from the autobahns to "Strength through Joy," held longer than loyalties to individual Nazi leaders, "Goebbels, Himmler, cowardly Goering and whatever their names are," who, with the possible exception of Hitler, had very little appeal to Germans after the war (Kempowski Archive, 5461, Elly Wilde diary entry for 4 May 1945). In this scenario, Hitler was doubly to blame: his war against the Jews had wrecked the cherished Third Reich and indelibly tarnished the idea of Germany.

With the advance of the Soviet army, bureaucrats began destroying their archives, particularly those documenting "anti-Jewish activity." Correspondents and diarists did the same: "When you have two military brothers and a like-minded brother-in-law, you can image what sort of stuff has collected around the house," wrote one woman in besieged Gleiwitz in late January 1945 as she tore up incriminating photographs before the arrival of the Russians (Walk 1981: 406; Kempowski 1999, 2: 650). In this way, much of the material evidence of Nazism's domestic setting, including evidence about the "Final Solution," was deliberately destroyed. Self-protection blocked the way to self-incrimination so that written admissions like the following, written on 10 May 1945, right after the end of the Third Reich, were rare indeed: "Yesterday I lay in bed the entire day. Over dinner, I read the KZ reports in the enemy newspaper. That turned my stomach so much that I woke up and had to throw up. Thereafter, I was better, but I was so depressed that I just stayed in bed" (Kempowski Archive, 6257/1, Ella to Erich Neuss, 10 May 1945).

Information about the "Final Solution" was passed most effectively in oral form. It is highly likely that Hitler gave oral authorizations for Himmler's step-by-step accomplishment of the "Final Solution": the expansion of the Einsatzgruppen killings in the Soviet Union in summer 1941, the construction of death camps in occupied Poland in fall 1941, and the European-wide implementation of the war against the Jews in winter 1942. News about the murder of Jews was passed along in German military canteens in Poland, in bars in Berlin, and in railway waiting rooms and train compartments. Neighbors persistently exchanged gossip and rumor about the deportations and the bombings as well. Diaries, letters, and the regime's security reports picked up some of this, but the conversations were certainly much more dense, extensive, and continuous than the fragments of their written transcription suggest. Historians can only imagine the conversations in German homes as soldiers arrived on leave in spring and summer 1942 for the first time after a year or more of fighting in the Soviet Union (Dürkefälden 1985: 110).

Even so, the archives that established themselves over the course of the Third Reich both in the German bureaucracy and in German homes indicate widespread knowledge and, to some extent, debate about the "Final Solution." From Goebbels' voluminous diary down to ordinary correspondents' reports on the deportation of Jews, the documents combine obfuscatory language and telling detail and shift from registers of shock to justification or detachment. Not even Himmler, in his two speeches to the party elite gathered in Posen in October 1943, made reference to death camps or gas chambers. Yet the documentary and commemorative enthusiasm of participants at all levels as well as the regime's efforts to create shared knowledge and responsibility for the "Final Solution" at the end of the war undermined the maintenance of secrecy and the format of camouflage. The Nazi regime never arrived at a consensus as to how public the success of the "Final

Solution" should become, along what timeline, and with what sort of detail. But drafts of the "pages of glory" of the Third Reich provided concrete and horrific evidence of Germany's murderous campaign against the Jews. At the beginning of the war, the rush to document history in the making put the accent on the full range of participation; by the end of the fighting, witnesses had composed more limited roles for themselves as bystanders and observers in a calamity beyond their control. As a result, memories laid down in 1943 or 1944 undoubtedly covered up much more frank knowledge about the "Final Solution" assembled in 1941 or 1942.

REFERENCES

ADAM, U. (1972). *Judenpolitik im Dritten Reich.* Düsseldorf: Droste.

ADLER, H. (1974). *Der verwaltete Mensch: Studien zur Deportation der Juden aus Deutschland.* Tübingen: Mohr.

ARAD, Y., KRAKOWSKI, S., and SPECTOR, S. (eds.) (1989). *The Einsatzgruppen Reports: Selections from the Dispatches of the Nazi Death Squads' Campaign Against the Jews, July 1941–January 1943.* New York: Holocaust Library.

ARENDT, H. (1978). *The Jew as Pariah.* New York: Grove Press.

BARTH, C. (2003). *Goebbels und die Juden.* Paderborn: Schöningh.

BECKER, F. (1994). *Gewalt und Gedächtnis: Erinnerungen an die nationalsozialistische Verfolgung einer jüdischen Landgemeinde.* Göttingen: V. Schmerse.

BROWNING, C. (2004). *The Origins of the Final Solution: The Evolution of Nazi Jewish Policy, September 1939–March 1942.* With contributions by J. Matthäus. Lincoln, NE: University of Nebraska Press.

BURLEIGH, M. (2000). *The Third Reich: A New History.* New York: Hill and Wang.

DÖRNER, B. (1998). *"Heimtücke": Das Gesetz als Waffe—Kontrolle, Abschreckung und Verfolgung in Deutschland 1933–1945.* Paderborn: Schöningh.

——(2007). *Die Deutschen und der Holocaust: Was niemand wissen wollte, aber jeder wissen konnte.* Berlin: Propyläen.

DÜRKEFÄLDEN, K. (1985). *"Schreiben wie es wirklich war . . ." Aufzeichnungen Karl Dürkefäldens aus den Jahren 1933–1945.* Ed. H. and S. Obenaus. Hannover: Fackelträger.

DÜSTERBERG, R. (2004). *Hanns Johst: "Der Barde der SS". Karrieren eines deutschen Dichters.* Paderborn: Schöningh.

DWORK, D. and VAN PELT, R. (2002). *Auschwitz.* New York: W. W. Norton.

EHRENREICH, E. (2007). *Nazi Ancestral Proof: Genealogy, Racial Science, and the Final Solution.* Bloomington, IN: Indiana University Press.

FRIEDLÄNDER, S. (ed.) (1992). *Probing the Limits of Representation: Nazism and the "Final Solution."* Cambridge, MA: Harvard University Press.

——(1997). *Nazi Germany and the Jews.* Vol. 1, *The Years of Persecution, 1933–1939.* New York: HarperCollins.

FRITZSCHE, P. (2008). *Life and Death in the Third Reich.* Cambridge, MA: Harvard University Press.

GAERTRINGEN, H. (ed.) (2007). *Die Auge des Dritten Reiches: Hitlers Kameramann und Fotograph Walter Frentz*. Munich: Deutscher Kunstverlag.

GERLACH, C. (1999). *Kalkulierte Morde: Die deutsche Wirtschafts- und Vernichtungspolitik in Weißrußland 1941 bis 1944*. Hamburg: Hamburger Edition.

GOEBBELS, J. (1943). "Die zwangsläufigen Schlüsse." *Das Reich*, 14 November.

——(1994). *Die Tagebücher von Joseph Goebbels: Sämtliche Fragmente*. Ed. E. Fröhlich. Munich: K. G. Saur.

GOTTWALDT, A. and SCHULLE, D. (2005). *Die "Judendeportationen" aus dem Deutschen Reich, 1941–1945*. Wiesbaden: Marixverlag.

GUTMAN, I. and GUTTERMAN, B. (eds.) (2002). *The Auschwitz Album: The Story of a Transport*. Jerusalem: Yad Vashem.

HAMMER, I. and NIEDEN, S. (eds.) (1992). *Sehr selten habe ich geweint: Briefe und Tagebücher aus dem Zweiten Weltkrieg von Menschen in Berlin*. Zurich: Schweizer Verlagshaus.

HILBERG, R. (2001). *Sources of Holocaust Research*. Chicago, IL: Ivan Dee Publishers.

——(2003). *The Destruction of the European Jews*. New Haven, CT: Yale University Press.

HITLER, A. (1980). *Monologe im Führerhauptquartier 1941–1944: Die Aufzeichnungen Heinrich Heims*. Ed. W. Jochmann. Hamburg: A. Knaus.

HOCKE, G. (1963). *Das europäische Tagebuch*. Wiesbaden: Limes.

INTERNATIONAL MILITARY TRIBUNAL (1947–49). *Trial of the Major War Criminals before the International Military Tribunal, Nuremberg 14 November 1945–1 October 1946*. 42 vols. Nuremberg.

JÜNGER, E. (1955). *Strahlungen*. Tübingen: Heliopolis.

KALSHOVEN, H. (ed.) (1995). *Ich denk so viel an Euch: Ein deutsch-holländischer Briefwechsel, 1920–1949*. Munich: Luchterhand.

KARDORFF, U. VON (1942). "Vom Tagebuch," in *Deutsche Allgemeine Zeitung*.

KEMPOWSKI, W. (1999). *Das Echolot: Fuga furiosa*. 4 vols. Munich: K.G. Saur.

Kempowski Archive, Akademie der Künste, Berlin.

KLEMPERER, V. (1998). *I Will Bear Witness 1933–1941: A Diary of the Nazi Years*. New York: Random House.

KLEPPER, J. (1955). *Unter dem Schatten Deiner Flügel: Aus den Tagebüchern der Jahre 1932–1942*. Stuttgart: Deutsche Verlags-Anstalt.

LACAPRA, D. (1994). *Representing the Holocaust: History, Theory, Trauma*. Ithaca, NY: Cornell University Press.

LONGERICH, P. (2006). *"Davon haben wir nichts gewusst!" Die Deutschen und die Judenverfolgung 1933–1945*. Berlin: Siedler.

——(2008). *Heinrich Himmler: Biographie*. Berlin: Siedler.

MÜLLER, R. (1988). *Stuttgart zur Zeit des Nationalsozialismus*. Stuttgart: K. Theiss.

NIEBUHR, H. and RUPPERT, A. (eds.) (1998). *Nationalsozialismus in Detmold: Dokumentation eines stadtgeschichtlichen Projekts*. Bielefeld: Aisthesis.

SCHULTHEIS, H. (1980). *Juden in Mainfranken 1933–1945*. Bad Neustadt: Rötter.

STARGARDT, N. (2006). *Witnesses of War: The Third Reich through Children's Eyes*. New York: Knopf.

STEINERT, M. (1977). *Hitler's War and the Germans: Public Mood and Attitude During the Second World War*. Athens, OH: Ohio University Press.

WALK, J. (ed.) (1981). *Das Sonderreicht für die Juden im NS-Staat.* Heidelberg: C.F. Mueller Juristischer Verlag.

WANTZEN, P. (2000). *Das Leben im Krieg, 1939–1946: Ein Tagebuch.* Bad Homburg: Verlag Das Dokument.

OTHER SUGGESTED READING

EVANS, R. (2009). *The Third Reich at War.* New York: Penguin Press.

FRIEDLÄNDER, S. (2007). *The Years of Extermination: Nazi Germany and the Jews, 1939–1945.* New York: HarperCollins.

GELLATELY, R. (2001). *Backing Hitler: Consent and Coercion in Nazi Germany.* New York: Oxford University Press.

JOHNSON, E. and REUBAND, K. (2005). *What We Knew: Terror, Murder and Everyday Life in Nazi Germany: An Oral History.* Cambridge, MA: Basic Books.

KLEE, E., DRESSEN, W., and RIESS, V. (eds.) (1991). *"The Good Old Days": The Holocaust as Seen by Its Perpetrators and Bystanders.* New York: Free Press.

KOONZ, C. (2003). *The Nazi Conscience.* Cambridge, MA: Harvard University Press.

CHAPTER 26

JEWS' DIARIES AND CHRONICLES

AMOS GOLDBERG

As a genre, the private journal stands on the margins of the literary canon and usually receives little academic attention. Such texts are regarded as a kind of first draft, lacking minimal form or organization (Pascal 1960: 5; Langford and West 1999: 6–7). Diaries also have been allotted second-class status as historical sources, considered suspect because of their writers' supposed personal biases and limited perspectives. As a result, research about diaries has been modest and sporadic (Schlissel 1982; Nussbaum in Olney 1988: 128–40; Bunkers and Huff 1996). Holocaust diaries have been subject to the same neglect, and discussion of them long occupied a marginal place in Holocaust studies. Several such diaries, however, are part of the canon of Holocaust literature, a few of them, such as those by Anne Frank (1929–1945) and Victor Klemperer (1881–1960), have helped shape Holocaust awareness worldwide, and the Holocaust diaries written by Jews are receiving increased scholarly attention.

Until recently, most studies of Holocaust diaries were written by literary scholars and within the framework of monographs that examine a range of literary and other forms of Holocaust representation (Ezrahi 1980; Rosenfeld 1980; Young 1988; Langer 1995; Waxman 2006). Extensive literary and historical research has been conducted on a few famous, even canonical diaries, such as those kept by Frank, Etty Hillesum (1914–1943), and Adam Czerniakow (1880–1942), but only since the mid-1990s have entire volumes devoted to diaries appeared, written from the perspective of a variety of disciplines (Feldhay-Brenner 1994; Heer 1997; De Costa 1998; Patterson 1999; Shapiro 1999; Goldberg 2004; Leociak 2004; Garbarini 2006).

Important as they are, these studies hardly exhaust this historical-cultural phenomenon. Holocaust diaries are being reprinted constantly in Hebrew, English,
and other languages. They are an essential element of the current "Era of the
Witness," in which historical consciousness, especially with regard to the Holocaust, is shaped by individual testimonies (Wieviorka 2006).

This chapter presents aspects of Jews' Holocaust diaries via a review of the
academic contexts in which they have been discussed. After a short survey of the
extent and general characteristics of diary writing, the chapter discusses three types
of diaries and concludes with a brief discussion of their reception and possible
directions for future research.

THE DIARIES

Jews wrote in most literary genres during the Holocaust, but the most typical is
surely the diary, either in the classical form of daily entries or in the more processed
form of memoirs and hybrids of chronicle and recollection. The memoir form
emerged mostly in the later years of the war (1943 onwards) in occupied Europe
and often from authors in hiding. The centrality of the genre is indicated by the
large number of diaries extant in archives and the certainty that these constitute
only a small portion of what was written. As Emanuel Ringelblum (1900–1944), the
historian of the Warsaw ghetto, noted, "In this war, everybody wrote, and in
particular kept diaries . . . most of these diaries were destroyed during the great
deportation . . . one may calculate that tens, or maybe even hundreds of diaries
were lost" (Ringelblum 1994: 19).

Indeed, all over Europe, in cities and villages, in ghettos and forests, in places of
hiding and concentration and labor camps, Jews of all ages (although elderly
people and mothers with young children are underrepresented), backgrounds,
identities, and cultures recorded in most European languages and in Hebrew and
Yiddish their experiences under Nazi rule. Naturally, more diaries were written
where conditions permitted, so that many more survived from the ghettos than the
camps, but even there diaries were kept and survived, including three by members
of the *Sonderkommando* in Auschwitz (Bezwinska 1973).

In general, autobiographical writing flourishes at times of crisis, when individuals are forced to rethink their identities (Weintraub 1966). The spread of diary
writing during the war in Germany and the rest of Europe is therefore not
surprising (Garbarini 2006: 1–3). The large number of diaries written by Jews is
less self-explanatory. Writing materials were often difficult to obtain (Ringelblum 1994:
313), and some diaries had to be written on any scraps of paper that came to hand,

as illustrated by three diaries from Łódź. An anonymous boy made his entries in the margins of a French textbook (Ben-Amos 2004), Menachem Oppenheim wrote his in the margins of a prayer book (Yad Vashem Archive 33/1032), and Abraham Kajzer penned his on scraps of brown paper from cement sacks (Leociak 2004: 68). More serious than such difficulties was the danger to which the act of writing sometimes exposed the authors and those around them. The widespread overcoming of these impediments attests to a drive to write and record that overcame all considerations of expediency, ethics, and Jewish law (*halacha*), which prioritizes the preservation of life above all else. Again, the chronicler of the Warsaw ghetto makes the point, observing in February 1941, "The drive to write memoirs is so strong that even in the labor camps young people wrote their memoirs. When they were caught, they were beaten, and the pages torn to shreds" (Ringelblum 1958: 133).

Although all diarists shared a drive to write, its impetus differed. Some writers acted on an internal imperative that became an addiction in the face of grim reality and extreme powerlessness. Others stressed their mission to document or bear witness, some also noting their obligation to raise the conscience of the world or aid future tribunals. Still others saw the act of writing as a form of revenge on their persecutors or memorializing their loved ones (Leociak 2004: 77–103).

Amidst the outpouring of diaries and memoirs during the Holocaust, the diary genre underwent a change. It evolved from texts inclined to focus on the writer's personal life, often without even assuming an external addressee, to ones that frequently seek to document historical events or at least include a documentary perspective. The diary as an autobiographical genre went from introspectively responding to the question "who am I?" (Schlaeger in Langford and West 1999: 22–36) to seeking to answer the questions "what have I seen?" (testimony) and "what are the external forces determining my and my community's fate?" This trend is most evident in prewar diaries that continued into the war years (e.g., Kaplan 1999; Klemperer 1999 and 2001), and it highlights the paradoxical nature of intensive first-person writing during the Holocaust. Such writing strongly presents the writer's "I" as an individuated self, yet at the same time attests to the diminishing of this very "I" and its vulnerability to external forces and atrocities that it can only record.

Holocaust diaries vary enormously in content and form, so typologizing them is difficult. They can be categorized according to place of origin, e.g., a ghetto or camp (Waxman 2006), or genre, e.g. journal, memoir, or chronicle (Leociak 2004), but these are technical distinctions that tell little about the nature of these texts. This chapter therefore will define three major types of diaries in relation to the distinct poetic-existential principles that predominate in each and examine the particular series of questions and thematic foci that each raises.

CONTINUOUS TEMPORALITY AND THE
DOCUMENTARY DIARY

Continuity and succession are crucial to human identity, and they stand at the very core of the autobiographical act. The life story text flows from page to page, from event to event, from entry to entry, and from day to day in an orderly fashion, expressing a constant search for meaning and imposing compositional order on the chaos of events (Fothergil 1974). This dynamic should not be taken for granted, however. Precisely because it expresses a basic vitality, a search for meaning and identity, it demands an effort that is revealed at the moments when writers feel obliged, almost against their will, to stop writing because continued confrontation with reality is unbearable. As Zelig Kalmanovitch (1885–1944) wrote on 25 April 1943 after one of the "actions" in the Vilna district: "More than a month passed since the last time I wrote . . . actually every day should be documented but I am so powerless" (Kalmanovitch 1977: 102). Or as Chaim Kaplan (1880–1942) wrote in the Warsaw ghetto on 26 November 1940: "Six days have passed without an entry. In these days . . . the sheer volume and numbers of impressions leave me without the literary power to record and organize them" (Kaplan 1999: 226).

Sometimes, continuity itself becomes the very purpose and goal of writing. Epistolary diaries written by parents trapped in Nazi Europe to children who had escaped are an interesting expression of this desire. When regular correspondence was cut off, parents compiled diaries of letters that were never sent. As the discoverer of these texts points out, "In recording family history and bridging the epistemological divide, diarists attempted to maintain the continuity of their families" (Garbarini 2006: 121).

At the same time, in many cases the family was where the breaking up of lives was felt most keenly. To cite three examples from the Łódź ghetto, David Sierako-wiak (1924–1943) tells how his father ate his children's bread ration (1996: 176–77), Josef Zelkowicz (1897–1944) how shame and modesty disappeared in families (2002), and Shlomo Frank (1902–1966) how a mother hid her child's rotting corpse in her house in order to keep receiving his ration cards (1958: 64).

The subject of the family is an example of how diaries expose the conflict between the continuity that writers tried to preserve in their world and their lives and the radical reality into which they were hurled. Thus, in many of the extensive diaries, such as those of Etty Hillesum of Amsterdam, Raymond Lambert (1894–1943) of France, Mihail Sebastian (1907–1945) of Bucharest, and Kalmano-vich of Vilna, issues of continuity and discontinuity of the writer's identity predominate. This tension is particularly acute in diaries that are self-consciously documentary in form.

Many diarists, perhaps most of them, intuited that their writings would be of great historical value. Some diarists actually wrote precisely in order to record history, to give as full an account as possible of events. *The Chronicle of the Lodz Ghetto* (Dobroszycki 1984) is an example, written by a team of writers on the initiative and under the supervision of Mordechai Chaim Rumkowski (1877–1944), the head of the Jewish Council (*Judenrat*) in the ghetto, who perhaps wished to document life there in order to burnish his image in the future. Most historical documentary diaries, however, were the work of individuals who sought through writing to transcend the daily details of their personal lives. These diaries—those of Herman Kruk (1897–1944) of Vilna, Ringelblum and Kaplan from Warsaw, and Klemperer from Dresden are examples—usually were written by highly educated people with established and sophisticated political and historical viewpoints. They brought to bear broad perspectives on the events around them and sought to lay the basis for historical understanding in the future. Structurally speaking, these diaries are very regular, with long entries daily or sometimes even several times a day. The writers seek to create a fine, continuous, and reliable network of outlooks, reports, and testimonies in order to provide the fullest possible picture of their experiences.

Continuity expresses itself in these diaries not only in form, but also in the fact that these writers continue in the tradition of writing from which they sprang and within whose framework they write. This prewar tradition provided a world of concepts and a discursive field to the writers' attempts to grasp events and organize them into a reality that, if incomprehensible, is at least describable (Feldhay-Brenner 2008). Thus, Kruk and Ringelblum followed the eastern European Jewish historiographical tradition that crystallized in the Yivo Institute during the 1920s and reflected their political agenda. They oriented their "Jewish historical craft toward the investigation . . . of the texture of everyday life, the routine of popular culture that proved Jews to be a people" (Kassow in Shapiro 1999: 173). They persisted with this approach in their wartime diaries and in Ringelblum's case in the huge *Oneg Shabbat* documentary project (Roskies in Hartman 1994: 37; Kassow 2007).

The historical documentary diary did not always follow the writer's intellectual tradition in a straightforward manner, however. The question of continuity often emerges from its being cut off or questioned. Klemperer's diary is particularly interesting in this context because it consciously emphasizes the struggle for personal and theoretical continuity perhaps more than any other such text. As that of a Jewish convert to Protestantism living in Dresden, Klemperer's life story is deeply rooted in the move from Jewishness to Germanhood typical of many German Jews after emancipation (Gerstenberger in Heer 1997: 14). The underpinning of the philosophical and cultural views and the nationalism that framed his literary research before World War II was *Völkerpsychologie* (the psychology of peoples), a field that assumed that a nationality's culture, literature, and language are expressions or realizations of its unique essence or spirit. Although this school of thought had its origins in liberal political philosophy, it took on increasingly nationalist and racist overtones in the course of the nineteenth century, which Klemperer adopted and echoed. His identity thus faced a terrible crisis during the Nazi period. He saw himself as deeply rooted in German tradition, culture, identity, and values, although he never denied his Jewish origins, yet the race laws cast him against his will back into the Jewish world and its fate. This situation, which intensified during the twelve years of Nazi rule, forced Klemperer to examine his life story and intellectual convictions. He was thrown into the whirl of doubt and inner contradictions that he articulated in the diary.

Klemperer's diary has provoked widespread commentary, especially in Germany, much of it seeking to move beyond Klemperer's "multiple identities" to discern in his identity line(s) of continuity (Aschheim 2001: 70–98). The scholarly emphasis on continuity is not unique to the Germans or to Klemperer's diary. Most works of Jewish studies, mainly in the United States, read Holocaust diaries from this perspective, reflecting a "constructivist approach" that sees the only legitimate interpretation of a text as one that emerges first and foremost from the cultural-linguistic context in which it was written (Mintz 2001: 36–84). Therefore, the meaning of the ghetto diaries is to be found primarily (if not exclusively) in the cultural context of eastern European Jewry in the pre-Holocaust period and in the richness of the Jewish languages of the time, Yiddish and Hebrew.

The problem with this approach is that it ignores elements that elude continuity. These traumatic elements, of which the diarists were acutely aware, involve excesses that tend to unravel continuity and identity (LaCapra 2001: 90–4). One of the writers of the *Lodz Ghetto Chronicle* wrote in his personal diary: "In the beginning God created the ghetto" (Rosenfeld 2002: 106), a phrase the publishers chose as the title for the English version. With these words he established an epistemological perspective utterly different from that of succession. He did not approach events from the point of view of cultural continuity and contiguity, but rather the opposite. His epistemology is shaped by the ghetto, which casts a shadow on the past and future and challenged not just an understanding of continuity, but continuity itself. The catastrophic and aberrant perspective undid a priori any continuity on which a solid continuous identity could be based.

Many diarists, even those who expressed or enacted continuity in their writing, were forced to adopt on occasion an approach that deconstructed continuity. As several scholars have shown, this break in the understanding of time as a linear progression often occurred during 1942, the year of greatest carnage (Garbarini 2006; Kassow in Shapiro 1999: 206–11). At these moments, almost all sense of temporality collapsed and the world lost meaning, as expressed in the following extract from an entry for 14 September 1944:

Only a few facts stick in the mind, dates not at all. One is overwhelmed by the present, time is not divided up, everything is infinitely long ago, everything is infinitely long in coming; there is no yesterday, no tomorrow, only an eternity. And that is yet another reason one knows nothing of the history one has experienced: The sense of time has been abolished; one is at once too blunted and too overexcited. (Klemperer 1999, 1: 357)

In order not to collapse altogether with the undermining or even abolition of time, writing often organized itself around a completely different temporal system based on the future, as expressed by Gustawa Jarecka (1908–1943) after observing deportations from the Warsaw ghetto:

One can lose all hopes except for one—that the suffering and destruction of this war will make sense when they are looked at from a distant, historical perspective. From sufferings, unparalleled in history, from bloody tears and bloody sweat, a chronicle of days of hell is being composed, in order that one may understand the historical reasons that shaped the human mind in this fashion, and created government systems which made possible the events through which we passed in our time. (Kermish 1986: 704)

Thus, the time structure of diaries was transformed from a continuity of past-present-future, which is typical of life-narratives, to a future perfect ("will have been"), in which the future determines the present retrospectively. This future is not in continuity with the present concerns of the writer. It is utterly different and unknown and will materialize only after the war. This means that the reality that the writer experiences does not exist in his present as a meaningful entity; on the contrary, it can exist only in the future and retrospectively, in a conceptual field determined by the future reader (the historian). It is as though, says the writer, at this time of catastrophe, I and the world do not exist and are not accessible by consciousness, but the future will enable our existence in retrospect.

Embedding History in One's Own Tragedy— the Synecdochical Diary

In synecdoche, a part represents the whole or vice versa, and in synecdochical diaries, the author writes about himself and his family. The story is of the way the whole (historical catastrophe) operates on the small part (the writer and his immediate surroundings). In many ways the synecdochical view is the authentic one of the victim whose main interest is survival. The author is focused on the self as a victim of history and has difficulty seeing beyond this situation. Such diaries tend to be shorter than documentary ones, sometimes only tens of pages. They are often concise and written in ascetic language, as though the writer's linguistic being is constricted. The language of personal record becomes a language of survival that wastes no energy on anything but the essential. Moshe Maltz kept a diary of this type in the town of Sokal (1993). The major part of the diary was written in hiding in a barn under constant threat of discovery. The diary tells of great dangers, chilling drama, generosity of heart, and enormous initiative, but is almost devoid of any reflective or emotional aspect, so that a reader learns almost nothing of what Jews felt as the drama was taking place. It focuses on the here and now of the writer, his struggle for his own and his family's survival.

Maltz describes an almost total war of all against all and the suspension of basic ethical norms in the face of the daily struggle for survival, although family units showed striking solidarity so long as they were intact. Following German sweeps through the ghetto, however, sexual mores deteriorated. Men whose wives had been murdered found other women overnight and dressed them in the murdered women's clothes, sometimes in return for a food ration that the new woman still obtained. Cultured women from important families kept company with members of the Jewish police in order to survive (1993: 68). Maltz's diary highlights typical features of texts of this kind—a focus on individual experience, prosaic language, terror, animal instincts, awareness, initiative, and blunted emotions—and displays an unusual facility in describing the struggle for survival.

Historiography has had difficulty relating to diaries that focus on microcosms and thus largely has ignored them. Most of these diaries have not been published and remain in archives. They are problematic as primary sources and even more so as objects of study because of their synecdochical viewpoint. Moreover, they highlight the extent to which the Holocaust is a single name for millions of individual experiences that resist historical generalization (Garbarini 2006; Waxman 2006). Only in recent years has research interest turned to these hundreds of diaries kept by ordinary Jews, and several historical works have focused attention on their synecdochical rendition of the way the catastrophe took place in the world of the individual.

Havi Dreifuss (née Ben-Sasson) makes extensive use of diaries, mostly from archives, to trace the image of the Poles among the Jews and how it changed during the war years. As with many historical studies of autobiographical writing, she is not interested in the reality presented in these texts, but rather in the consciousness that they reflect and that determines perceptions. She finds that at the outbreak of the war most of Polish Jewry had an impression of solidarity between Jews and Poles that collapsed only when the deportations and slaughter began in the spring and summer of 1942. Thereafter a fierce sense of betrayal, fury, and pain arose among the Jews (Ben-Sasson 2005: 180–8).

Whereas Dreifuss seeks to extract from Jews' diaries a broad generalization applicable to most of Polish Jewry, Alexandra Garbarini (2006) is interested in the diaries as a cultural phenomenon. She also deals with a wide range of texts, mostly from archives, using them to examine the various strategies that Jews employed in an attempt to explain their catastrophic reality and lend it meaning. Garbarini looks at subjects not previously studied, such as family, the impact of rumors, historical understanding, and the writers' understanding of self. She shows how some of the diarists adopted new epistemological paradigms in order to make reality comprehensible, while others relied on older structures. She also points out that some of the writers were aware of the crisis of language that they experienced in their attempts to represent such extreme events. In this the diarists prefigured theoretical discussions about representation of trauma that developed after the Holocaust (2006: 12–16). Finally, she argues that in contrast with other cultural practices that may have provided a momentary refuge, the diary brought the writer face to face with a painful reality over and over again. It was therefore both a distressing and a calming practice, and "diary writing could be self-effacing as well as self-legitimating" (2006: 163).

Jacek Leociak's research on Warsaw ghetto first-person documents (2004) presents another way to come to terms with the variety of synecdochical and other kinds of diaries. He uses poetic and anthropological guidelines to analyze these texts as forms of discourse. For example, he shows how personal and impersonal forms of narration intermingle and examines in a hermeneutical manner the discourse of life and death, indeed of religion in general.

Synecdochical diaries seem to challenge historiography at a deep level. Some contemporary thinkers argue that historical writing naturally tends to close off an event, even when that writing distinguishes between the event's various strata and is aware of the tensions and widely varying conflicting forces that operate within it (Brunner in Elm and Koessler 2007: 77). Historical writing therefore extracts from discussion some of the dynamic range, emotions, and local processes that are involved in any historical event. Much is lost in the process of generalization and construction of contextual and causal contiguity. From this perspective, diaries are the authentic embodiment of a multiplicity of directions, forces, voices, and silences that cannot be circumscribed or reduced. Thus, they present a problem for the historical and narrative procedures of generalization and organization (Nussbaum in Olney 1988: 128–40). The importance of the excess expressed in these chaotic texts increases precisely because something essential to the event of trauma is inscribed in that excess, namely an essence whose ungraspable character eludes any disciplined articulation. However, after the historical experience of Nazism, which pursued a course of radical exclusion, even destruction of all Otherness, some historians recognize an urgent need to open up historical narrative and procedures to potentially threatening aspects that undo artificial closure (2001: 148–50).

Saul Friedländer confronts this challenge in his *The Years of Extermination*, where quotations from diaries occupy a central place. He justifies that practice by arguing that diary excerpts pre-empt hasty generalizations and that:

An individual voice suddenly arising in the course of an ordinary historical narrative of events such as those presented here can ... pierce the (mostly involuntary) smugness of scholarly detachment and "objectivity." Such a disruptive function would hardly be necessary in a history of the price of wheat on the eve of the French Revolution, but it is essential to the historical representation of mass extermination. (Friedländer 2007: xxvi)

Later, Friedlander endorses disbelief as an authentic response to the world that historical practice attempts to tame by providing reasonable explanations: "In this book I wish to offer a thorough historical study of the extermination of the Jews of Europe without eliminating or domesticating that initial sense of disbelief" (2007: xxvi). The role of diaries is to preserve a degree of alienation and discomfort in his historical narrative. Worthy as the effort is, one might ask whether the technique of alienation through personal, contemporary voices still can disturb in an age when almost every current or historical event is immediately presented in the media via the individual witness. Might this technique actually achieve an opposite, comforting, and pleasurable effect nowadays, as the testimonies merely amplify the aesthetic and familiar status of historical narrative (Goldberg 2009)?

PROCESSES OF TRANSFORMATION—THE REFLECTIVE DIARY

Reflecting on the transformations that Jewish societies underwent under Nazi occupation, Oskar Rosenfeld (1884–1944) of the Łódź ghetto wrote, "the change of social, intellectual and economic functions brought with it a change in the most commonplace conceptions. Concepts that until then were understood unambiguously everywhere among Europeans underwent a complete transformation" (2002: 229). Many diaries reflect on this cultural transformation, and some make this reflection their major literary feature. Often the explicit or implicit theme of these diaries, most of them written in camps or during the terror and extermination from 1942 onwards, is the inability of an old conceptual world to express new reality. This observation, made during the great deportation from the Warsaw ghetto in summer 1942, may serve as a maxim for such texts: "The desire to write is as strong as the repugnance of words. We hate them, because they too often served as a cover for emptiness or meanness" (Kermish 1986: 704).

   This writing is born of a fundamentally ambivalent attitude toward language. It involves not only a wish to represent reality and experience, but also a competing sense that language betrays because it cannot match reality. Thus, Fela Szeps (1918–1945) wrote on 14 July 1942, while in the Gruenberg labor camp, "and if . . . someone calls what is happening to us 'a tragedy,' we laugh a bad, cynical laugh. No, this is not a tragedy, it has as yet no definition, a new term must be invented, non-existent and bloodcurdling like this reality" (2002: 23–4). At times this ambivalence reaches a crisis of confidence in language itself. As Abraham Lewin (1893–1943) wrote in the Warsaw ghetto on 25 May 1942, two months before the great deportations, "words are beyond us now" (1988: 97).

Diaries of this sort raise the question of the nature and perhaps even the existence of world, language, and even the human under the extreme conditions of the ghettos and the camps. In one of the last entries in her diary from Bergen-Belsen, Hanna Lévy-Hass (1913–2001) poignantly expresses this mood: "Everything manifest to one's eyes, all which occurs in front of one's eyes—raises doubts in one's heart about one's human qualities. Bit by bit, a hopeless and oppressive doubt establishes itself—doubt in the human" (2009: 90).

MEANING AND LOSS

All diaries present the victim as a polarized subject, disrupted by radical inner contradictions. Two interpretive approaches have evolved in response to this duality. The first highlights humanistic aspects of the diaries: the way the eternal human spirit is able to document and bear witness, to communicate with future readers, to hope and to lend meaning to reality even in the most catastrophic circumstances. Scholars of this approach often use the concept of resistance to emphasize the ability of the victim to stand up to the dehumanizing processes of Nazi persecution and murder through writing and to preserve his or her human identity. They celebrate diary writing as a victory of the human spirit and sometimes also of Jewish tradition (Gutman 1985: 72–90; Feldhay-Brenner 1994; Langford and West 1999; Wisse 2000; Waxman 2006).

Other researchers stress the pessimistic aspects of the diaries, including the deep fissures, melancholy tone, hopelessness, linguistic collapse, shocking content, and breakdown of solidarity expressed in the texts. Scholars adopting this approach do not see the diaries as an expression of victory of the human spirit, but argue that such a standpoint not only prettifies the reality of the Holocaust, but also constitutes a narcissistic attempt to retrieve a message of comfort for our own world and to avoid recognizing the atrocity that took place and the warning it gives about the fragility of humanity (Langer 1995; Patterson 1999). As the editor of a recent anthology of young people's Holocaust diaries states:

There are many fragments from history that can be regarded as evidence of humanity's achievements and its progress; these diaries unfortunately do not fall into that category . . . No celebration of the courage or grace of the writer's gesture can cover up the human fallibility and frailty that is captured within the diary pages. (Zapruder 2004: 9)

One might argue that until 1942 Jews' diaries told a story of resistance, continuity, and the preservation of meaning, but that after that date, the principal themes are chaos, breakage, and radical loss. But the matter is more complicated because the historical divide does not always match the individual experience expressed in the diaries. A more useful resolution of the controversy emphasizes that both readings are valid with reference to certain aspects of the diaries, and that precisely this duality is their most fundamental characteristic. These texts typically move between extremes that cannot be bridged, between the sharp narrating "I" and the powerless protagonist "I," between continuity and rupture, between awareness and numbness, between narrative and scream, between faith in words and frustration at their impotence, between temporality and trauma. The space between these poles, which dictates the poetics and dynamics of any autobiographical text, becomes in these diaries so extreme as to constitute a rupture that cannot be bridged, a theme that itself becomes a definitive feature of the Holocaust diary.

THE RECEPTION OF VICTIMS' DIARIES

A substantial body of recent scholarship has examined the reception of Holocaust diaries, since they have played an increasing role in the construction of Holocaust consciousness throughout the world. Naturally, the particular reception of any given text always reflects the local, cultural, and political context at the time of publication, as well as more universal factors. For example, the responses to the appearance of Anne Frank's diary in English in 1952, the Broadway play of 1955, and the Hollywood film of 1959 are connected closely to the situation of Jews and non-Jews in America during the 1950s and to the Cold War (Ezrahi 1980; Langer 1995; Loewy in Langford and West 1999: 156–74). Frank's diary was turned into a popular and uplifting consumer product that functioned as representative of the Holocaust for millions of people worldwide. Identification with the character of a young, charming, very western adolescent girl, whose diary was written in hiding and therefore omits the atrocities of the ghettos and the camps, smoothed and distorted the atrocious reality of the Holocaust in popular understanding. Thus Theodor Adorno (1903–1969) recalls a German woman saying after seeing the play, "yes, but at least this girl they should have allowed to live" (1998: 101). Most critics have targeted the happy ending given to the play, which makes one of the final entries in the diary (15 July 1944) into its (and the Holocaust's) entire message: "In spite of everything, I still believe that people are truly good at heart." Bruno Bettelheim (1903–1990) countered this succinctly: "If all men are good, there never was an Auschwitz" (1979: 254).

Victor Klemperer's diary, which appeared in print in 1995 and became a bestseller in Germany and abroad, is another fascinating case in point. The book's popularity stemmed in part from its usefulness as an antidote to the charges in Daniel Goldhagen's *Hitler's Willing Executioners*, which appeared in 1996. Goldhagen depicted

Germans as devotees of lethal antisemitism and charged them with eager ideological collaboration with the "Final Solution." Klemperer's diary presents a much more varied face of German society in the same period. As a result, in the course of German public discussion, an admiring view of Klemperer crystallized in Germany, and problematic aspects of the diary and his own conduct were suppressed. This view contributed to the configuration of Germany's western, humanistic identity during the period following unification (Traverso 1997). In particular, the diary was edited to give it a melodramatically happy ending: after 1,500 pages on the Nazi period, the journal leaves off, not at the end of the war on 8 May 1945 or at the end of that calendar year, but in June 1945 when the Klemperers return to the home in Dresden that they had fled after the fire-bombing of the city: "In the late afternoon, we walked up to Doelzschen" (Klemperer 1999, 1: 514). The remainder of the diary, which covers Klemperer's decisions to join the Communist Party and remain in East Germany, was published separately later.

Sometimes the wish to temper those discomfiting aspects of a diary that undermine identity leads to a radical rewriting of it. The most obvious example is the diary of Calek Perechodnik (1916–1944), a Jewish policeman from Otwock who helped round up Jews for deportation, including his own wife and daughter. Because the original diary records enormous self-loathing and distinctly anti-Polish feelings, both the English translation and the published Polish version omit major passages and drastically alter others in order to temper these aspects (Engel 1999). This tendency in translation is also typical of German diaries of the period (Langford and West 1999), and it undermines the credibility of even the English versions of classic texts, such as Chaim Kaplan's diary, whose translation is extremely biased and selective. Sometimes surviving diarists seem to have "corrected" their own diaries, tailoring them to their current worldview or to readers' tastes (Seidman 1997). Bowdlerization is so common as to appear to be a cultural trend. While different cultures are almost obsessive consumers of these diaries, as witnessed by their regular reprinting, those same cultures protect themselves by editing and rewriting to remove traumatic elements that disturb and disrupt identity.

CONCLUSION

Jews' diaries and chronicles of the Holocaust constitute both a source of information and a reflection of consciousness. They demonstrate strategies for creating meaning under traumatic conditions and how these fail. These texts provide a window into the world of the individual and the society of the time and embody the first literary response to catastrophe. Their reception is indicative of deep-seated cultural and political trends.

Three approaches to these texts deserve further exploration. The first is comparative analysis, particularly with autobiographical texts written during other catastrophes or extreme political events, such as other genocides. Comparing Holocaust diaries and their reception with diaries kept by soldiers during the World Wars or written during the Armenian genocide would be one potentially fruitful line of work. Post-colonialism also may provide an interesting framework in which to read the diaries, along the lines of several recent essays that compare post-Holocaust and post-colonial testimonies (Maier 2000; Rothberg 2006; Weiss in Zimmermann 2006: 161–76).

A second desideratum is a diachronic reading that situates Holocaust diaries in traditions of autobiographical writing in Europe in general and Jewish culture in particular. This approach entails not only literary criticism that notes themes and motifs taken from Jewish tradition, but also anthropological study that connects autobiographical writing with subjective understandings in various cultures, traditions, and periods.

A third new approach to the diaries would be in the spirit of anthropological history, the Annales School, and cultural history. Whereas current historical research into Jewish life during the Holocaust focuses mostly on formal and informal organizations, diaries could shift attention to the history of emotions, conceptualizations, consciousness, identities, and trauma and depict the experience of the individual and the meaning of social and cultural interactions under extreme circumstances and within a broad cultural context.

Such broad comparative and historical analysis would lend Jews' Holocaust diaries and chronicles widespread and even surprising significance, and thus would rescue them further from the marginality to which they have sometimes been relegated in Holocaust studies.

REFERENCES

ADORNO, T. (1998). *Critical Models*. New York: Columbia University Press.

ASCHHEIM, S. (2001). *Scholem, Arendt, Klemperer: Intimate Chronicles in Turbulent Times*. Bloomington, IN and Cincinnati, OH: Indiana University Press and Hebrew Union College.

BEN-AMOS, B. (2004). "A Multilingual Diary from the Lodz Ghetto." *Gal-Ed* 19: 51–74.

BEN-SASSON, H. (2005). *Poland and Poles in the Eyes of Polish Jews During the Second World War (1939–1944)*. Ph.D. thesis, Hebrew University of Jerusalem (in Hebrew).

BETTELHEIM, B. (1979). *Surviving, and Other Essays*. New York: Vintage Books.

BEZWINSKA, J. (ed.) (1973). *Amidst a Nightmare of Crime: Notes of Prisoners of Sonderkommando Found at Auschwitz*. Poland: State Museum at Oswiecim.

BUNKERS, S. and HUFF, C. (eds.) (1996). *Inscribing the Daily: Critical Essays on Women's Diaries*. Amherst, MA: University of Massachusetts Press.

DE COSTA, D. (1998). *Anne Frank and Etty Hillesum: Inscribing Spirituality and Sexuality*. New Brunswick, NJ: Rutgers University Press.

DOBROSZYCKI, L. (ed.) (1984). *The Chronicle of the Lodz Ghetto: 1941–1944*. New Haven, CT: Yale University Press.

ELM, M. and KOESSLER, G. (eds.) (2007). *Zeugenschaft des Holocaust: Zwischen Trauma, Tradierung und Ermittlung*. Frankfurt am Main: Campus Verlag.

ENGEL, D. (1999). "On the Bowdlerization of a Holocaust Testimony: The Wartime Journal of Calek Perechodnik." *Polin* 12: 316–29.

EZRAHI, S. (1980). *By Words Alone: The Holocaust in Literature*. Chicago, IL: University of Chicago Press.

FELDHAY-BRENNER, R. (1994). *Writing as Resistance: Four Women Confronting the Holocaust*. University Park, PA: The Pennsylvania State University Press.

——(2008). "Voices from Destruction: Two Eyewitness Testimonies from the Stanisławów Ghetto." *Holocaust and Genocide Studies* 22/2: 320–39.

FOTHERGIL, R. (1974). *Private Chronicles: A Study of English Diaries*. London: Oxford University Press.

FRANK, S. (1958). *A Diary from the Lodz Ghetto*. Tel Aviv: Menora (in Yiddish).

FRIEDLÄNDER, S. (2007). *The Years of Extermination: Nazi Germany and the Jews, 1939–1945*. New York: HarperCollins.

GARBARINI, A. (2006). *Numbered Days: Diaries and the Holocaust*. New Haven, CT: Yale University Press.

GOLDBERG, A. (2004). *The Helpless I: Diary Writing During the Holocaust*. Ph.D. thesis, Hebrew University of Jerusalem (in Hebrew).

——(2009). "The Victim's Voice and Melodramatic Aesthetics in History." *History and Theory* 48/3: 220–37.

GUTMAN, Y. (1985). *Struggles in Darkness: Studies in Holocaust and Resistance*. Israel: Moreshet & Sifriyat Po'alim and The Hebrew University (in Hebrew).

HARTMAN, G. (ed.) (1994). *Holocaust Remembrance: The Shapes of Memory*. Oxford: Blackwell.

HEER, H. (ed.) (1997). *Im Herzen der Finsternis: Victor Klemperer als Chronist der NS-Zeit*. Berlin: Aufbau Verlag.

KALMANOVITCH, Z. (1977). *A Diary from the Ghetto in Nazi Vilna*. Tel Aviv: Moreshet (in Hebrew).

KAPLAN, C. (1999). *Scroll of Agony: The Warsaw Diary of Chaim A. Kaplan*. Ed. A. Katsh. Bloomington, IN: Indiana University Press.

KASSOW, S. (2007). *Who Will Write Our History? Emanuel Ringelblum, the Warsaw Ghetto, and the Oyneg Shabes Archive*. Bloomington, IN: Indiana University Press.

KERMISH, J. (ed.) (1986). *To Live With Honor, To Die With Honor! Selected Documents from the Warsaw Ghetto Underground Archives "O.S."* ["Oneg Shabbath"]. Jerusalem: Yad Vashem.

KLEMPERER, V. (1999, 2001). *I Will Bear Witness: A Diary of the Nazi Years*. 2 vols. New York: The Modern Library.

LACAPRA, D. (2001). *Writing History Writing Trauma*. Baltimore, MD: The Johns Hopkins University Press.

LANGER, L. (1995). *Admitting the Holocaust: Collected Essays*. Oxford: Oxford University Press.

LANGFORD, R. and WEST, R. (eds.) (1999). *Marginal Voices, Marginal Forms: Diaries in European Literature and History*. Amsterdam: Rodopi B.V.

LEOCIAK, J. (2004). *Text in Face of Destruction: Accounts from the Warsaw Ghetto Reconsidered*. Warsaw: Żydowski Instytut Historyczny.

LÉVY-HASS, H. (2009). *Diary of Bergen-Belsen: 1944–1945*. Chicago: Haymarket Books.

LEWIN, A. (1988). *Cup of Tears: A Diary of the Warsaw Ghetto*. Oxford: Basil Blackwell.

MAIER, C. (2000). "Consigning the Twentieth Century to History: Alternative Narratives for the Modern Era." *American Historical Review* 105: 807–31.

MALTZ, M. (1993). *Years of Horror—Glimpse of Hope: The Diary of a Family in Hiding*. New York: Shengold.

MINTZ, A. (2001). *Popular Culture and the Shaping of Holocaust Memory in America*. Seattle, WA: University of Washington Press.

OLNEY, J. (ed.) (1988). *Studies in Autobiography*. New York and Oxford: Oxford University Press.

PASCAL, R. (1960). *Design and Truth in Autobiography*. Cambridge, MA: Harvard University Press.

PATTERSON, D. (1999). *Along the Edge of Annihilation: The Collapse and Recovery of Life in the Holocaust Diary*. Seattle, WA: University of Washington Press.

RINGELBLUM, E. (1958). *Notes from the Warsaw Ghetto*. New York: McGraw-Hill Book Company, Inc.

——(1994). *Last Writings & Polish–Jewish Relations: January 1943–April 1944*. Jerusalem: Yad Vashem (in Hebrew).

ROSENFELD, A. (1980). *A Double Dying: Reflections on Holocaust Literature*. Bloomington, IN: Indiana University Press.

ROSENFELD, O. (2002). *In the Beginning Was the Ghetto: Notebooks from Lodz*. Evanston, IL: Northwestern University Press.

ROTHBERG, M. (2006). "Between Auschwitz and Algeria: Multidirectional Memory and the Counterpublic Witness." *Critical Inquiry* 33: 158–84.

SCHLISSEL, L. (1982). *Women's Diaries of the Westward Journey*. New York: Schocken Books.

SEIDMAN, H. (1997). *The Warsaw Ghetto Diaries*. Southfield, MI: Targum.

SHAPIRO, M. (ed.) (1999). *Holocaust Chronicles: Individualizing the Holocaust through Diaries and other Contemporaneous Personal Accounts*. Hoboken, NJ: Yeshiva University Press and KTAV.

SIERAKOWIAK, D. (1996). *The Diary of Dawid Sierakowiak: Five Notebooks from the Lodz Ghetto*. New York: Oxford University Press.

SZEPS, F. (2002). *Blaze from Within: The Diary of Fela Szeps, the Greenberg Forced-Labor Camp*. Jerusalem: Yad Vashem (in Hebrew).

TRAVERSO, P. (1997). "Victor Klemperers Deutschlandbild." *Tel Aviver Jahrbuch für deutsche Geschichte* 26: 307–44.

WAXMAN, Z. (2006). *Writing the Holocaust: Identity, Testimony, Representation*. New York: Oxford University Press.

WEINTRAUB, K. (1966). *Visions of Culture*. Chicago, IL: University of Chicago Press.

WIEVIORKA, A. (2006). *The Era of the Witness*. Ithaca, NY: Cornell University Press.

WISSE, R. (2000). *The Modern Jewish Canon: A Journey through Language and Culture*. New York: The Free Press.

YAD VASHEM ARCHIVE, Jerusalem. 33/1032, Diary of Menachem Oppenheim.

YOUNG, J. (1988). *Writing and Rewriting the Holocaust.* Bloomington, IN: Indiana University Press.

ZAPRUDER, A. (2004). *Salvaged Pages: Young Writers' Diaries of the Holocaust.* New Haven, CT: Yale University Press.

ZELKOWICZ, J. (2002). *In Those Terrible Days: Notes from the Lodz Ghetto.* Jerusalem: Yad Vashem.

ZIMMERMANN, M. (ed.) (2006). *On Germans and Jews under the Nazi Regime: Essays by Three Generations of Historians.* Jerusalem: Hebrew University Magnes Press.

OTHER SUGGESTED READING

ADELSON, A. and LAPIDES, R. (ed.) (1989). *Lodz Ghetto: Inside a Community Under Siege.* New York: Viking Press.

FRIEDMAN, S. (ed.) (1992). *The Terezin Diary of Gonda Redlich.* Lexington, KY: The University Press of Kentucky.

HILBERG, R., STARON, S., and KERMISZ, J. (eds.) (1979). *The Warsaw Diary of Adam Czerniakow.* New York: Stein and Day.

KORCZAK, Y. (1978). *Ghetto Diary.* New Haven, CT: Yale University Press.

KRUK, H. (2002). *The Last Days of the Jerusalem of Lithuania: Chronicles from the Vilna Ghetto and the Camps 1939–1944.* Bloomington, IN: Indiana University Press.

LAMBERT, R. (2007). *Diary of a Witness.* Chicago, IL: Ivan R. Dee.

RUBINOWICZ, D. (1982). *The Diary of David Rubinowicz.* Edmonds, WA: Creative Options.

CHAPTER 27

SURVIVORS' ACCOUNTS

HENRY GREENSPAN

AT least 100,000 survivors' accounts have been collected since 1944 in many languages, contexts, and formats. Even among scholars and archivists who have spent their lives working with such texts, no one has engaged more than a tiny fraction of them. How our understanding will evolve as a result of listening to new voices or listening better to voices we already know is impossible to predict. In the meantime, readers have attended to survivors such as Charlotte Delbo (1913–1985), Primo Levi (1919–1987), and Elie Wiesel (b. 1928), whose works are the heart of the contemporary "canon." Their reflections, especially Levi's, figure centrally in this chapter, as do those of Abe, Agi, Leon, Lydia, and Reuben. Indispensable teachers and friends, they are survivors whom I have interviewed and re-interviewed many times since the mid-1970s.

Speaking generally, recounting can be considered as a noun or a verb, a product or a process. As a noun, recounting is a fixed and finished thing. It is what appears in archives, excerpts, and documentary films. Taken as a noun, recounting entails an external perspective. One might want to catalog: How many accounts have been published, where, and when? Or one might want to summarize applications: In what ways have survivors' accounts served historiography, psychology, or philosophical reflection? Approaching recounting as a verb, by contrast, means to focus on the process of retelling. How do survivors find words and forms for their memories? What motivates their attempts to do so? In what ways do survivors' listeners (and survivors' perceptions of their listeners) impact what survivors relay? What is the impact on retelling of literary precedents or survivors' wider life histories? This chapter considers recounting both as a noun and a verb, but the emphasis is on recounting as a process. That is, literally, "where the action is"; it foregrounds survivors' own perspectives, and it reflects the state of the field. Sixty years after liberation, scholars have learned much about how to use survivors' accounts— particularly in pedagogy, documentary film, and historiography—but understand far less about the accounts themselves; that is, about all that has shaped their creation (Hartman 1996; Kushner 2006).

A word about "accounts" rather than "testimonies," the more usual term. On one level, the choice reflects the sheer diversity of forms: memoirs and essays, postwar diaries and meditations, audio and video recordings for a wide variety of purposes. Within that multiplicity, "accounts" seems the more inclusive term, with "testimony" being one important subtype. Furthermore, reflecting its use in judicial and religious contexts to refer to formal declarations of witness or of faith, "testimony" suggests an account that is definitive, as fixed and finished as possible (Greenspan 2010). If one views recounting as a process, "accounts" leaves room for what is unfixed and unfinished, contingent and accidental—like surviving itself.

ORIGINS

In both oral and written recounting, Holocaust survivors do not just retell memories of the destruction. They also discuss the nature of memory, the limits of the communicable, the impact of listeners, and the vicissitudes of faith—in short, all the issues that have also occupied Holocaust scholars. Thus, survivors' accounts are not only, and often not primarily, "oral history." They are equally "oral psychology," "oral narratology," and more, an interweaving of narrative and non-narrative content. Primo Levi intended his *Survival in Auschwitz*, which was written immediately after World War II, not as another "account of atrocities," but rather "to furnish documentation for a quiet study of certain aspects of the human mind" (1996: 9). That said, more compelled Levi, especially then, than contributing to moral psychology. He recalled that "the need to tell our story to 'the rest,' to make 'the rest' participate in it, had taken on for us, before our liberation and after, the character of an immediate and violent impulse" (1996: 9). Of course, not every survivor was driven to tell and retell. But for those who were, the first recounting emerged as a kind of scream—simultaneously, an effort to awaken, to reverse traumatic muteness, and, above all, to call for help (Des Pres 1976). Auschwitz survivor Jean Améry (1912–1978) insisted, "The experience of the persecution was, at the very bottom, that of an extreme *loneliness*" (1980: 70). No one described better than Améry the hopelessness that comes when, scream as one may, nobody hears: for Améry, as for others, the feeling was both a personal experience and an archetype for the Holocaust as a whole.

On one level, then, survivors' earliest accounts sought out "the rest." The several large testimony projects (the right word here) that emerged before or immediately after liberation had similar goals: the crimes would be documented, the world would know, and justice (and sometimes vengeance) would be served (Greenspan 2001; Wieviorka 2006). Usually organized by survivors themselves, historical commissions and documentation centers were set up throughout Poland, in the displaced persons' camps, in Hungary, France, and elsewhere. By the end of 1947, more than 10,000 accounts had been collected, including transcribed oral interviews, responses to questionnaires, and freely written retelling, and hundreds of survivors independently had "set down their recollections, even before they rebuilt their homes" (Krakowski in Gutman and Avital 1985: 395). In this context, the 109 interviews of survivors conducted by American psychologist David Boder (1886–1961) in 1946 are noteworthy because they were done by an outsider and electronically recorded (Boder 1949; Niewyk 1998). Boder's work is often viewed as a precursor to the large audio and video testimony archives that were not founded until a generation later.

Survivors also looked back to the world that had been destroyed. Begun soon after liberation, hundreds of "memorial books" (*Yizkor Bikher*) were eventually created as collective remembrances of Yiddish culture and the communities that sustained it. Modeled on earlier memorial forms, the Yizkor books sought both to "reconstitute the lost object" and "to retrace its death throes" (Wieviorka 2006: 26). They were, in effect, the first Holocaust memorials (Young 1993).

Important for their own sake, the Yizkor books also represent one of the forms of remembrance that survivors created mainly among themselves. Behind public retelling, there was always a communal conversation—survivors recounting to each other—and it continues into the present. Indeed, before writing there was talk, both among survivors and sometimes more widely. Of his homecoming, Levi recalled: "Nobody could speak of anything else or permit others to speak of anything else . . . I repeated my stories dozens of times in just a few days . . . Then I realized that my tale was crystallizing into a definitive and unchanging form. All I needed in order to write it all down was paper, pen and time" (in Belpoliti 2005: 24). With regard to Levi's first memoir, one of his biographers summarizes: "Before he came to write each episode, he had already told it many times. He knew it worked—and not just for him. It worked on *them*" (Angier 2002: 443).

SURVIVORS AND THEIR LISTENERS

Despite different emphases and approaches, commentators have arrived at a general consensus about the key dimensions of survivors' recounting. To have survived the Holocaust means, at core, to live in two constantly juxtaposed but never integrated worlds. And to recount the Holocaust is, most essentially, an effort of translation: an attempt to use the terms of one world (the world survivors share with us) to describe the terms, and the negation of terms, of the other. Viewed from a different angle, recounting emerges from what survivors anticipate will be both tellable by them and hearable by their audience; it constitutes a "double transaction" comprising an "inner dialogue, always embattled, between survivors' speech and survivors' memories, and an outer dialogue, equally contested, between survivors and their listeners" (Greenspan 2010: 42). In actual retelling, survivors' assessments of the tellable and the hearable occur simultaneously; recounting always reflects both. But, for analytic purposes, this section focuses mainly on listeners and the following section deals with issues of the tellable. Either way, the point is that the part is not the whole. The account as given has to be measured against what was judged *not* tellable or hearable.

No such analysis can be more than tracks in a forest. The contingencies that shape retelling are so various that a complete description, even of a single instance, will always be beyond our grasp. As an eminent authority notes, even when survivors share very similar histories, "the details of recollection are so modified by so many distinct factors—memory, personality, extent of loss, duration of imprisonment, health, moral attitude, depth of spiritual commitment—that no unified view emerges from the testimony" (Langer 1985). Still, the absence of a "unified view" does not mean that we cannot learn important things.

For written accounts, the most obvious impact of the survivors' audience is simply upon getting published. Although very few of the earliest accounts, whether collected by historical commissions or written independently, ever appeared in print, more memoirs were published in 1945–1947 than in any three-year period until the 1960s. A substantial increase in memoir publication then took place during the 1970s, and the rate continued to climb through the 1990s (Rozett in Roth and Maxwell 2001). As of this writing, some 6–10,000 survivor memoirs have been printed worldwide. Even so, only a handful of survivor memoirs ever have been read widely. Whereas some writers, such as Robert Antelme (1917–1990) in France, enjoyed national prominence relatively early, only Viktor Frankl (1905–1997), Wiesel, and Levi have achieved international renown. The "academic canon" also includes Améry, Delbo, and, more recently, Ruth Kluger (b. 1931) (Baron in Jacobs 2009).

Even the now "classic" memoirs struggled to see the light. Levi's *Se questo è un uomo* (*If This is a Man*, widely known in English as *Survival in Auschwitz*) essentially disappeared after a small print run in 1947, gaining a precarious second life when Einaudi, without confidence, brought it out again in 1958 (Angier 2002: 502–4). Wiesel's *Night* (2006) was originally written in Yiddish and published in 1956 in Argentina. As its initial title suggests, *Un di Velt hot geshvign* (*And the World Was Silent*) was an angrier and more accusing book than the leaner *La Nuit* published in France in 1958, a change that has been interpreted variously (Seidman

1996; Mintz 2001; Wieviorka 2006). Delbo had written the first two volumes of her trilogy, *Auschwitz and After*, by 1947. But she held onto them until the 1960s, perhaps waiting for a more receptive time (Langer, introduction to Delbo 1995). In fact, a good many memoirs got "second lives" in republished or revised editions, often with the help of other media. Gerda Klein's (b. 1924) 1957 memoir, *All But My Life*, was virtually unknown until the 1995 (Oscar and Emmy) award-winning documentary, *One Survivor Remembers*. A number of memoirs have been complemented by dramatic adaptations, including radio and staged versions of *If This is a Man* in the 1960s (Levi in Belpoliti 2005) and, more recently, Antony Sher's 2005 dramatization, *Primo*. Delbo, always a dramatist, included parts of *None of Us Will Return* in her play *Who Will Carry the Word?*, written in the 1960s and first staged in 1974 (Skloot 1982).

While memoirs with universal and redemptive messages have certainly had an advantage—Frankl's *Man's Search for Meaning* (1971) is the clearest example—the wider point is that the public appetite for survivors' accounts has always been limited. The contemporary suggestion that there is a "glut" of such writing has been asserted many times since 1945 (Niewyk 1998: 5; Thomson 2002: 244, 444). Likewise, even the best-known memoirs have relied upon reissues, adaptations, and good fortune. Still, very few memoirists have simply tried to "please" their readers. Indeed, countering readers' expectations (which is also a way of taking them into consideration) has not been uncommon. The acid ironies of Améry come to mind, as does Kluger's remark to her readers that her memoir might require them "to rearrange a lot of furniture in their inner museum of the Holocaust" (2001: 73).

The impact of listeners is most evident in face-to-face retelling, particularly in the interviewing projects that blossomed in the 1980s and 1990s. Still, the history of these parallels that of written accounts in many respects. After the immediate post-liberation period, survivors were often actively silenced: "Don't talk about it," "Hush up your bad dreams" (Wiesel 1978; Bolkosky 2002; Greenspan 2010). While political culture played a selective role—in Israel, for example, stories of armed resistance were welcomed (Yablonka 2004)—the consistency of the silencing is more impressive than the differences. Whether motivated by listeners' guilt, anxiety, or good intentions ("it is healthier to forget"), the result was the same. The reversal of this situation, and the emergence of the survivor in the public role of "witness" has been variously described and explained (Greenspan in Flanzbaum 1999; Novick 1999; Wieviorka 2006), but most observers agree that the 1961 trial of Adolf Eichmann (1906–1962) played a pivotal role, particularly in Israel (Yablonka 2004), and that the 1978 television miniseries "Holocaust" marked another turning point. By the late 1970s, especially in the United States, survivors were increasingly celebrated as a group. The large survivor oral history projects both reflected and furthered the overall trend, generating nearly 80 percent of *all* survivors' accounts to date. Yale's Fortunoff Archive, founded in 1979, contains over 4,300 "video testimonies." Yad Vashem in Jerusalem possesses roughly 10,000 recorded accounts and the United States Holocaust Memorial Museum in Washington another 10,000. Founded in 1994, the Survivors of the Shoah Visual History Foundation (now the USC Shoah Foundation Institute for Visual History and Education) has yielded more than 50,000 video accounts.

As would be expected, survivors have responded variously to their new-found status. Speaking of his public recounting, Abe asks, "Am I doing it to show what kind of hero I was?" He answers his own question, "Well, let's be honest! Sure! Why not?! A little recognition!" (Greenspan 2010: 103). Abe's retelling never loses track of its wider context, but that does not prevent him from recalling episodes when guts and initiative did, indeed, seem to play a critical role. Other survivors comply with listener expectations outwardly but resist surreptitiously. Thus, Agi Rubin describes being put off by an interviewer's overly controlling format. In response, Agi reversed the field: "I am ashamed to tell you. I felt like I took over the whole thing . . . And she [the interviewer] says, 'You're wonderful! I didn't have to ask you anything!'" (Greenspan and Bolkosky 2006: 444). While the interviewer was grateful, what Agi said that day was itself preformatted—"the usual spiel," as she also described it. Still other survivors push back directly, for example Moses S., an interviewee who seemed driven to "offend our sense of order, reason, and civilized behavior" by retelling one degradation story after the other (Langer 1991: 28). Even after everyone else in the studio tried to end the interview, Moses S. is heard saying: "And more, and more, and more. Do you want to hear more?"

As these instances suggest, not only do survivors' responses to the perceived "hearable" vary enormously, but so also do the ways survivors approach the interview situation as a whole. In early descriptions of video testimony, much was said about its seeming immediacy, particularly in contrast with written accounts. "We quite literally watch the narrator organize his testimony," James Young noted. "[W]itness is quite literally being made before our eyes" (1988: 161). Clearly, there are many permutations. Some survivors do seem to create their accounts spontaneously, facilitated only by the presence of a willing listener. Others provide "the usual spiel," honed over multiple retellings. For many, probably most, what emerges is a complex co-creation *between* interviewer and interviewee (Young 1988). In any event, the spontaneous is neither inherently more authentic than the honed nor necessarily more representative of what a survivor has to convey.

Premising that the overall goal is the richest (most inclusive, detailed, and nuanced) possible representation of what different survivors have to convey, discussion is very much alive over what interview approaches are most likely to attain it: a single interview or several, on site or in the studio, open-ended questions or more specific ones, video recording or audio. These options and others have their advocates (Laub in Felman and Laub 1992; Hartman 1996; Greenspan and Bolkosky 2006; Jonker 2007), but even specialists know relatively little about what is substantively gained or lost through such alternative approaches. Particular goals, varied contexts, and different interviewers and interviewees affect the outcomes. Accumulated experience underscores the importance of knowing the survivor's specific history and engaging him or her with as much attentiveness and as little presumption as possible. Based on their varying experiences in different projects, survivors themselves also have remarked upon the importance of such interviewer "virtues" (Greenspan and Bolkosky 2006).

THE PROBLEM OF THE TELLABLE

Even with the most willing and responsive listeners, a survivor can convey only so much. The problem of the "incommunicable" in survivors' recounting is taken up by popular rhetoric about "unspeakable memories," by scholarly discourse on "the limits of representation," and by survivors themselves. For survivors, the question is two-sided. On the one hand, what of essential importance *can* be communicated? On the other hand, what may "work too well," creating only an illusion of coherence (Horowitz 1997: 43)? Survivors' accounts are, therefore, often characterized by simultaneous assertion and disclaimer. In spoken retelling, the disclaimer is often explicit. "I have told you nothing," "None of that is it," "And more, and more, and more." In memoirs, particularly those that are self-consciously literary, negation may be built into their form. Thus, one expert emphasizes the "revisionary and essentially antithetical nature of so much of Holocaust writing, which not only mimics and parodies but finally refutes and rejects its direct literary antecedents" (Rosenfeld 1980: 29). Although frames and analogies are employed, "in almost all cases the gains in perspective are only temporary," and "such analogies are introduced only to reveal their inadequacies" (21). Focusing on "the figure of muteness" in Holocaust fiction, another astute scholar describes narrative strategies that apply to many memoirs and to spoken recounting as well: "discontinuous plot and chronology," "a halting, stammering style," or a "hyperfluency that simultaneously tenders and denies all possibility of meaning" (Horowitz 1997: 39).

Of course, the deliberate use of a "halting, stammering style" differs from silences that reflect direct intrusions of memory. Although distinguishing between the practiced and the spontaneous in survivors' recounting is often impossible, distinguishing between what is mainly a literary challenge and what is more than that is important. One year after liberation, in April 1946, Agi Rubin awoke from an Auschwitz nightmare and tried to write about it. She and her diary were her only imagined readers.

This cannot be true. That I am here, on this earth, all by myself. That there is fire. That there are people. That there are bones. That there are the suffocated innocents . . .

My pen wants to go on and on, by itself. It is sliding from my hand. At times like this my strength leaves me. It leaves me each time I see it all again. It leaves me when I see the truth once more. (Rubin and Greenspan 2006: 102–3)

Langer (1982, 1991) has rightly warned against underestimating how much a dedicated listener *can* imagine what survivors attempt to retell. Still, there is a difference between directly remembering and what can be known even through the most attuned imagination. For Agi, that difference is reflected in a dropped pen and in consuming exhaustion.

For survivors, then, the problem of the tellable is, literally, embodied. Lydia, who endured the Lwów ghetto and several years in hiding, lost her voice during the war and only gradually retrieved it. Even now voids open in Lydia's speech that are more like holes than silences; for her, the "unspeakable" is not a literary problem (Greenspan 2010). Even Levi might not have been precise when he wrote that "those who saw the Gorgon . . . have not returned to tell about it, or have returned mute" (1988: 83–4). Some returned mute who do, indeed, also tell about it.

Being muted could be temporary but impact recounting and a survivor's understanding of what retelling requires. Leon attempted to describe a liquidated ghetto, with growing frustration over his inability to do so. He finally said:

Entering the ghetto in a dead silence . . . This is probably what makes it so unbelievable. This pure landscape of death . . . It appears to be devoid of the human element, of the redeeming feature of a human emotion. . . . Even sound, even sound would be out of place. There is no sound actually. There is no sound. (Greenspan 2010: 200)

Leon intends to evoke not only a "landscape of death" but also a psychologically-dead landscape. Levi evoked a similar landscape through the "atavistic anguish" that he associated with the second verse of Genesis: "a deserted and empty universe crushed under the spirit of God but from which the spirit of man is absent: not yet born or already extinguished" (1988: 85).

Descriptions like these may be understood more accurately as knowledge than as memory, a persisting awareness rather than the recollection of particular events. Indeed, Levi insisted that the hardest thing to convey was the all-pervasive "lack of events . . . because memory works in precisely the opposite way: the single, clamorous terrifying episodes, or conversely the happy moments, prevail and invade the canvas, whereas as one lives them they are a part of a totally disintegrated reality" (in Belpoliti and Gordon 2001: 251). "Totally disintegrated reality" was also Levi's recurring nightmare in the aftermath. Rather than terrifying episodes, what returned was disintegration itself, and the knowledge that it carried: "As the dream proceeds, slowly or brutally, each time in a different way, everything collapses and disintegrates around me . . . I am alone in the centre of a grey and turbid nothing, and now, I *know* what this thing means, and I know that I have always known it; I am in the Lager once more, and nothing is true outside the Lager" (1987: 193).

How does one recount "a totally disintegrated reality," a "grey and turbid nothing"? Written accounts conform to no specific set of genres. The best known writers tend to return to aspects that, to them, signify the whole: to Levi, moral devolution; to Delbo, the sensory agonies of thirst, exhaustion, and stench; and to Wiesel, betrayals between creators and creatures, fathers and sons. Most survivors confirm Levi's distinction between the retold and the actually remembered: they recount a series of "terrifying episodes" and "happy moments" (uncanny in context yet part of it), but also insist that none of that is what it was. That is why so many memoirs are organized by multiple short chapters, and spoken accounts by "encapsulated" episodes (Kraft 2002: 29), rather than by an overarching narrative. Typically, survivors retell in bits what they know as a disintegrated whole.

Preoccupied with the problem of the tellable, Leon described a further strategy that also echoes Levi: "How do you describe a nightmare? Something which is shapeless, amorphous . . . It is *not* a story. It has to be *made* a story. In order to convey it. And with all the frustration that implies" (Greenspan 2010: 199). One way survivors "make a story" of what is "not a story" is to tell their own story *as* recounters. Thus, Wiesel notes how often "the story of the messenger" becomes the story "of the messenger unable to deliver his message" (1972: 16). Horowitz similarly describes recounters who do not trust their capacity to "write successfully about the catastrophe" and instead write "only of their struggle to do so" (1997: 37). Much that we usually consider survivors' general reflections—accounts of lost faith or personal guilt, for example—also function as tellable and hearable narratives. Anguished as they may be, such accounts more closely resemble tragedy than atrocity, exactly because they are the stories of personal fates rather than attempts to describe an entirely impersonal destruction. "Tragedy is manifest in the individual, in his well-defined personal suffering," wrote Aharon Appelfeld (b. 1932). "The dimensions of our suffering could not be fully expressed in an individual soul" (1994: 33). Retelling atrocity as tragedy, as the particular suffering of a particular soul, thus becomes another way survivors "make a story" of what is "not a story" (Greenspan 2010: 197–202). All such stories point beyond themselves, often to an exhaustion or futility that they cannot contain. Once again, we must be wary of mistaking the made story for the whole story, terrifying episodes for an all-consuming disintegration.

BEYOND HISTORY AND MEMORY

The "oral psychology" in survivors' recounting is as essential as the "oral history." As one authority aptly writes, survivors' accounts "*can* be a source for historical information and confirmation, yet their real strength lies in recording the psychological and emotional milieu of the struggle for survival, not only then but also now" (Hartman 1996: 142). The converse point might apply to the work of survivors such as Saul Friedländer (b. 1932) or Israel Gutman (b. 1923), who became professional historians. For them, as for us, narrative history may also be a way to "make a story" for what is "not a story."

Still, the relationship between historiography and survivors' accounts has been uneasy. While a number of survivor-historians, such as Gutman or Yitzhak Arad (b. 1926), drew on such accounts from the beginning, the arguments against the documentary use of survivors' accounts are well known: survivors' memories are unreliable; they become even less reliable with time; and they are inevitably shaped by representations of the Holocaust in popular culture, especially in film.

Here, two issues tend to be conflated: the consistency of survivors' retelling and its historical accuracy; after all, people can be consistently inaccurate. Regarding the stability of survivors' accounts over time and within different cultural contexts, only a few small studies (Kraft 2002; Browning 2003; Schiff 2005) have occurred, but the evidence suggests a surprising degree of consistency both between accounts by the same survivor at different times and concerning the overall qualities (e.g., amount of detail) of early accounts and those collected decades later. Based on his study of the Starachowice slave labor camp, Christopher Browning observed that "survivor memories proved to be more stable and less malleable" than he had anticipated (2003: 47). As to accuracy, Yehuda Bauer (2001: 24) has suggested that aging may even have advantages: a memory more focused on early experiences, greater detachment, and fewer reasons to be selective (e.g., protecting others still alive) than in earlier years. Browning found that some events, indeed, seem to "require a passage of time and the appropriate setting before witnesses are willing to speak," while noting that his study generally counters the presumption that, as years pass, survivors' accounts become more "simplified and sanitized" (2003: 81).

None of this means that experiences are somehow "imprinted" in survivors' memories as they occurred. As in all eyewitness accounts, versions differ, and many do not accord with facts otherwise known. Browning (2003, 2010) describes the painstaking and uncertain process of weighing contrary accounts against each other and against other documentary sources. Likewise, consistency is always relative, and cultural, individual, and interview-related factors significantly affect it (Schiff 2005). Still, the consistency that emerges is noteworthy, particularly at the level of episodes recalled. It may reflect the honing of accounts over many retellings as well as features of traumatic memory in general (Schacter 1996; McNally 2003).

At this writing, the use of survivor accounts as one documentary source appears to be becoming less controversial. Such accounts have been essential in studies of slave labor, the *Sonderkommandos*, and a range of local "microhistories" (Browning 2003, 2010; Greif 2005). Studies of victims' perceptions and resulting actions necessarily rely on contemporaneous writing (diaries or letters) or on later recollection (Young 1988; Friedländer 2007). Above all, "an individual voice suddenly arising in the course of an ordinary historical narrative ... can tear through seamless interpretation and pierce the (mostly involuntary) smugness of scholarly detachment and 'objectivity'" (Friedländer 2007: xxvi). For Saul Friedländer, such disruptions are precisely what historical narratives of the Holocaust require: reminders of the extremity retold.

Tony Kushner (2006) worries that the inclusion of victims' voices typically does *not* disrupt historical narrative. On the contrary, as excerpts from accounts are woven into histories, museum exhibits, or documentary films, they are most often "illustrative" and subservient to a still seamless whole. What is missing, Kushner argues, is attention to the act of retelling itself and its "internal dynamics, especially in relation to the rest of the person's life story" (279). When manifest only in memory bits, "the totality of the individual concerned is at best obscured and at worst utterly removed" (291). Kushner thus calls for studies of recounting within the thick context of individual lives; he favors a "life story" approach that draws on history, psychology, and narrative analysis but is really a subdiscipline of its own. This perspective means choosing depth over breadth and welcoming life stories' inevitable contradictions and mythologies as informative in their own right (Roseman 2000; Rothberg 2000; Bolkosky 2002; Greenspan 2010).

Whether pursuing Kushner's approach or weighing multiple accounts as Browning has done, most recent work exhibits an empirical turn in the engagement of survivors' retelling. Indeed, every core issue raised in this chapter—the impact of audience and context, forms and strategies in retelling, consistency and contingency in memory, advantages and disadvantages of different interviewing approaches—calls out for more systematic examination. Even well known voices deserve closer attention. In his last book, *The Drowned and the Saved*, Levi concluded that "the worst survived, that is, the fittest; the best all died" (1988: 82). But in 1986, the year of the book's original publication in Italian, Levi also said: "In the camp to be a *Mensch* was a factor in survival" although "not every survivor was a *Mensch*" (in Belpoliti and Gordon 2001: 25). Fortunately perhaps, in the same year he *also* said (to Philip Roth), "Please grant me the right to inconsistency" (Levi 1996: 180). In granting inconsistency, we may honor Primo Levi most of all.

Meanwhile so many voices remain outside the known and the read. In recent years, the earliest accounts have received increasing attention. Ten thousand of them have been translated into Hebrew (Greif 2007). New work has appeared on the early accounts by children, as the experiences of child survivors in general have come to seem less marginal (Cohen 2007; Michlic 2007). And, of course, the great majority of survivors have not recounted at all except perhaps to each other. With their passing, we will never know what they might have told us.

REFERENCES

AMÉRY, J. (1980). *At the Mind's Limits: Contemplations by a Survivor on Auschwitz and its Realities*. Bloomington, IN: Indiana University Press.

ANGIER, C. (2002). *The Double Bond: Primo Levi—A Biography*. New York: Farrar, Straus & Giroux.

APPELFELD, A. (1994). *Beyond Despair*. New York: Fromm.

BAUER, Y. (2001). *Rethinking the Holocaust*. New Haven, CT: Yale University Press.

BELPOLITI, M. (ed.) (2005). *Primo Levi: The Black Hole of Auschwitz*. Cambridge: Polity Press.

——and GORDON, R. (eds.) (2001). *Primo Levi: The Voice of Memory, Interviews, 1961–1987*. New York: The New Press.

BODER, D. (1949). *I Did Not Interview the Dead*. Urbana, IL: University of Illinois Press.

BOLKOSKY, S. (2002). *Searching for Meaning in the Holocaust*. Westport, CT: Greenwood Press.

BROWNING, C. (2003). *Collected Memories: Holocaust History and Postwar Testimony*. Madison, WI: University of Wisconsin Press.

——(2010). *Remembering Survival: Inside a Nazi Slave-labor Camp*. New York: W. W. Norton.

COHEN, B. (2007). "The Children's Voice: Postwar Collection of Testimonies from Child Survivors of the Holocaust." *Holocaust and Genocide Studies* 21/1: 73–95.

DELBO, C. (1995). *Auschwitz and After*. New Haven, CT: Yale University Press.

DES PRES, T. (1976). *The Survivor: An Anatomy of Life in the Death Camps*. Oxford: Oxford University Press.

FELMAN, S. and LAUB, D. (1992). *Testimony: Crises of Witnessing in Literature, Psychoanalysis, and History*. New York: Routledge.

FLANZBAUM, H. (ed.) (1999). *The Americanization of the Holocaust*. Baltimore, MD: Johns Hopkins University Press.

FRANKL, V. (1971). *Man's Search for Meaning*. New York: Pocket Books.

FRIEDLÄNDER, S. (2007). *The Years of Extermination: Nazi Germany and the Jews, 1939–1945*. New York: HarperCollins.

GREENSPAN, H. (2001). "The Awakening of Memory: Survivor Testimony in the First Years after the Holocaust, and Today." *Center for Advanced Holocaust Studies*. Washington, DC: United States Holocaust Memorial Museum.

——(2010). *On Listening to Holocaust Survivors: Beyond Testimony*. 2nd edn. St. Paul, MN: Paragon House.

——and BOLKOSKY, S. (2006). "When Is an Interview an Interview? Notes from Listening to Holocaust Survivors." *Poetics Today* 27/2: 431–49.

GREIF, G. (2005). *We Wept Without Tears: Testimonies of the Jewish Sonderkommando from Auschwitz*. New Haven, CT: Yale University Press.

——(2007). "The Big Project of the Holocaust—Translating Testimonies at Yad Vashem." *International Journal on Audio-Visual Testimony* 12: 85–7.

GUTMAN, Y. and AVITAL, S. (eds.) (1985). *She'erit Haplaytah, 1944–1948: Rehabilitation and Political Struggle*. Jerusalem: Yad Vashem.

HARTMAN, G. (1996). *The Longest Shadow: In the Aftermath of the Holocaust*. Bloomington, IN: Indiana University Press.

HOROWITZ, S. (1997). *Voicing the Void: Muteness and Memory in Holocaust Fiction*. Albany, NY: State University of New York Press.

JACOBS, S. (ed.) (2009). *Maven in Blue Jeans: A Festschrift in Honor of Zev Garber*. West Lafayette, IN: Purdue University Press.

JONKER, E. (2007). "No Other Destiny: Turning the Holocaust Experience into a Central Theme in Life and Work." *International Journal on Audio-Visual Testimony* 12: 89–108.

KLEIN, G. (1957). *All But My Life*. New York: Hill and Wang.

KLUGER, R. (2001). *Still Alive: A Holocaust Girlhood Remembered*. New York: The Feminist Press at the City University of New York.

KUSHNER, T. (2006). "Holocaust Testimony, Ethics, and the Problem of Representation." *Poetics Today* 27/2: 275–95.

KRAFT, R. (2002). *Memory Perceived: Recalling the Holocaust*. Westport, CT: Praeger Publishers.

LANGER, L. (1982). *Versions of Survival: The Holocaust and the Human Spirit*. Albany, NY: State University of New York Press.

——(1985). "Preliminary Reflections on the Videotaped Interviews at the Yale Archive for Holocaust Testimonies." *Facing History and Ourselves News*, Winter 1985: 4–5.

——(1991). *Holocaust Testimonies: The Ruins of Memory*. New Haven, CT: Yale University Press.

LEVI, P. (1987). *The Reawakening*. New York: Collier Books.

——(1988). *The Drowned and the Saved*. New York: Vintage International.

——(1996). *Survival in Auschwitz: The Nazi Assault on Humanity*. New York: Simon & Schuster.

MCNALLY, R. (2003). *Remembering Trauma*. Cambridge, MA: Harvard University Press.

MICHLIC, J. (2007). "Who Am I? Jewish Children's Search for Identity in Post-War Poland." *Polin* 20: 98–121.

MINTZ, A. (2001). *Popular Culture and the Shaping of Holocaust Memory in America*. Seattle, WA: University of Washington Press.

NIEWYK, D. (1998). *Fresh Wounds: Early Narratives of Holocaust Survival*. Chapel Hill, NC: University of North Carolina Press.

NOVICK, P. (1999). *The Holocaust in American Life*. Boston, MA: Houghton Mifflin.

ROSEMAN, M. (2000). *A Past in Hiding: Memory and Survival in Nazi Germany*. New York: Picador.

ROSENFELD, A. (1980). *A Double Dying: Reflections on Holocaust Literature*. Bloomington, IN: Indiana University Press.

ROTH, J. and MAXWELL, E. (eds.) (2001). *Remembering for the Future: The Holocaust in an Age of Genocide*. 3 vols. New York: Palgrave Macmillan.

ROTHBERG, M. (2000). *Traumatic Realism: The Demands of Holocaust Representation*. Minneapolis, MN: University of Minnesota Press.

RUBIN, A. and GREENSPAN, H. (2006). *Reflections: Auschwitz, Memory, and a Life Recreated*. St. Paul, MN: Paragon House.

SCHACTER, D. (1996). *Searching for Memory*. New York: Basic Books.

SCHIFF, B. (2005). "Telling It in Time: Interpreting Consistency and Change in the Life Stories of Holocaust Survivors." *International Journal of Aging and Human Development* 60/3: 189–212.

SEIDMAN, N. (1996). "Elie Wiesel and the Scandal of Jewish Rage." *Jewish Social Studies* 3/1: 1–19.

SKLOOT, R. (1982). *The Theatre of the Holocaust*, Vol. 1. Madison, WI: University of Wisconsin Press.

THOMSON, I. (2002). *Primo Levi: A Life.* New York: Picador.

WIESEL, E. (1972). *One Generation After.* New York: Avon.

——(1978). *A Jew Today.* New York: Random House.

——(2006). *Night.* New York: Hill and Wang.

WIEVIORKA, A. (2006). *The Era of the Witness.* Ithaca, NY: Cornell University Press.

YABLONKA, H. (2004). *The State of Israel vs. Adolf Eichmann.* New York: Schocken Books.

YOUNG, J. (1988). *Writing and Rewriting the Holocaust: Narrative and the Consequences of Interpretation.* Bloomington, IN: Indiana University Press.

——(1993). *The Texture of Memory: Holocaust Memorials and Meaning.* New Haven, CT: Yale University Press.

OTHER SUGGESTED READING

DINER, H. (2009). *We Remember with Reverence and Love: American Jews and the Myth of Silence after the Holocaust, 1945–1962.* New York: New York University Press.

DWORK, D. and VAN PELT, R. (2009). *Flight from the Reich: Refugee Jews, 1933–1946.* New York: W. W. Norton.

HARTMAN, G. (2002). *Scars of the Spirit: The Struggle Against Inauthenticity.* New York: Palgrave Macmillan.

LACAPRA, D. (1994). *Representing the Holocaust: History, Theory, Trauma.* Ithaca, NY: Cornell University Press.

MATTHÄUS, J. (ed.) (2009). *Approaching an Auschwitz Survivor: Holocaust Testimony and Its Transformations.* New York: Oxford University Press.

OFER, D. and WEITZMAN, L. (eds.) (1998). *Women in the Holocaust.* New Haven, CT: Yale University Press.

RITTNER, C. and ROTH, J. (eds.) (1993). *Different Voices: Women and the Holocaust.* New York: Paragon House.

WEISSMAN, G. (2004). *Fantasies of Witnessing: Postwar Efforts to Experience the Holocaust.* Ithaca, NY: Cornell University Press.

CHAPTER 28

....

LITERATURE

....

SARA R. HOROWITZ

"THOSE who had no papers entitling them to live lined up to die." So begins Jakov Lind's novella *Soul of Wood* (1962), introducing without commentary a world whose norms have been radically inverted. The straightforward, sardonic tone contrasts with the outrageousness of what is described. In a brief sentence, Lind (1927–2007) conveys the pervasiveness of bureaucratized murder. Through the inner turbulence of an orderly assigned to assist in murdering sanitarium patients deemed unworthy of living and ambivalent about the possibility of rescuing a Jewish child, the narrative explores the capacity of language to depict atrocity and also to shroud issues of moral culpability in layers of obfuscation. The novella's incorporation of historical and imaginative elements is characteristic of Holocaust literature. Its location at the interstices of history and imagination, chronology and aesthetics, has both defined and problematized Holocaust literature, as it negotiates lived and remembered horror through the prism of the literary imagination.

Holocaust literature encompasses not only belles-lettres by and about victims and survivors of the Nazi genocide, but also lifewriting, including diaries, autobiography, letters, journals, journalism, and other self-referencing narratives written during or after the war (Langer 1975; Ezrahi 1987; Young 1988; Horowitz 1997). Some critics argue for a narrower definition that embraces only works by those with first-hand experience of Nazi atrocity. Others distinguish between Holocaust literature as the term for literary representations of the experiences only of the targets of genocide, and war or prison literature, consisting of writings by other victims of Nazism (Mintz 1984; Roskies 1984; Sicher 2005). Still others avoid the category altogether, contending that "Holocaust literature" artificially groups disparate works under a thematic rubric that dislodges them from national historical and cultural contexts. For most literary scholars, however, Holocaust literature connotes a wide range of works. No chapter can reference all that deserve citation, but the examples included here show that Holocaust literature encompasses many languages, genres, and perspectives that mediate life and death, survival and memory, during and after the Nazi genocide.

CRITICAL APPROACHES AND LITERARY STRATEGIES

Critical approaches to Holocaust literature reach beyond the boundaries of much literary scholarship, embracing issues that are historical, psychological, and ethical. Critics struggle with the ethical implications of bringing literary sensibilities and aesthetic concerns to bear on the extremities of historical atrocity and death (Rosenfeld 1980). In contrast to the precision demanded of historical accounts, literary language builds upon ambiguities and multiple readings, giving free rein to the imagination. While Holocaust-centered writing is not the first instance of historically based literature, the extremity and magnitude of suffering and cruelty during the destruction of much of European Jewry place special demands on Holocaust literature. The gravity of the subject caused early scholars in the field to interrogate the appropriateness of traditional critical methodologies as unseemly or irrelevant. They questioned whether classical literary forms and conventional language were adequate to representing the Holocaust and whether such massive suffering was appropriate material for the playfulness and pleasure associated with aesthetic production. Holocaust literature was seen as freighted with particular moral responsibilities not usually associated with literary production—to hew with fidelity to historical fact, to memorialize the victims, to respect the experiences of survivors, and to condemn perpetrators and their collaborators. The insights of psychology and trauma theory have been brought to bear to deepen debate about literary representation of the Holocaust. Since the traumatic experience is not fully registered or assimilated, its core cannot be narrated except through metaphor (Felman and Laub 1992).

The idea of a genre called Holocaust literature vexes not only critics and theorists but also many of the most significant authors whose work can be subsumed under it. They often express ambivalence about their own work. Some critics distinguish between literature written by Holocaust survivors, authorized by personal memory and experience, and literature about the Holocaust written by those with no personal experience of that event. But even novelists who are survivors have interrogated the appropriateness of fiction and the adequacy of language and literary forms. Elie Wiesel (b. 1928) points to an internal contradiction innate to Holocaust fiction: "A novel about Auschwitz is not a novel, or else it is not about Auschwitz" (1975: 314).

Another Holocaust survivor, Arnost Lustig (b. 1926), reflects, "To write of Auschwitz-Birkenau as it was—no one will do" (1982: 393). These reservations are not glosses on literary writings; they interrogate the capacity of memory and narrative representation and recall the absent voices of the murdered victims.

Characterizing much of Holocaust literature, this self-reflexive ambivalence about literary representations rests on a fundamental paradox: the drive to recount, describe, and remember clashes with a strong sense of the limitations facing any account. For this reason, literature of the Holocaust works by indirection. Rather than plunge readers into the dark heart of atrocity, it presents narratives that spiral around and toward moments of horror that are not fully narrated, or layers together fragments of imagery and narrative that suggest the whole, without claiming to fully represent it. The literary strategies and structures developed insist that much remains outside the framework of narration, unspoken and unspeakable, while pointing to what cannot be expressed directly.

Emblematic of literary criticism associated with Holocaust literature is a statement by the German social-cultural critic Theodor Adorno (1903–1969), "To write poetry after Auschwitz is barbaric" (1981: 34). Adorno's assertion is invoked both to support and to refute arguments about the appropriateness of literary representations of the Holocaust and scholarly analysis about them. The larger context of his writing reveals this statement less as a categorical dictum against Holocaust literature than as an indication of a far-ranging crisis of representation, culture, ethics, philosophical systems, and knowledge after the Holocaust. Adorno amplifies, "I do not want to soften my statement that it is barbaric to continue to write poetry after Auschwitz; . . . literature must resist precisely this verdict, that is, be such that it does not surrender to cynicism merely by existing after Auschwitz" (1992: 87–8). Like the central paradox that runs through much Holocaust literature—speaking the unspeakable, representing the unrepresentable—Adorno argues for a weighty literature that engages embattled cultural and ethical issues while acknowledging that the Holocaust may render such a literature impossible. French theorist Maurice Blanchot (1907–2003) notes that representation of the Holocaust is impossible because "the disaster de-scribes" (1980: 7). Following Blanchot, French philosopher Sarah Kofman (1934–1994) argues, "About Auschwitz and after Auschwitz no story is possible, if by a story one means: to tell a story of events which makes sense" (1987: 14). Neither can an ethical literature resist encountering the Holocaust; for Blanchot, "It is not you who will speak; let the disaster speak in you, even if it be by your forgetfulness or silence" (1980: 8).

WARTIME LITERATURE

Holocaust literature began during the war years to document and interpret ongoing events, resist dehumanization and despair, and mourn overwhelming losses. "Who can render the stages of the dying people?" Rachel Auerbach (1903–1976) asked in "*Yizkor 1943*" (in Roskies 1988: 459), her eloquent lament for murdered Jews of the Warsaw ghetto, whose fate she narrowly avoided. Even under great duress, displacement, and the pervasiveness of death, literary production flourished. Although difficult and often dangerous, Jews confined to overcrowded ghettos or pressed into slave labor used their scant energy and resources to write diaries, poems, plays, and fiction. This writing imparts a detailed sense of everyday life under unlivable conditions and the threat of genocide, conveying the effect of Nazi atrocity on one's inner life and close relationships, as well as the vain hopes of people who were doomed.

Fiction and poetry composed during the war find varied literary forms for the ongoing struggle against dehumanization and death. In 1941, for example, Leyb Goldin (1906–1942) wrote a short story in the Warsaw ghetto, where he later perished. "Chronicle of a Single Day" (in Roskies 1988: 424–34) conveys the desperate hunger in the ghetto and the starving man's struggle to maintain human dignity. Written as a dialogue between a ghetto inhabitant and his insistent stomach, the story explores the erosion of one's humanness in the face of extreme hunger. As the protagonist becomes "90 percent your stomach and a little bit you" (in Roskies 1988: 425), he documents the deterioration of his starving companions as well as his own degeneration. "You feel that today you have fallen a step lower. . . . All these people around you, apparently, began like that. You're on your way . . ." Goldin's story exemplifies the way that literary production maintains the author's sense of his own humanity so that the "little bit you" prevails provisionally over the "90 percent . . . stomach." Goldin's story was preserved in Emanuel Ringelblum's Oyneg Shabbes project; Ringelblum (1900–1944), who escaped the Warsaw ghetto but was murdered by the Nazis in 1944, saw such cultural production in the ghettos as evidence that "though we have been sentenced to death and know it, we have not lost our human features" (1958: 299).

The most sustained poetic corpus is that of the modernist Yiddish poet Abraham (Avrom) Sutzkever (1913–2010), who, during his two years in the Vilna ghetto, composed more than eighty poems reflecting personal loss and collective suffering and death. Active in the underground, Sutzkever writes of the meshing of spiritual and armed resistance, especially in his 1943 poem "The Lead Plates at the Rom Press" (in Howe et al. 1987: 678), inspired by a plan to melt down printing plates for use in manufacturing ammunition. Famous for its definitive edition of the Talmud, the Rom Press also had published Yiddish literature. In Sutzkever's poem, the molten lead carries "the spirit" of its original letters and the scope of Jewish creativity and experience: "Liquified bullets, gleamed with thoughts: / A verse from Babylon, a verse from Poland." Already then, and continuing in his postwar work, Sutzkever intuits what became a theme in later Holocaust literature—the limitations of language and the boundaries between living and dead. His 1943 poem "Burnt Pearls" utilizes the indirection of the title's metaphor to stand for the gruesome charred smile of the incinerated corpse of a woman. The poem reflects upon the impossible calling of the poet in the deadly confines of the ghetto, where "you, written word, substitute for my world" (Sutzkever 1981: 38). "Poem about a Herring" depicts a mother incongruously feeding her child at the edge of a mass grave, instants before they are shot to death. Deflecting direct description of the unbearable murder with the metaphor of "a fiery string of notes" that "jolt" the child to his death, the poet follows the body of the "child with a bloody herring in his mouth" into the mass grave. There the poem acknowledges the limitations of the living to comprehend the experience of the dead, as the poet searches "for that herring's salt / and still can not / find its taste on my lips" (1981: 46).

Other ghetto poets make parodic use of Jewish texts and traditions to criticize God and lament death, developing motifs that characterized Jewish literature after the war. For example, in his 1942 epic "Lekh Lekho," addressed to his 5-year-old daughter Blimele just before their deportation from the Łódź ghetto, Simcha Bunim Shayevitch (1907–1944) ironically compares their doomed destiny to the biblical past. Taking its title from the divine injunction to Abraham in Genesis to "Go forth" to an unknown locale to found a people and a faith, the poem castigates God for abandoning his people. The more somber "Spring 5702" builds on a contrast between the spring festival of Passover, with its promise of renewal and redemption, and the spiritual darkness of spring in the Łódź ghetto. The poem uses traditional Jewish images, such as the weeping matriarch Rachel and the lament of Jeremiah, to express grief and anger at the murder of Europe's Jews (in Teichman and Leder 1994: 408–19). Related themes are explored by Yitzhak Katzenelson (1886–1944), a veteran of the Warsaw ghetto uprising, who later managed to hide the manuscript of his epic Yiddish poem *The Song of the Murdered Jewish People* (1980) before being deported to Auschwitz and murdered. Retrieved after the war, the work eulogizes the murdered Jews of the Warsaw ghetto, among them his wife and two sons.

Outside the epicenter, Jewish poets who eluded the Nazi genocide also brought the Holocaust into their poetic oeuvre. In North America, reports of Nazi persecution had a particularly strong impact on Yiddish writers, whose language choice solidified a close connection with the Jewish communities of eastern Europe. Jacob Glatstein (1896–1971), who left Poland for New York in 1914, was part of the *In Zikh* movement of Yiddish poets dedicated to experimental, introspective, and universalist, rather than nationally driven, poetry. With the Nazi rise to power, Glatstein shifted his focus to the Jewish catastrophe, proclaiming in his 1938 "Good Night, World" that he "slam[s] the gate" on the "polluted cultures" of Europe, choosing the vilified and assaulted Jewish ghetto culture and the "deep-deep meaning" and ethics of Jewish learning over the "Jesusmarxes" (1987: 101–3). His later poetry salvages what remains of the Jewish God and sees the Holocaust as a counter-revelation, reversing the Sinai covenant. The Canadian poet A. M. Klein (1909–1972) also responded to the European crisis in a series of poems that traces

Jewish memory of antisemitism and the tightening of the genocidal net over the Jews of Europe. Adopting classical poetic forms, Klein (1990) condemns the hatred and irrationality of Nazism as a betrayal of the promise of European culture and Enlightenment ideals.

POSTWAR DEVELOPMENTS

While empirically based approaches to the Holocaust struggled with how to incorporate the subjectivity of lifewriting, literary scholars drew upon a complex theoretical framework for understanding autobiographical memory and narrative. Postwar developments included an aggregation of lifewriting and belles-lettres. Attempting to represent Holocaust experience and memory, and to grapple with their impact on Jewish life, culture, and faith, as well as on western culture, thought, and ethics, Holocaust literature was initially the province largely of authors with first-hand experience, but later encompassed writing by others who engaged—whether through research, familial connection, or imagination—with the Nazi genocide and its aftereffects. Eventually, as the Holocaust became part of common cultural discourse, it served as a metaphor for injustice and persecution elsewhere or for individual psychological conditions.

Several memoirs written during the first decades after the war had a significant impact on Holocaust literature: Elie Wiesel's *Night* (1958), Jean Améry's *At the Mind's Limits* (1966), Primo Levi's *Survival in Auschwitz* (1958), and Charlotte Delbo's trilogy *Auschwitz and After* (completed in 1971). The incapacity of language to represent Holocaust experience runs through these and other memoirs. Levi (1919–1987) reflects, for example, "our language lacks words to express this offense, the demolition of a man" (1996: 26). In contrast to wartime writing, which frequently manifests a confidence in the power of its testimonial language, postwar writing often self-consciously questions the nature of memory, language, and representation. Written in the early 1940s, the *Lodz Ghetto Chronicle* asserts, for instance, that "the hand does not waver in writing this down. The hand is guided by a brain that reliably preserves all impressions of the eye and the ear" (Dobroszycki 1984: 19). In contrast, postwar writing questions the capacity of language to represent the Holocaust and to communicate it to anyone not personally affected.

The four memoirs noted above mirror similar experiences and observations but utilize different interpretive frameworks. The son of an assimilated Jewish Austrian father, Améry (1912–1978) responded to the restrictiveness of antisemitic laws by repudiating his Austrian heritage and reclaiming his Jewish identity. Active in the Belgian resistance, he was captured and tortured by the Gestapo, then deported to

Auschwitz. His writing conveys the despair of the intellectual who suffers not only from the harshness of unaccustomed manual labor but also from the collapse of any cohesive system of meaning. His most famous essay, "Torture," anticipates later theoretical writing on pain and torture, describing the permanent shattering of trust in society and in one's selfhood, noting, most profoundly and most disturbingly, "torture has an indelible character. Whoever was tortured, stays tortured. Torture is ineradicably burned into him . . ." (1980: 34).

Levi, an Italian Jew and a chemist by training, documents not only the struggle against death but also the Germans' deliberate and relentless effort to humiliate and dehumanize the concentration camp inmates. He captures the atmosphere of violence, chaos, and randomness by using the motif of a descent to hell. Levi takes on the role of guide to Dante's Inferno, both drawing upon and challenging the values of European secular humanism.

Captured as a member of the French resistance, Delbo (1913–1985) was deported to Auschwitz on a convoy of 230 non-Jewish Frenchwomen. Her trilogy mixes prose and poetry, stretching the conventions of memoir as genre and powerfully capturing the bodily suffering and sensory memories of Auschwitz, the omnipresence of death, and the camaraderie among the prisoners. Anticipating later theorists, she dwells on the nature of traumatized memory, especially on the disparity between the remembering "I" and the remembered "I." Like Améry, Delbo probes the indelible marking of torment on those who outlived it, focusing on what her *Days and Memory* (1985) termed "deep memory . . . the memory of the senses" that cannot be put into words and is "swollen with emotional charge" (1990: 3). In the final and most daring volume of the trilogy, *The Measure of Our Days*, Delbo writes in the voices of thirteen women who survived Auschwitz with her, blurring the boundaries between memoir and fiction in conveying the complexity of their responses to their "insurmountable anguish" (1995: 298).

Wiesel's *Night* presents the memory of a religious young man's experience in Auschwitz. This memoir struggles with a God whose silence ruptures the Jewish faith in covenant and continuity. Time progresses through a double set of indicators, the Gregorian calendar that marks the chronology of war and deportation and the Jewish calendar that offers ironic commentary on the refuted meanings of Jewish time, such as liberation and atonement.

HOLOCAUST FICTION AND POETRY

Literature by survivors, war refugees, and other eyewitnesses spans many languages, reflecting the vast reach of the Nazi genocide across national and linguistic boundaries, as well as the massive displacement of its victims. Holocaust fiction is written in the native languages of its authors and also in languages acquired in countries of refuge and immigration. Some continue to write in their mother tongue while living in a place where that language is not spoken. The decision to write in an acquired tongue often repudiates languages of atrocity and victimization or affirms a language linked with liberation or identity. This welter of languages mirrors the authors' displacement and uprootedness, losses and reconstitutions.

Several recurrent themes characterize Holocaust fiction by survivors. Many works utilize the settings of ghettos, forests, labor camps, or situations of hiding to convey the texture and inner experience of Nazi persecution. Jurek Becker (1937–1997), for example, draws on memories of his native Łódź for his novel, *Jacob the Liar* (1969), which conveys the desperation of the Łódź ghetto for reliable information. Fenced in, lacking access to radios or outside newspapers, ghetto inhabitants were vulnerable to rumor and manipulation. Jacob spreads hope of an imminent Allied victory, based on made-up newscasts from a non-existent radio. The novel focuses on the reality and uncertainty of ghetto life and on acts of resistance that prove insufficient, if momentarily inspiring. It also underscores the dangers of creating Holocaust fiction that comforts by softening and falsifying the harshness of genocide. Ilona Karmel's novel, *An Estate of Memory* (1969), focuses on the relationship among four women in the labor camp Skarzysko-Kamienna. Written in English after the author's immigration to the United States, the novel examines the possibility for moral behavior even in extreme circumstances. Karmel (1925–2000) explores the tension between the fortifying impulse to bond with and support other prisoners and the desperate pull to save oneself, using one woman's pregnancy as the fulcrum by which to think through ethical issues. On the one hand, the shared effort to protect the unborn child symbolizes an inner resistance to Nazi brutality; on the other hand, it places special demands on women who already suffer from starvation and the harshness of slave labor. A collection of short stories by Tadeusz Borowski (1922–1951), *This Way for the Gas, Ladies and Gentlemen* (1967), looks at the brutalizing effects of atrocity on the more privileged non-Jewish prisoners at Auschwitz. The stories, whose style is unsentimental and sardonic, are based on the author's own experiences there as a political prisoner. As in Améry's case, suicide eventually followed Borowski's survival.

Holocaust fiction frequently reflects upon the place of imaginative literature in mediating memory and develops literary strategies that negotiate the difficulties of representing the traumatic past. The exquisitely powerful short stories of Polish-born Israeli writer Ida Fink (b. 1921) depict the inner lives of victims struggling with radical bereavement and the aftershock of atrocity, as well as the ambiguous motives of rescuers and other eyewitnesses (1987, 1997). Fink is the master of the very short story—some a scant three pages—whose brevity reflects the fragmentary nature of any Holocaust narrative. The stories focus on moments of revelation, when a character understands that the world has changed utterly and irretrievably or that death is imminent—such as when a father awakes to the sound of trucks coming to round up his family and "a terrible feeling of regret tore through him when he ... understood that he had overslept his life" (1987: 44). Born of intimacy, the stories expose the strain of persecution on even the closest of relationships. Several stories narrate the experience of the dying and the dead as though from the inside, suggesting that without the act of empathic imagination, their last moments would be lost save through callous remembrances of murderers and bystanders. The Spanish-born French writer Jorge Semprun (b. 1923) explores the nature of memory and the impossibility of its transmission in his novel *The Long Journey* (1963), which centers on the train ride to the Buchenwald, reaching both into the past and the future in conveying unspeakable memory. The novel imagines how stories of Buchenwald produce a range of distancing responses from outsiders, which silence the narrator.

Literature written by those who were children or adolescents during World War II narrates the Holocaust from that vantage point or contends with the aftereffects of bereavement, horror, and brutality inflicted during one's formative years. The Israeli writer Aharon Appelfeld (b. 1932), who wandered as a child alone through the forests and villages of Ukraine, has observed that for children, the Holocaust became foundational, a building block of the self. "[T]he children ... knew no other childhood....They ... had no previous life, or, if they had, it was now effaced. The Holocaust was the black milk, as the poet [Celan] said, that they sucked morning, noon, and night" (in Brown and Horowitz 2003: 9). His fiction, written in lean and elegant Hebrew, focuses on the illusions of the cultured assimilated Jews of central Europe, unwilling to recognize what was brewing (*Badenheim 1939* and *The Age of Wonders*); on the inner life of children (*Tzili: The Story of a Life*), and on traumatized, often mute survivors (*The Immortal Bartfus, For Every Sin, The Iron Tracks*) (Appelfeld 1975, 1981, 1983a, 1983b, 1987, 1991). Appelfeld's spare and impressionistic style probes the terrors of traumatized memory, the conflicts of survival, and the price of distancing oneself from one's past, however painful.

The novels of Hungarian Nobel laureate Imre Kertész (b. 1929) draw upon autobiographical material, describing an assimilated Jewish family in Budapest, much like his own. Deported first to Auschwitz in 1944 and then to Buchenwald, he addresses philosophical questions about human meaning in the wake of an event that destroyed previous systems of meaning. *Fatelessness* (1975) depicts an adolescent's struggle not only to survive but to make sense of the randomness of Nazi atrocity. *Kaddish for a Child Not Born* (1990) explores how a former Buchenwald prisoner contends with trauma and guilt, which are focused and even intensified by refusal to father children after the war. The postmodern *Liquidation* (2003) centers on a rescued manuscript by that name, elaborating themes found in Kertész's earlier works.

Dutch writer Harry Mulisch (1927–2010), son of an Austrian Nazi father and a Jewish mother whose family was deported and murdered, probes the impact of unacknowledged childhood trauma. *The Assault* (1982) is structured as a multi-layered mystery. The protagonist, a Dutch anesthesiologist, administers drugs that prevent not pain itself but the memory of pain, a symbol of his own predicament. When he was a boy, his family was killed after the body of an assassinated Nazi collaborator was dragged to their doorstep. Years later, the doctor seeks to know why the body was moved and, on a deeper level, how the unrecollected past shaped his life.

Drawing from his experiences, the Polish-born American writer Louis Begley (b. 1933) tells in *Wartime Lies* (1991) how a Jewish boy survives the war by assuming false identities. Framed by the reflections of the melancholy and erudite man whom the child becomes, *Wartime Lies* explores the toll of secrets, lies, fear, and shame on the child's evolving selfhood as well as on the adult's struggle to create a coherent life story: "our man has no childhood that he can bear to remember; he had had to invent one" (1991: 181). The disconnection between the child and the man comments on the need for mediating autobiography through fiction.

Years after its initial publication, Adorno qualified his frequently quoted statement about poetry after Auschwitz: "perennial suffering has as much right to expression as the tortured have to scream . . . hence it may have been wrong to say that no poem could be written after Auschwitz" (1973: 362). Holocaust poetry meditates on the nature of memory and testimony, and its special use of language gives expression to what falls outside the boundaries of ordinary speech. Paul Celan (1920–1970) and Dan Pagis (1930–1986) are among the most important post-Holocaust Jewish poets. Many of Celan's poems constitute a lament for his murdered mother. His most famous poem, "Todesfugue" or "Death Fugue," is a complex composition that captures the doom of the murdered Jews of Europe with the metaphor "black milk" imbibed endlessly. The SS officer who "plays with his serpents" orders the Jews to a macabre dance before their death and incineration (1972: 61). Celan's intricate poems take parodic liturgical, classical, or scriptural forms, expressing human and divine despair. Pagis survived alone as a young boy in labor camps in Transnistria, immigrating to Mandatory Palestine in 1946. By 1950, he was publishing poems in Hebrew, and he earned a doctorate in medieval Hebrew literature. His poems show his classical training. "Written in Pencil in a Sealed Railway Car" (1981: 23), his best-known poem, briefly presents an incomplete transmission from the murdered to the murderer, turning on an allusion to the biblical Cain and Abel. Grounded in his wartime memories, Pagis's poems about testimony ask humanistic questions about the nature of good, evil, and human behavior.

Fiction and poetry often address the Holocaust's challenge to Jewish concepts of God, covenant, and history. Elie Wiesel's novels, influenced by traditional Jewish texts and French existentialist writers, are illustrative. In *The Town Beyond the Wall* (1962), a Holocaust survivor returns to the town of his birth and confronts the memory of neighbors indifferent to the deportation of Jews. The novel addresses the presence of human evil and the possibility of human good in a world where values have been inverted. Subjected to a torturous interrogation known as "prayer," the survivor imagines that God and man have exchanged places, and reflects that such terms as sanity and madness become interchangeable in a world governed by cruel irrationality. Like the bystander, whose disengagement creates a moral vacuum, the novel intimates that God, too, "sees without being seen . . . He says nothing. He is there, but acts as if he were not" (1964: 151). Challenging Jewish concepts of God, covenant, and history, the novel contemplates a meaningless world of chaos, nihilism, and suffering. Instead of the promise of religious redemption, the novel offers the possibility of human friendship and solidarity among the suffering. *The Gates of the Forest* (1964) focuses on a Jewish boy who survives the Holocaust by hiding in a forest cave, but years later is incapable of loving another person or God. The novel develops but does not resolve questions of theodicy and of Christian antisemitism raised first in *Night*. In *A Beggar in Jerusalem* (1968), the protagonist struggles to reconcile the redemptive possibilities of Israel with the overwhelming losses of the Holocaust. The presence of itinerant storytellers and the invoking of the eighteenth-century Hassidic Reb Nachman of Bratslav paradoxically connect radical doubt with radical faith. All of Wiesel's novels insist on the imperatives to create human meaning in a world where God's presence is hidden.

Tracking the destiny of a Jewish family over many centuries, French writer André Schwarz-Bart's (1928–2006) epic novel *The Last of the Just* (1959) places the Holocaust in the context of the long history of Jewish suffering and European anti-semitism. Building on the Jewish legend of the *lamed-vav*, the thirty-six unknown righteous men on whose existence the world depends, Schwarz-Bart creates a dynastic chain of martyrs, which takes the novel from the Crusades to the Auschwitz gas chamber where the last just man is murdered. The novel infuses the legend with christological elements; each Just Man becomes an infinitely suffering saint whose pain redeems his people. Like many works that struggle with theodicy and Jewish meaning, the novel leaves ambiguous whether the Holocaust can be placed in the continuum of Jewish history, or whether it is a rupture with the past, a sign of God's permanent absence, treason, or abdication from the covenant. While poems such as Celan's and Pagis's or novels such as Wiesel's or Schwarz-Bart's may be read in the context of Judaism and Jewish history, they also pose universal questions about good and evil, human values, and meaningfulness in the wake of the Holocaust.

Although from a distance, American Jewish writers have been deeply affected by the Holocaust, not only struggling with its implications for Jewish life but also attempting to relate the Holocaust to American experience, particularly to issues of social justice. In *The Pawnbroker* (1961), for example, Edward Lewis Wallant (1926–1962) depicts the Holocaust's emotional impact on a survivor, alienated from faith in God and people, who tries to keep the past at bay but cannot do so. With its pawnshop's collection of once-cherished, now repudiated objects serving as metaphor for the protagonist's emotionally charged memories of love and bereavement, the novel superimposes Holocaust memories on New York scenes, connecting past and present injustice.

Some of Cynthia Ozick's (b. 1928) works are among a number that foreground gender-based suffering during the Holocaust. Her novella *The Shawl* (1989), for instance, consists of two interwoven stories, originally published separately. "The Shawl" focuses on a young mother in a labor camp. With the help of a seemingly magic shawl, she tries but fails to protect her infant from death. While Ozick relies on research about the Holocaust, she makes a point to distinguish her fictional creation from testimonial or historical narrative through the deliberate artifice of her literary style. In "Rosa," *The Shawl*'s second story, Ozick looks at the effects of the mother's bereavement, with the woman many years later transported to a Florida residence, her pawnshop business destroyed. As in Wallant's novel, the unsentimental prose that delineates a somewhat unlikeable survivor challenges the popular notion that suffering ennobles or confers special wisdom; in these works, survivors are simply tormented. Ozick's novella also criticizes Holocaust research that further dehumanizes survivors by turning them only into objects of study. Rosa resents "the special word they used: *survivor*. . . . As long as they didn't have to say *human*" (1989: 36).

In postwar decades, the Holocaust has also found a place in the works of American poets, sometimes reflecting their experience in the armed forces during World War II, sometimes reflecting the Holocaust's entry into American cultural discourse. Written in 1982, Irena Klepfisz's (b. 1941) best known poem, "Bashert," draws on her childhood wartime experience, lamenting her father, killed in the Warsaw ghetto uprising. Her later poems, such as "Di rayze aheyme/The Journey Home" (1991) meld her mother tongue, Yiddish, with her New York English to articulate an ethical imperative for social justice born of the Jewish historical experience. Several poems by Anthony Hecht (1923–2004), most notably "More Light! More Light!" (1967) and "The Book of Yolek" (1990) show the poet's memory haunted by what he witnessed as a member of an American army unit that liberated a concentration camp.

Similarly, Israeli writers often have addressed the Holocaust in relation to Israeli identity and nationhood. In his novella *The Chocolate Deal* (1965), Haim Gouri (b. 1923) examines the Holocaust's psychological toll on survivors. In *Not of This Time, Not of This Place* (1965), Yehuda Amichai (1924–2000) explores the resonances of the past on the present through a protagonist who travels to Europe where his childhood friend was murdered in the Nazi genocide. In *Adam Resurrected* (1968), Yoram Kaniuk (b. 1930) uses black humor to probe the humiliation and despair that haunt the memory of Holocaust survivors. *The Last Jew* (1982) and *Commander of the Exodus* (1999) examine the Israeli response to the Holocaust survivors who came to Israel after the war and the tensions between images of the new Israeli Jew and the old and allegedly passive European Jew.

Fiction by writers born after the war has come to be categorized as second generation literature. Whether or not its authors have familial links to the Holocaust, their fiction addresses such issues as inherited or transmitted memory and secondary trauma, reflecting a world already unmoored by the crises triggered by the Holocaust in psychology, religion, philosophy, culture, and other systems of meaning. The product of "memory shot through with holes," to use the words of French novelist Henri Raczymow (b. 1948) (1994), second generation literature contends with events that preceded the life of the author, who cannot personally recollect them but nonetheless is profoundly affected, even defined by them. Perhaps the best known work to capture the perspective of the second generation is Art Spiegelman's (b. 1948) graphic novel *Maus* (1986, 1991). It interweaves the cartoonist's recovery of his father's story of survival with the complicated relationship between father and son, which is shaped by past loss. In his novel *See Under: Love*, Israeli writer David Grossman (b. 1954) explores the effects of Holocaust memory on a child of survivors who grows up in a Jerusalem neighborhood populated by them (1986). The child weaves together fragments of overheard, misunderstood conversations about horrors "Over There" with more literary stories, constructing a memory narrative that links the European Jewish past with the Israeli present. The novel reflects a generational turn, a reversal of the older Israeli repudiation of the European diaspora experience and an exploration of internalized and unacknowledged European roots. German writers also confront the disturbing legacy of the Nazi genocide in fiction that looks back at the actions of the wartime generation. Among the best examples is the novel *Austerlitz* (2001) in which the German expatriate writer W. G. Sebald (1944–2001) probes the troubled memory of a German Jew orphaned during the war as a means to understanding postwar German cultural amnesia and ambivalent relationships to home.

THE FUTURE OF HOLOCAUST LITERATURE

Holocaust literature reminds readers that, as the German Jewish philosopher Walter Benjamin (1892–1940) observed, "The past can be seized only as an image which flashes up at the instant when it can be recognized and is never seen again" (1968: 255). Through its development as a body of writing and a subject for scholarship, Holocaust literature not only contends with the rigors and detritus of history but also complicates the historian's sense of the past, particularly with regard to narrative. Not altogether approvingly, the historian Yosef Hayim

Yerushalmi predicted that, notwithstanding an abundance of historical research on the Holocaust, "its image is being shaped, not at the historian's anvil, but in the novelist's crucible" (1982: 98). Increasingly, methodologies learned from literary studies have begun to reverse the historian's reluctance to bring survivor memories into the fabric of the historical record. The foregrounding of language that is so crucial to literary analysis—including narrative patterns and conventions, tropes and recurrent images, ambiguity and other literary devices—complicates and enriches the reading not only of literary works but of other kinds of documents, and offers diverse ways to understand the researcher's relationship to the past. Interdisciplinary approaches to Holocaust studies draw upon the insights of postmodernist analysis about the constructedness of any version of the past and at the same time insist that the past is not only constructed.

As the body of writing by Holocaust survivors reaches closure, scholars debate the composition of the literary canon, arguing the merits or flaws of particular works or reclaiming neglected ones. Literary scholars explore the cultural meanings of the Holocaust, the transmission and interpretation of the past to later generations, and the lasting effects of the Nazi genocide (Hirsch 1997; Flanzbaum 1999; Rothberg 2000; Hungerford 2003). The study of Holocaust literature incorporates new methodologies, such as increased attention to women's writing and the insights of gender analysis (Horowitz in Epstein and Lefkovitz 2001). These new approaches mirror contemporary developments in literary studies, but they also arise in response to the evolution of Holocaust literature. For example, at the end of the twentieth century and start of the twenty-first, belated memoirs by Holocaust survivors—many by women—introduce topics largely absent from earlier memoirs, such as sexual abuse, barter, and rape. As Holocaust representation increasingly permeates western culture, Holocaust literature sometimes pushes against the boundaries of aesthetic propriety, recapturing the shock and disturbance that can be lost through over-familiarity with its imagery. Increasingly, Holocaust literature engages the inner experience of perpetrators, collaborators, and others during the war years, while literary analysis addresses how the Holocaust both resists and achieves integration into the continuum of Jewish and western traditions.

REFERENCES

ADORNO, T. (1973). *Negative Dialectics*. New York: Seabury Press.
——(1981). *Prisms*. Cambridge, MA: MIT Press.
——(1992). *Notes to Literature*. 2 vols. New York: Columbia University Press.
APPELFELD, A. (1975). *Badenheim 1939*. New York: Washington Square-Simon.
——(1981). *Age of Wonders*. Boston: Godine Publishers.
——(1983a). *The Immortal Bartfuss*. New York: Weidenfeld & Nicolson.

APPELFELD, A. (1983b). *Tzili: The Story of a Life*. New York: Dutton.

——(1987). *For Every Sin*. New York: Grove Press.

——(1991). *The Iron Tracks*. New York: Schocken.

AMÉRY, J. (1980). *At the Mind's Limits: Contemplations by a Survivor on Auschwitz and Its Realities*. Bloomington, IN: Indiana University Press.

BEGLEY, L. (1991). *Wartime Lies*. New York: Knopf.

BENJAMIN, W. (1968). *Illuminations*. New York: Harcourt, Brace & World.

BLANCHOT, M. (1980). *The Writing of the Disaster*. Lincoln, NE: University of Nebraska Press.

BROWN, M. and HOROWITZ, S. R. (eds.) (2003). *Encounter with Aharon Appelfeld*. Toronto: Mosaic Press.

CELAN, P. (1972). *Poems of Paul Celan*. New York: Persea.

DELBO, C. (1990). *Days and Memory*. Marlboro, VT: Marlboro Press.

——(1995). *Auschwitz and After*. New Haven, CT: Yale University Press.

DOBROSZYCKI, L. (ed.) (1984). *The Chronicle of the Lodz Ghetto, 1941–1944*. New Haven, CT: Yale University Press.

EPSTEIN, J. and LEFKOVITZ, L. (eds.) (2001). *Shaping Losses: Cultural Memory and the Holocaust*. Urbana, IL: University of Illinois Press.

EZRAHI, S. (1987). *By Words Alone: The Holocaust in Literature*. Chicago, IL: University of Chicago Press.

FELMAN, S. and LAUB, D. (1992). *Testimony: Crises of Witnessing in Literature, Psychoanalysis, and History*. New York: Routledge.

FINK, I. (1987). *A Scrap of Time: Stories*. New York: Random House.

——(1997). *Traces: Stories*. New York: Henry Holt.

FLANZBAUM, H. (ed.) (1999). *The Americanization of the Holocaust*. Baltimore, MD: Johns Hopkins University Press.

GLATSTEIN, J. (1987). *Selected Poems of Yankev Glatsheyn*. Philadelphia: Jewish Publication Society.

HECHT, A. (1967). *The Hard Hours*. New York: Atheneum.

——(1990). *The Transparent Man*. New York: Knopf.

HIRSCH, M. (1997). *Family Frames: Photography, Narrative, and Postmemory*. Cambridge, MA: Harvard University Press.

HOROWITZ, S. (1997). *Voicing the Void: Muteness and Memory in Holocaust Fiction*. Albany, NY: State University of New York Press.

HOWE, I., WISSE, R., and SHMERUK, K. (eds.) (1987). *The Penguin Book of Modern Yiddish Verse*. New York: Viking.

HUNGERFORD, A. (2003). *The Holocaust of Texts: Genocide, Literature and Personification*. Chicago, IL: University of Chicago Press.

KATZENELSON, Y. (1980). *The Song of the Murdered Jewish People*. Ed. S. Derech. Tel Aviv: Hakibbutz Hameuchad.

KLEIN, A. (1990). *Complete Poems, Part 2: Original Poems 1937–1955*. Toronto: University of Toronto Press.

KOFMAN, S. (1987). *Smothered Words*. Evanston, IL: Northwestern University Press.

LANGER, L. (1975). *The Holocaust and the Literary Imagination*. New Haven, CT: Yale University Press.

LEVI, P. (1996). *Survival in Auschwitz: The Nazi Assault on Humanity*. New York: Collier.

LIND, J. (1962). *Soul of Wood and Other Stories*. New York: Grove Press.

Lustig, A. (1982). "Auschwitz-Birkenau." *Yale Review* 71: 393–403.

Mintz, A. (1984). *Hurban: Responses to Catastrophe in Hebrew Literature.* New York: Columbia University Press.

Ozick, C. (1989). *The Shawl.* New York: Knopf.

Pagis, D. (1981). *Points of Departure.* Philadelphia: Jewish Publication Society.

Raczymow, H. (1994). "Memory Shot through with Holes." *Yale French Studies* 85: 98–106.

Ringelblum, E. (1958). *Notes from the Warsaw Ghetto.* New York: McGraw Hill.

Rosenfeld, A. (1980). *A Double Dying: Reflections of Holocaust Literature.* Bloomington, IN: Indiana University Press.

Roskies, D. (1984). *Against the Apocalypse: Responses to Catastrophe in Modern Jewish Culture.* Cambridge, MA: Harvard University Press.

——(ed.) (1988). *The Literature of Destruction: Jewish Responses to Catastrophe.* Philadelphia: Jewish Publication Society.

Rothberg, M. (2000). *Traumatic Realism: The Demands of Holocaust Representation.* Minneapolis, MN: University of Minnesota Press.

Sicher, E. (2005). *The Holocaust Novel.* New York: Routledge.

Sutzkever, A. (1981). *Burnt Pearls: Ghetto Poems.* Oakville, Ontario: Mosaic Press.

Teichman, M. and Leder, S. (eds.) (1994). *Truth and Lamentation: Stories and Poems of the Holocaust.* Urbana, IL: University of Illinois Press.

Wiesel, E. (1964). *The Town Beyond the Wall.* New York: Avon.

——(1975). "For Some Measure of Humility." *Shma* 5/100: 314–15.

Yerushalmi, Y. (1982). *Zakhor: Jewish History and Jewish Memory.* Seattle, WA: University of Washington Press.

Young, J. (1988). *Writing and Rewriting the Holocaust: Narrative and the Consequences of Interpretation.* Bloomington, IN: University of Indiana Press.

Other Suggested Reading

Gubar, S. (2003). *Poetry after Auschwitz: Remembering What One Never Knew.* Bloomington, IN: Indiana University Press.

Hirsch, M. and Kacandes, I. (eds.) (2004). *Teaching the Representation of the Holocaust.* New York: Modern Language Association.

Kremer, S. (ed.) (2003). *Holocaust Literature: An Encyclopedia of Writers and Their Work.* New York: Routledge.

Langer, L. (ed.) (1995). *Art from the Ashes: A Holocaust Anthology.* New York: Oxford University Press.

Patterson, D., Berger, A., and Cargas, S. (eds.) (2002). *Encyclopedia of Holocaust Literature.* Westport, CT: Oryx Press.

Roth, J. (ed.) (2008). *Holocaust Literature.* 2 vols. Pasadena, CA: Salem Press.

Stier, O. (2003). *Committed to Memory: Cultural Mediations of the Holocaust.* Amherst, MA: University of Massachusetts Press.

CHAPTER 29

....

FILM

....

LAWRENCE BARON

DOCUMENTARY and feature films have played a crucial role in popularizing the emotions, images, sounds, and themes associated with the Holocaust. Nazi propaganda documentaries, such as *Triumph of the Will* (1935), directed by Leni Riefenstahl (1902–2003), and *The Eternal Jew* (1940), idealized the Third Reich's racial utopia and revealed the genocidal hatred at its core. Feature films, such as *Jew Süss* (1940), demonized the Jew as a conspirator against "Aryan" purity and values. Contemporary satires, such as *The Great Dictator* (1940), directed by Charlie Chaplin (1889–1977), and *To Be or Not to Be* (1942), ridiculed the megalomaniac pretensions of Adolf Hitler (1889–1945) and the Manichean ideology of Nazism.

Newsreels, newspapers, and periodicals rapidly disseminated the footage and photos shot by Allied camera crews and journalists as they recorded the liberation of concentration and death camps. The American prosecution team at the Nuremberg Trials compiled a documentary entitled *Nazi Concentration Camps* from this footage and entered it as evidence of the crimes of the German defendants. In the ensuing years, television documentaries and photographic exhibitions recycled these appalling images. The French documentary *Night and Fog* (1955), directed by Alain Resnais (b. 1922), intercut colored footage of abandoned concentration camps with black and white footage and photographs of Hitler's speeches, Nazi rallies, people boarding deportation trains, naked prisoners standing at attention, rotting corpses bulldozed into mass graves, the smoldering ashes of crematoria, and mounds of the victims' shorn hair and confiscated belongings (van der Knaap 2006). These indelible images established the cinematic iconography of the Holocaust.

A GATHERING BODY OF WORK

Most Holocaust scholars maintain that the initial outrage over the slaughter of European Jewry dissipated quickly. Witnesses to Nazi atrocities supposedly repressed these traumatic images. Awareness of the Holocaust diminished as Jewish losses were subsumed under the casualties for World War II and overshadowed by the atomic bombing of Japan, the Cold War, and the transition to peacetime economies. Countries allied with or occupied by Germany concealed their collaboration in the persecution and deportation of their Jewish compatriots. The USSR coerced the states it "liberated" to interpret World War II in ideological terms that cast the Nazis as agents of capitalist imperialism and the Soviets as defenders of egalitarianism. The United States downplayed Nazi crimes to enlist West Germany as a Cold War ally. Hollywood avoided highlighting the Holocaust to avert accusations it was promoting a pro-Jewish agenda.

Nevertheless, filmmakers gravitated to the dramatic potential of stories about innocent individuals confronting brutal bigotry, repression, and war crimes. Between 1945 and 1960, more than a hundred Holocaust-related feature films and television dramas were produced (Baron 2005: 12–18, 25, 240). This body of work included movies about groups subjected to discrimination, incarceration, sterilization, and liquidation by Nazi Germany and its allies. Other films in this category dealt with war crimes trials, the repatriation or emigration of victimized groups, the psychological impact of events on perpetrators, survivors, and their descendants, and collective memory or amnesia about the persecution or rescue of Jews. Early Holocaust films evaded, idealized, and rationalized national responses to Hitler's policies in order to ingratiate the countries of origin with their respective superpower patron. Thus, these movies often marginalized the Jewish ordeal as one of many injustices inflicted by the Third Reich.

Several films from the first wave of Holocaust films garnered acclaim. The Swiss movie *The Last Chance* (1945), which traced how freed Allied POWs shepherded refugees, many of them Jews, to asylum in Switzerland, won awards for promoting international understanding and peace (Insdorf 2003: 251–2). Polish director Wanda Jakubowska (1907–1998) shot *The Last Stop* (1948) at Auschwitz, cast it with female camp survivors, and dramatized their wartime plight (Loewy 2004). Fred Zinnemann (1907–1997) filmed *The Search* (1948) in the rubble of German cities and gave all but the leading roles to children from displaced person camps. Although the protagonist is a Gentile boy, the movie includes identifiable Jewish juveniles, some of whom are preparing to immigrate to Palestine. Zinnemann admitted to "soften[ing] the truth to a certain extent" for American audiences, and his film received an Oscar and two Golden Globe awards (Baron 2005: 29–33; Etheridge 2006).

The early global popularization of the Holocaust stemmed from Anne Frank's diary, which appeared in Dutch in 1947 and in American and British editions in 1952. Shortly thereafter, adaptations aired on American radio and television and in the form of a Broadway play in 1955. George Stevens (1904–1975), who had headed the U.S. Army's filming of the liberation of the camps, turned the play into a motion picture in 1959, and the diary has spawned numerous documentaries and feature films ever since.

Holocaust scholars have decried the diary, play, and film for attenuating the Jewish identity of Anne Frank (1929–1945), accentuating her optimism, and never showing audiences her eventual fate. Yet Frank's upbeat and universalistic outlook enabled people to conceive of the collective Jewish tragedy in individual terms. *The Diary of Anne Frank* served as the prototype for Holocaust films whose appeal transcends racial, national, and religious differences. These works reduced the Holocaust to its tragic impact on "small groups, families and friends, parents and children, brothers and sisters" so that "the victims of trauma became everyman and everywoman, every child and every parent" (Alexander 2002: 34–7). By doing so, they fostered a "cosmopolitan memory" of an event that globally denoted absolute evil but locally connoted multiple meanings (Levy and Sznaider 2006: 23–63).

The doubling of the number of feature films about the Holocaust released per decade in the 1960s and the 1970s reflected the perceived reciprocal relationship between current events and the Shoah. The trial of Adolf Eichmann (1906–1962) and Hannah Arendt's portrait of his bureaucratic complicity (Arendt 1963) foreshadowed how opponents of the Viet Nam War accounted for American war crimes like the massacre at My Lai in 1968. Based on a teleplay broadcast in 1959, *Judgment at Nuremberg* (1961) drew analogies between the Third Reich's transgressions and those committed by the Allies (Mintz 2001: 85–107). The consciousness of racial discrimination and urban poverty raised by the civil rights movement elicited thematic and visual analogies with the Holocaust in Sidney Lumet's portrait of an anguished survivor in the 1965 release *The Pawnbroker* (Mintz 2001: 107–25). The Czech movie *The Shop on Main Street* (1965) exposed Slovakian collaboration in the deportation of Jews and implied continued collusion with despotism under Soviet rule (Liehm 1974: 394–425). Documentaries such as *The Sorrow and the Pity* (1969) and feature films like *The Garden of the Finzi Continis* (1970) respectively exposed the extent of native complicity in antisemitic policies in France and Jewish passivity in reaction to the imposition of Italian racial laws.

Capitalizing on the popularity of the television slavery saga *Roots* (1977), the NBC miniseries *Holocaust* (1978) inscribed the tragedy of European Jewry in American minds. Covering the period from 1935 until 1945, *Holocaust* framed the lives of a middle-class German-Jewish family, their gentile relatives through intermarriage, and an SS officer within the context of the escalation of antisemitic discrimination into extermination. It ended with the sole survivor of the Jewish family immigrating to Palestine, the widowed gentile wife of a Jewish artist giving birth to their son, and the Eichmann-like SS officer evading postwar trial by committing suicide.

Despite its melodramatic storyline, *Holocaust* remained firmly anchored in historical reality. The fictional characters respond to actual events and interact with individuals playing historical personages. While the reenactments of atrocities seem sanitized, the recurring insertion of documentary photographs taken by the Germans during the war reminds viewers that these scenes are based on actual incidents. The miniseries presented its Jewish protagonists as acculturated middle-class Germans who resembled the European and American audiences who watched it, but did not stereotype its Jewish leads as naive or passive victims as often was done in movies about this topic.

Holocaust demonstrated the power of film and television to affect public opinion and policy. It influenced President Jimmy Carter (b. 1924) to appoint the commission that eventually decided to build the United States Holocaust Memorial Museum in Washington, DC. In West Germany, the broadcast of *Holocaust* in 1979 reversed West German public opinion that had favored a statute of limitations on charges of murder. The ensuing legislation by the *Bundestag* authorized future prosecutions of Nazi war criminals.

The high-profile debate over *Holocaust* broached issues that have informed scholarly studies of Holocaust cinema ever since. Reiterating his distrust of fictional portrayals of the annihilation of European Jewry, Elie Wiesel (b. 1928) declared that "Auschwitz cannot be explained nor can it be visualized." He resented the insensitive staging of how the Germans killed Jews: "To use special effects and gimmicks to describe the indescribable is to me morally objectionable." Wiesel castigated NBC for trivializing the Holocaust by turning "an ontological event into a soap opera" (Wiesel 1978: 2).

Defenders of *Holocaust* praised the program for educating an audience estimated at 120 million Americans (Shandler 1999: 164–75). Pollsters for the American Jewish Committee (1978) found that 60 percent of the program's viewers felt the film helped them understand what Hitler had done to the Jews and three-quarters believed it provided "an accurate picture of Nazi anti-Semitic policies." Andreas Huyssen (1980) attributed the docudrama's similarly powerful impact on West Germans to its melodramatic narrative, which allowed Germans to identify emotionally with Jewish characters.

The polarized responses to *Holocaust* illustrated two models for fictional representations of the Holocaust (Mintz 2001: 36–84). The exceptionalist model treats the Holocaust as unique. Thus, it is either futile to replicate the inhumanity manifested in the "Final Solution" or that inhumanity must be depicted with uncompromising realism, which would lack aesthetic beauty or positive meaning. The constructionist model assumes that "meaning is constructed by communities of interpretation—differently by different communities—out of their own motives and needs" (Mintz 2001: 40).

Director Claude Lanzmann (b. 1925) has been the most outspoken advocate of the first position (Lanzmann in Liebman 2007: 27–49). For him, the Holocaust "created a circle of flame around itself, a boundary not to be crossed, since horror in the absolute degree cannot be communicated." Consequently, neither the images filmed by the Germans and Allies nor fictional reenactments convey a semblance of the debasement and deaths of millions of Jews, and "to pretend that one has done so is to commit the gravest of transgressions" (Lanzmann in Liebman 2007: 30). In his celebrated documentary *Shoah* (1985), Lanzmann relied entirely upon interviews of German perpetrators, Polish bystanders, and Jewish survivors. Their testimonies often serve as the soundtrack for tracking shots of the effaced "nonsites" of memory as they appear in the present. Absence and prolonged periods of silence underscore the void left by the obliteration of the Jewish community in Poland.

FIRST SURVEYS, EARLY ASSESSMENTS

The first surveys of Holocaust cinema were published in the 1980s in the wake of the debates over *Holocaust* and *Shoah*. They tended to concentrate on the development and impact of Holocaust-related films in particular national settings. Annette Insdorf opened her study by criticizing "the Hollywood version of the Holocaust" (1983: 4). Agreeing with Wiesel, she stipulated "that filmmakers confronting the Holocaust must assume a special responsibility, commensurate with its gravity and enormity." While appreciative of the educational impact of the NBC miniseries, she objected to how it romanticized and trivialized the Holocaust. Insdorf faulted other popular American movies such as *The Diary of Anne Frank, Judgment at Nuremberg*, and *The Boys from Brazil* (1978) for their formulaic treatment of the topic. She contended that they domesticate unsettling subject material by casting stars whom audiences associate with prior roles, manipulating emotions musically and visually, scripting platitudinous dialogue, and tacking on uplifting endings. The second edition of her book expanded the category of "Hollywood film" to include foreign productions that manifest the same flaws (1989: 15–18). Insdorf qualified her dislike of typical American productions by praising exceptions like *Cabaret* (1972), *The Pawnbroker*, and *Sophie's Choice* (1982) (1983: 21–44).

Ilan Avisar doubted the possibility of authentic representations of the Holocaust in movies "designed to please large audiences by catering to escapist melodramas . . . and yielding to popular demands and conventional tastes to assure commercial success" (1988: viii–ix). He equated the latter with Hollywood productions that drew trite lessons from the Holocaust, interpreted it through Christian concepts of redemption, minimized the Jewish identity of its victims, and shielded audiences from its threatening implications. In his opinion, "American interest in the subject is motivated by other considerations which are not necessarily rooted in a genuine concern with the disturbing truth of the historical tragedy" (1988: 90–133).

Insdorf valued a wider range of cinematic styles, narrative strategies, and themes than Avisar because they made the Holocaust relevant to contemporary audiences. Hence, "visualizing the subjective memories of survivors of the camps and ghettos, for example, can have more consistency and integrity than a movie that purports to show the past in an objective way" (Insdorf 1983: 22). In the third edition of her book, Insdorf classified Holocaust cinema as a distinct genre and acknowledged that "most Holocaust films have engaged in creative confrontation, indeed imagining that which is unimaginable in terms of fact and figures" (2003: 245–9).

Judith Doneson's *The Holocaust in American Film* (1987) contextualized depictions of the Shoah within a single nation's cinematic culture and politics. She analyzed both the accuracy of Hollywood productions and their relevance to American audiences and tended to prioritize the educational and political messages delivered by these films over their faithfulness to real events (Doneson 1987: 59–83). Her discussion of Stevens's *The Diary of Anne Frank* situates its narrative strategy and themes within the attitudes and issues that concerned Americans during the 1950s. She appreciated how the similarities between Anne's entourage and middle-class Americans facilitated identification with the characters in the diary, play, and movie. The alteration of Anne's meditation on why Jews were perennial scapegoats into one on why various groups endured persecution in history established that the ordeal of the Jews "shows what can happen when racism prevails." Doneson saw in this shift a condemnation of discrimination against African-Americans and suggested that the betrayal of Anne and her compatriots by a thief was an allusion to the informer system employed by the U.S. House of Representatives Un-American Activities Committee to purge communists from the movie industry and government.

Doneson realized how easily films like *The Diary of Anne Frank* and *The Pawnbroker* fell into the trap of validating common stereotypes of Jews, reducing Jews to passive figures dependent on Christian benefactors and endowing gentiles with active masculine traits and Jews with submissive feminine ones. The Jewish protagonists were, respectively, a young girl and a man who impotently watches his son trampled to death and his wife made a prostitute for German guards at the concentration camp (1987: 73–9, 110–12).

Doneson (1987: 143–96) regarded the miniseries *Holocaust* as a cinematic watershed, because of both the record viewership and the presentation of a range of responses to the escalation of Nazi antisemitism. The Jewish characters engage in armed and cultural resistance or maintain their faith. The Germans include Nazi ideologues, efficient bureaucrats, obedient citizens, and pro-Jewish dissidents. The story introduces the failure of the Allies, neutral nations, and the Vatican to intervene on behalf of the Jews. Seeing how ordinary people responded to Nazi genocide helped viewers draw connections with the consequences of not opposing similar injustices in the present.

A few scholars have shared Doneson's enthusiasm for the educational and political role of films in shaping America's collective memory about the Holocaust, a role that probably reached its apex with *Schindler's List* (1993). Surveying American television's depiction of the Holocaust from the documentaries, ecumenical religious programs, and live theatrical productions of the 1950s through the docudramas, documentaries, and talk show interviews with survivors like Wiesel in the 1990s, Jeffrey Shandler asserted that "Americans would not be as widely familiar with the Holocaust, and in as complex, emotionally charged, and morally engaged a manner as they are, without television's many presentations of the subject" (Shandler 1999: 256). Alan Mintz has scrutinized signature American films about the Holocaust from both exceptionalist and constructivist perspectives, contrasting the initially relatively positive reviews of the first major films and the criticisms leveled at them subsequently by Holocaust scholars. Although he voiced serious reservations about the treatment of the Holocaust by Hollywood, he also praised it as "an agent of moral seriousness that changes people's lives for the better and confers on the American popular mind the possibility of escape from vulgarity" (Mintz 2001: 157).

Most Holocaust scholars, however, believe that the positive and universal spin Hollywood puts on the Holocaust strips it of historical particularity and irremediable inhumanity. Lawrence Langer, for example, lambasted Hollywood for failing to confront the numbing reality that millions of Jews had died in vain and for striving "to parlay hope, sacrifice, justice, and the future into a victory that will mitigate despair" (in Cohen 1983: 213–14). Similarly, Alvin Rosenfeld criticized American popular culture for equating the Holocaust with other manifestations of prejudice and for idealizing gentile rescuers and resilient Jewish survivors to the point of obscuring that both were the exception to the rule of complicity and indifference among gentiles and traumatic scarring and victimization among survivors (1997: 119–50).

Nowhere has the cinematic representation of the Holocaust been more controversial than in West Germany. During the 1970s, political liberalization, renewed interest in Hitler, outbreaks of domestic terrorism, violations of civil liberties to combat it, and the ostensible national catharsis occasioned by the airing of *Holocaust* served as catalysts for films, released primarily at the end of the decade and in the early 1980s, that dealt with the meaning of the Nazi legacy for the German present. Anton Kaes (1989) and Eric Santner (1990) analyzed whether these films succeed in coming to terms with the past. Both devote considerable attention to *Our Hitler* (1978), a film by Hans-Jürgen Syberberg (b. 1935), a pastiche of actors, newsreel footage, music, and puppets symbolizing the myriad of personae Germans projected onto their Führer, and to *Heimat* (1984) by Edgar Reitz (b. 1932), a fifteen-hour miniseries chronicling the lives of the inhabitants of a provincial German town from the end of World War I until 1982. Kaes and Santner concur that the two films mourn the excesses of Nazism for tarnishing postwar German identity and causing the victimization of the country by Allied bombings, military occupation, and partition. What happened to the Jews in both films is relegated to collateral damage emanating from the genocide that developed under the impetus of unrestricted warfare. To Santner, these films lamented the past without endorsing cultural pluralism to avert future genocides.

Robert and Carol Reimer's *Nazi-Retro Film* (1992) encompassed a broader sampling of German films. "Retro" refers to the two directions films about the Nazi era have taken—nostalgic normalization or progressive retrospection. The most acclaimed example of the latter is *The Tin Drum*, directed by Volker Schlöndorff (b. 1939), a film version of the novel by Günter Grass (b. 1927). In Schlöndorff's film, the first postwar German movie to win the Oscar for Best Foreign Language Film, a boy named Oskar refuses to grow up while the adults around him blindly follow Hitler. Soon after Oskar relates how Santa Claus was transformed into the "gas man," the film shows images of a synagogue in flames and the death of the beloved Jewish toy store owner who sold Oskar tin drums. When Russian troops overrun Germany, Oskar's father tosses his Nazi lapel pin away, but Oskar retrieves it. After his father swallows it and chokes to death, Oskar decides to begin growing again (Reimer and Reimer 1992: 123–9).

Significant work has also been done on Holocaust-related films that have emerged from and impacted French and Italian culture (Colombat 1993; Marcus 2007). In France, the early postwar celebration of resistance and vilification of traitors eventually was challenged by documentaries like *The Sorrow and the Pity* (1969) and a flurry of feature films about common forms of French betrayal or rescue of Jews. From the end of the war until 1990, the Holocaust exerted a relatively weak influence on Italian film with the exception of notable motion pictures such as *Kapo* (1959), *The Garden of the Finzi Continis* (1971), and *The Night Porter* (1974). The end of the Cold War, Pope John Paul II's conciliatory gestures toward Jews, and the influx of Third World immigrants into Italy generated a racist backlash, and all of these factors, which heightened liberal vigilance against a fascist revival, alerted Italian directors to the salience of the Holocaust for their society. As a result, films such as *Life Is Beautiful* (1998), *The Truce* (1998), and *Unfair Competition* (2001) have etched the Holocaust further into Italian collective memory.

Scholarship's Second Wave

Just as the first surveys of Holocaust cinema appeared shortly after landmark films like *Holocaust* and *Shoah*, the second wave of this scholarship emerged as a reaction primarily to *Schindler's List*, directed by Steven Spielberg (b. 1946), and *Life Is*

Beautiful, directed by Roberto Benigni (b. 1952). The panoply of awards conferred on these two films and the international success they achieved renewed the debates over how much creative license directors should exercise in representing the Holocaust, whether certain genres and themes inherently misrepresent its severity, and if media popularizations might eventually overshadow eyewitness accounts, primary sources, and scholarly research.

Yosefa Loshitzky's *Spielberg's Holocaust: Critical Perspectives on Schindler's List* (1997) explored many of these themes in one volume. Reactions to Spielberg's magnum opus fell into four categories: censure for blurring the boundary between dramatization and documentary; comparison of Spielberg's graphic reenactments of Nazi atrocities with Lanzmann's reliance on interviews of eyewitnesses; questions as to whether the scenario of a good German man rescuing passive Jews inadvertently perpetuates traditional stereotypes; and national receptions.

Spielberg employed rich black and white film stock, referenced iconic images from documentaries, feature films, newsreels, and photographs, shot the movie at the sites where the events occurred, and utilized a held camera to replicate the viewpoints of perpetrators and victims alike. He eschewed many of his signature special effects and imbued the film with a *cinéma-vérité* look. In interviews he declared his intent to bear witness to the slain Jews by creating a film that seemed more like a documentary than a docudrama (Friedman and Notbohm 2000: 157–92). Though the film's detractors dwelled on discrepancies between it and the historical novel about Oskar Schindler (1908–1974) by the Australian author Thomas Keneally (b. 1935), Spielberg's collapsing of characters, heightening of suspense, and simplifying of plot details did not violate standard cinematic practices of adaptation except toward the ending, when Schindler undergoes a moral catharsis and regrets that he had not saved enough of his workers.

For some Holocaust scholars, the accolades heaped upon *Schindler's List* as the definitive Holocaust film confirmed a nagging fear that "as the Hitler era slowly passes from the realm of experience and personal memory into the realm of images, will it also become a mere movie myth?" (Kaes 1989: 198). Barbie Zelizer advised viewers to "build again that distinction between the event-as-it happened and the event-as-it is retold" (Loshitzky 1997: 29–30). Bryan Cheyette observed that despite "the initial admiration of Spielberg's ambitious, often breathtaking naturalism, one also becomes aware of the overriding theatricality of *Schindler's List*" (Loshitzky 1997: 229–30). Sara Horowitz worried that the film's semblance of authenticity could become fodder for Holocaust deniers who would cite misleading scenes, like the one where Schindler's female workers get showers at Auschwitz rather than being gassed, as proof that Jews were never killed in gas chambers there (Loshitzky 1997: 128–9).

Claude Lanzmann denounced *Schindler's List* as the antithesis of *Shoah*. He excoriated Spielberg's directorial hubris of visualizing a moral void and offering salvation through the altruism of Schindler and the establishment of Israel.

Loshitzky preferred Lanzmann's strategy of forcing the viewer to imagine the inhumanity described by eyewitnesses and rejected Spielberg's pandering to "an audience hungry for the spectacle of atrocity." She accused Spielberg of sharing Schindler's flaws: "Both attempt to redeem the easy money they have made through the performance of 'a good deed'" (Loshitsky 1997: 110–15). Conversely, Miriam Bratu Hansen and several other commentators urged peers to transcend the binary oppositions between elite and popular culture, intellectual complexity and empathic melodrama, and non-representational and representational art and to concede that "different stories relating to the most traumatic and central event of the twentieth century will be and will have to be told, in a variety of media and genres, within an irrevocably multiple and hybrid public sphere" (Loshitzky 1997: 98–9).

The dependence of Jews on Schindler, their vulnerability to the sadism of Amon Goeth (1908–1946), the commandant of the Plaszow labor camp, and the displays of feminine sexuality struck many scholars as a reinforcement of Christian, Jewish, Nazi, and female stereotypes. Doneson discerned a Christian motif in the storyline of a Messianic savior of the Jews (Loshitzky 1997: 140–50). She coded Christian men, whether decent like Schindler or demonic like Goeth, as the masculine actors in this sacred drama, and Jews as the feminine recipients of their respective benevolence or malevolence. Horowitz rebuked Spielberg for continuing the trope of the eroticized female victims reminiscent of films like *The Night Porter* and *Sophie's Choice*, especially in two egregious scenes. In one, Goeth sees his maid's translucent naked body under a sheer nightgown, ponders yielding to his desires but then beats her for seducing him. In the other, which poses naked women in the showers, horror is transformed into voyeurism (Loshitzky 1997: 126–32).

Omer Bartov contended that *Schindler's List* validates common stereotypes by tapping into pre-existing audience attitudes (Loshitzky 1997: 48–50). Schindler's decency, the wickedness of Goeth, and the passivity of cowering Jews are caricatures that resonate with the preconceptions viewers harbor toward Jews and Nazis. Bartov went on to argue that the stereotypical traits ascribed to Jews are so deeply ingrained in western culture that even directors who attempt to depict complex Jewish characters inadvertently idealize or vilify them, depending on the prejudices held by audience members. His argument becomes strained, however, when he proffers readings that subvert the directorial intent of movies like *Europa, Europa* (1991). That its Jewish protagonist can dupe his Hitler Youth instructor into believing he is a pedigree "Aryan" discredits racist determinism. Yet Bartov insists that Solly's chameleonic skill also confirms antisemitic suspicions of the Jew as "an insubstantial, protean parasite" (2005: 161).

Life is Beautiful caused more critical consternation than *Schindler's List*. Its use of humor coincided with an increase in the number of Holocaust comedies released in the 1990s. Roberto Benigni begins his film with an adult's voiceover calling the tale he is about to tell a "fable," thus dispelling any pretence that the film is realistic. Benigni plays Guido, the narrator's father, who shields his son from the realities of a death camp by pretending that its hardships are part of a game to win a tank. Prisoners supposedly earn points by not succumbing to despair. Fabricating an assuring lie to cope with desperation provided the premise for other Holocaust comedies such as *Train of Life* (1998) and *Jakob the Liar* (1999). Unlike the brightly colored first half of *Life Is Beautiful*, which recounts Guido's courtship of his future wife, a bleaker bluish-grey filter casts a pall over the last half, which is set in a concentration camp. Since viewers know the fate awaiting the camp's inmates, Guido's innocuous explanations of frightful rumors sound ludicrous to the audience. When Guido stumbles upon a pit filled with corpses, he cradles his sleeping son to prevent him from glimpsing the abyss. After hiding the boy, Guido is captured and executed. When the Germans have fled, an American tank gives his son a ride. He rejoins his mother and exclaims, "We won!" The happy ending is tempered by the audience's awareness that he has lost his father, and she her husband.

Guido's ruse of a concentration camp as a game polarized film and literary critics. The *New Yorker*'s David Denby (1999: 96-9) abhorred the picture's happy ending as tantamount to Holocaust denial. Kobi Niv (2005: xxii) inveighed against Benigni for selecting "a very particular, doctored, cute little 'frame' out of the whole picture. . . . creating the impression that this fake reality is in fact what took place in the death camps." Italian film specialists traced *Life Is Beautiful*'s cinematic lineage to motion pictures like *Amarcord* (1974) and *Cinema Paradiso* (1988), which combined humor and tragedy to depict everyday life under fascism (Marcus 2002). Hilene Flanzbaum applauded Benigni's innovative approach: "For the parents in the audience who have lost sleep over what they might do to protect their own child, the film proved overwhelming. Benigni accomplishes a great deal when he defamiliarizes the Holocaust enough to make viewers feel it all over again" (2001: 283).

RECENT TRENDS AND INTERPRETATIONS

During the 1990s, the growing influence of trauma theory on cultural studies led to the examination of the psychological patterns evidenced in eyewitness accounts and creative representations of the Holocaust (Langer 1991; Felman and Laub 1992; LaCapra 1994). Criticism of the linear narrative of *Schindler's List* asserted that unedited videotapes of survivors recounting the random chain of events that contributed to their survival better conveyed what actually happened than any feature film (Hartman 1996: 82–98, 133–50). Oren Baruch Stier questioned whether even videotaped interviews elicit and transmit unmediated historical remembrance. He described how filmmakers and interviewers visually and verbally prompt respondents who censor themselves to repress personal shame and preempt misinterpretation by viewers or auditors (2003: 67–109).

Joshua Hirsch (2004) applies trauma theory to documentaries and feature films concerned with rationalizing, reliving, and repressing consciousness of the Holocaust. Focusing on such motion pictures as *Night and Fog, Shoah, The Pawnbroker,* and the Holocaust trilogy by the Hungarian director István Szabó (b. 1938), he elucidates the cinematic techniques utilized to replicate the fear and horror that survivors experienced and subconsciously transmitted to their children or the profound shock over the Shoah that humanity felt then and now. In these films, individual and public memory coalesce into a permeable barrier that allows the past, when extermination was state policy, to trespass into the present, when something similar could happen again.

Can duplicating the interplay between trauma and remembered and repressed "truth" provide a viable basis for a commercial mass medium? Trauma denotes a personal sense of degradation, impotence, loss, and pain experienced by survivors, victims, and eyewitnesses. Yet the vast majority of people living today are "nonwitnesses" who learn about the Holocaust primarily through artworks, documentaries, feature films, fictional narratives, history books, memoirs, and museums, sources that communicate a constructed approximation of the experience (Weissman 2004: 18–24). Alison Landsberg believes movies function as "prosthetic memories," acting like "artificial limbs" to mark the site of a traumatic event, enable us to touch a past we have not endured, and generate empathy for victims of another era (2004: 18–22). Libby Saxton (2008) distinguishes between films that render audiences voyeuristic spectators of atrocity and those that compel them to respond ethically to it.

Questions about the limits of realism have been raised especially by *The Grey Zone* (2001), directed by Tim Blake Nelson (b. 1964), which tried to take viewers directly into the gas chambers and crematoria as the *Sonderkommando* units at Auschwitz-Birkenau experienced them (Baron in Petropoulos and Roth 2005: 286–92). Recent studies, however, tend to evaluate Holocaust films by cinematic criteria rather than by their historical accuracy, examining, for instance, how the genres and themes of Holocaust films reflect contemporary trends in their respective movie industries (Baron 2005: 25, 66, 202, 240). Paralleling the rise of the docudrama, the biographical film, usually based on survivors' memoirs, emerged as the most popular genre for Holocaust films over the last thirty years. Such "biopics" lend themselves to genre hybridization, and thus *Schindler's List* follows the conventions of films about rogues with golden hearts à la *The Magnificent Seven* (1960) and *The Sting* (1973); *Nowhere in Africa's* (2001) plot about German-Jewish refugees finding a haven in Kenya harkens back to pioneer films about adapting to the wildness; and *The Pianist* (2002) combines the themes of an artist sustained by his talent, the isolated survivalist like Robinson Crusoe, and the fugitive staying one step ahead of his pursuers.

Changes in cinematic treatments of Holocaust-related love stories are among the developments clarified by recent scholarship (Baron 2005). In the 1980s and before, movies from this genre usually revolved around religiously mixed heterosexual couples whose commitment to each other was tested by Nazi racial laws. More recent movies about gay lovers, such as *Bent* (1997), *Aimée and Jaguar* (1999), and *Facing Windows* (2003), mirror new research about the Third Reich's persecution of homosexuals, the gains achieved by the gay rights movement, and the growth of a niche audience and venues for motion pictures about same-sex relationships. *Train of Life* (1999) and *The Man Who Cried* (2001) feature romances between Gypsy and Jewish characters. The focus on non-Jewish victims of Nazism parallels the rise of the multicultural paradigm in the west.

Contemporary scholars have also directed attention to similar cinematographic techniques and plot dynamics in horror movies, such as *Psycho* (1960) and *Silence of the Lambs* (1991), and Holocaust films, such as *Apt Pupil* (1998) and *Schindler's List* (Picart and Frank 2006). Like the famous American director Alfred Hitchcock (1899–1980), Spielberg uses a shower scene to induce dread. Goeth rivals Hannibal Lecter in his ability to morph from an affable drinking buddy to a remorseless mass murderer. Portrayals of Nazi villains as monsters tend to reinforce the intentionalist interpretation of the Holocaust and to divert attention from the less ideological, more self-interested impulses that encouraged participation in Nazi persecution (Picart and Frank 2006).

CONCLUSION

Partly because study of Holocaust cinema is a relatively young field, debates about the adequacy of film to represent the Holocaust and the appropriate genres for treatments of that event are unlikely to abate. Questions about film and the Holocaust are further complicated by differences of opinion over the way films sometimes use the Holocaust to rationalize Israeli security concerns and bolster American Jewish identity (Horowitz in Flanzbaum 1999: 142–66; Mart 2006; Ginsberg 2007). Since many Holocaust films have followed recent trends toward multinational productions and international marketing (Baron 2005: 240), current scholars need to keep considering how depictions of the event change to suit the collective memories of the countries where the Holocaust occurred (Brenner 2000; Levy and Sznaider 2006). National comparisons of the promotion, content, and reception of Holocaust films may help delineate the differential evolution of public memory about World War II and the Jewish genocide in various countries (Lichtner 2008; Paris 2008). Research that compares Holocaust films with those about other genocides and with severe personal traumas also remains vital (Haggith and Newman 2005: 255–87; Walker 2005; Mandel 2006). Pedagogical literature on using Holocaust films in classroom settings is another helpful research path (Hirsch and Kacandes 2004; Eaglestone and Langford 2008).

Unintended effects of proliferating Holocaust films—including *The Boy in Striped Pyjamas* (2008), *Defiance* (2008), *The Reader* (2008), *Valkyrie* (2008), and *Inglourious Basterds* (2009), with more on the way—may range from "Holocaust fatigue," on the one hand, to, on the other, inclining people to dismiss contemporary atrocities as less horrible than those inflicted on Jews during the Holocaust. Yet filmmakers return to Holocaust images and themes because they believe the event retains its power to touch human conscience. Time will tell whether that belief is well founded, but an explanation of why Hollywood recycles film genres is likely to remain applicable to Holocaust films as well: "Those icons, scenarios, visual conventions continue to carry with them some sort of cultural 'charge' or resonance that must be reworked according to the exigencies of the present" (Collins 1995: 147–8).

References

ALEXANDER, J. (2002). "On the Social Construction of Moral Universals: The Holocaust from Mass Murder to Trauma Drama." *European Journal of Social Theory* 5/1: 5–86.

AMERICAN JEWISH COMMITTEE (1978). *Americans Confront the Holocaust: A Study of the Reactions to NBC-TV's Four Part Drama of the Nazi Era*. New York: American Jewish Committee.

ARENDT, H. (1963). *Eichmann in Jerusalem: A Report on the Banality of Evil*. New York: Viking Press.

AVISAR, I. (1988). *Screening the Holocaust: Cinema's Images of the Unimaginable*. Bloomington, IN: Indiana University Press.

BARON, L. (2005). *Projecting the Holocaust into the Present: The Changing Focus of Contemporary Holocaust Cinema*. Lanham, MD: Rowman & Littlefield.

BARTOV, O. (2005). *The "Jew" in Cinema: From 'The Golem' to 'Don't Touch My Holocaust'*. Bloomington, IN: Indiana University Press.

BRENNER, D. (2000). "Working Through the Holocaust Blockbuster: From *Schindler's List* to Hitler's Willing Executioners, Globally and Locally." *Germanic Review* 75/4: 296–317.

COHEN, S. (ed.) (1983). *From Hester Street to Hollywood*. Bloomington, IN: Indiana University Press.

COLLINS, J. (1995). *Architectures of Excess: Cultural Life in the Information Age*. New York: Routledge.

COLOMBAT, A. (1993). *The Holocaust in French Film*. Metuchen, NJ: Scarecrow Press.

DENBY, D. (1999). "Life Is Beautiful." *New Yorker* 75/3: 96–9.

DONESON, J. (1987). *The Holocaust in American Film*. Philadelphia, PA: Jewish Publication Society.

EAGLESTONE, R. and LANGFORD, B. (2008). *Teaching Holocaust Literature and Film*. New York: Palgrave Macmillan.

ETHERIDGE, B. (2006). "In Search of Germans: Contexted Germany in the Production of *The Search.*" *Journal of Popular Film and Television* 34/1: 34–43.

FELMAN, S. and LAUB, D. (1992). *Testimony: Crises of Witnessing in Literature, Psychoanalysis, and History.* New York: Routledge.

FLANZBAUM, H. (ed.) (1999). *The Americanization of the Holocaust.* Baltimore, MD: Johns Hopkins University Press.

——(2001). "But Wasn't It Terrific? A Defense of Liking *Life Is Beautiful.*" *Yale Journal of Criticism* 14/1: 273–86.

FRIEDMAN, L. and NOTBOHM, B. (eds.) (2000). *Steven Spielberg: Interviews.* Jackson, MS: University Press of Mississippi.

GINSBERG, T. (2007). *Holocaust Film: The Political Aesthetics of Ideology.* Newcastle: Cambridge Scholars Publishing.

HAGGITH, T. and NEWMAN, J. (eds.) (2005). *Holocaust and the Moving Image: Representations in Film and Television Since 1933.* London: Wallflower Press.

HARTMAN, G. (1996). *The Longest Shadow: In the Aftermath of the Holocaust.* Bloomington, IN: Indiana University Press.

HIRSCH, J. (2004). *Afterimage: Film, Trauma, and the Holocaust.* Philadelphia, PA: Temple University Press.

HIRSCH, M. and KACANDES, I. (eds.) (2004). *Teaching the Representation of the Holocaust.* New York: Modern Language Association of America.

HUYSSEN, A. (1980). "The Politics of Identification: Holocaust and West German Drama." *New German Critique* 19: 117–136.

INSDORF, A. (1983). *Indelible Shadows: Film and the Holocaust.* New York: Random House.

——(1989). *Indelible Shadows: Film and the Holocaust.* 2nd edn. New York: Cambridge University Press.

——(2003). *Indelible Shadows: Film and the Holocaust.* 3rd edn. New York: Cambridge University Press.

KAES, A. (1989). *From* Heimat *to Hitler: The Return of History as Film.* Cambridge, MA: Harvard University Press.

KNAAP, E. VAN DER (2006). *Uncovering the Holocaust: The International Reception of* Night and Fog. London: Wallflower Press.

LACAPRA, D. (1994). *Representing the Holocaust: History, Theory, Trauma.* Ithaca, NY: Cornell University Press.

LANDSBERG, A. (2004). *Prosthetic Memory: The Transformation of American Remembrance in the Age of Mass Culture.* New York: Columbia University Press.

LANGER, L. (1991). *Holocaust Testimonies: The Ruins of Memory.* New Haven, CT: Yale University Press.

LEVY, D. and SZNAIDER, N. (2006). *The Holocaust and Memory in the Global Age.* Philadelphia, PA: Temple University Press.

LICHTNER, G. (2008). *Film and the Shoah in France and Italy.* London: Vallentine Mitchell.

LIEBMAN, S. (ed.) (2007). *Claude Lanzmann's* Shoah: *Key Essays.* New York: Oxford University Press.

LIEHM, A. (1974). *Closely Watched Films: The Czechoslovakian Experience.* White Plains, NY: International Arts and Science Press.

Loewy, H. (2004). "The Mother of All Holocaust Films: Wanda Jakabowska's Auschwitz Trilogy." *Historical Journal of Film, Radio, and Television* 24/2: 179–204.

Loshitzky, Y. (ed.) (1997). *Spielberg's Holocaust: Critical Perspectives on* Schindler's List. Bloomington, IN: Indiana University Press.

Mandel, N. (2006). *Against the Unspeakable: Complicity, the Holocaust, and Slavery in America.* Charlottesville, VA: University of Virginia Press.

Marcus, M. (2002). *After Fellini: National Cinema in the Postmodern Age.* Baltimore, MD: Johns Hopkins University Press.

——(2007). *Italian Film in the Shadow of Auschwitz.* Toronto: University of Toronto Press.

Mart, M. (2006). *Eye on Israel: How America Came to View Israel as an Ally.* Albany, NY: State University of New York.

Mintz, A. (2001). *Popular Culture and the Shaping of Holocaust Memory in America.* Seattle, WA: University of Washington Press.

Niv, K. (2005). *Life Is Beautiful, but Not For Jews: Another View of the Film by Benigni.* Lanham, MD: Scarecrow Press.

Paris, M. (ed.) (2008). *Repicturing the Second World War: Representations in Film and Television.* New York: Palgrave Macmillan.

Petropoulos, J. and Roth, J. (eds.) (2005). *Gray Zones: Ambiguity and Compromise in the Holocaust and Its Aftermath.* New York: Berghahn Books.

Picart, C. and Frank, D. (2006). *Frames of Evil: The Holocaust as Horror in American Film.* Carbondale, IL: Southern Illinois University Press.

Reimer, C. and Reimer, R. (1992). *Nazi Retro-Film: How German Narrative Cinema Remembers the Past.* New York: Twayne Publishers.

Rosenfeld, A. (ed.) (1997). *Thinking about the Holocaust: After Half a Century.* Bloomington, IN: Indiana University Press.

Santner, E. (1990). *Stranded Objects: Mourning, Memory, and Film in Postwar Germany.* Ithaca, NY: Cornell University Press.

Saxton, L. (2008). *Haunted Images: Film, Ethics, Testimony and the Holocaust.* London: Wallflower Press.

Shandler, J. (1999). *While America Watches: Televising the Holocaust.* New York: Oxford University Press.

Stier, O. (2003). *Committed to Memory: Cultural Mediations of the Holocaust.* Amherst, MA: University of Massachusetts Press.

Walker, J. (2005). *Trauma Cinema: Documenting Incest and the Holocaust.* Berkeley, CA: University of California Press.

Weissman, G. (2004). *Fantasies of Witnessing: Postwar Efforts to Experience the Holocaust.* Ithaca, NY: Cornell University Press.

Wiesel, E. (1978). "Trivializing the Holocaust: Semi-Fact and Semi-Fiction." *New York Times,* April 16, Sec.2, 1, 29.

Other Suggested Reading

Bathrick, D., Prager, B., and Richardson, M. (eds.) (2008). *Visualizing the Holocaust: Documents, Aesthetics, and Memories.* Lanham, MD: Rowman & Littlefield.

LANG, B. (2000). *Holocaust Representation: Art within the Limits of History and Ethics.* Baltimore, MD: Johns Hopkins University Press.

PICART, C. (ed.) (2004). *The Holocaust Film Sourcebook.* 2 vols. Westport, CT: Praeger.

RAPHAEL, M. (ed.) (2003, 2006). *The Representation of the Holocaust in Literature and Film.* 2 vols. Williamsburg, VA: Department of Religion of the College of William and Mary.

WILCOX, L. (2002). "The Holocaust on Film." *Film and History* 32, no. 1–2.

CHAPTER 30

···

ART

···

DORA APEL

FOCUSING on works by artists such as Rico Lebrun (1900–1964), George Segal (1924–2000), or Jerome Witkin (b. 1939), art critics and art historians have sometimes criticized too realistic art about the Holocaust for aestheticizing atrocity, presenting a gratuitous and repellent violence, and advancing a reductive and one-dimensional literalness. Similarly, curators have often preferred to show work that is abstracted or allusive, avoiding "morbidity, sentimentality, and overused visual stereotypes" that have lost their power to shock (Bohm-Duchen in Feinstein 2005: 56). The guiding mandate for post-Holocaust artistic practice was laid down by Theodore Adorno's (1903–1969) interdiction of "poetry after Auschwitz" (1981). Paradoxically, Adorno's refusal of aesthetics, which began as a refusal of art altogether, became the conventionalized, dominant aesthetic, or anti-aesthetic, although the negative and allusive Holocaust-related artwork that met this mandate took a wide variety of forms. More recently, however, younger artists have rebelled against this ethic of representation in provocative ways. This chapter explores the changing strategies of representation in the postwar era, moving from the modernist premise guided by Adorno's interdiction to the postmodernist rejection of that premise. The controversy surrounding the 2002 exhibition *Mirroring Evil* at the Jewish Museum in New York provides an exemplary case study that illuminates the continuing debate over visual representation of the Holocaust.

EVOLVING POST-HOLOCAUST CONTEXTS

···

Historical contexts condition art about the Holocaust. In her monumental survey of the Holocaust's influence on the visual arts, Ziva Amishai-Maisels (1993) demonstrates that in the immediate postwar period Jewish and non-Jewish artists such as

Pablo Picasso (1881–1973), Leonard Baskin (1922–2000), and Ben Shahn (1898–1969) sought to universalize the horror of the Nazi genocide by avoiding specific reference to Jewish victims, instead turning the victim into an Everyman. Artists such as Marc Chagall (1887–1985) and Francis Bacon (1909–1992) used Christian symbols as part of their universalizing imagery. Non-figurative artists such as Mark Rothko (1903–1970) and Barnett Newmann (1905–1970) used the universalizing gesture of abstract minimalism to create a "transcendental" space. The impulse to universalize stemmed from varied political factors: the concept of the Holocaust as a war against the Jews did not come into public discourse until the 1960s, following the 1961 trial of Adolf Eichmann (1906–1962) in Jerusalem; for Americans, the horror of the death camps was superseded by the horror of the bombings of Hiroshima and Nagasaki, in which Americans were perpetrators; Jews themselves wished to avoid the negative stereotype of the Jew as victim and strongly encouraged assimilation and forgetting of the past; American Cold War ideology shifted hatred of the Nazis to hatred of the communists as Germany ceased to be an enemy and became an ally, while the Soviet Union ceased to be an ally and became the new enemy. Nazis and communists were made coeval under the new rubric of "totalitarianism," which downplayed the genocide of the Jews as a central and defining feature of the Nazi regime in order to posit the essential identity between the Nazis and the Soviets. At the same time, Jews were identified with Bolshevism, as embodied by the Julius and Ethel Rosenberg trial in the United States in the early 1950s, and since only the American communists opposed accepting Germany as a Cold War ally, American Jews were reluctant to end up in the same camp with them, especially in the era of McCarthyism. To prove themselves good Americans, they downplayed the ethnic specificity of Europe's Jewish victims (Novick 1999).

At least until the 1980s, the Holocaust was generally regarded as indescribable, incomprehensible, and unrepresentable. This conviction corresponds to what Gene Ray calls Adorno's "'after Auschwitz' ethic of representation," which not only made aesthetic pleasure taboo but also refused all positive or direct representation of the disaster (Ray 2005). This ethic is perhaps most frequently associated with Anselm Kiefer (b. 1945) and Christian Boltanski (b. 1944), whose ambiguous and elegiac work nonetheless problematized the question of subject position (perpetrator, victim, bystander, secondary witness) in relation to the genocide in powerful and provocative ways. Although there are still those who question Kiefer for dwelling on the postwar German subject, or Boltanski for a lack of historical specificity (Kaplan 2007), most critics no longer question the moral integrity of their pioneering work (van Alphen 1997; Biro 1998; Saltzman 1999; Gumpert 2001). Often ironic, Kiefer ranges from his 1969 photographed performances giving the Hitler salute in *Occupations* to his later monumental paintings centering on German national identity. Kiefer, who "put the problem of German guilt on the agenda" (Amishai-Maisels in Feinstein 2005: 147), explored the taboos and limitations of Nazi and Holocaust subject matter, producing complex and multivalent works. Similarly, Boltanski (whose father was Jewish and mother Catholic) probes and deconstructs the borders that divide good and evil, transforming photographs of ordinary citizens into allusions to Holocaust victims and rephotographing the family album of a Nazi officer. From different subject positions, Kiefer and Boltanski are both concerned with the complex effects of the past on the present, depicting Holocaust-related content allusively, indirectly, and with a dark solemnity. Older artists such as Samuel Bak (b. 1933) and R. B. Kitaj (1932–2007) sought symbolic figurative approaches to the Holocaust, the former using allegorical, surreal, or biblical frameworks, the latter preoccupied with a "diasporist" mentality that grappled with the meaning of Jewishness in a post-Holocaust world.

As Jews embraced the Holocaust with a new self-confidence following the Israeli victories in the Arab–Israeli Six Day War of 1967 and the Yom Kippur War of 1973, many artists felt that the universalizing of the atrocities by an earlier generation of artists had undermined the ability of the works to function meaningfully. Younger artists turned to a more historically explicit treatment of the subject, as in the seminal *Maus* books by Art Spiegelman (b. 1948) (1986, 1991) and in the work of Rachel Whiteread (b. 1963), Jochen Gerz (b. 1940) and Esther Shalev-Gerz (b. 1948), David Levinthal (b. 1949), and Shimon Attie (b. 1957). Like Kiefer and Boltanski, they also problematized the question of subject position, sometimes touching off controversies.

By the 1990s, this growing trend among those born later was consolidated as artists began to challenge the anxiety of aesthetics in the visual exploration of difficult subject matter and to assert a new paradigm for what art about the Holocaust might be. With growing distance from the Holocaust itself as a historical "event," many younger artists became far more focused on its representation within contemporary media where "the Holocaust" as a flexible trope has become an adaptable cultural and political instrument. These latter uses—*abuses*, many would say—of the "idea" of the Holocaust draw responses from these artists, who produce their own forms of representation, while exploring its dilemmas.

In his important study, *At Memory's Edge*, James Young (2000) proposed that younger artists were no longer confronting the past but their own "vicarious memory" of the past in the present, with a loss of faith in redemptive meanings. Ernst van Alphen, myself, and others have also explored such contemporary memory work and examined the relationship between Holocaust documentary and the continuing artistic response to the disaster of the genocide (van Alphen 1997; Liss 1998; Apel 2002), or between family photographs and individual and cultural identity after the Holocaust (Hirsch 1997). Anthologies examine contemporary Holocaust representation in a variety of visual forms (Zelizer 2001; Hornstein and Jacobowitz 2003; Hornstein et al. 2003; Feinstein 2005). Postmodern artists reject the heroic gesture in favor of the anti-redemptive and approach Jewish identity not only in relation to the Judeocide but also as an evolving phenomenon. Gene Ray notes that increasingly the work of artists born later addresses questions of contemporary Jewish identity in the context of Zionism and Israeli politics, not only rejecting representational taboos, but daring to investigate issues such as "the mobilization of sexual desire in fascist imagery, and the survival of fascist logic in consumer capitalism" (Ray 2005: 63).

The first group exhibition of contemporary art devoted to representing the Holocaust did not take place until 1994. Organized by the Washington Project for the Arts in Washington, DC, *Burnt Whole: Contemporary Artists Reflect on the Holocaust* presented the work of thirty-one artists from six countries, the United States, Israel, Germany, France, England, and Argentina. The artists, including Kiefer, Boltanski, Spiegelman, Astrid Klein (b. 1951), Guillermo Kuitca (b. 1961), and Ellen Rothenberg (b. 1949), were all born after the war. The critical response was mixed. Donald Kuspit found the work "naïve" and judged the exhibition a failure because of its inability to comprehend the significance of the Holocaust (Kuspit 1995). But Martha McWilliams judged the exhibition a success because it radically altered the prevailing view of the Holocaust as incomprehensible and unrepresentable (McWilliams 1995: 12). Many exhibitions both large and small followed, such as *Witness and Legacy: Contemporary Art about the Holocaust* (1995), a traveling exhibition that originated at the Minnesota Museum of American Art, and *After Auschwitz: Responses to the Holocaust in Contemporary Art* (1995), at the Royal Festival Hall in London. By the mid-1990s, an explosion of Holocaust representation had occurred in the form of museums (the United States Holocaust Memorial Museum opened in 1993), films, monuments, hundreds of books, anthologies, memoirs, dissertations in a variety of disciplines, scholarly journals devoted to the Holocaust, and catalogs documenting artistic projects.

No exhibition sparked as much public controversy as *Mirroring Evil: Nazi Imagery/Recent Art*, which was on view at the Jewish Museum in New York from 17 March to 30 June 2002. The contents set off a barrage of criticism and condemnation among Holocaust survivors, politicians, and art critics, some of it coming even before the exhibition opened. The *New York Times* published nine articles about the show, including reports, editorials, guest opinion pieces, letters, and reviews. What made this exhibition so troubling? The controversy spawned by *Mirroring Evil* offers a view into the central conflicts in the debate over Holocaust representation.

WHO OWNS AUSCHWITZ?

Mirroring Evil included nineteen works by thirteen artists, Jewish and non-Jewish, all born after World War II: Boaz Arad, Roee Rosen (Israel), Christine Borland (Scotland), Mat Collishaw, Alan Schechner (England), Rudolf Herz, Mischa Kuball (Germany), Elke Krystufek (Austria), Zbigniew Libera, Maciej Toporowicz, Piotr Uklański (Poland), Tom Sachs (United States), and Alain Séchas (France). Norman Kleeblatt, the Jewish Museum's chief curator, organized the exhibition and edited its catalog, which included essays by respected scholars and museum professionals such as James Young, Sidra DeKoven Ezrahi, Ellen Handler Spitz, Lisa Saltzman, Ernst van Alphen, Reesa Greenberg, and Kleeblatt himself. The ensuing polemics in the press, radio, television, and university roundtables, which began with charges of irreverence and insensitivity, ultimately articulated more serious political issues.

Survivors were appalled to see Nazis such as Josef Mengele (1911–1979) represented by six differing sculptures in the classical tradition, a project by Christine Borland (*L'Homme Double*, 1997) that was meant to focus on the mythology of appearance and how "image" is constructed. Critics also regarded as trivializations of Holocaust experience works such as *LEGO Concentration Camp Set* (1996) by Zbigniew Libera, featuring seven boxes of Holocaust Legos—actual Lego pieces from other existing sets—with which to construct a death camp, or two works by Tom Sachs, *Giftgas Giftset* (1998), featuring Zyklon B canisters with Chanel, Hermes, and Tiffany logos, and *Prada Death Camp* (1998), a pop-up camp made from a Prada hatbox. In his exhibition catalog essay, Ernst van Alphen addressed the idea of "play" and the limits of a traditional moralizing pedagogy about the Holocaust for a new generation, defending the value of Holocaust "toys." He asks

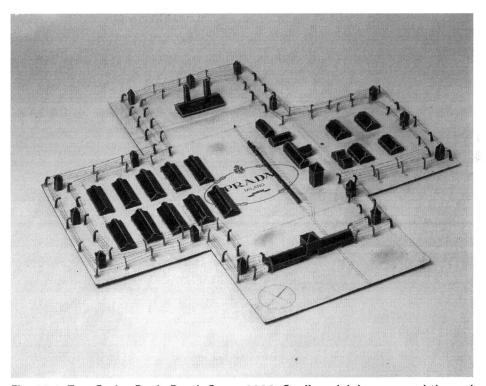

Fig. 30.1 Tom Sachs, *Prada Death Camp*, 1998. Cardboard, ink, paper and thermal adhesive, 11 3/4 x 17 1/2 x 12 1/4 inches.

Photo Credit: Courtesy of the Artist and Sperone Westwater, NY, USA

Fig. 30.2 Alan Schechner, *It's the Real Thing: Self-Portrait at Buchenwald*, 1993. Digital still.

www.dottycommies.com. Internet project. Photo Credit: Courtesy of Alan Schechner

how this work "can contribute to the cultural necessity to shake loose the traumatic fixation in victim positions that might be partly responsible for the 'poisonous' boredom that risks jeopardizing all efforts to teach the Holocaust under the emblem of 'never again'" (van Alphen in Kleeblatt 2002: 82).

Survivors were also dismayed by Alan Schechner's *It's the Real Thing: Self-Portrait at Buchenwald* (1993), in which Schechner digitally inserted himself into a well-known Margaret Bourke-White photo of the liberation of the camp. Schechner holds a Diet Coke can, the only color element in the image. *It's the Real Thing* refers to the commodification of Holocaust imagery, its loss of meaning through overuse, and its exploitation for political gain. Survivors took it far more literally or saw it as mockery. Elie Wiesel (b. 1928), a survivor of Auschwitz and Buchenwald, called the exhibition "a betrayal" (Goldstein 2002). Brooklyn Assemblyman Dov Hikind called for a citywide boycott of the exhibition and, along with Menachem Rosensaft of the Washington-based International Network of Children of Jewish Holocaust Survivors, led a protest outside the museum when the show opened to the public.

Many art critics wrote derisive reviews. Discussing Maciej Toporowicz's video *Obsession* (1991), which alternates sexualized images of women from Calvin Klein's

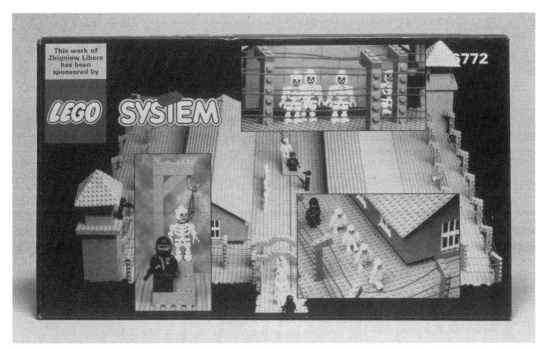

Fig. 30.3 Zbigniew Libera, *Lego Concentration Camp Set*, 1996. Seven boxes; sizes variable. Edition of 3.

Museum purchase with funds provided by the Fine Arts Acquisitions Committee and Thomas Healy and Fred Hochberg, 1997-163A-G. The Jewish Museum, New York, NY, U.S.A. Photo Credit: The Jewish Museum, New York / Art Resource, NY. The artistic product has not been endorsed by LEGO of Copenhagen, Denmark.

Eternity perfume advertisements with images of "Aryan" bodies in films by or about the Nazis, the *New York Times* critic Michael Kimmelman sarcastically noted "the fine line between being enticed to buy expensive lingerie and being persuaded to go along with state-sponsored mass murder." Kimmelman was "grumpy," he wrote, because of "anguished e-mail messages from Holocaust survivors and their relatives" (Kimmelman 2002). The *New Yorker*'s Peter Schjeldahl (2002) described the show as "trivial shock" whose references to childhood, commerce, and sex were "giddily eroticizing themes of cruel power" only to produce "solemn smut." "Over all," wrote Schjeldahl, "the show suggests an emergency ward for cases of toxic narcissism." Matters were not helped when Tom Sachs was interviewed by Deborah Solomon for the *New York Times Magazine* and asserted, "I'm using the iconography of the Holocaust to bring attention to fashion. Fashion, like fascism, is about loss of identity" (Solomon 2002).

Donald Kuspit took the critique of *Mirroring Evil* a step further, suggesting that the exhibition had entered sinister territory. Reprising his criticism of the *Burnt Whole* exhibition, Kuspit found the works "upsetting because the artists were tampering with something they didn't deeply understand, something they knew only superficially and secondhand—filtered through the media—and thus whose significance they failed to grasp." The exhibition, asserted Kuspit, "plays into the hands of the anti-Semites who deny the reality of the Holocaust." Moreover, because the show "relies on media art, the artists have little or no imagination of their own." Like others, Kuspit noted that various works, such as Sach's *Giftgas Giftset* and Toporowicz's *Obsession*, were "more anticapitalist than anti-Nazi" (2002: 8–9). Constituting what might be called a discourse of offense, the accusation that these artists were "tampering" with something not their own, "filtered through the media," most clearly articulates the fundamental view that the memory of Auschwitz is owned by its victims. Anyone else not only has no right to this memory but, through lack of understanding or failure of imagination, risks aiding and abetting those who deny the Holocaust altogether.

This notion led philosopher Peter-Wim Zuidhof to ask, ironically, "Should the use of 'Auschwitz' not be protected like a trademark™ or registered sign® only to be used by its 'owners'?" Drawing on French theorist Jean François Lyotard (1924–1998), Zuidhof argues that artistic discourses on Auschwitz, while still required to meet an ethical standard of "bearing witness," are not required to close off new meanings. On the contrary, Zuidhof emphasizes that the task is "to reformulate, make current again, rephrase and to keep on reformulating, updating, and rephrasing." Since all representations, however, are partial, and therefore violate "Auschwitz," which can never be truly or fully represented, one must distinguish between, "so to say, good violations and bad violations." Yet it is only possible to "access, address, and assess the good violations by new violations." Zuidhof accepted the art critics' claims that the works in *Mirroring Evil* are mostly "bad violations," but argued against the discourse of offense raised by those who would stabilize only one meaning of "Auschwitz" as "Auschwitz™" (Zuidhof 2002: 15–20).

The former director of the United States Holocaust Memorial Museum, Walter Reich, also took a stance at variance with the derisive views of many survivors and their supporters, addressing the issue of images "filtered through the media" by observing that Holocaust themes are "incorporated into the experiences, activities, products and reflections of life at every level—in movies, television, novels, religion, government, diplomacy, language, dreams, nightmares and art." The Jewish Museum exhibition, he observed, does not portray the Holocaust itself, but instead "attempts to highlight and present reflections on this process of incorporation" (Reich 2002). Far from "playing into the hands" of those who deny the Holocaust, then, the exhibition interrogated the effects of mainstreaming the Holocaust.

Along these lines, critic Jack Hitt asked whether we haven't "slowly flattened out the Holocaust's horror into something safely digestible? It's easy for politicians to denounce such work as deliberate provocation, but quick publicity is not why artists are examining notions of the sacred in America—the body, the image of divinity, the memory of history." When Hitt added that "variations of Auschwitz Legos lie all around, unnoticed until we get an elbow in the ribs," perhaps he had in mind commercialized and fetishized objects of Holocaust kitsch, such as the railway spikes from Treblinka preserved in Lucite that, at the time, one could receive—for a contribution of $5,000—from the Holocaust museum in St. Petersburg, Florida. Alluding to the failure of a sacralized post-Holocaust rhetoric, Hitt concluded, "It's not fun to think that the public response to the Holocaust—'never again' might more honestly be, 'again and again': Armenians, Kurds, Cambodians, Tutsis, Croats" (Hitt 2002).

A *New York Times* editorial that proclaimed the exhibition "banal" nonetheless observed, "In a way, the most these artists can do, when it comes to transforming the imagery of the Third Reich, is to suggest how profoundly our culture itself transformed that imagery since the early 1940s" ("The Art of Banality," *New York Times*, 22 March 2002: A24). From this perspective, we might better understand another comment made by Tom Sachs: "I am interested in the hardware of horror and death. The death camps are examples of amazing German engineering and design. And there are strong links between military products and consumer products. During World War II, Westinghouse developed parts for the atomic bombs, and I.B.M. made machine guns" (Solomon 2002). Indeed, most domesticated technologies employed today were originally developed for wartime use (Colomina 2007).

Artists who cannot address Holocaust experience directly because they were born later deal with the Holocaust at the level of representation, and more specifically, with the wholesale diffusion of "Auschwitz" as a social, cultural, and political signifier in contemporary life. As Israeli curator Tali Tamir observed in relation to *Wonderyears*, an exhibition of Holocaust art at Berlin's *Neue Gesellschaft für*

Bildende Kunst in 2003—it featured twenty-three post-Zionist Israeli artists, in-cluding Boaz Arad and Roee Rosen, who were in *Mirroring Evil*—she was shocked at first, but came to understand the way contemporary consumer culture formed the outlook of the artists: "The works draw their sources from official texts and collective memories, from familiar and recycled black-and-white photographs, and from exciting Hollywood epics. The result is sometimes humorous and amusing, and the Holocaust comes across as another image in the endless data bank offered by the New Age as part of a cinematic spectacle" (Gilerman 2003).

As a result of curating the *Wonderyears* exhibition, Tamir perceived what Kuspit and others failed to recognize in the artistic discourses of *Mirroring Evil*: the Holo-caust cannot be apprehended now except as "filtered through the media," since, for those born later, it can *only* be known through representation, which is therefore primary, not secondary experience, and these new artistic discourses are therefore valid attempts to examine the contemporary meanings of "Auschwitz." Elie Wiesel's sense of betrayal no doubt lies in his conception of "Auschwitz" as a sacred event, "equal to the revelation at Sinai" (Novick 1999: 201). Like Kuspit, Wiesel reads a subtle form of antisemitism into the attempts by contemporary artists to demystify the discourse of sacralization and to look, not at the Holocaust itself, but at the ways in which we have learned to "know" the Holocaust or the ways in which the effects of the Holocaust have filtered into everyday life. But these reactions depend on the belief in a fixed and stable meaning for "Auschwitz," one that is owned by the victim generation and cannot change no matter how much it is instrumentalized for other purposes.

Beyond these responses, hostility to the *Mirroring Evil* exhibition was political. Some read its anticapitalist motifs as anti-American and the catalog's ambiguity about perpetrator and victim as a critique of Israeli policy against the Palestinians (Ray 2005). Artist and Washington civil servant Steve Munson, writing for the conservative Jewish journal *Commentary*, was particularly indignant at the com-ments of Alan Schechner (*It's the Real Thing*) reproduced in the exhibition catalog: "Throughout my time in Israel, I became acutely aware of how the Holocaust was used to justify some of the unsavory aspects of Israeli policy. I was told more than once how: 'Whatever we do to them (the Palestinians) can never be as bad as what they (the Germans) did to us'" (Kleeblatt 2002: 115). For Munson, America and Israel are not "the worst"; those are found "among the contemporary acolytes of Hitler—those whom we can accurately describe as modern-day Nazis—in the Islamic world." At the time of the exhibition, then-Prime Minister Ariel Sharon's policy of city destruction and military strangulation was causing an escalation of violence in occupied Gaza and the West Bank. Hence Munson's conclusion regard-ing the exhibition: "This was not the best moment to be offering a morally undermining critique of American consumer culture and Israeli policies of self-defense." Echoing the efforts of the Bush/Cheney administration to chill dissent following 11 September 2001, Munson's implicit charge against the artists and exhibition organizers was a lack of patriotism in support of American and Israeli nationalism. Munson asserted that the exhibition, offensive in any case, should have been canceled or postponed following 9/11, alleging that *Mirroring Evil* reflected a trend in postmodern art "to create works that, for lack of a better term, may be described as against life" (Munson 2002). For Munson, apparently, *any* critique of capitalist or imperialist ideology is unacceptable.

Defending the exhibition in the pages of *Artforum*, art historian Linda Nochlin found *Mirroring Evil* "an uncommonly thoughtful if profoundly disturbing show" based on "irony, satire, playfulness, and send-up." Nochlin defined its postmodernist premise as "an art that emphasizes diversity rather than homogeneity; that rejects a single master narrative of history and its representation; that provides a potent critique of modernist orthodoxy in both theory and practice; and above all, that is inevitably imbricated in the world of the commodity and that of popular culture." Nochlin distinguished this postmodernist approach from the realism of documentary photographs and film footage and from the modernist approach to Holocaust representation characterized by "negation and silence" or a "refusal to represent"—Adorno's "after Auschwitz" interdiction. These are tropes still seen in the refusal of Claude Lanzmann (b. 1925) to use archival footage in his 1985 film *Shoah* (Nochlin 2002).

IMPLICATIONS FOR A NEW GENERATION

If *Mirroring Evil*'s works do not depict evil in elegiac terms of horror, loss, and darkness, territory already covered by the negative and allusive work of earlier decades, what does the shift in modes of representation to "irony, satire, playfulness, and send-up" mean for a new generation? What are the implications of rejecting the now ossified modernist conventions of Holocaust representation? How has the Holocaust been incorporated and transformed by the pressures of commerce and popular culture? How has it become a tool of contemporary political critique? These are the questions historians of art about the Holocaust need to explore. We need to consider how the Holocaust endures as an evolving signifier, the very success of the injunction to "never forget" perforce producing a cultural phenomenon in which "Auschwitz" has exceeded its boundaries of meaning and become a term that can be mobilized in many ways, including critiques of capitalist greed and Israeli foreign policy. At bottom, the question is not whether these are violations of a single fixed meaning, which of course they are, but how they reveal new ways of meaningfully engaging with the effects of the Holocaust after more than half a century.

Despite themselves, even the most mocking critics have been drawn to particular instances of these new strategies of representation in *Mirroring Evil*. Schjeldahl

Fig. 30.4 Piotr Uklański, *The Nazis*, 1998 (detail). 164 chromogenic, black and white and color photographs, 35.5 × 25.4 cm each. From left to right: Klaus Kinski in *Five Into Hell*, directed by Frank Kramer, 1969; George Mikell in *Victory*, directed by John Houston, 1981; Jan Englert in *Złoto Dezerterów*, directed by Jamusz Majewski, 1998; Robert Duvall in *The Eagle Has Landed*, directed by John Sturges, 1976; Hardy Krüger in *A Bridge Too Far*, directed by Richard Attenborough, 1977; Yul Brynner in *Triple Cross*, directed by Terence Young, 1966; Christopher Plummer in *The Scarlet and the Black*, directed by Jerry London, 1983; Cedric Hardwicke in *The Moon Is Down*, directed by Irving Pichel, 1943.

Installation Zachęta Gallery, Warsaw, 2000. Photo Credit: Courtesy of the Artist, Gagosian Gallery, Galerie Emmanuel Perrotin and Galleria Massimo De Carlo

praised Israeli artist Boaz Arad's *Hebrew Lesson* (2000), a repeating twelve-second video that splices together isolated words and syllables from films of Hitler's speeches to produce the Hebrew sentence, "Shalom, Yerushalayim, ani mitnatzel" ("Hello Jerusalem, I am deeply sorry"). Schjeldahl (2002) finds the work successful in dealing with "Nazism's aesthetic appeal" and even "delivering a touch of the sublime." Kimmelman found Arad's video "haunting" and described Alain Séchas's sculptures (*Enfants Gâtés*, 1997)—cat-like creatures with Hitler mustaches, lined up in little cribs and repeating endlessly in mirrors on the walls—as "memorable." Kimmelman also described Israeli artist Roee Rosen's *Live and Die as Eva Braun* (1995), a text, accompanied by sixty black and white drawings, that asks viewers to imagine themselves as Hitler's lover on the night of their suicides, as having "a novelistic imagination and psychological ambition that exceeds everything else in the show" (Kimmelman 2002: E33).

Village Voice critic Jerry Saltz singled out Piotr Uklański's *The Nazis*, a group of 166 small color and black-and-white photos of famous actors portraying Nazis, as a "simple, post-Pop gesture [that] explicitly illustrates our ongoing fascination with Nazis, and the ways we make them sexy" (Saltz 2002). Uklański's work, focusing on "the erotic charge of the Nazi uniform" (Nochlin 2002), created a scandal when

first shown at the Photographic Gallery in London, where the *Evening Standard* headlined, "Outrage in London Gallery Highlights 'Glamour of Nazism.'" The work evokes the sadomasochistic Nazi chic popularized in the 1970s (Goldstein 2002). From Liliana Cavani's *The Night Porter* (1974) to Steven Spielberg's *Schindler's List* (1993) and beyond, films continue to play an important role in teaching the postwar generations about Nazism, embodied by actors such as Dirk Bogarde and Ralph Fiennes, while blurring the line between representation and history, just as Arad's and Rosen's works blur the line between history and fantasy. Since it is not possible for those born later to recover a past that was never theirs, their works attempt to illuminate the effects of the past on the present, reacting to history rather than enshrining it.

Critic Ana Finel Honigman (2002) found Toporowicz's video *Obsession* "one of the show's strongest works," though she immediately disavowed her praise by suggesting that it "trivializes the issues behind both fashion and fascism." Yet the strength of this work, which combines clips from Leni Riefenstahl (1902–2003) films and movies such as Luchino Visconti's *The Damned* (1969) and Cavani's *The Night Porter* (1974) with Calvin Klein advertising, lies in the sexy seductiveness of the *white* body, the West's universal signifier of all bodies. The body of Calvin Klein model Kate Moss, which is "unmarked" and therefore does not read as "racialized," nonetheless depends upon the visual tropes of "whiteness" and notions of "purity" that can be traced to Greek classical statuary. Such works were the foundation for the hyper-classicized visual imagery of Nazi painting and sculpture that was meant to represent the Aryan ideal and have long served as the touchstone for the idealized beauty of contemporary advertising (Apel 2005). Despite critics who find a too glib parallel between Nazi imagery and contemporary advertising, Toporowicz's work does not imply that these images are the same but that the mobilization of a racialized sexual desire in fascist imagery survives in the logic of consumer capitalism.

In Israel, a split between the positive self-identity of the Israeli Jew and the concept of the weak and passive Diaspora Jew made the Holocaust a long-time taboo in Israeli art until the 1980s and 1990s (Katz-Freiman in Hornstein et al. 2003: 129–56; Manor in Feinstein 2005: 194–218). Roee Rosen's work, first shown in Israel in 1997–98, was the first to manifest Adolf Hitler in an Israeli exhibition space and provoked a public furor (Azoulay 2001: 48–75; Azoulay in Hornstein et al. 2003: 85–117). Boaz Arad's *Hebrew Lesson* not only represented Hitler, but showed him offering an apology to his audience. This apology, however, is barely comprehensible, based on the clipped syllables Arad has edited together, making both the "Hebrew lesson" and Hitler's difficulty in enunciating an apology laughable. Gene Ray observes that Arad's attempt to make the Führer apologize thus offers a different lesson, in which a deep yearning is made conscious by being simultaneously presented and subverted, both satisfying and ridiculous. Because such an apology can never be uttered, Arad makes apparent that the traumatic memory of victimhood and the unforgivability of the Nazi genocide are passed on in perpetuity, allowing Jews to justify and legitimize the power of violence they claim as a way to "erase the shame of victimhood even while maintaining it as a founding stone of identity" (Ray 2005: 126–8). This "shield of moral immunity" blinds the former victims to their contemporary potential as perpetrators, although Israeli writers, playwrights, and filmmakers have challenged this rationale for some time in postwar moral discourse (Ezrahi in Kleeblatt 2002: 17–38).

Schechner's Diet Coke image also may be understood as deliberately making visible the outrageous use to which the Holocaust can be put. On his website, Schechner posts a text by Alessandro Imperato that alludes to the Israeli government as it urges the viewer to "consider the society in which the Holocaust happened and in which it is now being used to justify further atrocities . . . to re-question power and responsibility in terms of modern politics and to question everything we assume and consume about the Holocaust be it the news media, Hollywood representations or state Museums and memorials" (www.dottycommies.com). Schechner also asserts that Holocaust images are "imbued with a sort of false religiosity; they become sacred. . . . By placing my well-fed self with a Diet Coke amongst the emaciated survivors of Buchenwald I was not only attacking Israeli society with its fetishistic fascination of all fads American, but also more importantly, saying that we (the Jewish people) need to put ourselves back in the shoes of those survivors" (Weinstein in Feinstein 2005: 88–9).

CONCLUSION

The debate over Holocaust representation may be understood as signifying two profoundly divergent approaches. Defenders of the ethic of representation first articulated by Adorno believe that Auschwitz is owned by its victims and regard postmodern conceptual sensibilities as opening the subject to exploitation and trivialization, disrespecting the memory of the victims and even paving the way for Holocaust denial. Postmodern artists, on the other hand, believe the Holocaust has already been exploited in invidious ways and respond to its proliferating cultural and political uses. As Gene Ray suggests, *Mirroring Evil* became politically explosive because it took place in the context of September 11 and the New York Jewish establishment's support for the Bush administration's "war on terror" and for Israel as Middle East tensions heated up. These circumstances made intolerable the exhibition's challenge to Jewish claims of a moral high ground that could justify all acts of atrocity.

Adorno's "after Auschwitz" ethic of representation must be historicized and understood as formulated in the context of Europe's postwar reconstruction culture, for which it was appropriate (Ray 2005). But contemporary works, in what may be seen as a generational debate, must be understood as producing new meanings in very differently constituted national and global contexts. The grave need to respect the victims and their memory continues to motivate contemporary artists, whose practices keep alive memory and meaning by replacing an ossified and sacralized pedagogy of the Holocaust with works that address the problematic logic of race and capitalism and resist exploitative uses of memory that provide a "moral alibi" for political and ethnic repression. Their work is emblematic of an updated ethic of representation for a newly dangerous era.

REFERENCES

ADORNO, T. W. (1981). *Prisms*. Cambridge, MA: MIT Press.

ALPHEN, E. VAN (1997). *Caught by History: Holocaust Effects in Contemporary Art, Literature, and Theory*. Stanford, CA: Stanford University Press.

AMISHAI-MAISELS, Z. (1993). *Depiction and Interpretation: The Influence of the Holocaust on the Visual Arts*. Newton, MA: Butterworth-Heinemann.

APEL, D. (2002). *Memory Effects: The Holocaust and the Art of Secondary Witnessing*. New Brunswick, NJ: Rutgers University Press.

——(2005). "Trespassing the Limits: Mirroring Evil—Nazi Imagery/Recent Art at the Jewish Museum." *Other Voices* 2/3. Available at: <http://www.othervoices.org>.

AZOULAY, A. (2001). *Death's Showcase: The Power of Image in Contemporary Democracy*. Cambridge, MA: MIT Press.

BIRO, M. (1998). *Anselm Kiefer and the Philosophy of Martin Heidegger*. Cambridge: Cambridge University Press.

COLOMINA, B. (2007). *Domesticity at War*. Cambridge, MA: MIT Press.

FEINSTEIN, S. (ed.) (2005). *Absence/Presence: Critical Essays on the Artistic Memory of the Holocaust*. Syracuse, NY: Syracuse University Press.

GILERMAN, D. (2003). "Declaring Post-Zionism in Berlin." *Haaretz*. Available at: <http://www.haaretz.com> Accessed May 2003.

GOLDSTEIN, R. (2002). "Managing the Unmanageable." *Village Voice*, 6–12 March 2002. Available at: <http://www.villagevoice.com>.

GUMPERT, L. (2001). *Christian Boltanski*. Paris: Flammarion.

HIRSCH, M. (1997). *Family Frames: Photography, Narrative, and Postmemory*. Cambridge, MA: Harvard University Press.

HITT, J. (2002). "America's Problem with Modern Art." *New York Times*, Week in Review, 17 March 2002: 3.

HONIGMAN, A. (2002). "Not Good: Mirroring Evil: Nazi Imagery/Recent Art." *Afterimage* 30/1: 17.

HORNSTEIN, S. and JACOBOWITZ, F. (eds.) (2003). *Image and Remembrance: Representation and the Holocaust*. Bloomington, IN: Indiana University Press.

——LEVITT, L., and SILBERSTEIN, L. (eds.) (2003). *Impossible Images: Contemporary Art after the Holocaust*. New York: New York University Press.

KAPLAN, B. (2007). *Unwanted Beauty: Aesthetic Pleasure in Holocaust Representation*. Urbana, IL: University of Illinois Press.

KIMMELMAN, M. (2002). "Evil, the Nazis and Shock Value." *New York Times*, 15 March 2002: E33.

KLEEBLATT, N. (ed.) (2002). *Mirroring Evil: Nazi Imagery/Recent Art*. New Brunswick, NJ: Rutgers University Press.

KUSPIT, D. (1995). "Reducing the Holocaust to Artistic One-Liners." *Forward*, 3 February 1995.

——(2002). "Mirroring Evil: Nazi Imagery in Recent Art at the Jewish Museum." *Art New England* 23/5: 8–9.

LISS, A. (1998). *Trespassing through Shadows: Memory, Photography, and the Holocaust*. Minneapolis, MN: University of Minnesota Press.

McWILLIAMS, M. (1995). "Order Out of Chaos: 'Burnt Whole: Contemporary Artists Reflect on the Holocaust.'" *New Art Examiner* 22/8: 12–17.

MUNSON, S. (2002). "Nazis, Jews, and 'Mirroring Evil.'" *Commentary* 113/5: 60–4.

NOCHLIN, L. (2002). "Mirroring Evil—Nazi Imagery/Recent Art." *Artforum* 40/10: 167.

NOVICK, P. (1999). *The Holocaust in American Life*. Boston, MA: Houghton Mifflin.

RAY, G. (2005). *Terror and the Sublime in Art and Critical Theory: From Auschwitz to Hiroshima to September 11*. New York: Palgrave MacMillan.

REICH, W. (2002). "Appropriating the Holocaust." *New York Times*, 15 March 2002: A23.

SALTZ, J. (2002). "Mild Thing." *Village Voice*, 27 March–2 April 2002. Available at: <http://radio.villagevoice.com>.

SALTZMAN, L. (1999). *Anselm Kiefer and Art after Auschwitz*. New York: Cambridge University Press.

SCHJELDAHL, P. (2002). "The Hitler Show." *New Yorker*. Available at: <http://www.new-yorker.com>.

SOLOMON, D. (2002). "The Way We Live Now: Questions for Tom Sachs." *New York Times Magazine*, 10 March 2002, 19.

SPIEGELMAN, A. (1986, 1991). *Maus: A Survivor's Tale*. Vol. 1, *My Father Bleeds History*; Vol. 2, *And Here My Troubles Began*. New York: Pantheon Books.

YOUNG, J. (2000). *At Memory's Edge: After-Images of the Holocaust in Contemporary Art and Architecture*. New Haven, CT: Yale University Press.

Zelizer, B. (ed.) (2001). *Visual Culture and the Holocaust*. New Brunswick, NJ: Rutgers University Press.

Zuidhof, P.-W. (2002). "Lyotard's Ethicality: Appeal without Sentiment; Ethics after 'Auschwitz' through the Exhibition 'Mirroring Evil.'" Unpublished manuscript.

Other Suggested Reading

Bathrick, D., Prager, B., and Richardson, M. (eds.) (2008). *Visualizing the Holocaust: Documents, Aesthetics, Memory*. Rochester, NY: Camden House.

Blatter, J. and Milton, S. (1981). *Art of the Holocaust*. London: Pan Macmillan.

Godfrey, M. (2007). *Abstraction and the Holocaust*. New Haven, CT: Yale University Press.

Sujo, G. (2003). *Legacies of Silence: The Visual Arts and Holocaust Memory*. London: Philip Wilson.

Wiedmer, C. (1999). *The Claims of Memory: Representation of the Holocaust in Contemporary Germany and France*. Ithaca, NY: Cornell University Press.

Zelizer, B. (2000). *Remembering to Forget: Holocaust Memory through the Camera's Eye*. Chicago, IL: University of Chicago Press.

CHAPTER 31

···

MUSIC

···

BRET WERB

MUSICAL works about the Holocaust range in style and scale from modest memento mori to portraits in sound of the apocalyptic end of the world. In the ghettos, camps, and hideaways of World War II, music served a utilitarian function. Newly fashioned topical songs acted as messengers and memory aids to pass along prison gossip or rumors of deportations, while "escapist" music, mostly songs popular before the war, offered a spell of relief from continuing daily trials. While liberation rendered such music-making contexts obsolete, an ongoing need remained for commemorative music, as the *Sh'erit ha-Pletah*, the "surviving remnant" of European Jewry, began to convene formally to mourn victims of the recent catastrophe.

EARLY REPRESENTATIONS

···

Some early musical representations of the Holocaust were created by survivors, often for an audience of their peers. The programmatic *Rhapsody 1939–1945* (1947) for piano and chamber ensemble by Leo Spellman (Poland/Canada; b. 1913) is marked by such immediacy. First heard in concert at the Bavarian Displaced Persons' Camp at Fürstenfeldbruck, the music evokes in turn the German invasion, Jewish misery, flying bullets, a basement hideaway, longing for rescue, liberation, and, at the end, hope for the future (telegraphed by the Zionist anthem "Hatikvah"). Larger in scale though similarly intentioned is the symphonic poem *Fantasie in Gelb* (Fantasy in Yellow) (1947) by Percy Haid (Germany/USA; 1913–1977). A former member of the Kovno ghetto orchestra, Haid conceived the work in 1944 in Dachau, naming it for the yellow Star of David patch that branded Jewish prisoners. Its three movements depict, in the composer's words, "tragedy, dispersion and death"; one section cites the melody to Haid's song "Mamele" (mother), written in Kovno after a devastating *Kinderaktion* ("selection" of children for destruction). Karel Berman (Czechoslovakia; 1919–1995) composed *Suite Terezín* (1944), for piano, while still a prisoner at Theresienstadt (Terezín). A rare *in situ* tone portrait of life in a Nazi camp, the suite at first comprised three movements, "Terezín," "Horror," and "Alone." Berman subsequently expanded the score to account for ordeals at Auschwitz and Kauffering, and still later rounded it off with evocations of his youth and "new life" after liberation.

Among survivors and returning refugees, the anniversary of the Warsaw ghetto uprising of April 1943 quickly became the focal point of memorial observation. In Warsaw, the uprising's fifth anniversary, notable for the unveiling of the monument by Nathan Rappaport (1911–1987), "To the Heroes of the Warsaw Ghetto," also occasioned the commission and premiere of a cantata, *Żydom Polskim* (To the Jews of Poland). Its text, by Polish soldier-poet Władysław Broniewski (1897–1962), was inscribed to the martyred Jewish political leader Szmuel Zygielbojm (1895–1943), who committed suicide in London on 12 May 1943 to protest the Allies' inaction against the destruction of Jewish life. Composer Leo Wajner (Poland/Argentina; 1898–1977) set the verses (translated into Yiddish) while still a refugee in the Soviet Union; his score bears a separate dedication: "to the memory of my wife and child, murdered in the Warsaw ghetto." Written for mixed choir and large orchestra, Wajner's musical setting echoes the poem's somber rhetoric, reserving its heroic, uplifting passages for final verses that herald the birth of a new and just society.

The ghetto, if not the uprising, also figures in Arnold Schoenberg's *A Survivor from Warsaw*, Op. 46 (1947). Forced from Germany after the Nazi takeover, Schoenberg (Austria/USA; 1874–1951) waited out the war in southern California increasingly obsessed with Jewish identity and the Zionist cause. Inspired by a survivor account, his *Survivor* scenario is less concerned with storyline than with projecting the narrator's delirium and disorientation—emotional extremes that Schoenberg's musical language (characterized by semi-spoken, semi-sung narration, twelve-tone melodies, and pervasive dissonance) brings into full relief. Scored for narrator, men's chorus, and large orchestra, *A Survivor from Warsaw* concludes as the chorus (representing doomed prisoners) rises to intone *Sh'ma Yisroel* (Hear, O Israel), the affirmation of faith that is Judaism's fundamental prayer. Days before the work's debut in Albuquerque, New Mexico, in November 1948, Schoenberg, reflecting on the survivor's story and still grappling with issues of identity, declared to a friend: "The miracle is, to me, that all these people who might have forgotten, for years, that they are Jews, suddenly facing death, remember who they are" (quoted in Muxeneder 2002).

Violinist, violist, and composer Artur Gelbrun (Poland/Israel; 1913–1985) escaped Warsaw just ahead of the German invasion, leaving behind family and friends who later perished in the ghetto. Taking refuge in Switzerland, he spent time in an internment camp, and on his release found work as an orchestral musician. Gelbrun's *Lament for the Victims of the Warsaw Ghetto* (1953), commissioned for the uprising's tenth anniversary, draws its text from one of the period's foremost literary testaments, *The Song of the Murdered Jewish People* by Yitzhak Katzenelson (1886–1944). Seeking a musical counterpart to Katzenelson's evocations of biblical verse, Gelbrun turned to the Passion settings of J. S. Bach (1685–1750). The Bachian model, evident in Gelbrun's baroque-styled deployment of vocalists and orchestra, extends also to the *Lament*'s overall ambience of religious solemnity, descended from common themes of suffering and martyrdom. First performed in Israel, the *Lament* was dedicated to the memory of the composer's mother, herself a casualty of the Warsaw ghetto.

Other early musical reflections on the Holocaust were created during wartime by politically committed noncombatants. Michael Tippett (United Kingdom; 1905–1997), a lifelong pacifist, conceived the oratorio *A Child of Our Time* (1941) after learning of the November 1938 *Kristallnacht* pogroms in Germany and Austria. He summarized his libretto in an essay: "Part I deals with the general state of oppression in our time; part II presents the particular story of a young man's attempt to seek justice by violence and the catastrophic consequences; while part III considers the moral to be drawn, if any" (Tippett 1995: 182). Rooted in the British oratorio tradition, the work innovatively substitutes African-American spirituals for the customary hymn settings, thereby broadening the social relevance of Tippett's themes of persecution and scapegoating. First performed in London in 1944, *A Child of Our Time* has proved an enduringly popular work.

In contrast, *The Battle of Warsaw* by Franz Waxman (Germany/USA; 1906–1967)—part of the musical pageant *We Will Never Die*—might have vanished with scarcely a trace had not its sole performance, at the Hollywood Bowl in July 1943, been recorded for radio broadcast. Created by screenwriter Ben Hecht (1894–1964) and composer Kurt Weill (1900–1950) to raise consciousness about the genocide in Europe (and fated to end its run after only seven showings), *We Will Never Die* had opened in New York the previous March. On reaching Los Angeles, however, the pageant's producers urgently needed to include an account of the recently suppressed Warsaw ghetto revolt. Waxman, a prominent film composer already enlisted to conduct the production, agreed to provide new music, underscoring Hecht's narration with a dramatic, stand-alone set piece driven by a leitmotif from the anthem "Deutschland über Alles." The episode climaxes, amid a clamor of martial sound effects, with "The Hymn of the Ghetto" (words by Frank Loesser, 1910–1969), its melody yet another transfiguration of the malevolent, Germanic theme.

A travesty of "Deutschland über Alles" also figures in the "Intermezzo Drammatico" (subtitled "massacre music") of *Den judiska sången* (The Jewish Song), a symphonic cantata by Moses Pergament (Finland/Sweden; 1893–1977). Written in response to war reports—and as an assertion of ethnic pride in the face of local antisemitism—the large scale work for chorus, soloists, and orchestra was given a partial performance in 1944. By the time of its full premiere in Stockholm three years later, Pergament had subtitled the Prelude: "In Memoriam. A lament for the six million Jews who fell victim to the cruelty of the Third Reich." The Viennese Eric Zeisl (Austria/USA; 1905–1959), his own life threatened during *Kristallnacht*, instinctively turned to music, jotting down the sketches that would be posthumously titled *November Pieces*. In the United States from 1939, Zeisl completed a major work of commemoration while the war still raged: *Requiem Ebraico* (1944/45), a setting of Psalm 92 for chorus and orchestra dedicated to the memory of his father and "of the other countless victims of the Jewish tragedy in Europe" (Zeisl 1946: reverse cover page).

The committed anti-fascist Karl Amadeus Hartmann (Germany; 1905–1963) remained in his native Munich throughout the war, an "inner exile" who withheld his music from performance in Germany. After witnessing a death march from nearby Dachau, he was moved to write the piano sonata "27. April 1945," inscribing his manuscript with the words: "Unending was the stream of humanity. Unending was the misery. Unending was the sorrow" (Hartmann 1983: 3). The sonata's centerpiece, a funeral march, depicts this procession as if from a bystander's perspective. But Hartmann took care to seed the work with musical cues that, deciphered, proclaim the prisoners' (and composer's) hidden defiance and hope: in the scherzo, where the communist anthem "The Internationale," camouflaged by busy figuration, is symbolically tapped out by the left hand; in the funeral march, which borrows a motif from an outlawed workers' hymn; and in the finale, where much of the musical substance derives from a Soviet partisan song.

In Palestine, with its burgeoning survivor and refugee populations, two works of a commemorative nature appeared in 1947. Named for the Hebrew prayer of remembrance for the souls of martyrs, *Yiskor* (in memoriam) for viola and string orchestra by Oedoen Partos (Hungary/Israel; 1907–1977) evokes an east European Jewish liturgical service, with the solo instrument, standing in for the cantor, declaiming quasi-improvisatory lines over an orchestral accompaniment suggestive of the cadences of a choir or congregation. Arranged for various instrumental combinations, the work has become a mainstay of commemoration programs. *Suite in memoriam* ("to the Polish martyrs") for piano trio by Yitzhak Edel (Poland/Israel; 1896–1973) cites rather than suggests Jewish traditional music. Insisting "no art can possibly express this tragedy," Edel demurred from musical portraiture, attempting instead "only to preserve the sounds inseparably bound to the spiritual life of millions of men, women and children who were cruelly slaughtered, suffocated and burnt by barbaric murderers for their one and only unforgivable crime—that of being Jews" (in Arnold 1992: 343).

CHANGING PERFORMANCE CONTEXTS

With the proclamation in 1951 of Yom Hashoah as an official day of Holocaust remembrance, the Israeli government provided a new performance context for commemorative music. Yet during the 1950s, as the war's immediacy receded, composers largely abandoned the Holocaust theme. An exception to this trend was Benjamin Frankel (United Kingdom; 1906–1973), who dedicated his *Concerto for Violin and Orchestra*, Op. 24 (1951) "to the memory of the six million." Best known for his film scores, Frankel, the child of Polish-Jewish immigrants, foreswore folklore and cinematic tone-painting in writing this abstract concert piece, concentrating the great part of its emotional weight on the slow movement (the work's longest), an elegiac *andante mesto* (sad andante). Also dating from this period is *Musik für vier Instrumente in memoriam: Lied der Moorsoldaten* (Music for four instruments in memoriam: Song of the Peat Bog Soldiers) (1952), by Hanning Schröder (Germany; 1896–1987). A political dissident married to a Jew, Schröder kept a low profile in Nazi Berlin, yet risked his life to hide a Jewish couple hunted by the Gestapo. *Musik für vier Instrumente* (scored for string quartet) pays homage to the Reich's internal opponents, employing the concentration camp song "Die Moorsoldaten" (The Peat Bog Soldiers) as a symbolic and melodic resource. Sounding from within a variety of musical contexts and textures (ostinato patterns, dissonant harmonies, pizzicato chords), the storied melody variously recalls (in Schröder's words) "the inexorability of events" and "the determination to survive" (cited in Eberle 1981).

Interest in the Holocaust as a topic for artistic treatment began to revive in the politically turbulent 1960s, with many works cast as object lessons relevant to the times. The cantata *Jüdische Chronik* (A Jewish Chronicle) (1961)—a collective effort by East Germans Paul Dessau (1894–1979) and Rudolf Wagner-Régeny (1903–1969), and West Germans Boris Blacher (1903–1975), Karl Amadeus Hartmann, and Hans Werner Henze (b. 1926)—came about in response to a fresh wave of antisemitic activity in Germany. Each composer had experienced the depredations of Nazism first-hand—Dessau, the group's only Jew, emigrated to the United States; the others remained in Germany, with Wagner-Régeny and Henze ultimately conscripted into military service—and each felt a moral imperative to protest the rise of neofascism publicly. Despite stylistic inconsistency, the cantata's five movements are unified by an unfolding narrative by East German poet Jens Gerlach (1926–1990), distinctive orchestration, and, to a lesser extent, a twelve-tone motif devised by Dessau, the project's instigator. The Jewish genocide is explicitly represented in Hartmann's "Getto" (set, however, in the death camp Treblinka), and Henze and Dessau's "Aufstand" (Uprising; set in the Warsaw ghetto). Yet, keeping to the mission of socially engaged art, a tone of admonition prevails throughout, culminating with the urgent declamation of Dessau's "Epilog": "Think about what occurred! The world of today and tomorrow is a picture of your own face! Be vigilant! Vigilant!!"

Cold War cultural politics were a key factor in canceling the first performance of *Jüdische Chronik*, scheduled to debut concurrently in East and West Germany in 1961 (the work would not be heard until 1966). Indeed, the cultural climate in many Eastern Bloc countries, where officials denied the local persistence of antisemitism and deemphasized the selective persecution of Jews during the war, was not favorable to the creation and reception of Holocaust-themed art. Given this context, the *Symphony no. 13 in B-flat Minor*, Op. 113 (1962), by Dmitri Shostakovich (Soviet Union; 1906–1975) stands as a sociological as well as a musical phenomenon. A symphonic song cycle to poems by Yevgeny Yevtushenko (b. 1933), its first and weightiest movement is a setting of "Babi Yar," Yevtushenko's meditation on the Nazi killing field near Kiev, where, the poet tellingly observes, the Soviets had not placed a memorial. As an unequivocal attack on antisemitism and complicity, the *Babi Yar Symphony* drew fire from Soviet authorities while in rehearsal and remained controversial even after Yevtushenko, at the behest of party officials, altered some lines to account for non-Jewish Russian and Ukrainian victims of fascism.

To the Memory of the Babi Yar Martyrs (1945) by the repatriated Ukrainian refugee Dmitri Klebanov (1907–1987) ranks as the earliest musical response to the mass killings. Based on Jewish folk motifs, the symphonic poem was performed in Kharkov and Kiev, then subsequently suppressed. The oratorio *Memorial to the Victims of Fascism* (1961) by ghetto and camp survivor Mendelis Bašs (Latvia; b. 1919), which features an inner movement based on the Soviet Yiddish song "Babi Yar" (described below), can also be considered a portent of the *Babi Yar Symphony*. However, the high profile example of Shostakovich and Yevtushenko evidently spurred Soviet composers to create memorial music, although their work often got uneasy receptions. The mono-opera (single character opera) *Diary of Anne Frank*, Op. 60, by Moscow-based Grigori Frid (b. 1915), completed in 1969, did not receive a staged performance until eight years later, and then only at a distant, provincial venue. Anticipating controversy, Leningrad composer David Finko (b. 1936) employed a generic title, *Heroic Ballad*, to mask the intent of his tone poem *Holocaust: An Uprising in the Ghetto* (the work's eventual published title) at its 1965 premiere.

Undoubtedly the most prolific contributor to the genre in the Soviet Union was Polish-born Mieczysław Weinberg (1919–1996), who fled east in 1939 and eventually settled in Moscow, where he became a close friend and musical confrère of Shostakovich. Having lost his entire immediate family in the Warsaw ghetto, Weinberg obsessively returned to the subject of the war and the Holocaust in his work. His *Symphony No. 6 in A minor*, Op. 79 (1962–63), focuses on children. At its core is the elegy "Deep Pits, Crimson Clay" by Yiddish writer Shmuel Halkin (1897–1960), which Weinberg had previously set to music in 1944 and now reworked for children's choir and large orchestra. The ten-movement *Symphony No. 8 in G major*, opus 83 (1964), for soloists, chorus, and orchestra, draws on the war-exiled Polish-Jewish poet Julian Tuwim's epic of nostalgia and loss, *Polish Flowers*. War-related writings by Tuwim (1894–1953), as well as Władisław Broniewski, compose the libretto to the *Symphony no. 9*, Op. 93 ("Lines That Escaped Destruction"), a quasi-oratorio conceived as early as 1940 and completed in 1967. Weinberg's cantata *Diary of Love* (1964), to words by Auschwitz survivor Stanisław Wygodzki (1907–1992), honors the memory of children martyred at that camp. Auschwitz also provides the setting for Weinberg's major opera *Passazhirka* (The Passenger), Op. 97 (1967–68), based on Zofia Posmysz's survivor memoir. Although performance opportunities were scarce, Weinberg never ceased mourning the Holocaust in his music; among his last and most personal compositions is the *Symphony no. 21*, Op. 152, "In Memory of the Victims of the Warsaw Ghetto" (1991), a work still awaiting its premiere.

By the late 1960s, as the number of Holocaust-related compositions began to steadily increase, three themes emerged that would be repeatedly elaborated in coming decades: Auschwitz, Anne Frank, and children's poetry from Theresienstadt. The widely publicized Frankfurt Trials of 1963–1965 anchored Auschwitz in the popular imagination as the archetypal death camp and universal byword for genocide. The proceedings inspired a cantata, *Die Asche von Birkenau* (The Ashes of Birkenau) (1965), by Günther Kochan (East Germany; b. 1930) to words by refugee poet Stephan Hermlin (1915–1997). They also gave rise to the highly influential stageplay *Die Ermittlung* (The Investigation) by Peter Weiss (1916–1982), featuring an incidental score by Luigi Nono (Italy; 1924–1990) that the composer soon refashioned into a concert piece, *Ricorda cosa ti hanno fatto in Auschwitz* (Remember what they did to you in Auschwitz) (1966). A Schoenberg disciple who proclaimed *A Survivor from Warsaw* "the aesthetic and musical manifesto of our epoch" (quoted in Muxeneder 2002), Nono had earlier responded to the war with *Il Canto Sospeso* (The Interrupted Song) (1956), a suite for choir and orchestra on writings by condemned resistance fighters. *Ricorda* dispenses entirely with conventional word setting and instrumentation: created in a recording studio on magnetic tape, the work employs textless, electronically distorted voices (including children's choir) and clamorous sound effects to evoke the death camp's chilling environs. With this brief, enigmatic work, Nono pioneered a style that many subsequent composers found well-suited to portraying the inhuman experience of the Holocaust.

The oratorio *Dies Irae* (1967) by Krzysztof Penderecki (Poland; b. 1933) builds on an approach akin to Nono's. Scored for solo voices, mixed choir, and orchestra, its musical texture is dominated by unorthodox sonorities—the choir shouts, buzzes, and whistles; scrapers, chains, whips, and sirens sound out from the instrumentarium—intended to graphically express (in the composer's words) "the ghastliness of history" (quoted in Tomaszewski 1989). Incorporating biblical verse and texts by

Aeschylus, Valéry, Aragon, Różewicz, and Broniewski and dedicated to the memory of those murdered at Auschwitz, *Dies Irae* premiered at the unveiling in 1967 of the International Monument to the Victims of Fascism at Birkenau.

Anne Frank (1929–1945), the surrogate face and voice of countless young victims, has long been a Holocaust icon, her writings and life story drawing responses from creative artists worldwide. Among the earliest musical tributes (in addition to the already-noted opera by Grigori Frid) were *Anne Frank, Symphony in One Movement for String Orchestra* (1964) by León Biriotti (Uruguay; b. 1929); *In Memoriam Anne Frank (A Song of Strength)* (1965), an homage for soprano and orchestra by Godfrey Ridout (Canada; 1918–1984); and *In Memoriam Annei Frank* (1966), a symphonic tone poem by Ludovic Feldman (Romania; 1893–1987). Two noteworthy works drawn from Frank's famous *Diary* appeared in 1970: *Le Journal d'Anne Frank*, an oratorio for female youth choir and chamber ensemble, by Edith Lejet (France; b. 1941); and *From the Diary of Anne Frank*, focused on Frank's anxiety over the fate of a friend, by war refugee Oskar Morawetz (Czechoslovakia/Canada; 1917–2007).

The subject continued (and continues) to inspire new works in diverse styles and genres, among them the aptly titled *Anna Frank, un símbol* (1971), for string orchestra, by Jordi Cervelló (Spain; b. 1935); *Diary of a Young Girl* (1973), for readers, rock group, and orchestra, by Peter Nero (USA; b. 1934); *Anne Frank Cantata: A Child of Light* (1984), for soloists, choir, and orchestra, by Hans Kox (Netherlands; b. 1930), whose collage of texts ranges from the Bible and classic German poetry to fragments from Hitler's speeches; *Elegy for Anne Frank* (1989), for piano, chamber orchestra, and optional narrator, by Lukas Foss (Germany/ USA; 1922–2009); and *Annelies: The Anne Frank Oratorio* (2004), for soprano, choir and orchestra, with libretto largely compiled from the *Diary*, by James Whitbourne (United Kingdom; b. 1963).

I Never Saw Another Butterfly, an anthology of children's poetry and art from Theresienstadt, has been mined for musical inspiration since its first publication in Prague in 1959. Czech composers quickly responded to the material, beginning with Karel Reiner (1910–1979), a Theresienstadt survivor who reworked his score to a documentary film about the child artists into a concert suite, *Motýli tady nežijí* (Butterflies Don't Live Here) (1960). Musical settings of the poems proliferated: the earliest, an oratorio by Gustav Křivinka (1928–1990) also titled *Motýli tady nežijí*, premiered in 1963. With the symphonically-scaled *Song of Terezin* (1964), Franz Waxman became the first to set the lyrics in English translation. Modeled after the orchestral song cycles of Richard Strauss (1864–1949) and Shostakovich, the work (scored for children's chorus, mixed chorus, solo voice, and orchestra) bears the dedication "to the memory of the thousands of children who have passed through the concentration camp of Terezin, but particularly to those whose poems I have set to music." Ensuing "Butterfly"-inspired compositions (entitled *I Never Saw Another Butterfly* unless otherwise noted) include art song settings by Srul Irving Glick (Canada, 1934–2002; 1968), Elwood Derr (USA, b. 1932; 1977), and Lori

Laitman (USA, b. 1955; 1995); choral suites by Joel Hardyk (USA, 1980) and Robert Convery (USA, b. 1954; *Songs of Children*, 1994); narrative oratorios by Ronald Senator (UK, b. 1926; *Kaddish for Terezin*, 1986) and Edoardo Brizio (Italy; *Ai bambini di Terezin*, 1987); and jazz and pop-inflected compositions by Jeanie Brindley-Barnett (USA; *Butterfly Songs*, 1993) and Daniel Dobiáš (Czech Republic; *K cemu je slunce, kdyz není den?* [Who Needs the Sun When There Is No Day?], 1994–97). The repertoire mainstay, however, has long been *I Never Saw Another Butterfly: A Musical Memorial* (1968) by Charles Davidson (USA; b. 1929), a melodically accessible, harmonically neo-impressionistic setting performable by school ensembles, for treble choir with piano or orchestral accompaniment.

A wide array of works, often reflecting personal or nationalist agendas, weighed against the tendency to reiterate themes. Greek Holocaust victims are memorialized by Mikis Theodorakis (Greece; b. 1925) in *Ballad of Mauthausen* (1965), a suite of folk-styled settings of poetry by camp survivor Iakovos Kambanellis (b. 1922); and by Daniel Akiva (Israel; b. 1953) in *Siniza i Fumo* (Smoke and Ashes) (1986; rev. 1996), to texts by Judeo-Spanish (Ladino) poet Avner Perez (b. 1942). The experience of Dutch deportees is portrayed in *Westerbork Symfonie* (1992) by Willem Stoppelenburg (Netherlands; b. 1943); and *3.62 Square Metres: 3 pieces for solo flute* (2000) by Robert Pot (Netherlands; b. 1961) evokes the ordeals of the composer's mother, a hidden child. Two recent works address the experiences of homosexuals during the Third Reich: the choral *Requiem for the Victims of Nazi Persecution* (2001) by Ståle Kleiberg (Norway; b. 1958) and the song cycle *For a Look or a Touch* (2007), based on journal entries by a gay man who did not survive, by Jake Heggie (USA; b. 1961). The ambitious *Requiem für Kaza Kathárinna* (1990) by Gerhard Rosenfeld (Germany; 1931–2003), for speaker, singer, Gypsy ensemble, and large orchestra, confronts the persecution and murder of European Sinti and Roma. Literary testaments by Nelly Sachs (1891–1970) and Moshe Prager (1909–1984) inspired, respectively, *O, the Chimneys* (1969), for voice, chamber ensemble, and electronics, by Shulamit Ran (Israel/USA; b. 1949); and *Sparks of Glory* (1995), a klezmer-influenced score by Paul Schoenfield (USA; b. 1947).

The legacy of Paul Celan (1920–1970) has also proved attractive to composers, perhaps due to the forceful music imagery in certain of his poems. Notable settings of Celan texts include works by Aribert Reimann (Germany; b. 1936) (1956 and 2001), Peter Ruzicka (Germany; b. 1948) (1969/70), Harrison Birtwistle (England; b. 1934) (1989/96), Michael Nyman (England; b. 1944) (1990), and Tzvi Avni (Germany/Israel; b. 1927) (1991). Elie Wiesel (b. 1928), the most widely influential survivor-memoirist, has contributed original librettos to two cantatas on Holocaust themes: *Ani Maamin: A Song Lost and Found Again* (1973), with music by French composer (and former war-exile) Darius Milhaud (1892–1974), and *A Song for Hope* (1987), with music by the American David Diamond (1915–2005).

NEW SENSIBILITIES

With *Different Trains* (1988), Steve Reich (USA; b. 1936) introduced a new sensibility to the Holocaust music genre. Rather than approach the subject as a dramatist or social critic, he drew on personal associations, contrasting happy childhood memories of cross-country train travel with reflections on the different sorts of journeys he might have made had he, a Jew, then lived in Nazi-ruled Europe. The musical language, too, is innovative: writing for string quartet and prerecorded tape, Reich thematically employs fragments of interviews (with his former governess; a retired Pullman porter; and three Holocaust survivors of the composer's own generation), cycling their words over a soundscape derived from recordings of World War II-era trains. Rhythmic ostinatos in the strings, characteristic of Reich's minimalist style but here conjuring railcars clattering over wooden ties, underpin and unify the entire work, which, the composer observed, marked a new direction in presenting "both a documentary and a musical reality" (Reich 1988).

Music bibliographers tracking the repertoire's exponential growth have, by intention, focused on art music compositions. Yet Holocaust history also resonates in the realm of popular culture, although its impact has not been similarly documented. Popular songs about the plight of displaced persons, for example, began appearing soon after the war's end. The best known of these, "Vu ahin zol ikh geyn?" (Where shall I go?)—adapted from a Warsaw ghetto song—became the unofficial anthem of Yiddish-speaking DPs and was published and recorded internationally. Other notable early songs include the Yiddish tango "Exodus 47" (1947) by Shmerke Kaczerginski (lyrics) and Sigmunt Berland (music), dramatizing the story of the refugee ship and voicing the anger of survivors still stranded in Europe, and, for an American audience, "Sleep My Child (Shloof Mein Kind)" (1948), by George Brown (lyrics) and recent Polish-Jewish émigré Henry Vars (music), "a lullaby for a displaced child" offering hope for the future and counseling the suppression of painful memories. In the Soviet Union, the harrowing Yiddish lullaby "Babi Yar" (1951), by Shike Driz (lyrics) and Rivke Boyarska (music), spread swiftly despite censorable allusions to Jewish suffering; the following decade Russian troubadour Alexandr Galich (1918–1977) faced exile for songs like "Rekviem po neubitym" (Requiem for those not killed) (1967), thoughts on the Nazis' Jewish victims provoked by Soviet anti-Israel propaganda, and the extended ballad "Kaddish" (c. 1969), inspired by the words and deeds of Dr. Janusz Korczak (1878–1942), who led an orphanage for Jewish children in the Warsaw ghetto and was murdered with them at Treblinka. Some European folksingers confronted the fate of Sinti and Roma: Wolf Biermann (Germany) with "Schlaflied für Tanepen" (Lullaby for little one) (1980), about a hunger strike at Dachau protesting the lack of a memorial to Sinti victims; and Peter Wagner (Austria) with "Waast Du, wo

Auschwitz liegt?" (Do you know where Auschwitz is?) (1981), a first-person portrait of an emotionally unbalanced camp survivor.

In the United States, balladeer Tom Paxton followed his graphic "Train for Auschwitz" (1961) with "We Didn't Know" (1965), an indictment of societal apathy linking the Holocaust to contemporary civil rights abuses and the Vietnam war. Subsequent American songs in popular genres include the admonitory "Dachau Blues" (1969) by rock experimentalist Captain Beefheart (Don Van Vliet); "Ride 'Em Jewboy" (1973), a country/western tribute to victims, by Richard S. "Kinky" Friedman; "Denmark 1943" (1988), a folk-styled ballad about the exodus of Danish Jews by flotilla to Sweden, by Fred Small; "Tattoo" (1992), a pop lyric exploring a female survivor's scarred psyche, by Janis Ian; and "This Train Revised" (1994), inescapably influenced by *Different Trains*, with lyrics detailing the horrors of deportation juxtaposed with musical echoes of a traditional American spiritual, by Amy Ray of the rock band Indigo Girls.

In 1988, singer-composer Yehuda Poliker and lyricist Yaacov Gilad, sons of survivors from Salonika and Warsaw, respectively, released *Efer ve'Avak* (Ashes and Dust), a Holocaust-themed concept album considered a landmark of Israeli popular music. Employing Greek rhythms and instrumentation, and incorporating selections of Polish poetry, songs such as "A Small Station Called Treblinka" and "Because" retell parental stories and probe their long-term aftereffects. Deeply personal, the album spoke to a generation of younger Israelis whose lives had been shadowed by the Holocaust.

Jazz musicians, too, have taken on the subject. Clarinetist Tony Scott included a *Portrait of Anne Frank* on his album *Sung Heroes* (1959); pianist Ran Blake's *Shoah!* (1985) is an improvisation on the Jewish Partisan anthem "Zog nit keynmol az du geyst dem letstn veg" (Never say that you have reached the final road"). Guitarist John Zorn and Austrian keyboardist Joe Zawinul each composed ambitious, multi-movement Holocaust-themed jazz suites. Zorn's *Kristallnacht* (1992), a panorama of twentieth-century Jewish experience scored for small ensemble, begins with serene klezmer melodies increasingly overlaid with a babel of menacing Germanic voices. Sounds of shattering glass dominate the work's second and longest movement, "Never Again," the sustained din meant to induce visceral recoil on the listener's part. Zawinul's *Mauthausen* (1998) uses prerecorded sequences as well as realistic sound effects in the service of a chronologically progressive series of snapshots of life in the concentration camp. Commissioned for the sixtieth anniversary of the camp's establishment, the work initially featured holographic projections and readings from the letters of prisoners.

Finally, American rap singer Remedy (Ross Filler) reached a new audience with "Never Again" (1998), a hip-hop manifesto inspired by stories of lost family members. Underscored by electronic samples of the *Theme from "Schindler's List,"* "Hatikvah," and *Sh'ma Yisroel*, the song presents a barrage of atrocities in a context of modern ethnic pride. "Never Again" (which has been embraced by the

Anti-Defamation League for its K-12 educational curricula) found a successor in *Adon Olam Ad Matai?* (God Almighty When Will It End?) (2007), a performance piece by Israeli hip-hop artist Subliminal (Ya'akov Shimoni). While such popular treatments of a subject as laden as the Holocaust may risk trivializing history or abusing the memory of victims, the aesthetic boundaries separating a work deemed acceptable from one considered to be in questionable taste are, in fact, no more easily determined with respect to popular music than with art music compositions.

REFERENCES

ARNOLD, B. (1992). "Art Music and the Holocaust." *Holocaust and Genocide Studies* 6: 335–49.
EBERLE, G. (1981). Note to Hanning Schroder, *Berliner Komponistenporträt 2*. LP. Thorofon Capella MTH 199.
HARTMANN, K. (1983). *Sonate "27. April 1945" für Klavier*. Mainz: Schott.
MUXENEDER, T. (2002). Program note to A. Schönberg, *A Survivor from Warsaw* Op. 46 (1947). Available at: <http://www.schoenberg.at/index.php?option=com_content&view=article&id=224&Itemid=391&lang=en> Accessed 23 May 2010.
REICH, S. (1988). Note to *Different Trains/Electric Counterpoint*. CD. Elektra/Nonesuch 79176-2.
TIPPETT, M. (1995). *Tippett on Music*. London: Oxford University Press.
TOMASZEWSKI, M. (1989). Note to Krzysztof Penderecki, *Dies Irae*. LP. Polskie Nagrania Muza PNCD 021.
ZEISL, E. (1946). *Requiem Ebraico: the 92nd Psalm*, for soli, mixed chorus and organ (or orchestra). New York: Transcontinental Music Corp.

OTHER SUGGESTED READING

Archives, United States Holocaust Memorial Museum, Washington, DC. Available at: <http://www.ushmm.org/research/collections/music/>.
ARNOLD, B. (1993). *Music and War: A Research and Information Guide*. New York: Garland.
BASART, A. (1986). "Music and the Holocaust: A Selective Bibliography," in *Cum notis variorum*: the newsletter of the Music Library, University of California, Berkeley, 101: 19–30.
BENARDE, S. (2003). *Stars of David: Rock'n'roll's Jewish Stories*. Hanover, NH: Brandeis University Press.
FETTHAUER, S. (2005). *Eine Liste mit Musikwerken der Holocaustrezeption*. Available at: <http://www.sophie.fetthauer.de/MusikundHolocaust06-05-20.pdf>. Accessed 19 February 2009.
GILBERT, S. (2007). *Music in the Holocaust: Confronting Life in the Nazi Ghettos and Camps*. New York: Oxford University Press.
SILVERMAN, J. (2002). *The Undying Flame: Ballads and Songs of the Holocaust*. Syracuse, NY: Syracuse University Press.

CHAPTER 32

....

MEMORIALS AND MUSEUMS

....

JAMES E. YOUNG

PUBLIC memorialization of the Holocaust era began early. Within days of liberation, former concentration camp inmates at Dachau, Buchenwald, and Bergen-
Belsen fashioned makeshift memorial towers from the bric-a-brac of their disman-
tled barracks. Soviet, American, and British soldiers inscribed stone markers
throughout Germany to the memory of their fallen comrades. Jewish, Catholic,
and Protestant clergy gathered in specially designated spaces to mourn their dead.
Memory of terror at the hands of the Nazis energized Social Democrats, communists, and other formerly persecuted parties, whose memorial ceremonies and
political rallies immediately after the war often melded together.

In America, the first public Holocaust commemoration took place even earlier,
at the very height of the killing. On 2 December 1942, some 500,000 Jews in
New York City stopped work for ten minutes, both to mourn those already killed
and to call attention to the ongoing massacre. In a gesture of sympathy, several
radio stations observed a two-minute silence before broadcasting memorial services at 4:30 that afternoon. Similar commemorations followed the next spring,
culminating in several mass public memorial ceremonies, including a pageant held
at Madison Square Garden in March 1943 called "We Will Never Die," which was
dedicated to "the two million Jews who perished at the hands of the Germans [by]
that year." The largest single Holocaust memorial event during the war took place
on 19 April 1944, the first anniversary of the Warsaw ghetto uprising. On the steps
of New York City Hall, some 30,000 Jews gathered to hear Mayor Fiorello La
Guardia (1882–1947) and prominent Jewish leaders honor the memory of fighters

and martyrs who had died in the uprising. Contemporaneous to the events they commemorated, the first "memorials" to the Holocaust thus marked the turn of history into public memory.

The further World War II and the Holocaust recede in time, the more prominent their museums and memorials become. Indeed, as survivors struggle to bequeath memory of their experiences to the next generations and governments strive to unify disparate polities with "common" national narratives, a veritable "Holocaust memorial and museums boom" has occurred. Since 1990, hundreds of museums and institutions dedicated to remembering and telling the history of Nazi Germany's destruction of the European Jews during World War II have sprung up around the world. Depending on their locations and patrons, these entities remember this past according to divergent national myths, ideals, and political needs. Some recall war dead, others resistance, and still others mass murder. All reflect both the past and present of their communities and countries. At a more specific level, the museums also reflect the temper of the time in which they were built, their architects' schools of design, and their physical locations in national memorial landscapes.

Public memory of the Holocaust, as found in these memorials and museums, is never shaped in a vacuum, its motives never pure. Both the reasons given for Holocaust memorial museums and the kinds of memory they generate are as various as the sites themselves. Some are built in response to traditional Jewish injunctions to remember, others according to a government's need to explain a nation's past to itself. Whereas the aim of some museums is to educate the next generation and to inculcate in it a sense of shared experience and destiny, others are conceived as expiations of guilt or as gestures of national self-aggrandizement. Still others are intended to attract tourists. In addition to traditional Jewish memorial iconography, every state has its own institutional forms of remembrance. As a result, Holocaust museums inevitably mix national and Jewish figures, political and religious imagery.

The aim of critical inquiry into Holocaust memorials and museums, therefore, has moved well beyond surveying or cataloging of these sites. Contemporary material-cultural and historical inquiry demands an exploration of the aesthetic, social, political, and performative dimensions underlying these sites' lives in the public mind: Who creates public memory of the Holocaust, under what circumstances, for which audiences? Which events are remembered, which forgotten, and how are they explained? What places do Holocaust museums occupy in national and religious commemorative cycles? How do memorial competitions, architects, and artists shape public memory? How do memorial representations of history both reflect and weave themselves into the course of ongoing events? What are the aims and consequences of these Holocaust museums, why does memory as found in these national institutions matter at all? This chapter explores such questions by focusing on Holocaust memorial histories and debates in Germany, Poland, Israel, and the United States.

GERMANY

As the first concentration camp in Germany, Dachau came to epitomize German memorialization of the "*KZ-Zeit*" (concentration camp time). Built in 1933 for political enemies of the Reich, Dachau housed and thereby created *German* victims, many of whom were also Jews. As horrifying as the conditions were at Dachau, its gas chamber was never used, so the crematoria burned "only" the remains of those who died of shootings, beatings, or most often, disease. Of the Dachau survivors still living in Germany, most are Christians, many of them clergymen and Social Democrats, whose own memories constitute the core of these memorial projects. There are, therefore, three religious memorials in the camp: one each for the Catholic Church, the Protestant Church, and the Jewish community.

As the name "The Trustees for the Monument of Atonement at the Concentration Camp Dachau" suggests, however, the reasons for the museum and memorials at Dachau differ for each group of victims. The Christian memorials were established not to mourn the loss of a Jewish population but to atone for Nazi sins against humanity. Stylized and cerebral, all of the monuments within the grounds of the camp tend to emphasize the great gulf between past and present. From well-scrubbed barracks floors, to the swept gravel walks outside, to the crematorium (open, a sign says, from 9 to 5), cleanliness and order now govern the "remembrance" of filth and chaos.

Over 900,000 visitors a year tour Dachau and its excellent museum. Most are Germans, but hundreds of thousands come from abroad on a pilgrimage to what is one of the most notorious tourist stops in Germany. What may not be apparent to many of the memory-tourists, however, is that Dachau's notoriety stems less from its having been one of the deadliest concentration camps (it was not) than from the widespread media coverage of its liberation, the on-site war trials, its proximity to Munich, and the accessible and concise narratives of its museum exhibitions. Dachau has become a Holocaust icon for western tourists, taking on a life of its own in the culture of travel.

If Dachau attests to the Federal Republic's effort to put its Nazi past behind, Buchenwald for many years demonstrated East Germany's determination to draw legitimacy from that past. At the behest of the Soviet liberators, East Germans recalled primarily the communist victory over fascism and the great redemption of socialist martyrs by the founding of the German Democratic Republic (GDR). Its national identity was rooted in the political memory of the Nazis as an occupying power that the progressive segments of the German people had to throw off. This self-idealization was enacted to great effect in the monuments and museum narrative at Buchenwald prior to 1989, which insisted that the camp was not liberated by American soldiers, but self-liberated by the camp underground, composed mostly of German communists. Of all the camps in Soviet-occupied Germany, only Buchenwald became a truly national East German memorial to the Nazi period. Indeed, as both place and idea, Buchenwald played a fundamental, nearly mythological role in the GDR's self-conceptualization. As an internment center for young German communists, the camp served as an enforced gathering site for debate and political formulation, a place where plans were drawn for the future and leaders were chosen to create the new order. As a site of suffering and resistance, Buchenwald became hallowed, sacred ground. Little wonder, then, that GDR officer cadets were awarded their bars at Buchenwald—where their political forebears had symbolically earned their own stripes as enemies of the Third Reich.

With the fall of the communist regime, however, this sort of Holocaust memory, one with the Jews virtually left out, became an embarrassing relic. Shortly after Germany's reunification on 3 October 1990, the museum at Buchenwald closed for physical and ideological renovation. It was now recalled that shortly after the war, some 130,000 Germans—some Nazis, some SS, some Social Democrats regarded as enemies by the Soviet Union—passed through eleven Soviet-run camps near Buchenwald and 50,000 died. In reconfiguring the museum to acknowledge the forgotten Soviet takeover of the Nazi camps at Buchenwald and other places, the post-reunification German state created a new form of memorialization. Now when the nation's leader lays flowers at Buchenwald to the victims of Nazi terror, he saves a wreath for the six new crosses commemorating the Germans who died there later as well. The accretion of memory has made Buchenwald a place where Germans were victimized by both sides. With further updating, Buchenwald may serve the new Germany as a national memorial as well as it did for the GDR.

Issues surrounding Holocaust memorialization come into the sharpest, most painful relief in Germany. In the land of "redemptive anti-Semitism" (Friedländer 1997: 3), the possibility that art might redeem mass murder with beauty (or with ugliness) or that memorials might somehow redeem this past with the instrumentalization of its memory continues to haunt a postwar generation of memory-artists. Moreover, these artists in Germany are both plagued and inspired by irreducible memorial questions: How does a state incorporate shame into its national memorial landscape? How does a state commemorate its misdeeds, making them part of its reason for being? Under what memorial aegis, whose rules, does a nation remember its own barbarity? Unlike state-sponsored memorials built by victimized nations and peoples to themselves in Poland, the Netherlands, or Israel, those in Germany are necessarily those of the persecutor remembering its victims. Facing this necessary breach in the conventional "memorial code," German national memory of the Holocaust remains torn and convoluted. Germany's "Jewish question" is now a two-pronged memorial question: How does a nation both mourn its victims and reunite on the bedrock memory of its horrendous crimes? These questions constitute the conflicted heart of Germany's struggle with its national memory of the Holocaust.

One of the most compelling results of Germany's memorial conundrum has been the advent of its "counter-monuments": brazen, painfully self-conscious memorial spaces conceived to challenge the very premises of their being. Contemporary German memory-artists are heirs to a double-edged postwar legacy: a deep distrust of monumental forms in light of their systematic exploitation by the Nazis and a profound desire to use memory to distinguish their generation from that of the killers. In these artists' eyes, the didactic logic of monuments—their demagogical rigidity and certainty of history—continues to recall too closely traits associated with fascism itself. A monument against fascism, therefore, has to be monument against itself: against the traditionally didactic function of monuments, against their tendency to displace the past they would have us contemplate, and against the authoritarian propensity in monumental spaces that reduces viewers to passive spectators.

Rather than attempt to resolve such memorial questions in their designs, contemporary artists and architects have striven for formal articulation of the questions themselves. An early critique of Germany's "memorial problem" is embodied in the *Exit-Dachau* project (1971) by Jochen Gerz (b. 1940) and in disappearing and invisible memorials in Harburg and Saarbrucken, among other installations. In 1986, for example, Gerz and Esther Shalev (b. 1948) created their "Monument against Fascism" in Harburg-Hamburg, a 12-meter-high lead-covered column that was sunk into the ground as people inscribed their names (and much else) onto its surface; on its complete disappearance in 1993, the artists hoped that it would return the burden of memory to those who came looking for it. With audacious simplicity, their "counter-monument" thus flouted a number of memorial conventions: its aim was not to console but to provoke, not to remain fixed but to change, not to be everlasting but to disappear, not to be ignored by its passers-by but to demand interaction, not to remain pristine but to invite its own violation, and not to accept graciously the burden of memory but to throw it back at the town's feet. How better to remember a now-absent people than by a vanishing monument?

In a similar vein, Horst Hoheisel (b. 1944) commemorated the void left behind by Europe's missing Jews in his "negative-form memorial" called Aschrott-Brunnen (1986) in Kassel. Through related installations, such as the empty underground library room on the Bebel Platz, created by Micha Ullman (b. 1939), or the cenotaph-like "Bibliotek" on the Juden Platz in Vienna, sculpted by Rachel Whiteread (b. 1963), artists have turned to bookish themes and negative spaces to represent the void left behind by the burning of books and of the "people of the book." Still other artists in Germany, such as the American Shimon Attie (b. 1957) in his "Writing on the Wall" series in Berlin, have attempted to reanimate otherwise amnesiac sites with the dark

Fig. 32.1 Almost vanished, the *Monument against Fascism* in Harburg by Jochen Gerz and Esther Shalev.

Photo credit: James Young.

light of their pasts. In this vein, Berlin artists Renata Stih (b. 1955) and Frieder Schnock affixed eighty double-sided metal signs to street light posts in Berlin's Bayerisches Viertel. Each includes a simple image of an everyday object on one side and a short text on the other, excerpted from Germany's anti-Jewish laws of the 1930s and 1940s. Where past citizens once navigated their lives according to these laws, present citizens may literally navigate by reminders of such laws.

For these and other artists and architects, the possibility that memory of events so grave might be reduced to exhibitions of public craftsmanship or cheap pathos remains intolerable. They reject art and architecture that console viewers, redeem such tragic events, indulge in a facile kind of *Wiedergutmachung* (reparation), or purport to mend the memory of a murdered people. Instead of searing memory into public consciousness, they fear, conventional memorials seal memory off from awareness altogether; instead of embodying memory, they find that memorials may only displace it. These artists fear that to the extent that we encourage monuments to do our memory-work for us, we become that much more forgetful. They believe, in effect, that the initial impulse to memorialize events like the Holocaust may actually spring from an opposite and equal desire to forget them.

Among the hundreds of submissions in the aborted 1995 competition for a German national "memorial for the murdered Jews of Europe," one seemed an especially uncanny embodiment of the intractable questions at the heart of Germany's memorial process. Hoheisel proposed a simple, if provocative anti-solution to the memorial competition: blow up the Brandenburg Gate, grind its stone into dust, sprinkle the remains over its former site, and then cover the entire memorial area with granite plates. How better to remember a people murdered in the name of the German nation than by destroying Germany's national monument? Rather than commemorating the destruction of a people with the construction of yet another edifice, Hoheisel wanted to mark one destruction with another. Rather than filling in the void left by a murdered people with a positive form, the artist intended to carve out an empty space in Berlin by which to recall a now absent people. Rather than concretizing and thereby displacing the memory of Europe's murdered Jews, the artist aimed to open a place in the landscape to be filled with the memories of those who come to remember Europe's murdered Jews. A landmark celebrating Prussian might and crowned by a chariot-borne Quadriga, the Roman goddess of peace, would be demolished to make room for the memory of Jewish victims of German might and peacelessness.

Of course, such a memorial undoing would never be sanctioned by the German government, and this was part of the artist's point. At least some of his polemic was directed against actually building any winning design, against ever finishing the monument at all. Hoheisel seemed to suggest that the surest engagement with Holocaust memory in Germany actually lay in its perpetual irresolution, that only an unfinished memorial process could guarantee the life of memory.

For a time, in fact, it looked as if Germany's national memorial would remain only an endless debate. But in 1997, with Chancellor Helmut Kohl's (b. 1930) blessing, the Bundestag and Berlin Senate appointed a *Findungskommission* to devise yet another process and competition. After much further debate, much of it politically infused, the jury recommended that the waving field of stelai designed by Peter Eisenman (b. 1932) be built in the five-acre site of the former ministerial gardens, between the Brandenburg Gate and Potsdamer Platz in the center of Berlin. Dedicated in 2005, Germany's national "Memorial to the Murdered Jews of Europe" provides no single vantage-point from which to view it. The memorial stretches like an Escherian grid in all directions and even echoes the rolling, horizontal plane of crypts covering Jerusalem's Mount of Olives. From its edges, the memorial is a somewhat forbidding forest of stelai, most of them between one and three meters in height, high enough to close us in, but not so high as to block out sunlight or the surrounding skyline. The color and texture of the stelai change with the cast of the sky, from steely gray on dark or overcast days, to sharp-edged black and white squares on sunny days, to a softly rolling field of wheat-colored stelai that glows almost pink in the sunset.

As one enters the field of stelai, light and sky come along, but the city's other sights and sounds are gradually occluded. Deep in the midst of the pillars, the thrum of traffic is muffled and all but disappears. Looking up and down the pitching rows, one catches glimpses of others who are within the memorial. Their appearance and disappearance, an interactive feature of the memorial, reminds one of absent Jews. One can feel very much alone in this vast space, almost desolate, even with hundreds of other mourners nearby. Depending on where one stands, the experience of the memorial varies—one feels reassurance on the sidewalk in the company of others, invigorated by the life of the city hurtling by,

Fig. 32.2 Field of Stelai, Berlin's *Denkmal* by Peter
Eisenman.

Photo credit: James Young.

but existential aloneness deep inside this dark forest of stone, oppressed and
depleted by the memory of mass murder, not reconciled to it.

Able to see over and around these pillars, visitors have to find their ways through
this field of stones even as they are never actually lost in or overcome by the
memorial act. In effect, they collectively make and choose individual spaces for
memory. The implied sense of motion in the gently undulating field also represents
a kind of memory that is neither frozen in time, nor static in space. The sense of
such instability helps visitors resist an impulse toward closure in the memorial act
and heightens one's own role in anchoring memory in oneself.

As one descends the stairs from the midst of the field into the "*Orte der
Information*," it becomes clear just how crucial a complement this underground
information center is to the field of pillars above. It neither duplicates the commemorative function, nor is it arbitrarily tacked on as an historical afterthought.
Rather, in tandem with the field of stelai, the center, as conceived and designed by
the architect Dagmar von Wilcken, completes the memorial's dual mandate as a
site of both memory and history, each shaped by the other.

POLAND

Between 1939 and 1945, the Nazis and their collaborators killed some 3 million of
Poland's 3.3 million Jews. During the same period, some 2 million ethnic Poles and
1 million other non-Jewish Polish citizens died as a result of concentration camp

internment, slave labor, mass executions, and military action. This means that some 6 million Polish nationals died during World War II, half of them Polish Jews murdered solely for having been Jews. To many Poles after World War II, the perceived symmetry of numbers (though not proportions) suggested a certain equivalency of suffering.

Moreover, with the mass exit of Poland's surviving Jewish remnant after the Kielce and other pogroms in 1946, Jewish memory also departed: memory of a thousand-year Jewish past, memory of good and bad relations with their Polish neighbors, memory of the Holocaust, and finally memory of Poland's own post-Holocaust pogroms. When Jewish Holocaust survivors next remembered, it was often to themselves in their new communities abroad—and to their new compatriots. The Poles were left alone with their own memory of events, uncontested until the survivors' return to Poland years later as tourists with their children in tow. In the interim, memory of this past reflected a characteristically Polish grasp of events, Polish ambivalence, and eventually even a Polish need for a Jewish past.

That the death camps were located on Polish soil was not viewed by Poles as evidence of local antisemitism or collaboration, but as a sign of the Germans' ultimate plans for the Polish people. In the Polish view, the killing centers in Poland were to have begun with the Jews and ended with the Poles. The mass murder of Jews became significant in Polish memory only insofar as it prefigured the Poles' own, narrowly averted genocide. Thus, the very first Holocaust memorials anywhere were the places of destruction themselves. Liberated by the Red Army in July 1944, the intact remains of the concentration camp at Majdanek, just outside Lublin, were turned into the first memorial and museum of its kind. Early the next year, the Polish Committee of National Liberation conferred similar status on the ruins of Stutthof, the earliest camp in Poland, and on the gargantuan complex at Auschwitz-Birkenau, commonly regarded as the "epicenter" of the Holocaust.

The memorials at Majdanek and Auschwitz are devastating in their impact, for they compel the visitor to accept the horrible fact that what they show is real. In both cases, the camps seem to have been preserved as the Russians found them decades ago. Guard towers, barbed wire, barracks, and crematoria—mythologized elsewhere—here stand palpably intact. In contrast to museums and memorials located away from the sites of destruction, the remnants here collapse the distinction between themselves and what they evoke. In the rhetoric of their ruins, these memorial sites do not merely gesture toward past events but present themselves as fragments of events, inviting us to mistake the debris of history for history itself.

The communist-era guidebook for the State Museum at Majdanek, for example, proclaimed the memorial's threefold aim: to preserve these buildings as material evidence of the crimes committed here; to analyze the facts of these crimes; and to present analyzed facts to the public (Marszalek and Wisniewska 1983: 3). As became clear, however, the Majdanek ruins were also material evidence of a state's reasons for remembering those crimes. Indeed, little reason to preserve these ruins existed outside of the meanings preservation imputed to them. Majdanek's remains thus

Fig. 32.3 Monument at Majdanek by Viktor Tolkin.

Photo credit: James Young.

were made to "tell" the story favored by the camp's Soviet liberators. As a result, the Jewish victims of Majdanek were assimilated twice over: once to the memory of Polish national suffering, and again to a stridently economic interpretation of the camp that was blind to the ethnic identity of the victims. At Majdanek, where Jews accounted for perhaps 40 percent of the 350,000 murdered victims, the memorial recalls Jews primarily as part of other persecuted groups, including Poles, communists, and Soviet POWs.

For years at Auschwitz-Birkenau, memorialization was a mix of ruins, museums, and sculpted art. Surrounded by a seemingly endless field of countless barracks' chimneys and piles of dynamited crematoria, a long row of block-like sarcophagi marks the end of the rail line, the beginning of the death zone inside Birkenau. In concert with the relics nearby, this monument provides material evidence for the simple message that used to be inscribed on twenty stone tablets in twenty different languages, including Yiddish and Hebrew: "Four million people suffered and died here at the hands of the Nazi murderers between the years 1940 and 1945." With Poland's regime change in 1989, these inscriptions were removed from the tablets, memory's slate wiped clean and corrected. The statistic was as wrong as it was round, arrived at by a combination of the camp commandant's self-aggrandizing exaggerations, Polish perceptions of their great losses, and the Soviet occupiers' desire to create socialist martyrs. Historians now generally believe the most accurate count is closer to 1.3 million, of whom about 1.1 million were Jews. The remaining 200,000 victims were Polish Catholics, Gypsies, and Russian POWs (Wellers 1983: 127).

The questions for the post-communist museum at Auschwitz became: What is required to create a commemorative space large enough to accommodate the

Fig. 32.4 Gate of Auschwitz.

Photo credit: James Young.

plural memories and symbols of disparate, occasionally competing groups? How should the correct proportions of space and significance be allotted? How can the Polish and Jewish narratives best be told? Are these decisions properly made by the museum itself? Resolution of these issues continues to be fraught because, by dint of its location, Auschwitz will always be a Polish memorial to both Polish and Jewish victims, a shared but contested shrine to both Jewish and Polish catastrophes.

ISRAEL

The national Holocaust remembrance day in Israel—Yom Hashoah Vehagvurah—commemorates both the mass murder of Europe's Jews and the heroism of ghetto fighters—all seemingly redeemed by the birth of the State. Like any state, Israel remembers the past according to its national myths, ideals, and current political needs. At times ambivalent, at times strident, the official approach to Holocaust memory in Israel has long been torn between the simultaneous need to remember and to forget, between the early founders' enormous state-building task and the reasons why such a state was necessary, between the Holocaust survivors' memory of victims and the Israeli soldiers' memory of resistance. On the one hand, early founders like David Ben-Gurion (1886–1973) regarded the Holocaust as the ultimate, bitter fruit of Jewish life in exile. On the other hand, such founders also recognized their perverse debt to the Holocaust: after all, it seemingly proved the

Zionist dictum that without a state and the power to defend themselves, Jews in exile would always be vulnerable to just this kind of destruction (Liebman and Don-Yehiya 1983: 24).

Ironically, however, by linking the state's *raison d'être* to the Holocaust, the early founders also located the Shoah at the center of national identity: Israel would be a nation condemned to defining itself in opposition to the very event that makes it necessary. The questions for the early state became: How to negate the Diaspora and put it behind the "new Jews" of Israel while basing the need for new Jews in the memory of Shoah? How to remember the Holocaust in Israel without allowing it to constitute the center of one's Jewish identity? In part, the answers entailed a forced distinction between the Israeli and the "*galut* (or exilic) Jew." According to this distinction, the Jew in exile has known only defenselessness and destruction, the Israeli has known fighting and self-preservation. Such a stereotype negates, of course, the early reality of Israel as an immigrant nation, whose population— approximately 800,000—at the state's founding in 1948 contained some 200,000 Holocaust survivors, including more than 20,000 who fought for Israel's independence. The Holocaust-related tensions in Israel's national narrative persist in the ubiquitous twinning of martyrs and heroes in memorial iconography. In this mixed figure, the victims are memorable primarily for the ways they demonstrate the need for fighters, who, in turn, are remembered for their part in the state's founding. The martyrs are not forgotten but are recollected heroically as the first to fall in defense of the state itself.

Whereas memorials and museums in Europe, especially those located at the sites of destruction, focus relentlessly on the annihilation of Jews and almost totally neglect the millennium of Jewish life in Europe before the war, those in Israel locate events in a historical continuum that includes Jewish life before and after the destruction. In Israeli museums at kibbutzim like Lohamei Hageta'ot, Tel Yitzchak, Givat Chaim, and Yad Mordechai, Jewish life before and during the Holocaust is emphasized over the killing itself—and Jewish life after the Holocaust is to be found primarily in Israel.

Over the years, the museums at these kibbutzim have changed little, continuing to reflect their early attachment to a strong Zionist ideology underlying their genesis. As a result, a new generation of Israelis often tends to see these (and almost all kibbutzim) as museums to both an actual historical past and to a past way of understanding the present. Such kibbutz museums often end up speaking more to tourists who come to see Israel itself as a museum to their own archaic and nostalgic longing for Israel's pioneering days.

Kibbutz Lohamei Hageta'ot (literally Fighters of the Ghettos) was founded by survivors of the camps and ghettos, many of them partisans and members of the Jewish Fighting Organization, as a living monument to what they had seen. Although the museum there is now dedicated to the memory of poet Yitzchak Katzenelson (1886–1944), in both its name and memorial configuration, the kibbutz commemorates less the dying of Jews during the war and more their fighting during the war and surviving afterward. Of the twelve museum halls, only two are devoted to the ghettos, concentration camps, and exterminations. One arrives at these halls only after visiting graphic reconstructions of Vilna, "the Jerusalem of Lithuania," and "The Shtetl, Olkieniki." If in this lay-out, the path to Holocaust lay through the centers and shtetls of diaspora life, then the road from Holocaust leads through resistance to survival, to the kibbutz itself and to the vibrant new self-sufficiency of Jews in their own land. Here the Holocaust is contextualized not only in aspects of life in exile but also in Jewish life before and after. The theme at Holocaust Remembrance Day ceremonies at Lohamei Hageta'ot is always the same: "From Destruction to Redemption."

Of all the memorial centers in Israel, only Yad Vashem Martyrs' and Heroes' Remembrance Authority bears the explicit imprimatur of the state. Conceived in the throes of the state's birth and building, Yad Vashem was regarded from the outset as an integral part of Israel's civic infrastructure. As one of the state's cornerstones, Yad Vashem both shared and buttressed the state's ideals and self-definition. In its eclectic amalgamation of outdoor monuments, exhibition halls, and massive archives, Yad Vashem functions as a national shrine to both Israeli pride in heroism and shame in victimization. Unlike memorials that attempt to hide their national origins and interests, Yad Vashem's legally mandated mission is to be simultaneously custodian and creator of national memory. The function of memory here is what it has always been for the Jewish nation: to bind present and past generations, to unify a world outlook, to create a vicariously shared national experience. These are the implied functions of every national memorial, of course, merely made visible in Israeli legislation.

At the same time, however, Yad Vashem was also conceived by the state's founders as an explicit tearing away from the traditional religious continuum and its meanings—another kind of counter-memorial. Its establishment was to inaugurate a new, civic religion simultaneously with the creation of the state, and events of the Holocaust and the state's founding were to be recalled quite literally side by side. The foundation stone for Yad Vashem was thus laid into the hillside just west of the national military cemetery at Mount Herzl on 29 July 1954 in a ceremony that turned this entire area into Har Hazikaron (Memorial Hill) (Handelman 1990: 201). In this way, Yad Vashem became a topographical extension of the national cemetery, where Israel's ideological founder, Theodor Herzl (1860–1904), lay alongside Israel's fallen soldiers, including Hannah Senesh (1921–1944), Israel's martyred ideal heroine of the Holocaust.

As if trying to keep pace with the state's own growth, Yad Vashem has continued to expand its reservoir of images, sculptures, and exhibitions. Almost every year has witnessed an unveiling of a new memorial piece or garden on the grounds, including reproductions of figures from the Warsaw ghetto and Dachau. A monument and plaza commemorating Jewish soldiers in the allied forces were added in

1985, a children's memorial in 1988, and a memorial sculpture commemorating four martyred women, heroines of the Auschwitz *Sonderkommando* uprising, in 1991. A huge project, "The Valley to the Destroyed Communities," was completed in 1992. Paralleling the state's self-construction, the construction of memory at Yad Vashem spans the entire history of the state itself.

Until its massive redesign in 2003, however, the historical museum at Yad Vashem concerned itself primarily with the destruction of Jews during the war, not with other groups murdered en masse by the Nazis. But as the state began to recognize the fact of its plural and multi-ethnic society and its own debt to globalization, its perception of the Holocaust has evolved to include non-Jewish victims of the Nazis. Yad Vashem thus has revamped its historical exhibition completely to reflect a new generation's reasons for remembering such history. The most significant of the many changes now in Yad Vashem's new Historical Museum, therefore, is a narrative that includes Gypsies, Jehovah's Witnesses, political prisoners, homosexuals, and even Polish clergy and German victims of the Nazis' T4 (euthanasia) program for the mass murder of the disabled and handicapped. In a land of immigrants, including Christian Russian spouses of Jewish immigrants from the former Soviet Union and Ethiopian Jews, and in a time when young people are increasingly looking outward at other groups of contemporary victims in the world around them, Yad Vashem now sees the need to tell the stories of victims other than Jews. With a new-found grasp of itself as a plural, immigrant nation, Israel's national institutions have begun to negate the traditional Zionist negation of the Diaspora.

THE UNITED STATES

In 1964, when a group of Jewish-American survivors of the Warsaw ghetto uprising submitted a design for a Holocaust memorial to New York City's Arts Commission, they were turned down for three reasons. First, the commissioners claimed that the design proposed by Nathan Rapoport (1911–1987), whose credits included the Warsaw ghetto memorial, was too big and not aesthetically tasteful. Second, such a monument might inspire other "special groups" to be similarly represented on public land—another regrettable precedent. And finally, the city had to ensure that "monuments in the parks ... be limited to events of American history" (Farrell 1965: 1). Apparently, the Holocaust was not an American experience.

For the Jewish survivors of the Holocaust who had immigrated to America after World War II and regarded themselves as typical "new Americans," such an answer challenged the very conception of what it meant to be an American. A distinction had been drawn between "events of American history" and those of "Americans' history." Did American history begin and end within the nation's geographical borders or did it, as most of these immigrants believed, begin in the experiences abroad that drove them to America's shores? With the April 1993 dedication of the United States Holocaust Memorial Museum (USHMM) in Washington, DC, America recognized the survivors' experiences as part of the nation's experience—and made the Holocaust part of American history.

Situated adjacent to the National Mall and within view of the Washington Monument and the Jefferson Memorial, USHMM is a neighbor to the National Museum of American History and other museums in the Smithsonian Institution complex. By dint of its placement, USHMM enshrines, not just the history of the Holocaust, but American democratic and egalitarian ideals as counterpoint to the Holocaust.

The official American justification for a national Holocaust museum in the nation's capital was provided by President Jimmy Carter (b. 1924) in April 1979. Not only would this museum depict the lives of "new Americans," he said, but it would reinforce America's self-idealization as a haven for the world's oppressed. It would thus serve as a universal warning against the bigotry and anti-democratic impulses underpinning such a catastrophe and call attention to the potential in other totalitarian systems for such slaughter (U.S. Holocaust Memorial Council Press Release, n.d.). Defined as the antithesis of America's Bill of Rights and American pluralism, the Holocaust epitomizes all the reasons immigrants—past, present, and future—ever had for seeking refuge in America.

Yet other levels of meaning can be found in the very design of the museum itself. "It is my view," the museum's architect, James Ingo Freed (1930–2005), once said, "that the Holocaust defines a radical...break with the optimistic conception of continuous social and political improvement underlying the material culture of the West" (Freed n.d.). This view led, in turn, to a fundamental architectural dilemma: How to represent the Holocaust as an irreparable breach in the western mind without violating the architectural harmony of the nation's capital? Freed's answer was an exterior that conformed to the Fine Arts Commission's strict guidelines and an interior that metaphorically removes visitors from the capital. In an echo of the brokenness already recalled in traditional Jewish mourning motifs, Freed's design includes skewed angles, exposed steel trusses, and jagged walls—all to suggest an architectural discontinuity, rawness, and an absence of reassuring forms.

The discontinuity and fragmentation preserved in the museum's interior architectural space cannot, however, be similarly conveyed in the permanent exhibition narrative. For that account depends on the continuous sequence of its telling, on chronological integration of historical events. Though housed in a structure reverberating with brokenness and the impossibility of repair, the exhibition operates on the internal logic of orderly, linear narration. While visitors to the permanent exhibition first encounter the Holocaust through the testimony of American liberators of Nazi concentration camps in 1945, including General and later President Dwight D. Eisenhower (1890–1969), the exhibition proper begins with the rise of Nazism in its post–World War I historical context. And then, because the American experience of Nazi Germany in the thirties was necessarily mediated by newsreels, papers, and radio broadcasts, that media experience is recreated in the next part of the permanent exhibition. Further sections focus on deportation, ghettoization, mass murder, concentration camps, resistance, and rescuers. Finally, like the museum narratives in Israel, where lives were rebuilt after the Holocaust, USHMM's permanent exhibit ends with the "return to life." This idealistic trope is shared by America and Israel because both see themselves as lands of refuge and freedom. USHMM's version of the "return to life" story emphasizes immigration, the long journey from "old world" antisemitism, ravaged towns, and "displaced persons" camps to the "new world" of American egalitarianism. The story underscores America's absorption of immigrants and their memories, including the gradual integration of Holocaust memory into American civic culture.

A similar appreciation for the richness of Jewish life in America is found in New York City's Museum of Jewish Heritage—A Living Memorial to the Holocaust, located on the Battery in downtown Manhattan within sight of the Statue of Liberty and Ellis Island and only blocks removed from Ground Zero of the 11 September 2001 World Trade Center attacks. Opened only in September 1997, the Museum of Jewish Heritage is the culmination of what was to be America's first Holocaust memorial. Years of city and state debates over where and how to commemorate the Holocaust in New York combined with numerous competing fundraising agendas to delay the construction. As its name suggests, the Museum of Jewish Heritage integrates the Holocaust into a Jewish past, present, and future, locating the Shoah in the long continuum of Jewish life in Europe before the war and then after the war in Israel and America.

Looking out over New York harbor from the museum's exhibition halls, visitors are able to hold in mind both the time of destruction in Europe and the safety of refuge in America, life before and after the catastrophe. With its much-lauded Memorial Garden of Stones, designed in 2003 by the landscape artist Andy Goldsworthy (b. 1956), the Museum of Jewish Heritage integrates the symbols of universal and Jewish material culture, each now grasped in terms of the other. Sapling trees of life and regeneration grow out of eighteen boulders to embody the miracle of new life taking hold wherever it can, the indomitable spirit of survivors, and by extension, all immigrants who have been cast voluntarily or involuntarily on America's shores.

REFERENCES

FARRELL, W. (1965). "City Rejects Park Memorials to Slain Jews." *New York Times*, 11 February 1965.

FREED, J. (n.d.) "The United States Holocaust Memorial Museum: What Can It Be?" Washington, DC: United States Holocaust Memorial Museum.

FRIEDLÄNDER, S. (1997). *Nazi Germany and the Jews*. Vol. 1, *The Years of Persecution, 1933–1939*. New York: HarperCollins.

HANDELMAN, D. (1990). *Models and Mirrors: Towards an Anthropology of Public Events*. Cambridge: Cambridge University Press.

LIEBMAN, C. and DON-YEHIYA, E. (1983). *Civil Religion in Israel: Traditional Judaism and Political Culture in the Jewish State*. Berkeley, CA: University of California Press.

MARSZALEK, J. and WISNIEWSKA, A. (eds.) (1983). *Majdanek*. Lublin: Krajowa Agencja Wydawnicza.

WELLERS, G. (1983). "Essai de Determination du nombre de Morts au Camp d'Auschwitz." *Le Monde Juif*, Fall 1983.

OTHER SUGGESTED READING

ALEXANDER, J. (2009). *Remembering the Holocaust: A Debate*. New York: Oxford University Press.

APEL, D. (2002). *Memory Effects: The Holocaust and the Art of Secondary Witnessing*. New Brunswick, NJ: Rutgers University Press.

BERNARD-DONALS, M. (2009). *Forgetful Memory: Representation and Remembrance in the Wake of the Holocaust*. Albany, NY: State University of New York Press.

LEVY, D. and SZNAIDER, N. (2005). *The Holocaust and Memory in the Global Age*. Philadelphia, PA: Temple University Press.

LINENTHAL, E. (1995). *Preserving Memory: The Struggle to Create America's Holocaust Museum*. New York: Viking.

STIER, O. (2003). *Committed to Memory: Cultural Mediations of the Holocaust*. Amherst, MA: University of Massachusetts Press.

WIEDMER, C. (1999). *The Claims of Memory: Representations of the Holocaust in Contemporary Germany and France*. Ithaca, NY: Cornell University Press.

YOUNG, J. (1993). *The Texture of Memory: Holocaust Memorials and Meaning*. New Haven, CT: Yale University Press.

——(ed.) (1994). *The Art of Memory: Holocaust Memorials in History*. New York and Munich: Prestal Verlag.

——(2000). *At Memory's Edge: After-Images of the Holocaust in Contemporary Art and Architecture*. New Haven, CT: Yale University Press.

PART V

AFTEREFFECTS

CHAPTER 33

......

LIBERATION AND DISPERSAL

......

ARIEH J. KOCHAVI

AFTER World War II, Jewish displaced persons (DPs) in Germany and Austria faced a situation similar to that of Jews in central Europe in the late 1930s. Western countries were unwilling to accept many immigrants, and Great Britain largely blocked entrance to Palestine. In both time periods, the policies arrived at by the various democracies stemmed from a mixture of antisemitism, xenophobia, geo-political interests, domestic political considerations, and economic priorities.

Preparations for dealing with the DP problem already had been set in motion during the war. In November 1943, representatives of forty-four countries met at the White House at the invitation of President Franklin D. Roosevelt (1882–1945) and established the United Nations Relief and Rehabilitation Administration (UNRRA). The objective of the organization was to provide food, clothing, medical supplies, and other forms of assistance to people awaiting repatriation. As Allied forces advanced toward Germany following the Normandy invasion in June 1944, the number of DPs increased constantly and soon overwhelmed the inadequately staffed and funded UNRRA. Primary responsibility for the millions of DPs and refugees fell on the Supreme Headquarters Allied Expeditionary Force (SHAEF).

When SHAEF ceased functioning in mid-July 1945, care of the DPs was trans-ferred to the four major victorious nations, the United States, Britain, the Soviet Union, and France, in their respective zones of occupation in Germany and Austria. Berlin, though located in the Russian zone, fell under the joint supervision of all four powers. All four powers favored the rapid repatriation of all DPs and refugees, as did the refugee organizations. Citizens of western European countries willingly and quickly returned home, and Russian nationals as of 1939 were forcibly repatriated, as had been agreed at the Yalta Conference in February. Nonetheless, in mid-September, approximately 1.2 million DPs remained in the British, American, and French zones in Germany and about 210,000 in their zones in Austria (Proudfoot 1956: 238–9).

Polish DPs formed the largest national group following the repatriation of Soviet nationals and thus the main problem for the American and British occupation authorities. Both occupying powers, though eager to solve the DP problem as quickly as possible, opposed forced repatriation in this instance, but did offer a modest economic incentive ("Operation Carolt") in the fall of 1946 for Poles to return home. The escalation of the Cold War during 1947, however, led Washington and London to appreciate the political and propaganda advantages of the refusal of most DPs from Poland, Ukraine, and the Baltic states to go back to countries now under Soviet influence. Moscow, for its part, was determined to repatriate all DPs from territories annexed by the Soviet Union following the war. Accusing the West of exploiting the DP issue for political purposes, the Soviets rejected any attempt to resettle DPs in other countries and demanded that UNRRA stop sustaining the DPs and thus encouraging them to stay in the camps. Controversy surrounding UNRRA's activities and the establishment of its successor, the International Refugee Organization (IRO), became part of the escalating Cold War.

Between November 1945 and the end of June 1947, when UNRRA ceased functioning, the organization helped repatriate approximately 742,000 DPs from Germany and about 202,000 from Austria. In the spring of 1947, UNRRA was operating 762 DP centers in Germany, 416 of which were in the American and 272 in the British zone. When IRO took over from UNRRA on 1 July 1947, the new organization had responsibility for the care of 712,000 refugees and DPs (Salomon 1991: 49–51; Marrus 1985: 343–4). IRO focused on resettlement, not on repatriation; as a result, the countries of the Soviet bloc refrained from joining the new refugee organization. As in the case of UNRRA, the United States financed the IRO's budget for the most part and, accordingly, determined its activities and priorities.

JEWISH DPs IN THE BRITISH OCCUPATION ZONE IN GERMANY

The escalation of the Cold War significantly affected the fate of the Jewish DPs, but in this case the West–East conflict did not pertain. The geopolitical interests of the Soviet Union and domestic political considerations of the White House drew the

Americans and the Soviets together against the British, though from completely different motives. When the war was over, Germany contained fewer than 60,000 Jewish survivors of the Holocaust from several European countries and approximately 28,000 German Jews. During the next two years, tens of thousands of Jews fled eastern Europe and the Balkans, raising the number of Jewish DPs in the western zones at the end of 1947 to approximately 230,000 or about 25 percent of the DP population there (Marrus 1985: 335). In many respects, the dramatic increase in the scope of the Jewish DP problem was caused by the policies of the Big Two Powers, the U.S. and the USSR.

When the western Allies formulated their displaced persons policy, it made no special provision for Jewish survivors, except that Jewish nationals of all former enemy countries could claim the same treatment accorded to DPs from Allied nations. The attitude was that Jews, like all other DPs, ought to return to their countries of origin and get on with their lives there as soon as possible. As DPs were brought together in hastily constructed camps and divided according to country of origin, victims of persecution and torture found themselves at times thrown together with inmates who, only a short time before, had been their persecutors and torturers. For the first few weeks after the war, the United States and Britain acted in tandem regarding Jewish displaced persons seeking refuge in those powers' respective zones of occupation. Very quickly, however, geopolitical and domestic political considerations overrode other concerns and determined Whitehall's and the White House's respective treatment of Jewish DPs.

Britain's policy toward the Jewish DPs stemmed first and foremost from its interests in the Middle East. Viewing the region as pivotal both economically and strategically, London was determined to obtain the cooperation of the Arab countries in the region. Because the latter had made Jewish immigration into Palestine a test case of Anglo–Arab relations, Whitehall decided to limit this immigration and to separate the Jewish DP problem from the Palestine question. Officially defining the Jews as a religious community, London argued that treating them otherwise would be tantamount to accepting the Nazi categorization of Jews as a separate race. Britain therefore refused to group the Jewish DPs as a distinct nationality irrespective of their countries of origin, to separate Jewish from other DPs, to appoint Jewish liaison officers, and to recognize a united body representing both Jewish DPs and German Jews in the British zone of Germany. Whitehall, furthermore, opposed any preferential treatment and special considerations for Jewish DPs, claiming that their suffering had been no different from that of other peoples during the war, and remained determined to resolve their status as part of the overall refugee issue (Reilly 1998: 86–8).

The overwhelming majority of the Jewish DPs in the British zone of Germany lived in Bergen-Belsen. When British soldiers captured the concentration camp on 15 April 1945, they faced a horrendous reality: heaps of dead bodies and about 60,000 Jewish and non-Jewish survivors, most of them barely alive. Some 35,000 inmates had died from starvation or disease during the preceding four months, and a further 14,000, most of them Jews, succumbed within a few weeks after the arrival of the British forces. Approximately 38,000 survivors needed urgent medical treatment (Lavski 2002: 42–5). Most critical was preventing a typhus epidemic; lice-infested barracks were therefore burned down and their inhabitants transferred to a former Wehrmacht camp a mile away. One of the first things the British did was to set up a hospital and mobilize about 250 medical students from London and from Belgium, who, among other things, began feeding intravenously the many survivors who were close to starvation. A number of deaths occurred as a result of overeating or inability to digest the food provided by the British soldiers. Given the debilitated physical and mental health of most of the survivors—about 14,000 of them were hospitalized by mid-May—the demand for more doctors, nurses, psychologists, and social workers became acute. The British therefore engaged German and POW doctors and nurses, though this caused the patients great emotional distress. Although the emergency measures taken by the British military saved the lives of thousands of the survivors, many others perished, and most of the military personnel mobilized in the effort were unqualified and unprepared to deal with such a situation.

Roughly 30,000 inmates of Bergen-Belsen were Jews on the day the camp was liberated. Close to 10,000 of them died soon after. About 4,000 others were fit enough to return to their home countries in western Europe. The British military authorities then transferred approximately 4,000 Jews of Polish origin to a DP camp in Lingen, near the German–Dutch border, until resistance by the Jewish DPs forced an end to that effort. By the end of summer 1945, the survivors from the Soviet Union, Czechoslovakia, Yugoslavia, Hungary, and Romania had been repatriated, and two groups of DPs were left in Bergen-Belsen, non-Jewish Poles and Jews. The majority of the approximately 12,000 remaining Jewish DPs were from Poland; another large group, numbering about 3,000, consisted of Orthodox Hungarian Jews who had survived Auschwitz. British military authorities, recognizing the mutual animosity between the Jews and the Poles, concentrated the 8,000 or so non-Jewish DPs in a different section of the camp (Reilly 1998: 81–2).

The relatively large number of Jews among the survivors of Bergen-Belsen had led other Jewish refugees in the British zone to move to the camp, since it held out the prospect of Jewish surroundings. Bergen-Belsen soon became the largest Jewish DP camp in all of Germany. In contrast to the American zone, most Jewish DPs in the British zone lived in this one camp. Relations between the Jewish DPs and their leaders and the British military authorities were tense almost from the beginning. When the Central Jewish Committee, under the leadership of Josef (Yossel) Rosensaft (1911–1975), saw that resettlement of the DPs was not imminent, the group strove to create a self-governing community that could live as normal a life as possible under abnormal conditions. This effort required much political skill and determination, since the Committee was wholly dependent on the reluctant

British military authorities, as well as on Jewish and gentile relief organizations, mainly the American Jewish Joint Distribution Committee (JDC) and UNRRA.

The Committee's main challenge, however, was mentally and physically rehabilitating DPs who for years had undergone unspeakable horrors, seen their families vanish, and lost faith in humanity. In many respects, the biographies of the Committee's leaders illustrate the tragedy experienced by survivors of the Holocaust: Rosensaft, born in Benzin, Poland, lost his family at Auschwitz and his deputy, Norbert Wollheim (1913–1998), born in Berlin, was a laborer at Auschwitz-Birkenau, where his wife and only son perished. The Committee had to contend with difficult conditions in Bergen-Belsen: shortage of food, density in the barracks, lack of privacy, unemployment, idleness, and above all demoralization. Nevertheless, a functional administration took shape that included Health, Economic, Rabbinical, and Cultural departments. With the aid and support of Jewish organizations from Britain, the United States, and Palestine, the Committee built a vital community life. One central focus was education. Bergen-Belsen contained about 500 children on the day of liberation and approximately 2,300 at the beginning of 1948, including 1,000 who were less than 3 years old. Institutions were established for both secular and orthodox children and students, as were a vocational school, a teachers' seminary, a yeshiva, a popular university, and educational and vocational programs for adults. Cultural and religious activities were also important. As early as summer 1945, a theater and a drama studio were set up, and the first Jewish newspaper in postwar Germany, *Unzer Sztyme* (Our Voice), was published. A year later, a library opened and a publishing house began work. A different manifestation of the camp's autonomy was the formation of a Jewish police force to protect the Jewish DPs from antisemitic assaults by non-Jewish DPs and to keep law and order, particularly regarding black market activities in the camp.

Essential as the activities of the Committee and the different refugee organizations were for recovery, the survivors needed strong wills and courage for the long process of rehabilitation. Many survivors were young men and women in their twenties and thirties whose families had been murdered. Their vitality found expression in starting new families. More than 1,000 weddings took place in Bergen-Belsen alone in 1946, and altogether about 1,000 babies were born that year in the British zone. The baby boom among Jewish DPs in both the American and British zones of occupation reflected first and foremost the personal will of each couple, but many also considered it the final victory over Nazism, which had tried to eradicate the Jewish people.

The political-ideological controversy between the DPs and the British military authorities determined the nature of the relationship between the two sides and considerably blunted empathy with the suffering that the Jewish DPs had undergone. The British were concerned about what they regarded as the Zionist militancy of the Central Jewish Committee of Bergen-Belsen. And, indeed, Zionism was a significant motive of the activities of the Central Committee from its inception. The schools taught in Hebrew and gave central attention to the study of Zionism and the Land of Israel. *Unzer Sztyme* extensively reported news from and about Palestine and Zionism, and DPs demonstrated on behalf of the Zionist cause. The First Congress of Holocaust survivors, convened at Bergen-Belsen in September 1945, reflected the strong Zionist convictions of the DP leadership. The gathering called upon Britain and the other Allied governments to designate Palestine a Jewish State and immediately let one million Jews enter it, adding that no obstacle would prevent the Jews from reaching the Holy Land. In response, the British military authorities refused to recognize the Central Committee as representing the DPs in Bergen-Belsen, let alone all Jewish DPs and German Jews in the British zone. Even the name of the camp became a source of political-propaganda contention. British officials spoke of the Höne camp while the DPs and Jewish and Zionist organizations kept the name Bergen-Belsen. Höne was the name of the nearby village where the British had turned former SS barracks into a DP camp.

Jewish DPs in American Occupation Zones

While geopolitical considerations predominated in shaping British policy toward the Jewish DPs, domestic political calculation was determinative in the case of the Americans. President Harry S. Truman (1884–1972) became involved personally in the problem of Jewish DPs in the fall of 1945, even though they made up a small proportion of the 600,000 DPs then in the American zones of Germany and Austria. Most significantly, Truman put an end to the tacit American–British understanding reached prior to the Evian Conference of July 1938 that Britain would not ask the U.S. to change its immigration laws and the U.S. would not insist that the British allow Jewish immigration into Palestine. Truman, like his predecessor Roosevelt, preferred not to contend with the domestic opposition to admitting Jewish immigrants into the United States; instead, he publicly demanded that Britain allow 100,000 Jewish DPs to enter Palestine.

This call occurred shortly after the President received on 24 August 1945 a report that Earl Harrison (1899–1955), dean of the University of Pennsylvania Law School, had been asked to prepare on the conditions of refugees who could not be repatriated, particularly Jews encamped in Germany and Austria. The document accused the U.S. Army of inhuman conduct toward the Jewish DPs and criticized the fact that Jewish DPs were still being kept in concentration camps behind barbed wire fences and under armed guard. Harrison also criticized American military officers for manifesting "the utmost reluctance" at "inconveniencing the German population," which enjoyed, particularly in the rural areas, better living conditions than did the DPs (Dinnerstein 1982: 301) His main recommendations called for recognizing the Jews as a distinct national group entitled to separate camps and preferential treatment, designating Palestine as the main destination of the Jewish DPs, separating the political issue of the future of Palestine from the humanitarian goal of rehabilitating Jewish refugees there, and transferring 100,000 displaced Jews to Palestine. The Harrison report conceded that the United States could not serve as a destination that would solve the Jewish DP problem, but encouraged American intervention with the British government to that end.

Harrison's recommendations, inspired by Joseph J. Schwartz (1899–1975) of the JDC and other American Jews participating in his mission, became the cornerstone of President Truman's policy toward the Jewish DPs. Although genuine compassion and sympathy toward Holocaust survivors probably played a role in this development, political calculations on Truman's part predominated. Not yet an elected president, Truman respected the electoral and financial significance of the American Jewish community. His appeal to Britain to allow 100,000 Jewish DPs to enter Palestine turned out to be pivotal because it created the linkage between the Jewish DP problem in Europe and the question of Palestine that British policy makers had striven to avoid. Moreover, the President's public demonstration of interest in the plight of the Jewish DPs transformed their treatment in the American zones of occupation and turned these zones into a haven for east European Jews.

Not all U.S. military commanders in Germany, however, favored Truman's policy toward Jewish DPs. While Dwight D. Eisenhower (1890–1969), the European theater commander, carefully followed Truman's instructions, some high-ranking servicemen displayed a lack of sympathy toward Jewish DPs that bordered on antisemitism. George S. Patton, Jr. (1885–1945), commander of the U.S. Third Army in southern Germany, was a conspicuous example. Patton resisted Eisenhower's instructions to evict Germans from their homes in order to house Jews. Referring to the Germans as decent people, he described the Jewish DPs as "lower than animals" (Blumenson 1974: 751–2). The rotation of officers and enlisted men only exacerbated relations between American soldiers and Jewish DPs. Newly arrived Army personnel lacked first-hand encounters with the suffering the Jews had endured and viewed them solely through the lens of daily confrontations. The Jewish DPs became regarded as troublemakers, extremists, and black-marketeers. A wide mental and psychological gap opened between the DPs and the young soldiers, whose past or training had not prepared them for such a complicated, sensitive mission. The horrors and torture experienced by the Jewish DPs had made them complicated people to handle, since they had lost basic trust in humankind in general and in gentiles in particular. In contrast, the Germans seemed well mannered and orderly. Furthermore, as time passed, strategic interests arising out of the intensifying tension between east and west, notably Washington's desire for Germany's economic recovery and integration into the anti-Soviet sphere, reinforced tendencies to satisfy the Germans at the expense of the DPs.

Nevertheless, the situation of Jewish DPs in the American zones of Germany, Austria, and Berlin improved considerably following Harrison's report. Still, given the disarray in Germany after the war and the enormous tasks confronting the military authorities, discrepancies between instructions and implementation remained. Jewish DPs had to struggle to improve conditions, to turn their camps into exclusively Jewish settings, and to take charge of their own lives. Official recognition by the American military authorities of the Central Committee of Liberated Jews for the U.S. Zone of Occupation, under the chairmanship of Dr. Zalman Grinberg (1912–1983), who also directed the Jewish hospital in St. Ottilien, did not come until September 1946. Like the Central Committee in Bergen-Belsen, the Central Committee in the American zone considered itself responsible for the rehabilitation and welfare of all Jewish DPs located there and as their sole representative vis-à-vis the military authorities, refugee organizations (both Jewish and non-Jewish), and international bodies. The Committee's Zionist inclination was demonstrated at the *She'erit Hapletah* (Surviving Remnant) Convention in Munich in January 1946. Convention delegates strongly condemned British policy in Palestine, particularly the limitation on Jewish immigration.

In contrast to the continuous decrease in the number of non-Jewish DPs, the number of Jewish DPs constantly increased as a result of the influx of Jews from eastern Europe in the first years after the war. In July 1945, most of the approximately 15,000 survivors of the Holocaust in the American zone were in Bavaria, mainly around Munich. By the end of the summer, the largest Jewish DP camps were Landsberg, Feldafing, and Föhernwald, the last established because of overcrowding in the first two camps. In October, some 3,000 DPs encamped in Föhernwald; three months later, this number reached about 5,300. January 1946 saw about 47,000 Jewish DPs in the American zone, of whom 30,000 lived in camps and about 17,000 in special sections in German cities. At that time, about 5,000 more Jewish DPs lived in five camps in the U.S. zone of Austria. By the end of the year, about 95,000 Jews inhabited camps in Germany, more than 36,000 in 143 different communities in the U.S. zone. In addition, more than 8,000 children and members of youth movements lived in children's houses and Zionist vocational training institutions, while 3,000 more were hospitalized (Mankowitz 2002: 20–2). Altogether about 520,000 Jewish and non-Jewish DPs were in Germany at the end of 1946. In the American zone in Austria, the number of Jewish DPs increased to 24,000 out of about 70,000 DPs, while the number of Jewish DPs in the British zone of Austria increased only slightly, from about 1,000 to 3,500 out of approximately 63,000 DPs in December 1946 (Bauer 1989: 130–1).

Although each DP camp was distinct in the size and the composition of the population, the overall conduct of the different camps in the American zone was highly similar. More research on the internal life in the camps from the perspective of the DPs is needed, however; missing or incomplete facets include personal feelings and thoughts on mourning, revenge, and humankind in general, as well as gender-related matters: pregnancy, childbirth, motherhood, social networks formed by women, and the roles women took upon themselves in the camps. Each camp sought to become an autonomous community, separate from the German economy and self-sufficient with regard to such necessities as a health care system, schools, kindergartens, vocational training, religious institutions, law courts, police, sport clubs, and cultural activities, including a theater, an orchestra, libraries, and newspapers. As in Bergen-Belsen, education, primarily for children, enjoyed first priority in the American-zone camps. Following the exodus from eastern Europe and the baby boom, the composition of the DP community changed significantly. In December 1945, for example, only 1,800 DP children were in the American zone; a year later, more than 25,000 were. In fifty-four schools, almost 600 teachers taught approximately 10,000 children between the ages of 6 and 17. Still, as many as 5,000 children in this age group found no suitable school or any Jewish educational institute in their area. More than 3,000 youths participated in Zionist pioneering training (*Kibbutzei Hachsharah*), and about 580 students studied in German universities, mainly in Munich (Mankowitz 2002: 131–6).

Political activity relating mainly to Zionism became a social-cultural focus of camp life. A majority of DPs hoped to immigrate to Palestine, but resettling in countries in the democratic world, most notably the United States, also appeared desirable. When in early 1946 the Anglo-American Committee of Inquiry Regarding the Problems of European Jewry and Palestine (AAC) asked Jewish DPs in the western zones of Germany for their preference, an overwhelming majority (118,570 of 138,320) listed Palestine. This was also the preferred destination of 18,700 of the 19,000 DPs in Italy whom UNRRA questioned (Wyman 1989: 139). Generally, polls conducted among the DPs manifested strong Zionist aspirations. Historians have debated heatedly whether the DPs were genuinely Zionist or merely manipulated by the Zionist leadership in Palestine and in the camps and whether the polls would have been different had the democratic countries opened their gates to Jewish DPs. Nonetheless, the majority of the DPs do appear to have been Zionists in the broad sense, although that does not mean that they all wanted to immigrate to Palestine/ Israel. Family considerations, especially the location of relatives, mental fatigue after long years of struggling for survival, the British blockade of Palestine, the fighting between Jews and Arabs after the UN resolution of 29 November 1947 on the creation of a Jewish state, and the harsh conditions in the embryonic State were factors weighing against immigration to Palestine/Israel, though not against Zionist goals. In fact, in the end, Rosensaft and several other fervent Zionist leaders of the DPs in both the British and American zones of occupation immigrated to countries other than Israel. Zionist history shows that there was always a gap between ardent support for the ideology and personal realization of it.

The dramatic increase in the number of Jewish DPs in the American zone resulted from the decision of the American military authorities to admit Jews fleeing eastern Europe and the Balkans to the American-controlled sectors of Germany, Austria, and Berlin. Although the U.S. commanders there and the U.S. secretaries of state and war wished to seal the borders of the American occupation zones, they refrained from doing so because of Truman's sensitivity to the problem of Jewish refugees and his electoral considerations. Thus, fleeing Jews were assigned DP status, with all the preferential treatment this entailed, once they reached the American zones of occupation. Moreover, in an effort to reduce their density in Austria and in Berlin, both of which served as important transit routes, tens of thousands of the incoming Jews were transferred to the U.S. zone in Germany. A change in policy on incoming refugees from eastern Europe occurred, however, in spring 1947, when General Lucius D. Clay (1897–1978), the American commander in Germany, attempted to hold down the number and the cost of DPs in the U.S. zones by announcing that no additional refugees would be accepted in DP camps or fed from American supplies after 21 April 1947. In the long run, Clay's directive proved inconsequential because it did not seal the borders; in the short term, however, the financial burden of maintaining new Jewish refugees fell upon the JDC. In the spring of 1947, approximately 250,000 Jewish DPs were in Europe, 182,000 of them in Germany, 44,000 in Austria, including about 12,000 in the western zones of Vienna, and 19,000 in Italy (Dinnerstein 1982: 278).

ILLEGAL IMMIGRATION

In keeping with their overall policy toward Jewish DPs, the British blamed the exodus of Jews from eastern Europe to Germany and Austria on Zionist agitation. As early as fall 1945, London asserted that the influx from Poland was part of a Zionist plot to embarrass the British military authorities in Germany and to prove to the world that Jews could no longer live in Europe and had to immigrate to Palestine. To dissuade further would-be infiltrators, as the British called them, London decided not to allow refugees who arrived after 1 July 1946 to remain in the DP camps and allocated food to each camp according to the register of refugees living there prior to that date (Königseder and Wetzel 2001: 51). In light of this policy, the overwhelming majority of the increasing number of fleeing Jews headed toward the American zones of occupation.

Although the number of Jewish DPs in the British zone of Germany was negligible in comparison with the overall DP population there of approximately 530,000 at the end of 1945 and about 368,000 in the summer of 1946, Whitehall ascribed disproportionate importance to the Jewish DP problem (Lavski 2002: 49). The salience of the issue reflected its impact on Anglo-American relations and on Britain's position in the

Middle East, particularly in Palestine. Publicly the British held to their policy of denying that Jewish DPs represented a separate nationality; in practice, however, they began to treat Jewish DPs, irrespective of country of origin, as one group. In April 1946, London appointed an advisor for Jewish affairs in Germany, thus acknowledging that a common denominator bound together all Jewish DPs, including German Jews. This concession was followed by another. Faced with continuing friction between Jewish and Polish DPs in Bergen-Belsen, British military authorities in the summer of 1946 removed the Polish DPs, with the result that the camp became an exclusively Jewish DP camp—the largest in Germany and Austria. When the British military authorities in April 1947 gave official recognition to the Central Committee in Bergen-Belsen as the camp's representative, they still refused to recognize it as speaking for all Jewish DPs in the British zone. This disinclination, though, was more symbolic than practical, since 10,346 of the 12,232 Jewish DPs in the British zone lived in Bergen-Belsen. Nonetheless, the British continued to exclude from the Committee's purview the 5,000 German Jews living in the British zone, in keeping with Britain's insistence that all Jewish DPs had to return to their countries of origin, where they could and should rebuild their lives (Kochavi 2001: 56).

Britain failed not only to put an end to the land exodus from eastern Europe, but also to halt illegal sailings of Jewish DPs to Palestine. The Zionists, rejecting the British Mandatory Authorities' offer of 1,500 visas per month, sent approximately 70,000 *ma'apilim* (in Hebrew), or illegal immigrants as the British called them, from ports on both sides of the Iron Curtain to Palestine between the end of the war and the establishment of the State of Israel in May 1948. About 46,000 of these immigrants were intercepted on the way to Palestine and deported to detention camps in Cyprus. More than half of the *ma'apilim* departed from Italian and French ports. Most were Polish Jews who had traveled via Germany and Austria. Of the fifty-six clandestine immigrant ships that sailed to Palestine, thirty-four set out from Italy, carrying more than 21,000 persons; approximately 16,000 Jewish refugees sailed from French ports (Naor 1978: appendix).

Polish Jews also composed the majority of the Jewish DPs gathered in the camps in Germany and Austria. Estimates of the number of Jews in Poland after the end of World War II vary between 55,000 in June and 80,000 in August of 1945, but the repatriation of approximately 150,000 Polish Jews from the Soviet Union during the first half of 1946 significantly increased this population. Zionist convictions, the sense of Poland as a graveyard, and the resurgence of indigenous antisemitism prompted thousands to escape to the DP camps in Germany and Austria. More than 30,000 Jews left Poland via Czechoslovakia by the end of 1945. The exodus accelerated significantly after the pogrom in Kielce on 4 July 1946, when 42 of the 250 Jews who lived in the city were murdered by a mob impelled by a blood libel. Within a year of the pogrom, between 100,000 and 122,000 more Jews left the country, most of them by the end of 1946 and with the tacit cooperation of the Polish authorities. In November 1946, Polish Jews composed more than 70 percent of all DPs in the American zone of Germany. Altogether, between 160,000 and 190,000 Jews left Poland after its liberation, about 70 percent of them with the help of Zionist emissaries (Engel 1996: 155 n. 7, 245 n. 33). In 1947, about 19,000 Romanian Jews succeeded the Polish ones as the largest group of arrivals at the DP camps in Austria and Germany (Bauer 1989: 140).

On the whole, more than a quarter of a million Jews fled to the west from eastern Europe and the Balkans after the end of World War II, and more than 29,000 Jews escaped the region via ports in the Balkan countries. Obviously, the mass departure of Jews by land and sea from Soviet bloc countries could have occurred only with the knowledge and consent of Moscow. This exodus was part of the Kremlin's efforts to cause a rupture in London's relations with both the Arab countries and the United States. In view of the Anglo-American dispute over transferring Jewish DPs to Palestine, the Soviet Union had an interest in exacerbating the problem of Jewish DPs in Germany and Austria and in allowing tens of thousands of Jews to sail to Palestine. Thus, the Kremlin suspended its usual practice of barring emigration from Soviet bloc countries and permitted Polish Jews who had found refuge in the Soviet Union during the war to return to Poland, even though most of them were likely to continue on to the DP camps in Germany and Austria (Kochavi 2004: 60–76). This exodus played a crucial role in transforming the Jewish DP problem, which had been negligible immediately after the war, into a matter that could not be solved without opening Palestine or the democratic countries to immigration.

UNWANTED

Even President Truman, who demonstrated concern and sympathy for the Jewish DPs, carefully avoided tampering with America's existing immigration regulations. When he outlined U.S. policy on the absorption of DPs and refugees from war-ravaged Europe on 22 December 1945, he categorically stated that U.S. policy would operate within the scope of current legislation, that unused immigration quotas would not accumulate, and that he would not ask Congress to change the law. The total quota for all central and eastern European and Balkan states, of which most of the potential immigrants were nationals, allowed only 39,000 persons to enter the United States each year, two-thirds of them from Germany. In other words, America's contribution to a solution of the DP problem would not go beyond giving preference to DPs within the existing immigration quotas. Polish Jewish DPs had especially little reason for optimism, since the annual immigration quota for Poland was 6,524. Truman's directive accorded with the mood of Congress and the prevailing attitude of the American public.

Summer 1946 saw the beginning of a campaign on the part of non-Zionist Jewish organizations in the United States to press for the entry of Jewish DPs into the United States. A new body, the Citizens Committee on Displaced Persons (CCDP), was set up to mobilize support among the American public and in Congress. The organization was financed mostly by Jews, but included prominent non-Jewish figures, among them Eleanor Roosevelt (1884–1962), and was headed by Earl Harrison in order to stress its non-sectarian character. Within a short period of time, the CCDP became one of the largest, most efficient pressure groups in the United States. Nevertheless, it failed to overcome resistance to opening the country's gates to DPs. Congress did not pass a bill introduced in April 1947 by Rep. William G. Stratton (1914–2001), Republican of Illinois, to allow the entry of 100,000 DPs annually over the next four years. Aware of widespread antisemitic sentiment, Stratton played down the Jewish aspect of the DP problem, and President Truman refrained from supporting Stratton's bill publicly.

On 25 June 1948, more than a month after the establishment of the State of Israel, Congress finally passed the Displaced Persons Act, allowing 200,000 DPs into the United States over a period of two years. This law, however, included restrictions that minimized the number of Jewish DPs eligible to enter the United States and gave priority to DPs from the former Baltic States and Poland east of the Curzon Line, regions that the Soviet Union had annexed. In effect, many former collaborators with the Nazis obtained preference over Holocaust survivors. Although he signed the legislation, President Truman condemned its discriminatory clauses, which prevented more than 90 percent of Jewish DPs from entering the United States. Only in June 1950 was new legislation passed to cancel the restrictions of the 1948 Act; by then, however, about 100,000 Jewish DPs from Germany, Austria, and Italy, in addition to the detainees in Cyprus, already had gone to the State of Israel. In all, approximately 28,000 Jewish DPs (15,000 of them German Jews) entered the United States between 22 December 1945, the date of Truman's directive, and 30 June 1948, when the first of the DP acts came into force; a further 68,000 arrived as a result of the DP Acts of 1948 and 1950 (Dinnerstein 1982: 251; Bauer 1989: 291–2).

Between the passage of the bill in 1948 and the end of the IRO's mandate on 30 December 1951, the U.S. admitted some 312,000 DPs or about 37 percent of the 830,000 DPs resettled worldwide through the IRO (Proudfoot 1956: 425). Compared to other absorbing countries, U.S. immigration policy toward Jewish DPs was generous. During the first three crucial years after the war, both Canada and Australia refrained altogether from absorbing Jewish DPs. After Israel was established, Canada took in 8,000 Jews in the summer of 1948, and Australia only 150 (out of 50,000 DPs accepted by September 1949). By 1954, however, about 17,000 survivors of the Holocaust migrated to Australia (Abella and Troper 1983: 274; Rutland 2001: 50, 61–2). The British Labour government not only blocked the immigration of Holocaust survivors, but also considered ways to rid the country of Jewish refugees who had entered before the war, even as Britain was admitting about 300,000 immigrants between 1946 and 1948 (Kochavi 2001: 30; Kushner and Knox 2001: 206).

The creation of the State of Israel and gradual changes in the immigration policy of several democratic countries marked the beginning of the end of the Jewish DP problem in Germany and Austria. In November 1949, about 30,000 Jews remained in the U.S. zone in Germany, half of them in nine camps, but by 1952, a single camp at Föhrenwald, which now came under German administration, could house all remaining Jewish DPs. The camp was closed toward the end of 1956, and the last few Jewish DPs left it in February 1957 (Königseder and Wetzel 2001: 163–6). In the British zone, about 7,000 Jewish DPs were in camps, mainly Bergen-Belsen, and about 4,500 in different cities in May 1948; a year later, fewer than 5,000 were left. In May 1950, the Jewish DPs of Bergen-Belsen were moved to Upjever, near the Dutch border. One year later, only 700 Jews lived in this last DP camp in the British zone, which finally closed in August 1951 (Lavski 2002: 210–11). Of the 21,000 Jews in Austria in May 1948, half were gone two years later, and among those left only 4,400 still lived in DP camps (Albrich 1998: 108, 130).

The majority of Jewish DPs seemed to have succeeded in reconstructing their lives in the absorbing countries, in the sense of establishing families and leading more or less normal lives. Still, the effects of the DP experience on their minds and the course of their everyday lives, as well as those of their families, have yet to be researched adequately. The semi-autonomous Jewish communities established in the DP camps appear to have contributed significantly to the mental and morale rehabilitation of the DPs. This is an ironic consequence of the policies of the democratic countries, showing how the lack of generosity and sensitivity that typified their attitude toward Jewish immigration before and even during World War II persisted well into the postwar era.

REFERENCES

ABELLA, I. and TROPER H. (1983). *None Is Too Many: Canada and the Jews of Europe, 1933–1948*. New York: Random House.

ALBRICH, T. (1998). "The Zionist Option: Israel and the Holocaust Survivors in Austria." *The Journal of Israeli History* 19/3: 105–31.

BAUER, Y. (1989). *Out of the Ashes: The Impact of American Jews on Post-Holocaust European Jewry*. Oxford: Pergamon Press.

BLUMENSON, M. (1974). *The Patton Papers: 1940–1945*. Boston, MA: Houghton Mifflin.

DINNERSTEIN, L. (1982). *America and the Survivors of the Holocaust*. New York: Columbia University Press.

ENGEL, D. (1996). *Between Liberation and Flight*. Tel Aviv: Am Oved Publishers Ltd (Hebrew).

KOCHAVI, A. (2001). *Post-Holocaust Politics: Britain, the United States and Jewish Refugees, 1945–1948*. Chapel Hill, NC: University of North Carolina Press.

——(2004). "Indirect Pressure: Moscow and the End of the British Mandate." *Israel Affairs* 10: 6–76.

KÖNIGSEDER, A. and WETZEL, J. (2001). *Waiting for Hope: Jewish Displaced Persons in Post-World War II Germany*. Evanston, IL: Northwestern University Press.

KUSHNER, T. and KNOX, K. (2001). *Refugees in an Age of Genocide: Global, National, and Local Perspectives during the Twentieth Century*. London: Frank Cass.

LAVSKI, H. (2002). *New Beginnings: Holocaust Survivors in Bergen-Belsen and the British Zone in Germany, 1945–1950*. Detroit, MI: Wayne State University Press.

MANKOWITZ, Z. (2002). *Life between Memory and Hope: The Survivors of the Holocaust in Occupied Germany*. Cambridge: Cambridge University Press.

MARRUS, M. (1985). *The Unwanted: European Refugees in the Twentieth Century*. New York: Oxford University Press.

NAOR, M. (1978). *The Ha'apala, 1934–1948*. Tel Aviv: Ministry of Defence Publications (Hebrew).

PROUDFOOT, M. (1956). *European Refugees, 1939–1945*. Evanston, IL: Northwestern University Press.

REILLY, J. (1998). *Belsen: The Liberation of a Concentration Camp*. London: Routledge.

RUTLAND, S. (2001). "Subtle Exclusions: Postwar Jewish Emigration to Australia and the Impact of the IRO Scheme." *Journal of Holocaust Education* 10: 50–66.

SALOMON, K. (1991). *Refugees in the Cold War*. Lund: Lund University Press.

WYMAN, M. (1989). *DP: Europe's Displaced Persons, 1945–1951*. Philadelphia, PA: The Balch Institute Press.

OTHER SUGGESTED READING

BANKIER, D. (ed.) (2005). *The Jews are Coming Back*. Jerusalem: Yad Vashem.

BRENNER, M. (1999). *After the Holocaust: Rebuilding Jewish Lives in Postwar Germany*. Princeton, NJ: Princeton University Press.

COHEN, B. (2007). *Case Closed: Holocaust Survivors in Postwar America*. New Brunswick, NJ: Rutgers University Press.

FEINSTEIN, M. (2010). *Holocaust Survivors in Postwar Germany, 1945–1957*. New York: Cambridge University Press.

GUTMAN, Y. and SAF, A. (eds.) (1990). *She'erit Hapletha, 1944–1948*. Jerusalem: Yad Vashem.

NACHMANI, A. (1987). *Great Power Discord in Palestine*. London: Frank Cass.

REILLY, J., CESARANI, D., and KUSHNER, T. (eds.) (1997). *Belsen in History and Memory*. London: Frank Cass.

SJÖBERG, T. (1991). *The Powers and the Persecuted: The Refugee Problem and the Intergovern-mental Committee on Refugees (IGCR), 1938–1947*. Lund: Lund University Press.

CHAPTER 34

··

PUNISHMENT

··

REBECCA WITTMANN

PUNISHMENT for the Holocaust brings trials to mind: the Nuremberg trial of 1945–46, the Eichmann trial in Israel in 1961, the Auschwitz trial in Germany in 1963–65, and the Papon trial in France in 1997, to name the best known. Yet, only one of these proceedings, the Eichmann trial, made the Holocaust the central crime. The others identified the offenses at issue as war crimes, crimes against peace, crimes against humanity, or ordinary murder and manslaughter.

What explains this pattern? First, genocide did not become a separate and distinct crime under international law until the United Nations Convention on the Prevention and Punishment of the Crime of Genocide was approved on 9 December 1948, two years after the largest of the Allied and U.S. tribunals dealing with Nazi crimes. The Convention, clearly a result of the Nazi atrocities committed during World War II, defines genocide in terms of specific acts—including but not limited to killing—"committed with intent to destroy, in whole or in part, a national, ethnical, racial or religious group" and requires that the contracting parties "undertake to prevent and to punish" the crime of genocide (United Nations 1948). Clearly, the Holocaust exemplified the UN's definition, but the Genocide Convention did not enter into force until 12 January 1951. Second, although West Germany adopted a charge of genocide in 1954, the charge was not made retroactive. Ironically, the Holocaust led to the criminalization of genocide, but with regard to the Holocaust nobody in Germany or elsewhere was indicted, let alone punished, for that specific crime. Various nations and international bodies brought other charges against accused perpetrators, whose trials resulted in death or life sentences for a few, prison terms for a larger number, fines and loss of political rights for some, and amnesty, exoneration, or acquittal for the vast majority.

Beginning in 1943, the Allies had discussed how to deal with Nazi war crimes after the fighting stopped. Both Joseph Stalin (1879–1953) and Winston Churchill (1874–1965) initially favored summarily executing a few thousand top Nazi officials by firing squad. This course was rejected in favor of trials in the Moscow Declaration on German Atrocities signed by the Allies on 1 November 1943. In April 1945, at the founding conference of the United Nations in San Francisco, the delegates discussed establishing an international tribunal and defined the due process that defendants were to receive.

The American dedication to a judicial process was evident from the subsequent prosecution of 1,885 war criminals in the U.S. occupation zone in Germany between 1945 and 1949. This prosecution took place in three settings: (1) U.S. army trials of low ranking war criminals; (2) the Nuremberg Trial of the Major War Criminals, conducted by the International Military Tribunal (IMT), which judged high ranking Nazi officials whose alleged crimes were not confined to a single legal jurisdiction; and (3) the subsequent or successor Nuremberg trials, staffed exclusively by Americans, which assessed the culpability of prominent figures in various professions, organizations, and institutions implicated in war crimes. The U.S. prosecutors saw these trials as essential parts of the process of turning Germany into a thriving democracy. Success in that regard remains debatable, however, since most Germans at the time rejected the results as "victor's justice."

THE U.S. ARMY TRIALS

Between 1945 and 1947, the U.S. Army prosecuted 1,676 lesser war criminals in 462 trials, held mainly at the former Dachau concentration camp, near Munich. Among the indicted were military and government officials, concentration camp personnel, and civilians accused of violations of the laws of war, primarily assaults on captured American soldiers and airmen. These trials were based on military law, including the Geneva and Hague conventions on the decent treatment of prisoners of war. For example, the Fourth Hague Convention of 1907 prescribed that prisoners of war "must be humanely treated" and not subjected to excessive forced labor in support of the machinery of war. The Third Geneva Convention, ratified by Germany and forty-three other nations in 1929, reinforced the Hague conventions with stipulations that captive soldiers must not be subjected to violence, could not be placed under "undue pressure" to make confessions or incriminate themselves, and had to receive a fair trial through a military court.

The crimes at issue during the first six months of the Army trials were acts that had been committed against American military personnel or Allied civilians within what became the American zone of occupation. In the course of proceedings against a total of 646 defendants, the courts established not only that official Nazi policy was to mistreat downed flyers and often to kill them immediately, but also that people who did so acted mainly out of desires for revenge that Nazi propaganda fostered. But the initial limitation of the jurisdiction of U.S. Army courts to crimes perpetrated against Allied citizens produced the oddity that seven doctors and nurses who had murdered thousands at the Hadamar euthanasia facility in the American zone could be charged with killing Polish and Soviet citizens who had died there but not the German ones. In October 1945, three of the defendants were sentenced to death and four to prison terms that ranged from twenty-five years to life (Heberer in Heberer and Matthäus 2008: 25–47).

During the second phase of the Army trials, which followed the promulgation of Allied Control Council Law 10, allowing military prosecutions of "crimes against humanity," the focus turned to 1,030 people accused of having committed atrocities at concentration camps. Needing to deal expeditiously with such a large number of defendants, the courts made use of two available legal shortcuts. First, military law permitted a charge of "common design" that allowed prosecutors to try as many as sixty-one people at a time. The charge operated on the principle of "vicarious liability," which meant that participation of any kind in an act that resulted in homicide was grounds for conviction. This charge differed fundamentally from indictments in other postwar trials. Unlike the conspiracy charge presented at the IMT, the common design charge did not require defendants to have engaged in a previously conceived plan to commit homicide. Simply being a part of the system that resulted in mass atrocity, i.e., working at a camp like Dachau or Mauthausen, made a defendant guilty of common design; intent and initiative did not matter. Furthermore, the U.S. Army trials used a "parent case" system. It entailed prosecuting one main case for each concentration camp, after which the basic proven evidence was accepted automatically without time-consuming restatement in all subsequent cases involving the same camp. Altogether, the U.S. Army trials produced 432 death sentences, of which 261 were carried out, along with 305 sentences to lifetime imprisonment, 794 impositions of prison terms ranging from two months to thirty years, and 258 acquittals (Yavnai in Heberer and Matthäus 2008: 49–71).

That these Army trials went largely unnoticed at the time and were quickly forgotten has two principal explanations. First, the trials were overshadowed by the concurrent proceedings against the major war criminals at Nuremberg. Second, at the time few people grasped the importance of the defendants on trial at Dachau, who were often seen merely as small cogs in a large machine or reluctant participants who had no choice but to follow orders. Only later did scholars show that most camp personnel chose concentration camp work to escape likely death on the battlefield. Only later did appreciation grow for a point that the prosecutors in the U.S. Army trials already knew and sought to prove: that cogs are vital for machinery to turn at all.

NUREMBERG

....

Allied representatives assembled in London in June 1945 to draft procedures for an International Military Tribunal to try the major Nazi war criminals. The resulting Nuremberg Charter laid down the most important governing condition of the trial: that only Nazi crimes would come under the jurisdiction of the court. The Soviets, for example, did not want to be charged with responsibility for the massacre of thousands of Polish officers at Katyn in 1940 and actually included reference to this crime in the indictment against the Germans. All of the Allies had killed civilians and wanted to avoid a *tu quoque* argument by the defense. The charter stipulated clearly that war crimes meant only crimes committed in connection with Germany's waging of aggressive war.

On 8 August 1945, the Allies ratified the Charter, whose paragraph 6 stated the four key charges against the defendants: (a) conspiracy to commit aggressive war; (b) crimes against peace, namely, planning and waging a war of aggression in violation of international treaties and agreements; (c) war crimes, i.e., violations of the laws or customs of war, such as murder, deportations or slave labor of civilians, ill-treatment of prisoners of war, killing of hostages, plunder of public or private property, and wanton destruction of cities, towns, or villages; and d) crimes against humanity, such as murder, extermination, enslavement, deportation, and other inhumane acts or persecutions on political, racial, or religious grounds. The wording of the charge of "crimes against humanity" provided that Germans could be charged with persecuting their own population only during the war, not before. The subcharge of "Crimes against the Jews," which included "Persecution on Political, Racial, and Religious Grounds in Execution of and in Connection with the Common Plan Mentioned in Count One [aggressive war]," was referred to rarely.

The Americans wanted to ensure that major leadership figures, especially members of the SS, were in the dock, but almost all of the most infamous Nazis were dead, including Adolf Hitler (1889–1945), Heinrich Himmler (1900–1945), and Joseph Goebbels (1897–1945). Still, a representative cross section of significant leaders remained to be indicted. They included Karl Dönitz (1891–1980), Commander in Chief of the German War Navy; Hans Frank (1900–1946), Governor General of Nazi-occupied Poland; Rudolf Hess (1894–1987), Deputy Party Leader of the Nazi Party until 1941; Alfred Jodl (1890–1945), Chief of the Armed Forces High Command Operational Staff; Ernst Kaltenbrunner (1903–1946), Chief of the Reich Security Main Office (RSHA) and Chief of Security Police 1943–45; Albert Speer (1905–1981), Hitler's architect and Reich Minister of Armaments and Munitions from 1942; Julius Streicher (1885–1946), propagandist and editor of *Der Stürmer*, an antisemitic newspaper; Alfred Rosenberg (1893–1946), chief Nazi philosopher and head of the civil administration in parts of the occupied Soviet Union; and the biggest catch, Hermann Göring (1893–1946), Commander in Chief of the Luftwaffe

(Air Force), President of the Reichstag, and Director of the Four Year Plan. For good measure, Martin Bormann (1900–1945?), Nazi Party secretary and chief aide to Hitler, whose whereabouts were unknown at the time, also was tried *in absentia*.

In many ways, the Allies failed at Nuremberg to paint a full picture of the atrocities committed by the Nazis. Because the prosecution chose to focus on aggressive war and especially conspiracy to engage in war crimes, evidence against the defendants centered on the planning and implementation of conquest rather than the extermination of Jews and others. The "Final Solution" was not ignored, since the crimes against humanity charge included an explicit reference to crimes against the Jews, and the Allies took pains during the trial to evoke the horrors of Nazi destruction by showing a grizzly film entitled "Nazi Concentration Camps" (Douglas 2001: 11–37). But the Holocaust was seldom prominent in the proceedings, all the more so because the prosecution chose to rely almost completely on documentary evidence generated by the Nazis and their allies, which alluded to the "Final Solution" only vaguely and rarely, and to exclude survivor and witness testimony. Nevertheless, the main Nuremberg trial put war crimes at the forefront of public consciousness for decades to come; and despite quarrels among the Allies, endless and often boring documentary reports, and recalcitrant and unhelpful defendants, the Trial of the Major War Criminals can be considered a success in its attempt to expose and punish Nazi crime (Douglas 2001).

When the Trial of the Major German War Criminals ended in October 1946, three defendants went free, twelve were sentenced to the gallows (though Bormann was never found, and Göring killed himself on the eve of his hanging), and seven received prison terms ranging from ten years to life. Fifteen of the defendants were convicted on the charge of crimes against humanity, but the verdicts reflected the imperfect understanding of the Holocaust at the time. Though hardly a policy maker, Streicher was seen as the ideologue behind the "Final Solution" and punished accordingly, whereas the murderous role of Göring was overshadowed by attention to his economic and territorial rapacity and that of Speer obscured by his pose as a repentant, contemplative intellectual.

The proceedings of the IMT at Nuremberg were the first and last joint Allied prosecution. Instead, as permitted in December 1945 by Control Council Law 10, each occupying power henceforth proceeded against Nazi criminals as it saw fit. Subsequent trials were conducted by all four occupying powers, but the largest and most famous were the twelve "successor" trials before American judges at Nuremberg in 1946–1949. The Americans grouped the defendants primarily by occupation, resulting in proceedings against doctors involved in human experimentation and the murder of the mentally and physically handicapped, Nazi lawyers and judges, corporate executives (those of Krupp and Flick, the coal, steel, and munitions giants, and of IG Farben, a huge chemical company that leased laborers from Auschwitz and co-owned the firm that controlled the distribution of Zyklon B), leading SS members and Einsatzgruppen commanders, the principal civil servants in a number of government ministries, and senior figures in the high command of the German armed forces.

Although the "Final Solution" was still not at the center of these trials, German atrocities were prominent themes, and the mass murder of the Jews began to come into relief, most notably in the trial of Oswald Pohl (1892–1951), the head of the Economic and Administrative Main Office or WVHA, and in proceedings against the Einsatzgruppen commanders and defendants accused of crimes against the inmates of concentration camps. All told, 185 Germans were indicted and 177 tried, resulting initially in 142 convictions, most of which were overturned on appeal or commuted by the American occupation authorities by 1951. Only twelve of the twenty-five Germans sentenced to death ultimately were executed (Friedman in Heberer and Matthäus 2008: 79, 88–95). Even in the case of the Einsatzgruppen trial, where the documentary evidence demonstrated direct involvement in mass murder, ten of the fourteen defendants initially sentenced to death managed to escape that fate and went free by 1958. As the Cold War intensified, American officials grew less insistent on punishment and more intent on winning the loyalty of a German populace weary of war crimes trials, admissions of guilt, and looking back.

OTHER POSTWAR TRIALS AND TRIBUNALS

The overwhelming majority of the other war crimes trials immediately after World War II involved lower-level personnel, such as concentration camp guards and commandants, police officers, members of the Einsatzgruppen, and doctors who had participated in medical experiments. Many of these proceedings took place in the British, French, and Soviet zones of occupied Germany and Austria and before military courts. For example, acting on a Royal Warrant issued by the British War Office in June 1945, British occupation authorities held 358 trials of 1,085 accused war criminals; 240 defendants received death sentences, including two executives of Tesch & Stabenow, the company that sold Zyklon B to the SS. British war crimes investigators also spearheaded investigations of medical atrocities at Bergen-Belsen and at Ravensbrück (Schmidt in Heberer and Matthäus 2008: 123–57).

In formerly Nazi-occupied countries, German war criminals captured there or extradited by the Allies also were prosecuted in significant numbers, along with many local collaborators. The Poles were especially active: between 1944 and 1946 special tribunals convicted 2,741 of approximately 10,000 defendants; 631 people received death sentences, almost all of which were carried out (*Urteil* 1947). One of the most famous defendants was Rudolf Höss (1900–1947), a former commandant of Auschwitz, who was sentenced to death by a Polish tribunal and hanged at the camp in a symbolic gesture of revenge and justice. A trial of forty other senior figures in the administration of Auschwitz resulted in the execution of Arthur Liebehenschel (1901–1948), another former commandant, Maximilian Grabner (1905–1948), a former head of the Political Department (the camp Gestapo), Hans Aumeier (1906–1948), also of the Political Department, and eighteen other individuals. In Czechoslovakia, approximately 19,000 people were brought to trial; most were native collaborators, above all Josef Tiso (1887–1947), the Catholic priest who had been wartime president of Slovakia, but the group included such prominent Germans as Dieter Wisliceny (1911–1948), an aide to Eichmann; Karl Frank (1898–1946), commander of the police and the SS in Bohemia-Moravia during the war; and Hanns Ludin (1905–1947), the former German envoy to Slovakia. Hungary, where a large number of collaborators had made the swift deportation of over 440,000 Jews possible, tried almost 40,000 suspects after 1948 (*Encyclopedia Judaica* 2008). Dutch prosecutions were launched in 1948–1952 against some 200 defendants, most of them collaborators, but including a few former ranking officials in the Nazi occupation, among them Hanns Rauter (1895–1949), the commander of the police and SS in the Netherlands from 1940 to 1945, who was executed (*Encyclopedia Judaica* 2008). Denmark tried almost 14,000 collaborators, but the most prominent defendant was Werner Best (1903–1989), Reich plenipotentiary and civil administrator in Denmark from November 1942 until the end of World War II. Sentenced to death in 1948 by a Danish court, he was released in 1951.

Among the states formerly occupied by Germany, France had the greatest difficulty dealing with the complicity of some of its own citizens in Nazi criminality. Defeated by the Germans in 1940, the country was left partially unoccupied and governed until 1943 from the city of Vichy by a French administration headed by Marshal Henri Philippe Pétain (1856–1951). That collaborationist regime had enacted the *Statut des Juifs* (Law of the Jews) in two parts in October 1940 and June 1941, excluding Jews from public life; requiring their dismissal from positions in the civil service, the army, commerce, and industry; and barring them from participation in the professions, including medicine, law, and teaching. Shortly thereafter, Vichy launched an extensive "Aryanization" program, confiscating Jewish-owned property for the French state and leaving many Jews destitute. Foreign Jews were particularly vulnerable. Thousands were sent to internment camps, such as Gurs near the Spanish border, where many died. Beginning in the summer of 1942, French police had rounded up Jews, mainly those without French citizenship, in both the occupied and unoccupied (Vichy) zones and delivered them for deportation to German camps.

Until recently, France preferred to let the memory of these events fade and to focus retrospection on the heroic acts of the resistance, a selective remembering aptly called the "Vichy Syndrome" (Rousso 2004). During the 1970s and 1980s, however, the brilliant film *The Sorrow and the Pity* (1969) by Marcel Ophuls (b. 1927) undermined this image of constant and broad resistance, and the work of several historians reinforced that effect (Marrus and Paxton 1981). Nonetheless, the French were long reluctant to find and prosecute French persecutors of Jews. Prosecutions began only after years of agitation by prominent French citizens and Nazi hunters such as Serge (b. 1935) and Beate (b. 1939) Klarsfeld. The most famous trials took place in the 1980s and 1990s. In 1971, Beate Klarsfeld tracked down Klaus Barbie (1913–1991), "the butcher of Lyon," who served as a Security Police official and SD (*Sicherheitsdienst*) station chief in that city during World War II, but more than fifteen years elapsed before he stood trial, charged with atrocities that included responsibility for a raid on the General Union of French Jews in Lyon, which resulted in the arrest and deportation to Auschwitz of eighty-five Jews. On 4 July 1987, Barbie was found guilty of crimes against humanity and sentenced to life in prison. In 1997, Maurice Papon (1910–2007), prefect of Paris in 1958–1967 and later a government minister, was tried for his deeds as the senior official responsible for Jewish affairs in Bordeaux during the Nazi occupation. Unlike Barbie, Papon had been a bureaucratic or desk killer: he signed the death warrants for 1,560 French Jews, including 223 children. Papon was found guilty of crimes against humanity and sentenced to ten years in jail. His release in 2002 on grounds of ill health aroused considerable controversy.

ISRAEL

Certainly the most famous trial of a Nazi since the major Nuremberg trial of 1945–46 was that of Adolf Eichmann (1906–1962) in Israel in 1961. On 11 May 1960, three members of the Israeli Security Service captured Eichmann near Buenos Aires, Argentina, where he had been in hiding since 1950. Eichmann had been in charge of deportations during the Nazi period, responsible for coordinating the transportation system that took millions of Jews to their death at concentration and death camps. That Israel could kidnap and try someone for crimes committed thousands of miles away remains a subject of some controversy, not least because the most famous depiction of the resulting trial is extremely critical of it (Arendt 1963). Eichmann faced multiple charges, including that of crimes against the Jewish people. His trial was a highly public spectacle during which he sat inside a glass booth in the courtroom. Ostensibly for his protection, this arrangement had the effect of turning him into a monster in a cage. Precisely this transformation irritated Hannah Arendt (1906–1975), who reported that Eichmann was not the animal he was made out to be, but a banal character with "no motives at all" beyond the desire to please his superiors and advance his career. Arendt's analysis of Eichmann as a clownish, pathetic figure angered many, including the thousands of survivors living in Israel at the time who had difficulty swallowing the implicit message that their fate had been at the hands of a relatively benign character.

During the trial itself, the prosecution's relentless introduction of seemingly irrelevant witness testimony exasperated the judges and infuriated onlookers like Arendt, who complained that the trial forfeited judicial legitimacy by straying from the usual concentration on establishing a factual record of the accused person's deeds. But the proceedings, which resulted in a death sentence for Eichmann, the only one imposed in Israeli history—it was carried out by hanging on 31 May 1962—resulted in new respect for Holocaust survivors and their testimonies. Thus, a more recent assessment of the trial is much more positive than Arendt's, arguing that it functioned as group therapy for hundreds of thousands of survivors by enabling them to unload their memories on a nation that had suppressed the stories of helpless Jews as incompatible with the image of Israel as a healthy and strong state (Douglas 2001).

SOVIET-OCCUPIED AND EAST GERMANY

The Soviets held hundred of tribunals in the early postwar years, but only that of guards at the Sachsenhausen concentration camp was public, and it had many of the classic features of a Soviet show trial (Friedman in Heberer and Matthäus 2008: 159–84). In the Soviet zone of occupied Germany, torture and privation often preceded quite brief tribunal proceedings that generally concluded with verdicts of guilty, but death sentences were hardly universal. The exact number of legal proceedings instituted by Soviet courts under Control Council Law 10 is unknown. One of the leading early researchers on Nazi trials believed that the number of individuals convicted vastly exceeded the number of defendants sentenced by all the tribunals in the western occupation zones put together (Rückerl 1979). The West German justice ministry estimated in 1965 that Soviet tribunals sentenced over 10,000 people. Those who had not died in Soviet custody were handed over to the East German regime three months after the founding of the German Democratic Republic (GDR) in October 1949.

Little scholarly work on East German prosecutions for war crimes has appeared to date, and contemporary reactions took predictable form: East German press reports hailed all trial results, and West German press reports looked askance at East German actions. Clearly, the trials were highly politicized and ideological: East Germans were most likely to prosecute crimes against communists and socialists. Much of the focus was on defendants accused of having denounced political opponents of the Nazi state. Early in its existence the GDR held thousands of trials and tribunals, meting out 3,224 sentences in the last two-and-a-half months of 1949 alone. In fact, the East German justice system prosecuted about the same number of suspected Nazis as the West Germans, but the figure bulked larger in the East because of its much smaller population and the fact that most defendants were tried in the East as principal actors, rather than as accessories, as in the West. The trials tapered off after the onset of the Cold War, and the average number dropped from about one hundred to seven per year (Friedman in Heberer and Matthäus 2008: 159–84) as the focus of East German justice became defectors and internal resisters.

Historians collecting German trial judgments at the invaluable *Justiz und NS Verbrechen* website think an accurate estimate of the number of trials conducted, the legal standards employed (they shifted throughout the GDR's existence), and the dismissals or acquittals granted is virtually impossible to obtain. The site has collected information on 933 trials concerning homicidal crimes, involving 1,716 court judgments of 1,637 defendants (*Justiz und NS Verbrechen* 2009). These figures do not include the notorious Waldheim trials of 1950, which were politically rather than judicially motivated proceedings that summarily convicted some 3,400 former officials of the Nazi state (de Mildt 1996: 19).

The state and particularly the security apparatus intervened often in the investigations of Nazis carried out in East Germany, and the ideological opposition of the two German states led to both successful and unsuccessful dialogue on the question of Nazi perpetrators. At the Frankfurt Auschwitz trial, co-plaintiff Karl Friedrich Kaul (1906–1981) represented East German Auschwitz survivors and raised his voice against the crass right-wing apologetics of the defense. In contrast, East Berlin prosecutors dragged their feet in the joint East/West investigation of the Main Reich Security Office (RSHA) and contributed to the perpetual delay and eventual suspension of that investigation (Weinke 2002).

WEST GERMAN COURTS

The years 1945–1950 marked a slow transition from Allied control of the German justice system to an autonomous German judiciary. At the start of the Allied occupation, German courts ceased to function, and they came back to life only gradually. The Allies took it upon themselves to determine the legal foundations of postwar Germany. They decided that laws instituted by the Nazis that were obviously criminal, such as those sanctioning racial discrimination, would be revoked. Allied Control Council Laws were designed to reconstruct the German state. Law 4 on "the Reorganization of the German Judicial System" prohibited German courts from trying crimes committed against the Allies, and Control Council Law 10 stipulated that the German courts could try only crimes "committed by persons of German citizenship or nationality against other persons of German citizenship or nationality, or stateless persons." As a result, the Allies prosecuted all crimes committed by the Germans against Allied nationals and all war crimes, including crimes against the Jews.

German jurists argued bitterly over the basic character of Control Council Law 10. Although useful in convicting defendants of genocide, the law drew no distinction between perpetrator and accomplice and seemed an example of *ex post facto* legislation, which the new West German constitution banned. Ultimately the Germans decided not to apply the laws of the Control Council, and Nazis were prosecuted after 1951 only according to the West German penal code of 1871, which is to say as common criminals. This practice accorded with the widespread German view that the Allied judicial proceedings were acts of political revenge rather than criminal justice. Germans were also skeptical toward the accompanying process of "denazification" by which the Allies sought to exclude former Nazis from public posts.

A large portion of the West German population did not want to pursue denazification or postwar judicial reckoning or even to remember the past (Herf 1997). Konrad Adenauer (1876–1967), West Germany's first chancellor (1949–1963), had a policy of integrating rather than alienating ex-Nazis. He argued that the Nuremberg trials and other Allied investigations had drawn public attention to the horrors of Nazism, and the time had come to concentrate on reconstruction, restitution to Jewish survivors, and reintegration of former Nazis. This less than satisfying posture was pragmatic and quite successful. Millions of former Nazi Party members lived in West Germany after the war, and the newly formed government could scarcely investigate all of them. Many of these people had high levels of education, training, and professional expertise; they possessed the experience and skill that were essential for a devastated country's recovery. The Allies largely acknowledged this reality and increasingly amnestied former Nazis or ignored their pasts, primarily because the United States needed its erstwhile enemy as an ally against the Soviets. Thus, most professions in West Germany were restocked with old Nazis.

Nonetheless, more than 6,000 Nazi defendants stood trial in West Germany. About 100,000 other people were investigated but never tried. The defendants faced regular criminal charges, not accusations of crimes against humanity. Many judges were former Nazi judges who interpreted the law in ways that generally led to lesser convictions. Furthermore, legal theorists introduced roadblocks to the conviction of former Nazis, which allowed some of the same jurists to avoid prosecution or severe punishment for their actions as law enforcers during the Nazi period. For example, facing postwar indictments for having sentenced anti-Nazi resistance fighters to death, most judges from the notorious *Volksgerichtshof* (People's Court) received mild treatment on the grounds that the National Socialist *Rechtsdenken* (attitude toward law and legality) was responsible for the death sentence, not the judge himself (Müller 1991; Perels 1999).

Growing awareness of a massive number of hitherto uninvestigated crimes and suspects led the regional judicial administrations of the West German federal states to found and fund the Central Office of the State Judicial Authorities for the Investigation of National Socialist Crimes (*Zentrale Stelle der Landesjustizverwaltung zur Aufklärung nationalsozialistischer Verbrechen*—ZdL) in Ludwigsburg in 1958. It was dedicated to investigating Nazi crimes and collecting documentary evidence and witness testimony concerning perpetrators. The findings were then made available to appropriate prosecutors' offices. Whereas most information initially collected came from previously examined documents and the Nuremberg trial records, the ZdL began to produce new evidence as well. In 1959 alone, the ZdL initiated four hundred investigations of crimes committed in occupied eastern Europe by the Einsatzgruppen and the guards at concentration and death camps. By the late 1980s, the ZdL had launched at least 13,000 proceedings (Weinke 2008).

Several peculiar features of the German penal code and postwar jurisprudence resulted in serious impediments to prosecuting crimes of mass murder (Wittmann 2005). First, a murder conviction required that the prosecution prove the defendant possessed "base motives," such as sexual or other lust to kill, treachery, malicious intent, cruelty, and race-hatred. Second, the penal code distinguished between perpetrator and accomplice and specified that a perpetrator must show individual initiative and knowledge of the illegality of the act in question. These provisions meant that a murder conviction required proof that the accused had acted individually, with personal initiative, and with knowledge that the act in question was illegal. In the Third Reich, the only unquestioned perpetrators of murder—those with the requisite base motives and individual initiative—were the people who conceived the "Final Solution": Hitler, Himmler, and Reinhard Heydrich (1904–1942). All other state functionaries, no matter their rank, could and did claim that they were simply doing their jobs, with limited autonomy and no "base motives." Third, the provision that knowledge of the act's illegality was required for a murder conviction opened further loopholes, for the more a defendant claimed that he believed in and identified with the Nazi world view, the less likely he was to be judged aware of the illegality of the acts in question. Thus, in the West German trials of Nazi doctors, some physicians who participated in euthanasia and experimented on humans were exculpated because of the prevalent medical norms in German society when those actions took place. Fourth, the statute of limitations even prevented the courts from using the manslaughter charge because any crimes with possible sentences of fifteen years or less could not be tried fifteen years after the crimes had been committed (de Mildt 1996; Pendas 2005). In short, the provisions and interpretations of the murder statute led to the condemnation only of those killers who had exceeded their orders, and even they usually were found guilty only as accomplices. After 1969, the statute of limitations applied to all charges other than murder, so accused accomplices no longer could be tried.

The Auschwitz trial of 1963–65 made apparent the impediments to prosecuting crimes of mass murder in West Germany. This enormous trial—probably the last major Nazi trial that the German press or public cared much about—had as defendants twenty Auschwitz perpetrators, ranging from a *kapo* (prisoner barrack guard) to two adjutants to the camp commander. The trial called more than 400 witnesses, drew upon and produced thousands of pages of documentation, and brought the inner workings of the Auschwitz concentration camp to the attention of a willfully uninformed German public. Fritz Bauer (1903–1968), the attorney general of the State of Hesse, led a team of determined and dedicated attorneys. Because of the narrow interpretation of the laws by a very conservative (and former Nazi) judge, however, only the most sadistic defendants, who had murdered people drunkenly, wantonly, and without official orders, were convicted of murder and sentenced to life in prison. The rest, the vast majority, got mild sentences that usually were reduced at the end of the trial to time served. They remained ordinary citizens who were basically seen as decent and reluctant Nazis, while the others, the sadists and "excess perpetrators," were monsters who in no way bore resemblance to the majority of society. The murder of millions in the gas chambers or the creation and execution of laws that allowed for the murder of Jews, the handicapped, and political prisoners became a lesser crime with a lighter sentence than the murder of one person without orders from superiors. The German public learned to chastise and denounce the sadistic "excess perpetrators" of Auschwitz and to forgive the order-followers whose complicity was never the true focus of the trial or of the extensive press coverage.

In the West German euthanasia trials, judges found innovative ways to exonerate the accused doctors. During the earliest proceedings in the 1950s, West German courts found doctors who participated in the program guilty of murder. But as defense lawyers grew more inventive, judges began to interpret the law in the defendants' favor. One example of successful legal maneuvering was the acceptance of the "collision of duties" defense, in which defendants argued that they participated in the program of murder in order to minimize the number of killings. Another example involved the "exertion of conscience" defense, in which defendants were taken at their word that they had searched their conscience and found that they had no choice but to participate. In these trials, defendants were elevated from killers to moral heroes for their decision to work in the euthanasia program and sabotage it from within, although little evidence indicated that any of the defendants had averted more deaths (Bryant 2005).

Over time, amendments to the German penal code increasingly enabled Nazi defendants to go free. One, in particular, had devastating effects for a massive investigation that was going on in Berlin in 1968. The Berlin Court of Appeal, in conjunction with East Berlin prosecutors, had opened an investigation of the high command of the RSHA or Main Reich Security Office. Located in Berlin, the RSHA was responsible for all aspects of state security, including the police, the Gestapo, the Einsatzgruppen, and the concentration camp administration. About 7,000 people worked for the organization, which Heydrich headed, and so the prosecution had daunting work to do. The RSHA investigation fell apart because defense attorneys could exploit the requirement that proof of "base motives"—in this case antisemitism—was necessary for a murder conviction.

The largest trial of the 1970s, the Majdanek trial in Düsseldorf, involved camp guards charged with crimes of excess and gruesome cruelty. The trial lasted from 1975 to 1981 and was plagued by legal limitations, endless debates about the statute of limitations on murder, aging and dying defendants, and survivors whose memories were fading and who were more and more reluctant to appear at yet another trial for fear of being branded "professional witnesses." Furthermore, the press was uninterested, and the German public felt that senior citizens who had lived productive lives for the last thirty years were harmless in comparison to the "state enemies" on trial in Stuttgart at the same time, namely the terrorists from the radical left-wing Red Army Faction (RAF). While efforts continue in Germany to find and prosecute former Nazi criminals, the heyday of German trials is long over and confrontation with the past in Germany now takes place through other channels, such as the press and scholarly inquiry.

CONCLUSION

Is rendering justice possible after a crime of such magnitude of the Holocaust? Can a legal system possibly come to terms with the atrocities committed by the Nazis and atone for the guilt of hundreds of thousands? The answer is obvious: no punishment exists that fits this crime. Sadly, only a minority of the many trials held after the Holocaust even attempted to punish the planning and implementation of the "Final Solution." Even after the establishment of the Genocide Convention, judicial processes did not produce widespread recognition of the sweeping nature of the Holocaust, its hundreds of thousands of perpetrators and their collaborators, and its distinct nature within the framework of war.

REFERENCES

ARENDT, H. (1963). *Eichmann in Jerusalem: A Report on the Banality of Evil.* New York: Viking Press.

BRYANT, M. (2005). *Confronting the "Good Death": Nazi Euthanasia on Trial, 1945–1953.* Boulder, CO: University Press of Colorado.

Douglas, L. (2001). *The Memory of Judgment: Making Law and History in the Trials of the Holocaust.* New Haven, CT: Yale University Press.

Encyclopedia Judaica (2008). "War Crimes Trials." Jewish Virtual Library: <http://www.jewishvirtuallibrary.org/jsource/judaica/ejud_0002_0020_0_20618.html>.

Heberer, P. and Matthäus, J. (eds.) (2008). *Atrocities on Trial: Historical Perspectives on the Politics of Prosecuting War Crimes.* Lincoln, NE: University of Nebraska Press.

Herf, J. (1997). *Divided Memory: The Nazi Past in the Two Germanys.* Cambridge, MA: Harvard University Press.

Justiz und NS Verbrechen. (2009)."DDR Justiz und Nazi Verbrechen": <http://www1.jur.uva.nl/junsv/JuNSVEng/JuNSV%20English%20homepage.htm>.

Marrus, M. and Paxton, R. (1981). *Vichy France and the Jews.* New York: Basic Books.

Mildt, D. de (1996). *In the Name of the People: Perpetrators of Genocide in the Reflection of Their Post-War Prosecution in West Germany—The "Euthanasia" and "Aktion Reinhard" Trial Cases.* The Hague: Martinus Nijhoff Publishers.

Müller, I. (1991). *Hitler's Justice: The Courts of the Third Reich.* Cambridge, MA: Harvard University Press.

Pendas, D. (2005). *The Frankfurt Auschwitz Trial.* London: Cambridge University Press.

Perels, J. (1999). *Das Juristische Erbe des "Dritten Reiches": Beschädigungen der Demokratischen Rechtsordnung.* Frankfurt am Main: Campus.

Rousso, H. (2004). *The Vichy Syndrome: History and Memory in France since 1944.* Cambridge, MA: Harvard University Press.

Rückerl, A. (1979). *The Investigation of Nazi Crimes 1945–1978: A Documentation.* Hamden, CT: Shoestring Press.

United Nations (1948). Genocide Convention: <http://www.un.org/millennium/law/iv-1.htm>.

Urteil und Urteilsbegründung im Verfahren gegen Liebehenschel und andere (Judgment and Explanation in the Proceedings against Liebehenschel and Others) (1947). Polish People's Tribunal 5/47, 22 December 1947, in *Pretrial Files of the First Frankfurt Auschwitz Trial.* Frankfurt am Main: The Public Prosecutor's Office at the District Court of Frankfurt am Main (4 Js 444/59), 49: 8291–513.

Weinke, A. (2002). *Die Verfolgung von NS-Tätern im Geteilten Deutschland: Vergangenheitsbewältigung 1949–1969, oder: Eine Deutsch-Deutsche Bezeihungsgeschichte im Kalten Krieg.* Paderborn: Ferdinand Schöningh.

——(2008). *Eine Gesellschaft ermittelt gegen sich selbst: Die Geschichte der Zentralen Stelle Ludwigsburg 1958–2008.* Darmstadt: Wissenschaftliche Buchgesellschaft.

Wittmann, R. (2005). *Beyond Justice: The Auschwitz Trial.* Cambridge, MA: Harvard University Press.

Other Suggested Reading

Bartov, O., Grossman, A., and Nolan, M. (eds.) (2002). *Crimes of War: Guilt and Denial in the Twentieth Century.* New York: New Press.

Bass, G. (2000). *Stay the Hand of Vengeance: The Politics of War Crimes Tribunals.* Princeton, NJ: Princeton University Press.

BLOXHAM, D. (2001). *Genocide on Trial: War Crimes Trials and the Formation of Holocaust History and Memory.* Oxford: Oxford University Press.

BURUMA, I. (1994). *The Wages of Guilt: Memories of War in Germany and Japan.* New York: Meridian.

COOPER, B. (ed.) (1998). *War Crimes: The Legacy of Nuremberg.* New York: TV Books.

EARL, H. (2009). *The Nuremberg SS-Einsatzgruppen Trial, 1945–1958.* New York: Cambridge University Press.

FREI, N. (2002). *Adenauer's Germany and the Nazi Past.* New York: Columbia University Press.

GODA, N. (2007). *Tales from Spandau: Nazi Criminals and the Cold War.* New York: Cambridge University Press.

MARRUS, M. (1997). *The Nuremberg War Crimes Trial 1945–46: A Documentary History.* London: Bedford Books.

OSIEL, M. (1997). *Mass Atrocity, Collective Memory, and the Law.* New Brunswick, NJ: Transaction Press.

ROSENBAUM, A. (1993). *Prosecuting Nazi War Criminals.* Boulder, CO: Westview Press.

SMITH, B. (1982). *The American Road to Nuremberg: The Documentary Record, 1944–1945.* Stanford: Hoover Institution Press.

TAYLOR, T. (1992). *The Anatomy of the Nuremberg Trials: A Personal Memoir.* New York: Alfred A. Knopf.

WILDT, M. (2009). *An Uncompromising Generation: The Nazi Leadership of the Reich Security Main Office.* Madison, WI: University of Wisconsin Press.

CHAPTER 35

PLUNDER AND RESTITUTION

PETER HAYES

IN Germany and most of eastern Europe during the late nineteenth and early twentieth centuries, Jews became disproportionately numerous in commercial and professional occupations and *on average* wealthier than the surrounding populations. Although a great many Jews remained poor, the community's relative collective prosperity gave rise to considerable envy and resentment, which translated into accusations that Jews had used emancipation and economic modernization to take advantage of the rest of the citizenry. Demands to make Jews disgorge their supposedly ill-gotten gains and "return" them to their allegedly rightful owners, the "host" populations, were the stock-in-trade of the antisemitic political parties that waxed and waned from the 1870s on. One of their poisonous legacies was growing support throughout the region after World War I for capping the percentage of Jews among university students and prospective or practicing bankers, brokers, lawyers, physicians, and professors. Wherever Germany's reach extended during World War II, a sense of entitlement to take "back" what Jews purportedly had pilfered served as a powerful inducement to persecution.

Given the prevalence of such ideas, the secondary importance that Nazism ascribed prior to 1933 to Jewish economic activity may seem surprising. In the first volume of *Mein Kampf*, which appeared in 1925, Adolf Hitler (1889–1945) laid out his explanation of how Jews had acquired first economic, then cultural, and finally political influence in Germany and made clear not only that he intended to roll back that process in the reverse order, but also that the economic dimension of Jewish power was far less serious than its other aspects (1943: 284–329). This sense of priorities, combined with reluctance to risk further economic disruption during the Depression, meant that the top Nazi leaders spoke and planned inconsistently regarding the future economic role of Jews in Germany. In consequence, during the first year of Nazi rule, intimidation and dismissal of Jewish political and cultural figures was more thorough than of Jewish business executives, except for those whose operations attracted particular attention from Party zealots, e.g., defense or other public contractors, department stores, publishing houses, and breweries. The infamous state-sanctioned boycott of Jewish businesses on 1 April 1933 was, in fact, testimony to the gap between the high importance attached to attacking Jewish commercial operations by the fervid Party rank-and-file and the more cautious attitude of the leaders in Berlin, since the event occurred in response to the agitation of the former, but lasted only one day because of the wishes of the latter.

In the ensuing years, however, the Nazi regime caught up with the lust of the Party faithful to impoverish and dispossess the Jews, developing ever more numerous and rapacious means of monetizing and/or confiscating their assets and turning most of these to the purposes of the German state. The result was robbery on a scale scarcely seen in European history, all the more so because the plunder of the Jews outside of Germany during World War II took place alongside the looting of even greater quantities of precious metals, stocks and bonds, cash, art works, enterprises, real estate, and labor from non-Jewish sources in the occupied countries. Tracing the booty after 1945 and returning it to or compensating the owners posed enormous challenges, partly because international law traditionally permitted only state-to-state claims for restitution or reparations, partly because the beneficiaries of plunder outnumbered the survivors of it, and partly because the Cold War inhibited the pursuit of numerous claims. The end result of this drawn-out and halting process was only "some measure of justice" (Marrus 2009), as many Jewish victims died before their claims were recognized and the monetary value of compensation payments rarely equaled the worth of what individuals had lost.

Learning How to Steal: Germany, 1933–1939

Because the Nazi Party came to office without a plan for the dispossession of the German Jews, the initial assaults on their livelihoods occurred in erratic and improvised fashion. While fervent antisemites in factories or businesses demanded the ouster of Jewish co-workers and managers, equally bigoted Party members installed themselves in municipal offices and began abrogating contracts with Jewish-owned suppliers, restricting the use of state welfare payments in stores owned by Jews, and expelling them from space in public market halls. These initiatives, like more violent or threatening visits to Jewish property owners by units of storm troopers and the public shaming of shoppers who continued to patronize Jewish-owned establishments, were intended to reduce the incomes or property values of Jews and induce them to emigrate. Although this "economic squeeze" was at first tighter in rural areas and small towns than in some cities and less strictly applied in some commercial sectors than in others, it gradually became more uniformly suffocating as a result of the exchange of information via such institutions as the German Council of Municipalities (*Deutscher Gemeindetag*) (Gruner 2002). By the end of 1937, 60 percent of the roughly 100,000 Jewish-owned businesses in Germany as of 1933 had been liquidated or "Aryanized' (i.e., taken over by non-Jews), the total wealth of German Jews had fallen by 40–50 percent, one-third of the German Jewish population had fled the country, and nearly all of the Jews remaining were working for themselves or each other or unemployed and dependent on the community's relief measures (Barkai 1989: 106–14).

That the spoliation of Germany's Jews had gone this far largely without central government direction did not mean that the German state had been uninvolved. On the contrary, it expelled about half of the Jewish members of the German civil service in April 1933 and the rest in the fall of 1935, and meanwhile barred Jews from the military and membership in the National Cultural Chamber, thus excluding them from work in theaters, orchestras, museums, publishing houses, and newspapers. Moreover, the Secret State Police (*Gestapo*) and the tax, customs, and currency control authorities discovered new ways to exert pressure on Jews' livelihoods and to obtain an increasing share of the proceeds on property that Jews sold or left behind. Suspicion that a Jewish property owner was engaged in the possession or transfer of foreign currency or contemplating emigration increasingly resulted in the freezing of his or her assets, followed by paralyzing and costly investigations, the assessment of supposedly outstanding tax payments, and potential fines. Just the threat of such proceedings frequently prompted owners to sell out cheaply.

Even Jews who found a buyer for their property at anything approaching its depressed nominal value and had a visa to leave the country found that they were stripped of at least half of their wealth upon exit. One-quarter of their assets went to pay the Reich Flight Tax, an invention of pre-Nazi governments that generated revenue of more than 900 million reichsmarks from 1933 to 1941, most of it from departing Jews (Kenkman in Feldman and Seibel 2005: 154). Another 20 percent (in 1934) to 96 percent (by 1939) of what was left was taken by the government as a fee for converting the remaining and increasingly tiny fraction of reichsmarks into the currency of the nation to which an emigrant was escaping (Dean 2008: 61).

Although severe, these extortions were but the prelude to the systematic expropriation of the Jews that the Third Reich devised between late 1937 and early 1939. Hitler believed that the Jews of Germany had played a subversive role during World

War I and that they could not be allowed to do so again once a new conflict erupted. Thus, from the moment he told his closest advisors in early November 1937 that the nation's war for living space was at hand, a wave of new restrictions on Jews' economic activities emanated from Berlin. The trend accelerated after the annexation of Austria in March 1938 because Hermann Göring (1893–1946), the Nazi leader charged with Germany's economic preparations for war, concluded that the uncoordinated plundering of Vienna's Jews by Party zealots was depriving the state of indispensable income and had to be regulated. Consequently, in April 1938, the Nazi regime ordered the dismissal of all remaining Jews from positions in industry and finance, the completion by each Jewish head of household of a detailed itemization of his or her property and its estimated value, and the subjection of all sales of Jewish-owned businesses to official review.

In the ensuing months, Jews lost the right to practice their professions through-out Germany, and enterprising bureaucrats developed "the Vienna model" for disposing of Austrian Jews' possessions. This entailed the establishment of two central organizations to arrange the liquidation or sale of low- and high-value properties, as well as the appointment of trustees to operate them in the meantime and of auditors to determine the lowest feasible sale prices and assess the "equal-ization" fees due to the state. Any proceeds to the seller went into a blocked account from which he or she could withdraw only subsistence amounts monthly, and the state could extract all taxes, fines, levies, emigration expenses, and other financial obligations assessed against the former owners (Dean 2008: 92–111). Those Jews lucky enough to obtain exit and entry visas then exchanged the paltry remaining account balances for foreign currency at the Reich's extortionist exchange rates and escaped largely penniless, unless they had assets abroad, while those who remained watched their blocked accounts dwindle. When their resources ran out, Jews were supported from the proceeds on the transfer of Jewish community property, such as synagogues and schools.

Following the *Kristallnacht* pogrom of November 1938, this system of disposses-sion was extended to the entire Reich and expanded in a variety of ways. All German Jews had to establish blocked accounts, the "Aryanization" of all Jewish-owned businesses became compulsory at terms set by politically appointed trust-ees, and a fine of one billion reichsmarks was imposed on the Jewish population. Each person who had registered his or her property in the summer of 1938 now had to pay 25 percent of its total value in installments to the national treasury by August 1939. Doing so became doubly difficult when the regime ordered Jews to put their stocks and bonds in safe deposit accounts from which sales could take place only with government permission and forced Jews to surrender virtually all their possessions containing precious metals to the state-run pawnshops in return for nominal compensation paid to the blocked accounts (Hayes 2004: 159–60). Such restrictions compelled Jews to convert as many of their other assets as possible to cash, often by selling their furniture, artworks, and household goods and by redeeming their insurance policies for their paid-in value, which went directly into the blocked accounts (Feldman 2001; Stiefel in Rathkolb 2002: 174–6).

By the summer of 1939, the Third Reich had reduced German Jews to penury and pocketed at least 3 billion of the 7.1 billion reichsmarks in property that they had registered the previous year ($12 billion of $28.4 billion in U.S. currency in the year 2000). In the succeeding years, the regime may have raked in as much as half of the remainder through additional impositions, the mandatory conversion of sums in blocked accounts into war bonds, and the terms of the Eleventh Decree to the Reich Citizenship Law, which declared that the property of German Jews "fell" to the state at the moment they exited the country, whether through emigration or deportation (Hayes in Berenbaum and Peck 1998: 208; Kenkmann in Feldman and Seibel 2005: 162). Over and above these sums were the proceeds from the deportation of Jews from the Protectorate of Bohemia and Moravia via Theresienstadt. Exact figures are lacking, but an indication of the Reich's gains from this process is provided by the relevant account balances recorded by the subsidiaries of the Dresdner and Deutsche banks in Prague: the former's already came to 53.5 million reichsmarks in February 1942 at a very early stage of the round ups; the latter's to almost 91 million in November 1943, by which time most of the Czech Jews were gone (James 2001: 171; Wixforth 2006: 393).

Despite the siphoning off of substantial amounts by the middlemen in property transfers—a diverse group that included corrupt Nazi officials, lawyers and real estate brokers who specialized in "Aryanization," art dealers and auction houses, and banks that matched buyers and new managers to properties—Göring thus succeeded in grasping the bulk of Jewish assets for the national treasury. But thousands of Germans also became complicit in the spoliation by taking advantage of the knocked-down purchase prices as businesses, homes, and possessions changed hands.

As the Reich discovered how to steal most of the assets of Jews, it devised new procedures for exploiting their physical energy as well. Forced labor began on German soil early in 1939, when the regime declared that Jews between the ages of 16 and 65 who were unable to support themselves would have to accept employment assigned by the official Labor Exchanges. Most of the work consisted initially of street cleaning, snow removal, and rubbish collection, but soon encompassed road construction, river or canal improvement, and factory labor, sometimes at considerable distance from home (Barkai 1989: 159–64; Hayes 2004: 236–7). By the outbreak of World War II in September 1939, 20,000 Jews were so occupied; by July 1941, more than 51,000 were (Gruner 2006: 8, 19). Although such workers received pay, it was much lower than that of their non-Jewish counterparts, subject to special deductions, and generally below the value of the labor provided. Compulsory work thus constituted another form of confiscation.

LOOTING THE JEWS OF EUROPE

In Poland, the Baltic states, and the conquered portions of the Soviet Union, where the Nazis found three-quarters of the Jews murdered in the Holocaust, the Third Reich did not trouble to employ the elaborate machinery of theft perfected at home. Instead, virtually upon arrival German forces looted and destroyed on a large scale and requisitioned labor as they wished. Even before Warsaw surrendered on 27 September 1939, the conquerors forbade Poland's Jews to sell their property, blocked their bank accounts, began seizing the contents of their safe deposit boxes, and ordered them to prepare to move into ghettos, leaving their businesses and most of their possessions behind. In October, the Reich created the Main Trusteeship Office East (*Haupttreuhandstelle Ost* or HTO) to receive and dispose of all property formerly owned by the Polish state, Polish Jews, and those Polish non-Jews who fled or were expelled from the part of the country that Germany annexed. The new organization promptly also took over Poland's insurance companies and directed them to pay all claims by Polish or Jewish clients to the German National Bank (Pohl in Dean et al. 2007: 72). By 1942, the HTO controlled assets valued at 6–7 billion reichsmarks and had developed a pattern of selling these off at an average of half their worth to German settlers and companies willing to locate in the annexed or occupied portions of the country (Rosenkötter 2003: 278). Meanwhile, what little wealth remained to the ghettoized Jews was drained away by the charges for food and raw materials that the German jailers exacted prior to deportation to the death camps.

Most of the household effects that the Germans took from the Jews of Poland and the USSR were requisitioned by the occupying administration, given or left to their non-Jewish neighbors in order to win their support, or collected for the use of the several hundred thousand ethnic Germans who were being brought "home to the Reich" from parts of eastern Europe. The latter group was also the principal beneficiary of the goods stripped from Jews brought to death camps in the German East: one itemization reported that 825 freight cars had left the Auschwitz and Majdanek camps by 6 February 1943, carrying, among other things, 188,000 pairs of shoes, 1,417,000 garments, and 450,000 pieces of bedding and table linen destined for the agency charged with the resettlement of these *Volksdeutsche* (Hayes 2003: 338). The 1,900 boxcars of clothing that went to Germany from the camps at Belzec, Sobibor, and Treblinka by the end of 1943 served different purposes, however: the contents went to foreign forced laborers or to textile plants for recycling (Hochstadt 2004: 171–2).

For the German state, the major material returns on mass murder in the East came in the form of money, precious metals and stones, and labor. Operation Reinhard, the murder of most of the Jews of Poland in 1942–43 at Belzec, Sobibor, and Treblinka, yielded gold, silver, and platinum valued by Nazi officials at nearly

9 million reichsmarks, foreign currencies worth over 6 million, jewelry and other valuables appraised at 43.7 million, and cash in German and Polish banknotes of almost 74 million—altogether some 133 million reichsmarks in fungible loot *after* deduction of expenses for deporting and killing the roughly 1.5 million victims (Hochstadt 2004: 170–8). Auschwitz sent to Berlin probably over half a metric ton of dental gold alone, worth about 2 million reichsmarks at the time, along with untold amounts of seized cash. The camp also earned a net profit of roughly 30 million reichsmarks by leasing its inmates to work for enterprises or government agencies (Hayes 2003: 337–8). At the Łódź ghetto with its many workshops, the gap between the income and expenses of the German administration was surely even greater, though estimates of how much so vary widely.

Staggering as these figures are, they record only the portion of what the German state stole that it processed and used. The total haul was vastly more. Corruption and theft on the part of guards of camps and ghettos soaked up incalculable sums. Moreover, as time passed, the Reich had increasing difficulty exploiting what it seized. When the Soviet Army approached Auschwitz in January 1945, for example, the so-called Canada barracks remained so full of luggage and other possessions taken from deportees that the buildings burned for five days after the SS set them alight (Hayes 2003: 338). Of the infamous seventy-six deliveries of precious metals from the death camps in Poland to the German National Bank between August 1942 and the end of 1944, only forty-three were sorted, smelted, and refined into negotiable forms; the remaining thirty-three were sent into storage in a salt mine in Thuringia, where the U.S. Army recovered them in 1945 (Hayes 2004: 181–2).

In occupied western Europe, plundering methods more closely resembled the bureaucratic, semi-camouflaged methods applied within Germany, and nowhere more so than in the Netherlands. Presumably because the country was slated for incorporation into the Greater German Reich, the Nazis subjected it to direct rule by veterans of the takeover of Austria. Schooled in the procedures for tabulating the assets of Jews and then converting them to cash, ostensibly to finance emigration, these individuals had laid the basis by the summer of 1941 for the "Aryanization" or liquidation of all 21,000 businesses owned by Dutch Jews (Aalders in Feldman and Seibel 2005: 188). Between August 1941 and May 1942, the Germans turned their attention to individuals, compelling the Dutch Jews, first, to deposit their liquid assets to accounts at a new puppet bank, then to redeem their insurance policies and put the proceeds in these accounts, and, finally, to turn over for auction all other valuables, including art works, jewelry, and precious metals, with the receipts also earmarked for deposit. After most of the victims had been deported, their dwellings were stripped of furniture, either for auction or for distribution to people who had been bombed out in Germany (Bajohr 2002: 278–80), and all the individual accounts disappeared into a collective one. A small portion of the enormous proceeds of some 700 million to 1.5 billion guilders at the time ($4–8 billion in the year 2000) paid the costs of the concentration camp at Westerbork and the deportations; the rest was used to buy Dutch government bonds (Aalders in Feldman and Seibel 2005: 168, 184–5, 188; Aly 2005: 210).

Although the despoliation of the Dutch Jews was especially harsh and thorough, Jews in Belgium, France, Denmark, and Norway also experienced substantial losses. In France, for example, the plunder began during 1940–41 with exclusion of Jews from key professions and the registration of Jewish-owned businesses. Appointed trustees subsequently liquidated most of these businesses, selling off the remainder in both the German-occupied and the nominally sovereign parts of the defeated country (Dreyfus in Rathkolb 2002: 147–50). As this sequence neared completion, another one commenced that imposed a collective fine on the Jewish community (in the occupied zone), monetized Jews' assets (except insurance policies), and put them in frozen accounts, which were centralized at the *Caisse des Depots et Consignations*, where the French state skimmed off a service charge of 10 percent. Between 1940 and 1944, some 50,000 formerly Jewish-owned enterprises were disposed of, and the spoliation had yielded between 3.3 and 5 billion French francs ($650 million to $1 billion in the early 1940s or ten times as much in U.S. dollars of the year 2000) (Baruch in Feldman and Seibel 2005: 196–7, 211). The despoilment of Jews in France differed from the process in the Netherlands partly because local officials assumed primary responsibility and strove to retain as much of the loot as possible, rather than let it fall into German hands (Verheyde in Feldman and Seibel 2005: 75–82). Most of the money, like the Jews' precious metals and jewels, remained in France, and the vast majority of the new owners of the sold-off assets were French (Dreyfus in Rathkolb 2002: 147–52).

The Axis-allied states of Bulgaria, Romania, Slovakia, and Hungary also labored to pillage the resident Jews without letting the Germans fill the economic vacuum thus created. In all these states, the goal translated into a succession of crushing collective levies on the Jewish population; outright confiscations of agricultural land, forests, and shops; blocked accounts and extensive liquidations; the imposition of forced labor; and anomalous delays in attacking large firms owned by Jews for fear that Germans would buy them up (Toensmeyer in Dean et al. 2007: 84–91).

Despite the apparent "success" of these Nazi-occupied and allied states in assuring that most of what was pillaged remained in country, with the conspicuous exception of the numerous works of art carried off by the *Einsatzstab Reichsleiter Rosenberg* (ERR), most of the proceeds of persecution ultimately found their way to Germany indirectly. In the Netherlands and France, the sums generated in government bonds or revenue helped to pay the enormous occupation charges that the Germans levied; there and in Greece, Hungary, Serbia, and the Protectorate, the gold taken from Jews propped up the local currencies in which the German troops were paid and which they used to buy enormous quantities of consumer goods that were shipped back to the Reich (Aly 2005).

Scholars have been able to assemble only the roughest estimates of the total value of the property once owned by Jews that the Nazi regime either used for its war effort (the equivalent of $60–80 billion in the year 2000, according to Aly 2005: 285) or seized (up to the equivalent of $99 billion in Germany, Austria, Poland, France, Holland, and Hungary, according to Junz 2002: 132). Such enormous sums are almost surely understatements, since they make no allowance for the value of the labor extorted, yet they are also misleading when read in isolation. Without recalling that even such vast totals made up but a fraction of what Nazi Germany stole from occupied and allied Europe—whether one is talking about gold and silver, stocks and bonds, cash or forced laborers, the portion of the loot taken by the Third Reich that came from Jews is generally about 10 percent—one cannot understand the difficulty of focusing public or official attention on Jewish claims to compensation in the immediate aftermath of World War II. These claims arose amidst massive material damage and loss, and in every formerly occupied country the non-Jewish majority both prioritized recompense for its own suffering and clung to any gains that the persecution of Jews had offered.

German Restitution and Compensation Payments

Lingering prejudice and prolonged preoccupation with their own losses of people and property during the war made most Germans slow to recognize their moral and material obligations to the victims of the Holocaust after 1945. The communist regime in East Germany from 1949 to 1989 simply proclaimed that its "anti-fascist" heritage exonerated it—and its populace—of any special responsibilities toward Jews. Although the West German state's claim to be the legal successor of its predecessors ruled out a similar stance, domestic economic and political concerns argued for trying to limit the bill for the nation's crimes. As a result, almost every form of redress extended by West Germany to Jews in the postwar period occurred in response to outside pressure and was confined to relieving it. The quest for recompense thus stretched over almost sixty years, produced remarkably uneven treatment of different categories of survivors, and left behind a sense of disappointment that overshadows the unprecedented sum involved, which by the year 2000 exceeded $100 billion.

The first form of redress forced upon the Germans concerned property that had been taken from Jews between 1935 and 1945 in any part of Germany that came under U.S., British, and French occupation. This was a comparatively easy matter to handle for both political and legal reasons. The victorious occupiers had the power to insist on this *restitution* (restoration of a good or its equivalent value) to owners or heirs as a condition of recognizing a new West German state, the Federal Republic; the leaders of this portion of the defeated country saw renewed self-government as worth the price; and reversing the consequences of intra-German dispossession raised no delicate issues of international law. Within West Germany, the return of "Aryanized" residences was facilitated by the fact that most had been rented, not sold, while the Nazi state reserved them for eventual allocation to war veterans. Although claims to businesses were often bitterly contested in court, most Jews who sought to recover their families' former holdings succeeded and/or obtained monetary settlements (Hayes 2004: 106–10).

By the mid-1950s, restitution for identifiable formerly Jewish-owned assets in West Germany and West Berlin had resulted in payments of 3.5 billion deutsch-marks. Because a great deal of what had been stolen had been destroyed or gone missing, the West German government also paid out an additional 4 billion deutschmarks by the mid-1960s as restitution for no longer identifiable property (e.g., jewelry, furniture, artworks) that could be proven to have been on the territory of the Federal Republic or West Berlin when seized or seemed likely to have reached these places (Goschler in Diefendorf 2004: 381, 383). In the 1990s, when these West German practices were applied in former East Germany, the yield on the restitution of heirless "Aryanized" property to a consortium of organizations called the Con-ference on Jewish Material Claims against Germany (Claims Conference, for short) totaled to another 1.6 billion deutschmarks (Henry 2007: 106).

The Western Allies also insisted on *compensation* for harm done to the lives, bodies and health, freedom, property, and professional and economic advance-ment of Holocaust survivors. Thus, in the late 1940s, the Allies gave to Jewish refugee organizations some 120 million deutschmarks of proceeds from seized German assets in Sweden, Switzerland, and Portugal and captured non-monetary gold—for example, the yield from the thirty-three hitherto unprocessed shipments of precious metals from the death camps in Poland (Hayes 2004: 184, 190–1). Washington, London, and Paris also looked on approvingly as Konrad Adenauer (1876–1967), pursuing his course of winning for West Germany a respected place in the western alliance, signed the Luxembourg Agreements of 1952 that obligated the Federal Republic to pay 3 billion deutschmarks to Israel and 450 million to the Claims Conference. Some 250,000 survivors in Israel received payments from these funds (Goschler in Diefendorf 2004: 385–8).

Both the Federal Compensation Law that went through numerous iterations between 1953 and 1965 and the Federal Restitution Law of 1957, under which most of the payments for unidentifiable property occurred, were responses to Allied wishes, but also reflections of the political effects of the Cold War. Wishing to bolster West Germany in the struggle over Europe with the Soviet Union, the Allies had little interest in adding to the Federal Republic's financial burden. Therefore, they accepted, first, the London Agreements of 1952 that largely postponed Ger-many's obligations to pay *reparations* (financial penalties for damages done to citizens of foreign countries on their soil) until the negotiation of a final peace treaty ending World War II, and second, the territorial restrictions contained in the West German restitution and compensation laws. The latter stipulated that claimants had (a) to have lived within Germany (as defined by the borders at the end of 1937) at some time between 1933 and 1945 or moved to the western occupation zones or West Berlin in 1945–52, and (b) to reside currently either there or in a country that had diplomatic relations with West Germany. People who had been victimized outside of German frontiers as of 1937 and never been on German soil, as well as those living in the communist states of eastern Europe prior to 1965 thus were ruled ineligible for any form of relief from the West German state.

Even for those whose losses appeared covered by the German compensation legislation, it had perverse consequences. The multiple agencies charged with processing individual claims often acted rudely and inconsistently toward claimants and placed unreasonable burdens of proof upon them (Pross 1998). Many claimants, such as those entitled to compensation for the lost value of insurance policies redeemed under duress, found that the process of calculating their worth and adjusting for the currency change from reichsmarks to deutschmarks resulted in insignificant payouts, unless the claimant could show that the money obtained for the policy had been used to pay the Flight Tax or other emigration charges (Feldman in Rathkolb 2002: 170–1).

Above all, compensation for different forms of loss diverged in a fashion that favored the well educated. Whereas former inmates of concentration camps could receive only 150 deutschmarks for each month of "loss of freedom," people prevented from completing qualifying exams for certain professions could obtain 10,000 deutschmarks for "damage to education," and those driven out of the law or the professorate could be granted the lifelong pension of someone who had reached the senior ranks of the judiciary or a university. Despite these flaws, by 1998 the total payout by the German federal and state governments under the terms of the compensation law had reached almost 106 billion deutschmarks; a few years later, approximately 100,000 people, nearly all of them Jews, still were receiving pensions (Goschler in Diefendorf 2004: 390–5, 409).

West Germany also agreed, when political considerations warranted, to relax both its exemption from paying reparations and the territorial restrictions laid down by its legislation. In 1958–61, the Federal Republic made a so-called "Global Treaty" with a group of eleven non-communist European states, later expanded to sixteen, that called for payments that eventually came to 2.5 billion deutschmarks, from which these nations could compensate Nazi victims who were ineligible for direct payments from West Germany. After 1960, 123 million deutschmarks were extended to people who had been subjected to Nazi medical experiments, regardless of where they lived. As part of the pursuit of normalizing relations with the countries of eastern Europe after the election of the Social Democratic–Liberal coalition in 1969, the Federal Republic began advancing low-interest loans to several eastern European states as a substitute for reparations or compensation payments. And, in 1980, the West German government allocated 440 million deutschmarks for a "Hardship Fund" under the auspices of the Claims Conference and the Central

Committee of Jews in Germany. The money was for grants of up to 5,000 deutsch-marks to previously uncompensated Jews, mostly people who had come to Germany from eastern Europe, had suffered physical harm or incarceration for two years or more under the Nazis, and were now in need (Goschler 2005: 309–44).

In the 1990s, after the 4+2 Agreements provided for German unification, officially ended World War II, and relieved Germany of all reparations obligations, the claims of two principal and overlapping categories of Holocaust victims remained unsatisfied: victims who still lived in the former communist bloc and those who had been compelled to work for private enterprises in the Third Reich. Many people in the former group were covered in 1991–1998 by a series of agreements modeled on the earlier Global Treaty. These pacts ultimately called for payments of 1.8 billion deutsch-marks to foundations in Poland, the Russian Federation, Belarus, Ukraine, the Baltic States, and the Czech Republic. But, since most of the recipients were non-Jewish former forced laborers and the individual payments quite small, the Hardship Fund of 1980 was extended in 1992 to provide payments to Holocaust survivors who had fled eastern Europe after 1965 and in 1998 to provide monthly allowances to severely injured survivors in eastern Europe. Total expenditures have exceeded one billion deutschmarks, but the demanding thresholds for the payments (minimum stays of six months in a camp or eighteen months in a ghetto) undercut much of the goodwill the Germans sought to create (Goschler 2005: 429–49).

German firms consistently maintained after 1945 that the Nazi regime had imposed the systems of forced (i.e., poorly paid) or slave (unpaid) labor, and hence the German state, not the erstwhile employers, was liable for compensation. Largely in order to control damage to their reputations in foreign markets, a few enterprises made token postwar payments as expressions of generosity, rather than legal obligation. Thus, IG Farben in Liquidation, Krupp, Siemens, AEG, and Rheinstahl agreed between 1957 and 1962 to pay some 51.5 million deutschmarks to the Claims Conference in order to aid approximately 15,000 Jewish former concentration camp inmates who had toiled for these enterprises during World War II; the average payout was a rather pitiful 3,433 deutschmarks per person or roughly $850 at the time (Ferencz 1979). More than two decades later and for similar reasons, Feldmühle Nobel, Daimler-Benz, and Volks-wagen offered a total of 37 million deutschmarks to the survivors among their workers drawn from camps, but not all of the money went to Jews (Goschler in Diefendorf 2004: 397; Henry 2007: 133).

The matter was brought to a head anew in the 1990s by a series of class action suits in the United States. Lawyers for former forced and slave laborers requested courts to award these victims compensation from the assets of American subsid-iaries of the German firms that had once been the beneficiaries of compulsory work. Although the claims ultimately failed in the only two cases decided, which involved the Degussa and Siemens corporations, by then the adverse publicity and the uncertainty of the judicial outcomes had prompted the governments of the United States and Germany to begin negotiating a deal that eventually called for the establishment of a new Memory, Responsibility, and the Future Foundation. Funded with 10 billion deutschmarks, half from the German state budget and half from corporate contributions to the Foundation Initiative of German Business (*Stiftungsinitiative der deutschen Wirtschaft*), the Foundation disbursed about 3 billion of the total to Jewish victims of the Holocaust, 2.3 billion via the Claims Conference to slave laborers and other survivors, and 500 million via the International Commission on Holocaust Era Insurance Claims (Eizenstat 2003: 243–78; Goschler in Diefendorf 2004: 401). In return, the U.S. government pledged to urge American courts to dismiss further cases related to the conduct of German firms during World War II.

In short, the history of recompense by Germany for the crimes of the Holocaust is an ambivalent one. On the one hand, buoyed by the extraordinary postwar revival of its economy and motivated by an initially self-interested desire for integration into the western alliance and the new Europe, Germany consented to pay an overall indemnity for the Holocaust that no one would have thought conceivable in 1945. On the other hand, the German record is clouded by the highly variable support provided to individuals, along with the halting, makeshift, and grudging way in which compensation expanded, which meant that hundreds of thousands of victims died before they became eligible.

RESTITUTION AND COMPENSATION
BY OTHER NATIONS

In broad outline, the postwar restitution and compensation policies of European countries on either side of the Iron Curtain paralleled those of their German counterparts. Like East Germany, the communist regimes in Poland, Czechoslovakia, Hungary, Romania, Bulgaria, and Yugoslavia, and the expanded Soviet Union preferred nationalizing private property to restoring it. As a result, most of their Jewish survivors got little back and emigrated as soon as they could. Soviet Jews were unable to leave in large numbers until the 1980s, but 90 percent of Bulgaria's Jews already had fled by 1949 (Dean 2008: 342), and the corresponding percentages and dates for the other Eastern Bloc states fell between these extremes. This trend had far-reaching effects after the collapse of communism, since some successor regimes, such as the Czech Republic, initially required residency as a prerequisite for belated compensation or restitution and some, such as Poland, still do (Kubu and Kuklik in Dean et al. 2007: 223–39; Stola in Dean et al. 2007: 240–55).

In Norway, the Netherlands, Belgium, Italy, France, and Austria, on the other hand, practices resembled those of West Germany in that an initial flurry of attention to restituting homes and physical assets—facilitated by the fact that many of these plundered items remained backlogged in the confiscation machinery at the war's end—soon gave way to insensitivity and indifference that lasted into the 1990s. Norway, for example, set about identifying and returning property swiftly after the war, but also imposed death taxes on estates at each discovery that someone in the chain of inheritance had been murdered. Such bureaucratic reflexes were among the reasons why the country indemnified its Jewish community with $60 million in 1998 (Dean 2008: 290). In the Netherlands, another nation from which the mortality rate of deported Jews was high, restitution of physical property whose owners could be traced proceeded rapidly and was nearly complete by the 1950s, and great care was taken to disaggregate the Nazis' collective bank account in order to return individual deposits to their surviving owners. But, apparently heirless goods, including thousands of artworks, remained in the possession of Dutch people or institutions, as did most of the plundered stocks that had been sold on Amsterdam's exchanges during the war, both of which became the subjects of new restitution programs during the 1990s (Aalders in Rathkolb 2002: 120–31; Eizenstat 2003: 197).

The notable defects of Belgium's postwar restitution process (van Doorslaer in Dean et al. 2007: 161–8) were recognized only even more recently: in March 2008, the national government and the nation's leading banks agreed to make $170 million available to Holocaust survivors and their families and to community institutions for commemorative projects (*New York Times*, 11 March 2008). Italy's shameful practices, which included requiring applicants for restitution to pay back taxes and administrative fees on property held by the Italian state between 1938 and 1945, and which enabled banks and the government to pocket assets unclaimed after the war, were still officially unacknowledged and unexpiated as late as 2007 (Pavan in Dean et al. 2007: 175–80).

In France, the relatively low rate of deportation made the postwar restitution process more complete than nearly anywhere else. Although the officials and offices in charge were often the same ones that had been responsible for the spoliation of Jews under the Vichy government (Baruch in Feldman and Seibel 2005: 208), "restitution was made with respect to 90 percent of the total value of businesses, real estate, shares, and bank accounts subjected to confiscation measures," and in 1948, the French state agreed to reimburse the French Jewish community for the fine the German occupiers had imposed (Andrieu in Dean et al. 2007: 136, 143). Still, the Matteoli Commission of 1997–2000 estimated the maximum value of unclaimed, formerly Jewish-owned property in France at 2.3 billion francs, and this became the basis for an appropriation of 2.5 billion as the endowment of the Foundation for the Memory of the Shoah. In addition, a new Commission for the Indemnification of Victims of Spoliation has been entrusted with recommending compensation for all previously unrecompensed thefts of property during the German occupation, and the country's banks have agreed to provide $22.5 million to pay back individuals or their heirs whose bank accounts had been confiscated under Vichy and never refunded (Eizenstat 2003: 315–37; Andrieu in Dean et al. 2007: 138–40).

Austria enacted no fewer than seven restitution laws during the Allied occupation, but they did not cover the more than 30,000 Jewish-owned businesses that had been liquidated under the Nazis, the value of goods that had been auctioned off, payments of the Flight Tax and other last-minute impositions, and insurance policies that owners had redeemed (Stiefel in Rathkolb 2002: 176; Eizenstat 2003: 302). Between 1961 and 1999, the enactment of successive stopgap measures, as in West Germany, provided some $96 million for various categories of losses and victims and extended the Austrian social benefit system to increasing numbers of Holocaust survivors (Henry 2007: 158–71), yet stopped well short of a comprehensive compensation scheme. The stage thus was set for intense negotiations at the beginning of this century about numerous plundered artworks in Austrian museums, as well as the glaring omissions in previous restitution arrangements. As a result, since 2001, Austria has returned more than 2,200 objects to their rightful owners, and a joint commitment by the Austrian government and industry, akin to the German Foundation Initiative, has begun providing almost $1.4 billion in per capita payments to Austrian Holocaust survivors worldwide, payments to former forced and slave laborers, pensions for Jews driven from Austria or their children, and settlements of assorted property claims (Eizenstat 2003: 200, 293–314; Henry 2007: 173–4).

Switzerland long represented a special case regarding restitution and compensation because the country had been formally neutral during World War II. The nation's liabilities, however, were substantial, as it had purchased considerable quantities of plundered gold from the Third Reich and had served as the salesroom for much of the art, furs, jewelry, and commercial paper that the Nazis stole from Jews. Moreover, Switzerland's banks were suspected of having pocketed the contents of numerous accounts opened by Jews who later were killed in the Holocaust. These issues were largely swept under the rug in the immediate postwar years, as the United States acceded to the Washington Agreement of 1946, by which the Swiss promised to liquidate frozen German assets in their country, transfer half their value to a fund for stateless Nazi victims, and hand over one-sixth of the gold acquired from Nazi Germany in return for rehabilitation as an acceptable trading partner (Ludi in Dean et al. 2007: 197). Although the Swiss government passed a law in 1946 that ordered restitution of stolen art even if the purchase had been made in good faith, the legislation allowed only a short interval for making claims and applied only to works bought after 1939 and in occupied areas, not Germany proper (Kreis in Rathkolb 2002: 142).

During the 1990s, the World Jewish Congress succeeded in turning a spotlight on Switzerland's involvement with the Nazi regime, especially the issues of stolen gold, dormant accounts, production of war materials, and hostility to refugees. A series of commissions of inquiry, notably one under Paul Volcker (b. 1927) on the conduct of Swiss banks and another led by Jean-Francois Bergier (1931–2009) on the broad subject of Swiss policy and actions during World War II, demonstrated that the number of bank accounts opened by Jews during the Nazi era probably was lower than Switzerland's critics had claimed, but that Swiss banks had conspired to frustrate postwar inquiries about them (Eizenstat 2003: 180–1; Dean 2008: 360–1). The Bergier Commission also found that the Swiss National Bank knowingly had accepted plundered gold from the Nazi regime and afterwards repeatedly mischaracterized its policies and conduct (Independent Commission of Experts 2002: 238–53).

These emergent findings played a significant role in setting the terms of the settlement of a U.S. court case against the United Bank of Switzerland in 1999 by which the Bank agreed to pay $1.25 billion into a fund administered by the Claims Conference: $800 million for restitution of dormant accounts; $100 million for compensation for looted assets; and $325 million for payments to former slave laborers at Swiss-owned companies or German firms that had put their revenue in Swiss banks and for refugees mistreated by the Swiss (Eizenstat 2003: 178). As of January 2005, the Claims Conference had disbursed $219 million to 2,800 bank account claimants, $255 million to 176,000 surviving Jewish and Roma former slave laborers, $11 million to 4,000 Jews and Roma barred from entrance to Switzerland or mistreated there, and $205 million to social welfare agencies (www.claimscon. org/index.asp?url=news/crt).

The United States restituted considerable amounts of property plundered by the Nazis to the countries of origin after 1945 and turned over numerous Jewish communal and liturgical objects and books to the Jewish Cultural Reconstruction and other organizations for distribution to libraries and congregations (Kurtz 2006). American occupation forces also carried off many valuable items and shipped thousands of publications formerly owned by Jews to American public and university libraries, and the U.S. made little effort to recover or even track such property. A Presidential Advisory Commission on Holocaust Era Assets existed from 1998 to 2000, but its purview was confined to the actions and possessions of the federal government, and its final report proved rushed and disappointing (2000). No thorough survey of victims' property that fell to individual American states via the legally mandated forfeit of dormant bank accounts after a given statutory period or that private enterprises acquired ever has taken place. With regard to art works, however, the record has improved, and several notable returns of objects to owners or their heirs have occurred in recent years (Eizenstat 2003: 200–3).

CONCLUSION

In retrospect, the recurrent pursuit of recompense for the victims of the Holocaust has been both impossible and necessary—impossible because so much of what was lost was intangible and irremediable, necessary because so little of what could be given back or paid for was treated as such in the early postwar years, when every European nation was preoccupied with reconstruction. Even now, the justice achieved remains incomplete, since thousands of victims died before being able to benefit, the monetization of loss is always approximate and grows more so as the interval between offense and redress increases, and many of the countries where the thefts were most extensive, notably Poland and Romania, have yet to grapple seriously with their obligations.

In other words, despite enormous expenditures, gaps still yawn between what people suffered and what they got back and between what a perpetrating entity did or gained and what it ultimately paid. Every major restitution or compensation settlement since 1950 has been an instance of "negotiated justice" (Barkan 2000) in which the amounts made available have had less to do with what real compensation required or real criminality deserved than with the momentary bargaining strength of the parties. This was as true of the sums distributed pursuant to the Luxembourg Agreements of 1953 as of those raised by the German Foundation Initiative of 2000. Political realities also explain why Switzerland never has been forced to indemnify any agency for making agreements with the governments of Poland and Hungary shortly after World War II that allowed the Alpine country to keep the heirless Swiss assets of dead Polish and Hungarian citizens, most of whom were Jews, as compensation for the nationalization of Swiss property in these newly communist states (Ludi in Dean et al. 2007: 199).

Moreover, the settlements involving corporations have been instances of "rough" justice in which the enterprises bought valuable advantages by paying arbitrarily determined sums that bore no relation to their earlier conduct, while sometimes guiltier parties walked away untouched. The United Bank of Switzerland, in effect, purchased the right to take over a major American bank and do further business in the United States in return for a payment that vastly exceeded the value of all Holocaust-related dormant bank accounts and gold deposits in the country's commercial banks, while the National Bank of Switzerland, the recipient of 92 percent of the Swiss gold that came from Nazi Germany (Independent Commission of Experts 2002: 238) escaped with its underpayment under the Washington Agreement because it had no business interests in the United States that later could be threatened. German companies are not obligated to contribute to the Foundation Initiative, regardless of their involvement in slave labor or other dimensions of the Holocaust, and the extent of their contributions not only is pegged to their annual sales totals, not their degree of culpability, but also is tax-deductible.

These are not the only blemishes on the quest for recompense. Although it precipitated many significant historical studies, it also spread misconceptions about the breadth, causes, and monetary worth of many forms of persecution and spoliation that historians will be busy correcting for a long time (Hayes in Petropoulos and Roth 2005: 7–25; Hayes in Bazyler and Alford 2006: 197–204). The admiring accounts of the role of American lawyers and courts that have appeared

(Bazyler 2003; Schapiro 2003) also need rebuttal, not least because many of the representatives of the plaintiffs in the American proceedings of the 1990s were censured, disbarred, forced to resign their positions, and sentenced to jail in subsequent years for legal and financial misconduct (Marrus 2009: 124–7). Finally, recent settlements have opened old wounds within the Jewish community world-wide regarding the propriety of accepting money as indemnification for death and whether funds received should go exclusively to survivors or, at least in part, to Jewish cultural undertakings.

All that said, hundreds of thousands of survivors and heirs have benefited from the persistence of people who refused to settle for the first round of restitution and compensation in the immediate postwar years, many others still deserve to do so, and all the pertinent questions have not yet been answered. Among the items still awaiting thorough research are the extent of property transfers in most eastern European countries, the volume of gold stolen from Jews still in the reserves of states such as Greece, and the number of unclaimed accounts of Holocaust victims in United States banks after World War II. Although detailed exploration of these and similar matters is not likely to result in further significant monetary settlements, it will reveal once more how ramified the consequences of the Holocaust have been.

REFERENCES

ALY, G. (2005). *Hitler's Beneficiaries: Plunder, Racial War, and the Nazi Welfare State.* New York: Henry Holt and Company.

BAJOHR, F. (2002). *"Aryanisation" in Hamburg.* New York: Berghahn Books.

BARKAI, A. (1989). *From Boycott to Annihilation: The Economic Struggle of German Jews 1933–1943.* Hanover, NH: University Press of New England.

BARKAN, E. (2000). *The Guilt of Nations.* New York: W. W. Norton & Co.

BAZYLER, M. (2003). *Holocaust Justice: The Battle for Restitution in America's Courts.* New York: New York University Press.

——and ALFORD, R. (eds.) (2006). *Holocaust Restitution: Perspectives on the Litigation and its Legacy.* New York: New York University Press.

BERENBAUM, M. and PECK, A. (eds.) (1998). *The Holocaust and History.* Bloomington, IN: Indiana University Press.

DEAN, M. (2008). *Robbing the Jews: The Confiscation of Jewish Property in the Holocaust, 1933–1945.* New York: Cambridge University Press.

——GOSCHLER, C., and THER, P. (eds.) (2007). *Robbery and Restitution: The Conflict over Jewish Property in Europe.* New York: Berghahn Books.

DIEFENDORF, J. (ed.) (2004). *Lessons and Legacies VI: New Currents in Holocaust Research.* Evanston, IL: Northwestern University Press.

EIZENSTAT, S. (2003). *Imperfect Justice: Looted Assets, Slave Labor, and the Unfinished Business of World War II.* New York: Public Affairs.

FELDMAN, G. (2001). *Allianz and the German Insurance Business 1933–1945.* New York: Cambridge University Press.

FELDMAN, G. and SEIBEL, W. (eds.) (2005). *Networks of Nazi Persecution*. New York: Berghahn Books.

FERENCZ, B. (1979). *Less Than Slaves: Jewish Forced Labor and the Quest for Compensation*. Cambridge, MA: Harvard University Press.

GOSCHLER, C. (2005). *Schuld und Schulden*. Göttingen: Wallstein Verlag.

GRUNER, W. (2002). *Oeffentliche Wohlfahrt und Judenverfolgung: Wechselwirkungen lokaler und zentraler Politik im NS-Staat (1933–1942)*. Munich: Oldenbourg.

——(2006). *Jewish Forced Labor Under the Nazis*. New York: Cambridge University Press.

HAYES, P. (2003). "Auschwitz, Capital of the Holocaust." *Holocaust and Genocide Studies* 17: 330–50.

——(2004). *From Cooperation to Complicity: Degussa in the Third Reich*. New York: Cambridge University Press.

HENRY, M. (2007). *Confronting the Perpetrators: A History of the Claims Conference*. London: Vallentine Mitchell.

HITLER, A. (1943). *Mein Kampf*. Boston, MA: Houghton Mifflin.

HOCHSTADT, S. (ed.) (2004). *Sources of the Holocaust*. New York: Palgrave Macmillan.

INDEPENDENT COMMISSION OF EXPERTS SWITZERLAND—SECOND WORLD WAR (2002). *Switzerland, National Socialism and the Second World War: Final Report*. Zurich: Pendo.

JAMES, H. (2001). *The Deutsche Bank and the Nazi Economic War against the Jews*. New York: Cambridge University Press.

JUNZ, H. (2002). *Where Did All the Money Go? Pre-Nazi Era Wealth of European Jewry*. Berne: Staempfli.

KURTZ, M. (2006). *America and the Return of Nazi Contraband*. New York: Cambridge University Press.

MARRUS, M. (2009). *Some Measure of Justice: The Holocaust Era Restitution Campaign of the 1990s*. Madison, WI: University of Wisconsin Press.

New York Times (2008). "Belgium to Pay Holocaust Survivors". 11 March. <http://www.nytimes.com>.

PETROPOULOS, J. and ROTH, J. (eds.) (2005). *Gray Zones: Ambiguity and Compromise in the Holocaust and its Aftermath*. New York: Berghahn Books.

PRESIDENTIAL ADVISORY COMMISSION ON HOLOCAUST ASSETS IN THE UNITED STATES (2000). *Plunder and Restitution: The U.S. and Holocaust Victims' Assets; Findings and Recommendations*. Washington, DC: U.S. Government Printing Office.

PROSS, C. (1998). *Paying for the Past*. Baltimore, MD: Johns Hopkins University Press.

RATHKOLB, O. (ed.) (2002). *Revisiting the National Socialist Legacy: Coming to Terms with Forced Labor, Expropriation, Compensation, and Restitution*. Innsbruck: Studien Verlag.

ROSENKÖTTER, B. (2003). *Treuhandpolitik: Die "Haupttreuhandstelle Ost" und der Raub polnischer Vermögen 1939–1945*. Essen: Klartext.

SCHAPIRO, J. (2003). *Inside a Class Action*. Madison, WI: University of Wisconsin Press.

WIXFORTH, H. (2006). *Die Expansion der Dresdner Bank in Europa*. Munich: Oldenbourg.

OTHER SUGGESTED READING

BALABKINS, N. (1971). *West German Reparations to Israel*. New Brunswick, NJ: Rutgers University Press.

FELICIANO, H. (1997). *The Lost Museum*. New York: Basic Books.

LEVIN, I. (2004). *Walls Around: The Plunder of Warsaw Jewry during World War II and Its Aftermath.* Westport, CT: Praeger.

NICHOLAS, L. (1995). *Rape of Europa: The Fate of Europe's Treasures in the Third Reich and the Second World War.* New York: Vintage.

SMITH, A. (1989). *Hitler's Gold: The Story of the Nazi War Loot.* Oxford: Berg.

ZIEGLER, J. (1998). *The Swiss, the Gold, and the Dead.* New York: Harcourt, Brace & Co.

ZWEIG, R. (2001). *German Reparations and the Jewish World: A History of the Claims Conference.* 2nd edn. London: Frank Cass.

CHAPTER 36

....

DENIAL

....

DEBORAH E. LIPSTADT

HOLOCAUST denial is the name used to describe the effort by a small but prolific group of writers—for example, Robert Faurisson (b. 1929), Arthur Butz (b. 1933), and David Irving (b. 1938)—to spread the notion that the Holocaust, the systematic annihilation of the European Jews by Germany's Third Reich, never happened. Though not all deniers propound the same arguments, certain ingredients are common to most of them (Lipstadt 1993, 2005). They include the following claims:

- No genocide took place. The Germans' "Final Solution" meant the expulsion of the Jews to eastern Europe. The Germans' objective was to uproot the Jewish community, not to kill or physically harm it.
- The gas chambers never existed, since those described in Holocaust narratives were incapable of functioning as such.
- The number of Jews actually killed by the Nazis and their allies is substantially smaller than six million. At most, it equaled the number of German civilians slain in Allied bombing raids.
- Hitler's Germany was not the instigator of World War II. The Allies and, even more so, the Jews must share responsibility for the war.
- The Jews invented the notion of a genocide perpetrated against them in order to win sympathy from the world, money from Germany, and land in the Middle East. This creation was a "hoax," a "swindle," and a propaganda effort with ramifications that continue to this day.
- Jews fabricated material and documentary evidence of a genocide and planted it to make the Germans look guilty.

- The Allies' primary foe in the 1930s and 1940s was the Soviet Union. Their focus should have been on defeating Stalin's regime, not Hitler's, but the Jews helped to maneuver the Allies into fighting the wrong war.
- Jews who were in fact murdered by the Germans, particularly by the mobile killing units on the eastern front, perished because they were partisans, criminals, spies, or subversives, and Germany was, therefore, justified in killing them.
- Rational and non-sinister explanations exist for much of what has been presented as "evidence" for a mass killing. The supposed gas chambers were, in fact, air raid shelters, the cans of Zyklon B gas found in places such as Auschwitz after the war were used to get rid of vermin that spread typhus, and terms, such as *"ausrotten,"* which have been given sinister explanations by the Jews, really mean uprooting.
- Classic works, such as *The Diary of Anne Frank*, are forgeries that have been deftly used by Jews to convince millions of young people throughout the world that the Holocaust occurred.
- After the war the Allies engaged in "victors' justice" at places such as Nuremberg, where they put innocent Germans on trial. Torture was used at these tribunals to elicit false confessions from the Germans.
- The Allies' investigatory teams contained a preponderance of Jews, who played pivotal roles in planting evidence and forcing confessions to non-existent crimes.

In short, deniers not only claim that Germans committed no crimes against Jews but also recast the Germans as the genuine victims. According to deniers, the real crimes against civilization were carried out, not by the Germans against the Jews, but by the Americans, Russians, British, and French against the Germans. Germans, stress the deniers, suffered through the bombing of Hamburg, Dresden, and other German cities. Germans endured wartime starvation, invasions, victors' vengeance at Nuremberg, and brutal occupation by both Soviet and Allied occupiers. Then, in the ultimate miscarriage of justice, Germans had to bear, not just the historical shame, but the financial burden of an act that has become emblematic of the concept of genocide.

But if the Holocaust is a hoax, why does postwar Germany accept responsibility for it? Why do Germans, who more than all other people should know that the Holocaust is an invention, not say so publicly? The deniers' response is that the Jews' success in spreading the myth of the Holocaust left Germans no option but to acquiesce to their supposed guilt. Doing so was the price of postwar Germany's readmission to the family of civilized nations. Denial of complicity in genocide would have relegated Germany to pariah status. Germans therefore shouldered both moral and financial burdens, including paying reparations to the putative victims and to the State of Israel.

At the heart of the deniers' assertions about the Holocaust is the assertion that Jews are victimizers, not victims. Not only have the Germans been victimized by the Holocaust myth, but also the nations of the world were made to feel responsible for failing to stop the Nazis. Jews won the world's sympathy and then used it to "displace" another people, the Palestinians, and establish the State of Israel. Holocaust denial has become a crucial arrow in the quiver of those who are opposed to the existence of the State of Israel. Consequently Holocaust denial has become widespread in much of the Arab and Muslim world, where journalists, governmental leaders, and academics engage in it.

For a prejudicial charge against any particular group to be convincing, it must be based on familiar stereotypic elements. The deniers' assertion that Jews created a vast Holocaust myth in order to gain political and economic advantages emerges from traditional antisemitic characterizations of Jews as constantly engaged in secret manipulations to benefit themselves at the majority population's expense. This stereotype has roots in the New Testament's narratives about the crucifixion of Jesus, which led to the claim that Jews had committed deicide. That allegation inflamed the long-standing and still-present conviction that Jews readily inflict harm on others—Christians or other ethnic or religious groups—to advance Jewish purposes. Holocaust denial expresses an extreme position on this antisemitic continuum, for it implies that even though the Germans did not murder Jews, the latter's evil ways made them deserve death.

Not only antisemitism motivates deniers. Many of them also want to rehabilitate the reputations of neo-fascist and far right extremist political ideologies, including National Socialism, by literally erasing their association with mass murder. Similarly, white racists who ignore the scientific baselessness of the category "Aryan" and believe that those encompassed by the term are genetically, socially, and culturally superior to other peoples see denial as enabling them to promote Aryan superiority without having to justify or defend the Holocaust.

Deniers' Tactics

Deniers use a variety of tactics. Among the most insidious are appeals to "immoral equivalencies." Faurisson, one of the movement's leaders, once began an interview by stating: "War is terrible. People do awful things in wars. All sides are guilty" (Interview with Deborah Lipstadt, Vichy, France, July 1986). The implication is that the wrongs of one side are equal to the wrongs of the other. But this gambit of bracketing, for example, Nazi concentration camps with the internment camps for Americans of Japanese descent, blurs the key difference that, while the camps for Japanese Americans reflected America's racist fears, the treatment experienced by the Japanese Americans was much less harsh than that inflicted on the inmates of German concentration camps.

Another form of "immoral equivalencies" appears when deniers deal with documents such as the "Death Books," the records of registered prisoners at Auschwitz who "died" in the camps (the books do not record those prisoners who were taken directly to the gas chambers). Comparing the deaths of registered prisoners with the deaths of German civilians in cities such as Hamburg and Dresden, deniers contend that more Germans were killed in one or two nights of bombing than Jews who "died" at Auschwitz over four years. In a speech in 1992, Irving, a British Holocaust denier, claimed that 100,000 people had died at Auschwitz, "most of them from epidemics" and "twenty-five thousands from shooting or hanging" (Evans 2001: 181). He then compared these losses to the suffering of the Germans.

Let me show you....in my book, a vivid picture of twenty-five thousand people being killed in twenty-five minutes by us British [in February 1945] in Pforzheim, a little town where they make jewelry and watches....Twenty-five thousand civilians are being burned alive in twenty-five minutes....You don't get it spelled out...like that. Except by us, their opponents....When you put things in perspective...it diminishes their Holocaust—that word with a capital letter. (Evans 2001: 179)

This statement is designed to give the impression that the Allied bombing of German cities was as bad as or worse than the Germans' killing of Jews in Auschwitz. To compound his minimization of Auschwitz, Irving not only understated the number of registered prisoners who died there but also inflated the Pforzheim death toll—as calculated by the city's Statistical Office—by 40 percent; the actual figure was 17,600, not 25,000 (Evans 2001: 180–1).

For many years, most Holocaust deniers presented their arguments rather crudely. Evoking Nazi-era publications, they included almost pornographic drawings of Jews designed to appeal to "skinheads," fascists, and neo-Nazis. But in the late 1970s, deniers adopted a dramatically different and more efficacious strategy aimed at a more educated and sophisticated audience. Now deniers cast themselves as academics engaged in a reasoned pursuit of historical truth, debunking errors of fact and interpretation in mainstream scholarship about the Holocaust.

This change was associated with the founding in 1978 of the California-based Institute for Historical Review (IHR). Funded primarily by Willis Carto (b. 1926), the founder of Noontide Press, which published books on the superiority of white people, antisemitism, and Holocaust denial, the IHR organized conferences that imitated academic gatherings but actually were devoted to Holocaust denial and published a journal that likewise mimicked the appearance and format of standard outlets for authentic scholarly research. The IHR presented itself as an advocate of historical "revisionism," thus appropriating a familiar term for the long-standing and respected practice of questioning and amending accepted historical conclusions in light of new evidence.

The IHR and its followers contend that, while all fields of history are appropriately subject to continuous revision, only the Holocaust is treated as sacrosanct and beyond further examination. This contention is easily disproven by examining the course of Holocaust historiography. Indeed, the volume containing this chapter records the advance of Holocaust studies thanks to repeated rounds of new research and reconsideration. Holocaust historians have repeatedly revised their conclusions, all the more so since the fall of the USSR and the opening of eastern European archives that were off limits to most historians until late in the twentieth century.

Key revisions in Holocaust historiography include modification of the notion that the Third Reich was a tightly organized bureaucratic system with all decisions flowing from the top—from Adolf Hitler (1889–1945)—down. Increasingly, historians' interpretations have been revised to underscore that, while Hitler determined that the European Jews must be destroyed, decisions about how to carry out the "Final Solution" were made at multiple levels and by many different officials. Another crucial revision concerns the role of Adolf Eichmann (1906–1962), the SS officer who facilitated the "Final Solution." When he was brought to trial in Jerusalem in 1961, Israeli prosecutors and the historians who helped prepare the case against Eichmann assumed that he was the main coordinator of the "Final Solution" and that all decisions regarding the destruction of the Jews flowed through him. Current scholarship shows that the role he played, while decisive, was not as all-inclusive or at as high a level as had been assumed. Yet another revision concerns the number of Jews killed at Auschwitz. Early postwar estimates were four million. Later research indicated that this number was far too high. Careful calculations revised the Jewish death toll downward to approximately one million. These "revisions" by Holocaust historians are based on archival research, judicious interpretation of documents, material evidence pertaining to the Auschwitz-Birkenau site, and the open exchange of ideas.

The deniers' methodology is quite different. Postwar testimony by Holocaust survivors is ignored, discredited, or dismissed unless it can be interpreted as indicating that the Holocaust did not happen. Incriminating postwar testimony by Nazis regarding the mass murder of the Jews, such as the memoir of Auschwitz commandant Rudolf Höss (1900–1947), is dismissed as having been coerced or forged. Deniers also rely on verbal obfuscation. They argue that because the terms *Endlösung* (final solution) and *Sonderbehandlung* (special treatment) sometimes were used by Germans in contexts that had nothing to do with mass killings, then these terms always had benign meanings, even when used in obviously genocidal contexts. In addition, minor errors, such as those in Auschwitz commandant Höss's memoirs, are cited to discredit all of a perpetrator's—or a survivor's—testimony.

Deniers turn to still other tactics when documentation leaves no doubt that the Germans killed large numbers of Jews. For example, even deniers cannot evade the murderous activities of the Einsatzgruppen, the mobile killing units on the eastern front, since these units prepared detailed daily and weekly reports on the locations, numbers, and sorts of their victims, and multiple copies of these summaries were distributed to other units, government officials, and, in certain instances, private individuals. Einsatzgruppe D, for instance, reported on 5 November 1941 that it had killed 11,037 Jews and 3 communist officials in the previous two weeks. In late October 1941, Einsatzgruppe C reported that it had "liquidated" some 80,000 people of which 75,000 were Jews. Another document, "Report to the Führer on Combating Partisans" (No. 51, December 1942), listed the number of Jews murdered as 363,211. The report, signed by the SS leader Heinrich Himmler (1900–1945), was typed in the large font favored by Hitler, who hated to wear his reading glasses, and bears the stamp "Shown to the Führer." Similar reports followed, including one that referenced 44,125 people murdered in one month with the notation: "mostly Jews" (Browning 2000).

Because the sheer abundance of such documents makes the claim of forgery implausible, deniers try to exonerate the Nazi regime by maintaining that these Jews were killed by rogue elements of the German forces or by German allies such as Lithuanians, Estonians, and Latvians and claiming that the killings were legitimate because the Jews were saboteurs and partisans. But why, then, were so many women and children slaughtered? And why do the reports often include two separate death tolls, one for partisans and one for Jews? Deniers' wriggling cannot stand up to such questions.

Another oft-repeated denial argument is that no one ever has produced a document signed by Adolf Hitler ordering the mass murder of the Jews. Nazi Germany, deniers contend, was such an authoritarian system that no German would have dared to undertake such an activity without a Hitler order. Acknowledging the existence of a document signed by Hitler, authorizing the T4 "euthanasia" program under which as many as 100,000 disabled and mentally ill German "Aryans" were gassed, the deniers ask, why has no one found a parallel document regarding the Holocaust? Irving has made the non-existence of this document a core principle of his denial arguments. He has "offered a thousand pounds to any person who could produce even one wartime document showing explicitly what Hitler knew, for example, of Auschwitz . . ." His website states that "nobody has yet claimed the widely publicized $1,000 reward . . . for even one page of wartime contemporary evidence that Hitler was even aware of Auschwitz ('the Holocaust'), let alone gave the order for the Final Solution" (www.fpp.co.uk/docs/Irving/cesspit/HSJP210898html). An article on the website for the Committee on Open Debate on the Holocaust (CODOH), a Holocaust denial organization, maintains that, if such an order was issued, "it would have been located . . . Since none has been found, the conclusion is inescapable: There was no policy to exterminate Jews by the Nazi government" (Weir n.d.).

Reputable historians seldom base their conclusions on the existence, let alone the absence, of a single document, particularly when dealing with an event like the Holocaust for which the paper trail is so long and thick. And in this instance, deniers ignore the fact that the Nazis' desire to conceal the "Final Solution" while it was happening made the absence of written orders from Hitler more probable than not. As Himmler told leading SS officers in Posen in 1943 regarding the mass killing of Jews: "We will never speak of it publicly....I mean the evacuation of the Jews, the extermination of the Jewish race....we're doing it, exterminating them... This is a page of glory in our history which has never been written and is never to be written..." (www.holocaust-history.org/himmler-poznan/speech-text.shtml). After the war, Rudolf Höss, the commandant of Auschwitz, wrote that "according to the orders of the Reichsführer-SS [Himmler], all other units which took part in any way [in the liquidation operations] had to destroy all records immediately" (State of Israel 1992, 3: 1005–6.).

Gas Chambers

Since the gas chambers at Auschwitz have become emblematic of the Holocaust, deniers make great efforts to convince the public that the relevant structures could not have been used to gas hundreds of thousands of Jews to death. "No holes, no Holocaust!" is a slogan frequently used by deniers, a reference to their contention that the roofs of the Auschwitz structures lacked holes and thus Zyklon B pellets could not have been put into the rooms below and no mass gassing of Jews could have taken place. For example, with reference to "Krema 2," one of the gassing facilities at Auschwitz-Birkenau, Faurisson said: "The caved-in roof of this supposed mass extermination 'gas chamber' has visibly never had any of the four special holes...through which, we are told, Zyklon B pellets were poured in. This being the case, how, simply, could an execution gassing operation have even begun here at Birkenau, the core of the so-called 'Holocaust'?" (Faurisson 1998).

Deniers make this claim about the allegedly missing holes despite a wide variety of evidence that attests to their existence and location. Significantly, Hans Stark (1921–1991), a member of the Auschwitz Gestapo, testified at the Auschwitz trial in Frankfurt in 1963 that in Auschwitz I, the Main Camp, gassings were carried out "in a room in the small crematorium which had been prepared for this purpose." Stark told the court that the roof above the gas chamber room was flat with openings through which "Zyklon B in granular form" was poured. On at least one occasion, Stark himself poured the Zyklon B through the holes. Stark recalled that the Zyklon B, trickled down over the people as it was being poured in. They then started to cry out terribly for they now knew what was happening to them . . . After a few minutes there was silence. After some time had passed, it may have been ten or fifteen minutes, the gas-chamber was opened. The dead lay higgledy-piggledy all over the place. It was a dreadful sight. (Klee et al. 1991: 255)

At Auschwitz, *Sonderkommando* units composed primarily of Jewish prisoners were forced to work in the gas chambers and crematoria. This assignment carried a death sentence because the Germans wanted no witnesses of this kind, and the testimony of the few survivors is therefore highly significant (Greif 2005). Filip Müller (b. 1922), a Slovak Jew who arrived in Auschwitz in April 1942, was put to work as an oven stoker in the main camp and made to drag corpses from the morgue-turned-gas-chamber to the ovens and to sort and remove valuables from the abandoned clothing. Later, he was transferred to work in the crematoria and burning pits at Birkenau. He recalled one gassing in Birkenau as follows:

When the last one had crossed the threshold, two SS leaders slammed shut the heavy iron-studded door which was fitted with a rubber seal, and bolted it . . . the Unterführers on duty had gone onto the crematorium roof . . . They removed the covers from the six camouflaged openings. There, protected by gas-masks, they poured the green-blue crystals of the deadly gas into the gas chamber. (Müller 1999: 38)

In 1944, Allied planes flew over Auschwitz, and on 25 August reconnaissance filming captured the camps' gas chambers and crematoria. The underground gas chambers in crematoria 2 and 3 are visible from the outline of the berm of earth and grass that covered them. The Zyklon B introduction chimneys are clearly visible on the roof as four dark squares staggered side to side down the length of the room. Holocaust deniers claim that these aerial photos have been tampered with and the black spots on the roof added. In 1996, experts at the National Aeronautics and Space Administration's (NASA) Jet Propulsion Laboratory in Pasadena, California, a leading center for the analysis of aerial and satellite images, examined the negatives and found no evidence of forgery or tampering. The markings on the roof were on the original negatives.

As the Germans built the gas chambers and crematoria at Auschwitz-Birkenau, they photographed the construction's progress. In December 1942, for instance, a picture of work on crematorium 2 showed the roof of the gas chamber shortly before its completion and covering with dirt and grass; chimneys protruding over the holes are clearly visible. Scientific studies have shown where the holes were placed and how the bars in the concrete roof were constructed to accommodate them (Keren et al. 2004).

In addition to rejecting the existence of gas chambers, deniers claim that the space they supposedly occupied had other uses, notably as air raid shelters. In 1997, Arthur Butz, a professor of electrical engineering at Northwestern University, stated that crematoria 2 and 3 in Birkenau were "ideal for adaptation as air raid shelters . . . there was no better choice at Auschwitz" (Butz 1997). Similarly, writing under the pseudonym Samuel Crowell, another denier claimed that the Germans, who had experienced poison gas attacks in World War I, designed air raid shelters that "were to be made secure from both bombs and poison gas" (Crowell 1997). The air raid shelter explanation attracts deniers because it offers a "benign" explanation with "no criminal significance at all" for a series of Auschwitz Central Construction Office documents dating from early 1943. These documents include orders for gas-tight doors (January 1943), twelve "gas-tight doors of 30/40 cm" (February 1943), ten gas detectors (February 1943), a gas-tight door (March 1943), and so forth (van Pelt 2002: 311, 312, 400, 401). If these sites were indeed to be, in Crowell's words, "secure from both bombs and poison gas," such items would have been needed. But for this explanation to be plausible, Butz, Crowell, and their fellow deniers must ignore the fact that the Central Construction Office at Auschwitz did not begin to construct air raid shelters in both Auschwitz I and Birkenau until late 1943, well *after* the gas-tight doors and detectors had been ordered. Even then, the camp authorities chose one- and two-person shelters, which were situated at regular intervals around the camp's perimeter, usually close to guard posts so that SS men could keep watch on the camp and prevent escapes during air raids. In Auschwitz I, as opposed to Birkenau, the gas chamber was turned into a shelter, since it was adjacent to the SS quarters and already had a gas-tight door. The conversion of the facility at Auschwitz I, however, lends no support to the deniers' contention that the structures at Birkenau were really air raid shelters.

Nevertheless, deniers such as Irving hold that the files of the Central Construction Office in Auschwitz showed the Germans' concern about taking precautions against Allied air raids "from mid-1942 onwards," when they "began to consider the construction at the camp of shelters, splinter trenches, and other Air Raid Precaution measures" (http://www.hdot.org/en/trial/transcripts/day32/pages176-180). But according to the Germans' records, they did not begin to plan shelters until October 1943 and did not begin to build them until the fall of 1944, when air raids actually took place in the area. No Auschwitz-related document prior to November 1943 refers to converting a morgue or a crematorium into an air raid shelter. In November 1943, representatives of the German regional air raid protection authority inspected Auschwitz and Birkenau to see what preparations had been made in the camp in case of an air raid. A memo detailing their meetings with senior SS officials notes that construction of a trench for a shelter had only just begun. To link the February 1943 requisitions of gas-tight equipment to the building of air raid shelters in the camp, as deniers want to do, is false. Deniers ignore the documentation from November 1943 because it shows that their theory—"the gas chambers were gas shelters"—is far-fetched.

The gas-tight "doors" ordered in February 1943 were actually window shutters and are of the precise size and number indicated on an architectural design for the gas chambers (van Pelt 2002: 336–7). Deniers offer no explanation why an underground air raid shelter would need gas-tight window shutters or why an air raid shelter would have windows. Even considered independently of the documentary record, the claim that the Birkenau gas chambers were air raid shelters is counterintuitive. The sites were about a mile from the SS barracks, the roofs were quite thin and susceptible to collapse, and the doors opened outward, making them impossible to open with debris in front of them. Moreover, a metal grill over the peephole in the door faced the inside of the room, not the outside to prevent the glass from breakage in case of an air raid: its purpose was to prevent those inside the room from breaking the glass. Similarly, the gas tight shutters—remnants of which are evident in Auschwitz today—had external window handles. People inside were not intended to open those windows.

"Disproving" Anne Frank's Diary

A crucial target for deniers has been the celebrated diary written by Anne Frank (1929–1945), which has become as emblematic of the Holocaust as the gas chambers at Auschwitz. Deniers dismiss it as a postwar creation or a novel. In 1974, a pseudonymous denier described Frank's diary as a "propaganda legend . . . just one more fraud in a whole series of frauds perpetrated in support of the 'Holocaust' legend and the saga of the Six Million" (Harwood 1974: 28). Irving subsequently called the book a "forgery" (Barnouw and van der Stroom 2003: 91) and "more of a novel than a personal diary, . . . written in ballpoint ink, which did not exist at the time of her tragic death. Her father Otto Frank played an obscure role in all this" (http://www.fpp.co.uk/Auschwitz/docs/controversies/AnneFrank/index. html). In 1978, an Austrian Holocaust denier dubbed the diary a "colossal hoax" and, because of Anne's feelings for her friend Peter, the "first child porno" in which the "Germans . . . are made out as being veritable beasts" (Felderer 1979: 4, 11, 57).

In light of these attacks, the Netherlands State Institute for War Documentation, which was given Anne's original diary by her father, Otto Frank (1889–1980), conducted a detailed forensic study, which included analysis of the diary's paper, ink, glue, handwriting, and all other material aspects. The specialists determined that all these elements dated clearly from the war years. Handwriting specialists compared Anne's diary sheets with other extant samples of her handwriting and concluded that all were written by the same person (Barnouw and van der Stroom 2003).

Deniers also have attacked the diary's content. Faurisson argues that the diary contains entries that could not have been written by someone in hiding. For example, on 5 August 1943 and 6 December 1943, Anne wrote about noise made by the occupants of the secret annex (Barnouw and van der Stroom 2003). Such entries, says Faurisson, demonstrate that Anne and the other occupants could not have been hiding in a secret place because the noise would have revealed their location. But examination of the text reveals that Faurisson quoted selectively and ignored Anne's comments, which explain why they were able to make noise on some occasions. In one of the entries, she notes, "The warehousemen have gone by now." On another occasion, when Anne describes noisy laughter, Faurisson fails to inform his readers that it was a Sunday evening and nobody else was in the building (Barnouw and van der Stroom 2003: 95).

DENIAL ON TRIAL

Various countries, primarily in Europe, have passed laws outlawing genocide denial and specifically, in certain cases, Holocaust denial. Among them are Austria, Belgium, the Czech Republic, France, Germany, Lithuania, Luxemburg, Poland, Spain, Switzerland, Romania, and the European Union. The EU's position with regard to those who grossly trivialize or deny genocide is that member nations "may choose to punish only conduct which is either carried out in a manner likely to disturb public order or which is threatening, abusive or insulting" (European Union 2008). Generally, legislation affecting Holocaust denial puts it in the category of hate speech. Supporters of efforts to criminalize Holocaust denial argue that it causes pain to Holocaust survivors, inculcates hatred, and attempts to revive a discredited and dangerous political system. Those who oppose such laws contend that they create sympathy for people charged with violating them. Even those who have no sympathy for deniers often oppose these laws, holding that they are not efficacious because deniers can and do claim that such legislation violates their freedom of speech. Moreover, opponents argue, the existence of such laws suggests that Holocaust denial cannot be fought adequately by appeals to historical evidence and documentation. Some opponents of these laws make an exception for places such as Germany and Austria, the birthplace of Nazism, where denial could have a uniquely noxious resonance.

   A number of countries have taken deniers to court. At this writing, Austria's 2005 case against Irving for having denied the existence of gas chambers remained the most prominent. He was convicted of Holocaust denial, sentenced to three years in jail, and released after serving approximately eleven months (http://news.bbc.co. uk/2/hi/uk_news/4578534.stm).

   A twist on the traditional way in which Holocaust denial has entered the legal arena took place in England in 2000, when Irving sued Deborah Lipstadt for libel for having called him a denier, an antisemite, and a right wing extremist who denied the Holocaust despite knowing that he was manipulating and fabricating historical data. The defense team's strategy was not to prove the Holocaust happened, which seemed superfluous, but rather to show that Lipstadt's charges were correct, that Irving not only denied the Holocaust but also was aware of the fact that he was twisting, distorting, and falsifying evidence to prove his claims. Lipstadt's defense "followed his footnotes," tracking his arguments back to the sources he cited and, he claimed, proved the Holocaust a myth. In every case the defense found distortion, falsification, invention, or misquotation. The defense team's lead witness, Richard Evans, described Irving's scholarship as a "tissue of lies" (http://www.hdot.org/en/trial/transcripts/day21/pages101–105).

The presiding judge, Charles Gray, wrote a lengthy judgment in which he described Irving's writings about the Holocaust with unambiguous words such as the following: "perverts," "distorts," "misleading," "unjustified," "travesty," and "unreal." Gray rejected Irving's self-justifying claim that he simply had made mistakes and had no intention to distort documentation. Gray disagreed, writing that Irving's "falsification of the historical record was deliberate and . . . motivated by a desire to present events in a manner consistent with his own ideological beliefs even if that involved distortion and manipulation of historical evidence" (Lipstadt 2005: 271). Since Irving's claims about the Holocaust include virtually all the central arguments made by deniers, the trial succeeded in exposing those arguments as fraudulent.

In recent years, Holocaust denial has evolved into what some call "soft" denial. Rather than dispute that the Holocaust occurred, false analogies are offered in attempts to distort and diminish what happened. The trend toward "soft" denial is evident in some former Soviet bloc countries where an effort is made not only to equate the wrongs of the Soviets and the Nazis but also to give greater prominence to the Soviet crimes. This step is taken, in part, because emphasizing Nazi wrongdoings entails highlighting the Soviets' heroic role in defeating Nazism. "Soft" denial has also become inherent to the anti-Israeli rhetoric sometimes voiced by the political left, particularly in Europe. This discourse equates Israelis with Nazis and their treatment of the Palestinians with genocide. By grossly distorting Israel's actions such comparisons deny the true nature of what the Germans did and what the Israelis are doing. Other manifestations of "soft" denial have occurred in Muslim countries, particularly those in the Middle East, where Holocaust denial has become closely connected to the Arab–Israeli conflict. Muslim denial of the Holocaust has been most closely associated with Iranian President Mahmoud Ahmadinejad (b. 1956), who hosted an international conference dedicated to the topic in December 2006.

In 2009, the Vatican had to deal with outrage and criticism from Christian as well as Jewish quarters when Pope Benedict XVI (b. 1927) lifted the excommunication of the illicitly ordained Bishop Richard Williamson (b. 1940), whose interview on Swedish television denied well-documented facts about the Holocaust (Rittner and Smith 2009). Extending antisemitic views frequently expressed by his fellow clerics in the traditionalist Society of St. Pius X, Williamson affirmed his belief that no Jews were killed in gas chambers, claimed that, at most, 200,000–300,000 Jews perished in Nazi concentration camps, and suggested that the notion of a Holocaust was created to pressure Germany to pay reparations (http://svtplay.se/v/1413831/webbextra_langre-intervju_med_williamson). With his May 2009 visit to Israel forthcoming, the pope's damage control included denunciation of Holocaust denial and a reaffirmation of the Roman Catholic Church's rejection of antisemitism. On 26 February 2009, Williamson apologized for his denial remarks but did not retract them, which the Vatican made a condition for his serving as a Catholic bishop (Donadio 2009). At the time, Williamson said that he would reassess Holocaust documentation, an intention that led him to contact Irving. At this writing, no closure had been reached regarding this episode in the history of Holocaust denial.

Although Holocaust denial has not, on the whole, been persuasive in public discourse, many people wonder whether it will have greater success when the last of the survivors has passed away. Concerns have also been expressed that denial will ultimately persist in a "yes-but" syndrome: yes, gas chambers existed, but probably not as many as is claimed; yes, Jews died, but probably not as many as they claim; yes, the Germans did wrong, but so did the Allies; and yes, the Jews may have been mistreated, but they deserved much of what they received. In years to come this "yes-but" revision of history—"soft" denial—is likely to be more prominent than outright denial of the Holocaust.

References

Barnouw, D. and van der Stroom, G. (eds.) (2003). *The Diary of Anne Frank: The Critical Edition.* New York: Doubleday.

Browning, C. (2000). "Evidence for the Implementation of the Final Solution, IV. Documentary Evidence for the Systematic Mass Killing of Jews by Shooting, (A) Scale of Killing." Expert Report prepared for the High Court, David Irving v. Penguin, UK and Deborah E. Lipstadt. See <http://www.hdot.org/en/trial/defense/browning>.

Butz, A. (1997). "Vergasungskeller." See <http://www.codoh.com/gcgv/gcvergas.html>.

Crowell, S. (1997). "Technique and Operation of German Anti-Gas Shelters in World War II: A Refutation of J. C. Pressac's 'Criminal Traces.'" See <http://www.codoh.com/incon/inconpressac.html>.

Donadio, R. (2009). "Vatican Calls the Apology of a Bishop Insufficient." *New York Times.* 28 February 2009: A10.

European Union (2008). Acts Adopted Under Title VI of the EU Treaty, Council Framework Decision 2008/913/JHA of 28 November 2008 on Combating Certain Forms and Expressions of Racism and Xenophobia by Means of Criminal Law.

Evans, R. (2001). *Lying About Hitler: History, Holocaust, and the David Irving Trial.* New York: Basic Books.

Faurisson, R. (1998). "The Gas Chambers of Auschwitz." See <http://www.ihr.org/jhr/v18/v18n5p12_Faurisson.html>.

Felderer, D. (1979). *Anne Frank's Diary: A Hoax.* Torrance, CA: Institute for Historical Review. See <http://www.vho.org/aaargh/fran/livres5/harwoodeng.pdf>.

Greif, G. (2005). *We Wept Without Tears: Testimonies of the Jewish Sonderkommando from Auschwitz.* New Haven, CT: Yale University Press.

Harwood, R. (1974). *Did Six Million Really Die? The Truth at Last.* Richmond: Historical Review Press. See <http://www.vho.org/aaargh/fran/livres5/harwoodeng.pdf>.

Holocaust History Project, The, <http://www.holocaust-history.org>

Keren, D., McCarthy, J., and Mazal, H. (2004). "The Ruins of the Gas Chambers: A Forensic Investigation of Crematoriums at Auschwitz I and Auschwitz-Birkenau." *Holocaust and Genocide Studies* 18: 68–103.

Klee, E., Dressen, W., and Riess, V. (eds.) (1991). *"The Good Old Days": The Holocaust as Seen by Its Perpetrators and Bystanders.* New York: Free Press.

Lipstadt, D. (1993). *Denying the Holocaust: The Growing Assault on Truth and Memory.* New York: Free Press.

——(2005). *History on Trial: My Day in Court with David Irving.* New York: Ecco.

Müller, F. (1999). *Eyewitness Auschwitz: Three Years in the Gas Chamber.* Ed. S. Flatauer. Chicago, IL: Ivan R. Dee.

Rittner, C. and Smith, S. (eds.) (2009). *No Going Back: Letters to Pope Benedict XVI on the Holocaust, Jewish–Christian Relations and Israel.* London: Quill Press.

State of Israel, Ministry of Justice. (1992). *The Trial of Adolf Eichmann: Record of Proceedings in the District Court of Jerusalem.* 5 vols. Jerusalem: The Trust for the Publication of the Eichmann Trial.

Van Pelt, R. (2002). *The Case for Auschwitz: Evidence from the Irving Trial.* Bloomington, IN: Indiana University Press.

Weir, J. (n.d.). "The Plum Cake." *The Revisionist.* See <http://www.codoh.com/revisionist/comment/tr08plumcake.html>.

Other Suggested Reading

Arad, Y. (1987). *Belzec, Sobibor, Treblinka: The Operation Reinhard Camps.* Bloomington, IN: Indiana University Press.

——Krakowski, S., and Spector, S. (eds.) (1989). *The Einsatzgruppen Reports: Selections from the Dispatches of the Nazi Death Squads' Campaign Against the Jews in Occupied Territories of the Soviet Union July 1941–January 1943.* New York: Holocaust Library.

Finkielkraut, A. (1998). *The Future of a Negation: Reflections on the Question of Genocide.* Lincoln, NE: University of Nebraska Press.

Pressac, J.-C. (1989). *Auschwitz: Technique and Operation of the Gas Chambers.* New York: The Beate Klarsfeld Foundation.

Shapiro, S. (1990). *Truth Prevails: Demolishing Holocaust Denial: The End of "The Leuchter Report."* New York: The Beate Klarsfeld Foundation and Holocaust Survivors & Friends in Pursuit of Justice.

SHERMER, M. and GROBMAN, A. (2000). *Denying History: Who Says the Holocaust Never Happened and Why Do They Say It?* Berkeley, CA: University of California Press.

STERN, K. (1993). *Holocaust Denial.* New York: American Jewish Committee.

VIDAL-NAQUET, P. (1993). *Assassins of Memory: Essays on Denial of the Holocaust.* New York: Columbia University Press.

ZIMMERMAN, J. (2000). *Holocaust Denial: Demographics, Testimonies, and Ideologies.* Lanham, MD: University Press of America.

CHAPTER 37

....

ISRAEL

....

BOAZ COHEN

ESTABLISHED in 1948, three years after the defeat of Nazi Germany, the State of Israel remains intrinsically connected to the Holocaust. It influences cultural norms, education, and political decision making. Neither the outlooks of Israelis nor the policies of the state can be understood without regard to the central role that the Holocaust plays in Israel's life. This chapter explores this pervasive impact on the State of Israel, whose existence has depended significantly on survivors and memories of the Nazi genocide against the Jewish people.

"SURVIVOR-LAND"

....

As expressed in Zionist movements of the late nineteenth and early twentieth centuries, the Jewish national revival aimed to reestablish a Jewish national home in Palestine (or *Eretz-Israel*, Land of Israel, as Jewish sources called that territory). Zionists thought that European Jews needed a Jewish state in order to escape oppression and suffering. The Balfour Declaration (1917), in which the British government expressed support for a Jewish national home in Palestine, and the subsequent conquest of Palestine by the British in World War I raised Zionist hopes. On 24 July 1922, the League of Nations placed Palestine under British mandate, but that September the British ceded 77 percent of the territory, the Transjordan, to the Hashemite dynasty. Following strong Arab opposition to

Jewish immigration, British "white papers" in 1922, 1930, and 1939 curtailed Jewish immigration and settlement. During the Mandate period, which lasted until 1948, the Jewish settlers organized themselves into the *Yishuv* (Hebrew for settlement). Its institutions and representative governing body eventually served as the infrastructure for the State of Israel.

By the late 1930s, the deteriorating situation of the Jews in Germany and eastern Europe made Jewish emigration a matter of life and death, a crisis that became even more acute when World War II began in September 1939. With escape routes to Palestine largely blocked, mainly by the British, the European Jews' desperate dilemmas raised a crucial question for the leadership in the Yishuv, namely, what should it do in response? David Ben-Gurion (1886–1973), who had arrived in Palestine in 1906 and later became the first prime minister of the State of Israel, articulated the governing maxim: Jews of the Yishuv should fight alongside the British as if there were no British restrictions on Jewish immigration to Palestine, but resistance against the British immigration restrictions should go forward as if there were no war.

Ben-Gurion's adroit maxim was by no means easy to implement, and numerous barriers stood in the way of effective help for Europe's Jews from the Yishuv. Nonetheless, before, during, and after the Holocaust, the leadership of the Yishuv was criticized for failing to do enough for Europe's Jews, and the issue is still contested in Israeli historiography and public discourse. Critics from the anti-Zionist left have joined those from ultra-orthodox circles and right-wing Zionists in castigating the leadership's alleged inaction, the lack of Jewish solidarity during the war, and politicians' manipulation of surviving Jews afterward (Beit-Zvi 1991; Grodzinsky 2004). The controversy led to intensified historical research that has presented a more complicated and nuanced picture of the choices and actions of the Zionist leadership in Palestine (Porat 1990; Bauer 1994; Friling 2005).

The focal point of the Zionist campaign for a Jewish state immediately after World War II was the plight of the Jewish remnant in the displaced persons (DP) camps in Europe. For hundreds of thousands of Jews, Europe had become a gigantic graveyard. Most soon learned that returning to their former homes meant facing their previous neighbors' hostility. A desirable alternative was immigration to a Jewish state in Palestine. British attempts to halt the Holocaust survivors' "illegal" entry to Palestine drew worldwide attention and sympathy to the refugees. But the extent to which the plight of the survivors or the Holocaust itself was a crucial factor in the establishment of the State of Israel remains a matter of debate among historians (Bauer 2001: 242–60; Michman 2003: 303–28).

The birth of the State of Israel took place in the context of a war of survival against the local Arab population and the armed forces of surrounding Arab countries. The 1948 war for independence underlined the importance of Holocaust survivors as a reservoir of manpower for the emerging Israeli armed forces. More than 20,000 survivors, about 10 percent of those in Israel in 1948, served in that capacity. Recruitment was widespread in DP camps; fighting-age survivors got priority for transportation to Palestine (Ofer 1996; Yablonka 1999). Replacing fallen or wounded soldiers, these survivors contributed importantly to Israel's victory, which brought many more survivors to the new state. By the late 1950s, about 500,000 Holocaust survivors and their children lived in Israel, almost 25 percent of the population (Yablonka 2003). The "veteran" Israelis assisting them were either early Zionists, who had roots in eastern Europe, or refugees, mostly from Poland and Germany, who had arrived in the 1930s. All of the survivors had lost immediate or extended family members in the Holocaust. Many Israeli citizens thus were affected personally by the Holocaust, for in the words of one survivor, Israel was "Survivor-land" (Dworzecki 1956). At the time of Israel's sixtieth anniversary in 2008, the survivor population was about 250,000, more and more of it consisting of senior citizens (Brodsky and DellaPergola 2005; Yablonka 2008). The number will decline rapidly as mortality takes its toll. Nevertheless, Israel's identification as "Survivor-land" remains apt.

THE HOLOCAUST IN ISRAEL'S PUBLIC SQUARE

Holocaust-related issues had a prominent place in Israeli public discourse during the first years of the State. The Knesset debated Holocaust memorial day in 1951, reparations from Germany in 1952, the establishment of Yad Vashem (the national Holocaust memorial) in 1953, and an enhanced Holocaust memorial day in 1959. The courts tried accused Nazi collaborators throughout the first decade and made headlines with the Kasztner trial in 1954 and the Eichmann trial in 1961 (Yablonka 2003).

Relations with postwar Germany, divided into the Federal Republic (West Germany) and the Democratic Republic (East Germany), and reparations in particular stood high on the agenda. Public opinion and government policy were both averse initially to any contact with postwar Germany. Israeli passports, for example, were stamped "not valid for Germany." Although the Israeli government wanted reparations, it did not wish to enter direct negotiations with German representatives and finally agreed to do so only after the western occupying powers refused to negotiate on Israel's behalf. Clandestine talks with the West German government led by Konrad Adenauer (1876–1967) began in April 1951 (Sagi 1986). The East German regime refused to negotiate on reparations, claiming that it was an anti-fascist state and therefore not responsible for Nazi crimes (Tim 1997).

To streamline the initial negotiations, the Israeli government and the World Jewish Congress, headed by Nahum Goldmann (1895–1982), established the Conference on Jewish Material Claims against Germany, which encompassed twenty-three Jewish organizations worldwide. Nevertheless, the prospect of German reparations split Israeli opinion. Opponents insisted that accepting reparations would allow Germans to cleanse their consciences too easily. The critics also contended that the preservation of Jewish honor required refusal of compensation for murdered Jews. Proponents claimed that the money in question had been stolen from European Jews and should not be allowed to remain in the murderers' hands. Furthermore, the reparations were needed to relieve Israeli finances, which were drained by the costs of absorbing the Holocaust survivors who had immigrated to Israel in large numbers. From the left, the right, and even his own Mapai (Labor) Party, opponents assailed Ben-Gurion, the prime minister. Led by Menachem Begin (1913–1992), head of the Herut Party, demonstrators stormed the Knesset during the debate on the ratification of the reparations agreement (Segev 1993: 189–252).

Ben-Gurion strove to normalize relations with what he called "the other Germany." He even cultivated military contacts with the Federal Republic, which was willing to help Israel's defense system when other western states would not. Israel's budding military industries sold mortars and Uzi sub-machine guns to Germany; in return, West Germany sold Israel M-48 Patton tanks (with American consent). These military connections, however, produced complications. In 1964, for example, a mission of Israeli officers, some of them sons of Holocaust survivors, went to West Germany for tank training. Their instructors included officers who had served in the Wehrmacht during World War II. This activity proceeded secretly, out of sight of the Israeli public, and even Ben-Gurion's cabinet was kept in the dark. But on at least two occasions in the 1950s, Israeli governments fell following disclosure of military relations with West Germany (Segev 1993: 311–20).

Holocaust-related issues inflamed emotions in 1954, when the government initiated a libel trial to redeem the reputation of Israel (Rezso) Kasztner (1906–1957), a Mapai official who had headed Hungarian Jewry's rescue commission during the Holocaust. Malchiel Gruenwald (1881–1958), a Hungarian Jew who had lost more than fifty family members in the Holocaust, accused Kasztner of collaboration with SS officer Adolf Eichmann (1906–1962) to misinform Hungarian Jews about the fate awaiting them, thus hindering their escape. Gruenwald claimed that Kasztner had done this to ensure that a privileged group of Jewish leaders and his own family would be spared deportation to Auschwitz and sent instead to safety in Switzerland aboard the so-called Kasztner train. Gruenwald contended further that Kasztner had made financial deals with Nazi officials and testified on their behalf in Nuremberg, thus ensuring their release.

The government sued Gruenwald but soon found itself in the role of the accused. With the help of Uri Avnery (b. 1923), editor of the inflammatory weekly *Ha'olam Hazeh* (This World), Shmuel Tamir (1923–1987), Gruenwald's lawyer, turned the proceedings into a public trial of not only Kasztner but also the entire Mapai

Zionist leadership for its failure to rescue Europe's Jews. The two-year trial, which resulted in Gruenwald's acquittal and the assessment of judge Benjamin Halevi (1910–1996) that Kasztner had "sold his soul to the devil," provoked heated debate about collaboration, rescue, and Jewish solidarity. On the government's appeal, the Supreme Court, which proved reluctant to pass judgment on moral choices people made during the Holocaust, reversed most of the lower court's decision in January 1958. Kasztner, however, got no comfort from that action, since he had been assassinated ten months earlier (Segev 1993: 253–310).

On 23 May 1960, Ben-Gurion announced Eichmann's capture by Mossad, the Israeli security service, in Argentina. His trial in Jerusalem began on 2 April 1961. When it ended on 14 August, the court found Eichmann guilty of crimes against the Jewish people and humanity and sentenced him to death. He was executed by hanging on 1 June 1962. The trial's significance went beyond the judgment against Eichmann, for it featured the testimony of numerous survivor-witnesses who told the story of the destruction of European Jewry.

That story got worldwide attention as international journalists covered the proceedings, which were held in a public venue, broadcast live by radio, and depicted at home and abroad in televised reports and cinema news reels. In Israel, a kind of national catharsis ensued as people avidly followed the trial, which in unprecedented ways put the Holocaust in the forefront of Israeli public discourse. Never before in Israel had survivor testimony been voiced so publicly, let alone broadcast to the nation on such a large scale. The trial helped to give the Holocaust a human face. It led to the survivors' receiving an iconic place in Israeli conscious-ness and proved especially important for Israeli young people who had no first-hand knowledge of the Holocaust.

Acknowledging these immediate outcomes, historians nonetheless debate the impact of the Eichmann trial on Israeli society. The trial often has been seen as a turning point in Israel's coming to terms with the Holocaust, a watershed between a time when the Holocaust was repressed and survivors estranged and a period in which Holocaust survivors not only were accepted fully but also placed, along with the Holocaust itself, at the center of Israeli consciousness (Weitz 1996; Shapira 1998). More recently, some scholars have questioned this analysis and stressed the continuity between pre- and post-trial time frames. In this perspective, the Eich-mann trial was a part—a climactic part to be sure—of an ongoing process of remembrance, which centrally involved survivors in preparing the trial, locating witnesses, and giving testimony (Yablonka 2004). Enlisting witnesses to tell the story of the Holocaust was survivor-driven and based on work survivors had done in preceding years (Cohen in Davies and Szejnmann 2007: 139–49). The public's receptiveness to the survivor testimonies and the trial's impact did not come out of the blue but depended on the fact that the Holocaust was already omnipresent in the State of Israel.

HOW TO REMEMBER?

When confirmation of the systematic extermination of European Jewry reached the Yishuv in November 1942, the Chief Rabbinate set the 10th of the Jewish month of Tevet as a day of mourning. In Jewish tradition, this day of fasting, which marks the fall of Jerusalem to the Babylonians in 586 BCE, includes recitation of the Kaddish, the Jewish prayer for the dead, for those whose place and date of death are unknown. Later, 19 April, the date of the outbreak of the Warsaw ghetto uprising in 1943, appealed to many Israelis, especially in secular and socialist circles, as an appropriate commemoration date. The need to remember and commemorate the fate of Europe's Jews was acknowledged early and never in doubt, but questions about the best ways of doing so were significant and contentious (Ofer 2000).

In 1951, a legislative initiative by left-wing Zionist politicians to set 19 April as the official Holocaust remembrance day brought about the establishment of a Knesset committee aimed at reaching an agreed date for the commemoration. Heading the committee was Rabbi Mordechai Nurok (1879–1962), a survivor who lost his family in the Holocaust and a leader of the Knesset's religious faction. After much deliberation, the compromise date of the 27th of the Jewish month of Nisan was accepted. That date is close to the anniversary of the beginning of the Warsaw ghetto uprising, but it also took religious and educational considerations into account. On 12 April 1951, the Knesset set this date as the *Yom Hazicaron la-Shoah Ve-Mered Hagetaot* (Holocaust and Ghetto Revolt Memorial Day). Later on, in 1953, the day was renamed *Yom Hazicaron la-Shoah Ve-Hagvurah* (Holocaust and Heroism Memorial Day), thus making the title more inclusive. Israeli Independence Day is celebrated on the 5th of the Jewish month of Iyyar, a date corresponding to 14 May 1948, the day when Israeli statehood was proclaimed, and that date falls shortly after the commemoration day. Although the proximity of the dates arose by accident, it has come to suggest that from ruin and resistance Jewish life has risen to renewed vitality in Israel.

At first, the Knesset set no mandatory events or restrictions for Yom Hashoah, and ceremonies took place in various venues, often as an occasion for speeches by the Israeli left, until a campaign by Holocaust survivors persuaded the Knesset in 1959 to require Holocaust ceremonies and appropriate cultural events in public institutions and schools. The protocol for the evening of Yom Hashoah entails that Israel's president and prime minister attend ceremonies at Yad Vashem, accompanied by a military honor guard, indicating Israel's capacity and intention to resist repetition of the Holocaust. No specific form of remembrance is required for ceremonies in schools and community centers, where cultural, religious, and even musical trends are controlling. Throughout Israel on Yom Hashoah, however, people pause at an appointed time for two minutes of respectful silence while sirens wail.

Early discussion about how the murdered Jews of Europe ought to be remembered included places as well as times. For example, in September 1942, Mordechai Shenhabi (1900–1983), a fervent left-oriented Zionist, offered a proposal for a massive monumental complex with two major features: a Hall of Memory for the murdered Jews and a Hall of Heroism dedicated to Jews who fought the Germans in the Allied armies and in the resistance. He called the complex *Yad Vashem* (a monument and a name), which he took from a biblical text, Isaiah 56:5, "I will give, in my house and within my walls, a monument and a name . . ." Infused by a view of the Yishuv as the center of world Jewry and thus of commemoration of the murdered Jews, Shenhabi's project was to be financed by donations from Jews who wanted to memorialize lost relatives.

Despite its Zionist underpinning, Shenhabi's plan did not win the instant support of the Yishuv's leaders and institutions. Available and prospective funds were earmarked for Jewish settlement projects in Palestine, attempts to rescue European Jews, and assistance for survivors of the Nazi onslaught. Commemoration projects seemed to be an unaffordable luxury, and Shenhabi's plan to finance commemoration by voluntary giving left the trustees of Zionist funds skeptical. Nor was opposition limited to economic considerations. Critics argued that the monumental character of Shenhabi's project was inspired more by Soviet architecture and ideology than by Jewish tradition, which commemorates the dead in memorial books and by "good deeds" of education and welfare.

In 1946, after long deliberation and numerous design changes, the National Council of the Yishuv and the Zionist Congress approved Shenhabi's project (Brog in Laqueur 2001: 697–701; Brog 2002). But approval did not ensure the building of Yad Vashem. More pressing postwar needs took priority. An important turn took place, however, when Zorach Warhaftig (1906–2002), a Lithuanian survivor and eventually a prominent Israeli political leader, joined the Yad Vashem directorate in 1946 and pushed successfully for an emphasis on documentation and research. This orientation proved to be immensely important, but it created enormous problems as well. The key documents were in faraway Europe; so were most of the survivors. Especially in Germany and Poland, Jewish historical commissions were already collecting documents, interviewing survivors, and publishing books and journals (Cohen in Dieter and Inge 2005: 290–300; Jockusch 2007).

If Yad Vashem's hopes to be the central site of Jewish Holocaust commemoration were not to be cut short, decisive steps had to be taken. Thus, the Yad Vashem directorate, prompted by Shenhabi, decided to hold an international Holocaust research conference, a plan made more urgent by news that a similar conference was being organized in Paris. With 150 participants representing European historical commissions and many Yishuv institutions, the "International Conference on the Holocaust and Martyrdom in Our Time" convened in Jerusalem in the summer of 1947. This conference, the first major forum for reports on Holocaust documentation and lectures on Holocaust research, concentrated on diverse issues, ranging from research methodology to questions about ideology and ethics. Even more importantly, the conference signaled Yad Vashem's importance in Holocaust research, particularly when the cooperation offered by many historical commissions included agreement to send their document collections to the Israeli institution. But ensuing events—Israel's war of independence in 1948 and the immigration of Jews from European DP camps and North Africa—stalled the momentum. By 1951, Yad Vashem almost had closed.

While Yad Vashem faltered, another Israeli institution commemorating the Holocaust was rising. Founded in 1949 and dedicated to the memory of Yitzhak Katzenelson (1886–1944), the Jewish poet who had lived in the Warsaw ghetto before he was murdered at Auschwitz, the Ghetto Fighters' House, established by survivors of the Warsaw ghetto uprising, was not only the centerpiece of Kibbutz Lohamei Hageta'ot but also the first museum devoted to the Holocaust. During the 1950s, the Ghetto Fighters' House, which early in the decade had opened an exhibition and assembled an archive, stepped ahead of Yad Vashem. Focusing on education as well as commemoration, its museum was inaugurated in 1955, two years before Yad Vashem opened its first building.

Although outwardly a monolithic, left-Zionist institution, the Ghetto Fighters' House faced controversy. Some of the founders wanted to feature the work of the Zionist *Hechalutz* (pioneer) movement whose members resisted the Germans. The House, as these proponents called it, should honor armed Jewish resistance. Others argued that the focus ought to be on the murdered Jewish people, their prewar lives and culture, and on the Jewish masses' fortitude against German oppression. They took inspiration from Katzenelson, who had devoted his writing during the Holocaust to "my people." In retrospect, the history of the Ghetto Fighters' House reflects the co-existence of both perspectives. Increasingly, armed resistance in ghetto revolts and partisan activities is seen as but one manifestation of Jewish resistance, standing side by side with other forms of resistance: moral, cultural, and social.

THE "NEW" YAD VASHEM

In 1953, the Knesset passed the "Law of Remembrance of Holocaust and Heroism, Yad Vashem," which established Yad Vashem as Israel's national Holocaust commemoration authority and detailed its mission. Contrary to conventional wisdom about the centrality of Jewish armed resistance in Israel's Holocaust narrative, the law used an inclusive definition of resistance and heroism. Rebuffing calls by the leftist parties to concentrate on the armed resistance of ghetto fighters and partisans, the Knesset's majority put spiritual resistance, rescue, and other nonviolent modes of behavior before armed resistance in the list of heroic activities to be commemorated (Stauber 2007: 66–77).

Behind the scenes, Shenhabi figured prominently in shaping this legislation. While the "old" Yad Vashem lost momentum, he worked to obtain posthumous Israeli citizenship for the murdered Jews of Europe, recruiting Ben-Zion Dinur (1884–1973), an eminent Zionist historian, to help him. In 1951, Dinur became minister of education and thus became well placed to lend crucial support when Shenhabi seized the opportunity provided by German reparations, some of which were earmarked for commemoration, and reintroduced his concept that Yad Vashem ought to be the central Israeli and Jewish memorial to the Holocaust. Amidst rising criticism about the inaction of Ben-Gurion's government regarding Holocaust commemoration, the "Law of Remembrance" went through the Knesset. Yad Vashem was established with Dinur at its head. Half of Yad Vashem's funding came from the international Conference of Jewish Material Claims against Germany. The State of Israel and other Jewish sources provided the rest. As the major underwriter, the Claims Conference maintained influence over Yad Vashem's plans and policies, which reflected not only Israeli memorial culture but also sensibilities and values of diaspora Jews and the American Jewish community in particular.

Dinur staffed Yad Vashem with his students from the Hebrew University and survivor historians who had worked in the Jewish historical commissions in liberated Europe. The interests and approaches of these groups collided. Dinur took Yad Vashem's responsibility to be research about the history of the Jews in Europe and treated the Holocaust as but the concluding chapter of that long story. His approach entailed studying each European Jewish community from its inception to its destruction. To encourage a new generation of historians to carry out this work, Dinur founded a joint research institute with the Hebrew University (Cohen 2005). A majority of its scholars there wrote on modern Jewish history, not on the Holocaust or the history of European Jewish communities. That outcome produced criticism, inflamed by the fact that the new institute's funding came from Yad Vashem.

Meanwhile, the survivor historians and their allies favored focusing on the Holocaust itself. They wanted research that concentrated on German policies and actions, Jewish life and choices, and Jewish resistance. Research, they argued, must deal with the "painful questions" raised by the Holocaust, including issues about human behavior, Jewish solidarity, society under stress, and the breakdown of western culture. The lack of Holocaust commemoration created more contention between Dinur and the survivor historians. Yad Vashem's first building housed its administration, library, and archive but provided no place for commemoration, a situation remedied in part by the opening of the Hall of Memory in 1961.

By 1957, the tension had reached a boiling point. The survivor historians—some of them ousted, others marginalized within Yad Vashem—went public, indicting the Yad Vashem directorate for no commemoration, no understanding of the special character and role of Holocaust research, no publication of Holocaust-related material, and, above all, the sidelining of the survivor historians who were the experts on the Holocaust (Cohen in Dieter and Inge 2005: 290–300; Cohen 2005; Cohen in Davies and Szejnmann 2007: 139–49). A commission of inquiry established by the Yad Vashem Council investigated the complaints. As a result, Dinur resigned, his students departed with him, and a new administration put Holocaust commemoration, public education, and relations with survivors at the top of Yad Vashem's agenda.

The upheaval sidetracked Holocaust research at Yad Vashem, but that work, along with teaching about the Holocaust, expanded at Hebrew University in Jerusalem and at Bar Ilan University, which in 1959 created Israel's first chair for Holocaust studies, an initiative funded by survivors. By the 1970s, all Israeli universities had courses and graduate students focused on Holocaust studies. Emphasis on research returned to Yad Vashem in 1993, when cooperation with Hebrew University led to the establishment of the International Institute for Holocaust Research, headed by Yehuda Bauer (b. 1926) and Israel Gutman (b. 1923), a survivor of the Warsaw ghetto uprising.

HOLOCAUST EDUCATION

Israel's educational structure developed step by step after the establishment of the state. Curricula were formulated very slowly. Only in 1953 was the history curriculum introduced, and it stipulated a mere two hours of teaching on the Holocaust, focused on eighth-graders (12-year-olds). The Israeli school system had no clear policy on the content and objectives of Holocaust education; teachers and educators were left to work on their own.

Eichmann's capture and the recognition that many young Israelis presumed that European Jews had been docile in the face of the Nazi onslaught increased awareness in the Ministry of Education and in wider circles that Holocaust education should be advanced. In November 1960, the Ministry established a public commission for the introduction of Holocaust teaching in the school system. Teaching materials were commissioned and written by veteran ghetto fighters and partisans, who had attained an iconic place in the Israeli pantheon. Centered on Jewish actions during the Holocaust, the books emphasized armed resistance, but also dealt with other forms of resistance (Cohen 2003). But no standard curriculum and textbooks were mandated, and teaching about the Holocaust still was left to the teachers' judgment and ability.

In April 1979, teaching about the Holocaust became mandatory throughout the Israeli school system. Since 1983, Israeli students have not been able to graduate from high school without passing an examination on the Holocaust. Three factors account for the intensification of Holocaust teaching requirements. First, anxiety grew in Israeli educational and cultural circles that the passage of time would diminish awareness of the Holocaust among young Israelis. Second, time's passage also facilitated a more balanced and nuanced educational approach. Third, by the 1980s, Israeli academic teaching and research about the Holocaust were becoming highly developed and thus were able to provide the materials that Holocaust teaching required.

Holocaust education in Israel extends well beyond school books and classrooms. Trips to Yad Vashem, the Ghetto Fighters' House, and other Holocaust-related institutions regularly take place. Young people participate in Yom Hashoah observances. Religious schools have special ceremonies and educational programs that focus on the Holocaust, especially around the 10th of Tevet. Among the more important components of Holocaust education in Israel are students' trips to Poland. During these trips, students explore prewar Jewish life and visit sites such as Auschwitz and Majdanek. Each tour is accompanied by one or more Holocaust survivors. The Israeli Ministry of Education trains guides, organizes multi-school trips the year round, and supervises the educational and psychological preparation of the students (Feldman 2008). The trips, however, are not required in school curricula, and students pay their own expenses. Thousands of Israeli students aged 16–17 make these pilgrimages. Evaluations indicate that the trips enhance the students' Jewish and Zionist identity.

Since the early 1990s, similar travel to Poland supplements the Holocaust education program, including seminars at Yad Vashem, provided by and for the Israeli Defense Forces (IDF). Accompanied by historians and survivors, military officers visit Holocaust sites and hold commemoration ceremonies in uniform. Such programs link Holocaust education and Israeli security, but whether the travel to Poland focuses on students or soldiers, it generates controversy. Proponents underscore the educational importance of the trips and the Jewish tradition of paying respect to the dead—in this case the murdered Jews of Europe. Opponents claim that the tours encourage overly particularistic and nationalistic worldviews. Especially in the case of students, critics add that the trips create psychological stress and encourage counterproductive identity formation by dwelling on the negativity of the Jew-as-victim rather than on the positive values and traditions of Jewish culture.

THE HOLOCAUST AND ISRAELI SECURITY

From its birth, the State of Israel has been embattled. During its first sixty years, Israel fought six wars with hostile neighboring states that often denied Israel's right to exist and clamored for its extinction. Terrorist attacks, many of them part of the ongoing Palestinian–Israeli conflict, have targeted Israel's civilian population. In multiple and complex ways, the Holocaust is embedded in these threats and Israel's responses to them.

Reflecting states of mind prevalent in the Israeli rank and file, Ben-Gurion's early appeals for arms from the French and Americans were accompanied by reminders that an attempt to exterminate the Jewish people had taken place not long ago and that military support was needed to prevent that intention from being enacted again. Ben-Gurion's effort to ensure Israel's military capacity reflected Israeli conviction, also influenced by the Holocaust, that the Jewish state would have to be prepared to stand alone—the world's powers would not go to war to safeguard Israel's existence. By no means have contemporary events put these Holocaust-related concerns to rest in Israel.

Israel's need for adequate self-defense drove Ben-Gurion's decision in the early 1950s to develop a nuclear capability, a crucial initiative for a small country whose economy was strained to the limit by mass immigration. Israel's nuclear development, moreover, had to be hidden from friend and foe alike. Ben-Gurion was not alone in linking the Holocaust to nuclear strategy. The Holocaust appears repeatedly in the writings of the politicians and scientists as they justify their support of Israel's nuclear project (Aronson 1992: 18–48; Cohen 1998).

In 1967, six Arab armies under unified command threatened Israel, whose Red Sea port at Eilat was blockaded by the Egyptians. Public morale plunged as Israelis anticipated a second Holocaust. Mass gravesites were prepared and consecrated, evacuation plans for children were under way, and requests for Red Cross surgeons were sent (Segev 1993: 387–93). The outcome of the Six Day War, however, was very different. The IDF routed the Arab armies, captured land, and reunified the city of Jerusalem. But only to some extent did the victory calm Israelis' Holocaust-related anxiety, which intensified when the Yom Kippur War broke out in 1973, and the coordinated surprise attacks by Egyptian and Syrian armies threatened Israel's existence. Although the IDF was again victorious, Israeli self-confidence was shaken. Photos of Israeli soldiers, their weapons lost and hands raised in surrender, recalled the Holocaust. An intriguing side effect of the recollection was that the stereotype that European Jews went "as lambs to the slaughter" was called into question as a more informed and realistic attitude emerged regarding the choices and actions of Jews during the Holocaust.

Memory of the Holocaust also influenced Israeli decision making during Menachem Begin's tenure as prime minister (1977–83). He insisted that he would "not be the man in whose time there will be a second Holocaust" (MBHC 2003: 31–2). Therefore, when the Iraqi dictator Saddam Hussein (1937–2006) tried to develop a nuclear capability, Begin sent the Israeli air force to destroy Iraq's nuclear reactor. The successful strike on 7 June 1981 incurred criticism at home and abroad, but Begin stood his ground, recalling the fate of Jewish children murdered in the

Holocaust: "We must protect our nation," he said, "a million and a half of whose children were murdered by the Nazis in gas chambers" (Segev 1993: 398).

The 1991 Gulf War set off other Holocaust reverberations, when justifiable fear of gas attacks forced Israeli civilians to don gas masks and take shelter in protected rooms as Iraqi missiles targeted Israel. The fact that the Iraqi gas stockpiles were of German origin made Holocaust-associated anxiety even stronger.

In the twenty-first century, the Holocaust continues to loom large in Israeli politics and public discourse, reminding Israelis that some repetition of that catastrophe could take place. Current threats to Israel range from a possibly nuclear-armed Iran to terrorist organizations whose inflammatory rhetoric about the Palestinian–Israeli conflict contradictorily denies that the Holocaust happened while depicting Israelis as Nazis and Palestinians as their victims. Although Israeli opinion is divided about the severity of such threats and how to cope with them, Israeli society remains profoundly affected by the Holocaust. Even as Israel's population of Holocaust survivors diminishes with each year of the twenty-first century, the Holocaust remains and will continue to be prominent in the state's politics and public discourse and in the private lives of Israel's people as well.

REFERENCES

ARONSON, S. (1992). *The Politics and Strategy on Nuclear Weapons in the Middle East: Opacity, Theory, and Reality, 1960–1991: An Israeli Perspective*. Albany, NY: State University of New York Press.

BAUER, Y. (1994). *Jews for Sale: Nazi–Jewish Negotiations 1933–1945*. New Haven, CT: Yale University Press.

——(2001). *Rethinking the Holocaust*. New Haven, CT: Yale University Press.

BEIT-ZVI, S. (1991). *Post-Ugandan Zionism On Trial: A Study of the Factors that Caused the Mistakes Made by the Zionist Movement during the Holocaust*. Tel Aviv: Zahala.

BRODSKY, J. and DELLAPERGOLA, S. (2005). *Health Problems and Socioeconomic Neediness Among Jewish Shoah Survivors in Israel*. Jerusalem: Myers-JDC-Brookdale Institute and the A. Harman Institute of Contemporary Jewry, The Hebrew University of Jerusalem.

BROG, M. (2002). "In Blessed Memory of a Dream: Mordechai Shenavi and Initial Holocaust Commemoration Ideas in Palestine 1942–1945." *Yad Vashem Studies* 30: 297–336.

COHEN, A. (1998). *Israel and the Bomb*. New York: Columbia University Press.

COHEN, B. (2003). "Holocaust Heroics: Ghetto Fighters and Partisans in Israeli Society and Historiography." *Journal of Political and Military Sociology* 31: 197–213.

——(2005). "The Birth Pangs of Holocaust Research in Israel." *Yad Vashem Studies* 33: 203–43.

DAVIES, M. and SZEJNMANN, C.-C. (eds.) (2007). *How the Holocaust Looks Now: International Perspectives*. New York: Palgrave Macmillan.

DIETER, J.-S. and INGE, W.-N. (eds.) (2005). *Beyond Camps and Forced Labour: Current International Research on Survivors of Nazi Persecution*. Osnabrück: Secolo Verlag.

DWORZECKI, M. (1956). "Holocaust Survivors in Israel – Research of Demographic and Biological Problems of Holocaust Survivors" (She'erit Hapleita Be'Israel – Mehkar ha'beayot ha'demographiot ve'ha' biologiot shell aliyat nitzolei ha'shoah). *Gesher* (year 2) 1: 83–114.

FELDMAN, J. (2008). *Above the Death Pits, Beneath the Flag: Youth Voyages to Poland and the Performance of Israeli National Identity.* New York: Berghahn Books.

FRILING, T. (2005). *Arrows in the Dark: David Ben-Gurion, the Yishuv Leadership, and Rescue Attempts during the Holocaust.* Madison, WI: University of Wisconsin Press.

GRODZINSKY, Y. (2004). *In the Shadow of the Holocaust: The Struggle between Jews and Zionists in the Aftermath of World War II.* Monroe, ME: Common Courage Press.

JOCKUSCH, L. (2007). "'Khurban Forshung': Jewish Historical Commissions in Europe 1945–1949." *Yearbook of the Simon Dubnow Institute* 6: 441–73.

LAQUEUR, W. (ed.) (2001). *The Holocaust Encyclopedia.* New Haven, CT: Yale University Press.

MBHC (MENACHEM BEGIN HERITAGE CENTER) (2003). "Israel's Strike against the Iraqi Nuclear Reactor 7 June, 1981." Jerusalem: MBHC.

MICHMAN, D. (2003). *Holocaust Historiography: A Jewish Perspective.* London: Vallentine Mitchell.

OFER, D. (1996). "Holocaust Survivors as Immigrants: The Case of Israel and the Cyprus Detainees." *Modern Judaism* 16/1: 1–23.

——(2000). "The Strength of Remembrance: Commemorating the Holocaust During the First Decade of Israel." *Jewish Social Studies* n.s. 6/2: 24–55.

PORAT, D. (1990). *The Blue and the Yellow Stars of David: The Zionist Leadership in Palestine and the Holocaust 1939–1945.* Cambridge, MA: Harvard University Press.

SAGI, N. (1986). *German Reparations: A History of the Negotiations.* New York: St. Martin's Press.

SEGEV, T. (1993). *The Seventh Million: The Israelis and the Holocaust.* New York: Hill and Wang.

SHAPIRA, A. (1998). "The Holocaust: Private Memories, Public Memory." *Jewish Social Studies* 4/2: 40–58.

STAUBER, R. (2007). *The Holocaust in Israeli Public Debate in the 1950s: Ideology and History.* London: Vallentine Mitchell.

TIM, A. (1997). *Jewish Claims against East Germany: Moral Obligations and Pragmatic Policy.* Budapest: Central European University Press.

WEITZ, Y. (1996). "The Holocaust on Trial: The Impact of the Kasztner and Eichmann Trials on Israeli Society." *Israel Studies* 1/2: 1–26.

YABLONKA, H. (1999). *Survivors of the Holocaust: Israel after the War.* London: Macmillan.

——(2003). "The Development of Holocaust Consciousness in Israel: The Nuremberg, Kapos, Kasztner, and Eichmann Trials." *Israel Studies* 8/3: 1–24.

——(2004). *The State of Israel vs. Adolf Eichmann.* New York: Schocken Books.

——(2008). Introduction to "My Homeland: Holocaust Survivors in Israel." Jerusalem: Yad Vashem, <http://www1.yadvashem.org/exhibitions/my_homeland/homepage.html>. Accessed 24 August 2009.

OTHER SUGGESTED READING

BANKIER, D. and MICHMAN, D. (eds.) (2009). *Holocaust Historiography in Context: Emergence, Challenges, Polemics and Achievements.* New York: Berghahn Books.

BAUMEL, J. (1997). *Kibbutz Buchenwald: Survivors and Pioneers*. New Brunswick, NJ: Rutgers University Press.

KENAN, O. (2003). *Between Memory and History: The Evolution of Israeli Historiography of the Holocaust, 1945–1961*. New York: Peter Lang.

OFER, D. (1990). *Escaping the Holocaust: Illegal Immigration to the Land of Israel, 1939–1944*. New York: Oxford University Press.

PENKOWER, M. (1994). *The Holocaust and Israel Reborn: From Catastrophe to Sovereignty*. Urbana, IL: University of Illinois Press.

PORAT, D. (2008). *Israeli Society, the Holocaust and Its Survivors*. London: Vallentine Mitchell.

YOUNG, J. (1993). *The Texture of Memory: Holocaust Memorials and Meaning*. New Haven, CT: Yale University Press.

CHAPTER 38

....

JEWISH CULTURE

....

JEFFREY SHANDLER

THE current prominence of the Holocaust in Jewish culture may seem self-evident
and straightforward. At the turn of the millennium, some surveys of Jews reported
that remembering the Holocaust was "the activity most important" for their sense
of self as Jews, surpassing their commitment to religious observance and support for
the State of Israel (American Jewish Committee 1998: 23). But the salience of the
Holocaust has not been a constant of postwar Jewish culture. Indeed, the place of
Holocaust remembrance in Jewish life since the end of World War II has been
variable and controversial. At different times, observers have voiced concern that the
subject has received either too little attention—especially in the early postwar
period, before the term "Holocaust" and its conceptualization as a discrete event
were widely familiar—or too much. In 1972, author Elie Wiesel (b. 1928) worried
that the Holocaust, "no longer taboo," was becoming discussed "sometimes too
freely"; he wondered whether so much public attention was imperiling remembrance precisely because the Holocaust was "doomed to remain in the limelight"
(Wiesel 1972). Others have questioned the implications of a salient Holocaust
remembrance for the quality of Jewish life, cautioning that more is known about
how Europe's Jews died during World War II than how they lived for centuries
beforehand.

Despite these concerns, Holocaust remembrance looms large across the geographic, political, and ideological spectra of Jewish cultural life and is often at the
forefront of the Jews' presence in the countries where they live. While some Jewish
forms of Holocaust remembrance are unprecedented, others relate to established
Jewish customs for remembering the past and responding to catastrophe. And as
extensive and prominent as Holocaust remembrance has become in Jewish life,

these efforts frequently provoke controversy and are sometimes dismissed as unseemly, if not impossible undertakings.

Jewish cultural engagements with the Holocaust are defined not only by the catastrophic events of World War II but also by more recent developments, ranging from international political transformations to the advent of new communications technologies. Notwithstanding their great diversity, Jewish cultural practices for recalling the Holocaust may be examined together as responses to circumstances that Jews believe demand new understandings of Jewishness and new means of realizing them.

New Demographics

As a consequence of the Nazi-led mass murder of European Jewry, many of the oldest and largest centers of Jewish culture, religious as well as secular, were destroyed or displaced. Along with millions of other civilians at the end of the war, Jewish survivors of the Holocaust relocated on a mass scale. Those who chose to remain in Europe seldom returned to their prewar homes, moving either to new urban centers in their countries of origin or to different countries altogether. The redrawn map of Europe and the establishment of new communist governments in the east had a profound impact on Jewish life. Of greatest consequence was the suppression of Jewish public culture in the Soviet Union, home to the largest number of Jews in postwar Europe; Soviet policies also affected Jews living in the countries it dominated. Several hundred thousand Jewish Holocaust survivors resettled beyond Europe's borders, mostly in the United States and Palestine/Israel, with significant migration to Canada, Argentina, and Australia as well. In the wake of other postwar political upheavals, Jews who had been living for centuries in Arab lands across northern Africa and the Middle East began immigrating in large numbers to Israel and western Europe.

Accompanying these geographic shifts were major changes in Jewish cultural life. During the early postwar years, the United States suddenly became home to the largest and most stable Jewish population in the world. For Jews, America went from being a cultural frontier to a major center (and, consequently, American Jewry has played a prominent role in Jewish remembrance of the Holocaust beyond the nation's borders). However, this transformation by default entailed considerable anxiousness. In particular, early postwar American Jewish culture bore the imprint of the sometimes virulent antisemitic rhetoric and policies prevalent before the war and the constraints imposed by the discourses of religiosity and loyalty to America of the early Cold War era. Concurrently, the State of Israel emerged as a new, if uncertain, center of Jewish life, defined by a largely secular and socialist Zionist political majority.

Jewish religious life witnessed marked changes during the early postwar period as the survivors of ultra-Orthodox rabbinic and Hasidic communities moved from generations-old bases in towns large and small across eastern Europe to major urban centers in North America, western Europe, Israel, and Australia. At the same time, Reform and Conservative Judaism experienced rapid institutional expansion in North America, while Orthodoxy became the officially recognized form of Judaism in the new State of Israel. The postwar period witnessed major shifts in language use by Jews as well, notably the decline of Yiddish, especially among secular Jews, the concomitant expansion of English as an international Jewish vernacular, and the consolidation of modern Hebrew as the state-mandated language in Israel. Such sweeping demographic developments form the basis for Jews' cultural engagements with the Holocaust, which entailed new narratives, practices, authorities, and discourses.

New Narratives and Practices

Central to Jewish responses to the Holocaust are new narratives, in which Jews have sought to situate the genocide of European Jewry in changing understandings of their history, religiosity, political convictions, and ethical principles. These narratives appear in print (as histories, memoirs, works of journalism, literature, and philosophy), in performances (spoken and musical; live, recorded, and broadcast), and in works of visual art and display. Some Holocaust narratives are produced by individuals, to be shared privately with family and close acquaintances; others are the work of numerous collaborators and presented on a grand scale to national or international audiences. Diverse as these narratives are in agency, form, and substance, they are all definitional works. Indeed, their creation, presentation, and discussion are all part of a larger cultural project of redefining a Jewish collective sense of self—assessing its past, remote as well as recent, and envisioning its future—in the wake of an event widely understood as demanding a new accounting.

The boundaries of Jewish Holocaust narratives vary considerably. They range from the stories of individual survivors or victims to large-scale histories and from accounts focusing on particular phases of Jewish persecution (e.g., dealing exclusively with mass murder at death camps) to those whose temporal boundaries extend beyond the Nazi era and World War II. Some of these narratives begin as far back as medieval Christian antisemitism; others conclude after the end of the war with accounts of restoration or retribution or in unresolved anxiety over further persecution.

Even though Jewish narratives typically characterize the Holocaust as a watershed in Jewish history, they conceptualize the event's place in this chronology differently: as an epoch-making event, comparable to the destruction of the ancient Temple in Jerusalem in 70 CE (Greenberg 1980); as "a novelty in extremis, severed from all normative connections to historical precedent and causality" (Cohen 1981: 12); or as the latest in a series of persecutions. Thus, Yiddish speakers often refer to the Holocaust as *der letster khurbn* (the last destruction), positioning it at the end of a chronology of persecutions of Jews reaching back to ancient times.

These narratives generally reflect their creators' orientation with regard to ideology or epistemology. Jewish theologians, for example, typically position the Holocaust in narratives that interrogate, redefine, or affirm their faith in God. Some Orthodox Jews grappling with the question of theodicy have offered Holocaust narratives in which God temporarily withdrew from Europe's Jews, in response to their errant modernism and secularism (Bauer 2001: 186–212). Sociologist Samuel Heilman argues that "for the Orthodox . . . the Holocaust not only set their future direction but also ex post facto reconsecrated and even more importantly reframed and redefined their past" (2006: 15).

In political narratives, many Jews have embraced what Jacob Neusner terms a "generative myth" beginning "in death, 'the Holocaust,' and completed by resurrection or rebirth, '[the State of] Israel.'" (1981: 1). This narrative rubric has evolved with the dynamics of Israel's political history. In particular, the 1967 war that Israel fought against Egypt, Jordan, and Syria galvanized diaspora Jewry's support for Israel as a response to both the precedent of the Holocaust and the fear of its recurrence (Lederhandler 2000). Similarly, Jews in the west often explained their activism on behalf of Soviet Jewry as acting on the admonition to prevent another Holocaust (Feingold 2007). In Israel, Holocaust narratives variously valorize or critique Zionist ideas and practices in relation to the dynamics of Israeli politics (Segev 1993; Zerubavel 1995). And while some Jews situate the Holocaust in narratives that strengthen a sense of Jewish exceptionalism, others position Holocaust remembrance in national or universal narratives. Thus, Michael Berenbaum, as director of the research institute of the United States Holocaust Memorial Museum in Washington, DC, asserted that this museum is an "American institution," which relates a chapter of history that "cuts against the grain of the American ethos" and is "a violation of every essential American value" (1993: 2).

Diverse as they are, all these narratives center on Jewish experiences, in contrast to other Holocaust narratives that focus on its perpetrators, the political or military history of modern Europe, or some other organizing principle. Jewish Holocaust narratives typically situate Jews at their center, not only as protagonists (exemplified by the title of Lucy Dawidowicz's 1975 history of the Holocaust, *The War Against the Jews*), but also as the primary storytellers. Beyond demonstrating a commitment to memorializing the dead, coming to terms with the consequences of this great loss, and offering cautionary lessons for the future, this assertion of narrative authority over the Holocaust may also be considered a means of redressing the profound loss of political power and social legitimacy that Jews experienced during the war.

This variety of Jewish Holocaust narratives has occasionally engendered controversy within the Jewish community. Early examples include Bruno Bettelheim's *The Informed Heart* (1960) and Hannah Arendt's *Eichmann in Jerusalem* (1963), both of which disparaged many European Jews' reactions to Nazi persecution. The latter work provoked an especially heated and prolonged debate among Jewish intellectual and community leaders (Robinson 1965). The proliferation of Jewish narratives centered on the Holocaust has also prompted counter-narratives of modern Jewish history, which caution against reading prewar Jewish experience retrospectively through "lenses tinted by nostalgia or horror" as a consequence of the Holocaust (Shandler 2002: xii) or seek to offer a narrative of modern European Jewry dedicated "to life, not to death" (Eliach 1998: 4).

Further enriching the diversity of these new Jewish narratives is their realization in a wide array of new cultural institutions and practices. Some of these efforts are related to familiar Jewish cultural endeavors, both religious (e.g., incorporating Holocaust remembrance into the Passover seder or communal worship on Tisha b'Av, the traditional day for mourning the destruction of the Temples in ancient Jerusalem) and secular (e.g., modernist Yiddish or Hebrew poetry reflecting on the Holocaust). Other practices engage general public culture or intergroup endeavors (e.g., national broadcasts or public memorials convened by governments or interfaith groups, in which Jews participate), and yet others are unprecedented and autonomous undertakings (e.g., the creation of Holocaust-themed travel or the erection of Holocaust museums). As they draw upon the familiar and the innovative, the religious and the secular, the specifically Jewish and the general, these practices of remembrance entail a complex interrelation of theology, politics, ethics, aesthetics, and citizenship.

Contrary to a widespread perception of Jewish silence in response to the Holocaust in the early postwar years (Mintz 2001), some of these practices date from the war years and their immediate aftermath (Diner 2009). Many of these early efforts were internal to local Jewish communities and, more specifically, confined to Holocaust survivors and refugees who had fled Europe shortly before the war. Survivors' early responses are exemplified by hundreds of *Yizker Bikher*, collaboratively produced memorial books, which began to appear in the early postwar decades. These volumes documented prewar Jewish life and its wartime destruction in individual communities, mostly small towns, across eastern Europe (Kugelmass and Boyarin 1983). Typically self-published and written largely in Yiddish and Hebrew, these works were produced for an audience consisting largely of their creators. The subsequent expansion of Holocaust memory practices in the Americas, Europe, Israel, and elsewhere reflects a growth in Jewish communal desires for more public engagement with the subject (and the willingness of governments to endorse this remembrance).

As a new component of Jewish culture, Holocaust remembrance has engendered new occasions, literacies, sites, and activities. Public rites of Holocaust remembrance have established new dates on the Jewish calendar (the anniversaries of *Kristallnacht* on 9–10 November and the start of the Warsaw ghetto uprising on 19 April, as well as the Israeli state holiday of Yom Hashoah), engendered a new canon of key texts (e.g., "The Butterfly," a poem written in Terezin concentration camp in 1942 by young Pavel Friedmann [1921–1944]), and new ritual protocols, notably lighting six candles in memory of the Holocaust's six million Jewish victims (Littell and Gutman 1996). Holocaust education has assumed a significant place in the lives of many young Jews, sometimes configured as a communal rite of passage. This activity is exemplified by group travel to sites associated with the Holocaust in Europe, such as the March of the Living, instituted in 1988 (Sheramy 2006). The Holocaust also figures prominently in Jewish fundraising and philanthropic activities, invoked not only for causes directly related to its remembrance but also to support Jewish scholarship, promote political advocacy, and combat antisemitism. Jonathan Woocher argues that, in response to the Holocaust, a new Jewish civil religion centered on philanthropy has flourished in America (and, one might add, elsewhere in the diaspora), in which a "commitment to Jewish survival" assumes "highest priority," superseding religious concerns and driving political and pedagogical agendas (1986: 73).

Across this wide array of undertakings, certain commonalities arise. For example, many of these memorial practices entail some form of collecting, ranging from Hasidic lore related to the Holocaust to recipes recalled by women interned in a concentration camp (Eliach 1982; de Silva 1996). These collecting efforts respond to desires to document Jews' prewar and wartime experiences, to demonstrate the enormity of the Holocaust, and to repair a broken Jewish past. Collections that manifest the vastness of the destruction of European Jewry include rosters of victims' names—printed in memorial publications, etched into monuments, recited at commemorative rituals—and the massing of items (such as shoes, suitcases, and other possessions confiscated from prisoners in concentration and death camps) in Holocaust museum displays. Exemplary of efforts to repair wartime destruction are projects to collect photographs of prewar Jewish life (e.g., Majewski and Bikont 1996) and "pastiche" monuments erected in Poland, formed from the fragments of vandalized Jewish tombstones (Young 1993: 185–208). While centered on the Jewish community, these undertakings often involve non-Jewish participation, thereby providing opportunities for forging new relationships between Jews and others.

An especially noteworthy common feature of Jewish practices of Holocaust remembrance is the attention Jews regularly pay to the challenges of mediating this subject across the distances of time, place, and experience, as reflected in their scrutiny of books, films, broadcasts, exhibitions, and other works engaging the Holocaust. The choice of medium and genre for these works not only informs how their creators articulate their narratives but also shapes audiences' engagement with them. In some instances, this choice has proved so provocative that it drives much of the public discussion of the works in question, as in the case of Roberto Begnini's film comedy *La Vita è Bella* (1997) or Art Spiegelman's comic book *Maus* (1997). High profile films dealing with the Holocaust, such as Claude Lanzmann's *Shoah* (1985) and Steven Spielberg's *Schindler's List* (1993), have engendered extensive discussion following their presentation to the public (Loshitzky 1997; Liebman 2007). Sometimes these works have been preceded by extensive debate, as was the case with the 1978 television miniseries *Holocaust: The Story of the Family Weiss* (Shandler 1999: 155–78) or the exhibition *Mirroring Evil: Nazi Imagery/Recent Art*, presented in 2002 at the Jewish Museum in New York (Kleeblatt 2002).

This ongoing scrutiny should be regarded as a Jewish practice of Holocaust remembrance in its own right, in which debating the merits of these works prompts the discussion of larger issues, including the interrelation of historical actuality and remembrance and the aesthetic possibilities and ethical implications of Holocaust culture, among others. Indeed, for decades the scholarly discussion of Holocaust representation has centered on the notion that its aesthetics are inherently problematic (Hornstein et al. 2003).

Both Jewish community leaders and scholars have addressed Holocaust remembrance and its impact on Jewish life as a topic unto itself. They sometimes do so with considerable opprobrium, as in the cases of historian Peter Novick (1999) and political scientist Norman G. Finkelstein (2000), both of whom fault what the latter terms "the Holocaust industry" as an "exploitation of Jewish suffering." Some recent fiction has also taken to task Jewish Holocaust memory practices, including museums (Hasak-Lowy 2005), tourism (Prose 1997), pedagogy (Bezmozgis 2004), and the videotaping of survivor testimonies (Bukiet 1995). These and similar works demand a rethinking of how Jews, especially in established community institutions, invest in Holocaust remembrance, question its intellectual, moral, political, and aesthetic assumptions, and implicitly call for more thoughtful engagement with the subject.

Complementing this attention to the challenges of mediating the Holocaust is a growing attraction to Jewish practices of Holocaust remembrance that entail some form of embodied experience. In addition to travel to the grounds of Nazi concentration camps and death camps or other European sites related to the Holocaust—especially organized visits that retrace the steps of victims of Nazi persecution as an act of mourning or retribution—are practices of embodiment that can be enacted anywhere. These include a proliferation of pedagogical simulations of Jews' stigmatization, hiding, hunger, and so on, despite the controversy these practices often provoke (Schweber 2003), or the wearing of yellow stars or simulated tattoos on days of Holocaust remembrance. Monuments and museums regularly situate visitors in environments that render Holocaust remembrance a kinetic experience. Perhaps the most elaborately conceived of these is Berlin's

Jewish Museum, designed by Daniel Libeskind (b. 1946), which materializes the Holocaust and the affect of its remembrance through twisting, narrow corridors, slanting, uneven walls, sloping floors, and empty spaces that visitors can see but cannot enter (*Jewish Museum, Berlin* 1999).

NEW AUTHORITIES

Within Jewish culture generally, Holocaust memory practices have engendered their own authoritative individuals and institutions. Over the past half century, Jewish communities in North America, Israel, and Europe have invested extensive resources in establishing institutions and supporting scholars devoted to the documentation and analysis of the Holocaust and its remembrance. These include research centers at state-supported institutions (e.g., the International School for Holocaust Studies, Yad Vashem, Jerusalem; the Center for Advanced Holocaust Studies, United States Holocaust Memorial Museum, Washington, DC) as well as privately established initiatives (the Simon Wiesenthal Center, Los Angeles; the Ghetto Fighters' House and Jewish Resistance Heritage Museum and Documentation Center, located on a kibbutz in the Western Galilee). Holocaust scholarship and remembrance have also become important tasks for Jewish advocacy and academic institutions that were established before the war, such as the Anti-Defamation League, founded in New York in 1913; the YIVO Institute for Jewish Research, founded in Vilna in 1925 and located since the 1940s in New York; and the Jewish Historical Institute, founded in 1928 (as the Institute of Judaic Studies) in Warsaw. In addition to gathering and archiving documentation, these institutions typically employ multiple means of addressing the public and establishing their authority through publications, films, exhibitions, websites, presentations, public relations campaigns, and educational programs.

At the same time, an array of individuals, including writers, artists, musicians, architects, filmmakers, and others producing works of Holocaust remembrance have assumed larger authoritative stature as keepers of Holocaust memory. An early example of this phenomenon is Otto Frank (1889–1980), who edited and arranged the publication of his murdered daughter Anne's wartime diary in 1947. Following its extraordinary reception—especially after being translated from Dutch into German, French, and English, and its highly popular dramatization (Goodrich and Hackett 1956)—Otto Frank achieved renown as a voice for Holocaust remembrance committed to a universalist vision of human rights activism by establishing the Anne Frank-Fonds in Basel, Switzerland, in 1963. Similarly, after the success of *Schindler's List*, Spielberg initiated a major project in 1994, the

Survivors of the Shoah Visual History Foundation, to film Holocaust survivor testimonies, and he established the Righteous Persons Foundation to support, in part, other efforts by Jews to combat intolerance.

Most telling is the authority of Holocaust survivors, which achieved a distinctive primacy by the turn of the millennium. Their dynamic stature is largely a consequence of the fact that most survivors were young adults at the end of World War II. As has sometimes been the case earlier in Jewish history (e.g., the advent of Hasidism in the mid-eighteenth century and of Zionism at the turn of the twentieth century), a group quickly moved from being outside the Jewish establishment to occupying positions of considerable communal influence. Although members of the survivor cohort were among the first to produce memoirs, memorials, and other works of Holocaust remembrance, they were seldom recognized as figures of authority by the larger Jewish community or the general population until decades after the end of the war. Indeed, to the extent that attention was paid to this community in the early postwar years—when they were referred to as "displaced persons," "Europe's homeless" or, in Yiddish, *sheyres-hapleyte* (the saved remnant)—they were more likely to be pathologized as victims of persecution in need of rehabilitation. As their cohort has aged, however, Holocaust survivors have attained greater respect, as is typical of elders generally and conforms to the rising stature of their peers who fought in World War II. Exemplifying this change in Holocaust survivors' public profile is the initiation of a series of projects to create film or video records of survivor testimonies, beginning in the late 1970s (e.g., the project that came to be known as the Fortunoff Video Archive for Holocaust Testimonies, now based at Yale University). The Shoah Foundation, the largest of these projects, has filmed interviews with over 50,000 survivors and other witnesses to the Holocaust. Beyond the evidentiary value of these testimonies, the process of engaging survivors in recalling their wartime experiences has itself been the subject of scrutiny (Greenspan 1998).

Since the end of the twentieth century, Holocaust survivors' authority has been widely celebrated in museums, films, memorial and pedagogical programs, many of which accord survivors pride of place over scholars, clergy, or political leaders. Some Holocaust survivors have become well-known figures through publications (e.g., Primo Levi [1919–1987], author of *If This Is a Man* [1959] and other memoirs), films (Gerda Weissman Klein, subject of the 1995 Academy Award-winning documentary *One Survivor Remembers*), institutions (the Wiesenthal Center in Los Angeles, established in 1977 and named in honor of Simon Wiesenthal [1908–2005], the renowned investigator of Nazi war criminals), or public service (Representative Tom Lantos [1928–2008], the only Holocaust survivor to serve in the U.S. Congress). Recognition of their wartime experiences and postwar responses to Nazi persecution has endowed these and other prominent Holocaust survivors with a paradigmatic value as embodiments of a moral force. Wiesel, for example, who was awarded the Nobel Peace Prize in 1986, has invoked his stature as a survivor to call attention to moral crises ranging from the nuclear arms race in the 1980s to ethnic cleansing operations in the Balkans in the 1990s and the twenty-first century genocidal atrocities in Darfur. The stature of Holocaust survivors in public culture has become so compelling that it has inspired more than one person to invent a false autobiography as a Jewish Holocaust survivor (Wilkomirski 1996; Defonseca 1997).

NEW PUBLIC PRESENCE AND DISCOURSES

Jews enjoyed new visibility in the postwar public cultures of the Americas and west European countries after World War II as a result of the Holocaust and related postwar events, including the resettlement of displaced persons, Nazi war crimes trials, and the establishment of the State of Israel. In the postwar United States, the organized Jewish community pursued new strategies against antisemitism, having often been reluctant before the war to respond forthrightly to anti-Jewish incidents and practices in American society, such as antisemitic attacks on the Hollywood film industry (Carr 2000) and quotas restricting Jews' enrollment in elite universities and professional schools (Oren 1985). Similarly, American Jewish leaders' political responses to the threat that Nazism posed to European Jews during the 1930s had been constrained by that period's heightened xenophobia, nativism, and isolationism (Arad 2000). But during the early postwar decades, the organized American Jewish community played a leading role in intergroup dialogue organizations devoted to eradicating prejudice generally in American society (Svonkin 1997). This new approach was exemplified by the Jewish Theological Seminary's production of ecumenical broadcasts in conjunction with major national networks. Its radio series *The Eternal Light*, for example, frequently aired programs (on NBC) dealing with the Holocaust and its aftermath (Shandler 2009: 56–94).

Following the dynamics of American identity politics generally, Jews have since asserted their difference more forthrightly in the national culture, often in conjunction with Holocaust remembrance as it acquired an increasing prominence in the American public sphere during the latter half of the twentieth century. Reactions to the official dramatization of Anne Frank's diary illustrate this shift. Widely praised when it premiered on Broadway (and was awarded the 1956 Pulitzer Prize for Best Drama), *The Diary of Anne Frank* has more recently been criticized for downplaying the Franks' Jewishness, in an effort to present their story as having universal value, and offering a problematically redemptive response to genocide (Rosenfeld in Hayes 1991: 243–78; Langer 2006: 16–29). For its most recent Broadway revival, the script was "newly adapted" by Wendy Kesselman (Goodrich and Hackett 2001), in part to address these concerns.

While inexorably tied to the Holocaust, the Jewish public presence in postwar Europe varies considerably from one nation to the next. In Poland, for example, Jews' public profile not only has reflected events directly concerning them—early postwar antisemitic violence, expulsions of the majority of Polish Jews in the late 1960s—but also has been shaped by the Soviet domination of Poland beginning in the late 1940s, the rise of Solidarity in the early 1980s, and the end of communist rule in 1989. In post-communist Poland, a small Jewish population tends to avoid public attention, even as remembrance of prewar Jewish life and its destruction looms large in national culture (Irwin-Zarecka 1989; Steinlauf 1997). Occasionally, Holocaust remembrance provokes national debate in Poland, as was the case with the 2001 publication of historian Jan Gross's *Neighbors*, an account of Poles' attacks on their Jewish neighbors in Jedwabne and nearby locations (Polonsky and Michlic 2004).

These changes in Jews' public presence reflect new postwar relationships between Jews and their neighbors that have been shaped by the Holocaust. In the west, antisemitism decreased markedly after the war and became widely recognized as an untenable sensibility with the gravest of consequences not only for Jews but also for the societies in which they live. Many Christian theologians have thus felt compelled to examine their faiths' ethical principles in light of the Holocaust, and this scrutiny has occasionally resulted in official changes of policy toward Jews, most notably among Roman Catholic reforms instituted at Vatican II and, more recently, in some formulations of Christian Zionism. Even as Jews generally welcome many of these developments, non-Jews' engagement with Holocaust remembrance sometimes proves provocative for Jews. Christian understandings of the Holocaust are often at odds with Jewish views of its theological or political significance. Thus, Jews and Catholics clashed publicly over efforts, beginning in the 1980s, to establish a convent and erect a cross at Auschwitz (Rittner and Roth 1991; Berger et al. 2004) In a study of late-twentieth-century Holocaust remembrance in Lincoln, Nebraska, historian Alan Steinweis observes that local Jews "often take umbrage" at Christians who invoke the Holocaust to argue against abortion rights, regarding such steps "as an appropriation of Jewish history . . . [and] of the very component of Jewish identity that in recent years has done the most to elicit Christian sympathy for the Jewish predicament" (in Flanzbaum 1999: 173).

Non-Jews also challenge Jews' notions of the relationship between peoplehood and culture by engaging in forms of prewar European Jewish culture—including playing klezmer music, studying Yiddish, restoring prewar synagogues and Jewish cemeteries—as acts of memorialization of these "lost" communities or atonement for their murder. Such examples of what Ruth Ellen Gruber terms "virtually Jewish" culture (2002), in which actual Jews are often absent, elicit ambivalent responses from Jewish observers, both in Europe and elsewhere, especially to the extent that these activities point up the disparity between actual Jewish life in Europe today and the recalled prewar past.

Alongside Jewish cultural practices responsive to the Holocaust, new public conversations on its significance and remembrance arise regularly among scholars, religious leaders, politicians, Holocaust survivors, public culture workers, artists, and the general public. These discussions, often extensive and prominent, should be considered part of the culture of Holocaust remembrance, even as they manifest a distinctive self-consciousness regarding these memory practices. Involving Jews as both participants and subjects, these discussions evince a range of understandings of Jews' place in public culture generally as well as in relation to the Holocaust.

The most conspicuous of these conversations debate contentious issues. Thus, even as Jews and others champion Holocaust remembrance, this moral imperative has frequently been implicated as a divisive issue in political controversies, juxtaposing the imperative of recalling the Holocaust against other principles. For example, the rights of neo-Nazis to stage a public demonstration in the Chicago suburb of Skokie, Illinois, in the late 1970s provoked an extended court battle and proved a limit-case test of American Jews' commitment to supporting civil liberties, seen by many in this case as inimical to Holocaust remembrance (Neier 1979). U.S. President Ronald Reagan's plan to visit a military cemetery in Bitburg, West Germany, in 1985, to mark the fortieth anniversary of the end of World War II, provoked outrage among both American Jews and American veterans' groups when they learned that soldiers in the Wehrmacht and SS were among those interred in Bitburg. An intended gesture of reconciliation, meant to bolster U.S. relations with a strategic Cold War ally, became instead the point of conflict between the cultural politics of public memory and the political exigencies of the moment (Hartman 1986).

The Holocaust remains a polarizing issue in public discourse as political paradigms have shifted following the Cold War. For example, official American recognition of the Turkish mass murder of Armenians during World War I has hinged on debates between the moral imperative of acknowledging and denouncing genocides, in which the Holocaust figures as paradigmatic, on one hand, and the strategic importance of Turkey as an ally of the United States and of Israel, on the other hand (Melson 2006). An Iranian newspaper's 2006 contest soliciting cartoons mocking the Holocaust (in response to cartoons insulting to Islam that had been published in the western press) elicited, among other reactions, an Israeli group's announcing its own contest for antisemitic cartoons, open to Jews only, in an effort both to defuse the assault on Holocaust remembrance (and, along with it, antisemitic and anti-Zionist sentiments) and to offer a provocative validation of freedom of speech.

For decades, Jews have debated the notion of proprietary rights to Holocaust remembrance, prompted occasionally by works of culture some perceive as provocative, even hostile. Examples include Sylvia Plath's use of Holocaust imagery in the early 1960s in her poem "Daddy"; the casting of anti-Zionist activist Vanessa Redgrave in the lead role of *Playing for Time*, Arthur Miller's 1980 television drama based on the memoir of a survivor of Auschwitz; and titling a 1998 exhibition on detention camps in which Japanese Americans were interned during World War II "America's Concentration Camps." This issue is part of a larger discourse on the "use and misuse/abuse" of Holocaust remembrance that has flourished alongside the expansion of Holocaust memory practices (Jick 1981; Marrus in Hayes 1991: 106–19; Langer 2006). Implying a distinct moral connoisseurship of Holocaust remembrance, this discourse is related to the rhetoric of Holocaust exceptionalism, concerning both the "uniqueness" of the event and its remembrance as challenging the limits of human scholarship, ethics, or artistry (Friedländer 1992; Lang 2000; Rosenbaum 2009).

These concerns with regulating understandings of and responses to the Holocaust are in tension with desires, sometimes voiced by the same parties, to see it widely recognized and the value of its remembrance honored. Indeed, largely because the Holocaust has been established so successfully as a fixture of public culture, it has become a paradigm for understanding other acts of genocide as well as other morally charged social issues, including global warming, the nuclear arms race, the AIDS pandemic, and animal rights. Jewish responses to Holocaust analogies vary considerably. For example, literary scholar Edward Alexander characterizes some analogies as "stealing the Holocaust" from Jews by transforming its Jewish-centered specificity into a metaphor that is sometimes directed against Jews, notably by analogizing Palestinians' conflict with Israelis and Jewish victimization by Nazi Germany (1994: 194–206). Conversely, many Jews have embraced public denunciations of "ethnic cleansing" operations in the Balkans during the 1990s and the early-twenty-first-century genocide in Darfur as "another Holocaust."

FUTURE STUDY OF THE HOLOCAUST
IN JEWISH CULTURE

Holocaust remembrance has a history of its own. Early in the twenty-first century, the cultural practices of remembering the Holocaust are at a critical point in this dynamic, tied to the aging and eventual passing of survivors and other eyewitnesses of wartime atrocities. Already much anticipated by educators and public historians, this transition has important implications for the children and grandchildren of Holocaust survivors, some of whom have assumed the onus (and authority) of remembrance (Bukiet 2002). Concurrently, mediations of the Holocaust are becoming increasingly central to these cultural practices, as exemplified by the extensive inventories of recorded testimonies by survivors and other eyewitnesses to the Holocaust, which are now being remediated through an array of documentary films, educational projects, and internet resources.

Holocaust remembrance has taken on new political significance as a consequence of recent developments, including the end of communist rule in eastern Europe, the establishment of the European Union, and the rise of Holocaust denial in some Muslim countries as part of anti-Zionist and anti-west policies. These developments can have complicated consequences for the cultural politics of Jewish engagements in Holocaust remembrance. For example, anthropologist Matti Bunzl notes that, since the establishment of the European Union, a new philosemitism has flourished among west European right-wing political parties, whose roots can be traced to pro-Nazi parties, in tandem with these parties' intensifying Islamophobia (Bunzl 2007). In Israel, the official public history of the Holocaust has recently been expanded to include the wartime experience of Mizrahi Jews in North Africa (as evinced in the new museum at Yad Vashem, which opened in 2005), reflecting the state's commitment to maintain the Holocaust as a defining historical event for all Israelis.

The value of Holocaust remembrance as a master moral paradigm continues to be asserted and debated as the inventory of genocides and other large-scale atrocities grows. These and other developments engage Jews, whether centrally or obliquely, and will inform Jewish culture for decades to come, as the Holocaust continues to play a leading role in defining Jews' sense of self.

REFERENCES

ALEXANDER, E. (1994). *The Holocaust and the War of Ideas.* New Brunswick, NJ: Transaction.

AMERICAN JEWISH COMMITTEE (1998). *1998 Annual Survey of American Jewish Opinion.* New York: American Jewish Committee.

ARAD, G. (2000). *America, Its Jews, and the Rise of Nazism.* Bloomington, IN: Indiana University Press.

BAUER, Y. (2001). *Rethinking the Holocaust.* New Haven, CT: Yale University Press.

BERENBAUM, M. (1993). *The World Must Know: The History of the Holocaust as Told in the United States Holocaust Memorial Museum.* Boston, MA: Little, Brown.

BERGER, A., CARGAS, H., and NOWAK, S. (eds.) (2004). *The Continuing Agony: From the Carmelite Convent to the Crosses at Auschwitz.* Lanham, MD: University Press of America.

BEZMOZGIS, D. (2004). *Natasha and Other Stories.* New York: Farrar, Straus and Giroux.

BUKIET, M. (1995). *While the Messiah Tarries.* New York: Harcourt Brace & Co.

——(ed.) (2002). *Nothing Makes You Free: Writings by Descendants of Jewish Holocaust Survivors.* New York: W. W. Norton.

BUNZL, M. (2007). *Anti-Semitism and Islamophobia: Hatreds Old and New in Europe.* Chicago, IL: University of Chicago Press.

CARR, S. (2000). *Hollywood and Anti-Semitism: A Cultural History Up to World War II.* Cambridge: Cambridge University Press.

604 JEFFREY SHANDLER

COHEN, A. (1981). *The Tremendum: A Theological Interpretation of the Holocaust*. New York: Crossroad.

DEFONSECA, M. (1997). *Misha: A Mémoire of the Holocaust Years*. Boston, MA: Mt. Ivy Press.

DINER, H. (2009). *We Remember with Reverence and Love: American Jews and the Myth of Silence after the Holocaust, 1945–1962*. New York: New York University Press.

ELIACH, Y. (1982). *Hasidic Tales of the Holocaust*. New York: Oxford University Press.

——(1998). *There Once Was a World: A 900-Year Chronicle of the Shtetl Eishyshok*. Boston, MA: Little, Brown.

FEINGOLD, H. (2007). *"Silent No More": Saving the Jews of Russia, the American Jewish Effort, 1967–1989*. Syracuse, NY: Syracuse University Press.

FINKELSTEIN, N. (2000). *The Holocaust Industry: Reflection on the Exploitation of Jewish Suffering*. London: Verso.

FLANZBAUM, H. (ed.) (1999). *The Americanization of the Holocaust*. Baltimore, MD: Johns Hopkins University Press.

FRIEDLÄNDER, S. (ed.) (1992). *Probing the Limits of Representation: Nazism and the "Final Solution."* Cambridge, MA: Harvard University Press.

GOODRICH, F. and HACKETT, A. (1956). *The Diary of Anne Frank*. New York: Random House.

————(2001). *The Diary of Anne Frank*. Newly adapted by W. Kesselman. New York: Dramatists Play Service.

GREENBERG, I. (1980). *On the Third Era in Jewish History: Power and Politics*. New York: National Jewish Resource Center.

GREENSPAN, H. (1998). *On Listening to Holocaust Survivors: Recounting and Life History*. Westport, CT: Praeger.

GRUBER, R. (2002). *Virtually Jewish: Reinventing Jewish Culture in Europe*. Berkeley, CA: University of California Press.

HARTMAN, G. (ed.) (1986). *Bitburg in Moral and Political Perspective*. Bloomington, IN: Indiana University Press.

HASAK-LOWY, T. (2005). *The Task of This Translator: Stories*. Orlando, FL: Harcourt.

HAYES, P. (ed.) (1991). *Lessons and Legacies: The Meaning of the Holocaust in a Changing World*. Evanston, IL: Northwestern University Press.

HEILMAN, S. (2006). *Sliding to the Right: The Contest for the Future of American Jewish Orthodoxy*. Berkeley, CA: University of California Press.

HORNSTEIN, S., LEVITT, L., and SILBERSTEIN, L. (eds.) (2003). *Impossible Images: Contemporary Art after the Holocaust*. New York: New York University Press.

IRWIN-ZARECKA, I. (1989). *Neutralizing Memory: The Jew in Contemporary Poland*. New Brunswick, NJ: Transaction.

Jewish Museum, Berlin, Architect Daniel Libeskind. (1999). Amsterdam: G + B Arts International.

JICK, L. A. (1981). "The Holocaust: Its Use and Abuse within the American Public." *Yad Vashem Studies* 14: 303–18.

KLEEBLATT, N. (ed.) (2002). *Mirroring Evil: Nazi Imagery/Recent Art*. New Brunswick, NJ: Rutgers University Press.

KUGELMASS, J. and BOYARIN, J. (eds.) (1983). *From a Ruined Garden: The Memorial Books of Polish Jewry*. New York: Schocken.

LANG, B. (2000). *Holocaust Representation: Art within the Limits of History and Ethics*. Baltimore, MD: Johns Hopkins University Press.

LANGER, L. (2006). *Using and Abusing the Holocaust*. Bloomington, IN: Indiana University Press.

LEDERHANDLER, E. (ed.) (2000). *The Six-Day War and World Jewry*. Bethesda, MD: University Press of Maryland.

LEVI, P. (1959). *If This Is a Man*. New York: Orion Press.

LIEBMAN, S. (ed.) (2007). *Claude Lanzmann's Shoah: Key Essays*. Oxford: Oxford University Press.

LITTELL, M. and GUTMAN, S. (eds.) (1996). *Liturgies on the Holocaust: An Interfaith Anthology*. Rev. edn. Valley Forge, PA: Trinity Press International.

LOSHITZKY, Y. (ed.) (1997). *Spielberg's Holocaust: Critical Perspectives on "Schindler's List."* Bloomington, IN: Indiana University Press.

MAJEWSKI, L. and BIKONT, A. (eds.) (1996). *And I Still See Their Faces: Images of Polish Jews/I ciagle widze ich twarze: Fotografia Zydów polskich*. Warsaw: Fundacja Shalom.

MELSON, R. (2006). "Responses to the Armenian Genocide: America, the Yishuv, Israel." *Holocaust and Genocide Studies* 20/1: 103–11.

MINTZ, A. (2001). *Popular Culture and the Shaping of Holocaust Memory in America*. Seattle, WA: University of Washington Press.

NEIER, A. (1979). *Defending My Enemy: American Nazis, the Skokie Case, and the Risks of Freedom*. New York: Dutton.

NEUSNER, J. (1981). *Stranger at Home: "The Holocaust," Zionism and American Judaism*. Chicago, IL: University of Chicago Press.

NOVICK, P. (1999). *The Holocaust in American Life*. Boston, MA: Houghton Mifflin.

OREN, D. (1985). *Joining the Club: A History of Jews and Yale*. New Haven, CT: Yale University Press.

POLONSKY, A. and MICHLIC, J. (eds.) (2004). *The Neighbors Respond: The Controversy over the Jedwabne Massacre in Poland*. Princeton, NJ: Princeton University Press.

PROSE, F. (1997). *Guided Tours of Hell: Novellas*. New York: Metropolitan Books/Henry Holt.

RITTNER, C. and ROTH, J. (eds.) (1991). *Memory Offended: The Auschwitz Convent Controversy*. New York: Praeger Publishers.

ROBINSON, J. (1965). *And the Crooked Shall Be Made Straight: The Eichmann Trial, the Jewish Catastrophe, and Hannah Arendt's Narrative*. New York: MacMillan.

ROSENBAUM, A. (ed.) (2009). *Is the Holocaust Unique?: Perspectives on Comparative Genocide*. 3rd edn. Boulder, CO: Westview Press.

SCHWEBER, S. (2003). "Simulating Survival." *Curriculum Inquiry* 33/2: 139–88.

SEGEV, T. (1993). *The Seventh Million: The Israelis and the Holocaust*. New York: Hill and Wang.

SHANDLER, J. (1999). *While America Watches: Televising the Holocaust*. New York: Oxford University Press.

——(ed.) (2002). *Awakening Lives: Autobiographies of Jewish Youth in Poland before the Holocaust*. New Haven, CT: Yale University Press.

——(2009). *Jews, God, and Videotape: Religion and Media in America*. New York: New York University Press.

SHERAMY, R. (2006). "From Auschwitz to Jerusalem: Re-enacting Jewish History on the March of the Living." *Polin: Studies in Polish Jewry* 19: 307–25.

SILVA, C. DE (ed.) (1996). *In Memory's Kitchen: A Legacy from the Women of Terezin*. Northvale, NJ: Jason Aronson.

SPIEGELMAN, A. (1997). *Maus: A Survivor's Tale*. New York: Pantheon Books.

STEINLAUF, M. (1997). *Bondage to the Dead: Poland and the Memory of the Holocaust.* Syracuse, NY: Syracuse University Press.

SVONKIN, S. (1997). *Jews Against Prejudice: American Jews and the Intergroup Relations Movement from World War to Cold War.* New York: Columbia University Press.

WIESEL, E. (1972). "The Telling of the War." *New York Times Book Review,* 5 November 1972, p. 3.

WILKOMIRSKI, B. (1996). *Fragments: Memories of a Wartime Childhood.* New York: Schocken.

WOOCHER, J. (1986). *Sacred Survival: The Civil Religion of American Jews.* Bloomington, IN: Indiana University Press.

YOUNG, J. (1993). *The Texture of Memory: Holocaust Memorials and Meaning.* New Haven, CT: Yale University Press.

ZERUBAVEL, Y. (1995). *Recovered Roots: Collective Memory and the Making of Israeli National Tradition.* Chicago, IL: University of Chicago Press.

OTHER SUGGESTED READING

FERMAGLICH, K. (2006). *American Dreams and Nazi Nightmares: Early Holocaust Consciousness and Liberal America, 1957–1965.* Hanover, NH: University Press of New England.

GROSS, J. (2001). *Neighbors: The Destruction of the Jewish Community in Jedwabne, Poland.* Princeton, NJ: Princeton University Press.

MORGAN, M. (2001). *Beyond Auschwitz: Post-Holocaust Jewish Thought in America.* New York: Oxford University Press.

RAPAPORT, L. (1997). *Jews in Germany after the Holocaust: Memory, Identity, and Jewish-German Relations.* Cambridge: Cambridge University Press.

ROTH, J. (2001). *Holocaust Politics.* Louisville, KY: Westminster John Knox Press.

STRATTON, J. (2008). *Jewish Identity in Western Pop Culture: The Holocaust and Trauma through Modernity.* New York: Palgrave Macmillan.

CHAPTER 39

....

JUDAISM

....

MICHAEL BERENBAUM

THE impact of the Holocaust on Judaism and particularly on Jewish theological
reflection did not reach full force until the 1960s. Since that time, attention to the
Shoah's implications for Jewish religious thought and practice has been intense and
widespread (Cohn-Sherbok 2002). As struggles persist to grasp what God's relationship to the Holocaust might be, confidence is not the lot of those who wrestle with the
Holocaust's significance for Judaism. The deeper the struggle to confront the Holocaust, the deeper the mystery, the more profound the humility and incomprehension.
The acclaimed Talmud scholar David Weiss Halivni (b. 1927) provides an instructive
example in *Breaking the Tablets: Jewish Theology after the Shoah* (2007).

FROM THE TALMUD TO AUSCHWITZ
....

Study of Talmud, the ancient and authoritative rabbinical exposition of the biblical
Pentateuch (Torah), is king in the Jewish sciences. From the most traditional yeshiva to
the theological seminary and even in many secular universities, unique authority is
granted to the Talmudic scholar—until recently all Talmudic scholars were men—and
singular respect is accorded to his branch of Jewish learning. A *talmid hahum* was the
traditional title of veneration for the gifted student of Talmud, a wise student, no
matter what the age. So when Halivni, a renowned Talmudist, employs his immense
learning to write a work of theology—traditional and radical, personal and philosophical—dealing with the question of God and the Holocaust, attention is due. When he
writes with the authority of a Holocaust survivor, that is all the more the case.

A child of Sighet, a Romanian city but part of Hungary during the Holocaust and made legendary by Elie Wiesel (b. 1928), Halivni's contemporary and friend, Weiss— he later added the name Halivni (the Hebrew word for "weiss" or "white")—was an *ilui*, a boy genius. He spent his youth studying from morning until night, and his Talmudic acuity brought him to the attention of the religious leaders of the city, who expected great things from him. They were not to be disappointed. He was ordained a rabbi at 17, just before the Germans and the Holocaust came to Hungary in March 1944. Ghettoized and then deported to Auschwitz, Weiss was shipped from there to Wolfsberg, a forced labor subcamp of Gross-Rosen, and eventually liberated at Ebensee. His autobiography *The Book and the Sword: A Life of Learning in the Shadows of Destruction* (1996) recounts his experience during the Shoah, including an episode when he saw a German soldier eating a lunch that was wrapped in a page of rabbinic commentary. Risking his life, Weiss begged the soldier for the wrapping. His risk embodied his love for Torah, the study of which helped him to endure the camps.

After liberation, Halivni came to the United States, attended college, and continued his religious studies, coming under the tutelage of Saul Lieberman (1898–1983), the preeminent Talmudist at the Jewish Theological Seminary (JTS) and also a teacher of Wiesel. Halivni received a second ordination, pursued a doctorate in Talmud, and taught at JTS for thirty years. But he left the seminary—according to his memoir— when he was not named Rector after Lieberman's death. This period coincided with the 1980s debate at JTS over the ordination of women, which the traditionalist Halivni opposed. He moved up Broadway to Columbia University and went on to do some of his finest work. After retiring from Columbia in 2005, he relocated to Israel, lecturing at the Hebrew University and at Bar-Ilan University and receiving the Israel Prize for his lifetime of scholarly accomplishments.

Halivni's religious response to the Holocaust is as radical as it is steeped in the most fundamental traditions of Judaism. Unlike Wiesel, who uses Midrash, a Jewish interpretive tradition that seeks the underlying and even hidden meaning of scripture, to create novel narratives that echo ancient texts but recreate them in ways necessitated by the Shoah, Halivni responds to the Holocaust by using close textual analysis to develop a traditional argument, but in ways that produce the most untraditional, perhaps even anti-traditional, results.

Sin Does Not Explain the Holocaust

Halivni critiques the simple explanation employed by traditionalists who feel required to justify God during the Holocaust: The Holocaust was God's punishment for Israel's—the Jewish people's—sin. Basing his claim on a detailed textual analysis of

Jewish scripture (Tanakh)—the Torah, the Prophets, and the Writings—and the reflection of revered Jewish sages, Halivni states his conclusion in a traditional way: "*Do we attribute the Shoah to sin?... It is written in the Torah, a second time in the Prophets, a third time in the Writings, and a fourth time in the words of our sages, that the Shoah was not the consequence of sin*" (2007: 17, italics his).

Halivni argues in rabbinic fashion, using texts to prove his point. His proof text from the Torah is Leviticus 26:44: "And yet for all that, and when they are in the land of their enemies, I will not loathe them to destroy them utterly, and to break my covenant with them." The key Hebrew word is *l'khalotam*. Those who interpret it to mean total annihilation argue that since there were survivors of the Holocaust, the covenant was not abrogated. Halivni is more radical: "*L'khalotam* does not mean total extermination, the killing of a people or a large part of it, but rather the irremediable destruction of a people's institutional infrastructure. And this is precisely what happened in the Shoah: institutional Jewish life in Eastern Europe was uprooted and almost totally erased; the only survivors were as brands snatched from the fire." The words "brands snatched from the fire" allude to Zechariah 3:2 in the Bible's prophetic writings. "The limits of *lo l'khalotam* [not to destroy them]," continues Halivni, "were blurred and suspended, and the covenant God made with Israel was shaken if not totally abrogated" (2007: 18).

Halivni's notion of the shattered covenant is widely shared among post-Holocaust thinkers, although he makes no mention of their work. "The Torah was given at Sinai and we gave it back at Lublin," said the great Yiddish poet Jacob Glatstein (1896–1971) in 1946 (in Curzon 1994: 165–7). For the Jewish philosopher Emil Fackenheim (1916–2003), the Holocaust was the great and almost total rupture of the traditional covenant between God and the Jewish people (1972). Richard L. Rubenstein (b. 1924), among the earliest Jewish thinkers to probe the radical theological implications of the Holocaust for traditional Judaism, added to these perspectives: "To see any purpose in the death camps, the traditional believer is forced to regard the most demonic, antihuman explosion in all history as a meaningful expression of God's purpose. The idea is simply too obscene for me to accept" (1966: 153). In a symposium on "Jewish Values in the Post-Holocaust Future," Wiesel contended that "for the very first time in our history, this very covenant was broken. That is why the Holocaust has terrifying theological implications. In the beginning there was the Holocaust. We must, therefore begin all over again" (1967: 285).

Halivni's primary concern is neither to break new ground nor to begin all over again, but he shatters conventional pieties. Turning the table on the traditionalists, he writes: "We must not blame such a catastrophe on the sins of its victims. Anyone who does so denies the promises God made to Israel and merits our careful scrutiny" (2007: 19). And if the Torah is insufficient, Halivni cites the Prophets in typical rabbinic fashion: "Chastise me, O Lord, but in measure, not according to Your anger, lest You reduce me to nothing" (Jeremiah 10:24). Jeremiah's prayer is answered: "I will indeed chastise you in measure and will not utterly destroy you" (Jeremiah 30:11, 46:28).

Unlike many Christians, especially Protestant fundamentalists, Jews do not approach scripture unmediated by commentary. So, for a more detailed understanding of what "in measure" means, Halivni turns to the sages' commentaries. Radak (1160–1235), the medieval commentator on the Prophets, said that "in measure" means in proportion that one can tolerate. Rashi (1040–1105), the great French commentator, interpreted "in measure" to exclude annihilation. As a traditionalist, Halivni considers their interpretations authoritative.

Turning to the biblical Writings, Halivni cites Nehemiah 9:27–8: "and you rescued them again and again." Tradition holds that God saves despite sin and insolence because God is gracious and merciful, long suffering, and of great kindness. While this passage indicates that God would not annihilate the Jewish people utterly, Halivni and others still contend that God did not save at Auschwitz. Rubenstein, for one, would rather reject the God of tradition than affirm God's presence at Auschwitz. Fackenheim's first extended articulation of a response to the Holocaust discarded the notion of a saving God and replaced it with a commanding God—more appropriately a teaching God—because God did not save at Auschwitz (1972). In Fackenheim's view, the divine "Voice of Auschwitz" says:

Jews are forbidden to hand Hitler posthumous victories. They are commanded to survive as Jews, lest the Jewish people perish. They are commanded to remember the victims of the Auschwitz, lest their memory perish. They are forbidden to despair of man and his world, and to escape into either cynicism or otherworldliness, lest they cooperate in delivering the world over to the forces of Auschwitz. Finally, they are forbidden to despair of the God of Israel, lest Judaism perish. (1972: 84)

Halivni's approach turns in different directions, emphasizing that a gracious, compassionate God could not be present at Auschwitz. He speaks of the absence of God; in the language of mysticism of *tsimtsum*, God's contraction, which leaves room for human freedom.

Unfortunately for their victims and for us, those who exercised this free will exercised it in the most evil of ways, while their victims remained unprotected and undefended, without any intervention from Above. *They suffered and died, but for nothing they had done. The cause of their suffering was cosmic.* (Halivni 2007: 34, italics his)

Questions persist, however:

Why during *our* generation in particular did God choose not to intervene, despite His having intervened in previous epochs to save Israel from annihilation? Why in *our* generation in particular did He choose not to interfere with the freedom and moral license of evildoers, when He did interfere in previous times and even hardened Pharaoh's heart? Why was our generation singled out? (Halivni 2007: 32)

Halivni acknowledges that he has no answers to such questions, but "must be instructed by Isaiah's words, when he rebuked King Hezekiah and said, according to Talmudic tradition, 'Why do you concern yourself with the secrets of the Merciful One?'" Nevertheless, Halivni still longs for "an appropriate metaphor," which is not the same thing as an explanation, "to capture the singular fate of our generation, who suffered so terribly, not because of anything they did or as a result of any misdeeds of their own." Halivni finds that metaphor in the "Divine Contraction," which resulted in a maximal human freedom that led tragically to the Shoah.

Halivni's glimpse of the *tsimtsum* finds it to be a cosmic process, one that requires periodic regenerating and reequalizing of

the normal balance between humanity's bounded freedom and the absolute freedom of God....Since God will continue to intervene in history, we should expect that it will be necessary, in the course of time, for the *tsimtsum* to be restored and adjusted once again. Let us hope that the free will that results from this restoration will be exercised for good and not as it was exercised in our generation. (2007: 32–3)

PRAYER AFTER THE HOLOCAUST?

Prayer is fundamental in Judaism. But how does one—Jewish or not—pray after Auschwitz? Wiesel recalls the observance there of Rosh Hashanah in 1944. The prayers said, "Blessed be the Almighty...Blessed be God's name...All the earth and the universe are God's!...All of creation bears witness to the Greatness of God!" Wiesel describes the prisoner who officiated at the solemn service:

He kept pausing, as though he lacked the strength to uncover the meaning beneath the text. The melody was stifled in his throat. (2006: 67–8)

Holocaust survivor Norbert Wollheim remembers his neighbor's prayer in Auschwitz:

I saw that friend of mine who was standing there not far from me praying, . . . I said, "What are you doing?" He said, "I am, uh, prai-praising God." I said, "Here! Are you out of your mind?" . . . and I said, "What are you thinking? What are you thanking God for?" He said, "I'm thanking God for the fact that he didn't make me like the murderers around us." (Wollheim 1991)

More recently, David Blumenthal has wrestled with prayer after the Holocaust, composing prayers that echo Wollheim and also Wiesel's protest when he says in *Night*, "I was the accuser, God the accused" (Blumenthal 1993; Wiesel 2006: 68).

Halivni considers prayer during and after the Shoah by asking *how* Jews prayed in Auschwitz—not how in a technical sense but how in the deepest sense: What did they say? What prayer could they recite? A passage in *Breaking the Tablets* offers Halivni's confession to God, expressing his grief for a moment when, in pleading for his life, he addressed an SS man with the "holy word, 'Merciful One' (*har-achamin*)—which appears in the sources only in relation to the Holy One" (2007: 37). What he perceives as a moment of personal weakness is theologically insightful, for those German "masters" played God, sometimes choosing Yom Kippur, the Day of Atonement, for "selections" that usurped God's place by deciding "who shall live and who shall die." Perhaps Halivni's tormenter even believed that he was being the "merciful one" by sparing a Jew's life, but Halivni ends this episode with a prayer of his own:

May it be Your will that, by virtue of my having understood the correct meaning of the prayer, *melokh al kil haolom kulo bekh'vodekha*, "Rule over all the world in your full glory," that all the world comes to eradicate the condition that ruled in the forced labor camp. May it be Your will to repair the damage I have caused by substituting the profane for the holy. And may we be worthy of beholding the fulfillment of the prayer, "And His dominion rules over all." (2007: 37–8)

What prayer can one offer in and after Auschwitz? For Halivni, sound responses to that question require awareness that there have been "two major theological events in Jewish history, 'Revelation' at Sinai and revelation at Auschwitz" (2007: 117). The former is of God's presence, the latter of God's absence. Halivni shares this position with Wiesel, Fackenheim, and Irving Greenberg (b. 1933). Fackenheim called the Holocaust an "epoch making event" (1982: 20). He tried to fill its void by invoking the Commanding Voice of Auschwitz, but he never removed crucial and perhaps unavoidable ambiguity as to whose voice that was: God's or the voice of Jewish history? And if this Voice spoke and was heard, did that action take place at Auschwitz or in its ashes and in the Shoah's aftermath? Fackenheim conceded that the saving God was not present at Auschwitz. He later attempted to fill the void by emphasizing *tikkun*, which he defined minimally as "mending" rather restoring it, or as reuniting the divine sparks, building on those elements that were not totally destroyed during the Shoah and may yet heal its great rupture (1982).

Greenberg also speaks of the shattering of the covenant in the Holocaust. Following Wiesel and Glatstein, Greenberg recognizes that the Holocaust altered our perceptions of God and humanity. He offers a powerful verification principle that, he argues, must become the test of religious integrity after the Holocaust. "No statement, theological or otherwise, should be made that would not be credible in the presence of burning children" (in Fleischner 1977: 23). Greenberg argues that the authority of the covenant was broken in the Holocaust, but the Jewish people, released from its obligations, chose voluntarily to renew it again. "We are in the age of the renewal of the covenant. God is no longer in a position to command, but the

Jewish people are so in love with the dream of redemption that it volunteered to carry out the mission" (1987: 35). Our choice to remain Jews, Greenberg argues, is our response to the covenant with God and between generations of Jews and our utterance of the response to Sinai, "we will do and we will hear" (Exodus 24:7, 19). The task of Jewish existence—and of all authentic religious existence after the Holocaust—is to recreate the divine and human images that were destroyed in the Holocaust, to respond to death by creating life, and to continue the Jewish people's journey in history. Jews must continue to labor to bring redemption.

For Halivni, how to conceive and participate in a Holocaust-shadowed relationship with God is the key challenge. Like Rubenstein, he says we live in a time of God's absence; like Rubenstein and Friedrich Nietzsche (1844–1900) before him, he believes that if God is absent (dead), anything is possible. Rejecting Nietzsche's celebration of the "death of God," which was amplified by some American Christian theologians in the 1960s, Halivni, along with Rubenstein, takes Auschwitz to be one of the consequences of a disrespect for and denial of divinity. Would that the fear of God had really existed, but in the Holocaust even that was absent.

Halivni experienced the Absence. In his generation it was Auschwitz. What then can be said? What words of prayer can be uttered? Consider the words of the Rosh Hashanah liturgy repeated in the silent devotion of each service:

Our God and God of our fathers, reign in your glory over the whole universe and be exalted in the whole earth so that whatever has been made may know that You made it, so that whatever has been created may know that You have created it: and so that whatever has breath in its nostrils may say: 'The Lord God of Israel is King and has dominion over all."

This affirmation was so distant from the experiences of those imprisoned in the *lagers* or those murdered in the Shoah. Halivni writes:

In the concentration camps and forced labor camps . . . the prisoners perceived the incomprehensible evil that happened as the consequence of the Holy One's abdicating His rule, of His transferring the reins of government into the cruel hands of blood suckers, and of His own decision not to intervene against them but to grant them unlimited authority. Against them, they prayed, "Rule over all the world in Your full glory. And may every creature know that you created it, and everything that moves know that you move it. . . ." And they said, Now these villains behave like gods. Life and death is in their hands; by their will life is given, and by their will life is taken away. Remove this power from them and punish them according to their deeds, and then, "Every soul will say, 'The Lord God of Israel is King and His dominion'"—the right and true One—"'rules over all.'" (2007: 36–7)

The point of such prayer, Halivni explains, is not to request directly that "the government of the world would be conducted according to justice and law." Instead, the prayer "Rule over all the world, in Your full glory" is "a petition for God's own good, that He would rule, that He would be glorified, that He would appear." If God would do so, "then the world would be conducted according to justice and law" (2007: 36).

Halivni's sober scholarship unmasks the shallowness of attempts to explain God's presence in catastrophe by a calculus of reward and punishment, sin and atonement. He insists that no form of Judaism can be credible, no matter what its momentary confidence and comfort, if it cannot stand the test of the events it purports to illuminate or explain. Therefore, Halivni underscores that history is the realm of human responsibility. The Holocaust's perpetrators, not God, are responsible for their deeds. But having seen what he has seen, having experienced what he has experienced, Halivni prays for God's dominion; he has seen enough of human dominion unchecked by the fear of God. Halivni's sense of Holocaust-related prayer holds God as well as humankind accountable. It beseeches God to be God.

Loss, Re-Creation, Legacy

What else shall Judaism say of the Holocaust? One response emphasizes the difference between tragedy and atrocity (Berenbaum 1990). In tragedy what is learned balances, to some extent, the price paid for such knowledge. Atrocity offers no possibility of such balance. At most, it leaves those left behind searching amidst the ashes to find some meaning in events that defy meaning, to confront the presence of an absence and the absence of presence, to grapple with the void. As Judaism goes forward after the Shoah, it cannot avoid asking, "Where was God in that abysmal time?" Whether the responses of Halivni, Fackenheim, Rubenstein, Greenberg, or any other post-Holocaust Jewish thinker will be sufficient remains to be seen.

As that process unfolds, it seems clear that God is not to be found in the acts of the Holocaust's perpetrators or in the selection of its victims, but amidst the destruction's rubble perhaps God's traces can be found in rescue, in sheltering, providing a meal, offering a haven, in moments of compassion and remnants of decency. God may be found as well in the courage of the Holocaust's victims and survivors. Rabbi Harold Schulweis (b. 1925) has written of God as a Predicate. To say that God is love, for example, means that loving is Godly. To say that God is just means that doing justice is Godly (1984: 124). As time passes, Judaism will continue to find little solace—quite the opposite—in the Holocaust. But in the lives of its victims, in those who helped and rescued them, and in the example of its survivors, doing justice and loving that are Godly can be found.

In *The Song of the Murdered Jewish People*, written in 1943 and 1944 shortly before his murder at Auschwitz, the great Yiddish writer Yitzhak Katzenelson (1886–1944) lamented for his people:

Never will the voice of Torah be heard from *yeshivoth* synagogues, and pale students...
Masters of Talmud and Codes, small Jews with great heads, high foreheads, bright eyes—all
     gone...
Never will a Jewish mother cradle a baby. Jews will not die or be born.
Never will plaintive songs of Jewish poets be sung. All's gone, gone...
Woe unto me, nobody is left...There was a people, and it is no more.
     There was a people and it is...Gone...(1980: 84–5)

In the fateful year of 1944, when the last living Jewish community in Hungary was
being eviscerated and the last ghetto in Poland destroyed, Katzenelson's vision
seemed almost a prophecy. Two of three European Jews were dead, one in three
Jews in the world. The great center of Jewish life, the reservoir of the Jewish culture,
which had given rise to the American Jewish community and planted seeds in
Palestine for emergent Jewish nationalism, was destroyed. The event now known as
the Holocaust nearly destroyed Yiddish as a daily and vibrant language as well as
the diverse expressions of Yiddish culture. The age-old Jewish village—the *shtetl*—
was wiped off the face of the earth. Europe was no longer the center of Jewish
leadership and learning. Judaism in Poland, which served as the biological and
spiritual center of Jewish life, was reduced to rubble, while other old European
Jewish centers suffered deeply. Jewish Vienna, Jewish Berlin, Jewish Prague, Jewish
Paris, Jewish Amsterdam, and Jewish Salonika were no more.

Nothing, it seemed, could arise from the ashes. Would Auschwitz be the graveyard not only of the Jews of Europe but of the Jewish people, Jewish history, and
even of a vibrant Judaism? In 1945, the fate of the Yishuv in Palestine seemed
precarious; what would become of this remnant? Soviet Jews had been depleted by
the German occupation; entire communities had been murdered one by one, day
after day, by the Einsatzgruppen and their collaborators. And those who had been
spared the rod of Hitler soon faced Stalin's purges and the Soviet Union's hostility
toward manifestations of Jewishness among its nationals. Would American Jews,
whose country had emerged triumphant from World War II, be able to fill the gap,
to provide the leadership necessary for regeneration? The sons and daughters of the
great 1881–1920 emigration to the United States were coming into their own, ready
to claim their rightful place as Americans first and foremost, but perhaps not as
Jews. During the 1930s and well into the early war years, antisemitism was at its all-
time high in the United States. Barriers were erected, sanctioned by law and
custom, social exclusion was not rare, and the desire for assimilation was rampant.
Would this community be able to assume responsibility for the Jewish future? Even
in 1945 after the liberation of the camps, the verdict was not clear. A remnant had
survived, truly a brand plucked from the fire, to use Zechariah's metaphor, yet
could these emaciated souls, who had seen and lost all, return to life and rebuild
their existence? Would they give up on Jewish history?

Illustrative responses to such questions are found in the narrative of Romana
Strochlitz Primus (b. 1946), who considers the mystery of her origin:

My parents, who had met briefly in Birkenau, were both liberated in Bergen-Belsen. My mother weighed 78 pounds and was delirious with typhus; she barely understood that she was liberated. My father weighed 88 pounds. They had lost their families, their communities, their way of life. And yet, I was born in a Bergen-Belsen DP camp less than 15 months after the liberation. (in Rosensaft 2001: 22)

In those fifteen months, survivors reconstituted themselves personally, politically, and Jewishly. They married, often out of loneliness rather than love, dared to have children even when their future was uncertain, even when they had lost their first families. Perhaps most dramatically, even while living in the lands of their oppression, they dared to circumcise their sons but months after the mark of the covenant could have condemned them to death.

In the aftermath of dehumanization and destruction, survivors reclaimed their lives and renewed the will to restore the Jewish people. Within three years of liberation Israel was born, but even then the future was uncertain. Would the fledgling state withstand the onslaught of war declared against it by its neighbors and would survivors of the *Churban* (the destruction)—it was not yet known as the Holocaust—dare to place themselves in danger once again?

Historians note that the period 1945–1967 was a period of Jewish rebirth, restoration, regeneration of life. One wonders if the motif of resurrection would have been used had it not been so central to Christianity, but the major response to overwhelming death was the fervent re-creation of Jewish life. Only later, however, did a language of Holocaust and Rebirth give voice to this phenomenon. Only later did the Jewish community begin to see what had been done.

The re-creation of Jewish life astonishingly reinvigorated the ultra-Orthodox community. Hasidism, the fervent pietism of eighteenth- and nineteenth-century Poland, long viewed as being in corrupt and inevitable decline, reasserted itself with new vigor in Brooklyn and Jerusalem as well as in places farther removed from large Jewish populations. Katzenelson's plaintive fear, well-grounded in 1944, that "all's gone, gone" has not been realized. On the contrary, Jewish communities and traditions have come back in remarkable ways.

Judaism is the ongoing creation of a living people wrestling with its traditions and shaping its future. Thus, it can be said that Judaism responded to the Holocaust by Zionism and the empowerment of the Jewish people. Jews and Judaism also responded by bearing witness about the Holocaust, by commemoration and remembrance, and by transforming the Shoah into a universal call to conscience. The Israeli scholar Yehuda Bauer (b. 1926) argued, "The reason why Holocaust survivors turned to Zionism is not hard to understand. The murder of the European Jews seemed to vindicate the Zionist argument that there was no future for Jews in Europe" (in Rosensaft 2001: 25). After World War I, Jews could imagine that they could find their future by appealing for the protection of minority rights within majority cultures. After World War II, that position was untenable. Even during World War II, the Biltmore Conference, convened in New York in May 1942, united Zionists in a program for the establishment of a Jewish State in Palestine.

Emphasis on empowerment for the Jewish people accompanied Zionist initiatives. Powerlessness invites victimization, and the experience of the Holocaust evoked a great upsurge in Jewish power and willingness to employ that power for specifically Jewish causes. During the second half of the twentieth century, the State of Israel became a regional military superpower and a dominant presence in the Middle East. It repeatedly demonstrates the link between the Holocaust and that accumulation of power by bringing state visitors to Yad Vashem, Israel's and the Jewish People's Memorial to the Holocaust, which is situated in Jerusalem, and by periodic flyovers from Tel Aviv to Auschwitz by the Israeli Air Force. The message is clear: Israel's task is to protect the Jewish people, and Israel has the power to do so. The accumulation of power, however, has not enabled Israel or the Jewish people to shake senses of vulnerability, at least not completely. How Judaism will and should respond to these realities is a chapter of Jewish life still in the making.

Survivors once proclaimed a simple message: *Never Again.* This impassioned cry of an anguished people said that no one—Jews or others—should have to suffer as they had suffered. Although mass atrocity crimes continue, the Holocaust has a central place in contemporary political and ethical consciousness. It has become the negative absolute, a cornerstone for consideration of values. Under the leadership of survivors, museums and memorials teaching and commemorating the Holocaust have been created throughout the world. Holocaust remembrance has become a basic part of the Jewish calendar and increasingly a part of the calendars of many nations affected by the Holocaust, including the United States, Germany, Poland, and Great Britain, as well as the United Nations. Because of Holocaust denial and antisemitism, many governments have placed increasing emphasis on Holocaust commemoration.

Utilizing state-of-the-art technologies, Holocaust survivor testimony has been gathered on an unprecedented scale, supplementing the many memoirs that survivors have written. These developments ensure that the survivors' witnessing voices will live long after their lives end, continuing to form cornerstones for films and educational programs for generations. The generation of Holocaust survivors responded to survival in the most biblical of ways: by remembering evil and suffering in order to strengthen the force of conscience, by enlarging memory and broadening responsibility. The ancient Israelites responded to slavery and the Exodus in that way. By transforming victimization into witness, dehumanization into a plea to deepen our humanity, survivors of the Shoah carry on traditions that are central to Judaism, the life of the Jewish people, and the future of humanity itself.

The narrative of the Jewish people has been altered. Shaped in slavery, biblical Jews and their descendants told of their enslavement and redemption, the Exodus from Egypt, and their standing before Sinai and hearing the revelation of God that demanded the best of humanity. Jews must now speak of their journey from freedom into slavery and to the revelation of the anti-man and anti-God that was Auschwitz. To live authentically after the Shoah, to journey forth into the future, to enliven post-Holocaust Judaism, they must testify to and struggle with these diverse and even conflicting moments in Jewish memory.

REFERENCES

BERENBAUM, M. (1990). *Beyond Tragedy and Triumph: Essays in Modern Jewish Thought and the American Experience.* Cambridge: Cambridge University Press.

BLUMENTHAL, D. (1993). *Facing the Abusing God: A Theology of Protest.* Louisville, KY: Westminster John Knox Press.

COHN-SHERBOK, D. (2002). *Holocaust Theology: A Reader.* New York: New York University Press.

CURZON, D. (ed.) (1994). *Modern Poems on the Bible.* Philadelphia, PA: Jewish Publication Society.

FACKENHEIM, E. (1972). *God's Presence in History: Jewish Affirmations and Philosophical Reflections.* New York: Harper Torchbooks.

——(1982). *To Mend the World: Foundations for Future Jewish Thought.* New York: Schocken Books.

FLEISCHNER, E. (ed.) (1977). *Auschwitz: Beginning of a New Era? Reflections on the Holocaust.* New York: Ktav.

GREENBERG, I. (1987). *Perspectives: Voluntary Covenant.* New York: CLAL-The National Jewish Center for Learning and Leadership.

HALIVNI, D. (1996). *The Book and the Sword: A Life of Learning in the Shadows of Destruction.* New York: Farrar, Straus and Giroux.

——(2007). *Breaking the Tablets: Jewish Theology After the Shoah.* Ed. and introd. P. Ochs. Lanham, MD: Rowman & Littlefield.

KATZENELSON, Y. (1980). *The Song of the Murdered Jewish People.* Ed. S. Derech. Tel Aviv: Hakibbutz Hameuchad Publishing House.

ROSENSAFT, M. (ed.) (2001). *Life Reborn: Jewish Displaced Persons 1945–1951.* Washington, DC: United States Holocaust Memorial Museum.

RUBENSTEIN, R. (1966). *After Auschwitz: Radical Theology and Contemporary Judaism* Indianapolis, IN: Bobbs-Merrill.

SCHULWEIS, H. (1984). *Evil and the Morality of God.* Cincinnati, OH: Hebrew Union College Press.

WIESEL, E. (1967). "On Jewish Values in the Post-Holocaust Future." *Judaism* 16/3: 281–84.

——(2006). *Night.* New York: Hill and Wang.

WOLLHEIM, N. (1991). Interview with N. Wollheim, 10 and 17 May 1991. Oral History Collection, United States Holocaust Memorial Museum.

OTHER SUGGESTED READING

BERKOVITS, E. (1973). *Faith After the Holocaust.* New York: Ktav.

BRAITERMAN, Z. (1998). *(God) After Auschwitz: Tradition and Change in Post-Holocaust Thought.* Princeton, NJ: Princeton University Press.

KATZ, S. (2005). *The Impact of the Holocaust on Jewish Theology.* New York: New York University Press.

——BIDERMAN, S., and GREENBERG, G. (eds.) (2007). *Wrestling with God: Jewish Theological Responses during and after the Holocaust.* New York: Oxford University Press.

PATTERSON, D. (2006). *Open Wounds: The Crisis of Jewish Thought in the Aftermath of the Holocaust.* Seattle, WA: University of Washington Press.

ROSKIES, D. (1999). *Against the Apocalypse: Responses to Catastrophe in Modern Jewish Culture.* Syracuse, NY: Syracuse University Press.

ROTH, J. and BERENBAUM, M. (eds.) (1989). *Holocaust: Religious and Philosophical Implications.* New York: Paragon House.

RUBENSTEIN, R. (1992). *After Auschwitz: History, Theology, and Contemporary Judaism.* 2nd edn. Baltimore, MD: Johns Hopkins University Press.

CHAPTER 40

CHRISTIANITY

STEPHEN R. HAYNES

CONSIDERATIONS of Christianity and the Holocaust have produced challenging questions, fierce debates, and a voluminous literature. As with Holocaust studies generally, perspectives have evolved steadily in the decades since the end of World War II, with new developments catalyzed by important publications.

Postwar church pronouncements on Christian–Jewish relations demonstrate that the Holocaust has caused a theological reorientation in much of contemporary Christianity. Many of these statements, which are accessible at <www.jcrelations. net>, acknowledge Christian co-responsibility for the Holocaust, illuminate the Jewish roots of Christianity, reaffirm Israel's election, condemn antisemitism, and call for understanding and cooperation between Christians and Jews. Evidence of a changing Christian stance toward Judaism also exists in the curricula of theological seminaries (some of which offer courses in Judaism and/or Christian–Jewish relations), commitments to dialogue, specialized centers dedicated to Christian–Jewish understanding, and the establishment of denominational agencies charged with maintaining positive relations with Jews.

Of course, denominational initiatives do not always represent the views of people in the pew. Some conservative Christians still believe that Jews suffer under divine judgment as reluctant witnesses to the truth of the gospel. But the extent of the Holocaust's impact on Christian faith is indicated by the fact that even Christians who seek the conversion of Jews are careful to preface their endorsements of such evangelism with condemnations of antisemitism and persecution (Lausanne Committee for World Evangelization 1989; Southern Baptist Convention 1996).

Milestones in the recognition of the Holocaust's significance for the churches extend from the Stuttgart Confession of Guilt (1945) and the Ten Points of

Seelisberg (1947) of the International Council of Christians and Jews, to the Second Vatican Council's "Declaration on the Relation of the Church to Non-Christian Religions" (1965), the pioneering work of Christians in developing Holocaust courses in North American colleges and universities, the founding of an annual Scholars' Conference on the Holocaust and the Churches (1970), the statement on "renovation" of Christian–Jewish relations by the Synod of the Evangelical Church of the Rhineland (1980), Pope John Paul II's visit to a Roman synagogue (1986), and the Vatican statement "We Remember: Reflections on the Shoah" (1998). Yet some insist that the post-Holocaust church has failed to sufficiently rethink Christian belief and practice. Christian hostility toward Jews over two millennia and culminating in the Nazi "Final Solution," they claim, reveals indisputably the church's "mass apostasy" from authentic Christianity (Littell 1975). Since the Holocaust is "the greatest tragedy for Christians since the crucifixion" (Cargas 1990: 1), a truly post-Holocaust faith must reassess every doctrine—every Christian affirmation— in the shadow of Auschwitz (Metz 1981). This challenge has been taken up by theologians from many traditions who feel an obligation to revise Christian thought and practice "after Auschwitz."

CHRISTIANITY AND ANTISEMITISM

Scholars continue to explore two long-standing and still vexing questions: What role has Christianity played in the origin and perpetuation of antisemitism? Is antipathy toward Jews fundamental to—or an unfortunate distortion of— Christian faith? The first question focuses on historical links between Christianity and persistent Jew-hatred, the second on whether the roots of antisemitism in the Christian tradition can be reliably identified.

The first question's persistence illustrates how the Holocaust has shaped perceptions of Christianity's historical legacy. A few studies addressing the relationship of Christian faith and Jew-hatred preceded full awareness of the Shoah (Parkes 1934; Trachtenberg 1943), but most accounts of Christianity's responsibility for anti-Jewish sentiment in the west, and thus for the beliefs and attitudes that made the Holocaust possible, responded directly to that catastrophe (Isaac 1964; Flannery 1965; Heer 1970; Ruether 1974; Littell 1975; Nicholls 1993; and Carroll 2001). Although these studies raised awareness of Christian Jew-hatred and its centrality to the church's history and theology, their authors' zeal to demonstrate Christian complicity in Jewish suffering sometimes led them to draw too straight a historical line between Christian ideas and Nazi deeds. For instance, Littell wrote that "the cornerstone of Christian Antisemitism is the superseding or displacement myth... [which] already rings with a genocidal note" (1975: 2); and Ruether claimed that modern racial antisemitism was simply a "secular mutation" of religious anti-Judaism. But most historians, cautious about positing a causal connection between Christianity and the Holocaust, have echoed Yosef Yerushalmi's response to Ruether: Even if "Christian teaching was a necessary cause leading to the Holocaust, it was surely not a sufficient one" (Yerushalmi in Fleischner 1977: 103; Rittner and Roth 1997: 46–7).

The distinction between necessary and sufficient conditions establishes helpful parameters for considering relationships between Christian antipathy for Jews and the Nazi "Final Solution" (Rubenstein and Roth 2003). The affirmation that Nazi genocide could not have occurred without Christian ideological contributions (i.e., that Christianity was a necessary condition for the Holocaust) accords religious prejudice the prominence it deserves, while the denial that Christianity alone can explain the Holocaust (i.e., it was not a sufficient condition) guards against obscuring other necessary conditions, including nationalism, anti-communism, class antagonism, economic deprivation, and world war.

Another conceptual tool for assessing Christian responsibility in the Holocaust is the distinction between anti-Judaism and antisemitism, the former term designating anti-Jewish religious polemic, the latter attitudes based in ethnic or "racial" prejudice. Although the terms are commonly employed in this way, the distinction can become apologetic when it implies that Christian expressions of hostility toward Jews are by definition discontinuous with modern forms of Jew-hatred. To emphasize continuity and deny a qualitative distinction between religious and secular forms of anti-Jewish prejudice, some utilize the phrase "Christian antisemitism." Each approach invites problems. The temptation in the first case is to effect a semantic denial of Christian responsibility for modern antisemitism and the Holocaust; in the second case it is to over-determine the relationship between Christian Jew-hatred and the "Final Solution," so that Christian *precedents* for Nazi anti-Jewish measures are assumed to be *causes* of Nazi antisemitism.

A mediating position defines anti-Judaism as "a nonrational reaction to overcome nonrational [religious] doubts," while antisemitism is "the hostility aroused by irrational thinking about 'Jews,'" whether or not it is expressed in a religious idiom (Langmuir 1990: 275–6). The bridge between the two, according to Langmuir, was established in nonrational reactions against Jews—including the accusation of deicide and the belief that Jews suffered divine punishment for this crime—that formed the core of Christian anti-Judaism and laid the groundwork for later antisemitism.

A second concern of scholars is whether antipathy for Jews, "racial" or otherwise, is foundational to Christianity or a contingent and even alien element that crept in with Christendom's construction. Seeking to document the tragic history of Jewish life in Christendom, some postwar Christian writers responded optimistically to this question. Emphasizing the persistence of anti-Jewish prejudice in the centuries preceding the Holocaust, they nevertheless assumed that Christian anti-Judaism had historical and theological roots that could be identified and extirpated. One new paradigm for interpreting the relationship between Christianity and Jew-hatred contended that Christian anti-Judaism was essential to the early Christian movement's understanding of itself as the "true Israel" and of Jesus as the Jewish Messiah (Ruether 1974). Scholarship that followed this lead holds that "the basic root of modern antisemitism lies squarely in the Gospels and the rest of the New Testament" (Parkes in Davies 1979: xi) but expresses hope that authentic faith in Jesus' message may be extricated from the church's christological dogma.

Some scholars reject such hope, contending that the impulse to hate and murder Jews is not aberrant but, arguably, essential to mainstream Christianity—perhaps not part of the Christian creed but an integral part of the Christian story (Maccoby 1982). In this perspective, the Holocaust was a long-delayed result of hostile teachings about Jews that are fundamental to the Christian narrative (Rosenbaum 1998). Suggesting that "Christianity" or "Christian faith" may be inherently anti-Jewish, Maccoby undermines the assumption that Jew-hatred is a corruption of the Christian gospel.

Whether or not anti-Judaism dwells at the heart of Christian faith, "volatile ambivalence" is undoubtedly to be found there (Rubenstein and Roth 2003: 52). In the patristic era, for instance, Christian identity was shaped both by the anti-Jewish polemic of the *adversus Judaeos* tradition as well as by popular philo-Judaism (Simon 1986). These paradoxical impulses were combined in the theology of Augustine (354–430), who claimed that Jewish existence testifies to the Jews' condemnation for killing Christ as well as to their divinely willed preservation (Haynes 1995). This conception of Jewish destiny as one of exile and oppression defined Jewish life in Christendom until the late eleventh century, when a marked increase in Christian hostility contributed to a diminishment of the physical security implied by Augustinian witness-people theology. While the official theological view persisted—as "living letters of Scripture" (Bernard of Clairvaux) Jews were not to be killed but preserved in miserable safety until the end of the age—tens of thousands of European Jews died at Christian hands during the late Middle Ages.

Scholars have long sought to understand the origins of this change. Langmuir (1990) identified the crucial ideological shift in irrational fantasies about Jews that emerged in the twelfth century, particularly the charge that Jews commit ritual murder against Christians. Jeremy Cohen (1982) saw a turning point in the thirteenth-century efforts of mendicant religious orders to rid Christendom of Jews. Bernard Lewis (1986) perceived a fateful change in the shift toward race-based antisemitism in fifteenth-century Spain, where Jews were first defined in terms of descent rather than belief. These *limpiezza de sangra* laws are widely viewed as foreshadowing the racial theories that led to the Holocaust (Nicholls 1993).

What is beyond doubt is that the Augustinian understanding of Jewish existence after the appearance of Christ was strained to the breaking point in Jewish massacres during the Crusades, the episodic popular hysteria over ritual murder charges, the conception and implementation of Spanish blood purity statutes, and the tirades of Martin Luther (1483–1546). Furthermore, the relevance of Augustinian witness-people theology was called into question by the disconcerting realization that Jews were not a People of the Book in the sense assumed by Augustine: While these "librarians" of the church bore "the law and the prophets as testimony to the tenets of the church," Jews' other books (the "oral Torah" codified in collections such as the Talmud) prohibited them from recognizing that "all that Moses wrote is of Christ." When it became clear that the practice of actual Jews did not conform to the model of the "hermeneutical Jew" constructed by Christian theology, the response included church-sanctioned public burnings of Jewish books (Cohen 1999: 2, 27).

By the eighteenth century, without discarding traditional notions of Jews as Christ-killers and conspirators against Christendom, European Christians began to adopt vague racial conceptions of Jews' essential otherness. While this volatile mixture of Christian Jew-hatred and "scientific" racism helped fuel the Holocaust, even in the Nazi era Augustinian ambivalence continued to animate the Christian mind, in which could be found ancient canards such as deicide and forced dispersion, pockets of intense theological philo-Semitism, and repeated invocations of the "mystery" of Israel.

CHRISTIANITY AND NAZISM

That Nazism was an anti-Christian movement has been an enduring but problematic truism. This view of National Socialism was forged in the 1930s, when American churchmen interpreted Nazism as an outbreak of "unbaptized nationalism" in the heart of Christendom, a "tribalism with religious overtones," a "new paganism" that "denied all the Christian and humanist presuppositions of our civilization" (Wentz 1954: 321, 323, 325). Awareness of Nazi crimes against Jews only intensified the perception among Christians in America and Great Britain that National Socialism was an "inversion of Christianity" that actively sought the "negation of a *Christian* God" (Lawson 2007: 406).

The conviction that Nazism was irreconcilable with western, Christian values has also been nurtured by historians, social scientists, and philosophers. In an influential interpretation of "Nazi culture," George Mosse analyzed a memorandum by Martin Bormann (1900–1945?) on the incompatibility of National Socialist and Christian concepts, concluding that Bormann's was the "real face of the leadership," his claim that "we can do without Christianity" a reflection of the Nazis' "real aims" (Mosse 1966: 237). When political religion theorists describe Nazism as an ersatz or surrogate religion complete with myths, rituals, prophets, martyrs, canonical texts, redemption through antisemitism, and a promised millennium (Langmuir 1990; Lease 1994), they sustain the portrait of a competing religious movement determined to replace, if not destroy, the churches. Endorsing this portrayal of Nazism are philosophers who interpret it as a spiritual assault on the western tradition—a rebellion against ethical monotheism, a promethean effort at self-liberation from the shackles of divine law, a grand subversion of western morality through the forging of a "Nazi ethic" (Haas 1988).

This image of National Socialism as a transvaluation of traditional values, profoundly if discreetly anti-Christian, lends credibility to claims that the Nazis were as anti-Christian as they were anti-Jewish and that suppression of the churches was an inevitable result of their success. But later scholarship has discredited these claims by challenging three crucial assumptions: (1) that Christians, paralyzed by the threat of victimization, were fearful bystanders in the state's war against Jews; (2) that the Christian solution to the "Jewish problem," however hatefully expressed, was incompatible with the Nazi "Final Solution"; and (3) that the Nazi worldview was fundamentally anti-Christian.

The first assumption finds support in the stories of prominent Christians whose faith led them to resist the Nazis sacrificially and of thousands of less-known gentile rescuers who are the subject of a growing literature (Gushee 2003). But the tragic reality is that the vast majority of Christians were not resisters, rescuers, or victims. Although most Christians did not perpetrate crimes against Jews, nearly all the people who did were shaped by one or another form of Christian faith. Whatever we might conclude about the depth or authenticity of this faith, the actions of Holocaust perpetrators reflect the moral and theological failures of the churches.

Scholarship in the past two decades shows that many German Christians welcomed the Nazi revolution as an opportunity for the resurgence of "Christian values" and that this hope in the culturally redemptive character of National Socialism led to active Christian collaboration with the Nazi state. Leading theologians and biblical scholars were among the most enthusiastic supporters of Nazism (Ericksen 1985). The pro-Nazi movement of "German Christians" (*Deutsche Christen*) was born not of government manipulation or Christian opportunism but from a deep affinity for National Socialism that was rarely invited or reciprocated (Bergen 1996). Christian scholars in Nazi Germany, laboring with and without official support, fashioned a so-called Aryan Jesus (Heschel 2008). The emerging scholarly consensus regarding Protestant reactions to Nazism is accurately summarized as follows: "For every Protestant who expressed misgivings privately, there was another who believed Nazism meant a return to Christianity" (Steigmann-Gall 2007: 205).

What of the Confessing Church (*Bekennende Kirche*) and the 1934 Barmen Declaration, high points in "the church's confession under Hitler" (Cochrane 1962)? For decades the confessing movement in the Protestant churches was considered the anti-Nazi resistance at prayer, the German "church struggle" a symbol of the inevitable conflict between paganism and Christianity. This conflict's stakes were dramatized by the stories of persecuted Confessing Church heroes, including Karl Barth (1886–1968), Martin Niemöller (1892–1984), and Dietrich Bonhoeffer (1906–1945). Later scholarship, however, has deflated heroic myths associated with the "confessors" by documenting the Confessing Church's endemic antisemitism, its fierce loyalty to the state, and its determination to maintain the privileges of an established church (Barnett 1992; Gerlach 2000).

Parallel developments characterize the scholarly picture of the Roman Catholic Church's response to Nazism. No longer preoccupied with Catholics as Nazi victims, more recent research focuses on Catholics who embraced the regime— church theologians who translated National Socialism into a Catholic idiom, as well as "brown priests" who commended Nazism to their parishioners (Spicer 2008). The wartime actions of Pope Pius XII (1876–1958) have also reignited controversy (Cornwell 1999). The official Catholic position states that Pius "personally or through his representatives . . . save[d] hundreds of thousands of Jewish lives" ("We Remember" 1998). Yet most scholars conclude that Pius could have done more to oppose Nazi genocide and save Jewish victims (Rittner and Roth 2002).

Explanations for Pius's shortcomings include charges that he was a power-hungry autocrat and/or an antisemite, that his moral vision was obscured by a determination to resist the spread of communism or to protect the Catholic Church from Nazi onslaughts, that he sought to maintain Vatican neutrality at any cost, and that he acted to preserve Christian domination in a Europe free of Jews (Phayer in Dietrich 2003: 87–98). Defenders argue that the pope spoke against Nazism and used his influence to rescue thousands of Jews, all the while saving the Catholic Church from potential destruction (Rychlak 2005). Despite condemning antisemitism and commemorating the Shoah, the post-Holocaust Catholic Church remains reluctant to implicate its leadership in errors committed by nameless "sons and daughters of the church." Concern grows that under Pope Benedict XVI Jewish–Catholic dialogue has begun to stagnate (Pawlikowski 2007).

Recent scholarship challenges a second assumption: namely, that Christian and Nazi solutions to the "Jewish problem" were incompatible because religious and racial forms of antisemitism are distinct. Some scholars have argued that this distinction is more appearance than reality since the church fathers indulged in racist thinking when they posited innate evil as the essence of Jewishness (Michael 2005). Others have called the distinction into question by pointing to Martin Luther's role in preparing the German soil from which Nazi antisemitism sprang. In addition to suggestive parallels between Nazi anti-Jewish measures and Luther's advice for curtailing Jews' "blasphemy," scholars have noted adumbrations of modern German antisemitism in Luther's "destructionist ideal of Jewish redemption" (Rose 1990: 5).

This provocative scholarly trajectory, however, relies on a dubious reading of Luther. Nazi leaders may have been influenced by Luther's volatile prescriptions in "On the Jews and Their Lies" (1543). Indisputably they utilized Luther's writings on the Jews to advance their antisemitic propaganda. But whether Luther shared the goal that motivated the architects of the "Final Solution" is far from clear. Even his conclusion that "we are at fault in not slaying [the Jews]" can be reasonably interpreted as expressing frustration at the limits of the church's (Augustinian) solution to the "Jewish problem" rather than an invitation to ignore it.

Recent scholarship also criticizes a third assumption—that the Nazi worldview was fundamentally anti-Christian (Steigmann-Gall 2004; Michael 2005). These studies focus not on Christians who wished to subject Nazism to forced baptism, but on the Christian character of the movement itself. Analyzing Christian and pagan impulses among the Nazi elite, Steigmann-Gall concludes that the paganist cohort, which never achieved dominance, "was highly ambivalent toward and quite partial in its rejection of Christianity" (2007: 187). "Although increasingly hostile to the churches," he argues, Nazism "never became uniformly anti-Christian" (2004: 12). Michael analyzes the religiosity of Adolf Hitler (1889–1945), whom he views as a predictable, if extreme, product of Christian antisemitism. Hitler's identity as a baptized (and never excommunicated) Catholic has long been a source of shame for Christians, many of whom have portrayed him as alienated from the church and fascinated by pagan myths and the occult. According to Michael, however, Hitler was socialized into Jew-hatred by an Austrian Catholicism that made him a "Christian antisemite" long before his arrival in Vienna. Hitler's private and public utterances, Michael contends, indicate that he thought of himself as a Christian informed by the Bible, the church fathers, and Martin Luther. Accordingly, Michael interprets the "Final Solution" as a modern Crusade in which Hitler "acted out an ideology of hatred that had been implicit in Christian religious and racial antisemitism for centuries" (2005: 184).

Invoking Jesus himself as an anti-Jewish crusader, Hitler and the Nazis undoubtedly saw in Christianity a crucial ideological ally in their struggle against "the Jew." Nevertheless, without denying Christianity's deep implication in antisemitism, the Christian rhetoric of Hitler and other Nazi ideologues was arguably cynical and self-serving, Christian symbols being "used and abused to make political points" (Poewe 2006: 143). Hitler's "Christianity" is particularly dubious, expressed in the vaguest references to the will of "the Lord"—a being interchangeable with "Providence," "the Almighty," or even "Nature." In any case, Hitler seemed to understand that because the church perpetuated the "big lie" that cast Jews as a religious rather than a racial community, Christian perceptions of the Jew were a mixed blessing. Claims for the "Christian" character of Nazism should be considered alongside evidence for the influence of the "German pagan faiths, expressed in countless new religions, by diverse leaders and adherents both inside and outside of the official church" (Poewe 2006: 1). Viewing Christianity as "dead—rejected, overcome, ineffectual," prominent National Socialists, including Hitler, were "uniformly ob-sessed" with overcoming it (Poewe 2006: 143, 150).

CHRISTIANITY AND THE JEWISH PEOPLE

As Christianity's relationship to Jews and Judaism has undergone reassessment in recent decades, scholars and church bodies have identified several tasks as crucial to developing a post-Holocaust Christian theology of Israel:

(1) *Establishing the Christian Significance of the Holocaust.* Many post-Holocaust Christian scholars regard "Auschwitz as an occasion for rethinking" the church's theology and practice (Mussner 1984: 1). For some, this rethinking is imperative and urgent. As Johann Baptist Metz contends, "Auschwitz is not really a matter of revising Christian theology with regard to Judaism, but a matter of revising Christian theology altogether" (1981: 22). "Never again should any theologian write anything that might even remotely reopen the path from supersession to genocide," writes Darrell Fasching (1992: 15). For still others, the Holocaust re-minds Christians of their intimate connection to Jews, Auschwitz serving as a "monumental sign of the intimate bond and unity between the Jewish martyrs . . . and the crucified Christ" (Thoma 1980: 159). As this statement suggests, however, the Christian significance of the Holocaust can be interpreted in many ways.

(2) *Identifying the Roots of Christian Jew-hatred.* Peering through the lens of the Holocaust, Christians have sought to uncover anti-Judaism's roots in the Christian tradition. But it is not clear how far these roots have sunk into the soil of Christian history. Is anti-Judaism "a function of Christian triumphalism" (Hall in Davies 1979: 168), spawned by the fateful alliance of church and state in the fourth century? Did it emerge in the second century as a Christian "teaching of contempt" evolved in patristic *adversus Judaeos* literature? Was the faith corrupted by a replacement theology that is already evident in the New Testament? These questions are more than theoretical. How they are answered determines the agenda for those who wish to revise Christian faith in the shadow of the Holocaust.

(3) *Retrieving Jesus' Jewishness.* Nineteenth-century biblical scholarship sought to illumine Jesus' universal qualities by removing him from the shadow of Judaism. During the Nazi era, some Christian scholars extended this trend, arguing that Jesus of Nazareth had not been Jewish at all, but "Aryan" (Heschel 2008). In the postwar period the anti-Jewish biases of Christian theology and biblical scholarship have gradually been acknowledged and condemned, partly as a result of the church's complicity in Jewish suffering. Today the standard portrait of Jesus emphasizes the Jewishness of his words, prayers, dress, customs, and thought

world. While he may have disputed with some of the Torah's interpreters, he "lived in solidarity with his people, their faith and ways of life" (Thoma 1980: 116). Significantly, traditional and progressive Christians tend to agree that exploring and recovering Jesus' Jewishness is a key to post-Holocaust Christian authenticity.

(4) *Reassessing Responsibility for Jesus' Death.* Who killed Jesus? In the wake of the Holocaust, this question has profound implications for Jewish life. The deicide charge is often seen as the taproot of Christian anti-Judaism, while New Testament accounts of Jesus' death are regarded as tendentious reflections of late first-century tensions between a fledgling Christian community and established Jewish groups (Pagels 1996). Some have encouraged Christians to adopt a historically corrected version of the gospel accounts of Jesus' relations with his Jewish contemporaries (Eckardt and Eckardt 1982); others have argued that, read in their proper context, Jesus' angry sayings in the Gospels are "nothing more than one Jew might say of another" (Nicholls 1993: 76). Yet there is general acknowledgment that the New Testament's portrait of Jesus as engaged in mortal conflict with other Jews can endanger Jewish life.

(5) *Affirming the Permanent Election of Israel.* If replacement theology is a root of Christian Jew-hatred, affirmation of Israel's divine election appears to be the surest way to extirpate that hostility. Many Christians have embraced this election by recovering the New Testament's metaphor of engraftment developed by Paul in Romans 11, where gentiles are "wild olive shoots" grafted onto a tree whose native branches have been "broken off through unbelief." Paul leaves the status of Jews who reject Christ somewhat uncertain, but post-Holocaust interpretation of Romans 9–11 has emphasized his declarations that "God has not rejected his people whom he foreknew" (11:2) and that "all Israel will be saved" (11:26). Rediscovery of Paul's theology of Israel, central to nearly every post-Holocaust attempt to rethink the relationship of church and synagogue, has provided Christians with a biblical basis for affirming the salvific character of the Jews' covenant and recognizing Judaism as a living religion.

(6) *Describing the Relationship.* Room for various descriptions of the Jewish–Christian relationship exists within the general scheme of a Christian theology that acknowledges Jews have their own route to God. But must a non-supersessionist model of the relationship stress continuity between Judaism and Christianity or can discontinuity be acknowledged as well (McGarry 1977)? Should Christians speak of a single covenant into which gentiles have been integrated, or is it better to refer to two covenants? Is it possible to imagine separate covenants while avoiding theological relativism? And can an integrationist model, according to which the church becomes the God of Israel's way of reaching non-Jews, avoid turning Christianity into "Judaism for gentiles"?

(7) *Redefining Christian Witness to Jews.* If Christians regard Judaism as a living religion with which they are to co-exist, what is to be their witness to Jews? Most post-Holocaust Christians have concluded that dialogue is normative for

encounters with Jews and that proselytizing is forbidden; but does this imply that *all* religious traditions are equally valid? Finding unacceptable post-Holocaust Christian theology's construal of witness as dialogue, some evangelical Christians have reaffirmed their commitment to evangelizing Jews. And what of so-called Jewish Christians? Some have argued they must be central to a theology of Christian–Jewish dialogue (Osten-Sacken 1986); others, recognizing that their status is one of the thorniest issues in the Christian–Jewish relationship, have ignored them.

(8) *Affirming the Promise of Land.* Many in the churches have come to view support for the modern State of Israel as an obligation rooted in the church's failure to protect Jews during their near extermination in Europe. Conservatives find a pro-Israel stance amenable to their eschatological hopes while many liberals see it as a reasonable response to the Holocaust and threats to Israel's security. But as disputes about the Palestinian–Israeli conflict and divestment controversies in several American denominations have shown, Christian promises to protect Jewish interests exist in tension with commitments to peacemaking and justice, as well as long-term alliances with Arab Christians.

(9) *Emphasizing What Jews and Christians Share.* Many post-Holocaust assessments of the relationship emphasize that modern Jews and Christians worship the same God, emerge from the same tradition, and share sacred texts. But each of these assertions raises questions. Is the one God of Israel the same God the church confesses to be triune? Does the concept of a Judeo-Christian tradition obscure important differences? How should the section of the Bible claimed by Jews and Christians be identified? "Old Testament" carries supersessionist connotations, "Hebrew Bible" does not indicate what this part of Scripture means to Christians, and "First Testament" has failed to catch on (as has "Apostolic Writings" as a proposed substitute for "New Testament"). A less complicated way of underscoring commonality is to conceive of Jews and Christians as partners engaged in "mending the world" as they await the fulfillment of messianic promises.

(10) *Doing Christology in a New Way.* Ever since Rosemary Ruether called anti-Judaic polemic "the left-hand" of the church's Christology (Ruether 1974: 121), Christians have displayed uncertainty about which of the church's christological affirmations are meaningful and appropriate in the post-Holocaust environment. No doubt Christology will remain "that which distinguishes and divides" Christians and Jews (Mussner 1984); but since christological affirmations have buttressed the church's anti-Judaism, Christian theologians have labored to develop a "Christology affirmative of Israel" (Osten-Sacken 1986: 41). The most fraught questions include whether it is necessary or acceptable for Christians to speak of Jesus as Messiah of Israel. While the term continues to appear in church statements, some scholars believe that "a Christianity continuing to claim that Jesus is or was the Messiah in any sense cannot avoid being opposed to the Jewish people and

the Jewish faith" (Nicholls 1993: 425). Others have suggested that Christian theology requires the Jewish "no" to Jesus as a reminder that the messianic age has not begun.

CONCLUSION

Christian wrestling with the Holocaust continues to produce new perspectives on the church's belief and practice. Scholars have offered thoroughgoing critiques of anti-Judaism and antisemitism in the Christian tradition, and major church bodies have attempted to guide their members in reflecting on the significance of the Holocaust for Christianity. In the process, they have endorsed novel conclusions: that God's election of Israel is eternal, that Jews should be engaged in dialogue rather than evangelized, that the church's christological claims may be in need of revision, and that sermons, catechetical texts, and the Scriptures themselves should be scrutinized for anti-Jewish stereotypes. The faithful do not embrace all of these conclusions, but they find some resonance in the pews of most Christian churches, which is perhaps the best gauge of the Holocaust's impact on Christianity.

REFERENCES

BARNETT, V. (1992). *For the Soul of the People: Protestant Protest against Hitler*. New York: Oxford University Press.

BERGEN, D. (1996). *Twisted Cross: The German Christian Movement in the Third Reich*. Chapel Hill, NC: University of North Carolina Press.

CARGAS, H. (1990). *Shadows of Auschwitz: A Christian Response to the Holocaust*. New York: Crossroad.

CARROLL, J. (2001). *Constantine's Sword: The Church and the Jews: A History*. Boston, MA: Houghton Mifflin.

COCHRANE, A. (1962). *The Church's Confession under Hitler*. Philadelphia, PA: Westminster.

COHEN, J. (1982). *The Friars and the Jews*. Ithaca, NY: Cornell University Press.

——(1999). *Living Letters of the Law: Ideas of the Jew in Medieval Christianity*. Berkeley, CA: University of California Press.

CORNWELL, J. (1999). *Hitler's Pope: The Secret History of Pius XII*. New York: Viking.

DAVIES, A. (ed.) (1979). *Antisemitism and the Foundations of Christianity*. New York: Paulist Press.

DIETRICH, D. (ed.) (2003). *Christian Responses to the Holocaust: Moral and Ethical Issues*. Syracuse: Syracuse University Press.

ECKARDT, A. R. with ECKARDT, A. (1982). *Long Night's Journey into Day: Life and Faith after the Holocaust*. Detroit, MI: Wayne State University Press.

ERICKSEN, R. (1985). *Theologians under Hitler: Gerhard Kittel, Paul Althaus, and Emanuel Hirsch.* New Haven, CT: Yale University Press.

FASCHING, D. (1992). *Narrative Theology after Auschwitz: From Alienation to Ethics.* Minneapolis, MN: Fortress.

FLANNERY, E. (1965). *The Anguish of the Jews: Twenty-Three Centuries of Anti-Semitism.* New York: Macmillan.

FLEISCHNER, E. (ed.) (1977). *Auschwitz: Beginning of A New Era? Reflections on the Holocaust.* New York: Ktav.

GERLACH, W. (2000). *And the Witnesses Were Silent: The Confessing Church and the Persecution of the Jews.* Ed. V. Barnett. Lincoln, NE: University of Nebraska Press.

GUSHEE, D. (2003). *Righteous Gentiles of the Holocaust: Genocide and Moral Obligation.* 2nd edn. St. Paul, MN: Paragon House.

HAAS, P. (1988). *Morality after Auschwitz: The Radical Challenge of the Nazi Ethic.* Philadelpia, PA: Fortress Press.

HAYNES, S. (1995). *Reluctant Witnesses: Jews and the Christian Imagination.* Louisville, KY: Westminster John Knox Press.

HEER, F. (1970). *God's First Love: Christians and Jews Over Two Thousand Years.* New York: Weybright and Talley.

HESCHEL, S. (2008). *The Aryan Jesus: Christian Theologians and the Bible in Nazi Germany.* Princeton, NJ: Princeton University Press.

ISAAC, J. (1964). *The Teaching of Contempt: Christian Roots of Anti-Semitism.* New York: Holt, Rinehart and Winston.

LANGMUIR, G. (1990). *History, Religion and Antisemitism.* Berkeley, CA: University of California Press.

LAUSANNE COMMITTEE FOR WORLD EVANGELIZATION. (1989). *The Willowbank Declaration on the Christian Gospel and the Jewish People.* Available at: <http://www.lcje.net/willow-bank.html>.

LAWSON, T. (2007). "Shaping the Holocaust: The Influence of Christian Discourse on Perceptions of the European Jewish Tragedy." *Holocaust and Genocide Studies* 21/3: 404–20.

LEASE, G. (1994). *"Odd Fellows" in the Politics of Religion: Modernism, National Socialism, and German Judaism.* Berlin: Mouton de Gruyter.

LEWIS, B. (1986). *Semites and Anti-Semites: An Inquiry into Conflict and Prejudice.* New York: Norton.

LITTELL, F. (1975). *The Crucifixion of the Jews.* New York: Harper and Row.

MACCOBY, H. (1982). *The Sacred Executioner: Human Sacrifice and the Legacy of Guilt.* London: Thames and Hudson.

McGARRY, M. (1977). *Christology After Auschwitz.* New York: Paulist.

METZ, J. (1981). *The Emergent Church: The Future of Christianity in a Postbourgeois World.* New York: Crossroad.

MICHAEL, R. (2005). *Holy Hatred: Christianity, Antisemitism and the Holocaust.* London: Palgrave Macmillan.

MOSSE, G. (1966). *Nazi Culture: Intellectual, Cultural and Social Life in the Third Reich.* New York: Schocken Books.

MUSSNER, F. (1984). *Tractate on the Jews: The Significance of Judaism for Christian Faith.* Philadelphia, PA: Fortress Press.

NICHOLLS, W. (1993). *Christian Antisemitism: A History of Hate.* Northvale, NJ: J. Aronson.

OSTEN-SACKEN, P. VON DER (1986). *Christian–Jewish Dialogue: Theological Foundations.* Philadelphia, PA: Fortress.

PAGELS, E. (1996). *The Origin of Satan.* New York: Vintage.

PARKES, J. (1934). *The Conflict of the Church and the Synagogue: A Study in the Origins of Antisemitism.* London: Soncino Press.

PAWLIKOWSKI, J. (2007). "Reviving the Dialogue: The Church Can Do More to Promote Catholic–Jewish Relations." *Celebration: A Comprehensive Worship Resource* (October 2007): 6–7.

POEWE, K. (2006). *New Religions and the Nazis.* New York and London. Routledge.

RITTNER, C. and ROTH, J. (eds.) (1997). *From the Unthinkable to the Unavoidable: American Christian and Jewish Scholars Encounter the Holocaust.* Westport, CT: Praeger.

————(2002). *Pope Pius XII and the Holocaust.* New York: Continuum.

ROSE, P. (1990). *German Question/Jewish Question: Revolutionary Antisemitism from Kant to Wagner.* Princeton, NJ: Princeton University Press.

ROSENBAUM, R. (1998). *Explaining Hitler: The Search for the Origins of His Evil.* New York: Random House.

RUBENSTEIN, R. and ROTH, J. (2003). *Approaches to Auschwitz: The Holocaust and Its Legacy.* Rev. edn. Louisville, KY: Westminster John Knox Press.

RUETHER, R. (1974). *Faith and Fratricide: The Theological Roots of Anti-Semitism.* New York: Seabury.

RYCHLAK, R. (2005). *Righteous Gentiles: How Pius XII and the Catholic Church Saved Half a Million Jews from the Nazis.* Dallas, TX: Spence Publishing Company.

SIMON, M. (1986). *Verus Israel: A Study of the Relations between Christians and Jews in the Roman Empire, 135–425.* New York: Oxford University Press.

SOUTHERN BAPTIST CONVENTION (1996). *Resolution On Jewish Evangelism.* Available at: <http://www.jcrelations.net/en/?item=987>.

SPICER, K. (2008). *Hitler's Priests: Catholic Clergy and National Socialism.* Dekalb, IL: Northern Illinois University Press.

STEIGMANN-GALL, R. (2004). *Holy Reich: Nazi Conceptions of Christianity, 1919–1945.* Cambridge: Cambridge University Press.

——(2007). "Christianity and the Nazi Movement: A Response." *Journal of Contemporary History* 42: 185–211.

THOMA, C. (1980). *A Christian Theology of Judaism.* New York: Paulist Press.

TRACHTENBERG, J. (1943). *The Devil and the Jews: The Medieval Conception of the Jew and Its Relation to Modern Anti-Semitism.* New Haven, CT: Yale University Press.

WENTZ, F. (1954). "American Protestant Journals and the Nazi Religious Assault." *Church History* 23/4: 321–38.

OTHER SUGGESTED READING

BERGER, A. and PATTERSON, D., with GUSHEE, D., PAWLIKOWSKI, J., and ROTH, J. (2008). *Jewish–Christian Dialogue: Drawing Honey from the Rock.* St. Paul, MN: Paragon House.

ERICKSEN, R. and HESCHEL, S. (eds.) (1999). *Betrayal: German Churches and the Holocaust.* Minneapolis, MN: Fortress Press.

GROB, L. and ROTH, J. (eds.) (2008). *Anguished Hope: Holocaust Scholars Confront the Palestinian–Israeli Conflict.* Grand Rapids, MI: Eerdmans.

HAYNES, S. (2006). *The Bonhoeffer Legacy: Post-Holocaust Perspectives.* Minneapolis, MN: Fortress Press.

PALDIEL, M. (2007). *The Righteous among the Nations: Rescuers of Jews during the Holocaust.* New York: HarperCollins.

PHAYER, M. (2000). *The Catholic Church and the Holocaust, 1930–1965.* Bloomington, IN: Indiana University Press.

——(2008). *Pius XII, The Holocaust, and the Cold War.* Bloomington, IN: Indiana University Press.

RITTNER, C. and ROTH, J. (2001). *"Good News" after Auschwitz? Christian Faith within a Post-Holocaust World.* Macon, GA: Mercer University Press.

WILLIAMSON, C. (1993). *A Guest in the House of Israel: Post-Holocaust Church Theology.* Louisville, KY: Westminster John Knox Press.

ZUCCOTTI, S. (2000). *Under His Very Windows: The Vatican and the Holocaust in Italy.* New Haven, CT: Yale University Press.

CHAPTER 41

GERMANY

JEFFREY HERF

In the past decade, historians have changed the terms of debate regarding the substance and scope of memory and public discussion of the Holocaust in both the Federal Republic of Germany (West Germany) and in the German Democratic Republic (East Germany) after their foundations in 1949. A previously conventional juxtaposition of silence to memory has been supplemented by an emphasis on the multiplicity of memories. Recent historical scholarship has drawn attention especially to the first postwar decade, when the political cultures of both Germanys and the contours of public memory of Nazi crimes took shape (Herf 1997). The historical distinctiveness of the West German process of "coming to terms with the past" (*Vergangenheitsbewältigung*) did not lie in the much discussed and recurrent phenomena of silence and avoidance. These reflexes are the norm in post-dictatorial societies. Rather, given the enormity of the crimes the Nazi regime committed against the Jewish people, what calls for explanation is the presence of any truthful memory and any consequential judicial reckoning in the country after 1945.

The emergence of a distinctive German tradition of grappling with the nation's past depended on several preconditions. First, the Allied governments won an unconditional victory over the Nazi regime followed by a four-year military occupation during which no sovereign German government or state existed. The abjectness of Germany's defeat made a new version of the "stab in the back" legend after World War I simply impossible and completed the discrediting of the Nazi Party as a serious political force. The victors' complete power made possible the arrest of approximately 100,000 officials of the Nazi regime, followed by the International Military Tribunal in Nuremberg as well as some 90,000 indictments of Germans for war crimes. These and other denazification measures in all zones of occupied Germany were more consequential than is often realized. Above all, the judicial proceedings brought the basic facts of the Holocaust and other Nazi crimes to the attention of the German public and left behind a massive documentary record. After Nuremberg, although many people in West, East, and united Germany sought to avoid discussion about the Holocaust or claim that such crimes were not unique to German history, blunt denial of the basic facts presented never extended beyond extremist fringe parties. Public debate has been about how and why the Holocaust was possible or whether and how it should be discussed, but not about whether or not the Nazi regime in fact murdered approximately six million Jews. In the meantime, examples were made of a substantial number of war criminals: In 1946–47 alone, the United States delivered 3,914 people for trial in sixteen European countries, two-thirds of them to France and Poland; in 1945–49, Allied courts handed down 6,500 convictions on war crimes charges (Götz 1986: 22). To be sure, many perpetrators escaped justice. Yet viewed in comparative perspective of other efforts to come to terms with criminal dictatorships, the Nuremberg era stands out as the most consequential such effort of modern history.

Second, thanks to escapes abroad or to "inner emigration," some German political opponents of Nazism during the Weimar era were alive in 1945 and able to return to politics. All of the leading political figures of early postwar West and East Germany came of political age between 1900 and 1930. They experienced Nazism, World War II, and the Holocaust in their mature, not their young and formative years and interpreted what had happened on the basis of long-held beliefs. The power or "hegemony" of the victors lay in their ability not only to impose their own interpretations on the Germans, but also to encourage some Germans to speak out and repress other, in this case Nazi, voices. The Allies thus helped to bring about "multiple restorations" of the political traditions that Nazism had crushed, including communism, social democracy, liberalism, and a mostly chastened and westernized West German conservatism. The resulting political language and culture of both West and East Germany was less the result of a zero hour or tabula rasa than of the support the victors extended to advocates of these pre-existing ideological outlooks. The power of the occupiers lay less in creating novel ideas about democracy and the rule of law in the west or anti-fascism and communism in the east than in lending aid to German actors who expressed such views. Furthermore, since a sizable German Jewish community no longer existed to force German politicians to take Jewish concerns into account, and a great many Germans had a personal interest in avoiding discussion of the past, Allied support for these prewar opponents of Nazism was indispensable for any postwar reckoning with the past.

Third, as public memory of Nazi crimes emerged, it diverged along the ideological spectrum both within West German politics and between West and East Germany. The Holocaust took center stage in the West, whereas in East Germany, the brutal Nazi invasion and occupation of the Soviet Union became the focus of attention. The self-declared "anti-fascist" East German regime repressed and marginalized the specifics of the Holocaust and became a supporter to the Arab states and of terrorist organizations at war with the State of Israel (Meuschel 1992; Herf 1997: 106–61).

WEST GERMANY

The key figures of the formative years in West Germany were Konrad Adenauer (1876–1967), the leader of the Christian Democrats and chancellor of the Federal Republic of Germany from 1949 to 1963, who had been mayor of Cologne from 1917 to 1933; Kurt Schumacher (1895–1952), the leader of the Social Democrats, who had served in the Reichstag during the Weimar Republic and spent the Nazi years in a concentration camp; Theodor Heuss (1884–1963), the first president of the Federal Republic, who had worked as a journalist, professor of politics, and in liberal politics in the Weimar years; and Ernst Reuter (1889–1953), the Mayor of West Berlin during the crucial early years of the Cold War, who had been a Social Democratic politician in the Weimar era and then a Nazi political prisoner and an exile in Turkey during the Third Reich. The communist leadership in East Germany also came of political age before 1933 and drew on an intact German political tradition. Walter Ulbricht (1893–1973), the effective head of the East German government until 1971, served in the Reichstag from 1928 to 1933, as did Wilhelm Pieck (1876–1960), a comrade and friend of Rosa Luxemburg (1870–1919) and the first President of the German Democratic Republic. Otto Grotewohl (1894–1964), co-chair of the Socialist Unity Party, did the like from 1925 to 1933, albeit as a Social Democrat, not a communist, and Paul Merker (1894–1969), whose unsuccessful efforts to raise the Jewish question in East Berlin led to his political downfall in 1950, had been a leading figure of the German Communist Party since 1920.

From 6 May 1945, two days before the Nazi surrender, until his death at the age of 57 on 20 August 1952, Schumacher repeatedly urged his fellow Germans to face up to the Nazi past, including the mass murder of European Jewry. Among postwar German political leaders, he was the first to support emphatically financial restitution to the Jewish survivors of the Holocaust (*Wiedergutmachung*) and diplomatic relations with the new State of Israel. A democratic socialist, Schumacher believed overcoming the Nazi past meant breaking with German capitalism, but he also stressed that Nazism had been more than a plot by a small group of capitalists and Nazi leaders. He recalled that it had mass support, that the Germans fought for Adolf Hitler (1889–1945) to the bitter end, and that the Nazi regime was destroyed only as a result of Allied arms. He rejected the idea of German collective guilt because the concept both ignored the anti-Nazi resistance and helped the most criminal Germans evade justice, since if everyone was guilty, no one could be held responsible. Yet he was blunt in his criticism of German passivity in the face of Nazi criminality. In 1945, he said that the Germans knew what was taking place in their midst. They "saw with their own eyes with what common bestiality the Nazis tortured, robbed, and hunted the Jews. Not only did they remain silent, but they would have preferred that Germany had won the Second World War, thus guaranteeing them peace and quiet and also a small profit." Because they had given themselves over to belief in dictatorship and violence, they had ended up occupied by others after 1945. "This political insight," he said, was "the precondition for a spiritual-intellectual and moral repentance and change" (in Albrecht 1985: 217). A vigorous advocate of removal of former Nazis from positions of power and influence, continuation of war crimes trials, restitution to Jews, and honesty about Nazi crimes, Schumacher lost West Germany's first parliamentary elections by a narrow margin to Adenauer, who held a very different view of the relationship between democratization and the Nazi past.

The distinctive West German government tradition of public remembrance of the crimes of the Nazi past began as elite practice that sounded a soft dissonant note in the larger West German silence. The founding father was Federal President Heuss, who throughout the occupation era articulated the importance of clear and honest memory of past crimes (Heuss 1966). From 1949 to 1959, he used the platform of the president's office and its insulation from electoral politics to urge Germans to remember the crimes of the Nazi era, especially the Holocaust. To his critics, he was the cultured veneer of the Adenauer restoration, whose emphasis on eloquent memory merely distracted attention from the absence of a thorough judicial reckoning. Yet in speeches about German history and extensive private correspondence with Jewish survivors, resistance veterans, and West German and foreign intellectuals, Heuss forged a tradition of political recollection that would eventually contribute to broader public discussion and action. The title of his most important speech regarding the Nazi past, delivered at memorial ceremonies at the former Nazi concentration camp at Bergen-Belsen on 29–30 November 1952, eloquently conveys his general position: "No One Will Lift This Shame from Us" (*Bulletin des Presse- und Informationsamtes der Bundesregierung* 189 [1 December 1952]: 1655–6). Broadcast on radio and extensively covered by the West German press, the speech was the most extensive statement to that date of national West German reflection on the mass murder of European Jewry. Heuss included among the virtues of patriotism a willingness to face an evil past honestly rather than to avoid doing so by pointing to the misdeeds of others. Following Heuss's Bergen-Belsen speech, commemoration of the Holocaust became a part of official West German political culture.

The memorial gathering at Bergen-Belsen was also important because for the first time after 1949 a representative of Jewish survivors, Nahum Goldmann (1894–1982) of the World Jewish Congress, spoke alongside an official of the West German government. Goldmann described the destruction of European Jewry in detail and recalled "the millions who found their tragic end in Auschwitz, Treblinka, Dachau, and in Warsaw and Vilna and Bialystok and in countless other places." In this very western ceremony during the Cold War, Goldmann drew attention to the eastern geography of the Holocaust. In so doing, he implicitly pointed out that the geography of memory did not coincide with the fault lines of the Cold War in the west. The Holocaust had largely taken place in a part of Europe that during the Cold War was "behind the Iron Curtain." Goldmann's recounting of the Holocaust inevitably called to mind German aggression on the eastern front during World War II, an invasion that eventually led to the presence of the Red Army in the center of Europe in May 1945 (Herf 1997: 318–19).

More than any other West German political leader, Adenauer shaped West German policy toward the Nazi past. In his speeches as the leader of the Christian Democratic Union between 1945 and 1949, he asserted that Nazism stemmed from profound flaws in German history and society, including Prussian authoritarianism, the weakness of individualism, Marxism, and an ideology of racial superiority that had arisen in place of the Christian notion of the dignity of all human beings. The antidote to these ills, he contended, was democracy resting on Christian natural right and the belief in the value of every individual that flowed from it (Herf 1997: 209–26). His belief in the importance of a Christian religious revival, however, did not make room for an interrogation of the place of antisemitism in Christian theology. Moreover, Adenauer's pessimism about the breadth and depth of Nazism's roots within German history and society paradoxically led him to favor reticence about the past lest a more confrontational stance set off a nationalist and anti-democratic backlash. He adopted a strategy of integrating former and hopefully disillusioned followers of Nazism into the new Federal Republic, even including government officials who had served in the Nazi regime, and he was reluctant to discuss the crimes of the past and in favor of amnesty for convicted war criminals. As early as the spring and summer of 1946, Adenauer told audiences in the British zone of occupation that "we finally should leave in peace the followers, those who did not oppress others, who did not enrich themselves, and who broke no laws" (in Schwarz 1975: 92). Convinced that liberal democracy could not be established in Germany against the will of the majority, he chose not to risk offending crucial groups that could make the difference between the success or failure of the Federal Republic, as well as his own electoral victory or defeat.

The result was a tension between the early emergence of democratic politics in post-Nazi Germany and the desire for clear memory and timely justice. West German politicians in the postwar decade were seeking the votes of many citizens who emphatically opposed trials for war crimes and crimes against humanity. Paradoxically, more democracy meant less judicial reckoning. Indeed, at the outset of the Federal Republic a broad consensus prevailed within the West German establishment in favor of amnesty and integration of ex-Nazis. From 1949 to

1954, when democratically elected German politicians first had a chance to act, they passed "a series of parliamentary initiatives, legislative acts, and administrative decisions aimed at" the "vitiation" of the denazification measures of the occupation era. The result of this "politics about the past" was "both an annulment of punishments and integrative measures on behalf of an army of millions of Nazi Party members. Virtually without exception, these people regained their social, professional, and civic, but not their political status," which they had lost in the course of denazification and internment after the war (Frei 2002: xii). The grand bargain of West German democratization entailed letting bygones be bygones in exchange for support for or at least acceptance of the new democratic political institutions. The results included striking continuities of personnel in important government ministries such as the foreign office, executive offices in industry, the universities, judiciary, medical profession, and other parts of the West German establishment (Döscher 1995; Remy 2002). Amnesty and integration for all but the unreconstructed was a formula that linked democratization with silence about Nazi era crimes in the crucial early years. As the philosopher and social theorist, Theodor Adorno (1903–1969) wrote in 1959, repression of the Nazi past was far less the product of unconscious processes or deficient memory than it was "the product of an all too wide awake consciousness" (in Hartman 1986: 114–29).

Yet, the postwar decade was also one of "de-radicalization" for some prominent German intellectuals who had joined the Nazi Party and become disillusioned as Hitler's successes turned into defeats and utter catastrophe. In this sphere as well, silence about the deeds of the past and convenient gaps in life histories accompanied acceptance of the new liberal democratic institutions (Muller 1987; Neaman 1999). Some prominent former Nazi supporters, such as the philosopher Martin Heidegger (1889–1976), made no effort at all to reflect critically on their pasts or Nazi era crimes. Instead, he continued and deepened a pessimism about modern society and technology that served to deflect questions of human responsibility onto impersonal—and non-indictable—phenomena such as western reason or modernity (Wolin 1993; Rabinbach 1997: 97–128). Albert Speer (1905–1981), the former armaments minister of the Nazi regime and close associate of Hitler, articulated this kind of "belated pessimism" and exculpation in his testimony at the Nuremberg War Crimes Trial and then in his bestselling memoirs (Herf in Ezrahi et al. 1994: 115–36).

Returned war veterans and West Germans expelled from eastern Europe had many "war stories" to tell in the postwar years. Overwhelmingly these were not narratives about German crimes committed against others but of suffering inflicted on Germans by the victors, especially by the Red Army (Moeller 2001). In the 1950s, German cities and towns, large and small, erected plaques to commemorate civilians who died in Allied bombing raids (Reichel 1995). Where given the opportunity to examine truthfully the history of concentration camps located near towns, such as the one in Dachau, local officials opted instead for what one historian has called myths of "victimization, ignorance and resistance" (Marcuse 2001).

Given Adenauer's view of the depth of Nazism's roots in the German past and its residues in the postwar era, he shifted the focus regarding the Holocaust away from war crimes trials and toward the somewhat less contentious matter of restitution payments to Jewish survivors and to the State of Israel. In September 1951, he announced to the federal parliament his willingness to support a restitution agreement. Against considerable opposition from his own Christian Democrats, but with the unanimous support of the opposition Social Democrats, he gained parliamentary support for the "Luxembourg agreement" of 10 September 1952. As a result, from 1953 to 1965, the Federal Republic delivered goods such as ships, machine tools, trains, autos, medical equipment, and telephone technology that amounted to 10 to 15 percent of annual Israeli imports. By the mid-1990s, the West German restitution payments to individual survivors of Nazi persecution, most of them Jewish survivors, totaled about 124 billion deutschmarks (Herf 1997: 288). While Adenauer's critics on the right railed that Germany had no financial obligations to Jews, and the communist government in East Berlin denounced the payments as a capitalist scheme to avoid learning the true lessons of the past, the payments made a difference both for the young State of Israel and in the lives of thousands of recovering Jewish survivors (Goschler 2005). To the conservative Adenauer, wary as he was of all grand schemes to remake the world, the abiding principle regarding the Jews was to do no more harm and to help where possible. He accomplished those modest, far from self-realizing goals.

Adenauer's unequivocal decision to integrate West Germany into the western alliance was another, at times ambiguous precondition for a German reckoning with the Holocaust (Schwartz 1991). The collapse of the anti-Hitler coalition and the emergence of the Cold War postponed a focus on Nazi Germany's conduct on the eastern front during World War II. Although rearmament and integration into the west facilitated the return of old, compromised elites, the latter process also meant that the Federal Republic was abandoning the anti-western traditions of decades past, which included assaults on liberal democracy, the primacy of individual rights, and anti-Americanism as well as antisemitism. The military presence of the western allies was a stabilizing factor both within West Germany, where they served as an insurance policy against an increasingly unlikely neo-Nazi revival, and in Europe as a whole, where they reassured Germany's former European victims that the country would not become aggressive again.

Scholarly examination of the origins and nature of the Nazi regime had been facilitated by the establishment of the Institute of Contemporary History in 1949 and its presence in Munich since 1950. Yet by the late 1950s, leaders in the West German parliament and several prosecutors at the state level recognized that a large number of persons suspected of having participated in the Holocaust and other war crimes remained at liberty. As a result, in 1958, the Central Office of the State Judicial Authorities for the Investigation of National Socialist Crimes was established in the town of Ludwigsburg. In the 1960s, the parliament (*Bundestag*) passed the first of several extensions of the statute of limitations on crimes of murder prior to its complete abolition in 1979 (Herf 1997: 337–42). Fritz Bauer (1903–1968), the attorney general of the State of Hesse, directed the efforts that led in 1964 to "the Auschwitz Trial" of guards at the former extermination camp (Wittmann 2005).

The 1960s did witness greater discussion of Nazi era crimes, stimulated in part by the trial of Adolf Eichmann (1906–1962) in Jerusalem. Yet the decade was not, as is sometimes claimed, the era when the memory of the Holocaust emerged on a broad scale in West German politics and intellectual life. In 1969, the new Eastern Policy (*Ostpolitik*) of Chancellor Willy Brandt (1913–1992) revived attention to the war on the eastern front, as did his famous gesture of kneeling at the memorial to the Jews of the Warsaw ghetto. Yet the primary objective was improving relations with the Soviet bloc, not recovering the memory of the Holocaust. The emergence of the new left in the universities in the 1960s inspired Marxist discussions about fascism and capitalism far more than examinations of the particularities of the Holocaust. The scholarly breakthrough began in 1965 with the appearance of historian Andreas Hillgrüber's ground-breaking study placing racial antisemitism at the center of Hitler's war strategy. Four years later, the German versions of Karl Bracher's *The German Dictatorship* (1970) and Eberhard Jaeckel's *Hitler's World View* (1981) detailed the link between Nazi antisemitism and the "Final Solution" of the Jewish question. Although the ten-volume work, *Germany and the Second World War*, by historians at the Military History Research Office in Freiburg and Potsdam did not address the Holocaust, some volumes have shed important light on the impact of racial antisemitism on the Nazi conduct of the war, especially on the eastern front (Boog et al. 1998). However, for most of the postwar decades, the bulk of major works of historical scholarship on the Holocaust and especially on its antisemitic ideological inspiration continued to be written by American, British, and Israeli scholars (Dawidowicz 1981; Berg 2003), and the significant German works that made original contributions appeared from historians who came of age well after the 1960s (Longerich 1998; Herbert 2000; Mallmann and Cuppers 2006; Wildt 2009).

Though historians, prosecutors, and producers of television documentaries had examined the Holocaust since the 1960s, it became a topic of debate and discussion by a wide public beyond the political, judicial, and intellectual elites only in the 1980s (Kansteiner 2006). The radical left marginalized the subject in the "red decade" of the late sixties and seventies and compared nuclear deterrence to a "nuclear Auschwitz" in the early eighties (Herf 1991: 185–92). In the middle of that decade, in what became known as "the historians dispute" (*der Historikerstreit*), conservative intellectuals also began to obscure the historical distinctiveness of the Holocaust by comparing it to other episodes of mass murder and inhumanity, such as the Soviet Union's Gulag (Maier 1988). On 8 May 1985, the fortieth anniversary of the end of World War II, following an extremely controversial visit by President Ronald Reagan (1911–2004) and Chancellor Helmut Kohl (b. 1930) to a West German military cemetery in Bitburg, the tradition inaugurated earlier by Heuss was reinvigorated and updated by Federal President Richard von Weizsäcker (b. 1920), whose speech to the Bundestag placed the memory of the Holocaust at the center of West German memory of the crimes of the Nazi era. The Weizsäcker speech, and the enormous outpouring of support and enthusiasm with which elites and the public greeted it, indicated that efforts on the left and right to marginalize or repress the memory of the Holocaust had failed and that it had become and would likely remain an enduring aspect of West German official understanding of the Nazi era (Hartman 1986; Herf 1997: 350–9).

East Germany

Following the collapse of the Soviet bloc, including the German Democratic Republic, in 1989 and German reunification in 1991, the archives of the former East German government became available for examination by historians. For the first time, they could document the history of what the communists called "the Jewish question" in East Germany. No less than in West Germany's "multiple restorations," the ideological prism through which East German Marxist-Leninist leaders viewed "the Jewish question" was inherited from the past. In the communist tradition, the fate of the Jews was peripheral to the central issue of class struggle. Communists viewed antisemitism less as an autonomous cultural tradition than as a tool used by ruling classes to divide the working class. As fascism—the term they used to describe the Nazi regime—was a product of capitalism, coming to terms with the fascist past meant, first and foremost, destroying capitalism. Moreover, since Karl Marx (1818–1883) had identified Jews with hated capitalism, an element of anti-Jewish sentiment lingered within communist attacks on capital. However, after the Nazi invasion of the Soviet Union in 1941, many communists viewed the Jews as allies against a Nazi Germany that labeled its enemy "Jewish Bolshevism." Yet after 1945, and especially after the onset of the Cold War by 1948, the power of the dominant traditions of German and European communist orthodoxy was reinforced by Stalin's definition of the political interests of the Soviet Union. The result was the repression and marginalization of the memory of the Holocaust for the entire postwar period and worse, the emergence of a mixture of anti-Zionism and antisemitism (Groehler and Kessler in Kocka 1993: 105–28, 149–68; Herf 1997: 13–39).

The East German archival record makes clear that in the first years after World War II a debate took place among East German communists about how an anti-fascist German government should deal with the "Final Solution" and its aftermath. Led by Ulbricht, the communists who had spent the war years in Moscow and returned to Berlin in June 1945 stressed the crimes the Nazi regime had committed against the peoples of the Soviet Union and celebrated the heroism of the Red Army that had brought liberation. The catastrophe of Europe's Jews found modest mention in such narratives (Meuschel 1992). For these returning exiles, memories of Nazi brutality and of the absence of a German uprising against Hitler's regime reinforced communist suspicions of liberal democracy and the political tendencies of their fellow Germans. The more communists remembered their persecution by the Nazi regime, the Nazi war on the eastern front, German popular support for the Third Reich, and the absence of effective resistance to the Hitler dictatorship, the more inclined they were to impose a second, this time Marxist-Leninist dictatorship on a people they regarded as dangerous.

A minority view regarding Jewish issues emerged, however, among communists who fled into western, especially Mexican exile. In wartime Mexico City, the Jewish question moved from the periphery to the center of the struggle against Nazism. Paul Merker (1894–1969), a member of the Politburo of the German Communist Party (KPD), was the leading proponent of this development. Upon returning to East Berlin, he and others advocated giving not only a central place in communist memory to the fate of the Jews, but also financial restitution to Jewish survivors and political support to the Zionist goal of a Jewish state in Palestine. As a consequence of a series of arrests, purges, and secret trials between 1950 and 1953 that constituted the East German chapter of the Soviet bloc's "anti-cosmopolitan campaign," Merker and others who shared his views ceased to be a factor in East German policy in these issues (Herf 1997: 40–161). Their defeat constituted a decisive blow to hopes for a distinctively East German communist confrontation with the Jewish catastrophe, restitution to Jewish survivors, close relations with Israel, and the continuation of wartime solidarities into the postwar era.

Indeed, the published documents that accompanied the purge smeared communists who advocated Jewish concerns as members of an international conspiracy of American imperialists, Zionists, Jewish capitalists, and counter-revolutionary communists, whose goal was to destroy communism in East Germany and eastern Europe. Such denunciation bizarrely echoed the Nazis' conspiracy theory of a powerful international Jewry (*Dokumente der Sozialistische Einheitspartei* 1954: 199–219). Once again, a German government attacked the Jews as cosmopolitans, defining them as other than true members of the nation. Once again, German nationalists, this time of communist hue, defined themselves in opposition to a western, capitalist, international, liberal, and Jewish conspiracy (Meuschel 1992: 101–16). Remarkably, at a moment of extreme Jewish weakness, Germany's anti-fascist regime denounced the Jews for their supposed power.

The Merker case and the anti-cosmopolitan purge led to the establishment of an East German orthodoxy regarding the memory of the "Final Solution" that remained largely intact until the collapse of the regime in 1989. Ironically, some of the leading architects of this orthodoxy were communists from Jewish backgrounds, such as Alexander Abusch (1902–1982), minister of culture in the 1950s and former Mexican émigré, and Albert Norden (1904–1982), the head of the East German office charged with propaganda offensives against West Germany. Both presented East Germany as the representative of a progressive, enlightened nation that had no more room for what they regarded as religious obscurantism or for religion of any kind. Communist tradition and a particular reading of German national identity provided mutually reinforcing reasons to marginalize Jewish concerns, including the memory of the Holocaust. In East Germany, coming to terms with the Nazi past meant abolishing capitalism and engaging in attacks on the allegedly "fascist" regime in West Germany. The German Democratic Republic made no restitution payments to Jewish survivors. The contributions of its historians and prosecutors to expanding knowledge about the Holocaust were modest, and the record of judicial reckoning was less impressive than that of the Federal Republic.

By the mid-1950s, communists had shifted their loyalties toward the Arab states and away from the Jewish state that they denounced as an ally and agent of western imperialism. From the late 1960s to 1989, the East German government not only gave diplomatic and military support to the Arab states at war with Israel, but also fervently supported the Palestine Liberation Organization as it engaged in violent attacks on Israel. To be sure, though the record of East German persecution of the Jews pales compared to that of the Nazi regime, the important moral and historical point is that such a record exists at all—and began in the decade following the Holocaust. In spring 1990, the first act of the first democratically elected parliament in the still existing East German state was to pass unanimously a resolution that asked "the Jews of the world to forgive us for the hypocrisy and hostility of the East German policies towards Israel and also for the persecution and degradation of Jewish citizens after 1945 in our country." The resolution also expressed "willingness to contribute as much as possible to the healing of mental and physical sufferings of survivors and to provide just compensation for material losses" (Herf 1997: 365). Although the suppression of the memory of the Holocaust accompanied the consolidation of dictatorship in East Germany in the early 1950s, the recovery of that memory was one aftereffect of the collapse of dictatorship and the return of democracy and human rights in 1991.

MEMORY AND THE POLITICS
OF THE PAST SINCE 1989

Beginning in the first months after the end of World War II and continuing in the seven decades since, some Germans have called for "finally" putting the past behind and forgetting about the Holocaust. With the collapse of communism in 1989 and German reunification a year later, some observers expected that a wave of nationalist triumphalism would help these voices achieve their goal. In 1995, however, the parliament of unified Germany designated 27 January, the day that the Red Army liberated Auschwitz-Birkenau in 1945, as the national day of remembrance for the victims of Nazi persecution and genocide. In 1999, the same parliament agreed to build a memorial to the murdered Jews of Europe within walking distance of the Bundestag and the Chancellor's office in Berlin, the new national capital (Heimrod et al. 1999). As unique as the Holocaust is in history, so is the West German and now German tradition of public memory of the most criminal and barbaric period of Germany's past.

In West Germany, the initial strategy of democratization through integration, amnesty, and a general silence about the crimes of the Nazi era meant that a large but difficult to ascertain number of individuals long avoided war crimes charges. Gradually a more vigorous judicial reckoning and, over time, greater scholarly engagement with the issue emerged. Despite periodic challenges, the Heussian tradition made acceptance of this burden of German history a key element of national self-definition. Conversely, despite years of anti-fascist discourse, the East German regime repressed the memory of the Jewish catastrophe and then moved on to anti-Zionist, at times antisemitic ideology and policy, both at home and in the Middle East. One can write the history of the aftereffects of the Holocaust in West and East Germany as one of avoidance, denial, repression, and myth making. Yet viewed from the comparative perspective of the aftereffects of other totalitarian and unjust regimes of modern history, the post-Nazi West German and then unified German confrontation with the crimes of the Nazi era is also a history of some truth telling, some judicial reckoning, some excellent historical scholarship, and some compassion for the victims of the previous regime.

As noted at the outset, the emergence and persistence of German attempts to come to terms with the Nazi past was made possible by the Allies' unconditional victory followed by four years of occupation and denazification and multiple restorations of pre-existing liberal democratic traditions by leaders with memories of a German-Jewish Germany destroyed by Nazism. Most barbaric regimes do not end so definitively, nor are they and their supporters driven from power so effectively. Although many escaped justice, a comparative perspective shows that the outcome could have been far worse. The distinctive character of the German political and intellectual confrontation with the crimes of the Nazi regime against Europe's Jews arose out of historically exceptional circumstances.

REFERENCES

ALBRECHT, W. (ed.) (1985). *Kurt Schumacher: Reden-Schriften-Korrespondenzen, 1945–1952*. Berlin: J. H. W. Dietz.

BERG, N. (2003). *Der Holocaust und die westdeutschen Historiker: Erforschung und Erinnerung*. Göttingen: Wallstein.

BOOG, H., FÖRSTER, J., HOFFMANN, J., KLINK, E., MÜLLER, R., and UEBERSCHÄR, G. (1998). *Germany and the Second World War*. Vol. 4, *The Attack on the Soviet Union*. New York: Oxford University Press.

BRACHER, K. (1970). *The German Dictatorship*. New York: Praeger.

DAWIDOWICZ, L. (1981). *The Holocaust and the Historians*. Cambridge, MA: Harvard University Press.

Dokumente der Sozialistische Einheitspartei, Band IV (1954). [East] Berlin: Dietz.

DÖSCHER, H.-J. (1995). *Verschworene Gesellschaft: Das Auswärtige Amt unter Adenauer zwischen Neubeginn und Kontinuität*. Berlin: Akademie Verlag.

EZRAHI, Y., MENDELSOHN, E., and SEGAL, H. (eds.) (1994). *Technology, Pessimism and Postmodernism*. Dordrecht: Kluwer Academic Publishers.

FREI, N. (2002). *Adenauer's Germany and the Nazi Past: The Politics of Amnesty and Integration*. New York: Columbia University Press.

GOSCHLER, C. (2005). *Schuld und Schulden: Die Politik der Wiedergutmachung für NS-Verfolgte seit 1945*. Göttingen: Wallstein Verlag.

GÖTZ, A. (1986). *Bilanz der Verfolgung von NS-Straftaten*. Cologne: Bundesanzeiger.

HARTMAN, G. (ed.) (1986). *Bitburg in Moral and Political Perspective*. Bloomington, IN: Indiana University Press.

HEIMROD, U., SCHLUSCHE, G., and SEFERENS, H. (eds.) (1999). *Der Denkmalstreit – das Denkmal? Die Debatte um das "Denkmal für die ermordeten Juden Europas": Eine Dokumentation*. Berlin: Philo Verlagsgesellschaft.

HERBERT, U. (ed.) (2000). *National Socialist Extermination Policies*. New York: Berghahn Books.

HERF, J. (1991). *War By Other Means: Soviet Power, West German Resistance and the Battle of the Euromissiles*. New York: The Free Press.

——(1997). *Divided Memory: The Nazi Past in the Two Germanys*. Cambridge, MA: Harvard University Press.

HEUSS, T. (1966). *Theodor Heuss: Aufzeichnungen, 1945–1947*. Tübingen: Rainer Wunderlich Verlag.

JAECKEL, E. (1981). *Hitler's World View*. Cambridge, MA: Harvard University Press.

KANSTEINER, W. (2006). *In Pursuit of German Memory: History, Television and Politics After Auschwitz*. Athens, OH: Ohio University Press.

KOCKA, J. (ed.) (1993). *Historische DDR-Forschung: Aufsätze und Studien*. Berlin: Akademie Verlag.

LONGERICH, P. (1998). *Politik der Vernichtung*. Munich: Piper.

MAIER, C. (1988). *The Unmasterable Past: History, Holocaust and German National Identity*. Cambridge, MA: Harvard University Press.

MALLMANN, K. and CUPPERS, M. (2006). *Halbmond und Hakenkreuz: Das Dritte Reich, Die Araber und Palästina*. Darmstadt: Wissenschaftliche Buchgesellschaft.

MARCUSE, H. (2001). *Legacies of Dachau: The Uses and Abuses of a Concentration Camp, 1933–2001*. New York: Cambridge University Press.

MEUSCHEL, S. (1992). *Legitimation und Parteiherrschaft in der DDR*. Frankfurt am Main: Suhrkamp Verlag.

MOELLER, R. (2001). *War Stories: The Search for a Usable Past in the Federal Republic of Germany*. Berkeley, CA: University of California Press.

MULLER, J. (1987). *The Other God That Failed: Hans Freyer and the Deradicalization of German Conservatism*. Princeton, NJ: Princeton University Press.

NEAMAN, E. (1999). *A Dubious Past: Ernst Jünger and the Politics of Literature and Nazism.* Berkeley, CA: University of California Press.

RABINBACH, A. (1997). *In the Shadow of Catastrophe: German Intellectuals between Apocalypse and Enlightenment.* Berkeley, CA: University of California Press.

REICHEL, P. (1995). *Politik mit der Erinnerung: Gedächnisorte im Streit um die national-sozialistische Vergangenheit.* Munich: Carl Hanser.

REMY, S. (2002). *The Heidelberg Myth: The Nazification and Denazification of a German University.* Cambridge, MA: Harvard University Press.

SCHWARTZ, T. (1991). *America's Germany: John J. McCloy and the Federal Republic of Germany.* Cambridge, MA: Harvard University Press.

SCHWARZ, H.-P. (ed.) (1975). *Konrad Adenauer: Reden, 1917–1967: Eine Auswahl.* Stuttgart: Deutsche Verlagsanstalt.

WILDT, M. (2009). *An Uncompromising Generation: The Nazi Leadership of the Reich Security Main Office.* Madison, WI: University of Wisconsin Press.

WITTMANN, R. (2005). *Beyond Justice: The Auschwitz Trial.* Cambridge, MA: Harvard University Press.

WOLIN, R. (ed.) (1993). *The Heidegger Controversy: A Critical Reader.* Cambridge, MA: MIT Press.

OTHER SUGGESTED READING

BROWN-FLEMING, S. (2006). *The Holocaust and the Catholic Conscience: Cardinal Aloisius Muench and the Guilt Question in Germany.* Notre Dame: University of Notre Dame Press.

BUSCHER, F. (1989). *The U.S. War Crimes Trial Program in Germany, 1946 to 1955.* New York: Greenwood Press.

CORNELISSEN, C., KINKHAMMER, L., and SCHWENTKER, W. (eds.) (2003). *Erinnerungskul-turen: Deutschland, Italien und Japan seit 1945.* Frankfurt am Main: Fischer Taschenbuch.

DINER, D. (2000). *Beyond the Conceivable:. Studies on Germany, Nazism, and the Holocaust.* Berkeley, CA: University of California Press.

DUBIEL, H. (1999). *Niemand ist frei von der Geschichte.* Munich: Carl Hanser.

EARL, H. (2009). *The Nuremberg SS-Einsatzgruppen Trial, 1945–1958: Atrocity, Law and History.* New York: Cambridge University Press.

FRIEDRICH, J. (1984). *Die kalte Amnestie: NS-Täter in der Bundesrepublik.* Frankfurt am Main: Fischer.

HENKE, K. and WOLLER, H. (eds.) (1991). *Politische Säuberung in Europa: Die Abrechnung mit Faschismus und Kollaboration nach den Zweiten Weltkrieg.* Munich: Deutscher Taschenbuch Verlag.

HEUSS, T. (1965). *Theodor Heuss: Der Grossen Reden: Der Staatsmann.* Tübingen: Rainer Wunderlich Verlag.

KÖHLER, H. (1994). *Adenauer: Eine politische Biographie.* Frankfurt am Main: Propyläen.

MARRUS, M. (1997). *The Nuremberg War Crimes Trial, 1945–56: A Documentary History.* Boston: Bedford Books.

MÜLLER, J.-W. (ed.) (2002). *Memory and Power in Postwar Europe: Studies in the Presence of the Past.* New York: Cambridge University Press.

PENDAS, D. (2005). *The Frankfurt Auschwitz Trial, 1963–1965: Genocide, History, and the Limits of the Law*. New York: Cambridge University Press.

SCHWARZ, H.-P. (1986). *Konrad Adenauer: Der Aufstieg, 1876–1952*. Stuttgart: Deutsche Verlagsanstalt.

VOLLNHALS, C. (1991). *Entnazifizierung: Politische Säuberung und Rehabilitierung in den vier Besatzungszonen, 1945–1949*. Munich: Deutscher Taschenbuch Verlag.

CHAPTER 42

EUROPE

JAN-WERNER MÜLLER

"EUROPE" can designate a geographical entity (with, to be sure, always contested boundaries), but it can also be shorthand for a set of values and practices (as in "European civilization" or, more recently, "European norms of democracy and human rights"). "Europe" is also increasingly used simply to stand for the European Union (EU), a cluster of institutions that certainly do not encompass the entirety of Europe in a geographical sense and that may not always live up to supposedly European values in an emphatic sense.

This chapter argues that the Holocaust took place within a distinct normative vision of Europe as a privileged embodiment of certain values, namely the Nazis' authoritarian and antisemitic "New European Order." While postwar European integration was justified with regard to national conflict in the past, the memory of the Holocaust played virtually no role in the initial construction of the European Community (or even the Council of Europe, for that matter). Even when there was increasing awareness of the Judeocide after the 1960s and 1970s, especially in the United States and Germany, neither individual European countries—with the obvious exception of the Federal Republic—nor the European Community as a whole felt compelled to define themselves in relation to it, let alone address their complicity in it.

However, this state of affairs changed markedly in the 1990s: partly because of the end of the Cold War, transnational political pressures, and a new emphasis on self-critical memorialization as a mode of legitimacy, European countries confronted their roles in the Holocaust directly and to such an extent that some scholars in fact have begun to speak of a "Europeanization of the Holocaust." Moreover, what was now known as the European Union attempted to define its identity with reference to the Holocaust. This undertaking culminated in sanctions against Austria in 2000 for including a party associated with Holocaust denial in its government and is, according to most observers, fraught with moral and political difficulties. Nevertheless, the meaning of an emphatic notion of "Europeanness," once invoked to justify Nazi rule as a defense against Bolshevism, had been completely reversed sixty years after the Holocaust: it now is supposed to stand for tolerance, non-discrimination, and appreciation of diversity.

THE HOLOCAUST AND THE NAZI NEW EUROPEAN ORDER

The Nazis frequently appealed to "Europe," both in the geographical sense and as a set of values and practices, to justify their conquests from September 1939 onwards (Mazower 2008). In 1939, Carl Schmitt (1888–1985), a leading Nazi legal theorist, called on the Führer to declare a "European Monroe doctrine" and make the Third Reich the center of a new *Großraum* (great space), from which extra-European powers, the Anglo-American ones in particular, were excluded. Alfred Rosenberg (1893–1946), the foremost ideologue of the Nazi movement, celebrated Germany as the "European force of order" and insisted time and again that war was, above all, about "Europe as a problem" (Piper 2005: 610). Such views conformed to the determination of Adolf Hitler (1889–1945) to create a European empire and prevent Germany from becoming a "second Holland," a "second Switzerland," or even a "slave people" and to defend Europe as a whole against Bolshevism in the east. At the heart of this "great European space" was to be the Greater German *Reich*, with other countries or "spaces" as dependencies surrounding it.

Above all, however, Europe was a racial or "blood-determined" concept in the Nazi imagination, as Hitler put it (Piper 2005: 598). The idea of such a Reich was entirely different from the older notion of a continental, multinational empire. Hitler had always railed against the Habsburg Empire, which he called "Babylonian" because of its multiplicity of nationalities and its lukewarm patriotism for the emperor. But the Nazis were even distrustful of the idea of the nation; to them, even nationalism still smacked of nineteenth-century liberalism. Instead, empire was to be entirely racialized, that is, defined by "racial blood," cleansed of Jews, and separated from Slavic Asia by a "blood wall" (Overy 2004: 574–7). As Hitler asserted on the very first page of *Mein Kampf*: "One blood demands one Reich" (1943: 1). Hence the Nazis set up a large "race bureaucracy" and tasked it during the war with classifying and certifying people, issuing "race cards," and gathering every last drop of German blood into a single political community.

Antisemitism was not incidental, but essential to this thoroughly racialized vision of a "great European space"; the entire Nazi "system that emerged after 1933 was fundamentally antisemitic in its outlook, purpose and practices" (Overy 2004: 583). Moreover, Hitler insisted from the beginning of the war he had unleashed that it would be both a "war of world views" (*Weltanschauungskrieg*) and a "Volk and race war": the elimination of the German Jews was a precondition of German victory in this war, and the destruction of European Jewry—to Hitler, the "anti-nation" as such—was to be its consequence. Perversely, Jews were blamed for having instigated the war; and even at the Nuremberg trials the defendants insisted that they had always been on the defensive, fighting for survival. Hitler claimed that "never before has there been a war so typically and at the same time so exclusively Jewish" (Overy 2004: 589). In short, racism thoroughly structured the inner life of the Nazi state, but also foreign policy, the approach to the war, and all plans for a "New Europe."

The idea of a new Europe that set itself against Bolshevism in the east and Anglo-American capitalist liberal democracy in the west appealed to many intellectuals across the continent; it was arguably the single most powerful attraction for collaborators in France and other countries who were not simply seeking material advantage. Non-German volunteers for fighting on the eastern front thought they were defending European culture and civilization in a "European civil war." They seemed genuinely to believe that the "New Europe" could be characterized by something other than total domination at the hands of Nazi Germany. Their illusions were reinforced by propaganda publications such as *Junges Europa: Blätter der akademischen Jugend Europas*, edited by Léon Degrelle (1906–1994) (Piper 2005: 598). The Germans even broadcast a "Song for Europe" and issued stamps with the motto "European United Front against Bolshevism" (Mazower 1998: 152). Continent-wide cultural diplomacy reinforced the European dimension of the war effort: the conference on "Poetry in the Future Europe" in Weimar in 1941 was one of the most prominent measures, and it attracted a large French delegation.

As the fortunes of the war turned against Nazi Germany, European rhetoric became more pronounced: according to many of Hitler's speeches after 1943, the fate of Europe as a whole was at stake in the fight against Bolshevism and capitalism (or, as Rosenberg often put it, "liberalism" and "Americanism") and the sinister force that was directing both, "international Jewry."

The European dimension of Nazism and the Holocaust was not entirely forgotten or repressed after 1945. Precisely because of this cluster of associations—Hitler, Europe, conquest, and also colonialism—a number of left-wing intellectuals after the war were opposed to the construction of the European Community. Only through the experience of decolonization was the idea of Europe "purified" (Morin 1987: 140–7). But overall, many of the countries that had in one way or another collaborated with Nazi Germany had an interest in downplaying the legitimacy that the "New European Order" had enjoyed and the continuities in public law and political personnel across the historical divide of 1945 (Joerges and Ghaleigh 2003). In a sense, a specifically European dimension of the Holocaust could begin to be emphasized only toward the end of the twentieth century; earlier, European integration was justified mostly with the argument that it would prevent another war among nation-states. This was certainly the case both among left-wing idealists within the Resistance, who wished for a socialist, anti-fascist Europe, and the Christian Democratic *Realpolitiker* who actually constructed the European Community.

European Integration—a Response to the Holocaust?

The postwar period in western Europe was characterized by an intense suspicion about popular sovereignty. The specter of the Weimar Republic's failure, that is, the apparent suicide of a liberal democracy, haunted politicians across the continent. Institutions were designed to keep an always potentially "totalitarian democracy" in check and to protect individual rights against both the state and illiberal majorities. An outstanding example was the spread of a new institution, the constitutional court, which was not simply a copy of the American Supreme Court, but a court specifically tasked with testing legislative acts for constitutionality. Mindful of the memory of mass atrocity and murder, such courts also viewed themselves as being primary instruments in defending the dignity of individuals.

European integration was, if anything, another symptom of the new postwar constitutionalist ethos and, in particular, the distrust of popular sovereignty or unrestricted parliamentary supremacy (Lindseth 2004). Countries sought to delegate powers to unelected institutions domestically and also to supranational bodies in order to "lock in" liberal democratic arrangements and the protection of individual rights and to prevent a backsliding toward authoritarianism (Moravcsik 2000). As is well known, the architects of the European Community followed an indirect way of gaining legitimacy for their project: rather than having the peoples of the initial member states vote for supranational arrangements, they relied on technocratic and administrative measures agreed among elites to yield what Jean Monnet (1888–1979) time and again called "concrete achievements"; these eventually convinced citizens that European integration was a good thing.

From the beginning, then, European integration was a political end pursued by economic and administrative means. The idea of small (economic and administrative) steps and grand (political) effects was designed to bring about lasting peace and prosperity on a ravaged continent—or at least the western half of it. Low-level technocratic measures, initially hardly visible for the peoples in the founding countries, were supposed eventually to spill over into high politics. The approach fit well with the fashion for technocracy, the "end of ideology," and the "politics of productivity" in the 1950s (Maier 1987). It was far removed, however, from any conception of grounding European unity in a collective political will and did not rely on common values or explicit human rights language and only to a very limited degree on a shared desire for international reconciliation.

None of this had anything to do with the memory of the Holocaust or, as another self-celebratory EU myth would later have it, with promoting democracy. Of course, the project was informed by the personal experiences and political convictions of the "founding fathers." Alcide de Gasperi (1881–1954), Konrad Adenauer (1876–1967), and Robert Schuman (1886–1963) were all Christian Democrats who hailed from the margins of their respective nation-states and had been marked by the brutal homogenization of the "late" nation-states Italy and Germany. All had directly experienced the politics of empire: de Gasperi had studied in Vienna and served in the pre-1918 Austrian Reichsrat; Adenauer had been mayor of Catholic Cologne; Schuman's family had fled Lorraine from the Germans to Luxembourg (Pulzer in Gehler et al. 2001: 62). All could speak German with each other, if they wished. National sovereignty was not a value in itself for them; if anything, it was something to be feared. Instead, they advocated federalism, decentralization, and subsidiarity, the principle derived from Catholic social doctrine according to which decisions should be taken at the lowest possible political and administrative level, and, less openly, a Europe united in its Christian-humanist heritage. The latter aspect was important, but, despite Pope Pius XII's (1876–1958) quasi-official endorsement of European integration, the Community was hardly a Catholic conspiracy. German Chancellor Adenauer was true to his convictions when he said that the role of the churches in politics was only to say amen.

And yet some of the structural features that came to characterize European integration—the judicialization of politics, for instance, and the emphasis on individual rights—arguably paved the way for the claim that the European Community as it took shape over the decades and the supposed "lessons from the Holocaust" fit together. Here, however, one must again beware of myth-making: Even when in the late 1960s an institution like the European Court of Justice bootstrapped itself into the role of protecting basic rights, this effort had little to do with memories of atrocity; rather, when the German and the Italian constitutional courts threatened to declare European law invalid in the name of defending the individual rights enshrined in their respective constitutions, the European court pre-empted such a move by declaring itself the guardian of individual rights vis-à-vis supranational European institutions, despite the fact that no such rights had been mentioned in the original European treaties. In other words, "European rights talk" was all about enhancing and safeguarding the supranational European legal order that had emerged since the Treaty of Rome (1957) and not a response to a past of systematic rights violations (Haltern 2005).

THE POLITICS OF REGRET AND THE "EUROPEANIZATION OF THE HOLOCAUST"

....

Only the last twenty years or so have seen what can plausibly be called a "European-ization of the Holocaust." Europeanization carries at least two meanings here: individual European countries have confronted their role in the Holocaust, and Europe as a whole (and, more specifically, the EU) has increasingly defined itself in relation to the Holocaust, a process that without a doubt happened only after the "Americanization of the Holocaust" and presumably as one step toward what some sociologists now call the "globalization" or "glocalization" of the Holocaust (Novick 1999; Levy and Sznaider 2001). This move was part of a larger shift toward what scholars now often summarize as "the politics of regret"—that is, the acknowledgment of atrocity, public apologies, and reparations as modes of polit-ical legitimacy (Knigge and Frei 2002; Olick 2007). But it also had to do with the perceptions that the European Union was in need of more legitimacy among its citizens and that such legitimacy could supposedly be furnished by a clearer sense of European identity, which was to be derived from particular interpretations of the European past.

In fact, toward the end of the twentieth century a pattern seemed to have emerged whereby individual European nations acknowledged their roles in the Holocaust and at the same time affirmed its universal significance. France, Italy, and Denmark, as well as the Netherlands and even the "neutrals" Sweden and Switzerland, went through extensive debates about collaboration, slave labor, and "Nazi Gold." After the collapse of communism, memories of World War II were "unfrozen" on both sides of the former Iron Curtain. This is not to say that some pristine, pre-representational memory, free of all political instrumentalization, could suddenly be recovered. But both personal and collective memories were liberated from constraints imposed by the need for state legitimation and by friend–enemy thinking associated with the Cold War and from what Dan Diner once called the mutual "neutralization" of memory (Diner 2003).

This process of re-engaging with the past was prompted partly by the string of half-century anniversaries stretching from 1989 to 1995, the general desire for "closure" or settling of historical records at the end of the last century, and, not least, the passing of the generation of survivors and direct witnesses to the Holocaust. Moreover, while a persistent anxiety remained that an engagement with the past would lead to a "competition in victimhood," a new willingness arose to confront other wrongs during and after World War II, such as the extensive retribution policies and the massive expulsions and resettlements that followed the Nazi occupation of Europe. Detailed studies have now demonstrated how punish-ment contributed to myths of national expiation and rebirth (Deák et al. 2000;

Lagrou 2000). Precisely these myths of resistance and retribution imploded in France and Italy, where local communist parties and the structure of the postwar party systems at least partially collapsed, thereby enabling a somewhat more dispassionate view of the past. In the same vein, Germany moved toward a more open engagement with the history of the expulsions of Germans from central and eastern Europe, while, for the most part, being careful not to question the centrality of the Holocaust to the commemoration of World War II.

In short, many myths of resistance and moral purity that had been created in the postwar period seem to have dissolved, which, obviously, is not to claim that guilt or responsibility are all of a sudden distributed equally across the continent. Arguably, European integration helped western European countries to gain some distance from their own pasts. Integration lessened the need for national self-assertion, for homogeneous narratives of national continuity, and for morally pristine pasts (Jeismann 2001: 57–8). Thus *la hantise du passé*—being haunted by the past—is certainly no longer a German peculiarity (Jeismann 2000: 59). Some European intellectuals even have gone so far as to claim that the impulse to "critically work through the past" is the essence of "European civilization" and to argue that "it is at the expense of his culture that the European individual has conquered, one by one, all his liberties, it is also, and more generally, the critique of tradition which constitutes the spiritual foundation of Europe" (Finkielkraut 1987: 143–4).

A process of "unfreezing" and simultaneously fragmenting memories has also taken place in central and east-central Europe. The painful Polish self-interrogation over the massacre at Jedwabne, the debates surrounding Budapest's House of Terror, and the German–Czech disputes over the Beneš decrees are only a few examples of intense recent historical controversies, in which Nazism, communism, and collaboration were at stake all at once. In each case, history and national identity have been linked more or less directly, and in each case, a European dimension was eventually added to the discussions. In fact, for some ex-communist eastern European countries set to join the EU, establishing Holocaust memorial days seems to have become almost a test case for their level of liberalism and democratic maturity. Again, European integration has arguably helped these processes of critical self-reflection: the prospect of inclusion has made central and eastern European politicians and intellectuals *more* willing to de-center and question national identities. The long-term security of "belonging to Europe"—even if sometimes on rather unfavorable terms—might make national self-questioning even more secure.

Nevertheless, British, French, German, and east-central European views of the Holocaust still remain deeply divided and will remain so as long as no illegitimate homogenization of historical narratives blurs the lines between victims, bystanders, and perpetrators. But certainly a common language of guilt, complicity, and regret now exists, along with a "method" of using apologies and reparations as a form of political legitimation.

THE HOLOCAUST AS A NEGATIVE "EUROPEAN IDENTITY"

The Holocaust probably would not have become central to debates in and about the EU but for the seemingly ever more urgent need for a common "European identity." The search for such an identity has had very specific political impulses: in the late 1980s and, in particular, the early 1990s, the process of European integration was gathering momentum but also encountering genuine doubts and even outright resistance on the part of various populations. The Single European Act that led to the completion of the Common European Market in 1992 significantly increased instances of majority voting among member states of the Community. National governments (and citizens) had to ask themselves whether they were really prepared to give what political scientists call "losers' consent" when they found themselves in a minority; and this in turn made the question about European identity much more real: Did majorities and minorities really share one single political space or identity so that minorities (who in some national contexts might themselves be in the majority) would accept being outvoted? This is the *realpolitische* background to the wide-ranging debates about specific "European lessons" from the Holocaust.

In a more theoretical or perhaps idealistic vein, a German social theorist argues that the Nuremberg trials and the goals of the anti-Nazi Resistance laid the normative foundations for European integration or what he calls "cosmopolitan Europe" (Beck 2003). According to this view, the idea that state sovereignty and national laws could not protect perpetrators when the charge was crimes against humanity foreshadowed a cosmopolitan (or at least pan-European) legal order, in which nation-states are no longer respected as containers sealed off from outside moral and legal claims. In short, the Holocaust de-nationalized and "European-ized" the Jews (as indicated by the commonly used phrase "European Jewry") and discredited traditional conceptions of the sovereign European nation-state. Or, as another inventive formulation has it, "Auschwitz from 1940 to January 1945 was a center of death and destruction, and of the Nazi project to destroy the Jews in Europe; the still living in the camps built a peculiar, multilingual tower of Babel, a dark and deformed version of European integration" (James 2003: 6).

As suggested above, the notion that Europe's collective memory of the Holocaust provides the basis of the EU is highly questionable from a historical perspective.

But no one can doubt that in the last few years references to the Holocaust have come to be linked explicitly in the EU with affirmations of tolerance, non-discrimination, and respect for diversity in the present. These references and invocations are part of a pattern in which a present-day political community reaffirms itself against an image of absolute moral evil in the past, thereby linking memory of past atrocity and present-day political morality.

But challenges and issues other than European integration made the choice of the Holocaust as a horizon of absolute political evil far from accidental: after the end of the communist "evil empire," the Third Reich appeared as a new (or old) standard of political evil. Moreover, in the presence of "rogue states" and geno-cide—the worst political specters of the immediate post-Cold War period—the Third Reich seemed the most "useful past." Thus, memories of the Holocaust served to legitimate both multicultural integration and humanitarian intervention. And, at least until 11 September 2001, integration and intervention seemed to be the two major political projects of Europe (and the west more generally) after the end of the Cold War (Jeismann 2001). In fact, they were connected, although often in complex ways. The wars of Yugoslav succession flooded the continent with refugees in a way not seen since World War II and its aftermath. Military intervention was designed partly to manage (and limit) the problems of integration at home, while the goals of intervention often included the reestablishment of an integrated multi-ethnic society (as had supposedly existed in Bosnia before 1992, for instance). For both of these purposes, the Holocaust proved a useful past. Tellingly, during the 1990s, Austria, France, and Switzerland made Holocaust denial a crime, and in 2001, Britain and Italy held their first Holocaust Memorial Days.

In the spring of 2000, the primarily diachronic adversary structure ("us" in the present versus "them" in the past) that informed "European identity" suddenly became a present one, when European countries decided on sanctions against an Austrian government that included the Freedom Party (FPÖ) led by Jörg Haider (1950–2008). Finally, a real political will seemed to be shared by a number of European leaders, notably Jacques Chirac (b. 1932) and Guy Verhofstadt (b. 1953), to show that Europe found its real limits not with any geographical borders, but with a certain kind of politics. In the European response to the participation of the FPÖ in the Austrian government, an emphatic notion of Europe as a set of values was deployed. That European leaders took steps against Austria almost immedi-ately after the Stockholm "Holocaust Forum" in January 2000, where they solemnly pledged "collective responsibility," was not an accident (Jeismann 2000). The moralization and memorialization of European politics went hand in hand, as memory was invoked as a motivational resource for moral action against Austria and for a renewed identification with universal norms. The Holocaust became what some scholars started calling a "negative foundation myth for Europe." Put more simply, Europe could be defined by the opposite of all the ideas and practices associated with the Holocaust: racism, hatred, cruelty, moral indifference.

Yet the sanctions against Austria were for the most part judged a failure. Charges of hypocrisy were leveled against European leaders, Chirac in particular, who were asked why they sanctioned Austria after having done nothing when the post-fascist *Alleanza Nazionale* had joined the first Berlusconi government in Italy in 1994. Were large countries that happened to be founding members of the Community judged by different standards? And was moral outrage not obviously calculated with domestic party political self-interest in mind? In other words, was Chirac not simply trying to weaken the extreme right-wing *Front National* and the Belgian government warning voters not to choose the extreme right-wing *Vlaams Blok*?

Another issue was the sense that Haider and similar right-wing parties, however problematic, might have been misjudged and that analogies with the past had been more misleading than helpful in understanding the political present. Sanctions against Austria were often presented as "negative republicanism"—that is, they were legitimated not as measures against extremist political movements and parties in general, but as a means to combat the return of a particular past, namely the Nazi one (Niesen in Avineri and Sternhell 2003: 249–68). Yet to many observers, arguing for an "essential affinity" between the Freedom Party and various European fascist parties in the past strained credulity. Establishing such an affinity, however, would have been the minimum condition for a party ban or other drastic measures within a particular country subscribing to negative republicanism.

Attempts to fashion a pan-European approach to remembrance and to combat political extremism by invoking the Holocaust did not end after the Austrian debacle. In 2002, the Council of Europe dedicated an annual "Day of Remembrance of the Holocaust and for the prevention of crimes against humanity." In 2005, the EU representative to the United Nations argued, "the significance of the Holocaust is universal. But it commands a place of special significance in European remembrance. It is in Europe that the Holocaust took place. And, like the United Nations, it is out of that dark episode that a new Europe was born" (EU Presidency Statement 2005). And in 2007, the German Presidency of the EU set itself the ambitious task of introducing an EU-wide ban on Holocaust denial by having the European Council adopt a "Framework Decision on Combating Racism and Xenophobia." This goal was greeted with considerable skepticism by liberal (and libertarian) intellectuals, primarily in Britain but also in a number of continental European countries. Free speech was one obvious counter-argument; a less obvious concern was with decentralized decision making: Every country, according to this line of reasoning, should decide by itself how to combat racism, xenophobia, and Holocaust denial, rather than being dictated an approach from Brussels.

At the same time, the political idea of making an admission of genocide (and apologies) a de facto precondition for entry to the EU was transferred from debates on the Holocaust to the question of the treatment of millions of Armenians at the hand of the Ottoman Empire during World War I. The existence of what the Germans might call *Vergangenheitsbewältigungswille* (determination to work critically through the past) became a barometer for the liberal democratic quality of a political culture. Like the ban on Holocaust denial, such an approach remained highly controversial—and again advocates of subsidiarity argued that each country had to deal with its own past in its own way.

At the beginning of the twenty-first century, toleration and respect for diversity kept being propounded as specifically European (and hard-won) virtues. Angela Merkel declared "tolerance" to be "Europe's soul" in an address to the European Parliament in January 2007; and many scholars of the EU continued to insist that it would remain a persistent plurality of peoples devoted to dealing with each other's differences in a civil manner, often proclaiming "constitutional tolerance" as a prime EU achievement (Weiler in Nicolaïdis and Howse 2001: 54–70).

Debating the "Europeanization of the Holocaust"

What is one to make of this definition of the EU as arising from a negation and the celebration of its achievements as a matter of lessons learned from the Holocaust? Certainly, as critics have long pointed out, the Holocaust is perhaps the last form of acceptable, albeit negative "Eurocentrism." In the eyes of some, its uniqueness in the annals of genocide is based precisely on the fact that it occurred in Europe and, in particular, that it originated in "highly cultured Germany," as the standard phrase goes: somehow the contrast with culture makes the barbarism even more barbaric.

But is it legitimate to argue that the European Union in particular has learnt the correct lessons from the Holocaust? To be sure, the Union's continuous expansion has been a highly successful method of democratizing and liberalizing entire countries. But such expansion surely can be justified without any reference to genocide; on the other hand, the EU as such has hardly distinguished itself, as far as actual humanitarian interventions and the prevention of genocide are concerned.

What about more specific policy debates? In general, invoking the Holocaust opens up the Pandora's Box of problems associated with historical analogies. James Bryce's (1838–1922) judgment that "the chief practical use of history is to deliver us from plausible historical analogies" will not deter politicians, intellectuals, and citizens from rummaging through the past. Yet analogical reasoning is likely to have poor results, for reasons rooted in cognitive psychology (Foong Khong 1992). Mostly, analogies simply serve to create "instant legitimacy"; they also are used to reduce moral and political complexity and, in the worst case, short-circuit critical reflection. Invocations of the Holocaust are not immune to these persistent problems.

Invoking the past often furnishes the participants in political debates with a moral certainty that otherwise hardly can be had in pluralist democratic societies. Drawing on memories for the justification of foreign and military policies, as frequently happened in the Kosovo War of 1999, can be designed simply to lend these policies a self-evident character and moral legitimacy. That legitimacy, however, may be facile and misleading because appeals to the past can function as a way to avoid political debate and rigorous moral argument. Perversely, perhaps, such appeals even can end up de-moralizing political argument. After all, reference to the Holocaust might set the standard for military intervention, for instance, far too high. One needs to find a language for the political present that relies on arguments instead of analogies and prepares the participants to live with the moral uncertainty that comes with even the most careful political judgments in complex and morally ambiguous situations.

The use of analogies raises an ethical question that has been debated most extensively in connection with extracting "lessons" from the Holocaust. As one scholar argues, "drawing lessons," as laudable as it might be in the abstract, can be part of a strategy of consolation, of deriving a comforting meaning from the past, rather than adopting a more painful strategy of confrontation with the past (Langer 1995: 5). But above all, what these lessons are is, of course, rather indeterminate. The Shoah can be as much a conclusive refutation of well-meaning universalist morality as its affirmation (Geras 1998; Agamben 1999). Auschwitz was philosophically or "conceptually" devastating and therefore resists any simple appropriation by different moral doctrines (Neiman 2002: 258–81; Roth 2005).

Finally, intensive remembrance can come at the cost of promoting universalist values in the present. Solidarity is a scarce good in politics, according to this line of reasoning, and what some scholars have called "anamnestic solidarity" could potentially crowd out present-day solidarity. In fact, the sheer enormity of the Holocaust, one could argue, might make perceiving injustice in the present actually more difficult. As has often been pointed out, the rise of a "politics of regret" has also been associated with a retreat from transformative politics and the replacement of a politics of mass mobilization with a "politics of legal disputation" (Torpey 2001). Some critics have gone so far as to claim that, like neoliberalism, the politics of regret and reparations is, above all, directed against the state, that it leads to a private cultivation of victimhood and a juridification of public life that are equally apolitical (Torpey 2001).

The validity of this quasi-empirical claim remains to be proven. Equally plausible is to argue that an engagement with even enormous past injustices can make societies as a whole more attentive to injustices in the present; to put the point differently, no prima facie reason explains why solidarity and compassion should be conceived as social and political zero-sum games.

Moreover, none of the foregoing arguments suggests placing a moral-cum-political *cordon sanitaire* around the Holocaust, even if that were possible. But they warn against facile analogies, the complacency of only recognizing familiar images, and misguided "strategies of consolation." After all, even if one holds the view that universally valid insights can be derived from the Holocaust, it does not follow that every universalism needs recourse to the Holocaust to be effective or even fully comprehended (Friedländer 1992: 19–20). Neither does it follow that the democratic experiment of the EU necessarily needs that recourse. After all, it would be "astonishing if Europe determined its future in response to some 'negationists,' who are fortunately marginal" (Lévy 2002: 45).

Yet references to the Holocaust also have played an important role in discussions about the future of the nation-state and the attractiveness of supranational forms of governance. Two kinds of political logic already clash on the world-stage ever more frequently: a post-national, universalist morality propounded and even enforced by international elites on the one hand, and a logic of popular national self-determination on the other. Put differently, normative notions of post-national power sharing and classical conceptions of sovereignty stand opposed to each other. Proponents of the former rely primarily on international law, the collaborations of experts, bureaucrats, and judges across borders, and "global governance" instead of national government. Its practitioners often act in a manner that they construe as "anticipating" a future cosmopolitan order. In such an order, state sovereignty is to be superseded by a global "domestic law," and policing will eventually replace foreign policy. Clearly, the EU is the most advanced practical realization of such a vision.

Opposed stand the notions that democracy cannot be had outside nation-states and that political action should not be left to bureaucrats, experts, and judges, no matter how accountable, but has to be grounded ultimately in a popular will. Constitutional government, advocates of this position hold, is ultimately incompatible with "global governance." Consequently, the EU, given that it was built on the basis of distrust of popular electoral democracy, is condemned to remain undemocratic.

One of the most sensitive points where these two "logics" clash is Israel (Lilla 2003). However, this clash is not simply between European post-nationalists and Israeli nationalists. Post-Zionists within Israel are subscribing to a universalist post-national orientation, just as much as many pro-Israeli Europeans have drawn the "lesson" from the Holocaust that the Jews need a politically independent homeland—or, in the extreme version, an "ethnic state" (Silberstein 1999; Levy and Sznaider 2001; Sznaider 2003). In the same vein, constitutional lawyers on the right of the American political spectrum criticize the EU as profoundly undemocratic, in order to oppose domestic advocates of "global governance" who in turn praise the Union for its advanced practices in transnational cooperation (Slaughter 2004; Rabkin 2005).

What is really a debate about Israel (or, sometimes, American domestic policy) has often been transferred onto the EU: its critics evoke Vichy and charge "the Europeans" (this is often the level of generality) with antisemitism; one book even asks, "Is the European Union's covert war against Israel, through its Palestinian

Arab allies, the secret schadenfreude fulfillment of an interrupted Holocaust?" (Ye'or 2005: 23). Others emphasize that the Holocaust was not perpetrated by a classical nation-state but by a transnational movement and that supranational institutions—as opposed to national, self-governing democracies—are not an effective means to prevent political injustice and violence (Rabkin 2005: 258–9).

The Union's advocates, on the other hand, perceive it as being precisely in the forefront in the struggle against nationalist intolerance and racism, with additional help provided by the Council of Europe (which sponsors institutions such as the European Commission against Racism and Intolerance, whereas the EU has campaigns such as "For Diversity – Against Discrimination"). At the extremes, alarmist visions of a Muslim-dominated "Eurabia," in which the Holocaust can no longer be taught in the schools of the *banlieus*, confront irenic scenarios of a pan-European multiculturalism, in which the Union's prime task (and achievement) is maintaining and "managing" diversity. Both are caricatures of today's Europe and its potential futures, but both increasingly dominate perceptions of the EU from within and from without. Very real, deep, and possibly irresolvable normative disagreements about political principles are at work behind them.

CONCLUSION

The Holocaust happened not just in, but at least to some degree in the name of Europe: the Nazis' "New European Order" was directed against Bolshevism, liberal capitalism, and "international Jewry" and persistently evoked specifically "European values." Postwar European integration was meant to prevent war among nation-states; memories of World War II were central to it, the Holocaust was not. Only in the 1980s and especially in the 1990s was the Holocaust "Europeanized" as individual European countries began critically to examine their role in it, and the European Union started to define itself against the background of the Holocaust. This also meant that the Judeocide became perceived as central to memories of World War II, yet also decontextualized and then recontextualized in the political present, most prominently in the sanctions against Austria in 2000.

Risks attend a strategy of a conscious "memorialization" within European politics. Despite the apparent "Europeanization of the Holocaust," European memories remain not just divided but also divisive. This point is not the same one that critics of the "memory industry" often have made, namely that memories are necessarily of a "liturgical" and non-negotiable character—that memory can become a secular religion (Maier 1993). A Europe that regards the Holocaust as a "negative foundation myth" can sentimentalize the past and, perversely, derive consolation from it, while remaining politically passive in the present. A shared public reasoning on Europe's pasts, their "admonitory meaning and moral purpose" (Judt 2005: 831), is profoundly desirable, but Euro-nation-building through negative memory as secular religion is not.

REFERENCES

AGAMBEN, G. (1999). *Remnants of Auschwitz: The Witness and the Archive*. New York: Zone Books.

AVINERI, S. and STERNHELL, Z. (eds.) (2003). *Europe's Century of Discontent: The Legacies of Fascism, Nazism and Communism*. Jerusalem: Magnes Press.

BECK, U. (2003). "Understanding the Real Europe." *Dissent* 50: 32–8.

DEÁK, I., GROSS, J., and JUDT, T. (eds.) (2000). *The Politics of Retribution in Europe: World War II and its Aftermath*. Princeton, NJ: Princeton University Press.

DINER, D. (2003). *Gedächtniszeiten: Über jüdische und andere Geschichten*. Munich: C. H. Beck.

EU PRESIDENCY STATEMENT (2005). Holocaust Remembrance: <http://www.europa-eu-un.org/articles/en/article_5224_en.htm>. Accessed 24 October 2007.

FINKIELKRAUT, A. (1987). *La défaite de la pensée*. Paris: Gallimard.

FOONG KHONG, Y. (1992). *Analogies at War: Korea, Munich, Dien Bien Phu and the Vietnam Decisions of 1965*. Princeton, NJ: Princeton University Press.

FRIEDLÄNDER, S. (1992). *Probing the Limits of Representation: Nazism and the "Final Solution"*. Cambridge, MA: Harvard University Press.

GEHLER, M., KAISER, W., and WOHNOUT, H. (eds.) (2001). *Christdemokratie im Europa im 20. Jahrhundert*. Vienna: Böhlau.

GERAS, N. (1998). *The Contract of Mutual Indifference: Political Philosophy after the Holocaust*. London: Verso.

HALTERN, U. (2005). *Europarecht: Dogmatik im Kontext*. Tübingen: Mohr Siebeck.

HITLER, A. (1943). *Mein Kampf*. Boston, MA: Houghton Mifflin Company.

JAMES, H. (2003). *Europe Reborn: A History 1914–2000*. London: Longman.

JEISMANN, M. (2000). "Die Weihe: Das Stockholmer Holocaust-Forum." *Frankfurter Allgemeine Zeitung*, 28 January 2000.

——(2001). *Auf Wiedersehen Gestern: Die deutsche Vergangenheit und die Politik von morgen*. Stuttgart: Deutsche Verlags-Anstalt.

JOERGES, C. and GHALEIGH, N. (eds.) (2003). *Darker Legacies of Law in Europe: The Shadow of National Socialism and Fascism over Europe and its Legal Traditions*. Oxford: Hart.

JUDT, T. (2005). *Postwar: A History of Europe since 1945*. New York: Penguin.

KNIGGE, V. and FREI, N. (eds.) (2002). *Verbrechen erinnern: Die Auseinandersetzung mit Holocaust und Völkermord*. Munich: C. H. Beck.

LAGROU, P. (2000). *The Legacy of Nazi Occupation: Patriotic Memory and National Recovery in Western Europe 1945–1965*. Cambridge: Cambridge University Press.

LANGER, L. (1995). *Admitting the Holocaust*. New York: Oxford University Press.

LEVY, D. and SZNAIDER, N. (2001). *Erinnerung im globalen Zeitalter: Der Holocaust*. Frankfurt/Main: Suhrkamp.

LÉVY, É. (2002). *Les Maîtres censeurs: Pour en finir avec la pensée unique*. Paris: Jean-Claude Lattès.

LILLA, M. (2003). "The End of Politics: Europe, the Nation-state, and the Jews." *The New Republic*, 23 June 2003.

LINDSETH, P. (2004). "The Paradox of Parliamentary Supremacy: Delegation, Democracy, and Dictatorship in Germany and France, 1920–1950s." *Yale Law Journal*, 113: 1341–1415.

MAIER, C. (1987). *In Search of Stability: Explorations in Historical Political Economy*. Cambridge: Cambridge University Press.

——(1993). "A Surfeit of Memory? Reflections on History, Melancholy and Denial." *History and Memory* 5: 136–52.

MAZOWER, M. (1998). *Dark Continent: Europe's Twentieth Century*. London: Penguin.

——(2008). *Hitler's Empire: How the Nazis Ruled Europe*. New York: Penguin.

MORAVCSIK, A. (2000). "The Origins of Human Rights Regimes: Democratic Delegation in Postwar Europe." *International Organization* 54: 217–52.

MORIN, E. (1987). *Penser l'Europe*. Paris: Gallimard.

NEIMAN, S. (2002). *Evil in Modern Thought: An Alternative History of Philosophy*. Princeton, NJ: Princeton University Press.

NICOLAÏDIS, K. and HOWSE, R. (eds.) (2001). *The Federal Vision: Legitimacy and Levels of Governance in the United States and the European Union*. Oxford: Oxford University Press.

NOVICK, P. (1999). *The Holocaust in American Life*. Boston, MA: Houghton Mifflin.

OLICK, J. (2007). *The Politics of Regret: Collective Memory and Historical Responsibility*. New York: Routledge.

OVERY, R. (2004). *The Dictators: Hitler's Germany, Stalin's Russia*. London: Penguin.

PIPER, E. (2005). *Alfred Rosenberg: Hitlers Chefideologe*. Munich: Karl Blessing.

RABKIN, J. (2005). *Law without Nations? Why Constitutional Government Requires Sovereign States*. Ithaca, NY: Cornell University Press.

ROTH, J. (2005). *Ethics During and After the Holocaust: In the Shadow of Birkenau*. New York: Palgrave Macmillan.

SILBERSTEIN, L. (ed.) (1999). *The Postzionism Debates: Knowledge and Power in Israeli Culture*. London: Routledge.

SLAUGHTER, A-M. (2004). *A New World Order*. Princeton, NJ: Princeton University Press.

SZNAIDER, N. (2003). "Israel: Ethnischer Staat und Pluralistische Gesellschaft." *Internationale Politik und Gesellschaft*, <http//www.fes.de/ipg/IPG1_2003/ARTSZNAIDER.HTM> (last accessed 28 October 2009).

TORPEY, J. (2001). "'Making Whole What Has Been Smashed': Reflections on Reparations." *Journal of Modern History* 73: 333–58.

YE'OR, B. (2005). *Eurabia: The Euro-Arab Axis*. Madison, NJ: Fairleigh Dickinson University Press.

OTHER SUGGESTED READING

BARKAN, E. (2000). *The Guilt of Nations: Restitution and Negotiating Historical Injustices*. New York: W. W. Norton.

LEBOW, R., KANSTEINER, W., and FOGU, C. (eds.) (2006). *The Politics of Memory in Postwar Europe*. Durham, NC: Duke University Press.

MÜLLER, J-W. (2000). *Another Country: German Intellectuals, Unification and National Identity*. New Haven, CT: Yale University Press.

——(2007). *Constitutional Patriotism*. Princeton, NJ: Princeton University Press.

——(2010). *The Democratic Age: Political Ideas in Twentieth Century Europe*. New Haven, CT: Yale University Press.

MÜLLER, J-W. (ed.) (2002). *Memory and Power in Postwar Europe*. Cambridge: Cambridge University Press.

PAKIER, M. and STRATH, B. (eds.) (2010). *A European Memory? Contested Histories and Politics of Remembrance*. New York: Berghahn Books.

CHAPTER 43

....

THE SOCIAL SCIENCES

....

JAMES E. WALLER

THE term "social science" first appeared in *An Inquiry into the Principles of the Distribution of Wealth Most Conducive to Human Happiness* (1824) by William Thompson (1775–1833), an Irish political and philosophical writer and social reformer. The French thinker Auguste Comte (1798–1857), however, was the first modern thinker to apply the scientific method of empirical observation, deduction, and generalization to the social world in systematic fashion. By 1830, he had coined the term "sociology" for the new academic field of study that he envisioned to be the "queen of the positive sciences." His ambition opened the door for mid-nineteenth-century thinkers to take a "scientific" approach to issues that had been the concerns of theology and philosophy, notably the relationship between human society and the individual and the sources and patterns of human thought, feeling, and behavior. Later in the nineteenth century, the new field of psychology joined sociology in applying quantitative analysis to human social behavior. By the 1930s, departments of "social research" were developing at prestigious universities around the world to meet the growing demand to quantify human interactions and produce predictive models for decision making. By the time of the Holocaust, social science was well established as a legitimate, if not uniform, collection of disciplines.

In 1949, the first issue of UNESCO's *International Social Science Bulletin* declared: "Immense things were expected of the social sciences by a world which felt that one of the fundamental reasons for the chaotic world in which we live consisted essentially in the social sciences not having kept pace with our knowledge in other fields" (1949a: 9). While this statement placed inordinate responsibility on the social sciences for the "chaotic" state of the post-Holocaust world, it also underscored their promise for comprehending and perhaps correcting the destructive nature of the recent past. Indeed, in the later pages of that same issue, UNESCO noted "a wide consensus of informed opinion that a progressive internationalisation of the social sciences is one of the great educational, scientific, and cultural needs of the present age" (1949b: 68).

Building on UNESCO's suggestions about the responsibility and potential of the social sciences, this chapter explores the impact of the Holocaust on subsequent social scientific research and the contribution of social scientific research to understanding the Holocaust and its aftereffects. The principal disciplines involved in this analysis are psychology, sociology, anthropology (particularly social and cultural anthropology), political science, and economics. Although some subfields of history deploy quantitative and qualitative methodologies similar to those of the social sciences, the emphasis here is on disciplinary and interdisciplinary work that seeks to go beyond the minutiae of thick description ("who," "what," "when," and "where") to arrive at formulations of explanation and understanding ("why" and "how") that reach beyond individual cases, i.e., that claim to know a little less and understand a little more.

The Holocaust presents challenges to such approaches because its seemingly unprecedented inhumanity questioned many social scientific presuppositions, paradigms, and theories. Comprehending the mind-boggling brutality of the people who perpetrated the atrocities and the dreadful suffering of their victims simply did not fit within the scope of pre-Holocaust social scientific understanding. As was the case in theology and philosophy, many believed that social science—to avoid being negated by history—had to be fundamentally reconstructed to deal with the Holocaust and its aftereffects (see, for instance, the 1969 piece by the eminent sociologist Kurt Wolff). At the same time, more contemporary sources of dread diverted social scientists' attention from the Holocaust.

In 1957, for example, the Jewish-American sociologist Irving Louis Horowitz published *The Idea of War and Peace in Contemporary Philosophy and Social Theory*. Although Horowitz eventually became an eminent scholar of genocide, his book said scarcely a word about the Holocaust and focused instead on the fears of nuclear destruction that animated much American discourse at the time. How, then, did the social sciences rise to the challenges that the Holocaust put before them?

SOCIAL SCIENCE AND HOLOCAUST STUDIES: A FIFTY-YEAR RETROSPECTIVE

In the first fifteen years following the Holocaust, only a few western social scientists—mainly those who could work with primary source documents and testimonies—were drawn to Holocaust studies. Since free exchanges with social scientists in eastern European universities were largely impossible during the Cold War, western social scientists worked in geographical as well as disciplinary isolation during these early years. Mirroring the world's fascination with the question of how the Holocaust could have happened, western social scientists generally homed in on the behavior of perpetrators, which was often presented as highly exceptional, and left aside issues concerning victims and bystanders. One notable exception was David Boder (1886–1961), a professor of psychology at the Illinois Institute of Technology, who traveled to Europe in 1946 and collected 109 interviews, totaling 120 hours, that recorded the experiences of displaced persons and Holocaust survivors (1949). The general tendency, however, was reflected in social scientific analyses during and after the Nuremberg Trials, which stressed that pathology had led the defendants to commit the horrific crimes for which they were indicted. The world seemed to want a simple lesson: Keep insane people out of high office and the atrocities of Nazi Germany will never happen again. In fact, for most of the mental health professionals assigned to Nuremberg, the question was not *if* they would find psychopathology among the defendants, but simply *how much* psychological disturbance they would find. In this "mad Nazi" thesis, the notion that any of the defendants would test as seemingly normal and ordinary people was simply not considered; by definition, no "normal" or "healthy" person could engage in such atrocities.

But how valid did the "mad Nazi" thesis prove to be? Millions waited in anticipation as a contingent of Allied mental health professionals, led by Douglas M. Kelley (1912–1958) and Gustave Gilbert (1911–1977), descended upon Nuremberg to plumb the depths of what most assumed to be the darkest psychopathology imaginable. Kelley and Gilbert administered psychological tests, primarily intelligence and Rorschach inkblot tests, to the accused war criminals. Although the two experts differed dramatically in their interpretations of the test results, as have subsequent analysts, the most thorough research indicates that the leaders of Nazi Germany were anything but "mad Nazis" (Zillmer et al. 1995). For the most part, they were extremely able, intelligent, high-functioning people, who presented no evidence of thought disorder or psychiatric conditions. In brief, the data from Nuremberg and other studies do not support the conclusion that the vast majority of Nazi perpetrators, whether of high or low rank, were significantly mentally abnormal. Nor do the data permit the identification of a personality structure common to Nazi perpetrators and abnormal in a clinical sense that would justify speaking of a psychological coherence or homogeneity among perpetrators as a group (Waller 2007: 59–97).

By the 1960s, even these futile searches for exceptionalism were directly challenging the social sciences' prevailing normative picture of human beings as rational creatures who could be expected to relate to and treat fellow humans with basic empathy, kindness, respect, and decency. Social scientists appeared conceptually and linguistically ill-equipped to grapple with the ubiquity of human inhumanity. Despite its universality in human affairs, and its particular manifestation in the Holocaust, "evil" was seen as an antiquated concept, heavy with archaic baggage, and was nearly absent from the vocabulary of the social sciences. In 1969, for instance, Wolff wrote, "To my knowledge, no social scientist, as a social scientist, has asked what evil is. 'What is evil?' is a question that rather has been raised (both in the West and in the East) by philosophers and theologians, as well as uncounted, unclassified, unrecorded people since time immemorial" (1969: 111).

Although social scientists did not often use the word "evil" in the 1960s, an increasing number turned their theoretical attention to the origins of human readiness to inflict deliberate harm. Rather than locating the origin of human atrocities in a pathological or faulty personality, social scientists began to focus on the power of social structures to shape the thoughts, feelings, and behaviors of ordinary actors. Central to this shift was the publication of the first edition of Raul Hilberg's *The Destruction of the European Jews* in 1961. Hilberg (1926–2007), a political scientist at the University of Vermont, wrote his doctoral dissertation at Columbia University under the supervision of Franz Neumann (1900–1954), a German left-liberal political activist and labor lawyer who became a political scientist in exile and is best-known for *Behemoth: The Structure and Practice of National Socialism 1933–1944*, a monumental analysis of National Socialism that appeared during World War II. Under Neumann's influence, Hilberg emphasized the bureaucratic "machinery of destruction" that underlay the Holocaust. His resulting three-volume work laid the groundwork for a paradigmatic shift that increasingly led Holocaust studies to highlight the far-reaching power of social structures (Hilberg 2003).

Hilberg's work was paralleled by the findings of Hannah Arendt (1906–1975), a political theorist whom *New Yorker* magazine commissioned in 1961 to cover the Jerusalem trial of Adolf Eichmann (1906–1962) in a series of five articles. Two years later, these appeared in revised and expanded form as the book *Eichmann in Jerusalem: A Report on the Banality of Evil* (1963). Arendt located the *why* of the Holocaust—its explanation—largely in the nature of the modern bureaucratic mind and its world of operations without consequences, information without knowledge, and perpetrators who followed orders uncritically and did what they were expected to do no matter how destructive the outcomes. Eichmann was frightening, Arendt argued, not because he was unusual or monstrous but because he was *ordinary*. Although the meaning of her phrase and thesis about "the banality of evil" remains controversial, her emphasis on the social structures that produced perpetrators of the Holocaust reinforced the emergent and crucial insight that, in certain circumstances, ordinary people can and often will perform extraordinarily evil deeds.

The emphasis that Hilberg and Arendt placed on the power of social structures received "experimental" validation in Stanley Milgram's three-year study (1960–1963) on obedience to authority. Milgram (1933–1984), a young social psychologist at Yale University, posed a simple, but intriguing, research question: How far would ordinary Americans go in inflicting harm on a perfectly innocent stranger if an authority figure told them to do so? To probe this question empirically, Milgram devised a "learning" experiment in which unwitting subjects were led to believe that they were administering increasingly severe but "corrective" electrical shocks to another "volunteer" subject (in reality, an accomplice of the experimenter). The experimenter/"authority figure" explained that the shocks were intended to test the effects of punishment on learning. In the initial experiment, twenty-six out of forty participants (65 percent) obeyed the experimenter's orders to shock the "learner," in steadily increasing magnitude, to the point of maximum, perhaps even life-threatening, punishment. In a series of more than twenty studies, Milgram could not devise a variation in which no subjects would obey the experimenter fully (Milgram 1963 and 1974). Testing more than a thousand individuals in a variety of settings, Milgram found that obedience to authority is deep-seated and often insidious in human behavior without regard to age, gender, or level of education. Moreover, his main findings have been replicated at least forty times in subsequent research around the world. Although the motivations and behaviors exhibited in Milgram's laboratory are not equivalent, morally or psychologically, to those of Holocaust perpetrators (Waller 2007: 111–12), his findings joined those of Hilberg and Arendt to show how social structures may produce immensely destructive behavior.

By the 1970s and 1980s, an emphasis on the power of social structures was so ingrained in social science that Milgram could write:

Many people, not knowing much about the experiment [obedience to authority], claim that subjects who go to the end of the board are sadistic. Nothing could be more foolish than an overall characterization of these persons. It is like saying that a person thrown into a swift-flowing stream is necessarily a fast swimmer, or that he has great stamina because he moves so rapidly relative to the bank. The context of action must always be considered. The individual, upon entering the laboratory, becomes integrated into a situation that carries its own momentum. (Milgram 1974: 118)

The prominence of such thinking in social scientific analyses of the Holocaust produced a new issue: the problem of "normalization." Does a strong focus on the context of action (as seen in social structures) lead to a normalization of evil, which risks replacing moral responsibility and judgment with overly deterministic social scientific insights? Or is the problem of normalization better understood as an inflicted insight about our human nature that is less problematic than astutely perceptive?

The social psychologist Philip Zimbardo explored these issues in his Stanford Prison Experiment (SPE), a simulation in which he investigated how the immediate social context of prison life—its roles, rules, and norms—might transform the people within it (Zimbardo 1972). Under realistic circumstances, each of twenty-one male undergraduates was assigned randomly to play the role of a prisoner or guard during the study. Although neither group received instructions about how to behave, some "prisoners" and "guards" soon acted like their real-world counterparts. Many of the prisoners grew resigned, ineffectual, apathetic, submissive, and depressed. Despite their knowledge that they might just as easily have been randomly assigned as prisoners, about a third of the eleven guards took on cruel, callous, sadistic, dominating, authoritarian, tyrannical, coercive, and aggressive roles. This moral drift and brutality escalated daily, demoralizing the mock prisoners to such an extent that Zimbardo aborted the study—planned to last two weeks—after only six days.

While reaffirming the power of social structures, the SPE also brought social scientists closer to "normalizing" and arguably "excusing" evil. Critics maintained that an inordinate focus on social structures transcended, even voided, the role of individual agency in perpetrating evil. For instance, the child psychologist Bruno Bettelheim (1903–1990), a survivor of Dachau and Buchenwald, wrote: "I restricted myself to trying to understand the psychology of the prisoners and I shied away from trying to understand the psychology of the SS—because of the ever-present danger that understanding fully may come close to forgiving" (1986). In response, social scientists had to reckon with this possibility, as well as the risk of exculpating perpetrators by reducing their intentionality and responsibility.

In the face of this challenge, social scientists would do well to follow the words of historian Christopher Browning: "Explaining is not excusing; understanding is not forgiving. Not trying to understand the perpetrators in human terms would make impossible not only this study but any history of Holocaust perpetrators that sought to go beyond one-dimensional caricature" (1992: xx). We must not confuse explanation with exoneration. Perpetrators are not just the hapless victims of the social structures in which they are immersed. Social scientific explanations, when presented responsibly and legitimately, are more probabilistic than deterministic. They show what people are *most likely* to do rather than what they *must* do. In willfully failing to exercise moral judgment, perpetrators remain morally and legally accountable for the atrocities they committed. No social scientific "insight" should ever remove or "normalize" that reality.

In the last two decades of the twentieth century, the social scientific emphasis on perpetrators was matched increasingly by interest in the Holocaust's victims and bystanders. A greater reliance on interdisciplinary analysis accompanied the expanding breadth of content. The political sociologist Helen Fein produced a landmark example in *Accounting for Genocide: National Responses and Jewish Victimization During the Holocaust* (1979), a work still noted for its innovative use of quantitative methods and its comparative approach. Her study was followed in 1980 by *The Holocaust and the Crisis of Human Behavior*, a distinctive interdisciplinary interpretation by the historian George H. Kren and the psychologist Leon Rappoport, which originated from a "conviction that neither conventional history nor psychology alone could provide an adequate basis for comprehension of the Holocaust" (Kren and Rappoport 1994: ix). The historian Frank Chalk and the sociologist Kurt Jonassohn advanced the scope of collaboration with *The History and Sociology of Genocide: Analyses and Case Studies* (1990), which became an influential textbook in the courses on the Holocaust and genocide that increasingly were offered outside departments of history and Jewish studies. Comparative social scientific study of genocide was further advanced by *Revolution and Genocide: On the Origins of the Armenian Genocide and the Holocaust* (1992), whose author, Robert Melson, is both a child survivor of the Holocaust and a political scientist. Finally, at the close of the twentieth century, Inga Clendinnen, an Australian anthropologist, published her wide-ranging *Reading the Holocaust* (1999), which brought anthropological methodologies and insights to bear on questions about eyewitness accounts, the Nazi mentality, and artistic representation of the Holocaust.

CURRENT TRENDS IN SOCIAL SCIENCE AND HOLOCAUST STUDIES

In the twenty-first century, social scientific study of the Holocaust engages a broad and expanding array of issues and approaches. For example, while continuing to nuance their understanding of perpetrator motivations and behavior, psychologists also are deepening their understanding of victims, survivors, bystanders, resisters, and rescuers (Welzer 2006 and Waller 2007). Among those who are unpacking issues related to the trauma of survival and remembering, Henry Greenspan, the author of *On Listening to Holocaust Survivors: Recounting and Life History* (1998), is notable. His unique oral history methodology involves interviews and reinterviews that he has done with the same group of Holocaust survivors for two decades. Peter Suedfeld, a child survivor of the Holocaust, has also studied the long-term adaptation of survivors, concentrating on the indomitable, resilient nature of humankind (2002). In addition, scholars in psychology-related fields are addressing the intergenerational trauma of surviving genocide (Lev-Wiesel 2007). Noteworthy psychological studies of bystanders, resisters, and rescuers include Eva Fogelman's *Conscience and Courage: Rescuers of Jews during the Holocaust* (1994), Daniel Bar-On's "The Bystander in Relation to the Victim and the Perpetrator: Today and During the Holocaust" (2001), and Norman Solkoff's *Beginnings, Mass Murder, and Aftermath of the Holocaust: Where History and Psychology Intersect* (2001).

Current trends in sociological analyses of the Holocaust and other genocides increasingly use comparative approaches to relate and distinguish the two topics. Specific lines of investigation include the roles of education, religion, and racial, class, and stratification systems; the impacts on families and kinship; diverse cultural and gender reactions; political, economic, demographic, and health-related effects; and social change, technology, and social movements related to genocide (Porter 2005: 969). Standing out among recent works by sociologists are Jan Gross's *Neighbors: The Destruction of the Jewish Community in Jedwabne, Poland* (2001), a provocative analysis of Polish–Jewish relations, and Vahakn Dadrian's *The History of the Armenian Genocide: Ethnic Conflict from the Balkans to Anatolia to the Caucasus* (2003), which draws detailed, comparative parallels with the Holocaust. An especially rich, well informed, and illuminating analysis is provided by Michael Mann's *The Dark Side of Democracy: Explaining Ethnic Cleansing* (2005).

Sociologists also are continuing a long line of research in which modernity, the primary analytic and normative framework for social theory, is called into question. Is the Holocaust part, even an inevitable outcome, of modernity and Enlightenment ideals? Or is the Holocaust better understood as a tragic aberration and a perversion of these ideals, a return to barbarism that represents the corrupting breakdown of modernity? Most influential here is Zygmunt Bauman's postmodernist work, stemming from his groundbreaking *Modernity and the Holocaust* (1989). That work explores the confluence of the Holocaust with modern rationalism, maintaining, according to two of his perceptive interpreters, that "the Holocaust is no longer a perversion of the principles of rationality but rather its direct outcome, insofar as it provides the necessary logistics for its execution" (Levy and Sznaider 2005: 380). The relationship between modernity and the Holocaust and genocide remains ground both contested and fertile for sociologists and social theorists.

In 1975, Ailon Shiloh called the entire anthropological discipline to task for ignoring the Holocaust as a legitimate and important field of anthropological study and research. He charged his profession with "culture blindness" in deliberately avoiding or tabooing the study of Nazi war crimes (Shiloh 1975). Perhaps because such study threatened the concept of cultural relativity, or perhaps because of the discipline's predisposition to focus on small-scale societal processes rather than large-scale political ones, few anthropologists wrote about the Holocaust and genocide prior to the mid-1980s. Since then, Alexander Hinton has taken a lead in laying a foundation for the "anthropology of genocide" (Hinton 2002a and 2002b). Because of their "experience-near" perspective, anthropologists can bring a local, intimate, micro-level focus to genocide studies that complements well the macro-level perspectives of other social scientific disciplines. As Hinton writes: "It is precisely because anthropologists can link macro-level analysis to the local-level understandings which help give genocide pattern, impetus, and meaning that they stand to make a unique and crucial contribution to our understanding of genocide" (2002b: 3). Indeed, the American Anthropological Association's extensive bibliography on "Genocide, Ethnocide, and Ecocide" testifies to the degree to which anthropologists are making those unique and crucial contributions (Hitchcock 2007).

Political scientists continue to contribute to Holocaust studies through their focus on theoretical analyses of mass violence, state racism, imperialism, and totalitarianism. R. J. Rummel's data-rich work on genocide and government mass murder (democide) argues that democracies commit genocide and mass murder less than other regimes (2000). Also significant are Enzo Traverso's *The Origins of Nazi Violence* (2003), Ira Katznelson's *Desolation and Enlightenment: Political Knowledge after Total War, Totalitarianism, and the Holocaust* (2003), Olivier LeCour Grandmaison's *Colonize, Exterminate* (2005), Scott Straus's *The Order of Genocide: Race, Power, and War in Rwanda* (2006), and Jacques Semelin's *Purify and Destroy: The Political Uses of Massacre and Genocide* (2007). In addition, Adam Jones has brought a political science perspective to bear on a web-based educational initiative, co-founded with Carla Bergman, that confronts gender-selective atrocities against men and women worldwide and explores the relevance of gender to genocide prevention and humanitarian intervention (Jones 2004 and Gendercide Watch 2007).

Economics is the most underrepresented of social scientific disciplines in Holocaust studies, but economists—approaching human behavior as a relationship between ends (wants and needs) and scarce resources—have an immense potential to contribute to the field. For instance, a recent master's thesis comparing the Armenian, Holocaust, and Rwandan genocides suggested that economic incentives are a motive for genocide and may play a more significant role than ideological explanations (Latham 2000). While far from conclusive, such research indicates how economists may make future contributions to Holocaust studies.

SOCIAL SCIENCE AND HOLOCAUST STUDIES: THE FULFILLMENT OF A PROMISE?

In the effort to understand how the Holocaust happened and to grasp its broader implications for the study of human social behavior, recognition of disciplinary interdependence is vital. Regardless of disciplinary perspective, those who engage in Holocaust studies are students in the slow business of comprehending what it means to be human and inhuman. Only in collaboration will they come to fuller insight about inhumanity. Social science complements, not replaces, other scholarly perspectives (historical, theological, philosophical, literary, and artistic) on the Holocaust.

In this light, to what degree has the promise of the "immense things" UNESCO expected of the social sciences been fulfilled for the "chaotic world in which we live"? Myriad challenges remain, but contemporary social scientists continue to build on the work of earlier generations in attempting to bring their analyses of social behavior to bear in repairing a broken world. The ways in which this effort unfolds are best understood in relation to the "scholar-activist" model.

Many social scientists, for example, complement their work in Holocaust studies by engaging in comparative analyses of genocide and mass killing. Such analyses have helped to clarify the concept of "genocide" as well as to identify its social, structural, and ideological components (Porter 2005: 969–70). In addition, the work of social scientists in comparative genocide has affirmed the universality of the potential for genocide, which is not confined to one culture, place, or time. Moreover, to make clear the synergetic relationship between comparative analysis and Holocaust studies, much of what we have studied in the former has been used to clarify or raise new issues in the latter. For instance, the study of sexual violence and rape as a tool of genocide in Bosnia pushed scholars to reexamine the role of such atrocities in the Holocaust. In this way, rather than detracting from the field of Holocaust studies, comparative analyses of genocide promise to deepen understanding of the Holocaust.

On the "activist" level, social scientists often have been at the forefront of organizations and movements aimed at predicting and preventing genocide by identifying social conditions that increase or decrease the likelihood of genocide. Quantitative work by the political scientist Barbara Harff has resulted in an influential structural model of the antecedents of genocide and politicide (political mass murder) (2003). Other scholar-activists, such as the sociologist Leo Kuper (1908–1994), have also focused on genocide prevention and the responsibility of the United Nations in that cause (1985). In 1994, social scientists (including Israel Charny, Helen Fein, Roger Smith, and Robert Melson) led in the formation of the International Association of Genocide Scholars (IAGS), an interdisciplinary, non-partisan organization that seeks to further research and teaching about the nature, causes, and consequences of genocide, and to advance policy studies on genocide prevention. In 1999, anthropologist Gregory Stanton founded Genocide Watch and the International Campaign to End Genocide, another example of how the model of the scholar-activist manifests itself in social scientific commitments to Holocaust and genocide studies.

A focus on genocide prevention has also led social scientists to play an "activist" role in applied studies of post-genocidal healing, reconciliation, and peacebuilding. Since 1999, for example, the social psychologist Ervin Staub, a child survivor of the Holocaust, and Laurie Anne Pearlman, a clinical psychologist and trauma specialist, have initiated programs to prevent violence and develop positive human values in post-genocidal Rwandan society. A quantitative evaluation of the effectiveness of their programs found that the community members who worked with the facilitators trained by Staub and Pearlman showed reduced trauma symptoms, both over time and in comparison with other groups. They also showed a more positive attitude toward members of the other "ethnic" group (Hutu or Tutsi) over time and in comparison with the other groups in the study (Staub 2003).

The persistence of inhumanity in human affairs is incontrovertible. Only blindness or arrogance would lead one to think that extraordinary human evil—including genocidal violence—is dissipating. To achieve, however, the goal of structuring a society in which the exercise of human evil is lessened, the social sciences must continue to pursue the promise of "immense things" called for by UNESCO in 1949. The potential for social scientific work to repair the "chaotic world in which we live" is immense and is held in trust for the coming generations of social scientists who work in Holocaust and genocide studies.

REFERENCES

BAR-ON, D. (2001). "The Bystander in Relation to the Victim and the Perpetrator: Today and During the Holocaust." *Social Justice Research* 14: 125–48.

BETTELHEIM, B. (1986). Review of Lifton's "The Nazi Doctors." *New York Times Book Review*, 5 October 1986, p. 62.

BODER, D. (1949). *I Did Not Interview the Dead*. Urbana, IL: University of Illinois Press.

BROWNING, C. (1992). *Ordinary Men: Reserve Police Battalion 101 and the Final Solution in Poland*. New York: HarperCollins.

GENDERCIDE WATCH (2007). <http://www.gendercide.org>. Accessed 24 February 2009.

GRANDMAISON, O. (2005). *Coloniser, Exterminer—Sur la guerre et l'Etat colonial (Colonize, Exterminate)*. Paris: Fayard.

HARFF, B. (2003). "No Lessons Learned from the Holocaust? Assessing Risks of Genocide and Political Mass Murder since 1955." *American Political Science Review* 97: 57–73.

HILBERG, R. (2003). *The Destruction of the European Jews*. 3 vols. 3rd edn. New Haven, CT: Yale University Press.

HINTON, A. (ed.) (2002a). *Annihilating Difference: The Anthropology of Genocide*. Berkeley, CA: University of California Press.

——(ed.) (2002b). *Genocide: An Anthropological Reader*. Malden, MA: Blackwell Publishers.

HITCHCOCK, R. (2007). *Genocide, Ethnocide, Ecocide, with Special Reference to Indigenous Peoples: A Bibliography*. <http://www.aaanet.org/committees/cfhr/bib_hitchcock_genocide.htm>. Accessed 24 February 2009.

JONES, A. (ed.) (2004). *Gendercide and Genocide*. Nashville, TN: Vanderbilt University Press.

KREN, G. and RAPPOPORT, L. (1994). *The Holocaust and the Crisis of Human Behavior*. Rev. edn. New York: Holmes & Meier.

KUPER, L. (1985). *The Prevention of Genocide*. New Haven, CT: Yale University Press.

LATHAM, M. (2000). "Economic Motives for Total Genocide: A Comparison of the Armenian, the Holocaust, and Rwandan Genocides." Unpublished Master's Thesis, Boston College, MA.

LEV-WIESEL, R. (2007). "Intergenerational Transmission of Trauma Across Three Generations: A Preliminary Study." *Qualitative Social Work* 6: 75–94.

LEVY, D. and SZNAIDER, N. (2005). "Holocaust". *Encyclopedia of Social Theory*. Thousand Oaks, CA: Sage Publications.

MILGRAM, S. (1963). "Behavioral Study of Obedience." *Journal of Abnormal and Social Psychology* 67: 371–8.

——(1974). *Obedience to Authority: An Experimental View.* New York: Harper and Row.

PORTER, J. (2005). "Sociology of Perpetrators." *Encyclopedia of Genocide and Crimes Against Humanity.* Detroit, MI: Macmillan Reference.

RUMMEL, R. (2000). *Death by Government.* 2nd paperback edn. New Brunswick, NJ: Transaction Publishers.

SHILOH, A. (1975). "Psychological Anthropology: A Case Study in Cultural Blindness." *Current Anthropology* 16: 618–20.

STAUB, E. (2003). "Preventing Violence and Generating Humane Values: Healing and Reconciliation in Rwanda." *International Review of the Red Cross* 852: 791–806.

SUEDFELD, P. (2002). "Life After the Ashes: The Postwar Pain, and Resilience, of Young Holocaust Survivors." Washington, DC: United States Holocaust Memorial Museum, Center for Advanced Studies.

UNESCO (United Nations Educational, Scientific and Cultural Organization) (1949a). "UNESCO and the Social Sciences." *International Social Science Bulletin* 1: 9–10.

——(1949b). "Draft Proposals for the Establishment of an International Institute of Social Sciences." *International Social Science Bulletin* 1: 68–72.

WALLER, J. (2007). *Becoming Evil: How Ordinary People Commit Genocide and Mass Killing.* 2nd edn. New York: Oxford University Press.

WELZER, H. (2006). *Täter: Wie aus ganz normalen Menschen Massenmörder werden.* Frankfurt am Main: Fischer.

WOLFF, K. (1969). "For a Sociology of Evil." *Journal of Social Issues* 25: 111–25.

ZILLMER, E., HARROWER, M., RITZLER, B., and ARCHER, R. (1995). *The Quest for the Nazi Personality: A Psychological Investigation of Nazi War Criminals.* Hillsdale, NJ: Lawrence Erlbaum.

ZIMBARDO, P. (1972). "Psychology of Imprisonment." *Society* 6: 4–8.

OTHER SUGGESTED READING

BLOXHAM, D. (2009). *The Final Solution: A Genocide.* Oxford: Oxford University Press.

——and MOSES, D. (eds.) (2010). *The Oxford Handbook of Genocide Studies.* New York: Oxford University Press.

GERSON, J. and WOLF, D. (eds.) (2007). *Sociology Confronts the Holocaust: Memories and Identities in Jewish Diasporas.* Durham, NC: Duke University Press.

NEWMAN, L. and ERBER, R. (2002). *Understanding Genocide: The Social Psychology of the Holocaust.* New York: Oxford University Press.

OLINER, S. and OLINER, P. (1988). *The Altruistic Personality: Rescuers of Jews in Nazi Europe.* New York: Free Press.

PAWELCZYNSKA, A. (1979). *Values and Violence in Auschwitz: A Sociologial Analysis.* Berkeley, CA: University of California Press.

SUEDFELD, P. (ed.) (2001). *Light from the Ashes: Social Science Careers of Young Holocaust Refugees and Survivors.* Ann Arbor, MI: University of Michigan Press.

TOTTEN, S. and JACOBS, S. (eds.) (2002). *Pioneers of Genocide Studies.* New Brunswick, NJ: Transaction.

VALENTINO, B. (2004). *Final Solutions: Mass Killing and Genocide in the 20th Century.* Ithaca, NY: Cornell University Press.

ZIMBARDO, P. (2007). *The Lucifer Effect: Understanding How Good People Turn Evil.* New York: Random House.

CHAPTER 44

....

THE HUMANITIES

....

BEREL LANG

THE title of "humanist" emerged as a recognizable if loosely defined norm in the "humanistic" Renaissance (on the elements, form, and afterlife of Renaissance humanism, see Kristeller 1964 and 1977; Grafton and Jardine 1986; and Grafton 1991). Vague as its boundaries were, the emphasis of that norm on human nature and history and thus *away* from God's nature and rule—both tendencies furthered by an ambitious retrieval of the classical past—distinguished its advocates from contemporaries who held fast to the theological anchor of scholastic learning. As with all paradigm shifts, the drama of this revolution gradually lost its edge; but its focus on the human as a *match* for nature (literally and figuratively) persisted, overcoming sporadic dissent and eventually being absorbed and advanced by the Enlightenment in the seventeenth and eighteenth centuries.

Near the end of the latter period, however, a counter-movement challenged the intellectual and moral optimism of this "enlightened" emergence into modernity. This reaction was largely motivated by "philosophers of suspicion" (Heller 1957) who, more or less independently and on other matters often at odds, launched themselves against the foundations of the humanist tradition (indeed, against the idea of foundations as such), pushing forward in virtually all areas of thought, within but also outside the humanities. (In contemporary discourse, the humanities typically refer to disciplines such as history, literature, philosophy, and religious studies.) In biology, economics, theology, geology, linguistics, philosophy, and psychology, an incipient skepticism gained momentum against the essentialist grounds on which the Renaissance and the Enlightenment had depended, protesting that the very concept of a human *nature* was contestable—and that even if one sidestepped this issue, the claims that had been asserted about the nature of humanity were tendentious and empty.

The "humane sciences" that emerged from this intervention focused increasingly on the *way* in which the world and its human inhabitants could be represented or known rather than on the existence of natures or essences that had been emphasized previously. This shift of attention—in effect, of commitment—spread broadly, extending from interpretations of physics to those of literary texts, from assessing business cycle "corrections" to justifications for human rights. It heralded a conceptual reformation: replacing substances or essences with an emphasis on method and perspective, forgoing the search for what was *real* in favor of the *means* by which knowledge might (or might not) emerge, subordinating historical or social or linguistic "facts" to systems-analysis of the signs or symbols in their representation. If achievements in the "hard" sciences and technology seemed to undermine these currents of skepticism and anti-foundationalism, they hardly interrupted the revisionary arguments for suspending or bracketing the claims of truth or fact.

Admittedly, this same reflexive impulse produced findings not inconsistent with certain traditional motifs of the humanities. The stipulation, for example, that humanistic (indeed, all) discourse must consider its own structure did not *entail* giving up the independence of either speaker or object: knower and known could still retain autonomy. But the rising suspicion often viewed even such minimal concessions as too generous. At the farthest extreme of this view, then, consciousness or reason would become "slaves of the passions," in David Hume's daring pronouncement, and the passions' newly extended reach, encompassing an indefinite variety of forces, familiar or not, meant that neither the autonomy of the self nor the objectivity of knowledge was safe from displacement.

THE HOLOCAUST'S BRUTE FACTICITY

Into this unstable setting, the brute facticity of the Holocaust has injected a conceptual dilemma. According to some accounts, the Holocaust *followed* from the narrative just described, whether directly or by its own version of the "transvaluation of all values," its own reduction of humanity (and human nature) to the "superfluity" underscored by Hannah Arendt (1906–1975) (1968). From this perspective, the Holocaust revealed crucial consequences, however unintended, of these historical developments, which continue to inform twenty-first-century life. On this view, the Renaissance commitment to human creativity and originality, complemented by the Enlightenment's faith in reason, struck down traditional moral and religious norms and paved the way for willful assertion and hubris that could harbor the intense dogmatism and depersonalized bureaucracy that eventually resulted in Nazi Germany's genocide against the Jews (Horkheimer and Adorno 1972; Bauman 1989; and Lang 1990).

This provocative hypothesis, however, revealed only one side of a two-sided narrative. The event and then the concept of the Holocaust make unavoidable a counter-move to the motif of suspicion that has come to be embedded in the humanities, disclosing in that same motif, for all its critical incisiveness, the seeds of its own deconstruction. An event of the Holocaust's enormity was not required to bring that outcome into the open. Nor did the Holocaust force that disclosure by itself (a disclosure still in process and still contested). But the moral and social impact of the Holocaust powerfully informs a dilemma for the humanities and human existence generally because its historical reality and weight are *beyond* suspicion. The Holocaust challenges the contemporary humanities and especially the role assigned, often assumed there, of a conceptual skepticism that has ignored the problems within its own conceptual foundations.

Both the event and the concept of Holocaust bring the meaning and status of truth to the fore. True to their Renaissance origins, contemporary humanities emphasize the centrality of the person as both the agent and subject of culture, at once shaping and shaped by it. One consequence of this emphasis is that truth becomes contextual and relative to time and place; the word itself appears, implicitly if not explicitly, in scare quotes. If the Holocaust is beyond suspicion, if this event cannot be credibly denied, should or can this largely assumed view of truth be maintained?

I am not in any way proposing that the humanities are implicated in, let alone responsible for, Holocaust denial. But it is important to note that since the latter turns not only on a particular set of historical data but also on a general concept of truth, it should not be surprising to find ramifications of the issue of truth in the humanities extending also to that extreme view. And still more specifically: it becomes part of my claim that a prominent conception of truth in the human-ities—the one challenged here—would ultimately have no grounds or basis for *disputing* assertions of Holocaust-denial. (That deficiency does not become the equivalent of affirming the claims of Holocaust deniers, but the deficiency is a serious matter nonetheless.)

The invocation of the Holocaust as an historical event is a crucial matter both in its particular role as a much-discussed subject in the humanities and as exemplary for the humanities because the reality of the Holocaust involves a standard of truth applicable more generally. In other words, I am suggesting that as much as we require conceptual instruments with which to view—to analyze, to understand, to assess—historical events and the moral issues to be found in them, those events themselves (here, specifically the Holocaust) are significant for shaping those instruments themselves. The Holocaust's contemporary presence in the humanities is found not only in the many works of history, philosophy, literature, religious thought, and the arts that explicitly address that event but also in its shadow-presence in many texts and much discourse that do not address the Holocaust directly. Wherever the Holocaust is present, issues about truth are close at hand, even if the humanities have evaded them, largely by failing to notice that the humanities' efforts at historical contextualization become incoherent unless they resist the view that no truth claim is ever beyond suspicion and that all truth claims are always questionable and disputable.

Especially in philosophy but also in literary theory and, odd as it may seem, in historical discourse itself, a wariness about and a distancing from the particularity and facticity of individual historical events predominate. Here the paradigm of "hard" science has been obtrusive, as the humanities have at times attempted to emulate the methods (also for them, hopefully, the success) of the sciences for which universal or general principles stand as ideals. The confidence of science in moving beyond individual "events" (including individual experiments) to more abstract generalizations drew much of its energy from the "covering law" model that thought to subsume particular occurrences under single, blanket formulas of explanation (Hempel 1965). The latter, then, represented a more fundamental claim on reality than the individual historical instances that they "covered." In supporting this formulation, any single occurrence would count only as an instance or example and did not have to be reckoned with for itself.

Unlikely as it might seem to find evidence of this same disposition in historical discourse, its influence has nonetheless been apparent there as well—in part, as a residual scientism sought to impose general patterns of explanation on disparate individual events; in part, through a reactive attentiveness to *alltäglich* history, which in its focus on the significant commonplace of daily life led on its *other* side to a blurring between major and lesser historical events (Ginzburg 1980 and 1989; Davis 1995).

On the other hand, history is also foremost among the humanities in marking and analyzing the complexities—the *facts*—of the Holocaust. This accomplishment, however, has taken place in the face of pressures from outside and inside the discipline—pressures progressively weakened by the tide of Holocaust scholarship but still persisting, at least on certain levels. For instance, debates continue about what place "the Holocaust" should have among academic disciplines and courses: In history departments in the context of modern German history? In German departments? As "Jewish history" in Judaic studies programs? In human rights programs in relation to other instances of genocide?

More is at stake in such discussions than bookkeeping or university and college catalogs. As recently as the 1960s, *any* reference to the Holocaust in academe was fraught. Vivid evidence of that fact appears in Raul Hilberg's memoir *The Politics of Memory* (1996). There Hilberg (1926–2007) recounts his advisor's discouraging reaction to Hilberg's doctoral dissertation proposal, which eventually, on Hilberg's insistence, gave way to Franz Neumann's grudging consent: "It's your funeral." That dissertation became *The Destruction of the European Jews* (1961), the path-breaking work for the field of Holocaust studies, but *then* only after difficulty in finding a publisher.

Not only in the still young field of Holocaust studies, the Holocaust itself, especially as the range of its planning and instrumental details and, still more, its ethical dimensions began to unfold, became increasingly important in historical analysis and in the humanities more generally. Attention focused increasingly and intensively on factual detail and on "getting it right" where the history of the Holocaust is concerned. Even when viewed at its highest possible level of abstraction, the Holocaust cast a shadow backward and forward from the mid-point of the twentieth century, magnified by its origin in a nation that was a center of the western humanistic tradition, and sustained in near- or full view of other nations sharing this tradition. It is too much to claim (and, at any rate, unverifiable) that since the Holocaust, *all* thinking about culture and the place of the human within it has been affected by the moral weight and consequences of that event. But it would be no less exaggerated to deny the impact of the Holocaust on the work of the humanities— overtly, with the Holocaust as an announced subject or participant, but also as it appears tacitly, in the form of moral and epistemic limits that impose a sub-textual, even silent, condition. The reality of the Holocaust, the truth that it happened and continues to reverberate, seems impossible to ignore any more than one can rightly deny the presence of a nearby mountain even when clouds or fog obscure it.

The effects of this presence, however, have sometimes fostered a notable distortion at the other extreme. Numerous literary, historical, and philosophical representations pronounce the Holocaust as extraterritorial. Finding it beyond understanding, they put the Holocaust *outside* history (or reason or psychology). Such accounts characterize the Holocaust as unique, incomparable, unclassifiable—modifiers that in the end are both confused and confusing in placing the Holocaust past the reach of history itself. In these interpretations, what was so determinately and emphatically historical in the motivating, planning, and implementing of the "Final Solution" appears as not *more* difficult to understand than other events but *impossible* to understand. The most serious attempt to establish the Holocaust's "uniqueness" on historical grounds blurs the distinction between *unique* and *unprecedented* (Katz 1994). Most other references to the Holocaust as unique rely as much on rhetorical as historical grounds (Steiner 1967; Rawls 1999; Rosenbaum 2009).

The Holocaust's Challenge

The field of Holocaust studies fosters, even depends upon, the view that there are events that really happened and that there are true and false judgments that can be made about them, judgments whose validity is not entirely dependent on one's time, place, or circumstance. If that outlook is credible, it constitutes a deep challenge to assumptions that govern much of modern intellectual history. Even an abbreviated account of that challenge requires revisiting the Enlightenment "project" and the turn that its evolution gave to the concept of truth. This development is epitomized in the 150-year span between the philosophers René Descartes (1596–1650) and Immanuel Kant (1724–1804). For Descartes, valid truth claims were fully representational, a gleaming "mirror of nature." Steeped in a growing self-consciousness and related skepticism, which undid Cartesian realism, Kant's version of the Copernican Revolution not only inextricably related the knower and the known but entailed that the knower unavoidably shaped the known. Kant became a founding source of what has since emerged as the "constructivist" theory of knowledge.

Radical as Kant's Revolution was, with human reason and understanding ingredient in whatever comes to be "known," it did not imply that the knowledge gained—its *content*—is individuated or, in the all-purpose term often applied now, "subjective." For Kant and the Enlightenment more generally, reason and judgment were, as human, *inter*-subjective, reaching beyond the individual so long as he or she put aside other accidental conditions. In this sense, Kant's Revolution traversed a half-, not a full turn, with knowers and the known linked in a common project but retaining a significant measure of independence. Post-Enlightenment philosophers of suspicion would propel Kant's half-turn into a full turn by enlarging further the domain of the knower to the point that what had persisted for Kant as *facts* of experience (and knowledge) also began to waver and vanish, apparently real but only as apparent, like the smile of Lewis Carroll's Cheshire Cat.

It might be objected that this linear and much condensed representation of modern intellectual history leaves out the totalizing impulse in the nineteenth-century combination of Idealism and Romanticism that acted to displace the rationalist optimism of the Enlightenment with an even more ambitious optimism of the will. But both these grandiose visions soon provoked their own reactions, which rejected the grandiosity but nonetheless expanded the role of the self or "knower." They did so by continuing to emphasize the role of the subject in the construction of knowledge and cultural institutions, but they went even further by claiming to dispense with the ladder—for instance, realities and facts that were not solely constructed by the knower and yet still knowable—that the subject (symbolically) had climbed to make its contribution to that construction, arriving at a full "inwardness" (Taylor 1989) for which history and its material means—let alone any metaphysical means—were quite irrelevant.

According to this philosophical view, truth became a function of language and "experience," not of events or actions or things that had an existence of their own. So the pragmatist philosopher William James (1842–1910) cited the "cash-value" of truth claims, with the rate of exchange set by the pragmatists' own bank of "experience"; the phenomenologists concentrated on experience but demurred to say what (if anything) existed outside it; existentialists, rejecting the moral and

conceptual force of general "principle" as such, placed the burden of all justification on individual assertion (*as* assertion); "ordinary language" analysis relied on
the context of discourse closest to the analysts themselves for the definition of truth
(or other key terms), effectively precluding any question of how linguistic or
cultural communities had come to assume the forms they had.

The common source—and it has to be said, truth—from which these views set
out is evident. It consisted of the flaws in traditional rationalistic claims for
certainty, for truth as self-evident, for a basis in "immaculate" perception or
knowledge—perception or knowledge as frictionless (or fictionless)—that skepticism made insurmountable. Skepticism's pendulum swung toward multiple versions of constructivism, which contextualized and relativized understandings of
truth and truth claims themselves. Contrary to the hope that the removal of
absolutist perspectives about truth, including its objectivity, would have the beneficial effect of checking dogmatism and tyrannical politics, neither abdicated the
field and both found aid and comfort in a cultural context where "triumphs of the
will" seemed all the more possible and crucial for determining what would be.
Those "triumphs" could even take the form of assertion that non-constructed
views of reality and truth remained in play. The Holocaust itself, with its proximate
origins in the industrialized killing of World War I that was then brought to a new
extreme in the extent, intensity, and single-mindedness of Nazi ideology, policy,
and action during the twelve years of the Hitler regime, reveals the staying power of
commitment to a "*non*-constructed" theory of truth, which characterized many
"true believers" in the Nazi regime and still finds adherents among those who
inflict genocidal atrocities in the post-Holocaust world.

Of course, the staying power of dogmatism has had to contend with the rising
tide of constructivism that it attempts to resist. (Force and power, it should be
noted, are not exclusively associated with dogmatic or essentialist traditions. In
philosophers such as Friedrich Nietzsche (1844–1900) and Michel Foucault (1926–
1984), for example, those realities are key for analyzing history and for interpreting
forecasts and prescriptions for the future. That a "will to power" or force can play a
common and central role in contradictory claims of principle must surely be
significant in assessing that alleged source.) In any event, the pendulum of history
plays no favorites, and at the point where the combination of self-assertion and
suspicion approached their contemporary apex a collision between that combination and the occurrence of the Holocaust has become evident. This collision is
warranted and even necessary. For, again, the constructivist view of history and
truth has been an urgent, if not entirely dominant, presence in the humanities, one
that trades not only in arguments but also in attempts to create a sense of shame in
those who, according to the constructivists, fail to have the courage or insight
required to look below the surface and to embrace the unending relativity of those
depths. (Strictly speaking, however, the constructivist view would be hard put to
speak of philosophical *arguments* at all. Richard Rorty (1931–2007) makes this point

explicitly, openly replacing the "argument," with its implications of truth or falsity as criteria, by "looking bad" or "looking good"—that is, by judging the "looks" of positions (Rorty 1989). His criteria for assessing "looks," however, remained an open and puzzling question.) The pressure from this culture of shaming has been especially prominent in literary theory, but it has extended also to historiography, cultural studies, psychology, and philosophy. Although contested on all these fronts, it has been and remains a force.

At this contested juncture the Holocaust as an event crucially makes its presence known—raising as dramatically and forcefully as ever the question of the status of truth. The very phrase "the Holocaust" has acquired an epistemic weight; its heft has been continuously reinforced as the details of the Holocaust's history have not only come to light but also been documented in depth: the development of the "Final Solution" in Nazi thinking; the organizing of the concentration camps and then the death camps—and the intricacies (sometimes the blunders) of experimentation in devising the latter (how *does* one invent a production line for the killing of millions?). The phrase "the six million" has become a metonymy for Holocaust history as such: the obviously imprecise number remains a shorthand aggregation for the willfully selected Jewish victims, joined in common by an identity and a fate that the Nazis and their collaborators determined.

The phenomenon of "Holocaust denial" is well-known, far exceeding the reach, number, or standing of its early postwar advocates as it reflects and inflames antisemitism in twenty-first-century politics. The issue of truth underlies these developments, too. With the historical and conceptual status of Holocaust denial as feeble as it is, why should this denial assert and sustain itself as it has? (For summaries and critiques of Holocaust denial, see Lipstadt 1993 and 2005; Evans 2001.) This question becomes the more pointed because of the divisions and vagaries in the denial itself: whether it is the number of Jews who were or were not killed in the (alleged) Holocaust; what was responsible for the deaths of those who were killed (or died); what the Nazi (or Hitler's) intentions *were* vis-à-vis the Jews. (A point typically left unstated in Holocaust-denial debates is the tacit concession by many deniers that *if* the Holocaust had occurred, it would have been evil and wrong—a shady difference between them and those who do not deny the event's occurrence but continue even now to defend or excuse it.)

The question of "truth" or "fact" in relation to Holocaust denial thus arises at a number of levels: most generally, in the ascription of intention, but more immediately in empirical questions such as whether there *were* gas chambers or crematoria and in which camps, and even if there were, whether they could have accomplished the killing attributed to them. That such questions are raised tendentiously does not mean that they are meaningless or trivial or do not require answers; in fact they bear directly on the status of truth and its standing for the humanities in the post-Holocaust world. For even after allowing for interpretive differences of the "fine" anatomy of the Holocaust (for example, the causal role of antisemitism in Nazi policy), as distinct from the Holocaust's "gross" anatomy, about which there is little to *argue*; and after acknowledging the obvious limitation of historical discourse insofar as it never brings back to life for scrutiny the events it purports to reconstruct (and typically does not *wish to*)—after all this, there remains a ground of fact about the Holocaust as strongly supported as any claim of fact ever has been. Indeed, for the post-Holocaust world, that ground serves as a *criterion* for truth. At this crucial point the Holocaust and the humanities converge or, as it seems, *collide*.

Consider the following statement: "At a meeting in Wannsee on 20 January 1942, fifteen Nazi officials discussed plans for implementing the 'Final Solution of the Jewish Question.'" This statement does not speculate on the meeting's background or the decisions leading to it; nor does the statement assume the implementation of plans discussed at the meeting. The statement itself, however, is attested by the protocol—the minutes—of the meeting, whose authenticity is attested by other evidence, much of it independent of the *Bespreschungsprotokoll* of the Wannsee Conference (Mendelsohn 1982; Browning 2004; Cesarani 2005). The weight of this documentary and supporting material does not mean that to deny the truth of the statement above is *impossible*; but it does mean that, if pushed further, denial of that assertion—which is, after all, one piece of a larger whole—is also a piece of a larger whole that would seem in the end to amount to denial of the concept of evidence or, no less fundamentally, of historical truth.

A Foundational "Ground Zero"

Interpretations of a sequence of events or acts are not identical to the facts that constitute such a sequence. The difference between a narrative and a chronicle reflects that distinction. This difference especially demands attention, reflection, and caution with respect to factual statements about the Holocaust and then to the ways in which those integral pieces are handled in the interpretations of how and why the Holocaust took place. The statement above about the Wannsee Conference formally resembles innumerable others in historical accounts that are much less highly charged than those about the Holocaust. Without claiming "uniqueness" for the Holocaust, the statement about the Wannsee Conference, along with the exemplary force of others (whether or not their subject is the Holocaust) provides a foundational "ground zero" for historical and, more generally, empirical assertions and then for their verification. That such assertions may *also* reflect various motivations (psychological, moral, ideological) is a consideration separate from the question of the truth or falsity of the claims registered, which also crosses the boundaries of different historical interpretations or narratives.

Again, it is not *necessary* to ground this position in the claim for the historicity of the Holocaust. But precisely because that event *is* so highly charged, it is an example that compels reflection on the discomfort in the humanities concerning questions about interpretation, the referentiality of texts (historical as well as literary), and the criteria by which narratives (grand or not-so-grand) can be assessed. As I have traced it through the centuries of its evolution, the pressure from one side has reached the point where, as Rorty asserted, so far as truth is concerned, "everything is up for grabs" (Collini 1992, especially Rorty's response to Umberto Eco and Eco's reply to Rorty's response). At this juncture, in the brute facts of the events of the Holocaust and in the either/or that those facts pose, the crux of the matter appears in bold relief: *either* the Nazis initiated a systematic genocide against the Jews *or* they did not; no third way is open for interrogation. The choice between the two alternatives thus appears itself as a matter of fact, as either matching or not matching a set of historical events that can be detailed, perhaps not fully but fully enough to require a decision.

The argument here is not "merely" historical. Literary representations of the Holocaust have less evidentiary or epistemic force than straightforward empirical claims; but that literary representations incorporate—in effect, *presuppose*—historical evidence, and commonly assumed historical evidence at that, adds their weight to the historical ground. Not, of course, because "fiction" cannot be inventive, but because the most inventive fictions also build on empirical and historical grounds: at one extreme, the details of human experience, at the other extreme and on a much larger scale, the historical settings from which individual characters emerge. The varied appearances of the Holocaust that figure in the works of writers as diverse as Jerszy Kosinski, Philip Roth, Bernard Schlink, Jakov Lind, Aharon Appelfeld, Paul Celan, Vassily Grossman, and Art Spiegelman all posit, tacitly but also unmistakably, a historical ground (thus also of truth) that assumes the view I have been proposing. Absent this empirical underpinning, their writings would be utterly different than they actually are. The interpretive space beyond that base, the space of the creative imagination (or even of ideology), is not at all at odds with this common starting point: the greatest artists do not, cannot, spin out of whole cloth. Nowhere is this clearer than in the imaginative diversity of the strongest examples of Holocaust "literature" viewed against the common background in non-literary fact from which they set out. Whatever view one has about the adequacy of literary (fictional, poetic) representation regarding an event with the dimensions of the Holocaust, the basis of that representation remains as a common feature of that representation and the key facts that comprise that feature are *beyond* interpretation, even if one agrees that there is indeterminacy wherever interpretation does apply.

By no means, it should be emphasized, is the status or role of truth in the humanities confined to the reach of literary analysis in relation to literature conventionally defined. That reach has been extended also to historiography.

Here, too, the alternatives are stark, and the issue of historical truth hangs in the balance. Either the Wannsee Conference, for example, took place or it did not. The evidence that it did take place is overwhelming. If it can be credibly maintained—it cannot—that it is false (evidentially, causally, and consequentially) to say that that meeting took place, then it would not be too much of a stretch to say that the Holocaust did not occur. But the Holocaust happened and so did the Wannsee Conference that was a key factor in the genocide. Historiography and philosophies of history that abandon this empirical and epistemological base also entail the pernicious outcome that everything is up for grabs.

That truth as such and not only one or another particular claim is at stake here indicates that what may seem exclusively an epistemic or cognitive issue is also, and no less basically, an ethical one. The Holocaust has influenced a broad variety of political and social legislation and institution-building in the post-Holocaust period A sample includes the Nuremberg Trials (1945), the United Nations Convention on the Prevention and Punishment of the Crime of Genocide (1948), and establishment of the International Criminal Court (2002), which is empowered to try and punish genocide and related crimes. Even Raphael Lemkin's coining of the term *genocide*, which has been so fully absorbed into social discourse as to serve as a synonym for atrocity as such, cannot be fully understood apart from the Holocaust's facticity. Drawn from aspects of the Holocaust, a broader vocabulary has entered the language (for both use and abuse) as metaphors: "Auschwitz," "Nazi," "Kapo," "Final Solution," "Musselman," "Hitler"—all recur, standing on their own, with their individual complex histories *assumed* as sub-texts for use in ethically charged statements in which they are typically invoked.

As these examples attest to the Holocaust by *their* consequences, they also converge on the characterization I have given here of that event's serving now as a criterion of truth as such, most pointedly in the areas of the humanities where that criterion has come to be placed at risk. But there is also a more basic issue at stake here, which is the common assumption of a sharp line between fact and value, between theoretical and moral reasoning. The classic formulation of this distinction is the "naturalistic fallacy," named and defined by G. E. Moore (1873–1958) (1903). These divisions, too, have circulated as virtual shibboleths in contemporary discourse in the humanities, but their conceptual authority has reached its ethical as well as epistemic limits when confronted by the Holocaust. To say that the Holocaust happened does not inspire confidence that a neat separation can be maintained between fact and value or that there is a fallacy in moving from a factual statement to a moral judgment. Plato found an intrinsic relation between the True and the Good by way of his "theory of forms," but the connection can be demonstrated apart from that theory, and not only by considering the moral *consequences* of the difference between truth and its opposite. The claim that the Holocaust occurred does not refer only to an assembly of individual historical assertions (like that about the Wannsee Conference), since both the assembly and indeed the individual assertions incorporate a valuation in themselves. What they refer to includes and warrants ethical considerations. The moral outrage provoked by claims that the Holocaust did not occur is not merely a protest against historical or empirical misrepresentation, nor is it motivated only by concern for particular individuals—the remaining survivors or their descendants. The fact that is at risk has *itself* moral standing. If the evidence for this view seems more intense or striking in the affirmation or denial of the occurrence of the Holocaust than in many other claims, such evidence remains an aspect of the findings of truth (or falsity), wherever they occur.

It may be objected that this account of the relation between the humanities and the Holocaust is less descriptive than prescriptive, that it identifies turning points or shifts of which their agents either have been unaware or even that they explicitly rejected, that I am *formulating* an argument rather than describing one. The objection may go on to say that the premise that the Holocaust has been and continues to be a large and moving presence in the humanities is difficult to verify even in principle let alone in fact: the humanities are too scattered, various, multi-tasking, to subside readily under such a characterization—and certainly the efforts made here, themselves piecemeal and unsystematic, do not advance the claim very far. And then, too, even if my claims are granted for the sake of argument, the conclusion I have drawn from them can be read as an apologia for reaction, a plea for return to the Enlightenment project, with all the baggage of essentialism, dominance, and master narratives associated with that project, at times for better, but certainly, at other times, for worse.

Well, perhaps—and then at most, in part. To be sure, the account here affirms as well as describes the contention that where truth is at risk, as it has been placed in the contemporary humanities, the occurrence of the Holocaust exemplifies a ground from which truth, *wherever* its presence is in question, pushes off. And that truth could not do without some such ground. But here "prescription" merges with "description": either the claim for such a ground is warranted or it is not; if it is, then it must be acknowledged (here the prescription), whatever else is subsequently built on it or taken from it. No particular epistemic assertion is at issue here, nor is the possibility of disagreement, as in conflicts of evidence, ruled out. But that there is a *ground-zero* in any such procedure, and that the occurrence of the Holocaust has come—for good reasons—to hold that position in much contemporary discourse is also a matter of fact. That fact endures not because the Holocaust is "unique" and not because no other event *could* serve, but because in the context of our own presence, the combination of the dimensions of the Holocaust, its proximity, and the threatening repetition of certain of its features commands attention and recognition.

A GROUNDING FOR THE HUMANITIES

My analysis of the Holocaust and its relation to truth claims proposes a grounding for the humanities wherever the claims made in its fields of discourse are subject to assessment as true or false. That grounding entails that an either/or must be faced and a decision made about it—for example, the Holocaust happened or it did not—with no third or intermediate way. That there are *some* such cruxes would not often be denied, but they are typically set aside as exotic or special cases, remote from everyday life as well as from the abstract findings or conclusions that recur in the work of the humanities, in literary or historical or philosophical accounts and judgments. But epistemic skepticism and moral openness must themselves concede limits if they are to be intelligible or applicable (beginning with self-referentiality, their willingness to question their own questions), and one can see the force of this stricture as clearly as it can be seen in the superficially simple move that would put the Holocaust in scare quotes, as "the Holocaust": that is, as the "so-called" Holocaust, the Holocaust "as it were," or, more deeply, "as it is claimed to have been."

The classic imperative, "Know thyself," resonated in directing human vision and understanding to the person whose vision and understanding it was. The humanities have grown through and past that ideal, recognizing its contingency and thus also disputing the vacuum or airlessness of the "view from nowhere" by means of which Enlightenment thinking had thought to elevate both humanity and knowledge. A path followed in the aftermath of that period did make the effort to introduce inhabitants of flesh and blood, particular ones, but these corrections were themselves deficient because they provided those inhabitants insufficient means for sustenance and survival. The alternative that I have been proposing adds to the latter adjustment the stark irony that recognition of the Holocaust, symbol of death and brutality as it is, also conveys and sustain the life of truth. The basic question for the fields of the humanities, now as ever, is not how to redo or reimagine history, but how to countenance and imagine the present through and after history, through and after real events that actually happened and that can be known as such. The fact that individual historical events are entirely contingent does not mean that our view of them, including the frame by which we grasp them, is contingent in the same way and to the same extent. The Holocaust in its twofold role—as fact and as a fundamental grounding for our understanding—exemplifies this reality. The humanities can look to the Holocaust not only to learn from history but also as a guide for learning and understanding as such, which is, after all, a key reason for caring about the humanities and their links to the Holocaust and Holocaust studies in particular.

REFERENCES

ARENDT, H. (1968). *The Origins of Totalitarianism*. New York: Harcourt, Brace, and World.

BAUMAN, Z. (1989). *Modernity and the Holocaust*. Ithaca, NY: Cornell University Press.

BROWNING, C. (2004). *The Origins of the Final Solution: The Evolution of Nazi Jewish Policy, September 1939–March 1942*. With contributions by J. Matthäus. Lincoln, NE: University of Nebraska Press.

CESARANI, D. (2005). *Eichmann: His Life and Crimes*. New York: Vintage.

COLLINI, S. (ed.) (1992). *Umberto Eco: Interpretation and Overinterpretation*. Cambridge: Cambridge University Press.

DAVIS, N. (1995). *Women on the Margins*. Cambridge, MA: Harvard University Press.

EVANS, R. (2001). *Lying about Hitler: History, Holocaust, and the David Irving Trial*. New York: Basic Books.

GINZBURG, C. (1980). *The Cheese and the Worms: The Cosmos of a Sixteenth Century Miller*. Baltimore, MD: Johns Hopkins University Press.

——(1989). *Clues, Myths and the Historical Method*. Baltimore, MD: Johns Hopkins University Press.

GRAFTON, A. (1991). *Defenders of the Text: Traditions of Scholarship in the Age of Science, 1450–1800*. Cambridge: Cambridge University Press.

——and JARDINE, L. (1986). *From Humanism to the Humanities*. London: Duckworth.

HELLER, E. (1957). *The Disinherited Mind*. London: Bower & Bower.

HEMPEL, C. (1965). *Aspects of Scientific Explanation*. New York: Free Press.

HILBERG, R. (1961). *The Destruction of the European Jews*. 1st edn. Chicago, IL: Quadrangle Books.

——(1996). *The Politics of Memory* Chicago, IL: Ivan Dee.

HORKHEIMER, M. and ADORNO, T. (1972). *Dialectic of Enlightenment*. New York: Herder & Herder.

KATZ, S. (1994). *The Holocaust in Historical Context*. New York: Oxford University Press.

KRISTELLER, P. (1964). *Eight Philosophers of the Italian Renaissance*. Stanford, CA: Stanford University Press.

——(1977). *Renaissance Concepts of Man*. New York: Harper & Row.

LANG, B. (1990). *Act and Idea in the Nazi Genocide*. Chicago, IL: University of Chicago Press.

LIPSTADT, D. (1993). *Denying the Holocaust: The Growing Assault on Truth and Memory*. New York: Free Press.

——(2005). *History on Trial: My Day in Court with David Irving*. New York: Harper-Collins.

MENDELSOHN, J. (ed.) (1982). *Documents of the Holocaust*. Vol. 11. New York: Garland.

MOORE, G. (1903). *Principia Ethica*. Cambridge: Cambridge University Press.

RAWLS, J. (1999). *The Law of Peoples*. Cambridge, MA: Harvard University Press.

RORTY, R. (1989). *Contingency, Irony, and Solidarity*. Cambridge: Cambridge University Press.

ROSENBAUM, A. (ed.) (2009). *Is the Holocaust Unique?* 3rd edn. Boulder, CO: Westview Press.

STEINER, G. (1967). *Language and Silence*. New York: Atheneum.

TAYLOR, C. (1989). *Sources of the Self: Making of the Modern Identity*. Cambridge, MA: Harvard University Press.

OTHER SUGGESTED READING

BIALAS, W. and RABINBACH, A. (eds.) (2006). *Nazi Germany and the Humanities*. Oxford: Oneworld Publications.
CLENDINNEN, I. (2002). *Reading the Holocaust*. Cambridge: Cambridge University Press.
KANT, I. (1987). *Critique of Judgment*. Indianapolis, IN: Hackett.
LANG, B. (1995). "Is It Possible to *Mis*represent the Holocaust." *History and Theory* 34: 84–89.
LEVI, N. and ROTHENBERG, M. (eds.) (2003). *The Holocaust: Theoretical Readings*. New Brunswick, NJ: Rutgers University Press.
RUBENSTEIN, R. and ROTH, J. (2003). *Approaches to Auschwitz: The Holocaust and Its Legacy*. Rev. edn. Louisville, KY: Westminster John Knox Press.
SHERMER, M. and GROBMAN, A. (2000). *Denying History: Who Says the Holocaust Never Happened and Why Do They Say It?* Berkeley, CA: University of California Press.
SLUGA, H. (1993). *Heidegger's Crisis: Philosophy and Politics in Nazi Germany*. Cambridge, MA: Harvard University Press.
SOKOL, A. (1996). "Trangressing the Boundaries: Towards a Transformative Hermeneutics of Quantum Gravity." *Social Text* 46–47: 217–52.
STEINWEIS, A. (2006). *Studying the Jew: Scholarly Antisemitism in Nazi Germany*. Cambridge, MA: Harvard University Press.

CHAPTER 45

....

EDUCATION

....

SIMONE SCHWEBER

THOUSANDS of publications have addressed teaching and learning about the Holo-caust, but rigorous research about Holocaust education did not emerge until the 1990s. Previously, historians, teachers, museum educators, survivors, curriculum writers, reporters, parents, psychologists, and even students argued about why the Holocaust should (or should not) be taught, when, in which contexts, by whom, what ought to be included in or left out of the curriculum, and what students ought to learn. Often strongly opinionated, frequently providing important insights, many of these early discussions nevertheless lacked or overlooked empirical data. Even when the literature explored Holocaust education in specific contexts, the analysis was more often anecdotal than research-based.

This early lack of a solid evidentiary foundation on which to base Holocaust education is explained, at least in part, by the relatively recent incorporation of the Holocaust in school curricula and by the particular national contexts in which teaching and learning occur. In Israel, for example, where the Holocaust was "a meaningful factor in the creation of the new Jewish identity after World War II" (Shamai et al. 2004: 766), Holocaust education began in the 1950s, but teaching often reflected the ideologies of the reigning political parties. Not until the late 1970s did Holocaust education become mandatory in Israeli public education. In the United States, the Holocaust was taught in Jewish congregational schools prior to the 1970s, but only in that decade did it become a topic for study in American public schools (Sheramy 2003; Fallace 2008). In Germany, the history of Holocaust education is especially complicated and multifaceted because it took different paths in the West and East. Reunited Germany continues to struggle with the generational implications of the Holocaust. As these examples suggest, Holocaust education is inextricably bound up in national discourses over the meaning of being a citizen, not just of a country but of the world. Research on Holocaust education thus has rich possibilities, though it has taken time to develop, partly owing to philosophical divides.

PHILOSOPHICAL DIVIDES

Early on, researchers of Holocaust education divided over the Holocaust's unique-ness and the extent to which it had "universal" implications that could serve as a basis for encouraging civic engagement (Friedlander 1979). Critics of the "univer-sal" camp bemoaned approaches that seemed to strip the Holocaust of its distinct-ive power, diminishing "its unique significance . . . instead of making students sensitive to [its] abnormalities" (Schatzker 1982: 80). This polarization of unique-ness and universality affected educational researchers' discussions about the activ-ities, goals, and outcomes of Holocaust education. Those inclined to emphasize the Holocaust's uniqueness warned teachers about the impossibilities inherent in teaching about the Holocaust, including the event's "incomprehensibility." They emphasized the dangers of drawing comparisons between the Holocaust and other historical events and argued for maintaining Holocaust exceptionalism in relation to other genocides. After examining an array of American curricula, the historian Lucy Dawidowicz (1915–1990) recapitulated this position. Railing against "how *they* teach the Holocaust," she found that many of the school materials bastardized the Holocaust, misrepresenting its root causes and central victims (1992: 65–83).

Like Dawidowicz, those who stress the Holocaust's particularity have tended to argue that teaching about the Holocaust demands specialized knowledge and careful handling—beyond that which might be involved in teaching about other events. Karen Shawn has therefore claimed that teaching about the Holocaust should involve expert certification for teachers (Shawn 1995). And Samuel Totten has argued that young children should not be taught about the Holocaust, that Holocaust simulations should never be enacted, and that teachers ought to rely on survivor testimonies and historical documents over fanciful or fictional accounts (Totten 1999, 2000, 2002).

Totten and William Parsons wrote the United States Holocaust Memorial Museum's (USHMM) *Guidelines for Teaching about the Holocaust*, published in 1993 to coincide with the museum's opening. The guidelines helped enshrine the Holocaust's uniqueness as the official position of USHMM, which exerts consider-able influence on Holocaust education worldwide. As the museum has matured, administrators have begun to revisit the uniqueness perspective, taking other genocides more fully into account.

At Yad Vashem, the national Israeli Holocaust Memorial, the emphasis on the Holocaust's particularity is similar to USHMM's, though its socio-political context and educational purposes are very different. Critics argue that the ideological commitment to uniqueness, which can be found in most Israeli textbooks, encourages prejudice, racism, and a questionable nationalistic siege mentality (Firer 1998). Supporters of the Holocaust's "uniqueness" defend the legitimacy of that outlook in light of Israel's security interests. Debates about these matters reveal the complex relationships between Holocaust education and national politics in Israel (Porat 2004).

Debates about the Holocaust's uniqueness have affected Holocaust memory and education in Germany, too. For some in Germany, denial of the Holocaust's uniqueness seems tantamount to a morally indefensible denial of German responsibility (Brumlik 1995). A variation on that theme holds that the Holocaust should not be treated "like any other topic in the curriculum," a rejection of relativizing trends that might insert study of the Holocaust "after biology and right before the test in math" (Schweitzer 2000: 371).

Disputes about the Holocaust's uniqueness have not been laid to rest, and strong advocates of that uniqueness are still to be found among educational researchers (Totten and Riley 2005), but they no longer exert the influence they enjoyed in the 1990s. Increasingly those who teach about the Holocaust or conduct research on Holocaust education do not stress the event's uniqueness, even if they agree that its particularities require close attention. These educators often maintain that learning about the Holocaust may contribute to students' developing skills, attitudes, and dispositions conducive to humanitarian, democratic, and global citizenship (Carrington and Short 1997; Short 2003). Rejecting the quasi-religious and anti-historical implications of much argumentation in defense of Holocaust uniqueness, these teachers and researchers question the morality of cordoning the Holocaust off from other genocides and crimes against humanity. The hagiography of Holocaust uniqueness, they argue, not only inhibits inquiry but also reinstates the "hierarchy of suffering" that one of USHMM's guidelines urges teachers to avoid. Rather than respecting the Holocaust, isolation from other events trivializes it.

In the United States, this group of educators includes researchers whose empirical studies explore what actually takes place in classes where the Holocaust is taught (Fine 1995; Greenbaum 2001; Schweber and Irwin 2003; Schweber 2004; Schweber and Findling 2007). Such studies upend some normative assumptions about Holocaust education—often those associated with the Holocaust's purported uniqueness—while also reinforcing other concerns. For example, simulations can be educative, even if they are risky pedagogical formats (Schweber 2004). At the same time, Dawidowicz's trenchant critique of published curricula pertains to the lived experiences in numerous classrooms: research shows that antisemitism often has been glossed over as a root cause of the Holocaust, and Jewishness has received simplistic treatment. One study examined students who interpreted the

Holocaust through the lens of fundamentalist Christian theology. Problematically, some thought the Holocaust was a necessary part of God's plan for the redemption of the world, and they believed that Elie Wiesel's religious faith sustained him in Auschwitz and Buchenwald (Spector 2007). Research on middle schools found that teachers' and students' language positioned Jews during the Holocaust as objects rather than subjects, as victims of actions rather than actors in history (Juzwik 2009).

Though wide-ranging, this body of classroom-based studies stands on one side of another important philosophical divide among educational researchers. Described as post-positivistic or constructionist, these studies all share the assumption that "reality," including history and the Holocaust in particular, has some independence from individual or social experience, even if that experience helps to construct what is real. Fascinating work on Holocaust education has also been done from postmodern positions that blur the conventional boundaries between what is considered "real" and what is "performed" as such. These researchers explore trauma theory, what testimony teaches, and how curricula can be "dystopic" in the wake of the Holocaust (i.e., how curricula can promote non-utopian worlds since utopian worlds "conceal othering") (Bernard-Donals and Glejzer 2001; Morris 2001: 197). Generally speaking, for these researchers the development of theory tends to trump the demand for empirical investigation, though exceptions occur.

Using a psychoanalytic lens to view her university-level teaching, Shoshana Felman took her students' difficulty in learning about the Holocaust as an occasion to reimagine pedagogy itself, concluding that "if teaching does not hit upon some sort of crisis, if it does not encounter either the vulnerability or the explosiveness of a . . . critical and unpredictable dimension, it has perhaps not truly taught" (Felman in Caruth 1995: 55). Other interpreters stress that the Holocaust produces "difficult knowledge" that challenges people's senses of themselves, that brings to the fore all implicit power relations, or that exceeds the conventional parameters of educational discourse itself (Britzman 1998; Ellsworth 2005).

Where Is the Holocaust Taught?

The venues for Holocaust education can be delimited in three intersecting ways: schooling level, geographic locale, and structure (formal or informal). In the United States after the late 1970s, if students studied the Holocaust before entering colleges or universities, they usually did so in high school. Over time, however, American middle and elementary schools increasingly have become sites for

Holocaust education, a movement referred to as "curricular creep" (Schweber 2008b: 2075), whose speed and reach are difficult to gauge because the U.S. has no intra-state content consistency, let alone a national Holocaust curriculum.

Studies of Holocaust education aimed at 8-to-12-year-olds in British schools revealed assets and liabilities, thus raising questions about when students should start learning about the Holocaust in formal school settings (Maitles and Cowan 1999; Short and Reed 2004; Cowan and Maitles 2007; Schweber 2008b). In some cases, young children who studied the Holocaust experienced nightmares and incomprehension. Lack of awareness about Jews signaled the need for substantial preparation before undertaking education about the Holocaust. Evidence could also be found that the learning of students in the 10-to-12-year-old range included at least short-term positive effects on their civic engagement, an outcome suggesting that formal schooling about the Holocaust can be beneficial for that age cohort but perhaps not earlier.

No one-size-fits-all template should or even can exist in these matters, however. German and Israeli children, for example, often learn about the Holocaust early on—through friends, older siblings, family members, memorial spaces, and commemoration days. Thus, questions about the ideal age to begin Holocaust education are sometimes rendered moot by circumstances beyond the schoolroom. In any case, more research needs to be directed to what children actually learn about the Holocaust—formally and informally—and how their abilities, genders, ethnic identities, religious and social class positions, capacities for identification, and national and local contexts affect learning outcomes.

The need for research on Holocaust education also looms large for middle-school students, whose ages span the late pre-teen and early teen years, when children's capacities for intellectual understanding, ethical judgment, and emotional awareness are at crucial stages of development. The few systematic studies of Holocaust education for this age group show that much work remains to be done to develop curricula for contexts that range from ultra-orthodox yeshivas and conservative Christian academies to state-sponsored public schools (Mansilla 1998; Schweber 2008a).

Far more numerous are studies that consider Holocaust education within high schools. One of these focused on the American state of Illinois, one of a minority of states that mandates Holocaust education (Ellison and Pisapia 2006). The survey found that teachers in Illinois high schools spend an average of eight hours of instruction on the Holocaust per year, usually in the students' year before graduation. Aimed at encouraging multicultural awareness and tolerance, this instruction tends to use the Holocaust as an occasion to explore stereotyping, but not necessarily antisemitism. A national survey commissioned by USHMM in 2003–2004 found that the Holocaust usually was covered somewhere in the high school curriculum and that "the vast majority of teachers (72 percent) reported that [it] was addressed in one or more of their [English and social studies] courses" (Donnelly 2006: 51). British students usually learn about the Holocaust in Key

Stage 3, in history classes of Year 9, when the students are 14–15 years old. Though required by the national curriculum, the Holocaust's positioning in the history curriculum is less than ideal because that subject's "status" is lower than that of other disciplines (Brown and Davies 1998). The Council for Cultural Cooperation (CDCC), the Council of Europe's educational arm, has published useful booklets on teaching the Holocaust to secondary students, a sign that such instruction is encouraged among its forty-nation membership.

High school instruction about the Holocaust has maintained a strong curricular presence in Germany and Israel, but in many places such education—at whatever grade level—is still in early stages of development. The Holocaust was not taught in Poland until 1996, and in Ukraine, Belarus, Hungary, and Slovakia, Holocaust education "remains in its infancy" (Crawford and Foster 2007: 22). Although Holocaust education existed earlier in some parts of South Africa, the province of KwaZulu-Natal initiated it as recently as 2006 (Schneider 2006).

Though on the rise in some parts of the world, Holocaust education scarcely enjoys favor everywhere. In some state-sponsored schools outside of Paris that contain large numbers of North African immigrants, teachers stopped teaching about the Holocaust because such instruction was taken to imply support for the State of Israel. Georges Bensoussan, the author of a 2004 report on antisemitism in French schools, declared during an interview, "I know of cases in which the teacher mentioned Auschwitz and Treblinka, and students clapped" (2004). Such hostile learners certainly discouraged teachers from continuing. In countries that oppose the existence of the State of Israel, the Holocaust is taught about as though it were fabricated propaganda rather than historical reality. In 2007, a false rumor that the Holocaust was being removed from the United Kingdom's national curriculum prompted multiple organizations to clarify British policy. Meanwhile, Holocaust education can be found in Romania and Ukraine, but continuing antisemitism impedes its progress in both of those countries (Ivanova 2004; Misco 2008). More hopeful research includes comparative analyses of Israeli and German adolescents' views of Nazism, the Holocaust, and each other, finding that the more students in both countries knew about Nazism and the Holocaust, the more they were interested in meeting youth from the other country (Shamai et al. 2004).

Though the Holocaust is regularly taught on college and university campuses, too little is known about the impact of such efforts. A survey of post-secondary, U.S.-based Holocaust courses found a high degree of diversity in the materials and strategies instructors employed. Until quite recently, many of those who teach the subject had little or no formal preparation to do so and therefore "neither their perspective on the subject matter nor their pedagogical style [was] necessarily informed by any coherent philosophy of Holocaust education" (Haynes 1998: 282). Consequently, much writing in this area has focused on university teachers' own ideas and practices, wherein authors make claims about the utility of their teaching. Thus, for example, the claim is made that Holocaust education confronts apathy and the "tension between obedience and critical thinking" (Wink 2006: 84). Or, emphasis falls on the idea that a Holocaust course can highlight relations between the Holocaust and German culture or between the Holocaust and gender issues (Faber 1996; Baumel 2002). Sometimes these discussions explore how Holocaust education can and should be responsive to the particularity of the institutions in which it takes place—e.g., military academies, community colleges, church-based campuses, and state universities (Farnham 1983; Halperin 1986; Friedrichs 1996; Westermann 1996; Berlak 1999; Braiterman 1999). The identity, teaching philosophy, and disciplinary training of the professor also affect the content, objectives, and assessment of Holocaust-related teaching (Hirsch and Kacandes 2004; Tinberg 2005). The profusion of self-studies within post-secondary education, many of them more anecdotal than systematic, calls attention to the need for research devoted specifically to analysis of the expectations, practices, and outcomes of Holocaust education in colleges and universities.

Alongside schooling level, research must consider venue type, whether Holocaust education occurs formally, through classroom-based learning, or informally, through pilgrimage tours, museum visits, or extracurricular activities. In Israel, for example, Holocaust-related youth missions to Poland have flourished, reflecting various ideological biases and producing highly varied, sometimes problematic, experiences for participants (Kugelmass 1993; Feldman in Schreier and Heyl 1997: 117–32; Hazan 2001). One study of these trips reports that they tend to emphasize Zionist over Jewish or universalistic goals, which could be viewed as endorsement of a "'new Israeli religion,' based on the notion that since the Jews were weak during the Holocaust, there is a need to ensure that Israel remains strong" (Lazar et al. 2004: 190). Another study, which surveyed students five years after they had experienced such trips, showed that participants favored increased support for a militarily strong state (Romi and Lev 2007). Other studies indicate that this type of travel can encourage universalistic values, too (Spalding et al. 2007).

Museum visits, which often accompany formal Holocaust education programs, have not been studied sufficiently. While many publications discuss the displays or exhibits of various Holocaust museums, few focus on how specific audiences learn from the presentations and what they learn in particular (Ellsworth 2005 provides an exception). Comparative research remains to be done on the educational effects of visits to actual Holocaust sites and visits to museums that are not authentic sites of Holocaust events.

So-called Holocaust Days or memorial days can be powerful informal educational occasions, but research needs to determine what participants learn from them. When students organize Holocaust remembrance activities on their university campuses, what do they choose to do, why, and with what effects? In the United Kingdom, some research has been done regarding the impact of Holocaust Memorial Day, which has been observed in British schools since 27 January 2001 (Burtonwood 2002; Cowan and Maitles 2002), but this work marks only a beginning.

Summer camps for American Jewish youth often include commemorative events meant to teach about the Holocaust, but thus far scarcely any research has documented or analyzed these efforts. How do Jewish youth camps from different denominational and political positions commemorate the Holocaust, toward what ends, and with what effects? How do commemorative events differ from place to place and country to country? Comparative research could be informative, especially as the importance of educating young people for global citizenship gains momentum.

How: Curriculum and Pedagogy

Textbooks remain the primary information source for most history teachers and their students. Because textbooks are always political documents, the results of compromises among commercial, political, and (occasionally) academic interests, they are also windows into national narratives and ideological aims. A careful study of British and German textbook treatments of the Holocaust found them to contain not only similar content but also "generic educational objectives couched in the all too often cliché-ridden language of democracy, freedom, and human rights" (Crawford and Foster 2007: 26). This study also highlighted many of the dilemmas faced by Holocaust educators and Holocaust-related textbooks: Should Adolf Hitler (1889–1945) be in the fore- or background? Should testimony include the voices of Holocaust perpetrators or only those of victims? How should resistance be depicted? What connections should be made between the Holocaust and present-day human rights violations? On this last point, British textbooks have tended to shy away from applying the Holocaust to contemporary issues while German textbooks have not (Crawford and Foster 2007). Much more research remains to be done in the comparative analysis of Holocaust-related educational texts, including the history of their development (Porat 2004), students' receptions of them, and how, in particular, students' complex identities influence their textual interpretations.

The most commonly assigned literature on the Holocaust, not only in the United States but also worldwide, remains *The Diary of Anne Frank* for younger students and Elie Wiesel's *Night* for older ones. Over-reliance on these works can produce what has been called "victim as curriculum," wherein students' attention focuses exclusively on the diaries, memoirs, and perspectives of Holocaust victims and survivors (Wineburg 1999). The most frequently assigned film in classrooms has been *Schindler's List*, which encourages students to empathize with a rescuer. The popularity of these materials has resulted in a curricular emphasis on victims and rescuers, an orientation that deserves scrutiny because, in extreme form, it can render invisible the perpetrators, collaborators, and on-lookers, which, combined with the typical downplaying of antisemitism and the oversimplification of Jews and Jewishness, leaves significant gaps in Holocaust education efforts.

A "literature of atrocity" for young readers has been growing as "curricular creep" has moved the Holocaust into lower grade levels (Baer 2000). Careful readings of these materials highlight their complexities (Kertzer 2002; Kokkola 2003). For example, Holocaust fiction for young people tends to cast girls (and not boys) as victims. It also tends to include emotional uplift to buffer children's confrontations with historical tragedy. Adrienne Kertzer concludes that "if we persist in thinking that children need hope and happy endings . . . then we will need to consider narrative strategies . . . that give child[ren] a double narrative, one that simultaneously respects our need for hope and happy endings even as it teaches a different lesson about history" (2002: 74–5). As Holocaust education extends into lower grades, another issue that demands study is whether and when students' repeated encounters with the Holocaust—through books, films, and classes—produce "Holocaust fatigue" (Short and Reed 2004: 67).

Packaged curricula are another mainstay of Holocaust education, and they have been variously evaluated. The U.S.-based organization Facing History and Ourselves (FHAO) is the largest supplier of Holocaust-related curricular packages, replete with print material, videos, and internet resources for teachers and students. It has been criticized for drawing loose comparisons, being overly universalistic, and for instrumentalizing the Holocaust (Lipstadt 1995). Other criticisms center on the costs of the FHAO program, which prohibit poorer schools from utilizing it, but teachers tend to respond favorably to the FHAO approach and the support its staff provides. The USC Shoah Foundation Institute for Visual History and Education has made a wide variety of Holocaust-related testimonies accessible for classroom use. And Yad Vashem and USHMM provide many curricular materials and educational services, as do smaller, city-based Holocaust centers. In Texas, for example, Holocaust Museum Houston provides "teaching trunks" that contain Spanish-language materials about the Holocaust. How these kinds of materials affect student learning deserves rigorous research.

Other initiatives besides full-fledged curricular packages aim to support Holocaust education. Among the newer trends are collecting activities in which student groups "accumulate six million of a particular object (such as paper clips, buttons, or shoes) to symbolize the murdered" (Magilow 2007: 23). These projects, though well-intentioned grassroots efforts aimed at engendering empathy, can become fetishistic exercises in accounting. Also new are internet-based education efforts, which remain understudied. These include on-line interactive geographic maps, streamed testimony excerpts, and discussion, social-networking, and social action sites (Manfra and Stoddard 2008). In one study of a web-based instructional site for teachers, the site's impact on teachers' knowledge and attitudes was found to be minimal (Calandra et al. 2002), indicating that more than a superficial encounter with new technologies is required to change teachers' practices significantly (Kern 2001; Lincoln 2003). Particularly troublesome, most Holocaust video games available on-line are racist, antisemitic, and anti-democratic. When interactive video environments are designed to educate toward worthwhile goals, these will merit research as well.

CONCLUSION

Much research on Holocaust education remains to be done, especially on how such education affects students. Ideally, such research ought to embrace comparative, international perspectives rather than insular, local orientations. As for its content, Holocaust education has primarily focused on victims' and rescuers' experiences. Increased attention to perpetrators, collaborators, and on-lookers would be helpful for students to grasp the complexity of decision-making faced by all of the Holocaust's protagonists. In this era of continued genocidal violence, Holocaust education can and should be used to promote greater compassion and global citizenship.

REFERENCES

BAER, E. (2000). "A New Algorithm in Evil: Children's Literature in a Post-Holocaust World." *The Lion and the Unicorn* 24: 378–401.

BAUMEL, J. (2002). "'Can Two Walk Together If They Do Not Agree?' Reflections on Holocaust Studies and Gender Studies." *Women: A Cultural Review* 13/2: 195–206.

BENSOUSSAN, G. (2004). "It Began with Students Denying the Holocaust." *Jerusalem Report*, 13 December 2004.

BERLAK, A. (1999). "Teaching and Testimony: Witnessing and Bearing Witness to Racisms in Culturally Diverse Classrooms." *Curriculum Inquiry* 29/1: 99–127.

BERNARD-DONALS, M. and GLEJZER, R. (2001). *Between Witness and Testimony: The Holocaust and the Limits of Representation*. Albany, NY: State University of New York Press.

BRAITERMAN, Z. (1999). "Teaching Jewish Studies in a Radically Gentile Space: Some Personal Reflections." *Religious Education* 94/4: 396–409.

BRITZMAN, D. (1998). *Lost Subjects, Contested Objects: Toward a Psychoanalytic Inquiry of Learning*. Albany, NY: State University of New York Press.

BROWN, M. and DAVIES, I. (1998). "The Holocaust and Education for Citizenship: The Teaching of History, Religion and Human Rights in England." *Educational Review* 50/1: 75–83.

BRUMLIK, M. (1995). "Erziehung nach Molln oder in Gedenken unterweisen." *Erziehung and Wissenschaft* 4: 6–10.

BURTONWOOD, N. (2002). "Holocaust Memorial Day in Schools—Context, Process and Content: A Review of Research into Holocaust Education." *Educational Research* 44/1: 69–82.

CALANDRA, B., FITZPATRICK, J., and BARRON, A. (2002). "A Holocaust Website: Effects on Preservice Teachers' Factual Knowledge and Attitudes Toward Traditionally Marginalized Groups." *Journal of Technology and Teacher Education* 10/1: 75–93.

CARRINGTON, B. and SHORT, G. (1997). "Holocaust Education, Anti-Racism and Citizenship." *Educational Research* 49/3: 271–82.

CARUTH, C. (ed.) (1995). *Trauma: Explorations in Memory*. Baltimore, MD: Johns Hopkins University Press.

COWAN, P. and MAITLES, H. (2002). "Developing Positive Values: A Case Study of Holocaust Memorial Day in the Primary Schools of One Local Authority in Scotland." *Educational Review* 54/3: 219–29.

————(2007). "Does Addressing Prejudice and Discrimination through Holocaust Education Produce Better Citizens?" *Educational Review* 59/2: 115–30.

CRAWFORD, K. and FOSTER, S. (2007). *War, Nation, Memory: International Perspectives on World War II in School History Textbooks*. Charlotte, NC: Information Age Publishing, Inc.

DAWIDOWICZ, L. (1992). *What Is the Use of Jewish History?: Essays*. Ed. N. Kozodoy. New York: Schocken Books.

DONNELLY, M. (2006). "Educating Students about the Holocaust: A Survey of Teaching Practices." *Social Education* 70/1: 51–54.

ELLISON, J. and PISAPIA, J. (2006). "The State of Holocaust Education in Illinois." *IDEA: A Journal of Social Issues* 11/1 (September 7). <http://www.ideajournal.com/articles.php?id=41>. Accessed 25 August 2009.

ELLSWORTH, E. (2005). *Places of Learning: Media, Architecture, Pedagogy*. New York: RoutledgeFalmer.

FABER, M. (1996). "Teaching a Multidisciplinary Course on the Holocaust and German Culture." *Annals of the American Academy of Political and Social Science* 548: 105–15.

FALLACE, T. (2008). *The Emergence of Holocaust Education in American Schools*. New York: Palgrave Macmillan.

FARNHAM, J. (1983). "Ethical Ambiguity and the Teaching of the Holocaust." *English Journal* 72/4: 63–8.

FINE, M. (1995). *Habits of Mind: Struggling Over Values in America's Classrooms*. San Francisco, CA: Jossey-Bass.

FIRER, R. (1998). "Human Rights in History and Civics Textbooks: The Case of Israel." *Curriculum Inquiry* 28/2: 195–208.

FRIEDLANDER, H. (1979). "Toward a Methodology of Teaching about the Holocaust." *Teacher's College Record* 81/3: 519–42.

FRIEDRICHS, C. (1996). "Teaching the Unteachable: A Canadian Perspective." *Annals of the American Academy of Political and Social Science* 548: 94–104.

GREENBAUM, B. (2001). *Bearing Witness: Teaching about the Holocaust*. Portsmouth, NH: Boynton/Cook.

HALPERIN, I. (1986). "Teaching the Holocaust by Indirection." *Judaism* 35: 441–6.

HAYNES, S. (1998). "Holocaust Education at American Colleges and Universities: A Report on the Current Situation." *Holocaust and Genocide Studies* 12/2: 282–307.

HAZAN, H. (2001). "The Three Faces of the Holocaust: A Comparative Discussion on the Preparation of Students of Different Schools for the Voyages to Poland." *Panim* 11: 66–75.

HIRSCH, M. and KACANDES, I. (eds.) (2004). *Teaching the Representation of the Holocaust.* New York: Modern Languages Association.

IVANOVA, E. (2004). "Ukrainian High School Students' Understanding of the Holocaust." *Holocaust and Genocide Studies* 18/3: 402–20.

JUZWIK, M. (2009). *The Rhetoric of Teaching: Understanding the Dynamics of Holocaust Narratives in an English Classroom.* Cresskill, NJ: Michigan State University.

KERN, H. (2001). "An End to Intolerance: Exploring the Holocaust and Genocide." *English Journal* 91/2: 100–3.

KERTZER, A. (2002). *My Mother's Voice: Children, Literature, and the Holocaust.* Peterborough, Ontario: Broadview Press.

KOKKOLA, L. (2003). *Representing the Holocaust in Children's Literature.* New York: Routledge.

KUGELMASS, J. (1993). "The Rites of the Tribe: The Meaning of Poland for American Jewish Tourists." *YIVO Annual* 10: *Going Home.* Evanston, IL: Northwestern University Press.

LAZAR, A., CHAITLIN, J., GROSS, T., and BAR-ON, D. (2004). "Jewish Israeli Teenagers, National Identity, and the Lessons of the Holocaust." *Holocaust and Genocide Studies* 18/2: 188–204.

LINCOLN, M. (2003). "The Holocaust Project: A Media Specialist's Success Story in Online Resource Use, Staff Collaboration, and Community Outreach." *MultiMedia Schools* 10/4: 32–6.

LIPSTADT, D. (1995). "Not Facing History." *New Republic* 212/26: 26–29.

MAGILOW, D. (2007). "Counting to Six Million: Collecting Projects and Holocaust Memorialization." *Jewish Social Studies* 14/1: 23–40.

MAITLES, H. and COWAN, P. (1999). "Teaching the Holocaust in Primary Schools in Scotland: Modes, Methodology and Content." *Educational Review* 51/3: 263–72.

MANFRA, M. and STODDARD, J. (2008). "Powerful and Authentic Digital Media and Strategies for Teaching about Genocide and the Holocaust." *The Social Studies* 99/6: 260–4.

MANSILLA, V. (1998). "Beyond the Lessons from the Cognitive Revolution." *Canadian Social Studies* 32: 49–51.

MISCO, T. (2008). "'We did also save people': A Study of Holocaust Education in Romania after Decades of Historical Silence." *Theory and Research in Social Education* 36/2: 61–94.

MORRIS, M. (2001). *Curriculum and the Holocaust: Competing Sites of Memory and Representation.* Mahwah, NJ: Lawrence Erlbaum.

PORAT, D. (2004). "From the Scandal to the Holocaust in Israeli Education." *Journal of Contemporary History* 39/4: 619–36.

ROMI, S. and LEV, M. (2007). "Experiential Learning of History through Youth Journeys to Poland: Israeli Jewish Youth and the Holocaust." *Research in Education* 78: 88–102.

SCHATZKER, C. (1982). "The Holocaust in Israeli Education." *International Journal of Political Education* 5/1: 75–82.

SCHNEIDER, M. (2006). "Holocaust Education Now Mandatory in South African Province." <http://www.jewishinstlouis.org/page.aspx?id=136904>, October 11.

SCHREIER, H. and HEYL, M. (eds.) (1997). *Never Again!: The Holocaust's Challenge for Educators.* Hamburg: Krämer.

SCHWEBER, S. (2004). *Making Sense of the Holocaust: Lessons from Classroom Practice.* New York: Teacher's College Press.

——(2008a). "'Here There Is No Why': Holocaust Education at a Lubavitch Girls' Yeshivah." *Jewish Social Studies* 14/2: 156–85.

——(2008b). "'What Happened to Their Pets?': Third Graders Encounter the Holocaust." *Teacher's College Record* 110/10: 2073–115.

——and FINDLING, D. (2007). *Teaching the Holocaust.* Los Angeles, CA: Torah Aura Productions.

——and IRWIN, R. (2003). "'Especially Special': Learning about Jews in a Fundamentalist Christian School." *Teacher's College Record* 105/9: 1693–719.

SCHWEITZER, F. (2000). "'Education After Auschwitz'—Perspectives from Germany." *Religious Education* 95/4: 360–70.

SHAMAI, S., YARDENI, E., and KLAGES, B. (2004). "Multicultural Education: Israeli and German Adolescents' Knowledge and Views Regarding the Holocaust." *Adolescence* 39/156: 765–78.

SHAWN, K. (1995). "Current Issues in Holocaust Education." *Dimensions: A Journal of Holocaust Studies* 9/2: 15–18.

SHERAMY, R. (2003). "'Resistance and War': The Holocaust in American Jewish Education, 1945–1960." *American Jewish History* 91/2: 287–313.

SHORT, G. (2003). "Lessons of the Holocaust: A Response to the Critics." *Educational Review* 55/3: 277–87.

——and REED, C. (2004). *Issues in Holocaust Education.* Hampshire: Ashgate.

SPALDING, E., SAVAGE, T., and GARCIA, J. (2007). "The March of Remembrance and Hope: Teaching and Learning about Diversity and Social Justice through the Holocaust." *Teacher's College Record* 109/6: 1423–56.

SPECTOR, K. (2007). "God on the Gallows: Reading the Holocaust through Narratives of Redemption." *Research in the Teaching of English* 55/1: 7–55.

TINBERG, H. (2005). "Taking (and Teaching) the Shoah Personally." *College English* 68/1: 72–89.

TOTTEN, S. (1999). "Should There Be Holocaust Education for K-4 Students? The Answer Is No." *Social Science and the Young Learner* 121: 36–39.

——(2000). "Diminishing the Complexity and Horror of the Holocaust: Using Simulations in an Attempt to Convey Historical Experiences." *Social Education* 64/3: 170.

——(2002). *Holocaust Education: Issues and Approaches.* Boston, MA: Allyn & Bacon.

——and RILEY, K. (2005). "Authentic Pedagogy and the Holocaust: A Critical Review of State Sponsored Holocaust Curricula." *Theory and Research in Social Education* 33: 120–41.

WESTERMANN, E. (1996). "The Holocaust Course at the United States Air Force Academy." *Annals of the American Academy of Political and Social Science* 548: 116–22.

WINEBURG, S. (1999). "Historical Thinking and Other Unnatural Acts." *Phi Delta Kappan* 80/7: 488–99.

WINK, K. (2006). "A Lesson from the Holocaust: From Bystander to Advocate in the Classroom." *English Journal* 96/1: 84–9.

OTHER SUGGESTED READING

AURON, Y. (2005). *The Pain of Knowledge: Holocaust and Genocide Issues in Education.* Trans. R. Ruzga. New Brunswick, NJ: Transaction Publishers.

DAVIES, I. (ed.) (2000). *Teaching the Holocaust: Educational Dimensions, Principles and Practice.* London: Continuum.

GOLDENBERG, M. and MILLEN, R. (eds.) (2007). *Testimony, Tensions, and* Tikkun: *Teaching the Holocaust in Colleges and Universities.* Seattle, WA: University of Washington Press.

HAYNES, S. (1997). *Holocaust Education in the Church-related College: Restoring Ruptured Traditions.* Westport, CT: Greenwood Press.

SIMON, K. (2001). *Moral Questions in the Classroom: How to Get Kids to Think Deeply about Real Life and Their Schoolwork.* New Haven, CT: Yale University Press.

TOTTEN, S. and FEINBERG, S. (eds.) (2001). *Teaching and Studying about the Holocaust.* Boston, MA: Allyn & Bacon.

WIEVIORKA, A. (2002). *Auschwitz Explained to My Child.* New York: Marlowe & Company.

....

CHAPTER 46

HUMAN RIGHTS LAW

....

DAVID H. JONES

THIS chapter assesses the aftereffects of the Holocaust on human rights law. Such an assessment must begin by noting that the Holocaust played a direct causal role in the emergence of what promised to be a distinctively new era in international human rights law that began with the Charter of the International Military Tribunal. This historic document provided the legal justification for the trial of the major Nazi war criminals at Nuremberg in 1945–46, as well as for the trials of lesser offenders that followed. The moral evil of the Holocaust was not consistently recognized or emphasized in public pronouncements by the Allied Powers during World War II, largely because they feared that focusing on it would undermine the policy of victory first (Hilberg 2003: 1138) and play into the hands of Nazi propaganda that consistently depicted Germany's enemies as fighting for the Jews (Aronson 2004). However, by mid-to-late 1942 the governments of both the United States and Great Britain were fully aware of the ongoing genocide. In December 1942, these powers and their European allies publicly accused Nazi Germany of a "bestial policy of extermination of the Jewish people in Europe" (Taylor 1992: 26). Plans for a postwar trial of major war criminals reached the discussion stage as early as 1943, but final agreement to hold the trials occurred only after the end of the war two years later. Although the main focus of the first trial was on crimes against peace and war crimes, the defendants were also charged with crimes against humanity, including extermination. Moreover, at the end of the proceedings, the Tribunal took judicial notice of the persecution of the Jews, noting that in this respect, the Nazi "record of consistent and systematic inhumanity [was] on the greatest scale" (Ball 1999: 59).

Perhaps the greatest difficulty in assessing the aftereffects of the Holocaust lies in explaining why its initially powerful and positive effects on the drafting of the Nuremberg Charter and the Nuremberg Trials marked the apex of the Holocaust's direct influence on the development of human rights law. Consequently, this chapter has three goals: (1) to describe and explain what can be called the Promise of Nuremberg, namely, the conviction that bringing the leaders of the Nazi regime to trial and punishing them for their crimes signaled a turning point in the long struggle to bring the actions of sovereign states and their leaders under the rule of law and to assure that in the future human rights would be protected and promoted; (2) to show that the Promise of Nuremberg remains unfulfilled, despite such recent positive developments as the permanent International Criminal Court, largely because of the flawed structure of the United Nations Security Council and the lack of law enforcement and crime prevention mechanisms in international human rights law; and (3) to present some of the more promising recent proposals about ways to bring about a higher degree of human rights protection and promotion, including reform of the Security Council and long-term strategies to encourage and support the spread of democracy.

THE PROMISE OF NUREMBERG

The modern system of international law stems from the Peace of Westphalia in 1648, a treaty designed to outlaw aggressive war by granting all sovereign powers equal rights to non-interference in their domestic affairs. A "sovereign power" is one that has legal authority over a domain, defined as the unrestricted power to make law and enforce it by virtue of possessing a monopoly of coercive capacity and the general acceptance of those governed (Nagel 2005).

From a post-Nuremberg perspective, three features of this traditional system of international law are noteworthy. First, only states were subjects of and possessed legal rights under international law; individual human beings did not have international legal rights as such. But some limits on the manner in which states could treat their nationals came to be recognized. For example, the doctrine of humanitarian intervention allowed the use of force to stop the maltreatment of the populace of another state when the abuse was so extensive and brutal as to shock human conscience (Buergenthal et al. 2002: 2–3). However, such doctrines did not contemplate criminal trials of the heads of state or their agents who inflicted such maltreatment. Second, under the doctrine of "sovereign immunity," a head of state could not be held legally responsible for official actions taken in the interest of his or her commonwealth. The head of state enjoyed a kind of immunity analogous to that of the state itself (May 2005: 152). Third, soldiers in the army of a sovereign state generally were considered legally obligated to obey "lawful" superior orders and immune from prosecution for actions taken in compliance with such orders (Christopher 1999: 132–3). Had these features of traditional international law been treated as settled law in 1945, they would have precluded the Charter of the International Military Tribunal under which the Nazi leaders were tried and convicted and the trials of subordinate offenders that followed. However, outrage and revulsion at Nazi Germany's atrocities overcame the Allies' initial ambivalence about conducting postwar trials (Taylor 1992: 56–77).

A more dramatic repudiation of the traditional system with respect to human rights law than the Charter of the International Military Tribunal is difficult to imagine. In this chapter, "human rights law" refers only to security rights that protect people from such crimes as murder, massacre, torture, and rape (Nickel 2007: 93), i.e., crimes that cause serious harm, are done intentionally and knowingly, and for which punishment is imposed (Buergenthal et al. 2002: 71–2; Schabas 2004: 108). The Charter gave the Tribunal the power to try and punish persons acting in the interests of the European Axis countries who committed crimes falling into one or more of three categories: *crimes against peace*, primarily planning and waging wars of aggression; *war crimes*, i.e., violations of the laws or customs of war, including murder or ill-treatment of civilians, prisoners of war, and hostages; and *crimes against humanity*, including murder, extermination, enslavement, and deportation of civilians. The Charter explicitly stated that "there shall be individual responsibility" for all such crimes and that legal defenses based on sovereign immunity and superior orders would not be accepted as sufficient to avoid guilt (Ball 1999: 52–3).

The conduct of the Nuremberg trial of the major war criminals and the series of subsequent trials of "lesser offenders" involved significant concessions to the practical constraints of time, funding, and available legal resources. The most troublesome consequence was a highly selective prosecution. For example, only twenty-one major offenders were put on trial, with Martin Bormann (1900–1945?) tried *in absentia*, while an original list of some 5,000 "lesser" offenders was whittled down to fewer than 200 defendants (Hilberg 2003: 1152–6). Many critics at the time and since also have contended that the Nuremberg trials were politically motivated exercises of *ex post facto* law and thus amounted to "victor's justice" (Minow 1998: 25–51). Nevertheless, the promise of Nuremberg was clear: henceforth, war criminals and violators of international law could not assume that they would be immune to criminal responsibility. The momentum toward a genuine system of international human rights law increased in the years immediately after Nuremberg, when an impressive set of declarations and treaties was adopted by the United Nations. Unfortunately, none of these documents provided for meaningful enforcement or crime prevention. (The account that follows does not include regional systems of human rights law developed by the Council of Europe, the Organization of American States, and the Organization of African Unity; see Buergenthal et al. 2002: 34–125).

The United Nations Charter, also adopted in 1945, states that one of the UN's purposes is to achieve international cooperation in "promoting and encouraging respect for human rights and fundamental freedoms for all without distinction as to race, sex, language, or religion." Although the Charter declares that member states have an obligation to promote these human rights and fundamental freedoms (Buergenthal et al. 2002: 29–30), the document does not provide an enforcement system. Because each of the major powers pursued policies that could be challenged as infractions of human rights, none had an interest in establishing an effectively protective system (Buergenthal et al. 2002: 28). In December 1946, when the Nuremberg Principles (including the categories of crime and the doctrine of individual responsibility) were codified and made part of international law by the UN General Assembly (Ball 1999: 86–7), once more no steps toward enforcement were taken.

What has come to be known as the International Bill of Human Rights consists of two parts. The first is the Universal Declaration of Human Rights, which some writers characterize as "a hortatory declaration," that was passed by the UN General Assembly in December 1948; it is not a treaty and has no force of law. The second consists of the codification over the next eighteen years of the rights covered by the Universal Declaration in two International Covenants on Human Rights and in some Optional Protocols. One of these documents, the Convention on Civil and Political Rights, deals with the most serious harms to human life, security, and well-being. The Covenants and Protocols are treaties that entered into force in 1976 (Buergenthal et al. 2002: 34–5). Although they contain detailed provisions for "enforcing" the human rights codified, these consist largely of self-reporting to a UN oversight committee regarding compliance (for example, concerning enactment of domestic legislation needed to put the human rights into effect). The committee can, in turn, direct "serious compliance problems" to the UN General Assembly in its annual report (Buergenthal et al. 2002: 49–51). In practice, this UN reporting system supplies nothing in the way of effective international law enforcement or crime prevention.

The UN Convention for the Prevention and Punishment of the Crime of Genocide was adopted by the UN General Assembly in December 1948 and entered into force in January 1951. The Convention not only defines the crime of genocide as acts that are intended "to destroy in whole or in part, a national, ethnical, racial, or religious group" but also makes conspiracy, incitement, and complicity to commit genocide punishable as well, whether these acts are committed in peace or war. Moreover, the Convention provides that "persons committing genocide . . . shall be punished, whether they are constitutionally responsible rulers, public officials or private individuals." Interestingly, the Convention recognizes the possibility that persons charged with genocide might be tried by an international criminal court, but it does not establish such a tribunal. Moreover, despite the name of the Convention, it provides no mechanism for the prevention of genocide; it merely asserts that "the Contracting Parties confirm that genocide...is a crime...which they undertake to prevent and to punish." The sole means of enforcement available from 1951 until 1993 was the possibility (never realized) of punishment in a competent national court (Buergenthal et al. 2002: 71–4).

WHY THE PROMISE OF NUREMBERG REMAINS UNFULFILLED

Not until 1993 did the UN create its first court, an *ad hoc* International Criminal Tribunal for the Former Yugoslavia, which was established in response to ethnic cleansing and genocide in that European region. Prior to that date, the member nations, especially the five permanent members of the Security Council, lacked the political will to create institutional mechanisms to head off or punish human rights violations. Instead, international human rights "law" up to 1993 consisted entirely of declarations of rights, codifications of crimes, and largely toothless self-reporting procedures. Although "the system has helped to create an international climate in which most countries are willing to discuss and address human rights issues" (Nickel 2007: 20), actual protection is another matter.

The world has paid a very high price for this lack of effective human rights law enforcement and crime prevention. Since Nuremberg more than 15 million people, largely defenseless civilians, have been killed by state-sponsored genocidal projects and mass killings. The long and familiar list of these atrocities includes Indonesia (1965) under Sukarno (1901–1970), Uganda (1971–1979) under Idi Amin (*c.* 1925–2003), Cambodia (1975–1979) under Pol Pot (1928–1998), and Rwanda (1994) under the Hutus (Harff in Fein 1992). Perpetrators of these crimes killed with impunity. On paper, states that are signatories to the Convention on the Prevention and Punishment of Genocide are "obligated" to take action to fulfill the terms of the Convention, but the salient feature of international law in this period was the phenomenon of bystander states, which included the permanent members of the Security Council that are supposed to oversee human rights security (Kuper 1985). The Nuremberg trials began to look more and more like an historical aberration that was not likely to be repeated; after all, in 1945 the victorious Allies, unchallenged occupiers of an utterly devastated Germany, were in an almost unique position to put human rights criminals on trial and punish them. Dwelling on the precedents set by the Nuremberg trials, however, may not be the most fruitful way to think about ways to achieve human rights law enforcement.

Analysis of the structure of the Security Council and the way in which it operates reveals a major additional flaw that hampers enforcement of human rights law: no executive authority can take timely and effective action against imminent or ongoing criminal activity by a state. To begin with, only the Security Council has the power to authorize the use of military force against a sovereign nation. The General Assembly's actions in this area are strictly advisory, while the office of the Secretary General is confined to executing the decisions of the Security Council. Moreover, the Security Council cannot approve a military intervention without the unanimous agreement of the five permanent members (Great Britain, France, the Soviet Union [now Russia], China, and the United States). The threat of a veto means that obtaining Security Council approval for a specific armed intervention is often difficult, if not impossible.

Even when the Security Council agrees to authorize military intervention, nothing guarantees that the intervention will take place in a timely and effective manner. Since the UN has no standing military forces of its own, these must be volunteered by member nations, most of which are reluctant to risk their troops to stop aggression or genocide unless doing so is in their national interest. Usually an *ad hoc* coalition of states must take shape through time-consuming negotiations. Finally, military personnel, weapons, and logistical support must reach the scene of the intervention, a process that can take weeks, or even months, as in Rwanda in 1994 (Jones in Roth 2005: 268–9).

THE PERMANENT INTERNATIONAL CRIMINAL COURT (ICC)

Not only does the international system of human rights law lack an effective executive authority, but from 1945 until 1993 a judicial authority or responsible criminal court also was absent. *Ad hoc* International Criminal Tribunals for the former Yugoslavia (ICTY) and for Rwanda (ICTR) were created in 1993 and 1994, respectively, but the most significant improvement in the system's judicial capabilities was the establishment of the permanent International Criminal Court (ICC) by the Rome Statute in 1998, which went into force in 2002. A permanent institution, the ICC is intended to deal with "not only 'the most serious crimes,' but also the most serious criminals, generally leaders, organizers and instigators" (Schabas 2004: 29). Accordingly, the ICC has jurisdiction over genocide, crimes against humanity, war crimes, and aggression committed by nationals of state parties or on their territories. However, the Court can be prevented from exercising jurisdiction when so directed by the Security Council and is prohibited from prosecuting when a case is already being dealt with appropriately by a national legal system (Schabas 2004: 72–85). Because the ICC has the codification of international crimes in the UN Convention on Civil and Political Rights at its disposal, together with its own elaborate set of trial procedures to protect defendants, it has the potential to play a significant role in human rights law enforcement and deterrence of human rights abuses.

However, a number of factors throw doubt on the ICC's ability to realize its potential. Because international law is treaty-based, it binds only the states that are signatories. As of 1 June 2008, 108 members of the UN had accepted the Rome Statute, so that the ICC began to become fully operational, but three permanent members of the Security Council (China, Russia, and the United States) are not yet parties to the ICC treaty. Indeed, the United States has vigorously opposed the ICC, concluded a number of bilateral treaties that grant immunity from ICC prosecution to United States nationals, and threatened to veto UN peace-keeping missions unless the participants in them also have immunity from ICC prosecution (Schabas 2004: 21–3, 83–5). Over eighty more UN members are not parties to the ICC, including Cuba, North Korea, Egypt, India, Iran, Israel, Pakistan, Saudi Arabia, and Turkey. Thus, hundreds of millions of human beings live in countries where the ICC has no jurisdiction over human rights crimes inflicted by the government on its own people.

If the foregoing analysis is sound, the ICC is unlikely to have a noticeable deterrent effect on potential perpetrators any time soon. A credible threat of punishment can only be created by a proven track record of prosecutions and penalties. Moreover, to make a significant contribution to human rights law enforcement, the ICC must target major perpetrators, such as heads of state, since political leaders are the people who have the authority to initiate mass killing and genocide, which require bureaucratic planning and implementation, personnel, and other resources (Smith 1999).

Some Promising Developments

Grounds for guarded optimism arise from some recent examples of heads of state and other high-level officials who have been tried and convicted for human rights crimes in UN *ad hoc* tribunals as well as in domestic courts. Jean Kambanda (b. 1955), the former prime minister of Rwanda, became the first head of state to be convicted of genocide when he was found guilty by the ICTR in 1998 and sentenced to life imprisonment. The ICTR also found a local Rwandan mayor, Jean-Paul Akayesu (b. 1953), guilty of directing local killings of Tutsis and sentenced him to life imprisonment (Ball 1999: 176–81). Slobodan Milosevic (1941–2006), the former President of Serbia, was put on trial in 2002 by the ICTY for war crimes in Kosovo, Croatia, and Bosnia but died before the proceedings concluded. On 2 August 2001, the ICTY found the former Bosnian Serb general Radislav Krstic (b. 1948) guilty of genocide for his part in the massacre of Bosnia Muslims at Srebrenica in July 1995. He was the first person convicted of genocide by an international tribunal in Europe. On appeal in April 2004, his sentence was reduced from 46 to 35 years on the ground that he had "aided and abetted genocide" but not been a full-fledged perpetrator of that crime. Charles Taylor (b. 1948), the former President of Liberia, was charged with war crimes by the Special Court for Sierra Leone in 2007.

The ICC has also begun to take action against certain political leaders. In 2005, the UN Security Council conferred jurisdiction over Darfur in Sudan on the ICC, and in March 2009 the Court issued its first indictment of a sitting head of state, charging President of Sudan Omar al-Bashir (b. 1944) with crimes against humanity (including extermination) and war crimes. In May 2009, the ICC also indicted a Sudanese rebel leader, Bahr Idriss Abu Garda, on charges of murder, pillaging, and attacking African Union peacekeepers. Although these prosecutions are encouraging, whether they presage a new era of more aggressive law enforcement of human rights laws under the ICC is difficult to judge at present.

The case of General Augusto Pinochet (1915–2006), the former President of Chile, did not involve a trial by a UN tribunal, yet it managed to set important precedents in international law. Since 1978, Pinochet had managed to evade those who sought to prosecute him for human rights violations in Chilean courts, but while he was in England for medical treatment in 1998, he was arrested on a Spanish warrant and held for possible extradition to Spain for trial on such charges. Although Pinochet was eventually judged too ill to undergo extradition and allowed to leave England and return to Chile, his arrest in the United Kingdom, which was upheld by the House of Lords, challenged the tradition of immunity to criminal liability for former heads of state (May 2005: 148–50). Even so, little evidence presently exists that UN *ad hoc* tribunals deter potential perpetrators; the same can be said with even more confidence with regard to the ICC, since, at the time of this writing, it had yet to conduct its first trial. Thus, the post-Holocaust future of human rights law enforcement and deterrence remains very much in doubt.

Despite the gloomy outlook for effective deterrence, the ICC can promote human rights by dispensing *retributive justice* (Feinberg and Gross 1995: 613–52), which is also an essential purpose of criminal law. Retributive justice has at least four interrelated purposes and rationales: (1) *Vindicating the rule of law*, since a system of criminal law must demonstrate that it has the power and the will to make its laws "binding" in the elementary sense that crimes are in fact punished; (2) *Providing defendants found guilty with their "just desserts"* in the form of a punishment proportional to their blameworthiness as established by a fair trial based on objective evidence, impartially assessed; (3) *Recognizing and assuaging the justified feelings of victims, their families, and the community as a whole*, all of which are affronted and insulted whenever perpetrators are allowed to live their lives in freedom; and (4) *Fulfilling the "expressive function" of punishment* by providing emphatic communal disapproval of criminal behavior (Feinberg 1970: 95–118).

The benefits of retributive justice are real in that they make the world less awful than it would be without them. But they will not by themselves ensure that human rights are protected. Since the goals of deterrence and prevention of human rights abuses by means of criminal justice remain remote, greater attention should focus on reforms of the UN Security Council and political and economic strategies that can make the world safer for human rights.

NEEDED CHANGES

Among the urgently needed institutional reforms are changes in the procedures of the UN Security Council that would greatly reduce the problem of bystander states, a problem largely caused by the lack of an executive authority capable of taking timely and effective action to meet human rights emergencies. Disasters like the 1994 genocide in Rwanda, which claimed 800,000 lives, illustrate the problem. Even with advance warnings that the governing Hutus were planning genocide against the Tutsis, the Security Council failed to act decisively until too late. The delay was caused partly by opposing views among the permanent members of the Council, but even after these differences had been worked out, the logistical problems of getting the needed troops and equipment to Rwanda in time proved too great (Power 2002: 329–89).

A number of proposals have been advanced in order to avoid a repetition of such failure (Mendlovitz and Fousek in Riemer 2000: 105–22). First, the Security Council could delegate to the Secretary General's Office limited executive authority to authorize military intervention in human rights emergencies like the genocide in Rwanda. The criteria for authorizing such interventions would be formulated in a standing procedure drawn up by the Security Council, while the mandate for each particular intervention would be drafted by the Secretary General. Permanent members of the Security Council would retain the veto but could not exercise it until a specified period of time had elapsed, e.g., ninety days. Second, the Secretary General could be supported by a Crime Watch Advisory Board, which would develop an early warning system to identify signs of imminent human rights violations and monitor conflict situations in order to be able to make timely recommendations to the Secretary General. Third, a permanent UN Rapid Response Force (RRF) could be created and kept at a sufficient state of readiness to intervene quickly in human rights emergencies. The RRF would have to be large enough to be militarily effective but small enough to be quickly mobilized and transported, i.e., probably it would contain 5,000–15,000 troops. The European Union already has its own operational Rapid Reaction Force for peace-keeping and humanitarian assistance, as in Bosnia in 1994 (Trybus and White: 2007). The UN's RRF would consist of volunteer international civil servants individually recruited and paid by the UN, much like its weapons inspectors. Ideally they would come from a wide range of UN member states and receive training not only in combat skills but also in policing and human rights enforcement.

History suggests that, everything else being equal, human rights are much more likely to be protected and promoted by democratic liberal states (hereafter "democracies") than by non-democracies. A study of "democide" (intentional government killing of unarmed persons) in the years 1900–87 concludes that democracies killed just one percent of the nearly 170 million victims worldwide. The author correctly insists that the explanation lies not just in the fact that democracies have liberal political institutions designed to limit the power of the state, but also in the values and attitudes fostered by democratic culture, such as tolerance and pluralism (Rummel 1994: 14–20, 22–3). Moreover, democracies rarely go to war with each other (Lipson 2003: 1). They do clash with non-democracies, and such conflicts account for most of the rare cases in which democracies engage in democide. In fact, genocide and democide, as in the case of the Holocaust, generally occur under the cover of war. If the peace that prevails among democracies could be expanded to include more and more of the world's states, a gradual decline in the number of wars and democides would be probable. If this reasoning is sound, then democracies should engage in a long-term effort to do everything in their power (short of aggressive war and other violations of international law reminiscent of imperialism) to foster the spread of liberal political institutions and democratic culture. An urgent need exists for empirical research about the most effective ways to pursue this goal.

Economically underdeveloped countries experience high rates of poverty, which undermine the protection or promotion of human rights. Systematic discrimination against women is widespread in non-democratic states, but especially prevalent in poor countries where women often receive little or no education and are subjected to sexual abuse and cruel practices such as genital mutilation (Neft 1997; Kristoff 2007). These examples underscore the ineffectiveness of current international human rights law, especially the Convention on the Elimination of All Forms of Discrimination Against Women, which has been in force since 1981 (Buergenthal et al. 2002: 82–7). The continued subjection of women is doubly tragic since evidence indicates that women in poor countries manage family spending better than the men do: "women invest in food, children, and small businesses—and men squander funds on cigarettes, alcohol, video halls, and prostitution" (Kristoff 2007: 35). Economists have identified a number of effective ways to reduce poverty, such as micro-financing, but the main propellants of dramatic reductions in world poverty may be globalization and integration into the world economy (Banerjee et al. 2006: ch. 1). Given the central role of poverty in the denial of human rights, wealthy democracies and non-governmental organizations should be doing much more than at present to accelerate economic development in poor countries (Sachs 2005).

Conclusion

The goal of this chapter has been to assess the impact of the Holocaust on the development of an international criminal justice system capable of protecting individual human rights. For such a criminal justice system to function properly, it must possess three aspects: a competent *legislative* authority to make human rights law, an effective *executive* authority to enforce the law and prevent its violation, and a *judicial* authority to punish law-breakers in the names of deterrence and retribution.

What effect, if any, did the Holocaust have on the development of these three authorities required for a functioning system of human rights law? With regard to legislative authority, the most important direct result was a radically new and positive direction in the development of human rights law that has been called the Promise of Nuremberg. After Nuremberg, the focus of international criminal law shifted away from codifying the rights of sovereign states and toward acknowledging and protecting individual human rights. Starting with the hortatory Universal Declaration of Human Rights, the United Nations went on to ratify a series of legal treaties that created and defined the crime of genocide, war crimes, and crimes against humanity and to establish an obligation on the part of member states to "punish and prevent" these crimes.

Concerning executive authority, the Allies' revulsion in 1945 at the cruelty and inhumanity of the Holocaust was not strong enough to override their determination to maintain the power they had achieved with the victory over the Axis. Consequently, UN executive authority resides exclusively in the Security Council, where control is in the hands of the five permanent members, each of which can veto the use of force against any member state. Moreover, without armed forces of its own, the UN must rely on the willingness of member states to volunteer troops to carry out Security Council resolutions that involve intervention, peace-keeping, and arrest of human rights criminals. These facts go a long way to explain the shameful history of UN inaction in the face of genocide and other human rights violations, and the recurring phenomenon of bystander states that make a mockery of the post-Holocaust slogan, "Never again!"

Finally, as to judicial authority, the creation of international criminal courts (especially the ICC) has been an essential and welcome first step. However, much more will be required to create a truly effective judicial authority in the human rights legal system. First, the limited jurisdiction of the ICC would have to be expanded to include all members of the UN, and the ICC will have to build a track record of consistently and successfully punishing political and military leaders who commit genocide and other atrocities. But without the correction of fundamental flaws in the executive authority of the Security Council, even a greatly improved UN judiciary will not be enough to make the UN human rights legal system an effective protector of human rights worldwide.

References

ARONSON, S. (2004). *Hitler, the Allies, and the Jews.* New York: Cambridge University Press.

BALL, H. (1999). *Prosecuting War Crimes and Genocide: The Twentieth Century Experience.* Lawrence, KS: University Press of Kansas.

BANERJEE, A., BENABOU, R., and MOOKHERJEE, D. (eds.) (2006). *Understanding Poverty.* New York: Oxford University Press.

BUERGENTHAL, T., SHELTON, D., and STEWART D. (2002). *International Human Rights in a Nutshell.* 3rd edn. St. Paul, MN: West Group.

CHRISTOPHER, P. (1999). *The Ethics of War and Peace: An Introduction to Legal and Moral Issues.* 2nd edn. Upper Saddle River, NJ: Prentice Hall.

FEIN, H. (ed.) (1992). *Genocide Watch.* New Haven, CT: Yale University Press.

FEINBERG, J. (1970). *Doing and Deserving.* Princeton, NJ: Princeton University Press.

——and GROSS, H. (eds.) (1995). *Philosophy of Law.* 5th edn. Belmont, CA: Wadsworth.

HILBERG, R. (2003). *The Destruction of the European Jews.* 3 vols. 3rd edn. New Haven, CT: Yale University Press.

KRISTOFF, N. (2007). "Wretched of the Earth." *New York Review of Books,* 31 May: 34–6.

KUPER, L. (1985). *The Prevention of Genocide.* New Haven, CT: Yale University Press.

LIPSON, C. (2003). *Reliable Partners: How Democracies Have Made a Separate Peace.* Princeton, NJ: Princeton University Press.

MAY, L. (2005). *Crimes Against Humanity: A Normative Account.* Cambridge: Cambridge University Press.

MINOW, M. (1998). *Between Vengeance and Forgiveness: Facing History after Genocide and Mass Violence.* Boston, MA: Beacon Press.

NAGEL, T. (2005). "The Need for Nations." *New Republic,* 27 July.

NEFT, N. (1997). *Where Women Stand: An International Report on the Status of Women in 140 Countries 1997–1998.* New York: Random House.

NICKEL, J. (2007). *Making Sense of Human Rights.* 2nd edn. Oxford: Blackwell.

Power, S. (2002). *"A Problem from Hell": America and the Age of Genocide.* New York: Basic Books.

Riemer, N. (ed.) (2000). *Protection Against Genocide: Mission Impossible?* Westport, CT: Praeger.

Roth, J. (ed.) (2005). *Genocide and Human Rights: A Philosophical Guide.* New York: Palgrave Macmillan.

Rummel, R. (1994). *Death by Government.* New Brunswick, NJ: Transaction.

Sachs, J. (2005). *The End of Poverty: Economic Possibilities for Our Time.* New York: Penguin Press.

Schabas, W. (2004). *An Introduction to the International Criminal Court.* 2nd edn. Cambridge: Cambridge University Press.

Smith, R. (ed.) (1999). *Genocide: Essays Toward Understanding, Early-Warning, and Prevention.* Williamsburg, VA: Association of Genocide Scholars.

Taylor, T. (1992). *The Anatomy of the Nuremberg Trials: A Personal Memoir.* New York: Knopf.

Trybus, M. and White, N. (2007). *European Security Law.* New York: Oxford University Press.

Other Suggested Reading

Bloxham, D. (2003). *Genocide on Trial: War Crimes and the Formation of Holocaust History and Memory.* New York: Oxford University Press.

Evans, G. (2008). *The Responsibility to Protect: Ending Mass Atrocity Crimes Once and For All.* Washington, DC: Brookings Institution Press.

Geras, N. (1999). *The Contract of Mutual Indifference: Political Philosophy after the Holocaust.* London: Verso.

Heberer, P. and Matthäus, J. (eds.) (2008). *Atrocities on Trial: Historical Perspectives on the Politics of Prosecuting War Crimes.* Lincoln, NE: University of Nebraska Press.

Heidenrich, J. (2001). *How to Prevent Genocide: A Guide for Policymakers, Scholars, and the Concerned Citizen.* Westport, CT: Praeger.

Ronayne, P. (2001). *Never Again?: The United States and the Prevention and Punishment of Genocide since the Holocaust.* Westport, CT: Praeger.

CHAPTER 47

....

ETHICS

....

JOHN K. ROTH

ABSENT the overriding of moral sensibilities, if not the collapse or collaboration of ethical traditions, the Holocaust could not have happened. Although the Shoah did not pronounce the death of ethics, it showed that ethics is vulnerable, subject to misuse and perversion, and that no simple reaffirmation of pre-Holocaust ethics, as if nothing disastrous had happened, will do. To focus those realities and some of the most important issues they contain, a few words about ethics itself are necessary.

THE MEANINGS OF ETHICS
....

Abilities to think, make judgments, and remember are among the defining character-istics of human life. Persons are also identified by relationships, including families and societies. History puts us in political and religious traditions; we are citizens of countries, too. Enriched and complicated by environmental factors and survival needs as well as by memories of past actions and their consequences, human beings have to evaluate and choose. People deal constantly with factual matters, but we also make value judgments, issue prescriptive statements, formulate normative appraisals, and aim to take decisions and act accordingly. In short, we try to figure out what we ought to do, for few of us are always and entirely content with the way events happen to turn out. Thus, human existence is inseparable from distinctions between what is right and wrong, just and unjust, good and evil.

The defining words of ethics are *should* and *ought, right* and *wrong, justice* and *injustice, good* and *evil.* Whenever such concepts are used, ethics appears in at least three ways. Many factors enter into the evaluations that people make. They include cultural backgrounds, political and economic circumstances, religious training or the lack of it, the influences of parents, teachers, and friends. So ethics can refer, first, to the value judgments that people make and to the beliefs that people hold—individually and collectively—about what should or should not be done, what is right and just or wrong and unjust, what is good or evil. From this descriptive perspective, it can be argued that every person, community, and nation is ethical. All of them have normative beliefs, make evaluative judgments, try to act accordingly, and face accountability for failure.

Ethics, however, includes much more than a primarily descriptive use of that term suggests. A second dimension of ethics involves the study of value judgments and the ways in which they influence—and are influenced by—institutions. Such study has historical dimensions; it may concentrate, for instance, on how a society's values have changed or developed over time. In one way or another, such work has gone on for centuries. Its roots are in the earliest human awareness that groups and persons are not identical, that they think and act differently.

Important though they are, neither description nor historical study of human belief and action forms the core of ethics. Its third and most fundamental dimension emphasizes critical inquiry about the values people hold and sustained effort to strengthen action that reflects and supports such inquiry. People make value judgments when they say, for example, that "abortion is wrong" or that "the death penalty is right." But does the variety of values, and especially the arguments, policies, and actions that conflicting evaluations can produce mean that value judgments are culturally relative and even personally subjective? Or are at least some value judgments—for example, "the Holocaust was wrong" or "genocide should never happen"—objectively grounded and true in every time and place?

For centuries debate has swirled around normative questions of that kind. Agreement about how to answer them is not universal, but ethics would not be *ethics* if it failed to emphasize the importance of critical inquiry about the values that people hold. The need for such inquiry is rooted in awareness that people's value judgments can be mistaken—nothing is truly good or right simply because someone desires or values it—and in the fact that another feature of human life remains deeply entrenched, namely, that human beings often make faulty judgments, inflict unwarranted suffering, lay waste to things that are good, treat each other brutally, rob, rape, and murder. Thus, expanding its scope beyond intellect and inquiry, ethics attempts to check and correct humanity's destructive tendencies by showing how human life can be more just and promising and by urging and encouraging us to make life more caring and humane.

Ethics tries to bring the human will into conformity with sound ethical judgment. Unfortunately, this juncture between thought and action, theory and practice, is also where the failure(s) of ethics become most obvious and fraught. The Holocaust did immense harm to ethics by highlighting its shortcomings. In those ruins, the crucial, lingering questions include: what should ethics be and what can it do after the Holocaust?

GOOD DAYS AND BAD

After World War II and the Holocaust, good days for ethics occurred on 9 and 10 December 1948 when the General Assembly of the United Nations adopted the Convention on the Prevention and Punishment of the Crime of Genocide and the Universal Declaration of Human Rights. The Convention criminalized specific "acts committed with intent to destroy, in whole or in part, a national, ethnical, racial or religious group, as such," which the contracting parties would "undertake to prevent and punish." Proclaiming that "recognition of the inherent dignity and of the equal and inalienable rights of all members of the human family is the foundation of freedom, justice and peace in the world," the Declaration aimed to become a standard for all peoples and nations, securing "universal and effective" respect for "the right to life, liberty and security of person" and rejection of slavery, torture, and other forms of "cruel, inhuman or degrading treatment or punishment." Two good days for ethics in December 1948 called for more of the same, but as far as the Holocaust is concerned, such days—during and after that disaster—have been relatively few and far between.

Notwithstanding the UN Declaration, the Holocaust had ruptured the notion of universal human rights as the Third Reich's genocidal policies trapped Jews and other victim groups in one "choiceless choice" and lethal dilemma after another (Rosenbaum 1976; Langer 1980, 1991; Browning 2010). Jean Améry (1912–1978), a Jewish philosopher who endured Nazi torture and survived Auschwitz before eventually taking his own life, experienced and reflected on that breach. The gravest loss produced by the Holocaust, he suggested, was that it destroyed "trust in the world, . . . the certainty that by reason of written or unwritten social contracts the other person will spare me—more precisely stated, that he will respect my physical, and with it also my metaphysical being" (1980: 28). Much as he yearned for the right to live, which he equated with dignity itself, Améry found that "it is certainly true that dignity can be bestowed only by society, whether it be the dignity of some office, a professional or, very generally speaking, civil dignity; and the merely individual, subjective claim (I am a human being and as such I have my dignity, no matter what you may do or say!) is an empty academic game, or madness" (1980: 89). Each morning Améry saw the tattooed Auschwitz number on his arm, making it impossible to "feel at home in the world" and convincing him that "declarations of human rights, democratic constitutions, the free world and the free press, nothing can lull me into the slumber of security from which I awoke in 1935" (1980: 40, 95). Améry's philosophy is not necessarily a postmortem for human rights, but its assessment tests every affirmation of them.

As the "Final Solution" unfolded, the most fundamental moral imperative of all—the sixth of the biblical Ten Commandments, "Thou shalt not murder"—was overridden and eclipsed by a "Nazi ethic" whose antisemitic and racist sense of progress depicted the destruction of Jewish life and other "inferior" groups as morally right and good (Haas 1988; Koonz 2003; Roth in Van Harn 2007: 113–26; Waller 2007; Weikart 2009). While shooting squadrons and gas chambers took their toll, ethical traditions that urged people to aid those in need and to resist injustice proved insufficient to interrupt the power of peer pressure among the German rank and file, disrupt the business interests of German corporations that utilized slave labor, or challenge the ways of on-lookers and opportunists (Browning 1992; Jones 1999; Barnett 2000; Gushee 2003; Hayes 2004).

After the Holocaust, postwar trials convicted and punished some of the major perpetrators, but justice was scarcely served by the proceedings and the commuted sentences that freed the guilty (Marrus 1997; Wittmann 2005; Earl 2009). Holocaust museums, memorials, and education programs—worthy initiatives all—proliferated, but the "lessons of the Holocaust" could not prevent a resurgence of antisemitism and Holocaust denial let alone forestall the mass atrocities, including ethnic cleansing and genocide in Cambodia, the Balkans, Rwanda, and Darfur, that have raised questions about how to situate the Holocaust in comparative genocide studies and mocked the slogan "Never again!" (Valentino 2004; Lipstadt 2005; Kiernan 2007; Berenbaum 2008; Bloxham 2009; Totten and Parsons 2009). As the twentieth century closed, belated efforts to restitute property looted and stolen during the Holocaust were accompanied by initiatives to expand reparations for the survivors of Nazi slave labor and concentration camps (Bayzler 2003; Eizenstat 2003; Henry 2007; Marrus 2009). Legal and political wrangling and arguments about property rights, payment distributions, and lawyers' fees left this post-Holocaust chapter bereft of satisfying closure.

Ethics requires philosophical reflection, often intensified when events go badly wrong. Forty years after World War II, the Jewish philosopher Emil Fackenheim (1916–2003) made an exaggerated but still valid point when he asserted that "philosophers have all but ignored the Holocaust" (1985: 505). Fackenheim, who fled Nazi Germany, was prominent among the notable exceptions to that judgment (Camus 1948; Jaspers 1948; Heschel 1951; Arendt 1951, 1963; Buber 1967; Adorno 1967, 1973; Levinas 1969; Fackenheim 1970; Améry 1980). Nevertheless, the Holocaust has never attracted as much philosophical and specifically ethical inquiry as might be expected after an event of such devastating proportions. Again, notable contributions exist, many of them quite recent, and their number may continue to grow (Blanchot 1986; Bauman 1989; Jonas 1996; Rose 1996; Hallie 1997; Geras 1998; Agamben 1999; Glover 2000; Badiou 2001; Bernstein 2002; Margalit 2002; Neiman 2002; Roth 2005; Morgan 2008; Geddes et al. 2009; Lang 2009).

Probably no contributions have been more influential than those made by the Jewish philosopher Emmanuel Levinas (1906–1995), who lost most of his family in the Holocaust. He developed an important post-Holocaust ethical perspective by arguing that previous ethical theory had failed to concentrate on something as obvious and profound as the human face. Close attention to the face of the other person, Levinas affirmed, could produce a reorientation not only of ethics but also of human life itself, for our deepest seeing of the other person's face drives home how closely human beings are connected and how much the existence of the other person confers responsibility upon us (Levinas 1985; 1998). Unfortunately, neither the influence of Levinas nor that of any other post-Holocaust ethical theorist has dramatically changed the world for the better.

THE HOLOCAUST AS AN ETHICAL ABSOLUTE

A widely shared conviction persists that the Holocaust was *wrong* or nothing could be. An assault not only against Jewish life but also against goodness itself, the Holocaust should not have happened, and nothing akin to it should ever happen again. Michael Berenbaum echoes these points when he says that the Holocaust has become a "negative absolute" (2000: 60). Even if people remain skeptical that rational agreement can be obtained about what is right, just, and good, the Holocaust seems to reestablish conviction that what happened at Auschwitz and Treblinka was wrong, unjust, and evil—period. More than that, the scale of the wrongdoing, the magnitude of the injustice, and the devastation of the Holocaust's evil are so radical that humankind can ill afford not to have its ethical sensibilities informed and oriented by them.

Although the Holocaust scholar Raul Hilberg (1926–2007) did not consider himself a philosopher, his ethical outlook resonated with Berenbaum's view of the Holocaust as negative absolute. Hilberg affirmed that ethics is the same today as it was yesterday and even the day before yesterday; it is the same after Auschwitz as it was before and during the lethal operations at that place. Especially with regard to needless and wanton killing, he emphasized, ethics is the same for everyone, everywhere. Hilberg left no unclarity. Such killing is wrong. We know that "in our bones," he said, for such knowledge is the heritage of many years (Roth 2005: 70, 193–4).

Hilberg was a self-identified atheist. If asked about the foundations or grounding for his ethical outlook, he neither would nor could locate them in any divine source. Equally clear, Hilberg was no ethical relativist. He did not think that might makes right. Nor did he follow Friedrich Nietzsche (1844–1900) in claiming that the human will is the source of values and evaluations. But how should one understand the tantalizing idea that ethical sensibilities like Hilberg's are "in our bones," especially if something such as "the heritage of many years," which implies a social formation of the ethical, has put them there? In addition, how would that outlook square with the idea that ethics is the same today as it was yesterday and even the day before yesterday?

Hilberg's perspective seems to be grounded in the view that social history or evolution produces a deep-seated ethical consciousness that has universal and, in that sense, timeless qualities. Ethical outlooks do have a history, and they are socially formed. Those elements can fuse to make ethical outlooks, at least some of them, so widely accepted that the appearance of universality, timelessness, and absoluteness attaches to them. Developments of this kind may be at work in making the Holocaust a negative absolute. Thus, the Holocaust's ethical absoluteness, its role in claims that universal moral truth exists, may be a social construction (Alexander et al. 2009).

The social construction of ethics can be powerful. At the end of the day, such construction may be the best hope for ethics, but with the Holocaust and other mass atrocities so recent and ongoing, one can scarcely take moral comfort in that conclusion. The Holocaust may have deepened conviction that a fundamental, nonrelativistic difference exists between right and wrong. Its destruction may have renewed awareness of the importance of ethical standards and conduct. Nevertheless, the Holocaust continues to cast disturbing shadows over basic beliefs concerning right and wrong, human rights, and the hope that human beings will learn from the past. Identification of the Holocaust as a negative absolute that reinstates confidence in moral absolutes is a step that cannot be taken easily, precisely because social construction may be at work in every aspect of such thinking. One may argue that ethical injunctions against needless and wanton killing, for example, obtain normative status because collective experience shows them to have social utility. Such killing is wrong, on this view, because it threatens individual and social well-being. Over time this lesson may be experienced, taught, and driven home so that the ethical norm becomes embedded "in our bones." Something akin to this development might happen with the Holocaust's becoming a universal moral norm, a negative absolute or something more robust. But what if individuals or groups do not understand wanton and needless killing in the same way?

Heinrich Himmler (1900–1945) and his associates could agree that wanton and needless killing was wrong, but they did not think that the destruction of the European Jews fitted that description. They can and should be held accountable for ethical wrongdoing of the most devastating kind, but their deviation from the norm raises suspicion about ethical groundings of the kind that Hilberg seems to have had in mind, let alone appeals that would situate ethical truth confidently in divinity or in universal rationality. None of these "foundations," including appeals to the social construction of morality, deterred the "Final Solution," which did not end until massive Allied violence brought the Third Reich to its knees. Such realities gnaw at making one of the Holocaust's aftereffects the elevation of that disaster as a confidence-inspiring ethical absolute. "No obstruction stopped the German machine of destruction," Hilberg observed. "No problem proved insur-mountable. . . . The old moral order did not break through anywhere along the line. This is a phenomenon of the greatest magnitude" (2003: 1085). Hilberg may have exaggerated but not by much.

FAILURES AND FRAGMENTS

The Holocaust signifies the singular failure of ethics, which is that ethics has not made human beings better than we are. What we are, moreover, is often far from being what should make us proud to be human. Human-inflicted abuse of human life and the world that is our home, including inaction and indifference in the face of that abuse, is often so great that shame about our humanity ought to take precedence over our pride in it. One implication is that ethics seems too fragile and weak to do what we hope, at least in our better moments, it can accomplish.

An objection to this analysis might say that the failure(s) attributed to ethics are misplaced. The Holocaust does not signify the failure of ethics but the failures of men and women, of groups and communities, that failed to follow the light and to heed the insight that ethical reflection provides, at least when that reflection is sound. But this objection fails because it depends upon a distinction between the ethical and the human that cannot pass scrutiny. Ethics is not independent of human existence but is instead an expression, a reflection, of it. Ethics may correspond to or embody transcendent or transcendental realities that are not entirely human alone, but even then, ethics remains a human project, if not a human projection. The gap between thought and action, between theory and practice, where ethics is concerned is about *our* failure, but our *failure* includes the failure(s) of ethics, which are not separable from our human existence. Our reason and freedom have crucial parts to play in establishing the ethical. Our reason and our freedom also outstrip the ethical, and the ethical struggles, usually in vain, to keep reason and freedom under its less than fully persuasive sway.

Ethical theory and teaching have a long history, but it is hard to say with confidence that humankind has been forever making moral progress. Arguably the twentieth century was the most murderous in human history. No assurance exists that the twenty-first will be an improvement, in spite of the fact that talk about ethics and our need for it may be more widespread than ever. Human life is so full of discouragement, cynicism, and despair produced by folly, miscalculation, and wrongdoing that one can scarcely call ethics successful. Absent ethics we would be much worse than we are, but the slaughter bench of history, as the philosopher G. W. F. Hegel (1770–1831) rightly called it, does not allow much comfort to be taken from that fact.

The philosopher Sarah Kofman (1934–1994), a Holocaust survivor who, like Améry, committed suicide, anticipated and prompted such thinking when she asked, "How is it possible to speak, when you feel . . . a strange *double bind*: an infinite claim to speak, *a duty to speak infinitely*, imposing itself with irrepressible force, and at the same time, an almost physical impossibility to speak, a *choking* feeling" (1998: 39). Writing those words in 1985, she primarily focused the dilemma of the survivor who tries to transmit experiences and insights that cannot be voiced, but her words also identify a quandary that impacts post-Holocaust ethics.

One may feel a duty to speak, an obligation to make ethics stronger and less subject to overriding or subversion, an insistence not only to drive home the difference between right and wrong but also to influence action accordingly. Yet such work can produce a choking feeling, a sense that too much harm has been done for a good recovery to be made, a suspicion that ethics may be overwhelmed by the challenges it faces. The bind is double, for the sense of ethical responsibility, real though it is, remains hopelessly optimistic and naive unless it grapples with the despair that encounters with the Holocaust are bound to produce. To be touched by that despair, however, scarcely encourages one to believe that ethical responsibilities will be sufficiently accepted and met. Caught between the post-Holocaust need to speak for ethics and above all to speak ethically and boldly, on the one hand, and the feeling that the key elements of ethics—words, arguments, appeals to reason, persuasion through the example of moral action, even the legislation and implementation of law—may be inadequate, on the other, awareness intensifies about the fragility of ethics and the folly of taking anything good for granted.

As Kofman tried to salvage ethical fragments from the ruins of the Holocaust, she spoke of "the possibility of a new ethics" (1998: 73). Kofman's post-Holocaust ethical fragments only hinted at what she may have had in mind, but her insights are particularly important. She was convinced, for example, that "no community is possible with the SS" (1998: 70). With a vengeance, Nazi ideology rejected the idea of an inclusively shared humanity. Regarding difference—especially alleged racial difference—as profoundly threatening, its genocidal impulses took the world to Treblinka and Auschwitz. Nazi Germany, of course, took pride in its own sense of community, which underscores the fact that community is not necessarily human-ity's ally, especially if humanity is understood to be pluralistic and diverse. So Kofman emphasized the importance of supporting "the community (of those) without community" (1998: 70).

Those without community are outsiders, but Kofman's thinking did not stop with a call to defend and protect those who are threatened and harmed because they are left out. More radically and fundamentally, she rejects all senses of community that are based on "any specific difference or on a shared essence" (1998: 70). The right forms of community, she seems to be saying, are those that consciously accept a double bind. This bind acknowledges that every community is particular, different, finite, even exclusive in one way or another, but no community should rest on assumptions about immutable superiority or inferiority. On the contrary, the particularity of one community ought to affirm, protect, and encourage the particularity of others.

At its best, Kofman contends, community depends on "a shared power to choose, to make incompatible though correlative choices, the power to kill *and* the power to respect and safeguard the incommensurable distance, the relation without relation" (1998: 70). These hints, allusions, signposts point toward an ethical outlook that would not be the same as old humanisms that appealed to human nature, to the essence of humanity, or to reason as humankind's most decisive characteristics. Instead, Kofman suggests that everyday realities and actions—things such as choices and keeping or betraying one's word—reveal our humanity and make all the difference. The Holocaust reaffirmed that all of those caught in it—perpetrators, victims, on-lookers, and more—were human. Humanity survived the Holocaust, if only to testify, as the philosopher Maurice Blanchot (1907–2003) put it, how human indestructibility reveals "that there is no limit to the destruction of man" (1993: 135). But if humanity is to mean more than that, if humanity is to be what Kofman thought it ought to become, then the destruction of old humanisms may make possible the willful reconstitution of a "new kind of 'we,'" even "a new 'humanism' one might say, if it were still acceptable to use this trite and idyllic word" (1998: 73).

The status of ethics after the Holocaust is far from settled. One might argue that Nazi Germany's downfall shows that right defeated wrong and that goodness subdued evil, thus revealing that reality has a fundamentally moral underpinning. The Holocaust, however, is far too awesome for such facile triumphalism. The Nazis did not win, but they came too close for comfort. Even though the Third Reich was destroyed, it is not so easy to say that its defeat was a clear and decisive triumph for goodness, truth, and justice over evil, falsehood, and corruption. Add to those realizations the fact that the Nazis themselves were idealists. They had positive beliefs about right and wrong, good and evil, duty and responsibility. The "Final Solution" was a key part of those outlooks, which were put into practice with a zealous and apocalyptic vengeance.

The "Final Solution" still threatens the status, practical and theoretical, of moral norms that are contrary to the Nazi ethic, whose deadly way failed but still prevailed long enough to call into question virtually all moral assumptions and religious hopes. Adolf Hitler (1889–1945) and his regime intended the annihilation of Jewish life to signify the destruction of the very idea of a common humanity that all people share. Jean Améry was thinking in a vein akin to Sarah Kofman's when he wrote that the Nazis "hated the word 'humanity'" (1980: 31). He amplified his point when he said, "Torture was no invention of National Socialism. But it was its apotheosis" (1980: 30). Améry meant that the Third Reich aimed to produce men, women, and children whose hardness would transcend humanity in favor of a so-called racially pure and culturally superior form of life that could still be appropriately called "Aryan" or German but not merely "human."

Insofar as *humanity* referred to universal equality, suggested a shared and even divine source of life, or implied any of the other trappings of weakness and sentimentality that Hitler and his most dedicated followers attributed to such concepts, National Socialism intentionally tried to go beyond humanity. Such steps entailed more than killing allegedly inferior forms of life that were thought to threaten German superiority. Moving beyond humanity made it essential to inflict torture—not only to show that "humanity" or "subhumanity" deserved no respect in and of itself, but also to ensure that those who had moved beyond humanity, and thus were recognizing the respect deserved only by Germans or "Aryans," had really done so. Hitler and his followers did not succeed completely in implementing their antisemitism, but they went far enough in establishing what Améry aptly called "the rule of the antiman" that none of our fondest hopes about humanity can be taken for granted (1980: 31).

As Améry and Kofman help to show, our senses of moral and religious authority have been fragmented and weakened by the accumulated ruins of history and the depersonalized advances of civilization that have taken us from a bloody twentieth century into an even more problematic twenty-first. A moral spirit and religious commitment that have the courage to persist *in spite of* humankind's self-inflicted destructiveness are essential, but the question remains how effective these dispositions can be in salvaging moral fragments within a world where power, and especially the power of governments, stands at the heart of that destructiveness. To find ways to salvage the fragments, to affect "the powers that be" so that their tendencies to lay waste to human life are checked, ethics after Auschwitz will need to draw on every resource it can find: appeals to human rights, calls for renewed religious sensitivity, respect and honor for people who save lives and resist atrocity, and attention to the Holocaust's warnings, to name only a few. Those efforts will need to be accompanied by determination to build these concerns into our educational, religious, business, and political institutions. Further exploration of these needs and prospects forms a key part of the agenda for future work to salvage ethics in the context of Holocaust studies.

That humankind will ever reach full agreement on a single worldview that will ground belief in human rights is extremely unlikely. But that does not mean that appeals to human rights are dashed as well. If people feel the need to ground appeals to human rights, a variety of options—philosophical and religious—may remain credible, even though they will not be universally accepted. More import-antly, there may be considerable agreement—especially after the Holocaust—about what the functional interpretation of human rights ought to be. Here, too, agree-ment will not be universal, but the Holocaust itself has had an important impact on helping to clarify what ought not to happen to human beings. If we think about what ought not to happen to human beings—here an echo of Berenbaum's idea of the Holocaust as negative absolute is appropriate—we may find considerable agreement about what should happen.

CONCLUSION: ETHICAL BEHAVIOR IS HARD

The eloquent Auschwitz survivor Primo Levi (1919–1987) said of philosophy, "no, it's not for me," but as his explorations of "the gray zone" and other Holocaust realities make clear, he had a keen philosophical mind, which he often brought to bear on ethical questions (1988: 36–69; 2001: 175). Levi, who thought that "each of us is a mixture of good and not so good," lacked trust in "the moral instinct of humanity, in mankind as 'naturally' good" (2001: 180, 232). In an essay called "News from the Sky," for example, he notes that the great German philosopher Immanuel Kant (1724–1804) emphasized two wonders in creation: the starry sky above and the moral law within. "I don't know about the moral law," mused Levi, "does it dwell in everyone? . . . Every passing year augments our doubts" (1989: 20). The starry sky seemed to be another matter, but even those considerations gave Levi pause. The stars remain, but the sky—the territory of bombers, hijacked planes, and missiles that can unleash terror and horror capable of annihilating human existence itself—has become an ominous place because of World War II, the Holocaust, and their aftereffects.

Levi was not sure that ethics could be salvaged after Auschwitz, but he knew that the failure to try would exact a price higher than humankind could pay. "The universe is strange to us, we are strange in the universe," he wrote, and "the future of humanity is uncertain" (1989: 22–3). Nevertheless, Levi had his hopes. "There are no problems that cannot be solved around a table," he said, "provided there is good will and reciprocal trust" (1988: 200). Probably Levi was too optimistic, for much hinges on his qualification about good will and reciprocal trust. Their scarcity remains one of the Holocaust's most confounding results.

When asked what Holocaust studies research has taught him about ethics, the historian Peter Hayes responded simply but profoundly: "ethical behavior is hard" (Hayes in Petropoulos et al. 2010: 302). The Holocaust did not have to happen. It emerged from human choices and decisions. Those facts mean that nothing human, natural, or divine guarantees respect for the ethical values and commitments that are most needed in contemporary human existence, but nothing is more important than our commitment to defend them, for they remain as fundamental as they are fragile, as precious as they are endangered. Ethics may not be enough. It may be what the American poet William Stafford (1914–1993) called a "forlorn cause" (1998: 85), but failures and all, ethics still provides our best compass.

REFERENCES

ADORNO, T. (1967). *Prisms*. London: Neville Spearman.

——(1973). *Negative Dialectics*. New York: Seabury Press.

AGAMBEN, G. (1999). *Remnants of Auschwitz: The Witness and the Archive*. New York: Zone Books.

ALEXANDER, J., with commentaries by JAY, M., GIESEN, B., ROTHBERG, M., MANNE, R., GLAZER, N., KATZ, E., and KATZ, R. (2009). *Remembering the Holocaust: A Debate*. New York: Oxford University Press.

AMÉRY, J. (1980). *At the Mind's Limits: Contemplations by a Survivor on Auschwitz and Its Realities*. Bloomington, IN: Indiana University Press.

ARENDT, H. (1951). *The Origins of Totalitarianism*. New York: Harcourt.

——(1963). *Eichmann in Jerusalem: A Report on the Banality of Evil*. New York: Viking Press.

BADIOU, A. (2001). *Ethics: An Essay on the Understanding of Evil*. London: Verso.

BARNETT, V. (2000). *Bystanders: Conscience and Complicity during the Holocaust*. Westport, CT: Praeger.

BAUMAN, Z. (1989). *Modernity and the Holocaust*. Ithaca, NY: Cornell University Press.

BAYZLER, M. (2003). *Holocaust Justice: The Battle for Restitution in America's Courts*. New York: New York University Press.

BERENBAUM, M. (2000). "Who Owns the Holocaust?" *Moment* 25/6: 60.

——(ed.) (2008). *Not Your Father's Antisemitism: Hatred of Jews in the Twenty-first Century*. St. Paul, MN: Paragon House.

BERNSTEIN, R. (2002). *Radical Evil: A Philosophical Interrogation*. Cambridge: Polity Press.

BLANCHOT, M. (1986). *The Writing of the Disaster*. Lincoln, NE: University of Nebraska Press.

BLOXHAM, D. (2009). *The Final Solution: A Genocide*. New York: Oxford University Press.

——(1993). *The Infinite Conversation*. Minneapolis, MN: University of Minnesota Press.

BROWNING, C. (1992). *Ordinary Men: Reserve Police Battalion 101 and the Final Solution in Poland*. New York: HarperCollins.

——(2010). *Remembering Survival: Inside a Nazi Slave-labor Camp*. New York: W. W. Norton.

BUBER, M. (1967). *On Judaism*. Ed. N. Glazer. New York: Schocken Books.

CAMUS, A. (1948). *The Plague*. New York: Modern Library.

EARL, H. (2009). *The Nuremberg SS-Einsatzgruppen Trial, 1945–1958*. Cambridge: Cambridge University Press.

EIZENSTAT, S. (2003). *Imperfect Justice: Looted Assets, Slave Labor, and the Unfinished Business of World War II*. New York: Public Affairs.

FACKENHEIM, E. (1970). *God's Presence in History: Jewish Affirmations and Philosophical Reflections*. New York: New York University Press.

——(1985). "The Holocaust and Philosophy." *Journal of Philosophy* 82: 505–14.

GEDDES, J., ROTH, J., and SIMON, J. (eds.) (2009). *The Double Binds of Ethics after the Holocaust: Salvaging the Fragments*. New York: Palgrave Macmillan.

GERAS, N. (1998). *The Contract of Mutual Indifference: Political Philosophy after the Holocaust*. London: Verso.

GLOVER, J. (2000). *Humanity: A Moral History of the Twentieth Century*. New Haven, CT: Yale University Press.

GUSHEE, D. (2003). *Righteous Gentiles of the Holocaust: Genocide and Moral Obligation*. 2nd edn. St. Paul, MN: Paragon House.

HAAS, P. (1988). *Morality after Auschwitz: The Radical Challenge of the Nazi Ethic*. Philadelphia, PA: Fortress Press.

HALLIE, P. (1997). *Tales of Good and Evil, Help and Harm*. New York: HarperCollins.

HAYES, P. (2004). *From Cooperation to Complicity: Degussa in the Third Reich*. Cambridge: Cambridge University Press.

HENRY, M. (2007). *Confronting the Perpetrators: A History of the Claims Conference*. London: Vallentine Mitchell.

HESCHEL, A. (1951). *Man Is Not Alone: A Philosophy of Religion*. New York: Farrar, Straus & Young.

HILBERG, R. (2003). *The Destruction of the European Jews*. 3rd edn. 3 vols. New Haven, CT: Yale University Press.

JASPERS, K. (1948). *The Question of German Guilt*. New York: Dial Press.

JONAS, H. (1996). *Mortality and Morality: A Search for the Good after Auschwitz*. Ed. L. Vogel. Evanston, IL: Northwestern University Press.

JONES, D. (1999). *Moral Responsibility in the Holocaust: A Study in the Ethics of Character*. Lanham, MD: Rowman & Littlefield.

KIERNAN, B. (2007). *Blood and Soil: A World History of Genocide and Extermination from Sparta to Darfur*. New Haven, CT: Yale University Press.

KOFMAN, S. (1998). *Smothered Words*. Evanston, IL: Northwestern University Press.

KOONZ, C. (2003). *The Nazi Conscience*. Cambridge, MA: Harvard University Press.

LANG, B. (2009). *Philosophical Witnessing: The Holocaust as Presence*. Hanover, NH: University Press of New England.

LANGER, L. (1980). "The Dilemma of Choice in the Death Camps." *Centerpoint* 4: 53–9.

——(1991). *Holocaust Testimonies: The Ruins of Memory*. New Haven, CT: Yale University Press.

LEVI, P. (1988). *The Drowned and the Saved*. New York: Summit Books.

——(1989). *Other People's Trades*. New York: Summit Books.

——(2001). *The Voice of Memory: Interviews, 1961–1987*. Ed. M. Belpolit and R. Gordon. New York: New Press.

LEVINAS, E. (1969). *Totality and Infinity: An Essay on Exteriority*. Pittsburgh, PA: Duquesne University Press.

——(1985). *Ethics and Infinity*. Pittsburgh, PA: Duquesne University Press.

——(1998). *Entre Nous: On Thinking-of-the-Other*. New York: Columbia University Press.

LIPSTADT, D. (2005). *History on Trial: My Day in Court with David Irving*. New York: Ecco.

MARGALIT, A. (2002). *The Ethics of Memory*. Cambridge, MA: Harvard University Press.

MARRUS, M. (1997). *The Nuremberg War Crimes Trial, 1945–46: A Documentary History.* Boston, MA: Bedford Books.

——(2009). *Some Measure of Justice: The Holocaust Era Restitution Campaign of the 1990s.* Madison, WI: University of Wisconsin Press.

MORGAN, M. (2008). *On Shame.* New York: Routledge.

NEIMAN, S. (2002). *Evil in Modern Thought: An Alternative History of Philosophy.* Princeton, NJ: Princeton University Press.

PETROPOULOS, J., RAPAPORT, L., and ROTH, J. (eds.) (2010). *Lessons and Legacies IX: Memory, History, and Responsibility: Reassessments of the Holocaust, Implications for the Future.* Evanston, IL: Northwestern University Press.

ROSE, G. (1996). *Mourning Becomes the Law: Philosophy and Representation.* Cambridge: Cambridge University Press.

ROSENBAUM, I. (1976). *The Holocaust and Halakhah.* New York: Ktav.

ROTH, J. (2005). *Ethics During and After the Holocaust: In the Shadow of Birkenau.* New York: Palgrave Macmillan.

STAFFORD, W. (1998). *The Way It Is: New & Selected Poems.* St. Paul, MN: Graywolf Press.

TOTTEN, S. and PARSONS. W. (eds.) (2009). *Century of Genocide: Critical Essays and Eyewitness Accounts.* New York: Routledge.

VALENTINO, B. (2004). *Final Solutions: Mass Killing and Genocide in the Twentieth Century.* Ithaca, NY: Cornell University Press.

VAN HARN, R. (2007). *The Ten Commandments for Jews, Christians, and Others.* Grand Rapids, MI: Eerdmans.

WALLER, J. (2007). *Becoming Evil: How Ordinary People Commit Genocide and Mass Killing.* 2nd edn. New York: Oxford University Press.

WEIKART, R. (2009). *Hitler's Ethic: The Nazi Pursuit of Evolutionary Progress.* New York: Palgrave Macmillan.

WITTMANN, R. (2005). *Beyond Justice: The Auschwitz Trial.* Cambridge, MA: Harvard University Press.

OTHER SUGGESTED READING

BRUDHOLM, T. (2008). *Resentment's Virtue: Jean Améry and the Refusal to Forgive.* Philadelphia, PA: Temple University Press.

——and CUSHMAN, T. (eds.) (2009). *The Religious in Response to Mass Atrocity: Interdisciplinary Responses.* Cambridge: Cambridge University Press.

EVANS, G. (2008). *The Responsibility to Protect: Ending Mass Atrocity Crimes Once and For All.* Washington, DC: The Brookings Institution.

GARRARD, E. and SCARRE, G. (eds.) (2003). *Moral Philosophy and the Holocaust.* Burlington, VT: Ashgate Publishing Company.

LEVI, N. and ROTHBERG, M. (eds.) (2003). *The Holocaust: Theoretical Readings.* New Brunswick, NJ: Rutgers University Press.

PATTERSON, D. and ROTH, J. (eds.) (2004). *After-Words: Post-Holocaust Struggles with Forgiveness, Reconciliation, Justice.* Seattle, WA: University of Washington Press.

PETROPOULOS, J. and ROTH, J. (eds.) (2005). *Gray Zones: Ambiguity and Compromise in the Holocaust and Its Aftermath.* New York: Berghahn Books.

ROTH, J. (ed.) (1999). *Ethics after the Holocaust: Perspectives, Critiques, and Responses.* St. Paul, MN: Paragon House.

——(2005). *Genocide and Human Rights: A Philosophical Guide.* New York: Palgrave Macmillan.

EPILOGUE

PETER HAYES

JOHN K. ROTH

EVERY book draws to a close, but its final pages scarcely determine the ending(s). Reader responses influence a book's destiny and fate. In the case of this *Handbook of Holocaust Studies*, unfinished and future events also will affect its durability. These prospects reflect a governing principle in the field: desires for finality and closure never should trump critical inquiry that corrects and reformulates what is "known" and searches for discoveries about what is still unknown. That principle means not only that no book can claim finality and closure regarding Holocaust studies but also that the ending(s) of the Holocaust itself have not yet reached finality and closure and, arguably, never will. As work on *The Oxford Handbook of Holocaust Studies* approached its conclusion at the end of 2009, four Holocaust-related incidents illustrated that fact.

On 30 November 2009, a trial began in Munich. The accused, John Demjanjuk (b. 1920), a retired autoworker stripped of American citizenship and deported, faced charges that he was an accessory in the murder of more than 27,000 Jews at the Sobibor death camp in Nazi-occupied Poland in 1943, where he worked as a guard. Two decades earlier, in 1988, Demjanjuk had been convicted of Holocaust-related crimes and sentenced to death by an Israeli court, but then he was set free in 1993 when new evidence revealed that he had not been the sadistic Treblinka functionary known as "Ivan the Terrible." Although mistaken identity will not intervene in Demjanjuk's favor at his Munich trial, a verdict had not been reached at the time of this writing. Doctors found the ailing defendant fit enough to stand trial, but whether he would live to hear the court proclaim his guilt or innocence remained to be seen. Clearly, however, Demjanjuk's trial is among the last of its kind, for a rapidly diminishing number of the Holocaust's perpetrators and accessories remain alive. Scholars will write the last chapter of the Demjanjuk saga, but the ending of his trial and his life will bring little finality and closure because no one can say for certain, once and for all, what the significance of his or any Holocaust trial will turn out to be. If that claim is plausible, similar quandaries about the significance of the Holocaust and Holocaust studies also arise in connection with three other episodes.

On 2 October 2009, about two months before the Demjanjuk trial began in Munich, a physician named Marek Edelman (b. 1919) died in Warsaw. In 1943, while Demjanjuk worked at Sobibor, Edelman was among the tens of thousands of Jews crammed into the Warsaw ghetto. A witness to the deportations that escalated in the summer of 1942, Edelman was often present at the *Umschlagplatz*, where the trains were loaded with Jews destined for the gas chambers at Treblinka. The Germans tried to reassure the deportees that they were being resettled to more favorable circumstances, a ruse that sometimes included temporarily excusing ill Jews from the journey. Edelman's job as a messenger for the ghetto hospital gave him opportunities to rescue some Jews by presenting documents certifying that they were too ill to travel. He used these opportunities to save people useful to the ghetto resistance movement in which he increasingly was involved.

When the Warsaw ghetto uprising began on 19 April 1943, Edelman was one of its leaders. By escaping with others through the ghetto's sewers as the Germans put down the uprising several weeks later, Edelman lived to resist the Nazis again in the 1944 Polish uprising in Warsaw. After the war, he took up his medical studies, became a highly respected cardiologist in Łódź, endured the upsurge of antisemitism in communist Poland, and became a leader in the Solidarity movement. News reports at the time of Edelman's death said that he had been the last surviving commander of the Warsaw ghetto uprising. His passing drives home awareness that only a few years hence no survivors of the Holocaust will be alive. No one can say for sure, once and for all, what the significance of that reality will be, but its approach assures that the Holocaust will no longer be a first-hand memory, let alone an immediate experience, of anyone on earth. The unfolding of Holocaust studies will have to take that fact into account.

On 19 December 2009, Pope Benedict XVI (b. 1927) confirmed the 2007 findings of a Vatican committee that attributed "heroic virtues" to the controversial Holocaust-era pontiff Pius XII (1876–1958), moving him a significant step forward in a vetting process that can culminate in Roman Catholic sainthood. Pius XII now can be beatified when a miracle attributed to his intercession is officially acknowledged, and the recognition of a second miracle would set the stage for canonization. For decades, few if any Holocaust-related controversies have been more fraught than that surrounding Pius XII's behavior during and toward the Holocaust, a matter exacerbated by the delay in the opening of the Vatican's archives pertinent to his reign (1939–1958). At this writing, no one can be certain that sainthood will be conferred on Pius XII, let alone precisely what the reverberations, one way or the other, will be. It seems likely, however, that his canonization is coming and that understanding of the Holocaust itself will be different as a result. The implications—historical and political, ethical and religious—of the Vatican's posture and decision in this matter are that important.

Probably the timing was a sheer coincidence, but in the predawn hours of 18 December 2009—one day after Germany announced an $87 million contribution to the Auschwitz-Birkenau Foundation to enhance preservation of the death camp as a museum and memorial and one day before Pope Benedict XVI affirmed Pius XII's "heroic virtues"—another highly symbolic act took place: thieves stole the historic "Arbeit Macht Frei" sign that mockingly spanned the entrance of Auschwitz I. Within hours of the theft's discovery, police dragnets sought the robbers, rewards were offered for the sign's recovery, and news reports and bloggers' commentaries rapidly multiplied in print and electronic outlets. International shock and outrage erupted. The lack of video surveillance tapes aroused comment and hindered detection of the thieves, but early conjectures dismissed the notion that they were thoughtless vandals and focused instead on the likelihood that they must be neo-Nazis or opportunists aiming for profit in sales of Nazi memorabilia.

About seventy-two hours after discovery of the theft, police in northern Poland recovered the metal sign, which the thieves had cut into three pieces, one for each of its infamous words. Five Polish men were taken into custody and sent to Kraków for questioning, but early stages of the investigation suggested that someone outside of Poland orchestrated the theft. "Case closed" may soon be said, but in crucial ways that judgment will be premature. Conviction of the thieves and restoration of the sign to its proper place are unlikely to put an end to the matter. Beyond the obvious question—how could such a theft happen?—the aftereffects of this episode may expand in ways that influence Holocaust studies and understanding of the Holocaust itself. The last words have not been written about the history behind the Auschwitz sign, its meaning before, during, and after the Holocaust, and the people who erected it and suffered under it. Furthermore, what difference will it make that the "Arbeit Macht Frei" sign was stolen from Auschwitz I? What importance will that episode have ten, twenty, or a hundred years from now? Much depends on what investigators discover about the motives behind the crime.

Questions of this kind lead to the much larger, much more important one that this handbook cannot answer: What importance will the Holocaust and Holocaust studies have ten, twenty, a hundred years, a millennium from now? Presently, as this book's chapters document, the Holocaust and study about it are deeply embedded in human memory, memorialization, scholarship, and teaching. A generation of younger scholars will carry forward the work that those before them have begun. But the world will not be the same as time passes. Holocaust scholars and Holocaust-related institutions and education programs will continue their work. Assessment of their accomplishments will be needed, too, but to what end(s) all of this effort will be expended is less than clear.

Will "Holocaust fatigue" eventually dissipate widespread interest in the history of the Holocaust and its implications? What will happen to the "warnings" and "lessons" of the Holocaust in a world where mass atrocities and genocides show few signs of abating? Who can say with certainty that catastrophes worse than the Holocaust are not in store? What of the Holocaust's status—so often claimed—as a watershed event unprecedented, if not unique, in human history? Events may be in play that will lead eventually to the extinction of much or all of human life. What would the Holocaust and studies about it amount to then?

Like the Holocaust itself, the field of Holocaust studies does little to encourage optimism about humanity's future and progress. Both entail darkness and invite despair. *The Oxford Handbook of Holocaust Studies* is but a fleeting episode in history's unfolding, and the ending(s) of both will come only with time's passage. How the Holocaust is studied, the care given to that work, may or may not affect the outcomes that await, but if this book and its ending(s) keep summoning inquiry and discovery, resisting finality and closure in the process, then perhaps the intellectual and creative labor recorded in and by these pages will not have been in vain.

INDEX

....

Note: page numbers in *italics* refer to figures.

AAC (Anglo-American Committee of Inquiry
    Regarding the Problems of European
    Jewry and Palestine) 517
Abe (survivor) 419
abortion 208
Abusch, Alexander 644–5
Activist Front, Lithuania 318
Adam, Uwe Dietrich 129
Adam Resurrected (Kaniuk) 439
Adenauer, Konrad 534, 549, 577, 637, 638, 654
    and policy towards Nazi past 639, 641
Adler, Hans 386
Adon Olam Ad Matai? (Subliminal) 488–9
Adorno, Theodor 408, 461, 640
    on Holocaust literature 430, 437
    postwar rejection of aesthetics 14, 462
adversus Judaeos tradition 623, 628
AEG compensation payments 551
AELKZ (Allgemeine Evangelisch-Lutherische
    Kirchenzeitung) 254
Africans 56, 61, 62–3
    in French army, murder of 101, 142
    see also Herero people; Nama people
*After Auschwitz: Responses to the Holocaust in
    Contemporary Art* (exhibition) 464
Age of Wonders, The (Appelfeld) 436
Agrarian League, Germany 34, 61–2
Agudath Israel 192
Ahmadinejad, Mahmoud 571
Ahnenerbe (Ancestral Heritage) 42
Ahnenpässe (racial passports) 383, 384
Ai bambini di Terezin (Brizio) 485–6
Aimée and Jaguar (film) 456
Akayesu, Jean-Paul 716
Akiva, Daniel 486
Alexander, Edward 602
All But My Life (G. Klein) 418
Alleanza Nazionale, Italy 659
Allen, Michael Thad 139
Allgemeine Evangelisch-Lutherische
    Kirchenzeitung (*AELKZ*) 254

Alliance against the Arrogance of Jewry,
    Germany 34
Allied bombing raids 391, 568, 640
    Pforzheim death toll 563
    possible Allied bombing of Auschwitz 160,
        192, 272
Allied Control Council Laws 526, 533–4
Allies 9, 265–72
    assessment of Holocaust 108
    bombing raids 391, 563, 568, 640
    knowledge of mass murder in Soviet
        Union 104
    military planning 104
    occupation 635–6
    responses to forced emigration policy 266–7
    and world Jewry, Nazi propaganda and 265–6
    see also United Kingdom; United States; USSR
Althaus, Paul 253
Aly, Götz 138–9
Amarcord (film) 454
America, *see* United States of America
American Anthropological Association 674
American Congregationalists 180
American Jewish Joint Distribution Committee
    (JDC) 512–13, 518
American Relief Organization 178
"America's Concentration Camps"
    (exhibition) 602
Améry, Jean 415, 417, 433–4, 724–5, 731
Amichai, Yehuda 439
Amishai-Maisels, Ziva 461–2
Anatolia 62
Ancestral Heritage (*Ahnenerbe*) 42
Anger, Per 163
Anglo-American Committee of Inquiry
    Regarding the Problems of European
    Jewry and Palestine (AAC) 517
Ani Maamin: A Song Lost and Found Again
    (Milhaud and Wiesel) 486
Anna Frank, un símbol (Cervelló) 485
Anne Frank Cantata: A Child of Light (Kox) 485

Anne Frank, Symphony in One Movement for String Orchestra (Biriotti) 485
Anne Frank-Fonds, Basel 597
Annelies: The Anne Frank Oratorio (Whitbourne) 485
Antelme, Robert 417
anthropology 56, 674
anti-bourgeois campaign, Italy 89
Anti-Comintern Pact 285
Anti-Defamation League 488–9, 597
anti-Jewish policies
    evolution of 187–8
    stages of 189–90
anti-Judaism 622–3, 628
Antisemites' League 24
antisemitism 11, 23–37
    antisemitic political parties, electoral history of 31–3
    Catholic Church and 9, 233–4
    characteristics of antisemites 28–30
    Christianity and 30, 621–4
    colonialism and 71–3
    communism and 643–4
    as cultural code 28
    definitions of 23–4, 622
    and fascism 5, 82–4
    growth of 24
    Imperial Germany and 63
    introduction of word 58
    as necessary enabling condition for Holocaust 4, 5
    origins of 25–8
    redemptive 116
    revolutionary 33–7
    situational 29
    strategies of 30–3
    university students and 29–30, 34–5
Antonescu, Ion 88, 327–8
Antonescu, Mihai 329
apartheid 62
Apel, Dora 14, 461–75
Appelfeld, Aharon 422, 436, 689
Apt Pupil (film) 456
Arab–Israeli conflict 630
    Holocaust denial and 571
Arad, Boaz 464, 470, 471–2, 474
Arad, Yitzhak 423
Arbeitskommandos 356: *see also* concentration camps: forced labor in
archives 196, 197, 401
Arendt, Hannah 54, 63, 446, 594, 670, 681
    and Eichmann trial 531–2
    on Jewish leadership 193

armaments industry 358, 369
Armenian genocide 96, 601, 659
Aronson, Shlomo 9, 265–72
Arrow Cross Party, Hungary 83, 179, 279, 330, 331
art 14, 196–7, 461–75
    children's pictures 222–3
    contemporary exhibitions 463–4
    and Jewish identity 463–4
    looted artworks 547, 554
    universalization of horror 461–2, 463
"Aryan physics" 42–3
"Aryanization" 117–18, 129–30, 297, 298–9
    of businesses 542–3, 546
    confiscation of Jewish property 98, 544
    in Italy 91, 92
    in Protectorate of Bohemia and Moravia 300
Asche von Birkenau, Die (Kochan) 484
Aschrott-Brunnen, Kassel 494
asocials 48, 279, 280
Assault, The (Mulisch) 437
assimilation 61, 91, 256, 286
Atatürk, Mustafa Kemal 161
atrocity propaganda 6
Attie, Shimon 463, 494–5
attritionism 133–4, 343
Auerbach, Rachel 430–1
Auerswald, Heinz 134
Augustine of Hippo, St. 623–4
Aumeier, Hans 530
"Auschwitz Album" 382, 388
Auschwitz and After (Delbo) 418
Auschwitz concentration and death camp 40, 105, 138, 218, 366
    Central Construction Office 568
    crematoria as gas chambers 566–7
    Death Books 563
    death toll 564
    deportation of Jews to, from France 334
    deportation of Jews to, from Hungary 331
    deportation of Jews to, from Italy 337–8
    deportation of Jews to, from Netherlands 335–6
    evacuation of 374
    experimental gas killings 123, 136
    gas chambers 106
    Gypsies in 106, 280, 373
    human experimentation at 40, 51–2
    medical professionals and genocide 50
    murder of Gypsies 106, 278
    possible Allied bombing of 160, 192, 272
    Sonnderkommando units 398, 423, 567
    Sonnderkommando uprising 503

theft of "Arbeit Macht Frei" sign 739
transfer of Slav prisoners to work camps 106
transports to 315–16
Zyklon B as killing agent 370–1
see also Auschwitz-Birkenau
Auschwitz trial 524, 536
Auschwitz-Birkenau 50, 160
    Birkenau Family Camp 221, 222
    children's games 221
    genocide in 373
    Gypsy Camp 106, 280, 373
    as holding camp for Soviet prisoners 367
    memorial 485, 498, 499–500, *500*
    mothers with small children, treatment of 207
    murder of European Jews 371
    Sonderkommando uprising 373
    transports to 105–6
Aussenlager (satellite camps) 356
Austerlitz (Sebald) 440
Australia 192, 521
Austria 132, 194
    antisemitic political parties in 33
    antisemitism in 24
    Christian Socialists 33
    industrial capitalism in 25
    legislation against genocide and Holocaust
        denial 570
    Pan-German Party 33
    and restitution/compensation 552–3, 554
    sanctions against 651, 658, 659
    segregation of Jews in education 297–8
    trial of Irving 570
    university students and antisemitism 29–30
Austro-Hungarian Empire, *see* Habsburg
    Empire
auxiliary police units (*Schutzmannschaften*) 135,
    150, 152
Avisar, Ilan 448–9
Avnery, Uri 578
Avni, Tzvi 486
Axis powers 105, 152: *see also* Germany; Italy

"Babi Yar" (Boyarska) 487
Babi Yar massacre 102, 317
Bacon, Francis 462
Badenheim (Appelfeld) 436
Badoglio, Pietro 84
Baeck, Leo 295
Bak, Samuel 463
Baker, Philip 172
Balfour Declaration 575
Balkans
    brutality in 101

genocide in 602, 725
    see also Bosnia-Herzegovina; Bulgaria; Croatia;
        Greece; Macedonia; Serbia; Yugoslavia
Ballad of Mauthausen (Theodorakis) 486
Baltic states 317
    concentration camps, evacuation of 374
    ethnic Germans in 100
    ghettos in 345–6
    invasion of 102
    mass murder in 102
    reparations 551
    see also Estonia; Latvia; Lithuania
Banat, Serbia 333
bank accounts, Jewish
    blocked 543–4, 545
    in Switzerland 554–5, 556
Bankier, David 165
Bar-On, Daniel 673
Baranowicze ghetto 346, 347
Barash, Ephraim 350–1
Barbie, Klaus 531
Barmen Declaration 252–3, 625–6
Baron, Lawrence 13–14, 444–57
Barth, Karl 252, 253, 626
Bartov, Omer 150, 453
"Bashert" (Klepfisz) 439
al-Bashir, Omar 716
Baskin, Leonard 461–2
Bašs, Mendelis 483
Battle of Warsaw, The (Waxman) 480
Bauer, Fritz 536, 642
Bauer, Yehuda 159–60, 423, 584, 616
Bauman, Janina 228
Bauman, Zygmunt 674
Bazan, Heinrich Banniza von 73
Becker, Jurek 435
Becker, Paul and Edmund 318, 323
Beggar in Jerusalem, A (Wiesel) 438
Begin, Menachem 578, 586–7
Begley, Louis 437
Beitz, Berthold 361
Bekennende Kirche, see Confessing Church
Belarus 71, 302
    Einsatzgruppen in 318
    Germanization of 317, 318, 321
    ghettos in 321, 346–7
    Holocaust education in 700
    mass murders in 102, 135, 317
    reparations 551
    and starvation policy 147
Belev, Alexander 331
Belgium 133
    Gypsies in 280

Belgium (*cont.*)
  legislation against genocide and Holocaust
    denial 570
  under occupation 335
  and restitution/compensation 552–3
Belorussia, *see* Belarus
Belzec death camp 50, 345, 370
  gassing of Jews 122
  murder of Gypsies in 280
  prototype death camp with stationary gas
    chambers 136
Ben-Gurion, David 500, 576, 578
  and Israel's nuclear capability 586
Bendin ghetto: women in 212–13
Benedict XVI, Pope 626, 738, 739
  and Holocaust denial 571–2
Beneš decrees 656
Benigni, Roberto 451–2, 453–4, 596
Benjamin, Walter 440
Bensoussan, Georges 700
Bent (film) 456
Berenbaum, Michael 17, 593, 607–18, 726
Berg, Mary 206
Bergen, Doris L. 6, 95–108
Bergen-Belsen camp 374, 375
  memorial ceremonies at 638–9
  music in 196
  post-liberation 511–14
Bergier, Jean-Francois 554
Bergier Commission 554–5
Bergman, Carla 675
Berk, Leon 346
Berland, Sigmunt 487
Berlin Court of Appeal 536–7
Berlusconi government, Italy 659
Berman, Karel 479
Bermuda Conference 160, 177–8, 269
Bernadotte, Folke 163, 374–5
Bernard of Clairvaux 623
Bernburg euthanasia institution 367
Bernheim petition 191
Bertram, Adolf 237, 238, 239, 240
Bessarabia 138, 327
Best, Werner 174, 530
Bettelheim, Bruno 408, 594, 672
Beyerchen, Alan 42–3
Białystok ghetto 96, 350–1
"Bibliotek" (Whiteread) 494
Biebow, Hans 133, 343
Bielefeld Archive 259
Biermann, Wolf 487
Biltmore Conference 617
Binding, Karl 48–9

biographical films (biopics) 455
Biriotti, León 485
Birkenau concentration and death camp,
    see Auschwitz-Birkenau
Birtwistle, Harrison 486
Bischof, Max 134
Bismarck, Otto von 60, 70, 234, 283
Bitburg controversy 642
Bitburg military cemetery, West Germany 601
BK, *see* Confessing Church
Blacher, Boris 482–3
Black Thursday 206
Blake, Ran 488
Blanchot, Maurice 430, 730
Blue Division, Spain 164
Blumenbach, Johann Friedrich von 56
Blumenthal, David 611
Boder, David 415, 669
Bolchover, Richard 161
Bolshevism 74, 652
  Bolshevik revolution, Jews as scapegoats
    for 82–3
  Judeo-Bolshevism 76, 121, 125, 148–9
Boltanski, Christian 462–3, 464
Bolzano 92
Bonaparte, Napoleon 59
Bondy, Ruth 204
Bonhoeffer, Dietrich 250, 253, 257, 626
Boogaard, Hannis 175
Boogaard family 175
"Book of Yolek, The" (Hecht) 439
Boris III, King of Bulgaria 332
Borland, Christine 464, 465
Bormann, Martin 528, 624, 711
Borowski, Tadeusz 435
Bosnia-Herzegovina 101, 284, 676
Boss, Arthur 318, 323
Bouhler, Philipp 49
Boyarska, Rivke 487
Boys from Brazil, The (film) 448
Bracher, Karl 642
Brack, Viktor 49
Brackmann, Albert 285–6
Brandt, Karl 49, 50
Brandt, Willy 642
Bratianu, Constantin I. C. 329
Breitman, Richard 159–60
Brindley-Barnett, Jeanie 485–6
Britain, *see* United Kingdom
British Empire 73–4
British Union of Fascists 86
Brizio, Edoardo 485–6
Bromberg (Bydgoszcz) 218

Broniewski, Władysław 479, 484
brothels in concentration camps 106
Brown, George 487
Brown-Fleming, Suzanne 242
Browning, Christopher R. 7, 128–40, 144, 423, 672
   on Order Police 145
   on origins of "Final Solution" 121
Brückner, Helmuth 282
Bryce, James 660
Buchenwald concentration camp 365, 375
   deportation of Gypsies to 276, 279
   memorial and museum 492–3
Bukovina 138, 327
Bulgaria 11, 138, 284
   antisemitic policies 331–2
   and deportation of Jews 104, 327, 331–2
   and Gypsies 278, 279
   and restitution/compensation 552
Bullock, Alan 114
Bülow, Bernhard von 130
Bülow-Schwante, Vicco von 130
Bund (Polish Jewish Socialist Party) 190
Bunzl, Matti 603
Bürckel, Joseph 298
Burckhardt, Carl J. 374
bureaucracy: paper trails 383–6
"Burnt Pearls" (Sutzkever) 431–2
Burnt Whole: Contemporary Artists Reflect on the Holocaust (exhibition) 464
Burzio, Giuseppe 332–3
Business Administration Main Office (WVHA) 11, 144–5, 369
Butterfly Songs (Brindley-Barnett) 485–6
Butz, Arthur 560, 567–8
bystanders, see on-lookers

Cabaret (film) 448
Cadogan, Alexander 266
Caisse des Depots et Consignations 547
Cambodian genocide 713, 725
Cameroon 62
camp sisters (Lager-Schwestern) 215
camp system 364–76
   14 f. 13: 367
   in 1945: 372–4
   death rates: and nationality 367
   and forced labor 356, 369–70, 371
   and genocide 369, 370–2
   mass killings in 367–8, 373
   subterranean factory camps 373
   survival: factors affecting 370
   T4: 367

   treatment in: and nationality 366–7
   see also concentration camps;
      death camps; forced labor camps;
      transit camps
Campbell, Ronald I. 268
Canada 521
Canaris, Wilhelm 250
Canaris Conspiracy 258
Canto Sospeso, Il (Nono) 484
Captain Beefheart (Don Van Vliet) 488
Carpatho-Ruthenia, see Felvidek
Carter, Jimmy 447, 504
Carto, Willis 563
Catholic Church 233–45
   and antisemitism 9, 26, 233–4
   and Auschwitz 600
   and denunciation of euthanasia 240
   hiding children 228
   and Nazi Party 234–6
   and Nazism 626
   and Nuremberg Laws 237–8
   as on-looker 9
   and persecution of German Jews 237–41
   and rescue of Jews 178, 180
   scandals involving clergy 238
CCDP (Citizens Committee on Displaced Persons) 521
CDCC (Council for Cultural Cooperation) 700
Celan, Paul 437, 486, 689
CENTOS (Federation of Associations for the Care of Orphans in Poland) 176
Central Committee of Jews in Germany 550–1
Central Committee of Liberated Jews for the U.S. Zone of Occupation 516
Central Immigration Office 314
Central Jewish Committee, Bergen-Belsen 512–14
Central Office for Jewish Emigration 298
Central Office for Jewish Emigration, Prague 300
Central Office of the State Judicial Authorities for the Investigation of National Socialist Crimes (Zentrale Stelle der Landesjustiz-verwaltung zur Aufklärung nationalsozia-listischer Verbrechen, ZdL) 535, 641
Central Resettlement Office for ethnic Germans, Łódź 314
Central Trading Society East 321
Cervelló, Jordi 485
Chagall, Marc 462
Chalk, Frank 673
Chaplin, Charlie 444
Charny, Israel 676

Charter of the International Military Tribunal, Nuremberg 527, 709, 711
Chelmno death camp 370–1
  carbon monoxide as killing agent 370
  gas vans 122–3, 136
  Gypsies at 277
Cheyette, Bryan 452
child beggars 224
Child of Our Time, A (Tippett) 480
child rescue 176
children 8–9, 218–30
  adaptability of 224–5
  attraction of Catholicism 228
  cult of the child 229–30
  disabled 49
  euthanasia programs 49, 218
  games 220–1, 225
  Germanization of 226–7
  hiding of 176–7, 228
  medical experiments on 219
  responsibilities of 224–5
  sense of identity 226–8
Children's Aid Organization (*Oeuvre de Secours aux Enfants*, OSE) 176–7, 228
Children's Bureau, Poland 176
China 62, 715
Chirac, Jacques 658, 659
Chocolate Deal, The (Gouri) 439
Christianity 620–31
  and antisemitism 30, 621–4
  and "Aryan Jesus" 9, 257, 261–2, 626, 628
  and democracy 30
  impact of Holocaust on 17–18
  and Jewish people 628–31
  and Nazism 624–8
  Positive Christianity 234, 254
  see also Catholic Church; Protestant Church
Christian–Jewish relations 620–1, 629–30
Christian Socialists, Austria 33
Christology 630–1
"Chronicle of a Single Day" (Goldin) 431
Chronicle of the Lodz Ghetto, The 401, 402, 433
Church Struggle (*Kirchenkampf*) 9
Churchill, Winston 267, 269, 525
Cinema Paradiso (film) 454
Citizens Committee on Displaced Persons (CCDP) 521
civil rights movement 446
Civil Service Law (7 April 1933): "Aryan paragraph" 251–2, 295
Claims Conference, *see* Conference on Jewish Material Claims against Germany
Class, Heinrich 35, 71

Clauberg, Karl 52
Clay, Lucius D. 518
Clendinnen, Inga 673
CODOH (Committee on Open Debate on the Holocaust) 565
Cohen, Boaz 17, 576–87
Cohen, Jeremy 623
Cold War 510, 601
collaboration 11, 93, 445, 446
  Christians and 625
  and culpability 40
  in mass murders 102, 103–4, 149
  motivation for 323, 652
  Norway and 336–7
  Poland and 285
  Switzerland and 162
  trials of 530, 577, 578–9
  see also Arrow Cross Party
collections of Jewish items 595
Collishaw, Mat 464
colonial culture 63
colonialism 11, 57, 68–77
  and antisemitism 71–3
  as necessary enabling condition for Holocaust 5
  reverse colonization 73
  see also living space
coming to terms with the past (*Vergangenheitsbewältigung*) 635, 659–60
Commander of the Exodus (Kaniuk) 439–40
Commission for the Indemnification of Victims of Spoliation 553
Committee for Jewish Refugees, Holland 171
Committee on Open Debate on the Holocaust (CODOH) 565
common design charge, US Army trials 526
communism 243
  and antisemitism 643–4
  mass murder of communists, in Latvia 149
  support for Palestine Liberation Organization 645
comparative genocide studies 2, 676
compensation 548–55
  Germany 549–51
  other nations 552–5
compulsory sterilization 40, 47–8
Compulsory Sterilization Law, *see* Law for the Prevention of Progeny with Hereditary Diseases
Comte, Auguste 667
concentration camps 11–12, 136
  Africans in 62
  brothels in 106

children's games 221
coping strategies in 211–15
evacuation of 374–5
forced labor in 356, 358, 369–70, 371
homosexuals in 282
inmate labor 139
liberation footage 13, 446
mass shootings 368
mothers with small children, treatment of 207
selection processes 207, 208, 215
see also individual camps
Concerto for Violin and Orchestra (Frankel) 482
Conference on Jewish Material Claims against
    Germany (Claims Conference) 549,
    550–1, 552, 555, 577–8, 583
Confessing Church (Bekennende Kirche,
    BK) 251, 252–3, 258, 259, 625–6
and antisemitism 256
as on-looker 9
Provisional Church Administration (Dahle-
    mites, Niemöller wing) 255
Connelly, John 10, 274–88
constitutional courts 653
constructivism 686
Convention on the Elimination of All Forms of
    Discrimination Against Women 718
Convention on the Prevention and Punishment
    of the Crime of Genocide, United
    Nations 20, 524, 690, 712–13, 724
Convery, Robert 485–6
Coppa, Frank J. 241
Cornwell, John 242
Council for Aid to Jews (Rada Pomocy Żydom,
    RPŻ) 166, 175–6
Council for British Jewry 172
Council for Cultural Cooperation (CDCC) 700
Council of Europe 659, 663, 700
Council of German Municipalities 130
Covenant on Civil and Political Rights 712
Crime Watch Advisory Board 717–18
Crimea 317
crimes against humanity 526, 527, 711
crimes against peace 711
Criminal Police (Kripo) 365
Croatia 11, 284, 286
antisemitic policies 333
and Gypsies 278
mass murder of Croats 101
Ustasha fascist movement 83, 284
Crowell, Samuel (pseudonym of Holocaust
    denier) 568
culture war (Kulturkampf) 234
Czech Republic

legislation against genocide and Holocaust
    denial 570
reparations 551
and restitution/compensation 552
Czechoslovakia 286
and refugees 171
and restitution/compensation 552
Sudetenland crisis 98
trials 530
see also Czech Republic; Protectorate of
    Bohemia and Moravia; Slovakia
Czerniakow, Adam 205, 225, 397

DAAD (German Academic Exchange
    Service) 284–5
"Dachau Blues" (Captain Beefheart) 488
Dachau concentration camp 119–20, 364, 365,
    375
deportation of Gypsies to 276
memorials and museum 492
"Daddy" (Plath) 601
Dadrian, Vahakn 674
Dahlemites 255
Daimler-Benz compensation payments 551
Dallin, Alexander 147
Danielsson, Carl Ivan 163
Danish Jews 163
Danish Red Cross 337
Danmarks Nationalsocialistiske Arbejderparti
    (DNSAP, National Socialist Workers'
    Party of Denmark) 83
Dannecker, Theo 137
Darfur genocide 602, 725
Darquier de Pellepoix, Louis 334
Darré, Richard Walther 42
Darwin, Charles 58
Davenport, Charles 45
Davidson, Charles 485–6
DAW (German Armaments Works) 371–2
Dawidowicz, Lucy 696, 697
Day of Remembrance of the Holocaust and
    for the prevention of crimes against
    humanity 659
Days and Memory (Delbo) 434
DC, see Deutsche Christen
de Jong, Lies 175
de Swaan-Willems, Truus 175
Dean, Martin C. 11, 340–51
death camps 333: see also Auschwitz-Birkenau;
    Belzec; Chelmno; Majdanek; Sobibor;
    Treblinka
"Death Fugue" ("Todesfugue", Celan) 437
death marches 107, 374

death squads, *see* Einsatzgruppen
Death's Head formations 142
Declaration of the Rights of Man and Citizen
      (1789) 56
"Declaration on the Relation of the Church to
      Non-Christian Religions," Vatican II 621
"Deep Pits, Crimson Clay" (Halkin) 483–4
Degrelle, Léon 652
Degussa compensation payments 551
Delbo, Charlotte 414, 417, 418, 422, 434
Demjanjuk, John 737–8
demographic engineering 54, 132–4, 138–9
Demorazza (Italian race agency) 91
denazification measures 635–6, 639–40
denazification process 260
Denby, David 454
Denmark 133, 174, 337, 530
"Denmark 1943" (Small) 488
dental gold 546
department stores 25, 62
Derr, Elwood 485
Desbuquois, Gustave 241
Descartes, René 685
Descent of Man, The (Darwin) 58
Dessau, Paul 482–3
Deutsche Bank 544
Deutsche Christen (DC, German Christians) 9,
      251–2, 257, 261–2, 625
Deutsche Forschungsgemeinschaft (German Re-
      search Foundation, DFG) 40
Deutsche Gesellschaft für Rassenhygiene (German
      Society for Racial Hygiene) 46
Deutscher Gemeindetag (German Council of
      Municipalities) 295, 296
Deutschtum 65
Diamond, David 486
diaries 6, 196–7, 204, 206, 209, 397–410
   Berg 206
   documentary diaries 12, 400–3
   documenting "Final Solution" 388–9, 390, 392
   Frank 229, 446, 569–70
   interpretive approaches 407–8
   Kaplan 189, 401, 409
   Klemperer 401–3, 408–9
   reception of 408–9
   reflective diaries 13, 406–7
   status as historical source 397
   synecdochical diaries 12, 403–6
Diary of a Young Girl (Nero) 485
Diary of Anne Frank, The (film) 446, 448, 449
Diary of Anne Frank, The (Frank) 229, 446, 569–
      70, 702
Diary of Anne Frank, The (Frid) 483

Diary of Anne Frank, The (Kesselman) 599
Diary of Love (Weinberg) 484
diaspora 185–7
Dibelius, Otto 256
Dies Irae (Penderecki) 484–5
Different Trains (S. Reich) 487
Diner, Dan 655
Dinur, Ben-Zion 583–4
disabled children 49
disabled people 45–6, 47
displaced persons (DPs) 15–16, 509–10
   and campaign for Jewish state 576–7
   camps 512–14, 516–17
   Jewish
      in American occupation zones 514–18
      in British occupation zone 510–14
      Polish 510, 512, 519
Displaced Persons Act, USA 521
DNSAP (Danmarks Nationalsocialistiske Arbej-
      derparti, National Socialist Workers'
      Party of Denmark) 83
Dobiáš, Daniel 485–6
doctrine of humanitarian intervention 710
docudramas 447, 455
documentaries 14, 446, 448, 451, 455, 596
Dolchstoß (stab-in-the-back) myth 6, 46, 65, 97
Doneson, Judith 449–50, 453
Dönitz, Karl 527
Dora-Mittelbau 107
Drägerwerke, Lübeck 360
dragnet operations (*razzias*) 175, 177
Drancy transit camp, France 334
Dreifuss, Havi (née Ben-Sasson) 404
Dresdner Bank 544
Dreyfus Affair 32
Driz, Shike 487
Drowned and the Saved, The (Levi) 424
DuBois, Josiah, Jr. 271
Duckwitz, Georg 174
Dwinger, Edwin Erich 387
Dwork, Debórah 8, 170–81

East Africa 62
East Germany 492–3
   and anti-cosmopolitan purge 644
   and Jewish question 643–5
   trials 532–3
Eastern Galicia 284, 320
   ghettos 345
economic crash (Krach) of 1873 25–6
economics 675
Edel, Yitzhak 481
Edelman, Marek 738

Eden, Anthony 268
education
    Jews banned from public schools 299
    segregation of Jews, in Austria 297–8
    see also Holocaust education
Education Ministry, Italy 91
Efer ve'Avak (Poliker and Gilad) 488
Eichmann, Adolf 98, 131, 243
    and Central Office for Jewish Emigration 298
    and deportation of Jews/Poles 314
    and "Final Solution" 136–7
    and Jewish desk of Gestapo 119
    and mass deportations 136, 303–4
    ordinariness of 670
    and resettlement of Jews in Poland 300
    and transports of Jews 105–6, 132
    trial of 446, 524, 531–2, 564, 579, 642
Eicke, Theodor 364, 365
Eingabenpolitik (policy of suggestion) 238
Einsatzgruppen 102, 134–5, 142, 149, 317
    in Belarus 318
    and "Final Solution" 121, 386–7
    murder of Soviet Jews 76
    and pogroms 148
    reports on killings 565
    targets 146
Einsatzstab Reichsleiter Rosenberg (ERR) 547
Einstein, Albert 42
Eisenhower, Dwight D. 515
Eisenman, Peter 496–7, 497
Eisner, Kurt 115
electrotechnical industry: forced labor in 356
Elegy for Anne Frank (Foss) 485
Elena, Queen Mother, Romania 329
Eleventh Decree to the Reich Citizenship
        Law 544
Eliaš, Alois 300
emancipation: and antisemitism 26–7
Emergency Rescue Committee (ERC), USA 178
emigration 131, 194
    forced emigration policy 266–7, 298, 300
Endlösung, see "Final Solution"
Enfants Gâtés (Séchas) 472
England, *see* United Kingdom
Engzel, Gösta 163
Enlightenment 56
Epp, Franz Ritter von 68
Erbgesundheitsgerichte (hereditary health
        courts) 48, 276
ERC (Emergency Rescue Committee), USA 178
Eretz-Israel, see Israel
Ericksen, Robert P. 9, 250–62
Erlebnis 140

Ermittlung, Die (Weiss) 484
Erntefest (Operation Harvest Festival) 138, 358,
        371
ERO (Eugenics Record Office), New York 46
ERR (*Einsatzstab Reichsleiter Rosenberg*) 547
Estate of Memory, An (Karmel) 435
Estonia 102, 317
Eternal Jew, The (film) 444
ethics 20, 722–33
    duty to speak 729
    failure of 728
    Holocaust as ethical absolute 726–8
    meaning of 722–4
Ethiopia 87, 88, 90
Ethnic German Liaison Office
        (*Volksdeutsche Mittelstelle*) 313
ethnic Germans (*Volksdeutsche*) 142, 149
    in Baltic states 100
    Hitler–Stalin Pact and 100
    in Poland 100, 132, 149, 313, 315
    resettlement of 100, 313–16, 321, 322–3, 545
    in Waffen-SS 149
eugenics 39, 45–6, 58
Eugenics Record Office (ERO), New York 46
Europa, Europa (film) 453
European Council: "Framework Decision on
        Combating Racism and
        Xenophobia" 659
European Union (EU) 650–64
    German presidency 659
    Holocaust
        Europeanization of 655–7, 660–3
        as founding myth for 658
        impact on 18
        integration as response to 653–4
        as negative "European identity" 657–60
    legislation against genocide and Holocaust
        denial 570
    meaning of 650–1
    politics of regret 655–7
euthanasia programs 48–51, 99–100, 219, 382
    adults 49–50
    Catholic Church's denunciation of 240
    children 49, 218
    handicapped people 99–100
    mentally ill people 100, 120
    T4 program 49–50, 120, 165, 367
    West German trials 536
Evangelical Church of the Rhineland Synod 621
Evangelische Sonntagsblatt, Berlin 256
Evans, Richard 571
Evian Conference 160, 177, 269
evolution, theory of 58

exhibitions
   After Auschwitz 464
   "America's Concentration Camps" 602
   Burnt Whole 464
   Wehrmacht photographic exhibition 150
   Witness and Legacy 464
   Wonderyears 469–70
   see also *Mirroring Evil: Nazi Imagery/ Recent
      Art* (exhibition)
existentialism 685–6
Exit-Dachau project (Gerz) 494
"Exodus 47" (Berland) 487
experimentation, human 40, 51–2
  on children 219
  on homosexuals 282
Expert Advisory Council on Questions of
      Population and Racial Policy 47
Ezrahi, Sidra DeKoven 464–5

Facing History and Ourselves (FHAO), USA 703
Fackenheim, Emil 609, 610, 612, 725
Fantasie in Gelb (Haid) 478–9
Fasching, Darrell 628
fascism 81–93
  and antisemitism 5, 82–4
  demographic policy 84–5
  racism and 82
fascist racism 86–9
Fascist Social Republic, Italy 92
Fatelessness (Kertész) 436
Fatherland Party 32, 64
Faulhaber, Michael von 237
Faurisson, Robert 560, 562, 566–7, 569–70
Federal Bureau of Investigation 178
Federal Compensation Law 549
Federal Republic of Germany, *see* West Germany
Federal Restitution Law 549
Federation of Associations for the Care of
      Orphans in Poland (CENTOS) 176
Fein, Helen 672, 676
Feingold, Henry 159–60
Feldgendarmerie (military police) 152
Feldman, Ludovic 485
Feldmühle Nobel compensation payments 551
Felman, Shoshana 698
Felvidek (Carpatho-Ruthenia) 327, 329–30, 331
Ferencz, Benjamin 362
Ferramonti di Tarsia, Italy 92
FHAO (Facing History and Ourselves), USA 703
Fichte, Johann Gottlieb 55
Fiehler, Karl 294
Fighter Staff Program (*Jägerstab-Programm*)-
      358, 373

films 13–14, 444–57, 473
  American 448–50
  documentaries 14, 446, 448, 451, 455, 596
  documenting "Final Solution" 387
  European 13
  French 451
  Golden Globe awards 445
  Gypsies in 456
  Hollywood and 13–14
  homosexuals in 456
  Italian 451
  liberation footage 13, 446
  Oscars 445, 451
  propaganda films 13
  scholarship
    first wave of 448–51
    second wave of 451–4
    latest wave of 454–6
  and stereotypes of Jews 449, 453
  trauma theory and 454–5
  West German 450–1
"Final Solution"
  commemoration of 386–9
  demographic reconfiguration and 138–9
  development of 134–7
  Gestapo and 119
  justification for 392
  moves towards 119–24
  "part-timers" and 384, 385
  SD and 119
  Wehrmacht and 150–2
Fink, Ida 435–6
Finkelstein, Norman G. 596
Finko, David 483
Finland 317, 321
First Congress of Holocaust survivors, Bergen-
      Belsen 514
Fischer, Eugen 39, 68–9
Fleischmann, Gisi 207
Flossenbürg concentration camp 365, 375
Fogelman, Eva 673
For a Look or a Touch (Heggie) 486
For Every Sin (Appelfeld) 436
forced emigration policy 266–7, 298
  Protectorate of Bohemia and Moravia 300
forced labor 11, 107, 354–62, 544
  civilian workers 356–7
  compensation payments 551–2
  concentration camps and 356, 358, 369–70, 371
  conditions at sites of 361
  destruction through work 359
  economic motives for 360–1
  in ghettos 349–50, 356

Hungarian Jews' survival rates 358
    profits from 546
    survival, influences on 358–9
forced labor camps (*Zwangsarbeitlager*)
        356, 372
forced labor policy 301–2, 303
forced labor sites 11, 361
Ford, Henry 29
Foreign Office, Germany 130
    documents 384
    Jewish desk 137
    and resettlement of Jews 133
Fortunoff Archive, Yale 419, 598
Forty Days of Musa Dagh (Werfel) 96
Foss, Lukas 485
Fossoli di Carpi transit camp 337–8
Foucault, Michel 686
Foundation for the Memory of the Shoah 553
Foundation Initiative of German Business
        (*Stiftungsinitiative der deutschen
        Wirtschaft*) 552
4+2 Agreements 551
Fourth Hague Convention (1907) 525
FPÖ (Freedom Party), Austria 658, 659
"Framework Decision on Combating Racism
        and Xenophobia" 659
France 11
    antisemitic political parties in 32
    antisemitism in 24, 27
    deportation of Jews 334
    emancipation of Jews in 27
    execution of black French colonial troops
        101, 142
    Gypsies in 280–1
    Holocaust education in 700
    Jews in 27
    legislation against genocide and Holocaust
        denial 570
    under occupation 334–5
    plundering of Jews 547
    and refugees 171
    reprisal policies 142
    and rescue of Jews 180
    and restitution/compensation 552–3
    trials 530
    see also Vichy France
Francisme, France 83
Franco, Francisco 163–4
Frank, Anne 227, 408, 485
    diary 229, 446, 569–70, 702
Frank, Hans 75, 122, 132–3, 277, 382, 527
Frank, Karl 530
Frank, Otto 569, 597

Frank, Shlomo 400
Frankel, Benjamin 482
Frankfurt Trials 484
Frankl, Viktor 417, 418
Freed, James Ingo 504
Freedom Party (FPÖ), Austria 658, 659
Freigabe der Vernichtung lebensunwerten Lebens
        (The Authorization of the Destruction of
        Life Unworthy of Life, Binding and
        Hoche) 48–9
French Revolution 56
Freud, Sigmund 42
Frick, Wilhelm 295
Fricke, Otto 260
Frid, Grigori 483
Friedländer, Saul 95, 129, 228, 405–6, 423, 424
Friedman, Richard S. "Kinky" 488
Fritsch, Theodor 35
Fritzsche, Peter 12, 381–94
From the Diary of Anne Frank (Morawetz) 485
Front for Reborn Poland 175
Front National, France 659
Fry, Varian 178
functionalism 129, 143, 275

Galich, Alexandr 487
Galton, Francis 45, 58
Garbarini, Alexandra 404–5
Garda, Bahr Idriss Abu 716
Garden of the Finzi Continis, The (film) 446, 451
Garel, Georges 177
gas chambers 566–9
    claimed to be air raid shelters 567–9
Gasperi, Alcide de 654
Gates of the Forest, The (Wiesel) 438
Gebhardt, Karl 51
Geehr, Richard 33
Gelbrun, Artur 480
Gellately, Robert 165
gender differences: and roles of Jews 8
General Commissariat White Russia 321
General Government (*Generalgouvernement*)
    ghettos in 11, 341, 342
    Jewish reservation 313
    Ukraine and 284–5
General-Siedlungsplan 75
Generalplan Ost (General Plan East, GPO)
        44, 75, 286, 287–8, 314, 320–1
Geneva Conventions 525
genocide
    anthropology of 674
    camp system and 369, 370–2
    definition of 524

genocide (*cont.*)
  legislation against 570
  non-cooperation of German allies 137–8
genocide prevention 676
genocide studies 2, 19
Genocide Watch 676
Genschel, Helmut 129–30
Gerlach, Jens 482
German Academic Exchange Service
    (DAAD) 284–5
German Armaments Works (DAW) 371–2
German Christians, see *Deutsche Christen*
German Communist Party (KPD) 644
German Confederation 59
German Council of Municipalities (*Deutscher
    Gemeindetag*) 295, 296
German Democratic Republic (GDR),
    see East Germany
German Empire 60–1
German Research Foundation (*Deutsche For-
    schungsgemeinschaft*, DFG) 40
German Society for Racial Hygiene (*Deutsche
    Gesellschaft für Rassenhygiene*) 46
German Union 34
German–Finnish treaty on population
    exchange 321
Germanization policy 44
  Poland 315–16
  USSR 101, 316–21
German–Soviet Nonaggression Pact,
    see Hitler–Stalin Pact
Germany 194, 635–46
  1848 revolution 59–60
  1871 constitution 61
  antisemitic organizations in 25–6
  antisemitic political parties in 32
  democracy in 64
  Holocaust education 695, 697, 699, 702
  industrial capitalism in 25
  and Israel 577–8
  legislation against genocide and Holocaust
    denial 570
  memorials and museums 492–7
  nationalism in 59–61
  post-reunification 645–6
  and restitution/compensation 556
  university students and antisemitism 29–30
  see also East Germany; West Germany
Gerz, Jochen 463, 494, 495
Gesetz zur Verhütung erbkranken Nachwuchses
    (Law for the Prevention of Progeny with
    Hereditary Diseases, 1933) 47–8, 276
Gestapa (Prussian Secret State Police Office) 364

Gestapo (*Geheime Staatspolizei*, Secret State Po-
    lice) 119, 384
Ghetto Fighters' House 582, 585, 597
ghettoization
  attritionist policy 133, 134
  patterns of 340–2
  productionist policy 133
ghettos 11, 133–4, 340–51
  in Baltic States 345–6, 349
  bartering 342, 349
  in Belarus 346–7
  black market in 343
  children's games 220–1
  conditions in 349
  coping strategies in 211–13
  economic restrictions 343
  forced labor 349–50, 356
  ghettoization, patterns of 340–2
  mortality rates in 342
  music in 14, 196
  open ghettos 343–4, 344–5, 348
  in Poland 11, 96–7, 119, 123, 137, 194, 341, 343–5
  resistance in 346–7, 350–1
  in Ukraine 347–9
  see also individual ghettos; Jewish councils
Giftgas Giftset (Sachs) 467, 468
Gilad, Yaacov 488
Gilbert, Gustave 669
Gilbert, Martin 159–60
Glatstein, Jacob 432, 609
Gleichschaltung (synchronization) 42
Glick, Srul Irving 485
Gliniany, Eastern Galicia 345
Global Treaty 550
Globke, Hans 276
Globocnik, Odilo 122, 315–16, 322
Glowno ghetto 343
Godesberg Declaration 257
Goebbels, Joseph 284, 286
  diaries 114, 122, 123, 392
  on Hitler's prophecies 122, 123
  and *Kristallnacht* pogrom 118
  propaganda 97, 103
  scandals involving Catholic clergy 238
gold 545–6, 547, 554, 555, 556
Goldberg, Amos 12–13, 397–410
Goldfein, Olia (Olga) 207
Goldhagen, Daniel J. 143–4, 408–9
"Goldhagen controversy" 143–4
Goldin, Leyb 431
Goldmann, Nahum 577–8, 638–9
Goldsworthy, Andy 505
"Good Night, World" (Glatstein) 432

Göring, Heinrich 68
Göring, Hermann 132–3, 527–8
  centralization of anti-Jewish policy 298
  decree on Catholic Church 238
  demand for Jew-free Vienna 297
  expropriation of Jewish property 129
  and "Final Solution" 136
  Four Year Plan for USSR 317
  and ghettos 340
  and Poland 285
Gottberg, Curt von 76
Gouri, Haim 439
GPO, see Generalplan Ost
Grabner, Alexander 530
Grandmaison, Olivier LeCour 675
Grass, Günter 451
Gray, Charles 571
Graziani, Rodolfo 84
Great Britain, see United Kingdom
Great Depression
  Jews as scapegoats for 82–3
  and refugees 170–1
Great Dictator, The (film) 444
Great War, see World War I
Greater Germany 10, 293–306
  coordination of anti-Jewish policy 298–300
  creation of 297–304
Greece: Sephardic Jews in 105
Greenberg, Irving 612–13
Greenberg, Reesa 464–5
Greenspan, Henry 13, 414–24, 673
Grey Zone, The (film) 455
Grimm, Hans 70
Grinberg, Zalman 516
Gröber, Conrad 239
Groß-Rosen concentration camp 366, 374
Gross, Jan 166, 600, 674
Gross, Walter 130, 131
Grossman, David 440
Grossman, Vassily 689
Grotewohl, Otto 637
Gruber, Ruth Ellen 600
Gruenwald, Malchiel 578–9
Grundmann, Walter 257
Gruner, Wolf 10, 293–306
Gulf War (1991) 587
Gundlach, Gustav 241
Günther, Hans F. K. 47
Gutman, Israel 165, 423, 584
Gütt, Arthur 47
gymnastics associations 59
Gypsies 65, 274, 275–81
  in concentration/death camps 276

deported to Auschwitz 280
deported to Buchenwald 276, 279
in films 456
mass murder of, in Latvia 149
and partisans 277
in Wehrmacht 277–8
see also Roma; Sinti

H-K-T Society (Hakatisten, Society for the
      Support of Germandom in the Eastern
      Marches) 70
Ha'avara ("Transfer") agreement 191
Habsburg Empire 26–7, 60: see also Austria;
      Hungary
Hadamar psychiatric asylum 226, 526
Hague Conventions 525
Haid, Percy 478–9
Haider, Jörg 658, 659
Halachic treatises and responsa 196–7
Halbstadt Colony 319
Halevi, Benjamin 579
Halivni, David Weiss 17, 607–14
  on prayer during/after Holocaust 612, 613
  on sin as cause of Holocaust 608–10
Halkin, Shmuel 483–4
handicapped people: murder of 99–100
Hanf, Anna, Marie, and Vaclav 226
Hannemann, Kurt 276
Hansen, Miriam Bratu 453
Hardship Fund 550–1
Hardyk, Joel 485–6
Harff, Barbara 676
Harrison, Earl 514–15, 521
Harrison report 514–15
Hartheim euthanasia institution 367
Hartmann, Karl Amadeus 481, 482–3
HASAG (Hugo Schneider AG) 357–8
Hasler, Alfred A. 162
Haupt, Joachim 282
Haupttreuhandstelle Ost (HTO, Main
      Trusteeship Office East) 545
Hayes, Peter 1–20, 540–57, 732, 737–40
Haynes, Stephen R. 17–18, 620–31
Heberer, Patricia 4–5, 39–52
Hebrew Lesson (Arad) 471–2, 474
Hechalutz (pioneer) movement 582
Hecht, Anthony 439
Hecht, Ben 480
Hegel, G. W. F. 729
Hegewald Colony 319
Heggie, Jake 486
Heidegger, Martin 640
Heilman, Samuel 593

Heimat (film miniseries) 450–1

Henze, Hans Werner 482–3

hereditary health courts (*Erbgesundheitsgerichte*) 48, 276

Herero people 62, 69

Herf, Jeffrey 18, 635–46

Hering, Ernst 319, 323

Hermlin, Stephan 484

Heroic Ballad (Finko) 483

Herz, Rudolf 464

Herzl, Theodor 502

Herzogenbusch concentration camp,
Netherlands 372, 374

Hess, Rudolf 71, 130, 527

Heuss, Theodor 637
"No One Will Lift This Shame from Us"
(Bergen-Belsen speech) 638

Heydrich, Reinhard 75, 129, 300
assassination of 304
and deportation of Jews 133, 301
and "Final Solution" 122, 136, 137
gas vans for Chelmno 122–3
and ghettos 340
and Gypsies in Protectorate of Bohemia and
Moravia 280
Jewish desk in SD 131
and resettlement of ethnic Germans 314
and RSHA 119
and Wannsee Conference 303

Hikind, Dov 467

Hilberg, Raul 140, 157, 159, 188, 326, 670, 683
and ethics 726–7, 728
on France 334
on Romania 328

Hilfswerk beim bischöflichen Ordinariat Berlin
(Relief Agency of the Berlin
Chancery) 239

Hilgenfeldt, Erich 219

Hillesum, Etty 400

Hillgrüber, Andreas 642

Himmler, Heinrich 6–7, 75, 114, 116, 129, 276
as architect of genocide 113
brothels in concentration camps 106
demographic engineering 132–3
and Eichmann's Nisko experiment 132
and ethics of killing 727
euphemistic genocidal terminology 381–2
and "Final Solution" 121–2, 124, 125, 566
and Gypsies 277, 278
military experience 115
move from selective to mass murder 135
and murder of women and children 388
and Operation Harvest Festival 358

and persecution of homosexuals 282
personality/background 114–15
Posen speech justifying destruction of Jews 97
and problem solvers 128
as Reich Commissar for the Strengthening of
Germandom 313, 317
and resettlement of ethnic Germans 313
and RSHA 119
on Slav work force 287
and SS 116–17
suspension of transports to Poland 301
unification of Reich political police
forces 364–5
and *völkisch* movement 116
and *Welteislehre* (World Ice Theory) 41–2

Hindenburg, Paul von 65, 252

Hinton, Alexander 674

Hinzert concentration camp 366

hip-hop music 488–9

Hirsch, Joshua 455

historians dispute (*Historikerstreit*) 642

historical discourse 683

historiography
and diaries 404–6
survivor testimonies and 422–4

Hitler, Adolf 6, 33, 34
assessment of 143
and Austrian Catholicism 627
and British Empire, admiration for 73–4
and camp system 365
and Catholic Church 234
and colonialism 68
and euthanasia programs 50, 382
and "Final Solution" 116, 118–19, 121–2, 123
and German "Garden of Eden" 135, 317
and humanity 730–1
imperialism of 73–6
and Jews as hostages in peace
negotiations 374
living space theory 311, 312–13, 314
and mass murder as military necessity 100–1
military experience 115
and new European order 651
and Nuremberg Laws 117
and persecution policies 305
personality/background 114–15
on Polish intelligentsia 287
Political Testament 124, 272
and problem solvers 128
prophecies and visions 122, 139
annihilation of Jewish race in Europe 99,
118–19, 123, 131
and Protestant Church 252

and racial hygiene 47
and racism 86
redemptive antisemitism of 116
responsibility for Jewish policy 113–14
view of Jews 115–16, 124, 187
and war of world views
     (*Weltanschauungskrieg*) 652
and World War I, lessons of 96
see also Mein Kampf
Hitler Youth 252
Hitler–Stalin Pact 100, 102, 132
Hitt, Jack 469
Hoare, Samuel 172
Hoche, Alfred 48–9
Hocke, Gustav René 388
Hodonin, Moravia 280
Hoheisel, Horst 494, 495–6
Hohenlychen 51
Holland, *see* Netherlands
Holocaust
    analogies 660–1
    antisemitism as necessary enabling condition
         for 4, 5
    awareness, diminution of 445
    and Christianity, impact on 17–18
    commemoration of 580–2
    consequences of 197–8
    as ethical absolute 726–8
    European integration as response to 653–4
    Europeanization of 655–7
         debate about 660–3
    as filtered through media 469–70
    as founding myth for a united Europe 658
    German documentation 381–94
         destruction of 393
    God and 607–9, 614
    in Israeli art 473–4
    in Israeli education 584–5, 595
    and Israeli security 585–7
    and Judaism, impact on 17, 611–14
    and Nazi Party's New European Order 651–3
    as negative "European identity" 657–60
    number of victims, estimated 197–8, 375–6
    ownership of memory of 468
    postwar Germany, impact on 18
    sin and 608–11
    and State of Israel, establishment of 198,
         561–2, 575–6
    and truth issues 681–91
    uniqueness of 696–7
    universality of 696
    and Zionism 198, 616–17
Holocaust: An Uprising in the Ghetto (Finko) 483

Holocaust and Ghetto Revolt Memorial Day
     (*Yom Hazicaron la-Shoah Ve-Mered
     Hagetaot*) 580
Holocaust and Heroism Memorial Day
     (*Yom Hazicaron la-Shoah
     Ve-Hagvurah*) 580
Holocaust commemoration 490–1: *see also*
     memorials and museums
Holocaust denial 16, 452, 454, 468, 560–72, 682,
     687–8
    and Arab–Israeli conflict 571
    arguments for 560–1
    legislation against 570, 658
    soft denial 571–2
    tactics of 562–6
         immoral equivalencies 562–3
    trials 570–2
Holocaust education 19, 695–704
    approaches to 696–8
    information sources 702–4
    schooling level 698–701
    venue type 701–2
Holocaust Forum, Stockholm 658
Holocaust Memorial Days 658, 701
    Knesset and 577, 580
Holocaust Museum Houston 703
Holocaust remembrance: new cultural practices
     of 17
Holocaust representation 475
    constructionist model 447
    exceptionalist model 447–8
    see also art; films; literature
Holocaust studies 1–20, 684–5, 737–40
Holocaust survivors 598–9
    and Israeli army 576–7
    see also survivor testimonies
Holocaust: The Story of the Family Weiss
     (television miniseries) 14, 418, 446–7,
     448, 449–50, 596
Homme Double, L' (Borland) 465
homosexuals 98, 106, 274, 275, 281–3
    castration of 283
    in films 456
    in music 486
Höne camp (Bergen-Belsen) 512–14
Honigman, Ana Finel 473
Hörbiger, Hanns 41
Horochów ghetto 349
Horowitz, Irving Louis 668
Horowitz, Sara R. 13, 422, 428–41, 452, 453
horror movies 456
Horthy, Miklos 329, 330, 331
Höss, Rudolf 119–20, 529–30, 564, 566

House of Terror, Budapest 656
HTO (*Haupttreuhandstelle Ost,* Main
    Trusteeship Office East) 545
Hudal, Alois 243
Hugo Schneider AG (HASAG) 357–8
Hull, Isabel 69
human rights law 709–20
    implementation of 713–14
    International Criminal Court 690, 714–15
    poverty and 718–19
Humani Generis Unitas (The Unity of the
    Human Race, encyclical) 241
humanities 680–92
    effect of Holocaust on 19
Hume, David 681
Hungarism 83
Hungary 11, 83, 327
    antisemitic political parties in 32
    antisemitism in 29–30, 32, 329–31
    Arrow Cross Party 83, 179, 279, 330, 331
    ghettos 341
    and Gypsies 278, 279
    Holocaust education in 700
    industrial capitalism in 25
    Jews in 27
        deportation of 104, 331
        enforced emigration of 88, 138
        mass murder of 331
        rescue of 178–9
        survival rates 358
    as on-looker 166–7
    and restitution/compensation 552
    transports to Auschwitz-Birkenau 105–6
    university students and antisemitism 29–30
Hunke, Heinrich 311–12
Al-Husseini, Hajj Amin (Mufti of
    Jerusalem) 105
Huyssen, Andreas 447
"Hymn of the Ghetto, The" (Loesser) 480

I Never Saw Another Butterfly (anthology of
    children's poetry and art from
    Theresienstadt) 485–6
IAGS (International Association of Genocide
    Scholars) 676
Ian, Janis 488
Iasi pogrom 318
ICRC, *see* International Committee of the Red
    Cross (ICRC)
ICTR, *see* International Criminal Tribunal for
    Rwanda
ICTY, *see* International Criminal Tribunal for the
    former Yugoslavia

identity
    children and 226–8
    Holocaust as negative European 657–60
    Jewish, and art 463–4
IDF (Israeli Defense Forces) 585, 586
If This is a Man (*Survival in Auschwitz,*
    Levi) 415, 417, 418, 433, 598
IG Farben 316, 357, 361, 368, 528
    compensation payments 551
IHR (Institute for Historical Review) 563–4
IKL, *see* Inspectorate of Concentration Camps;
    Patriotic People's Movement, Finland
immigration, illegal 518–20
Immortal Bartfuss, The (Appelfeld) 436
Imperial Germany 33–5
    and antisemitism 63
    as first racial German state 62
    German army 62
imperialism 60, 62–3
    of Hitler 73–6
IMT (International Military Tribunal) 526
In Memoriam Anne Frank (A Song of Strength)
    (Ridout) 485
In Memoriam Annei Frank (Feldman) 485
In Zikh movement 432
Independent Commission of Experts
    Switzerland–Second World War 162–3
Indigo Girls rock band 488
Indonesian genocide 713
informed consent 51
Insdorf, Annette 448, 449
Inspectorate of Concentration Camps (IKL) 11,
    364–5
Institute for Hereditary Biology and Racial
    Hygiene, Frankfurt 39
Institute for Historical Review (IHR) 563–4
Institute for the History of the
    New Germany 257
Institute for the Study and Eradication of Jewish
    Influence in German Religious Life 257
Institute of Contemporary History, Munich 641
insurance policies 543–4, 546, 547, 550
intentionalism 129, 143, 275
Interior Ministry, Germany 130
Interior Ministry, Italy 91–2
International Association of Genocide Scholars
    (IAGS) 676
International Bill of Human Rights 712
International Campaign to End Genocide 676
International Commission on Holocaust Era
    Insurance Claims 552
International Committee of the Red Cross
    (ICRC) 167, 329, 374

International Conference on the Holocaust and
    Martyrdom in Our Time 581–2
International Council of Christians and
    Jews 620–1
International Covenants on Human Rights 712
International Criminal Court (ICC) 690, 714–15
International Criminal Tribunal for Rwanda
    (ICTR) 714, 715–16
International Criminal Tribunal for the former
    Yugoslavia (ICTY) 713, 714, 716
International Institute for Holocaust
    Research 584
international legal rights 710
International Military Tribunal (IMT) 197, 526,
    527, 709, 711
International Monument to the Victims of
    Fascism, Birkenau 485
International Refugee Organization (IRO) 510,
    521
International Social Science Bulletin
    (UNESCO) 667–8
Ioanid, Radu 11, 326–38
Iran 601
Iraq 586–7
Ireland: neutrality of 161
IRO (International Refugee Organization) 510,
    521
Iron Guard, Romania 82, 86, 88, 328, 330
Iron Tracks, The (Appelfeld) 436
Irving, David 16, 560, 563, 565
    on Anne Frank's diary 569
    libel suit against Penguin UK and Lipstadt
        570–1
    trial of, in Austria 570
Islamophobia 603
Israel 17, 576–87
    Benedict XVI's visit to 572
    and Germany 577–8
    Holocaust
        education system and 584–5, 595
        and establishment of State of Israel 561–2,
            575–6
        in Israeli art 473–4
        and Israeli security 585–7
        as *raison d'être* of state 500–1
        survivors of, and Israeli army 576–7
    Holocaust education 695, 697, 699, 701
    and Iraq 586–7
    memorials and museums 500–3
    nuclear capability 586
    post-Zionism 662
    punishment in 531–2
    State of Israel as "Survivor-land" 575–7

Israeli Defense Forces (IDF) 585, 586
Israeli Independence Day 580
Italian Fascist regime 83–4
Italian Social Republic (RSI) 81
Italy 11, 84, 659
    African empire 89–90
    as ally of Germany 337–8
    "Aryanization" in 91, 92
    assimilation in 91
    deportation of Jews 337–8
    fascist antisemitism 5
    holding camps 92
    Jews
        measures against 90–1
        native Jews 138
        refugees 180
        rescue of 179
        wartime internment of 87–8
    measures against miscegenation 89–90, 91
    reprisal policies 142
    and restitution/compensation 552–3
It's the Real Thing: Self-Portrait at Buchenwald
    (Schechner) 466, 467

Jacob, Erich 282
Jacob, Lili 382
Jacob the Liar (J. Becker) 435
Jaeckel, Eberhard 642
Jäger, August 254
Jägerstab-Programm (Fighter Staff
    Program) 358, 373
Jahn, Friedrich Ludwig 59
Jakob the Liar (film) 454
Jakubowska, Wanda 445
James, William 685
Japan: and rescue of Jews 178
Jarecka, Gustawa 403
Jasenovac death camp, Croatia 278, 333
jazz 488
JDC (American Jewish Joint Distribution
    Committee) 190, 191, 192, 512–13, 518
Jedwabne, Poland 102, 318, 656
Jehovah's Witnesses 98
Jew Süss (film) 444
Jewish Agency 190
Jewish Anti-Fascist Committee, USSR
    192–3
Jewish-Bolshevist system 102–3
Jewish chroniclers 96–7, 108
Jewish Community (*Kultusgemeinde*),
    Vienna 173
Jewish Councils (*Judenräte*) 134, 193–5, 207, 341,
    346–50

Jewish Councils (*Judenräte*) (*cont.*)
  and underground organizations 346–7
Jewish Cultural Reconstruction 555
Jewish culture 590–603
  authority figures 597–9
  changes in narratives 592–4
  changes in practices 595–7
  effect of demographics on 591–2
  Holocaust remembrance controversies 601–2
  narratives, controversy over 594
  public profile 599–602
  "virtually Jewish" culture 600
Jewish desk(s) (*Judenreferat*) 130–1, 384
Jewish emigration 136
  Eichmann and 119
  forced 88, 103, 138, 266–7, 298, 300
  Madagascar Plan 133, 301
"Jewish experts" 130–1, 133
Jewish Fighting Organization 501
Jewish Historical Institute, Warsaw 597
Jewish identity: art and 463–4
Jewish Kulturbund, Germany 196
Jewish leadership 193–4
Jewish Museum, Berlin 596–7
Jewish Museum, New York: *Mirroring Evil: Nazi Imagery/Recent Art* (exhibition) 14, 461, 464–71
Jewish Partisan anthem ("Zog nit keynmol az du geyst dem letstn veg") 488
Jewish people 185–98
  1938 census of, in Italy 91
  assimilation of 115–16
  attacks on 98–9
  blocked bank accounts 543–4, 545
  and Bolshevism 76, 82–3
  Christianity and 628–31
  as colonizers of Germany 72, 77
  conversion of 115–16
  and crucifixion of Jesus 562
  crises of faith 195
  economic exclusion 129–30, 296–7, 298, 299, 383, 386, 542–3
    boycott of Jewish businesses 237, 294–5, 541
  emancipation of 26–8, 61
  enforced emigration of 88, 103, 138, 266–7, 298, 300
  flight from Germany 99
  history of 185–7
  mass deportations of 303–4
  measures against, in Italy 90–1
  obligatory middle names 384
  Orthodox 195

persecution of 187–8
  central/local policies 294–7
  gendered German policies 206–9, 215
  gendered response to 204–6
  intervention initiatives 191–3
  and preparations for World War II: 98–9
  property, seizure of 139
  in Protectorate of Bohemia and Moravia 299–300
  perseverance strategies 194–5
  postwar recovery 615–16
  racial definition 296
  Reform/liberal 195
  resettlement of 300–3
  rise of 27–8
  segregation of 301
    in education 297–8, 299
    in housing 299
  social exclusion 129, 296, 299, 386
  Star of David badge 103, 302
  youth movements 195–6
  see also Judaism
Jewish Question (*Judenfrage*) 128
  Protestant Church and 256–8
Jewish Refugees Committee (JRC), Great Britain 171
Jewish reservation, Lublin District 132, 133
Jewish Residential District (*Jüdischer Wohnbezirk*), *see* ghettos
Jewish resistance 8, 14, 213, 346–7, 350–1
Jewish Resistance Heritage Museum and Documentation Center, Western Galilee 597
Jewish Theological Seminary (JTS) of America 599, 608
Jodl, Alfred 383, 527
John, Gospel of 233
John Paul II, Pope 621
Johst, Hanns 387
Joint Distribution Committee, *see* JDC
Jonassohn, Kurt 673
Jones, Adam 675
Jones, David H. 19–20, 709–20
Joodsche Raad (Jewish Council), Amsterdam 191
Journal d'Anne Frank, Le (Lejet) 485
Journal for Racial and Social Biology 58
JRC (Jewish Refugees Committee), Great Britain 171
JTS (Jewish Theological Seminary) of America 599, 608
Judaism 607–18
  impact of Holocaust on 17

and prayer after Holocaust 611–14
  see also Jewish people
Judenfrage, see Jewish Question
Judenhäuser 299
Judenräte, see Jewish Councils
Judenreferat (Jewish desk(s)) 130–1, 384
Judeo-Bolshevism 76, 121, 125, 148–9
Judgment at Nuremberg (film) 446, 448
Jüdische Chronik (Dessau, Wagner-Régeny,
    Blacher, Hartmann and Henze) 482–3
Jüdischer Wohnbezirk (Jewish Residential
    District), *see* ghettos
judiska sången, Den (Pergament) 480–1
Jünger, Ernst 387

K cemu je slunce, kdyz není den? (Dobiáš)
    485–6
Kaczerginski, Shmerke 487
"Kaddish" (Galich) 487
Kaddish for a Child Not Born (Kertész) 436
Kaddish for Terezin (Senator) 485–6
Kaes, Anton 450–1
Kaiser Wilhelm Institute for Anthropology 39
Kaiser Wilhelm Society 44
Kajzer, Abraham 399
Kaller, Maximilian 233
Kalmanovitch, Zelig 400
Kaltenbrunner, Ernst 527
Kambanda, Jean 715–16
Kambanellis, Iakovos 486
Kamianets'- Podil's'kyi massacre 317
Kamiński, Aleksander 229
Kammler, Hans 373
Kaniuk, Yoram 439–40
Kant, Immanuel 56, 685, 732
Kaplan, Chaim 189, 400
  diary 401, 409
Karay, Felicja 208, 210, 215
Kardorff, Ursula von 388
Karmel, Ilona 435
Karsai, Laszlo 279
kashariyot (couriers) 213
Kasztner, Israel (Rezso) 578–9
Katowice: transports of Jews to Nisko 132
Katz, Esther 203
Katzenelson, Yitzhak 432, 480, 501, 582, 614–15
Katznelson, Ira 675
Kaul, Karl Friedrich 533
Kaunas (Kovno) concentration camp,
    Lithuania 334, 372
Kaunas (Kovno) ghetto 96, 349
  Kaunas (Kovno) pogrom 148, 318
Kelley, Douglas M. 669

Keneally, Thomas 452
Kennkarte (required identification) 176
Kerrl, Hanns 255
Kershaw, Ian 288
Kertész, Imre 436
Kertzer, Adrienne 702
Kertzer, David I. 242
Kesselman, Wendy 599
kibbutzim museums 501
Kiefer, Anselm 462, 463, 464
Kielce pogrom 519
killers 103–4, 106–7, 122, 142–52
  see also Einsatzgruppen; Order Police
killing centers, *see* death camps
Kimmelman, Michael 467–8, 472
Kindertransports 173, 267
Kirchenkampf (Church Struggle) 9
Kitaj, R. B. 463
Kittel, Gerhard 256, 257–8
Klarsfeld, Serge and Beate 531
Klausener, Erich 236
Klebanov, Dmitri 483
Klee, Ernst 260
Kleeblatt, Norman 464–5
Kleiberg, Ståle 486
Klein, A. M. 432–3
Klein, Astrid 464
Klein, Cecilie 209
Klein, Gerda Weissman 418, 598
Klemperer, Victor 384, 401–3, 408–9
Klepfisz, Irena 439
Kluger, Ruth 417, 418
Knesset
  Holocaust memorial day committee 580
  Holocaust memorial day debates 577
  Law of Remembrance of Holocaust and
    Heroism, Yad Vashem 582–3
Koblik, Steven 162
Koch, Erich 284, 347
Kochan, Günther 484
Kochavi, Arieh J. 15–16, 509–22
Kofman, Sarah 430, 729–30
Kohl, Helmut 496, 642
Kook, Hillel (alias Peter Bergson) 192
Korczak, Janusz 487
Korherr, Richard 381
Kosinski, Jerszy 689
Kosmala, Beate 166
Kosovo War 661
Kossak-Szczucka, Zofia 175
Köster, Adolf 72
Kovner, Abba 190–1, 197
Kovno, *see* Kaunas

Kox, Hans 485
Koylnbrener (Jewish Council chairman) 348
KPD (German Communist Party) 644
Krahelska-Filipowiczowa, Wanda 175
Krause, Reinhold 252
Kraut, Alan 159–60
Kreisau Circle 258
Kren, George H. 672–3
Kripo (Criminal Police) 365
Kristallnacht (Zorn) 488
Kristallnacht pogrom 98, 118, 129, 172, 206, 298, 365, 480
Křivinka, Gustav 485
Krstic, Radislav 716
Krüger, Wilhelm 345
Kruk, Herman 95–6, 401
Krupp compensation payments 551
Krystufek, Elke 464
Kuball, Mischa 464
Kuchenbuch letter 390–1
Kuitca, Guillermo 464
Kulturkampf (culture war) 234
Kultusgemeinde (Jewish Community), Vienna 173
Kuper, Leo 676
Kushner, Tony 160, 424
Kuspit, Donald 464, 468
Kvaternik, Slavko 122
Kwiek, Rudolf 280
KZ der Verlagerungsprojekte (subterranean factory camps) 373

La Guardia, Fiorello 490–1
labor camps 106, 138, 276, 279
LaFarge, John 241
Lager-Schwestern (camp sisters) 215
Laitman, Lori 485–6
Lambert, Raymond 400
Lament for the Victims of the Warsaw Ghetto (Gelbrun) 480
Lampe, Friedo 283
Landesarchiv Berlin 384
Landsberg, Alison 455
Landser (infantrymen) 150–1
Lang, Berel 19, 680–92
Langer, Lawrence 421, 450
Langlet, Valdemar 163
Langmuir, Gavin 622, 623
language: as marker of nationalism 57
Lantos, Tom 598
Lanzmann, Claude 14, 448, 452, 596
Laqueur, Walter 159–60
Last Chance, The (film) 445

Last Jew, The (Kaniuk) 439–40
Last of the Just, The (Schwarz-Bart) 438
Last Stop, The (film) 445
Latvia
  Germanization of 317, 320
  invasion of 102
  mass murders in 149, 317
Law for Combating Gypsies, Vagabonds and Work-shy (1926) 275
Law for the Prevention of Progeny with Hereditary Diseases (*Gesetz zur Verhütung erbkranken Nachwuchses*, 1933) 47–8, 276
Law for the Protection of German Blood and Honor 383
Law for the Restoration of the Professional Civil Service (1933) 43–4, 295, 383
Law of Remembrance of Holocaust and Heroism, Yad Vashem 582–3
Law of the Jews (*Statut des Juifs*), Vichy France 530
Le Chambon-sur-Lignon (Huguenot village) 180–1
"Lead Plates at the Rom Press, The" (Sutzkever) 431
League of Nations
  High Commissioner for Refugees Coming from Germany (Jewish and Other) 191
  and Israel 575
Lebensborn scheme 226–7
Lebensraum, see living space
Legion of the Archangel Michael (Iron Guard), Romania 82, 86, 88, 328, 330
LEGO Concentration Camp Set (Libera) 465, 467
Lejet, Edith 485
"Lekh Lekho" (Shayevitch) 432
Lemkin, Raphael 690
Lenard, Philipp 42
Lengyel, Olga 214
Leociak, Jacek 405
Leon (survivor) 421, 422
letters 12, 196–7, 400
  documenting "Final Solution" 388, 389, 390–1
Lety, Bohemia 280
Levi, Primo 92, 156, 203, 414, 416, 422, 434
  The Drowned and the Saved 424
  "News from the Sky" 732
  on unspeakable memories 421
  see also *If This is a Man* (*Survival in Auschwitz*)
Levinas, Emmanuel 726
Levine, Paul A. 7, 156–68
Levinthal, David 463
Levy, Richard S. 4, 23–37
Lévy-Hass, Hanna 407

Lewin, Abraham 406
Lewis, Bernard 623
Lewy, Guenter 278
Libera, Zbigniew 464, 465, 467
liberation and dispersal 509–22
Libeskind, Daniel 596–7
Libya 84, 87
Lichtenberg, Bernhard 165, 239
Lidice massacre 227
Liebehenschel, Arthur 530
Lieberman, Saul 608
Life Is Beautiful (*La Vita é Bella*, film) 14, 451–2,
    453–4, 596
limpiezza de sangra laws 623
Lind, Jakov 428, 689
Lindberg, Hans 162
Lindemann, Albert 27
Linnaeus, Carolus 56
Lippert, Julius 294
Lipstadt, Deborah E. 16, 159, 560–72
    Irving's libel suit against 570–1
Liquidation (Kertész) 436
literary theory 683
literature 13, 196–7, 428–41
    critical approaches to 429–30
    language, limitations of 433–4
    lifewriting 433–4
    novellas 439
    novels 435, 436–8, 440
    poetry 431–3, 437, 439
    postwar 433–4
    second generation literature 440
    short stories 435–6
    survivors, fiction by 434–40
    wartime 430–3
Lithuania 317, 318
    ghettos in 208, 345–6, 349
    invasion of 102
    legislation against genocide and Holocaust
        denial 570
    mass murders in 317
    pogroms 148–9
Littell, Franklin 621–2
    Live and Die as Eva Braun (Rosen) 472
living space (*Lebensraum*) 70–1, 310–23
    in eastern Europe 116
    expansion of 10–11
    Germanization of Poland 315–16
    Germanization of USSR 316–21
    Ratzel's concept of 310–11
Ljubljana 87
Łódź (Litzmannstadt) ghetto 133, 138, 342, 343
    children's games 221

deportation of Jews to 302
diaries 398–9, 400, 401, 402, 406
Gypsies in 277
women in labor force 212
see also Chelmno
Loesser, Frank 480
Lohamei Hageta'ot 501–2, 582
Lohse, Heinrich 277
Łokacze ghetto 348
London, Louise 160
London Agreements 549
Long Journey, The (Semprun) 436
Longerich, Peter 129
Lösener, Bernhard 130–1
Loshitzky, Yosefa 452, 453
Lower, Wendy 10–11, 310–23
Lublin ghettos 343–4
Luckner, Gertrud 239
Ludendorff, Erich 65, 70, 72
Ludin, Hanns 530
Lueger, Karl 33
Lumet, Sidney 446
Lupu, Nicolae 329
Lustig, Arnost 430
Luther, Martin 623, 626–7
Lutheran church 234
Lutz, Karl 163
Luxembourg 570
Luxembourg Agreements 549, 641
Lwów, Eastern Galicia 102, 318
Lydia (survivor) 421
Lysenkoism 41

Macedonia 138, 327, 331
McWilliams, Martha 464
Madagascar Plan 133, 301
Maglione, Luigi 244
Magnis, Gabriele Gräfin 239
Mährisch Ostrau 132
Main Trusteeship Office East
        (*Haupttreuhandstelle Ost*, HTO) 545
Majdanek concentration camp 218, 358, 366
    deportation of Jews to, from France 334
    evacuation of 374
    as holding camp for Soviet prisoners 367
    as killing center 371
    as memorial 498–9
    murder of Gypsies in 280
    Zyklon B as killing agent 370–1
Majdanek monument (Tolkin) 499
Majdanek trial, Düsseldorf 537
Malines transit camp, Belgium 335
Maltz, Moshe 403–4

Maly Trostinets 321
Man Who Cried, The (film) 456
Maniu, Iuliu 329
Mann, Michael 674
Man's Search for Meaning (Frankl) 418
Marahrens, August 252, 255
March of the Living 595
Marr, Wilhelm 58
Marrus, Michael 242, 245
Marx, Karl 643
mass mortality camps 373–4
Matteoli Commission 553
Matthäus, Jürgen 145
Maus (Spiegelman) 440, 463, 596
Mauthausen (Zawinul) 488
Mauthausen concentration camp 365
Measure of Our Days, The (Delbo) 434
media 237
    19th-century 57
    newspapers 25, 32, 513, 514
medicine
    as necessary enabling condition for
        Holocaust 4–5
    see also eugenics; experimentation, human;
        racial hygiene
Meierhofer, Marie 227
Mein Kampf (Hitler) 33, 143, 540–1
    land policy 311
    murder of Jews 116
    occupation of Germany by Jews 72–3
    racial policy 651
Meiser, Hans 252, 254, 255
Meisinger, Josef 282
Melchior, Marcus 174
Melson, Robert 673, 676
memoirs 12, 203, 204
    camp sisters 215
    coping strategies 214
    hiding 228
    humiliation of Jewish women 209
Memorial Garden of Stones, Museum of Jewish
        Heritage, New York 505
"Memorial to the Murdered Jews of Europe"
        (Eisenman), Berlin 496–7, 497
Memorial to the Victims of Fascism (Bašs) 483
memorials and museums 14–15, 490–505
    Germany 492–7
        counter-monuments 494–6
    Israel 500–3
    Poland 497–500
    USA 503–5
Memory, Responsibility, and the Future
        Foundation 551–2

Mengele, Josef 40, 51–2, 243, 465
mentally ill people 45–6, 47, 48, 102
mercy killing 48
Merkel, Angela 660
Merker, Paul 637, 644
Metz, Johann Baptist 628
Meyer, Konrad 314
Michael, Robert 627
Michman, Dan 8, 185–202
Middle East 62, 585–7
Milgram, Stanley 670–1
Milhaud, Darius 486
Military History Research Office, Freiburg and
        Potsdam 642
military police *(Feldgendarmerie)* 152
Miller, Arthur 601–2
Milosevic, Slobodan 716
Ministry of Church Affairs 255
Ministry of Eastern Territories 278
Ministry of Finance, Germany 384
Ministry of Food and Agriculture, Germany 384
Ministry of Popular Culture, Italy 91
Ministry of the Interior, Germany 384
Ministry of the Interior, Protectorate of Bohemia
        and Moravia 300
Minkovski, Eugène 177
Minnesota Museum of American Art: *Witness
        and Legacy: Contemporary Art about the
        Holocaust* (exhibition) 464
Minsk ghetto 321
Mintz, Alan 450
Mir ghetto 347
Mirroring Evil: Nazi Imagery/Recent Art
        (exhibition) 14, 461, 464–71, 596
    artists 464
    as critique of Israeli policy against
        Palestinians 470
    new strategies of representation 471–3
    and political hostility 470–1
    postmodern interpretation 471
    reaction of art critics 467–9
    reaction of survivors 465–7
    and war on terror 470–1, 475
miscegenation 85
    Italian measures against 89–90, 91
Mischlinge 226, 274, 275–6, 383
Mit brennender Sorge (With Burning Concern,
        encyclical) 238
Mittelbau-Dora camp 373, 375
Mizrahi Jews 603
Mogilev, Belarus 136
Molotov, Vyacheslav 190
Moltke, Helmuth James Count von 258

Monnet, Jean 653
Monowitz satellite camp 357
"Monument against Fascism" (Gerz and Shalev),
      Harburg-Hamburg 494, 495
monuments 479, 596–7
Moore, G. E. 690
Morawetz, Oskar 485
"More Light! More Light!" (Hecht) 439
Morgan, Philip 5, 81–93
Morgenthau, Henry, Jr. 192, 271
Morley, John F. 244
Morse, Arthur 158
Moscow Declaration on German
      Atrocities 525
Moses, A. Dirk 5, 68–77
Moses S. (survivor) 419
Mosse, George 624
Motýli tady nezijí (Křivinka) 485
Motýli tady nezijí (Reiner) 485
Movement for the Care of Children from
      Germany, UK 173
Mszana Dolna ghetto 345
Mulisch, Harry 437
Müller, Filip 567
Müller, Heinrich 386
Müller, Jan-Werner 18, 650–64
Müller, Ludwig 251, 252, 254
Münchener Post 281
Munich Conference 98
Munich Putsch 116
munitions industry 357–8
Munson, Steve 470–1
Münster war chronicles 387, 388
Museum of Jewish Heritage—A Living Memorial
      to the Holocaust, New York 505
museums 14–15, 596–7: see also memorials and
      museums
music 14, 196–7, 478–89
   early art music 478–81
   in ghettoes 14, 196
   Gypsies and 486, 487
   and Jewish resistance 14
   later art music 482–6
   popular music 487–9
Musik für vier Instrumente in memoriam: Lied
      der Moorsoldaten (Schröder) 482
Mussolini, Benito 81, 84
   and demographic policy 85
   on race laws 88
   and racism 86

Nama people 62, 69
Napoleon Bonaparte 59

NASA (National Aeronautics and Space
      Administration): Jet Propulsion
      Laboratory 567
National Bank of Switzerland 556
National Cultural Chamber 542
National Representation of German Jews
      (Reichsvertretung der deutschen
      Juden) 173, 191, 295
National Socialism/National Socialist German
      Workers' Party (NSDAP) 4–5, 81
   Catholic Church and 234–6
   Christianity and 624–8
   definitions of nation and race 55
   and homosexuality 281
   and humanity 730–1
   Jewish policy: phases of 7
   and New European Order 651–3
   occupation policy in eastern Europe 74–5
   and positive Christianity 234, 254
   and science 41–4
National Socialist Movement (NSB),
      Netherlands 83
National Socialist Office for Enlightenment on
      Population Policy and Racial Welfare 130
National Socialist Union of Doctors 276
National Socialist Workers' Party of Denmark
      (Danmarks Nationalsocialistiske
      Arbejderparti, DNSAP) 83
National Zeitung, Basel 237
nationalism 54–66
   in Germany 59–61
   language as marker of 57
   as necessary enabling condition for
      Holocaust 5
   rise of 55–7
naturalistic fallacy 690
Natzweiler concentration camp 366, 374
Navy League, Germany 61–2
Nazi Concentration Camps (documentary
      film) 444
"Nazi Concentration Camps" (film) 528
Nazi Party, see National Socialism/National
      Socialist German Workers' Party (NSDAP)
Nazis, The (Uklański) 472–3, 472–3
Nedic, Milan 333
Neighbors (J. Gross) 600
Nelson, Tim Blake 455
neo-Nazis: in Chicago 601
Nero, Peter 485
Netherlands 11, 133, 194, 372
   Committee for Jewish Refugees 171
   deportation of Jews 335–6
   Gypsies in 280

Netherlands (*cont.*)
  under occupation 335–6
  plundering of Jews 546–7
  and refugees 171, 173, 175
  and restitution/compensation 552–3
  transit camps 335–6, 372, 546
  trials 530
Netherlands State Institute for War
    Documentation 569
Neubacher, Hermann 297
Neue Gesellschaft für Bildende Kunst:
    Wonderyears (exhibition) 469–70
Neuengamme concentration camp 366, 375
Neumann, Franz 670, 683
Neurath, Konstantin von 300
Neusner, Jacob 593
"Never Again" (Remedy) 488–9
New Deal 270
Newmann, Barnett 462
"News from the Sky" (Levi) 732
newspapers 25, 32, 513, 514
Niedernhagen concentration camp 366
Niemöller, Martin 250, 251–2, 253, 259, 626
Niemöller, Wilhelm 258–9
Nietzsche, Friedrich 686, 727
Night (Wiesel) 417–18, 434, 611, 702
Night and Fog (documentary film) 444, 455
Night of the Long Knives 119
Night Porter, The (film) 451
Nisko: transports of Jews to 132
Niv, Kobi 454
Nochlin, Linda 471
Nono, Luigi 484
Noontide Press 563
Norden, Albert 644–5
North Africa 105, 603
Northern Transylvania 327, 331
Norway 133, 163
  under occupation 336–7
  and restitution/compensation 552–3
Not of This Time, Not of This Place (Amichai) 439
November Pieces (Zeisl) 481
Novick, Peter 161, 596
Nowhere in Africa (film) 455
NSB (National Socialist Movement),
    Netherlands 83
NSDAP, *see* National Socialist German Workers
    Party
Nuremberg Charter, *see* Charter of the
    International Military Tribunal,
    Nuremberg
Nuremberg Laws 47, 98, 117, 129, 130–1, 160, 276,
    296, 383

Catholic Church and 237–8
Nuremberg Principles 19–20, 712
Nuremberg Trials 524, 527–9, 690, 711, 713–14
  American successor trials 528–9
  "Doctors' Trial" 52
  Einsatzgruppen trial 529
  German documents 382
  punishment 527–9
Nurok, Mordechai 580
Nussbaum, Felix 196
Nyman, Michael 486

O, the Chimneys (Ran) 486
Obsession (Toporowicz) 467–8, 473
Occupations (Kiefer) 462
Oeuvre de Secours aux Enfants (OSE, Children's
    Aid Organization) 176–7, 228
Ofer, Dalia 161
Omaheke desert 62
on-lookers 7, 156–68
  bystander guilt 157
  European neutrality 161–4
  Greater German Reich 164–6
  Nazi-occupied Europe 166–7
  UK as 158–61
  USA as 158–61
On the Origin of Species (Darwin) 58
One Survivor Remembers (G. Klein) 598
One Survivor Remembers (documentary film) 418
Oneg Shabbat archive 196, 401
open ghettos 343–4, 344–5, 348
Operation Barbarossa 101, 134, 146–7
  invasion of Poland as rehearsal for 145–6
  and starvation of Slavs 316–17
Operation Carolt 510
Operation Harvest Festival (*Erntefest*) 138, 358, 371
Operation Reinhard 218, 315, 545–6
  camps 370–1
  carbon monoxide as killing agent 370
  see also Belzec; Sobibor; Treblinka
Operation T4, *see* T4 program
Operation Werwolf 316
Ophuls, Marcel 530
Oppenheim, Menachem 399
Order Police 102, 135, 142
  and "Final Solution" 121–2
  and mass murder in east 145
Organisation Schmelt 360
Organisation Todt 373
Orth, Karin 11–12, 364–76
Orthodox Church 178, 332
OSE (*Oeuvre de Secours aux Enfants*, Children's
    Aid Organization) 176–7, 228

L' Osservatore Romano 237–8
Ostara (racist publication) 115
Ostheer 146
Ostpolitik 70
Otwock ghetto 96–7
Our Hitler (film) 450–1
outmarriage 61
Oyneg Shabbes project 431
Ozick, Cynthia 439

Pacelli, Eugenio 233, 237: *see also* Pius XII, Pope
Pagis, Dan 437
Palestine 105, 198
    Arab opposition to Jewish immigration
        to 575–6
    and British mandate 575–6
    emigration of Jews to 171–2, 266, 268, 514, 515
    illegal emigration of Jews to 519
    Jewish national home in 575
    musical works 481
Palestine Liberation Organization 645
Palfinger, Alexander 133–4
Pan-German League 35, 71
Pan-Germany Party, Austria 33
paper walls 162
Papon, Maurice 531
Papon trial 524
Parsons, William 696
partisans 101
    action against 106–7
    anti-partisan campaign in southeast
        Europe 142
    Gypsies and 277
    Jewish anthem 488
    Jews and 195–6, 347
Partisans' Song 14
Partos, Oedoen 481
Passazhirka (Weinberg) 484
Pastors' Emergency League 251, 252, 257
Patriotic People's Movement (Isänmaallinen
        kansanliike, IKL), Finland 83
Patton, George S., Jr. 515
Paul, Randolph 271
Paul, St. 629
Paulsson, G. Steven 166
Pawnbroker, The (film) 446, 448, 449, 455
Pawnbroker, The (Wallant) 438–9
Paxton, Tom 488
Peace of Westphalia (1648) 710
Pearlman, Laurie Anne 676–7
pedagogy 596
Pehle, John W. 271
Penderecki, Krzysztof 484–5

Penguin UK: Irving's libel suit against 570–1
Penkower, M. N. 159
Perechodnik, Calel (Calek) 96–7, 108, 409
Peretz, Aharon 208
Perez, Avner 486
Pergament, Moses 480–1
Perl, Gisella 214
perpetrator motivation 143–5
perseverance strategies 194–5
Persilscheine 260
Peshev, Dimiter 332
Pétain, Henri Philippe 530
Peters, Carl 71
Pforzheim death toll 563
Pfundtner, Hans 130
Phayer, Michael 242–3
phenomenology 685
philanthropy 595
philo-Judaism 623
philosemitism 603
philosophers of suspicion 680, 685
philosophy 683–8, 725–7
Photographic Gallery, London 472–3
photographs 463, 595
    documenting "Final Solution" 387, 389–90
physicians: and euthanasia programs 49–51
Pianist, The (film) 455
Picard, Jacques 163
Picasso, Pablo 461–2
Pilsudski, Jozef 285
Pinochet, Augusto 716
Pinsk ghetto 349
Piotrków-Trybunalski ghetto 341
Pius XI, Pope 238, 241
Pius XII, Pope 180, 626, 654, 738–9
    and communism 243
    doctrine of supersession 242
    and European Jews 241–5
Plaszow labor camp 138
Plath, Sylvia 601
Plato 690
Playing for Time (Miller) 601–2
Ploetz, Alfred 45, 47, 58
"Poem about a Herring" (Sutzkever) 432
"Poetry in the Future Europe" conference,
        Weimar 652
pogroms 102, 131, 138, 148–9, 160, 318, 519:
        see also *Kristallnacht* pogrom
Pohl, Oswald 365, 369, 371, 372, 374, 529
Poland
    antisemitism in 27
    Germanization of 75, 315–16
    ghettos in 11, 96–7, 119, 123, 137, 194, 341, 343–5

Poland (*cont.*)
  Gypsies in 280
  Holocaust education in 700
  invasion of 98, 102, 132, 315
    as rehearsal for invasion of USSR 145–6
  Jews
    emancipation of in 27
    enforced emigration of 88
    flight of, to USSR 173–4
    looting of 545–8
    persecution of 189–90
    public profile of 600
    refugees 175–6, 180
  legislation against genocide and Holocaust
      denial 570
  mass murders in 100, 105
  memorials and museums 497–500
  nationalization of Polish victims 229
  Nazi campaign against 69
  occupation of 100
  as on-looker 166
  reparations 551
  and restitution/compensation 552
  university students and antisemitism 29–30
  Volksdeutsche in 100, 132, 149, 313, 315
  Volkstumskampf (ethnic battle) in 146
  wartime losses 287
  see also General Government; *Warthegau*
Polesje-Prypiat marshland 321
police forces
  anti-partisan campaign in USSR 146–7
  Feldgendarmerie (military police) 152
  Gestapo 119, 384
  Kripo (criminal police) 365
  Order Police 102, 121–2, 135, 142, 145
  and Poland, invasion of 146
  Secret Field Police 152
  Security Police (*Sipo*) 142, 365
  unification of 364–5
Poliker, Yehuda 488
Polish Committee of National Liberation 498
Polish Flowers (Tuwim) 484
Polish State Institute of Mental Hygiene 229–30
political science 675
politicide 676
politics of legal disputation 661
politics of regret 655–7, 661
Poniatowa camp 358, 371
Porajmos (the Devouring) 281
Porat, Dina 160
Portrait of Anne Frank (Scott) 488
Portugal 161, 178
Positive Christianity 234, 254

Posmysz, Zofia 484
Pot, Robert 486
poverty: and human rights law 718–19
POWs, *see* prisoners of war
Prada Death Camp (Sachs) 465, 465
Prager, Moshe 486
precious metals 545–6, 549
pregnancy 207–8, 219
Presidential Advisory Commission on
      Holocaust Era Assets, USA 555
Prevention of Genetically Diseased Offspring law
      (1933) 47–8, 276
preventive medicine 43
Preysing, Konrad von 238, 239, 240, 241, 244
Primo (Sher) 418
Primus, Romana Strochlitz 615–16
Prinz, Joachim 295–6
prisoners of war, Soviet 103, 106, 134, 147, 367–8
  as forced labor 368
  Hilfswillige 286–7
  starvation policy 147
problem solvers 7, 128–40
  motivation of 139–40
productionism 133–4, 343
Professional Civil Service Law (1933) 43–4, 295,
      383
propaganda 36–7, 296
  atrocity propaganda 6
  Goebbels and 97, 103
Protectorate of Bohemia and Moravia 173, 284
  "Aryanization" in 300
  Gypsies in 279–80
  persecution of Jews 299–300
Protestant Church
  and "Aryan Jesus" 257, 261–2
  Bavarian 253–4, 261
  Hanoverian 261
  hiding children 228
  national 251
  as on-looker 9
  regional churches (*Landeskirchen*) 251
  Reich Bishop 251
  and rescue of Jews 178, 180
Protestants 250–62
  and antisemitism 26
  and Jewish Question 256–8
  Kirchenkampf (church struggle) 251–3
  war-time attitudes, distortion of 258–61
Prussia 60
Prussian Secret State Police Office (*Gestapa*) 364
Przekrój (Warsaw illustrated magazine) 229
Psycho (film) 456
psychology 42, 673

psychotherapy 42
public health measures 43
punishment 524–37
    East German trials 532–3
    Israel 531–2
    Nuremberg 527–9
    other postwar trials/tribunals 529–31
    Soviet trials 525
    US Army trials 525–6
    West German trials 533–7

Quisling, Vidkun 336

race: rise of concept 56, 57–8
Race Manifesto (1938) 90
racial hygiene (*Rassenhygiene*) 39–40, 45, 47
racial imperialism: as necessary enabling
        condition for Holocaust 5
racial passports (*Ahnenpässe*) 383, 384
racial shame (*Rassenschande*) 209
racism 61, 82, 86–9
Raczymow, Henri 440
Rada Pomocy Żydom (RPZ, Council for Aid to
        Jews) 166, 175–6
Radak (David Kimhi) 610
Rademacher, Franz 133
Radom District 138, 344, 357–8
Ran, Shulamit 486
rap music 488
rape 8, 209–11, 676
Rapid Response Force (RRF), EU 718
Rapid Response Force (RRF), UN 718
Rapoport, Nathan 479, 503
Rappaport, Leon 672–3
Rarkowski, Franz 240
Rascher, Siegfried 51
Rashi (Shlomo Yitzhaki) 610
Rassenhygiene (racial hygiene) 39–40, 45, 47
Rassenschande (racial shame) 209
Ratzel, Friedrich 70, 310–11
Rauter, Hanns 530
Ravensbrück concentration camp 51, 365, 375
    Gypsies deported to 279
    human experimentation at 52
Ray, Amy 488
Ray, Gene 462, 463, 474, 475
"rayze aheyme, Di/The Journey Home"
        (Klepfisz) 439
razzias (dragnet operations) 175, 177
Reagan, Ronald 601, 642
Rechtman, Eva 176
redemptive antisemitism 116
Redgrave, Vanessa 601

refugees 174, 175
    children 172–3
    Great Depression and 170–1
    USA and 271
Reich, Steve 487
Reich, Walter 469
Reich Central Office for Combating
        Homosexuality and Abortion 282
Reich Citizenship Law: Eleventh Decree 544
Reich Flight Tax 542, 550, 554
Reich Imperial League 34
Reich Interior Ministry: killing of disabled
        children 49
Reich Labor Service 296
Reich legal code (1871): Paragraph 175: 281, 282
Reich–Vatican Concordat 234, 238
Reichenau, Walter von 102
Reichsvereinigung der Juden in Deutschland 299,
        304
Reichsvertretung der deutschen Juden (National
        Representation of German Jews) 173, 191,
        295
Reimann, Aribert 486
Reimer, Robert and Carol 451
Reiner, Karl 485
Reinhardt, Angela 226
Reitz, Edgar 450
"Rekviem po neubitym" (Galich) 487
Relief Agency of the Berlin Chancery (*Hilfswerk
        beim bischöflichen Ordinariat Berlin*) 239
religious commentaries on scriptures 196–7
Remedy (Ross Filler) 488
reparations 549, 550, 551
Report to the Führer on Combating Partisans
        (No. 51, December 1942) 565
Requiem Ebraico (Zeisl) 481
Requiem for the Victims of Nazi Persecution
        (Kleiberg) 486
Requiem für Kaza Kathárinna (G. Rosenfeld) 486
rescuers 8, 170–81, 351, 482, 738
    Beitz 361
    in Denmak 174, 337
    false papers for Jews 176
    at forced labor sites 361
    hiding Jews 175–7, 195, 227–8, 336
    pre-war 170–3
    Schindler, Oskar 361, 453
    Research Institute for Racial Hygiene and
        Population Biology 276
resistance 8, 14, 213, 346–7, 350–1: *see also*
        partisans
Resnais, Alain 444
restitution (*Wiedergutmachung*) 548–55, 637

restitution *(Wiedergutmachung)* *(cont.)*
  Germany 548–9
  other nations 551, 552–5
retributive justice 716–17
Reuter, Ernst 637
revisionism 563–4
revolutionary antisemitism 33–7
Rhapsody (Spellman) 478
Rheinstahl compensation payments 551
Ribbentrop, Joachim von 332
Ricorda cosa ti hanno fatto in Auschwitz
    (Nono) 484
"Ride 'Em Jewboy" (Friedman) 488
Ridout, Godfrey 485
Riefenstahl, Leni 444
Riga concentration camp 372
  deportation of Jews to 302
  and experimental gassing 136
Righteous Gentiles 258
Righteous Persons Foundation 598
Ringelblum, Emanuel 190, 196, 204, 221–2
  on diaries 398, 399
  diary of 401
  on gendered response to persecution of
    Jews 205
  on Holocaust literature 431
Ringelheim, Joan 203
Ritter, Heinz 344
Ritter, Robert 275–6
road construction schemes: and destruction of
    Jews through work 359
Röhm, Ernst 274, 281–2
Röhm Purge 236
Roma 47, 219
  in Auschwitz 106, 280, 373
  deportation to Transnistria 278–9, 327
  and human experimentation 40
  mass murder of 101, 102
  and music 486, 487
  and restitution 555
  see also Gypsies; Sinti
Romania 11
  deportation of Gypsies to Transnistria
    278–9, 327
  deportation of Jews 104, 327, 328–9
  ethnic Germans in 100
  forced emigration of Jews 88, 103
  ghettos 341
  Holocaust education in 700
  Iron Guard 82, 86, 88, 328, 330
  legislation against genocide and Holocaust
    denial 570
  mass murder of Jews 138, 327

and restitution/compensation 552
university students and antisemitism 29–30
Romberg, Hans 51
Roosevelt, Eleanor 229, 521
Roosevelt, Franklin D. 160, 178, 269–71, 509
Rorty, Richard 686–7, 689
"Rosa" (Ozick) 439
Roschmann, Eduard 243
Rosen, Roee 464, 470, 472, 474
Rosenberg, Alfred 71, 238, 255, 277, 527, 651, 652
  and euphemistic genocidal terminology 382
  justification for "Final Solution" 392
  and living space policy 311, 320
Rosenberg, Hans 25
Rosenfeld, Alvin 450
Rosenfeld, Gerhard 486
Rosenfeld, Oskar 406
Rosensaft, Josef (Yossel) 512, 513, 517
Rosensaft, Menachem 467
Ross, Henryk 221
Rossino, Alexander 146
Roth, John K. 1–20, 722–33, 737–40
Roth, Philip 689
Rothenberg, Ellen 464
Rothko, Mark 462
Rotta, Angelo 163, 179
Royal Festival Hall, London: *After Auschwitz:*
    Responses to the Holocaust in Contempo-
    rary Art (exhibition) 464
Royal Prussian Colonization Commission 70
RPZ (*Rada Pomocy Żydom*, Council for Aid to
    Jews) 175–6
RRF (Rapid Response Force), EU 718
RRF (Rapid Response Force), UN 718
RSHA (*Reichssicherheitshauptamt*, Reich
    Security Main Office) 119, 144–5, 174, 299
  documents 384–5, 386
  and "Final Solution" 122
  investigation into 533, 536–7
  and mass deportations 300, 301, 303, 304
RSI (Italian Social Republic) 81
Rubenstein, Richard 242, 609, 610
Rubin, Agi 419, 420–1
Rüdin, Ernst 47
Ruether, Rosemary 622, 630
Rufeisen, Oswald 347
Ruff, Siegfried 51
Rumkowski, Mordecai Chaim 401
Rummel, R. J. 675
Rürup, Reinhard 26–7
Russian Empire
  antisemitism in 24, 27
  Bolshevik revolution 82–3

emancipation of Jews in 27
Russian Federation
    and ICC 715
    reparations 551
Ruzicka, Peter 486
Rwandan genocide 676–7, 713, 717, 725

SA (*Sturmabteilung*) 118, 281–2, 294–5
Saar region 296
Sachs, Nelly 486
Sachs, Tom 464, 465, *465*, 467, 468, 469
Sachsenhausen concentration camp
    119–20, 276, 365, 375, 532
Saddam Hussein 586
St. Francis Waldbreitbach religious
    community 238
St. Josefspflege children's home 226
Saliège, Jules-Gérard 180, 228
Salomon, Andrée 177
Saltz, Jerry 472–3
Saltzmann, Lisa 464–5
Samoa 62
Sánchez, José 243–4
Sandomierz ghetto 344
Santi Quattro Coronati, Rome 245
Santner, Eric 450–1
Sanz Briz, Angel 164
"sardine-packing" 135
satellite camps (*Aussenlager*) 356
satellite states
    controlled 332–3: *see also* Croatia; Serbia;
        Slovakia
    opportunistic 326–32: *see also* Bulgaria;
        Hungary; Romania
Sauckel, Fritz 369
Saxton, Libby 455
Scandinavian Jews 163
Schacht, Hjalmar 118
Schechner, Alan 464, 466, 467, 470, 474
Schindler, Oskar 361, 453
Schindler's List (film) 14, 450, 451–3, 455, 456,
    596, 702
Schjeldahl, Peter 468, 471–2
"Schlaflied für Tanepen" (Biermann) 487
Schleunes, Karl 129
Schlink, Bernard 689
Schlöndorff, Volker 451
Schmitt, Carl 651
Schmitz, Elisabeth 258
Schnock, Frieder 495
Schoenberg, Arnold 479, 484
Schoenfield, Paul 486

Scholars' Conference on the Holocaust and the
    Churches 621
Schön, Waldemar 134
Schönerer, Georg von 33
Schönhaus, Cioma 258
Schreiber, Christian 236
Schröder, Hanning 482
Schubert, Franz 235–6
Schultz, Bruno 196
Schultz, Irena 176
Schulweis, Harold 614
Schumacher, Kurt 637–8
Schuman, Robert 654
Schumann, Hirst 52
Schutzmannschaften (auxiliary police units) 135,
    150, 152
Schutzstaffel, *see* SS
Schwartz, Erna 226
Schwartz, Joseph J. 515
Schwarz-Bart, André 438
Schweber, Simone 19, 695–704
science 39–52
    as necessary enabling condition for
        Holocaust 4–5
Scott, Tony 488
SD (*Sicherheitsdienst*, Security Service) 119, 131,
    193
    documents 384
Search, The (film) 445
Sebald, W. G. 440
Sebastian, Mihail 400
Séchas, Alain 464, 472
Second Vienna Award 322
Second World War, *see* World War II
Secours Suisse aux Enfants (Swiss Relief for
    Children) 180
Secret Field Police 152
Secret State Police, *see* Gestapo
Security Council, United Nations 713–14, 717–18
Security Police (*Sipo*) 142, 365
See Under: Love (D. Grossman) 440
self-determination 662
Semelin, Jacques 675
Semprun, Jorge 436
Senator, Ronald 485–6
Sendlerowa, Irena 176
Senesh, Hannah 502
Sephardic Jews 105
Serbia 135, 278, 284, 333
    mass murder of Serbs 101
Sergi, Giuseppe 86
sermons 196–7

settler colonialism 11
sexual violence 209–11, 676
SHAEF (Supreme Headquarters Allied
    Expeditionary Force) 509
Shahn, Ben 461–2
Shalav-Gerz, Esther 463
Shalev, Esther 494, 495
Shandler, Jeffrey 17, 450, 590–603
Sharf, Andrew 158
Shawl, The (Ozick) 439
Shawn, Karen 696
Shayevitch, Simcha Bunim 432
She'erit Hapletah (Surviving Remnant)
    Convention, Munich 516
Shenhabi, Mordechai 581, 583
Sher, Anthony 418
Shik, Na'ama 214–15
Shiloh, Ailon 674
Shoah! (Blake) 488
Shoah (documentary film) 14, 448, 455, 596
Shop on Main Street, The (film) 446
Shostakovich, Dmitri 483
Sicily 105
Sidor, Charles 244
Siemens compensation payments 551
Sierakowiak, David 400
Sieyès, Abbé 57
Silence of the Lambs (film) 456
Simon Wiesenthal Center, Los Angeles 597
sin: and Holocaust 608–11
Siniza i Fumo (Akiva) 486
Sinti 48
    children 219, 226
    and music 486, 487
    see also Gypsies; Roma
Sipo (Security Police) 142, 365
situational antisemitism 29
Six Day War 586, 593
Sixth Army: defeat of 104
Skarzisko-Kamienna plant, Poland 357–8
Skarzysko labor camp 210, 215
skepticism 686
slander laws 381
slave labor, see forced labor
slavery 56, 57
Slavs 65, 274–5, 283–7
    assimilation of 286
    in Italy 84
    starvation of, in order to feed Germans 317
    transfer of prisoners to work camps 106
    see also Bulgaria; Croatia; Czechoslovakia;
        Poland; Protectorate of Bohemia and
        Moravia; Slovakia; USSR

"Sleep My Child" (Vars) 487
Slepak, Cecilia 212
Slovakia 244, 284
    antisemitic policies 332–3
    collaboration 446
    and Gypsies 278, 279
    Holocaust education in 700
Slovenia 87
Small, Fred 488
Smith, Roger 676
smuggling: children and 225
Sobibor death camp 50, 106, 280, 334, 336, 370
Social Darwinism 58, 85
Social Democratic Party (SPD), Germany 61, 281
social sciences 667–77
    21st-century 673–5
    effect of Holocaust on 18–19
    and evil 670
    postwar 668–73
Society for the Support of Germandom in the
    Eastern Marches 70
Society of Friends 180
Society of St. Pius X 572
sociology 673–4
Solkoff, Norman 673
Sommer, Karl 260
Sommer, Margarete 239
Sonderbehandlung (special treatment) 564
Sonderkommando R (Special Command
    Russia) 318
Sonderkommandos 398, 423
Song for Hope, A (Diamond) 486
Song of Terezin (Waxman) 485
Song of the Murdered Jewish People, The
    (Katzenelson) 432, 480, 614–15
Songs of Children (Convery) 485–6
Sonnenstein euthanasia institution 367
Sophie's Choice (film) 448
Sorrow and the Pity, The (documentary
    film) 446, 451, 530
Soul of Wood (Lind) 428
Sousa Mendes, Aristedes de 161, 178
South Africa 172, 700
South America 172, 192
Southwest Africa 62, 69
sovereign immunity 710–11
sovereign power: definition of 710
Soviet Union, see USSR
Spain 163–4, 570
Sparks of Glory (Schoenfield) 486
SPE (Stanford Prison Experiment) 671–2
Speer, Albert 369, 527, 528, 640
Spellman, Leo 478

Spicer, Kevin P. 9, 233–45
Spiegelman, Art 440, 463, 464, 596, 689
Spielberg, Steven 451–3, 456, 596, 597–8
Spitz, Ellen Handler 464–5
Spoerer, Mark 11, 354–62
Sports Palace scandal 252
"Spring 5702" (Shayevitch) 432
SS (*Schutzstaffel*) 7
    anti-partisan campaign in USSR 146–7
    "Aryan race" research, funding for 42
    Business Administration Main Office
        (WVHA) 11, 144–5, 369
    and Central Office for Jewish Emigration 298
    Himmler and 116–17
    and invasion of Poland 146
    and resettlement of Jews 133
    see also Einsatzgruppen
stab-in-the-back (*Dolchstoß*) myth 6, 46, 65, 97
Stafford, William 732
Stahlecker, Franz Walter 148
Stalin, Josef 160, 268, 269, 525
Stalingrad: defeat at 104
Stanford Prison Experiment (SPE) 671–2
Stangl, Franz 106, 243
Stanton, Gregory 676
Stara Gradiska death camp, Croatia 333
Stargardt, Nicholas 8–9, 218–30
Stark, Hans 566–7
Stark, Johannes 42
starvation policy 147
Statut des Juifs (Law of the Jews), Vichy
    France 530
Staub, Ervin 676–7
Steigmann-Gall, Richard 627
Steinmetz, G. 70
Steinweis, Alan E. 6–7, 113–25, 600
Stevens, George 446, 449
Steyr-Daimler-Puch AG 368
Stier, Oren Baruch 454–5
Stiftungsinitiative der deutschen Wirtschaft
    (Foundation Initiative of German
    Business) 552
Stih, Renata 495
Stoecker, Adolf 29
Stoppelenburg, Willem 486
Stratton, William G. 521
Strauch, Eduard 321
Straus, Scott 675
Streicher, Julius 129, 131, 527, 528
Stroop, Jürgen 388
Stroop Report 382, 388
student associations 59
Sturmabteilung, see SA (*Sturmabteilung*)

Stuttgart Declaration of Guilt 260–1, 620
Stutthof labor camp 368, 374, 375, 498
Subliminal (Ya'akov Shimoni) 488–9
subterranean factory camps (*KZ der
    Verlagerungsprojekte*) 373
Sudetenland crisis 98
Suedfeld, Peter 673
Sugihara, Chiune 178
Suite in memoriam (Edel) 481
Suite Terezín (Berman) 479
Summi Pontificatus (On the Unity of Human
    Society, encyclical) 241
Sung Heroes (Scott) 488
supersessionism 242–3, 257, 628
Supreme Headquarters Allied Expeditionary
    Force (SHAEF) 509
*Survival in Auschwitz, see If This is a Man
    (Survival in Auschwitz*, Levi)
Survivor from Warsaw, A (Schoenberg) 484
survivor testimonies 13, 414–24, 596, 617
    and audience 416–20
    and historiography 422–4
    origins of 415–16
    unspeakable memories 420–2
Survivors of the Shoah Visual History
    Foundation 419, 597–8
Sutzkever, Abraham (Avrom) 431–2
Sweden 321
    and Jewish refugees 174
    neutrality of 161–3
    paper walls 162
Swedish Red Cross 374–5
Swiss National Bank 555
Swiss Relief for Children (*Secours Suisse aux
    Enfants*) 180
Switzerland
    legislation against genocide and Holocaust
        denial 570
    neutrality of 161–3
    paper walls 162
    and restitution/compensation 554–5, 556
Syberberg, Hans-Jürgen 450
Symphony No. 6 in A minor, Op. 79
    (Weinberg) 483–4
Symphony No. 8 in G major, opus 83
    (Weinberg) 484
Symphony no. 9 ("Lines That Escaped
    Destruction"), Op. 93 (Weinberg) 484
*Symphony no. 13 in B-flat Minor (Babi Yar
    Symphony)*, Op. 113 (Shostakovich) 483
Symphony no. 21 ("In Memory of the Victims of
    the Warsaw Ghetto"), Op. 152
    (Weinberg) 484

synchronization (*Gleichschaltung*) 42
Szabó, István 455
Szálasi, Ferenc 83, 331
Szawernowski, Andrej 228
Szeps, Fela 406
Sztojay, Dome 331

T4 program 120, 165, 367
    physicians and 49–50
Talmud 607
Tamir, Shmuel 578–9
Tamir, Tali 469–70
"Tattoo" (Ian) 488
Taylor, A. J. P. 114
Taylor, Charles 716
teenagers: effects of war on 230
Temporary Committee to Help Jews,
    Poland 175–6
Ten Points of Seelisberg 620–1
Tesch & Stabenow (company) 529: *see also*
    Zyklon B gas
theft 16, 541–8
theodicy 593, 607–11
Theodorakis, Mikis 486
Theological Dictionary of the New Testament,
    The 256
Theresienstadt Family Camp 373
Theresienstadt ghetto 304, 336, 337, 341
    abortion in 208
    children's pictures 222–3
    music in 14, 196
Thessaloniki 341
Third Geneva Convention (1929) 525
"This Train Revised" (Ray) 488
This Way for the Gas, Ladies and Gentlemen
    (Borowski) 435
Thompson, William 667
Thrace 138, 327, 331
3.62 Square Metres: 3 pieces for solo flute
    (Pot) 486
Tin Drum, The (film) 451
Tippett, Michael 480
Tiso, Josef 244, 333, 530
To Be or Not to Be (film) 444
"To the Heroes of the Warsaw Ghetto"
    (N. Rapoport) 479
To the Memory of the Babi Yar Martyrs
    (Klebanov) 483
"Todesfugue" ("Death Fugue," Celan) 437
Togo 62
Tolkin, Viktor 499
Toll, Nelly 227
Toporowicz, Maciej 464, 467–8, 473

"Torture" (Améry) 434
totalitarianism theory 114
Totten, Samuel 696
tourism 596
Town Beyond the Wall, The (Wiesel) 437–8
"Train for Auschwitz" (Paxton) 488
Train of Life (film) 454, 456
transit camps 334–5, 337–8, 372, 546
transit ghettos 344
Transjordan 575
Transnistria, Ukraine 103, 138, 278–9, 327, 341
trauma theory 454–5
Traverso, Enzo 675
Trawniki camp 358, 371
Treblinka death camp 50, 106, 137, 280, 370
Trial of the Major German War Criminals
    527–8
Triumph of the Will (film) 444
Trocmé, André 180
Truce, The (film) 451
Truman, Harry S. 514, 515, 520, 521
"Trustees for the Monument of Atonement at
    the Concentration Camp Dachau,
    The" 492
truth issues 681–91
Tuka, Vojtech 332–3
Tunisia 105
Turkey 161
Tuwim, Julian 484
"27. April 1945" (Hartmann) 481
twin research 39, 40, 51–2
221st Security Division 151
253rd Infantry Division 151
Tzili: The Story of a Life (Appelfeld) 436

Ugandan genocide 713
Uklański, Piotr 464, 472–3, 472–3
Ukraine 71
    and General Government 284–5
    Germanization of 317, 318–19
    ghettos 347–9
    Holocaust education in 700
    mass murders in 102, 317, 318, 319
    pogroms 102, 149, 318
    reparations 551
    and starvation policy 147
Ukrainian Relief Committee 284
Ulbricht, Walter 637, 643
Ullman, Micha 494
UNESCO (United Nations Educational, Scien-
    tific and Cultural Organization) 667–8
Unfair Competition (film) 451
United Bank of Switzerland 555, 556

United Kingdom 173
and antisemitism 24
Holocaust education 699–700, 702
and Jewish DP problem 171, 172–3, 518–19
Jewish Refugees Committee (JRC) 171
and Middle East 511
as on-looker 158–61
response to Holocaust 267–8
United Nations (UN) 19–20, 525, 659
Convention on the Elimination of All
    Forms of Discrimination Against
    Women 718
Convention on the Prevention and
    Punishment of the Crime of
    Genocide 20, 524, 690, 712–13, 724
Covenant on Civil and Political Rights 712
Nuremberg Principles 19–20
Rapid Response Force (RRF) 718
Relief and Rehabilitation Administration
    (UNRRA) 509, 510, 512–13
Universal Declaration of Human Rights 20,
    712, 724
United Nations Charter 712
United States Holocaust Memorial Museum
    (USHMM), Washington, DC 419, 447,
    464, 504–5, 593, 696, 703
Center for Advanced Holocaust Studies 597
Holocaust education survey 699
United States of America (USA)
compulsory sterilization in 48
and eugenics 45
Holocaust education 695, 697–8, 698–9
and ICC 715
immigration policy 515, 520–1
internment of Japanese Americans 562, 602
Jewish youth camps 702
memorials and museums 503–5
as on-looker 158–61
public profile of Jews 599
and rescue of Jews 178
response to Holocaust 269–72
and restitution 555
US Army trials 525–6
Universal Declaration of Human Rights 20, 712,
    724
universalism 662
university students: and antisemitism 29–30,
    34–5
UNRRA (United Nations Relief and
    Rehabilitation Administration)
    509, 510, 512–13
Unzer Sztyme (Our Voice) newspaper 513, 514
Upper Silesia 107, 132, 138

USC Shoah Foundation Institute for Visual
    History and Education 419, 703
USSR (Union of Soviet Socialist Republics) 160,
    192–3, 284
criminalization of civilian population 76
emergence of 82
exacerbation of Jewish DP problem 520
forced labor in 359
Four Year Plan 317
Germanization of 75, 101, 316–21
ghettos 341
and Jewish refugees 173–4
mass murders in 104, 135, 317
Nazi campaign against 69
Operation Barbarossa 101, 134, 145–7
response to Holocaust 269
and restitution/compensation 552
suppression of Jewish public culture 591
trials 532
Ustasha fascist movement, Croatia 83, 284

Vaivara concentration camp 372
Vaks, Yosef 348
Vallat, Xavier 334
van Alphen, Ernst 463, 464–7
Vars, Henry 487
Vatican 329, 621
and Holocaust denial 571–2
neutrality of 161
Reich-Vatican Concordat 234, 238
Vatican II 600, 621
Vergangenheitsbewältigung (coming to terms
    with the past) 635, 659–60
Verhofstadt, Guy 658
Vernichtungskreig (war of destruction) 134–5
Versailles, Treaty of 64–5, 73
Verschuer, Otmar Freiherr von 39–40, 41, 260
Vichy France 105, 334
Statut des Juifs (Law of the Jews) 530
Vichy Syndrome 530
vigilante groups 148
village ghettos 341
Vilna ghetto 220–1, 431
*Vita é Bella, La, see Life Is Beautiful (La Vita é
    Bella, film)*
Vlaams Blok, Belgium 659
Voievodina 327
Volcker, Paul 554
Volk ohne Raum (Grimm) 70
Völkel, Alfred 226
Völkerpsychologie (psychology of peoples) 401–2
völkisch movement 42, 43, 116
Volkov, Shulamit 28

Volksdeutsche, see ethnic Germans
Volksdeutsche Mittelstelle (Ethnic German
    Liaison Office) 313
Volksgerichtshof (People's Court) 534
Volkskörper 65
Volkstum 65
Volkswagen compensation payments 551
Vollnhals, Clemens 259
von Galen, Clemens August Graf 165, 240, 254
"Vu ahin zol ikh geyn?" (Warsaw ghetto
    song) 487
Vught transit camp, Netherlands 335–6

"Waast Du, wo Auschwitz liegt?"
    (P. Wagner) 487–8
Waffen-SS 121, 142, 149
Wagner, Gerhard 47, 98
Wagner, Peter 487–8
Wagner, Richard 14, 29
Wagner-Régeny, Rudolf 482–3
Wajner, Leo 479
Walk, Falk 177
Wallant, Edward Lewis 438–9
Wallenberg, Raoul 163, 179
Waller, James E. 18–19, 144, 667–77
Wannsee Conference 123, 137, 303, 688
war of destruction (*Vernichtungskrieg*) 134–5
war on terror 470–1, 475
War Refugee Board (WRB), USA 160, 179, 192,
    271–2, 329
Warhaftig, Zorach 581
Warsaw ghetto 96, 133, 176, 342
    1943 uprising 195–6, 388, 479
    black market 343
    Gypsies in 280
    women in 212–13
Warschau concentration camp 372
Warthegau 132, 313, 341–2
Wartime Lies (Begley) 437
Washington Project for the Arts: *Burnt Whole:
    Contemporary Artists Reflect on the
    Holocaust* (exhibition) 464
Wassermann, Oscar 237
Wasserstein, Bernard 159–60
Waxman, Franz 480, 485
"We Didn't Know" (Paxton) 488
"We Remember: Reflections on the Shoah"
    (Vatican statement) 621
"We Will Never Die" (pageant), New York 480,
    490
Wehrmacht 142
    anti-partisan campaign in USSR 146–7
    and "Final Solution" 150–2

Gypsies in 277–8
    and invasion of Poland 146
    and mass murders 100–1, 135, 146–7
    Secret Field Police 152
    Wehrmacht Exhibition 150
Weill, Kurt 480
Weimar Republic 34, 35, 36, 64
    euthanasia programs 48–51
    Gypsies in 275
Weinberg, Mieczysław 483–4
Weiss, Peter 484
Weissler, Friedrich 255
Weissová, Ilona 223
Weissruthenien, *see* Belarus
Weitz, Eric D. 5, 54–66
Weitzman, Lenore J. 8, 203–15
Weizmann, Chaim 268
Weizsäcker, Richard von 642–3
Weltanschauungskrieg (war of world views) 652
Welteislehre (World Ice Theory) 41–2
Weltpolitik 70, 74
Welzer, Harald 144
Werb, Bret 14, 478–89
Werfel, Franz 96
West German Bishops' Conference 240
West Germany
    attitude to Nazi past 637–43
    extensions of statute of limitations on crimes
        of murder 641–2
    films 450–1
    trials 533–7
    restitution 641
West Prussia 132
Westerbork Symfonie (Stoppelenburg) 486
Westerbork transit camp, Netherlands 196, 335,
    546
Westermann, Edward B. 7, 142–52
Wetzel, Erhard 287–8
Whitbourne, James 485
White Busses expedition 163
White Collar Employees Association,
    German-National 34
Whiteread, Rachel 463, 494
Who Will Carry the Word? (Delbo) 418
WHVA (Economic Administration Main
    Office), SS 11, 369
Widmann, Albert 136
Wiedergutmachung, see restitution
    (*Wiedergutmachung*)
Wiener, Alfred 191
Wiener Library 191
Wiesel, Elie 203, 414, 422, 434, 598–9, 698
    and contemporary art 470

on Holocaust literature 429
on *Holocaust* miniseries 447
on Holocaust remembrance 590
librettos 486
on *Mirroring Evil* (exhibition) 467
novels 437–8
on prayers in Auschwitz 611
on sin as cause of Holocaust 609
see also *Night*
Wiesenthal, Simon 598
Wiesenthal Center, Los Angeles 598
Wilcken, Dagmar von *497*
Wildt, Michael 144
Wilhelm I, Kaiser 60
Wilhelm II, Kaiser 61, 62, 64
Williamson, Richard 571–2
Winterová, Zuzana 223
Winton, Nicholas 173
Wirth, Christian 106, 136
Wisliceny, Dieter 137, 187, 530
Witaszek, Alusia and Darya 226
Witness and Legacy: Contemporary Art about the Holocaust (exhibition) 464
Wittmann, Rebecca 16, 524–37
Wolff, Kurt H. 670
Wolhynien-Podolien, Ukraine 347–8
Wollheim, Norbert 513
women 203–15
    abortion 208
    coping strategies in camps and ghettos 211–15
    humiliation of 206, 208–9
    and norms of chivalry 205–6
    pregnancy 207–8, 219
    rape 8, 209–11, 676
    and resistance movement 213
Wonderyears (exhibition) 469–70
Woocher, Jonathan 595
work camps, *see* labor camps
World Council of Churches 260
World Ice Theory (*Welteislehre*) 41–2
World Jewish Congress 191, 192, 237, 554, 577–8
World War I: 63–4
    Armenian genocide 96, 601, 659
    lessons of 96–7
    stab-in-the-back myth 6, 46, 65, 97
World War II: preparations for, and persecution of Jews 98–9
"Writing on the Wall" (Attie) 494–5
"Written in Pencil in a Sealed Railway Car" (Pagis) 437"
Wurm, Theophil 252, 254, 255, 260
WVHA (Business Administration Main Office) 11, 369, 144–5

Wygodzki, Stanisław 484
Wyman, David 158, 159

Yad Vashem, Israeli Holocaust Memorial 178, 197, 419, 502–3, 580, 581–2, 617, 697, 703
    International School for Holocaust Studies 597
    new 582–4, 603
Yad Vashem Council 584
Yalta Conference 510
Yerushalmi, Yosef Hayim 440–1, 622
Yevtushenko, Yevgeny 483
Yiddishe Sotziale Alaynhilf, Poland 194
Yishuv (Jewish organized community), Palestine 190, 192, 575–6, 581
Yiskor (Partos) 481
YIVO Institute for Jewish Research, Vilna 597
Yizkor (memorial) books 348, 416, 594
"*Yizkor* 1943" (Auerbach) 430–1
Yom Hashoah Vehagvurah 500
Yom Hazicaron la-Shoah Ve-Mered Hagetaot (Holocaust and Ghetto Revolt Memorial Day) 580
Yom Hazicaron la-Shoah Ve-Hagvurah (Holocaust and Heroism Memorial Day) 580
Yom Kippur War 586
Young, James E. 14–15, 419, 463, 464–5, 490–505
Yugoslavia 87, 101, 105, 552, 658

Zamosc action 315–16
Zawinul, Joe 488
ZdL (*Zentrale Stelle der Landesjustizverwaltung zur Aufklärung nationalsozialistischer Verbrechen*, Central Office of the State Judicial Authorities for the Investigation of National Socialist Crimes) 535, 641
Zegota, see Council for Aid to Jews
Zeisl, Eric 481
Zelizer, Barbie 452
Zelkowicz, Josef 225, 400
Zentrale Stelle der Landesjustizverwaltung zur Aufklärung nationalsozialistischer Verbrechen (ZdL, Central Office of the State Judicial Authorities for the Investigation of National Socialist Crimes) 535, 641
Zhytomyr massacre 318
Ziel und Weg (Goal and Path) magazine 276
Zimbardo, Philip 671–2
Zimmerer, Jürgen 69
Zinnemann, Fred 445

Zionism 61, 192, 198, 600
    campaign for Jewish state 576–7
    Hechalutz (pioneer) movement 582
    as response to Holocaust 616–17
Zionist Congress 581
"Zog nit keynmol az du geyst dem letstn veg"
        (Jewish Partisan anthem) 488
Zollverein 59

Zorn, John 488
Zuccotti, Susan 244–5
Zucker, B. A. 160
Zuidhof, Peter-Wim 468–9
Zwangsarbeitlager (forced labor camps) 356, 372
Żydom Polskim (Wajner and Broniewski) 479
Zygielbojm, Szmul 190, 479
Zyklon B gas 50, 136, 370–1, 566–7

Printed and bound by CPI Group (UK) Ltd, Croydon, CR0 4YY